Ethics in Practice

BLACKWELL PHILOSOPHY ANTHOLOGIES

Each volume in this outstanding series provides an authoritative and comprehensive collection of the essential primary readings from philosophy's main fields of study. Designed to complement the *Blackwell Companions to Philosophy* series, each volume represents an unparalleled resource in its own right, and will provide the ideal platform for course use.

Ethics in Practice
An Anthology

Third Edition

Edited by

Hugh LaFollette

Blackwell
Publishing

BLACKWELL PUBLISHING
350 Main Street, Malden, MA 02148-5020, USA
9600 Garsington Road, Oxford OX4 2DQ, UK
550 Swanston Street, Carlton, Victoria 3053, Australia

First published 2007 by Blackwell Publishing Ltd

4   2008

Library of Congress Cataloging-in-Publication Data

Ethics in practice : an anthology / edited by Hugh LaFollette.—3rd ed.
     p. cm.—(Blackwell philosophy anthologies ; 3)
  Includes bibliographical references.
  ISBN: 978-1-4051-2945-9 (pbk. : alk. paper)   1. Applied ethics. 2. Ethical problems. I. LaFollette, Hugh, 1948– II. Series.

BJ1031.E854 2006
170—dc22

                              2006009885

A catalogue record for this title is available from the British Library.

Set in 9.5/11.5pt, Ehrhardt
by SPi Publisher Services, Pondicherry, India
Printed and bound in Singapore
by C.O.S. Printers Pte Ltd

The publisher's policy is to use permanent paper from mills that operate a sustainable forestry policy, and which has been manufactured from pulp processed using acid-free and elementary chlorine-free practices. Furthermore, the publisher ensures that the text paper and cover board used have met acceptable environmental accreditation standards.

For further information on
Blackwell Publishing, visit our website:
www.blackwellpublishing.com

Contents

Contents

Contents

Contents

Preface for Instructors

This anthology seeks to provide engagingly written, carefully argued philosophical essays, on a wide range of important, contemporary ethical issues. When I had trouble finding essays that suited those purposes, I commissioned new essays – seven for this edition. I also invited a number of philosophers to revise their "classic" essays – six for this edition. The result is a tasty blend of the old and the new, the familiar and the unfamiliar. I have organized the book into five thematic sections and fifteen topics to give you the greatest flexibility to construct the course you want. When feasible, I begin or end sections with essays that bridge to preceding or following sections.

Although I have included essays I think introductory students can read and comprehend, no one would believe me if I claimed all the essays were easy to read. We all know many students have trouble reading philosophical essays. That is not surprising. Many of these essays were written originally for other professional philosophers, not first-year undergraduates. Moreover, even when philosophers write expressly for introductory audiences, their ideas, vocabularies, and styles are often foreign to the introductory student. So I have included a brief introduction on READING PHILOSOPHY to advise students on how to read and understand philosophical essays.

I want this volume to be suitable for a variety of courses. The most straightforward way to use the text is to assign essays on six of seven of your favorite practical issues. If you want a more topical course, you could emphasize issues in one or more of the major thematic sections. You could also focus on practical and theoretical issues spanning individual topics and major divisions of the book. If, for instance, you want to focus on gender, you could select most essays from five sections: ABORTION, FAMILY AND REPRODUCTIVE TECHNOLOGY, SEXUALITY, SEXUAL AND RACIAL DISCRIMINATION, and AFFIRMATIVE ACTION, and combine these with some specific articles scattered throughout, e.g., Young's "Displacing the Distributive Paradigm" (ECONOMIC JUSTICE). Finally, you can also give your course a decided theoretical flavor by using the new section on ETHICAL THEORY, and then selecting essays that address, in diverse contexts, significant theoretical issues like the act/omission distinction, the determination of moral status, or the limits of morality, etc. You can also direct your students to THEORIZING ABOUT ETHICS. This brief introductory essay is designed to help them understand why we should theorize and to give them a snapshot of some major theories.

One distinctive feature of the anthology is the section introductions. Some anthologies do not include them; those that do often use introductions simply to summarize the articles in that section. The introductions here do indicate the main thrust of the essays. However, that is not their primary purpose. Their purpose is (1) to focus students' attention on the theoretical issues at stake, and (2) to relate those issues to the discussion of the same or related issues in other sections. All too often students (and philosophers) see practical ethics as a hodgepodge of largely (or wholly) unrelated problems. The introductions should go some way toward remedying this tendency. They show students that practical questions are not discrete, but intricately connected with one another. Thinking carefully about any problem invariably illuminates (and is illuminated by) others. Thus, the overarching aim of these introductions is to give the book a coherence some anthologies lack.

There are consequences of this strategy you might mention to your students. I organized the order of the papers within each section to maximize the students' understanding of that practical issue – nothing more. However, I wrote the introductions and organized the summaries to maximize the understanding of theoretical issues. Often the order of the discussion of essays in the introduction matches the order of essays in that section; occasionally it does not. Moreover, I spend more time "summarizing" some essays to the exclusion of others. That in no way suggests that the essays on which I focus are more cogent, useful, or in any way better than the others. Rather, I found it easier to use them as *entrées* into the theoretical questions.

Finally, since I do not know which sections you will use, you should be aware that the introductions will likely refer to essays the student will not read. When that happens, they will not realize one aim of the introductions. They

may still be valuable. For even if the student does not read the essays to which an introduction refers, she can better appreciate the interconnections between issues. It might even have the delicious consequence of encouraging the student to read an essay that you did not assign.

One last note about the criteria for selecting essays. Many practical ethics anthologies include essays on opposing sides of every issue. For most topics I think that is a laudable aim that an editor can normally achieve. But not always. I include essays that discuss the issue as we currently frame and understand it. Sometimes that understanding precludes some positions that might have once been part of the debate. For instance, early practical ethics anthologies included essays that argued that an individual should always choose to prolong her life, by any medical means whatever. On this view, euthanasia of any sort and for any reason was immoral. Although that was once a viable position, virtually no one now advocates or even discusses it. Even the author of the essay with serious misgivings about a "right to die" would not embrace *that* position. The current euthanasia debate largely concerns *when* people might choose not to sustain their lives, *how* they might carry out their wishes, and with *whose* assistance. Those are the questions addressed by these essays on euthanasia.

Likewise, I do not have any essays that argue that women and blacks ought to be relegated to the bedroom or to manual labor. Although everyone acknowledges that racism and sexism are still alive and well in the United States, few people openly advocate making blacks and women second-class citizens. No one seriously discusses these proposals in academic circles. Instead, I include essays that highlight current issues concerning the treatment of minorities and women (sexual harassment, date rape, etc.).

Acknowledgments

I would like to thank three people who, through their work, encouraged me to think about practical moral issues and who, through their lives, encouraged me to act on what I found: Joel Feinberg, James Rachels, and Richard Wasserstrom.

I would like to thank Eva LaFollette for her insight and her comments on the structure and content of this volume.

I would like to thank Jeff Dean, who is everything one could possibly want in an editor. He is knowledgable, thoughtful, and efficient. Finally I would like to thank the staff at Blackwell for making my job as editor easier. I am especially grateful to Danielle Descoteaux, who made my job so much easier than it would have been otherwise.

Text Credits

New material [*NW*]:

I would like to thank the following authors who have written material especially for this edition:

1   Peter Vallentyne, "Consequentialism"
2   David McNaughton and Piers Rawling, "Deontology"
3   Rosalind Hursthouse, "Virtue Theory"

48   John M. Doris, "Out of Character: On the Psychology of Excuses in the Criminal Law"
49   John Paul Wright, Francis T. Cullen, and Kevin M. Beaver, "Does Punishment Work?"
65   Douglas P. Lackey, "Nipping Evil "
67   William J. Hawk, "Pacifism"

Material written for Ethics in Practice [*W*]:

I would like to thank those authors who have granted permission for material they had written for previous editions to be used in this third edition:

4   Brad Hooker, "Rule-Utilitarianism and Euthanasia"
5   Tom L. Beauchamp, "Justifying-Physician Assisted Deaths"
7   John Hardwig, "Dying at the Right Time"
11   Don Marquis, "An Argument that Abortion is Wrong"
27   John Corvino, "Homosexuality and the Moral Relevance of Experience"
37   John Arthur, "Sticks and Stones"
38   Andrew Altman, "Speech Codes and Expressive Harm"

46 Luke Charles Harris and Uma Narayan, "Affirmative Action as Equalizing Opportunity: Challenging the Myth of Preferential Treatment"

47 James Rachels, "Punishment and Desert" (reprinted with the kind permission of David Rachels, son of James Rachels)

50 Louis P. Pojman, "In Defense of the Death Penalty"

55 Jonathan Wolff, "Economic Competition: Should We Care about the Losers?"

57 John Arthur, "Famine Relief and the Ideal Moral Code"

63 Alan Carter, "Hume and Nature"

Previously published material including some essays that were revised for Ethics in Practice [*R*]:

I would like to thank publishers who granted permission for their copyright material to be used or reused in this edition:

6 J. David Velleman, revised version of pp. 665–81 from "Against the Right to Die," *Journal of Medicine and Philosophy* 17:6 (1992). Reprinted by permission of Taylor & Francis and the author.

8 Felicia Cohn and Joanne Lynn, "A Duty to Care Revisited," pp. 145–54 from J. Hardwig, *Is There a Duty to Die?* New York: Routledge, 2000.

9 Judith Jarvis Thompson, "A Defense of Abortion," pp. 47–62, 65–6 from *Philosophy and Public Affairs* 1(1). Reprinted with permission of Blackwell Publishing Ltd.

10 Mary Anne Warren, revised version of "On the Moral and Legal Status of Abortion," pp. 43–61 from *The Monist* 57, 1973. © 1973 by The Monist: An International Quarterly Journal of General Philosophical Inquiry, Peru, Illinois, USA 61354. Reprinted by permission.

12 Margaret Olivia Little, "The Moral Permissibility of Abortion," pp. 27–39 from Christopher Heath Wellman and Andrew Cohen (eds.), *Contemporary Debates in Applied Ethics*. Oxford: Blackwell, 2004. Reprinted with permission of Blackwell Publishing Ltd.

13 Rosalind Hursthouse, revised version of "Virtue Theory and Abortion," pp. 223–46 from *Philosophy and Public Affairs* 20. Princeton University Press, 1991. Reprinted with permission of Blackwell Publishing Ltd.

14 Peter Singer, "All Animals are Equal," from *Philosophical Exchange* 1, 1974. © by Peter Singer.

15 Michael Allen Fox, "The Moral Community," pp. 49–63 from *Case for Animal Experimentation: An Evolutionary and Ethical Perspective*. University of California Press, 1986. © 1986 by The Regents of the University of California.

16 R. G. Frey, "Moral Standing, the Value of Lives, and Speciesism," pp. 191–201 from *Between the Species* 4 (1988). Reprinted with permission of the journal and the author.

17 Tom Regan, "The Case for Animal Rights," pp. 13–26 from Peter Singer (ed.), *In Defense of Animals*. Oxford: Basil Blackwell, 1985. Reprinted by permission of Blackwell Publishing Ltd.

18 Jane English, "What Do Grown Children Owe their Parents?," pp. 351–6 from William Ruddick and Onora O'Neill (eds.), *Having Children*. © Oxford University Press, 1979.

19 James Rachels, "Morality, Parents, and Children," pp. 46–62 from George Graham and Hugh LaFollette, *Person to Person*. Temple University Press, 1989. Reprinted with the kind permission of David Rachels, son of James Rachels.

20 Ruth Macklin, "Artificial Means of Reproduction and Our Understanding of the Family." Reprinted by permission of The Hastings Center.

21 Elizabeth S. Anderson, "Is Women's Labor a Commodity?," pp. 71–92 from *Philosophy and Public Affairs* (1990). Reprinted by permission of Blackwell Publishing Ltd.

22 John Harris, " 'Goodbye Dolly': the Ethics of Human Cloning," pp. 353–60 from *Journal of Medical Ethics.* BMJ Publishing Group, 1997. Reprinted with permission of the BMJ.

23 Leon R. Kass, "The Wisdom of Repugnance," pp. 17–27 from *The New Republic*, June 2, 1997. Reprinted with the kind permission of the author.

24 Vincent C. Punzo, "Morality and Human Sexuality," from Vincent Punzo, *Reflective Naturalism.* Macmillan, 1969. Reprinted with permission of Pearson Education, Upper Saddle River, NJ.

25 Alan H. Goldman, "Plain Sex," pp. 267–87 from *Philosophy and Public Affairs*, 1977. Reprinted by permission of Blackwell Publishing Ltd.

26 Michael Levin, revised version of "Why Homosexuality Is Abnormal," pp. 251–83 from *The Monist* 67/2, 1984. © 1984 The Monist, An International Quarterly Journal of General Philosophical Inquiry, Peru, Illinois, 61354. Reprinted by permission.

29 Lester H. Hunt, "On Improving People by Political Means," pp. 61–76 *from Reason Papers*, 1985. Reprinted with permission of Reason Papers and the author.

30 James Q. Wilson, "Against the Legalization of Drugs," from *Commentary* (February 1990). Reprinted by permission. All rights reserved.

31 Douglas Husak, "Why We Should Decriminalize Drug Use," pp. 21–9 from *Criminal Justice Ethics* 22 (1), Winter/ Spring 2003. Reprinted with the kind permission of the author.

32 Todd C. Hughes and Lester H. Hunt, revised version of "The Liberal Basis of the Right to Bear Arms," pp. 1–25 from *Public Affairs Quarterly* 14, 2000. Reprinted with permission of Public Affairs Quarterly.

33 Hugh Lafollette, "Gun Control." This essay first appeared *in Ethics* 110 (2000).

Reprinted with permission of The University of Chicago Press © 2000.

35 Susan J. Brison, revised version of "The Price We Pay?," pp. 236–50 from Christopher Heath Wellman and Andrew Cohen (eds.) *Contemporary Debates in Applied Ethics*, 1. Malden, MA: Blackwell 2004. Reprinted with permission of Blackwell Publishing Ltd.

36 Andrew Altman, "The Right to Get Turned On: Pornography, Autonomy, Equality," pp. 223–35 from Christopher Heath Wellman and Andrew Cohen, *Contemporary Debates in Applied Ethics*, 1. Malden, MA: Blackwell 2004. Reprinted with permission of Blackwell Publishing Ltd.

39 Michele Moody-Adams, "Racism," pp. 89–101 from R. G. Frey and C. H. Wellman, *Blackwell Companion to Applied Ethics.* Malden: Blackwell 2003. Reprinted with permission of Blackwell Publishing Ltd.

40 Thomas E. Hill Jr., "Servility and Self-Respect," pp. 87–104 from *The Monist*, 1974. © 1974 The Monist: An International Quarterly Journal of General Philosophical Inquiry, Peru, Illinois, 61354. Reprinted by permission.

41 Anita M. Superson, "Sexual Harassment," pp. 51–64 from *Journal of Social Philosophy* 24/3, 1993. Reprinted with permission of Blackwell Publishing Ltd.

42 Louis Pineau, "Date Rape," pp. 217–43 from *Law and Philosophy* 8. Kluwer Acedemic Publishers, 1989. Reprinted with permission of Springer Verlag.

43 Larry May and Robert Strikwerda, revised version of "Men in Groups: Collective Responsibility for Rape," pp. 134–51 from *Hypatia* 9, 1994.

44 Louis P. Pojman, revised version of "The Case Against Affirmative Action," *International Journal of Applied Philosophy* 12 (1998). Reprinted courtesy of the author, Louis Pojman.

45 Ronald Dworkin, "The Rights of Allan Bakke," from *The New York Review of*

Books, 1977. Reprinted with permission of New York Review of Books.

51 Jeffrey Reiman, "Against the Death Penalty," pp. 553–62 from S. Luper, *Living Well*. Harcourt Brace and Company, 2000. Reprinted by permission of the author.

52 John Rawls, "A Theory of Justice," pp. 11–21, 60–4, 150–6 from Belknap Press of Harvard University Press, 1971. © 1971, 1999 by the President and Fellows of Harvard College. Reprinted with permission of Harvard University Press.

53 Robert Nozick, "The Entitlement Theory of Justice," pp. 140–64, 167–74 from *Anarchy, State, and Utopia*. Basic Books, 1974. © 1974 by Basic Books, Inc. Reprinted with permission.

54 Iris Marion Young, "Displacing the Distributive Paradigm," pp. 15–16, 18–30, 33–4, 37–8 from *Justice and the Politics of Difference*. Princeton University Press, 1990. © 1990 Princeton University Press. Reprinted by permission of Princeton University Press.

56 Peter Singer, "Famine, Affluence, and Morality," pp. 229–43 from *Philosophy and Public Affairs*. Princeton University Press, 1972. © 1990 Princeton University Press. Reprinted by permission of Princeton University Press.

58 Thomas W. Pogge, revised version of "Eradicating Systemic Poverty: Brief for a Global Resources Dividend," pp. 501–38 from D. Crocker and T. Linden, *Ethics of Consumption*. Rowman Littlefield Publishers, Inc, 1997. Reprinted by permission of Rowman & Littlefield Publishers Inc.

59 Holmes Rolston III, revised version of "Feeding People versus Saving Nature," pp. 248–67 from W. Aiken and Hugh LaFollette, *World Hunger and Morality*. Prentice Hall, 1996.

60 Aldo Leopold, "The Land Ethic," pp. 129–33 from Aldo Leopold, *A Sand County Almanac: With Other Essays on Conservation from Round River*. Oxford University Press, 1981. © 1949, 1953, 1966 renewed 1977, 1981 by Oxford University Press Inc, Used by permission of Oxford University Press Inc.

61 David Schmidtz, revised version of "A Place for Cost-Benefit Analysis," pp. 148–71 from *Philosophical Issues* 11. Supplement to *Noûs*, 2001. Reprinted by permission of Blackwell Publishing Ltd.

62 Thomas E. Hill, Jr., "Ideals of Human Excellence and Preserving Natural Environments," pp. 211–24 from *Environmental Ethics* 5, 1983. Reprinted with the kind permission of the author.

64 Joseph Boyle, revised version of "Just War Doctrine and the Military Response to Terrorism," from *Journal of Philosophy*, 2003. Reprinted by permission of Blackwell Publishing Ltd.

66 Charles Beitz, revised version of "The Justifiability of Humanitarian Intervention." Reprinted by permission of Bowdoin College.

The following material is taken from the public domain:

28 John Stuart Mill, "Freedom of Action"
34 John Stuart Mill, "Freedom of Thought and Discussion"

General Introduction

All of us make choices. Some of these appear to concern only ourselves: what to wear, when to sleep, what to read, where to live, how to decorate our homes, and what to eat. Under most circumstances these choices are purely personal. Purely personal concerns are beyond the scope of morality and will not be discussed in this book. Other choices demonstrably affect others: whether to prolong the life of our comatose grandmother, when and with whom to have sex, how to relate to people of different races, and whether to support capital punishment or laws against cloning. These choices clearly affect others and are normally thought to be choices we should assess, at least in part, on moral grounds.

Upon closer examination, however, we see that it is not always obvious whether a choice affects only us. Is choosing to view pornography personal or does it support the degradation of women? Is eating meat purely personal or does it encourage and sustain the inhumane treatment of animals or the depletion of resources that we could use to feed the starving? Is choosing where to live purely personal or does it sometimes support racist practices that confine African-Americans or Hispanics or Asians to

inadequate housing? If so, then some choices that *seem* purely personal turn out to affect others in morally significant ways.

In short, once we reflect carefully on our choices, we discover that many might profoundly affect others, and therefore, that we ought to evaluate them morally. By choosing to buy a new stereo rather than send money for famine relief, children in India may starve. By choosing to support political candidates who oppose or support abortion, tough drug laws, affirmative action, or lax environmental protection, I affect others in demonstrably significant ways. Of course, knowing that our choices affect others does not yet tell us how we should behave. It does, however, confirm that we should evaluate those choices morally. Unfortunately many of us are individually and collectively near-sighted: we fail to see or appreciate the moral significance of our choices, thereby increasing the evil in the world. Often we talk and think as if evil resulted solely from the conscious choices of wholly evil people. I suspect, however, that evil results more often from ignorance and inattention: we just don't notice or attend to the significance of what we do. A central aim of this book is to improve our moral vision: to help us notice and comprehend the moral significance of what we do.

The primary means of achieving this end is to present essays that carefully and critically discuss a range of practical moral issues. These essays will supply information you likely do not have and perspectives you may not have not considered. Many of you may find that your education has ill-prepared you to think carefully about these issues. Far too many public schools in the United States neither expect nor even permit students to think critically. Many of them will not have expected or wanted you to develop and defend your own views. Instead, they will have demanded that you memorize the content of your texts and the assertions of your teachers.

Philosophy professors, in contrast, do not standardly expect you to memorize what they or someone else says. Still less will they want you to parrot them or the texts. They require you to read what others have said, but not because they want you to recite it. Instead, these professors think that critically reading the arguments of others will help you better reach your own conclusions. For those of you who find that your high school education, with its premium on memorization and blind adherence to authority, did not prepare you to read philosophical essays, I have included a brief section on READING PHILOSOPHY.

I also include a brief introductory essay on ethical theorizing. Philosophers do not discuss practical issues in a vacuum. They place their discussions in larger contexts that help clarify and define the practical issues. Thus, they discuss not only the details peculiar to the issue, but also more general features that are relevant to many practical moral quandaries. That introductory essay will explain the purpose of THEORIZING ABOUT ETHICS: the benefits of placing a practical question in a larger framework. The essay will also briefly describe some prominent ethical theories that you will encounter in these pages. You will also notice, as you read the essays, that some authors provide more detailed explanations of these theories.

To augment your understanding of theory, I will, in the introductions to each section, not only summarize the central themes of the essays, I will also spotlight some general theoretical questions and explain how these are relevant to other issues discussed in this volume. It is important to appreciate the myriad ways in which practical moral issues are woven together by common theoretical threads. Practical ethics is not a random collection of unconnected issues, but a systematic exploration of how we can most responsibly act in a variety of practical moral contexts.

Consequently, this is not a recipe book that answers all moral questions. Rather, it is a chronicle of how a number of philosophers have thought about these significant practical moral issues. If you absorb the information the authors supply, attend to their arguments, and consider the diverse perspectives they offer, you will find, when the course is over, that you are better able to think carefully and critically about practical and theoretical moral issues.

Theorizing about Ethics

When deciding how to act, we often face uncertainty over, confusions about, or conflicts between, our inclinations, desires, interests, and beliefs. These can arise even when we want only to promote our self-interests. We may not know what is in our best interests: we may have simply adopted some mistaken ideas of our parents, our friends, or our culture. For instance, were our parents Nazis we might believe that maintaining racial purity is our most important personal aim. We may also confuse our wants and our interests: we want to manipulate others for our own end and therefore infer that caring for others systematically undermines our interests. Even when we know some of our interests, we may be unable to determine their relative importance: we may assume that wealth is more important than developing character and having close relationships. Other times we may know our interests, but be unsure of how to resolve conflicts between them: I may need to write a paper, yet want to hike the local mountain. Finally, even if I know the best choice, I may not act on it: I may know precisely that it is in my best long-term interest to lose weight, yet inhale that scrumptious pie instead.

These complications show why I can best pursue my self-interests only if I rationally deliberate about them, only if I theorize about them. I must sometimes step back and think more abstractly about (a) what it means for something to be an interest (rather than a mere desire); (b) to detect which objects or behavior or goals are most likely to advance those interests; (c) to understand the interconnections between my interests (e.g., the ways that health enhances my chance of achieving other interests); (d) to find a procedure for coping with conflicts; and (e) to learn how to act on the outcome of rational deliberation. Such theorizing can guide practice: it can help us act more prudently.

Of course, many – perhaps most – actions do not concern simply us; they also concern others, and they do so in myriad ways. Some of my actions may benefit others while other actions may harm them; I may benefit or harm others directly or indirectly, intentionally or unintentionally. I might directly harm Joe by pushing him. I might push him because I am angry with him or because I want his place in the queue. I could indirectly harm Joe by landing the promotion he needs to finance nursing care for his dying mother. Or I might offend Joe by privately engaging in what he considers "kinky sex." If so, my bedroom antics affect him, although only indirectly, and only because of his particular moral beliefs. Arguably it is inappropriate to say that I harmed Joe in these last two cases, although I did choose to act while knowing my actions might affect him (or someone else) in these ways.

In choosing how to act, I should acknowledge that many of my actions affect others, even if only indirectly. In these circumstances, I must choose whether to pursue my self-interest or whether to pursue (or at least not harm) the interests of others. Other times I must choose to act in ways that may harm some people while benefiting others. I might occasionally find ways to promote everyone's interests without harming anyone's. Occasionally, but not always.

Knowing this does not settle the question of how I should act. It only sets the arena within which morality operates. Morality, traditionally understood, involves primarily, and perhaps exclusively, behavior that affects others. I say "perhaps" because some people (e.g., Kant) think anyone who harms herself, for instance, by squandering her talents or abusing her body, has done something morally wrong. For present purposes, though, we can leave this issue to the side. For what everyone acknowledges is that actions that indisputably affect others should be evaluated morally.

We might disagree about how the fact that an action negatively affects others should shape our decision about how to act. We might also disagree whether and to what extent actions that affect others only indirectly should be evaluated morally. We might further disagree about how to distinguish direct from indirect harm. Nonetheless, if someone's action directly and substantially affects others (either benefits or harms them), then even if we do not yet know whether the action is right or wrong, we can agree that we should evaluate it morally. How we should evaluate it I will discuss in a moment.

First, I should note related but opposite dangers here that we should avoid. We might infer from the previous discussion that most moral decisions are complicated or confusing. That is a mistake. For many moral "decisions" are

quite easy to make – so easy that we never think about them. No one seriously debates whether morally someone should drug a classmate so she can have sex with him, whether she should steal money from her co-workers to finance a vacation on the Riviera, or whether she should knowingly infect someone with AIDS. This is not the stuff of which moral disagreement is made. We know quite well that such actions are wrong. In fact, I dare say that most moral questions are so easily answered that we never ask them. Rather than discuss these obvious "questions," we focus on, think about, and debate only those that are unclear, those about which there is genuine disagreement.

However, we are also sometimes guilty of assuming that a decision is easy to make, when, in fact, it is not. This is an equally (or arguably more) serious mistake. We may fail to see the conflicts, confusions, or uncertainties: the issue may be so complicated that we overlook, fail to understand, or do not appreciate how (and how profoundly) our actions affect others. We may be so preoccupied with our self-interest that we either do not see the ways our behavior significantly affects others or else it leads us to give inadequate weight to others' interests. Finally, our unquestioning acceptance of the moral status quo can blind us to just how wrong some of our individual behaviors and social institutions are.

The Need for Theory

We may think that an action is grossly immoral, but not really know why. Or we may think we know why, only to discover, upon careful examination, that we are just parroting the "reasons" offered by our friends, teachers, parents, or preachers. There is nothing wrong with considering how others think and how they have decided similar moral questions. We would be fools not to absorb and benefit from the wisdom of others. However, anyone even faintly aware of history will acknowledge that collective wisdom, like individual wisdom, is sometimes mistaken. Our ancestors held slaves, denied women the right to vote, practiced genocide, and burned witches at the stake. I suspect most of them were generally morally decent people who were firmly convinced that their actions were moral. They acted wrongly because they failed to be sufficiently self-critical. They did not evaluate their own beliefs; they unquestioningly adopted the outlook of their ancestors, political leaders, teachers, friends, and community. In this they were not unique. This is a "sin" of which we are all guilty. The resounding lesson of history is that we must scrutinize our beliefs, our choices, and our actions to ensure that we are informed, consistent, imaginative, unbiased, and not mindlessly repeating the views of others. Otherwise we may perpetrate evils we could avoid, evils for which future generations will rightly condemn us.

To critically evaluate our moral views we should theorize about ethics: we should think about moral issues more abstractly, more coherently, and more consistently. Theorizing is not some enterprise divorced from practice, but is simply the careful, systematic, and thoughtful reflection on practice. Theorizing in this sense will not insulate us from error. However, it will empower us to shed ill-conceived, uninformed, and irrelevant considerations. To explain what I mean, let's think briefly about a matter dear to most students: grades. My grading of students' work can go awry in at least three different ways.

1 I might use an inconsistent grading standard. That is, I might use different standards for different students: Joan gets an A because she has a pleasant smile; Ralph, because he works hard; Rachel, because her paper was exceptional. Of course, knowing that I should use a unified grading standard does not tell me what standards I should have employed or what grades the specific students should have received. Perhaps they all deserved the A's they received. However, it is not enough that I accidentally gave them the grades they deserved. I should have given them A's *because they deserved them*, not because of some irrelevant considerations. If I employ irrelevant considerations, I will usually give students the wrong grades, even if, in some cases, I give them the right grades.

2 I might have improper grading standards. It is not enough that I have an invariant standard. I might have a flawed standard to which I adhere unwaveringly. For instance, I might consistently give students I like higher grades than students I dislike. If so, I grade the papers inappropriately, even if consistently.
3 I might apply the standards inappropriately. I might have appropriate and consistent grading standards, yet misapply them because I am ignorant, close-minded, exhausted, preoccupied, or inattentive.

I can make parallel "mistakes" in ethical deliberations. For instance:

1 I might use inconsistent ethical principles.
2 I might have inappropriate moral standards.
3 I might apply moral standards inappropriately.

Let us look at each deliberative mistake in more detail:

Consistency. We should treat two creatures the same unless they are relevantly different – different in ways that justify treating them differently. Just as students expect teachers to grade consistently, we expect others (and hopefully ourselves) to be morally consistent. The demand for consistency pervades our moral thinking. A common strategy for defending our moral views is to claim that we are consistent; a common strategy for criticizing others' views is to charge that they are not.

The argumentative role of consistency is evident in the discussion of every practical moral issue. Consider its role in the ABORTION debate. Disputants spend considerable effort arguing that their own positions are consistent while charging that their opponents' positions are inconsistent. Each side labors to show why abortion is (or is not) relevantly similar to standard cases of murder. Most of those who think abortion is immoral (and likely all of those who think it should be illegal) claim abortion is relevantly similar to murder, while those who think abortion should be legal claim it differs relevantly from murder. What we do not find are people who think abortion is murder and yet wholly moral.

Consistency likewise plays central roles in debates over FREE SPEECH and PATERNALISM AND RISK. Those opposed to censorship often argue that books, pictures, movies, plays, or sculptures that some people want to censor are relevantly similar to other art that most people do not want censored. They further claim that pornography is a form of speech, and if we can prohibit it because the majority finds it offensive, then we must censor any speech that offends the majority. Conversely, those who claim we can legitimately censor pornography go to some pains to explain why pornography is relevantly different from other forms of speech we want to protect. Both sides want to show that their position is consistent and that their opponent's position is inconsistent.

Although consistency is generally recognized as a requirement of morality, in specific cases it is difficult to detect if someone is (has been) (in)-consistent. Someone may appear to act (in)consistently, but only because we do not appreciate the complexity of her moral reasoning or fail to understand the morally relevant features framing her action. Nonetheless, what everyone acknowledges is that *if* someone is being inconsistent, then that is a compelling reason to reject her position unless she can find some way to eliminate that inconsistency.

Correct principles. It is not enough to be consistent. We must also employ the appropriate guidelines, principles, standards, or make the appropriate judgments. Theorizing about ethics is one good way to discern the best (most defensible) standards or guidelines, to identify the morally relevant features of our actions, to enhance our ability to make good judgments. Later I discuss how to select and defend these principles – how we determine what is morally relevant.

Correct "application." Even when we "know" what is morally relevant, and even when we reason consistently, we may still make moral mistakes. Consider the ways I might misapply the "rules" prohibiting (a) lying and (b) harming another's feelings. Suppose my wife comes home wearing a gaudy sweater. She wants to

know if I like it. Presumably I should neither lie nor intentionally hurt another person's feelings. What, in these circumstances, should I do? There are any number of ways in which I might act inappropriately. (1) *I may not see viable alternatives*: I may assume, for example, that I must baldly lie or else substantially hurt her feelings. (2) *I may be insufficiently attentive to her needs and interests*: I may over- or underestimate how much she will be hurt by my honesty (or lack of it). (3) *I may be unduly influenced by self-interest or personal bias*: I may lie not to protect her feelings, but because I don't want her to be angry with me. (4) *I may know precisely what I should do, but be insufficiently motivated to do it:* I may lie because I just don't want the hassle. (5) Or, *I may be motivated to act as I should, but lack the talent or skill to do it*: I may want to be honest, but lack the verbal and personal skills to be honest in a way that will not hurt her feelings.

These are all failings with practical moral significance. We would all be better off if we had the personal traits to avoid these and other moral errors. Ultimately we should learn how to make ourselves more attentive, more informed, and better motivated. However, although these are vitally important practical concerns, they are not the primary focus of most essays in this book. What these authors do here is provide relevant information, careful logical analysis, and a clear account of what they take to be the morally relevant features of practical ethical questions.

Is It Just a Matter of Opinion?

Many of you may find talk of moral standards – and the application of those standards – troubling. You may think – certainly many people talk as if they think – that moral judgments are just "matters of opinion." All of us have overheard people "conclude" a debate about a contentious moral issue by saying: "Well, it is all just a matter of opinion anyway!" I suspect the real function of this claim is to signal the speaker's desire to terminate the debate. Unfortunately this claim implies more. It suggests that since moral judgments are just opinions, then all opinions are equally good (or equally bad). It implies that we cannot criticize or rationally scrutinize our (or anyone else's) moral judgments. After all, we don't rationally criticize *mere* opinions.

Is this a defensible implication? I don't see how. Even if no (contentious) moral judgment were indisputably correct, we should not conclude that all moral judgments are equally (un)reliable. Although we have no clear way of deciding with certainty which actions are best, we have excellent ways of showing that some are defective. We know, for instance, that moral judgments are flawed if they are based on misinformation, shortsightedness, bias, lack of understanding, or wholly bizarre moral principles. Conversely, judgments are more plausible, more defensible, if based on full information, careful calculation, astute perception, and if they have successfully survived the criticism of others in the marketplace of ideas.

Consider the following analogy: no grammatical or stylistic rules will determine precisely the way I should phrase the next sentence. However, from that we should not conclude that I may properly use just any string of words. Some clumps of words are not sentences while some sentences are complete gibberish. Other sentences might be grammatically well formed – even stylish – yet inappropriate because they are disconnected from the sentences that precede or follow them. All these collections of words are clearly unacceptable in these circumstances, although in another context(s) the same words might be wholly appropriate. Many other sentences are grammatically well formed, relevant and minimally clear, yet are nonetheless lacking in some way. They might, for instance, be somewhat vague or imprecise. Others may be comprehensible, relevant, and generally precise, yet still be gaudy or at least bereft of style. Some array of others might be wholly adequate, sufficiently adequate so that there is no strong reason to prefer one to the others. Perhaps some would be uniquely brilliant. No grammar book will enable us to make all those distinctions nor could it empower us to clearly identify the best sentence(s). And even if ordinary folks

or accomplished writers discussed the merits and demerits of each, they are unlikely to decide that one is uniquely best. Nonetheless, we have no problem distinguishing the trashy or the unacceptably vague from the linguistically sublime. In short, we needn't think that one sentence is uniquely good to acknowledge that some are better and some are worse. Likewise for ethics. We may not always know how to act; we may find substantial disagreement about some highly contentious ethical issues. But from that we should not infer that all moral ideas are created equal (LaFollette 1991).

We should also not ignore the obvious fact that circumstances often demand that we act even if there is no (or we cannot discern a) uniquely appropriate moral action. Nonetheless, our uncertainty does not lead us to think that – or act as if – all views are equal. We do not toss a coin to decide whether to remove our parents from life support, whom to marry, which job to take, or whether someone charged with a felony is guilty. We (should) strive to make an informed decision based on the best evidence and then act accordingly, even though the best evidence will never guarantee certainty. To make an informed decision we should understand the relevant issues, take a longer-term perspective, set aside irrational biases, and inculcate a willingness to subject our tentative conclusions to the criticisms of others.

After all, our actions sometimes do profoundly affect others and circumstances may demand that we act. We should not bemoan our inability to be certain that we have found the uniquely best action; we must simply make the best choice we can. We should, of course, acknowledge our uncertainty, admit our fallibility, and be prepared to consider new ideas, especially when they are supported by strong arguments. However, we have no need to embrace any pernicious forms of relativism. That would be not only misguided, but a moral mistake.

The Role of Theory

Even when people agree that an issue should be evaluated by criteria of morality, they may disagree about how to evaluate it. Using the language of the previous section, they may disagree about the best principles or judgments, about how those are to be interpreted, or about how they should be applied. Anti-abortionists argue that abortion should be illegal because the fetus has the same right to life as a normal adult, while pro-abortionists argue that it should be legal since the woman has the right to decide what happens in and to her body. Supporters of capital punishment argue that executions deter crime, while opponents argue that it is cruel and inhumane. Those who want to censor pornography claim it degrades women, while supporters argue that it is a form of free speech that should be protected by law.

In giving reasons for their judgments, people cite some features of the action they think explain or support their evaluation. This function of reasons is not confined to ethical disagreements. I may justify my claim that "*Fargo* is a good movie" by claiming that it has well-defined characters, an interesting plot, and the appropriate dramatic tension. That is, I identify features of the movie that I think justify my evaluation. The features I cite, however, are not unique to this movie. In giving these reasons I imply that "having well-defined characters" or "having an interesting plot" or "having the appropriate dramatic tension" are important characteristics of good movies, period. That is not to say these are the only or the most important characteristics. Nor is it yet to decide how weighty these characteristics are. However, it is to say that we have *a* reason to think that a movie with any of these characteristics is a good movie.

You can challenge my evaluation of the movie in three ways: you can challenge my criteria, the weight I give those criteria, or my application of the criteria (the claim that the movie satisfies the criteria). For instance, you could argue that having well-defined characters is not a relevant criterion, that I have given that criterion too much weight, or, that *Fargo* does not have well-defined characters. In defense, I could explain why I think it is a relevant criterion, why I have given the criterion the appropriate weight, and why the movie's characters are well developed. At this point we are discussing two distinct issues at different "levels." We are debating how to evaluate a particular movie and debating competing criteria of good movies.

Likewise, when discussing a practical ethical issue, we are discussing not only that particular issue but also underlying theoretical issues. We do not want to know only whether capital punishment deters crime, we also want to know whether deterrence is morally important, and, if so, just how important. When theorizing reaches a certain level or complexity, we begin to speak of someone's "having a theory." Ethical theories are simply formal and more systematic discussions of second-level, theoretical discussions. These are philosophers' efforts to identify the relevant moral criteria, decide the weight or significance of each criterion, and to offer some guidance about how to determine whether an action satisfies those criteria. In the next section, I will briefly outline some more familiar ethical theories. But before I do, let me first offer a warning. In thinking about ethical theories, we may be tempted to assume that people who hold the same theory will make the same practical ethical judgments, and that people who make the same practical ethical judgments will embrace the same theory. Not so. That is not true of any evaluative judgments. For instance, two people with similar criteria for good movies may differently evaluate *Fargo*, while two people who loved *Fargo* may have (somewhat) different criteria for good movies. Likewise for ethics. Two people with different ethical theories may nonetheless agree that abortion is morally permitted (or grossly immoral), while two adherents of the same moral theory may differently evaluate abortion. Knowing someone's theoretical commitments does not tell us precisely what actions she thinks are right or wrong. It tells us only how she thinks about moral issues – about her criteria of relevance and the weight she gives to them.

Main Types of Theory

Two broad classes of ethical theory – consequentialist and deontological – have shaped most people's understanding of ethics.

Consequentialists hold that we should choose the available action with the best overall consequences, while deontologists hold that we should act in ways circumscribed by moral rules or rights, and that these rules or rights are defined (at least partly) independently of consequences. Since this book includes a separate section on ETHICAL THEORIES, this exposition will be brief. Nonetheless, these descriptions should be sufficient to help you understand the broad outlines of each theory.

Consequentialism

Consequentialists claim that we are morally obligated to act in ways that produce the best consequences. It is not difficult to see why this is an appealing theory. It employs the same style of reasoning we use in purely prudential (wise, self-interested) decisions. If you are trying to prudently select a major, you will consider the available options, predict which one will likely lead to the best overall outcome, and then choose that major. If you are trying to decide to keep your present job or take a new one, you will consider consequences of each option (working conditions, location, salary, chance of advancement, how the change might alter your personal and family relations, etc.), and then choose the one with the best overall consequences.

Despite these similarities, prudence and morality are importantly different. Whereas prudence requires that we wisely advance only our own personal interests, consequentialism requires us to consider the interests of all affected. When facing a moral decision, we should consider available alternative actions, trace the likely consequences of each for all affected, and then select the one with the best overall consequences.

Of course, a consequentialist need not consider every consequence of an action, nor must she consider them all equally. Two consequences of my typing this introduction are that I am strengthening the muscles in my hands and increasing my eye–hand coordination. However, barring unusual circumstances, these are not morally relevant: they are neither a means to

nor a constituent of my or anyone else's welfare, happiness, or well-being. That is why they play no role in moral deliberation. However, different consequentialists profoundly disagree about whether or how much some consequences are morally relevant. That is why any adequate consequentialist theory must specify (a) which consequences are morally relevant (i.e., which we should consider when morally deliberating) and (b) how much weight we should give them.

Utilitarians, for instance, claim we should choose the option that maximizes "the greatest happiness of the greatest number." They also advocate complete equality: "each to count as one and no more than one." Of course we might disagree about exactly what it means to maximize the greatest happiness of the greatest number; still more, we might be unsure about how this is to be achieved. Act utilitarians claim that we determine the rightness of an action if we can decide which action, in those circumstances, would be most likely to promote the greatest happiness of the greatest number. Rule utilitarians reject the idea that moral decisions should be case-by-case (see Hooker, EUTHANASIA). On their view, we should decide not whether a *particular* action is likely to promote the greatest happiness of the greatest number, but whether a particular *type* of action would, if done by most people, promote the greatest happiness of the greatest number.

This theory is discussed in more detail by Vallentyne (ETHICAL THEORY).

Deontology

Deontological theories are most easily understood in contrast to consequentialist theories. Whereas consequentialists claim we should always strive to promote the best consequences, deontologists claim that our moral obligations – whatever they are – are in some ways independent of consequences. Thus, if I have obligations not to kill or steal or lie, those obligations are justified not simply on the ground that following such rules will always produce the best consequences.

That is why many people find deontological theories so attractive. For example, most of us would be offended if someone lied to us, even if the lie produced the greatest happiness for the greatest number. I would certainly be offended if someone killed me, even if my death might produce the greatest happiness for the greatest number (you use my kidneys to save two people's lives, my heart to save someone else's life, etc.) The rightness or wrongness of lying or killing cannot be explained, the deontologist claims, simply by its consequences. Of course, deontologists disagree about which rules are true and about how to determine these rules. Some claim abstract reason shows us how we should act (Kant 2002/1785). Others talk about discovering principles that are justified in *reflective equilibrium* (Rawls, e.g., in the selection on ECONOMIC JUSTICE), while some claim we should seek principles that might be adopted by an ideal observer (Arthur in WORLD HUNGER).

These theories are discussed in more detail by McNaughton and Rawling (ETHICAL THEORY).

Alternatives

There are numerous alternatives to these theories. To call them "alternatives" does not imply that they are inferior, only that they have not played the same role in shaping contemporary ethical thought. Two are especially worth mention since they have become highly influential in the past two decades; they also play pivotal roles in several essays in this book.

Virtue theory

Virtue theory predates both consequentialism and deontology as a formal theory. It was the dominant theory of the ancient Greeks, reaching its clearest expression in Aristotle's *Nicomachean Ethics*. For many centuries it was neither discussed nor advocated as a serious competitor. But by the late 1950s, it was starting to reappear in the philosophical literature (the history of this re-emergence is traced in the essays reprinted in Crisp and Slote 1997).

Much of the appeal of virtue theory arises from the perceived failings of the standard alternatives. Deontology and consequentialism, virtue theorists claim, put inadequate (or no) emphasis on the agent – on the ways she should *be*, or the kinds of *character* she should develop. Relatedly, they fail to give appropriate scope to personal judgment and put too much emphasis on following rules (whether deontological or consequentialistic).

Certainly on some readings of deontology and utilitarianism, it sounds as if advocates of these theories believed that a moral decision was the mindless application of a moral rule. If the rule says, "Be honest," then we should be honest. If the rule says: "Always act to promote the greatest happiness of the greatest number," then we need only figure out which action has the most desirable consequences, and then do it. Ethics thus seems to resemble math. The calculations may require patience and care, but they do not depend on judgment.

Many advocates of the standard theories find these objections by virtue theorists telling and, over the past two decades, have modified their respective theories to (partially) accommodate them. The result, says Rosalind Hursthouse, is "that the lines of demarcation between these three approaches have become blurred. . . . Deontology and utilitarianism are no longer perspicuously identified by describing them as emphasizing rules or consequences in contrast to character" (Hursthouse 1999: 4). Both put more emphasis on judgment and character. For instance, Hill, who is a deontologist, describes the proper attitude toward the ENVIRONMENT in a way that emphasizes excellence or character, while May and Strikwerda (SEXUAL AND RACIAL DISCRIMINATION), who do not generally embrace virtue theory, emphasize the need for men to feel shame for their complicity in the rape of women. However, although judgment and character may play an increasingly important role in contemporary versions of deontology or consequentialism, it does not play the central role it does in virtue theory. This is evident, for instance, in Hursthouse's discussion of ABORTION and in her essay on virtue ethics (ETHICAL THEORY). For a different view, see Doris (PUNISHMENT). He thinks any robust virtue theory rests on a flawed moral psychology.

Feminist theory

Historically most philosophers were men; most embraced the sexism of their respective cultures. Thus, it is not surprising that women's interests and perspectives played no role in the development of standard ethical theories. Does that mean these theories are useless? Or can they be salvaged? Can we merely prune Aristotle's explicit sexism from his theory and still have an Aristotelian theory that is adequate for a less sexist age? Can we remove Kant's sexism and have a non-sexist deontology?

In the early years of feminism, many thinkers thought so. They claimed that the standard ethical theories' emphasis on justice, equality, and fairness offer all the argumentative ammunition women need to claim their rightful place in the public world. Others were not so sure. Carol Gilligan (1982) argued that women have different moral experiences and different moral reasoning, and that these differences must be incorporated into our understanding of morality. She advocated an "Ethics of Care," which best exemplified women's experience and thinking. However, other feminists claimed this view too closely resembles old-fashioned views of women. What we need instead, they claim, are theories that have a keen awareness of gender and a concern to develop all people's unique human capacities (Jaggar 2000).

Observe the ways that issues concerning woman are discussed (SEXUAL AND RACIAL DISCRIMINATION, AFFIRMATIVE ACTION, and ABORTION, FREE SPEECH, and FAMILY AND REPRODUCTIVE TECHNOLOGY). See whether the reasons used differ from those employed in other essays. If so, how?

Conclusion

As you read the following essays, you will see how these different ways of thinking about ethics shape our deliberations about particular moral issues. Be alert to these theoretical differences. They will help you better understand the essays. Also, pay close attention to the section introductions. These highlight the theoretical issues that play a central role within that section.

References

Crisp, R. and Slote, M. A. (eds.) (1997) *Virtue Ethics*. Oxford: Oxford University Press.

Gilligan, C. (1982) *In a Different Voice: Psychological Theory and Women's Development*. Cambridge, MA: Harvard University Press.

Hursthouse, R. (1999) *On Virtue Ethics*. Oxford: Oxford University Press.

Jaggar, A. M. (2000) "Feminist Ethics." In H. LaFollette (ed.), *The Blackwell Guide to Ethical Theory*. Oxford: Blackwell Publishers, pp. 348–74.

Kant, I. (2002/1785) *Groundwork for the Metaphysics of Morals*. Oxford: Oxford University Press.

LaFollette, H. (1991) "The Truth in Ethical Relativism," *Journal of Social Philosophy* 20: 146–54.

Rachels, J. (1986) *The Elements of Moral Philosophy*. New York: Random House.

Scheffler, S. (1992) *Human Morality*. Oxford: Oxford University Press.

Singer, P. (1993) *Practical Ethics*, 2nd edn. Cambridge: Cambridge University Press.

Reading Philosophy

Reading philosophy differs from reading science fiction or the daily newspaper. The subjects are different; the purposes are different; the styles are different. Science fiction attempts to transport us imaginatively to distant worlds of larger-than-life heroes and villains. It aims to entertain us, to divert us from the doldrums of our daily lives, and perhaps even to empower us: having seen the glories or evils of worlds not yet experienced, we may be better equipped to live in our everyday world. Science fiction achieves these aims by spinning a convincing narrative of creatures living in previously unknown worlds; it evokes our imaginative powers through expressive language.

Newspapers inform us of significant political, social, cultural, economic, and climatic events. Once we are informed, we can presumably make better decisions about our leaders, our finances, and our social lives. The media typically achieves these aims by giving us the facts, just the facts. They usually present these facts in a pithy writing style.

Philosophers have neither the direct aims of the journalist nor the airy aims of the science fiction novelist. Their primary function is not to inform or to inspire, but to help us explore competing ideas and the reasons for them. The philosopher achieves these aims by employing a writing style that tends to be neither pithy nor expressive. The style likely differs from any to which you are accustomed.

Philosophical Language

While the reporter and the novelist write for the public, philosophers usually write for one other. Thus, while most newspapers and some science fiction are written for an eighth grade audience, philosophical essays are written for people with university training. That is why you will need a more robust vocabulary to understand a philosophical essay than you need to understand the latest novel or a column in the local paper. So keep a dictionary handy to look up "ordinary" words you may not yet know. You will also face an additional problem with these essays' vocabularies. Philosophy, like all academic disciplines, employs specialized terms. Some of these are familiar words with specialized meanings; others are words unique to the discipline. To fully grasp philosophical writing, you will need to understand both. Do not despair. Often you can roughly determine the term's meaning from its context. If, after doing your best, you still cannot understand its meaning, ask your instructor. Most of these words can be explained in a clear, non-technical way. You can also consult the on-line philosophical dictionary (see the link on this book's supporting web page: http://www.stpt.usf.edu/hhl/eip/).

Philosophical writing also tends to be more complex than the writings of reporters and novelists. Occasionally it is more complex than it needs to be: the author may not know how to write clearly. Sometimes the essay *seems* more complex than it is since the author wrote decades or even centuries ago, when most writers penned long, intricate sentences. You can often break down these long sentences into their component parts, e.g., by treating a semicolon as a period. You may also need to reread the essay several times to get a sense of the author's rhythm, much in the way that you may need to listen to a musician several times before you find it easy to appreciate her music.

Often, though, the writing is complex simply because the ideas expressed are complex. We cannot always render profound thoughts into intellectual pabulum. The only way to grasp such essays is to generally improve one's reading skills, in large part by reading and rereading essays until you understand them.

The Centrality of Argument

Philosophical writing is complex also because it contains and evaluates *arguments*. Philosophers forward their own arguments and critique the arguments of others. "Arguments," in this context, have a particular philosophical sense: An argument is a connected series of statements with some central claim the writer is trying to defend (the conclusion), supported by evidence (the premises) the author offers on behalf of the conclusion. The evidence philosophers use varies. They may proffer empirical data, forward imaginative examples, pose suggestions, and critique alternatives. Make certain you have identified the author's conclusion and her premises before you evaluate her work. Do not

fall into the trap of judging that an argument is bad simply because you dislike the conclusion.

This tendency to dismiss views we dislike helps explain philosophers' concern with arguments. Each of us is constantly bombarded with claims. Some of these claims are true, some false. Some offer sage wisdom; some, dreadful advice. How do we distinguish the true from the false, the wise from the stupid – especially when the topic is some controversial moral, political, and social issue? How do we know the proper moral response to abortion, world hunger, homosexuality, and affirmative action? Do we just pick the one we like? The one our parents, preachers, teachers, friends, or society advocate? Often that is exactly what we do. But we shouldn't. Even a cursory glance at history reveals that many horrendous evils were committed by those who embraced their views steadfastly and uncritically. Most Nazis, slaveholders, and commanders of Russian gulags did not think they were immoral; they assumed they were doing the right thing. They simply accepted their society's views without subjecting them to rational scrutiny. That we should not do – at least not if we are responsible individuals. After all, people's lives, welfare, and happiness may depend on our decisions, and the decisions of people like us.

What is our option? We can look for claims supported by the best evidence. We should examine the *reasons* offered for alternative beliefs. Doing so will not insure that we make the best decision, but it will increase the odds that we do. It will lessen the possibility that we make highly objectionable decisions, decisions we will later come to regret. Philosophers offer arguments for their views to help themselves and others make better decisions.

Most people are unaccustomed to scrutinizing arguments. Since most of us were taught to believe what our parents, our priests, our teachers, and our pals told us, we are disinclined to consider the arguments of others seriously, or to rationally criticize our own views. Moreover, although all of us have offered some arguments for our views, we have rarely done so with the care and depth that are the staples of good philosophy. Philosophers strive to offer a clear, unambiguous conclusion supported by reasons that even those disinclined to believe their conclusions are likely to find persuasive. That is not to say that philosophers never make bad arguments or say stupid things. Of course we do. However, it is to say that the explicit aim of philosophy is a *clear, careful assessment of the reasons for and against our and others' views*. That is why a key to understanding philosophy is being able to spot arguments, and then to critique them. That is something you will learn, at least in part, by practice.

Looking at Others' Views

Since part of the task of defending one's view is to show that it is rationally superior to alternatives, a philosopher usually not only (a) provides arguments for her view, she will also (b) respond to criticisms of that view, and (c) consider alternative perspectives. Sometimes those other views and criticisms are advocated by a specific philosopher whose work the author cites. Often, though, the view the author discusses is not that of any particular philosopher, but rather the view of some hypothetical advocate of a position (e.g., conservatism or theism or pro-life). This is often double trouble for a student. You may be unfamiliar with the view being discussed. Since you do not know if the view has been accurately represented, you cannot judge if the criticisms (and responses to criticisms) are telling. Worse, you may have trouble distinguishing the author's view from the views of those she discusses. Many students do.

If you read it quickly, and without concentrating, you will probably be confused. However, usually you can spot this practice if you read the essay carefully. After all, most authors give argumentative road signs that show when they are arguing for a view and when they are stating or discussing someone else's view. Of course the student may also miss these signs because she does not know what to look for. But simply knowing that this is a common argumentative strategy should lessen the difficulty. You can also look for specific cues.

For instance, authors who discuss another's views frequently use the third person to suggest that another person is speaking (or arguing). At other times the author may explicitly say something like "others may disagree . . . " and then go on to discuss someone else's view. In still other cases, the distinction may be more subtle, likely picked up only after carefully reading the essay several times. In the end there is no single or simple way to distinguish the author's view from other views the author is discussing. However, if you read the essays carefully, using the general strategy just outlined, you will increase the likelihood that you will not be confused.

The Rational Consequences of What We Say

The philosopher's discussion of examples or cases – especially fictional cases – sometimes confuses students. The use of such cases, though, builds upon a central pillar of philosophical argument, namely, that we should consider the implications or rational consequences of our beliefs and actions. The following fictional example explains what I mean. Suppose a teacher gives you an "A" because she likes you, and gives Robert – your worst enemy – an "F" because she dislikes him. You might be ecstatic that you received an "A"; you may also be thrilled to know that your worst enemy failed. However, do you want to say that what the teacher did was morally acceptable? No. There are implications of saying that, implications you would likely be loathe to accept.

If you said that the teacher's *reason* for giving those grades was legitimate, you would be saying, in effect, that teachers should be able to give students they like good grades and students they dislike bad grades. Thus, you would be rationally committed to saying that if you had a teacher who disliked you, then she could legitimately fail you. That, of course, is a consequence you are unwilling to accept. Therefore, you (and we) have reason to suspect that your original acceptance of the teacher's grading scheme was inappropriate. This is a common argumentative strategy. Trace the implications

– the rational consequences – of a person's *reasons* for action and then see if you (or others) would be willing to accept those consequences.

A Final Word

These suggestions will not make reading philosophical essays easy. My hope, though, is that it will make it easier. In the end the key to success is practice. If you have never read philosophical arguments before, you are unlikely to be able to glance at an essay and understand it: you will likely miss the central idea, its relation to alternatives, and you will almost certainly fail to comprehend the author's argument. To fully understand the essay, you must read the assignment carefully, and more than once. Most essays are too difficult in style and content for you to grasp in a single reading. Not even most professional philosophers can do that.

Here is a good strategy. Read the essay once. Identify confusing or unusual terms. Try to get a general sense of the argument: what is the point the author wants to establish, what reason does she offer for this claim? What arguments does she discuss? Identify the points about which you are still unclear. After you have a general sense of the essay, reread it more carefully. Strive for a thorough understanding of the argument. Come to class prepared to ask for help in clarifying any remaining confusions about the author's views. If you are accustomed to reading an assignment once – and then only quickly – this expectation will seem overly demanding. Yet, it is important that you learn to read carefully and critically.

Herein lies the key to success: persistence and practice. There may be times you find the reading so difficult that you will be tempted to stop, to wait for the instructor to explain it. Yield not to temptation. Press on. It is better and more rewarding to understand the reading for yourself. Think, for a moment, about what happens when someone "explains" a joke that you could (with time and effort) have understood on your own. It spoils the joke.

Learning to read more complex essays is a skill, and, like any skill, it is not acquired all at once or without effort. Little in life that is valuable is acquired effortlessly. Getting in physical shape requires vigorous exercise and more than a little perspiration. Establishing and maintaining a vibrant relationship requires effort, understanding, and sacrifice. Learning to play a musical instrument does not come quickly, and is, at times, exceedingly frustrating. Learning to read sophisticated essays is no different. If you persist, however, you will find that with time it becomes easier to read and understand philosophical essays. The payoff is substantial and enduring. You will better understand the day's reading assignment, which will most assuredly improve your grade. But more important, you will also expand your vocabulary and hone your reading skills. You will increase your ability to understand more complex and important writing. Most of the world's great books are inaccessible to those with minimal reading and argumentative skills. Learning to read methodically, critically, and in depth will expand your mental horizons. It will increase your understanding of others' views. And it will enhance your ability to refine and defend your own views.

PART I

Ethical Theory

Ethical Theory

In THEORIZING ABOUT ETHICS, I briefly outlined several ethical theories. In this section, new to the third edition, I include essays that explain and defend the three most prominent ones: Deontology, Consequentialism, and Virtue Theory.

Peter Vallentyne explains the basic forms of consequentialism. He begins by describing the most familiar versions: act and rule utilitarianism. Both forms claim that what is right is determined by the consequences on people's happiness or well-being. The idea is one that, in various ways and to various degrees, plays an important role in ordinary moral deliberation and in many of these essays. However, as you will see, that role is often not explicitly stated. Many authors discuss and evaluate the effects of an action or policy. However, they rarely do so in ways that specifically appeal to utilitarian principles. The one exception is Hooker's discussion of "Rule Utilitarianism and Euthanasia."

To explore the subtleties of the theories, Vallentyne explains – and responds to – a variety of objections to and questions about utilitarianism; this helps to illuminate several discussions of particular practical issues. For instance, one common criticism of act utilitarianism (and of consequentialism more generally) is that the theory is too demanding: that "under most realistic conditions, it typically requires agents to make significant sacrifices of their own wellbeing to maximize moral goodness." You will see this concern at play in several essays, most especially in John Arthur's criticism of Singer's claim that we are morally obligated to help the poor of the world, even if we thereby make ourselves substantially worse off (WORLD HUNGER).

A second common criticism of utilitarianism is that it "leaves no room for agents to favor their loved ones or others with whom they have special relationships. If one can save either one's own child (or friend) or a stranger, one is required to produce the morally best consequences." On this objection, common to most deontological theories, utilitarianism fails to acknowledge that individuals have *options* they are morally permitted to pursue, even when they thereby fail to maximize the good. This challenge is explicitly discussed by Rachels (FAMILY AND REPRODUCTIVE TECHNOLOGY). A variant of this criticism – the claim that utilitarians are insufficiently concerned about human choices – is used by Husak to criticize current drug laws (PATERNALISM AND RISK).

A third objection is that utilitarians are unconcerned about the equality of distributions (e.g., of economic goods) and, thus, cannot give appropriate moral attention to the plight of those who are especially disadvantaged. This and other objections can be adequately met, Vallentyne argues, only by jettisoning utilitarianism and its concern for total happiness or well-being. Act and rule *consequentialism* are more viable theories. They have the virtues of utilitarianism (focusing on the consequences of our action), without many of its problems. In particular, they specify that in our quest to bring about the best outcomes, we must find ways of accommodating considerations of equality and desert.

McNaughton and Rawling explain the second major ethical theory: deontology. They identify three key features of such theories: options, constraints, and special relationships. Deontologists claim that individuals have some options to pursue their own projects and interests, even if they thereby fail to promote the good (a view explicitly endorsed by Arthur in WORLD HUNGER). Deontologists also claim that individuals are morally constrained against harming others, even if in so doing they could thereby promote more good. Often this idea is expressed in the language of rights: that individuals have rights that limit what could be done to them, no matter what the benefits (or costs) to others. This idea plays a central role in many of the issues we discuss. For instance, Anderson argues that commercial surrogacy treats children and women as mere commodities and thereby violates moral constraints against their being used by others. The third element is the moral significance of special relationships: the claim that people can (or should) be more concerned about their friends and family than about others – even if others have more substantial and more pressing needs. This is an issue Rachels explicitly discusses in FAMILY AND REPRODUCTIVE TECHNOLOGY.

Despite these commonalities, deontologists disagree about exactly which constraints and options are in place, to whom they apply, and

precisely how strong they are. For instance, Hawk argues that the moral constraint against killing others is absolute. That is why he claims WAR is never morally permissible. Clearly most deontologists disagree. To that extent, they deny that constraints are absolute. If constraints are not absolute, it is incumbent upon the theorists to explain precisely when other moral considerations – say, the consequences of our actions – can override constraints against killing, truth telling, etc.

Other deontologists – most especially Tom Regan – argue that the same constraints that bar us from harming humans also bar us from harming non-human animals, e.g., by eating them or using them in experiments. Many deontologists would disagree. This illustrates my earlier claim (THEORIZING ABOUT ETHICS) that it is best not to think of theories as prescriptions for moral action, but rather as describing different ways of reasoning about morality.

Hursthouse describes the third major theory: virtue ethics. Virtue theory differs significantly from the other standard theories. While consequentialists and deontologists are concerned about what people morally ought to do, virtue theory is primarily concerned about how each of us should live. Virtue theorists hold that any life worth living must be one in which people inculcate the virtues. The excellent person is one who not only does what the virtuous person does, but does so for the right reasons. She must also enjoy doing it.

As you can see, this is a very different kind of theory. So much so, that you might wonder if it will give us much, if any, guidance in knowing how to act. Many virtue theorists think it does. For instance, in her essay on abortion, Hursthouse claims that the current debate over abortion, being dominated by consequentialists and deontologists, unduly narrows the moral questions. She claims we should be asking not only what a woman should be permitted to do, but what a virtuous person would do. In a somewhat similar way, Hill argues that thinking about the virtues (human excellences) could lead one to cherish non-sentient nature in ways that could not be defended on standard ethical grounds (ENVIRONMENT).

At least one author has serious misgivings about the adequacy of virtue ethics. Doris (PUNISHMENT) claims that our best empirical evidence shows that few if any humans have the developed character traits or virtues which are the centerpiece of this ethic. That suggests that few if any people can develop robust virtues. Therefore, trying to encourage people to do so is counterproductive. It would be far better, he argues, if we worked to change our environments in ways that are likely to make us act better.

These three essays do not cover all the theoretical territory. However, they do provide a broad map of the principal theories. And they do so in a way that helps the reader better see the interrelationship between theory and practice.

1

Consequentialism

Peter Vallentyne

Introduction

The three main general approaches to moral theory are consequentialism, deontology, and virtue theory. I shall describe and assess consequentialism. First, however, I shall make a few background remarks on morality.

Morality is normative. It is concerned with how the world should be – as opposed to how it is. More specifically, it is normative in the sense of being concerned with what is permissible (right, acceptable) and with what is good (desirable) and bad (undesirable). There are, however, many normative perspectives. There is, for example, permissibility and goodness from the perspective of rational self-interest, legal permissibility, and aesthetic goodness. Throughout, unless otherwise specified, permissibility and goodness should be understood as moral permissibility and goodness.

Morality can assess many different kinds of things: actions, states of affairs, character traits, social institutions, policies, and so on. To simplify our task, we will focus on the moral assessment of *actions*, which is arguably the most central form of moral assessment. Moreover, we shall focus primarily on the moral *permissibility* (as opposed to goodness) of actions. An action is

permissible if and only if it is acceptable (not wrong) to perform it.[1] Our central question, then, is, "What determines whether an action is morally permissible?"

Act Consequentialism holds that the permissibility of an action is determined by how good its consequences are. For example, if shooting an innocent person would have very good overall consequences compared to its alternatives (e.g., because it saves millions of lives), then it is permissible to do so, but it is not permissible to do so if it would have relatively very bad consequences. We shall explore this and related ideas.

Act Utilitarianism

Act Consequentialism holds that the permissibility of an action is based on how good its consequences are compared with those of its feasible alternatives. The idea is that, in a given choice situation, an agent has some number of actions that she can perform. These actions are the set of feasible alternatives and each alternative action has different consequences. The consequences include *everything* that will happen *in the world* if the action is performed. These include events in the distant future and in distant places. Suppose, for example, that if I help a young child with her homework, she will go on to become President of the United States, avert nuclear war, and thereby ensure that a certain island still exists a thousand years from now. These are all part of the consequences of my action. The effects on everything everywhere are part of its consequences. One qualification is in order: Given that the effects of actions are typically probabilistic, the consequences of an action must be understood as specifying the probability of various states of affairs (10 percent chance of peace and 90 percent chance of war if I do this). For simplicity, however, we will typically consider simple cases where the actions produce their effects with certainty.

The historically best-known Act Consequentialist theory is *Act Utilitarianism*. It arose primarily in Great Britain during the 1600s and 1700s, when social thinkers were beginning to challenge the traditional social, economic, and political systems (e.g., monarchies) and their justifications in terms of God's commands. The utilitarian emphasis was on designing and justifying social structures in terms of promoting human *well-being*, where a person's *well-being* is a matter of how well her life goes for her overall. (Utilitarians use "utility" as a synonym for well-being, but we'll generally use the latter term.) The most famous proponents are Jeremy Bentham (1748–1832), and John Stuart Mill (1806–73).[2]

Act Utilitarianism consists of the following two claims:

1. *Maximizing Act Consequentialism*: An action is permissible if and only if its consequences are morally maximally good (i.e., at least as good as those of its feasible alternatives).
2. *Utilitarian Value*: One state of affairs is morally at least as good as another if and only if the total individual well-being it includes is at least as great as the total individual well-being included in the other.[3]

We can clarify the nature of these claims by considering the following example, where there are just three feasible actions and just three people in the world:

Table 1.1 Consequences for well-being: Example 1

	Jane	Mary	John	Total
Action 1	40	30	20	90
Action 2	30	20	40	90
Action 3	0	10	20	30

Here, for example, Action 1 produces 40 units of well-being (e.g., happiness) for Jane, 30 for Mary, and 20 units for John. Utilitarian Value assumes that individual well-being can be measured on such a quantitative scale (which is controversial, and will be discussed below). Moreover, it tells us that the moral value of actions is determined by the *total* well-being, and thus we can consider only the total column in this example. Maximizing Act Consequentialism then tells us that Action 3 is impermissible (wrong) because it is less good than Action 1 (and also less good than Action 2). Action 1 and Action 2 are each judged permissible, because each produces as much well-being as possible (90). Because each is permissible, neither is obligatory (required). Each is optional (permitted but not required). The agent is required to choose either Action 1 or Action 2, but she is morally free to decide which.

We shall assess Maximizing Act Consequentialism below. First, however, we shall assess Utilitarian Value. One attractive feature of this view is that it holds that the moral goodness of states of affairs depends on how well people's lives go (i.e., their well-being). More specifically, it holds that making everyone better off makes things morally better. A second attractive feature is that everyone's well-being is given equal consideration. All individuals – rich or poor, man or woman, black or white – are given the same weight. In the above example, for instance, the well-being of Jane, Mary, and John counts equally, no matter what their race, religion, sex, etc.[4] It's important to note that Utilitarian Value leaves open what determines a person's well-being. Early utilitarians (e.g., Bentham) took well-being to be something like the quantitative net balance of pleasure over pain, but this takes an unduly narrow view of the types of joy and sorrow that are relevant for well-being. Later utilitarians (e.g., Mill) distinguished between higher and lower pleasures and emphasized that the quality of the pleasure and pains must also be factored in. For example, because humans typically have more sophisticated cognitive faculties, they typically are capable of much higher-quality pleasures and pains. Thus, in Mill's famous words (in Ch. 2 of *Utilitarianism*), "It is <typically> better to be a human being dissatisfied than a pig satisfied." Contemporary utilitarians tend to take a still broader view of well-being. They claim that happiness matters a lot, but it is not the only thing that matters for well-being. For most people, decreasing their happiness just slightly and significantly increasing their accomplishments and the quality of their relationships with others makes their lives go better. Consider, for example, a man who is very happy, but doesn't know that his wife, whom he adores, doesn't love him and cheats on him regularly. Wouldn't his life be better if his wife loved him and didn't cheat on him, even if his happiness (for other reasons) were slightly lower? Well-being, on this account, is not *purely subjective* in the sense that it does not depend solely on the individual's state of mind.

The issues are complex, and I'll here simply mention two of the main accounts of well-being that have been developed. *Preference Utilitarianism* claims that well-being is a matter of how well a person's informed self-regarding preferences are satisfied. This is partly subjective (the preferences) and partly objective (how well the world satisfies those preferences). The husband in the above case would probably prefer to be slightly less happy and have his wife love him more and be faithful to him. *Perfectionistic (or Ideal) Utilitarianism* claims that there are some things that are objectively good for a person even if she doesn't care about them (in her preferences). For example, one might claim that increasing a person's accomplishments or positive intimate relationships makes her life go better even if she doesn't care about them. In what follows, we'll leave open what the correct account of well-being is.

Utilitarian Value faces several important objections. One is that it presupposes that well-being can be *quantified very precisely*. In the above example, for instance, it does not merely assume (as is plausible) that there are facts about when Jane has more well-being (e.g., that Action 1 gives her more well-being than Action 2). Utilitarian Value also presupposes that there are facts about *how much more* well-being Jane has (e.g., that the difference in well-being for Jane between Action 1 (40 units) and Action 2 (30 units) is less than the difference in well-being for her between Action 2 (30 units) and Action 3 (0 units). Moreover, it further assumes that well-being is *interpersonally comparable* in the sense that there are facts about how one person's increase in well-being compares with that of another. Utilitarian Value presupposes, for instance, that, in moving from Action 2 to Action 1, Jane gains less well-being (10 units) than John loses (20 units). It's not clear, however, that such precise quantitative measurement of well-being is possible even in principle. Of course, the possibility of such measurement depends on how exactly well-being is understood. Defenders of Utilitarian Value must thus supply a clear account of well-being that is quantitatively measurable and interpersonally comparable. If no such account can be given, then Utilitarian Value rests on a false presupposition.

A second objection to Utilitarian Value is that, because it focuses solely on *total* well-being, it is *insensitive to how well-being is distributed among individuals*. To see this, consider the following example:

Table 1.2 Consequences for Well-being: Example 2

	Jane	Mary	John	Total
Action 1	0	0	99	99
Action 2	33	33	33	99
Action 3	50	10	20	80

Here, for example, Action 1 produces 0 units of well-being for Jane and Mary and 99 units of well-being for John. Utilitarian Value tells us that the moral value of these actions is determined by the total well-being, and thus we can consider only the total column. Action 1 and Action 2 are equally good (with a total of 99 each) and each is morally better than Action 3. Let us here grant that Action 3 is worse than the other two. Is it true that the first two actions are equally good? They have the same total, but well-being is more equally distributed in Action 2. If no one has any special claim to more well-being (e.g., because of working harder), the more equal distribution, it seems, is better. Utilitarian Value, however, leaves no room for distributive considerations such as equality or priority for those who are worse off. Given that some kind of distributive consideration seems relevant, this is a very significant objection to utilitarianism.

Utilitarians have a partial reply to the charge that they give no priority to the worse off and no consideration to equality. They appeal to *decreasing marginal well-being (utility)* from resources (or money). The idea is that, for a given person, the increase in well-being that results from having an additional unit of the resource (e.g., additional apple or additional dollar) decreases the more resources that individual has. Thus, for example, if a person has no money, acquiring a dollar gives a significant benefit in well-being (e.g., makes the difference between starving and not starving), but, if that person already has a million dollars, acquiring an additional dollar has a trivial impact on well-being. Given that individuals have roughly the same dispositions for decreasing marginal well-being, this means that, all else being equal, utilitarians will favor (because it will increase total well-being) shifting resources from the rich to the poor (and thus favor equality). Of course, there are other factors, such as incentive effects, that must be factored in as well, and they may push in the opposite direction. (For example, providing aid to the poor may reduce their incentive to work, and their reduction in work may reduce the total well-being.) Still, in light of the roughly equal decreasing marginal well-being of all, utilitarianism has some significant tendency to favor more equal distributions of resources over less equal ones.

The important point to note, however, is that equality of resources (e.g., money) is not equality of well-being. A person who regularly suffers severe depression may have the same amount of money (and other resources) as someone with a joyful disposition, but her level of well-being will be very different. Thus, utilitarianism's sensitivity to the distribution of resources does not automatically make it suitably sensitive to the distribution of well-being.

A third and related objection to Utilitarian Value is that it is *insensitive to what choices individuals make*. It doesn't care, for example, what good or bad deeds an individual performs. Everyone's well-being counts equally. Thus, for example, it views 100 units of well-being for a do-gooder and 0 units for an evildoer as equally as good as 0 units for the do-gooder and 100 for the evildoer (since they have the same total). There is no room for some individuals *deserving* more than others because of their choices.

In light of the last two objections, many consequentialists have abandoned Utilitarian Value. Instead, they appeal to some other theory of moral value (of what makes one state of affairs morally better than another). Their preferred theory of value might be sensitive equality of well-being, how well well-being matches desert, or even appeal to considerations that have nothing to do with well-being (e.g., the promotion of knowledge and beauty). In abandoning Utilitarian Value, such consequentialists are abandoning utilitarianism, but they are not abandoning the Act Consequentialist idea that the permissibility of actions is determined by how good their consequences are. In what follows, then, we shall assume that some suitable theory of value has been adopted, but leave open its exact content. We shall thus focus on consequentialism in general (as opposed to the utilitarian version thereof).

Act Consequentialism

Act Utilitarianism, we saw above, consists of Utilitarian Value plus the following thesis:

Maximizing Act Consequentialism: An action is permissible if and only if its consequences are morally maximally good (i.e., at least as good as those of its feasible alternatives).[5]

We shall now focus on this principle (which leaves open how moral goodness is determined).

Maximizing Act Consequentialism has two main attractive features. First, it is hardheaded and focuses on what the consequences of actions will be. It rightly holds that the permissibility of an action depends on how morally good its effects would be. Second, Maximizing Act Consequentialism requires agents to do the best they can. It requires them to perform the morally best action (in terms of consequences) that they can. Something about that seems right.

Maximizing Act Consequentialism faces, however, several important objections. One is that it is impossible, or at least counterproductive, to calculate the consequences of one's actions each time one makes a choice. To do this adequately, after all, one would have to have knowledge of all the consequences of one's actions for the entire world for all of time. No one has anything close to this knowledge, and thus it is practically impossible to apply a Maximizing Act Consequentialist principle with any reliability. This objection, however, is easily met. First, note that Maximizing Act Consequentialism is not a *decision procedure* that agents are supposed to follow consciously when making choices. It is instead a *criterion of permissibility*. It specifies the conditions that determine whether an action is permissible. Thus, for example, an agent might steal someone's yacht with the sole aim of getting rich by selling it. If the yacht belongs to terrorists who were going to use it to kill thousands of people, this action might have the morally best consequences, and thus be judged permissible. The fact that the agent was not consciously attempting to accomplish the moral good is not deemed relevant.

This reply, however, does not get Maximizing Act Consequentialism completely off the hook. After all, agents should at least sometimes consciously reflect upon what will have the best consequences, and, given their limited time and information, this seems practically impossible or counterproductive. Given all the needed information, for example, agents could spend all their time gathering and processing information and never make a substantive choice. Maximizing Act Consequentialists have, however, an answer to this problem. It is that we should adopt various rules of thumb (e.g., don't kill, don't steal,

don't lie), the application of which generally produce the best results. Under normal circumstances, there is no need to perform consequentialist calculations. Indeed, to do so will normally be wrong (since it will waste time and not produce the best consequences). Instead, one typically just applies the rules of thumb. It is only in special circumstances – in which one has special reason to think that one's choice will have unusual or unusually important consequences – that one should perform consequentialist calculations. Of course, agents will make lots of mistakes (i.e., perform impermissible actions), but this is just a fact of life. Morality, consequentialists claim, is very complex, and human beings have only limited time and knowledge. It is therefore not surprising that we often make mistakes. We should simply do the best we can.

This reply, I believe, adequately meets the objection. The next objection, however, is more powerful. It claims that Maximizing Act Consequentialism is *too demanding* in that it typically judges permissible only a very small percentage of an agent's feasible options. Indeed, if there is just one action that has the best consequences, there will be just one action that is permissible. Assuming (as we shall) that ties in moral value are relatively rare, then there will typically be only a few permissible actions in any given choice situation. There are two aspects of the demandingness objection. One is that, under most realistic conditions, it typically requires agents to make significant sacrifices of their own well-being to maximize moral goodness. The objection here is *not* that Maximizing Act Consequentialism *sometimes* requires agents to make significant sacrifices; all plausible moral theories have this feature. Any plausible theory, for example, will typically judge it impermissible to steal a million dollars, even though one can get away with it and would greatly benefit from the result. The objection here is that Maximizing Act Consequentialism *frequently* requires significant sacrifices from agents. It holds that typically it is wrong to spend money (e.g., for restaurants, clothes, or CDs) or time (e.g., watching TV, talking with friends) for one's own enjoyment, since morally better consequences can be obtained by using this money or time in other ways (e.g., helping the needy). Of course, such activities are not always wrong, since the most effective way of promoting moral goodness typically involves occasionally pampering oneself (e.g., to recharge one's batteries). Most of the time, however, Maximizing Act Consequentialism judges it impermissible to devote more than minimal time or resources to oneself.

A second aspect of the demandingness objection is that Maximizing Act Consequentialism leaves no room for agents to favor their loved ones or others with whom they have special relationships. If one can save either one's own child (or friend) or a stranger, one is required to produce the morally best consequences. There is no room (except in rare cases of ties in goodness) to choose among various permissible options and favor one's loved ones.

In light of the demandingness objection, some consequentialists have rejected Maximizing Act Consequentialism in favor of:

Satisficing Act Consequentialism: An action is permissible if and only if its consequences are morally adequate.

The idea is that morality requires that the consequences be adequate but not that they be maximally good. There are different kinds of criteria for adequacy. Consequences might be judged adequate if they are better than those of at least 50 percent of the alternatives, or if they do not make things worse than doing nothing. We shall not explore the important task of developing plausible criteria of adequacy. The important point is that, as long as the criterion requires significantly less than the best consequences, there will be significantly more moral freedom for agents to promote their own well-being or that of their loved ones. As long as the criterion of adequacy is sufficiently weak, the objection of demandingness can be avoided.

Let us therefore focus on the following broader class of theories:

Act Consequentialism: An action is permissible if and only if its consequences are morally good enough.

Maximizing Act Consequentialism and Satisficing Act Consequentialism are each forms of Act Consequentialism. The former hold that only the best possible consequences are good enough, whereas the latter hold that adequate consequences are good enough.

Act Consequentialism is subject to the objection that it gives little protection to individuals from gross interference from others. It judges it permissible to kill, torture, lie to, and steal from innocent individuals, whenever this produces sufficiently good outcomes. All that matters is the overall result. If it is good enough, then it is permissible to do whatever it takes to produce that result. The ends can justify any means. Nothing is ruled out in principle.[6] Most of us recoil at this idea. Even assuming that there is some kind of duty to promote good consequences, surely there are limits on the permissible means of how we treat others.

Of course, things are not quite so straightforward. Typically, treating people in horrible ways (killing, torturing, etc.) has very bad consequences. For example, it will cause people in general to fear being a victim of abuse. Thus, as a rule of thumb, Act Consequentialism will not favor such treatment. It will be only under special circumstances that Act Consequentialism will judge such treatment permissible. If circumstances are truly extraordinary (e.g., it is necessary to kill an innocent person to save 100,000 innocent people), then perhaps it is not wrong to do so.

Nonetheless, Act Consequentialism faces a problem here. Let us grant for the sake of argument that, under truly extraordinary circumstances, it is permissible to treat innocents in horrible ways and that, as a rule of thumb, Act Consequentialists will not favor gross mistreatment of individuals. The important point is that, all else being equal, Act Consequentialism will, for example, judge it permissible to torture and kill *one* innocent person when this is the only way to avoid *two* innocent people from being comparably tortured and killed by others. Of course, in practice Act Consequentialists will apply rules of thumb and be cautious about torturing and killing innocents. The point here is that the circumstances under which Act

Consequentialism judges it permissible to engage in such abuses is not limited to rare and extraordinary cases of avoiding social catastrophe. Most of us doubt that the ends justify the means as frequently as Act Consequentialism says they do.

Constrained Act Consequentialism and Rule Consequentialism

In response to the above criticism about the ends not always justifying the means, one might consider adopting the following modification:

Constrained Act Consequentialism: An action is permissible if and only if, of those actions that satisfy certain specified constraints, it has consequences that are sufficiently morally good.

Here we suppose that there are some independently supplied constraints that actions must respect. They might rule out, for example, killing and harming innocents, lying, breaking promises and agreements, and theft. These constraints might be based on the rights of individuals or they might have some other source.

With an appropriate set of constraints, Constrained Act Consequentialism avoids the problem of readily sacrificing individuals for the greater moral good. Moreover, if it takes a non-maximizing form, it avoids the problem of being excessively demanding of agents. More generally, it can capture at least the broad outlines of commonsense morality. We have some obligation to promote moral goodness, but we are left a fair amount of liberty in how we do so. We are not frequently required to make major sacrifices of our own well-being and are typically permitted to give special treatment to our friends and loved ones. Moreover, the ends do not always justify the means: there are some constraints on the permissible ways of promoting the moral good.

The important point to note is that Constrained Act Consequentialism is not a form of Act Consequentialism. It is rather a mixed theory: It has a deontological component (the constraints) and a consequentialist component (the duty to promote the good). To see that it is not a form of Act Consequentialism, it suffices to note that it sometimes judges impermissible the action with the best consequences. Suppose, for example, that all else is equal, and that, by killing one innocent person, you could save ten innocent people from being killed by a terrorist. We may suppose here that it is morally better that one innocent person be killed than that ten innocent people (with comparable lives) are killed. Thus, killing one innocent person has the best outcome, but Constrained Act Consequentialism judges it impermissible. This is, of course, just an example of the fact that it rejects the view that the ends always justify the means.

If one accepts Constrained Act Consequentialism, then one is a *deontic pluralist* in that one holds that there is more than one fundamental moral consideration for determining what is permissible. One such consideration is how well an action promotes the moral value of the consequences, but another is whether the action respects certain deontological constraints. Many people find such pluralism plausible, but Act Consequentialists do not. Although they can allow that there may be many considerations that are relevant for moral goodness, Act Consequentialists insist that the only moral consideration relevant for moral permissibility is how well moral goodness is promoted. Thus, the belief that there are some deontological constraints on how the good may be promoted has led some to reject Act Consequentialism.

So far, we have focused on *Act* Consequentialism. It grounds the permissibility of actions on their consequences. We shall now consider a form of consequentialism that appeals to the consequences of adopting (normative) *rules* (as opposed to actions). Such rules consist of practical dos and don'ts, such as "Never tell a lie," "Keep your promises," and more complex variations. Consider, then:

Rule Maximizing Consequentialism: An action is permissible if and only if it conforms to rules that, if generally followed (internalized, upheld, etc.), would have consequences that are at least as good as any feasible alternative set of rules.

Rule Maximizing Consequentialism does not assess actions on the basis of the value of their consequences. Instead, it assesses them on the basis of their compliance with selected rules, and it selects rules on the basis of the value of the consequences of their being generally followed (internalized, upheld, etc.). Rule Maximizing Consequentialism has the potential to avoid all the objections raised above. Because it does not assume Utilitarian Value, it can be sensitive to distributive considerations of various sorts (e.g., equality or desert). Because the rules with the best consequences are likely to leave agents a reasonable amount of moral freedom, Rule Maximizing Consequentialism will typically not require excessive sacrifices from agents and will leave them some significant freedom to favor their loved ones. Finally, because the rules with the best consequences are likely to give a certain basic protection to agents against interference from others, Rule Maximizing Consequentialism will recognize various constraints on how individuals may be treated.

Does this seem too good to be true? Many philosophers believe so. The main objection to Rule Maximizing Consequentialism is that it is inadequately sensitive to the consequences of actions. Suppose, for example, that the best set of rules prohibits lying, and you can either lie to the terrorist – which will thwart her plans, thereby saving thousands – or you can do something else (tell the truth, say nothing, be evasive, etc.), in which case the terrorist will succeed in killing thousands. Rule Maximizing Consequentialism says that you must obey the best set of rules, and that set of rules prohibits lying. Hence, Rule Maximizing Consequentialism says that lying is impermissible in this case. Act Consequentialists think that this is crazy. It is the consequences of our actions that matter, and it seems quite wrong not to lie in this case. The fact that some set of rules has the best

consequences if generally followed seems irrelevant. Rule Maximizing Consequentialism seems guilty of "rule worship."

Of course, the rules that have the best consequences may not be as simple as in the above example. Maybe, all the prohibitions are qualified by "unless doing so would have unusually good consequences" and maybe there is some kind of overriding master requirement to do whatever has unusually good consequences. This would, of course, reduce the objection of rule worship, but it also creates the danger that Rule Maximizing Consequentialism collapses into Maximizing Act Consequentialism. Whether it does so collapse is something that has been much debated, and we shall not attempt to resolve the issue here.[7]

Conclusion

We have surveyed some of the main forms of consequentialism. Each has its problems. This, however, does not establish that no version of consequentialism is correct. Once one examines the issues carefully, every moral theory seems to have problems of some sort. This is because our *untutored* moral judgments – which guide our judgments about what answers are correct – are not perfectly coherent. They are often based on false assumptions, confused notions, or failure to see the full implications of a view. The real test of a theory is how good its answers are relative to our *reflective* moral judgments, which are (roughly) the judgments that we have after we have thoroughly investigated all moral and related empirical issues. Thus, given that some of our current moral judgments may be mistaken, some of the seemingly powerful objections to consequentialism may be mistaken. If so, then some version of consequentialism might be the correct theory of morality.[8]

Notes

1 Some permissible actions are optional (permissible to perform but also permissible not to perform) and some are obligatory (permissible to perform and not permissible not to perform). Most people think that, under

normal circumstances, scratching one's head is morally optional but keeping a contract is morally obligatory.

2 See Jeremy Bentham, *Introduction to the Principles of Morals and Legislation* (London, 1789) and John Stuart

Mill, *Utilitarianism* (London, 1863). An excellent introduction to utilitarianism is J. J. C. Smart and Bernard Williams, *Utilitarianism: For and Against* (Cambridge: Cambridge University Press, 1973).

3 For simplicity, I here focus on Total Utilitarianism. Another version is Average Utilitarianism, according to which a state of affairs is morally at least as good as another if and only if its average well-being is at least as great. If the number of people is the same in both states of affairs, there is no difference between these two views. Where the number of people is different, however, the two views can diverge. The total view says, for example, that three people with 1 unit (total of 3, average of 1) is better than one person with 2, whereas the average view says the opposite.

4 Utilitarian Value is sometimes described as calling for "the greatest good for the greatest number," but this is a mistake – and indeed is incoherent. Utilitarian Value says that 99 people with 0 and one person with 100 (total 100) is better than 99 people with 1 and one person with 0 (total 99) – even though the latter is better for 99 of the 100 people.

5 Consequentialism is sometimes characterized more broadly so as to include moral egoism – the thesis that an action is permissible if and only if its consequences are maximally *prudentially* good *for the agent*. This view, however, is a non-starter as a moral theory – given that morality is concerned with everyone's well-being. More generally, the most plausible versions of consequentialism are based on moral goodness, and hence I shall focus on them.

6 It's worth noting that the satisficing version of Act Consequentialism is especially prone to this objection, since it sets the bar lower for the consequences to be good enough.

7 For a state-of-the-art defense of Rule Consequentialism, see Brad Hooker, *Ideal Code, Real World* (Oxford: Oxford University Press, 2000).

8 For helpful comments, I thank Hugh LaFollette, Eric Roark, and Alan Tomhave.

2

Deontology

David McNaughton and Piers Rawling

1 Introduction

When people try to decide how they should act, they often think about the consequences of their actions: they try to find the action that leads to the best overall outcome. That surely explains the appeal of act consequentialism (advocated by Vallentyne in the previous essay). But that is only one part of everyday, commonsense morality. Although we should be concerned to make things go as well as possible for everyone, most people do not think that this exhausts morality, or even identifies some of its most crucial elements. Are we not, for instance, sometimes required to aid our loved ones, even if we do not thereby produce the most good overall? And are there no limits on what we may do to produce good, or limits on what we must do to produce it? Deontology contrasts with consequentialism in its answers to these questions, and is, in one of its versions, our favored theory.

2 Classification

There are three areas of ordinary moral thought in which considerations other than the amount of good our actions would produce are taken to be relevant to what we morally ought to do.

2.1 Options

Act consequentialism appears very demanding. Given the amount of suffering in the world and the disparities in wealth, maximizing the good would require enormous sacrifice from anyone with more than a minimal standard of living. Most people believe that, though they should do something to help those less fortunate, there is nothing wrong with devoting a lot of time, effort, and money to one's own happiness, and the happiness of those one cares about. There is some point, perhaps hard to determine, at which someone has done all that they are *required* to do by way of helping strangers. At that point they are morally permitted, or have an *option*, to decline to do more. We admire those who make the extra sacrifice, but it is supererogatory – more than morality requires. Act consequentialism seems to leave no room for supererogation.

Deontologists don't deny that morality can be demanding. We may be obliged to make significant sacrifices – even of our lives – rather than breach a serious constraint (see below) or betray a friend. And we have a duty to do good. But, unlike act consequentialists, most deontologists see this latter duty as limited.

2.2 Duties of special relationship (or special obligations)

Many people believe that not only are we *permitted* to do more for those close to us, but we are often *required* to put their interests first. We *owe* things to those with whom we have special relationships – such as our friends, colleagues, and family members – that we do not owe to strangers. Each of us has, for example, a special obligation to our own children: they have a claim on our attention and resources that other people's children do not. It follows that it would be wrong to neglect our own children, even if we could thereby do slightly more good for other children.

2.3 Constraints

In addition to our special obligations, many people believe that we have a duty to avoid harming *anyone* unless, perhaps, they are a threat or deserve punishment. We should not lie, kill innocent people, or torture. These prohibitions *constrain* us in what we may do to *any* person (not just those close to us), even in pursuit of good ends. People differ in how stringent these constraints are. Some think them absolute or exceptionless. Roman Catholic moral theology has traditionally held that one may never intentionally kill an innocent person, even to prevent, say, two other innocents from being intentionally killed. Kant infamously argued that it would be wrong to lie, even to prevent murder. Others hold that though constraints are always a significant consideration, they may be overridden, especially to avoid catastrophe. Either way, such constraints would sometimes *require* us not to maximize the good.

2.4 Distinguishing deontology from act consequentialism

Traditionally, consequentialism and deontology are distinguished by their differing accounts of the relation between the right (in the sense of what is morally required) and the good. Act consequentialism holds that the good determines the right – the only consideration relevant to the rightness of an act is the amount of goodness it produces. Deontologists maintain, in contrast, that other considerations, of the kind discussed under 2.1–2.3, are also relevant. They accuse act consequentialism of oversimplifying moral thinking by giving exclusive attention only to the goodness produced. How might an act consequentialist respond to this charge?

She might claim that ordinary moral thinking is confused and unreliable. Since consequentialism is the correct theory, we should eliminate elements in our moral thinking that don't conform to it.

Alternatively, she might argue that her view is not only compatible with, but actually explains, those elements of our moral thinking to which the deontologist appeals. Consider special obligations: there might be good consequentialist reasons for encouraging people to do more for those close to them than for strangers. We are in a better position to benefit our nearest and dearest since we know their needs and we are more motivated to help them. Or consider constraints: the consequentialist might argue that we should discourage people from killing one innocent to save two when we consider, first, that it is often unclear that the two will be saved, and, second, that encouraging such killing might weaken the valuable reluctance to kill. In short, from a consequentialist perspective, things might go better if people were guided by commonsense morality, rather than making decisions using consequentialist criteria.

Whether consequentialism can align its prescriptions with those of commonsense morality in this way is a matter of dispute we have no room to address here. Even if this strategy were successful, however, act consequentialism would still differ from deontology concerning what is relevant to rightness. The former continues to maintain that the only relevant consideration is the amount of goodness that an act will produce, while the latter thinks that other considerations, such as that I have made a promise, or that some person is my friend, are themselves relevant to whether an act is right. This act consequentialist strategy points out that in less than perfect conditions – imperfect knowledge and imperfect motivation to be moral – we may well do better to act in accordance with the dictates of ordinary morality than to try to produce the best results and thereby inadvertently make things worse. But under ideal conditions of knowledge and motivation, the virtuous agent should never produce less good than she could. The deontologist disagrees: she believes that we are sometimes permitted, and even required, to do just that.

The three elements of commonsense morality to which we have drawn attention are distinct, so that it would be possible, for example, to believe (like Ross) that there are special obligations and constraints, but no options. Or (as we are inclined to do) one might accept that there are special obligations and options, but deny that there are constraints. Or (like some Kantians) one might accept constraints and (perhaps) options, while leaving less room for special obligations. Or (like Scheffler) one might accept only options. Which elements must one accept in order to qualify as a deontologist? There is no clear agreement among moral philosophers so we shall stipulate. What seems most distinctive of deontology is the claim that we are sometimes *required* not to maximize the good. So we count as deontological any theory that believes in duties of special relationships or in constraints (or, of course, both). Options only give us *permission* not to maximize the good and so, on our view, belief in them is not definitive of deontology: options are optional.

We have given a negative definition of deontology – it *denies* that the rightness of an act depends solely on the amount of good produced. We gestured toward a positive account by listing some of the other considerations deontology takes to be relevant. But is there anything that these have in common, or are they just a disparate list? In terms of *content* no unifying theme is apparent. Ross, for example, thought that, apart from producing good, there were a number of considerations that are relevant to the rightness of an act: fidelity

(to promises and commitments), gratitude, reparation, avoiding harming others. These considerations, he plausibly maintained, were distinct, and none is reducible to any of the others. Nevertheless, it has been suggested (Nagel, 1986, ch. 9, sect. 1) that the considerations that fall under our three headings do share a common *form*: they are all *agent-relative*.

2.5 Agent-relativity and agent-neutrality

The distinction between the agent-neutral and the agent-relative may be introduced by reference to reasons for acting.[1] Roughly, someone's reason is agent-relative if, at base, there is reference within it to her. For example, egoism is an agent-relative theory – it holds that each agent has reason to promote only *her own* good – whereas act consequentialism is an agent-neutral theory – it holds that each of us has reason to promote *everyone's* good. Another way of making this point (which we owe to Parfit, 1987, p. 27) is that consequentialism gives us the *common* aim of promoting the general or impersonal good, whereas according to egoism each of us has the *distinct* aim of promoting his personal good: I have reason to pursue my good, you yours. In contrast to act consequentialism, deontology is an agent-relative theory: at its base, there are agent-relative as well as agent-neutral moral reasons. Each of the three elements in deontology incorporates agent-relativity.

Special obligations are obviously agent-relative. I am required to care for *my* family, you for *yours*: we have distinct aims. Act consequentialism might allow that parental caregiving is valuable, but on this view we would have the common aim of promoting parental caregiving in general. That would require that I neglect my own children if I can thereby increase the total amount of parental caregiving – a claim that deontology denies.

Constraints are also agent-relative. Suppose I can only prevent you killing two innocents by killing one myself. If there are constraints, then each of us has strong (or even overriding) moral reason not to kill anyone ourselves. Constraints give each of us distinct aims: I have reason not to kill anyone *myself*, you have reason not to kill anyone *yourself*. Thus although you will do wrong in killing the two, I should not kill the one in order to prevent you. Consequentialism, by contrast, holds that, everything else equal, it is right to kill an innocent myself to save two: killing innocents is bad, so I have an agent-neutral moral reason to contribute to the common aim of minimizing such killing.

Options need not be agent-relative in their formulation. They simply permit us not to maximize the good. But the standard rationale for admitting options into a moral theory is agent-relative. Each of us is morally permitted to give special weight to *our own* interests, just because they are ours.

2.6   Rule consequentialism: a deontology in disguise?

Act consequentialism is not the only version of consequentialism. Perhaps its most popular rival is rule consequentialism, which offers a "two-stage" account of justification. Rule consequentialism assesses acts, not in terms of their contribution to the good, but by whether they are in accordance with the best set of rules governing human conduct. Rules, however, are assessed by their contribution to the good. The best set of rules is the one whose general adoption would maximize the good. Thus, according to rule consequentialism, "an act is wrong if and only if it is forbidden by the code of rules whose internalization by the overwhelming majority . . . has maximum expected value" (Hooker, 2000, p. 32). Which rules are best is determined, in part, by the psychological make-up of human beings. They must, for example, be simple enough for ordinary people to learn, and sufficiently appealing that the majority of people can be persuaded to follow them. Given these restrictions, acceptable rules will probably be close to the rules of commonsense morality. In particular, rule consequentialism is likely to include constraints, options, and special obligations. There will, for example, be a fairly simple rule against killing the innocent, since the adoption of a more complicated rule that allowed killing in pursuit of the good would be hard to follow. Given our natural concern for our nearest and dearest, and the need for companionship and security, there will also be rules permitting, and even requiring, us to give priority to the claims of friends and family.

Rule consequentialism raises a question for the classificatory scheme we are employing. For, despite its name, rule consequentialism might seem to have more in common with deontology. It agrees with deontology that it is often wrong to do the act that will produce the most good, and that some of the moral rules we should follow are agent-relative in form. However, we follow Hooker, a leading rule consequentialist, in classifying this theory as fundamentally agent-neutral and thus consequentialist. Each form of consequentialism assesses something, at its base, in terms of impersonal value. But what they assess varies: act consequentialism assesses acts, while rule consequentialism assesses rules. Impersonal value does not, however, vary with the perspective of the agent, and so is agent-neutral. As Hooker notes: "the agent-relativity in rule consequentialism is derivative. Agent-relative rules are justified by their role in promoting agent-neutral value" (Hooker, 2000, p. 110). Deontology, by contrast, holds that some agent-relative considerations are *underivatively* relevant. They have weight in their own right, not merely in virtue of their serving some further purpose.

3   Varieties of Deontology

3.1   Kant

There are a number of deontological theories. We look at three, beginning with Kant, who is often seen as the exemplar of deontology. His theory is remarkably rich and complex, and its interpretation is the subject of much scholarly dispute. Summarizing it, therefore, is especially tricky, but here is a brief attempt.

Kant contrasts theoretical and practical reasoning. The former endeavors to discover what we should believe; the latter to find out what we should do. Morality is thus a species of practical reasoning, which, like all reasoning, is subject to certain formal constraints. Theoretical reasoning, for example, is subject to rules of deductive and inductive inference.

In the practical sphere, we are guided by what Kant calls maxims. These are general principles of action we adopt, such as "Never volunteer." One important restriction governing practical reasoning is that our maxims are universalizable: we should only act only on maxims that everyone could adopt. Why? Because, as rational beings, we cannot make exceptions in our own case that could not be extended to everyone else. So Kant's first formulation of what he calls the Categorical Imperative, which is his test for whether an action is morally acceptable, reads as follows: "Act only according to that maxim by which you can at the same time will that it should become a universal law" (Kant, 1993, p. 30). Acts that fail this test are wrong.

Let us take Kant's best and most famous example. Suppose I obtain money from you by making a lying promise (i.e., one I intend to break) to repay it. Then my maxim seems to be: I will make lying promises whenever it benefits me. Kant's test then asks whether I could will this maxim to be a universal law. However, the maxim to make lying promises whenever it benefits me cannot be universally willed: its universal adoption would lead to the demise of the very practice on which it relies – namely the practice of promising. Promising could not exist in a world in which there was a universal and publicly acknowledged policy of making deceitful promises, since no one would believe anyone had made a promise, but would regard such attempted assurances as "vain pretenses" (Kant, 1993, p. 31). I can only achieve my aim by being an exception to the general rule of trustworthiness and honest dealing. (Kant seems to have thought that this argument is generalizable to show that lying in any circumstance is wrong.)

In this example, Kant's claim is that there is an implicit contradiction in a supposed description of a world in which everyone makes lying promises, since the practice of promising would be unsustainable in such circumstances. We might call this the contradiction-in-conception test. But, Kant suggests, even if a maxim passed

that test, it might still not be possible for me to will that there exist a world in which everyone acted on the maxim. Kant's clearest example is that of adopting the maxim: I will help nobody. A world in which no one helps anyone is conceivable – it contains no contradiction. But, Kant claims, a rational being could not possibly *will* that such a world exist, because she has all sorts of legitimate projects that may require the help of others. If she were to will that no one help anyone then her will would, as it were, be in contradiction with itself: she would be willing both that no one help anyone and that she receive help with her projects. Let us call this the contradiction-in-the-will test (see O'Neill, 2004, p. 103).

Kant also offers us a second formulation of the Categorical Imperative (the formula of the end-in-itself): "Act in such a way that you treat humanity, whether in your own person or in the person of another, always at the same time as an end and never simply as a means" (Kant, 1993, p. 36). To treat someone *simply* as a means to one's end is to ignore his right as a rational being to act autonomously – to make decisions for himself. Force and deceit are objectionable insofar as they attempt to subvert or circumvent, and thus fail to show respect for, people's autonomy.

Despite the scholarly controversy over what exactly the Categorical Imperative entails, there is general agreement that Kant's ethics has a deontological structure, for it incorporates agent-relative principles without seeking to establish them by appeal to the value of adopting them. The test yields constraints, for agents are forbidden, for example, to lie or kill the innocent, even to minimize lying and the killing of innocents. To kill an innocent yourself to prevent other killings would be to use your victim as a means to minimize victimization. Kant's system is also often thought to admit options, and thus to allow room for supererogation. If the universalized maxim, "Let no one help anyone," is unacceptable, then it follows that each of us should help someone or, as Kant puts it, we should make the ends of some others our own. But that does not entail that we should help as many as we can as much as we can.[2]

One of the striking features of Kant's theory is its scope. It not only defends our deontological intuitions, but also answers many of the questions that have traditionally perplexed moral philosophers. How can we show the selfish or the skeptical that they have good reason to be moral? And how are we to test which moral convictions are the right ones, given the degree of moral disagreement between different outlooks? In answering these questions, Kant's theory appeals to something as apparently rationally compelling and simple as the idea of non-contradiction. How are we to deal with moral conflicts – cases where there are morally relevant considerations on both sides? At least in some cases, Kant offers a clear-cut answer by coming down on one side – we are never, for instance, to lie, or kill the innocent. Finally, Kant offers an answer to the question of what distinguishes moral questions from others: they are all concerned with respect for the autonomy of other rational agents.

These strengths may, however, be more apparent than real. Is the Categorical Imperative test rationally compelling, and does it yield plausible results? We have space here only to outline some objections.

1 Does the test (in its first formulation) rule out maxims that are morally acceptable? Consider this maxim of generosity (which we owe to Parfit): I will give more to charity than the average. Clearly, this maxim cannot be universalized without contradiction. Does it follow that it is *morally wrong* of me to follow this rule myself? Scarcely. Indeed, it seems both rationally acceptable and morally admirable to adopt such a maxim.
2 Does the test fail to rule out maxims that are not morally acceptable? Does it, for example, rule out the use of violence or victimization to attain one's ends? Kantians point out that not everyone could adopt such a policy, because some of the victims would, as a result of the coercion used against them, be unable successfully to follow the policy themselves.[3] But this is not true of all morally objectionable policies of victimization. Take, for example, the ritualized bullying

("hazing") directed toward new members of certain institutions. Such policies seem to pass the Kantian test, since as each victim in turn rises to seniority he gets to take his turn in carrying out the policy. A Kantian might respond that this hierarchical victimization falls foul of the second formulation of the Categorical Imperative: it fails to show respect for others as ends in themselves. If true, that would simply raise another difficulty for the Kantian approach, since the two formulations are supposed to be equivalent, at least in the sense that they deliver the same results.

In other cases, a maxim that it would clearly be wrong for one person to adopt would be acceptable if universally followed. Consider two shipwrecked sailors on an otherwise uninhabited island. Suppose one considers whether to adopt the maxim of stealing from the other in amounts too small to be noticed. Does this maxim pass the Kantian test? Assuming they would be equally adept at this practice, the mutual adoption of such policies would cancel each other out and neither would be disadvantaged. However, it would clearly be wrong for either to adopt this policy if the other did not. Although the policy of unnoticeable theft is not objectionable when universally adopted, it is objectionable when some follow it while others do not. A Kantian might object to testing the maxim in such restricted circumstances. To be acceptable, she might claim, a maxim must pass the test in all possible circumstances. That response, however, is likely to make the test too stringent, since maxims that might be acceptable in our circumstances might have to be rejected because they would fail the test in some scenario far distant from our own.

3 On Kant's view, only other persons have moral claims on us; non-rational creatures, such as animals, and perhaps babies and the severely mentally retarded, have no independent moral standing.
4 Some conclusions that Kant draws from his test seem unduly rigorist – for example, that we should never lie.

Kantians may have acceptable responses to these and other objections. But suppose they succeed in bringing the results of the test into line with our moral intuitions – is that sufficient to vindicate the theory? No. There remain two concerns, the first about justification and the second about explanation. First, if the test is genuinely to justify our intuitions we must have a sense that its application has not been gerrymandered to yield the very intuitions for which we are seeking justification. Second, we need to be persuaded that Kant has uncovered, in the Categorical Imperative, the "supreme principle of morality" (Kant, 1993, p. 5) – the ultimate explanation of what makes wrong acts wrong. We might reasonably doubt whether Kant's test does explain our objection to various kinds of act. What is wrong with policies of lying, or victimization, is the harm they cause, not that they cannot be universalized.

3.2 Rossian deontology

Ross holds that moral philosophy uncovers what considerations are ultimately morally relevant by reflecting on our intuitions about a variety of cases and discovering what features we regard as having, at bottom, a crucial bearing on how we ought to act. Such reflection, he claims, reveals a number of basic moral considerations, which he formulates as a list of moral principles or duties. As we have seen, his suggested list includes agent-relative duties of promise keeping, gratitude, reparation, and not harming others,[4] as well as an agent-neutral requirement to promote the good. This latter includes, for Ross, justice, which consists in the distribution of benefits according to desert. These duties are, he says, only *prima facie* (or, as we prefer, *pro tanto*) since, though each is relevant to determining what is right, no duty automatically trumps any of the others in cases where they conflict – indeed, there is no decision algorithm: which duty is the weightier depends on the complexities of the particular circumstance. Where keeping a promise will harm someone, for example, what we ought to do will depend on how serious the promise is, to whom it was made, the size of the

potential harm, and so on. To weigh all these factors correctly requires discernment and judgment.

The items on Ross's list are intended to be basic in two ways. First, they are *underivative*, in that they are not instances of some more general principle. So, for example, the duty to pay one's debts is derivative because it is an instance of the more general duty to keep promises. But the latter duty is underivative since it is not itself an instance of some yet more general duty. Second, they are basic in the sense that they are *self-evident* and need no justification. We can see their truth directly, without reasoning from further premises. Indeed, Ross strongly implies that they not only require no further justification but that none is available. He thus rejects the Kantian claim that such basic principles rest on a common foundation. For Ross there is no test that principles must pass to earn their place on the list.

Of the two deontological theories we have looked at so far, Kant's and Ross's, which is the more attractive? This depends, in part, on what one is looking for in a moral theory. Kant's program is remarkably ambitious; Ross's is very modest. Kant seeks a *grounding* for common-sense morality, whereas Ross holds that none is available – but none is needed. Kant supposes that, at bottom, there is some one thing that morality is about; Ross makes no such assumption. Kant offers a test that purports to show that acting immorally is indisputably *irrational*, rather in the way that it is irrational to contradict oneself. Ross holds that there are moral reasons, but failure to appreciate them would be a sign of moral insensitivity or immaturity, rather than a gross failure of reasoning. Kant maintains that certain kinds of action, such as lying, are morally unacceptable in all cases; Ross rules nothing out in advance – it all depends on the facts of the particular case. Ambitious theories may be exciting and stimulating in a way that modest ones are not, but that does not make them correct. Not only may they fail to realize their ambitions, but those ambitions may themselves be misguided. It may, for example, be an error to suppose that our moral thought stands in need of special justification, or that a successful moral theory should provide un-equivocal guidance in perplexing cases. In our view, the modesty of Ross's account marks a strength, not a weakness.

Modest as it is, Ross's theory is not immune to objections. For example, he assumes that if a consideration is underivatively morally relevant in one case, then it is similarly relevant in all cases. Thus, if there is a *prima facie* duty not to harm, then the fact that an act would cause harm is *always* a moral reason not to do it, though not necessarily an overriding one. Bor-rowing a term from chemistry, we might say that harmfulness always has negative *moral valence*. Ross nowhere defends this assumption, but perhaps he reasoned thus. Any feature of an action may be morally relevant to its rightness, but many features are merely derivatively rele-vant. That it is Tuesday is morally relevant if I have promised to do something on Tuesday, but its relevance derives from the content of my promise. What is underivatively relevant, however, cannot derive its moral force from elsewhere, and so must have it essentially. Its valence will not vary.

This argument is, however, invalid. A moral consideration may be basic, in that wherever it counts its moral force is underivative. Yet its force may be conditional on the presence of other features – it might not count in all cases. Take promise keeping. Ross claims that my having promised to do an act always counts in favor of doing it. But this is mistaken. Promises extracted by fraud or force are null and void, as are promises to do something immoral. Suppose I promise to perform a contract killing. It is implausible to hold that though, all things con-sidered, I ought not to do it, yet the fact that I promised gives me *some* moral reason to do it. The duty to keep promises is not derivative – when we have reason to keep a promise, there is no more basic moral reason that explains why – but it is conditional.

Perhaps Ross can save his claim that there are exceptionless principles by building relevant exceptions into the principle. Particularists, however, reject this strategy. They hold that deontologists can dispense with principles altogether.

3.3 Particularism

To what extent can morality be codified into a set of rules or principles? Some moral theorists think that there are *strong* moral principles that tell us that we are always forbidden (or re-quired) to act in certain ways. Thus Kant claimed that lying is always wrong. Others, such as Ross, think there are only *weak* prin-ciples that tell us that certain features have invariant moral valence: they always count for (or against) the rightness of an act. Particular-ists, however, doubt the existence of even weak principles, and deny that we need them to engage in moral thinking. Whether and how a feature is morally relevant depends on the context. So, for example, the fact that an act brings pleasure often counts in its favor, but not, perhaps, when the pleasure is sadistic. That it would bring sadistic pleasure is *no* reason to perform an act.

Are there, as Ross supposes, any features with invariant valence? Particularists have been rather successful in showing that there are no *non-moral* features of an action – such as bring-ing pleasure, or the telling of an untruth – that always count morally the same way in every context. Ross's list, however, typically claims invariant valence for *moral* features as justice, fidelity, loyalty, and reparation. Here the par-ticularist seems to be on weaker ground; how could an act's being just, for example, not count in its favor, morally speaking?

4 Defending Deontology

We have seen that commonsense moral thinking seems to favor deontology, in that both recog-nize duties of special relationship, options, and constraints. And we have mentioned two con-sequentialist responses: consequentialism can either reject commonsense morality as mis-guided, or it can endorse it, claiming a conse-quentialist justification for that morality. Whether or not either of these two strategies, or some combination, is successful, consequen-tialism must deny deontology's claim that there is an *underivative* agent-relative component to morality. There is nothing puzzling about the claim that value is morally relevant. But how, consequentialism might enquire, can the *mere* fact that some act will be good or bad for *me*, or for *my* nearest and dearest, itself make a moral difference? Isn't this moral favoritism, implying that I and mine are more important than others? In what follows we try to meet this challenge in the case of special relationships and options, while conceding that it is harder to meet it in the case of constraints.

4.1 *Special relationships and the ties that bind*

To see how considerations other than value can constitute moral reasons, we need to understand the notion of a personal moral tie. Our favored brand of deontology holds that there are under-ivative agent-relative moral ties between those who stand in certain social relationships to each other. *Agent-relative*, because reference to the fact that each is in the relationship is an ineliminable part of the reason why each should do something for the other: "she owes it to him because he is *her* colleague, friend etc." *Under-ivative*, because such reasons do not rest on considerations about the general value of people being in such relationships, or behaving in certain ways when they are. You have a right, for example, to expect that I will come because I promised to, and not because of the general utility of supporting the institution of promise keeping. A *moral* tie, because it is *pro tanto wrong* not to fulfill our special obligations.

We might concede to act consequentialism that we only have reason to act when it will do some good. But goodness is not the only consideration. Some have stronger claims than others to my good offices, so that which act would be right depends on two factors: the good I can do someone and the strength of the claim she has on me in virtue of our relationship.

Consider the tie of friendship. It is not just that friends like and support each other. In addition, your friend has the right to expect *your* loyalty and support because she is *your* friend. If you betray her, she has a moral complaint against you that no one else has. More-over, the (tacit) acknowledgment of a moral tie between friends appears essential to friendship. Friends come through for one another; someone who neither came through for you, nor believed she should, would not be loyal and so would not be a friend.

If this is right, then consequentialism has a serious strike against it. Loyalty is essential to friendship. Loyalty involves the recognition of an underivative agent-relative obligation to one's friends. Consequentialism has no place for underivative agent-relative obligations; thus it has no room for friendship. But friendship, as is generally acknowledged by consequentialists, is an important intrinsic good. Consequentialism holds that the good is to be promoted; but here is a good that it apparently cannot accommodate.

Act consequentialism has no room for moral ties, and hence for friendship, because it has no place for agent-relative moral reasons. But can it accommodate a different account of friendship based on the idea that there are special psychological (and non-moral) bonds of affection between friends? We contend not. Even if we abandon the thought that we are *required* to favor friends, surely we must be *permitted* to favor them if our bonds to them are to be special. That is, we must be morally permitted to favor our friends even when we could do more good overall by not doing so. But act consequentialism denies us this permission: an act is wrong if it fails to maximize the good.

The act consequentialist might try a different tack. She might concede that friendship requires loyalty, but then maintain that loyalty does not require that there actually be moral ties, only that people *believe* there to be. We saw earlier (2.4) that an agent might do better in achieving consequentialist goals if she did not think about which act is right on each occasion, but instead had dispositions to favor friends and family. So act consequentialism might encourage people falsely to believe that they have special obligations.

A serious objection to this strategy, however, is that it pictures the ideal moral agent as someone who has quite erroneous views about what makes acts right or wrong. And in addition, these dispositions to favor friends and family may lead one to act wrongly by consequentialist lights. At the least, this consequentialist strategy is unappealing, if not incoherent.[5] *If* there were serious objections to the very idea of one person having a moral claim on another in virtue of their relationship, then we might be forced to adopt this consequentialist strategy as the least unsatisfactory account. However, we see no objection to a deontological picture that features special obligations.

Can rule consequentialism accommodate friendship? No. Unlike act consequentialism, it acknowledges that favoring friends can be right, but it fails to capture friendship because it maintains that preferential treatment of friends can be justified only by appeal to the general good:

> Moral requirements of loyalty are . . . needed . . . when affection isn't up to the job. . . . <S>pecial moral obligations towards family and friends can then be justified on the ground that internalization of these obligations gives people some assurance that some others will consistently take a special interest in them. Such assurance answers a powerful psychological need. (Hooker, 2000, p. 141)

This does not yield genuine loyalty. Friends have moral reason not to let us down, and assurance is engendered in part by a belief that they will respond to this reason. (This is not to say that the only reasons here are moral.) But for rule consequentialism, the *moral* reason for John not to let Mary down is the general assurance that results from the internalization of a rule requiring the special treatment of "friends," not anything special about his relationship with Mary.

Rule consequentialism's position is that, given human psychology, it is best if each of us has special others who can be relied upon to reciprocate. The best set of rules takes account of this. And given the human tendency to feel special psychological connections to our nearest and dearest, the least costly option is to inculcate a rule requiring their preferential treatment. However, if we now contemplate our reasons to favor them, we see that these reasons rest not on our putative special relationships with those others, but on the impersonal calculus of costs and needs.

A final objection to our account. Morality requires us to be impartial, but don't duties of special relationship require us to be *partial* to our friends, etc.? No. In our view, we show partiality in allocating goods only if we give the claims of one person or group more weight than we are *warranted* in doing. If, as we are claiming, we have moral ties to friends and family, we are not showing partiality to them merely in virtue of putting their interests above those of others. We act partially only if, like the nepotist or Mafioso, we give *undue* or *inappropriate* weight to those interests – if we show favor in ways not warranted by the relationship.

4.2 Options

Does someone have special personal reason to pursue her own benefit, just in virtue of it being hers? We think she does. These agent-relative personal reasons arise because each of us has our own point of view. I have personal reason to care about my pain that I cannot have to care about yours, namely that it is mine. This does not mean that I have no reason to care about your pain, nor does it commit me to denying that pain is equally bad whoever has it. Options can be justified by appeal to the personal perspective. Each agent has moral permission not to maximize the good when the cost to *her* would be significant.[6] An agent is allowed, in determining what she is morally required to do, to accord greater weight to the cost borne by her than is warranted by its impersonal badness.

How can this be? Since I am a creature with a personal point of view, a morality that required me to transcend that point of view and think of the world as if I had no particular place in it would not merely be unreasonably demanding, it would deny all moral significance to the fact that my life is, in a sense, all I have. There has, therefore, to be some balance between the demands that the needs of others put on us and our right to live our own lives. Determining where that balance lies is notoriously difficult. But this does not entail that there is no balance to be struck.

Act consequentialism cannot allow *moral* significance to the personal point of view, because whether an act is morally permitted depends solely on the amount of impersonal value it would produce. It might try to argue that if too much is required of agents they will become disillusioned or exhausted and so do less good than they would if they had more modest targets. If true, however, that justification rests, not on the fact that each of us has our own life to lead, but solely on the claim that giving some priority to our own concerns will, because of our imperfections, bring about better long-term results than if we try to act rightly on each occasion. And that does not give any weight to our legitimate concern for our own welfare. Act consequentialism denies room for supererogation (acting beyond the call of duty): the person who bears great personal cost in maximizing the good, although admirable in the extreme, would be doing something morally wrong if she did otherwise.

Rule consequentialism does better. An agent who follows the rules does not act wrongly: she does enough good – to do more would be meritorious but is not required. The presence of this personal space, however, stems from impersonal costs: we are psychologically resistant to making significant sacrifices, and this makes it too expensive to inculcate a more demanding rule. But this resistance is a regrettable flaw, not a mark of personal reasons. Even if rule consequentialism concedes that the resistance has a rational basis, it is still committed to denying the *moral* significance of personal reasons at the fundamental level. They matter morally only because of the cost of training people to ignore them.

4.3 Constraints

Constraints, though often regarded as the most distinctive feature of deontology, seem harder to justify than options or duties of special relationship. Consider an absolute constraint (C) against (intentionally) killing an innocent person. Suppose Anne and several other innocents are about to be shot by Bert, but he agrees to let the others go if you shoot Anne. (C) forbids you

to do it. Yet, as Scheffler (1994) points out, this appears inexplicable: Anne is going to be shot, but at least you can prevent the other shootings.

Some advocates of constraints might concede that you should shoot Anne in this case, but they would object to your shooting some unthreatened innocent in order to save Bert's target group. But even this weaker position does not, in the end, evade the standard "irrationality objection" to constraints: that they forbid their own violation *even to minimize such violation*. (See McNaughton and Rawling, 1993.)

An important feature of constraints, as understood by traditional deontology, is that they are underivative. Rule consequentialism incorporates prohibitions against, say, killing the innocent, but these are *derivatively* "justified by their role in promoting agent-neutral value" (Hooker 2000, p. 110). In that sense, rule consequentialism does not include constraints.

We have defended special obligations and options by contending that, in addition to the amount of good we do, what we might call positional facts – that the good would accrue to *my* friends or to *me* – are also morally relevant. Constraints, however, cannot be similarly defended. Constraints, unlike duties of special relationship, single out no group on the basis of my relationship to its members, thus they cannot rest on my being more closely related to some than others. Could they be justified on the grounds that my violating a constraint, even to prevent worse actions by others, is a bad thing *for me*, and so something I have personal reason to avoid? Although such a violation may matter to me, since I have an understandable, if not always commendable, reluctance to get my hands dirty, this, at best, *might* ground a *permission* not to violate the constraint. It cannot ground a *requirement* not to do so: if constraint violation were impermissible simply because we are averse to it, why doesn't the same apply to, say, exercise on the part of the lazy?

Constraints, then, embody as fundamental the fact of your agency. It is the bare fact that you would be doing the killing that rules out your killing an innocent as a means to preventing other innocents suffering a like fate. Since constraints are fundamental, we should not expect to find a deeper justification for them. Their being fundamental does not, however, preclude our defending constraints, as we did with special obligations and options, by explicating their nature in ways that make their force clearer. The problem is that we can find no explication of constraints that dispels their air of irrationality.

Given that air of irrationality, it is not surprising that many deontologists have nevertheless attempted to find a deeper justification, but such attempts to explain why agency matters seem to presuppose the very point at issue (see Scheffler, 1994, chapter 4). Thus it is said (in a Kantian vein) that persons deserve respect in view of their unique importance as rational moral agents. But why does such respect forbid you to harm others rather than requiring you to minimize harm? It may be said that, just as we owe particular duties to others in view of our special relationships with them, so we owe to everyone else a duty not to harm them because of our general relationship with them. But what is that relationship? Perhaps that of being fellow humans, or fellow persons. Whatever the answer, the problem remains: why does our standing in that relationship ground a *constraint* against harming as opposed to a duty to minimize harm? Similarly, Natural Law theorists move from the claim that there are certain basic values, including life, to the claim that we should never act directly against a basic value, even in seeking to protect that value elsewhere. But how is that move to be justified?

Some defenders of constraints[7] have complained that, in seeing constraints as *agent*-relative, recent attempts to ground constraints have wrongly focused on agency. Rather, they claim, we should focus on a *patient*-centered justification – on what it is about innocents that entails the existence of constraints against harming them. But this does not seem to help. By the nature of innocence, innocents do not deserve to be harmed, so that, ideally, we should not harm them. But what are we to do in our non-ideal world in which innocents are under threat?

If we deny the existence of constraints, however, won't we have to abandon intuitions that seem to lend them credence? Not necessarily. First, many intuitions that appear to be support constraints may actually rest on other features. We may, for example, think it wrong to take $10 from one person in order to enrich another by $20. But our grounds for that (depending on the circumstances) might be that the harm of taking $10 *honestly possessed* outweighs the benefit of bestowing $20 *unearned*. Second, we may think it wrong to do considerable harm to one person in order to prevent small harms to a large number. But that may have nothing to do with agency but be explained by the fact that no number of small harms to different people, when added together, is as bad as a serious harm to one person. Finally, acts that are considered by traditional deontologists to be violations of serious constraints will increase good only in dire circumstances, so that the chances of our ever being required to, say, kill one innocent to save two are low.

We are tentatively proposing, then, a morality devoid of constraints (as traditionally understood) but incorporating duties of special obligation and options.[8] Is such a theory worthy of the name of deontology? Yes. A theory with special obligations and options, but without constraints, is still deontology: agent-relative considerations are underivatively relevant, and agents are forbidden in certain circumstances to maximize the good.

4.4 Virtue ethics

Consequentialism and deontology do not exhaust the options for a moral theory. Virtue ethics rejects what it sees as serious defects in both approaches, particularly their focus on the deontic status of acts, and their belief that moral theory should formulate precise moral principles from which to read off conclusions about what to do. Good moral judgment requires sensitivity, experience, and discernment, rather than slavish adherence to predetermined rules. The virtues are valuable in their own right, and not just as a guarantor of reliably choosing the right act. And only those who possess them can discern what is morally salient in any particular situation. The moral emotions play a crucial role not only in determining how one should act but also in motivating the agent; the sense of duty is to be harnessed only when better motives fail. Moral philosophy should focus more, therefore, on what kind of person it is best to be, rather than on what principles we should invoke to solve artificially constructed moral dilemmas.

There are two views concerning the purport of virtue ethics. On the less radical, virtue ethics is proposed as a welcome corrective to various distortions that have afflicted many versions of both deontology and consequentialism. On the more radical, it is put forward as an alternative theory in its own right. With the less radical approach we are entirely in sympathy. The deontological theory we favor, which is broadly Rossian in spirit, takes the above points on board. We see overly principled approaches as distorting moral

thinking by downplaying the need for judgment and imagination in discerning, in a particular case, which features are relevant, how they interact with each other, and what weight should be given to each. And it has often been pointed out that deontology and virtue ethics make common cause against consequentialism. But we are skeptical of the more radical approach, which maintains that the right is metaphysically dependent upon the judgments of the virtuous. In difficult cases we may have no *epistemic* access to which act is right other than via the judgment of virtuous agents. But the virtuous agent judges an act right because it is right, not the other way around. Otherwise, on what does she base her judgment? It must be responsive to reasons, and those reasons, if she is appropriately sensitive, lead her to the truth. The latter is there for her to find; she does not construct it. Virtue ethics is thus best seen as a crucial part of the best deontological theory.

Notes

1 But see McNaughton and Rawling (1991) for discussion of some problems for this approach.
2 This interpretation is disputed (see, for example, Hill, forthcoming, esp. fn. 2).
3 See O'Neill (2004, p. 102).
4 This last is, we think, agent-relative for Ross: he does not appear to countenance doing harm oneself in order to minimize the total amount of harm. (For a rebuttal of the complaint that this is an unsystematic list, see McNaughton, 1996.)

5 See Smart and Williams (1973, section 6).
6 For an extended defense of this approach, see Scheffler (1994, *passim*).
7 See for instance Brook (1991), Kamm (2000). For discussion see McNaughton and Rawling (1993).
8 Kagan (1984) argues that options require constraints. Scheffler responds in Scheffler (1994, pp. 167–92). For further discussion see McNaughton and Rawling (forthcoming).

Further Reading

Audi, R. (1996) "Intuitionism, Pluralism, and the Foundations of Ethics." In W. Sinnott-Armstrong and M. Timmons (eds.), *Moral Knowledge: New Readings in Moral Epistemology*. Oxford: Oxford University Press, pp. 101–36.

Dancy, J. (1983) "Ethical Particularism and Morally Relevant Properties," *Mind* 92: 530–47.

Dancy, J. (1993) "An Ethic of *Prima Facie* Duties." In P. Singer (ed.), *A Companion to Ethics*. Oxford: Blackwell Publishers, pp. 230–40.

Darwall, S. (1986) "Agent-centered Restrictions from the Inside Out," *Philosophical Studies* 50: 291–319.

Hooker, B. and Little, M. (eds.) (2000) *Moral Particularism*. Oxford: Clarendon Press.

McNaughton, D. (1988) *Moral Vision*. Oxford: Blackwell Publishers.

McNaughton, D. (1999) "Intuitionism." In H. LaFollette (ed.), *The Blackwell Guide to Ethical Theory*. Oxford: Blackwell Publishers, pp. 268–87.

McNaughton, D. and Rawling, P. (forthcoming) "Deontology." In D. Copp (ed.), *The Oxford Handbook of Moral Theory*. Oxford: Oxford University Press.

References

Brook, R. (1991) "Agency and Morality," *Journal of Philosophy* 88: 190–212.

Copp, D. (ed.) (forthcoming) *The Oxford Handbook of Moral Theory*. Oxford: Oxford University Press.

Dancy, J. (1993) *Moral Reasons*. Oxford: Blackwell Publishers.

Hill, T. (forthcoming) "Kantian Normative Ethics." In D. Copp (forthcoming), *The Oxford Handbook of Moral Theory*. Oxford: Oxford University Press.

Hooker, B. (2000) *Ideal Code, Real World*. Oxford: Clarendon Press.

Kagan, S. (1984) "Does Consequentialism Demand too Much?" *Philosophy and Public Affairs* 13: 239–54.

Kagan, S. (1989) *The Limits of Morality*. Oxford: Clarendon Press.

Kamm, F. (1999) "Nonconsequentialism." In H. LaFollette (ed.), *The Blackwell Guide to Ethical Theory*. Oxford: Blackwell, pp. 205–26.

Kamm, F. M. (2000) "Nonconsequentialism." In H. LaFollette (ed.), *The Blackwell Guide to Ethical Theory*. Oxford: Blackwell Publishers, pp. 205–26.

Kant, I. (1993) *Grounding of the Metaphysics of Morals*, trans. J. Ellington. Indianapolis: Hackett Publishing Company. (Originally published 1785.)

Korsgaard, C. M. (1996) *Creating the Kingdom of Ends*. Cambridge: Cambridge University Press.

LaFollette, H. (1999) *The Blackwell Guide to Ethical Theory*. Oxford: Blackwell Publishers.

McNaughton, D. (1996) "An Unconnected Heap of Duties?" *Philosophical Quarterly* 46: 433–47.

McNaughton, D. and Rawling, P. (1991) "Agent-relativity and the Doing–Happening Distinction," *Philosophical Studies* 63: 167–85.

McNaughton, D. and Rawling, P. (1993) "Deontology and Agency," *The Monist* 76: 81–100.

McNaughton, D. and Rawling, P. (2000) "Unprincipled Ethics." In B. Hooker and M. Little (eds.), *Moral Particularism*. Oxford: Clarendon Press, pp. 256–75.

Nagel, T. (1986) *The View from Nowhere*. Oxford: Oxford University Press.

O'Neill, O. (2004) "Kant: Rationality as Practical Reason." In A. Mele and P. Rawling (eds.), *The Oxford Handbook of Rationality*. Oxford: Oxford University Press, pp. 93–109.

Parfit, D. (1984) *Reasons and Persons*. Oxford: Oxford University Press.

Parfit, D. (1987) *Reasons and Persons*, rev. edn. Oxford: Clarendon Press.

Ross, W. D. (1930) *The Right and the Good*. Oxford: Clarendon Press.

Scheffler, S. (1994). *The Rejection of Consequentialism*, rev. edn. Oxford: Clarendon Press.

Smart, J. J. C. and Williams, B. (1973) "A Critique of Utilitarianism," in *Utilitarianism: For and Against*. Cambridge: Cambridge University Press.

3

Virtue Theory

Rosalind Hursthouse

Introduction

"Virtue ethics" is a technical term in contemporary Western analytical moral philosophy, used to distinguish a normative ethical theory focused on the virtues, or moral character, from others such as deontology (or contractarianism) and consequentialism. Imagine a case in which it is agreed by every sort of theorist that I should, say, help someone in need. A deontologist will emphasize the fact that in offering help, I will be acting in accordance with a moral rule or principle such as "Do unto others as you would be done by"; a consequentialist will point out that the consequences of helping will maximize well-being; and a virtue ethicist will emphasize the fact that providing help would be charitable or benevolent – charity and benevolence being virtues.

In Western philosophy, virtue ethics goes back to the ancient Greeks, but in Eastern philosophy, its origins are much older. Siddhartha Gautama, the Buddha, recognizes such virtues – perfections of character – as forbearance, self-restraint, contentment, compassion, generosity, mildness, courage, meditation, and wisdom. In Confucianism we find a focus on virtues, that is,

character traits that typify the good or noble person (the *junzi*). Confucianism also focuses on the good or worthwhile life. These two features are essentially connected – possession of the virtues is necessary for living a good life. And how one should live and how one should act is taught not by the giving of general rules or principles but through very particularized, illustrative examples of virtue in action.

The virtues most clearly identified are humanity/benevolence/compassion (*ren*), wisdom (*zhi*), righteousness (*yi*), courage (though this falls under righteousness in Mencius), trustworthiness, filial piety (*xiao*), and acting in accordance with ceremonial ritual, or "propriety" (*yi*). Although neither of the latter has ever appeared on any traditional Western list of the virtues, when we read the illustrative examples of them, most of us, even across the gap of over 2,500 years, can recognize them as such, notwithstanding the fact that nowadays and in Western society, our paradigm examples of these virtues in action might be rather different.

The Western origins of virtue ethics are not limited to Plato and Aristotle: the Stoics and Epicureans developed distinctively different versions; and individual Christian writers took up different strands, eventually, in Aquinas, interweaving virtue ethics with natural law theory.

Given the above, it would obviously be a mistake to think of neo-Aristotelianism as the only viable version of modern virtue ethics. Recent virtue ethicists have revived the Stoics, and also, turning to later writers, have found much to inspire them in Hume and Nietzsche. But the modern philosophers who have put virtue ethics on the map (Anscombe, Foot, MacIntyre, Williams, McDowell, Nussbaum, Slote, Hursthouse, and Swanton) had all absorbed Aristotle and he is still the natural starting point for an introduction to the virtue ethics approach.

Emergence of modern virtue ethics

Modern virtue ethics was barely recognized until the 1980s, despite the fact that Anscombe and Foot's first papers on it, at least, came out 20 years earlier than that. Only very recently has it been accepted as a genuine rival to consequentialism and deontology. (In the second edition (2002) of this anthology, for example, the latter two occur under the heading "Main Types of Theory" and virtue ethics under the subheading "Alternatives.") At least part of the reason why it took so long lay in the above fact – that Aristotle is the natural starting point for the virtue ethics approach – because it is from his ethical writings that virtue ethicists acquired various positions, interests, distinctions, and concepts which were all quite alien to modern analytical philosophy until virtue ethics became established.

One might think, not unreasonably, that surely these alien features would be things that modern philosophy had rightly discarded – as it has, indeed, discarded Aristotle's quite appalling misogyny, his defense of slavery, and his lamentable attitude to the other animals ("Plants exist for the sake of animals, and animals for the sake of man; the tame for our use and provision, the wild, at least the greater part, for our provision also or for some other advantageous purpose . . . " *Politics* 1256b). But in fact this is not so; rather the features were alien because the orthodoxy prevailing at the time had forgotten

about, or sidelined, a number of topics that had always previously been part and parcel of moral philosophy. Under the influence of the virtue ethicists, most of these have been welcomed back, but they were rarely discussed in the 1960s and 1970s. As examples we might cite: moral education, moral wisdom or discernment, friendship and family relationships, a rich concept of happiness, the moral significance of the emotions, and the virtues themselves.

Prior to the re-emergence of these Aristotelian topics, what was discussed was basically limited to the right and the good, famously identified by Rawls as "the two main concepts of ethics" (Rawls assumed that the concept of the "morally worthy person," which is as near as he comes to speaking of the virtuous person, "is derived from them"). There were, correspondingly, just two types of ethical theories: those that defined the right in terms of the good (consequentialist) and those that did not (deontological). And the purpose of both types of theory was to enable a moral agent to answer the question, "What should I do?" to show us how to resolve our moral problems or quandaries on "rational" grounds. In fact, as late as the 1980s, moral philosophers were still saying that a serious normative theory aimed to formulate a determinate decision procedure, consequently dismissing virtue ethics for its failure to do so.

Aristotle's *Ethics*

Against such a background, Aristotle did look very alien. His *Nicomachean Ethics* (NE) does indeed open with a discussion of the nature of the chief or highest good for man *sic*, namely *eudaimonia* (usually translated as "happiness"). But it immediately becomes clear that the purpose of this is not at all to identify the good which right action can be defined as maximizing. Rather, *eudaimonia* or "the good life" is what each of us is seeking, hence

> knowledge of this good is very important for our lives if like archers, we have a target, are we not more likely to hit the right mark? If so, we must try at least roughly to comprehend what it is . . .
>
> (NE 1094a23–25)

So the starting point is not, "How do I resolve my moral dilemmas (on rational grounds)?" nor even, at first sight, "How (morally) should I live?" but the apparently egocentric question: "How am I to achieve *eudaimonia*, to live happily or well?"

This doesn't look as though it has anything to do with ethics, as we understand it, at all. But the answer Aristotle gives brings us back to more familiar terrain. *Eudaimonia* is "activity of the soul in accordance with *arete* (virtue)" so the *eudaimon* (happy) life is the life of virtue. "The good life" that we all seek turns out to be what we would nowadays call "the morally good life."

This gives us some idea of our target: in order to achieve *eudaimonia* we need to acquire and exercise the virtues; and to get a better idea of it, Aristotle says, we should look at virtue. And this he proceeds to do, for most of the rest of the *Ethics*. But just before he begins, he says something about the nature of the "soul" or psyche, which we need to look at.

Most contemporary philosophy of mind draws a hard and fast distinction between belief and desire, and a correspondingly stark distinction between the rational and the non-rational. These distinctions are also common in modern meta-ethics, wherein there is a long-running debate about whether we can be motivated to act by reason (belief) alone, as the Kantians maintain, or whether action also requires the presence of a desire, as Hume maintained. But Aristotle (and his modern followers) see things differently.

Aristotle begins by saying, broadly, that the human psyche has two parts or aspects; one possesses reason and the other lacks it. The non-rational part is then further subdivided into the "nutritive" part, which is the cause of nutrition and growth (and which we share with all living things), and the "appetitive and generally desiring part." But then he notes that this latter part does partake in reason after all, for "in the self-controlled person it is obedient to reason, and in the temperate and the courageous person it is still more ready to listen, since in their case it is in total harmony with reason." So the "appetitive/desiderative" part, unlike the nutritive part, does possess reason in a way.

Contrasting the way in which this supposedly non-rational part of the soul has reason with the way in which the identified rational part has it, Aristotle says the former has it "in the sense that a person who listens to the reason of his father or friends is said to have reason, not reason in the mathematical sense." So, he concludes insouciantly, we could divide the human psyche differently, saying that the non-rational part just consists of the "nutritive" and that it is the rational part of the soul that has subdivisions, one which possesses reason "in the strict sense, in itself" and another, the "desiderative" part, which possesses reason in the other sense.

So our desires and emotions (the emotions are in the "desiderative" part) are not purely rational but they are not purely non-rational either. Our emotional reactions are up for assessment as in accordance with or contrary to reason, just as our beliefs are, and, like our beliefs, can be criticized for being incorrect, mistaken, wrong, when they are not in accordance with reason.

As we shall see shortly, it is an essential aspect of Aristotle's, and the modern virtue ethics', approach.

Virtue (*Arete*) as Excellence

The initial difficulties in establishing virtue ethics as a robust rival to consequentialism and deontology owed much to the fact that modern readers unacquainted with ancient philosophy took the standard translation of *arete*, namely "virtue," as perfectly adequate and, to some extent, the difficulty persists to this day. Its less standard, but more accurate, translation is "excellence," and *ethikai aretai* are excellences of character (as opposed to what Aristotle calls "intellectual excellences" such as wisdom and scientific understanding).

Here is how the "excellence" translation makes a difference. Something that is excellent is as good of its kind as it could (be reasonably expected to) be – think of an excellent first-year philosophy essay – and we do not say that anything is "too excellent." But the modern usage of "virtue" doesn't work in quite the same way. We may say that someone has the virtues of compassion and generosity but deny that, in these areas, he is as good as anyone could be. He would, we say, be better if he were not so virtuous; he is *too* compassionate or generous, liable to, for example, lie rather than hurt someone's feelings, find himself unable to kill the bird his cat has mauled, or impoverish himself and his family through giving too lavishly to others.

Now it would be foolish to maintain that it is incorrect to talk this way. It is, however, incorrect to talk that way if you are trying to talk about *arete* or virtue-as-excellence. What you say instead is that the agent in question does not have the excellence of compassion or generosity. Though seemingly well on the way to being excellent in these ways, with his heart in the right place, he is not yet as good as he could be. We know of, or can readily imagine, people who are compassionate without being dishonest or squeamish, and generous without being prodigal – and they are better than he is.

As a character trait involving dispositions to certain feelings as well as actions

Moreover, if you look up "virtue" in a modern dictionary, it won't tell you the essential thing about its genus, namely that a virtue-as-excellence (in ethical contexts) is a character trait; if you have *ethike arete* you are excellent in character. An excellent character trait is a well-entrenched or settled state of a person – a certain sort of way they are, through and through, all the way down – which involves a disposition of a very complex sort. It is not just a tendency to act in certain ways for, as Aristotle constantly asserts, excellences of character are to do with actions *and* feelings (or emotions). But neither is it just being prone to feel, and be prompted to action by feeling, for example, compassion, or an impulse to give; this brings feelings in the wrong way. Quite small children can have that tendency, and when adults have the same tendency to act on emotional impulse, like children, they are not, as we saw above, excellent in character but, for example, "too" compassionate or generous.

The Aristotelian way to bring in feelings is as follows.

> The pleasure or pain that supervenes on what people do should be taken as a sign of their dispositions; for someone who holds back from bodily pleasure and does so cheerfully is a temperate person, while someone who is upset at doing so is self-indulgent, and someone who withstands frightening things and does so cheerfully, or anyway without distress, is a courageous person, while someone who is distressed at them is cowardly. For excellence of character has to do with pleasures and pains . . . this is why we must have been brought up in a certain way from childhood onwards, as Plato says, so as to delight in and be distressed by the things we should. (NE 1104b3–12)

Excellence of character involves a disposition to act in certain ways for certain *reasons*, not just on emotional impulse, and feelings are involved particularly because of the relevance of how the agent feels about what she does. Doing what one should, reliably, for appropriate reasons, is not enough for excellence of character, because someone who gives to, or aids another reluctantly, unwillingly, with difficulty, is not as good as the one who does the same things gladly and easily. The best way for us to be is with our emotions/feelings in harmony with our reason, so they do not pull in opposite directions; someone whose reason characteristically conquers her bad impulses and who acts as she should is good; someone whose impulses are in harmony with their reason is excellent. (In Aristotelian vocabulary, this is the contrast between mere continence, or strength of will, and virtue.)

The commonest mistake amongst opponents of virtue ethics has been to take just one or perhaps two aspects of this complex disposition and identify it as (a) virtue. So, as we just saw, those who complain that the "virtue" of compassion may lead its possessor to act wrongly are assuming that it is no more than the strong tendency to be prompted to action by the emotion of compassion, ignoring the role that acting for certain sorts of reasons plays in the concept of a character trait. Those who think that virtue ethics is covertly relying on deontology assume that a virtue is a settled tendency to act in accordance with deontological rules because they are right, even if you do so with difficulty, ignoring the distinction between continence and virtue.

The importance of the point that the virtues or excellences are character traits comes up again in relation to various arguments that are brought against some of its versions. In one, naturalistic, version, it is claimed that the virtues are those character traits that perfect our nature as rational social animals. Some philosophers object on the grounds that this entails that homosexuality is a vice and that it cannot do justice to the idea that vegetarianism may well be a virtue. But neither homosexuality nor vegetarianism are character traits, and so the objection does not get off the ground.

A good test for whether or not Xness is a character trait is to ask yourself: "If I know that someone is X, do I thereby know quite a lot about what that person does and would do in certain circumstances *and* what they would think and feel about so doing *and* for what reasons *and* how they would think about and react to certain actions and emotions of others?"

Try this on honesty and you see it working easily. If (which is of course a big "if") I know that someone is really honest, then I do indeed know a lot about all those things. But now try it on homosexuality. If I knew, somehow, that someone was homosexual, what would follow from that about what they do and would do and so on? Well, I might make the mistake of thinking that they went in for homosexual activity, because they found it desirable. But we know that some homosexuals, like some heterosexuals, find their own sexual activity disgusting. And we know that many homosexuals – particularly female ones in the past – have perforce gone in for nothing but heterosexual activity or not gone in for sexual activity at all. Homosexuality, like heterosexuality, is not a character trait, for sex is such a mysterious force in our lives, so subject to being shaped by our individual and cultural beliefs, that there is just no knowing at all in what ways people are disposed to act and think and feel from their sexual orientation.

Vegetarianism is a little different. You can't be a vegetarian without practicing vegetarianism, so if I know someone is vegetarian I know that much about them. But that is all I know. I don't know anything about their reasons for not eating meat. Is it on moral, religious, or health grounds? Simply because they don't like meat? A whim? Hence I don't know under what circumstances, if any, they would eat meat, nor what they feel about refraining or about other people not refraining, nor whether or not they are happy about animals being killed for sport or experimented on, nor whether they mightn't cease to be vegetarian tomorrow.

As a disposition to act for certain reasons

For what sort(s) of reasons does someone with the excellences of character do the things they characteristically do? In a famous passage, Aristotle draws a distinction between doing what *is* temperate or just (or, as we might say, "right") and doing it temperate*ly* or just*ly* (or "right*ly*").

> Actions count as done justly or temperately not merely because they themselves are of a certain kind (i.e. just or temperate) but also because of facts about the agent doing them – first if he does them knowingly, secondly if he "chooses" to do them, and "chooses" to do them for their own sake, and thirdly if he does them from a firm and unchanging character. (NE 1105a30–35)

"Choice" (*prohairesis*) is a technical term in Aristotle. It is sometimes translated as "rational choice," which helps to capture his idea that the other animals, and children, although they act voluntarily, do not "choose," because they lack, or have not yet reached the age of, reason. Your "choices" manifest your own views on what is worth having and pursuing and avoiding and doing (your "values," we would say); the other animals do not have such views, and those of children are not yet their own. (If we used Aristotle's term, we would be able to say of children who commit murder that they did not "choose" to murder, rather than being forced to say that, in some sense, they "didn't know what they were doing.")

However, we need not go deeply into "choice" to understand this passage. To act virtuous*ly*/excellent*ly* on a particular occasion you must do what is, say, just or temperate intentionally (not by accident) and you must do it for a reason (not just on emotional impulse) and your reason must be, in some sense, that the action is worth doing for its own sake. (And you must be acting from the relevant character trait, which is what will make it the case that your feelings about what you do are the right ones.)

The most significant clause is "chooses to do them for their own sake," for it is this that rules out, as we would say, "doing the right thing for the wrong reason."

> We say that some people who do just actions are not yet just; for example, those who do what is laid down by the laws either unwillingly, or through ignorance or for some other reason, and not for the sake of the actions themselves (though they do indeed do what they should and what a good person is required to do). (NE 1144a13–16)

It is a truism in virtue ethics that the excellent (virtuous) person is excellent (virtuous) in acting and feeling. The excellent/virtuous person "gets things right" in both action and feeling. We can now start to make a list of the ways in which, on a particular occasion, we can fall short of this ideal. Take honesty as the example of the virtue-as-excellence in question. We can fall short in at least the following ways:

1 Most obviously, you do what you know to be dishonest instead of what is honest (either because you are dishonest or because of *akrasia*, weakness of will).
2 You do what is honest but not for the right reason(s). Your reason might be a wrong/ wicked reason – think of a blackmailer revealing the truth about a victim who has defied him in order to show his other victims that he is not just bluffing. Or it might be in itself innocuous but nevertheless not the sort of reason appropriate to honesty. For example, you might own up to something not simply because it is true that you did whatever it was, but because you can see you are going to be found out and there is no point in lying.
3 You do what is honest with the wrong emotions. You might act unwillingly or grudgingly, instead of readily and gladly, as someone with the virtue would in those

circumstances (strength of will but not full virtue). Or you might, for example, reveal a truth which the virtuous agent would also reveal in the same circumstances, but you do it with spiteful pleasure, whereas they would regret having to do it.

But, particularly with respect to action, there are other ways of "falling short" as well, which come about through lack of *phronesis* or "wisdom," to which we shall turn shortly.

As a mean

Before we do, something must be said about Aristotle's famous "doctrine of the mean." In fact, he has two such "doctrines." One is the rather odd thesis that to each virtue/excellence there correspond precisely two opposing vices/ defects, with the virtue "lying in a mean" between them. So, for example, he says (roughly) that courage is a mean – an intermediate state – between cowardice and rashness, and that temperance is a mean between self-indulgence and a kind of insensibility. Modern virtue ethicists have not been very interested in this doctrine, reserving most of their enthusiasm for the second.

"Excellence/virtue," Aristotle says, "is a kind of mean insofar as it is effective at hitting upon the mean" in actions and feelings, and he describes what is involved in this with respect to feelings, as follows:

> To have [such feelings as fear, confidence, appetite, anger, and in general pleasure and pain] on the right occasions, about the right things, towards the right people, for the right end and in the right way, is the mean and best; and this is the business of excellence/ virtue. (NE 1106b21–2)

He repeats these same requirements (right occasion, right things and/or people, right end, right way) with minor variations with respect to actions – or actions and feelings – again and again.

Having identified this range of requirements, he points out

> there are many ways of going astray . . . whereas there is only one way of getting it right (which is

exactly why the one is easy and the other difficult – missing the target is easy, but hitting it is difficult). (1106b29–33)

He reminds us that, "Excellence/virtue is effective at hitting upon the mean in actions and feelings," and continues:

> This is why being excellent/virtuous is difficult, because in any context it is difficult to find the mean; for instance, not everyone can find the mean (i.e. the centre) of a circle, but only the person with knowledge. So too, anyone can get angry or give and spend money – these are easy; but doing them in relation to the right person, in the right amount, on the right occasion, with the right end and in the right way – that is not something anyone can do, nor is it easy. (1109a2029)

(For reasons best known to themselves, translators of Aristotle always conceal the fact that the word *meson*, standardly translated as "mean," and sometimes as "midpoint," can also, as in this passage, be translated as "centre.")

The reason virtue ethicists are so enthusiastic about this is that it encapsulates their rejection of the view that normative ethical theory is supposed to provide a decision procedure or a code of rules or principles, which we could all use to work out what we should do, on any occasion. When, guided by Aristotle, we really take on board just how many different factors should be taken into account when we act and how they will vary with the circumstances, we see (so virtue ethicists claim) that it is utterly implausible to suppose that such complexities could be catered for by usable rules or principles.

This is not to deny that there may well be some absolute prohibitions – Aristotle himself cites the one against murder – but, few and far between as they are, they hardly provide us with much action guidance day by day. Moreover, faced with the situation in which killing someone seems right, as, perhaps, in some cases of euthanasia, of what use is the rule prohibiting murder? How do we know whether it applies to this case? And supposing we somehow determine that it does, what are we to do then? Not any old way of avoiding murder, in the tragic situation imagined, will do; some will be better than others – but how do we find out which? There are, no doubt, many different factors that should be taken into account – but what is involved in *recognizing* them in the first place?

According to Aristotle, excellence of character, in its fully developed form, involves *phronesis* or wisdom (sometimes translated as "practical" or "moral" wisdom), an excellence/virtue of the rational part of the psyche, and it is this, not the use of a code provided by academic philosophers, that enables the excellent/virtuous agent to "hit upon the mean in actions," notwithstanding the complexities.

Phronesis (Wisdom)

Like *arete*, this was an almost unrecognized concept in modern moral philosophy until the virtue ethicists brought it back. "Wisdom" is a very ordinary word, but one can read the classical utilitarian and Kantian texts without noticing any use of it, and search for it in vain in the index of hundreds of contemporary philosophy books (including the earlier editions of this one). So one might wonder how it could be relevant to modern ethics at all.

But outside the context of academic philosophy, it is still common currency and used pretty much the way Aristotle uses *phronesis*. "Google" it, and you find people saying that unlike cleverness or one's IQ, which one is born with, it is knowledge born of experience of life. It is a form of knowledge that enables you to make sound choices or good decisions in and about your life. The wise are the sort of people you would turn to for advice about *what to do*, not in areas that call for special expertise, where you need to consult a doctor or an engineer or an electrician, but in the general area of the day-to-day business of living your life with other people. The wise would be the best people to give you advice because they would know about how to act and how to live.

And so says Aristotle. Contrasting *phronesis* with mathematical knowledge, he says,

> Geometricians and mathematricians and those accomplished at such things, develop when young, while this is not thought to be the case with a wise

person; and the reason is that the objects of wisdom also include particulars, which come to be known through experience, and a young person is not an experienced one. (NE 1142a12–15)

Emphasizing the importance of the correct perception, or sizing up of situations, he says: "One should pay attention to the undemonstrated assertions and judgments of experienced and older people or wise ones no less than to demonstrations; because they have an eye, formed from experience, than enables them to see correctly" (1143b11–13). (The "seeing" here is not, of course, just ordinary sense perception, as he also notes.)

What does *phronesis* enable one to do, in detail? We saw above at least three ways in which we could fall short of excellence/virtue in action and feeling. But we can go wrong in other ways too, through failures in wisdom. As just noted, we do not expect to find wisdom in adolescents, however decent and high-minded they may be, because they lack experience of life, and the way to interpret the following examples is to think of them as innocent mistakes made, on a particular occasion, by (basically) honest adolescents.

4 They do what is in fact dishonest, not believing or realizing or "seeing" that it is.
5 They fail to do what is honest, on an occasion that called for a particular honest action, because they failed to see that such action was called for.
6 They do what is honest when they should not have, for example in circumstances such that doing what was honest was contrary to some other virtue.
7 They do what is honest but botch the manner of doing it.

Here are some examples to fill these out. (It doesn't matter if you disagree with the details; you should be able to find other examples of your own.)

Example for (4) above: Our basically honest adolescent doesn't think it is dishonest to tell white lies, and, on this occasion, he tells what he thinks is just a white lie, which is in fact a distinctly grey one.

Example for (5) above: Another falls under the sway of a convincing confidence trickster, and goes along with what he is doing because she doesn't see clearly that he is cheating other people.

Example for (6) above: He tells the truth without noting the fact that in doing so he is betraying a confidence, acting contrary to friendship, loyalty, and fidelity. (Someone with the virtue of "fidelity" typically keeps faith, is true to her word, keeps promises, etc.) Or, another case, he blurts out the truth when it would have been discreet or polite to remain silent, believing that discretion or courtesy do not matter in comparison with honesty.

Example for (7) above: She reveals the truth either on such an inappropriate occasion that the person who needs to know it can't take it in, or too bluntly, so that the recipient is unnecessarily hurt or shocked. (This used to be a common failure amongst doctors, until it was realized that they needed to be trained in how to deliver bad news in the *right* way, on the *right* occasion.)

Under pressure from the virtue ethicists, most proponents of the other two major approaches have abandoned the idea that a normative theory should provide a decision procedure and accepted the necessity for something akin to *prognosis* to enable an agent to apply their principles correctly. Can a young person brought up in a WASP environment, however well-intentioned, apply "Treat other persons with respect" or "Don't hurt other people's feelings needlessly" correctly? They may try, but the Afro-Americans, and the Amer-Indians, and the Asian Indians and the Middle Eastern Muslims will assure you that they fail, badly. They need, deontologists and consequentialists now recognize, sensitivity, imagination, perception, judgment, and experience before they can do it.

Although, within the context of ethics in practice, stressing the necessity for sensitivity, imagination, and so on is probably enough to give you the idea of *phronesis*, I should just briefly outline what is still explicitly lacking in it from the Aristotelian perspective.

As we have seen, Aristotle holds that you cannot have full virtue/excellence of character without *phronesis*. And when we think of the mistakes high-minded, "virtuous," adolescents are still prone to make, that seems obvious. But, more tendentiously, he also claims that you cannot have *phronesis* without virtue/excellence of character. When virtuous character is fully developed, it, and *phronesis*, are just two sides of the same coin. Why should he say such a thing?

> There is an ability that people call "cleverness"; and this is of a sort that, when it comes to the things that conduce to a proposed goal, it is able to carry these out and do so successfully. If the aim is a fine one, this ability is to be praised, but if the aim is a bad one, then it is villainy. This is why both wise and villainous people are called clever. Wisdom is not the same as this ability though it does involve it. [And this is because] a wise person <is> able to deliberate well about the sorts of things that conduce to the good life in general, i.e. *eudaimonia*. (NE 1140a24–29)

Shakespeare's Iago is, on any ordinary understanding of the terms, sensitive, imaginative, perceptive, experienced, and with excellent judgment. It is just those characteristics that enable him to manipulate Othello so cleverly and to hit his wicked target bang on. But he is not wise; you wouldn't go to him for guidance about how to live well.

Contemporary Virtue Ethics

In the early days of twentieth-century virtue ethics, the major problem was finding a way to get the Aristotelian material to engage with the contemporary debates about euthanasia, abortion, racism, and sexism, and our treatment of animals. (Our treatment of the environment was not yet an issue then.) Not only does Aristotle not discuss any of these in his ethical works (though we know only too well what he thought about racism, sexism, and killing animals from the *Politics*) but he does not give an extended discussion of *any* moral issue. Lacking an authoritative example of what the virtue ethics approach looked like in practice, its proponents found themselves driven to reiterating their Aristotelian claim that what it was right for a particular agent to do in a particular situation (and, necessarily, an actual action is always done by a particular agent in a particular situation) was far too complex a matter to be captured by the application of rules or principles, and that you should do what the fully virtuous agent would do in the circumstances, using your *phronesis*. And, not unnaturally, the proponents of the other approaches regarded this with contempt. "Where, in practice, are we going to find this hypothetical agent?" they asked. "And how, in practice, would we recognize one if we did?"

However, taking up a suggestion from Anscombe's 1958 paper, which is generally regarded as heralding the re-emergence of virtue ethics, its proponents found a way to preserve the Aristotelian idea that, "The right action is what a (fully) virtuous person would do in the circumstances," while deflecting the contemptuous questions. By and large, we do not need to find a virtuous agent, because in one way, we know what she does and would do. She does, and would do, what is virtuous, not vicious, that is, she does what is courageous, just, honest, charitable, loyal, kind, generous . . . and does not do what is cowardly or reckless, unjust, dishonest, uncharitable, malevolent, disloyal, unkind, stingy. Thus each virtue generates a prescription –"Do what is courageous, just, etc." – and every vice a prohibition – "Do not do what is cowardly or reckless, unjust, etc." and in order to do what the virtuous agent would do in the circumstances, one acts in accordance with these – which are called "v-rules."

Do I hear you ask, "How do we know that courage, justice, honesty, etc. are virtues and the others vices?" Students usually do ask this, but without noticing that they *don't* ask, "How do we know that equal interests should be equally respected or that people have a right to life, or to decide what happens to their own body?" when they read articles such as those in this collection. The fact is, all argument has to start somewhere, with premises that are not argued for in *that* context, and, in the context of applied ethics, or ethics in practice, everyone starts with unargued-for moral premises, such as "courage is a virtue" or "people have a right to life." Philosophers address the "How do we know?" question in the more abstract context of theoretical ethics.

That same abstract context is also the proper home for debates about cultural relativism. It is often claimed that the v-rules are inherently culturally specific and conservative because they are developed within existing traditions and societies. Indeed, in an early work, MacIntyre defined the virtues as specific to a tradition, rather than as rooted in human nature, as those who follow Aristotle (as MacIntyre later came to do) claim. But of course what the other approaches find "reasonable" or "rationally acceptable" about their principles is just as likely to have been shaped by modern Western culture and (predominantly) American society. We all need to admit that none of us has reason to suppose that our lists of rules are complete or beyond revision, though virtue ethicists may take heart from the empirical fact of the existence of the Virtues Project (go to www.virtuesproject.com). It is an international educational program based on 52 (!) virtues found to be common to seven of the world's major cultural traditions, which has been translated into numerous languages and successfully used in schools all over the world.

Mention of the Virtues Project brings us to an interesting feature of the v-rules. They are not the product of academic philosophers. They are not available because philosophers have theorized about everyday discussions of practical ethical issues and abstracted the morally relevant criteria from those discussions. They are, as the Virtues Project shows, simply the product of the common or garden, grassroots, moral vocabulary of the virtues and vices. In modern Western society, it is quite likely that much of this will be part of your reading rather than your spoken vocabulary – when did you last use the words "humble" or "prodigal"? – but it is still your vocabulary, sitting there waiting to be used. And, insofar as virtue ethics "tells you what to do," it tells you to use it, claiming that if you use it honestly and thoughtfully, it will give you *much* better guidance about what to do, day to day, in your life with other people, than the principles the other approaches come up with.

Part of the reason why (according to virtue ethicists) the v-rules offer much better guidance is that the vocabulary is *huge* and mostly remarkably specific. This is perhaps most noticeable with respect to rules couched in terms that connote, if not strictly vices, at least ways of falling seriously short of virtue. Much invaluable action guidance comes from avoiding actions that are irresponsible, feckless, lazy, inconsiderate, uncooperative, harsh, intolerant, indiscreet, tactless, arrogant, unsympathetic, cold, incautious, unenterprising, pusillanimous, feeble, presumptuous, hypocritical, self-indulgent, materialistic, grasping, short-sighted, punitive, disloyal, calculating, ungrateful, grudging, disingenuous, phony, rude, insensitive, spiteful, untrustworthy, treacherous, sneaky, manipulative . . . and on and on. It is no accident that we have all these terms. Every one of them has a correct use in some situation to which none of the others applies so well, and every time they single out a morally relevant feature of that situation. Such a feature may easily be overlooked if one doesn't make a point of using this vocabulary and relies instead on general principles that encapsulate only rather general morally relevant features.

Another reason they offer better guidance is that, long before we have reached the age of wisdom, we have a surprisingly subtle and nuanced understanding of them. However young you may be, you already know (though perhaps without realizing it) that the wide range of actions that honest people characteristically do, and refrain from, is far from being captured by, for example, "Do not lie." That still allows being "economical with the truth" in the way that some dishonest, cunning people are; so far we have set the standards for what counts as doing what is honest too low. So should we add, "Don't be economical with the truth, always tell it"? No, because now we have gone too far, specifying not honesty but brutal frankness or candor or ingenuousness. (How one dreads those frank, candid people who so typically begin, "I hope you won't mind my saying this but . . . ") So should we add, "Eschew being economical with the truth, tell it not always but when . . . "? But when what? There is, virtue ethicists think, no better way to capture when one must speak out and when one should remain discreetly silent, when one should tell the whole truth and when one should tell only part of it, than by saying "when an honest person characteristically would." And you already understand that so well that you could think of lots of examples of when they would and when they wouldn't – and thereby of when you should and when you shouldn't.

This is not, of course, to say that your – or my – understanding is complete. It is as true of the v-rules as of any others that *phronesis* is needed to apply them correctly in tricky situations; this brings us to the question of dilemmas. It is obvious that the requirements of the different virtues may, at least apparently, conflict. Honesty points to telling the hurtful truth, kindness or compassion to remaining silent or even lying. But so too do the related deontologists' and rule-consequentialists' rules, rightly reflecting the fact (ignored by the old act utilitarians) that life does present us with dilemmas whose resolution, even if correct, should leave us with a remainder of regret. Like the proponents of the other two approaches, virtue ethicists seek resolutions of such conflicts in a more refined or nuanced understanding or application of the rules involved; and, as with the other approaches, its proponents may disagree about the correct resolution.

In the case of virtue ethics, this "more nuanced understanding" does not standardly involve adding exception clauses to the v-rules. Rather it consists in such claims as, "One does people no kindness in concealing this sort of truth from them," or "The importance of the truth in this situation puts the consideration of hurt feelings out of court," or "You wouldn't say someone lacked honesty because she remained silent about that sort of thing in these circumstances." Hence it is very difficult to do virtue ethics in practice because only (the beginnings of) *phronesis* enables one to come up with such claims and to articulate what makes them plausible.

But this, virtue ethicists say, is just as it should be. Getting things right, hitting the target, *is* difficult, and not merely in the way that philosophy is difficult. Outside ethics, you can get difficult things right in philosophy if you are clever. In ethics, in practice, cleverness is not enough.

Eudaimonia

The agent with *phronesis* has a true grasp of *eudaimonia*, of "the good life" or how to live well. Under the influence of virtue ethics, this concept is more familiar than it was ten years ago. Many moral philosophers now use the term "objective well-being," which is certainly closer to *eudaimonia* than "happiness" is. The trouble with "happiness" as a translation is that, on any contemporary understanding of it uninfluenced by classically trained writers, it connotes something that is entirely subjectively determined. If I think I am happy then I am, and if I think I am not, then I am not – it's not something I can be wrong about. But this holds of *eudaimonia* only in part. I can't be wrong about my feeling of misery, and I can't be miserable and *eudaimon* (the adjective from *eudaimonia*) (nor miserable and in a state of well-being) so here, too, if I think I am not *eudaimon* then I am not; I can't be wrong about that. But I may well think that I am *eudaimon* and be just plain wrong, not because I am deceiving myself about my suppressed misery, but because I have the wrong conception of *eudaimonia*, believing it to consist largely in physical pleasure or luxury or "feeling good." Similarly, lying around in a state of drug-induced bliss, or hooked up to Nozick's pleasure-machine, I may think that I am in a state of objective well-being, but if I do, I am simply mistaken; it is something I can be wrong about.

However, the modern notion of "objective well-being" is perhaps still not quite equivalent to that of Aristotelian *eudaimonia*. It is often stipulated as consisting in some set of "non-moral" goods, which does not include virtuous activity, whereas *eudaimonia* is an explicitly moralized concept; virtue is, at least partly, constitutive of it.

On this picture, the familiar modern distinction between the dictates of prudence, or self-interest, and those of morality vanishes. Although, if I am virtuous, I choose virtuous actions for their own sake, not for ulterior reasons, *nothing* is more beneficial to me than acting virtuously.

PART II

Life and Death

Euthanasia

Should individuals, especially terminally ill people in excruciating pain, be able to end their lives? If so, may they hasten their deaths only by refusing medical treatment designed to sustain their lives, or may they take active measures to kill themselves? If they can take measures to kill themselves, can they ask others to assist them? Who can they ask: their spouses? close friends? their doctors? Should the law support their decisions?

Many people think that (at least) terminally ill people have the moral authority to decide whether and how to end their lives. If people have the freedom to choose how to live, they ask, why should they not also have the freedom to choose how to die? Many authors in this section think people should have that choice. If we respect individuals then we should give them this control over their lives. That view reflects the general public's. Most people now acknowledge that it is sometimes acceptable for an individual to act (or refuse to act) in ways that hasten her death.

Here the broad consensus ends. There is still considerable disagreement about when, where, and how a person may do so. Some claim only the terminally ill have the moral authority to

end their lives, while others claim that anyone who finds her life no longer worth living may kill herself. Some claim an individual can hasten her death only by refusing medical treatment that sustains her life, while others claim that an individual can legitimately take active measures to end her life. In short, many people disagree about the conditions under which a person may legitimately seek death, and about what such a person can legitimately do, or entice others to do, to achieve that end.

Even this broad consensus is fairly recent. Historically many people thought it was immoral for anyone to hasten her death, either by actively killing herself or by failing to take heroic measures to keep herself alive. They believed a person must preserve her life, even if it were, in some important sense, no longer worth living. Although few people now embrace this view in its strongest form, a significant number of people, like Velleman, have serious misgivings about the claim that people have a right to end their own lives, even if they are terminally ill and in considerable pain.

Velleman critiques the claim common to three of these essays: that we can justify the right to die by appealing to individual autonomy.

Having options, he argues, is not an unadulterated good. Options may make us vulnerable to unwanted pressure from others. For example, having the option of working for less than the minimum wage increases the chances that employers will offer people less than the minimum wage. Options also close off the possibility that we can maintain the status quo (in this case, continuing to live) without having to choose it. Autonomy is not the only good nor is it invariably desirable.

Most people, Velleman included, believe autonomy is a significant element of morality that the law must respect. They disagree profoundly, however, about the scope of autonomy, about the specific role it plays in a proper understanding of morality and the law. For instance, should the law always respect our explicit wishes, even when we wish to act in a way that would normally be considered harmful – as killing oneself would be? Should we have autonomy to do only those things that society considers to be in our own best interests?

Concern for autonomy is also critical for many moral issues, especially questions about PATERNALISM AND RISK. Should an individual be able to choose how she wants to live, even if others think those choices are detrimental to her? Suppose the action is likely detrimental, e.g. through the use of mind-altering drugs. Does that justify the state's making such use illegal?

Just as virtually everyone recognizes that autonomy is morally significant, most also acknowledge that it is not the only relevant moral consideration. Among other things, a single-minded attention on autonomy may mask the ways in which our choices (or lack of them) are shaped by our legal, political, social, and economic environments. For instance, an individual may decide that her life is no longer worth living because she is suffering from an extremely painful and debilitating disease. However, as Cohn and Lynn argue, the disease may be especially painful and debilitating only because she cannot afford first-rate medical care. Under these circumstances, death may be her best option. However, death may be the best option only because of the reigning

political and economic structures. In a different economic and political world other options might be preferable.

The emphasis on autonomy may also lead us to overlook the ways that our dying – or continuing to live – profoundly affects our families. Suppose I decide to have doctors use every conceivable means to keep me alive. That choice does not affect only me. Family and friends must inevitably bear the emotional trauma of seeing me debilitated and in pain. Likely they must also bear substantial financial costs. Often they must make considerable personal sacrifices since they likely would be expected – at least in our society – to care for me. In short, my decision to live or die substantially affects the interests of friends and family. Should they therefore, as Hardwig argues, be centrally involved in making the decision about my death? Or should they, as Hooker argues, be explicitly excluded from making such decisions since they are likely biased precisely because their interests are so heavily affected?

This disagreement between Hooker and Hardwig hints at a deep divide in ethical perspectives between individualists, who hold that personal autonomy is perhaps the highest, moral good, and communitarians, who stress our relationships with others. Put differently, individualists focus on our separateness from (and often conflicts with) others, while communitarians focus on our relationships with, dependence on, and responsibilities to, others. This fundamental difference in moral outlook weaves through many issues discussed in this volume.

Despite these differences, virtually all ethicists acknowledge that in addition to determining whether it would be moral to end one's life, we must also ask whether these choices should be legally protected. For instance, Beauchamp, Hooker, and Cohn/Lynn argue (for different reasons) that we must be concerned about the broader effects of legalizing assisted suicide. What are the likely consequences of legally permitting physician-assisted suicide? Beauchamp is worried that it would damage the doctor–patient relationship; in particular, he fears it would make doctors less committed to saving life and less sensitive to their patients' pain. Cohn and Lynn think this consequence is likely if one speaks, as Hardwig does, about a duty to die. If this were a consequence of legalizing the practice, it would be a powerful reason to oppose its legalization, even if we might think individuals have the right to take their own lives.

The issue of euthanasia is further complicated by the injection of the act/omission (or doing/allowing) distinction. Most people think there is a significant moral difference between things we do and things we permit: it is worse to kill Robert than (merely) to let him die. Some people employ that distinction to explain why passive euthanasia (removing medical measures sustaining a person's life) is morally acceptable, while active euthanasia, (an individual's – or some person acting for the individual – taking active steps to hasten her death) is morally objectionable. Most people who oppose active euthanasia rest their case on the purported moral significance of the act/omission distinction.

We will see this distinction at work in several moral issues. For example, most people think

that while killing Bengali children would be morally heinous, refusing to provide these same children with food, medical, and economic assistance is not immoral (WORLD HUNGER). This distinction is often associated with a deep theoretical divide between deontological and consequentialist moral theories. Consequentialists, being more concerned with the outcome or consequences of actions, will tend to see no strong reason to think that acts are morally more significant than omissions. As Beauchamp argues, although it sometimes appears that acts are morally more significant than omissions, that is usually because this distinction is conjoined with morally relevant differences that explain the different moral evaluations.

Deontologists, on the other hand, are more likely to think the act/omission distinction is fundamentally important. Since they think the consequences of our actions are, at most, only a portion of the moral story, they are prone to put moral emphasis on what we explicitly do rather than on what we permit.

Further Reading

Arras, J. D. (1999) "Physician-Assisted Suicide: A Tragic View." In J. D. Arras and B. Steinbock (eds.), *Ethical Issues in Modern Medicine*, 5th edn. Palo Alto, CA: Mayfield Publishing Company, pp. 274–80.

Battin, M. P. (2000) "Euthanasia and Physician-Assisted Suicide." In H. LaFollette (ed.), *Oxford Handbook of Practical Ethics*. Oxford: Oxford University Press, pp. 673–704.

Beauchamp, T. (ed.) (1996) *Intending Death: The Ethics of Assisted Suicide and Euthanasia*. Englewood Cliffs, NJ: Prentice-Hall.

Beauchamp, T. and Childress, J. (1983) *Principles of Biomedical Ethics*, 2nd edn. Oxford: Oxford University Press.

Beauchamp, T. and Walters, L. (eds.) (1994) *Contemporary Issues in Biomedical Ethics*. Belmont, CA: Wadsworth.

Pence, G. (1995) "Comas: Karen Quinlan and Nancy Cruzan," in *Classic Cases in Medical Ethics*. New York: McGraw-Hill.

Quill, T. (1991) " 'Death and Dignity': A Case of Individualized Decision Making," *New England Journal of Medicine* 324: 691–4.

Quill, T. and Cassell, C. (1995) "Nonabandonment: A Central Obligation for Physicians," *Annals of Internal Medicine* 122: 368–74.

Steinbock, B. (1980) *Killing and Letting Die*. Englewood Cliffs, NJ: Prentice-Hall.

Veatch, R. (ed.) (1989) *Medical Ethics*. Boston: Jones and Bartlett Publishers.

4

Rule-Utilitarianism and Euthanasia

Brad Hooker

1 Introduction

As scientific and technological advances enable the medical profession to keep people alive longer, the question arises whether this is always a good thing. Should those who could prolong life step back under certain conditions and allow a very ill person to die? And if allowing to die is sometimes right, then what about actively killing patients when this would be better for the patients than allowing them to die more slowly and painfully?

Such questions are debated under the heading of euthanasia. The term "euthanasia" derives from the Greek term for an easy, painless death. However, we often now hear the term "passive euthanasia," which refers to passing up opportunities to save an individual from death, out of concern for that individual. If passive euthanasia is indeed one kind of euthanasia, then "euthanasia" cannot mean "killing painlessly"; for to pass up an opportunity to save someone, i.e., passive euthanasia, is arguably not *killing*. Furthermore, the death involved in passive euthanasia is often *painful*. So let us take the term "euthanasia" to mean "either killing or passing up opportunities to save someone, out of concern for that person." (Note that, on this definition, what the Nazis called "euthanasia" was not euthanasia, because it was not done out of concern for the patients.)

Different moral theories will of course approach questions about the moral status of euthanasia in different ways, though some of these theories will end up with the same conclusions. This essay considers euthanasia from the perspective of just one moral theory. The theory is rule-utilitarianism. Rule-utilitarianism assesses possible rules in terms of their expected utility. It then tells us to follow the rules with the greatest expected utility. (Expected utility is calculated by multiplying the utility of each possible outcome by the probability that it will occur.)

In the next section, I explain what the term "utility" means. Then I outline another utilitarian theory – act-utilitarianism. I do this in order to contrast rule-utilitarianism with this perhaps more familiar theory. I then outline the distinctions between different kinds of euthanasia. The final sections of the paper consider the various factors that would go into a rule-utilitarian decision about euthanasia.

2   Utility

A moral theory is utilitarian if and only if it assesses acts and/or rules in terms of nothing but their utility. Classical utilitarianism took "utility" to refer to the well-being of sentient creatures. And classical utilitarianism took the well-being of sentient creatures to consist in pleasure and the absence of pain (Bentham, 1823; Mill, 1863; Sidgwick, 1877). On this view, people's level of well-being is determined *solely* by how much pleasure and pain they experience.

If anything is desirable for its own sake, pleasure is. But most utilitarians now think that pleasure, even if construed as widely as possible, is not the *only* thing desirable in itself, and pain not the *only* thing undesirable in itself (Moore, 1903, ch. 6; Hare, 1981, 101ff; Parfit, 1984, appendix I; Griffin, 1986, Part One; Goodin, 1991, p. 244; Harsanyi, 1993). Utilitarians can think that things that are desirable for their own sake include not only pleasure but also important knowledge, friendship, autonomy, achievement, and so on. Indeed, many utilitarians now construe utility just as the fulfillment of desire or the satisfaction of preferences, with relatively few restrictions on what the desires or preferences are for.

One reason most utilitarians have moved away from a version of utilitarianism that focuses exclusively on pleasure has to do with knowledge. Many of us care about certain things over and above the pleasure they typically bring, and one of these things is knowing the important truths (e.g., about the nature of the universe and about oneself), even if not knowing the truth would be more pleasant for us. Bliss isn't everything – for example, if purchased at the cost of ignorance. To be sure, knowledge does not always constitute a more significant addition to well-being than does pleasure. But sometimes it does.

People also care about autonomy, by which I mean control over one's own life. Many of us would be willing to trade away some pleasure for the sake of an increase in autonomy. Again, this is not to say that even a tiny increase in autonomy is more important than a great deal of pleasure; rather, the point is that pleasure is not always more important to our well-being than autonomy. Neither value is always more important than the other.

I agree with such convictions. Knowledge, autonomy, and other things can be beneficial to us, can increase our well-being, over and beyond whatever pleasure they directly or indirectly bring us. I shall presuppose this in what follows.

I shall also follow conventional philosophical opinion in supposing that it is possible to be in such a bad condition that death would be a welcome release. Severe pain can be unremitting, and indeed so overpowering that the person experiencing it can think of nothing else. If the rest of my life would consist of nothing but excruciating physical pain, then I might be better off dead. Indeed, if the rest of my life would consist wholly of intense psychological suffering, I'd be better off dead. Of course, we may argue about where to draw the line between being better off dead and being better off alive (Mitchell, 1995). But it seems deeply unreasonable to insist that there are never any instances of patients who would be better off dead.

Now, what about *divinely bestowed* benefits and harms? Most utilitarians, and all utilitarian writers of our era, have written as if there were no rewards or punishments granted by a god or gods. This is not to say that all utilitarians have been atheists. In fact, many have been religious believers (perhaps most notably, Bishop Berkeley, 1712). Nor would *any* utilitarians – theistic or agnostic or atheistic – hold that a person's religious beliefs are completely irrelevant to the morality of how he or she is treated. For any utilitarian would recognize that people's religious beliefs can have an effect on what brings them pleasure and on what preferences they form. So utilitarianism will favor, for example, freedom of religion and even the neutrality of the state with respect to religion.[1] But while utilitarians can think that people's religious beliefs are often relevant to moral argument about how these people should be treated, modern utilitarians eschew basing any moral argument on the *truth* of any religious belief. And this prohibition on assuming the truth of any religious belief applies to the belief that there are divinely bestowed benefits and harms.

That said, we must also note that utilitarianism is also often said to assume a god's-eye point of view. The main respect in which this is true is that the utilitarian approach prescribes a totally impartial calculation of well-being. To be more specific, in the calculation of utility, benefits or harms to any one person are to count for just as much as the same amount of benefit or harm to anyone else – that is, count the same without regard to race, religion, gender, social class, or the like.

It is a mistake to think that utilitarians hold that what benefits more people is *necessarily* better than what benefits fewer. Utilitarians focus on the greatest aggregate good. What results in the greatest aggregate good is sometimes not what benefits the majority. This is because the benefits to each of the smaller number may be large and the benefits to each of the greater number small. And large benefits to each of a minority can add up to more than small benefits to each of a majority. Thus, utilitarians will favor what benefits the minority if (but only if) what benefits the minority results in the greatest good overall.

On the other hand, many philosophers have pointed out that utilitarianism gives no intrinsic weight to how equally or fairly benefits are distributed. I myself accept that this is an important potential problem with utilitarianism. But because I don't think these worries about distribution are relevant to euthanasia, I shall ignore them in this paper.

3   Act-utilitarianism

The most direct and most discussed form of utilitarianism is act-utilitarianism. There are different versions of this theory. One version holds that an act is right if and only if its *actual consequences* would contain at least as much utility as those of any other act open to the agent. Another version claims that an act is right if and only if its *expected* utility is at least as great as that of any alternative.

But there are many familiar counter-examples to both versions of act-utilitarianism.

Some of these counter-examples have to do with moral prohibitions. For example, both versions of act-utilitarianism imply that killing an innocent person, or stealing, or breaking a promise would be morally right if the expected and actual utility of the act would be greater, even if just slightly greater, than that of any alternative act. We might think that normally prohibited acts could be right in very rare circumstances in which doing such acts is the only way to prevent something much worse. But we don't think such acts are permissible when the expected and actual utility of such an act would be only slightly greater than that of complying with the prohibition.

Another problem with act-utilitarianism is that it seems unreasonably demanding, requiring acts of self-sacrifice that seem beyond the call of duty. Think how much a middle-class individual in a relatively affluent country would have to give to CARE or Oxfam before further sacrifices on her part would constitute a larger loss to her than the benefit to the starving that CARE or Oxfam would produce with that contribution. Making sacrifices for strangers up to the point that act-utilitarianism requires would be saintly. But morality, most of us think, does not *require* sainthood.

4   Rule-utilitarianism

Rule-utilitarianism differs from act-utilitarianism in that rule-utilitarianism does *not* assess each act solely by its utility. Rather, rule-utilitarianism assesses acts in terms of rules, and rules in terms of their utility. Rule-utilitarianism holds that an act is morally permissible if and only if the rules with the greatest expected utility would allow it. The expected utility of rules is a matter of the utility of their "general" internalization, i.e., internalization by the overwhelming majority. For a code of rules to be internalized is for people to believe these rules justified and to be disposed to act and react in accordance with them. Assume I have internalized a rule against killing people against their will. If this assumption is correct, I will (a) think this kind of act wrong, (b) be disposed not to do this kind of act, and (c) be disposed to react negatively to those who I think have done it.

To say that rule-utilitarians focus on the consequences of the general internalization of rules does not mean that they consider only rules that existing people *already* accept. Rather, the question rule-utilitarians ask about each possible code is what the effects on utility would be of the code's being successfully inculcated in people who had no prior moral beliefs or attitudes. At least in principle, the code of rules best from a utilitarian point of view might be very different from those now accepted in any given society. (For developments of this sort of theory, see Brandt, 1963, 1967, 1979, part two; 1988; Harsanyi, 1982; Johnson, 1991; Barrow, 1991; Hooker, 1995, 2000.)

The intuitive attractions of rule-utilitarianism become clear as we notice the ways in which this theory seems superior to act-utilitarianism. For unlike act-utilitarianism, rule-utilitarianism agrees with common conviction that individual acts of murder, torture, promise-breaking, and so on can be wrong even when they produce somewhat more good than their omission would produce. For the general internalization of rules prohibiting murder, torture, promise-breaking, and the like would clearly result in more good than the general internalization of rules that did not prohibit such acts. Thus, on the rule-utilitarian criterion of moral permissibility, acts of murder, torture, and so on, can be impermissible even in rare cases where they really would produce better consequences than any alternative act.

Likewise, rule-utilitarianism will not require the level of self-sacrifice act-utilitarianism requires. For, crudely, rule-utilitarianism approaches this problem by asking how much each relatively well-off person would have to contribute in order for there to be enough to overcome world hunger and severe poverty. If *the overwhelming majority of the world's relatively well-off* made regular contributions to the most efficient famine relief organizations, no one would have to make severe self-sacrifices. Thus, rule-utilitarianism is not excessively demanding (Hooker, 1991, 2000; cf. Carson, 1991).

The advantages of rule-utilitarianism over act-utilitarianism are often construed as utilitarian advantages. In other words, some philosophers have argued that rule-utilitarianism will in fact produce more utility than act-utilitarianism (Brandt, 1979, pp. 271–7; Harsanyi, 1982, pp. 56–61; and Johnson, 1991, especially chs. 3, 4, 9; Haslett, 1994, p. 21; but compare Hooker, 1995, section III). I am *not* running that argument. Instead, I am merely pointing out that rule-utilitarianism seems to have implications that are more intuitively acceptable than those of act-utilitarianism (Brandt, 1963; 1967).

5 Kinds of Euthanasia

We need to distinguish three different kinds of euthanasia, or rather three different ways euthanasia can be related to the will of the person killed. Suppose I ask you to either kill me or let me die should my medical condition get so bad that I am delirious and won't recover. If you then comply with my request, we have what is commonly called *voluntary euthanasia*. It is voluntary because the person killed asked that this be done.

Now suppose that I slip into an irreversible coma without ever telling anyone whether I wanted to be killed in such circumstances. If I am then killed or let die, we have what is commonly called *non-voluntary euthanasia*. The distinguishing characteristic of non-voluntary euthanasia is that it is euthanasia on someone who did not express a desire on the matter.

But what if I do express a desire not to be killed no matter how bad my condition gets? Then killing me would constitute what is called *involuntary euthanasia*. Quite apart from its moral status, involuntary euthanasia can seem puzzling. To be euthanasia, it must be done for the good of the person killed. Yet if the person concerned expresses a desire that it not be done, how can it be done for this person's own good? Well, involuntary euthanasia may be morally wrong (we will discuss why in a moment), but we must start by acknowledging that people are *not always* in the best position to know what is best for themselves. Someone could be mistaken even about whether he or she would be better off dead than alive in a certain state. And other people could think that the person in front of them had made just this kind of mistake. If they not only thought this but also were motivated to do what was best for this person, they might contemplate euthanasia. What they would then be contemplating would be involuntary euthanasia.

Another important distinction is the distinction between active and passive euthanasia. Active euthanasia involves actively killing some one out of a concern for that person's own good. Passive euthanasia involves passing up opportunities to prevent the death of someone out of concern for that person's own good.

The distinction between active and passive euthanasia cuts across the distinction between voluntary, non-voluntary, and involuntary euthanasia. In other words, either with my consent, or without knowing what my wishes are or were, or against my wishes, you might kill me. Likewise, either with my consent, or without knowing what my wishes are or were, or against my wishes, you might pass up an opportunity to keep me from dying. Thus we have:

Active Voluntary Euthanasia
Active Non-voluntary Euthanasia
Active Involuntary Euthanasia
Passive Voluntary Euthanasia
Passive Non-voluntary Euthanasia
Passive Involuntary Euthanasia

6 Law and Morality

We also need to distinguish between questions about law and questions about moral rightness, permissibility, and wrongness. Utilitarians, as well as moral philosophers of many other stripes, can think that there may be some moral requirements that the law should not try to enforce. A relatively uncontroversial example concerns the moral requirement forbidding breaking verbal promises to your spouse. There may be good utilitarian reasons for not bothering the law with such matters – to police the give and take of such relationships might be

too difficult and too invasive. This isn't to deny that breaking verbal promises to spouses is usually morally wrong, only that the law shouldn't poke its nose into this matter.

So, initially at least, there is the potential for divergence in what the rule-utilitarian says about the law and about morality. There is less scope for this on rule-utilitarianism, however, than there is on some other theories. For both in the case of law and in the case of morality, the first thing rule-utilitarianism considers is the consequences of our *collective* compliance with rules. (See Mill, 1863, ch. 5.)

With respect to euthanasia, rule-utilitarianism is especially likely to take the same line on law as it does on morality. That is, if rule-utilitarians think that people's being allowed in certain circumstances to kill or let die would have generally good consequences, then they will think such acts are *morally* allowed in the specified circumstances. They will also think the *law* should allow them in the specified conditions. And if they think the consequences would be generally bad, then they will think morality does, and the law should, prohibit the acts in question.

Thus, in the following discussion of the rule-utilitarian approach to euthanasia, I will focus on just one realm and assume that the other follows suit. The realm on which I shall focus is the law. The question, then, is: what kinds of euthanasia (if any) should the law allow?

7 The Potential Benefits of Euthanasia

Perhaps the most obvious potential benefit of permitting euthanasia is that it could be used to prevent the unnecessary elongation of the suffering experienced by many terminally ill people and their families. What about painkilling drugs? Some kinds of pain cannot be eliminated with drugs, or at least not with drugs that leave the patient conscious and mentally coherent. And in addition to physical agony, there is often overwhelming emotional suffering for the patient, and derivatively for friends and family in attendance. All this could be shortened if euthanasia were allowed.

To the extent that the point is speedy termination of physical and emotional suffering, active rather than passive euthanasia can seem desirable. For passive euthanasia would often involve a slow and painful death, whereas active euthanasia could end the patient's suffering immediately. There may, however, be especially large costs associated with allowing active euthanasia. I shall consider these later.

Another advantage of permitting euthanasia – and again the advantage is even more pronounced in the case of permitting active euthanasia – concerns resource allocation. The resources, both economic and human, that are now devoted to keeping alive people who have incurable and debilitating diseases could often more cost-effectively be devoted to curing people of curable diseases, or to funding preventive medicine, or even just to feeding the starving. What I mean by saying that the change in resource allocation would be more cost effective is that this would increase average life-expectancy and quality of life.

For utilitarians who count personal autonomy as a value over and above whatever feelings of satisfaction it brings and frustration it prevents, there is an additional consideration. It is that *voluntary* euthanasia must increase personal autonomy, in that it gives people some control over *when* their lives end. And if active voluntary euthanasia were allowed, this would give people some control over *how* their lives end. Concern for people's autonomy obviously counts only in favor of *voluntary* euthanasia. It is irrelevant to the discussion of non-voluntary euthanasia of any kind, and opposes involuntary euthanasia of any kind.

8   The Potential Harms of Allowing Involuntary Euthanasia

A law permitting active *involuntary* euthanasia is likely to be strongly opposed by rule-utilitarians for other reasons as well. One such reason is that many people would be scared away from hospitals and doctors if they thought that they might be killed against their wishes. I cannot imagine how allowing involuntary euthanasia

could generate benefits large enough even to begin to offset this loss. The last thing a public policy should do is scare people away from trained medical experts. A related point is that allowing involuntary euthanasia would terrify many people taken to a hospital while unconscious. Imagine waking up to find that you had been taken to a hospital where people can, *against your wishes*, kill you, as long as they (claim to) think this would be best for you.

Furthermore, to allow the killing of innocent people against their wishes would be difficult to square with other moral prohibitions of supreme importance. In particular, the general feeling of abhorrence for the killing of innocent people against their wishes is, as Hobbes (1651) insisted, the bedrock of social existence. Without communal acceptance of that prohibition, life would be precarious and insecure. No law should be passed which genuinely threatens to undermine people's commitment to the general prohibition on killing the innocent against their wishes.

At this point someone might say, "Ah, but we can distinguish between killing innocent people against their wishes but *for their own good*, and killing them *for some other reason*." True, we can make that distinction. But is it a distinction whose enshrinement in law would be felicitous? No, again because people would not feel secure in a society where they might be, against their wishes, killed for their own good.

These points about insecurity add up to a very persuasive rule-utilitarian argument against permitting *active* involuntary euthanasia. But do they count against *passive* involuntary euthanasia? In the case of passive euthanasia, there isn't such a risk that people will stay away from doctors and hospitals for fear of being made worse off than they are already. Suppose you had a serious illness and found yourself in a society where active involuntary euthanasia was neither permitted nor practiced, but passive involuntary euthanasia was permitted and practiced. Then, you would not need fear that going to the hospital would get you killed against your wishes. But you might worry that the doctors or hospital would, against your wishes, pass up opportunities to prolong your life. Yet you probably wouldn't live longer if you stayed out of the hospitals. Indeed, if you were under the care of a doctor, you would probably suffer less. Thus, you have less to lose by going into the hospital in a society where passive involuntary euthanasia is permitted than you do in a society where active involuntary euthanasia is permitted. If passive involuntary euthanasia only were legally and morally permitted, the consequence would not be that everyone who thought they had or might have a fatal disease would avoid doctors. So the disadvantages of allowing passive involuntary euthanasia are clearly less than the disadvantages of allowing active involuntary euthanasia.

The disadvantages of allowing passive involuntary euthanasia may nevertheless be enough to convince rule-utilitarians to oppose it. Utilitarians have long argued that their doctrine is generally anti-paternalistic (Mill, 1859). Grown-up human beings are generally the ones who know which of the ways their lives might unfold would be best for themselves, because they are generally the ones who know best their own aspirations, tastes, talents, sensitivities, vulnerabilities, etc. Of course there are general exceptions – e.g., people with permanent or temporary mental impairments. But, by and large, people are the best guardians of their own well-being.

As noted at the very end of the previous section, rule-utilitarians can have another reason for opposing involuntary euthanasia, passive just as much as active. This reason comes from the idea that autonomy is an important component of well-being. Indeed, this seems to be the strongest rule-utilitarian reason for disallowing passive involuntary euthanasia.

9 The Potential Harms of Allowing Voluntary and Non-voluntary Euthanasia

Turn now to the harms that voluntary and non-voluntary euthanasia might involve. Suppose the doctors tell Jones he has disease X. This disease almost immediately produces excruciating pain, dementia, and then death. Jones asks

to be killed, or at least allowed to die, before the pain gets too severe. The doctors comply with Jones's wishes. Later, however, a post-mortem reveals that he didn't have disease X at all, but instead some curable condition. As this story illustrates, euthanasia can inappropriately take a life after a mistaken diagnosis.

And yet how often do medical experts misdiagnose a condition as a terminal illness when it isn't? And how wise is it now to go against expert medical opinion? And are there ways of minimizing the risk of doctors acting on misdiagnoses? Euthanasia could be restricted to cases where three independent medical experts – and I mean *real* experts – make the same diagnosis. With such a restriction, the worry about misdiagnoses seems overblown.

But closely associated with the point that doctors sometimes misdiagnose someone's condition is the point that doctors are sometimes wrong about what will happen to someone whose condition is correctly diagnosed. Suppose the doctors rightly believe that there is now no treatment known to prevent the disease some people have from bringing acute pain followed by a painful death. But a cure or more effective pain block might soon be discovered. If people are killed or allowed to die today and the medical breakthrough comes tomorrow, euthanasia will have amounted to giving up on those people too soon – with obviously tragic results.

However, again restrictions could be put in place to prevent the losses envisaged. One restriction could specify that euthanasia is completely out of the question until someone is fairly near the final stages of a disease, where new cures or treatments are very unlikely to be able to change the fatal path of the disease. (And one way of approximating this restriction would be to allow *passive* but not *active* euthanasia. But this seems an unnecessarily crude way of ensuring that people aren't killed before they could be cured.) Another restriction could specify that euthanasia be out of the question until after a thorough and disinterested investigation into the state of research on cures and treatments. When this investigation shows that the development of a cure or new treatment is a *realistic* possibility during the life of the patient, euthanasia would again be prohibited.

From a rule-utilitarian perspective, the points about mistaken diagnoses and future cures seem to mandate restrictions on when euthanasia would be considered, but they don't preclude euthanasia altogether – even active euthanasia. Something else, however, does threaten to add up to a conclusive case against allowing any kind of euthanasia, especially active euthanasia. This is the danger of intentional abuse.

Think of the people who might be in a hurry for some ill person's death. Some of these might be people who have to care for the ill person, or pay for the care and medicine the person receives. Another group, often overlapping with the first, is made up of the person's heirs. The heirs might even include the hospital in which the person lies. With so much to gain from an early death of the ill person, these people might easily convince themselves that the ill person would be better off dead. If it were left up to these people, many ill people might unnecessarily be killed or allowed to die. A system which allowed this would both result in unnecessary deaths and terrify the ill.

Even without these points about intentional abuse, rule-utilitarians have enough reason to disallow *involuntary* euthanasia. But do the points about intentional abuse add up to a compelling rule-utilitarian argument against *voluntary* euthanasia? Certainly they necessitate severe restrictions at the very least.

One sensible restriction would be that, with a single exception, the people given authority in the decision about euthanasia must be people with nothing to gain directly or indirectly from their decision. The single exception is of course the patient himself or herself. But heirs and those who stand to benefit from heirs could be denied any authoritative say in the matter. Thus if a hospital is itself an heir, its doctors could be precluded from having any role, including that of making or confirming the diagnosis. The law could be designed to ensure that the decision to perform euthanasia on a patient is made by people focusing on the wishes and best interests of the patient. Of course the patient may ask

loved and trusted others, including heirs, what they think. But the law could insist that doctors with nothing to gain certify that the patient really would be, at the time of the euthanasia, better off dead. And the law could insist that the patient be asked on a number of occasions whether he or she really does want euthanasia. Patients will need the law to protect them against coercive pressures by family and other heirs (not that the law can ever entirely protect us from our families).

Focus now on *non-voluntary* euthanasia – euthanasia performed on people who have not indicated whether or not they want their lives to be prolonged. Some patients have never been in a position to give or withhold consent. This is true of individuals who never developed sufficient rationality to be capable of consenting. Any euthanasia performed on such people will be non-voluntary euthanasia. Rule-utilitarians might well think that a cost–benefit analysis of this sort of euthanasia would end up supporting it – given that the law is designed so as to ensure that the people making the final decision are experts with nothing but the best interests of the patient in mind.

But what about patients who were once rational enough to consent or withhold consent but never made their wishes known and now are incapable of prolonged rationality? Rule-utilitarians can think that to allow euthanasia would be best here too. A more important question, however, might be whether the law should require adults now in possession of their faculties to indicate formally whether they want euthanasia if they become terminally ill and are plagued by acute pain which can be mollified only by severely mind-altering drugs. It might actually increase autonomy to get people to decide whether they would want euthanasia for themselves before they are unable to make such decisions. Obviously, the system for doing this would have to involve informing people what they were being asked to decide about. It would also need to be designed so as to make sure people's decisions are their own, i.e., not the result of some sort of coercion. Furthermore, ideally the system would annually ask for confirmation that people haven't changed their minds (there could be a box to check on annual tax returns).

Some people will think that, no matter how clever rule-utilitarians are in adding safeguards to a law allowing euthanasia, there will be at least a few people who manage to subvert it, and so abuses will occur. Rule-utilitarians may grant this, but then ask how many such abuses there would be. Would there be so many abuses as to terrify the general population? These questions are ones of sociology and social psychology. If the answers to them are that the abuses would be extremely rare and the general population would not become paranoid over them, then a rule-utilitarian might be willing to accept that, if some abuse is inevitable, this cost of a few abuses would be worth the benefits of allowing euthanasia.

There is one more potential harm associated with allowing voluntary and non-voluntary *active* euthanasia. To allow them might seem to be a step onto a slippery slope to a very undesirable position. As I have already noted, the prohibition on killing the innocent against their will is an immensely valuable, indeed essential, prohibition. Would people slide away from a firm commitment to that prohibition if they came to accept the permissibility of voluntary and non-voluntary active euthanasia?

This question, like the question of whether the level of intentional abuse would be unacceptably high, is really one for social scientists. Any answers to such questions have to be partly speculative. We ought to know by now that large social, economic, or legal changes often have unexpected results. We cannot be *certain* what the results of allowing voluntary and non-voluntary active euthanasia would be. Rule-utilitarians have to make a judgment based on what they think the probabilities are. And with respect to the sorts of changes under discussion here, reasonable people can disagree about the probabilities. Thus, reasonable rule-utilitarians can come down on different sides about the permissibility of voluntary and non-voluntary active euthanasia.

But even where there is reasonable disagreement, there can be a right answer. The success of voluntary active euthanasia in Holland suggests that the worries about abuse and slippery slopes can be answered. Of course any law allowing euthanasia (especially, active euthanasia) would need to be very carefully drafted. And the law would have to be rigorously policed, to prevent abuse. Though not certain, I am confident these things could be done. And, undeniably, the benefits, mainly in terms of the decrease of suffering and the increase in autonomy, are potentially enormous.

Notes

Thanks to John Cottingham, Hugh LaFollette, and Andrew Leggett for helpful comments on an earlier draft of this chapter.

1   Though utilitarians may also favor some restrictions on this. I remember that in Tennessee in the 1960s there was a Christian sect using rattlesnakes in church services. As I remember, the government stopped the practice after it led to a few deaths, and the courts upheld that freedom of religion did not extend to persuading people to submit to lethal dangers during worship. These decisions could well be supported on utilitarian grounds.

References

Barrow, R. (1991) *Utilitarianism*. London: Edward Elgar).

Bentham, J. (1823) *An Introduction to the Principles of Morals and Legislation*.

Berkeley, G. (1712) *Passive Obedience, or the Christian Doctrine of Not Resisting the Supreme Power, Proved and Vindicated upon the Principles of the Law of Nature*.

Brandt, R. B. (1963) "Toward a Credible Form of Utilitarianism," *Morality and the Language of Conduct*, ed. H.-N. Castañeda and G. Nakhnikian. Detroit: Wayne State University Press, pp. 107–43.

—— (1967) "Some Merits of One Form of Rule-Utilitarianism," *University of Colorado Studies in Philosophy* pp. 39–65. Reprinted in Brandt, 1992, pp. 111–36.

—— (1979) *A Theory of the Good and the Right*. Oxford: Clarendon Press.

—— (1988) "Fairness to Indirect Optimific Theories in Ethics," *Ethics* 98: 341–60. Reprinted in Brandt, 1992, pp. 137–57.

—— (1992) *Morality, Utilitarianism, and Rights*. New York: Cambridge University Press.

Carson, T. (1991) "A Note on Hooker's 'Rule Consequentialism'," *Mind* 100: 117–21.

Goodin, R. (1991) "Utility and the Good," *A Companion to Ethics*, ed. P. Singer. Oxford: Blackwell, pp. 241–8.

Griffin, J. (1986) *Well-Being: Its Meaning, Measurement and Moral Importance*. Oxford: Clarendon Press.

Hare, R. M. (1981) *Moral Thinking*. Oxford: Clarendon Press.

Harsanyi, J. (1982) "Morality and the Theory of Rational Behaviour," *Utilitarianism and Beyond*, ed. A. Sen and B. Williams. Cambridge: Cambridge University Press, pp. 39–62.

—— (1993) "Expectation Effects, Individual Utilities, and Rational Desires," in Hooker, 1993, pp. 115–26.

Haslett, D. W. (1994) *Capitalism with Morality*. Oxford: Clarendon Press.

Hobbes, T. (1651) *Leviathan*

Hooker, B. (1991) "Rule-Consequentialism and Demandingness: Reply to Carson," *Mind* 100: 270–6.

—— (ed.), (1993) *Rationality, Rules, and Utility: New Essays on the Moral Philosophy of Richard Brandt*. Boulder, CO: Westview Press.

—— (1995) "Rule-Consequentialism, Incoherence, Fairness," *Proceedings of the Aristotelian Society* 95: 19–35.

—— (2000) *Ideal Code, Real World: A Rule-Consequentialist Theory of Morality*. Oxford: Oxford University Press.

Johnson, C. (1991) *Moral Legislation*. New York: Cambridge University Press.

Mill, J. S. (1859) *On Liberty*.

—— (1863) *Utilitarianism*

Mitchell, D. (1995) "The Importance of Being Important: Euthanasia and Critical Interests in Dworkin's *Life's Dominion*," *Utilitas* 7: 301–14.

Moore, G. E. (1903) *Principia Ethica*. Cambridge: Cambridge University Press.

Parfit, D. (1984) *Reasons and Persons*. Oxford: Clarendon Press.

Sidgwick, H. (1877) *The Methods of Ethics*. London: Macmillan, 1874.

5

Justifying Physician-Assisted Deaths

Tom L. Beauchamp

Some recent developments in law encourage more discretion in the ways physicians are permitted to help patients die, despite traditional prohibitions in medicine against assisting in suicide and causing the death of patients. Among the most striking developments was the Canadian Supreme Court's decision in the case of Sue Rodriguez. She attempted to strike down section 241 of the Criminal Code of Canada, which prohibits physician-assisted suicide. The court did not find in her favor, but several justices delivered opinions that give strong support to the moral justifiability of Rodriguez's goal of dying with a physician's direct assistance.[1] A few legal developments in the United States have likewise suggested that prohibitions of assisted suicide are unconstitutional,[2] that certain acts of assistance in dying do not constitute manslaughter,[3] and that a physician's writing of a lethal prescription is acceptable.[4]

These legal developments encourage us to think of the primary moral questions about euthanasia as questions of legalization. The morality of what physicians do in particular cases is thereby demoted in importance, and

it is left unclear whether the fundamental moral issue is the justification of *individual acts* of killing and letting-die or the justification of institutional rules and public laws – *policies* – that permit or prohibit such acts. In due course I will argue that certain acts by physicians in assisting persons to die are justified. This argument will not, however, be sufficient to support conclusions about the legalization of physician-assisted suicide or voluntary active euthanasia.

The Troubled Distinction between Killing and Letting-die

Those who claim that physician-assisted suicide is fundamentally wrong typically assume that there is a basic distinction between acts of killing and acts of merely letting-die. This distinction is troubled. The problem is illustrated by the many cases in which parents, surrogates, and physicians evaluate their intentional omissions of treatment as justifiable acts of *letting-die*, whereas their critics charge that they have unjustifiably *killed* by intentionally allowing to die. For example, in one recent case, Dr Gregory Messenger was charged with manslaughter after he terminated his own premature infant son's life support system by disconnecting the ventilator. In his view, he merely allowed his son to die.

Ordinary language, law, and traditional medical ethics afford no clear answer whether such cases should be described as "allowing to die" or "letting-die," rather than "killing." Moreover, in neither ordinary language nor law does the word "killing" entail a wrongful act or a crime or an intentional action. For example, we can say that persons are killed in accidental shootings and automobile collisions. In ordinary language, *killing* represents a set of related ideas whose central condition is causal intervention to bring about another's death, whereas *allowing to die* represents another family of ideas whose central condition is intentional avoidance of causal intervention so that disease, system failure, or injury causes death.

But if we are to retain this distinction between killing and letting-die, we need clearer, more precise meanings for these notions. For example, the term "killing" could be restricted entirely to circumstances in which one person *intentionally and unjustifiably* causes the death of another human being – a usage that limits and reconstructs the ordinary meaning of the term. "Killing" would then be morally loaded, so that *justified* acts of arranging for death in medicine logically could not be instances of killing; they would always be cases of allowing to die. Under this stipulative meaning of "killing," physicians logically cannot kill when they justifiably remove a life-sustaining treatment in accordance with a patient's refusal of treatment, and patients cannot kill themselves when they justifiably forgo treatment.

I want to resist this simple move to redefine "killing" – or at least to refine its meaning. It is little more than stipulation that evades the moral and conceptual problems. Although I am skeptical that there is or can be a morally neutral analysis of either "killing" or "letting-die," I prefer to start with the neutral assumption that the term "killing" refers only to certain ways in which death is caused.

When Does a Role in Bringing About Death Constitute Killing?

Under this assumption, which captures more or less the ordinary sense of "killing," the justifiability of any particular type of killing is an open question and we cannot assert without looking at a particular case that killing is morally worse than allowing to die. That is, to apply the label "killing" or the label "letting-die" correctly (as morally neutral terms) to a set of events cannot determine whether one type of action is better or worse than the other, or whether either is acceptable or unacceptable.[5] Of course, killing may in most cases be worse than allowing to die, but this is not because of the meaning of the words. Some particular act of killing (a callous murder, say) may be morally worse than some particular act of allowing to die (forgoing treatment for a dying and comatose patient, say); but some act of letting-die (not resuscitating a patient who could easily be saved, but who has refused treatment because of a series of mistaken assumptions, say) also may be morally worse than some particular act of killing (mercy killing at the request of a seriously ill and suffering patient, say).

The point is this: Nothing about either killing or allowing to die, construed as morally neutral, entails judgments about the wrongness or rightness of either type of action, or about the acceptability of the intentions of the actor in performing the act. Rightness and wrongness depend exclusively on the merit of the justification underlying the action, not on the type of action it is. A judgment that an act of either killing or letting-die is justified or unjustified therefore entails that something else be known about the act besides its being an instance of killing or an instance of allowing to die. The actor's intention or motive (whether benevolent or malicious, for example), the patient's refusal of treatment or request of assistance, the balance of benefits over burdens to the patient, and the consequences of the act are all relevant to questions of justification, and some such additional factor is required to make a normative judgment.

Some writers who apparently accept the morally neutral character of "killing" have attempted to reach conclusions about the moral acceptability of letting-die, as follows:[6] They construe omission of treatment as letting-die rather than killing whenever an underlying disease or injury is the cause of death. By contrast, they argue, killings require that acts of persons be the causes of death. Accordingly, a natural death occurs when a respirator is removed, because natural conditions simply do what they would have done without the respirator. They conclude that one acts appropriately in many cases of intentionally allowing persons to die (one is no cause of death at all), but inappropriately in intentionally killing.

This argument does not support the moral conclusions that many draw from it. To make the argument plausible, one must add that the omission of treatment that allows a person to die is a *justified* omission. But what justifies an omission of treatment? The mere fact that a natural cause brings about death is not sufficient to justify not treating someone. To see why merely citing natural causes (of disease, etc.) is unsatisfactory without an additional justification, consider the following example: Mr Mafia comes into a hospital and maliciously detaches a patient, Mr Policeman, from a respirator. This act of detaching the patient from the respirator is causally no different from the acts physicians perform all the time in allowing patients to die. Some features in the circumstance other than omitting treatment, disconnecting the respirator, and the presence of disease or injury must be considered, to arrive at moral conclusions.

If Mr Mafia killed Mr Policeman – and he did – then physicians who do the same thing with their patients likewise kill their patients, unless we introduce a condition about the justifiability of the one omission of treatment and the unjustifiability of the other omission. Without some feature in the circumstances that renders their omissions of treatment justified, doctors cannot justifiably say "We do not kill our patients, only the underlying diseases and injuries do," any more than Mr Mafia can say, "It was the disease, not me, that killed him." An account of killing and letting-die restricted to omitting treatment, disconnecting machines, and disease-caused death leads to the absurd conclusion either that Mr Mafia did not kill the patient or that doctors always kill their patients when the patients die from such omissions of treatment. To solve this problem we must provide a more plausible account of justified omissions and justified actions.

Valid Refusal as the Basis of Letting-die

What justifies a physician's omission of treatment and disconnection of the respirator that does not justify Mr Mafia's "omission" of treatment and disconnection? Typically what validates the physician's omission is an *authoritative refusal of treatment* by a patient or authorized surrogate. It would be both immoral and illegal of the physician not to omit treatment in the face of a competent, authoritative refusal. It therefore seems attractive to say that what sorts the physician's act into the category of allowing to die rather than killing, and makes Mr Mafia's act one of killing rather than allowing to die, is nothing but the competent authoritative refusal of treatment present when the physician acts and absent when Mr Mafia and others act.

This claim has been defended by James L. Bernat, Bernard Gert, and R. Peter Mogielnicki.[7] They apparently believe that the type of action – killing or letting-die – depends on whether there is a valid refusal warranting an omission of treatment, rather than the validity of an omission of treatment (disconnection of the respirator, etc.) depending on the type of action it is. This clarification is insightful. Traditionally we have thought that the distinction between killing and letting-die is to be accounted for in terms of either the *intention* of persons (whether they intend someone's death) or the *causation* of persons (whether they cause someone's death). But the patient-refusal hypothesis provides a third way and demotes causation and intention in importance, giving the pivotal role to *valid refusal*.

A refusal is valid when the patient, who has rightful authority, autonomously refuses the proposed treatment (or an authorized surrogate does so). This account of the validity of a refusal is intimately tied to a larger account of the limits of professional authority and duty. The physician has a duty to follow an appropriate refusal and is required by society to do so; a bystander or someone like Mr Mafia has no comparable duty or social recognition. This duty and the corresponding limits of physician authority give us a reason for saying that the physician's actions *do not cause death*, whereas Mr Mafia's actions do cause death.

This theory shapes the meaning of the pivotal terms "killing" and "letting-die" in a way that protects the conventional moral thesis in law and medicine that it is justifiable to allow to die and unjustifiable to kill. This is exactly what Bernat, Gert, and Mogielnicki argue. But do they beg a central moral question by assuming that only letting-die, not killing, is justified? My own preference is to avoid this conclusion by independently looking at acts of killing to see if they can be justified on grounds other than a valid refusal. I believe we cannot decide the critical moral questions about physician-assisted suicide and euthanasia entirely by appeals to valid refusals and the letting-die-killing distinction. The critical question is whether there is an adequate justification for the action taken, whatever *type* of action it is and whether or not there has been a refusal of treatment.

I do agree with Bernat, Gert, and Mogielnicki that justification turns on having a valid *authorization*, but I would not limit the notion of a valid authorization to a valid refusal, and I would not make the account turn in any significant way on the distinction between killing and letting-die. I will now explain why.

Valid Refusals and Valid Requests

The problem with the analysis of Bernat, Gert, and Mogielnicki is not with their views about valid refusals, but with what they say about valid requests. They are correct in saying that a valid refusal of treatment always justifies a corresponding omission of the treatment, even if it is a refusal of hydration and nutrition that will result in death by starvation. Whenever

valid refusals occur, how death occurs is not decisive, and it is never a moral offense to comply with a valid refusal. My disagreement with their analysis comes when they insist that a *request* for help by a competent patient has no legitimate role to play in the justification of an action of physician-assisted suicide or voluntary active euthanasia. They believe the moral and legal requirement to honor a refusal does not extend to honoring a request. My view, by contrast, is the following: (1) physicians are both morally and legally required to honor refusals; (2) they are not legally required to honor requests; (3) whether they are either morally required or morally permitted to honor requests depends on the nature of the request and the nature of the patient-physician relationship.

In some of the clearest cases of justified compliance with requests, the patient and the physician discuss what is in the patient's best interest, under the assumption that the physician will not abandon the patient or resist what they jointly decide to be in the patient's best interests. A physician with these professional commitments has made a moral commitment to help patients that differs from the commitment made by a physician who rigidly draws the line in opposition to any form of euthanasia or assistance in suicide.[8] In some cases, a patient both refuses to start or continue a possible treatment and requests help in dying in order that the death be less painful; refusal and request are combined as parts of a single plan, and, in many of these cases, the physician agrees with the plan. In this way assisted suicide or active euthanasia grows naturally out of a close patient–physician relationship.

In cases in which patients make reasonable requests for assistance in dying, it is a misconception to suppose that doctors can escape responsibility for their decisions if they refrain from helping their patients die. No physician can say "I am not responsible for outcomes when I choose not to act on a patient's request." There has long been a vague sense in the physician and legal community that if only the doctor lets nature take its course, then one is not responsible for the outcome of death. But a physician is always responsible for any decision taken and the consequent action or inaction. The physician who complies with a patient's request is therefore responsible in exactly the way physicians who refuse to comply with the request are responsible.

Physicians who refuse to comply with a request cannot magically pass responsibility to the patient's condition of disease. The only relevant matter is whether the path the physician chooses, including what is rejected and omitted, has an adequate justification. Doctors cannot evade responsibility for acting in the best interests of the patient, and they cannot turn their backs on what the patient believes to be in his or her best interests. Of course, doctors often reject courses of action requested by patients and have good and sufficient reasons for doing so. That is not in dispute. The question is whether the physician who conscientiously believes that the patient's request for assistance in dying is reasonable and justified and assumes responsibility for any assistance undertaken does wrong in complying with the request.

Bernat, Gert, and Mogielnicki will object that I am confusing moral obligations and (non-required) moral ideals. They regard the physicians I just described as moving beyond professional obligations of providing medical care, into the domain of optional moral ideals of assistance in dying. In important respects, I do not want to resist this classification of the physician's commitment as a moral ideal, but the distinction can be misleading without further qualification. As Gert himself has argued, moral ideals sometimes legitimately override moral obligations in cases of contingent conflict. This position will do well enough for our purposes. If a physician *justifiably* believes that his or her moral ideals of patient-assistance override all other moral obligations (to avoid killing, to not violate laws, etc.), this conclusion is all I need to support the argument in this section.

The Wrongness in Causing or Assisting in Death

But is the act the physician believes to be justified really justified? Could assistance in someone's self-requested death be wrong, even if the physician conscientiously believes it is right?

The only way to decide whether killing is wrong and letting-die not wrong in some cases, though wrong in others, is to determine what *makes* them wrong when they are wrong. By longstanding convention, a person is not guilty of a crime or a wrongful act merely because he or she killed someone. Legitimate defenses for killing (excusable homicide) include killing in self-defense and killing by misadventure (accidental and non-negligent killing while engaged in a lawful act). From a moral point of view, causing a person's death is wrong *when it is wrong* not because the death is *intended* or because it is *caused*, but because an unjustified harm or loss to the person occurs. Therefore, what makes a physician's act of killing or "assisting" in causing a death wrong, when it is wrong, is that a person is unjustifiably harmed – that is, unjustifiably suffers a setback to interests that the person otherwise would not have experienced.

The critical question for acts both of killing and of letting-die in medicine is whether an act of assisting persons in bringing about their deaths causes them a loss or, rather, provides a benefit. If a person chooses death and sees that event as a personal benefit, then helping that person bring about death neither harms nor wrongs the person and may provide a benefit or at least fulfill the person's last important goal.

This helping might harm society by setting back its interests, and therefore might be a reason against *legalization*, but this form of harm does not alter conclusions about the justifiability of the *act* of helping. Not helping persons of this description in their dying, on the analysis I have presented, can interrupt or frustrate their goals and, from their perspective, cause them harm, indignity, or despair – even if, at the same time, it protects society's interests.

The Key Argument in Defense of Euthanasia and Assisted Suicide

These conclusions can now be joined with the previous reflections on valid refusals and requests. If passive letting-die based on valid refusals does not harm or wrong persons or violate their rights, then how can assisted suicide and voluntary active euthanasia harm or wrong the person who dies? In both cases – active killing and passive letting-die – the person is, in effect, refusing to go on and is seeking the best means to the end of quitting life. The judgment is that the best obtainable information about the future indicates that continuing life is, on balance, worse than not continuing it. The person who attempts suicide, the person who seeks active euthanasia, and the person who forgoes life-sustaining treatment are identically situated except that they select different means to bring about the end of life. Each intends to quit life because of its bleak possibilities.[9] Therefore, those who believe it is morally acceptable to let people die when they refuse treatment, but not to take active steps to help them die when they request assistance, must give a different account of the wrongfulness of killing and letting-die than I have offered.

To insist on continued treatment (or even palliation, in many cases) while refusing to comply with a patient's request for assistance in dying is to burden rather than help the patient and, of course, to reject their autonomous wishes. As the autonomy interests in this choice increase on the scale of interests, denial of help to the patient increasingly burdens the patient; and to increase the burden is to increase the harm done to the person.

The core of the argument in favor of the moral justifiability of acts of physician-assisted suicide and voluntary active euthanasia is that relief from suffering and a voluntary request justify our doing what we otherwise would not do: implement a plan to end a human life. This action has its strongest defense when: (1) a condition is extremely burdensome and the burden outweighs any benefits, (2) pain management cannot be made adequate, (3) only a physician is capable of bringing relief, and (4) the patient makes an informed request.

Medicine and law seem now to say to many patients, "If you were on life-sustaining treatment, you could withdraw the treatment and we could let you die. But since you are not, we can only give you palliative care until you die a natural death." This position condemns the patient to live out a life he or she does not want – a form of cruelty that violates the patient's rights and prevents discharge of the fiduciary obligations of the physician. To use this argument is not to claim that physicians face large numbers of desperately ill patients. Pain management has made circumstances at least bearable for most of today's patients, but some patients still cannot be satisfactorily relieved, and, even if they could, questions would remain about the autonomy rights of patients: If there is a right to stop a medical treatment that sustains life, why is there not a right to stop one's life by arrangement with a physician?

Dr Kevorkian's "patients" raise profound questions about the lack of a support system in medicine or elsewhere for handling their problems. Having thought for over a year about her future, Adkins decided that her suffering would exceed the benefits of continuing to live. She apparently had firm views about what she wanted, and she carefully calculated both the costs and the benefits. She faced a bleak future from her perspective as a person who had lived an unusually vigorous life. She believed that her brain would be slowly destroyed, with progressive and devastating cognitive loss and confusion, fading memory, immense frustration, and lack of all capacity to take care of herself. She also believed that her family would have to assume the full burden of responsibility for her care. From her perspective, what Kevorkian offered was better than other physicians offered, which, to her, was no help at all.

Current social institutions, including the medical system, have not proved adequate for patients like Adkins. Dying persons often face inadequate counseling, emotional support, pain information, or pain control. Their condition is intolerable from their perspective, and without any avenue of hope. To maintain that these persons act immorally by arranging for death is a harsh judgment that needs to be backed by a more persuasive argument than I have seen.

If this argument is sound, then the burden of justification for prescriptions of acts of voluntary active euthanasia and physician-assisted suicide rests on those who refuse or hinder assistance to patients who express a competent and rational wish to die, rather than on those who would help them die. Associations of medical professionals in the US have, I believe, reversed the proper burden of justification by placing it on physicians who want to help patients.[10]

Justifying Policies and Justifying Acts

The argument thus far leads to the conclusion that physicians' acts of honoring valid refusals and complying with valid requests can both be justified under specifiable circumstances. However, I said at the beginning that my argument is not strong enough to show that *policies*, such as the law passed in Oregon, are justified. I want now to explain how one can consistently hold strong views about the justifiability of some acts of physician-assisted suicide and voluntary active euthanasia, while simultaneously having deep-seated reservations about revising public policies that prohibit these acts. The point is that one can consistently judge acts morally acceptable that one cannot support legalizing.

The backbone of the resistance to physician-assisted euthanasia and voluntary active euthanasia has long been an argument referred to as the wedge argument or "slippery slope" argument. It proceeds roughly as follows:[11] Although particular acts of assistance in dying might be morally justified on some occasions, the social consequences of sanctioning practices of killing would involve serious risks of abuse and misuse and, on balance, would cause more harm than benefit to society. Attitudes, not merely guidelines, can be eroded by shifts in public policy. Prohibitions are often symbolically important, and their removal could weaken the fabric of restraints and beneficial attitudes. The argument is not that these negative consequences will occur immediately after legalization, but that they will grow incrementally over time. Society might start with innocent beginnings by developing policies that carefully restrict the number of patients who qualify for assistance in suicide or euthanasia. Whatever restrictions are initially built into our policies

will be revised and expanded over time, with ever-increasing possibilities in the system for unjustified killing. Unscrupulous persons will learn how to abuse the system, just as they do with methods of tax evasion that operate on the margins of the system of legitimate tax avoidance.

Slippery slope arguments depend on speculative predictions of a progressive erosion of moral restraints. If the dire and unmanageable consequences that they predict actually will flow from the legal legitimation of assisted suicide or voluntary active euthanasia, then slippery slope arguments do convincingly show that practices should be legally prohibited. But how good is the evidence that dire consequences will occur? Is there a sufficient reason to think that we cannot maintain control over and even improve public policy? Every reasonable person would agree that these difficult empirical questions are among the primary questions in the current moral controversy about euthanasia.

All that needs to be said here, I believe, is that even if slippery slope arguments provide solid reasons against legalization, they provide no moral basis for the conclusion that acts of euthanasia and physician-assisted suicide are morally wrong (unless one's only moral basis is identical to one's basis for opposing legalization). I will now explain why.

Slippery slope arguments conclude that patients such as Sue Rodriguez and the patrons of Jack Kevorkian cannot be justifiably helped by physicians because to help them, even if they deserve our help, would open the floodgates to killing persons who should not be killed. All patients should be denied help not because of anything they have done or because of any demerit in their cases or in their wishes, but because acts of assistance in dying would hurt others if legalized and therefore should not be tolerated under any circumstances.

There is something that seems both very right and very wrong about this slippery slope argument – right because the argument points to dangers of the most profound sort, wrong because at least some patients deserve to be helped and their physicians do nothing morally wrong in helping them. It may therefore be necessary to prohibit these acts of assistance in our public policies while acknowledging that there is nothing morally wrong with the acts other than their potentially far-reaching social consequences. They are truly "innocent beginnings."

In conclusion, I want to throw a final wrinkle into this already wrinkled picture. Despite my concerns about slippery slopes, I believe the legislation in Oregon is a promising development (which is not to say it is good legislation as it was passed), and I think that we should welcome some version of it. This suggestion may seem to contradict what I just argued about legalization, but concerns about slippery slopes ought not to be so paralyzing that we are not open to social experiments that will help us see whether empirical predictions are correct and which system works best.[12] The Oregon legislation could be viewed as a social experiment that gives us a good perspective on both risks and benefits – a trial that may or may not succeed. I would hope that research will be carried out to evaluate our experimental programs in upcoming years and that we will learn about the benefits and risks in a comprehensive, timely, and objective manner. Perhaps then we can be positioned to decide from evidence whether the slippery slope is as slippery as some fear it could be.

Notes

1   Supreme Court of Canada, *Sue Rodriguez* v. *Attorney General of Canada*, September 30, 1993, File No. 23476; on appeal from British Columbia Court of Appeal, *Rodriguez* v. *British Columbia (Attorney General)* [1993], B.C.J. No. 641 (Q.L.) (B.C.C.A.). In early 1994, with broad public support, Sue Rodriguez killed herself with the assistance of an anonymous physician.

2   *Compassion in Dying* v. *State of Washington*, 850 F. Supp. 1454 (W.D. Wash. 1994); overturned March 9, 1995, by the United States Court of Appeals for the Ninth Circuit in an opinion written by Judge John T. Noonan. *Compassion in Dying* v. *Washington*, No. 94–35534 (US App. March 9, 1995) (available March 1995, on LEXIS).

3   State of Michigan in the Circuit Court for the County of Oakland, *People of the State of Michigan* v. *Jack Kevorkian*, Case No. CR-92–115190–FC (July 21, 1992); Court of Appeals of Michigan, *Hobbins* v. *Attorney General* and *People of the State of Michigan* v. *Jack Kevorkian*, 518 N.W.2d 487 (Mich. App. 1994).

4   See *Oregon Death with Dignity Act* (1994). Under this Act, terminally ill adults are allowed to obtain lethal drugs from physicians in order to hasten death and escape unbearable suffering. This initiative, when scheduled to become law, faced legal challenges.

5   In effect, this proposal is made in James Rachels, "Active and Passive Euthanasia," *New England Journal of Medicine* 292/2 (January 9, 1975): 78–80; and Dan Brock, "Voluntary Active Euthanasia," *Hastings Center Report* 22/2 (March/April 1992): 10–22.

6   See: In the Matter of *Claire C. Conroy*, 190 N.J. Sup. 453, 464 A.2d 303 (App. Div. 1983); In the Matter of *Claire C. Conroy*, 486 A.2d 1209 (New Jersey Supreme Court, 1985), at 1222–3, 1236; *In re Estate of Greenspan*, 558 N.E.2d 1194, at 1203 (Ill. 1990); Daniel Callahan, "Vital Distinctions, Mortal Questions," *Commonweal*, 115 (July 15, 1988): 399–402; and several articles in Joanne Lynn (ed.), *By No Extraordinary Means* (Bloomington, IN: Indiana University Press, 1986), pp. 227–66.

7   James L. Bernat, Bernard Gert, and R. Peter Mogielnicki, "Patient Refusal of Hydration and Nutrition," *Archives of Internal Medicine* 153 (1993): 2723–8; Bernard Gert, *Morality: A New Justification of the Moral Rules* (New York: Oxford University Press, 1988), pp. 294–300.

8   Cf. Sidney H. Wanzer, Daniel D. Federman, S. James Adelstein et al., "The Physician's Responsibility toward Hopelessly Ill Patients: A Second Look," *New England Journal of Medicine* 320 (March 30, 1989): 844–9.

9   For the extension to suicide, see Dan Brock, "Death and Dying," in *Medical Ethics*, ed. Robert M. Veatch (Boston: Jones and Bartlett, 1989), p. 345.

10 American Medical Association, Council on Ethical and Judicial Affairs, *Euthanasia: Report C*, in *Proceedings of the House of Delegates* (Chicago: American Medical Association, June 1988): 258–60 (and see *Current Opinions*, § 2.20, p. 13, 1989); "Decisions Near the End of Life," *Report B*, adopted by the House of Delegates (1991), pp. 11–15; and see the abridged version in "Decisions Near the End of Life," *Journal of the American Medical Association* 267 (April 22/29, 1992): 2229–33.

11 Cf. Alan J. Weisbard and Mark Siegler, "On Killing Patients with Kindness: An Appeal for Caution," in J. Arras and N. Rhoden, *Ethical Issues in Modern Medicine*, 3rd edn. (Mountain View, CA: Mayfield,

1989), esp. p. 218; Douglas Walton, *Slippery Slope Arguments* (Oxford: Clarendon Press, 1992); Trudy Govier, "What's Wrong with Slippery Slope Arguments?," *Canadian Journal of Philosophy* 12 (June 1982): 303–16; Frederick Schauer, "Slippery Slopes," *Harvard Law Review* 99 (1985): 361–83; and James Rachels, *The End of Life: Euthanasia and* *Morality* (Oxford: Oxford University Press, 1986), ch. 10.

12 Cf. Franklin G. Miller, Timothy Quill, Howard Brody, John C. Fletcher, Lawrence O. Gostin, and D. E. Meier, "Regulating Physician-Assisted Death," *New England Journal of Medicine* 331 (1994): 119–23.

6

Against the Right to Die

J. David Velleman

In this chapter I offer an argument against establishing an institutional right to die, but I do not consider how my argument fares against countervailing considerations, and so I do not draw any final conclusion on the subject. The argument laid out in this paper has certainly inhibited me from favoring a right to die, and it has also led me to recoil from many of the arguments offered for such a right. But I am very far from an all-things-considered judgment.

My argument is addressed to a question of public policy – namely, whether the law or the canons of medical practice should include a rule requiring, under specified circumstances, that caregivers honor a patient's request to be allowed or perhaps even helped to die. This question is distinct from the question whether anyone is ever morally entitled to be allowed or helped to die. I believe that the answer to the latter question is yes, but I doubt whether our moral obligation to facilitate some people's deaths is best discharged through the establishment of an institutional right to die.

I

Although I believe in our obligation to facilitate some deaths, I want to dissociate myself from some of the arguments that are frequently offered for such an obligation. These arguments, like many arguments in medical ethics, rely on terms borrowed from Kantian moral theory – terms such as "dignity" and "autonomy." Various kinds of life-preserving treatment are said to violate a patient's dignity or to detain him in an undignified state; and the patient's right of autonomy is said to require that we respect his competent and considered wishes, including a wish to die. There may or may not be some truth in each of these claims. Yet when we evaluate such claims, we must take care not to assume that terms like "dignity" and "autonomy" always express the same concepts, or carry the same normative force, as they do in a particular moral theory.

When Kant speaks, for example, of the dignity that belongs to persons by virtue of their rational nature, and that places them beyond all price (Kant, 1964, p. 102), he is not invoking anything that requires the ability to walk unaided, to feed oneself, or to control one's bowels. Hence the dignity invoked in discussions of medical ethics – a status supposedly threatened by physical deterioration and dependency – cannot be the status whose claim on our moral concern is so fundamental to Kantian thought. We must therefore ask whether this other sort of dignity, whatever it may be, embodies a value that's equally worthy of protection.

My worry, in particular, is that the word "dignity" is sometimes used to dignify, so to speak, our culture's obsession with independence, physical strength, and youth. To my mind, the dignity defined by these values – a dignity that is ultimately incompatible with *being cared for* at all – is a dignity not worth having.[1]

I have similar worries about the values expressed by the phrase "patient autonomy"; for there are two very different senses in which a person's autonomy can become a value for us. On the one hand, we can obey the categorical imperative, by declining to act for reasons that we could not rationally propose as valid for all rational beings, including those who are affected by our action, such as the patient. What we value in that case is the patent's *capacity* for self-determination, and we value it in a particular way – namely, by according it *respect*. We respect the patient's autonomy by regarding the necessity of sharing our reasons with him, among others, as a constraint on what decisions we permit ourselves to reach.

On the other hand, we can value the patient's autonomy by making it our goal to maximize his effective options. What we value, in that case, is not the patient's capacity but his *opportunities* for self-determination – his having choices to make and the means with which to implement them; and we value these opportunities for self-determination by regarding them as *goods* – as objects of desire and pursuit rather than respect.

These two ways of valuing autonomy are fundamentally different. Respecting people's autonomy, in the Kantian sense, is not just a matter of giving them effective options. To make our own decisions only for reasons that we could rationally share with others is not necessarily to give *them* decisions to make, nor is it to give them the means to implement their actual decisions.[2]

As with the term "dignity," then, we must not assume that the term "autonomy" is always being used in the sense made familiar by Kantian moral theory; and we must therefore ask ourselves what sort of autonomy is being invoked, and whether it is indeed something worthy of our moral concern. I believe that, as with the term "dignity," the answer to the latter question may be "no" in some cases, including the case of the right to die.

II

Despite my qualms about the use of Kantian language to justify euthanasia, I do believe that euthanasia can be justified, and on Kantian grounds. In particular, I believe that respect for a person's dignity, properly conceived, can require us to facilitate his death when that dignity is being irremediably compromised. I also believe, however, that a person's dignity can be so compromised only by circumstances that are likely to compromise his capacity for fully rational and autonomous decision making. So although I do not favor euthanizing people against their wills, of course, neither do I favor a policy of euthanizing people for the sake of deferring to their wills, since I think that people's wills are usually impaired in the circumstances required to make euthanasia permissible. The sense in which I oppose a right to die, then, is that I oppose treating euthanasia as a protected option for the patient.

One reason for my opposition is the associated belief (also Kantian) that so long as patients would be fully competent to exercise an option of being euthanized, their doing so would be immoral, in the majority of cases, because their dignity as persons would still be intact. I discuss this argument elsewhere, but I do not return to it in the present paper.[3] In this chapter I discuss a second reason for opposing euthanasia as a protected option for the patient. This reason, unlike the first, is consequentialist.

What consequentialist arguments could there be against giving the option of euthanasia to patients? One argument, of course, would be that giving this option to patients, even under carefully defined conditions, would entail providing euthanasia to some patients for whom it would be a harm rather than a benefit (Kamisar, 1970). But the argument that interests me does not depend on this strategy. My consequential-ist worry about the right to die is not that some patients might mistakenly choose to die when they would be better off living.

In order to demonstrate that I am not pri-marily worried about mistaken request to die, I shall assume, from this point forward, that pa-tients are infallible, and that euthanasia would therefore be chosen only by those for whom it would be a benefit. Even so, I believe, the establishment of a right to die would harm many patients, by increasing their autonomy in a sense that is not only un-Kantian but also very undesirable.

This belief is sometimes expressed in public debate, although it is rarely developed in any detail. Here, for example, is Yale Kamisar's argument against "euthanasia legislation":

> Is this the kind of choice . . . that we want to offer a gravely ill person? Will we not sweep up, in the process, some who are not really tired of life, but think others are tired of them; some who do not really want to die, but who feel they should not live on, because to do so when there looms the legal alterna-tive of euthanasia is to do a selfish or a cowardly act? Will not some feel an obligation to have themselves "eliminated" . . . ? (Kamisar, 1970)

Note that these considerations do not, strictly speaking, militate against euthanasia itself. Rather, they militate against a particular deci-sion procedure for euthanasia – namely, the procedure of placing the choice of euthanasia in the patient's hands. What Kamisar is ques-tioning in this particular passage is not the practice of helping some patients to die, but rather the practice of asking them to choose whether to die. The feature of legalized eutha-nasia that troubles him is precisely its being an option offered to patients – the very feature for which it's touted, by its proponents, as an enhancement of the patients' autonomy. Kamisar's remarks thus betray the suspicion that this particular enhancement of one's autonomy is not to be welcomed.

But what exactly is the point of Kamisar's rhetorical questions? The whole purpose of giv-ing people choices, surely, is to allow those choices to be determined by their reasons and preferences rather than ours. Kamisar may think that finding one's life tiresome is a good reason for dying whereas thinking that others find one tiresome is not. But if others honestly think otherwise, why should we stand in their way? Whose life is it anyway?

IV

A theoretical framework for addressing this question can be found in Thomas Schelling's book *The Strategy of Conflict* (1960), and in Gerald Dworkin's paper "Is More Choice Bet-ter than Less?" (1982). These authors have shown that our intuitions about the value of options are often mistaken, and their work can help us to understand the point of arguments like Kamisar's.

We are inclined to think that, unless we are likely to make mistakes about whether to exer-cise an option (as I am assuming we are not), the value of having the option is as high as the value of exercising it and no lower than zero. Exer-cising an option can of course be worse than nothing, if it causes harm. But if we are not prone to mistakes, then we will not exercise a harmful option; and we tend to think that sim-ply *having* the unexercised option cannot be harmful. And insofar as exercising an option would make us better off than we are, having the option must have made us better off than we were before we had it – or so we tend to think.

What Schelling showed, however, is that hav-ing an option can be harmful even if we do not exercise it and – more surprisingly – even if we exercise it and gain by doing so. Schelling's examples of this phenomenon were drawn pri-marily from the world of negotiation, where the only way to induce one's opponent to settle for less may be by proving that one doesn't have the option of giving him more. Schelling pointed out that in such circumstances, a lack of options can be an advantage. The union leader who cannot persuade his membership to approve a pay-cut, or the ambassador who cannot contact his head of state for a change of brief, negotiates from a position of strength; whereas the nego-tiator for whom all concessions are possible deals from weakness. If the rank-and-file give their leader the option of offering a pay-cut, then management may not settle for anything less, whereas they might have settled for less if he hadn't had the option of making the offer. The union leader will then have to decide whether to take the option and reach an agreement or to leave the option and call a strike. But no matter which of these outcomes would make him better off, choosing it will still leave him worse off than he would have been if he had never had the option at all.

Dworkin has expanded on Schelling's point by exploring other respects in which options can be undesirable. Just as options can subject one to pressure from an opponent in negotiation, for example, they can subject one to pressure from other sources as well. The night cashier in a convenience store doesn't want the option of opening the safe – and not because he fears that he'd make mistakes about when to open it. It is precisely because the cashier would know when he'd better open the safe that his having the option would make him an attractive target for robbers; and it's because having the option would make him a target for robbers that he'd be better off without it. The cashier who finds himself opening the safe at gunpoint can consistently think that he's doing what's best while wishing that he'd never been given the option of doing it.

Options can be undesirable, then, because they subject one to various kinds of pressure; but they can be undesirable for other reasons, too. Offering someone an alternative to the status quo makes two outcomes possible for him, but neither of them is the outcome that was possible before. He can now choose the status quo or choose the alternative, but he can no longer *have* the status quo without *choosing* it. And having the status quo by default may have been what was best for him, even though choosing the status quo is now worst. If I invite you to a dinner party, I leave you the possibilities of choosing to come or choosing to stay away; but I deprive you of something that you otherwise would have had – namely, the possibility of being absent from my table by default, as you are on all other occasions. Surely, preferring to

accept an invitation is consistent with wishing you had never received it. These attitudes are consistent because refusing to attend a party is a different outcome from *not* attending without having to refuse; and even if the former of these outcomes is worse than attending, the latter may still have been better. Having choices can thus deprive one of desirable outcomes whose desirability depends on their being unchosen.

The offer of an option can also be undesirable because of what it expresses. To offer a student the option of receiving remedial instruction after class is to imply that he is not keeping up. If the student needs help but doesn't know it, the offer may clue him in. But even if the student does not need any help, to begin with, the offer may so undermine his confidence that he will need help before long. In the latter case, the student may ultimately benefit from accepting the offer, even though he would have been better off not receiving it at all.

Note that in each of these cases, a person can be harmed by having a choice, even if he chooses what's best for him. Once the option of offering a concession has undermined one's bargaining position, once the option of opening the safe has made one the target of a robbery, once the invitation to a party has eliminated the possibility of absence by default, once the offer of remedial instruction has implied that one needs it – in short, once one has been offered a problematic choice – one's situation has already been altered for the worse, and choosing what's best cannot remedy the harm that one has already suffered. Choosing what's best in these cases is simply a way of cutting one's losses.

Note, finally, that we cannot always avoid burdening people with options by offering them a second-order option as to which options they are to be offered. If issuing you an invitation to dinner would put you in an awkward position, then asking you whether you want to be invited would usually do so as well; if offering you the option of remedial instruction would send you a message, then so would asking you whether you'd like that option. In order to avoid doing harm, then, we are sometimes required not only to withhold options, but also to take the initiative for withholding them.

V

Of course, the options that I have discussed can also be unproblematic for many people in many circumstances. Sometimes one has good reason to welcome a dinner invitation or an offer of remedial instruction. Similarly, some patients will welcome the option of euthanasia, and rightly so. The problem is how to offer the option only to those patients who will have reason to welcome it. Arguments like Kamisar's are best understood, I think, as warning that the option of euthanasia may unavoidably be offered to some who will be harmed simply by having the option, even if they go on to choose what is best.

I think that the option of euthanasia may harm some patients in all of the ways canvassed above; but I will focus my attention on only a few of those ways. The most important way in which the option of euthanasia may harm patients, I think, is that it will deny them the possibility of staying alive by default.

Now, the idea of surviving by default will be anathema to existentialists, who will insist that the choice between life and death is a choice that we have to make every day, perhaps every moment.[4] Yet even if there is a deep, philosophical sense in which we do continually choose to go on living, it is not reflected in our ordinary self-understanding. That is, we do not ordinarily think of ourselves or others as continually rejecting the option of suicide and staying alive by choice. Thus, even if the option of euthanasia won't alter a patient's existential situation, it will certainly alter the way in which his situation is generally perceived. And changes in the perception of a patient's situation will be sufficient to produce many of the problems that Schelling and Dworkin have described, since those problems are often created not just by *having* options but by *being seen* to have them.

Once a person is given the choice between life and death, he will rightly be perceived as the agent of his own survival. Whereas his existence is ordinarily viewed as a given for him – as a fixed condition with which he must cope – formally offering him the option of euthanasia will cause his existence thereafter to be viewed as his doing.

The problem with this perception is that if others regard you as choosing a state of affairs, they will hold you responsible for it; and if they hold you responsible for a state of affairs, they can ask you to justify it. Hence if people ever come to regard you as existing by choice, they may expect you to justify your continued existence. If your daily arrival in the office is interpreted as meaning that you have once again declined to kill yourself, you may feel obliged to arrive with an answer to the question, "Why not?"

I think that our perception of one another's existence as a given is so deeply ingrained that we can hardly imagine what life would be like without it. When someone shows impatience or displeasure with us, we jokingly say, "Well, excuse me for living!" But imagine that it were no joke; imagine that living were something for which one might reasonably be thought to need an excuse. The burden of justifying one's existence might make existence unbearable – and hence unjustifiable.

VI

I assume that people care, and are right to care, about whether they can justify their choices to others. Of course, this concern can easily seem like slavishness or neurotic insecurity; but it should not be dismissed too lightly. Our ability to justify our choices to the people around us is what enables us to sustain the role of rational agent in our dealings with them; and it is therefore essential to our remaining, in their eyes, an eligible partner in cooperation and conversation, or an appropriate object of respect.

Retaining one's status as a person among others is especially important to those who are ill or infirm. I imagine that when illness or infirmity denies one the rewards of independent activity, then the rewards of personal intercourse may be all that make life worth living. To the ill or infirm, then, the ability to sustain the role of rational person may rightly seem essential to retaining what remains of value in life. Being unable to account for one's choices may seem to entail the risk of being perceived as unreasonable – as not worth reasoning with – and consequently being cut off from meaningful intercourse with others, which is life's only remaining consolation.

Forcing a patient to take responsibility for his continued existence may therefore be tantamount to confronting him with the following prospect: unless he can explain, to the satisfaction of others, why he chooses to exist, his only remaining reasons for existence may vanish.

VII

Unfortunately, our culture is extremely hostile to any attempt at justifying an existence of passivity and dependence. The burden of proof will lie heavily on the patient who thinks that his terminal illness or chronic disability is not a sufficient reason for dying.

What is worse, the people with whom a patient wants to maintain intercourse, and to whom he therefore wants to justify his choices, are often in a position to incur several financial and emotional costs from any prolongation of his life. Many of the reasons in favor of his death are therefore likely to be exquisitely salient in their minds. I believe that some of these people may actively pressure the patient to exercise the option of dying. (Students who hear me say this usually object that no one would ever do such a thing. My reply is that no one would ever do such a thing as abuse his own children or parents – except that many people do.)

In practice, however, friends and relatives of a patient will not have to utter a word of encouragement, much less exert any overt pressure, once the option of euthanasia is offered. For in the discussion of a subject so hedged by taboos and inhibitions, the patient will have to make some assumptions about what they think and how they feel, irrespective of what they say (see Schelling, 1984). And the rational assumption for him to make will be that they are especially sensible of the considerations in favor of his exercising the option.

Thus, even if a patient antecedently believes that his life is worth living, he may have good reason to assume that many of the people around him do not, and that his efforts to convince them will be frustrated by prevailing opinions about lives like his, or by the biases inherent in their perspective. Indeed, he can reasonably assume that the offer of euthanasia is itself an expression of attitudes that are likely to frustrate his efforts to justify declining it. He can therefore assume that his refusal to take the option of euthanasia will threaten his standing as rational person in the eyes of friends and family, thereby threatening the very things that make his life worthwhile. This patient may rationally judge that he's better off taking the option of euthanasia, even though he would have been best off not having the option at all.

Establishing a right to die in our culture may thus be like establishing a right to duel in a culture obsessed with personal honor.[5] If someone defended the right to duel by arguing that a duel is a private transaction between consenting adults, he would have missed the point of laws against dueling. What makes it rational for someone to throw down or pick up a gauntlet may be the social costs of choosing not to, costs that result from failing to duel only if one fails to duel by choice. Such costs disappear if the choice of dueling can be removed. By eliminating the option of dueling (if we can), we eliminate the reasons that make it rational for people to duel in most cases. To restore the option of dueling would be to give people reasons for dueling that they didn't previously have. Similarly, I believe, to offer the option of dying may be to give people new reasons for dying.

VIII

Do not attempt to refute this argument against the right to die by labeling it paternalistic. The argument is not paternalistic – at last, not in any derogatory sense of the word. Paternalism, in the derogatory sense, is the policy of saving people from self-inflicted harms, by denying them options that they might exercise unwisely. Such a policy is distasteful because it expresses a lack of respect for others' ability to make their own decisions.

But my argument is not paternalistic in this sense. My reason for withholding the option of euthanasia is not that others cannot be trusted to exercise it wisely. On the contrary, I have assumed from the outset that patients will be infallible in their deliberations. What I have argued is, not that people to whom we offer the option of euthanasia might harm themselves, but rather that in offering them this option, *we* will do them harm. My argument is therefore based on a simple policy of non-malfeasance rather than on the policy of paternalism. I am arguing that we must not harm others by giving them choices – not that we must withhold the choices from them lest they harm themselves.

Of course, harming some people by giving them choices may be unavoidable if we could not withhold those choices from them without unjustly withholding the same choices from others. If a significant number of patients were both competent and morally entitled to choose euthanasia, then we might be obligated to make that option available even if, in doing so, we would inevitably give it to some who would be harmed by having it. Consider here a closely related option.[6] People are morally entitled to refuse treatment, because they are morally entitled not to be drugged, punctured, or irradiated against their wills – in short, not to be assaulted. Protecting the right not to be assaulted entails giving some patients what amounts to the option of ending their lives. And for some subset of these patients, having the option of ending their lives by refusing treatment may be just as harmful as having the option of electing active euthanasia. Nevertheless, these harms must be tolerated as an inevitable byproduct of protecting the right not to be assaulted.

Similarly, if I believed that people had a moral right to end their lives, I would not entertain consequentialist arguments against protecting that right. But I don't believe in such a moral right, for reasons to which I have briefly alluded but cannot fully expound in this essay. My willingness to entertain the arguments expounded here thus depends on reasons that are explained elsewhere.[7]

IX

I have been assuming, in deference to existentialists, that a right to die would not alter the options available to a patient but would, at most, alter the social perception of his options. What would follow, however, if we assumed that death was not ordinarily a genuine option? In that case, offering someone the choice of euthanasia would not only cause his existence to be perceived as his responsibility; it would actually cause his existence to become his responsibility for the first time. And this new responsibility might entail new and potentially burdensome obligations.

That options can be undesirable because they entail obligations is a familiar principle in one area of everyday life – namely, the practice of offering, accepting, and declining gifts and favors. When we decline a gift or a favor that someone has spontaneously offered, we deny him an option, the option of providing us with a particular benefit. And our reason for declining is often that he could not have the option of providing the benefit without being obligated to exercise that option. Indeed, we sometimes feel obligated, on our part, to decline a benefit precisely in order to prevent someone from being obligated, on his part, to provide it.[8] We thus recognize that giving or leaving someone the option of providing a benefit to us may be a way of harming him, by burdening him with an obligation.

When we decline a gift or favor, our would-be benefactor sometimes protests in language similar to that used by proponents of the right to die. "I know what I'm doing," he says, "and no one is twisting my arm. It's my money, and I want you to have it." If he's unaware of the lurking allusion, he might even put it like this: "Whose money is it, anyway?"

Well, it is his money (or whatever); and we do believe that he's entitled to dispose of his money as he likes. Yet his right of personal autonomy in disposing of his money doesn't always require that we let him dispose of it on us. We are entitled – and, as I have suggested, sometimes obligated – to restrict his freedom in spending his money for our benefit, insofar as that freedom may entail burdensome obligations.

The language in which favors are declined is equally as interesting as that in which they are offered. What we often say when declining a favor is, "I can't let you do that for me: it would be too much to ask." The phrase "too much to ask" is interesting because it is used only when we haven't in fact asked for anything. Precisely because the favor in question would be too much to ask, we haven't asked for it, and now our prospective benefactor is offering it spontaneously. Why, then, do we give our reason for not having solicited the favor as a reason for declining when it's offered unsolicited?

The answer, I think, is that we recognize how little distance there is between permitting someone to do us a favor and asking him to do it. Because leaving someone the option of doing us a favor can place him under an obligation to do it, it has all the consequences of asking for the favor. To say, "I'm leaving you the option of helping me but I'm not asking you to help," is to draw a distinction without a difference, since options can be just as burdensome as requests.

X

Clearly, a patient's decision to die will sometimes be a gift or a favor bestowed on loved ones whose financial or emotional resources are being drained by his condition. And clearly, death is the sort of gift that one might well want to decline, by denying others the option of giving it. Yet protections for the option of euthanasia would in effect protect the option of giving this gift, and they would thereby prevent the prospective beneficiaries from declining it. Establishing a right to die would thus be tantamount to adopting the public policy that death is never too much to ask.

I don't pretend to understand fully the ethics of gifts and favors. It's one of those subjects that gets neglected in philosophical ethics, perhaps because it has more to do with the supererogatory than the obligatory. One question that puzzles me is whether we are permitted to restrict people's freedom to benefit us in ways that require no active participation on our part. Someone cannot successfully give us a gift, in most cases, unless we

cooperate by taking it into our possession; and denying someone the option of giving us a gift usually consists of refusing to do our part in the transaction. But what about cases in which someone can do us a good turn without any cooperation from us? To what extent are we entitled to decline the favor by means of restrictions on his behavior rather than omissions in ours?

Another question, of course, is whether we wouldn't, in fact, play some part in the deaths of patients who received socially sanctioned euthanasia. Would a medically assisted or supervised death be a gift that we truly took no part in accepting? What if "we" – the intended beneficiary of the gift – were society as a whole, the body that established the right to die and trained physicians in its implementation? Surely, establishing the right to die is tantamount to saying, to those who might contemplate dying for the social good, that such favors will never be refused.

These considerations, inconclusive though they are, show how the theoretical framework developed by Schelling and Dworkin might support remarks like Kamisar's about patients' "obligation to have themselves 'eliminated.'" The worry that a right to die would become an obligation to die is of a piece with other worries about euthanasia, not in itself, but as a problematic option for the patient.

XI

As I have said, I favor euthanasia in some cases. And, of course, I believe that euthanasia must not be administered to competent patients without their consent. To that extent, I think that the option of dying will have to be presented to some patients, so that they can receive the benefit of a good death.

On the basis of the foregoing arguments, however, I doubt whether policy makers can formulate a general definition that distinguishes the circumstances in which the option of dying would be beneficial from those in which it would be harmful. The factors that make an option problematic are too subtle and too various to be defined in a statute or regulation. How will the option of euthanasia be perceived by the patient and his loved ones? How will it affect the relations among them? Is he likely to fear being spurned for declining the option? Would he exercise the option merely as a favor to them? And are they genuinely willing to accept that favor? Sensitivity to these and related questions could never be incorporated into an institutional rule defining conditions under which the option must be offered.

Insofar as I am swayed by the foregoing arguments, then, I am inclined to think that society should at most permit, and never require, health professionals to offer the option of euthanasia or to grant patients' requests for it. We can probably define some conditions under which the option should never be offered; but we are not in a position to define conditions under which it should always be offered; and so we can at most define a legal permission rather than a legal requirement to offer it. The resulting rule would leave caregivers free to withhold the option whenever they see fit, even if it is explicitly and spontaneously requested. And so long as caregivers are permitted to withhold the option of euthanasia, patients will not have a right to die.

XII

The foregoing arguments make me worry even about an explicitly formulated permission for the practice of euthanasia, since an explicit law or regulation to this effect would already invite patients, and hence potentially pressure them, to request that the permission be exercised in their case. I feel most comfortable with a policy of permitting euthanasia by default – that is, by a tacit failure to enforce the institutional rules that currently serve as barriers to justified euthanasia, or a gradual elimination of those rules without fanfare. The best public policy of euthanasia, I sometimes think, is no policy at all.

This suggestion will surely strike some readers as scandalous, because of the trust that it would place in the individual judgment of physicians and patients. But I suspect that to place one's life in the hands of another person, in the way that one does today when placing oneself in the care of a physician, may simply be to enter a relationship in which such trust is essential, because it cannot be replaced or even underwritten by institutional guarantees. Although I do not share the conventional view that advances in medical technology have outrun our moral understanding of how they should be applied, I am indeed tempted to think they have outrun the capacity of institutional rules to regulate their application. I am therefore tempted to think that public policy regulating the relation between physician and patient should be weak and vague by design; and that insofar as the aim of medical ethics is to strengthen or sharpen such policy, medical ethics itself is a bad idea.

Notes

This is a revised version of a paper that was originally published in *The Journal of Medicine and Philosophy* (1992). That paper began as a comment on a paper by Dan Brock, presented at the Central Division of the APA in 1991. See his "Voluntary Active Euthanasia" (Brock, 1992). I received help in writing that paper from: Dan Brock, Elizabeth Anderson, David Hills, Yale Kamisar, and Patricia White. The present version of the paper replaces sections II and III of the original paper with a new and substantially different section II.

1 Here I echo some excellent remarks on the subject by Felicia Ackerman (Ackerman, 1990). I discuss the issue of "dying with dignity" in Velleman (1999a).

2 I discuss this issue further in Velleman (1999b, pp. 356–8, esp. nn. 69, 72).

3 See Velleman (1999a).

4 The *locus classicus* for this point is of course Camus's essay, "The Myth of Sisyphus" (Camus, 1956).

5 For this analogy, see Stell (1979). Stell argues – implausibly, in my view – that one has the right to die for the same reason that one has a right to duel.

6 The analogy is suggested, in the form of an objection to my arguments, by Dan Brock in Brock (1992).

7 See my paper, "A Right of Self-Termination?" (1999a).

8 Of course, there are many other reasons for declining gifts and favors, such as pride, embarrassment, or a desire not to be in someone else's debt. My point is simply that there are cases in which these reasons are absent and a very different reason is present – namely, our desire not to burden someone else with obligations.

References

Ackerman, Felicia (1990) "No, thanks, I don't want to die with dignity," *Providence Journal-Bulletin*, April 19, 1990.

Brock, Dan (1992) "Voluntary Active Euthanasia," *Hastings Center Report* 22: 10–22; reprinted in *Life and Death: Philosophical Essays in Biomedical Ethics* (Cambridge: Cambridge University Press, 1993).

Camus, Albert (1956) "The Myth of Sisyphus," in *The Myth of Sisyphus and Other Essays*, trans. Justin O'Brien. New York: Vintage Books.

Dworkin, Gerald (1982) "Is More Choice Better than Less?" *Midwest Studies in Philosophy* 7: 47–61.

Kamisar, Yale (1970) "Euthanasia Legislation: Some Non-religious Objections."In A. B. Downing (ed.), *Euthanasia and the Right to Die*. New York: Humanities Press, pp. 85–133.

Kant, I. (1964) *Groundwork of the Metaphysic of Morals*, trans. H. J. Paton. New York: Harper and Row.

Schelling, Thomas (1960) *The Strategy of Conflict*. Cambridge, MA: Harvard University Press.

Schelling, Thomas (1984) "Strategic Relationships in Dying," in *Choice and Consequence*. Cambridge, MA: Harvard University Press.

Stell, Lance K. (1979) "Dueling and the Right to Life," *Ethics* 90: 7–26.

Velleman, J. David (1991) "Well-being and Time," *Pacific Philosophical Quarterly* 72: 48–77.

Velleman, J. David (1999a) "A Right of Self-Termination?" *Ethics* 109: 606–28.

Velleman, J. David (1999b) "Love as a Moral Emotion," *Ethics* 109: 338–74.

7

Dying at the Right Time: Reflections on (Un)Assisted Suicide

John Hardwig

Let us begin with two observations about chronic illness and death:

1 Death does not always come at the right time. We are all aware of the tragedies involved when death comes too soon. We are afraid that it might come too soon for us. By contrast, we may sometimes be tempted to deny that death can come too late – wouldn't everyone want to live longer? But in our more sober moments, most of us know perfectly well that death can come too late.

2 Discussions of death and dying usually proceed as if death came only to hermits – or others who are all alone. But most of the time, death is a death in the family. We are connected to family and loved ones. We are sustained by these connections. They are a major part of what makes life worth living for most of us.

Because of these connections, when death comes too soon, the tragedy is often two-fold: a tragedy both for the person who is now dead and for those of us to whom she was connected. We grieve both for our loved one who is gone and for ourselves who have lost her. On one hand, there is the unrealized good that life would have been for the dead person herself – what she could have become, what she could have experienced, what she wanted for herself. On the other, there is the contribution she would have made to others and the ways *their* lives would have been enriched by her.

We are less familiar with the idea that death can come too late. But here, too, the tragedy can be two-fold. Death can come too late because of what living on means to the person herself. There are times when someone does not (or would not) want to live like this, times when she believes she would be better off dead. At times like these, suicide or assisted suicide becomes a perfectly rational choice, perhaps even the best available option for her. We are then forced to ask, "Does someone have a right to die?" Assisted suicide may then be an act of compassion, no more than relieving her misery.

There are also, sadly, times when death comes too late because *others* – family and loved ones – would be better off if someone were dead. (Better off overall, despite the loss of a loved one.) Since lives are deeply intertwined, the lives of the rest of the family can be dragged down, impoverished, compromised, perhaps even ruined because of what they must go through if she lives on. When death comes too late because of the effect of someone's life on her loved ones, we are, I think, forced to ask, "Can someone have a duty to die?" Suicide may then be an attempt to do what is right; it may be the only loving thing to do. Assisted suicide would then be helping someone do the right thing.

Most professional ethicists – philosophers, theologians, and bioethicists – react with horror at the very idea of a duty to die. Many of them even argue that euthanasia and physician-assisted suicide should not be legalized because then some people might somehow get the idea that they have a duty to die. To this way of thinking, someone who got that idea could only be the victim of vicious social pressure or perverse moral reasoning. But when I ask my classes for examples of times when death would come too late, one of the first conditions students always mention is: "when I become a burden to my family." I think there is more moral wisdom here than in the dismay of these ethicists.

Death does not always come at the right time. I believe there are conditions under which I would prefer not to live, situations in which I would be better off dead. But I am also absolutely convinced that I may one day face a duty or responsibility to die. In fact, as I will explain later, I think many of us will one day have this duty.

To my way of thinking, the really serious questions relating to euthanasia and assisted suicide are: Who would be better off dead? Who has a duty to die? *When* is the right time to die? And if my life should be over, who should kill me?[1] However, I know that others find much of what I have said here surprising, shocking, even morally offensive. So before turning to these questions that I want us to think about, I need to explain why I think someone can be better off dead and why someone can have a duty to die. (The explanation of the latter will have to be longer, since it is by far the less familiar and more controversial idea.)

When Someone Would be Better Off Dead

Others have discussed euthanasia or physician-assisted suicide when the patient would be bet-

ter off dead.[2] Here I wish to emphasize two points often omitted from discussion: (1) Unrelieved pain is not the only reason someone would be better off dead. (2) Someone can be better off dead even if she has no terminal illness.

(1) If we think about it for even a little while, most of us can come up with a list of conditions under which we believe we would rather be dead than continue to live. Severe and unrelieved pain is one item on that list. Permanent unconsciousness may be another. Dementia so severe that we no longer recognize ourselves or our loved ones is yet another. There are some people who prefer not to live with quadriplegia. A future shaped by severe deterioration (such as that which accompanies MS, ALS, AIDS, or Huntington's chorea) is a future that some people prefer not to live out.

(Our lists would be different because our lives and values are different. The fact that some people would not or do not want to live with quadriplegia or AIDS, for example, does not mean that others should not want to live like that, much less that their lives are not worth living. That is very important. The point here is that almost all of us can make a list of conditions under which we would rather not live, and that uncontrolled pain is not the only item on most of our lists.)

Focusing the discussion of euthanasia and assisted suicide on pain ignores the many other varieties of suffering that often accompany chronic illness and dying: dehumanization, loss of independence, loss of control, a sense of meaninglessness or purposelessness, loss of mental capabilities, loss of mobility, disorientation and confusion, sorrow over the impact of one's illness and death on one's family, loss of ability even to recognize loved ones, and more. Often, these causes of suffering are compounded by the awareness that the future will be even bleaker. Unrelieved pain is simply not the only condition under which death is preferable to life, nor the only legitimate reason for a desire to end one's life.

(2) In cases of terminal illness, death eventually offers the dying person relief from all her suffering. Consequently, things can be even

worse when there is *NO* terminal illness, for then there is no end in sight. Both pain and suffering are often much worse when they are *not* accompanied by a terminal illness. People with progressive dementia, for example, often suffer much more if they are otherwise quite healthy. I personally know several old people who would be delighted to learn that they have a terminal illness. They feel they have lived long enough – long enough to have outlived all their loved ones and all sense of a purpose for living. For them, even daily existence is much worse because there is no end in sight.

Discussions of euthanasia and physician-assisted suicide cannot, then, be restricted to those with unrelieved pain and terminal illness. We must also consider requests made by those who have no untreatable pain and no terminal illness. Often, their case for relief is even more compelling.

Sometimes, a refusal of medical treatment will be enough to bring relief. Competent adults who are suffering from an illness have a well-established moral and legal right to decline any form of medical treatment, including life-prolonging medical treatment. Family members who must make medical decisions for incompetent people also have the right to refuse any form of medical treatment on their behalf, so long as they are acting in accordance with the known wishes or best interests of their loved one. No form of medical treatment is compulsory when someone would be better off dead.[3]

But those who would be better off dead do not always have terminal illnesses; they will not always need any form of medical treatment, not even medically-supplied food and water. The right to refuse medical treatment will not help these people. Moreover, death due to untreated illness can be agonizingly slow, dehumanizing, painful, and very costly, both in financial and emotional terms. It is often very hard. Refusing medical treatment simply will not always ensure a dignified, peaceful, timely death. We would not be having a national debate about physician-assisted suicide and euthanasia if refusal of medical treatment were always enough to lead to a reasonably good death. When death comes too late, we may need to do more than refuse medical treatment.

Religion and Ending a Life

Some people can easily see that there are people who would be better off dead. But they still cannot accept suicide or physician-assisted suicide because they believe we have a duty to God not to take our own lives. For them, human life is a gift from God and it remains a gift no matter how much pain and suffering it may bring. It is a sin or an offense against God, the giver of life, to take your own life or to help someone else end theirs. Such believers may also feel that no one should be allowed to end their lives – every life is a gift from God, even the lives of those who do not believe that this is so.

I do not understand this position for two reasons. First, it involves the assumption that it is possible to take a human life (our own or someone else's) *before* God wants it ended, but we cannot possibly preserve it *after* God wants it ended. For if we do not make that assumption, we face *two* dangers – the danger that we are prolonging human life beyond its divine purpose, as well as the danger that we are ending it too soon. If we can extend life longer than God intends, suicide and physician-assisted suicide may be more in accord with God's wishes than attempts to preserve that life.

I can understand the view that everyone dies at precisely the right time, the moment God intends. If that is so, people who commit suicide or who are intentionally killed by physicians also die at precisely the moment God wants them to die. I can also understand the view that we can take life before God wants it ended but we can also extend life longer than God wants it prolonged. But I cannot make sense of the view that we can end a human life too soon but not preserve it too long. Surely, God has given us both abilities or neither one.

I also have a second difficulty with this religious objection to suicide, assisted suicide and euthanasia. Suppose there is a right time to die, a divinely-ordained moment when God wants each life to end. Even so, we have no right to assume that God will "take my life" when it's the right time for me to die. In fact, we cannot even assume that God will send a terminal illness that will kill me at the right time. There could be a religious test – God may want me to take my own life and the question is whether I will meet this final challenge. Or a God who loves me might see that I would benefit spiritually from the process of coming to the conclusion that I should end my own life and then preparing to take it. That might be a fitting ending for me, the culminating step in my spiritual growth or development.

In short, a God not totally obsessed with the sheer quantity of our lives may well have purposes for us that are incompatible with longer life – even if we want to live longer. So, I think we should not believe that we always have a duty to God not to take our lives or to assist others in ending theirs. God may want me to step up and assume the responsibility for ending my own life or for seeing that someone else's suffering is ended. This observation leads to our next question: Can there be a responsibility or duty to die?

The Duty to Die

I may well one day have a duty to die, a duty most likely to arise out of my connections with my family and loved ones.[4] Sometimes preserving my life can only devastate the lives of those who care about me. I do not believe I am idiosyncratic, morbid or morally perverse in believing this. I am trying to take steps to prepare myself mentally and spiritually to make sure that I will be able to take my life if I should one day have such a duty. I need to prepare myself; it might be a very difficult thing for me to do.

Our individualistic fantasy about ourselves sometimes leads us to imagine that lives are separate and unconnected, or that they could be so if we chose. If lives were unconnected, then things that happen in my life would not or need not affect others. And if others were not (much) affected by my life, I would have no duty to consider the impact of my life on others. I would then be morally free to choose whatever life and death I prefer for myself. I certainly would have no duty to die when I would prefer to live.

Most discussions of assisted suicide and euthanasia implicitly share this individualistic fantasy: they just ignore the fact that people are connected and lives intertwined. As a result, they approach issues of life or death as if the only person affected is the one who lives or dies. They mistakenly assume the pivotal issue is simply whether the person *herself* prefers not to live like this and whether *she herself* would be better off dead.[5]

But this is morally obtuse. The fact is we are not a race of hermits – most of us are connected to family and loved ones. We prefer it that way. We would not want to be all alone, especially when we are seriously ill, as we age, and when we are dying. But being with others is not all benefits and pleasures; it brings responsibilities, as well. For then what happens to us and the choices we make can dramatically affect the lives of our loved ones. It is these connections that can, tragically, generate obligations to die, as continuing to live takes too much of a toll on the lives of those connected to us.[6]

The lives of our loved ones can, we know, be seriously compromised by caring for us. The burdens of providing care or even just supervision 24 hours a day, 7 days a week, are often overwhelming.[7] But it can also be emotionally devastating simply to be married to a spouse who is increasingly distant, uncommunicative, unresponsive, foreign and unreachable. A local newspaper tells the story of a woman with Alzheimer's who came running into her den screaming: "That man's trying to have sex with me! He's trying to have sex with me! Who *IS* that man?!" That man was her loving husband of more than 40 years who had devoted the past 10 years of his life to caring for her (Smith, 1995). How terrible that experience must have been for her. But how terrible those years must be for him, too.

We must also acknowledge that the lives of our loved ones can also be devastated just by having to *pay* for health care for us. A recent study documented the financial aspects of caring for a dying member of a family. Only those who had illnesses severe enough to give them less than a 50 percent chance to live six more months were included in this study. When these patients survived their initial hospitalization and were discharged, about one-third required considerable caregiving from their families; in 20 percent of cases a family member had to quit work or make some other major lifestyle change; almost one-third of these families lost all of their savings, and just under 30 percent lost a major source of income (Covinsky et al., 1994).

A chronic illness or debilitating injury in a family is a misfortune. It is, most often, nobody's fault; no one is responsible for this illness or injury. But then we face choices about how we will respond to this misfortune. That is where the responsibility comes in and fault can arise. Those of us with families and loved ones always have a responsibility not to make selfish or self-centered decisions about our lives. We should not do just what we want or just what is best for *us*. Often, we should choose in light of what is best for all concerned.

Our families and loved ones have obligations to stand by us and to support us through debilitating illness and death. They must be prepared to make sacrifices to respond to an illness in the family. We are well aware of this responsibility and most families meet it rather well. In fact, families deliver more than 80 percent of the long-term care in the US, almost always at great personal cost.

But responsibility in a family is not a one-way street. When we become seriously ill or debilitated, we too may have to make sacrifices. There are limits to what we can ask our loved ones to do to support us, even in sickness. There are limits to what they should be prepared to do for us – only rarely and for a limited period of time should they do all they can for us.

Somehow we forget that sick, infirm, and dying adults also have obligations to their families and loved ones: a responsibility, for example, to try to protect the lives of loved ones from serious threats or greatly impoverished quality, or an obligation to avoid making choices that will jeopardize or seriously compromise their futures. Our obligations to our loved ones must be taken into consideration in making decisions about the end of life. It is out

of these responsibilities that a duty to die can develop.

Tragically, sometimes the best thing you can do for your loved ones is to remove yourself from their lives. And the only way you can do that may be to remove yourself from existence. This is not a happy thought. Yet we must recognize that suicides and requests for assisted suicide may be motivated by love. Sometimes, it's simply the only loving thing to do.

Who Has a Duty to Die?

Sometimes it is clear when someone has a duty to die. But more often, not. *WHO* has a duty to die? And *WHEN* – under what conditions? To my mind, these are the right questions, the questions we should be asking. Many of us may one day badly need answers to just these questions.

But I cannot supply answers here, for two reasons. In the first place, answers will have to be very particular and individualized . . . to the person, to the situation of her family, to the relationships within the family, etc. There will not be simple answers that apply to everyone.

Secondly and perhaps even more importantly, those of us with family and loved ones should not define our duties unilaterally. Especially not a decision about a duty to die. It would be isolating and distance-creating for me to decide without consulting them what is too much of a burden for my loved ones to bear. That way of deciding about my moral duties is not only atomistic, it also treats my family and loved ones paternalistically – *THEY* must be allowed to speak for themselves about the burdens my life imposes on them and how they feel about bearing those burdens.

I believe in family decision making. Important decisions for those whose lives are interwoven should be made *together*, in a family discussion. Granted, a conversation about whether I have a duty to die would often be a tremendously difficult conversation. The temptations to be dishonest in such conversations could be enormous. Nevertheless, if we can, we should have just such an agonizing discussion – partly because it will act as a check on the information, perceptions and reasoning of all of us; but perhaps even more importantly, because it affirms our connectedness at a critical juncture in our lives. Honest talk about difficult matters almost always strengthens relationships.

But many families seem to be unable to talk about death at all, much less a duty to die. Certainly most families could not have this discussion all at once, in one sitting. It might well take a number of discussions to be able to approach this topic. But even if talking about death is impossible, there are always behavioral clues – about your caregiver's tiredness, physical condition, health, prevailing mood, anxiety, outlook, overall well-being etc. And families unable to talk about death can often talk about those clues. There can be conversations about how the caregiver is feeling, about finances, about tensions within the family resulting from the illness, about concerns for the future. Deciding whether you have a duty to die based on these behavioral clues and conversation about them is more relational than deciding on your own about how burdensome this relationship and care must be.[8]

For these two reasons, I cannot say when someone has a duty to die. But I can suggest a few ideas for discussion of this question. I present them here without much elaboration or explanation.

1 There is more duty to die when prolonging your life will impose greater burdens – emotional burdens, caregiving, disruption of life plans, and, yes, financial hardship – on your family and loved ones. This is the fundamental insight underlying a duty to die.
2 There is greater duty to die if your loved ones' lives have already been difficult or impoverished (not just financially) – if they have had only a small share of the good things that life has to offer.
3 There is more duty to die to the extent that your loved ones have already made great contributions – perhaps even sacrifices – to make your life a good one. Especially if you have not made similar sacrifices for their well-being.

4 There is more duty to die to the extent that you have *already* lived a full and rich life. You have already had a full share of the good things life offers.
5 Even if you have not lived a full and rich life, there is more duty to die as you grow older. As we become older, there is a diminishing chance that we will be able to make the changes that would now be required to turn our lives around. As we age, we will also be giving up less by giving up our lives, if only because we will sacrifice fewer years of life.
6 There is less duty to die to the extent that you can make a good adjustment to your illness or handicapping condition, for a good adjustment means that smaller sacrifice will be required of loved ones and there is more compensating interaction for them. (However, we must also recognize that some diseases – Alzheimer's or Huntington's chorea – will eventually take their toll on your loved ones no matter how courageously, resolutely, even cheerfully you manage to face that illness.)
7 There is more duty to die to the extent that the part of you that is loved will soon be gone or seriously compromised. There is also more duty to die when you are no longer capable of giving love. Part of the horror of Alzheimer's or Huntington's, again, is that it destroys the person we loved, leaving a stranger and eventually only a shell behind. By contrast, someone can be seriously debilitated and yet clearly still the person we love.

In an old person, "I am not ready to die yet" does not excuse one from a duty to die. To have reached the age of, say, 80 years without being ready to die is itself a moral failing, the sign of a life out of touch with life's basic realities.

A duty to die seems very harsh, and sometimes it is. But if I really do care for my family, a duty to protect their lives will often be accompanied by a deep desire to do so. I will normally *want* to protect those I love. This is not only my duty, it is also my desire. In fact, I can easily imagine wanting to spare my loved ones the burden of my existence more than I want anything else.

If I Should Be Dead, Who Should Kill Me?

We need to reframe our discussions of euthanasia and physician-assisted suicide. For we must recognize that pleas for assisted suicide are sometimes requests for relief from pain and suffering, sometimes requests for help in fulfilling one's obligations, and sometimes both. If I should be dead for either of these reasons, who should kill me?

Like a responsible life, a responsible death requires that we think about our choices in the context of the web of relationships of love and care that surround us. We must be sensitive to the suffering as well as the joys we cause others, to the hardships as well as the benefits we create for them. So, when we ask, "Who should kill me?", we must remember that we are asking for a death that will reduce the suffering of *both* me and my family as much as possible. We are searching for the best ending, not only for me, but for *everyone concerned*–in the preparation for death, the moment of death, and afterwards, in the memory and on-going lives of loved ones and family.

Although we could perhaps define a new profession to assist in suicides – euthanasians?? – there are now really only three answers to the question, "Who should kill me?" (1) I should kill myself. (2) A loved one or family member should kill me. (3) A physician should kill me. I will consider these three possibilities. I will call these *unassisted* suicide, *family*-assisted suicide, and *physician*-assisted suicide.

1 Unassisted suicide: I should kill myself

The basic intuition here is that each of us should take responsibility for herself. I am primarily the one who wants relief from my pain and suffering, or it is fundamentally my own duty to die and *I* should be the one to do my duty. Moreover, intentionally ending a life is a very messy business – a heavy, difficult thing for anyone to have to do. If possible, I should not drag others into it. Often, I think, this is the right idea – I should be the one to kill myself.

But not always. We must remember that some people are physically unable to do so – they are too weak or incapacitated to commit suicide without assistance. Less persuasive perhaps are those who just can't bring themselves to do it. Without the assistance of someone, many lack the know-how or means to end their lives in a peaceful, dignified fashion. Finally, many attempted suicides – even serious attempts at suicide – fail or result in terrible deaths. Those who have worked in hospitals are familiar with suicide attempts that leave people with permanent brain damage or their faces shot off. There are also fairly common stories of people eating their own vomit after throwing up the medicine they hoped would end their lives.

Even more importantly, if I must be the one to kill myself, that may force me to take my life earlier than would otherwise be necessary. I cannot wait until I become physically debilitated or mentally incompetent, for then it will be too late for me to kill myself. I might be able to live quite comfortably for a couple more years, if I could count on someone else to take my life later. But if I cannot count on help from anyone, I will feel pressure to kill myself when unavoidable suffering for myself or my loved ones appears on the horizon, instead of waiting until it actually arrives.

Finally, many suicides are isolating – I can't die with my loved ones around me if I am planning to use carbon monoxide from automobile exhaust to end my life. For most of us, a meaningful end of life requires an affirmation of our connection with loved ones and so we do not want to die alone.

The social taboo against ending your own life promotes another type of isolation. The secrecy preceding many suicides creates conditions for misunderstanding or lack of understanding on the part of loved ones – Why did she do it? Why didn't I see that she was going to kill herself? Why didn't I do something to help? Secrecy and lack of understanding often compound the suffering family and loved ones go through when someone ends their life.

Unassisted suicide – I should kill myself – is not always the answer. Perhaps, then, my loved ones should participate in ending my life.

2   Family-assisted suicide: A member of my family should kill me

At times, we may have a moral obligation to help others end their lives, especially those close to us, those we love. I can easily imagine myself having an obligation to help a loved one end her life and I hope my family will come to my assistance if my death does not come at the right time. What should be the role of family and loved ones in ending a life?

They might help me get information about reliable and peaceful methods for ending my life. They might also be able to help me get the drugs I need, if that is the method I choose. Like most people, I would also very much want my loved ones to participate, at least to the extent of being there with me when I die.

For reasons already mentioned, I would hope I could talk over my plans with my loved ones, both to reassure myself and check on my reasoning, and also to help them work through some of the emotional reaction to my death. Some people believe that families should not be involved in decisions about the end of life because they are in the grips of powerful emotions that lead to wildly inappropriate decisions. (A familiar example is the difficulty many families have in deciding to withdraw medical treatment even when their loved one is clearly dying.) Families will always be gripped by powerful emotions over a death in the family. But appropriate decisions are not necessarily unemotional or uninvolved decisions. And I think inappropriate reactions or decisions stem largely from lack of the discussions I advocate or from an attempt to compress them into one, brief, pressure-packed conversation, often in the uncomfortable setting of a hospital.

So, a good death for all concerned would usually involve my family – the preparation for taking my life, at least, would be family-assisted. My loved ones should know; they should, if possible, understand. They should not be surprised. Hopefully my loved ones could come to agree with my decision. They should have had time to come to terms with the fact that I plan to end my life. Indeed, I should have helped them begin to deal emotionally with my death. All that would help to ease

their suffering and also my concern about how my death will affect them. It would reaffirm our connectedness. It would also comfort me greatly to feel that I am understood and known by my loved ones as I take this important step.

More than this I cannot ask of them, for two related reasons. The first is that actually killing a loved one would usually be extremely difficult. It would be a searing and unforgettable experience that could well prove very hard to live with afterwards. Killing a loved one at her request *might* leave you feeling relieved – it could give you the satisfaction of feeling you had done what needed to be done. In cases of extreme debility or great suffering, family-assisted suicide might be experienced as a loving act of kindness, compassion and mercy. It would still be very hard. Much harder would be killing me because I have a duty to die, a duty to die because my life is too great a burden *for the one who now must kill me*. I cannot ask that of someone I love. I fear that they would suffer too much from taking my life.

I might be wrong about this, however. It might be that, though difficult indeed, being killed lovingly and with your consent by your spouse or your child would be a final testimonial to a solid, trusting, and caring relationship. There might be no more powerful reaffirmation of the strength of your relationship, even in the face of death. The traumatic experience for the family members who assist in the suicide might be a healing experience for them, as well. We know so little about family-assisted suicide.

But in any case, there is also a second reason: I cannot ask for family-assisted suicide because it is not legally protected – a loved one who killed me might well be charged with murder. I could not ask my family to subject themselves to such a risk. Moreover, unlike physician-assisted suicide, we would not want to legalize family-assisted suicide. The lives of families are just too complex and too often laced with strong negative emotions – guilt, resentment, hatred, anger, desire for revenge. Family members also often have multiple motives stemming from deeply conflicting interests. As a result, there would be just too many cases in which family-assisted suicide would be indistinguishable from murder.[9]

Finally, family members may also fail. They also may lack know-how or bungle the job. Caught in the compelling emotions of grief and/or guilt, they may be unable to end a life that should be ended.

All this notwithstanding, family-assisted suicide may be the right choice, especially if physician-assisted suicide is unavailable. But should it be unavailable?

3 Physician-assisted suicide: My doctor should kill me

There are, then, important difficulties with both unassisted suicide and family-assisted suicide. These difficulties are arguments for physician-assisted suicide and euthanasia. If my death comes too late, a physician is often the best candidate to kill me . . . or at the very least, to help me kill myself.

Perhaps the main argument for physician-assisted suicide grows out of the physician's extensive knowledge of disease and of dying. If it is a medical condition that leads me to contemplate ending my life, a key question for determining *when* or even *whether* I should end my life is: What is the prognosis? To what extent can my illness be treated or at least alleviated? How long do I have to live with my condition? How much worse will it get and how soon? What will life with that condition be like for me and my family? Few besides physicians possess all this critical information. I will be more likely to reach the right decision at the right time if a trusted physician is in on my plans to end my life.

A related point is physicians' knowledge of and access to drugs. Few of us know what drugs to take and in what amounts without the advice of a physician. Often, only a physician will know what to do to ensure that I do not vomit up the "suicide pill" or what to do if it fails. Physicians also have a monopoly on access to drugs. If my physician were more closely involved in the process, I could be more certain – and thus reassured – that my death will be peaceful and dignified, a death that permits reaffirmation of my connections with family and close friends.

A second argument for physician-assisted suicide grows out of physicians' greater experience with death and dying. Physicians know what to expect; those of us outside the health professions often do not. Granted, few physicians nowadays will know *me* and *my* family. For this reason, physicians should seldom make unilateral decisions about assisted suicide. Still, most physicians could provide a rich source of information about death and about strategies to minimize the trauma, suffering, and agony of a death, both for the dying person and for the family.

Thirdly, physician-assisted suicide does not carry the same social stigma that unassisted suicide carries and physicians are not exposed to the legal risks involved in family-assisted suicide. Although many physicians are unwilling to take *any* risks to help someone end her life, there is really very little legal risk in physician-assisted suicide, especially if the family is in agreement. Physicians are also not morally censored the way family members would be for ending a life.

Finally, physicians ought not to abandon their patients, certainly not at the moment of death. Much has been made of the possibility that Americans would lose their trust in physicians if they knew that physicians sometimes kill. But many of us would trust our physicians *more* if we knew that we could count on them when death is needed or required (Quill and Cassell, 1995).

We have come, then, by a very round-about route to another argument for *physician*-assisted suicide. Often it is simply better – safer, more secure, more peaceful, less emotionally-damaging for others – than unassisted suicide or family-assisted suicide. If physicians refuse to assist or are not permitted to do so, families and seriously ill people will be forced back on their own resources. And many deaths will be much worse than they need to be. When death comes too late, a physician will often be the best candidate to kill me.

And yet, physician-assisted suicide is not always the answer, either. Many physicians take themselves to be sworn to preserve human life in all its forms. Also, many people want doctors who are sworn not to kill, for fear that physicians might start making presumptuous, single-handed decisions about when death comes too late. Moreover, in a time when most people lack a significant personal relationship with their physicians, physician-assisted suicide is often a death that is remote, isolated, disconnected from the relationships that gave meaning to life. It is not always the best death. At times, then, family-assisted suicide and unassisted suicide remain the best answers.

Conclusion

We have a long cultural tradition of attempts to deal with the problems of death that comes too soon. Modern medicine, with its dramatic high-tech rescue attempts in the emergency room and the intensive care unit, is our society's attempt to prevent death from coming too soon. On a more personal level, we are bombarded with advice about ways to avoid a death that would be too soon – sooner than we wished, before we were ready for it.

We have much less cultural wisdom about the problems of a death that comes too late. It is almost as if we had spent all our cultural resources trying to avoid deaths that come too soon, only to find that we then had no resources left to help us when death comes too late.

Deaths that come too soon usually raise no difficult moral problems, however difficult they may be in other ways. Such deaths normally occur despite our best attempts to prevent them. "There's nothing more we can do," we say to the dying person, her family, and ourselves. And there is ethical solace in this, despite the tragedy of the death itself. We admit our failure. But our failure is not a moral failure – we did what we could.

Deaths that come too late are ethically much more troubling. They call on us to assume responsibility – to make difficult decisions and to do difficult things. We can try to hide from this responsibility by claiming that we should always try to prolong life, no matter what. Or by not deciding anything. But we know that not to decide is to decide. And it is very often just

not clear what we should do. The weight of life-or-death decision pushes down upon us.

The recognition that the lives of members of families are intertwined makes the moral problems of a death that comes too late even more difficult. For they deprive us of our easiest and most comfortable answers – "it's up to the individual," "whatever the patient wants." But we do know that measures to improve or lengthen one life often compromise the quality of the lives of those to whom that person is connected.

So, we are morally troubled by deaths that come too late. We don't know what to do. Beyond that, the whole idea is unfamiliar to us. But in other societies – primarily technologically primitive and especially nomadic societies – almost everyone knew that death could come too late. People in those cultures knew that if they managed to live long enough, death would come too late and they would have to do something about it. They were prepared by their cultural traditions to find meaning in death and to do what needed to be done.

We have largely lost those traditions. Perhaps we have supposed that our wealth and technological sophistication have purchased exemption for us from any need to worry about living too long, from any need to live less than every minute we enjoy living. For a while it looked that way. But we must now face the fact: deaths that come too late are only the other side of our miraculous life-prolonging modern medicine.

We have so far avoided looking at this dark side of our medical triumphs. Our modern medicine saves many lives and enables us to live longer. That is wonderful, indeed. But it thereby also enables more of us to survive longer than we are able to care for ourselves, longer than we know what to do with ourselves, longer than we even *are* ourselves. Moreover, if further medical advances wipe out many of today's "killer diseases" – cancers, AIDS, heart attacks, etc. – then most of us will one day find that death is coming too late. And there will be a very common duty to die.

Our political system and health-care reform (in the USA) are also moving in a direction that will put many more of us in the position of having a duty to die. Measures designed to control costs (for the government, and for employers who pay for retirement benefits and health insurance) often switch the burdens of care onto families. We are dismantling our welfare system and attempting to shift the costs of long-term health care onto families. One important consequence of these measures is that more of us will one day find ourselves a burden to our families and loved ones.[10]

Finally, we ourselves make choices that increase the odds that death will come too late. Patient autonomy gives us the right to make choices about our own medical treatment. We use that right to opt again and again for life-prolonging treatment – even when we have chronic illnesses, when we are debilitated, and as we begin to die. Despite this autonomy, we may feel we really have no choice, perhaps because we are unable to find meaning in death or to bring our lives to a meaningful close. But if we repeatedly opt for life-prolong-ing treatment, we thereby also increase the chances that death will come too late. This is the cost of patient autonomy, combined with powerful life-prolonging medical technology and inability to give meaning to death or even to accept it.

Death is very difficult for us. I have tried here to speak about it in plain language; I have used hard words and harsh tones to try to make us attend to troubling realities. We may question the arguments and conclusions of this paper. We should do so. But this questioning must not be fueled by denial or lead to evasion. For one thing seems very clear: We had better start learning how to deal with the problems of a death that comes too late. Some day, many of us will find that we should be dead or that one of our loved ones should be dead. What should we do then? We had better prepare ourselves – mentally, morally, culturally, spiritually, and socially. For many of us, if we are to die at the right time, it will be up to us.

Notes

I get by with a little help from my friends. I wish to thank Hilde and Jim Nelson, Mary English, Tom Townsend, and Hugh LaFollette for helpful comments on earlier versions of this essay. And more: these friends have been my companions and guides throughout my attempt to think through the meaning of love and family in our lives.

1 A note about language: I will be using "responsibility," "obligation," and "duty" interchangeably, despite significant differences in meaning. I generally use the word "duty" because it strikes me as a hard word for what can be a hard reality. (It also echoes Richard Lamm's famous statement: "Old people have a duty to die and get out of the way to give the next generation a chance.") Similarly, I use "kill" despite its connotations of destruction because I think we should not attempt to soften what we are doing. War and capital punishment have already taught us too much about how to talk in sweet and attractive ways about what we do. So I have resisted talking about "bringing my life to a close" and similar expressions. I have tried to use the plain, hard words.

2 There are many articles on this topic. Perhaps the classic article is Rachels (1975). It has been widely reprinted. A good collection of articles can be found in the *Journal of Medicine and Philosophy* (June 1993), which was devoted to the topic, "Legal Euthanasia: Ethical Issues in an Era of Legalized Aid in Dying." Recent anthologies include Beauchamp (1996) and Moreno (1995).

3 A few states in the US – currently (January 1996) New York, Missouri, Delaware, and Michigan – do require that family members be able to supply "clear and convincing evidence" that withdrawal of treatment is what their loved one would have wanted. This can be hard to prove. So it is especially important for those who live in these states to put their wishes about the kind of treatment they would want (if they become unable to decide for themselves) in writing. For information about the laws that apply in your state, write to Choice in Dying, 200 Varick Street, New York, NY 10014, or call them at 212–366–5540.

4 I believe we may also have a duty to ourselves to die, or a duty to the environment or a duty to the next generation to die. But I think for most of us, the strongest duty to die comes from our connections to family and loved ones, and this is the only source of a duty to die that I will consider here.

5 Most bioethicists advocate a "patient-centered ethics" – an ethics which claims only the patient's interests should be considered in making medical treatment decisions. Most health-care professionals

have been trained to accept this ethic and to see themselves as patient advocates. I have argued elsewhere that a patient-centered ethic is deeply mistaken. See Hardwig (1989, 1993).

6 I am considering only mentally competent adults. I do not think those who have never been competent – young children and those with severe retardation – can have moral duties. I do not know whether formerly competent people – e.g., those who have become severely demented – can still have moral duties. But if they cannot, I think some of us may face a duty to die even sooner – before we lose our moral agency.

7 A good account of the burdens of caregiving can be found in Brody (1990). To a large extent, care of the elderly is a women's issue. Most people who live to be 75 or older are women. But care for the elderly is almost always provided by women, as well – even when the person who needs care is the husband's parent.

8 Ultimately, in cases of deep and unresolvable disagreement between yourself and your loved ones, you may have to act on *your own* conception of your duty and your own conception of the burdens on them. But that is a fall-back position to resort to when the better, more relational ways of arriving at a belief in a duty to die fail or are unavailable.

9 Although this is true, we also need to rethink our reactions to the motives of the family. Because lives are intertwined, if someone "wants Dad to be dead" and is relieved when he dies, this does not necessarily mean that she did not genuinely love him. Or that she is greedy, selfish, or self-centered. Her relief may stem from awareness of his suffering. It could also grow out of recognition of the sad fact that his life was destroying the lives of other family members whom she also loved.

10 Perhaps a more generous political system and a more equitable health-care system could counteract the trend toward a more and more common duty to die. For now, at least, we could pay for the care of those who would otherwise be a burden on their families. If we were prepared to do so, far fewer would face a duty to die. But we (in the US, at least) are not prepared to pay. Moreover, as medical advances enable more people to live longer (though also in various states of disability), it may be that the costs would overwhelm any society. Even if we could afford it, we should not continue to try to buy our way out of the problems of deaths that come too late. We would be foolish to devote all our resources to creating a society dedicated solely to helping all of us live just as long as we want.

References

Beauchamp, T. L. (ed.), (1996) *Intending Death: The Ethics of Assisted Suicide and Euthanasia*. Englewood Cliffs, NJ: Prentice-Hall.

Brody, Elaine M., (1990) *Women in the Middle: Their Parent-Care Years*. New York: Springer.

Covinsky, Kenneth E., Goldman, Less et al., (1994) "The Impact of Serious Illness on Patients' Families," *Journal of the American Medical Association* 272: 1839–44.

Hardwig, John (1989) "What about the Family?," *Hastings Center Report* 20 (March/April): 5–10.

—— (1993) "The Problem of Proxies with Interests of Their Own: Toward a Better Theory of Proxy

Decisions," *Journal of Clinical Ethics* 4 (Spring): 20–7.

Moreno, Jonathan (ed.) (1995) *Arguing Euthanasia*. New York: Simon Schuster.

Quill, Timothy E. and Cassell, Christine K. (1995) "Non-abandonment: a Central Obligation for Physicians," *Annals of Internal Medicine* 122: 368–74.

Rachels, James (1975) "Active and Passive Euthanasia," *New England Journal of Medicine* 292 (1995): 78–80.

Smith, V. P. [pen name of Val Prendergrast] (1995) "At Home with Alzheimer's" *Knoxville Metro Pulse* 5/30: 7, 27.

8

A Duty to Care Revisited

Felicia Cohn and Joanne Lynn

The notion of a "duty to die" is not foreign either to our medical culture or to society. Indeed, patients often say, "I just don't want to be a terrible burden," and they mean it, emotionally, physically, and financially. Certainly, patients do turn down potentially beneficial treatment to avoid family impoverishment and hardship. In asking if we have a "duty to die," John Hardwig raises an important question. His ruminations may have succeeded in "clarifying his own convictions," and he may even have helped some readers find personal answers.

However, despite its familiarity and Hardwig's earnest argument, the claim is no less demeaning to the elderly, frail, and sick in our society. Not wanting to be a burden might best translate to a hope for a merciful fate, neither imposing guilt because you are alive, nor pushing for deliberate action to die more quickly. That Hardwig is able to argue for a "duty to die" reveals much about our attitudes toward life, health care, and death. He builds his arguments on a number of troubling assumptions, neglects some important concepts, and sidesteps some problematic implications. First, Hardwig fails to consider the full impact of a "duty to die" on society and those who are

actually coming to the end of life. Second, he takes for granted common fears and misperceptions about dying. Third, he misinterprets the response to his proposal as emotional recoil, when it may be more disheartening dismay. Fourth, he constructs the debate in socially hollow terms of rights and limited choices. Examination of Hardwig's claims suggests that the better social policy lies not in encouraging an obligation to die, but in ensuring an obligation to care for the dying.

The Impact of a "Duty to Die": The Price of Dying and Public Policy

A duty to die has some serious policy implications. Hardwig paints the issue too cleanly, without considering the broad spectrum of circumstances in which people die. He neglects the impact on the dying, particularly the elderly, and the relationship between a duty to die and other policy initiatives, such as those related to health care reform and assisted suicide.

Hardwig's argument shortchanges the possibility of meaningful existence in the last phase of life. He goes so far as to suggest that even those who are not yet categorized as "dying" might incur a duty to die in order to avoid the tribulations associated with longer survival before their eventual deaths. This reflects a society-wide undervaluation and trivialization of life's final journey. The elderly, the sick, and the dying have much to contribute and to gain. Acknowledging a duty to die would serve to reinforce the negative evaluation surrounding aging and pervasive age-based biases.

In American cultures, individuals have not been called on to justify their continued existence. In this respect, Hardwig seems not to recognize the profound culture shift he is advocating. Accepting a duty to die means that the burden of proof will shift. While a duty to die is likely not to be enforceable or absolute, societal or family pressure and personal expectations are almost certainly coercive. Instead of an ongoing presumption in favor of life, any member of society could be required to make a case for his/her continued existence. It is not clear how anyone could actually make that case. No one can specify what counts as "enough" productivity, social relationships, enjoyment of life, or other valued aspects of life to make the case to stay alive.

Moreover, such a radical shift in thinking about aging could have a profound impact in many arenas: from how we spend our health care dollars to how we arrange services for health care and other community needs. A duty to die could affect entitlement payments or supportive housing arrangements for those who refuse to acquiesce, who refuse to give up living. For example, the adverse impact of that expectation may fall disproportionately on specific persons or classes of persons, such as those dependent on Social Security and Medicaid payments. While such consequences may be unintended, they might result if acceptance of a duty to die comes to shape cultural expectations and public policy. Protection from such implications would be impossible to achieve by legislative fiat or availability of supportive services alone.

Drawing practical boundaries to confine this duty would be a perplexing task, since the disabilities and limitations of serious illness in old age regularly fluctuate and gradually progress, and since the sum of shortcomings is so challenging to articulate. Nevertheless, the outcome would affect health care practices and research. Few would support forgoing treatment that costs little, dramatically improves life prospects, and is rather ordinary in nature. However, definitions of little cost, improvement, and ordinary treatment are already controversial. Accepting a duty to die might make physicians into the stewards of our deaths instead of our lives, and thereby create relationships of distrust, just when trust and confidence is so important. Health care policy makers might expect to fund less hospice and palliative care. Research priorities may radically shift away from life-extending treatments for chronic illnesses.

Directly implicated in this decision-making process is the debate over aid-in-dying. Hardwig's discussion fails to consider the nature and meaning of death and the current debate over assisted death. If we are to do away with ourselves prior to becoming burdensome, then we must have a means to ensure a more convenient fatality than the ordinary dying process. For some, this could mean forgoing a life-sustaining treatment; but for many, other forms of assistance will be necessary. For example, an otherwise healthy person might expect, and be expected, to stop eating and drinking after recognizing the early signs of Alzheimer's disease or to commit suicide preemptively to avoid declining cognitive ability. Assisted suicide and even euthanasia may become regularly accepted practices. The experience with physician-assisted suicide in Oregon has persisted for years now with few using this option (Department of Human Services, 2005).[1] A widespread assumption that the very sick have a duty to die could lead to much more widespread use.

Further, while Hardwig recognizes that death happens to families, not just to individuals, he does not account for the burden on survivors from even a "justifiable" suicide. Family and friends will almost certainly be troubled by feelings of grief, inadequacy, and guilt following a family member's suicide, even if they understand the rationale for that suicide. The balance between the burdens experienced by a family due to the premature and unnatural death of a loved one and the burdens imposed on a family in taking care of that elderly or dying loved one is often incommensurate and unclear.

Even if a duty to die could sometimes be appropriate, its impact on community commitment to support the seriously disabled, especially those with immense service needs, must be confronted. Negative perceptions of their lives already are major barriers to obtaining services or even to gaining attention for adequate support and life opportunities. Particularly troubling among Hardwig's conditions for invoking a duty to die is his claim that the duty increases as "the part of you that is loved will soon be gone or seriously compromised" (Hardwig, 2000, p. 90). Conceptions that certain persons are better off dead, while perhaps reasonable in some cases, are still a troubling basis for public policy or medical practice, and may result in backlash. Perhaps Pope John Paul II's revised thinking about artificial nutrition and hydration (2004) reflects a backlash.[2] Artificial nutrition and hydration are, in the Pope's view, no longer extraordinary treatment, but ordinary treatment owed to all as all life is to be valued. Similarly, the varied and complex public response to Mrs. Terri Schiavo's situation may also reflect perceptions of worthwhile life.[3] Among those who supported the withdrawal of her feeding tube, the arguments were based primarily on an understanding of what Mrs. Schiavo's wishes would have been and the unlikelihood of her recovery to meaningful existence. These arguments reflected deeply held beliefs about the meaning and value of life rather than a sense that the issue was whether she and society would be better off with her dead.

Hardwig admits that better palliative and supportive care of the dying might make a duty to die unnecessary or irrelevant. Instead of pressing for such reforms, though, he appears to accept that current arrangements need not change. Of course, considering that a sick neighbor or family member might feel obliged to be dead or to pursue assisted suicide because others were not ready to help should incite us to improve the care available at the end of life. Concerns about unimaginable suffering, overburdened family caregivers, and bankrupting expenses, speak not to a need for a duty to die but to a need for reliable services. These changes need not increase expenditures on medical care in the last phase of life. Rather, the funds now used could be redirected at ensuring affordable caregiving, easing the suffering of patients, relieving the physical and emotional burden on caregivers, and mitigating the risks of bankruptcy for the family. Invoking a duty to die in essence victimizes the victim of illness. Responsibility is "not a one-way street" (Hardwig, 2000, p. 87), as Hardwig notes, but it is not merely a two-way street traversed only by patient and family either. The intersections of life require societal intervention and oversight to function effectively. Love for your family, expressed in an act to spare them the burden of caregiving, need not involve a suicidal crash. Public policy always reflects the culture, but it also shapes that culture. Just as we need not impose an extended dying process on the ill, assaulting them with unwanted medical technologies, we also need not impose death on those who wish to live longer. New programs to provide care for dying persons and their families would not only address the array of problems most of us will face as we approach the end of life, but will also send a message: The final phase of life can be meaningful and valuable. As these values and meanings are more likely spiritual or relational rather than conventional productivity, they are fragile and require societal approval to flourish. For this to be possible, aging and chronic illness must become social and political priorities, advance care planning must be routine, and supportive care must be available. Rather than accepting a duty to die, policy makers and health care practitioners must be accountable for making a duty to care practical and affordable.[4]

Common Fears and Misperceptions: Fear of Death and the Technological Imperative

Hardwig's argument is symptomatic of the misperceptions about dying that pervade society.

He buys into the expectations that society has come to have for health care: that aggressive medical care can conquer death and that families must bear the costs of these battles. Common pictures of the dying – tethered to a hospital bed with tubes from every orifice and subject to every available medical technology, or homebound and completely dependent on loved ones for every need – evoke fear. Hardwig laments the current health care system, but he accepts society and health care as is. His response to the current context is a duty to avoid becoming a burden. The real burden, however, lies in this acceptance of poor quality care for those living with fatal illness. The goal need not be to eliminate those who become burdensome, but to decrease or share the burden. Patients, or their loved ones for them, may already refuse treatment they believe inappropriate, excessive, or unwanted. However, the moral and legal right to refuse life-sustaining treatment should not become a duty to do so. We should expect health care to enhance our final years, not to encumber or eliminate them.

Hardwig's arguments take for granted the current areas of focus and neglect in American medicine. While highlighting the use of technology to increase the length of life, we have ignored some of the implications of this usage. We have heralded longer life, but have not addressed the effects of a longer lifespan. We have not accepted that longer life does not mean extended youth or health. Nor have we recognized that while our health care system can extend life, it also can inflict too long a life on a person better served by accepting death.

The health care system reinforces the common practice of prizing youth and posing aging as a disease to be cured. In the United States, the primary end of medicine appears to be the avoidance of death or the extension of life.[5] However, our health care system has yet to do much to address the complex needs of those who face the relatively new health problems associated with longer life, e.g., chronic heart disease, dementing illness, or worsening functional dependency for many years. A side-effect of the great success of modern medicine is the advent of almost ubiquitous chronic illness.

Most of us will suffer for some years before we die in the expensive hands of modern medical care.[6] These are the roots of a duty to die, as Hardwig explains: "A fairly common duty to die might turn out to be only the dark side of our life-prolonging medicine and the uses we choose to make of it" (Hardwig, 1997, p. 35; Hardwig, 2000). Hardwig's misperception lies in his response to managing this dark side. The answer is not a duty to die but the addressing of the fallacy that "can" implies "ought." That we can use medical technology to extend life does not necessarily mean that we should. A duty to die is not the only or the best way of avoiding excessive medical treatment. Empowering patients/loved ones as partners in the medical decision-making process and building a health care system responsive to the needs of those with chronic and terminal illnesses may address the systemic problems in our health care system, without victimizing the dying.

Hardwig is correct in recognizing that pain is not the only stimulus for a sense that one might be better off dead. Illness and dying are accompanied by a host of other symptoms such as fatigue and shortness of breath, and problems such as time-consuming and expensive treatments. Polls regularly note concerns about other forms of suffering, including loss of independence and financial burdens. Many illnesses may create suffering without appreciably shortening life. Yet doing away with ourselves only curtails the symptoms, without addressing the larger challenge of living with chronic illness and dying well. The goal is increased quality of life, not longer life, or, as Hardwig seems to suggest, shorter life.

Since suffering involves more than pain, proposals for legalizing physician-assisted suicide (or even euthanasia) generally fall short. The availability of legal suicide turns on proving unrelenting pain and terminal prognosis in a person who can direct his or her care. The requirements for pain and prognosis that serve as safeguards in such a public policy run counter to the goal of providing an accessible option for the relief of suffering. If one waits until the suffering is too great, the capacity for taking one's own life is also likely diminished. For

Hardwig, this provides justification for demanding assisted suicide, in addition to what he calls "unassisted" suicide. Yet, as capacity dwindles, the law steps in to protect us. Assisted suicide would not be available to anyone without the mental capacity to make a timely request or the physical capacity to execute the final life-taking act.[7] A duty to die, then, would necessarily mean a preemptive suicide while one retains the capacity to decide and implement the decision. While one may wish to avoid experiencing the effects of physical or mental decline, one may not wish to cut life short prior to that decline.

Further, Hardwig's assumptions about the necessary role of the physician are overstated. Physicians do not have "a monopoly on access to drugs" (Hardwig, 2000, p. 95). Someone wishing to die can find all she needs on the shelves at the drug store. In addition, physicians are no experts on death and dying and becoming so may radically transform their professional role. No classes in medical school teach the skills and attitudes necessary to end life. In fact, most often we want our physicians to respond to our illnesses rather automatically, giving us every last chance at survival. Bringing about death is generally construed as a harm, something physicians bear a Hippocratic obligation to avoid, an ethical obligation legally reinforced in a number of states that explicitly ban physician-assisted suicide.

Only when mere continued existence is so highly and unconditionally prized could a duty to die evolve to the point of overwhelming a presumptive duty to live. Recognizing a duty to die indicates an acceptance of a dominant but narrow ethic: a technological imperative that requires cure despite the associated costs, both economic and human. Death is medicalized, transformed into a problem to be treated. The metaphor of war is pervasive in this context. We fight the enemy of disease with an arsenal of medicines. Death is seen as the ultimate defeat. Fighting the war, especially a losing war, does take a toll; when every day is a battle, a patient may prefer to surrender. Our health care system must learn to cater to the living of life even in the final phases rather than merely fighting

death. This qualitative difference would render a duty to die moot. Should dying become comfortable and meaningful, there would be no battles to fight and no need to hasten the process.

If dying is miserable and expensive, it is because we have allowed it to become that way. In 1900, we would likely have died at an age we now would consider young and would have experienced a relatively sudden death due to acute infection, childbirth, accident, or rapidly progressing disease. Now, we are more likely to die older, having lived with chronic illness for months or years. Our health care system has not responded to the technological advances of the last 40 years, retaining a system that is not prepared to handle the myriad needs of those living long while approaching the end of life. Thus, we have come to fear the process of dying perhaps more so than death itself. The real duty, then, lies not in doing away with ourselves when available resources become inadequate, but in facing those inadequacies. Rather than necessitating a duty to die, suffering should increase our willingness to care, to address the real needs of seriously ill and dying people. We can all imagine situations in which we might prefer not to live. The challenge is to imagine – and implement – societal conditions supportive of our needs and granting meaning to our lives, despite illness and death. We must come to appreciate and facilitate the changes that occur in our bodies and minds throughout the course of life. We must change our response to dying. Recognizing and acting in accord with a duty to die could deflect attention from this larger goal or create a disincentive for working toward that more difficult goal.

Not Horror but Dismay

Hardwig believes his invocation of a duty to die has been met with horror. Worrisome visions of a Huxleyan Brave New World replete with death conditioning and death automatic at a certain age may haunt the thoughts of some critics. But the "wisdom of repugnance" (Kass, 1997) only goes so far. Emotions and science fiction often trump rational debate and reasoned policy making, obscuring the important social conditions that give rise to claims of a duty to die. Real burdens – to individuals, families, and societies – accrue to ill-timed deaths. These burdens are social, emotional, financial, and physical.

The reactions Hardwig perceived to his proposal arise in part from his willingness to put into words what others have probably felt: that sometimes lives go on too long. Articulating beliefs about obligations to die in a society that at least pays lip service to the pricelessness of life may indeed seem shocking. Our society consistently rejects placing an explicit price on life, yet Hardwig's arguments violate the notion that life is invaluable or sacred. As a matter of practicality, we do implicitly place values on continued existence, at least considering it as one good competing among others. Accepting an explicit duty to die, however, would unmask our euphemistic discussions, which are significant for maintaining our illusion that human life is priceless. The illusion is not dishonest; it reflects fundamental beliefs about the value of life. Nor is the illusion a silly vanity; it conditions our attitudes and actions. We work hard to provide health care services to those in need, despite socioeconomic status. We do not let emergencies go unattended or allow individuals to die on the street. In accepting a duty to die, we would explicitly devalue life under certain circumstances and undermine an important cultural value. Society is more humane, kind, and protective when its members hold that every life is precious, even when nearing the end. In the words of one member of the generation that has outlived the conventional life span: "There's a growing number of oldsters still full of creaking vitality. Don't begrudge us respect" (Tresidder, 1998).

Given current conditions, a sense that sometimes death is the best option is neither shocking nor surprising. A common response to Mrs. Schiavo's situation was disbelief that she had survived so long. The public debate addressed the appropriate use of medical resources, the value of her existence, likelihood of improvement or recovery, and who should make decisions on her behalf, among other issues. Yet, few were willing to publicly acknowledge that she might have been better off dead. The family, policy makers, and members of the public, even those supportive of withdrawing her feeding tube, may well have been shocked by a suggestion that she had a duty to die. Willingness to let someone go does not necessarily mean acceptance of an obligation to die. An unreadiness to die or to let someone die is not a "moral failing" (Hardwig, 2000, p. 90) but an artifact of the promise of modern medicine and society's faith in the possibilities of extending life. Calling for an individual's death, no matter how ill or how overdue, seems unworthy of a wealthy and civil society.

More surprising than calling for a duty to die is actually giving into the implications of such a public duty. First, it suggests that we are stuck with the current conditions. Second, if we are to operationalize a duty to die, then public policy would have to arbitrate determinations as to who is better off dead, specifying the conditions that trigger it. If left to practice rather than policy, an informal, and arbitrarily utilized, set of conditions still would arise. While the duty would be technically unenforceable, the societal or family pressure, or the internalized expectations, would create coercive conditions. Thus the emotion that Hardwig's proposal engenders might best be characterized as a deep sense of dismay. Some people do live on beyond the time that seems optimal to bring life's projects to a close, or they live with illnesses that make them wish for the relief of death. Our health care system is ill equipped to support and cherish such people. We typically respond to these truths with a sense of responsibility for the difficult life-or-death choices confronting individual patients. The individual, the ill or dying person (or a surrogate decision maker), is forced to bear the real burden for our society's failure to prepare for his/her needs. Other than the few who experience unexpected, sudden death, all of us will eventually meet whatever criteria are established for exercising the duty to die. Hardwig is correct in suggesting that we should make choices that are best for all concerned, but he shortchanges society in recognizing who counts as "all." Given his concern about our "individualistic fantasy" (Hardwig, 2000, p. 86), that we live our lives as unconnected beings, it is odd that for him the answer lies in an individualistic duty.

Decisions and Choices: Rights Language and False Dichotomies

Hardwig chooses to frame the issue of dying as a matter of dichotomous choices and decisions. The language he uses defines and constructs the questions and their answers. Rather than focus on the process of dying and the needs of those living through that process, the debate turns on decisions to be made in response to limited choices. Hardwig's use of the term "duty" reflects the "rights" language that has become so prevalent in health care issues.[8] Rights, we learned in civics class, have correlative responsibilities. For example, if I have a right to drive, I also bear a responsibility to drive safely. Similarly, a right to die may entail a duty to die in a timely and reasonably convenient way. That is, if I have a right to die, a just and proper claim to have my life end, then I might incur a responsibility to end that life appropriately. In a note, Hardwig disavows the "legalistic overtones" of this language (Hardwig, 1997, p. 41). He acknowledges that no law grounds this duty, but, as a moral duty, the obligation is no less real. Whether legal or moral, reference to something as a duty entails obligation. This is a fear associated with calls for legalized physician-assisted suicide: that rather than existing as an option to be selected at will, it will quickly become a coercive offer, one that must be accepted because no other services are actually available or because others will harshly evaluate one's choice to stay alive. While the experience in Oregon has not borne out that fear, as a national laboratory, all eyes in the nation watched – and watchdogged – the experience there. No one is set to provide oversight, prevent abuses, and maintain choices

with a broader duty to die. The Netherlands experience of legalized assisted suicide and euthanasia has resulted in reports of abuses, which, though controversial, should serve as a cautionary tale.[9]

Moreover, the use of rights language makes death begin to look like it is appropriately held out as merely a choice; i.e., one may choose to live *or* choose to die at a particular time. The circumstances of death might seem to be within our discretion: to suffer with the disease health care professionals cannot treat or the patient will not treat *or* to bring about an end to life. Even suffering becomes a choice: to seek comfort from suffering in the form of continued medical attention, possibly at the risk of impoverishing one's family, *or* to suffer silently while maintaining the family's resources. Decisions at the end of life take on a "me versus them" quality, which seems at least undesirable and largely avoidable.

Hardwig does not consider the reciprocity possibly involved in family caregiving arrangements or account for arguments from family responsibility. Family members, particularly adult children, may believe they owe a sick parent care, as a reciprocal exchange for the care they received while growing up, or just as a mark of what it is to belong to a family. Refusing care to avoid burdening loved ones may undermine the very relationship(s) one hopes to protect (Gunderson, 2004). Some family members, after a lifetime supporting their families, may believe they are entitled to care in their golden years. The very nature of human bonds is necessarily wrought with burdens: "Is this not in large measure what it means to belong to a family: to burden each other – and to find, almost miraculously, that others are willing, even happy, to carry such burdens?"[10] (Meilander, 1991, p. 12). Yet, Hardwig trades on a particular notion of fairness that grows out of a Kantian sense of duty and a notion of family obligations. He appears to believe that such an obligation is a matter of universalizable law: that we should will all others in like situations to act similarly. Further, to expect one's family to bear the burden of one's preference for continued existence, he believes, renders family members as merely means to the dying person's end (i.e., living). Despite these explanations, Hardwig's analysis still appears to come down to a balance of burdens (Hardwig, 1997, p. 38).[11] He even provides a list of considerations that must be weighed in considering the duty to die (Hardwig, 1997, pp. 38–9).[12] This is not a simple utilitarian calculus, but it is utilitarian nonetheless and does not account for other fundamental notions of duty, such as those borne out of love and familial ties. It is the "consequences for his loved ones" about which he appears to be most concerned (Hardwig, 1997, p. 40).[13] A duty not to impose hardship on your family may exist. Certainly many patients express this feeling. But, as Hardwig admits, the duty to die is not incumbent upon those who are not wreaking havoc on their family's lives. The duty to die is contingent. When, exactly, does death become an obligation? For whom? Under what circumstances?

Matters of life and death are not best framed in terms of duties and choices. Even reframing a duty to die in terms of a "right" time to die suggests that someone can determine when the right time is, and can make an error in failing to make the correct determination. Death appears to be a matter of decision making. Reliance on autonomy, individual decision making, or exercise of rights rarely seems to afford the answers we need, and in fact may come back to haunt us. The principle of autonomy has been stretched almost beyond recognition. Respect for autonomy supports patients' rights to refuse treatment. This right to refuse suggests a responsibility to use health care resources appropriately, but a right to refuse treatment should not be confused with a duty to do so. Clinicians appear increasingly comfortable with conflating the right and the duty, requesting legal or ethical intervention when patients or families refuse to withdraw treatment. The collapsing of right and duty offers a testament to the adage admonishing that we be careful what we ask for. The patients' rights movement sought to increase individual input into and control over medical care, specifically to avoid

unwanted treatments. Yet, physicians appear also to have been empowered, now able to impose withdrawal as well as initiation of treatment.

Death is neither a duty nor a choice so much as it is a fact. It may be more helpful to consider that we all reach a "time to die" rather than that we have a duty to die and to try to make death happen at the "right" time. One can alter the probabilities of the timing and circumstances of death, e.g., via refusal of care, without acquiring an obligation to die at a particular time and in a particular way. The mere existence of technology does not command its use. Even acknowledging an obligation to justly distribute resources does not amount to having an obligation to die. The choice is not "to be or not to be," but how to use our resources appropriately as we "are." Furthermore, our choices are not stark: either to suffer and go bankrupt or to die; either to treat or not to treat; either to cure or to comfort. The options include treating sometimes and not treating sometimes, curing as well as comforting, and seeking to forge a balance among competing beneficial and burdensome aspects of the situation.

Conclusion

The issues Hardwig raises are and should be difficult. His arguments deserve both respect and criticism, and our criticism has as much to do with our health care system and public attitudes as with Hardwig's proposition. The concerns are not limited to health care professionals or policy makers. We will all face death one day, and very few of us will be fortunate enough to die suddenly, painlessly in our sleep, after a rich 80 or 90 years of life. The inadequacies of the current health care system are not somebody else's problem. We will be stuck with the system we create – or the system we neglect. Hardwig's arguments and conclusions deserve attention, but we must work to ensure that criticism is constructive. We owe it to ourselves, and our society's future, to establish a duty to care.[14]

Notes

An earlier version of this paper originally appeared as a commentary in response to John Hardwig's essay, "A Duty to Die." See F. Cohn and J. Lynn, "A Duty to Care," in J. Hardwig, *Is There a Duty to Die?* (New York: Routledge, 2000), pp. 145–54.

1 According to the "Seventh Annual Report on Oregon's Death With Dignity Act," a total of only 208 patients took lethal medications in the first seven years under the legal provisions allowing physician-assisted suicide.

2 Pope John Paul II stated:

In opposition to such trends of thought, I feel the duty to reaffirm strongly that the intrinsic value and personal dignity of every human being do not change, no matter what the concrete circumstances of his or her life. *A man, even if seriously ill or disabled in the exercise of his highest functions, is and always will be a man*, and he will never become a "vegetable" or an "animal" . . . Medical doctors and health-care personnel, society and the Church have moral duties toward these persons from which they cannot exempt themselves without lessening the demands both of professional ethics and human and Christian solidarity. The sick person in a vegetative state, awaiting recovery or a natural end, still has the right to basic health care (nutrition, hydration, cleanliness, warmth, etc.), and to the prevention of complications related to his confinement to bed. He also has the right to appropriate rehabilitative care and to be monitored for clinical signs of eventual recovery. I should like particularly to underline how the administration of water and food, even when provided by artificial means, always represents a *natural means* of preserving life, not a *medical act*. Its use, furthermore, should be considered, in principle, *ordinary* and *proportionate*, and as such morally obligatory, insofar as and until it is seen to have attained its proper finality, which in the present case consists in providing nourishment to the patient and alleviation of his suffering.

3 Theresa Marie Schiavo was 26 years old in February 1990 when she suffered a hypoxic event, probably from a heart attack as a result of a potassium imbalance. She never regained consciousness. Unable to speak, see, hear, eat, or interact with her environment in any meaningful way, physicians diagnosed her condition as a persistent vegetative state, a state of being permanently unconscious. Cases of recovery or improvement from a long-term state of PVS are rare. Mrs. Schiavo survived with a feeding tube which delivered nutrition and hydration directly into her stomach. In 1998, her husband, Michael Schiavo, petitioned a Florida trial court to allow him to discontinue his wife's artificial life support, which in her case was plastic tubing surgically implanted in her abdomen. He argued that she would not wish to be kept alive under her current circumstances. The request, contested by Mrs. Schiavo's parents, Robert and Mary Schindler, was reviewed by lower, intermediate, and high courts in Florida. Her parents contended that she was not in a persistent vegetative state, was able to interact with them, and would not have wanted her treatment withdrawn. After a series of court decisions favoring Michael Schiavo's position, and a series of stays, Mrs. Schiavo's parents appealed to Florida Governor Jeb Bush in 2003. The Florida Legislature and Senate met in special session to pass "Terri's Law" specifically to prevent removal of her feeding tube. Governor Bush, supported by his brother, President George W. Bush, signed an executive order reinstating the use of the feeding tube. In 2005, the Florida courts overturned Terri's Law as unconstitutional. A similar episode involving Congress and President Bush also was set aside by the US Supreme Court. Her feeding tube was withdrawn on March 17, 2005, and she died on March 31. An autopsy revealed that recovery and meaningful interaction with others would have been unlikely if not impossible.

4 In *Sick to Death and Not Going to Take It Anymore!* (2004), Joanne Lynn offers a series of practical suggestions for building a public policy agenda to reform the care of those with serious chronic illness in the last phase of life.

5 Hardwig claims a duty to die is common in other, largely poor and technologically unsophisticated cultures. This may not be a duty so much as a reality. Without the ability or resources to extend life, individuals have choices only with regard to the attitudes they express toward dying. Death comes not as an imposition on a life too costly to continue, but as an acceptance, even a graceful acceptance, of mortality.

6 For a comprehensive description of the state of end-of-life care in the United States, see Institute of Medicine (1997).

7 The current Oregon law and proposals in other states (e.g., California, 2005) contain language to this effect. See the Oregon Revised Statute, California Compassionate Choices Act (AB 654).

8 In discussing "rights language," we are drawing on Mary Ann Glendon's concept of "rights talk." She says:

A tendency to frame nearly every social controversy in terms of a clash of rights (a woman's right to her own body vs. a fetus's right to life) impedes compromise, mutual understanding, and the discovery of common ground. A penchant for absolute formulations ("I have the right to do whatever I want with my property") promotes unrealistic expectations and ignores both social costs and the rights of others. . . . I have endeavored to demonstrate how our simplistic rights talk simultaneously reflects and distorts American culture. It captures our devotion to individualism and liberty, but omits our traditions of hospitality and care for the community.

Like Glendon, we seek the "indigenous languages of relationship and responsibility that could help to refine our language of rights" and to build on our tradition of care. It is in the recognition of responsibility within relationships that a duty to care lies. This duty extends beyond family, as it involves creating a community context in which the final phase of life can be comfortable and meaningful. See Glendon (1991, pp. xi–xii).

9 Hendin (2002) describes the results of studies sanctioned by the Dutch government which reveal that guidelines established for the regulation of assisted suicide and euthanasia (i.e., a voluntary, well-considered, persistent request, intolerable suffering that cannot be relieved, consultation with a colleague, and reporting of cases) are often violated. Patients sometimes are given lethal medication without their consent, including children without capacity to consent, and persons suffering from illnesses that might be alleviated (e.g, depression) have been afforded access to assisted dying. Hendin suggests that euthanasia has become acceptable rather than exceptional. Further, he notes that palliative care has suffered as a result and lags behind what is available in other countries.

10 Meilander's comments are based on consideration of the burden of decision making at the end of life, but suggest broader implications for care at the end of life.

11 Hardwig states: "A duty to die is more likely when continuing to live will impose significant burdens – emotional burdens, extensive caregiving, destruction of life plans, and yes, financial hardship – on your family and loved ones. This is the fundamental insight underlying a duty to die."

12 The factors to be considered include burdens imposed on family and loved ones, age, fullness of life, difficulties already faced by loved ones, previous contributions and sacrifices of loved ones, loss of mind and identity, and depleted savings.

13 Hardwig later states: "Ending my life if my duty required might still be difficult. But for me, a far greater horror would be dying alone or stealing the futures of my loved ones in order to buy a little more time for myself" (Hardwig, 1997, p. 41). His expression of "greater horror" again suggests that he is pitting the value of his extended life against his family's future.

14 A duty to care involves more than a commitment by families to care for their elderly members. It would entail reform of our current health care system, including changes in health care financing mechanisms, service array, service sites, and eligible patient population. Hospice care is a step in the right direction, but it serves only about 20 percent of those who die in the Medicare program. New programs have been proposed to address the complex array of needs individuals develop as they approach the end of life. See, for example, Lynn and Wilkinson (1998); Lynn et al. (1996); Lynn (2004).

References

California Compassionate Choices Act (AB 654), http://www.leginfo.ca.gov/pub/bill/asm/ab_06510700/ab_654_bill_20050526_amended_asm.pdf, accessed 6/7/05.

Glendon, Mary Ann (1991) *Rights Talk: The Impoverishment of Political Discourse*. New York: The Free Press, pp. xi–xii.

Gunderson, Martin (2004) "Being a Burden: Reflections on Refusing Medical Care," *Hastings Center Report* (September–October) 34(5): 37–43.

Hardwig, John (1997) "Is There a Duty to Die?" *Hastings Center Report* (March–April 1997) 27(2): 34–42.

Hardwig, John (2000) "Dying at the Right Time: Reflections on (Un)assisted Suicide." In J. Hardwig, *Is There a Duty to Die?* New York: Routledge, pp. 81–100.

Hendin, Herb (2002) "The Dutch Experience," *Issues Law Med.* (Spring) 17(3): 223–46.

Institute of Medicine (1997) *Approaching Death: Improving Care at the End of Life*. Washington, DC: National Academy Press.

John Paul II (2004) Address to the Participants in the International Congress on "Life-sustaining Treatments and Vegetative State: Scientific Advances and Ethical Dilemmas," March 20, 2004, http://www.vatican.va/holy_father/john_paul_ii/speeches/2004/march/documents/hf_jp-ii_spe_20040320_congress-fiamc_en.html, accessed 6/1/05.

Kass, Leon R. (1997) "The Wisdom of Repugnance: Why We Should Ban the Cloning of Humans," *New Republic* (June) 2; 216(22):17–26.

Lynn, Joanne (2004) *Sick to Death and Not Going to Take It Anymore!* Berkeley, CA: University of California Press.

Lynn, Joanne and Wilkinson, Anne (1998) "Quality End of Life Care: The Case for a MediCaring Demonstration." In Joan K. Harrold and Joanne Lynn(eds.), *A Good Dying: Shaping Health Care for the Last Months of Life*. New York: Haworth Press, Inc.

Lynn, Joanne, Wilkinson, Anne, Cohn, Felicia, and Jones, Stanley (1996) "Capitated Risk-Bearing Managed Care Systems Could Improve End-of-Life Care," *Journal of the American Geriatrics Society* 46: 322–30.

Meilander, Gilbert (1991) "I Want to Burden My Loved Ones," *First Things* (October): 12–14.

Oregon Death with Dignity Act, http://egov.oregon.gov/DHS/ph/pas/ors.shtml, accessed 6/7/05.

Tresidder, Argus J. (1998) "Longevity and Livability," *Newsweek* (March 2): 17.

Abortion

The public debate over abortion in the United States has intensified since the Supreme Court's decision in *Roe v. Wade* (410 US 113, 1973). Advocates on each side of the debate often hint that we must select between two stark options: "Pro-life" and "Pro-choice." Strong pro-life advocates claim that abortion is immoral (except perhaps in a few cases) because the fetus is a human being from the moment of conception, while strong pro-choice advocates claim women must have a (virtually unlimited) legal right to an abortion until well into the third trimester.

Most authors in this section reject central tenets of the debate so characterized. They think it seriously oversimplifies the issues. Warren, Marquis, Little, and Hursthouse all reject elements of both positions, albeit for different reasons. Pro-lifers claim that abortion is immoral simply because the fetus is a human being. Since killing an innocent human being is murder, then abortion is murder. Warren and Marquis respond that calling a creature a "human being" is simply to identify its biological pedigree, not its moral status. We must first determine what it is about human life that makes it valuable, that grounds its right to life. Hursthouse would not only reject the standard

characterizations; she would equally object to Warren's and Marquis's claims. All make the mistake, she claims, of resting ordinary moral decisions on complicated metaphysical assertions about the status of the fetus. And Little thinks all these views, to varying degrees, fail to appreciate both the nature of fetal development and the precise relationship between the fetus and the mother.

On the other hand, pro-choicers like Thomson claim that abortion should be legal simply because women should have the right to choose what happens in and to their bodies. Warren and Marquis respond that this position illicitly ignores the status of the fetus. If the fetus has full moral status, they claim, there is something profoundly wrong with abortion. Hursthouse objects, but for a very different reason. Although claims about women's rights might be sufficient to settle the legal question of abortion, it is basically irrelevant to its moral evaluation. People who act within their legal rights may still act very badly. The moral question is whether and when a virtuous person might have an abortion, and that issue is settled independently of either the ascription of women's rights or metaphysical findings about the status of the fetus.

What is clear is that we have substantial disagreement over two issues: (a) the moral status of the fetus and (b) whether moral status is even relevant to this debate. Warren and Marquis think the issue *is* critical, but reach radically different conclusions about the fetus's status. Although they agree that the pro-lifer's emphasis on biological humanity is misplaced, they disagree about how to determine if a creature has full moral status. Warren argues that the proper moral question is not: "Is it human?" but "Is it a person?" Some creatures that are biologically human are not persons. For instance, we may say of someone in a persistent vegetative state: "She's a vegetable," thereby indicating that the body is no longer the person we once knew. Moreover, some non-humans might be persons: were we to find intelligent, caring, and sensitive aliens elsewhere in the universe, we should conclude they have full moral status.

Marquis accepts Warren's core insight: humanity is not the proper criterion of moral status. He does not, however, think the category of "person" does the moral trick. He claims we must first ascertain what it is about normal adult human beings that makes it wrong to kill them, and then determine if fetuses have those same characteristics. Killing a normal adult is wrong, he argues, because the adult is thereby deprived of a valuable future. Since fetuses have a *future like ours*, they, too, have moral status. Specifically, they have a right to life.

The idea that we must first establish criteria of moral status is not restricted to the issue of abortion. It also plays a role in debates over the proper treatment of non-human ANIMALS. Someone might argue that since some animals have a *future like ours*, we should not kill them without compelling reasons. This move employs a common strategy of philosophical argumentation, a strategy built upon the criterion of consistency, discussed in THEORIZING ABOUT ETHICS. Philosophers often support their arguments by showing how their views are consistent with widely held views on other moral topics.

However, as both Thomson, Little, and Hursthouse argue, albeit in different ways, settling the issue of moral status does not settle the question of how we should behave. Thomson claims that even if we knew the fetus had full moral status and a serious right to life, abortion would be morally, and should be legally, permissible. The central issue, according to Thomson, is not the status of the fetus, but whether the woman has an obligation to carry and care for the fetus. We have obligations to help others only if we explicitly agree to help them. Since women do not explicitly agree to carry their fetuses to term, then they have no such obligations toward them. Little is sympathetic with Thomson's claims but argues that the best way to explain the rights of the woman is by understanding the character of the relationship between the fetus and the woman. This relationship is deeply intimate, and it is not the place of morality or the state to require that women be intimate, in this case by carrying a fetus to term.

One related question concerns the limits of morality: just how much can morality demand of us? This is an issue explicitly discussed by Rachels (FAMILY AND REPRODUCTIVE TECHNOLOGY) and Arthur (WORLD HUNGER). This question about the nature and limits of our obligations is deeply intertwined with the *act/omission* distinction, mentioned in the previous introduction. Why? Everyone acknowledges we have obligations not to harm others directly (even perfect strangers), even if fulfilling that obligation comes at considerable personal cost, and even if we did not explicitly assume these obligations. Thus, when people describe the limits of morality, they are usually talking about the limits only on our obligations to help or benefit others.

Hursthouse not only rejects the standard characterizations of the abortion debate, but as an advocate of virtue theory she also rejects a central presumption undergirding this debate about the limits of morality. That debate assumes that morality constrains us from doing what we really want to do. Given this assumption, the question then becomes: how constraining can morality properly be? However, the virtue theorist sees the virtuous life not as an imposition on the good life, but as a prescription for it. That does not mean that there are no occasions in which morality might demand that we must act in ways that may work against our immediate interests. It is only to say that that is not the norm.

Hursthouse also differs from the other authors in this section because she does not address the legal issue. However, practically speaking, most people are interested not only in the moral question, but also in the legal one. What can the state properly force us to do, or prohibit us from doing? In the abortion debate, I frequently hear people say, "Although I am personally opposed to abortion, I am also opposed to legally forbidding abortions." Even if you think this is an untenable position in the abortion debate, sometimes it is an appropriate response. There are many actions we morally should not do but which the state should not

punish. Although it is wrong to be callous to a grieving parent, I would argue that we should not make such callousness criminal.

The problem, of course, is that although many people might agree that callousness should not be criminalized, other cases are not so clear. How can we reasonably distinguish between actions that are immoral, but should not be criminalized, from actions that are immoral (e.g., murder) and should be criminalized? Clearly this is a central question of PUNISHMENT; it also plays a central role in the issues of PATERNALISM AND RISK, where Hunt discusses "On Improving People by Political Means." Hunt acknowledges the importance of political authority, but argues that there are limits on whether and how we should use that authority to try to make people more virtuous.

Further Reading

Beckwith, F. (1993) *Politically Correct Death: Answering Arguments for Abortion Rights*. Grand Rapids, MI: Baker Books.

Callahan, J. and Knight, J. (1989) *Preventing Birth: Contemporary Methods and Related Moral Controversies*. Salt Lake City: University of Utah Press.

Feinberg, J. (ed.) (1973) *The Problem of Abortion*. Belmont, CA: Wadsworth.

Feldman, F. (1992) *Confrontations with the Reaper: A Philosophical Study of the Nature and Value of Death*. New York: Oxford University Press.

Hursthouse, R. (1999) *On Virtue Ethics*. Oxford: Oxford University Press.

Pojman, L. and Beckwith, F. (1994) *The Abortion Controversy: A Reader*. Boston, MA: Jones & Bartlett Publishers.

Rothman, B. (1989) *Recreating Motherhood: Ideology and Technology and a Patriarchal Society*. New York: W. W. Norton and Company.

Steinbock, B. (1992) *Life Before Birth: The Moral and Legal Status of Embryos and Fetuses*. New York: Oxford University Press.

9

A Defense of Abortion

Judith Jarvis Thomson

Most opposition to abortion relies on the premise that the fetus is a human being, a person, from the moment of conception. The premise is argued for, but, as I think, not well. Take, for example, the most common argument. We are asked to notice that the development of a human being from conception through birth into childhood is continuous; then it is said that to draw a line, to choose a point in this development and say "before this point the thing is not a person, after this point it is a person" is to make an arbitrary choice, a choice for which in the nature of things no good reason can be given. It is concluded that the fetus is, or anyway we had better say it is, a person from the moment of conception. But this conclusion does not follow. Similar things might be said about the development of an acorn into an oak tree, and it does not follow that acorns are oak trees or that we had better say they are. Arguments of this form are sometimes called "slippery slope arguments" – the phrase is perhaps self-explanatory – and it is dismaying that opponents of abortion rely on them so heavily and uncritically.

I am inclined to agree, however, that the prospects for "drawing a line" in the development of the fetus look dim. I am inclined to think also that we shall probably have to agree that the fetus has already become a human person well before birth. Indeed, it comes as a surprise when one first learns how early in its life it begins to acquire human characteristics. By the tenth week, for example, it already has a face, arms and legs, fingers and toes; it has internal organs, and brain activity is detectable.[1] On the other hand, I think that the premise is false, that the fetus is not a person from the moment of conception. A newly fertilized ovum, a newly implanted clump of cells, is no more a person than an acorn is an oak tree. But I shall not discuss any of this. For it seems to me to be of great interest to ask what happens if, for the sake of argument, we allow the premise. How, precisely, are we supposed to get from there to the conclusion that abortion is morally impermissible? Opponents of abortion commonly spend most of their time establishing that the fetus is a person, and hardly any time explaining the step from there to the impermissibility of abortion. Perhaps they ⟨ ⟩ the step too simple and obvious to requi⟨ ⟩ ⟨ ⟩ment. Or perhaps instead they ⟨ ⟩ economical in argument. Ma⟨ ⟩ defend abortion rely on the ⟨ ⟩ fetus is not a person, but ⟨ ⟩

that will become a person at birth; and why pay out more arguments than you have to? Whatever the explanation, I suggest that the step they take is neither easy nor obvious, that it calls for closer examination than it is commonly given, and that when we do give it this closer examination we shall feel inclined to reject it.

I propose, then, that we grant that the fetus is a person from the moment of conception. How does the argument go from here? Something like this, I take it. Every person has a right to life. So the fetus has a right to life. No doubt the mother has a right to decide what shall happen in and to her body; everyone would grant that. But surely a person's right to life is stronger and more stringent than the mother's right to decide what happens in and to her body, and so outweighs it. So the fetus may not be killed; an abortion may not be performed.

It sounds plausible. But now let me ask you to imagine this. You wake up in the morning and find yourself back to back in bed with an unconscious violinist. A famous unconscious violinist. He has been found to have a fatal kidney ailment, and the Society of Music Lovers has canvassed all the available medical records and found that you alone have the right blood type to help. They have therefore kidnapped you, and last night the violinist's circulatory system was plugged into yours, so that your kidneys can be used to extract poisons from his blood as well as your own. The director of the hospital now tells you, "Look, we're sorry the Society of Music Lovers did this to you – we would never have permitted it if we- had known. But still, they did it, and the violinist now is plugged into you. To unplug you would be to kill him. But never mind, it's only for nine months. By then he will have recovered from his ailment, and can safely be unplugged from you." Is it morally incumbent on you to accede to this situation? No doubt it would be very nice of you if you did, a great kindness. But do you have to accede to it? What if it were not nine months, but nine years? Or longer still? What if the director of the hospital says, "Tough luck, I agree, but you've now got to stay in bed, with the violinist plugged into you, for the rest of your life. Because remember this. All persons have a right to life, and violinists are persons. Granted you have a right to decide what happens in and to your body, but a person's right to life outweighs your right to decide what happens in and to your body. So you cannot ever be unplugged from him." I imagine you would regard this as outrageous, which suggests that something really is wrong with that plausible-sounding argument I mentioned a moment ago.

In this case, of course, you were kidnapped; you didn't volunteer for the operation that plugged the violinist into your kidneys. Can those who oppose abortion on the ground I mentioned make an exception for a pregnancy due to rape? Certainly. They can say that persons have a right to life only if they didn't come into existence because of rape; or they can say that all persons have a right to life, but that some have less of a right to life than others, in particular, that those who came into existence because of rape have less. But these statements have a rather unpleasant sound. Surely the question of whether you have a right to life at all, or how much of it you have, shouldn't turn on the question of whether or not you are the product of a rape. And in fact the people who oppose abortion on the ground I mentioned do not make this distinction, and hence do not make an exception in case of rape.

Nor do they make an exception for a case in which the mother has to spend the nine months of her pregnancy in bed. They would agree that would be a great pity, and hard on the mother; but all the same, all persons have a right to life, the fetus is a person, and so on. I suspect, in fact, that they would not make an exception for a case in which, miraculously enough, the pregnancy went on for nine years, or even the rest of the mother's life.

Some won't even make an exception for a case in which continuation of the pregnancy is likely to shorten the mother's life; they regard abortion as impermissible even to save the mother's life. Such cases are nowadays very rare, and many opponents of abortion do not accept this extreme view. All the same, it is a good place to begin: a number of points of interest come out in respect to it.

(1) Let us call the view that abortion is impermissible even to save the mother's life "the extreme view." I want to suggest first that it does not issue from the argument I mentioned earlier without the addition of some fairly powerful premises. Suppose a woman has become pregnant, and now learns that she has a cardiac condition such that she will die if she carries the baby to term. What may be done for her? The fetus, being a person, has a right to life, but as the mother is a person too, so has she a right to life. Presumably they have an equal right to life. How is it supposed to come out that an abortion may not be performed? If mother and child have an equal right to life, shouldn't we perhaps flip a coin? Or should we add to the mother's right to life her right to decide what happens in and to her body, which everybody seems to be ready to grant – the sum of her rights now outweighing the fetus's right to life?

The most familiar argument here is the following. We are told that performing the abortion would be directly killing[2] the child, whereas doing nothing would not be killing the mother, but only letting her die. Moreover, in killing the child, one would be killing an innocent person, for the child has committed no crime, and is not aiming at his mother's death. And then there are a variety of ways in which this might be continued. (1) But as directly killing an innocent person is always and absolutely impermissible, an abortion may not be performed. Or, (2) as directly killing an innocent person is murder, and murder is always and absolutely impermissible, an abortion may not be performed.[3] Or, (3) as one's duty to refrain from directly killing an innocent person is more stringent than one's duty to keep a person from dying, an abortion may not be performed. Or, (4) if one's only options are directly killing an innocent person or letting a person die, one must prefer letting the person die, and thus an abortion may not be performed.[4]

Some people seem to have thought that these are not further premises which must be added if the conclusion is to be reached, but that they follow from the very fact that an innocent person has a right to life.[5] But this seems to me to

be a mistake, and perhaps the simplest way to show this is to bring out that while we must certainly grant that innocent persons have a right to life, the theses in (1) through (4) are all false. Take (2), for example. If directly killing an innocent person is murder, and thus is impermissible, then the mother's directly killing the innocent person inside her is murder, and thus is impermissible. But it cannot seriously be thought to be murder if the mother performs an abortion on herself to save her life. It cannot seriously be said that she must refrain, that she must sit passively by and wait for her death. Let us look again at the case of you and the violinist. There you are, in bed with the violinist, and the director of the hospital says to you, "It's all most distressing, and I deeply sympathize, but you see this is putting an additional strain on your kidneys, and you'll be dead within the month. But you have to stay where you are all the same. Because unplugging you would be directly killing an innocent violinist, and that's murder, and that's impermissible." If anything in the world is true, it is that you do not commit murder, you do not do what is impermissible, if you reach around to your back and unplug yourself from that violinist to save your life.

The main focus of attention in writings on abortion has been on what a third party may or may not do in answer to a request from a woman for an abortion. This is in a way understandable. Things being as they are, there isn't much a woman can safely do to abort herself. So the question asked is what a third party may do; and what the mother may do, if it is mentioned at all, is deduced, almost as an afterthought, from what it is concluded that the third parties may do. But it seems to me that to treat the matter in this way is to refuse to grant to the mother that very status of person which is so firmly insisted on for the fetus. For we cannot simply read off what a person may do from what a third party may do. Suppose you find yourself trapped in a tiny house with a growing child. I mean a very tiny house, and a rapidly growing child – you are already up against the wall of the house and in a few minutes you'll be crushed to death. The child on the other hand won't be crushed to death; if nothing is done to stop him from growing he'll be hurt, but in the end he'll simply burst open the house and walk out a free man. Now I could well understand it if a bystander were to say, "There's nothing we can do for you. We cannot choose between your life and his, we cannot be the ones to decide who is to live, we cannot intervene." But it cannot be concluded that you too can do nothing, that you cannot attack it to save your life. However innocent the child may be, you do not have to wait passively while it crushes you to death. Perhaps a pregnant woman is vaguely felt to have the status of a house, to which we don't allow the right of self-defense. But if the woman houses the child, it should be remembered that she is a person who houses it.

I should perhaps stop to say explicitly that I am not claiming that people have a right to do anything whatever to save their lives. I think, rather, that there are drastic limits to the right of self-defense. If someone threatens you with death unless you torture someone else to death, I think you have not the right, even to save your life, to do so. But the case under consideration here is very different. In our case there are only two people involved, one whose life is threatened, and one who threatens it. Both are innocent: the one who is threatened is not threatened because of any fault, the one who threatens does not threaten because of any fault. For this reason we may feel that we bystanders cannot intervene. But the person threatened can.

In sum, a woman surely can defend her life against the threat to it posed by the unborn child, even if doing so involves its death. And this shows not merely that the theses in (1) through (4) are false; it shows also that the extreme view of abortion is false, and so we need not canvass any other possible ways of arriving at it from the argument I mentioned at the outset.

(2) The extreme view could of course be weakened to say that while abortion is permissible to save the mother's life, it may not be performed by a third party, but only by the mother herself. But this cannot be right either. For what we have to keep in mind is that the mother and the unborn child are not like two tenants in a small house which has, by an unfortunate mistake, been rented to both: the mother owns the house. The fact that she does adds to the offensiveness of deducing that the mother can do nothing from the supposition that third parties can do nothing. But it does more than this: it casts a bright light on the supposition that third parties can do nothing. Certainly it lets us see that a third party who says "I cannot choose between you" is fooling himself if he thinks this is impartiality. If Jones has found and fastened on a certain coat, which he needs to keep him from freezing, but which Smith also needs to keep him from freezing, then it is not impartiality that says "I cannot choose between you" when Smith owns the coat. Women have said again and again "This body is my body!" and they have reason to feel angry, reason to feel that it has been like shouting into the wind. Smith, after all, is hardly likely to bless us if we say to him, "Of course it's your coat, anybody would grant that it is. But no one may choose between you and Jones who is to have it . . . "

(3) Where the mother's life is not at stake, the argument I mentioned at the outset seems to have a much stronger pull. "Everyone has a right to life, so the unborn person has a right to life." And isn't the child's right to life weightier than anything other than the mother's own right to life, which she might put forward as ground for an abortion?

This argument treats the right to life as if it were unproblematic. It is not, and this seems to me to be precisely the source of the mistake.

For we should now, at long last, ask what it comes to, to have a right to life. In some views having a right to life includes having a right to be given at least the bare minimum one needs for continued life. But suppose that what in fact is the bare minimum a man needs for continued life is something he has no right at all to be given? If I am sick unto death, and the only thing that will save my life is the touch of Henry Fonda's cool hand on my fevered brow, then all the same, I have no right to be given the touch of Henry Fonda's cool hand on my fevered brow. It would be frightfully nice of him to fly in from the West Coast to provide it. It would be less nice, though no doubt well meant, if my friends flew out to the West Coast and carried Henry Fonda back with them. But I have no right at all against anybody that he should do this for me. Or again, to return to the story I told earlier, the fact that for continued life that violinist needs the continued use of your kidneys does not establish that he has a right to be given the continued use of your kidneys. He certainly has no right against you that you should give him continued use of your kidneys. For nobody has any right to use your kidneys unless you give him such a right; and nobody has the right against you that you shall give him this right – if you do allow him to go on using your kidneys, this is a kindness on your part, and not something he can claim from you as his due. Nor has he any right against anybody else that they should give him continued use of your kidneys. Certainly he had no right against the Society of Music Lovers that they should plug him into you in the first place. And if you now start to unplug yourself, having learned that you will otherwise have to spend nine years in bed with him, there is nobody in the world who must try to prevent you, in order to see to it that he is given something he has a right to be given.

Some people are rather stricter about the right to life. In their view, it does not include the right to be given anything, but amounts to, and only to, the right not to be killed by anybody. But here a related difficulty arises. If everybody is to refrain from killing that violinist, then everybody must refrain from doing a great many different sorts of things. Everybody must refrain from slitting his throat, everybody must refrain from shooting him – and everybody must refrain from unplugging you from him. But does he have a right against everybody that they shall refrain from unplugging you from him? To refrain from doing this is to allow him to continue to use your kidneys. It could be argued that he has a right against us that we should allow him to continue to use your kidneys. That is, while he had no right against us that we should give him the use of

your kidneys, it might be argued that he anyway has a right against us that we shall not now intervene and deprive him of the use of your kidneys. I shall come back to third–party interventions later. But certainly the violinist has no right against you that you shall allow him to continue to use your kidneys. As I said, if you do allow him to use them, it is a kindness on your part, and not something you owe him.

The difficulty I point to here is not peculiar to the right to life. It reappears in connection with all the other natural rights; and it is something which an adequate account of rights must deal with. For present purposes it is enough just to draw attention to it. But I would stress that I am not arguing that people do not have a right to life – quite to the contrary, it seems to me that the primary control we must place on the acceptability of an account of rights is that it should turn out in that account to be a truth that all persons have a right to life. I am arguing only that having a right to life does not guarantee having either a right to be given the use of or a right to be allowed continued use of another person's body – even if one needs it for life itself. So the right to life will not serve the opponents of abortion in the very simple and clear way in which they seem to have thought it would.

(4) There is another way to bring out the difficulty. In the most ordinary sort of case, to deprive someone of what he has a right to is to treat him unjustly. Suppose a boy and his small brother are jointly given a box of chocolates for Christmas. If the older boy takes the box and refuses to give his brother any of the chocolates, he is unjust to him, for the brother has been given a right to half of them. But suppose that, having learned that otherwise it means nine years in bed with that violinist, you unplug yourself from him. You surely are not being unjust to him, for you gave him no right to use your kidneys, and no one else can have given him any such right. But we have to notice that in unplugging yourself, you are killing him; and violinists, like everybody else, have a right to life, and thus in the view we were considering just now, the right not to be killed.

So here you do what he supposedly has a right you shall not do, but you do not act unjustly to him in doing it.

The emendation which may be made at this point is this: the right to life consists not in the right not to be killed, but rather in the right not to be killed unjustly. This runs a risk of circularity, but never mind: it would enable us to square the fact that the violinist has a right to life with the fact that you do not act unjustly toward him in unplugging yourself, thereby killing him. For if you do not kill him unjustly, you do not violate his right to life, and so it is no wonder you do him no injustice.

But if this emendation is accepted, the gap in the argument against abortion stares us plainly in the face: it is by no means enough to show that the fetus is a person, and to remind us that all persons have a right to life – we need to be shown also that killing the fetus violates its right to life, i.e., that abortion is unjust killing. And is it?

I suppose we may take it as a datum that in a case of pregnancy due to rape the mother has not given the unborn person a right to the use of her body for food and shelter. Indeed, in what pregnancy could it be supposed that the mother has given the unborn person such a right? It is not as if there were unborn persons drifting about the world, to whom a woman who wants a child says "I invite you in."

But it might be argued that there are other ways one can have acquired a right to the use of another person's body than by having been invited to use it by that person. Suppose a woman voluntarily indulges in intercourse, knowing of the chance it will issue in pregnancy, and then she does become pregnant; is she not in part responsible for the presence, in fact the very existence, of the unborn person inside her? No doubt she did not invite it in. But doesn't her partial responsibility for its being there itself give it a right to the use of her body? If so, then her aborting it would be more like the boy's taking away the chocolates, and less like your unplugging yourself from the violinist – doing so would be depriving it of what it does have a right to, and thus would be doing it an injustice.

And then, too, it might be asked whether or not she can kill it even to save her own life: If she voluntarily called it into existence, how can she now kill it, even in self-defense?

The first thing to be said about this is that it is something new. Opponents of abortion have been so concerned to make out the independence of the fetus, in order to establish that it has a right to life, just as its mother does, that they have tended to overlook the possible support they might gain from making out that the fetus is dependent on the mother, in order to establish that she has a special kind of responsibility for it, a responsibility that gives it rights against her which are not possessed by any independent person – such as an ailing violinist who is a stranger to her.

On the other hand, this argument would give the unborn person a right to its mother's body only if her pregnancy resulted from a voluntary act, undertaken in full knowledge of the chance a pregnancy might result from it. It would leave out entirely the unborn person whose existence is due to rape. Pending the availability of some further argument, then, we would be left with the conclusion that unborn persons whose existence is due to rape have no right to the use of their mothers' bodies, and thus that aborting them is not depriving them of anything they have a right to and hence is not unjust killing.

And we should also notice that it is not at all plain that this argument really does go even as far as it purports to. For there are cases and cases, and the details make a difference. If the room is stuffy, and I therefore open a window to air it, and a burglar climbs in, it would be absurd to say, "Ah, now he can stay, she's given him a right to the use of her house – for she is partially responsible for his presence there, having voluntarily done what enabled him to get in, in full knowledge that there are such things as burglars, and that burglars burgle." It would be still more absurd to say this if I had had bars installed outside my windows, precisely to prevent burglars from getting in, and a burglar got in only because of a defect in the bars. It remains equally absurd if we imagine it is not a burglar who climbs in, but an innocent person who blunders or falls in. Again, suppose it were like this: people-seeds drift about in the air like pollen, and if you open your windows, one may drift in and take root in your carpets or upholstery. You don't want children, so you fix up your windows with fine mesh screens, the very best you can buy. As can happen, however, and on very, very rare occasions does happen, one of the screens is defective; and a seed drifts in and takes root. Does the person-plant who now develops have a right to the use of your house? Surely not – despite the fact that you voluntarily opened your windows, you knowingly kept carpets and upholstered furniture, and you knew that screens were sometimes defective. Someone may argue that you are responsible for its rooting, that it does have a right to your house, because after all you could have lived out your life with bare floors and furniture, or with sealed windows and doors. But this won't do – for by the same token anyone can avoid a pregnancy due to rape by having a hysterectomy, or anyway by never leaving home without a (reliable!) army.

It seems to me that the argument we are looking at can establish at most that there are some cases in which the unborn person has a right to the use of its mother's body, and therefore some cases in which abortion is unjust killing. There is room for much discussion and argument as to precisely which, if any. But I think we should sidestep this issue and leave it open, for at any rate the argument certainly does not establish that all abortion is unjust killing.

(5) There is room for yet another argument here, however. We surely must all grant that there may be cases in which it would be morally indecent to detach a person from your body at the cost of his life. Suppose you learn that what the violinist needs is not nine years of your life, but only one hour: all you need do to save his life is to spend one hour in that bed with him. Suppose also that letting him use your kidneys for that one hour would not affect your health in the slightest. Admittedly you were kidnapped. Admittedly you did not give anyone permission to plug him into you. Nevertheless it seems to me plain you ought to allow him to use your kidneys for that hour – it would be indecent to refuse.

Again, suppose pregnancy lasted only an hour, and constituted no threat to life or health. And suppose that a woman becomes pregnant as a result of rape. Admittedly she did not voluntarily do anything to bring about the existence of a child. Admittedly she did nothing at all which would give the unborn person a right to the use of her body. All the same it might well be said, as in the newly emended violinist story, that she ought to allow it to remain for that hour – that it would be indecent in her to refuse.

Now some people are inclined to use the term "right" in such a way that it follows from the fact that you ought to allow a person to use your body for the hour he needs, that he has a right to use your body for the hour he needs, even though he has not been given that right by any person or act. They may say that it follows also that if you refuse, you act unjustly toward him. This use of the term is perhaps so common that it cannot be called wrong; nevertheless it seems to me to be an unfortunate loosening of what we would do better to keep a right rein on. Suppose that box of chocolates I mentioned earlier had not been given to both boys jointly, but was given only to the older boy. There he sits, stolidly eating his way through the box, his small brother watching enviously. Here we are likely to say "You ought not to be so mean. You ought to give your brother some of those chocolates." My own view is that it just does not follow from the truth of this that the brother has any right to any of the chocolates. If the boy refuses to give his brother any, he is greedy, stingy, callous – but not unjust. I suppose that the people I have in mind will say it does follow that the brother has a right to some of the chocolates, and thus that the boy does act unjustly if he refuses to give his brother any. But the effect of saying this is to obscure what we should keep distinct, namely the difference between the boy's refusal in this case and the boy's refusal in the earlier case, in which the box was given to both boys jointly, and in which the small brother thus had what was from any point of view clear title to half.

A further objection to so using the term "right" is that from the fact that A ought to do a thing for B, it follows that B has a right against A that A do it for him; it makes the question of whether or not a man has a right to a thing turn on how easy it is to provide him with it; and this seems not merely unfortunate, but morally unacceptable. Take the case of Henry Fonda again. I said earlier that I had no right to the touch of his cool hand on my fevered brow, even though I needed it to save my life. I said it would be frightfully nice of him to fly in from the West Coast to provide me with it, but that I had no right against him that he should do so. But suppose he isn't on the West Coast. Suppose he has only to walk across the room, place a hand briefly on my brow – and lo, my life is saved. Then surely he ought to do it, it would be indecent to refuse. Is it to be said "Ah, well, it follows that in this case she has a right to the touch of his hand on her brow, and so it would be an injustice in him to refuse"? So that I have a right to it when it is easy for him to provide it, though no right when it's hard? It's rather a shocking idea that anyone's rights should fade away and disappear as it gets harder and harder to accord them to him.

So my own view is that even though you ought to let the violinist use your kidneys for the one hour he needs, we should not conclude that he has a right to do so – we should say that if you refuse, you are, like the boy who owns all the chocolates and will give none away, self-centered and callous, indecent in fact, but not unjust. And similarly, that even supposing a case in which a woman pregnant due to rape ought to allow the unborn person to use her body for the hour he needs, we should not conclude that he has a right to do so; we should conclude that she is self-centered, callous, indecent, but not unjust, if she refuses. The complaints are no less grave; they are just different. However, there is no need to insist on this point. If anyone does wish to deduce "he has a right" from "you ought," then all the same he must surely grant that there are cases in which it is not morally required of you that you allow that violinist to use your kidneys, and in which he does not have a right to use them, and in

which you do not do him injustice if you refuse. And so also for mother and unborn child. Except in such cases as where the unborn person has a right to demand it – and we were leaving open the possibility that there may be such cases – nobody is morally required to make large sacrifices, of health, of all other interests and concerns, of all other duties and commitments, for nine years, or even for nine months, in order to keep another person alive . . . .

(6) My argument will be found unsatisfactory on two counts by many of those who want to regard abortion as morally permissible. First, while I do argue that abortion is not impermissible, I do not argue that it is always permissible. I am inclined to think it a merit of my account precisely that it does not give a general yes or a general no. It allows for and supports our sense that, for example, a sick and desperately frightened fourteen-year-old schoolgirl, pregnant due to rape, may of course choose abortion, and that any law which rules this out is an insane law. And it also allows for and supports our sense that in other cases resort to abortion is even positively indecent. It would be indecent in the woman to request an abortion, and indecent in a doctor to perform it, if she is in her seventh month, and wants the abortion just to avoid the nuisance of postponing a trip abroad. The very fact that the arguments I have been drawing attention to treat all cases of abortion, or even all cases of abortion in which the mother's life is not at stake, as morally on a par ought to have made them suspect at the outset.

Secondly, while I am arguing for the permissibility of abortion in some cases, I am not arguing for the right to secure the death of the unborn child. It is easy to confuse these two things in that up to a certain point in the life of the fetus it is not able to survive outside the mother's body; hence removing it from her body guarantees its death. But they are importantly different. I have argued that you are not morally required to spend nine months in bed, sustaining the life of that violinist; but to say this is by no means to say that if, when you unplug yourself, there is a miracle and he survives, you then have a right to turn round and slit his throat. You may detach yourself even if this costs him his life; you have no right to be guaranteed his death, by some other means, if unplugging yourself does not kill him. There are some people who will feel dissatisfied by this feature of my argument. A woman may be utterly devastated by the thought of a child, a bit of herself, put out for adoption and never seen or heard of again. She may therefore want not merely that the child be detached from her, but more, that it die. Some opponents of abortion are inclined to regard this as beneath contempt –

thereby showing insensitivity to what is surely a powerful source of despair. All the same, I agree that the desire for the child's death is not one which anybody may gratify, should it turn out to be possible to detach the child alive.

At this place, however, it should be remembered that we have only been pretending throughout that the fetus is a human being from the moment of conception. A very early abortion is surely not the killing of a person, and so is not dealt with by anything I have said here.

Notes

1 Daniel Callahan, *Abortion: Law, Choice and Morality* (New York, 1970), p. 373. This book gives a fascinating survey of the available information on abortion. The Jewish tradition is surveyed in David M. Feldman, *Birth Control in Jewish Law* (New York, 1968), Part 5; the Catholic tradition in John T. Noonan, Jr, "An Almost Absolute Value in History," in *The Morality of Abortion*, ed. John T. Noonan, Jr (Cambridge, MA, 1970).

2 The term "direct" in the arguments I refer to is a technical one. Roughly, what is meant by "direct killing" is either killing as an end in itself, or killing as a means to some end, for example, the end of saving someone else's life. See note 5, below, for an example of its use.

3 Cf. *Encyclical Letter of Pope Pius XI on Christian Marriage*, St Paul Editions (Boston, n.d.), p. 32: "however much we may pity the mother whose health and even life is gravely imperiled in the performance of the duty allotted to her by nature, nevertheless what could ever be a sufficient reason for excusing in any way the direct murder of the innocent? This is precisely what we are dealing with here." Noonan (*The Morality of Abortion*, p. 43)

reads this as follows: "What cause can ever avail to excuse in any way the direct killing of the innocent? For it is a question of that."

4 The thesis in (4) is in an interesting way weaker than those in (1), (2), and (3): they rule out abortion even in cases in which both mother and child will die if the abortion is not performed. By contrast, one who held the view expressed in (4) could consistently say that one needn't prefer letting two persons die to killing one.

5 Cf. the following passage from Pius XII, Address to the Italian Catholic Society of Midwives: "The baby in the maternal breast has the right to life immediately from God. – Hence there is no man, no human authority, no science, no medical, eugenic, social, economic or moral 'indication' which can establish or grant a valid juridical ground for a direct deliberate disposition of an innocent human life, that is a disposition which looks to its destruction either as an end or as a means to another end perhaps in itself not illicit. – The baby, still not born, is a man in the same degree and for the same reason as the mother" (quoted in Noonan, *The Morality of Abortion*, p. 45).

10

On the Moral and Legal Status of Abortion

Mary Anne Warren

For our purposes, abortion may be defined as the act a woman performs in deliberately terminating her pregnancy before it comes to term, or in allowing another person to terminate it. Abortion usually entails the death of a fetus.[1] Nevertheless, I will argue that it is morally permissible, and should be neither legally prohibited nor made needlessly difficult to obtain, e.g., by obstructive legal regulations.[2]

Some philosophers have argued that the moral status of abortion cannot be resolved by rational means.[3] If this is so then liberty should prevail; for it is not a proper function of the law to enforce prohibitions upon personal behavior that cannot clearly be shown to be morally objectionable, and seriously so. But the advocates of prohibition believe that their position is objectively correct, and not merely a result of religious beliefs or personal prejudices. They argue that the humanity of the fetus is a matter of scientific fact, and that abortion is therefore the moral equivalent of murder, and must be prohibited in all or most cases. (Some would make an exception when the woman's life is in danger, or when the pregnancy is due to rape or incest; others would prohibit abortion even in these cases.)

In response, advocates of a right to choose abortion point to the terrible consequences of prohibiting it, especially while contraception is still unreliable, and is financially beyond the reach of much of the world's population. Worldwide, hundreds of thousands of women die each year from illegal abortions, and many more suffer from complications that may leave them injured or infertile. Women who are poor, under-age, disabled, or otherwise vulnerable, suffer most from the absence of safe and legal abortion. Advocates of choice also argue that to deny a woman access to abortion is to deprive her of the right to control her own body – a right so fundamental that without it other rights are often all but meaningless.

These arguments do not convince abortion opponents. The tragic consequences of prohibition leave them unmoved, because they regard the deliberate killing of fetuses as even more tragic. Nor do appeals to the right to control one's own body impress them, since they deny that this right includes the right to destroy a fetus. We cannot hope to persuade those who equate abortion with murder that they are mistaken, unless we can refute the standard anti-abortion argument: that because fetuses are human beings, they have a right to life equal to that of any other human being. Unfortunately, confusion has prevailed with respect to the two important questions which that argument raises: (1) Is a human fetus really a human being at all stages of prenatal development? and (2) If so, what (if anything) follows about the moral and legal status of abortion?

John Noonan says that "the fundamental question in the long history of abortion is: How do you determine the humanity of a being?"[4] His anti-abortion argument is essentially that of the Roman Catholic Church. In his words:

> it is wrong to kill humans, however poor, weak, defenseless, and lacking in opportunity to develop their potential they may be. It is therefore morally wrong to kill Biafrans. Similarly, it is morally wrong to kill embryos.[5]

Noonan bases his claim that fetuses are human beings from the time of conception upon what he calls the theologians' criterion of humanity: that whoever is conceived of human beings is a human being. But although he argues at length for the appropriateness of this criterion of humanity, he does not question the assumption that if a fetus is a human being then abortion is almost always immoral.[6]

Judith Thomson has questioned this assumption. She argues that, even if we grant the anti-abortionist the claim that a fetus is a human being with the same right to life as any other human being, we can still demonstrate that women are not morally obliged to complete every unwanted pregnancy.[7] Her argument is worth examining, because if it is sound it may enable us to establish the moral permissibility of abortion without having to decide just what makes an entity a human being, or what entitles it to full moral rights. This would represent a considerable gain in the power and simplicity of the pro-choice position.

Even if Thomson's argument does not hold up, her essential insight – that it requires *argument* to show that if fetuses are human beings then abortion is murder – is a valuable one. The assumption that she attacks is invidious, for it requires that in our deliberations about the ethics of abortion we must ignore almost entirely the needs of the pregnant woman and other persons for whom she is responsible. This will not do; determining what moral rights a fetus has is only one step in determining the moral status of abortion. The next step is finding a just solution to conflicts between whatever rights the fetus has, and the rights and responsibilities of the woman who is unwillingly pregnant.

My own inquiry will also have two stages. In Section I, I consider whether abortion can be shown to be morally permissible even on the assumption that a fetus is a human being with a strong right to life. I argue that this cannot be established, except in special cases. Consequently, we cannot avoid facing the question of whether or not a fetus has the same right to life as any human being.

In Section II, I propose an answer to this question, namely, that a fetus is not a member of the moral community – the set of beings with full and equal moral rights. The reason that a fetus is not a member of the moral community is that it is not yet a person, nor is it enough like a person in the morally relevant respects to be regarded the equal of those human beings who are persons. I argue that it is personhood, and not genetic humanity, which is the fundamental basis for membership in the moral community. A fetus, especially in the early stages of its development, satisfies none of the criteria of personhood. Consequently, it makes no sense to grant it moral rights strong enough to override the woman's moral rights to liberty, bodily integrity, and sometimes life itself. Unlike an infant who has already been born, a fetus cannot be granted full and equal moral rights without severely threatening the rights and well-being of women. Nor, as we will see, is a fetus's *potential* personhood a threat to the moral permissibility of abortion, since merely potential persons do not have a moral right to become actual – or none that is strong enough to override the fundamental moral rights of actual persons.

I

Judith Thomson argues that, even if a fetus has a right to life, abortion is often morally permissible. Her argument is based upon an imaginative analogy. She asks you to picture yourself waking up one day, in bed with a famous violinist, who is a stranger to you. Imagine that you have been kidnapped, and your bloodstream connected to that of the violinist, who has an ailment that will kill him unless he is permitted to share your kidneys for nine months. No one else can save him, since you alone have the right type of blood. Consequently, the Society of Music Lovers has arranged for you to be kidnapped and hooked up. If you unhook yourself, he will die. But if you remain in bed with him, then after nine months he will be cured and able to survive without further assistance from you.

Now, Thomson asks, what are your obligations in this situation? To be consistent, the anti-abortionist must say that you are obliged to stay in bed with the violinist: for violinists are human beings, and all human beings have a right to life.[8] But this is outrageous; thus, there must be something very wrong with the same argument when it is applied to abortion. It would be extremely generous of you to agree to stay in bed with the violinist; but it is absurd to suggest that your refusal to do so would be the moral equivalent of murder. The violinist's right to life does not oblige you to do whatever is required to keep him alive; still less does it justify anyone else in forcing you to do so. A law which required you to stay in bed with the violinist would be an unjust law, since unwilling persons ought not to be required to be Extremely Good Samaritans, i.e., to make enormous personal sacrifices for the sake of other individuals towards whom they have no special prior obligation.

Thomson concludes that we can grant the anti-abortionist his claim that a fetus is a human being with a right to life, and still hold that a pregnant woman is morally entitled to refuse to be an Extremely Good Samaritan toward the fetus. For there is a great gap between the claim that a human being has a right to life, and the claim that other human beings are morally obligated to do whatever is necessary to keep him alive. One has no duty to keep another human being alive *at great personal cost*, unless one has somehow contracted a special obligation

toward that individual; and a woman who is pregnant may have done nothing that morally obliges her to make the burdensome personal sacrifices necessary to preserve the life of the fetus.

This argument is plausible, and in the case of pregnancy due to rape it is probably conclusive. Difficulties arise, however, when we attempt to specify the larger range of cases in which abortion can be justified on the basis of this argument. Thomson considers it a virtue of her argument that it does not imply that abortion is *always* morally permissible. It would, she says, be indecent for a woman in her seventh month of pregnancy to have an abortion in order to embark on a trip to Europe. On the other hand, the violinist analogy shows that, "a sick and desperately frightened fourteen-year-old schoolgirl, pregnant due to rape, may *of course* choose abortion, and that any law which rules this out is an insane law."[9] So far, so good; but what are we to say about the woman who becomes pregnant not through rape but because she and her partner did not use available forms of contraception, or because their attempts at contraception failed? What about a woman who becomes pregnant intentionally, but then re-evaluates the wisdom of having a child? In such cases, the violinist analogy is considerably less useful to advocates of the right to choose abortion.

It is perhaps only when a woman's pregnancy is due to rape, or some other form of coercion, that the situation is sufficiently analogous to the violinist case for our moral intuitions to transfer convincingly from the one case to the other. One difference between a pregnancy caused by rape and most unwanted pregnancies is that only in the former case is it perfectly clear that the woman is in no way responsible for her predicament. In the other cases, she *might* have been able to avoid becoming pregnant, e.g., by taking birth control pills (more faithfully), or insisting upon the use of high-quality condoms, or even avoiding heterosexual intercourse altogether throughout her fertile years. In contrast, if you are suddenly kidnapped by strange music lovers and hooked up to a sick violinist, then you are in no way responsible for your situation, which you could not have foreseen or prevented. And responsibility does seem to matter here. If a person behaves in a way which she could have avoided, and which she knows might bring into existence a human being who will depend upon her for survival, then it is not entirely clear that if and when that happens she may rightly refuse to do what she must in order to keep that human being alive.

This argument shows that the violinist analogy provides a persuasive defense of a woman's right to choose abortion only in cases where she is in no way morally responsible for her own pregnancy. In all other cases, the assumption that a fetus has a strong right to life makes it necessary to look carefully at the particular circumstances in order to determine the extent of the woman's responsibility, and hence the extent of her obligation. This outcome is unsatisfactory to advocates of the right to choose abortion, because it suggests that the decision should not be left in the woman's own hands, but should be supervised by other persons, who will inquire into the most intimate aspects of her personal life in order to determine whether or not she is entitled to choose abortion.

A supporter of the violinist analogy might reply that it is absurd to suggest that forgetting her pill one day might be sufficient to morally oblige a woman to complete an unwanted pregnancy. And indeed it is absurd to suggest this. As we will see, a woman's moral right to choose abortion does not depend upon the extent to which she might be thought to be morally responsible for her own pregnancy. But once we allow the assumption that a fetus has a strong right to life, we cannot avoid taking this absurd suggestion seriously. On this assumption, it is a vexing question whether and when abortion is morally justifiable. The violinist analogy can at best show that aborting a pregnancy is a deeply tragic act, though one that is sometimes morally justified.

My conviction is that an abortion is not always this deeply tragic, because a fetus is not yet a person, and therefore does not yet have a strong moral right to life. Although the truth of this conviction may not be self-evident, it does, I believe, follow from some highly plausible claims about the appropriate grounds for ascribing moral rights. It is worth examining these grounds, since this has not been adequately done before.

II

The question we must answer in order to determine the moral status of abortion is: How are we to define the moral community, the set of beings with full and equal moral rights? What sort of entity has the inalienable moral rights to life, liberty, and the pursuit of happiness? Thomas Jefferson attributed these rights to all *men*, and he may have intended to attribute them *only* to men. Perhaps he ought to have attributed them to all human beings. If so, then we arrive, first, at Noonan's problem of defining what makes an entity a human being, and second, at the question which Noonan does not consider: What reason is there for identifying the moral community with the set of all human beings, in whatever way we have chosen to define that term?

On the definition of "human"

The term "human being" has two distinct, but not often distinguished, senses. This results in a slide of meaning, which serves to conceal the fallacy in the traditional argument that, since (1) it is wrong to kill innocent human beings, and (2) fetuses are innocent human beings, therefore (3) it is wrong to kill fetuses. For if "human being" is used in the same sense in both (1) and (2), then whichever of the two senses is meant, one of these premises is question-begging. And if it is used in different senses then the conclusion does not follow.

Thus, (1) is a generally accepted moral truth,[10] and one that does not beg the question about abortion, only if "human being" is used to mean something like "a full-fledged member of the moral community, who is also a member of the human species." I will call this the *moral* sense of "human being." It is not to be confused with what I will call the *genetic* sense, i.e., the sense in which any individual entity that belongs to the human species is a human being, regardless of whether or not it is rightly considered to be an equal member of the moral community. Premise (1) avoids begging the question only if the moral sense is intended; while premise (2) avoids it only if what is intended is the genetic sense.

Noonan argues for the classification of fetuses with human beings by pointing, first, to the presence of the human genome in the cell nuclei of the human conceptus from conception onwards; and secondly, to the potential capacity for rational thought.[11] But what he needs to show, in order to support his version of the traditional anti-abortion argument, is that fetuses are human beings in the moral sense – the sense in which all human beings have full and equal moral rights. In the absence of any argument showing that whatever is genetically human is also morally human – and he gives none – nothing more than genetic humanity can be demonstrated by the presence of human chromosomes in the fetus's cell nuclei. And, as we will see, the strictly potential capacity for rational thought can at most show that the fetus may later *become* human in the moral sense.

Defining the moral community

Is genetic humanity sufficient for moral humanity? There are good reasons for not defining the moral community in this way. I would suggest that the moral community consists, in the first instance, of all *persons*, rather than all genetically human entities.[12] It is persons who invent moral rights, and who are (sometimes) capable of respecting them. It does not follow from this that only persons can have moral rights. However, persons are wise not to ascribe to entities that clearly are not persons moral rights that cannot in practice be respected without severely undercutting the fundamental moral rights of those who clearly are.

What characteristics entitle an entity to be considered a person? This is not the place to attempt a complete analysis of the concept of personhood; but we do not need such an analysis to explain why a fetus is not a person. All we need is an approximate list of the most basic

criteria of personhood. In searching for these criteria, it is useful to look beyond the set of people with whom we are acquainted, all of whom are human. Imagine, then, a space traveler who lands on a new planet, and encounters organisms unlike any she has ever seen or heard of. If she wants to behave morally toward these organisms, she has somehow to determine whether they are people and thus have full moral rights, or whether they are things that she need not feel guilty about treating, for instance, as a source of food.

How should she go about making this determination? If she has some anthropological background, she might look for signs of religion, art, and the manufacturing of tools, weapons, or shelters, since these cultural traits have frequently been used to distinguish our human ancestors from prehuman beings, in what seems to be closer to the moral than the genetic sense of "human being." She would be right to take the presence of such traits as evidence that the extraterrestrials were persons. It would, however, be anthropocentric of her to take the absence of these traits as proof that they were not, since they could be people who have progressed beyond, or who have never needed, these particular cultural traits.

I suggest that among the characteristics which are central to the concept of personhood are the following:

1 *sentience* – the capacity to have conscious experiences, usually including the capacity to experience pain and pleasure;
2 *emotionality* – the capacity to feel happy, sad, angry, loving, etc.;
3 *reason* – the capacity to solve new and relatively complex problems;
4 *the capacity to communicate*, by whatever means, messages of an indefinite variety of types; that is, not just with an indefinite number of possible contents, but on indefinitely many possible topics;
5 *self-awareness* – having a concept of oneself, as an individual and/or as a member of a social group; and finally
6 *moral agency* – the capacity to regulate one's own actions through moral principles or ideals.

It is difficult to produce precise definitions of these traits, let alone to specify universally valid behavioral indications that these traits are present. But let us assume that our explorer knows approximately what these six characteristics mean, and that she is able to observe whether or not the extraterrestrials possess these mental and behavioral capacities. How should she use her findings to decide whether or not they are persons?

An entity need not have *all* of these attributes to be a person. And perhaps none of them is absolutely necessary. For instance, the absence of emotion would not disqualify a being that was person-like in all other ways. Think, for instance, of two of the *Star Trek* characters, Mr Spock (who is half human and half alien), and Data (who is an android). Both are depicted as lacking the capacity to feel emotion; yet both are sentient, reasoning, communicative, self-aware moral agents, and unquestionably persons. Some people are unemotional; some cannot communicate well; some lack self-awareness; and some are not moral agents. It should not surprise us that many people do not meet all of the criteria of personhood. Criteria for the applicability of complex concepts are often like this: none may be logically necessary, but the more criteria that are satisfied, the more confident we are that the concept is applicable. Conversely, the fewer criteria are satisfied, the less plausible it is to hold that the concept applies. And if none of the relevant criteria are met, then we may be confident that it does not.

Thus, to demonstrate that a fetus is not a person, all I need to claim is that an entity that has *none* of these six characteristics is not a person. Sentience is the most basic mental capacity, and the one that may have the best claim to being a necessary (though not sufficient) condition for personhood. Sentience can establish a claim to moral considerability, since sentient beings can be harmed in ways that matter to them; for instance, they can be caused to feel pain, or deprived of the continuation of a life that is pleasant to them. It is unlikely that an entirely insentient organism could develop the other mental and behavioral capacities that are characteristic of persons. Consequently, it is odd to claim that an entity that is not sentient, and that has never been sentient, is nevertheless a person. Persons who have permanently and irreparably lost all capacity for sentience, but who remain biologically alive, arguably still have strong moral rights by virtue of what they have been in the past. But small fetuses, which have not yet begun to have experiences, are not persons yet and do not have the rights that persons do.

The presumption that all persons have full and equal basic moral rights may be part of the very concept of a person. If this is so, then the concept of a person is in part a moral one; once we have admitted that X is a person, we have implicitly committed ourselves to recognizing X's right to be treated as a member of the moral community.[13] The claim that X is a *human being* may also be voiced as an appeal to treat X decently; but this is usually either because "human being" is used in the moral sense, or because of a confusion between genetic and moral humanity.

If (1)–(6) are the primary criteria of personhood, then genetic humanity is neither necessary nor sufficient for personhood. Some genetically human entities are not persons, and there may be persons who belong to other species. A man or woman whose consciousness has been permanently obliterated but who remains biologically alive is a human entity who may no longer be a person; and some unfortunate humans, who have never had any sensory or cognitive capacities at all, may not be people either. Similarly, an early fetus is a human entity which is not yet a person. It is not even minimally sentient, let alone capable of emotion, reason, sophisticated communication, self-awareness, or moral agency.[14] Thus, while it may be greatly valued as a future child, it does not yet have the claim to moral consideration that it may come to have later.

Moral agency matters to moral status, because it is moral agents who invent moral rights, and who can be obliged to respect them. Human beings have become moral agents from social necessity. Most social animals exist well enough, with no evident notion of a moral right. But human beings need moral rights, because we are not only highly social, but also sufficiently clever and self-interested to be capable of undermining our societies through violence and duplicity. For human persons, moral rights are essential for peaceful and mutually beneficial social life. So long as some moral agents are denied basic rights, peaceful existence is difficult, since moral agents justly resent being treated as something less. If animals of some terrestrial species are found to be persons, or if alien persons come from other worlds, or if human beings someday invent machines whose mental and behavioral capacities make them persons, then we will be morally obliged to respect the moral rights of these nonhuman persons – at least to the extent that they are willing and able to respect ours in turn.

Although only those persons who are moral agents can participate directly in the shaping and enforcement of moral rights, they need not and usually do not ascribe moral rights only to themselves and other moral agents. Human beings are social creatures who naturally care for small children, and other members of the social community who are not currently capable of moral agency. Moreover, we are all vulnerable to the temporary or permanent loss of the mental capacities necessary for moral agency. Thus, we have self-interested as well as altruistic reasons for extending basic moral rights to infants and other sentient human beings who have already been born, but who currently lack some of these other mental capacities. These human beings, despite their current disabilities, are persons and members of the moral community.

But in extending moral rights to beings (human or otherwise) that have few or none of the morally significant characteristics of persons, we need to be careful not to burden human moral agents with obligations that they cannot possibly fulfill, except at unacceptably great cost to their own well-being and that of those they care about. Women often cannot complete unwanted pregnancies, except at intolerable mental, physical, and economic cost to themselves and their families. And heterosexual intercourse is too important a part of the social lives of most men and women to be reserved for

times when pregnancy is an acceptable outcome. Furthermore, the world cannot afford the continued rapid population growth which is the inevitable consequence of prohibiting abortion, so long as contraception is neither very reliable nor available to everyone. If fetuses were persons, then they would have rights that must be respected, even at great social or personal cost. But given that early fetuses, at least, are unlike persons in the morally relevant respects, it is unreasonable to insist that they be accorded exactly the same moral and legal status.

Fetal development and the right to life

Two questions arise regarding the application of these suggestions to the moral status of the fetus. First, if indeed fetuses are not yet persons, then might they nevertheless have strong moral rights based upon the degree to which they *resemble* persons? Secondly, to what extent, if any, does a fetus's potential to *become* a person imply that we ought to accord to it some of the same moral rights? Each of these questions requires comment.

It is reasonable to suggest that the more like a person something is – the more it appears to meet at least some of the criteria of personhood – the stronger is the case for according it a right to life, and perhaps the stronger its right to life is. That being the case, perhaps the fetus gradually gains a stronger right to life as it develops. We should take seriously the suggestion that, just as

> the human individual develops biologically in a continuous fashion the rights of a human person . . . develop in the same way.[15]

A seven-month fetus can apparently feel pain, and can respond to such stimuli as light and sound. Thus, it may have a rudimentary form of consciousness. Nevertheless, it is probably not as conscious, or as capable of emotion, as even a very young infant is; and it has as yet little or no capacity for reason, sophisticated intentional communication, or self-awareness. In these respects, even a late-term fetus is arguably less like a person than are many nonhuman animals.

Many animals (e.g., large-brained mammals such as elephants, cetaceans, or apes) are not only sentient, but clearly possessed of a degree of reason, and perhaps even of self-awareness. Thus, on the basis of its resemblance to a person, even a late-term fetus can have no more right to life than do these animals.

Animals may, indeed, plausibly be held to have some moral rights, and perhaps rather strong ones.[16] But it is impossible in practice to accord full and equal moral rights to all animals. When an animal poses a serious threat to the life or well-being of a person, we do not, as a rule, greatly blame the person for killing it; and there are good reasons for this species-based discrimination. Animals, however intelligent in their own domains, are generally not beings with whom we can reason; we cannot persuade mice not to invade our dwellings or consume our food. That is why their rights are necessarily weaker than those of a being who can understand and respect the rights of other beings.

But the probable sentience of late-term fetuses is not the only argument in favor of treating late abortion as a morally more serious matter than early abortion. Many – perhaps most – people are repulsed by the thought of needlessly aborting a late-term fetus. The late-term fetus has features which cause it to arouse in us almost the same powerful protective instinct as does a small infant.

This response needs to be taken seriously. If it were impossible to perform abortions early in pregnancy, then we might have to tolerate the mental and physical trauma that would be occasioned by the routine resort to late abortion. But where early abortion is safe, legal, and readily available to all women, it is not unreasonable to expect most women who wish to end a pregnancy to do so prior to the third trimester. Most women strongly prefer early to late abortion, because it is far less physically painful and emotionally traumatic. Other things being equal, it is better for all concerned that pregnancies that are not to be completed should be ended as early as possible. Few women would consider ending a pregnancy in the seventh month in order to take a trip to Europe. If, however, a woman's

own life or health is at stake, or if the fetus has been found to be so severely abnormal as to be unlikely to survive or to have a life worth living, then late abortion may be the morally best choice. For even a late-term fetus is not a person yet, and its rights must yield to those of the woman whenever it is impossible for both to be respected.

Potential personhood and the right to life

We have seen that a presentient fetus does not yet resemble a person in ways which support the claim that it has strong moral rights. But what about its *potential*, the fact that if nurtured and allowed to develop it may eventually become a person? Doesn't that potential give it at least some right to life? The fact that something is a potential person may be a reason for not destroying it; but we need not conclude from this that potential people have a strong right to life. It may be that the feeling that it is better not to destroy a potential person is largely due to the fact that potential people are felt to be an invaluable resource, not to be lightly squandered. If every speck of dust were a potential person, we would be less apt to suppose that all potential persons have a right to become actual.

We do not need to insist that a potential person has no right to life whatever. There may be something immoral, and not just imprudent, about wantonly destroying potential people, when doing so isn't necessary. But even if a potential person does have some right to life, that right could not outweigh the right of a woman to obtain an abortion; for the basic moral rights of an actual person outweigh the rights of a merely potential person, whenever the two conflict. Since this may not be immediately obvious in the case of a human fetus, let us look at another case.

Suppose that our space explorer falls into the hands of an extraterrestrial civilization, whose scientists decide to create a few thousand new human beings by killing her and using some of her cells to create clones. We may imagine that each of these newly created women will have all of the original woman's abilities, skills, knowledge, and so on, and will also have an individual self-concept; in short, that each of them will be a bona fide (though not genetically unique) person. Imagine, further, that our explorer knows all of this, and knows that these people will be treated kindly and fairly. I maintain that in such a situation she would have the right to escape if she could, thus depriving all of these potential people of their potential lives. For her right to life outweighs all of theirs put together, even though they are all genetically human, and have a high probability of becoming people, if only she refrains from acting.

Indeed, I think that our space traveler would have a right to escape even if it were not her life which the aliens planned to take, but only a year of her freedom, or only a day. She would not be obliged to stay, even if she had been captured because of her own lack of caution – or even if she had done so deliberately, knowing the possible consequences. Regardless of why she was captured, she is not obliged to remain in captivity for *any* period of time in order to permit merely potential people to become actual people. By the same token, a woman's rights to liberty and the control of her own body outweigh whatever right to life a fetus may have merely by virtue of its potential personhood.

The objection from infanticide

One objection to my argument is that it appears to justify not only abortion, but also infanticide. A newborn infant is not much more personlike than a nine-month fetus, and thus it might appear that if late-term abortion is sometimes justified, then infanticide must also sometimes be justified. Yet most people believe that infanticide is a form of murder, and virtually never justified.

This objection is less telling than it may seem. There are many reasons why infanticide is more difficult to justify than abortion, even though neither fetuses nor newborn infants are clearly persons. In this period of history, the deliberate killing of newborns is virtually never justified. This is in part because newborns are so close to being persons that to kill them requires a very strong moral justification – as does the killing of dolphins, chimpanzees, and other highly person-like creatures. It is certainly wrong to kill such beings for the sake of convenience, or financial profit, or "sport." Only the most vital human needs, such as the need to defend one's own life and physical integrity, can provide a plausible justification for killing such beings.

In the case of an infant, there is no such vital need, since in the contemporary world there are usually other people who are eager to provide a good home for an infant whose own parents are unable or unwilling to care for it. Many people wait years for the opportunity to adopt a child, and some are unable to do so, even though there is every reason to believe that they would be good parents. The needless destruction of a viable infant not only deprives a sentient human being of life, but also deprives other persons of a source of great satisfaction, perhaps severely impoverishing *their* lives.

Even if an infant is unadoptable (e.g., because of some severe physical disability), it is still wrong to kill it. For most of us value the lives of infants, and would greatly prefer to pay taxes to support foster care and state institutions for disabled children, rather than to allow them to be killed or abandoned. So long as most people feel this way, and so long as it is possible to provide care for infants who are unwanted, or who have special needs that their parents cannot meet without assistance, it is wrong to let any infant die who has a chance of living a reasonably good life.

If these arguments show that infanticide is wrong, at least in today's world, then why don't they also show that late-term abortion is always wrong? After all, third-trimester fetuses are almost as personlike as infants, and many people value them and would prefer that they be preserved. As a potential source of pleasure to some family, a fetus is just as valuable as an infant. But there is an important difference between these two cases: once the infant is born, its continued life cannot pose any serious threat to the woman's life or health, since she is free to put it up for adoption or to place it in foster care. While she might, in rare cases, prefer that the child die rather than being raised by others, such a preference would not establish a right on her part.

In contrast, a pregnant woman's right to protect her own life and health outweighs other people's desire that the fetus be preserved – just as, when a person's life or health is threatened by an animal, and when the threat cannot be removed without killing the animal, that person's right to self-defense outweighs the desires of those who would prefer that the animal not be killed. Thus, while the moment of birth may mark no sharp discontinuity in the degree to which an infant resembles a person, it does mark the end of the mother's right to determine its fate. Indeed, if a late abortion can be safely performed without harming the fetus, the mother has in most cases no right to insist upon its death, for the same reason that she has no right to insist that a viable infant be killed or allowed to die.

It remains true that, on my view, neither abortion nor the killing of newborns is obviously a form of murder. Perhaps our legal system is correct in its classification of infanticide as murder, since no other legal category adequately expresses the force of our disapproval of this action. But some moral distinction remains, and it has important consequences. When a society cannot possibly care for all of the children who are born, without endangering the survival of adults and older children, allowing some infants to die may be the best of a bad set of options. Throughout history, most societies – from those that lived by gathering and hunting to the highly civilized Chinese, Japanese, Greeks, and Romans – have permitted infanticide under such unfortunate circumstances, regarding it as a necessary evil. It shows a lack of understanding to condemn these societies as morally benighted for this reason alone, since in the absence of safe and effective means of contraception and abortion, parents must sometimes have had no morally better options.

Conclusion

I have argued that fetuses are neither persons nor members of the moral community. Furthermore, neither a fetus's resemblance to a person, nor its potential for becoming a person, provides an adequate basis for the claim that it has a full and equal right to life. At the same time, there are medical as well as moral reasons for preferring early to late abortion when the pregnancy is unwanted.

Women, unlike fetuses, are undeniably persons and members of the human moral community. If unwanted or medically dangerous pregnancies never occurred, then it might be possible to respect women's basic moral rights, while at the same time extending the same basic rights to fetuses. But in the real world such pregnancies do occur – often despite the woman's best efforts to prevent them. Even if the perfect contraceptive were universally available, the continued occurrence of rape and incest would make access to abortion a vital human need. Because women are persons, and fetuses are not, women's rights to life, liberty, and physical integrity morally override whatever right to life it may be appropriate to ascribe to a fetus. Consequently, laws that deny women the right to obtain abortions, or that make safe early abortions difficult or impossible for some women to obtain, are an unjustified violation of basic moral and constitutional rights.

Notes

1 Strictly speaking, a human conceptus does not become a fetus until the primary organ systems have formed, at about six to eight weeks gestational age. However, for simplicity I shall refer to the conceptus as a fetus at every stage of its prenatal development.

2 The views defended in this article are set forth in greater depth in my book *Moral Status*, Oxford University Press, 2000.

3 For example, Roger Wertheimer argues, in "Understanding the Abortion Argument," *Philosophy and Public Affairs* 1 (Fall, 1971), that the moral status of abortion is not a question of fact, but only of how one responds to the facts.

4 John Noonan, "Abortion and the Catholic Church: A Summary History," *Natural Law Forum* 12 (1967): p. 125.

5 John Noonan, "Deciding Who is Human," *Natural Law Forum* 13 (1968): 134.

6 Noonan deviates from the current position of the Roman Catholic Church in that he thinks that abortion is morally permissible when it is the only way of saving the woman's life. See "An Almost Absolute Value in History," in *Contemporary Issues in Bioethics*, edited by Tom L. Beauchamp and LeRoy Walters (Belmont, California: Wadsworth, 1994), p. 283.

7 Judith Jarvis Thomson, "A Defense of Abortion," *Philosophy and Public Affairs* 11 (Fall, 1971): 173–8.

8 Ibid., p. 174.

9 Ibid., p. 187.

10 The principle that it is always wrong to kill innocent human beings may be in need of other modifications, e.g., that it may be permissible to kill innocent human beings in order to save a larger number of equally innocent human beings; but we may ignore these complications here.

11 Noonan, "Deciding Who is Human," p. 135.

12 From here on, I will use "human" to mean "genetically human," since the moral sense of the term seems closely connected to, and perhaps derived from, the assumption that genetic humanity is both necessary and sufficient for membership in the moral community.

13 Alan Gewirth defends a similar claim, in *Reason and Morality* (Chicago: University of Chicago Press, 1978).

14 Fetal sentience is impossible prior to the development of neurological connections between the sense organs and the brain, and between the various parts of the brain involved in the processing of conscious experience. This stage of neurological development is currently thought to occur at some point in the late second or early third trimester.

15 Thomas L. Hayes, "A Biological View," *Commonweal*, 85 (March 17, 1967): 677–8; cited by Daniel Callahan, in *Abortion: Law, Choice, and Morality* (London: Macmillan, 1970).

16 See, for instance, Tom Regan, *The Case for Animal Rights* (Berkeley: University of California Press, 1983).

11

An Argument that Abortion is Wrong

Don Marquis

The purpose of this essay is to set out an argument for the claim that abortion, except perhaps in rare instances, is seriously wrong. One reason for these exceptions is to eliminate from consideration cases whose ethical analysis should be controversial and detailed for clear-headed opponents of abortion. Such cases include abortion after rape and abortion during the first fourteen days after conception when there is an argument that the fetus is not definitely an individual. Another reason for making these exceptions is to allow for those cases in which the permissibility of abortion is compatible with the argument of this essay. Such cases include abortion when continuation of a pregnancy endangers a woman's life and abortion when the fetus is anencephalic. When I speak of the wrongness of abortion in this essay, a reader should presume the above qualifications. I mean by an abortion an action intended to bring about the death of a fetus for the sake of the woman who carries it. (Thus, as is standard on the literature on this subject, I eliminate spontaneous abortions from consideration.) I mean by a fetus a developing human being from the time of conception to the time of birth. (Thus, as is standard, I call embryos and zygotes, fetuses.)

The argument of this essay will establish that abortion is wrong for the same reason as killing a reader of this essay is wrong. I shall just assume, rather than establish, that killing you is seriously wrong. I shall make no attempt to offer a complete ethics of killing. Finally, I shall make no attempt to resolve some very fundamental and difficult general philosophical issues into which this analysis of the ethics of abortion might lead.

Why the Debate Over Abortion Seems Intractable

Symmetries that emerge from the analysis of the major arguments on either side of the abortion debate may explain why the abortion debate seems intractable. Consider the following standard anti-abortion argument: Fetuses are both human and alive. Humans have the right to life. Therefore, fetuses have the right to life. Of course, women have the right to control their own bodies, but the right to life overrides the right of a woman to control her own body. Therefore, abortion is wrong.

Thomson's view

Judith Thomson (1971) has argued that even if one grants (for the sake of argument only) that fetuses have the right to life, this argument fails. Thomson invites you to imagine that you have been connected while sleeping, bloodstream to bloodstream, to a famous violinist. The violinist, who suffers from a rare blood disease, will die if disconnected. Thomson argues that you surely have the right to disconnect yourself. She appeals to our intuition that having to lie in bed with a violinist for an indefinite period is too much for morality to demand. She supports this claim by noting that the body being used is *your* body, not the violinist's body. She distinguishes the right to life, which the violinist clearly has, from the right to use someone else's body when necessary to preserve one's life, which it is not at all obvious the violinist has. Because the case of pregnancy is like the case of the violinist, one is no more morally obligated to remain attached to a fetus than to remain attached to the violinist.

It is widely conceded that one can generate from Thomson's vivid case the conclusion that abortion is morally permissible when a pregnancy is due to rape (Warren, 1973, p. 49; and Steinbock, 1992, p. 79). But this is hardly a general right to abortion. Do Thomson's more general theses generate a more general right to an abortion? Thomson draws our attention to the fact that in a pregnancy, although a fetus uses a woman's body as a life-support system, a pregnant woman does not use a fetus's body as a life-support system. However, an opponent of abortion might draw our attention to the fact that in an abortion the life that is lost is the fetus's, not the woman's. This symmetry seems to leave us with a stand-off.

Thomson points out that a fetus's right to life does not entail its right to use someone else's body to preserve its life. However, an opponent of abortion might point out that a woman's right to use her own body does not entail her right to end someone else's life in order to do what she wants with her body. In reply, one might argue that a pregnant woman's right to control her own body doesn't come to much if it is wrong for her to take any action that ends the life of the fetus within her. However, an opponent of abortion can argue that the fetus's right to life doesn't come to much if a pregnant woman can end it when she chooses. The consequence of all of these symmetries seems to be a stand-off. But if we have the stand-off, then one might argue that we are left with a conflict of rights: a fetal right to life versus the right of a woman to control her own body. One might then argue that the right to life seems to be a stronger right than the right to control one's own body in the case of abortion because the loss of one's life is a greater loss than the loss of the right to control one's own body in one respect for nine months. Therefore, the right to life overrides the right to control one's own body and abortion is wrong. Considerations like these have suggested to both opponents of abortion and supporters of choice that a Thomsonian strategy for defending a general right to abortion will not succeed (Tooley, 1972; Warren, 1973; and Steinbock, 1992). In fairness, one must note that Thomson did not intend her strategy to generate a general moral permissibility of abortion.

Do fetuses have the right to life?

The above considerations suggest that whether abortion is morally permissible boils down to the question of whether fetuses have the right to life. An argument that fetuses either have or lack the right to life must be based upon some general criterion for having or lacking the right to life. Opponents of abortion, on the one hand, look around for the broadest possible plausible criterion, so that fetuses will fall under it. This explains why classic arguments against abortion appeal to the criterion of being human (Noonan, 1970; Beckwith, 1993). This criterion appears plausible: The claim that all humans, whatever their race, gender, religion or *age*, have the right to life seems evident enough. In addition, because the fetuses we are concerned with do not, after all, belong to another species, they are clearly human. Thus, the syllogism that generates the conclusion that fetuses have the right to life is apparently sound.

On the other hand, those who believe abortion is morally permissible wish to find a narrow, but plausible, criterion for possession of the right to life so that fetuses will fall outside of it. This explains, in part, why the standard pro-choice arguments in the philosophical literature appeal to the criterion of being a person (Feinberg, 1986; Tooley, 1972; Warren, 1973; Benn, 1973; Engelhardt, 1986). This criterion appears plausible: The claim that only persons have the right to life seems evident enough. Furthermore, because fetuses neither are rational nor possess the capacity to communicate in complex ways nor possess a concept of self that continues through time, no fetus is a person. Thus, the syllogism needed to generate the conclusion that no fetus possesses the right to life is apparently sound. Given that no fetus possesses the right to life, a woman's right to control her own body easily generates the general right to abortion. The existence of two apparently defensible syllogisms which support contrary conclusions helps to explain why partisans on both sides of the abortion dispute often regard their opponents as either morally depraved or mentally deficient.

Which syllogism should we reject? The anti-abortion syllogism is usually attacked by attacking its major premise: the claim that whatever is biologically human has the right to life. This premise is subject to scope problems because the class of the biologically human includes too much: human cancer-cell cultures are biologically human, but they do not have the right to life. Moreover, this premise also is subject to moral-relevance problems: the connection between the biological and the moral is merely assumed. It is hard to think of a good *argument* for such a connection. If one wishes to consider the category of "human" a moral category, as some people find it plausible to do in other contexts, then one is left with no way of showing that the fetus is fully human without begging the question. Thus, the classic anti-abortion argument appears subject to fatal difficulties.

These difficulties with the classic anti-abortion argument are well known and thought by many to be conclusive. The symmetrical difficulties with the classic pro-choice syllogism are not as well recognized. The pro-choice syllogism can be attacked by attacking its major premise: Only persons have the right to life. This premise is subject to scope problems because the class of persons includes too little: infants, the severely retarded, and some of the mentally ill seem to fall outside the class of persons as the supporter of choice understands the concept. The premise is also subject to moral-relevance problems: Being a person is understood by the pro-choicer as having certain psychological attributes. If the pro-choicer questions the connection between the biological and the moral, the opponent of abortion can question the connection between the psychological and the moral. If one wishes to consider "person" a moral category, as is often done, then one is left with no way of showing that the fetus is not a person without begging the question.

Pro-choicers appear to have resources for dealing with their difficulties that opponents of abortion lack. Consider their moral-relevance problem. A pro-choicer might argue that morality rests on contractual foundations and that only those who have the psychological attributes of persons are capable of entering into the moral contract and, as a consequence, being a member of the moral community. (This is essentially Engelhardt's [1986] view.) The great advantage of this contractarian approach to morality is that it seems far more plausible than any approach the anti-abortionist can provide. The great disadvantage of this contractarian approach to morality is that it adds to our earlier scope problems by leaving it unclear how we can have the duty not to inflict pain and suffering on animals.

Contractarians have tried to deal with their scope problems by arguing that duties to some individuals who are not persons can be justified even though those individuals are not contracting members of the moral community. For example, Kant argued that, although we do not have direct duties to animals, we "must practice kindness towards animals, for he who is cruel to animals becomes hard also in his dealings with men" (Kant, 1963, p. 240). Feinberg argues that infanticide is wrong, not because infants have the right to life, but because our society's protection of infants has social utility. If we do not treat infants with tenderness and consideration, then when they are persons they will be worse off and we will be worse off also (Feinberg, 1986, p. 271).

These moves only stave off the difficulties with the pro-choice view; they do not resolve them. Consider Kant's account of our obligations to animals. Kantians certainly know the difference between persons and animals. Therefore, no true Kantian would treat persons as she would treat animals. Thus, Kant's defense of our duties to animals fails to show that Kantians have a duty not to be cruel to animals. Consider Feinberg's attempt to show that infanticide is wrong even though no infant is a person. All Feinberg really shows is that it is a good idea to treat with care and consideration the infants we intend to keep. That is quite compatible with killing the infants we intend to discard. This point can be supported by an analogy with which any pro-choicer will agree. There are plainly good reasons to treat with care and consideration the fetuses we intend to keep. This is quite compatible with aborting those fetuses we intend to discard. Thus, Feinberg's account of the wrongness of infanticide is inadequate.

Accordingly, we can see that a contractarian defense of the pro-choice personhood syllogism fails. The problem arises because the contractarian cannot account for our duties to individuals who are not persons, whether these individuals are animals or infants. Because the pro-choicer wishes to adopt a narrow criterion for the right to life so that fetuses will not be included, the scope of her major premise is too narrow. Her problem is the opposite of the problem the classic opponent of abortion faces.

The argument of this section has attempted to establish, albeit briefly, that the classic anti-abortion argument and the pro-choice argument favored by most philosophers both face problems that are mirror images of one another. A standoff results. The abortion debate requires a different strategy.

The "Future Like Ours" Account of the Wrongness of Killing

Why do the standard arguments in the abortion debate fail to resolve the issue? The general principles to which partisans in the debate appeal are either truisms most persons would affirm in the absence of much reflection, or very general moral theories. All are subject to major problems. A different approach is needed.

Opponents of abortion claim that abortion is wrong because abortion involves killing someone like us, a human being who just happens to be very young. Supporters of choice claim that ending the life of a fetus is not in the same moral category as ending the life of an adult human being. Surely this controversy cannot be resolved in the absence of an account of what it is about killing us that makes killing us wrong. On the one hand, if we know what property we possess that makes killing us wrong, then we can ask whether fetuses have the same property. On the other hand, suppose that we do not know what it is about us that makes killing us wrong. If this is so, we do not understand even easy cases in which killing is wrong. Surely, we will not understand the ethics of killing fetuses, for if we do not understand easy cases, then we will not understand hard cases. Both pro-choicer and anti-abortionist agree that it is obvious that it is wrong to kill us. Thus, a discussion of what it is about us that makes killing us not only wrong, but seriously wrong, seems to be the right place to begin a discussion of the abortion issue.

Who is primarily wronged by a killing? The wrong of killing is not primarily explained in terms of the loss to the family and friends of the victim. Perhaps the victim is a hermit. Perhaps one's friends find it easy to make new friends. The wrong of killing is not primarily explained in terms of the brutalization of the killer. The great wrong to the victim explains the brutalization, not the other way around. The wrongness of killing us is understood in terms of what killing does to us. Killing us imposes on us the misfortune of premature death. That misfortune underlies the wrongness.

Premature death is a misfortune because when one is dead, one has been deprived of life. This misfortune can be more precisely specified. Premature death cannot deprive me of my past life. That part of my life is already gone. If I die tomorrow or if I live thirty more years my past life will be no different. It has occurred on either alternative. Rather than my past, my death deprives me of my future, of the life that I would have lived if I had lived out my natural life span.

The loss of a future biological life does not explain the misfortune of death. Compare two scenarios: In the former I now fall into a coma from which I do not recover until my death in thirty years. In the latter I die now. The latter scenario does not seem to describe a greater misfortune than the former.

The loss of our future conscious life is what underlies the misfortune of premature death. Not any future conscious life qualifies, however. Suppose that I am terminally ill with cancer. Suppose also that pain and suffering would dominate my future conscious life. If so, then death would not be a misfortune for me.

Thus, the misfortune of premature death consists of the loss to use of the future goods of consciousness. What are these goods? Much can be said about this issue, but a simple answer will do for the purposes of this essay. The goods of life are whatever we get out of life. The goods of life are those items toward which we take a "pro" attitude. They are completed projects of which we are proud, the pursuit of our goals, aesthetic enjoyments, friendships, intellectual pursuits, and physical pleasures of various sorts. The goods of life are what makes life worth living. In general, what makes life worth living for one person will not be the same as what makes life worth living for another. Nevertheless, the list of goods in each of our lives will overlap. The lists are usually different in different stages of our lives.

What makes the goods of my future good for me? One possible, but wrong, answer is my desire for those goods now. This answer does not account for those aspects of my future life that I now believe I will later value, but about which I am wrong. Neither does it account for those aspects of my future that I will come to value, but which I don't value now. What is valuable to the young may not be valuable to the middle-aged. What is valuable to the middle-aged may not be valuable to the old. Some of life's values for the elderly are best appreciated by the elderly. Thus it is wrong to say that the value of my future to me is just what I value now. What makes my future valuable to me are those aspects of my future that I will (or would) value when I will (or would) experience them, whether I value them now or not.

It follows that a person can believe that she will have a valuable future and be wrong. Furthermore, a person can believe that he will not have a valuable future and also be wrong. This is confirmed by our attitude toward many of the suicidal. We attempt to save the lives of the suicidal and to convince them that they have made an error in judgment. This does not mean that the future of an individual obtains value from the value that others confer on it. It means that, in some cases, others can make a clearer judgment of the value of a person's future *to that person* than the person herself. This often happens when one's judgment concerning the value of one's own future is clouded by personal tragedy. (Compare the views of McInerney, 1990, and Shirley, 1995.)

Thus, what is sufficient to make killing us wrong, in general, is that it causes premature death. Premature death is a misfortune. Premature death is a misfortune, in general, because it deprives an individual of a future of value. An individual's future will be valuable to that individual if that individual will come, or would come, to value it. We know that killing us is wrong. What makes killing us wrong, in general, is that it deprives us of a future of value. Thus, killing someone is wrong, in general, when it deprives her of a future like ours. I shall call this "an FLO."

Arguments in Favor of the FLO Theory

At least four arguments support this FLO account of the wrongness of killing.

The considered judgment argument

The FLO account of the wrongness of killing is correct because it fits with our considered judgment concerning the nature of the misfortune of death. The analysis of the previous section is an exposition of the nature of this considered judgment. This judgment can be confirmed. If one were to ask individuals with AIDS or with incurable cancer about the nature of their misfortune, I believe that they would say or imply that their impending loss of an FLO makes their premature death a misfortune. If they would not, then the FLO account would plainly be wrong.

The worst of crimes argument

The FLO account of the wrongness of killing is correct because it explains why we believe that killing is one of the worst of crimes. My being killed deprives me of more than does my being robbed or beaten or harmed in some other way because my being killed deprives me of all of the value of my future, not merely part of it. This explains why we make the penalty for murder greater than the penalty for other crimes.

As a corollary the FLO account of the wrongness of killing also explains why killing an adult human being is justified only in the most extreme circumstances, only in circumstances in which the loss of life to an individual is outweighed by a worse outcome if that life is not taken. Thus, we are willing to justify killing in self-defense, killing in order to save one's own life, because one's loss if one does not kill in that situation is so very great. We justify killing in a just war for similar reasons. We believe that capital punishment would be justified if, by having such an institution, fewer premature deaths would occur. The FLO account of the wrongness of killing does not entail that killing is always wrong. Nevertheless, the FLO account explains both why killing is one of the worst of crimes and, as a corollary, why the exceptions to the wrongness of killing are so very rare. A correct theory of the wrongness of killing should have these features.

The appeal to cases argument

The FLO account of the wrongness of killing is correct because it yields the correct answers in many life-and-death cases that arise in medicine and have interested philosophers.

Consider medicine first. Most people believe that it is not wrong deliberately to end the life of a person who is permanently unconscious. Thus we believe that it is not wrong to remove a feeding tube or a ventilator from a permanently comatose patient, knowing that such a removal will cause death. The FLO account of the wrongness of killing explains why this is so. A patient who is permanently unconscious cannot have a future that she would come to value, whatever her values. Therefore, according to the FLO theory of the wrongness of killing, death could not, *ceteris paribus*, be a misfortune to her. Therefore, removing the feeding tube or ventilator does not wrong her.

By contrast, almost all people believe that it is wrong, *ceteris paribus*, to withdraw medical treatment from patients who are temporarily unconscious. The FLO account of the wrongness of killing also explains why this is so. Furthermore, these two unconsciousness cases explain why the FLO account of the wrongness of killing does not include present consciousness as a necessary condition for the wrongness of killing.

Consider now the issue of the morality of legalizing active euthanasia. Proponents of active euthanasia argue that if a patient faces a future of intractable pain and wants to die, then, *ceteris paribus*, it would not be wrong for a physician to give him medicine that she knows would result in his death. This view is so universally accepted that even the strongest *opponents* of active euthanasia hold it. The official Vatican view (Sacred Congregation, 1980) is that it is permissible for a physician to administer to a patient morphine sufficient (although no more than sufficient) to control his pain even if she foresees that the morphine will result in his death. Notice how nicely the FLO account of the wrongness of killing explains this unanimity of opinion. A patient known to be in severe intractable pain is presumed to have a future without positive value. Accordingly, death would not be a misfortune for him and an action that would (foreseeably) end his life would not be wrong.

Contrast this with the standard emergency medical treatment of the suicidal. Even though the suicidal have indicated that they want to die, medical personnel will act to save their lives. This supports the view that it is not the mere *desire* to enjoy an FLO which is crucial to our understanding of the wrongness of killing. *Having* an FLO is what is crucial to the account, although one would, of course, want to make an exception in the case of fully autonomous people who refuse life-saving medical treatment. Opponents of abortion can, of course, be willing to make an exception for fully autonomous fetuses who refuse life support.

The FLO theory of the wrongness of killing also deals correctly with issues that have concerned philosophers. It implies that it would be wrong to kill (peaceful) persons from outer space who come to visit our planet even though they are biologically utterly unlike us. Presumably, if they are persons, then they will have futures that are sufficiently like ours so that it would be wrong to kill them. The FLO account of the wrongness of killing shares this feature with the personhood views of the supporters of choice. Classical opponents of abortion who locate the wrongness of abortion somehow in the biological humanity of a fetus cannot explain this.

The FLO account does not entail that there is another species of animals whose members ought not to be killed. Neither does it entail that it is permissible to kill any non-human animal. On the one hand, a supporter of animals' rights might argue that since some non-human animals have a future of value, it is wrong to kill them also, or at least it is wrong to kill them without a far better reason than we usually have for killing non-human animals. On the other hand, one might argue that the futures of non-human animals are not sufficiently like ours for the FLO account to entail that it is wrong to kill them. Since the FLO account does not specify which properties a future of another individual must possess so that killing that individual is wrong, the FLO account is indeterminate with respect to this issue. The fact that the FLO account of the wrongness of killing does not give a determinate answer to this question is not a flaw in the theory. A sound ethical account should yield the right answers in the obvious cases; it should not be required to resolve every disputed question.

A major respect in which the FLO account is superior to accounts that appeal to the concept of person is the explanation the FLO account provides of the wrongness of killing infants. There was a class of infants who had futures that included a class of events that were identical to the futures of the readers of this essay. Thus, reader, the FLO account explains why it was as wrong to kill you when you were an infant as it is to kill you now. This account can be generalized to almost all infants. Notice that the wrongness of killing infants can be explained in the absence of an account of what makes the future of an individual sufficiently valuable so that it is wrong to kill that individual. The absence of such an account explains why the FLO account is indeterminate with respect to the wrongness of killing non-human animals.

If the FLO account is the correct theory of the wrongness of killing, then because abortion involves killing fetuses and fetuses have FLOs for exactly the same reasons that infants have FLOs, abortion is presumptively seriously immoral. This inference lays the necessary groundwork for a fourth argument in favor of the FLO account that shows that abortion is wrong.

The analogy with animals argument

Why do we believe it is wrong to cause animals suffering? We believe that, in our own case and in the case of other adults and children, suffering is a misfortune. It would be as morally arbitrary to refuse to acknowledge that animal suffering is wrong as it would be to refuse to acknowledge that the suffering of persons of another race is wrong. It is, on reflection, suffering that is a misfortune, not the suffering of white males or the suffering of humans. Therefore, infliction of suffering is presumptively wrong no matter on whom it is inflicted and whether it is inflicted on persons or nonpersons. Arbitrary restrictions on the wrongness of suffering count as racism or speciesism. Not only is this argument convincing on its own, but it is the only way of justifying the wrongness of animal cruelty. Cruelty toward animals is clearly wrong. (This famous argument is due to Singer, 1979.)

The FLO account of the wrongness of abortion is analogous. We believe that, in our own case and the cases of other adults and children, the loss of a future of value is a misfortune. It would be as morally arbitrary to refuse to acknowledge that the loss of a future of value to a fetus is wrong as to refuse to acknowledge that the loss of a future of value to Jews (to take a relevant twentieth-century example) is wrong. It is, on reflection, the loss of a future of value that is a misfortune; not the loss of a future of value to adults or loss of a future of value to non-Jews. To deprive someone of a future of value is wrong no matter on whom the deprivation is inflicted and no matter whether the deprivation is inflicted on persons or nonpersons. Arbitrary restrictions on the wrongness of this deprivation count as racism, genocide or ageism. Therefore, abortion is wrong. This argument that abortion is wrong should be convincing because it has the same form as the argument for the claim that causing pain and suffering to non-human animals is wrong. Since the latter argument is convincing, the former argument should be also. Thus, an analogy with animals supports the thesis that abortion is wrong.

Replies to Objections

The four arguments in the previous section establish that abortion is, except in rare cases, seriously immoral. Not surprisingly, there are objections to this view. There are replies to the four most important objections to the FLO argument for the immorality of abortion.

The potentiality objection

The FLO account of the wrongness of abortion is a potentiality argument. To claim that a fetus *has* an FLO is to claim that a fetus now has the potential to be in a state of a certain kind in the future. It is not claim that all ordinary fetuses *will* have FLOs. Fetuses who are aborted, of course, will not. To say that a standard fetus has an FLO is to say that a standard fetus either will have or would have a life it will or would value. To say that a standard fetus would have a life it would value is to say that it will have a life it will value if it does not die prematurely. The truth of this conditional is based upon the nature of fetuses (including the fact that they naturally age) and this nature concerns their potential.

Some appeals to potentiality in the abortion debate rest on unsound inferences. For example, one may try to generate an argument against abortion by arguing that because persons have the right to life, potential persons also have the right to life. Such an argument is plainly invalid as it stands. The premise one needs to add to make it valid would have to be something like: "If Xs have the right to Y, then potential Xs have the right to Y." This premise is plainly false. Potential presidents don't have the rights of the presidency; potential voters don't have the right to vote.

In the FLO argument potentiality is not used in order to bridge the gap between adults and fetuses as is done in the argument in the above paragraph. The FLO theory of the wrongness of killing adults is based upon the adult's potentiality to have a future of value. Potentiality is in the argument from the very beginning. Thus, the plainly false premise is not required. Accordingly, the use of potentiality in the FLO theory is not a sign of an illegitimate inference.

The argument from interests

A second objection to the FLO account of the immorality of abortion involves arguing that even though fetuses have FLOs, nonsentient fetuses do not meet the minimum conditions for having any moral standing at all because they lack interests. Steinbock (1992, p. 5) has presented this argument clearly:

> Beings that have moral status must be capable of caring about what is done to them. They must be capable of being made, if only in a rudimentary sense, happy or miserable, comfortable or distressed.

Whatever reasons we may have for preserving or protecting non-sentient beings, these reasons do not refer to their own interests. For without conscious awareness, beings cannot have interests. Without interests, they cannot have a welfare of their own. Without a welfare of their own, nothing can be done for their sake. Hence, they lack moral standing or status.

Medical researchers have argued that fetuses do not become sentient until after 22 weeks of gestation (Steinbock, 1992, p. 50). If they are correct, and if Steinbock's argument is sound, then we have both an objection to the FLO account of the wrongness of abortion and a basis for a view on abortion minimally acceptable to most supporters of choice.

Steinbock's conclusion conflicts with our settled moral beliefs. Temporarily unconscious human beings are nonsentient, yet no one believes that they lack either interests or moral standing. Accordingly, neither conscious awareness nor the capacity for conscious awareness is a necessary condition for having interests.

The counter-example of the temporarily unconscious human being shows that there is something internally wrong with Steinbock's argument. The difficulty stems from an ambiguity. One cannot *take* an interest in something without being capable of caring about what is done to it. However, something can be *in* someone's interest without that individual being capable of caring about it, or about anything. Thus, life support can be *in* the interests of a temporarily unconscious patient even though the temporarily unconscious patient is incapable of *taking* an interest in that life support. If this can be so for the temporarily unconscious patient, then it is hard to see why it cannot be so for the temporarily unconscious (that is, nonsentient) fetus who requires placental life support. Thus the objection based on interests fails.

The problem of equality

The FLO account of the wrongness of killing seems to imply that the degree of wrongness associated with each killing varies inversely with the victim's age. Thus, the FLO account of the wrongness of killing seems to suggest that

it is far worse to kill a five-year-old than an 89-year-old because the former is deprived of far more than the latter. However, we believe that all persons have an equal right to life. Thus, it appears that the FLO account of the wrongness of killing entails an obviously false view (Paske, 1994).

However, the FLO account of the wrongness of killing does not, strictly speaking, imply that it is worse to kill younger people than older people. The FLO account provides an explanation of the wrongness of killing that is sufficient to account for the serious presumptive wrongness of killing. It does not follow that killings cannot be wrong in other ways. For example, one might hold, as does Feldman (1992, p. 184), that in addition to the wrongness of killing that has its basis in the future life of which the victim is deprived, killing an individual is also made wrong by the admirability of an individual's past behavior. Now the amount of admirability will presumably vary directly with age, whereas the amount of deprivation will vary inversely with age. This tends to equalize the wrongness of murder.

However, even if, *ceteris paribus*, it is worse to kill younger persons than older persons, there are good reasons for adopting a doctrine of the legal equality of murder. Suppose that we tried to estimate the seriousness of a crime of murder by appraising the value of the FLO of which the victim had been deprived. How would one go about doing this? In the first place, one would be confronted by the old problem of interpersonal comparisons of utility. In the second place, estimation of the value of a future would involve putting oneself, not into the shoes of the victim at the time she was killed, but rather into the shoes the victim would have worn had the victim survived, and then estimating from that perspective the worth of that person's future. This task seems difficult, if not impossible. Accordingly, there are reasons to adopt a convention that murders are equally wrong.

Furthermore, the FLO theory, in a way, explains why we do adopt the doctrine of the legal equality of murder. The FLO theory explains why we regard murder as one of the worst of crimes, since depriving someone of a future like ours deprives her of more than depriving her of anything else. This gives us a reason for making the punishment for murder very harsh, as harsh as is compatible with civilized society. One should not make the punishment for younger victims harsher than that. Thus, the doctrine of the equal legal right to life does not seem to be incompatible with the FLO theory.

The contraception objection

The strongest objection to the FLO argument for the immorality of abortion is based on the claim that, because contraception results in one less FLO, the FLO argument entails that contraception, indeed, abstention from sex when conception is possible, is immoral. Because neither contraception nor abstention from sex when conception is possible is immoral, the FLO account is flawed.

There is a cogent reply to this objection. If the argument of the early part of this essay is correct, then the central issue concerning the morality of abortion is the problem of whether fetuses are individuals who are members of the class of individuals whom it is seriously presumptively wrong to kill. The properties of being human and alive, of being a person, and of having an FLO are criteria that participants in the abortion debate have offered to mark off the relevant class of individuals. The central claim of this essay is that having an FLO marks off the relevant class of individuals. A defender of the FLO view could, therefore, reply that since, at the time of contraception, there is no individual to have an FLO, the FLO account does not entail that contraception is wrong. The wrong of killing is primarily a wrong to the individual who is killed; at the time of contraception there is no individual to be wronged.

However, someone who presses the contraception objection might have an answer to this reply. She might say that the sperm and egg are the individuals deprived of an FLO at the time of contraception. Thus, there are individuals whom contraception deprives of an FLO and if depriving an individual of an FLO is what makes killing wrong, then the FLO theory entails that contraception is wrong.

There is also a reply to this move. In the case of abortion, an objectively determinate individual is the subject of harm caused by the loss of an FLO. This individual is a fetus. In the case of contraception, there are far more candidates (see Norcross, 1990). Let us consider some possible candidates in order of the increasing number of individuals harmed: (1) The single harmed individual might be the combination of the particular sperm and the particular egg that would have united to form a zygote if contraception had not been used. (2) The two harmed individuals might be the particular sperm itself, and, in addition, the ovum itself that would have physically combined to form the zygote. (This is modeled on the double homicide of two persons who would otherwise in a short time fuse. (1) is modeled on harm to a single entity some of whose parts are not physically contiguous, such as a university.) (3) The many harmed individuals might be the millions of *combinations* of sperm and the released ovum whose (small) chances of having an FLO were reduced by the successful contraception. (4) The even larger class of harmed individuals (larger by one) might be the class consisting of all of the individual sperm in an ejaculate and, in addition, the individual ovum released at the time of the successful contraception. (1) through (4) are all candidates for being the subject(s) of harm in the case of successful contraception or abstinence from sex. Which should be chosen? Should we hold a lottery? There seems to be no non-arbitrarily determinate subject of harm in the case of successful contraception. But if there is no such subject of harm, then no determinate thing was harmed. If no determinate thing was harmed, then (in the case of contraception) no wrong has been done. Thus, the FLO account of the wrongness of abortion does not entail that contraception is wrong.

Conclusion

This essay contains an argument for the view that, except in unusual circumstances, abortion is seriously wrong. Deprivation of an FLO explains why killing adults and children is wrong. Abortion deprives fetuses of FLOs. Therefore, abortion is wrong. This argument is based on an account of the wrongness of killing that is a result of our considered judgment of the nature of the misfortune of premature death. It accounts for why we regard killing as one of the worst of crimes. It is superior to alternative account of the wrongness of killing that are intended to provide insight into the ethics of abortion. This account of the wrongness of killing is supported by the way it handles cases in which our moral judgments are settled. This account has an analogue in the most plausible account of the wrongness of causing animals to suffer. This account makes no appeal to religion. Therefore, the FLO account shows that abortion, except in rare instances, is seriously wrong.

Acknowledgment

This essay is an updated version of a view that first appeared in the *Journal of Philosophy* (1989). This essay incorporates attempts to deal with the objections of McInerney (1990), Norcross (1990), Shirley (1995), Steinbock (1992), and Paske (1994) to the original version of the view.

References

Beckwith, F. J. (1993) *Politically Correct Death: Answering Arguments for Abortion Rights*. Grand Rapids, Michigan: Baker Books.

Benn, S. I. (1973) "Abortion, Infanticide, and Respect for Persons," *The Problem of Abortion*, ed. J. Feinberg. Belmont, CA: Wadsworth, pp. 92–104.

Engelhardt, Jr, H. T. (1986) *The Foundations of Bioethics*. New York: Oxford University Press.

Feinberg, J. (1986) "Abortion," *Matters of Life and Death: New Introductory Essays in Moral Philosophy*, ed. T. Regan. New York: Random House.

Feldman, F. (1992) *Confrontations with the Reaper: A Philosophical Study of the Nature and Value of Death*. New York: Oxford University Press.

Kant, I. (1963) *Lectures on Ethics*, trans. L. Infeld. New York: Harper.

Marquis, D. B. (1994) "A Future like Ours and the Concept of Person: a Reply to Mcinerney and Paske," *The Abortion Controversy: A Reader*, ed. L. P. Pojman and F. J. Beckwith. Boston: Jones and Bartlett, pp. 354–68.

—— (1995) "Fetuses, Futures and Values: a Reply to Shirley," *Southwest Philosophy Review* 11: 263–5.

—— (1989) "Why Abortion Is Immoral," *Journal of Philosophy* 86: 183–202.

McInerney, P. (1990) "Does a Fetus Already Have a Future like Ours?," *Journal of Philosophy* 87: 264–8.

Noonan, J. (1970) "An Almost Absolute Value in History," in *The Morality of Abortion*, ed. J. Noonan. Cambridge, MA: Harvard University Press.

Norcross, A. (1990) "Killing, Abortion, and Contraception: a Reply to Marquis," *Journal of Philosophy* 87: 268–77.

Paske, G. (1994) "Abortion and the Neo-natal Right to Life: a Critique of Marquis's Futurist Argument," *The Abortion Controversy: A Reader*, ed. L. P. Pojman and F. J. Beckwith. Boston: Jones and Bartlett, pp. 343–53.

Sacred Congregation for the Propagation of the Faith (1980) *Declaration on Euthanasia*. Vatican City.

Shirley, E. S. (1995) "Marquis' Argument Against Abortion: a Critique," *Southwest Philosophy Review* 11: 79–89.

Singer, P. (1979) "Not for Humans Only: the Place of Nonhumans in Environmental Issues," *Ethics and Problems of the 21st Century*, ed. K. E. Goodpaster and K. M. Sayre. South Bend: Notre Dame University Press.

Steinbock, B. (1992) *Life Before Birth: The Moral and Legal Status of Embryos and Fetuses*. New York: Oxford University Press.

Thomson, J. J. (1971) "A Defense of Abortion," *Philosophy and Public Affairs* 1: 47–66.

Tooley, M. (1972) "Abortion and Infanticide," *Philosophy and Public Affairs* 2: 37–65.

Warren, M. A. (1973) "On the Moral and Legal Status of Abortion," *Monist* 57: 43–61.

12

The Moral Permissibility of Abortion

Margaret Olivia Little

Introduction

When a woman or girl finds herself pregnant, is it morally permissible for her to end that pregnancy? One dominant tradition says "no"; its close cousin says "rarely" – exceptions may be made where the burdens on the individual girl or woman are exceptionally dire, or, for some, when the pregnancy results from rape. On both views, though, there is an enormous presumption against aborting, for abortion involves destruction of something we've no right to destroy. Those who reject this claim, it is said, do so by denying the dignity of early human life – and imperiling their own.

I think these views deeply flawed. They are, I believe, based on a problematic conception of how we should value early human life; more than that, they are based on a profoundly misleading view of gestation and a deontologically crude picture of morality. I believe that early abortion is fully permissible, widely decent, and, indeed, can be honorable. This is not, though, because I regard burgeoning human life as "mere tissue": to the contrary, I think it has a value worthy of special respect. It is, rather, because I believe that the right *way* to value early human life – and the right way

to value what is involved in and at stake with its development – leads to a view that regards abortion as both morally sober and morally permissible. Abortion at later stages of pregnancy becomes, for reasons I'll outline, multiply more complicated; but then it is early abortions – say, abortions in the first half of pregnancy – that are most at stake for women.

The Moral Status of Embryos and Early Fetuses

According to one tradition, the moral case against abortion is easily stated: abortion is morally impermissible because it is murder. The fetus, it's claimed, is a *person* – not just a life (a frog is a life), or an organism worthy of special regard, but a creature of full moral status imbued with fundamental rights. Abortion, in turn, constitutes a gross violation of one of that person's central-most such rights, namely, its right to life.

Now, for a great many people, the idea of a two-week blastocyst, or six-week embryo, or 12-week fetus counting as an equivalent rights-bearer to more usual persons is just an enormous stretch. It makes puzzles of widely shared intuitions, including the greater sense of loss most feel at later rather than earlier miscarriages, or again the greater priority we place on preventing childhood diseases than on preventing miscarriages. However else we may think such life worthy of regard, an embryo or early fetus is so far removed from our paradigmatic notion of a person that regarding it as such seems an extreme view.

The question is why some feel pushed to such an extreme. It's in part a reflection of just how inadequate our usual theories are when they bump up against reproduction. Surely part of the urge to cast a blastocyst as a full-fledged person, for instance, is a byproduct of the impoverished resources our inherited theory has for valuing germinating human life: if the only category of moral status one has is a person or rights-holder, then the only way to capture our sense of the kind of respect or honor that embryos might deserve (the only way to capture the loss many feel at early miscarriage, for instance, or the queasiness over certain aspects of human embryo research) is to insist on fetal personhood from the moment of conception. The alternative, of course, is to challenge the assumption: instead of making the fetus match those terms of moral status, we ask what our theory of value should look like to accommodate the value of an entity like the fetus.

Or again, part of the urge to cast the embryo as a person is the worry that drawing subsequent distinctions in moral status over the course of fetal development would be fatally ad hoc. But such a worry already presupposes a certain metaphysics: it is only if one believes that discrete events and steady states are the fundamental explanatory classifications that distinctions of stages will feel troublingly arbitrary. A metaphysics that accommodates *becoming* or *continua* as fundamental explanatory classifications will be more likely to regard the distinction between zygote and matured person as inherently graduated. It wouldn't expect to find – because it wouldn't think to need – any distinction between discrete properties adequate to the job.

This is not to say that everything about moral status is degreed. But if we expand our moral categories beyond *rights* to notions of *value*, and accept *continua* as everyday phenomena rather than special puzzles, the road is paved for a picture of burgeoning human life that accords far better with the intuitions of so many: burgeoning human life has a status and worth that deepen as its development progresses.

But, it will be said, such an account misses something crucial. Unlike other inherently gradualist processes – the building of a house, say – there is here something already extant that should ground full moral status to the embryo: namely, a potential or *telos* for personhood. The only gradualist element in the picture is its unfolding. This, it will be urged, is what really grounds the moral standing of early human life: it's not because the embryo or early fetus *is* a person, but because the right way to value potential persons is to regard them as deserving the same deference *as* persons.

Now, I think there is a very important sense in which we should regard human embryos and fetuses as potential persons. We are in part biological animals, and biology classifies organisms as the types of creatures they are by giving explanatory primacy to certain trajectories over others. While there are an infinite number of trajectories that fish eggs, for instance, could take – from developing into fish, to being eaten as caviar, to being enucleated with sheep DNA and becoming a sheep – they are understood as the kind of biological organism they are by privileging the first as its "matured state" and expressive of its "nature." It is in this sense that a fish egg is a potential fish while a salamander egg – which could in principle be turned into a fish with enough laboratory machinations – is only thereby a possible one. Similarly, a human embryo is understood biologically as the kind of organism it is by giving explanatory primacy to the trajectory of its developing into a matured human, i.e. a person – something that cannot be said of a given sperm or egg.[1]

Lest we hang too much on this point, though, we need to remember that biology is not the only rubric that matters here. There is no direct isomorphism from the idea of a biological potential to a normative end – something that should or must be realized. Indeed, on one view, biological potential is only a candidate for normative for creatures who independently count as having moral standing – the above view turns out to have things exactly backwards. More deeply, though, the particular classification at issue here carries an intrinsic tension. For the trajectory in virtue of which we connect this sort of organism with that further state is a trajectory that depends on what *another person –* the pregnant woman – is able and willing to do. That is, *unlike* most biological organisms, the trajectory we privilege as the fetus's "natural" development – against which we classify its "potential" and measure when its existence is "truncated" – depends on the actions and resources of an autonomous *agent*, not the events and conditions of a *habitat*. Knowing what to think of the fetus thus requires assessing moves that have their home in biology (classifying organisms based on privileging certain environmental counterfactuals), applied when the biological "environment" is, at one and the same time, an autonomous agent subsumable under normative, not just biological, categories.

If this is easy to miss, it's in part because of how human gestation itself tends to get depicted. Metaphors abound of passive carriage; the pregnancy is a project of nature. The woman is, perhaps, an especially close witness to that project, or again its setting, but the project is not her own. Her agency is thus noticed when she cuts off the pregnancy but passes unnoticed when she continues it. If, though, gestation belongs to the *woman*, if its essential resources are hers – her blood, her hormones, her energy, all resources that could be going to other of her bodily projects – then the concept of potential person is a hybrid concept from the start, not something we can read off from the neutral lessons of biology. In an important sense, then, talk of the fetus as potential person is dangerously misleading. For it encourages us to think of the embryo's development as mere *unfolding* – as though all that's needed other than the passage of time is already intrinsically there, or at least there independently of the woman.

In my own view, the biological capacities of early human life provide, once again, a degreed

basis for according regard. Such biological potential marks out early human life as especially *respect-worthy* – which is why we should try to avoid conception where children are not what is sought (or again, why we don't think we should tack up human embryos on the wall for art, or provide them for children to dissect at school if fertilized chicken eggs get too pricey). To say that such life is respect-worthy, though, is not the same as claiming we are charged to defer as we would those with moral status.

Abortion and Gestational Assistance

Thus far, I've argued that morally restrictive views of abortion ride atop a problematic view of how we should value early human life. I now want to argue that they also ride atop a problematic misconception of the act of aborting itself. Let me illustrate first by returning to the claim that, if the fetus *were* a person, abortion would be a violation of its right to life.

We noted above that, while certain metaphors depict gestation as passive carriage (as though the fetus were simply occupying a room until it is born), the truth is of course far different. One who is gestating is providing the fetus with sustenance – donating nourishment, creating blood, delivering oxygen, providing hormonal triggers for development – without which it could not live. For a fetus, as the phrase goes, to live *is* to be receiving aid. And whether the assistance is delivered by way of intentional activity (as when the woman eats or takes her prenatal vitamins) or by way of biological mechanism, assistance it plainly is. But this has crucial implications for abortion's alleged status as murder. To put it simply, the right to life, as Judith Thomson famously put it, does not include the right to have all assistance needed to maintain that life (Thomson, 1971). Ending gestation will, at early stages at least, certainly lead to the fetus's demise, but that does not mean that doing so would violate its right to life.

Now Thomson herself illustrated the point with an (in)famous thought experiment in which one person is kidnapped and used as life support for another: staying connected to the Famous Violinist, she points out, may be the kind thing to do, but disconnecting oneself does not violate the Violinist's rights. The details of this rather esoteric example have led to widespread charges that Thomson's point ignores the distinction between killing and letting die, and would apply at any rate only to cases in which the woman was not responsible for procreation occurring. In fact, though, I think the central insight here is broader than the example, or Thomson's own analysis, indicates.[2]

As Frances Kamm's work points out (Kamm, 1992), in the usual case of a killing – if you stab a person on the street, for instance – you interfere with the trajectory the person had independently of you. She faced a happy enough future, we'll say; your action changed that, taking away from her something she would have had but for your action. In ending gestation, though, what you are taking away from this person is something she wouldn't have had to begin with without your aid. She comes to you with a downward trajectory, as it were: but for you she would already be dead. In removing that assistance, you are not violating the person's right to life, judged in the traditional terms of a right against interference. While all killings are tragedies, then, not all are alike: some killings, as Kamm puts it, share the crucial "formal" feature of letting die, which is that they leave the person no worse off than before she encountered you. Of course, if one *could* end the assistance without effecting death, then, absent extraordinary circumstances, one should. (Part of the debate over so-called partial birth abortions is whether and when we encounter such circumstances.)[3]

The argument is not some crude utilitarian one, according to which you get to kill the person because you saved her life (as though, having given you a nice lamp for your birthday, I may therefore later steal it with impunity). The point, rather, is that where I am still in the process of saving – or sustaining or enabling – your life, and that life cannot be thusly saved or sustained by anyone else, ending that assistance, even by active means, does not violate your right to life.

Some, of course, will argue that matters change when the woman is causally responsible for procreation. In such cases, it will be said, she is responsible for introducing the person's need. She isn't like someone happening by an accident on the highway who knows CPR; she's like the person who *caused* the accident. Her actions introduced a set of vulnerabilities or needs, and we have a special duty to lessen vulnerabilities and repair harms we have inflicted on others.

But there is a deep disanalogy between causing the accident and procreating. The fact of causing a crash itself introduces a harm to surrounding drivers: they are in a worse position for having encountered that driver. But the simple act of procreating does not worsen the fetus's position: without procreation, the fetus wouldn't exist at all; and the mere fact of being brought into existence is not a bad thing. To be sure, creating a human is creating someone who comes with needs. But this, crucially, is not the same as inflicting a need *onto* someone (see Silverstein, 1987). It isn't as though the fetus already existed with one level of needs and the woman added a new one (as does happen, for instance, if a woman takes a drug after conception that increases the fetus's vulnerability to, say, certain cancers). The woman is (partially) responsible for creating a life, and it's a life that necessarily includes needs, but that is not the same as being responsible for the person being needy rather than not. The pregnant woman has not made the fetus more vulnerable than it would otherwise have been: absent her procreative actions, it wouldn't have existed at all.

Even if the fetus were a person, then, abortion would not be murder. More broadly, abortion isn't a species of *wrongful interference*. This isn't to say that abortion is thereby necessarily unproblematic. It is to argue, instead, that the crucial moral issue needs to be relocated to the question of what, if any, positive obligations pregnant women have to continue gestational assistance. The question abortion really asks us to address, that is, is about the *ethics of gestation*. But this is a question that takes us into far richer, and far more interesting, territory than that occupied by discussions of murder. In particular, it requires us to discuss and assess claimed grounds of obligation, and to assess the very specific kinds of burdens and sacrifice involved in rendering *this* type of assistance.

I've argued elsewhere that if, or when, the fetus is a person, then the question of when a woman might have some obligation to provide use of her body to save its life turns out to be a fascinatingly deep matter, and one which is ultimately deeply contextual. The issue I want to turn my attention to here is what picture we get when we join the two views I've outlined: a view that regards burgeoning human life as respect-worthy but not endowed with moral status, and a view that recognizes abortion as ending of gestational support. Abortion, I want to argue, is both permissible and widely decent, for reasons involving what we might call *authorship* and *stewardship*. Let me take them each in turn.

Intimacy, Pregnancy, and Motherhood

When people first ask what's at stake in asking a woman to continue a pregnancy, what usually get emphasized are the physical and medical risks. And, indeed, they're worth emphasizing. While many pregnancies go smoothly, many do not; and the neutral language of an obstetrics text hardly captures the lived reality. I think of a friend I visited who'd been put in lock-down on the psychiatric ward from pregnancy-related psychosis (and whose physician wouldn't discuss inducing at 39 weeks because there was no "obstetrical indication"). Or my sister, whose two-trimester "morning sickness" – actually gut-wrenching dry heaves every 20 minutes and three hospitalizations – was the equal of many an experience of chemotherapy. Or another acquaintance, whose sudden onset of eclampsia during delivery brought her so close to dying that it left us all breathless. Asking women to take on the ex ante medical risks of pregnancy is asking a lot.

Then there are the social risks pregnancy can represent for some women – risks it is very hard for those of us in more comfortable lives to fully appreciate. Pregnancy is a marker for increased domestic violence. It leads for many to aban-

donment by family and community, even as it can lead the woman to feel tied to a relationship she would otherwise leave.

All of these burdens are important to appreciate. But there is something incomplete in such renditions of pregnancy's stakes. For a great many women, it's another set of issues that motivate the desire to end a pregnancy – issues having to do with the extraordinarily *personal* nature of gestation.

To be pregnant is to allow another living creature to live in and off one's body for nine months. It's to have one's every physical system shaped by its needs, rather than one's own. It is to share one's body in an extraordinarily intimate and extensive – and often radically unpredictable – way. Then there is the aftermath of the nine months: for gestation doesn't just turn cells into a person; it turns the woman into a mother. One of the most common reasons women give for wanting to abort is that they do not want to become a mother – now, ever, again, with this partner, or no reliable partner, with these few resources, or these many that are now, after so many years of mothering, slated finally to another cause. Not because motherhood would bring with it such burdens – though it can – but because motherhood would so thoroughly change what we might call one's fundamental practical identity. The enterprise of mothering restructures the self – changing the shape of one's heart, the primary commitments by which one lives one's life, the terms by which one judges one's life a success or a failure. If the enterprise is eschewed and one decides to give the child over to another, the identity of mother still changes the normative facts that are true of one, as there is now someone by whom one does well or poorly. And either way – whether one rears the child or lets it go – to continue a pregnancy means that a piece of one's heart, as the saying goes, will forever walk outside one's body.

Gestation, in short, is not just any activity. It involves sharing one's very body. It brings with it an emotional intertwinement that can reshape one's entire life. It brings another person into one's family. Deciding whether to continue a pregnancy isn't like being asked to write a check for charity, however large; it's an enormous undertaking that has reverberations for an entire lifetime. To argue that women may permissibly decline this need not trade on a view that grants no value to early life; it is, in essence, to argue about the right way to value *pregnancy* and *parenthood*. It is to recognize a level of moral prerogative based not just on the concretely understood burdens of the activity in question, but in its deep connection to authoring a life.

Imagine that the partner of your family's dreams is wildly in love with you and asks for your hand in marriage. As it turns out, substantial utility would accrue by your accepting him: his connections would seal your father's bid for political office, raise the family profile yet higher and add nicely to its coffers just as your eldest brother faces expensive restoration of the family estate. It would also, and not incidentally, keep the fellow himself from falling into a pit of despair, as it's clear you're the only one for him.

All of this utility notwithstanding, many will believe that you don't thereby have a moral *obligation* – even a *prima facie* one – to accept the proposal. You might have a responsibility to give the proposal serious thought; but if, on reflection, you realize that marriage to this man – or to any man – is not what you want, then there we are. And this, even if we stipulate that marriage would not be a setback to your happiness: the utility function you'd enjoy following acceptance might, indeed, surpass the one that would follow refusal. This, even if we think that the needs presented would have coalesced to form a duty if the assistance required had been burdensome (say, writing a big check) rather than intimate.[4] Nor, finally, need we think the resistance must trace to a conviction that it would be morally wrong to accept the proposal – that it would in some way transgress the norms governing marriage. It is, we'll imagine, quite obvious to you that you would come to have an enduring love if you accept; he understands this and relishes the prospective courtship. It isn't that you would *use* him if you accept; it's that you don't *want* to have an enduring love with him, or now, or at all.

Or again, imagine that your providing sexual service would help comfort and inspire the soldiers readying for battle. Many will believe this does not ground a requirement, even *prima facie*, to offer intercourse. This, even if you're the only one around capable of offering such service, and even if doing so wouldn't actually be distressful to you. Such an intuition, again, needn't trade thinking it would be wrong to give sex for such a purpose. Those with more permissive views of sexuality might well think someone who authentically and with full self-respect wanted to share her body to this purpose would be doing something generous and fine. One just doesn't want to make doing so the subject of obligation.

Now, not all agree to these intuitions. If Victorian novels are to be believed, the upper classes of Regency England believed that both marriage and sex were fair candidates for obligation (especially when the family estate was at stake!). But for many, there is something about marriage as a relationship, and sexual intercourse as a bodily connection, that makes them deserving of some special kind of deference when assessing moral obligation. The deference is doubtless limited: one need be absolutist here no more than elsewhere. But it is, crucially, out of proportion to the plain disutility the action might cause the candidate agent, and here, juxtaposed with these sorts of stakes, may respectfully decline.

An important aspect of being a self is that the boundaries of one's self – the borders and use of one's body, the identity by which one knows oneself as oneself – are matters over which one deserves special moral deference. We might say it's on pain of imposing alienation. But the point is not to urge some fetishism about the evil of alienation (morality, after all, doesn't give a whit if you feel alienated when returning the borrowed library book), but to insist that there are some activities that can have a sufficiently tight connection to self that alienation with respect to *them* is especially problematic to maintaining our status *as* selves. One's self is not always implicated in sexual intercourse and marriage; where it is, one may not care. But where it is, and you do, that fact is worthy of a deference or protection in a way that caring about how one's garden grows is not.

Gestation, like sex, is a bodily intimacy of the first order. Motherhood, like marriage, is a relational intimacy of the first order. If one believes that decisions about whether to continue a pregnancy are deserving of moral prerogative, it need not be because one believes early human life has no value – any more than assigning prerogatives over sex and marriage denies the value of one's family, the boys in fighting blue, or the relationship of marriage. Such views instead stem from conviction that the proper way to value the relationship of motherhood and the bodily connection of pregnancy is to view them as intimacies deserving of special deference. Even if continuing a pregnancy represents *no* welfare setback to the woman, classically construed, we should recognize a strong moral prerogative over whether to continue that pregnancy.

This isn't a claim that any reason to abort is a good one. Human life, even in nascent forms, should not be extinguished lightly; one who decides to end a pregnancy because she wants to fit into a party dress, say, is getting wrong the value of burgeoning human life. To abort for such reasons is to act indecently. But this doesn't mean that such a woman now has an obligation to continue the pregnancy. What it means, in the first instance, is that she should not regard such a reason as adequate for the conclusion; not that the conclusion is not available to her.

It's not that decency is some optional ideal. Quite to the contrary: if one realizes that an action is indecent, one mustn't do it. But the "it" in question is, as Barbara Herman puts it, an action–reason pair; it is, though it makes our deliberations sound more formal than they are, a piece of practical syllogism. To say that a practical syllogism is indecent means one should discard it, but that doesn't yet comment on what action one should do. More specifically, it doesn't mean one can't decently arrive at its conclusion, for there may well be decent reasons waiting in the wings.

Take a standard example. A soldier, we might well decide, doesn't have an obligation to risk death falling on the grenade that threatens his comrades. Nonetheless, if the reason he declines has nothing to do with wanting to live and everything with wanting his hated comrades to die, his refusal is indecent. Such betrays a dreadful understanding of what is here at stake; he shouldn't refuse on that basis. But this doesn't mean he thereby faces now an obligation or imperative to fall on the grenade. For there is extant a reason the soldier can deploy as an honorable basis for declining – namely, that doing so would sacrifice his life.

Or again, to return to our fanciful example, if the reason you decide not to marry the suitor is not because you don't want at this stage of your life to enter such a commitment, say, but because you don't like the wart on his big toe, or the color of the drawing room walls in his mansion, or if you decline sexual intercourse for racist reasons, your behavior is indecent. To think these acceptable reasons – to think them adequate premises to support a practical conclusion of declining – is to fundamentally misappreciate the various values here implicated. But we don't thereby conclude that the person is now under a requirement to accept (as though it's the woman with the dreadful reasons who now has an obligation to have sex!). For there is extant a reason that would be honorable to deploy as a basis for declining – that one doesn't want to have sex, or enter marriage. Similarly, the fact that a given woman might deploy a genuinely trivial or offensive basis for aborting doesn't mean she is now obliged to continue the pregnancy. For there are available reasons – about sharing her body and entering motherhood – she may deploy as a basis for honorably declining.

Norms of Responsible Creation

Now some will urge that those who are (at least jointly) responsible for procreation thereby have a heightened obligation to continue gestating. People, of course, disagree over what it takes to count as "responsible" here – whether voluntary but contracepted intercourse is different from intercourse without use of birth control, and again from intentionally deciding to become pregnant at the IVF clinic. But those who satisfy the relevant criteria, it's often said, must thereby face greater duty to "see the pregnancy through." Unease is expressed at the thought of heterosexual intercourse conducted in callous disregard of procreative potential, of creating only to let wither. If you're going to allow a new life to begin, it's thought, you'd better see it through to fruition.

I think these intuitions point to important issues, but not the ones usually thought. Let's start with that notion of sexual irresponsibility. For many people, there is something troubling about the idea of couples engaging in heterosexual intercourse in complete disregard of contraception – say, when one is highly fertile and birth control is just an arm's reach away. Such a view points to an important set of intuitions about another layer of respect, namely, respect for creation itself. Respect for burgeoning human life carries implications, not just for the accommodation we might owe such life once extant, but for the conditions under which we should undertake activities with procreative potential in the first place. To regard something as having value sometimes means we should produce as much of it as possible; other times, as when the valuable thing is "person," it tells us to take care about the conditions in which we produce any.[5]

There are, as we might put it, norms of responsible creation. Such a view seems exactly right to me. Part of what I imagine teaching my own children about sexuality is that human life as such deserves respect (whatever the metaphysical details), and respect requires that one not treat one's procreative capacities in a cavalier way. But none of this means that one has a special responsibility to gestate if one *does* get pregnant. For one thing, these norms, while very important (and far too little emphasized in our current culture), are norms about the activities that can lead to procreation, not what one owes should procreation take place. They specify, as it were, the good faith conditions one should meet for engaging in certain activities. Even if the norms are broached – one has sex in callous disregard to its potential to lead to new human life – that doesn't itself imply that one now (as punishment?) must gestate: it says one

shouldn't have had that sort of sex. Indeed, for many of us, the thought that negligence here means one should continue a pregnancy has an internal disconnect: that one had irresponsible sex is no reason at all to bring a new person into the world.

This last point begins to point to a very different approach to the ethics of creation. The salience of responsibility for procreation to the responsibilities of gestation is not just complex: decisions about abortion are often located *within* the norms of responsible creation. Let me explain.

Many people have deeply felt convictions about the circumstances under which they feel it right for them to bring a child into the world – can it be brought into a decent world, an intact family, a society that can minimally respect its agency? These considerations can persist even after conception has taken place, for while the embryo has already been created, a person has not. That is, some women decide to abort not because they do not *want* the resulting child – indeed, they may yearn for nothing more, and desperately wish that their circumstances were otherwise – but because they do not think bringing a child into the world is the right thing for them to do.

As Barbara Katz Rothman (1989) puts it, decisions to abort often represent not a decision to destroy, but a refusal to create. These are abortions marked by moral language. A woman wants to abort because she knows she couldn't give up a child for adoption but feels she couldn't give the child the sort of life, or be the sort of parent, she thinks a child *deserves*; a woman who would have to give up the child thinks it would be *unfair* to bring a child into existence already burdened by rejection, however well grounded its reasons; a woman living in a country marked by poverty and gender apartheid wants to abort because she decides it would be *wrong* for her to bear a daughter whose life, like hers, would be filled with so much injustice and hardship.

Some have thought that such decisions betray a simple fallacy: unless the child's life were literally going to be worse than non-existence, how can one abort out of concern for the future child? But the worry here isn't that one would be imposing a *harm* on the child by bringing it into existence. The claim is that bringing about a person's life in these circumstances would do violence to her ideals of creating and parenthood. She does not want to bring into existence a daughter she cannot love and care for; she does not want to bring into existence a person whose life will be marked by disrespect or rejection. In struggling with these issues, the worry is not that the child would have been better off never to have been born – as though children who are in the situations just mentioned have lives that aren't worth living[6]; it's that continuing a pregnancy in such circumstances would violate the woman's commitments of respectful creation.

Nor does the claim imply judgment on women who *do* continue pregnancies in similar circumstances – as though there were here an obligation to abort. For the norms in question need not be impersonally authoritative moral claims. Like ideals of good parenting, they mark out considerations all should be sensitive to, perhaps, but equally reasonable people may adhere to different variations and weightings. Still, they are normative for those who do have them; far from expressing mere matters of taste, the ideals one does accept carry an important kind of categoricity, issuing imperatives whose authority is not reducible to mere desire. These are, at root, issues about *integrity*, and the importance of maintaining integrity over one's participation in this enterprise precisely because it is so normatively weighty.

Some will protest the thought of our deciding such matters. We have no dominion, it will be said, to pick and choose the conditions under which human life, once started, proceeds. On what we might call a "stewardship" view of creation, in contrast, this dominion is precisely *part* of the responsibility involved in creation. It's a grave matter to end a developing human life by not aiding it; but it can be an equally grave decision to continue a process that will result in creation of a person. The present case, note, is thus importantly different from the other area of controversy over dominion over

life, namely, actions intending to hasten death. Whatever one thinks of that matter, it diverges in a key respect from abortion. When we stand by rather than hastening death, we are allowing a trajectory independent of us to proceed without our influence. Not to abort, though, *is* to do something else – namely, to create a person.

Gestation is *itself* a creative endeavor – not in the sense that its constitutive activities are each or mostly intentional (as if the issue were whether the pregnant woman, like an athlete, deserves credit for the bodily activity involved); but if personhood emerges through pregnancy, and one has choices about whether to continue pregnancy, then decisions to do so themselves involve norms of respect. And not all norms of respect for creation, it turns out, tell in favor of continuing.

None of this is to say that abortion is morally neutral. Abortion involves loss – not just loss of the hope various parties have invested in the pregnancy, but loss of something valuable in its own right. Abortion is thus a sober matter, an occasion, often, for moral emotions such as grief and regret. Given the value at stake, it is only fitting to feel grief – a sorrow that life begun is now ended, or to feel moral regret – that the actions needed to help these cells develop into a person would have compromised too significantly the life of someone who already was one. Such regret, that is, can signal appreciation of the fact, not that the action was indecent, but that decent actions sometimes involve loss.

It takes enormous investment to develop early human life into a human being. Understanding the morality of early abortion involves assessing not just welfare, but intimacy, not just destruction, but creation. With the profound respect we should have for burgeoning human life, we should acknowledge moral prerogatives over associations such as having another inhabit and use one's body in such an extraordinarily enmeshed way, over identity-constituting commitments and enterprises as profound as motherhood, and over the weighty responsibility of bringing a new person into the world.

Notes

1 At least, one of a couple weeks' standing: earlier blastocysts' trajectories turn out to be fascinatingly underdetermined. There is, for instance, no fact of the matter internal to its own cellular information as to whether a one-week blastocyst will be one person or more; and at very early stages there is no fact of the matter as to which cells will become the fetus and which will become the placenta.

2 RU-486, which essentially interrupts the production of progesterone needed to maintain a placenta, provides a good example of an abortion method that is more straightforwardly a "letting die" rather than an active killing.

3 Later abortions are thus multiply complicated: fetal status increases even as its dependencies decline. On the one hand, later fetuses much closer to, and at some stage likely count as, persons; on the other hand, they are no longer solely and fully dependent on gestational assistance for life, hence enlarging

possibilities for removing assistance without effecting death.

4 That is, the action is not simply a token that falls under an imperfect duty. It's a fascinating question how to parse the structure of imperfect duties, a question I here leave aside.

5 Of course, just how much "care" one must exert to avoid conception will be heartily contested. Those, like myself, who value spontaneity in sexual relations and have mild views about the value of burgeoning human life will advance something quite modest – urging, say, good faith attempts to use birth control if it is safe, easily obtained, and immediately convenient. Others will advance stringent principles indeed, requiring, say, that one ought not to have sex at all until one is prepared to parent.

6 My thanks to Adrienne Asche for this way of putting the point.

Further Reading

Callahan, J. (986) "The Fetus and Fundamental Rights," *Commonweal*, April 11, 1986: 203–9.

Crittenden, A. (2001) *The Price of Motherhood*. New York: Henry Holt and Co.

Denes, M. (1976) *In Necessity and Sorrow: Life and Death in an Abortion Hospital*, New York: Basic Books, Inc.

Dworkin, R. (1993) *Life's Dominion: An Argument about Abortion, Euthanasia, and Individual Freedom*. New York: Alfred A. Knopf.

Dwyer, S. and J. Feinberg (eds.) (1997) *The Problem of Abortion*, 3rd edn. Belmont, CA: Wadsworth Pub.

Feinberg, J. (1992) "Abortion." In his *Freedom and Fulfillment: Philosophical Essays*. Princeton, NJ: Princeton University Press.

Hursthouse, R. (1987). *Beginning Lives*. Oxford: Open University.

MacKinnon, C. A. (1991) "Reflections on Sex Equality under Law," *The Yale Law Journal* 100:5 (March 1991): 1281–328, p. 1314.

McDonaugh, E. (1996) *Breaking the Abortion Deadlock: From Choice to Consent*. New York: Oxford University Press.

Quinn, W. (1993) "Abortion: Identity and Loss." In his *Morality and Action*. New York: Cambridge University Press.

Steinbock, B. (1992) *Life Before Birth: The Moral and Legal Status of Embryos and Fetuses*. New York: Oxford University Press.

Wertheimer, R. (1974) "Understanding the Abortion Argument." In M. Cohen, T. Nagel, and T. Scanlon (eds.), *The Rights and Wrongs of Abortion*. Princeton: Princeton University Press, pp. 23–51.

West, R. (1993) "Jurisprudence and Gender." In D. Kelly Weisberg (ed.), *Feminist Legal Theory: Foundations*. Philadelphia: Temple University Press, pp. 75–98.

References

Kamm, F. M. (1992) *Creation and Abortion: A Study in Moral and Legal Philosophy*. New York: Oxford University Press.

Rothman, B. K. (1989) *Recreating Motherhood: Ideology and Technology in a Patriarchal Society*. New York: Norton.

Silverstein, H. S. (1987) "On a Woman's 'Responsibility' for the Fetus," *Social Theory and Practice* 13: 103–19.

Thomson, J. J. (1971) "A Defense of Abortion," *Philosophy and Public Affairs* 1: 47–66.

13

Virtue Theory and Abortion

Rosalind Hursthouse

Virtue ethics is now widely recognized as a rival to deontological and utilitarian theories. With recognition has come criticism, much of which betrays an inadequate understanding of the theory's structure or of how it is to be applied. In the first half of this chapter I argue (very briefly) against eight standard criticisms of virtue ethics; in the second half, I aim to deepen our understanding of the theory by illustrating how it might be applied to a particular issue, namely, abortion.

Virtue Theory

I offer a framework that exposes some of the essential similarities and differences between virtue ethics and some versions of deontological and utilitarian theories. I begin with a rough sketch of the latter two, whose familiarity will provide a helpful contrast with virtue theory. Suppose a deontological theory begins with a premise specifying right action.

P.1 An action is right if and only if it is in accordance with a correct moral rule or principle.

This is a purely formal specification, forging a link between the concepts of *right action* and *moral rule*, and gives one no guidance until one

knows what a correct moral rule is. So the next thing the theory needs is a premise about that:

P.2 A correct moral rule is one that . . .

In many current versions of deontology, an acceptable completion of P.2 would be something like

(i) is required by rationality

or

(ii) would command rational acceptance from behind the veil of ignorance

and so on. Such a specification forges a second conceptual link, between the concepts of *moral rule* and *rationality*.

This skeleton of deontological theory links *right action, moral rule*, and *rationality*. The same basic structure can be discerned in act-utilitarianism.

Act-utilitarianism begins with a premise that specifies right action.

P.1 An action is right if and only if it promotes the best consequences.

It thereby forges a link between the concepts of *right action* and *consequences*. It goes on to specify what the best consequences are in its second premise:

P.2 The best consequences are those in which happiness is maximized.

It thereby forges a link between *consequences* and *happiness*.

Now let us consider what a skeletal virtue theory looks like. It begins with a specification of right action:

P.1 An action is right if and only if it is what a virtuous agent would, characteristically, do in the circumstances.

This, like the first premises of the other two sorts of theory, is a purely formal principle, giving one no guidance as to what to do, which forges a conceptual link between *right action* and *virtuous agent*. Like the other theories, it must, of course, go on to specify what the latter is. The first step toward this may appear quite trivial, but is needed to correct a prevailing tendency among many critics to define the virtuous agent as one who is disposed to act in accordance with a deontologist's moral rules.

P.1a A virtuous agent is one who acts virtuously, that is, one who has and exercises the virtues.

This subsidiary premise makes room for a non-deontological second premise:

P.2 A virtue is a character trait a human being needs to flourish or live well.

This premise forges a conceptual link between *virtue* and *flourishing* (or living well or *eudaimonia*). And just as deontology, in theory, goes on to argue that each favored moral rule meets its specification, so virtue ethics, in theory, goes on to argue that each favored character trait meets its.

Seven criticisms briskly dismissed

(i) *Flourishing* (or *eudaimonia*) is an obscure concept, so virtue theory is obscure in a way the other theories are not. I think this is clearly false. Both *rationality* and *happiness*, as they figure in their respective theories, are rich and difficult concepts – hence all the disputes about the various tests for a rule's being rational, and about what constitutes happiness.

(ii) The theory is trivially circular. This is a misunderstanding. Virtue ethics does not specify right action in terms of the virtuous agent and then immediately specify the virtuous agent in terms of right action. Rather, it specifies her

in terms of the virtues, and then specifies these, not merely as dispositions to right action, but as the character traits (which are dispositions to feel and react as well as act in certain ways) required for *eudaimonia*.

(iii) It does not answer the question "What should I do?" because

(iv) It does not come up with any rules or principles. Another misunderstanding. It does answer this question and, to a certain extent, by coming up with rules or principles. Every virtue generates a positive instruction (act justly, kindly, courageously, honestly, etc.) and every vice a prohibition (do not act unjustly, cruelly, like a coward, dishonestly, etc.) So trying to decide what to do within the framework of virtue theory does not require asking what one's favored candidate for a virtuous person would do in these circumstances (as if the raped 15-year-old girl were supposed to ask "Would Socrates have an abortion if he were in my circumstances?") The agent asks herself "If I were to do such and such now, would I be acting justly or unjustly (or neither), kindly or unkindly [and so on]?"

(v) Virtue ethics cannot define all our moral concepts in terms of the virtuous agent. Another misunderstanding; no virtue theorist who takes her inspiration from Aristotle would even contemplate aiming at such reductionism.[1] For example, a charitable or benevolent person is concerned with the good of others. That concept of *good is related to the concept of evil or harm, and both are related to the concepts of the worthwhile, the advantageous, and the pleasant.* Virtue ethics aims to relate these concepts to that of the virtuous agent (she is the one who has the correct conception of them) but not to define them away.

(vi) We do not know which character traits are the virtues, and disagreements about the virtues are particularly subject to the threat of moral skepticism, "pluralism," or cultural relativism. True, perhaps, but the parallel roles played by the second premises of both deontological and virtue theories show that both have this problem. Rule deontologists know they want to get "don't kill," "keep promises," "cherish your children," among the rules their theory sanctions. Yet they know that any of these can be disputed, that some philosopher may claim that it is "rational" to reject any one of them. Similarly, the virtue theorists know that they want to get justice, charity fidelity, courage, and so on as character traits needed for *eudaimonia*, and they know that any of these can be disputed.

This is a problem for both theories, and the virtue theorist certainly does not find it any harder to argue against moral skepticism, "pluralism," or cultural relativism than does the deontologist. Each theory has to stick out its neck and say, in some cases, "This person/these people/other cultures are (or would be) in error," and find some grounds for saying this. Utilitarianism initially fares somewhat better but, I would maintain, is eventually landed with the same problem when disputes about the nature of happiness (especially those that are grounded in religious belief) break out.

(vii) Virtue ethics has unresolvable conflicts built into it. "It is common knowledge," it is said, "that the requirements of the virtues can conflict; charity may prompt me to end the frightful suffering of the person in my care by killing him, but justice bids me to stay my hand, since he says he does not want to die. To tell my dedicated graduate student that he will never succeed as a philosopher would be honest, but it would be kinder to keep quiet about it."

The obvious reply is that deontology notoriously faces the same conflicts. These arise not only from conflicts between rules, but also from the fact that a rule (e.g., preserve life) can apparently yield contrary instructions in a particular case.[2] Although this is a problem for virtue theory, it is not unique to it, and act-utilitarianism, notoriously, avoids the problem only by resolving various moral dilemmas in ways that non-utilitarians find hair-raising.

A major criticism

The eighth criticism – perhaps because it reflects a general discomfort with the theory – is difficult to state clearly. But here is an attempt:

> Virtue theory can't help us resolve real moral issues. The virtue theorist can only assert her claims; she

cannot defend them. The best action-guiding rules she can offer (such as "act charitably," "don't act cruelly") rely on the virtue concepts, and these concepts presuppose concepts such as the good, the worthwhile, and so on. Consequently, any virtue theorist writing about real moral issues must assume that her audience agrees with her application of these concepts while other virtue theorists may apply them differently and reach different conclusions. Within the terms of the theory we cannot adjudicate between them.

I shall divide this criticism into two objections. The first concerns the virtue theorist's use of the concepts enshrined in her rules – act charitably, honestly, and so on – and the second, her use of concepts such as the *worthwhile*. Each objection relies on a certain condition of adequacy for a normative moral theory, a condition of adequacy, that once made explicit, is utterly implausible.

It is true that, when discussing moral issues, the virtue theorist must assert that certain actions are honest, dishonest, or neither; charitable, uncharitable, or neither. Certainly this is often difficult to decide. However, this is a telling criticism of virtue theory only if we assume that an adequate action-guiding theory must give clear and easily comprehensible instructions on how to act. But this is an implausible demand. The correct condition of adequacy – which virtue theory emphatically meets – is that it should encapsulate Aristotle's insight: that moral knowledge cannot be acquired merely by attending lectures, nor can we find it in people with little experience of life. Young people might be mathematical geniuses, but they will rarely, if ever, be moral geniuses. This tells us something significant about the nature of moral knowledge. Acting rightly *is* difficult and calls for moral wisdom. Virtue ethics captures this by relying on rules whose application manifestly may require the most delicate and sensitive judgment.[3]

Suppose someone "youthful in character," misapplies the relevant terms and mistakenly infers that she faces a real conflict. Then she will not be able to decide what to do (unless she knows a virtuous agent from whom to seek guidance). But her quandary is (*ex hypothesi*) the result of her lack of wisdom and just what virtue theory expects. Someone who hesitates to reveal a hurtful truth because she thinks it would be kind to lie, may need to realize, in these particular circumstances, not that kindness is more (or less) important than honesty or justice, nor that honesty or justice sometimes require one to act unkindly or cruelly, but that one does people no kindness by concealing this sort of truth from them, hurtful as it may be. This is the type of thing people with moral wisdom know, involving the correct application of *kind*, and that people without such wisdom find difficult.

What about the virtue theorist's reliance on concepts such as the worthwhile? Is this a problem for the theory? If it is, it must be because the objector thinks any good normative theory should provide guidance to real moral issues without in any way employing claims about what is worthwhile. Now although people are initially inclined to reject the claim that the practical conclusions of a normative moral theory must rely on premises about what is truly worthwhile, the alternative, once it is made explicit, may look even more unacceptable. Consider what this condition of adequacy entails. If truths about what is good, serious, or worthwhile in human life are irrelevant to resolving real moral issues, then I could sensibly seek guidance from someone who claimed to know nothing about such matters, or from someone who had opinions about them but claimed that they had no determining role in her advice.

Let us remember that we are talking about real moral issues and real guidance; I want to know whether I should have an abortion, take my mother off the life-support machine, leave academic life and become a doctor in the Third World, tell my father he has cancer. Would I go for advice to someone who says she has no views about what is worthwhile in life? Or to someone who says she thinks that the only thing that matters is having a good time but that her normative theory is quite independent of this belief? Surely this is absurd. The relevant condition of adequacy should be that the practical conclusions of a normative theory must rely, in part, on premises about what is worthwhile, import-

ant, and so on. Thus I reject this "major criticism" of virtue theory.

As promised, I now turn to the discussion of applying virtue theory to abortion. Before I embark on this tendentious business, I should remind the reader of my aims. I am not trying to solve "the problem of abortion"; I am illustrating how virtue theory directs us to think about it. Moreover, I am not assuming that all of my readers will agree with everything I say. On the contrary, given the plausible assumption that some are morally wiser than I am, and some less so, virtue ethics *expects* disagreement. For instance, we may well disagree about the particular application of some of the virtue and vice terms; and we may disagree about what is worthwhile or serious, worthless or trivial. But my aim is to make clear how these concepts might be employed in discussing abortion.

Abortion

As everyone knows, the morality of abortion is commonly discussed in relation to just two considerations: first, the status of the fetus and whether or not it is the sort of thing that may or may not be innocuously or justifiably killed; second, and less predominantly (when, that is, the discussion concerns the morality of abortion rather than the question of permissible legislation in a just society), women's rights. If one thinks within this familiar framework, one may well be puzzled about what virtue theory, as such, could contribute. Some people assume the discussion will be conducted solely in terms of what the virtuous agent would or would not do (cf. the third, fourth, and fifth criticisms above). Others assume that only justice, or at most justice and charity, will be applied to the issue, generating a discussion similar to Judith Jarvis Thomson's.[4]

Now if this is the way the virtue theorist's discussion of abortion is imagined to be, no wonder people think little of it. It seems obvious in advance that in any such discussion there must be either a great deal of extremely tendentious application of the terms just, charitable, and so on or a lot of rhetorical appeal to "this is what only the virtuous agent knows." But these are caricatures; they fail to appreciate the way in which virtue theory quite transforms the discussion of abortion by dismissing the two familiar dominating considerations as, in a way, fundamentally irrelevant. In what ways, I hope to make both clear and plausible.

Let us first consider women's rights. Let me emphasize again that we are discussing the morality of abortion, not the rights and wrongs of laws prohibiting or permitting it. If we suppose that women do have a moral right to do as they choose with their own bodies, or, more particularly, to terminate their pregnancies, then it may well follow that a law forbidding abortion would be unjust. Indeed, even if they have no such right, such a law might be, as things stand at the moment, unjust, or impractical, or inhumane: on this issue I have nothing to say in this article. But, putting all questions about the justice or injustice of laws to one side, and supposing only that women have such a moral right, nothing follows from this supposition about the morality of abortion, according to virtue theory, once it is noted (quite generally, not with particular reference to abortion) that in exercising a moral right I can do something cruel, or callous, or selfish, light-minded, self-righteous, stupid, inconsiderate, disloyal, dishonest – that is, act viciously. Love and friendship do not survive their parties' constantly insisting on their rights, nor do people live well when they think that getting what they have a right to is of preeminent importance; they harm others, and they harm themselves. So whether women have a moral right to terminate their pregnancies is irrelevant within virtue theory, for it is irrelevant to the question "In having an abortion in these circumstances, would the agent be acting virtuously or viciously or neither?"

What about the consideration of the status of the fetus – what can virtue theory say about that? Isn't this a metaphysical question, and an extremely difficult one at that? Must virtue theory then wait upon metaphysics to come up with the answer?

At first sight it might seem so. For virtue is said to involve knowledge, and part of this knowledge consists in having the right – i.e.,

accurate, true – attitude to things. And this suggests that if the status of the fetus is relevant to the rightness or wrongness of abortion, its status must be known, as a truth, to the fully wise and virtuous person.

But the sort of wisdom that the fully virtuous person has is not supposed to be recondite; it does not call for fancy philosophical sophistication, and it does not depend upon, let alone wait upon, the discoveries of academic philosophers. And this entails the following, rather startling, conclusion: that the status of the fetus – that issue over which so much ink has been spilt – is, according to virtue theory, simply not relevant to the rightness or wrongness of abortion (within, that is, a secular morality).

Or rather, since that is clearly too radical a conclusion, it is in a sense relevant, but only in the sense that the familiar biological facts are relevant. By "the familiar biological facts" I mean those that we are familiar with – that, standardly (but not invariably), pregnancy occurs as the result of sexual intercourse, that it lasts about nine months, during which time the fetus grows and develops, that standardly it terminates in the birth of a living baby, and that this is how we come to be.

It might be thought that this distinction – between the familiar biological facts and the status of the fetus – is a distinction without a difference. But this is not so. To attach relevance to the status of the fetus, in the way in which virtue theory rejects, is to be gripped by the conviction that we must go beyond the familiar biological facts, deriving some sort of conclusion from them, such as that the fetus has rights, or is not a person, or something similar. It is also to believe that this exhausts the relevance of the familiar biological facts, that all they are relevant to is the status of the fetus and whether or not it is the sort of thing that may or may not be killed.

These convictions have resulted in what should surely strike any nonphilosopher as a most bizarre aspect of nearly all the current philosophical literature on abortion, namely, that, far from treating abortion as a unique moral problem, markedly unlike any other, nearly everything written on the status of the fetus and its bearing on the abortion issue would be consistent with the human reproductive facts (to say nothing of family life) being totally different from what they are. Imagine that you are an alien extraterrestrial anthropologist who does not know that the human race is roughly 50 percent female and 50 percent male, or that our only (natural) form of reproduction involves heterosexual intercourse, viviparous birth, and the female's (and only the female's) being pregnant for nine months, or that females are capable of childbearing from late childhood to late middle age, or that childbearing is painful, dangerous, and emotionally charged – do you think you would pick up these facts from the hundreds of articles written on the status of the fetus? I am quite sure you would not. And that, I think, shows that the current philosophical literature on abortion has got badly out of touch with reality.

Now if we are using virtue theory, our first question is not "What do the familiar biological facts show – what can be derived from them about the status of the fetus?" but "How do these facts figure in the practical reasoning, actions and passions, thoughts and reactions, of the virtuous and the nonvirtuous? What is the mark of having the right attitude to these facts and what manifests having the wrong attitude to them?" This immediately makes essentially relevant not only all the facts about human reproduction I mentioned above, but a whole range of facts about our emotions in relation to them as well. I mean such facts as that human parents, both male and female, tend to care passionately about their offspring, and that family relationships are among the deepest and strongest in our lives – and, significantly, among the longest-lasting.

These facts make it obvious that pregnancy is not just one among many other physical conditions; and hence that anyone who believes that an abortion is comparable to a haircut or appendectomy is mistaken. The fact that the premature termination of a pregnancy is, in some sense, the cutting off of a new human life, and thereby connects with our thoughts about the procreation of a new human life, and about death, parenthood, and family relationships,

must make it a serious matter. To disregard this fact, to think of abortion as nothing but the killing of something that does not matter, or as nothing but the exercise of some right one has, or as the incidental means to some desirable state of affairs, is to do something callous and light-minded, the sort of thing that no virtuous and wise person would do. It is to have the wrong attitude not only to fetuses, but more generally to human life and death, parenthood, and family relationships.

Although I say that the facts make this obvious, I know that this is one of my tendentious points. In partial support of it I note that even the most dedicated proponents of the view that deliberate abortion is just like an appendectomy or haircut rarely hold the same view of spontaneous abortion, that is, miscarriage. It is not so tendentious of me to claim that to react to people's grief over miscarriage by saying, or even thinking, "What a fuss about nothing!" would be callous and light-minded, whereas to try to laugh someone out of grief over an appendectomy scar or a botched haircut would not be.

To say that the cutting off of a human life is always a matter of some seriousness, at any stage, is not to deny the relevance of gradual fetal development. Notwithstanding the well-worn point that clear boundary lines cannot be drawn, our emotions and attitudes regarding the fetus do change as it develops, and again when it is born, and indeed further as the baby grows. Abortion for shallow reasons in the later stages is much more shocking than abortion for the same reasons in the early stages in a way that matches the fact that deep grief over miscarriage in the later stages is more appropriate than it is over miscarriage in the earlier stages (when, that is, the grief is solely about the loss of this child, not about, as might be the case, the loss of one's only hope of having a child or of having one's husband's child). Imagine a woman who already has children; who finds herself unexpectedly pregnant. Though contrary to her plans, the pregnancy, once established, is welcomed – and then she loses the embryo almost immediately. If this were bemoaned as a tragedy, it would, I think, be a misapplication of the concept of what is tragic. But it may still properly be mourned as a loss. The grief is expressed in such terms as "I shall always wonder how she or he would have turned out" or "When I look at the others, I shall think, 'How different their lives would have been if this other had been part of them.' " It would, I take it, be callous and light-minded to say, or think, "Well she has already got four children; what's the problem?"; it would be neither, nor arrogantly intrusive in the case of a close friend, to try to correct prolonged mourning by saying, "I know it's sad, but it's not a tragedy; rejoice in the ones you have." The application of *tragic* becomes more appropriate as the fetus grows, for the mere fact that one has lived with it for longer, conscious of its existence, makes a difference. To shrug off an early abortion is understandable just because it is very hard to be fully conscious of the fetus's existence in the early stages and hence hard to appreciate that an early abortion is the destruction of life. It is particularly hard for the young and inexperienced to appreciate this, because appreciation of it usually comes only with age and experience.

The fact that pregnancy is not just one among many physical conditions does not mean that one can never regard it in that light without manifesting a vice. When women are in very poor physical health, or worn out from childbearing, or forced to do very physically demanding jobs, then they cannot be described as self-indulgent, callous, irresponsible, or light-minded if they seek abortions mainly with a view to avoiding pregnancy as the physical condition that it is. To go through with a pregnancy when one is utterly exhausted, or when one's job consists of crawling along tunnels hauling coal, as women in the nineteenth century were obliged to do, is perhaps heroic, but people who do not achieve heroism are not necessarily vicious. That they can view the pregnancy only as eight months of misery, followed by agony and exhaustion, and abortion only as the blessed escape from this prospect, is entirely understandable and does not manifest any lack of serious respect for human life or a shallow attitude to motherhood. What it does show is that something is terribly amiss in the conditions of their lives, which make it so hard to recognize pregnancy and childbearing as the good that they can be.

The foregoing discussion, in sofar as it emphasizes the right attitude to human life and death, parallels those standard discussions of abortion that concentrate on it solely as an issue of killing. But it does not, as those discussions do, gloss over the fact, emphasized by those who discuss the morality of abortion in terms of women's rights, that abortion, wildly unlike any other form of killing, is the termination of a pregnancy, which is a condition of a woman's body and results in her having a child if it is not aborted. This fact is given due recognition not by appeal to women's rights but by emphasizing the relevance of the familiar biological and psychological facts and their connection with having the right attitude to parenthood and family relationships. But it may well be thought that failing to bring in women's rights still leaves some important aspects of the problem of abortion untouched.

Speaking in terms of women's rights, people sometimes say, "Well, it's her life you're talking about too, you know; she's got a right to her own life, her own happiness." And the discussion stops there. But in the context of virtue theory, given that we are particularly concerned with what constitutes a good human life, with what true happiness or *eudaimonia* is, this is no place to stop. We go on to ask, "And is this life of hers a good one? Is she living well?"

If we are to go on to talk about living well, in the context of abortion, we have to bring in our thoughts about the value of love and family life, and our proper emotional development through a natural life cycle. The familiar facts support the view that parenthood in general, and motherhood and childbearing in particular, are intrinsically worthwhile, are amongst the things that can be correctly thought to be partially constitutive of a flourishing human life. If this is right, then a woman who opts for not being a mother (at all, or again, or now) by opting for abortion may thereby be manifesting a flawed grasp of what her life should be about – a grasp that is childish, or grossly materialistic, or shortsighted, or shallow.

I said "*may* thereby": this need not be so. Consider, for instance, a woman who has already had several children and fears that to have another will seriously affect her capacity to be a good mother to the ones she has – she does not show a lack of appreciation of the intrinsic value of being a parent by opting for abortion. Nor does a woman who has been a good mother and is approaching the age at which she may be looking forward to being a good grandmother. Nor does a woman who discovers that her pregnancy may well kill her, and opts for abortion and adoption. Nor, necessarily, does a woman who has decided to lead a life centered around some other worthwhile activity or activities with which motherhood would compete.

People who are childless by choice are sometimes described as "irresponsible," or "selfish," or "refusing to grow up," or "not knowing what life is all about." But one can hold that having children is intrinsically worthwhile without endorsing this, for we are, after all, in the happy position of there being more worthwhile things to do than can be fitted into one lifetime. Parenthood, and motherhood in particular, even if granted to be intrinsically worthwhile, undoubtedly take up a lot of one's adult life, leaving no room for some other worthwhile pursuits. But some women who choose abortion rather than have their first child are not avoiding motherhood for the sake of other worthwhile pursuits, but for the worthless one of "having a good time," or for the pursuit of some false vision of the ideals of freedom or self-realization. And some others who say "I am not ready for parenthood yet" are making some sort of mistake about the extent to which one can manipulate the circumstances of one's life so as to make it fulfill some dream that one has. Perhaps one's dream is to have two perfect children, a girl and a boy, within a perfect marriage, in financially secure circumstances, with an interesting job of one's own. But to care too much about that dream, to demand of life that it give it to one and act accordingly, may be both greedy and foolish, and is to run the risk of missing out on happiness entirely. Not only may fate make the dream impossible, or destroy it, but one's own attachment to it may make it impossible. Good marriages, and the most promising children, can be destroyed by just one adult's excessive demand for perfection.

Once again, this is not to deny that girls may quite properly say "I am not ready for motherhood yet," especially in our society, and, far from manifesting irresponsibility or light-mindedness, show an appropriate modesty or humility, or a fearfulness that does not amount to cowardice. However, even when the decision to have an abortion is the right decision – one that does not itself fall under a vice-related term and thereby one that the perfectly virtuous could recommend – it does not follow that there is no sense in which having the abortion is wrong, or guilt inappropriate. For, by virtue of the fact that a human life has been cut short, some evil has probably been brought about, and that circumstances make the decision to bring about some evil the right decision will be a ground for guilt if getting into those circumstances in the first place itself manifested a flaw in character.

What "gets one into those circumstances" in the case of abortion is, except in the case of rape, one's sexual activity and one's choices, or the lack of them, about one's sexual partner and about contraception. The virtuous woman (which here of course does not mean simply "chaste woman" but "woman with the virtues") has such character traits as strength, independence, resoluteness, decisiveness, self-confidence, responsibility, serious-mindedness, and self-determination – and no one, I think, could deny that many women become pregnant in circumstances in which they cannot welcome or cannot face the thought of having this child precisely because they lack one or some of these character traits. So, even in the cases where the decision to have an abortion is the right one, it can still be the reflection of a moral failing – not because the decision itself is weak or cowardly or irresolute or irresponsible or light-minded, but because lack of the requisite opposite of these failings landed one in the circumstances in the first place. Hence the common universalized claim that guilt and remorse are never appropriate emotions about abortion is denied.

They may be appropriate, and appropriately inculcated, even when the decision was the right one.

Another motivation for bringing women's rights into the discussion may be to attempt to correct the implication, carried by the killing-centered approach, that insofar as abortion is wrong, it is a wrong that only women do, or at least (given the preponderance of male doctors) that only women instigate. I do not myself believe that we can thus escape the fact that nature bears harder on women that it does on men, but virtue theory can certainly correct many of the injustices that the emphasis on women's rights is rightly concerned about. With very little amendment, everything that has been said above applies to boys and men too. Although the abortion decision is, in a natural sense, the woman's decision, proper to her, boys and men are often party to it, for well or ill, and even when they are not, they are bound to have been party to the circumstances that brought it up. No less than girls and women, boys and men can, in their actions, manifest self-centeredness, callousness, and light-mindedness about life and parenthood in relation to abortion. They can be self-centered or courageous about the possibility of disability in their offspring; they need to reflect on their sexual activity and their choices, or the lack of them, about their sexual partner and contraception; they need to grow up and take responsibility for their own actions and life in relation to fatherhood. If it is true, as I maintain, that insofar as motherhood is intrinsically worthwhile, being a mother is an important purpose in women's lives, being a father (rather than a mere generator) is an important purpose in men's lives too, and it is adolescent of men to turn a blind eye to this and pretend that they have many more important things to do.

Conclusion

Much more might be said, but I shall end the actual discussion of the problem of abortion here, and conclude by highlighting what I take to be its significant features. These hark back to many of the criticisms of virtue theory discussed earlier.

The discussion does not proceed simply by our trying to answer the question "Would a perfectly virtuous agent ever have an abortion and, if so, when?"; virtue theory is not limited to considering "Would Socrates have had an abortion if he were a raped, pregnant fifteen-year-old?" nor automatically stumped when we are considering circumstances into which no virtuous agent would have got herself. Instead, much of the discussion proceeds in the virtue- and vice-related terms whose application, in several cases, yields practical conclusions (cf. the third and fourth criticisms above). These terms are difficult to apply correctly, and anyone might challenge my application of any one of them. So, for example, I have claimed that some abortions, done for certain reasons, would be callous or light-minded; that others might indicate an appropriate modesty or humility; that others would reflect a greedy and foolish attitude to what one could expect out of life. Any of these examples may be disputed, but what is at issue is, should these difficult terms be there, or should the discussion be couched in terms that all clever adolescents can apply directly? (Cf. the first half of the "major criticism" above.)

Proceeding as it does in the virtue- and vice-related terms, the discussion thereby, inevitably, also contains claims about what is worthwhile, serious and important, good and evil, in our lives. So, for example, I claimed that parenthood is intrinsically worthwhile, and that having a good time was a worthless end (in life, not on individual occasions); that losing a fetus is always a serious matter (albeit not a tragedy in itself in the first trimester) whereas acquiring an appendectomy scar is a trivial one; that (human) death is an evil. Once again, these are difficult matters, and anyone might challenge any one of my claims. But what is at issue is, as before, should those difficult claims be there or can one reach practical conclusions about real moral issues that are in no way determined by premises about such matters? (Cf. the fifth criticism, and the second half of the "major criticism.")

The discussion also thereby, inevitably, contains claims about what life is like (e.g., my claim that love and friendship do not survive their parties' constantly insisting on their rights; or the claim that to demand perfection of life is to fun the risk of missing out on happiness entirely). What is at issue is, should those disputable claims be there, or is our knowledge (or are our false opinions) about what life is like irrelevant to our understanding of real moral issues? (Cf. both halves of the "major criticism.")

Naturally, my own view is that all these concepts should be there in any discussion of real moral issues and that virtue theory, which uses all of them, is the right theory to apply to them. I do not pretend to have shown this. I realize that proponents of rival theories may say that, now that they have understood how virtue theory uses the range of concepts it draws on, they are more convinced than ever that such concepts should not figure in an adequate normative theory, because they are sectarian, or vague, or too particular, or improperly anthropocentric, and reinstate what I called the "major criticism." Or, finding many of the details of the discussion appropriate, they may agree that such concepts should be present but argue that their theory provides a better account of how they fit in. (That would be interesting to see.) Moreover, I admitted that there were at least two problems for virtue theory: that it has to argue against moral skepticism, "pluralism," and cultural relativism, and that it has to find something to say about conflicting requirements of different virtues. Proponents of rival theories might argue that their favored theory provides better solutions to these problems than virtue theory can.

Defending virtue theory against all possible, or even likely, criticisms of it would be a lifelong task. I have aimed to defend it against some that I thought arose from an inadequate understanding of it, and to improve that understanding. If I have succeeded, we may hope for more comprehending criticisms of virtue theory than have appeared hitherto.

Notes

This is a considerably abridged version of "Virtue Theory and Abortion," *Philosophy and Public Affairs* 20 (1991): 223–46.

1 Cf. Bernard Williams' point in *Ethics and the Limits of Philosophy* (London: William Collins, 1985) that we need an enriched ethical vocabulary, not a cutdown one.

2 E.g., in Williams' Jim and Pedro case in J. J. C. Smart and Bernard Williams, *Utilitarianism: For and Against* (London: Cambridge University Press, 1973).

3 Aristotle, *Nicomachean Ethics* 1142a12–16.

4 Judith Jarvis Thompson, "A Defence of Abortion," *Philosophy & Public Affairs* 1, no. 1 (Fall 1971): 47–6.

Animals

Many people think the morality of abortion hinges entirely on the nature of the fetus: that once we know its moral status, then we will know if abortion is moral and if it ought to be legal. Several authors in the previous section repudiated this rendition of the debate. Nonetheless, it is safe to say that the moral status of the fetus is *an* element of that debate. Parallel questions play a significant role in determining our moral obligations, if any, to non-human animals. Do non-human animals have substantial or full moral status? If so, why? If not, why not? A central tenet of morality is that we should treat like cases alike. That is, morality requires that we should treat two creatures the same unless there is some general and relevant difference between them that morally justifies a difference in treatment. Thus, I can properly treat a pebble differently than I treat my friend George, because George and the pebble are relevantly different, different in ways that justify a difference in treatment.

We know there are serious moral limitations on how we should treat humans. We generally have no moral qualms about what we do to and with pebbles. What about non-human animals? Are they more like the pebble or more like George? Seems they are more like us in all sorts of important ways: they are alive, most of them are capable of suffering, some can arguably think and even have emotions. Are they sufficiently like us that they merit moral status? If so, how much status? Or are non-human animals sufficiently different from us that we can treat them as we wish, in the ways we might treat a pebble?

Of course, since not all animals are the same, it would be more precise to ask how we should treat those non-human animals (mostly mammals and birds) that we standardly use for food, for product and biomedical testing, and for their skins. Once, people assumed these animals had no moral worth – that we could morally do to them whatever we wanted, whenever we wanted, for any reason we wanted. For instance, nineteenth-century scientists would demonstrate the circulation of the blood by nailing a fully conscious dog to a large board, and then dissecting it. They cavalierly dismissed the dog's yelps as squeaks in the animal "machine."

Most philosophers, scientists, and laypeople have long since abandoned those views. Virtually everyone now agrees that it would be wrong to torture or kill (at least) a mammal or bird just for fun. Certainly all the authors in this section would agree. The issue for them is not whether these animals have moral status, but rather how much status they have – and why.

In the section on ABORTION, the authors disagreed about the proper criteria for moral status. One strong strand of popular opinion holds that a fetus has moral status because it is a human being. In contrast, Warren thought only persons had moral status, while Marquis thought only creatures with a Future Like Ours had moral status. Although the authors discussing animals do not use the same criteria of moral status, their criteria do resemble those used in the abortion debate.

For instance, Fox claims that only creatures who have rights and responsibilities can have full moral status, can be members of the moral community. Moreover, only creatures with critical self-awareness and the ability to manipulate complex concepts can have rights and responsibilities. That is why, on his view, humans – but not animals – are members of the moral community. Although his criteria of moral status are stronger than Warren's, they are conceptual kin.

Regan, though, argues that Fox's (and therefore Warren's) criteria are too stringent. Were we to adopt such rigorous criteria of moral status, we would exclude many humans (infants and retarded adults, etc.) from the moral community. Regan claims that infants and retarded adults have moral status although they are neither full persons (in Warren's sense) nor moral agents. Rather, they are moral patients – creatures who have morally significant interests, even if they cannot protect or even advocate those interests themselves. Moral patients must rely on others (moral agents) to speak for them. On his view, animals, like infants and retarded humans, are moral patients.

Why, exactly, does Regan think animals are moral patients? They are, he claims, "subjects of a life": they have a life that matters to them. This criterion of moral status is at least reminiscent of Marquis's. Both philosophers claim some creatures have serious moral status even if they do not have a hint of moral agency.

Although he does not employ the language of "moral status," Singer would claim all the aforementioned criteria are too strict. He thinks creatures deserve moral consideration if they can suffer. Since many non-human animals can suffer, then they have moral status, they have interests we should morally consider. For him the central ethical question is: how heavily should we weigh their interests, and how much moral status do they have? Do they have equal status with humans?

Suppose we can alleviate the suffering of only one of the following: a college professor, an infant, or an adult with Down's Syndrome. Whom should we assist? Singer would claim that even if we couldn't decide on the best answer, we know full well that some answers would be unacceptable. It would be morally intolerable to favor the college professor simply because she is more intelligent, autonomous, or learned than the others. Equality demands that the similar suffering of each counts similarly. That is true whether we are comparing the college professor with the infant, or whether we are comparing the infant to a rat.

Frey acknowledges the moral importance of suffering and grants the importance of equality. Like Singer, he is an act utilitarian who claims we should maximize the greatest happiness of the greatest number. Since non-human animals suffer, then they, as well as humans, count morally. "Higher" animals (mammals and birds) deserve additional moral respect because they have cognitive and emotional abilities that make them even more similar to us. That is why, Frey argues, there are moral limits on what we can do to animals. They are not ours to use however we wish.

Nonetheless, Frey interprets the demands of equality rather differently than does Singer. Since animals are not as cognitively or emotionally sophisticated as (most) humans, then their lives are not as rich. A creature's moral status, Frey claims, varies according to the richness of its life. Since (most) animals' lives are not as rich as the lives of (most) humans, then equality does not require that we treat them the same. Put differently, although they count morally, they do not count as much as normal humans.

Consequently, we can use non-human animals for our purposes, if the benefits of using them outweigh the costs. Of course, as a consistent utilitarian, Frey claims we could also use humans if the benefits are substantial enough, and the costs sufficiently slight. This vividly illustrates a profound difference between consequentialists and deontologists. Deontologists claim there are things we can't do to creatures with moral standing (usually humans) even if the action had substantial benefits for others. Most consequentialists disagree, and their disagreement is related to the purported moral difference between acts and omissions (recall the discussion in the section on eutha-nasia). If by failing to act, I permit more evil than I would cause by acting, then I should act, no matter how objectionable that action might seem. If I fail to act, then I am failing to act in a way that maximizes the greatest happiness for the greatest number. For instance, if experimenting on a seriously retarded human would produce a cure for AIDS, and there is no other way to find that cure and there are no countervailing costs, then Frey would claim we should experiment on the human. If we do not experiment, then we will permit more evil than we would cause by doing it.

Further Reading

Carruthers, P. (1992) *The Animals Issue*. Cambridge: Cambridge University Press.

Clark, S. (1977) *The Moral Status of Animals*. Oxford: Oxford University Press.

Fox, M. (1986) *The Case for Animal Experimentation*. Berkeley: University of California Press.

Frey, R. (1983) *Rights, Killing, and Suffering*. Oxford: Blackwell Publishers.

—— (1980) *Rights and Interests*. Oxford: Oxford University Press.

LaFollette, H. and Shanks, N. (1996) *Brute Science: The Dilemmas of Animal Experimentation*. London: Routledge.

Rachels, J. (1990) *Created From Animals*. Oxford: Oxford University Press.

Regan, T. 1983: *The Case for Animal Rights*. Berkeley: University of California Press.

Singer, P. (1990) *Animal Liberation*, 2nd edn. New York: Avon Books.

14

All Animals are Equal

Peter Singer

In recent years a number of oppressed groups have campaigned vigorously for equality. The classic instance is the Black Liberation movement, which demands an end to the prejudice and discrimination that has made blacks second-class citizens. The immediate appeal of the Black Liberation movement and its initial, if limited, success made it a model for other oppressed groups to follow. We became familiar with liberation movements for Spanish-Americans, gay people, and a variety of other minorities. When a majority group – women – began their campaign, some thought we had come to the end of the road. Discrimination on the basis of sex, it has been said, is the last universally accepted form of discrimination, practiced without secrecy or pretense even in those liberal circles that have long prided themselves on their freedom from prejudice against racial minorities.

One should always be wary of talking of "the last remaining form of discrimination." If we have learnt anything from the liberation movements, we should have learnt how difficult it is to be aware of latent prejudice in our attitudes to particular groups until this prejudice is forcefully pointed out.

A liberation movement demands an expansion of our moral horizons and an extension or reinterpretation of the basic moral principle of equality. Practices that were previously regarded as natural and inevitable come to be seen as the result of an unjustifiable prejudice. Who can say with confidence that all his or her attitudes and practices are beyond criticism? If we wish to avoid being numbered amongst the oppressors, we must be prepared to re-think even our most fundamental attitudes. We need to consider them from the point of view of those most disadvantaged by our attitudes, and the practices that follow from these attitudes. If we can make this unaccustomed mental switch we may discover a pattern in our attitudes and practices that consistently operates so as to benefit one group – usually the one to which we ourselves belong – at the expense of another. In this way we may come to see that there is a case for a new liberation movement. My aim is to advocate that we make this mental switch in respect of our attitudes and practices towards a very large group of beings: members of species other than our own – or, as we popularly though misleadingly call them, animals. In other words, I am urging that we extend to other species the basic principle of equality that most of us recognize should be extended to all members of our own species.

All this may sound a little far-fetched, more like a parody of other liberation movements than a serious objective. In fact, in the past the idea of "The Rights of Animals" really has been used to parody the case for women's rights. When Mary Wollstonecraft, a forerunner of later feminists, published her Vindication of the Rights of Women in 1792, her ideas were widely regarded as absurd, and they were satirized in an anonymous publication entitled A Vindication of the Rights of Brutes. The author of this satire (actually Thomas Taylor, a distinguished Cambridge philosopher) tried to refute Wollstonecraft's reasonings by showing that they could be carried one stage further. If sound when applied to women, why should the arguments not be applied to dogs, cats, and horses? They seemed to hold equally well for these "brutes"; yet to hold that brutes had rights was manifestly absurd; therefore the reasoning by which this conclusion had been reached must be unsound, and if unsound when applied to brutes, it must also be unsound when applied to women, since the very same arguments had been used in each case.

One way in which we might reply to this argument is by saying that the case for equality between men and women cannot validly be extended to nonhuman animals. Women have a right to vote, for instance, because they are just as capable of making rational decisions as men are; dogs, on the other hand, are incapable of understanding the significance of voting, so they cannot have the right to vote. There are many other obvious ways in which men and women resemble each other closely, while humans and other animals differ greatly. So, it might be said, men and women are similar beings and should have equal rights, while humans and nonhumans are different and should not have equal rights.

The thought behind this reply to Taylor's analogy is correct up to a point, but it does not go far enough. There are important differences between humans and other animals, and these differences must give rise to some differences in the rights that each have. Recognizing this obvious fact, however, is no barrier to the case for extending the basic principle of equality to nonhuman animals. The differences that exist between men and women are equally undeniable, and the supporters of Women's Liberation are aware that these differences may give rise to different rights. Many feminists hold that women have the right to an abortion on request. It does not follow that since these same people are campaigning for equality between men and women they must support the right of men to have abortions too. Since a man cannot have an abortion, it is meaningless to talk of his right to have one. Since a pig can't vote, it is meaningless to talk of its right to vote. There is no reason why either Women's Liberation or Animal Liberation should get involved in such nonsense. The extension of the basic principle of equality from one group to another does not imply that we must treat both groups in exactly the same way, or grant exactly the same rights to both groups. Whether we should do so will depend on the nature of the members of the two groups. The basic principle of equality, I shall argue, is equality of consideration; and equal consideration for different beings may lead to different treatment and different rights.

So there is a different way of replying to Taylor's attempt to parody Wollstonecraft's arguments, a way which does not deny the differences between humans and nonhumans, but goes more deeply into the question of equality and concludes, by finding nothing absurd in the idea, that the basic principle of equality applies to so-called "brutes." I believe that we reach this conclusion if we examine the basis on which our opposition to discrimination on grounds of race or sex ultimately rests. We will then see that we would be on shaky ground if we were to demand equality for blacks, women, and other groups of oppressed humans while denying equal consideration to nonhumans.

When we say that all human beings, whatever their race, creed, or sex, are equal, what is it that we are asserting? Those who wish to defend a hierarchical, inegalitarian society have often pointed out that by whatever test we choose, it simply is not true that all humans are equal.

Like it or not, we must face the fact that humans come in different shapes and sizes; they come with differing moral capacities, differing intellectual abilities, differing amounts of benevolent feeling and sensitivity to the needs of others, differing abilities to communicate effectively, and differing capacities to experience pleasure and pain. In short, if the demand for equality were based on the actual equality of all human beings, we would have to stop demanding equality. It would be an unjustifiable demand.

Still, one might cling to the view that the demand for equality among human beings is based on the actual equality of the different races and sexes. Although humans differ as individuals in various ways, there are no differences between the races and sexes as such. From the mere fact that a person is black, or a woman, we cannot infer anything else about that person. This, it may be said, is what is wrong with racism and sexism. The white racist claims that whites are superior to blacks, but this is false – although there are differences between individuals, some blacks are superior to some whites in all of the capacities and abilities that could conceivably be relevant. The opponent of sexism would say the same: a person's sex is no guide to his or her abilities, and this is why it is unjustifiable to discriminate on the basis of sex.

This is a possible line of objection to racial and sexual discrimination. It is not, however, the way that someone really concerned about equality would choose, because taking this line could, in some circumstances, force one to accept a most inegalitarian society. The fact that humans differ as individuals, rather than as races or sexes, is a valid reply to someone who defends a hierarchical society like, say, South Africa, in which all whites are superior in status to all blacks. The existence of individual variations that cut across the lines of race or sex, however, provides us with no defence at all against a more sophisticated opponent of equality, one who proposes that, say, the interests of those with I.Q. ratings above 100 be preferred to the interests of those with I.Q.s below 100. Would a hierarchical society of this sort really be so much better than one based on race or sex?

I think not. But if we tie the moral principle of equality to the factual equality of the different races or sexes, taken as a whole, our opposition to racism and sexism does not provide us with any basis for objecting to this kind of inegalitarianism.

There is a second important reason why we ought not to base our opposition to racism and sexism on any kind of factual equality, even the limited kind which asserts that variations in capacities and abilities are spread evenly between the different races and sexes: we can have no absolute guarantee that these abilities and capacities really are distributed evenly, without regard to race or sex, among human beings. So far as actual abilities are concerned, there do seem to be certain measurable differences between both races and sexes. These differences do not, of course, appear in each case, but only when averages are taken. More important still, we do not yet know how much of these differences is really due to the different genetic endowments of the various races and sexes, and how much is due to environmental differences that are the result of past and continuing discrimination. Perhaps all of the important differences will eventually prove to be environmental rather than genetic. Anyone opposed to racism and sexism will certainly hope that this will be so, for it will make the task of ending discrimination a lot easier; nevertheless it would be dangerous to rest the case against racism and sexism on the belief that all significant differences are environmental in origin. The opponent of, say, racism who takes this line will be unable to avoid conceding that if differences in ability did after all prove to have some genetic connection with race, racism would in some way be defensible.

It would be folly for the opponent of racism to stake his whole case on a dogmatic commitment to one particular outcome of a difficult scientific issue which is still a long way from being settled. While attempts to prove that differences in certain selected abilities between races and sexes are primarily genetic in origin have certainly not been conclusive, the same must be said of attempts to prove that these differences are largely the result of environment. At this stage of the investigation we cannot be certain which view is correct, however much we may hope it is the latter.

Fortunately, there is no need to pin the case for equality to one particular outcome of this scientific investigation. The appropriate response to those who claim to have found evidence of genetically-based differences in ability between the races or sexes is not to stick to the belief that the genetic explanation must be wrong, whatever evidence to the contrary may turn up: instead we should make it quite clear that the claim to equality does not depend on intelligence, moral capacity, physical strength, or similar matters of fact. Equality is a moral ideal, not a simple assertion of fact. There is no logically compelling reason for assuming that a factual difference in ability between two people justifies any difference in the amount of consideration we give to satisfying their needs and interests. The principle of the equality of human beings is not a description of an alleged actual equality among humans: it is a prescription of how we should treat animals.

Jeremy Bentham incorporated the essential basis of moral equality into his utilitarian system of ethics in the formula: "Each to count for one and none for more than one." In other words, the interests of every being affected by an action are to be taken into account and given the same weight as the like interests of any other being. A later utilitarian, Henry Sidgwick, put the point in this way: "The good of any one individual is of no more importance, from the point of view (if I may say so) of the Universe, than the good of any other."[1] More recently, the leading figures in contemporary moral philosophy have shown a great deal of agreement in specifying as a fundamental presupposition of their moral theories some similar requirement which operates so as to give everyone's interests equal consideration – although they cannot agree on how this requirement is best formulated.[2]

It is an implication of this principle of equality that our concern for others ought not to depend on what they are like, or what abilities they possess – although precisely what this concern requires us to do may vary according to the characteristics of those affected by what we do. It is on this basis that the case against racism and the case against sexism must both ultimately rest; and it is in accordance with this principle that speciesism is also to be condemned. If possessing a higher degree of intelligence does not entitle one human to use another for his own ends, how can it entitle humans to exploit nonhumans?

Many philosophers have proposed the principle of equal consideration of interests, in some form or other, as a basic moral principle; but, as we shall see in more detail shortly, not many of them have recognized that this principle applies to members of other species as well as to our own. Bentham was one of the few who did realize this. In a forward-looking passage, written at a time when black slaves in the British dominions were still being treated much as we now treat nonhuman animals, Bentham wrote:

> The day may come when the rest of the animal creation may acquire those rights which never could have been witholden from them but by the hand of tyranny. The French have already discovered that the blackness of the skin is no reason why a human being should be abandoned without redress to the caprice of a tormentor. It may one day come to be recognized that the number of the legs, the villosity of the skin, or the termination of the os sacrum, are reasons equally insufficient for abandoning a sensitive being to the same fate. What else is it that should trace the insuperable line? Is it the faculty of reason, or perhaps the faculty of discourse? But a full-grown horse or dog is beyond comparison a more rational, as well as a more conversable animal, than an infant of a day, or a week, or even a month, old. But suppose they were otherwise, what would it avail? The question is not, Can they reason? nor Can they talk? but, Can they suffer?[3]

In this passage Bentham points to the capacity for suffering as the vital characteristic that gives a being the right to equal consideration. The capacity for suffering – or more strictly, for suffering and/or enjoyment or happiness – is not just another characteristic like the capacity for language, or for higher mathematics. Bentham is not saying that those who try to mark "the insuperable line" that determines whether the interests of a being should be considered happen to have selected the wrong characteristic. The capacity for suffering and enjoying things is a prerequisite for having interests at all, a condition that must be satisfied before we can speak of interests in any meaningful way. It would be nonsense to say that it was not in the interests of a stone to be kicked along the road by a schoolboy. A stone does not have interests because it cannot suffer. Nothing that we can do to it could possibly make any difference to its welfare. A mouse, on the other hand, does have an interest in not being tormented, because it will suffer if it is.

If a being suffers, there can be no moral justification for refusing to take that suffering into consideration. No matter what the nature of the being, the principle of equality requires that its suffering be counted equally with the like suffering – in so far as rough comparisons can be made – of any other being. If a being is not capable of suffering, or of experiencing enjoyment or happiness, there is nothing to be taken into account. This is why the limit of sentience (using the term as a convenient, if not strictly accurate, shorthand for the capacity to suffer or experience enjoyment or happiness) is the only defensible boundary of concern for the interests of others. To mark this boundary by some characteristic like intelligence or rationality would be to mark it in an arbitrary way. Why not choose some other characteristic, like skin color?

The racist violates the principle of equality by giving greater weight to the interests of members of his own race, when there is a clash between their interests and the interests of those of another race. Similarly the speciesist allows the interests of his own species to override the greater interests of members of other species.[4] The pattern is the same in each case. Most human beings are speciesists. I shall now very briefly describe some of the practices that show this.

For the great majority of human beings, especially in urban, industrialized societies, the most direct form of contact with members of other species is at mealtimes: we eat them. In doing so we treat them purely as means to our ends. We regard their life and well-being as subordinate to our taste for a particular kind of dish. I say "taste" deliberately – this is purely a matter of pleasing our palate. There can be no defence of eating flesh in terms of satisfying nutritional needs, since it has been established beyond doubt that we could satisfy our need for protein and other essential nutrients far more efficiently with a diet that replaced animal flesh by soy beans, or products derived from soy beans, and other high-protein vegetable products.[5]

It is not merely the act of killing that indicates what we are ready to do to other species in order to gratify our tastes. The suffering we inflict on the animals while they are alive is perhaps an even clearer indication of our speciesism than the fact that we are prepared to kill them.[6] In order to have meat on the table at a price that people can afford, our society tolerates methods of meat production that confine sentient animals in cramped, unsuitable conditions for the entire durations of their lives. Animals are treated like machines that convert fodder into flesh, and any innovation that results in a higher "conversion ratio" is liable to be adopted. As one authority on the subject has said, "cruelty is acknowledged only when profitability ceases."[7] . . .

Since, as I have said, none of these practices cater for anything more than our pleasures of taste, our practice of rearing and killing other animals in order to eat them is a clear instance of the sacrifice of the most important interests of other beings in order to satisfy trivial interests of our own. To avoid speciesism we must stop this practice, and each of us has a moral obligation to cease supporting the practice. Our custom is all the support that the meat-industry needs. The decision to cease giving it that support may be difficult, but it is no more difficult than it would have been for a white Southerner to go against the traditions of his society and free his slaves: if we do not change our dietary habits, how can we censure those slaveholders who would not change their own way of living?

The same form of discrimination may be observed in the widespread practice of experimenting on other species in order to see if certain substances are safe for human beings, or to test some psychological theory about the effect of severe punishment on learning, or to try out various new compounds just in case something turns up . . . .

In the past, argument about vivisection has often missed the point, because it has been put in absolutist terms: Would the abolitionist be prepared to let thousands die if they could be saved by experimenting on a single animal? The way to reply to this purely hypothetical question is to pose another: Would the experimenter be prepared to perform his experiment on an orphaned human infant, if that were the only way to save many lives? (I say "orphan" to avoid the complication of parental feelings, although in doing so I am being overfair to the experimenter, since the nonhuman subjects of experiments are not orphans.) If the experimenter is not prepared to use an orphaned human infant, then his readiness to use nonhumans is simple discrimination, since adult apes, cats, mice, and other mammals are more aware of what is happening to them, more self-directing and, so far as we can tell, at least as sensitive to pain, as any human infant. There seems to be no relevant characteristic that human infants possess that adult mammals do not have to the same or a higher degree. (Someone might try to argue that what makes it wrong to experiment on a human infant is that the infant will, in time and if left alone, develop into more than the nonhuman, but one would then, to be consistent, have to oppose abortion, since the fetus has the same potential as the infant – indeed, even contraception and abstinence might be wrong on this ground, since the egg and sperm, considered jointly, also have the same potential. In any case, this argument still gives us no reason for selecting a nonhuman, rather than a human with severe and irreversible brain damage, as the subject for our experiments.)

The experimenter, then, shows a bias in favor of his own species whenever he carries out an experiment on a nonhuman for a purpose that he would not think justified him in using a human being at an equal or lower level of sentience, awareness, ability to be self-directing, etc. No one familiar with the kind of results yielded by most experiments on animals can have the slightest doubt that if this bias were eliminated the number of experiments performed would be a minute fraction of the number performed today.

Experimenting on animals, and eating their flesh, are perhaps the two major forms of speciesism in our society. By comparison, the third and last form of speciesism is so minor as to be insignificant, but it is perhaps of some special interest to those for whom this article was written. I am referring to speciesism in contemporary philosophy.

Philosophy ought to question the basic assumptions of the age. Thinking through, critically and carefully, what most people take for granted is, I believe, the chief task of philosophy, and it is this task that makes philosophy a worthwhile activity. Regrettably, philosophy does not always live up to its historic role. Philosophers are human beings, and they are subject to all the preconceptions of the society to which they belong. Sometimes they succeed in breaking free of the prevailing ideology: more often they become its most sophisticated defenders. So, in this case, philosophy as practiced in the universities today does not challenge anyone's preconceptions about our relations with other species. By their writings, those philosophers who tackle problems that touch upon the issue reveal that they make the same unquestioned assumptions as most other humans, and what they say tends to confirm the reader in his or her comfortable speciesist habits.

I could illustrate this claim by referring to the writings of philosophers in various fields – for instance, the attempts that have been made by those interested in rights to draw the boundary of the sphere of rights so that it runs parallel to the biological boundaries of the species homo sapiens, including infants and even mental defectives, but excluding those other beings of equal or greater capacity who are so useful to us at mealtimes and in our laboratories. I think it would be a more appropriate conclusion to this article, however, if I concentrated on the problem with which we have been centrally concerned, the problem of equality.

It is significant that the problem of equality, in moral and political philosophy, is invariably formulated in terms of human equality. The effect of this is that the question of the equality of other animals does not confront the philosopher, or student, as an issue itself – and this is already an indication of the failure of philosophy to challenge accepted beliefs. Still, philosophers have found it difficult to discuss the issue of human equality without raising, in a paragraph or two, the question of the status of other animals. The reason for this, which should be apparent from what I have said already, is that if humans are to be regarded as equal to one another, we need some sense of "equal" that does not require any actual, descriptive equality of capacities, talents or other qualities. If equality is to be related to any actual characteristics of humans, these characteristics must be some lowest common denominator, pitched so low that no human lacks them – but then the philosopher comes up against the catch that any such set of characteristics which covers all humans will not be possessed only by humans. In other words, it turns out that in the only sense in which we can truly say, as an assertion of fact, that all humans are equal, at least some members of other species are also equal – equal, that is, to each other and to humans. If, on the other hand, we regard the statement "All humans are equal" in some nonfactual way, perhaps as a prescription, then, as I have already argued, it is even more difficult to exclude nonhumans from the sphere of equality.

This result is not what the egalitarian philosopher originally intended to assert. Instead of accepting the radical outcome to which their own reasonings naturally point, however, most philosophers try to reconcile their beliefs in human equality and animal inequality by arguments that can only be described as devious.

As a first example, I take William Frankena's well-known article "The Concept of Social Justice." Frankena opposes the idea of basing justice on merit, because he sees that this could lead to highly inegalitarian results. Instead he proposes the principle that: all men are to be treated as equals, not because they are equal, in any respect, but simply because they are human. They are human because they have emotions and desires, and are able to think,

and hence are capable of enjoying a good life in a sense in which other animals are not.[8]

But what is this capacity to enjoy the good life which all humans have, but no other animals? Other animals have emotions and desires and appear to be capable of enjoying a good life. We may doubt that they can think – although the behavior of some apes, dolphins, and even dogs suggests that some of them can – but what is the relevance of thinking? Frankena goes on to admit that by "the good life" he means "not so much the morally good life as the happy or satisfactory life," so thought would appear to be unnecessary for enjoying the good life; in fact to emphasize the need for thought would make difficulties for the egalitarian since only some people are capable of leading intellectually satisfying lives, or morally good lives. This makes it difficult to see what Frankena's principle of equality has to do with simply being human. Surely every sentient being is capable of leading a life that is happier or less miserable than some alternative life, and hence has a claim to be taken into account. In this respect the distinction between humans and nonhumans is not a sharp division, but rather a continuum along which we move gradually, and with overlaps between the species, from simple capacities for enjoyment and satisfaction, or pain and suffering, to more complex ones.

Faced with a situation in which they see a need for some basis for the moral gulf that is commonly thought to separate humans and animals, but can find no concrete difference that will do the job without undermining the equality of humans, philosophers tend to waffle. They resort to high-sounding phrases like "the intrinsic dignity of the human individual";[9] they talk of the "intrinsic worth of all men" as if men (humans?) had some worth that other beings did not,[10] or they say that humans, and only humans, are "ends in themselves," while "everything other than a person can only have value for a person."[11]

This idea of a distinctive human dignity and worth has a long history; it can be traced back directly to the Renaissance humanists, for instance to Pico della Mirandola's Oration on the Dignity of Man. Pico and other humanists based their estimate of human dignity on the idea that man possessed the central, pivotal position in the "Great Chain of Being" that led from the lowliest forms of matter to God himself; this view of the universe, in turn, goes back to both classical and Judeo-Christian doctrines. Contemporary philosophers have cast off these metaphysical and religious shackles and freely invoke the dignity of mankind without needing to justify the idea at all. Why should we not attribute "intrinsic dignity" or "intrinsic worth" to ourselves? Fellow-humans are unlikely to reject the accolades we so generously bestow on them, and those to whom we deny the honor are unable to object. Indeed, when one thinks only of humans, it can be very liberal, very progressive, to talk of the dignity of all human beings. In so doing, we implicitly condemn slavery, racism, and other violations of human rights. We admit that we ourselves are in some fundamental sense on a par with the poorest, most ignorant members of our own species. It is only when we think of humans as no more than a small sub-group of all the beings that inhabit our planet that we may realize that in elevating our own species we are at the same time lowering the relative status of all other species.

The truth is that the appeal to the intrinsic dignity of human beings appears to solve the egalitarian's problems only as long as it goes unchallenged. Once we ask why it should be that all humans – including infants, mental defectives, psychopaths, Hitler, Stalin, and the rest – have some kind of dignity or worth that no elephant, pig, or chimpanzee can ever achieve, we see that this question is as difficult to answer as our original request for some relevant fact that justifies the inequality of humans and other animals. In fact, these two questions are really one: talk of intrinsic dignity or moral worth only takes the problem back one step, because any satisfactory defence of the claim that all and only humans have intrinsic dignity would need to refer to some relevant capacities or characteristics that all and only humans possess. Philosophers frequently introduce ideas of dignity, respect, and worth at the point at which other reasons appear to be lacking, but this is

hardly good enough. Fine phrases are the last resource of those who have run out of arguments.

In case there are those who still think it may be possible to find some relevant characteristic that distinguishes all humans from all members of other species, I shall refer again, before I conclude, to the existence of some humans who quite clearly are below the level of awareness, self-consciousness, intelligence, and sentience, of many nonhumans. I am thinking of humans with severe and irreparable brain damage, and also of infant humans. To avoid the complication of the relevance of a being's potential, however, I shall henceforth concentrate on permanently retarded humans.

Philosophers who set out to find a characteristic that will distinguish humans from other animals rarely take the course of abandoning these groups of humans by lumping them in with the other animals. It is easy to see why they do not. To take this line without re-thinking our attitudes to other animals would entail that we have the right to perform painful experiments on retarded humans for trivial reasons; similarly it would follow that we had the right to rear and kill these humans for food. To most philosophers these consequences are as unacceptable as the view that we should stop treating nonhumans in this way.

Of course, when discussing the problem of equality it is possible to ignore the problem of mental defectives, or brush it aside as if somehow insignificant.[12] This is the easiest way out. What else remains? My final example of speciesism in contemporary philosophy has been selected to show what happens when a writer is prepared to face the question of human equality and animal inequality without ignoring the existence of mental defectives, and without resorting to obscurantist mumbo-jumbo. Stanley Benn's clear and honest article "Egalitarianism and Equal Consideration of Interests"[13] fits this description.

Benn, after noting the usual "evident human inequalities," argues, correctly I think, for equality of consideration as the only possible basis for egalitarianism. Yet Benn, like other writers, is thinking only of "equal consideration of human interests." Benn is quite open in his defence of this restriction of equal consideration:

> not to possess human shape is a disqualifying condition. However faithful or intelligent a dog may be, it would be a monstrous sentimentality to attribute to him interests that could be weighed in an equal balance with those of human beings . . . if, for instance, one had to decide between feeding a hungry baby or a hungry dog, anyone who chose the dog would generally be reckoned morally defective, unable to recognize a fundamental inequality of claims.

This is what distinguishes our attitude to animals from our attitude to imbeciles. It would be odd to say that we ought to respect equally the dignity or personality of the imbecile and of the rational man . . . but there is nothing odd about saying that we should respect their interests equally, that is, that we should give to the interests of each the same serious consideration as claims to considerations necessary for some standard of well-being that we can recognize and endorse.

Benn's statement of the basis of the consideration we should have for imbeciles seems to me correct, but why should there be any fundamental inequality of claims between a dog and a human imbecile? Benn sees that if equal consideration depended on rationality, no reason could be given against using imbeciles for research purposes, as we now use dogs and guinea pigs. This will not do: "But of course we do distinguish imbeciles from animals in this regard," he says. That the common distinction is justifiable is something Benn does not question; his problem is how it is to be justified. The answer he gives is this:

> we respect the interests of men and give them priority over dogs not insofar as they are rational, but because rationality is the human norm. We say it is unfair to exploit the deficiencies of the imbecile who falls short of the norm, just as it would be unfair, and not just ordinarily dishonest, to steal from a blind man. If we do not think in this way about dogs, it is because we do not see the irrationality of the dog as a deficiency or a handicap, but as normal for the species. The characteristics, therefore, that distinguish the normal man from the normal dog make it intelligible for us to talk of other men having interests and

capacities, and therefore claims, of precisely the same kind as we make on our own behalf. But although these characteristics may provide the point of the distinction between men and other species, they are not in fact the qualifying conditions for membership, or the distinguishing criteria of the class of morally considerable persons; and this is precisely because a man does not become a member of a different species, with its own standards of normality, by reason of not possessing these characteristics.

The final sentence of this passage gives the argument away. An imbecile, Benn concedes, may have no characteristics superior to those of a dog; nevertheless this does not make the imbecile a member of "a different species" as the dog is. Therefore it would be "unfair" to use the imbecile for medical research as we use the dog. But why? That the imbecile is not rational is just the way things have worked out, and the same is true of the dog – neither is any more responsible for their mental level. If it is unfair to take advantage of an isolated defect, why is it fair to take advantage of a more general limitation? I find it hard to see anything in this argument except a defence of preferring the interests of members of our own species because they are members of our own species. To those who think there might be more to it, I suggest the following mental exercise. Assume that it has been proven that there is a difference in the average, or normal, intelligence quotient for two different races, say whites and blacks. Then substitute the term "white" for every occurrence of "men" and "black" for every occurrence of "dog" in the passage quoted; and substitute "high I.Q." for "rationality" and when Benn talks of "imbeciles" replace this term by "dumb whites" – that is, whites who fall well below the normal white I.Q. score. Finally, change "species" to "race." Now re-read the passage. It has become a defence of a rigid, no-exceptions division between whites and blacks, based on I.Q. scores, not withstanding an admitted overlap between whites and blacks in this respect. The revised passage is, of course, outrageous, and this is not only because we have made fictitious assumptions in our substitutions. The point is that in the original passage Benn was defending a rigid division in the amount of consideration due to members of different species, despite admitted cases of overlap. If the original did not, at first reading, strike us as being as outrageous as the revised version does, this is largely because although we are not racists ourselves, most of us are speciesists. Like the other articles, Benn's stands as a warning of the ease with which the best minds can fall victim to a prevailing ideology.

Notes

1 Henry Sidgwick, *The Methods of Ethics* (7th edn), p. 382.

2 For example, R. M. Hare, *Freedom and Reason* (Oxford, 1963), and J. Rawls, *A Theory of Justice* (Harvard, 1972); for a brief account of the essential agreement on this issue between these and other positions, see R. M. Hare, "Rules of War and Moral Reasoning," *Philosophy and Public Affairs*, 1/2 (1972).

3 Jeremy Bentham, *Introduction to the Principles of Morals and Legislation*, ch. XVII.

4 I owe the term speciesism to Richard Ryder.

5 In order to produce 1 lb of protein in the form of beef or veal, we must feed 21 lbs of protein to the animal. Other forms of livestock are slightly less inefficient, but the average ratio in the United States is still 1:8. It has been estimated that the amount of protein lost to humans in this way is equivalent to 90 percent of the annual world protein deficit. For a brief account, see Frances Moore Lappé, *Diet for a Small Planet* (Friends of The Earth/Ballantine, New York, 1971), pp. 4–11.

6 Although one might think that killing a being is obviously the ultimate wrong one can do to it, I think that the infliction of suffering is a clearer indication of speciesism because it might be argued that at least part of what is wrong with killing a human is that most humans are conscious of their existence over time and have desires and purposes that extend into the future – see, for instance, M. Tooley, "Abortion and Infanticide," *Philosophy and Public Affairs*, 2/1 (1972). Of course, if one took this view one would have to hold – as Tooley does – that killing a human infant or mental defective is not in itself wrong and is less serious than killing certain higher mammals that probably do have a sense of their own existence over time.

7 Ruth Harrison, *Animal Machines* (Stuart, London, 1964). For an account of farming conditions, see my *Animal Liberation* (New York Review Company, 1975).

8 In R. Brandt (ed.), *Social Justice* (Prentice-Hall, Englewood Cliffs, 1962), p. 19.

9 William Frankena, "The Concept of Social Justice," in R. Brandt, *Social Justice*, p. 19.

10 H. A. Bedau, "Egalitarianism and the Idea of Equality," in *Nomos IX: Equality*, ed. J. R. Pennock and J. W. Chapman (New York, 1967).

11 G. Vlastos, "Justice and Equality," in Brandt, *Social Justice*, p. 48.

12 For example, Bernard Williams, "The Idea of Equality," in *Philosophy, Politics, and Society* (2nd series), ed. P. Laslett and W. Runciman (Blackwell, Oxford, 1962), p. 118; J. Rawls, *A Theory of Justice*, pp. 509–10.

13 *Nomos IX: Equality*; the passages quoted are on pp. 62ff.

15

The Moral Community

Michael Allen Fox

Another view that is currently popular among spokespersons for animal welfare is that which endorses the notion of animal rights. To different individuals, the ascription of rights to animals means different things. To some, it is a way of expressing their conviction that animals' lives have intrinsic value or value to themselves. I have already shown . . . that no meaning can be attached to the notion of anything's having totally self-contained value; and as animals cannot reflectively examine their lives to arrive at qualitative assessments about them, their lives also cannot have intrinsic value or value to themselves. Others seem to think that granting rights to animals is like waving a magic wand or uttering incantations, as if by doing so they could change overnight the attitudes and behavior of their fellow human beings.

The origin of the idea of animal rights is not easy to trace. One view is that this notion is a natural spin-off or even a logical extension of the civil rights and women's rights movements; another is that it represents nothing more than another symptom of the tendency, particularly prevalent in the United States, to couch all demands for change in the language of rights. Arthur L. Caplan has referred to this contem-

porary phenomenon as the "hortatory or political usage of rights," remarking on "rights language . . . as a politically expedient device to focus social concern on any ethical or political question."[1] Thus we hear daily of employees' rights, students' rights, the right to die with dignity, a bill of rights for nonsmokers, the right to work, the right to strike, tenants' rights, landlords' rights, the right to a safe environment, prisoners' rights, gay rights, the rights of future generations, the rights of the handicapped, and so on. Lately, even the rights of left-handers and the right of parents to spank their children have been defended in the media! Some of these rights claims are surely legitimate. But there is little doubt that the concept of rights has been much abused, having been stretched almost beyond recognition and frequently invoked when other terminology would do just as well or when basic constitutional or civil rights could be cited instead. In any event, a sizable and growing number of people think that animals have (or should have) rights, such as the right to life, the right not to suffer, and the right to a certain minimum quality of life, and that it makes perfectly good sense to talk this way.

I think it can be shown that both the utilitarian position on animals and the advocacy of animal rights are fundamentally mistaken. To see why and to develop a sensible alternative position on the moral status of animals, it is necessary to examine the foundations of our system of moral beliefs. This in turn requires that we consider the nature of a moral community, for only within such a social organization can the basic concepts and principles of morality arise.

Foundations of the Moral Community: Preliminaries

Few people will dispute the statement that we all belong to a moral community, though we may have different ideas about the nature of such a community (for example, whether it is rooted in religion or in purely secular precepts) and its scope (such as whether morality is relative to a given culture or is universal; whether it includes only human beings or other species as well). What, then, is a moral community? Most generally, it is a group of beings that shares certain characteristics and whose members are or consider themselves to be bound to observe certain rules of conduct in relation to one another because of their mutual likeness. These rules create what we call obligations and derive in some intimate way from the characteristics which the beings composing the moral community have in common. Thus a moral community is a society in the broadest sense of the word, and the beings belonging to it are related by natural bonds, whereas their conduct is regulated by bonds of obligation – that is, the beings in question possess certain salient characteristics, are capable of recognizing these in other, similar beings, and acknowledge possession by other beings of the characteristics in question as grounds for following certain rules of conduct toward them.

Note, however, that not all people who are members of a moral community necessarily accept that they are bound to follow specifiable standard rules of conduct even by virtue of recognizing and acknowledging that others

share important characteristics with them. Sociopaths and terrorists, for instance, do not. Most moral theorists, however (as well as most laypersons), would argue that such exceptions do not seriously undermine our moral community or threaten to destroy the bond of association that holds it together, any more than the occasional act of anarchism or civil disobedience harmfully erodes the basic principles of political obligation and community.

Membership in the Moral Community

Now what sorts of beings do actually belong to a moral community such as I have just described? Clearly, they must be beings that, by their nature, are capable of functioning within one. This means, in effect, that they must possess the sorts of characteristics that we have already discussed: critical self-awareness; the ability to manipulate complex concepts and to use a sophisticated language (especially for the purpose of communicating wishes, desires, needs, decisions, choices, and so on);[2] and the capacity to reflect, plan, deliberate, choose, and accept responsibility for acting. The importance of these attributes in humans' evolutionary adaptation and in establishing their uniqueness has already been stressed. What we need to emphasize here is that these characteristics make humans autonomous or self-directing and capable of functioning as rational moral agents. It is because they are capable of long-range planning, anticipating consequences, choosing among alternative courses of action, taking responsibility, making and following rules, and the like that humans can engage in moral behavior, or behavior that affects others as well as themselves and that is subject to moral appraisal. Furthermore, the possession of these characteristics, plus the capacity to recognize them in others and to care about others, goes a long way toward explaining what we mean by speaking of ourselves as *persons*. Thus it appears that a moral community is a social group composed of interacting autonomous beings where moral concepts and precepts can evolve and be understood. It is also a social group in which the mutual recognition of autonomy and person-hood exists. The latter feature is equally important and indeed inseparable from the former, since the development of moral institutions (such as promise keeping, truth telling, making contractual agreements, and giving mutual aid in emergencies) is contingent on recognition of and respect for persons.

A number of animal-protectionist authors have attempted to refute the approach I have followed here, claiming that when we examine critically each of the characteristics differentiating humans from animals, which I have identified as morally relevant differences, we find that none of them succeeds in establishing the moral superiority of humans.[3] But I am not arguing that any one of these characteristics taken in isolation establishes the moral superiority of humans (or better, of autonomous agents or persons), rather that all of them do, when taken together. This is a crucial point: It is the whole cluster of interrelated capacities, and this alone, that constitutes the nature of an autonomous being. The piecemeal approach taken by animal welfarists to undermine, as they suppose, the position advocated here, simply succeeds in trivializing the claim being advanced on behalf of autonomy as the focus of full moral status and discourse. Their argument amounts in fact to an illicit *reductio*, much like one that might be offered, say, to "prove" that there is no politically relevant difference between democracy and other forms of government and hence no superiority of the former over the latter. We could imagine such an argument, cast in Socratic form, to run as follows: " 'Does freedom of speech, which you claim to be a politically relevant difference between democracy and other forms of government, establish the superiority of democracy over these other forms?' 'No, not taken by itself.' 'Well, then, what about freedom of assembly?' 'Also inadequate taken by itself.' 'Freedom from arbitrary arrest?' 'Not by itself.' 'The right to vote?' 'No.' 'It appears, then, that democracy is not superior to other forms of government because under examination each of its essential characteristics shows itself to be a politically irrelevant difference.' " But, of course, no one

would think to defend democracy by placing the entire weight of the argument on one isolated feature. In like manner, no one would seek to support the claim that autonomous beings are morally superior by building the case on a single characteristic of such beings.

On Rights

I wish to argue now that only within the context of a moral community do rights and obligations (duties) arise at all. This is so first of all because rights are possessed solely by persons. As a preliminary, I want to stress that I am speaking here of basic moral rights as distinct from legal rights. Defenders of animal rights are often unclear in their own minds, as well as in the presentation of their case to the public, whether they are endorsing moral or legal rights for animals or indeed both. This is an important distinction to which I return in the final chapter. For the moment, however, let us concentrate on moral rights. Why are moral rights possessed only by persons? The short answer is that rights are accorded to persons (that is, reflectively self-valuing beings) by other persons in recognition of their inherent independence, dignity, and worth *as persons* (rather than as individuals who have attained or failed to attain some level of moral development in their lives).

Much has been written over the past few centuries on the subject of rights, and a good deal of this literature has mystified rather than clarified the concept. Probably the principal factor in this mystification lies in the traditional doctrine of natural rights. Natural rights are "rights we are alleged to have in a state of nature, independently of human institutions and conventions, simply by virtue of our humanity (or some other set of attributes). Such rights are typically indefeasible, that is, they cannot be overridden (except maybe in great catastrophes . . .)."[4] Now the idea of a "state of nature" is notoriously vague, and for all we know one may never have existed, at least in the way envisioned by natural-rights theorists, since *Homo sapiens* and their ancestral hominids have always been highly social creatures. In addition, it has never been made plain what it means to say that we possess rights "by virtue of our humanity." Some have claimed that rights are God-given, others that no grounds can be given for the possession of rights; it is simply self-evident that all humans have them. Still others have asserted both, as in the famous passage from the Declaration of Independence of the United States of America, which reads, "We hold these truths to be self-evident, that all men are created equal, that they are endowed by their Creator with certain unalienable Rights, that among these are Life, Liberty and the pursuit of Happiness."

Because of these and other difficulties with the notion of rights, many philosophers have become convinced that talk of rights, although useful in a civil libertarian (that is, legal) context, has no value in moral theory and in fact should be avoided altogether in our discussion of moral issues. Some have also said that the British libertarian/egalitarian tradition in morality and the law does not depend on a strong conception of rights and that the American system is the exception, rights have been initially enshrined in the Declaration and then later in the Bill of Rights. However, in my view the idea of basic moral rights lies at the core of our system of moral beliefs and is an essential feature of the moral community. In an article on "Rights, Human Rights, and Racial Discrimination," Richard Wasserstrom observes that if the question be raised why ought anyone have a right to anything? or why not have a system in which there are not rights at all? the answer is that such a system would be a morally impoverished one . . . [for] one ought to be able to claim as entitlements those minimal things without which it is impossible to develop one's capabilities and to live a life as a human being.[5]

Wasserstrom helps to bring out here the crucial role that rights have to play by indicating that they serve to express the moral equality of autonomous beings, each of which has an equal claim to be provided the conditions necessary for self-development as a being of that kind. Rights also serve in this context to protect the interests of each in having certain goods and services on which self-development depends,

and this sets the stage for the many compromises and trade-offs that society must assure are justly arrived at and implemented. Some additional points may also be worth noting here.

First, the fact that scores of nations are signatories to the Universal Declaration of the Rights of Man, on which the United Nations was founded, indicates, prima facie at least, that the concept of rights is understandable and significant to people of diverse experience and cultural backgrounds. This remains true in spite of the egregious and often shocking violations of human rights in all parts of the globe that are characteristic of our era. Whether people in general live up to their moral precepts or only pay lip service to them is surely independent of considerations of their validity and significance, for moral beliefs as such are not invalidated by immoral behavior, however widespread.

Second, it seems highly unlikely that an account of fundamental legal or otherwise institutionalized rights (such as the rights of habeas corpus, trial by jury, suffrage, freedom of speech and assembly, and property) could even be formulated if there were no moral rights on which they could rest. One kind of legal right in fact serves the sole function of guaranteeing the exercise of basic moral rights in society and establishes grounds for protecting individuals against violations of their moral rights (in essence, their persons) in practical situations. In other words, this subclass of legal rights gives concrete definition to moral rights within a political framework. (Bills of rights and guarantees of civil liberties are of this type.)

Third, it is questionable whether morality can dispense with a strong assertion of rights. Persistent violation of persons' autonomy in some countries could be said to underscore the necessity of ascribing rights to individuals to serve as a declaration of the dignity and inviolability of the person, as well as some kind of protection against the arbitrary use of power over the person and as a foundation for international laws to protect individuals everywhere against such abuses.

With these points in mind, then, I wish to consider what it means to ascribe moral rights to human beings.

The idea of basic moral rights (the rights to life, liberty, happiness or well-being, freedom from suffering, and the like) need not remain a mystery, because it is possible to retain the attractive features of the traditional natural-rights theory while avoiding its pitfalls. To begin with, the possession of those characteristics that make humans members of a moral community also makes them the possessors of rights. It would be a mistake, however, to construe this as simply another way of expressing the natural-rights theorist's claim that rights are possessed by virtue of our being humans. Whereas I have endorsed the view that the possession of certain *attributes* is crucial to both autonomy and having rights, there are two important differences between the position I am defending and the traditional natural-rights theory. One is that having rights and ascribing them to others are functions of the mutual recognition that occurs within a social group of autonomous beings, that is, of the recognition that they manifest the sorts of characteristics that identify them as autonomous agents. In other words, members of the social group recognize and acknowledge, either explicitly or tacitly, that others in the group, like themselves, possess the prerequisites for autonomous, rational behavior and hence for moral personhood. The ascription of rights, then, is an act signifying the recognition that others are beings of this sort and expresses in symbolic form the resolve that they shall be treated in a manner appropriate to the autonomy and personhood thus perceived. Among other things, this resolve means that each undertakes to guarantee everyone else adequate scope for independent self-expression, responsibility, self-determination, and an equal opportunity to develop to his or her fullest potential. From the standpoint of the individual, rights may be seen, inversely, as claims on others to be recognized and respected in accordance with one's natural capacities, autonomy, and personhood.[6]

Thus rights belong to beings because they are moral agents functioning within a community of which responsibility and accountability are central features and where they are acknowledged to be such. Rights therefore do not need to be thought of as arising in some nebulous "state of nature, independently of human institutions and conventions, simply by virtue of our humanity," even though they do require that we conceive of them by reference to the possession of a certain set of attributes. Nor do rights need to be described or defended as God-given or as self-evidently attached to being a member of the genus *Homo sapiens* or even as self-evidently attached to manifestations of autonomy, personhood, and agency (although they are so attached). As we have seen, criteria for the assignment and possession of rights can be specified, so that religious and intuitionist considerations are unnecessary to give substance to the notion of universal moral rights, as belonging properly to a certain class of beings.

The second principal difference between the position put forward here and traditional natural-rights theory is that I have generally avoided speaking of humans or referring to "our humanness" in considering the notions of moral community and rights, opting instead for speaking in more species-neutral terms – of "beings" of a certain type (autonomous beings). In discussing such questions as the comparative moral status of humans and animals, we should try to avoid the sort of species chauvinism or narrow anthropocentrism argued against . . . . Many scientists now believe it is very probable that intelligent life exists elsewhere in the universe. If so, we may well come into contact some day with extraterrestrial forms of intelligent life with which we can communicate and interact at a high level of complexity. We have no reason to suppose that such extraterrestrials would belong to our own or a similar species or even resemble anything with which we are familiar.[7] But by the same token, there appears to be no good reason to assume that they would not share the same sorts of aspirations and have many of the same fundamental needs and interests as we or that they would be instinctively hostile to us. We should therefore recast our moral precepts in a form that could be extended to such creatures, which might very well be like us in all morally relevant respects.

Another reason for framing our moral precepts more cautiously has to do with other species that inhabit the earth. Though I do not think anyone can honestly assert, on the basis of the evidence available, that it is at all likely we shall learn to communicate at a high level with any terrestrial animals (such as chimpanzees, whales, or dolphins), it is at least possible. It is possible too that they are so very similar to us in all important respects that we should be prepared to extend our moral community to include them as equals if this turned out to be the case. However remote these prospects may be, it would be foolishly shortsighted to exclude animals from the moral community merely as a matter of principle or definition. Speaking of "beings" rather than "humans" avoids just these problems.[8]

The argument thus far has been that human beings have basic moral rights because they are beings of the requisite kind, that is, autonomous beings, persons, or moral agents. Even though other species have not been systematically excluded from possible membership in the moral community, I have not hesitated to characterize the central concepts that define the moral community in human or humanly understandable terms. For this I offer no apology. Since the only species we know of that has developed the notions of rights and obligations (and the institutions associated with them) is *Homo sapiens*, there must be something about this peculiar sort of social being that accounts for the phenomenon in question. My claim is that the attributes of humans that explain why they have developed such concepts and institutions are humans' possession of a particular kind of reflexive consciousness, unique cognitive and linguistic abilities, and the capacity to comprehend, undertake, and carry out obligations and to expect the same of similarly constituted beings. Furthermore, it is important to note that autonomous beings have certain types of interests which these institutions exist to ensure are recognized and respected. Only in this manner can such agents' well-being be protected and facilitated.

Autonomy and Rights

Why do only autonomous beings have rights? The answer can now be given quite briefly: (1)

Autonomous beings are capable of free (self-determining, voluntary), deliberative, responsible action and have the sort of awareness necessary to see this kind of action as essential to their nature, well-being, and development as individuals. (2) Autonomous beings are capable of recognizing autonomy in others and of full participation in the moral community, as already described.[9] It is not arbitrary to hold that all and only such beings qualify for the possession of rights. Once we demystify the notion of natural rights, we can see that the ascription of rights to other beings and to ourselves is the keystone of the mutual recognition process on which the moral community is founded. Assigning rights to others and claiming them for oneself is tantamount to issuing a declaration of nonintervention in the self-governing lives of others, by acknowledging the sort of being they are, and acquiring mutual guarantees of this type by tacit agreement (that is, "All things being equal, I agree to recognize your autonomy and not interfere with its free expression and development if you agree to do the same for me").

This is why philosophers have generally regarded rights and obligations as logically connected or correlative. If I have a right, then others are deemed to have a duty to respect that right, which means either to refrain from interfering with my free exercise of it or to assist me in attaining what I have a right to, as the case may be and as the circumstances require and permit. It does not follow, of course, that all such rights are absolute, inalienable, or indefeasible, and here the present account departs once more from traditional natural-rights theory. Normally, basic moral rights cannot be forfeited, compromised, suspended, or overridden by the acts of others or even of oneself. Under exceptional conditions, such as self-defense, imprisonment for crimes, or declarations of legal incompetence, certain rights justifiably may be abrogated. In addition, conflicts between individuals are commonplace in society and moral principles and institutions have to be evolved to deal with them in ways that are fair to those concerned. (A good deal of our political machinery serves just this function.)

The Position of Animals *vis-à-vis* the Moral Community

The conclusion to be drawn from the foregoing discussion, so far as it pertains to animals, is that lacking in various degrees the possession of capacities on which moral autonomy or agency depends, animals fail to meet the conditions specified for full membership in the moral community and likewise fail to qualify for having rights. Joel Feinberg has, I believe, stated fairly clearly why this is so with particular reference to dogs, but his point is generalizable to all animals.

Well-trained dogs sometimes let their masters down; they anticipate punishment or other manifestations of displeasure; they grovel and whimper, and they even make crude efforts at redress and reconciliation. But do they feel remorse and bad conscience? They have been conditioned to associate manifestations of displeasure with departures from a norm, and this is a useful way of keeping them in line, but they haven't the slightest inkling of the *reasons* for the norm. They don't *understand* why departures from the norm are wrong, or why their masters become angry or disappointed. They have a concept perhaps of the *mala prohibita* – the act that is wrong because it is prohibited, but they have no notion of the *mala in se* – the act that is prohibited because it is wrong. Even in respect to the *mala prohibita* their understanding is grossly deficient, for they have no conception of rightful authority. For dogs, the only basis of their master's "right" to be obeyed is his *de facto* power over them. Even when one master steals a beast from another, or when an original owner deprives it of its natural freedom in the wild, the animal will feel no moralized emotion, such as outraged propriety or indignation. These complex feelings involve cognitive elements beyond an animal's ken. Similarly, to suffer a guilty conscience is to be more than merely unhappy or anxious; it is to be in such a state because one has violated an "internalized standard," a principle of one's own, the rationale of which one can fully appreciate and the correctness of which one can, but in fact does not, doubt.[10]

Since animals could not begin to function as equals in a society of autonomous beings, they cannot be counted within the bond of association that makes morality and its institutions viable and gives them vitality. It should be apparent by now that the intent of this sort of judgment is not to portray the moral community as an exclusive club for membership within which "no animals need apply." Rather, it is to take a realistic look at the considerations that are relevant to regarding a being as having (or lacking) full moral status.

It should also be evident that any attempt to equate the "animal liberation" movement, which claims that animals and humans have equal moral status, with the civil rights and feminist movements is preposterous and indeed insulting to those who have worked long and hard to advance the cause of blacks and women (and children and other underprivileged groups). Blacks and women have been systematically denied full and equal moral status with whites and men. In effect, they have been prevented from enjoying the full membership in the moral community that is their due, on the basis of morally irrelevant differences – skin color and sex. It is precisely this sort of discrimination that we describe as unjust treatment. Animals, however, are denied full and equal moral status (and hence full membership in the moral community) for reasons that *are* morally relevant, namely, their lack of autonomy and moral agency. When women and blacks are granted their rights, these are not invented or "given" to them; rather, granting their rights is simply belatedly acknowledging that women and blacks are the sorts of beings that should have been perceived as autonomous all along and that therefore can claim to have been oppressed.

The characteristics on which this judgment or admission is made do not reduce merely to the capacity to experience pleasure and to suffer but are much more complex, as we have seen. If these characteristics are lacking in animals, then it makes no sense to speak of animals as "oppressed" and as deserving of equal moral concern. Failure to apprehend this crucial difference between animals and humans not only displays moral insensitivity but also denigrates and, by introducing conceptual confusion, weakens the legitimate case of those who genuinely are oppressed by trivializing it and making it appear ridiculous.[11]

I have tried to show why it is inappropriate to think of animals in terms that have meaningful application only to persons and to argue for this position rather than make a stand on faith or dogma. We may now turn to other issues to arrive at a resolution of the question of animals' proper moral status.

The Position of Deficient Humans *vis-à-vis* the Moral Community

Before we can make any progress on defining animals' moral status, however, we must face an extremely difficult question that is raised by the foregoing analysis and immediately presses itself on our attention. This is the problem of how to classify in relation to the moral community those beings that fall short of autonomy but which we should still consider candidates for rights and therefore to which we have obligations. Examples here would include infants, the severely mentally retarded, and those who are senile, autistic, mentally ill, badly brain damaged, comatose, and so on. Any theory linking full moral status to the possession of rights and the possession of rights in turn to autonomy is bound to encounter this issue and to stand or fall by how well it comes to terms with it.[12] This problem is also relevant because some might contend that certain animals are among those beings that fall short of autonomy but possess in varying degrees at least some of the capacities believed essential to autonomy. If deficient humans qualify for rights in spite of what they lack, it may then be asked, why not also higher animals? The difficulty is aggravated by the previous admission that it is not necessary to membership in the moral community that one be a member of the genus *Homo sapiens*; and if the stress falls on the possession of certain crucial traits, then it would seem that it is also not sufficient for membership that one be human.

Do human beings deficient in autonomy fail to qualify for rights, and do we as a result cease to have moral obligations toward them? Some anti-vivisectionists maintain that underdeveloped or deficient humans are no more and often less similar to normal humans in morally relevant respects than healthy and mature members of certain other species. Thus, it is claimed, a fully developed horse may be more reflective than a brain-damaged child; a chimpanzee more skilled in language than a newborn infant; a cat better able to reason than a comatose accident victim. It has even been suggested that to be consistent we should consider ourselves morally bound not to use such animals for any purpose for which we would not feel equally justified in using an underdeveloped or deficient human being.[13] However, this line of reasoning seems to me to betray a degree of moral insensitivity which we should all wish to reject.

If, as most would agree, natural emotional responses to and feelings of kinship with other species are allowed to count as factors in shaping our assessment of their moral status, then such responses and feelings should count equally in our dealings with members of our own species. We must also acknowledge differences among the sorts of cases under consideration. Infants are appropriately related to as potential fully autonomous beings, possessing in latency those attributes that will later (typically at maturity, given normal development) find expression, whereas those who are senile, comatose, mentally ill, or incapacitated by disease or accident are generally individuals who have achieved autonomy but whose full functioning is now blocked by conditions or circumstances beyond their control. In the case of children who are severely retarded, autistic, and so on, however, we are dealing with people who may never achieve a semblance of autonomy. In deciding how we ought to look on all these classes of individuals, a reasonable position to take would seem to be that here membership in our own species ought to count for something, in the sense in which a charitable attitude toward those less developed or less fortunate than ourselves, for whom we feel some especially close kinship, is particularly compelling to a morally mature person. Just as our untutored moral sense tells us that we have very strong obligations to members of our immediate families, so it seems that preferential treatment should, under certain circumstances, accordingly be granted to members of the human family.[14]

John Passmore, writing on the subject of our obligations to future generations, has argued that "a chain of love and concern" extends from our children and grandchildren to our grandchildren's grandchildren, and that it also embraces the "places, institutions and forms of activity" that shape our daily life. As Passmore notes, "Such links are sufficiently common and persistent to lend continuity to a civilization" and to explain sacrificing for future human beings.[15] Such a "chain" surely accounts for our concern for those among us who are severely handicapped or grievously disadvantaged. This is not to deny, of course, that a similar chain connects us to the animals, but the latter is not, I think, naturally so strong, direct, or morally compelling. (I have more to say on this important topic later in this chapter.)

Admittedly, for many it is not an easy matter to feel a close kinship to those less fortunate or often even to see them as human. Many cannot even establish an empathetic relationship with a normal, healthy human infant. Probably almost all of us would prefer and choose to spend time with responsive, sociable animals than with humans whose faculties are severely compromised. But none of these facts obviates the responsibility of each of us (whether religious or not) to develop and incorporate into our moral outlook the spirit behind the old saying, "There, but for the grace of God, go I." Let us say, then, that although underdeveloped or deficient humans are also, like animals, not full members of the moral community because they lack autonomy, they must nevertheless fall within the most immediate extension of the moral community and as such are subject to its protection. This sensibility is indeed a cornerstone of civilized society, for failure to cultivate and preserve this frail thread leaves the way open to systematic abuses of the dignity and rights of those designated as second-class citizens. Under certain all-too-common circumstances, it may also lead to Nazi-like genocidal campaigns to eliminate "undesirables," "defectives," or "unworthy lives."

We might add that it is also a matter of prudence that we cultivate such a sentiment; for each of us knows that under certain unforeseeable circumstances he or she might suffer an injury or illness that could severely limit or even terminate his or her autonomy.

Membership in the moral community is not a cut-and-dried matter. How many and what kinds of affinities with ourselves a creature must exhibit before being counted as autonomous is not something that can be decided in the abstract but rather has to be examined on a case-by-case basis. Just as animals cannot be looked on as an undifferentiated or virtually identical collection of beings, so too there is no uniform class of underdeveloped or deficient human beings. Because of this, a comparison of such individuals would array them variably according to the presence or absence in them of capacities that are essential for autonomy. At one end of the scale would be those whom we sometimes (less than charitably) identify as hopeless "human vegetables" or "basket cases," whereas at the other end could be found normal infants, less severe retardates, and others who manifest to a greater or lesser degree psychological attributes that are typical of personhood.

To add further complexity to this already very difficult issue, we must bear in mind that conditions considered irremediable at present may yield to scientific inroads with astonishing suddenness. Autism is a case in point. Once considered completely impervious to all therapies and treatments, techniques have been devised in the past few years that promise to give autistic children a semblance of a normal life.[16] This sort of breakthrough, of course, does not happen as often as some try to make out. A cure is not just around the corner for every severe handicap. But the examples that can be cited should give us pause when we feel inclined to lump together as without hope a whole range of diverse conditions affecting normal human functioning and autonomy.

In view of this, it appears that drawing a line to separate human beings who are full members of the moral community from those who are not is probably not only an impossible task but also, even if feasible, extremely dangerous and unwise. If we must nevertheless give a rule that will rationalize including such borderline cases within the framework of the moral community, it might reasonably take the following form:

All underdeveloped, deficient, or seriously impaired human beings are to be considered members of an immediately extended moral community and therefore as deserving of equal moral concern. To whatever degree seems reasonable, they should be treated according to either (a) their potential for full agency (and hence as potentially full participants in the moral community, taking into account their past participation, if any) or (b) the degree to which their behavior and capacities approximate what is generally considered to be characteristically human (that is, typically the case at maturity, given normal development) and the extent to which their behavior and capacities permit full participation in the moral community.

This benefit-of-the-doubt principle might be looked on by critics as speciesist, but it seems to me that charity, benevolence, humaneness, and prudence require such an extension and that it is not inconsistent with a theory of morality that makes rights and autonomy central or, more important, with the way we in fact treat such cases in everyday life. Finally, dealing with these cases in the way I have suggested here, if properly labeled speciesist at all, is not unacceptably so; for extending the moral community to take account of exceptional cases does not exclude other species in principle from being treated in a similar manner or bar them from full membership in the moral community if they so qualify. So-called borderline cases or marginal humans – those where we are unsure whether to call something a human being or person or where our moral principles come under severe strain – are notoriously difficult to deal with. There seems to be no justification, however, for condemning a theory holding persons (not species) to be the central focus of moral concern on the grounds that it favors *Homo sapiens* over other known species in fringe areas where the applicability of our usual moral categories is bound to be far from clear-cut.

Notes

1 Arthur L. Caplan, "Rights Language and the Ethical Treatment of Animals," in Laurence B. McCullough and James Polk Morris, III, eds., *Implications of History and Ethics to Medicine – Veterinary and Human* (College Station, Texas: Centennial Academic Assembly, Texas A & M University, 1978), p. 129.

2 Cf. H. J. McCloskey, "The Right to Life," *Mind* 84 (1975): 413.

3 This strategy is followed by Bernard E. Rollin in *Animal Rights and Human Morality* (Buffalo, NY: Prometheus Books, 1981), pt. 1; but it is also a central feature of Singer's *Animal Liberation* and of other works. Indeed, the archetype of the argument is Bentham's frequently cited remark which I quoted at the beginning of the chapter from which this excerpt is taken.

4 Christopher W. Morris, "Comments on 'Rights and Autonomy,' by David Richards, and 'Autonomy and Rights: A Case for Ethical Socialism,' by Michael McDonald," paper presented to Conference on Human Rights, University of Waterloo, Waterloo, Ontario, April 17–19, 1980, 2.

5 Richard Wasserstrom, "Rights, Human Rights, and Racial Discrimination," in A. I. Melden, ed., *Human Rights* (Belmont, CA.: Wadsworth, 1970), pp. 104, 105.

   As Alan Goldman has written, rights "carve out a moral space in which persons can develop as distinct individuals free from the constant intrusion of demands from others" ("The Source and Extent of a Patient's Right to the Truth," *Queen's Quarterly* 91 [1984]: 126).

6 It may be objected that agents' autonomy is protected by the traditional right to liberty and that therefore there is no reason why animals should not be seen as possessing other rights, such as the right not to suffer or the right to live. (I owe this objection to Christine Pierce.) But the argument offered here is that rights only arise and make sense within a framework in which mutual recognition and accountability are typical characteristics of

relationships, and it is clear that animals have no place in such a conceptual environment.

7 Carl Sagan, *The Cosmic Connection: An Extraterrestrial Perspective* (New York: Dell, 1975); John W. Macvey, *Interstellar Travel: Past, Present, and Future* (New York: Stein and Day, 1977).

8 For more on this interesting subject, see Roland Puccetti, *Persons: A Study of Possible Moral Agents in the Universe* (London: Macmillan, 1968), ch. 4.

9 A largely psychogenetic account has been given here of the reasons why the possession of autonomy or personhood (and only this) confers moral rights on a being or entitles it to respect and equal moral concern; that is, the ascription of rights to such beings has been explained in terms of the conditions under which autonomous beings are disposed to ascribe rights to themselves and to other like beings. It may be argued therefore that a clinching philosophical argument for such ascriptions has not been provided; that it has not been shown why the possession of autonomy is a peculiarly relevant consideration, whereas possession of other characteristics, such as the capacity to suffer, are not.

I am not sure this kind of argument can be supplied, though I think that further reflections on the nature of autonomy, like those that occupy much of the rest of this chapter, go a good distance toward satisfying this demand. The reason such an argument cannot be given is that here we are up against the same problem of the fact–value gap that plagues all moral theories. By the same token, for instance, utilitarians cannot defend their key claim that the capacity to suffer is the singularly relevant criterion for the assignment of rights or the entitlement to respect and equal moral concern.

10 Joel Feinberg, "Human Duties and Animal Rights," in Morris and Fox, *On the Fifth Day*, 50 (author's italics).

11 For reasons of this sort, some critics of animal liberation have denied that speciesism constitutes a form of immorality comparable to racism and sexism – indeed, that it is immoral at all. For good arguments against the claim that speciesism is im-moral, see the following: Leslie Pickering Francis and Richard Norman, "Some Animals Are More Equal Than Others," *Philosophy* 53, no. 206 (October 1978): 507–27; Cigman, "Death, Misfortune, and Species Inequality"; Meredith Williams, "Rights, Interests, and Moral Equality," *Environmental Ethics* 2 (1980): 149–61; Richard A. Watson, "Self-Consciousness and the Rights of Nonhuman Animals and Nature," *Environmental Ethics* 1 (1979): 99–129; Michael Wreen, "In Defense of Speciesism," *Ethics and Animals* 53 (September 1984): 47–60.

12 Any alternative moral theory will have to confront the same problem; for since no society's resources are unlimited, the interests of disadvantaged individuals must always be weighed against those of everyone else.

13 For example, Singer, *Animal Liberation*, 80 f.

14 For a closer look at the family-of-man argument and a perceptive discussion, from a different perspective, of its bearing on the ethical problem of according preferential treatment to defective humans over animals, see Vinit Haksar, *Equality, Liberty, and Perfectability* (Oxford: Oxford University Press, 1979), 38–45, 71–9. See also Wreen, "In Defense of Speciesism," 53; United States Congress, Office of Technology Assessment, *Alternatives to Animal Use in Testing, Research, and Education* (Washington, D.C.: US Government Printing Office, 1985), ch. 4.

15 Passmore, *Man's Responsibility for Nature*, 88–9.

16 See Helen Kohl, "The Strange Ones," *Canadian Magazine*, April 7, 1979, pp. 10–12, 14; Laura Schreibman and Robert L. Koegel, "Autism: A Defeatable Horror," *Psychology Today* 8/10 (March 1975): 61–7; O. Ivar Lovaas, "Behavioral Treatment of Autistic Children," in Janet T. Spence et al., eds., *Behavioral Approaches to Therapy* (Morristown, NJ: General Learning Press, 1976), pp. 185–201. The techniques described by Kohl and others, it should be noted, are based largely on knowledge about the efficacy of rewards and punishments in learning acquired initially through animal experiments.

16

Moral Standing, the Value of Lives, and Speciesism

R. G. Frey

The question of who or what has moral standing, of who or what is a member of the moral community, has received wide exposure in recent years. Various answers have been extensively canvassed; and though controversy still envelops claims for the inclusion of the inanimate environment within the moral community, such claims on behalf of animals (or, at least, the "higher" animals) are now widely accepted. Morally, then, animals count. I do not myself think that we have needed a great deal of argument to establish this point; but numerous writers, obviously, have thought otherwise. In any event, no work of mine has ever denied that animals count. In order to suffer, animals do not have to be self-conscious, to have interests or beliefs or language, to have desires and desires related to their own future, to exercise self-critical control of their behaviour, or to possess rights; and I, a utilitarian, take their sufferings into account, morally. Thus, the scope of the moral community, at least so far as ("higher") animals are concerned, is not something I contest. I may disagree with some particular way of trying to show that animals possess moral standing, e.g., by ascribing them some variant of moral rights, but I have no quarrel with the general claim that they possess such standing. Indeed, my reformist position with respect to vegetarianism, vivisection, and our general use of animals in part turns upon this very fact.

As I have indicated in my two books and numerous articles on animal issues,[1] my reservations come elsewhere. Some of these doubts and criticisms I have explored and developed in a recent series of articles.[2] There, I have focused upon the comparative value of human and animal life; I have taken the notion of autonomy to be central to this issue, since the exercise of autonomy by normal adult humans is the source of an immense part of the value of their lives. Here, I want to sketch one way this concern with the comparative value of human and animal life comes to have importance and to interact with the charge of speciesism.

I

Those who concern themselves with the moral considerability of animals may well be tempted to suppose that their work is finished, once they successfully envelop animals within the moral community. Yet, to stop there is never *per se* to address the issue of the value of animal life and so never to engage the position that I, and others, hold on certain issues. Thus, I am a restricted vivisectionist,[3] not because I think animals are outside the moral community but because of views I hold about the value of their lives. Again, I think it is permissible to use animal parts in human transplants,[4] not because I think animals lack moral standing but because I think animal life is less valuable than human life. (As some readers may know, I argue that experiments upon animals and the use of animal parts in human transplants are only permissible if one is prepared to sanction such experiments upon, and the use of, certain humans. I think the benefits to be derived from these practices are *sometimes* substantial enough to compel me to endorse the practices in the human case, unless the side-effects of any such decision offset these benefits.[5] I return to this matter of our use of humans below.)

I have written of views that I hold; the fact is, I think, that the vast majority of people share my view of the differing value of human and animal life. This view we might capture in the form of three propositions:

1 Animal life has some value;
2 Not all animal life has the same value;
3 Human life is more valuable than animal life.

Very few people today would seem to believe that animal life is without value and that, therefore, we need not trouble ourselves morally about taking it. Equally few people, however, would seem to believe that all animal life has the same value. Certainly, the lives of dogs, cats, and chimps are very widely held to be more valuable than the lives of mice, rats, and worms, and the legal protections we accord these different creatures, for example, reflect this fact. Finally, whatever value we take the lives of dogs and cats to have, most of us believe human life to be more valuable than animal life. We believe this, moreover, even as we oppose cruelty to animals and acknowledge value in the case of some animals, considerable value to their lives. I shall call this claim about the comparative value of human and animal life the unequalvalue

thesis. A crucial question, obviously, is whether we who hold this thesis can defend it.

Many "animal rightists" themselves seem inclined to accept something like the unequal-value thesis. With respect to the oft-cited raft example, in which one can save a man or a dog but not both, animal rightists often concede that other things being equal, one ought to save the man. To be sure, this result only says something about our intuitions and about those *in extremis*; yet, what it is ordinarily taken to say about them that we take human life to be more valuable than animal life is not something we think in extreme circumstances only. Our intuitions about the greater value of human life seem apparent in and affect all our relations with animals, from the differences in the ways we regard, treat, and even bury humans and animals to the differences in the safeguards for their protection that we construct and the differences in penalties we exact for violation of those safeguards.

In a word, the unequal-value thesis seems very much a part of the approach that most of us adopt towards animal issues. We oppose cruelty to animals as well as humans, but this does not lead us to suppose that the lives of humans and animals have the same value. Nor is there any entailment in the matter: one can perfectly consistently oppose cruelty to all sentient creatures without having to suppose that the lives of all such creatures are equally valuable.

We might note in passing that if this is right about our intuitions, then it is far from clear that it is the defender of the unequal-value thesis who must assume the burden of proof in the present discussion. Our intuitions about pain and suffering are such that if a theorist today suggested that animal suffering did not count morally, then he would quickly find himself on the defensive. If I am right about our intuitions over the comparative value of human and animal life, why is the same not true in the case of the theorist who urges or assumes that these lives are of equal value? If, over suffering, our intuitions force the exclusion of the pains of animals to be defended, why, over the value of life, do they not force an *equal*-value thesis to be defended? In any event, I have not left this matter of the burden of proof to chance in my other work (see also below), where I have *argued* for the unequal-value thesis. Here, I want only to stress that our intuitions *do not obviously endorse*, as it were, a starting-point of equality of value in the lives of humans and animals.[6] On the strength of this consideration alone, we seem justified in at least treating sceptically arguments and claims that proceed from or implicitly rely upon some initial presumption of equal value, in order to undermine the unequalvalue thesis from the outset.

Where pain and suffering are the central issue, most of us tend to think of the human and animal cases in the same way; thus, cruelty to a child and cruelty to a dog are wrong and wrong for the same reason.[7] Pain is pain; it is an evil, and the evidence suggests that it is as much an evil for dogs as for humans.[8] Furthermore, autonomy or agency (or the lack thereof) does not seem a relevant factor here, since the pains of non-autonomous creatures count as well as the pains of autonomous ones. Neither the child nor the dog is autonomous, at least in any sense that captures why autonomy is such an immensely important value; but the pains of both child and dog count and affect our judgements of rightness and wrongness with respect to what is done to them.

Where the value of life is the central issue, however, we do not tend to think of the human and animal cases alike. Here, we come down in favour of humans, as when we regularly experiment upon and kill animals in our laboratories for (typically) human benefit; and a main justification reflective people give for according humans such advantage invokes directly a difference in value between human and animal life. Autonomy or agency is now, moreover, of the utmost significance, since the exercise of autonomy by normal adult humans is one of the central ways they make possible further, important dimensions of value to their lives.

Arguably, even the extended justification of animal suffering in, say, medical research may make indirect appeal to the unequal-value thesis. Though pain remains an evil, the nature and size of some benefit determines whether its infliction is justified in the particular cases. Nothing precludes this benefit from accruing to human beings, and when it does, we need an independent defence of the appeal to benefit in this kind of case. For the appeal is typically invoked in cases where those who suffer are those who benefit, as when we go to the dentist, and in the present instance human beings are the beneficiaries of animal suffering. Possibly the unequal-value thesis can provide the requisite defence: what justifies the infliction of pain, if anything does, is the appeal to benefit; but what justifies use of the appeal in those cases where humans are the beneficiaries of animal suffering is, arguably, that human life is more valuable than animal life. Thus, while the unequal-value thesis cannot alter the character of pain, which remains an evil, and cannot directly, independently of benefit, justify the infliction of pain, it can, the suggestion is, anchor a particular use of the appeal to benefit.

I do not have space to discuss what constitutes a benefit, the magnitude of benefit required in order to justify the infliction of pain, and some principle of proportionality that rejects even a significant benefit at a cost of immense and excruciating suffering. In general, my views on these matters favour animals, especially when further commercial products are in question but also even when much medical/scientific research is under consideration. More broadly, I think a presumption, not in favour of, but against the use of animals in medical/scientific research would be desirable. Its intended effect would be to force researchers as a matter of routine to argue in depth a case for animal use.[9] Such a presumption coheres with my earlier remarks. The unequal-value thesis in no way compels its adherents to deny that animal lives have value; the destruction or impairment of such lives, therefore, needs to be argued for, which a presumption against use of animals would force researchers to do.

Clearly, a presumption against use is not the same thing as a bar; I allow, therefore, that researchers can make a case. That they must do so, that they must seek to justify the destruction or impairment of lives that have value, is the point.

II

How might we defend the unequal-value thesis? At least the beginnings of what I take to be the most promising option in this regard can be briefly sketched.

Pain is one thing, killing is another, and what makes killing wrong – a killing could be free of pain and suffering – seems to be the fact that it consists in the destruction of something of value. That is, killing and the value of life seem straightforwardly connected, since it is difficult to understand why taking a particular life would be wrong if it had no value. If few people consider animal life to be without value, equally few, I think, consider it to have the same value as normal (adult) human life. They need not be speciesists as a result: in my view, normal (adult) human life is of a much higher quality than animal life, not because of species, but because of richness; and the value of a life is a function of its quality.

Part of the richness of our lives involves activities that we have in common with animals but there are as well whole dimensions to our lives – love, marriage, educating children, jobs, hobbies, sporting events, cultural pursuits, intellectual development and striving, etc. – that greatly expand our range of absorbing endeavours and so significantly deepen the texture of our lives. An impoverished life for *us* need not be one in which food or sex or liberty is absent; it can equally well be a life in which these other dimensions have not taken root or have done so only minimally. When we look back over our lives and regret that we did not make more of them, we rarely have in mind only the kinds of activities that we share with animals; rather, we think much more in terms of precisely these other dimensions of our lives that equally go to make up a rich, full life.

The lives of normal (adult) humans betray a variety and richness that the lives of rabbits do not; certainly, we do not think of ourselves as constrained to live out our lives according to some (conception of a) life deemed appropriate to our species. Other conceptions of a life for ourselves are within our reach, and we can try to understand and appreciate them and to choose among them. Some of us are artists, others educators, still others mechanics; the richness of our lives is easily enhanced through developing and moulding our talents so as to enable us to live out these conceptions of the good life. Importantly, also, we are not condemned to embrace in our lifetimes only a single conception of such a life; in the sense intended, the artist can choose to become an educator and the educator a mechanic. We can embrace at different times different conceptions of how we want to live.

Choosing among conceptions of the good life and trying to live out such a conception are not so intellectualized a set of tasks that only an elite few can manage them. Some reflection upon the life one wants to live is necessary, and some reflection is required in order to organize one's life to live out such a conception; but virtually all of us manage to engage in this degree of reflection. (One of the tragic aspects of Alzheimer's disease is how it undoes a person in just this regard, once it has reached advanced stages.) Even an uneducated man can see the choice between the army and professional boxing as one that requires him to sit down and ponder what he wants to do, whether he has the talents to do it, and what his other, perhaps conflicting desires come to in strength. Even an habitual street person, if free long enough from the influence of drink or drugs to be capable of addressing himself to the choice, can see the life the Salvation Army holds out before him as different in certain respects, some appealing, others perhaps not, from his present life. Choosing how one will live one's life can often be a matter of simply focusing upon these particulars and trying to gauge one's desires with respect to them.

Now, in the case of the rabbit the point is not that the activities which enrich an adult human's life are different from those which enrich its life; it is that the scope or potentiality for enrichment is truncated or severely diminished in the rabbit's case. The quality of a life is a function of its richness, which is a function of its scope or potentiality for enrichment; the scope or potentiality for enrichment in the rabbit's case never approaches that of the human.

Nothing we have ever observed about rabbits, nothing we know of them, leads us to make judgements about the variety and richness of their life in anything even remotely comparable to the judgements we make in the human case. To assume as present in the rabbit's life dimensions that supply the full variety and richness of ours, only that these dimensions are hidden from us, provides no real answer, especially when the evidence we have about their lives runs in the other direction.

Autonomy is an important part of the human case. By exercising our autonomy we can mould our lives to fit a conception of the good life that we have decided upon for ourselves; we can then try to live out this conception, with all the sense of achievement, self-fulfilment, and satisfaction that this can bring. Some of us pursue athletic or cultural or intellectual endeavours; some of us are good with our hands and enjoy mechanical tasks and manual labour; and all of us see a job – be it the one we have or the one we should like to have – as an important part of a full life. (This is why unemployment affects more than just our incomes.) The emphasis is upon agency: we can *make* ourselves into repairmen, pianists, and accountants; by exercising our autonomy, we can *impose* upon our lives a conception of the good life that we have for the moment embraced. We can then try to live out this conception, with the consequent sense of fulfilment and achievement that this makes possible. Even failure can be part of the picture: a woman can try to make herself into an Olympic athlete and fail; but her efforts to develop and shape her talents and to take control of and to mould her life in the appropriate ways can enrich her life. Thus, by exercising our autonomy and trying to live out some conception of how we want to live, we make possible further, important dimensions of value to our lives.

We still share certain activities with rabbits, but no mere record of those activities would come anywhere near accounting for the richness of our lives. What is missing in the rabbit's case is the same scope or potentiality for enrichment; and lives of less richness have less value.

The kind of story that would have to be told to make us think that the rabbit's life *was* as rich as the life of a normal (adult) human is one that either postulates in the rabbit potentialities and abilities vastly beyond what we observe and take it to have, or lapses into a rigorous scepticism. By the latter, I mean that we should have to say either that we know nothing of the rabbit's life (and so can know nothing of that life's richness and quality) or that what we know can never be construed as adequate for grounding judgements about the rabbit's quality of life.[10] Such sceptical claims, particularly after Ryle and Wittgenstein on the one hand and much scientific work on the other, may strike many as misplaced, and those who have recourse to them, at least in my experience, have little difficulty in pronouncing pain and suffering, stress, loss of liberty, monotony, and a host of other things to be detrimental to an animal quality of life. But the real puzzle is how this recourse to scepticism is supposed to make us think that a rabbit's life is as varied and rich as a human's life. If I can know nothing of the rabbit's life, presumably because I do not live that life and so cannot experience it from the inside (this whole way of putting the matter sets ill with a post-Ryle, post-Wittgenstein understanding of psychological concepts and inner processes), then how do I know that the rabbit's life is as rich as a human's life? Plainly, if I cannot know this, I must for the argument's sake assume it. But why should I do this? Nothing I observe and experience leads me to assume it; all the evidence I have about rabbits and humans seems to run entirely in the opposite direction. So, why make this assumption? Most especially, why assume animal lives are as rich as human lives, when we do not even assume, or so I suggest below, that all human lives have the same richness?

III

I have taken autonomy to be or to imply agency, and I have elsewhere considered two ways animal rightists might try to move on this issue. On the one hand, I have in my paper "The Significance of Agency and Marginal Cases" considered attempts to work animals into the class of the autonomous by appeal to (i) some distinction between potential and actual autonomy, (ii) some notion of impaired autonomy, (iii) some attempt to loosen the requirements for possessing one or more of the components of agency, and (iv) some notion of proxy agency. On the other hand, both in that paper and in "Autonomy and the Value of Animal Life", I have considered the attempt, notably by Tom Regan,[11] to sever autonomy from agency altogether. Both paths I have argued against and tried to show why they will not substantiate the claims that animal lives are as rich as human lives and that animal lives have roughly the same value as human lives. In Regan's case in particular, I have been concerned to show that any sense of autonomy that severs the concept from agency has been drained of virtually all the significance for the value of a life that we take autonomy to have.

Agency matters to the value of a life, and animals are not agents. Thus, we require some argument to show that their lack of agency notwithstanding, animals have lives of roughly equal richness and value to the lives of normal (adult) humans. The view that they are members of the moral community will not supply it, the demand is compatible with acknowledging that not all life has the same value; and as we shall see, the argument from the value of the lives of defective humans will not supply it. Any *assumption* that they have lives of equal richness and value to ours seems to run up against, quite apart from the evidence we take ourselves to have about the lives of animals, the fact that, as we shall see, not all human lives have the same richness and value.

Most importantly, it will not do to claim that the rabbit's life is as valuable as the normal (adult) human's life because it is the only life each has. This claim does not as yet say that the rabbit's life has any particular value. If the rabbit and man are dead, they have no life which they can carry on living, at some quality or other; but this *per se* does not show that the lives of the man and the rabbit have a particular value as such, let alone that they have the same value. Put differently, both creatures must be alive in order to have a quality of life, but

nothing at all in this shows that they have the same richness and quality of life and, therefore, value of life.[12] I am not disputing that animals can have *a* quality of life and that their lives, as a result, can have value; I am disputing that the richness, quality, and value of their lives is that of normal (adult) humans.

IV

Not all members of the moral community have lives of equal value. Human life is more valuable than animal life. That is our intuition, and as I have assumed, we must defend it. How we defend it is, however, a vitally important affair. For I take the charge of speciesism, the attempt to justify either different treatment or the attribution of a different value of life by appeal to species membership very seriously. In my view, if a defence of the unequal-value thesis is open to that charge, then it is no defence at all.

As a result, one's options for grounding the unequal-value thesis become limited; no ground will suffice that appeals, either in whole or in part, to species membership. Certainly, some ways of trying to differentiate the value of human from animal life in the past seem pretty clearly to be speciesist. But not all ways are; the important option set out above – one that construes the value of a life as a function of its quality, its quality as a function of its richness, and its richness as a function of its capacity of enrichment – does not use species membership to determine the value of lives. Indeed, it quite explicitly allows for the possibility that some animal life may be more valuable than some human life.

To see this, we have only to realize that the claim that not all members of the moral community have lives of equal value encompasses not only animals but also some humans. Some human lives have less value than others. An infant born without a brain, or any very severely handicapped infant, seems a case in point, as does an elderly person fully in the grip of Alzheimer's disease or some highly degenerative brain, nervous, or physiological disorder. In other words, I think we are compelled to admit that some human life is of a much lower quality and so value than normal (adult) human life. (This is true as well of infants generally, though readers may think in their cases, unlike the cases of seriously defective infants and adults, some argument from potentiality may be adduced to place them in a separate category. The fact remains, however, that the lives of normal (adult) humans betray a variety and richness that the lives of animals, defective humans, and infants do not.)

Accordingly, we must understand the unequal-value thesis to claim that normal (adult) human life is more valuable than animal life. If we justify this claim by appeal to the quality and richness of normal (adult) human life and if we at the same time acknowledge that some human life is of a much lower quality and value than normal (adult) human life, then it seems quite clear that we are not using species membership to determine the value of a life.

Moreover, because some human lives fall drastically below the quality of life of normal (adult) human life, we must face the prospect that the lives of some perfectly healthy animals have a higher quality and greater value than the lives of some humans. And we must face this prospect, with all the implications it may have for the use of these unfortunate humans by others, at least if we continue to justify the use of animals in medical/scientific research by appeal to the lower quality and value of their lives.[13]

What justifies the medical/scientific use of perfectly healthy rabbits instead of humans with a low quality of life? If, for example, experiments on retinas are suggested, why use rabbits or chimps instead of defective humans with otherwise excellent retinas? I know of nothing that cedes human life of any quality, however low, greater value than animal life of any quality, however high. If, therefore, we are going to justify medical/scientific uses of animals by appeal to the value of their lives, we open up directly the possibility of our having to envisage the use of humans of a lower quality of life in preference to animals of a higher quality of life. It is important to bear in mind as well that other factors then come under consideration, such as

(i) the nature and size of benefit to be achieved, (ii) the side-effects that any decision to use humans in preference to animals may evoke, (iii) the degree to which education and explanation can dissipate any such negative side-effects, and (iv) the projected reliability of animal results for the human case (as opposed to the projected reliability of human results for the human case). All these things may, in the particular case, work in favour of the use of humans.

The point, of course, is not that we *must* use humans; it is that we cannot invariably use animals in preference to humans, if appeal to the quality and value of lives is the ground we give for using animals. The only way we could justifiably do this is if we could cite something that always, no matter what, cedes human life greater value than animal life. I know of no such thing.

Always in the background, of course, are the benefits that medical/scientific research confers: if we desire to continue to obtain these benefits, are we prepared to pay the price of the use of defective humans? The answer, I think, must be positive, at least until the time comes when we no longer have to use either humans or animals for research purposes. Obviously, this deliberate use of some of the weakest members of our society is distasteful to contemplate and is not something, in the absence of substantial benefit, that we could condone; yet, we presently condone the use of perfectly healthy animals on an absolutely massive scale, and benefit is the justification we employ.

I remain a vivisectionist, therefore, because of the benefits medical/scientific research can bestow. Support for vivisection, however, exacts a cost: it forces us to envisage the use of defective humans in such research. Paradoxically, then, to the extent that one cannot bring oneself to envisage and consent to their use, to that extent, in my view, the case for anti-vivisectionism becomes stronger.

V

The fact that not even all human life has the same value explains why some argument from marginal cases, one of the most common arguments in support of an equal-value thesis, comes unstuck. Such an argument would only be possible if human life of a much lower quality were ceded equal value with normal (adult) human life. In that case, the same concession could be requested for animal life, and an argument from marginal or defective humans could get underway. On the account of the value of a life set out above, however, the initial concession is not made; it is not true that defective human life has the same quality and value as normal (adult) human life. Nor is this result unfamiliar to us today; it is widely employed in much theoretical and practical work in medical ethics.

This fate of the argument from marginal cases matters; for unless one adopts a reverence-for-life principle (a possibility that I considered and rejected in *Rights, Killing, and Suffering*[14]) or adopts some form of holistic ethic, the supposed equal value of human and animal life, if it is not to be merely assumed, is often made to turn upon some variant of the argument from marginal cases.

As for an holistic account of value, wherein the value of the parts of an eco-system turns upon the value of the whole, this is much too large an issue for me to address here. Suffice it to say that I have elsewhere expressed doubts about any such account.[15] I have no very clear idea of exactly how one sets about uncovering the value of an entire eco-system, in order to arrive at some view of the value of humans and animals within it, or how one knows one has ascertained that value correctly. There seems no touchstone of error in any such uncovering; that is, there seems no clear way to contest one's claim that some eco-system in some particular state has whatever value one says it has.

This leaves the argument from marginal cases to try to force the admission of the equal value of human and animal life. Tom Regan has long relied upon this argument, and though I have given my objections to his position in another place,[16] a word on his use of the argument may help in part to clarify why I reject it.

In a recent article Regan wonders what could be the basis for the view that human life is more valuable than animal life and moves at once to invoke the argument from marginal cases to dispel any such possibility:

> What could be the basis of our having more inherent value than animals? Their lack of reason, or autonomy, or intellect? Only if we are willing to make the same judgment in the case of humans who are similarly deficient. But it is not true that some humans – the retarded child, for example, or the mentally retarded child, for example, or the mentally deranged – have less inherent value than you or I.[17]

Regan provides no argument for this claim (and, for that matter, no analysis of "inherent value"), but it seems at least to involve, if not to depend upon, our agreeing that human life of any quality, however low, has the same value as normal (adult) human life. I can see no reason whatever to accept this. Some human lives are so very deficient in quality that we would not wish those lives upon anyone, and there are few lengths to which we would not go in order to avoid such lives for ourselves and our loved ones. I can see little point in pretending that lives which we would do everything we could to avoid are of equal value to those normal (adult) human lives that we are presently living.

Of course, it is always possible to draw up, say, six different senses in which lives may be said to be valuable and to try to make out that deficient human life is as valuable as normal (adult) human life in four or five of them. I suspect that most of us, however, would see such an exercise as just that. For in however many senses human lives may be said to be valuable, the fact remains that we would do everything we could to avoid a life of severe derangement or mental enfeebleness or physical paralysis. It is hard to believe, as a result, that normal (adult) humans would consider such a life to be as valuable as their present life or to be a life – think of a life in the advanced stages of AIDS – that they would even remotely regard as a life as desirable to live as their present one.

So far as I can see, the quality of some lives can plummet so disastrously that those lives can cease to have much value at all, can cease to be lives, that is, that are any longer worth living. I acknowledge the difficulty in determining in many cases when a life is no longer worth living; in other cases, however, such as an elderly person completely undone by Alzheimer's disease or an infant born with no or only half a brain, the matter seems far less problematic.

VI

Is an involved defence of the unequal-value thesis, however, really necessary? Is there not a much more direct and uncomplicated defence readily to hand? I have space for only a few words on several possibilities in this regard.

The defence of the unequal-value thesis that I have begun to sketch, whether in its positive or negative aspect, does not make reference to religion; yet, it is true that certain religious beliefs seem to favour the thesis. The doctrine of the sanctity of life has normally been held with respect to human life alone; the belief in human dominion over the rest of creation has traditionally been held to set humans apart; and the belief that humans but not animals are possessed of an immortal soul seems plainly to allude to a further dimension of significance to human life. I am not myself religious, however, and I do not adopt a religious approach to questions about the value of lives. Any such approach would seem to tie one's defence of the unequal-value thesis to the adequacy of one's theological views, something which a non-religious person can scarcely endorse. I seek a defence of the unequal-value thesis, whatever the status of God's existence or the adequacy of this or that religion or religious doctrine. I do not pre-judge the issue of whether a religious person can accept a quality-of-life defence of the sort I have favoured; my point is simply that that defence does not rely upon theological premises.

It may be asked, however, why we need anything quite so sophisticated as a *defence* of the unequal-value thesis at all. Why can we not just express a preference for our own kind and be done with the matter? After all, when a father gives a kidney to save his daughter's life, we perfectly well understand why he did not choose to give the kidney to a stranger *in preference to* his daughter. This "natural bias" we

do not condemn and do not take to point to a moral defect in the father. Why, therefore, is not something similar possible in the case of our interaction with animals? Why, that is, can we not appeal to a natural bias in favour of members of our own species? There are a number of things that can be said in response, only several of which I shall notice here.

There is the problem, if one takes the charge of speciesism seriously, of how to articulate this bias in favour of members of our species in such a way as to avoid that charge. Then there is the problem of how to articulate this preference for our own kind in such a way as to exclude interpretations of "our own kind" that express preferences for one's own race, gender, or religion. Otherwise, one is going to let such preferences do considerable work in one's moral decision-making. I do not wish to foreclose all possibilities in these two cases, however; it may well be that a preference for our own kind *can* be articulated in a way that avoids these and some other problems.

Even so, I believe that there is another and deeper level of problem that this preference for our own kind encounters. On the one hand, we can understand the preference to express a bond we feel with members of our own species *over and above* the bond that we (or most of us) feel with ("higher") animals. Such a bond, if it exists, poses no direct problem, if its existence is being used to explain, for example, instances of behaviour where we obviously exhibit sympathy for human beings. (We must be careful not to *undervalue* the sympathy most people exhibit towards animals, especially domesticated ones.) On the other hand, we can understand this preference for our own kind to express the claim that we stand in a special moral relationship to members of our own species. This claim does pose a problem, since, if we systematically favour humans over animals on the basis of it, it does considerable moral work – work, obviously, that would not be done if the claim were rejected. I have elsewhere commented on this claim;[18] a word on one facet of it must suffice here.

I cannot see that species membership is a ground for holding that we stand in a special moral relationship to our fellow humans. The father obviously stands in such a relationship to his daughter, and his decision to marry and to have children is how he comes to have or to stand in that relationship. But how, through merely being born, does one come to stand in a special moral relationship to humans generally? Typically, I can step in and out of special moral relationships; in the case of species membership, that is not true. In that case, so long as I live, nothing can change my relationship to others, so long as they live. If this were true, my morality would to an extent no longer express my view of myself at large in a world filled with other people but would be something foisted upon me simply through being born.

Since we do not choose our species membership, a special moral relationship I am supposed to stand in to humans generally would lie outside my control; whereas it is precisely the voluntary nature of such relationships that seems most central to their character. And it is precisely because of this voluntary nature, of, as it were, our ability to take on and shed such relationships, that these relationships can be read as expressing *my* view of myself at large in a world filled with other people.

We often do stand in special moral relationships to others; but mere species membership would have us stand in such a relationship to all others. There is something too sweeping about this, as if birth alone can give the rest of human creation a moral hold over me. In a real sense, such a view would sever me from my morality; for my morality would no longer consist in expressions of how I see myself interacting with others and how I choose to interact with them. My own choices and decisions have no effect upon species membership and so on a moral relationship that I am supposed to stand in to each and every living, human being. Such a view is at odds not only with how we typically understand special moral relationships but also with how we typically understand our relationship to our own morality.

VII

It may well be tempting, I suppose, to try to develop another sense of "speciesism" and to

hold that a position such as mine is speciesist in that sense. I have space here for only a few comments on one such sense.

If to be a *direct* speciesist is to discriminate among the value of lives solely on the basis of species membership, as it is, for example, for Peter Singer, then I am not, as I have tried to show, a direct speciesist. But am I not, it might be suggested, an *indirect* speciesist, in that, in order to determine the quality and value of a life, I use human-centred criteria as if they were appropriate for assessing the quality and value of all life? Thus, for instance, when I emphasize cultural and artistic endeavours, when I emphasize autonomy and mental development and achievement, when I emphasize making choices, directing one's life, and selecting and living out conceptions of the good life, the effect is to widen the gulf between animals and humans by using human-centred criteria for assessing the quality and value of a life as if they were appropriate to appreciating the quality and value of animal life. And this will not do; for it amounts to trying to judge animals and animal lives by human standards. What one should do, presumably, is to judge the quality and value of animal life by criteria appropriate to each separate species of animals.

I stress again that the argument of this essay is not about whether rabbits have lives of value (I think that they do) but rather about whether they have lives of equal value to normal (adult) human life. It is unclear to me how the charge of indirect speciesism addresses this argument.

We must distinguish this charge of an indirect speciesism from the claim, noted earlier, that we can know nothing of animal lives and so nothing about their quality and value; indeed, the two claims may conflict. The point behind the speciesism charge is that I am not using criteria appropriate to a species of animal for assessing its quality of life, which presumably means that there *are* appropriate criteria available for selection. Knowledge of appropriate criteria seems to require that we know something of an animal's life, in order to make the judgement of appropriateness. Yet, the whole point behind the lack-of-knowledge claim is that we can know nothing of an animal's life, nothing of how it experiences the world, nothing, in essence, about how well or how badly its life is going. It would seem, therefore, as if the two views can conflict.

The crucial thing here about both claims, however, is this: both are advanced against my defence of the unequal-value thesis and on behalf of the equality of value of human and animal life without it being in any wise clear how they show this equality.

The ignorance claim would seem to have it that, because we can know nothing of the animal case, we must assume that animal and human life have the same value. But why should we fall in with this assumption? The ignorance claim would have us start from the idea, presumably, that all life, irrespective of its level of development and complexity, has the same value; but why should we start from that particular idea? Surely there must be some *reason* for thinking all life whatever has the same value. It is this reason that needs to be stated and assessed.

The indirect speciesist claim would seem to have it that, were we only to select criteria for assessing the quality and value of life appropriate to animals' species, we must agree that animal and human life are of equal value. The temptation is to inquire after what these criteria might be in rabbits, but any such concern must be firmly understood in the light of the earlier discussion of the richness of our lives. What the unequal-value thesis represents is our quest to gain some understanding of (i) the capacities of animals and humans, (ii) the differences among these various capacities, (iii) the complexity of lives, (iv) the role of agency in this complexity, and (v) the way agency enables humans to add further dimensions of value to their lives. The richness of our lives encompasses these multifacted aspects of our being and is a function of them. The point is not that a rabbit may not have a keener sense of smell than we do and may not derive intense, pleasurable sensations through that sense of smell; it is that we have to believe that something like this, augmented, perhaps, by other things we might say in the rabbit's case of like kind, suffices to make the rabbit's case of like as rich and as full as ours. If one thinks of our various capacities and of the different levels on which they operate, physical, mental, emotional, imaginative, then pointing out that rabbits can have as pleasurable sensations as we do in certain regards does not meet the point.

When we say of a woman that she has "tasted life to the full", we do not make a point about (or solely about) pleasurable sensations; we refer to the different dimensions of our being and to the woman's attempt to develop these in herself and to actualize them in the course of her daily life. And an important aspect in all this is what agency means to the woman: in the sense intended, she is not condemned to live the life that all of her ancestors have lived; she can mould and shape her life to "fit" her own conception of how she should live, thereby enabling her to add further dimensions of value to her life. It is this diversity and complexity in us that needs to be made good in the rabbit's case and that no mere catalogue of its pleasures through the sense of smell seems likely to accomplish.

Again, it is not that the rabbit cannot do things that we are unable to do and not that it has capacities which we lack; what has to be shown is how this sort of thing, given how rabbits behave and live out their days, so enriches their lives that the quality and value of them approach those of humans. And what is one going to say in the rabbit's case that makes good the role agency plays in ours? The absence of agency from a human life is a terrible thing; it deeply impoverishes a life and forestalls completely one's making one's life into the life one wants to live. Yet, this must be the natural condition of rabbits. It is this gulf that agency creates, the gulf between living out the life appropriate to one's species and living out a life one has chosen for oneself and has moulded and shaped accordingly, that is one of the things that it is difficult to understand what rabbits can do to overcome.

VIII

In sum, I think the unequal-value thesis is defensible and can be defended even as its adherent takes seriously the charge of speciesism.

And it is the unequal-value thesis that figures centrally in the justification of our use of animals in medical and scientific research. If, as I have done here, we assume that the thesis must be defended, then the character of that defence, I think, requires that *if* we are to continue to use animals for research purposes, then we must begin to envisage the use of some humans for those same purposes. The cost of holding the unequal-value thesis, and most of us, I suggest, do hold it, is to realize that, upon a quality-of-life defence of it, it encompasses the lives of some humans as well as animals. I cannot at the moment see that any other defence of it both meets the charge of speciesism and yet does indeed amount to a defence.

Notes

An earlier version of this essay was read in 1986 as my contribution to a debate with Stephen R. L. Clark, in a Wolfson College, Oxford, debate series on *Animal Rights and Wrongs*. It was especially pleasing to be able to join my old friend and colleague in starting off the series.

1   See especially my books *Interests and Rights: The Case Against Animals* (Oxford: Clarendon Press, 1980), and *Rights, Killing, and Suffering* (Oxford: Basil Blackwell, 1983). These give a reasonably full listing of my articles relevant to the subject of this paper, when taken together with those articles mentioned below.

2   "Autonomy and The Value of Animal Life", *The Monist* (1986); "The Significance of Agency and Marginal Cases", *Philosophica* (1986); "Autonomy and Conceptions of the Good Life", in L. W. Sumner, T. Attig, D. Callen (eds), *Values and Moral Standing* (Bowling Green Studies in Applied Philosophy, 1986); and "Animal Parts, Human Wholes: On the Use of Animals as a Source of Organs for Human Transplants", in J. Humber, R. Almeder (eds), *Biomedical Reviews 1987* (New Jersey: Humana Press, 1988).

3   See my "Vivisection, Medicine, and Morals", *Journal of Medical Ethics* (1983), and *Rights, Killing, and Suffering*, ch. 12.

4   See "Animal Parts, Human Wholes".

5   For a brief discussion of these side-effects, see my "Vivisection, Medicine, and Morals".

6   One might want to advance some vast generality here, of the order, for example, that all living things, just because and to the extent that they are living, have value and, perhaps, even equal value; but this generality will need argument in its support. I have heard such a generality advanced often in discussion, almost always, it eventually turned out, as a fundamental assumption about value; but I have not come across any good reason to grant such an assumption. Besides, most of us are going to need convincing that the lives of "lower" animals, such as agricultural pests, are as valuable as human lives. This whole way of talking, however, is alien to the discussion of the value of a life I advance below, in which richness and quality of life figure prominently.

7   This is not to say, of course, that there may not be ways in which normal (adult) humans can suffer that animals do not.

8   Suffering is a wider notion than pain; but I drop the distinction here, since it is not relevant to what follows.

9   In Britain, such a presumption increasingly receives support among the public, scientific bodies, and government, where the use of animals in medical/scientific research is on the whole already subject to more severe examination than in the United States. And the matter is under continuous review. I am at present part of a working party in the Institute of Medical Ethics in London that is examining the ethics of our use of animals in medical research. The members come from government, industry, the medical establishment, academia, religious organizations, and animal-welfare societies, and our aim is to produce a report that will assist and perhaps even direct discussion on all levels about our present, simply massive use of animals in medical research.

10   Something along these sceptical lines has been suggested to me by S. F. Sapontzis, a line of argument that doubtless his book *Morals, Reason, and Animals* (Philadelphia: Temple University Press, 1987) will pursue. (I have only now, May 1988, received Sapontzis' book for review.)

11   Tom Regan, *The Case for Animal Rights* (Berkeley: University of California Press, 1983).

12   For a discussion of this point, see *Rights, Killing, and Suffering*, p. 110.

13   I discuss this matter of our use of humans, in the context of a discussion of xenograph, in some detail in "Animal Parts, Human Wholes". See also my "Vivisection, Medicine, and Morals", and *Rights, Killing, and Suffering*, ch. 12.

14   *Rights, Killing, and Suffering*, ch. 12.

15   See *Rights, Killing, and Suffering*, ch. 14. This discussion is preliminary only and does not fully address a worked-out, holistic theory, if there be such.

16   See "Autonomy and The Value of Animal Life".
17   Tom Regan, "The Case for Animal Rights", in Peter Singer (ed.), *In Defence of Animals* (Oxford: Basil Blackwell, 1985), p. 23. This article mirrors some central claims of Regan's book of the same name.
18   See "Animal Parts, Human Wholes".

17

The Case for Animal Rights

Tom Regan

How to proceed? We begin by asking how the moral status of animals has been understood by thinkers who deny that animals have rights. Then we test the mettle of their ideas by seeing how well they stand up under the heat of fair criticism. If we start our thinking in this way, we soon find that some people believe that we have no duties directly to animals, that we owe nothing to them, that we can do nothing that wrongs them. Rather, we can do wrong acts that involve animals, and so we have duties regarding them, though none to them. Such views may be called *indirect duty views*. By way of illustration: suppose your neighbor kicks your dog. Then your neighbor has done something wrong. But not to your dog. The wrong that has been done is a wrong to you. After all, it is wrong to upset people, and your neighbor's kicking your dog upsets you. So you are the one who is wronged, not your dog. Or again: by kicking your dog your neighbor damages your property. And since it is wrong to damage another person's property, your neighbor has done something wrong – to you, of course, not to your dog. Your neighbor no more wrongs your dog than your car would be wronged if the windshield were smashed. Your neighbor's

duties involving your dog are indirect duties to you. More generally, all of our duties regarding animals are indirect duties to one another – to humanity.

How could someone try to justify such a view? Someone might say that your dog doesn't feel anything and so isn't hurt by your neighbor's kick, doesn't care about the pain since none is felt, is as unaware of anything as is your windshield. Someone might say this, but no rational person will, since, among other considerations, such a view will commit anyone who holds it to the position that no human beings feel pain either – that human beings also don't care about what happens to them. A second possibility is that though both humans and your dog are hurt when kicked, it is only human pain that matters. But, again, no rational person can believe this. Pain is pain wherever it occurs. If your neighbor's causing you pain is wrong because of the pain that is caused, we cannot rationally ignore or dismiss the moral relevance of the pain that your dog feels.

Philosophers who hold indirect duty views – and many still do – have come to understand that they must avoid the two defects just noted: that is, both the view that animals don't feel anything as well as the idea that only human pain can be morally relevant. Among such thinkers the sort of view now favored is one or another form of what is called *contractarianism*.

Here, very crudely, is the root idea: morality consists of a set of rules that individuals voluntarily agree to abide by, as we do when we sign a contract (hence the name contractarianism). Those who understand and accept the terms of the contract are covered directly; they have rights created and recognized by, and protected in, the contract. And these contractors can also have protection spelled out for others who, though they lack the ability to understand morality and so cannot sign the contract themselves, are loved or cherished by those who can. Thus young children, for example, are unable to sign contracts and lack rights. But they are protected by the contract nonetheless because of the sentimental interests of others, most notably their parents. So we have, then, duties involving these children, duties regarding them, but no duties to them. Our duties in their case are indirect duties to other human beings, usually their parents.

As for animals, since they cannot understand contracts, they obviously cannot sign; and since they cannot sign, they have no rights. Like children, however, some animals are the object of the sentimental interest of others. You, for example, love your dog or cat. So those animals that enough people care about (companion animals, whales, baby seals, the American bald eagle), though they lack rights themselves, will be protected because of the sentimental interests of people. I have, then, according to contractarianism, no duty directly to your dog or any other animal, not even the duty not to cause them pain or suffering; my duty not to hurt them is a duty I have to those people who care about what happens to them. As for other animals, where no or little sentimental interest is present – in the case of farm animals, for example, or laboratory rats – what duties we have grow weaker and weaker, perhaps to the vanishing point. The pain and death they endure, though real, are not wrong if no one cares about them.

When it comes to the moral status of animals, contractarianism could be a hard view to refute if it were an adequate theoretical approach to the moral status of human beings. It is not adequate in this latter respect, however, which makes the question of its adequacy in the former case, regarding animals, utterly moot. For consider: morality, according to the (crude) contractarian position before us, consists of rules that people agree to abide by. What people? Well, enough to make a difference – enough, that is, *collectively* to have the power to enforce the rules that are drawn up in the contract. That is very well and good for the signatories but not so good for anyone who is not asked to sign. And there is nothing in contractarianism of the sort we are discussing that guarantees or requires that everyone will have a chance to participate equally in framing rules of morality. The result is that this approach to ethics could sanction the most blatant forms of social, economic, moral, and political injustice, ranging from a repressive caste system to systematic racial or sexual discrimination. Might, according to this theory, does make right. Let those who are the victims of injustice suffer as they will. It matters not so long as no one else – no contractor, or too few of them – cares about it. Such a theory takes one's moral breath away . . . as if, for example, there would be nothing wrong with apartheid in South Africa if few white South Africans were upset by it. A theory with so little to recommend it at the level of the ethics of our treatment of our fellow humans cannot have anything more to recommend it when it comes to the ethics of how we treat our fellow animals.

The version of contractarianism just examined is, as I have noted, a crude variety, and in fairness to those of a contractarian persuasion, it must be noted that much more refined, subtle, and ingenious varieties are possible. For example, John Rawls, in his *A Theory of Justice*, sets forth a version of contractarianism that forces contractors to ignore the accidental features of being a human being – for example, whether one is white or black, male or female, a genius or of modest intellect. Only by ignoring such features, Rawls believes, can we ensure that the principles of justice that contractors would agree upon are not based on bias or prejudice. Despite the improvement a view such as Rawls's represents over the cruder forms of contractarianism, it remains deficient: it systematically denies that we have direct duties to those human beings who do not have a sense of justice – young children, for instance, and many mentally retarded humans. And yet it seems reasonably certain that, were we to torture a young child or a retarded elder, we would be doing something that wronged him or her, not something that would be wrong if (and only if) other humans with a sense of justice were upset. And since this is true in the case of these humans, we cannot rationally deny the same in the case of animals.

Indirect duty views, then, including the best among them, fail to command our rational assent. Whatever ethical theory we should accept rationally, therefore, it must at least recognize that we have some duties directly to animals, just as we have some duties directly to each other. The next two theories I'll sketch attempt to meet this requirement.

The first I call the cruelty–kindness view. Simply stated, this says that we have a direct duty to be kind to animals and a direct duty not to be cruel to them. Despite the familiar, reassuring ring of these ideas, I do not believe that this view offers an adequate theory. To make this clearer, consider kindness. A kind person acts from a certain type of motive – compassion or concern, for example. And that is a virtue. But there is no guarantee that a kind act is a right act. If I am a generous racist, for example, I will be inclined to act kindly towards members of my own race, favoring their interests above those of others. My kindness would be real and, so far as it goes, good. But I trust it is too obvious to require argument that my kind acts may not be above moral reproach – may, in fact, be positively wrong because rooted in injustice. So kindness, notwithstanding its status as a virtue to be encouraged, simply will not carry the weight of a theory of right action.

Cruelty fares no better. People or their acts are cruel if they display either a lack of sympathy for or, worse, the presence of enjoyment in another's suffering. Cruelty in all its guises is a bad thing, a tragic human failing. But just as a

person's being motivated by kindness does not guarantee that he or she does what is right, so the absence of cruelty does not ensure that he or she avoids doing what is wrong. Many people who perform abortions, for example, are not cruel, sadistic people. But that fact alone does not settle the terribly difficult question of the morality of abortion. The case is no different when we examine the ethics of our treatment of animals. So, yes, let us be for kindness and against cruelty. But let us not suppose that being for the one and against the other answers questions about moral right and wrong.

Some people think that the theory we are looking for is *utilitarianism*. A utilitarian accepts two moral principles. The first is that of equality: everyone's interests count, and similar interests must be counted as having similar weight or importance. White or black, American or Iranian, human or animal – everyone's pain or frustration matters, and matters just as much as the equivalent pain or frustration of anyone else. The second principle a utilitarian accepts is that of utility: do the act that will bring about the best balance between satisfaction and frustration for everyone affected by the outcome.

As a utilitarian, then, here is how I am to approach the task of deciding what I morally ought to do: I must ask who will be affected if I choose to do one thing rather than another, how much each individual will be affected, and where the best results are most likely to lie – which option, in other words, is most likely to bring about the best results, the best balance between satisfaction and frustration. That option, whatever it may be, is the one I ought to choose. That is where my moral duty lies.

The great appeal of utilitarianism rests with its uncompromising *egalitarianism*: everyone's interests count and count as much as the like interests of everyone else. The kind of odious discrimination that some forms of contractarianism can justify – discrimination based on race or sex, for example – seems disallowed in principle by utilitarianism, as is speciesism, systematic discrimination based on species membership.

The equality we find in utilitarianism, however, is not the sort an advocate of animal or human rights should have in mind. Utilitarianism has no room for the equal rights of different individuals because it has no room for their equal inherent value or worth. What has value for the utilitarian is the satisfaction of an individual's interests, not the individual whose interests they are. A universe in which you satisfy your desire for water, food, and warmth is, other things being equal, better than a universe in which these desires are frustrated. And the same is true in the case of an animal with similar desires. But neither you nor the animal have any value in your own right. Only your feelings do.

Here is an analogy to help make the philosophical point clearer: a cup contains different liquids, sometimes sweet, sometimes bitter, sometimes a mixture of the two. What has value is the liquids: the sweeter the better, the bitterer the worse. The cup, the container, has no value. It is what goes into it, not what it goes into, that has value. For the utilitarian, you and I are like the cup; we have no value as individuals and thus no equal value. What has value is what goes into us, what we serve as receptacles for; our feelings of satisfaction have positive value, our feelings of frustration negative value.

Serious problems arise for utilitarianism when we remind ourselves that it enjoins us to bring about the best consequences. What does this mean? It doesn't mean the best consequences for me alone, or for my family or friends, or any other person taken individually. No, what we must do is, roughly, as follows: we must add up (somehow!) the separate satisfactions and frustrations of everyone likely to be affected by our choice, the satisfactions in one column, the frustrations in the other. We must total each column for each of the options before us. That is what it means to say the theory is aggregative. And then we must choose that option which is most likely to bring about the best balance of totalled satisfactions over totalled frustrations. Whatever act would lead to this outcome is the one we ought morally to perform – it is where our moral duty lies. And that act quite clearly might not be the same one that would bring about the best results for me personally, or for my family or friends, or for a lab animal. The best aggregated consequences for everyone concerned are not necessarily the best for each individual.

That utilitarianism is an aggregative theory – different individuals' satisfactions or frustrations are added, or summed, or totalled – is the key objection to this theory. My Aunt Bea is old, inactive, a cranky, sour person, though not physically ill. She prefers to go on living. She is also rather rich, I could make a fortune if I could get my hands on her money, money she intends to give me in any event, after she dies, but which she refuses to give me now. In order to avoid a huge tax bite, I plan to donate a handsome sum of my profits to a local children's hospital. Many, many children will benefit from my generosity, and much joy will be brought to their parents, relatives, and friends. If I don't get the money rather soon, all these ambitions will come to naught. The once-in-a-lifetime opportunity to make a real killing will be gone. Why, then, not kill my Aunt Bea? Oh, of course I *might* get caught. But I'm no fool and, besides, her doctor can be counted on to cooperate (he has an eye for the same investment and I happen to know a good deal about his shady past). The deed can be done . . . professionally, shall we say. There is *very* little chance of getting caught. And as for my conscience being guiltridden, I am a resourceful sort of fellow and will take more than sufficient comfort – as I lie on the beach at Acapulco – in contemplating the joy and health I have brought to so many others.

Suppose Aunt Bea is killed and the rest of the story comes out as told. Would I have done anything wrong? Anything immoral? One would have thought that I had. Not according to utilitarianism. Since what I have done has brought about the best balance between totalled satisfaction and frustration for all those affected by the outcome, my action is not wrong. Indeed, in killing Aunt Bea the physician and I did what duty required.

This same kind of argument can be repeated in all sorts of cases, illustrating, time after time, how the utilitarian's position leads to results that impartial people find morally callous. It *is* wrong to kill my Aunt Bea in the name of bringing about the best results for others. A good end does not justify an evil means. Any adequate moral theory will have to explain why this is so. Utilitarianism fails in this respect and so cannot be the theory we seek.

What to do? Where to begin anew? The place to begin, I think, is with the utilitarian's view of the value of the individual – or, rather, the lack of value. In its place, suppose we consider that you and I, for example, do have value as individuals – what we'll call *inherent value.* To say we have such value is to say that we are something more than, something different from, mere receptacles. Moreover, to ensure that we do not pave the way for such injustices as slavery or sexual discrimination, we must believe that all who have inherent value have it equally, regardless of their sex, race, religion, birthplace, and so on. Similarly to be discarded as irrelevant are one's talents or skills, intelligence and wealth, personality or pathology, whether one is loved and admired or despised and loathed. The genius and the retarded child, the prince and the pauper, the brain surgeon and the fruit vendor, Mother Teresa and the most unscrupulous used-car salesman – all have inherent value, all possess it equally, and all have an equal right to be treated with respect, to be treated in ways that do not reduce them to the status of things, as if they existed as resources for others. My value as an individual is independent of my usefulness to you. Yours is not dependent on your usefulness to me. For either of us to treat the other in ways that fail to show respect for the other's independent value is to act immorally, to violate the individual's rights.

Some of the rational virtues of this view – what I call the *rights view* – should be evident. Unlike (crude) contractarianism, for example, the rights view *in principle* denies the moral tolerability of any and all forms of racial, sexual, or social discrimination; and unlike utilitarianism, the view *in principle* denies that we can justify good results by using evil means that violate an individual's rights – denies, for example, that it could be moral to kill my Aunt Bea to harvest beneficial consequences for others. That would be to sanction the disrespectful treatment of the individual in the name of the social good, something the rights view will not – categorically will not – ever allow.

The rights view, I believe, is rationally the most satisfactory moral theory. It surpasses all other theories in the degree to which it illuminates and explains the foundation of our duties to one another – the domain of human morality. On this score it has the best reasons, the best arguments, on its side. Of course, if it were possible to show that only human beings are included within its scope, then a person like myself, who believes in animal rights, would be obliged to look elsewhere.

But attempts to limit its scope to humans only can be shown to be rationally defective. Animals, it is true, lack many of the abilities humans possess. The can't read, do higher mathematics, build a bookcase, or make *baba ghanoush.* Neither can many human beings, however, and yet we don't (and shouldn't) say that they (these humans) therefore have less inherent value, less of a right to be treated with respect, than do others. It is the *similarities* between those human beings who most clearly, most noncontroversially have such value (the people reading this, for example), not our differences, that matter most. And the really crucial, the basic similarity is simply this: we are each of us the experiencing subject of a life, a conscious creature having an individual welfare that has importance to us whatever our usefulness to others. We want and prefer things, believe and feel things, recall and expect things. And all these dimensions of our life, including our pleasure and pain, our enjoyment and suffering, our satisfaction and frustration, our continued existence or our untimely death – all make a difference to the quality of our life as lived, as experienced, by us as individuals. As the same is true of those animals that concern us (the ones that are eaten and trapped, for example), they too must be viewed as the experiencing subjects of a life, with inherent value of their own.

Some there are who resist the idea that animals have inherent value. "Only humans have such value," they profess. How might this narrow view be defended? Shall we say that only humans have the requisite intelligence, or autonomy, or reason? But there are many, many humans who fail to meet these standards and yet are reasonably viewed as having value above and beyond their usefulness to others. Shall we claim that only humans belong to the right species, the species *Homo sapiens?* But this is blatant speciesism. Will it be said, then, that all – and only – humans have immortal souls? Then our opponents have their work cut out for them. I am myself not ill-disposed to the proposition that there are immortal souls. Personally, I profoundly hope I have one. But I would not want to rest my position on a controversial ethical issue on the even more controversial question about who or what has an immortal soul. That is to dig one's hole deeper, not to climb out. Rationally, it is better to resolve moral issues without making more controversial assumptions than are needed. The question of who has inherent value is such a question, one that is resolved more rationally without the introduction of the idea of immortal souls than by its use.

Well, perhaps some will say that animals have some inherent value, only less than we have. Once again, however, attempts to defend this view can be shown to lack rational justification. What could be the basis of our having more inherent value than animals? Their lack of reason, or autonomy, or intellect? Only if we are willing to make the same judgment in the case of humans who are similarly deficient. But it is not true that such humans – the retarded child, for example, or the mentally deranged – have less inherent value than you or I. Neither, then, can we rationally sustain the view that animals that are like them in being the experiencing subjects of a life have less inherent value. *All who have inherent value have it equally,* whether they be human animals or not.

Inherent value, then, belongs equally to those who are the experiencing subjects of a life. Whether it belongs to others – to rocks and rivers, trees and glaciers, for example – we do not know and may never know. But neither do we need to know, if we are to make the case for animal rights. We do not need to know, for example, how many people are eligible to vote in the next presidential election before we can

know whether I am. Similarly, we do not need to know how many individuals have inherent value before we can know that some do. When it comes to the case for animal rights, then, what we need to know is whether the animals that, in our culture, are routinely eaten, hunted, and used in our laboratories, for example, are like us in being subjects of a life. And we do know this. We do know that many – literally, billions and billions – of these animals are the subjects of a life in the sense explained and so have inherent value if we do. And since, in order to arrive at the best theory of our duties to one another, we must recognize our equal inherent value as individuals, reason – not sentiment, not emotion – reason compels us to recognize the equal inherent value of these animals and, with this, their equal right to be treated with respect.

That, *very* roughly, is the shape and feel of the case for animal rights. Most of the details of the supporting argument are missing. They are to be found in the book that bears the same title as this essay.[1] Here, the details go begging, and I must, in closing, limit myself to two final points.

The first is how the theory that underlies the case for animal rights shows that the animal rights movement is a part of, not antagonistic to, the human rights movement. The theory that rationally grounds the rights of animals also grounds the rights of humans. Thus those involved in the animal rights movement are partners in the struggle to secure respect for human rights – the rights of women, for example, or minorities, or workers. The animal rights movement is cut from the same moral cloth as these.

Secondly, having set out the broad outlines of the rights view, I can now say why its implications for farming and science, among other fields, are both clear and uncompromising. In the case of the use of animals in science, the rights view is categorically abolitionist. Lab animals are not our tasters; we are not their kings. Because these animals are treated routinely, systematically as if their value were reducible to their usefulness to others, they are routinely, systematically treated with a lack of respect, and thus are their rights routinely, systematically violated. This is just as true when they are used in trivial, duplicative, unnecessary or unwise research as it is when they are used in studies that hold out real promise of human benefits. We can't justify harming or killing a human being (my Aunt Bea, for example) just for these sorts of reason. Neither can we do so even in the case of so lowly a creature as a laboratory rat. It is not just refinement or reduction that is called for, not just larger, cleaner cages, not just more generous use of anesthesia or the elimination of multiple surgery, not just tidying up the system. It is complete replacement. The best we can do when it comes to using animals in science is – not to use them. That is where our duty lies, according to the rights view.

As for commercial animal agriculture, the rights view takes a similar abolitionist position. The fundamental moral wrong here is not that animals are kept in stressful close confinement or in isolation, or that their pain and suffering, their needs and preferences are ignored or discounted. All these *are* wrong, of course, but they are not the fundamental wrong. They are symptoms and effects of the deeper, systematic wrong that allows these animals to be viewed and treated as lacking independent value, as resources for us – as, indeed, a renewable resource. Giving farm animals more space, more natural environments, more companions does not right the fundamental wrong, any more than giving lab animals more anesthesia or bigger, cleaner cages would right the fundamental wrong in their case. Nothing less than the total dissolution of commercial animal agriculture will do this, just as, for similar reasons I won't develop at length here, morality requires nothing less than the total elimination of hunting and trapping for commercial and sporting ends. The rights view's implications, then, as I have said, are clear and uncompromising.

Note

Reprinted by permission from *In Defense of Animals* (Oxford: Basil Blackwell). Paper presented at the national conference, "Animals and Humans: Ethical Perspectives," Moorhead State University, Moorhead, MN, April 21–23, 1986.

1   *The Case for Animal Rights* (Berkeley: University of California Press, 1983).

PART III

The Personal Life

Family and Reproductive Technology

For most of us, our families are very important. Although they can cause discomfort, anguish, and pain, they often infuse our lives with meaning, bring us great joy, and heighten our contentment. When relationships with family are flourishing, it is difficult to envision life without them. At those times we don't really think about what we owe them or what they owe us. We care for them, we seek to promote their interests; they do likewise. In this idyllic world, ordinary moral principles have no clear role. Likely that is why we have few principles for morally evaluating close relationships. Those we do have – e.g., against incest and child or spousal abuse – concern only egregious behavior.

According to English, this is as it should be. If family members constantly harp on about their rights, if they repeatedly remind each other of their duties, we would infer that they were not, in fact, intimate. Although we may speak loosely of "filial obligations," these are not obligations as we ordinarily conceive of them. If I obtain a bank loan, the bank explicitly agrees to provide the money I desire, and I explicitly agree to repay the loan, with interest. In making the loan, the bank is not being generous, nor does it care for me. In repaying the

loan, I am not being generous or exhibiting my love for the bank. By making the loan, bank officials were merely promoting their interests; by repaying the loan I am simply promoting mine.

We are differently motivated when interacting with our families. Strong family relationships are based on love. Love is a gift, and, as when giving a gift, we do not demand that it be reciprocated. That explains why, English claims, grown children do not owe anything to their parents. Healthy family relationships are not governed by moral rules, but by care. Of course, if parents had good relationships with their children, then we would anticipate that the children would care for and help their ailing parents. However, that is a prediction of how we think the children will act, not a moral principle.

Since relationships with family and friends do not seem to be neatly captured or governed by ordinary accounts of morality, this might suggest that morality is at odds with close personal relationships. After all, personal relationships are deeply partial while morality is impartial. If so, what happens when the demands of morality appear to conflict with our desires to please or promote the interests of our friends? Morality does permit close friendships and familial relationships. However, Rachels argues, it does not permit us to favor our friends and family in trivial ways if doing so means others are substantially worse off.

Rachels' argument here resembles Singer's argument that we are obligated to feed the starving (WORLD HUNGER). One common feature of both is that they deny that there is a fundamental moral distinction between acts and omissions, between things we do and things we "allow." A failure to care for starving and impoverished children when we can easily do so is morally equivalent to directly harming those children. In contrast, Arthur (WORLD HUNGER) claims we can legitimately take a special interest in ourselves and in those we love. This disagreement has implications for virtually every moral issue. Determining whether an action is purely personal, or whether we should evaluate it by criteria of morality, also pervades the discussions of ABORTION, SEXUALITY, PATERNALISM AND RISK, and FREE SPEECH.

Lurking behind the discussion so far is an assumption that we all know perfectly well what constitutes a family: a (married) man and woman along with their biological offspring. Macklin, though, thinks a confluence of social changes and new reproductive technologies have appropriately forced us to rethink our understanding of the family. The appearance of same-sex marriages (SEXUALITY), surrogate mothers, and especially the possibility of human cloning requires us to rethink our conception of the family. Is the surrogate mother a part of the family? Would a single person with his/her cloned offspring constitute a family?

Kass agrees that we have rethought our understanding of the family; he just thinks we shouldn't have. There is wisdom in the norm of heterosexual marriage and "normal" procreation. To think we can just ignore them is one of many "excesses of human willfulness." Although she would likely reject many of Kass's ideas, Anderson does share his misgiv-

ings about some new forms of procreation. In particular, she objects to surrogacy contracts: paying someone else to carry a child to term. Such contracts, she argues, treat children and women's labor as commodities. Treating children and women's labor the way we treat shoes and refrigerators – as objects with a monetary value – fails to value them appropriately. Humans are not mere means but are ends in themselves. Anderson's argument – to object to practices because they "use people" – is quite common. The strategy, also used by Wolff to condemn certain forms of competition (ECONOMIC JUSTICE), derives from Kant's deontology (ETHICAL THEORY).

Although many people accept forms of surrogacy, most object to human cloning. Harris claims these objections are misplaced. Most arise because people do not understand the nature of genetics and, therefore, are confused about what cloning can and cannot accomplish. Other objections arise because they mistakenly assume cloning will undermine human dignity. Moreover, Harris argues, people should have reproductive autonomy, and that includes the right to have themselves cloned. Kass disagrees. Cloning would be a form of unacceptable experimentation on the created child. It also raises serious questions about personal identity: would this person really differ from the person from whom she is cloned? However, Kass's core reason for opposing cloning is simply that we find the idea repugnant. Although this does not sound like an especially compelling reason, Kass argues that there is profound moral wisdom in repugnance. We cannot muster wholly adequate arguments for much that we find wrong. No argument, he claims, is sufficient to explain just how wrong incest, bestiality, and cannibalism are. Our horror at such acts is sufficient to tell us that they are morally unacceptable. To this extent his argument relies on an appeal to intuition, described in the chapter on deontology (ETHICAL THEORY), but decried by Harris.

Further Reading

Badhwar, N. (ed.) (1993) *Friendship: A Philosophical Reader*. Ithaca, NY: Cornell University Press.

Bartky, S. (1990) *Femininity and Domination: Studies in the Phenomenology of Oppression*. New York: Routledge.

Graham, G. and LaFollette, H. (eds.) (1989) *Person to Person*. Philadelphia: Temple University Press.

Hardwig, J. (1984) "Should Women Think in Terms of Rights?" *Ethics* 91: 441–5.

Harris, J. (1998) *Clones, Genes, and Immortality : Ethics and the Genetic Revolution*. Oxford: Oxford University Press.

Kass, L. R. (2002) *Life, Liberty and the Defense of Dignity: The Challenge for Bioethics*. San Francisco, CA: Encounter Books.

LaFollette, H. (1996) *Personal Relationships: Love, Identity, and Morality*. Oxford: Blackwell Publishers.

Noddings, N. (1984) *Caring: A Feminine Approach to Ethics and Moral Education*. Berkeley, CA: University of California Press.

O'Neill, O. and Ruddick, W. (1979) *Having Children: Philosophical and Legal Reflections on Parenthood*. New York: Oxford University Press.

Williams, B. (1985) *Ethics and the Limits of Philosophy*. London: Williams Collins & Sons.

18

What Do Grown Children Owe Their Parents?

Jane English

What do grown children owe their parents? I will contend that the answer is "nothing." Although I agree that there are many things that children *ought* to do for their parents, I will argue that it is inappropriate and misleading to describe them as things "owed." I will maintain that parents' voluntary sacrifices, rather than creating "debts" to be "repaid," tend to create love or "friendship." The duties of grown children are those of friends and result from love between them and their parents, rather than being things owed in repayment for the parents' earlier sacrifices. Thus, I will oppose those philosophers who use the word "owe" whenever a duty or obligation exists. Although the "debt" metaphor is appropriate in some moral circumstances, my argument is that a love relationship is not such a case.

Misunderstandings about the proper relationship between parents and their grown children have resulted from reliance on the "owing" terminology. For instance, we hear parents complain, "You owe it to us to write home (keep up your piano playing, not adopt a hippie lifestyle), because of all we sacrificed for you (paying for piano lessons, sending you to college)." The child is sometimes even heard to reply, "I didn't ask to be born (to be given piano lessons, to be sent to college)." This inappropriate idiom of ordinary language tends to obscure, or even to undermine, the love that is the correct ground of filial obligation.

1 Favors Create Debts

There are some cases, other than literal debts, in which talk of "owing," though metaphorical, is apt. New to the neighborhood, Max barely knows his neighbor, Nina, but he asks her if she will take in his mail while he is gone for a month's vacation. She agrees. If, subsequently, Nina asks Max to do the same for her, it seems that Max has a moral obligation to agree (greater than the one he would have had if Nina had not done the same for him), unless for some reason it would be a burden far out of proportion to the one Nina bore for him. I will call this a *favor*: when A, at B's request, bears some burden for B, then B incurs an obligation to reciprocate. Here the metaphor of Max's "owing" Nina is appropriate. It is not literally a debt, of course, nor can Nina pass this IOU on to heirs, demand payment in the form of Max's taking out her garbage, or sue Max. Nonetheless, since Max ought to perform one act of similar nature and amount of sacrifice in return, the term is suggestive. Once he reciprocates, the debt is "discharged" – that is, their obligations revert to the condition they were in before Max's initial request.

Contrast a situation in which Max simply goes on vacation and, to his surprise, finds upon his return that his neighbor has mowed his grass twice weekly in his absence. This is a voluntary sacrifice rather than a favor, and Max has no duty to reciprocate. It would be nice for him to volunteer to do so, but this would be supererogatory on his part. Rather than a favor, Nina's action is a friendly gesture. As a result, she might expect Max to chat over the back fence, help her catch her straying dog, or something similar – she might expect the development of a friendship. But Max would be chatting (or whatever) out of friendship, rather than in repayment for mown grass. If he did not return her gesture, she might feel rebuffed or miffed, but not unjustly treated or indignant, since Max has not failed to perform a duty. Talk of "owing" would be out of place in this case.

It is sometimes difficult to distinguish between favors and non-favors, because friends tend to do favors for each other, and those who exchange favors tend to become friends. But one test is to ask how Max is motivated. Is it "to be nice to Nina" or "because she did x for me"? Favors are frequently performed by total strangers without any friendship developing. Nevertheless, a temporary obligation is created, even if the chance for repayment never arises. For instance, suppose that Oscar and Matilda, total strangers, are waiting in a long checkout line at the supermarket. Oscar, having forgotten the oregano, asks Matilda to watch his cart for a second. She does. If Matilda now asks Oscar to return the favor while she picks up some tomato sauce, he is obligated to agree. Even if she had not watched his cart, it would be inconsiderate of him to refuse, claiming he was too busy reading the magazines. He may have had a duty to help others, but he would not "owe" it to her. But if she has done the same for him, he incurs an additional obligation to help, and talk of "owing" is apt. It suggests an agreement to perform equal, reciprocal, canceling sacrifices.

2   The Duties of Friendship

The terms "owe" and "repay" are helpful in the case of favors, because the sameness of the amount of sacrifice on the two sides is important; the monetary metaphor suggests equal quantities of sacrifice. But friendship ought to be characterized by *mutuality* rather than reciprocity: friends offer what they can give and accept what they need, without regard for the total amounts of benefits exchanged. And friends are motivated by love rather than by the prospect of repayment. Hence, talk of "owing" is singularly out of place in friendship.

For example, suppose Alfred takes Beatrice out for an expensive dinner and a movie. Beatrice incurs no obligation to "repay" him with a goodnight kiss or a return engagement. If Alfred complains that she "owes" him something, he is operating under the assumption that she should repay a favor, but on the contrary his was a generous gesture done in the hopes of developing a friendship. We hope that he would not want her repayment in the form of sex or attention if this was done to discharge a debt rather than from friendship. Since, if Alfred is prone to reasoning in this way, Beatrice may well decline the invitation or request to pay for her own dinner, his attitude of expecting a "return" on his "investment" could hinder the development of a friendship. Beatrice should return the gesture only if she is motivated by friendship.

Another common misuse of the "owing" idiom occurs when the Smiths have dined at the Joneses' four times, but the Joneses at the Smiths' only once. People often say, "We owe them three dinners." This line of thinking may be appropriate between business acquaintances, but not between friends. After all, the Joneses invited the Smiths not in order to feed them or to be fed in turn, but because of the friendly contact presumably enjoyed by all on such occasions. If the Smiths do not feel friendship toward the Joneses, they can decline future invitations and not invite the Joneses; they owe them nothing. Of course, between friends of equal resources and needs, roughly equal sacrifices (though not necessarily roughly equal dinners) will typically occur. If the sacrifices are highly out of proportion to the resources, the relationship is closer to servility than to friendship.[1]

Another difference between favors and friendship is that after a friendship ends, the duties of friendship end. The party that has sacrificed less owes the other nothing. For instance, suppose Elmer donated a pint of blood that his wife Doris needed during an operation. Years after their divorce, Elmer is in an accident and needs one pint of blood. His new wife, Cora, is also of the same blood type. It seems not only that Doris does not "owe" Elmer blood, but that she should actually refrain from coming forward if Cora has volunteered to donate. To insist on donating not only interferes with the newlyweds' friendship, but it belittles Doris and Elmer's former relationship by suggesting that Elmer gave blood in hopes of favors returned instead of simply out of love for Doris. It is one of the heart-rending features of divorce that it attends to quantity in relationship previously characterized by mutuality. If Cora could not donate, Doris's obligation is the same as that for any former spouse in need of blood; it is not increased by the fact that Elmer similarly aided her. It *is* affected by the degree to which they are still friends, which in turn may (or may not) have been influenced by Elmer's donation.

In short, unlike the debts created by favors, the duties of friendship do not require equal quantities of sacrifice. Performing equal sacrifices does not cancel the duties of friendship, as it does the debts of favors. Unrequested sacrifices do not themselves create debts, but friends have duties regardless of whether they requested or initiated the friendship. Those who perform favors may be motivated by mutual gain, whereas friends should be motivated by affection. These characteristics of the friendship relation are distorted by talk of "owing."

3   Parents and Children

The relationship between children and their parents should be one of friendship characterized by mutuality rather than one of reciprocal favors. The quantity of parental sacrifice is not relevant in determining what duties the grown child has. The medical assistance grown children ought to offer their ill mothers in old age depends upon the mothers' need, not upon whether they endured a difficult pregnancy, for example. Nor do one's duties to one's parents cease once an equal quantity of sacrifice has been performed, as the phrase "discharging a debt" may lead us to think.

Rather, what children ought to do for their parents (and parents for children) depends upon (1) their respective needs, abilities, and resources and (2) the extent to which there is an ongoing friendship between them. Thus, regardless of the quantity of childhood sacrifices, an able, wealthy child has an obligation to help his needy parents more than does a needy child. To illustrate, suppose sisters Cecile and Dana are equally loved by their parents, even though Cecile was an easy child to care for, seldom ill, while Dana was often sick and caused some trouble as a juvenile delinquent. As adults, Dana is a struggling artist living far away, while Cecile is a wealthy lawyer living nearby. When the parents need visits and financial aid, Cecile has an obligation to bear a higher proportion of these burdens than her sister. This results from her abilities, rather than from the quantities of sacrifice made by the parents earlier.

Sacrifices have an important causal role in creating an ongoing friendship, which may lead us to assume incorrectly that it is the sacrifices that are the source of obligation. That the source is the friendship instead can be seen by examining cases in which the sacrifices occurred but the friendship, for some reason, did not develop or persist. For example, if a woman gives up her newborn child for adoption, and if no feelings of love ever develop on either side, it seems that the grown child does not have an obligation to "repay" her for her sacrifices in pregnancy. For that matter, if the adopted child has an unimpaired love relationship with the adoptive parents, he or she has the same obligations to help them as a natural child would have.

The filial obligations of grown children are a result of friendship, rather than owed for services rendered. Suppose that Vance married Lola despite his parents' strong wish that he marry within their religion, and that as a result, the parents refuse to speak to him again. As the years pass, the parents are unaware of Vance's problems, his accomplishments, the birth of his children. The love that once existed between them, let us suppose, has been completely destroyed by this event and thirty years of desuetude. At this point, it seems, Vance is under no obligation to pay his parents' medical bills in their old age, beyond his general duty to help those in need. An additional, filial obligation would only arise from whatever love he may still feel for them. It would be irrelevant for his parents to argue, "But look how much we sacrificed for you when you were young," for that sacrifice was not a favor but occurred as part of a friendship which existed at the time but is now, we have supposed, defunct. A more appropriate message would be, "We still love you, and we would like to renew our friendship."

I hope this helps to set the question of what children ought to do for their parents in a new light. The parental argument, "You ought to do *x* because we did *y* for you," should be replaced by, "We love you and you will be happier if you do *x*," or "We believe you love us, and anyone who loved us would do *x*." If the parents' sacrifice had been a favor, the child's reply, "I never asked you to do *y* for me," would have been relevant; to the revised parental remarks, this reply is clearly irrelevant. The child can either do *x* or dispute one of the parents' claims: by showing that a love relationship does not exist, or that love for someone does not motivate doing *x*, or that he or she will not be happier doing *x*.

Seen in this light, parental requests for children to write home, visit, and offer them a reasonable amount of emotional and financial support in life's crises are well founded, so long as a friendship still exists. Love for others does call for caring about and caring for them. Some other parental requests, such as for more sweeping changes in the child's lifestyle or life goals, can be seen to be insupportable, once we shift the justification from debts owed to love. The terminology of favors suggests the reasoning, "Since we paid for your college education, you owe it to us to make a career of engineering, rather than becoming a rock musician." This tends to alienate affection even further, since the tuition payments are depicted as investments for a return rather than done from love, as though the child's life goals could be "bought." Basing the argument on love leads to different reasoning patterns. The suppressed premise, "If A loves B, then A follows B's wishes as to A's lifelong career" is simply false. Love does not even dictate that the child adopt the parents' values as to the desirability of alternative life goals. So the parents' strongest available argument here is, "We love you, we are deeply concerned about your happiness, and in the long run you will be happier as an engineer." This makes it clear that an empirical claim is really the subject of the debate.

The function of these examples is to draw out our considered judgments as to the proper relation between parents and their grown children, and to show how poorly they fit the model of favors. What is relevant is the ongoing friendship that exists between parents and children. Although that relationship developed partly as a result of parental sacrifices for the child, the duties that grown children have to their parents result from the friendship rather than from the sacrifices. The idiom of owing favors to one's parents can actually be destructive if it undermines the role of mutuality and leads us to think in terms of quantitative reciprocal favors.

Note

1 Cf. Thomas E. Hill, Jr, "Servility and Self-respect," *Monist* 57 (1973). Thus, during childhood, most of the sacrifices will come from the parents, since they have most of the resources and the child has most of the needs. When children are grown, the situation is usually reversed.

19

Morality, Parents, and Children

James Rachels

The Problem

At about the same time Socrates was being put to death for corrupting the youth of Athens, the great Chinese sage Mo Tzu was also antagonizing his community. Unlike the Confucianists, who were the social conservatives of the day, Mo and his followers were sharply critical of traditional institutions and practices. One of Mo's controversial teachings was that human relationships should be governed by an "all-embracing love" that makes no distinctions between friends, family, and humanity at large. "Partiality," he said, "is to be replaced by universality" (Fung, 1960, p. 92). To his followers, these were the words of a moral visionary. To the Confucianists, however, they were the words of a man out of touch with moral reality. In particular, Mo's doctrine was said to subvert the family, for it recommended that one have as much regard for strangers as for one's own kin. Meng Tzu summed up the complaint when he wrote that "Mo Tzu, by preaching universal love, has repudiated the family" (Rubin, 1976, p. 36). Mo did not deny it. Instead, he argued that universal love is a higher ideal than family loyalty, and that obligations within families can be properly understood only as particular instances of obligations to all mankind.

This ancient dispute has not disappeared. Do parents have special obligations to their own children? Or, to put the question a bit differently: Do they have obligations to their own children that they do not have to other children, or to children in general? Our instincts are with the Confucianists. Surely, we think, parents do have a special obligation to care for their own. Parents must love and protect their children; they must feed and clothe them; they must see to their medical needs, their education, and a hundred other things. Who could deny it? At the same time, we do not believe that we have such duties toward strangers. Perhaps we do have a general duty of beneficence toward them, but that duty is not nearly so extensive or specific as the duties we have toward our own young sons and daughters. If faced with a choice between feeding our own children and sending food to orphans in a foreign country, we would prefer our own, without hesitation.

Yet the Mohist objection is still with us. The idea that morality requires us to be impartial, clearly articulated by Mo Tzu, is a recurring theme of Western moral philosophy. Perhaps the most famous expression of this idea was Bentham's formula, "Each to count for one and none for more than one." Mill's formulation was less memorable but no less emphatic: He urged that, when weighing the interests of different people, we should be "as strictly impartial as a disinterested and benevolent spectator" (Mill, 1957, p. 22). Utilitarianism of the kind espoused by Bentham and Mill has, of course, often been criticized for conflicting with common-sense morality, and so it will probably come as no great surprise that utilitarian notions clash with the common-sense idea of special parental obligations. However, the idea that morality requires impartiality is by no means exclusively a utilitarian doctrine. It is common ground to a considerable range of theories and thinkers.[1]

The problem, in its most general form, is this. As moral agents, we cannot play favorites, at least not according to the conception of morality as impartiality. But as parents, we do play favorites. Parental love is partial through and through. And we think there is nothing wrong with this; in fact, we normally think there is something wrong with the parent who is *not* deeply partial where his own children are concerned. Therefore, it would seem, one or the other of these conceptions has to be modified or abandoned.

Of course, exactly the same is true of our relations with friends, spouses, and lovers. All these relationships, and others like them, seem to include, as part of their very nature, special obligations. Friends, spouses, and lovers are not just members of the great crowd of humanity. They are all special, at least to the one who loves them. The problem is that the conception of morality as impartiality seems to conflict with *any* kind of loving personal relationship. Mo Tzu notwithstanding, it seems to conflict with love itself.[2] In this essay I discuss only the question of parental obligations to children, but it should be kept in mind that the deeper issue has to do with personal relationships in general.

Possible Solutions

There are three obvious approaches to solving our problem: first, we might reject the idea of morality as impartiality; second, we might reject the idea of special parental obligations; or third, we might try to find some way of understanding the two notions that would make them consistent. The first approach has recently attracted some support among philosophers, who think that although the conception of morality as impartiality seems plausible when stated abstractly, it is refuted by such counter-examples as parental obligation. Their thought is that we should reject this conception and look for a new theory of morality, one that would acknowledge from the outset that personal relationships can be the source of special obligations.

Rejecting the idea of impartiality has a certain appeal, for it is always exciting to learn that some popular philosophical view is no good and that there is interesting work to be done in formulating an alternative. However, we should not be too quick here. It is no accident that the conception of morality as impartiality has been so widely accepted. It seems to express something deeply important that we should be reluctant to give up. It is useful, for example, in explaining why egoism, racism, and sexism are morally odious, and if we abandon this conception we lose our most natural and persuasive means of combating those doctrines. (The idea of morality as impartiality is closely connected to modern thoughts about human equality. That humans are in some sense equals would never have occurred to the Confucianists, which perhaps explains why they saw nothing plausible in Mo's teaching.) Therefore, it seems desirable to retain the notion of moral impartiality in some form. The question is, can we find some way of keeping both ideas – morality as impartiality, and special parental obligations? Can we understand them in a way that makes them compatible with one another?

As it turns out, this is not a difficult task. It is fairly easy to interpret impartiality in such a way that it no longer conflicts with special parental obligations. We can say, for example, that impartiality requires us to treat people in the same way *only when there are no relevant differences between them*. This qualification is obviously needed, quite apart from any considerations about parents and children. For example, it is not a failure of impartiality to imprison a convicted criminal, while innocent citizens go free, because there is a relevant difference between them (one has committed a crime; the others have not) to which we can appeal to justify the difference in treatment. Similar examples come easily to mind. But once we have admitted the need for this qualification, we can make use of it to resolve our problem about parental obligations: We can say that there is a relevant difference between one's own children and other children that justifies treating one's own children better. The difference will have something to do with the fact that they are one's own.

We might call this the compromise view. It is appealing because it allows us to retain the plausible idea of morality as impartiality, without having to give up the equally plausible idea that we have special obligations to our own children. Having found this solution to our problem, we might be tempted to stop here. That, however, would be premature. There is a further issue that needs to be addressed, and when we do address it, the compromise view will begin to look less attractive.

We are not free to call just any differences between individuals relevant. Suppose a racist claimed that there is a relevant difference between blacks and whites that justifies treating whites better – the difference being that they are members of different races. We would think this mere bluster and demand to know why *that* difference should count for anything. Similarly, it is only hand-waving to say that there is a relevant difference between one's own children and others that justifies treating one's own better – the difference being that they are one's own. We need to ask why *that* difference matters.

Why Should it Matter that a Child is One's Own?

Why should it matter, from a moral point of view, that a child is one's own? Our natural tendency is to assume that it *does* matter and to take it as a mere philosophical puzzle to figure out why. Why should anyone want to

resist this tendency? The feeling that our own children have a superior natural claim on our attention is among the deepest moral instincts we have. Can it possibly be doubted? I believe there is a powerful reason for doubting that this feeling is morally legitimate. The fact that a child is one's own may *not* matter, or at least it may not matter nearly as much as we usually assume. That reason has to do with luck.

The point about luck can be brought out like this. Suppose a parent believes that, when faced with a choice between feeding his own children and feeding starving orphans, he should give preference to his own. This is natural enough. But the orphans need the food just as much, and they are no less deserving. It is only their bad luck that they were not born to affluent parents; and why should luck count, from a moral point of view? Why should we think that a moral view is correct, if it implies that some children should be fed, while others starve, for no better reason than that some were unlucky in the circumstances of their birth? This seems to me to be an extremely important matter important enough, perhaps, that we should take seriously the possibility that a child's being one's own does not have the moral importance that we usually assume it has.

With this in mind, let us look at some of the arguments that support the Compromise View. The idea that one's own children have a superior claim to one's care might be defended in various ways. Let us consider the three arguments that seem most important.

1   The argument from social roles

The first line of reasoning begins with some observations about social roles. It is not possible for an isolated individual to have anything resembling a normal human life. For that, a social setting is required. The social setting provides roles for us to fill thus in the context of society we are able to be citizens, friends, husbands and wives, hospital patients, construction workers, scientists, teachers, customers, sports fans, and all the rest. None of us (with rare heroic exceptions) creates the roles we play; they have evolved over many centuries of human life, and we encounter them as simply the raw materials out of which we must fashion our individual lives.

These roles define, in large measure, our relations with other people. They specify how we should behave toward others. Teachers must wisely guide their students; friends must be loyal; husbands should be faithful; and so on. To the extent that you fail in these respects, you will be an inferior teacher, a bad friend, a poor husband. You can avoid these obligations by declining to enter into these roles: Not everyone will be a teacher, not everyone will marry, and some unfortunate people will not even have friends. But you can hardly avoid *all* social roles, and you cannot fill a social role without at the same time acknowledging the special responsibilities that go with it.

Now, parenthood is a social role, and like other such roles it includes special duties as part of its very nature. You can choose not to have children, or, having had a child, you may give it up for adoption. But if you *are* a parent, you are stuck with the responsibilities that go with the role. A parent who doesn't see to his children's needs is a bad parent, just as a disloyal friend is a bad friend, and an unfaithful husband is a poor husband. And that is why (according to this argument) we have obligations to our own children that we do not have to other children.

The argument from social roles is plausible; but how far should we be persuaded by it? The argument has at least four apparent weaknesses.

1 We need to distinguish two claims: first, that our obligations to our own children *have a different basis* from our obligations to other children; and second, that our obligations to our own children *are stronger than* (take precedence over) our obligations to other children. If successful, the argument from social roles would show only that our obligations to our own children are based on different considerations than are our obligations to other children. We have a social relationship with our own children that is the basis of our obligation to them, while our obligations to other children are based on a general duty of

beneficence. The argument would not show that the former obligations are *stronger*. Thus a critic of the idea of special parental obligations could continue the dispute at another level. It could be argued that, even if one's duties to one's own children have a different basis, they nevertheless are *no stronger than* one's duties to other children.

2 The second point is related to the first. The argument from social roles trades on the notion of what it means to be a bad father or a bad mother. Now, suppose we admit that a man who ignores the needs of his own children is a bad father. It may also be observed that a man who ignores the cries of orphans, when he could help, is a bad *man*, a man lacking a proper regard for the needs of others. While it is undesirable to be a bad father (or mother), it is also undesirable to be a bad man (or woman). So, once again, the argument from social roles does nothing to show that our obligations to other children are weaker.

3 Third, there is the point about luck that I have already mentioned. The system of social roles acknowledged in our society makes special provision for children lucky enough to live in homes with parents. This system favors even more those lucky enough to have affluent parents who can provide more for them than less affluent parents are able to provide. Even granting this, we can still ask: Is it a morally decent system? The system itself can be subject to criticism.

We do not have to look far to find an obvious objection to the system. The system does well enough in providing for some children; but it does miserably where others are concerned. There is no social role comparable to the parent–child relationship that targets the interests of orphans, or the interests of children whose parents are unable or unwilling to provide for them. Thus in this system luck plays an unacceptably important part.

4 Finally, students of social history might find the argument from social roles rather naïve. The argument draws much of its strength from the fact that contemporary American and European ideals favor families bound

together by love. Anyone who is likely to read these words will have been influenced by that ideal – consider how the reader will have passed over the second paragraph of this essay, with its easy talk of parents loving and protecting their children, without a pause. Yet the cozy nuclear family, nourished by affectionate relationships, is a relatively recent development. The norm throughout most of Western history has been very different.

In his acclaimed book *The Family, Sex and Marriage in England 1500–1800*, Lawrence Stone points out that as recently as the seventeenth century affectionate relations between husbands and wives were so rare as to be virtually nonexistent, and certainly were not expected within normal marriages. Among the upper classes, husbands and wives occupied separate stations within large households and rarely saw one another in private. Children were sent away immediately after birth to be looked after by wet-nurses for 12 to 18 months; then, returning home, they would be raised largely by nurses, governesses, and tutors. Finally they would be sent away to boarding school when they were between 7 and 13, with 10 the commonest age (Stone, 1979, pp. 83–4). The children of the poor were of course worse off: they would leave home at an equally early age, often to go and work in the houses of the rich. Stone writes,

> About all that can be said with confidence on the matter of emotional relations within the sixteenth- and early seventeenth-century family at all social levels is that there was a general psychological atmosphere of distance, manipulation, and deference. . . . Family relationships were characterized by interchangeability, so that substitution of another wife or another child was easy. . . . It was a structure held together not by affective bonds but by mutual economic interests. (Stone, 1979, p. 88)

And what of parental duties? Of course there has always been a recognition of *some* special parental duties, but in earlier times these were much more restricted and were not associated with bonds of affection. Until some time in the eighteenth century, it seems, the emphasis in European morals was almost entirely on the duties owed

by children to parents, rather than the other way around. Children were commonly said to owe their parents absolute obedience, in gratitude for having been given life. The French historian Jean Flandrin notes that "In Brittany the son remained subject to the authority of his father until the age of sixty, but marriage contracted with the father's consent emancipated him" (Flandrin, 1979, p. 130). Pity the man whose father lived to a ripe old age and refused consent for marriage – his only emancipation would be to flee. Both Stone and Flandrin make it clear that, while parental *rights* is an old idea, the idea of extensive parental *obligations* is a notion of much more recent vintage. (The debate between Mo Tzu and the Confucians was also conducted in such terms – for them, the primary issue was whether children had special duties to their fathers, not the other way around.)

These observations about social history should be approached with care. Of course they do not refute the idea of special parental obligations. However, they do go some way toward undermining our easy confidence that present-day social arrangements only institutionalize our natural duties. That is the only moral to be drawn from them, but it is an important one. In this area, as in so many others, what seems natural just depends on the conventions of one's society.

2 The argument from proximity

The second argument goes like this. It is reasonable to accept a social arrangement in which parents are assigned special responsibility for their own children because parents are *better situated* to look after their own. Granted, all children need help and protection. But other children are remote, and their needs are less clear, while a parent's own children live in the same house, and the parent is (or ought to be) intimately familiar with their needs. Other things being equal, it makes sense to think that *A* has a greater responsibility for helping *B* than for helping *C*, if *A* is better situated to help *B*. This is true in the case of helping one's own children versus helping other children; therefore, one's obligation in the first instance is greater.

This argument is plausible if we concentrate on certain kinds of aid. Children wake up sick in the middle of the night; someone must attend to them, and that someone is usually Mother or Father. The parents are in a position to do so, and (most of the time) no one else is. The complaint that you nursed your own children, but you didn't help the other children who woke up sick elsewhere in the world, is obviously misguided. The same goes for countless other ways that parents assist their children: by making them take their medicine, by stopping them from playing in the roadway, by bundling them up against the cold, and so on. These are all matters of what we might call *day-to-day care*.

Day-to-day care involves a kind of personal attention that a parent *could not* provide for many others, because it is physically impossible. The importance of physical proximity is that it makes these kinds of caring behaviors possible; the impossibility of doing the same for other children is just the impossibility of being in two places at once. So if there is partiality here, it is a partiality that we need not worry about because it cannot be avoided. There is little doubt, then, that parents are normally in a better position to provide day-to-day care for their own children than for others.

This type of argument is less plausible, however, when we consider more general, fundamental needs, such as food. Is a parent in a better position to feed his own children than to provide for others? At one time this might have been the case. Before the advent of modern communications and transportation, and before the creation of efficient relief agencies, people might have been able to say that while they could feed their own, they were unable to do much about the plight of children elsewhere. But that is no longer true. Today, with relief agencies ready to take our assistance all over the world, needing only sufficient resources to do so, it is almost as easy to provide food for a child in Africa as to provide for one's own. The same goes for providing basic medical care: international relief agencies carry medical assistance around the world on the same basis.

Therefore, the argument from proximity is, at best, only partially successful. Some forms of assistance (such as getting up in the middle of the night to attend to sick children) do require proximity but others (such as providing food) do not. The argument might show that, where day-to-day care is concerned, parents have special duties. But the same cannot be said for the provision of fundamental needs.

3 The argument from personal goods

The third argument hinges on the idea that loving relationships are personal goods of great importance: To love other people and be loved in return are part of what is involved in having a rich and satisfying human life. A loving relationship with one's children is, for many parents, a source of such happiness that they would sacrifice almost anything else to preserve it. But as we have already observed, love necessarily involves having a special concern for the well-being of the loved one, and so it is not impartial. An ethic that required absolute impartiality would therefore require forgoing a great personal good.

The intuitive idea behind this argument may seem plain enough. Nevertheless, it is difficult to formulate the argument with any precision. Why, exactly, is a loving relationship with another person such a great good? Part of the answer may be that pacts of mutual assistance enable all of us to fare better. If A and B have this sort of relationship, then A can count on B's assistance when it is needed, and vice versa. They are both better off. Of course, deals of this kind could be made between people who are not joined by bonds of affection, but affection makes the arrangement more dependable: People who love one another are more apt to remain faithful when the going is hard. But there is more. Bonds of affection are more than just instrumentally good. To be loved is to have one's own value affirmed; thus it is a source of self-esteem. This is important for all of us, but especially for children, who are more helpless and vulnerable than adults. Moreover, there is, at a deep level, a connection between love and the meaning of life (although I cannot go into this very deeply here). We question whether our lives have meaning when we find nothing worth valuing, when it seems to us that "all is vanity." Loving relationships provide individuals with things to value, and so give their lives this kind of meaning. That is why parents who love their children, and who strive to see that they do well, can find, in this, meaning for their lives.

These are important points, but they do not prove as much as they are sometimes taken to prove. In the first place, there is a lot about parental love that *is* consistent with a large measure of impartiality. Loving someone is not only a matter of preferring their interests. Love involves, among other things, intimacy and the sharing of experiences. A parent shows his love by listening to the child's jokes, by talking, by being a considerate companion, by praising, and even by scolding when that is needed. It may be objected that these kinds of behavior also show partiality, since the parent does not do these things for all children. But these are only further instances of the day-to-day care that requires proximity; again, if this is partiality, it is partiality that cannot be avoided. And there is another difference between these kinds of support and such things as providing food and medical care. The companionship, the listening, the talking, and the praising and scolding are what make personal relationships *personal*. That is why the psychic benefits that accompany such relationships are more closely associated with these matters than with such relatively impersonal things as being fed.

Moreover, it is not necessary, in order to have a loving relationship with one's children and to derive from it the benefits that the argument from personal goods envisions, to regard their interests as *always* having priority, especially when the interests in question are not comparable. One could have a loving relationship that involves all the intimacies of day-to-day care and the provision of life's necessities, while acknowledging at the same time that when it comes to choosing between luxuries for them and food for orphans, the orphans' needs should prevail. At the very least, there is nothing in the argument from personal goods that rules out such an approach.

The Moral Point of Utopian Thinking

There is another approach to our problem, favored by the Mohists, that we have not yet considered: Clinging to the ideal of impartiality, we could simply reject the idea of special parental duties. This goes against our intuitions, and it is opposed by the (partially successful) arguments we have just examined. Nevertheless, we may ask whether there is anything to be said in favor of this approach.

In fact, there is a lot that might be said in its favor. Suppose we forget, for a moment, the imperfections of actual human life, and try to imagine what it would be like if everyone behaved in a morally blameless manner. What would relations between adults and children be like in such a utopia? Here is one plausible picture of such a world. In it, children with living parents able to provide for them would be raised by their parents, who would give them all the love and care they needed. Parents who through no fault of their own were unable to provide for their children would be given whatever assistance they needed. Orphans would be taken in by families who would raise and love them as their own. The burdens involved in such adoptions would be shared by all.

It is fair to say that, in such a world, the ideal of impartiality is realized. In this world people do not act as if any child is more deserving than any other: one way or another, equal provision is made for the needs of all. Moreover, luck plays no part in how children will fare: the orphans' needs are satisfied too. When it is said by the Mohists that "love is universal," or by their modern counterparts, the utilitarians, that we should "promote impartially the interests of everyone alike," this might be the point: In the morally best world, we would not recognize many of the distinctions that we do recognize in the real world we inhabit.

But the idea of special obligations has crept back in. In the utopian world I have sketched, some special obligations are acknowledged, because particular adults (most often parents) are assigned special responsibility for looking after particular children. However, two points need to be emphasized: First, the *reason* for this arrangement is consistent with the principle of impartiality (and inconsistent with the thought that one's own children somehow have a natural superior claim on one's attention); the reason is that this is the best way to see that the needs of all children are satisfied. Second, the recognition of some special obligations might be *welcomed*, even in utopia; it need not be merely something that is grudgingly admitted. The arguments we have already considered suggest that there are special benefits to be derived from a social system in which particular adults are assigned responsibility for particular children – the benefits that go with loving personal relationships. This gives us reason to think that such an assignment would be part of the best social system a system that would at the same time make adequate provision for all.

Of course we do not live in a utopia, and it might be objected that, in the real world we inhabit, it would be either silly or disastrous to start telling parents to stop favoring their own children: silly because no one would listen, or disastrous because if some did, their children would suffer greatly. (There might be, in current terms, a coordination problem: It might not be wise for some to adopt the best strategy unless all do.) So what is the point of thinking about utopia? I suggest this: A picture of utopia gives us an idea, not only of what we should strive for, but of what is in one sense objectively right and wrong. Conditions may exist in our own world that make it wrong, in some circumstances, to act as though we lived in utopia. But that is only because in our world human behavior is flawed. It may nevertheless be true that, in a deep sense, the utopian behavior is morally best.

Let me try to make this clearer by giving a different sort of example. It has been argued by many philosophers that there is nothing immoral in mercy-killing, when it is requested by a dying person as a humane alternative to a slow, painful death. Others have objected that if mercy-killing were permitted it would lead to further killings that we would not want – we might begin by killing people at their own request to put them out of misery, it is said, but then we would begin to pressure sick people

into making such requests, and that would lead to killing old people who have not requested it (for their own good, of course), and then we would go on to killing the feeble-minded, and so on. I do not believe these things would happen.[3] But suppose they would. What would follow? It would not follow that mercy-killing is immoral in the original case. The objection would show, paradoxically, that there are good reasons why we should not perform actions that *are* moral and humane. Those reasons would have to do with the imperfections of human beings – the claim is that people are so flawed that they would slide down the slippery slope from the (moral) practice of euthanasia to the additional (immoral) practices described.

This suggests that moral philosophy might be idealistic in a way that applied ethics is not. Moral philosophy describes the ideals that motivate perfect conduct, the conduct of people in utopia.[4] In utopia, as Thomas More observed in his book of that name, euthanasia would be accepted (More, 1965, p. 102), and the slippery-slope argument would be irrelevant because people in utopia do not abuse humane practices. Applied ethics, however, takes into account the messy details of the real world, including the prejudices, faults, and vices of real human beings, and recommends how we should behave considering all *that* as well as the ideals of perfect conduct.

What does this mean for the question of special parental obligations? It means that there is a point to the philosophical insistence that all children are equal, even if in the real world it would be unwise to urge particular parents to stop providing preferential care for their own. The practical question is, therefore, how nearly we can expect to approach the ideal system in the real world and what specific recommendations should be made, in light of this, to particular parents.

Practical Implications

How should parents, living not in utopia but in our society, who are concerned to do what is morally best, conceive of the relation between their obligations to their own children and their obligations to other children? Here are three contrasting views; each is implausible, but for different reasons.

1   Extreme bias

On this view, parents have obligations to provide for their own children, but they have *no obligations at all* to other children. Anything done for other children is at best supererogatory – good and praiseworthy if one chooses to do it, but in no way morally mandatory. On this view, parents may provide not only necessities but also luxuries for their own children, while other children starve, and yet be immune from moral criticism.

Extreme bias is not plausible, because it makes no provision whatever for a duty of general beneficence. It is hard to believe that we do not have *some* obligation to be concerned with the plight of the starving, whoever they are, even if that obligation is less extensive than our obligations to our own kin.[5] Thus it will not be surprising if this view turns out to be unacceptable.

2   Complete equality

The opposite view seems to be implied by the idea of morality as impartiality the view that all children are equal and that there is no difference at all between one's moral obligations toward one's own children and one's moral obligations toward other children. This view denies that there are any good moral grounds for preferring to feed one's own child rather than an orphan in a foreign country. In our society anyone who accepted and acted on such a view would seem to his neighbors to be morally deranged, for doing so would seem to involve a rejection of one's children a refusal to treat them with the love that is appropriate to the parent–child relationship.

3   The most common view

What, in fact, do people in our society seem to believe? Most people seem to believe that one

has an obligation to provide the necessities of life for other children only after one has already provided a great range of luxuries for one's own. On this view, it is permissible to provide one's own children with virtually everything they need in order to have a good start in life – not only food and clothing, but, if possible, a good education, opportunities for travel, opportunities for enjoyable leisure, and so forth. In the United States children of affluent families often have TV sets, stereos, and now computers, all laid out in their own rooms. They drive their own cars to high school. Few people seem to think there is anything wrong with this – parents who are unable to provide their children with such luxuries nevertheless aspire to do so.

The most common view imposes *some* duty regarding other children, but not much. In practical terms, it imposes a duty only on the very rich, who have resources left over even after they have provided ample luxuries for their own children. The rest of us, who have nothing left after doing as much as we can for our own, are off the hook. It takes only a little reflection to see that this view is also implausible. How can it be right to spend money on luxuries for some children, even one's own buying them the latest trendy toys, for example, while others do not have enough to eat? Perhaps, when confronted with this, many people might come to doubt whether it is correct. But certainly most affluent people act as if it were correct.

Is there a better alternative? Is there a view that escapes the difficulties of extreme bias, complete equality, and the most common view, and is consistent with the various other points that have been made in our discussion? I suggest the following.

4   Partial bias

We might say that, while we do have a substantial obligation to be concerned about the welfare of all children, our own nevertheless come first. This vague thought needs to be sharpened. One way of making it more precise is this. When considering similar needs, you may permissibly prefer to provide for the needs of your own children. For example, if you were faced with a choice between feeding your own children or contributing the money to provide food for other children, you could rightly choose to feed your own. But if the choice were between some relatively trivial thing for your own and necessities for other children, preference should be given to helping the others. Thus if the choice were between providing trendy toys for your own already well-fed children or feeding the starving, you should feed the starving.

This view will turn out to be more or less demanding, depending on what one counts as a "relatively trivial thing." We might agree that buying trendy toys for some children, even for one's own, while other children starve is indefensible. But what about buying them nice clothes? Or a college education? Am I justified in sending my children to an expensive college? Clearly, the line between the trivial and the important can be drawn at different places. (One will be pushed toward a more demanding interpretation as one takes more seriously the point about the moral irrelevance of luck.) Nevertheless, the intuitive idea is plain enough. On this view, you may provide the necessities for your own children first, but you are not justified in providing them luxuries while other children lack necessities. Even in a fairly weak form, this view would still require much greater concern for others than the view that is most common in our society.

From the point of view of the various arguments we have considered, partial bias clearly stands out as the superior view. It is closer to the utopian ideal than either extreme bias or the most common view; it is morally superior in that it makes greater provision for children who have no loving parents; it is consistent with the arguments we have considered concerning the benefits to be derived from loving relationships; and it is perhaps as much as we could expect from people in the real world. It is not, in fact, very far from the utopian ideal. If we begin with complete equality, and then modify it in the ways suggested in our discussion of utopia, we end up with something very much like partial bias.

What would the adoption of partial bias mean for actual families? It would mean that parents could continue to provide loving day-to-day care for their own children, with all that this involves, while giving them preferential treatment in the provision of life's necessities. But it would also mean preferring to provide the necessities for needier children, rather than luxuries for their own. Children in such families would be worse off, in an obvious sense, than the children of affluent parents who continued to live according to the dictates of extreme bias or the most common view. However, we might hope that they would not regard themselves as deprived, for they might learn the moral value of giving up their luxuries so that the other children do not starve. They might even come to see their parents as morally admirable people. That hope is itself utopian enough.

Notes

1 "The good of any one individual is of no more importance, from the point of view (if I may say so) of the Universe, than the good of any other," says Sidgwick (1907, p. 382). "We [must] give equal weight in our moral deliberations to the like interests of all those affected by our actions," says Singer (1972, p. 197). "Moral rules must be for the good of everyone alike," says Baier (1958, p. 200). "A rational and impartial sympathetic spectator is a person who takes up a general perspective: he assumes a position where his own interests are not at stake and he possesses all the requisite information and powers of reasoning. So situated he is equally responsive and sympathetic to the desires and satisfactions of every-

one affected by the social system. . . . Responding to the interests of each person in the same way, an impartial spectator gives free reign to his capacity for sympathetic identification by viewing each person's situation as it affects that person," says Rawls (1971, p. 186). In an interesting discussion, R. M. Hare (1972) argues that virtually all the major moral theories incorporate a requirement of impartiality and adds that his own "universal prescriptivism" is no exception.

2 The point is a familiar one that pops up in all sorts of philosophical contexts. For example: In his recent book *On the Plurality of Worlds*, David Lewis discusses an ethical objection to his thesis that all

possible worlds are equally real, a thesis he calls modal realism. The objection is that, if modal realism is true, then our actions will have no effect whatever on the total amount of good or evil that exists. If we prevented an evil from occurring in *this* world, it would still exist in some *other* world. As Lewis puts it, "The sum total of good throughout the plurality of worlds is non-contingently fixed and depends not at all on what we do." Thus we might as well forget about trying to maximize the good. Lewis comments, "But if modal realism subverts only a 'truly universalistic ethics,' I cannot see that as a damaging objection. What collapses is a philosopher's invention, no less remote from common sense than modal realism itself. An ethics of our own world is quite universalistic enough. Indeed, I dare say that it is already far too universalistic; it is a betrayal of our particular affections" (1986, p. 128).

3   For a complete discussion see Rachels (1986, ch. 10).
4   On this point I am following Richard Brandt, although he does not put it in just this way. Brandt writes: "What I mean by 'is objectively wrong' or 'is morally unjustified' is 'would be prohibited by the set of moral rules which a rational person would prefer to have current or subscribed to in the consciences of persons in the society in which he expected to live a whole life, as compared with any other set of moral rules or none at all' " (1975, 367). Clearly, this is a set of rules appropriate for a utopia, where it is assumed that people will actually live according to the rules. In the real world we can make no such assumption, and sometimes this will mean we should do things that, according to this definition, would be objectively wrong.
5   For arguments concerning the extensiveness of our obligations toward others, see Singer (1972) and Rachels (1979).

References

Baier, Kurt. (1958). *The Moral Point of View*. Ithaca: Cornell University Press).

Brandt, Richard B. (1975) "The Morality and Rationality of Suicide." In James Rachels (ed.), *Moral Problems*. New York: Harper & Row.

Flandrin, Jean. (1979) *Families in Former Times*. trans. Richard Southern. Cambridge: Cambridge University Press.

Fung Yu-lan. (1960) *A Short History of Chinese Philosophy*. New York: Macmillan.

Hare, R. M. (1972) "Rules of War and Moral Reasoning," *Philosophy and Public Affairs* 1: 166–81.

Lewis, David (1986) *On the Plurality of Worlds*. Oxford: Blackwell.

Mill, John Stuart (1957) *Utilitarianism*. Indianapolis: Bobbs-Merrill. This work, first published in 1861, is today available in many editions.

More, Thomas (1965) *Utopia*. Harmondsworth: Penguin. This work, first published in Latin in 1516, is today available in many editions. The Penguin translation is by Paul Turner.

Rachels, James (1979) "Killing and Starving to Death," *Philosophy* 54: 159–71.

—— (1986) *The End of Life: Euthanasia and Morality*. Oxford: Oxford University Press.

Rawls, John (1971) *A Theory of Justice*. Cambridge, MA: Harvard University Press.

Rubin, Vitaly A. (1976) *Individual and State in Ancient China*. New York: Columbia University Press.

Sidgwick, Henry (1907) *The Methods of Ethics*, 7th edn. London: Macmillan.

Singer, Peter (1972) "Famine, Affluence, and Morality," *Philosophy and Public Affairs* 1: 229–43.

—— (1978) "Is Racial Discrimination Arbitrary?" *Philosophia* 8: 185–203.

Stone, Lawrence (1979) *The Family, Sex and Marriage in England 1500–1800*. New York: Harper & Row.

20

Artificial Means of Reproduction and Our Understanding of the Family

Ruth Macklin

It is an obvious truth that scientific and techno-logic innovations produce changes in our trad-itional way of perceiving the world around us. We have only to think of the telescope, the microscope, and space travel to recall that here-tofore unimagined perceptions of the macro-cosm and the microcosm have become commonplace. Yet it is not only perceptions, but also conceptions of the familiar that become altered by advances in science and technology. As a beginning student of philosophy, I first encountered problems in epistemology gener-ated by scientific knowledge: If physical objects are really comprised of molecules in motion, how is it that we perceive them as solid? Why is it that objects placed on a table don't slip through the empty spaces between the mol-ecules? If the mind is nothing but electrical processes occurring in the brain, how can we explain Einstein's ability to create the special theory of relativity or Bach's ability to compose the Brandenburg Concertos?

Now questions are being raised about how a variety of modes of artificial means of repro-duction might alter our conception of the fam-ily. George Annas has observed: "Dependable birth control made sex without reproduction possible. . . . Now medicine is closing the circle . . . by offering methods of reproduction without sex; including artificial insemination by donor (AID), in vitro fertilization (IVF), and surrogate embryo transfer (SET). As with birth control, artificial reproduction is defended as life-affirming and loving by its proponents, and denounced as unnatural by its detractors."[1]

Opponents of artificial reproduction have ex-pressed concerns about its effects on the family. This concern has centered largely but not en-tirely on surrogacy arrangements. Among the objections to surrogacy made by the Roman Catholic Church is the charge that "the practice of surrogate motherhood is a threat to the stability of the family."[2] But before the conse-quences for the family of surrogacy arrange-ments or other new reproductive practices can be assessed, we need to inquire into our under-standing of the family. Is there a single, incon-trovertible conception of the family? And who are the "we" presupposed in the phrase, "our understanding"? To begin, I offer three brief anecdotes . . .

The Biological Concept of Family

It is possible, of course, to settle these conceptual matters simply and objectively by adopting a biological criterion for determining what counts as a family. According to this criterion, people who are genetically related to one another would constitute a family, with the type and degree of relatedness described in the manner of a family tree. This sense of "family" is important and interesting for many purposes, but it does not and cannot encompass everything that is actually meant by "family," nor does it reflect the broader cultural customs and kinship systems that also define family ties . . . .

Newly developed artificial means of reproduction have rendered the term "biological" inadequate for making some critical conceptual distinctions, along with consequent moral decisions. The capability of separating the process of producing eggs from the act of gestation renders obsolete the use of the word "biological" to modify the word "mother." In the past, it was possible to distinguish only the biological mother (sometimes called the "natural" mother) from the rearing or adoptive mother. The techniques of egg retrieval, in vitro fertilization, and gamete intrafallopian transfer (GIFT), now make it possible for two different women to make a biological contribution to the creation of a new life. It would be a prescriptive, rather than a descriptive definition to maintain that the egg donor should properly be called the "biological mother." The woman who contributes her womb during gestation – whether she is acting as a surrogate or is the intended rearing mother – is also a biological mother. We have only to reflect on the many ways that the intrauterine environment and maternal behavior during pregnancy can influence fetal and later child development to acknowledge that a gestating woman is also a biological mother. I will return to this issue later in considering how much genetic contributions should count in disputed surrogacy arrangements.

Additional Determinants of the Meaning of "Family"

In addition to the biological meaning, there appear to be three chief determinants of what is meant by "family." These are law, custom, and what I shall call "subjective intentions." All three contribute to our understanding of the family. The effect of artificial means of reproduction on our understanding of the family will vary, depending on which of these three determinants is chosen to have priority. There is no way to assign a priori precedence to any one of the three. Let me illustrate each briefly.

Law as a determinant of family

Legal scholars can elaborate with precision and detail the categories and provisions of family law. This area of law encompasses legal rules governing adoption, artificial insemination by donor, foster placement, custody arrangements, and removal of children from a home in which they have been abused or neglected. For present purposes, it will suffice to summarize the relevant areas in which legal definitions or decisions have determined what is to count as a "family."

Laws governing adoption and donor insemination stipulate what counts as a family. In the case of adoption, a person or couple genetically unrelated to a child is deemed that child's legal parent or parents. By this legal rule, a new family is created. The biological parent or parents of the child never cease to be genetically related, of course. But by virtue of law, custom, and usually emotional ties, the adoptive parents become the child's family.

The Uniform Parentage Act holds that a husband who consents to AID of his wife by a physician is the legal father of the child. Many states have enacted laws in conformity with this legal rule. I am not aware of any laws that have been enacted making an analogous stipulation in the case of egg donation, but it is reasonable to assume that there will be symmetry of reasoning and legislation.

Commenting on the bearing of family law on the practice of surrogacy, Alexander M. Capron and Margaret J. Radin contend that the "legal rules of greatest immediate relevance" to surrogacy are those on adoption. These authors identify a number of provisions of state laws on adoption that should apply in the case of surrogacy. The provisions include allowing time for a "change of heart" period after the agreement to release a child, and prohibition of agreements to relinquish parental rights prior to the child's birth.[5]

Capron and Radin observe that in the context of adoption, "permitting the birth mother to reclaim a child manifests society's traditional respect for biological ties."[6] But how does this observation bear on artificial reproduction where the "biological" tie can be either genetic or gestational?

Consider first the case of the gestational surrogate who is genetically unrelated to the child. Does society's traditional respect for biological ties give her or the genetic mother the right to "reclaim" (or "claim" in the first place) the child? Society's traditional respect is more likely a concern for genetic inheritance than a recognition of the depth of the bond a woman may feel toward a child she has given birth to.

Secondly, consider the case of egg donation and embryo transfer to the wife of the man whose sperm was used in IVF. If the sperm donor and egg recipient were known to the egg donor, could the donor base her claim to the child on "society's traditional respect for biological ties"? As I surmised earlier, it seems reasonable to assume that any laws enacted for egg donation will be similar to those now in place for donor insemination. In the latter context, society's traditional respect for biological ties gave way to other considerations arising out of the desire of couples to have a child who is genetically related to at least one of the parents.

Custom as a determinant of family

The most telling examples of custom as a determinant of family are drawn from cultural anthropology. Kinship systems and incest taboos dictated by folkways and mores differ so radically that few generalizations are possible.

Ruth Benedict writes: "No known people regard all women as possible mates. This is not in an effort, as is so often supposed, to prevent inbreeding in our sense, for over great parts of the world it is an own cousin, often the daughter of one's mother's brother, who is the predestined spouse."[7]

In contrast, Benedict notes, some incest taboos are

> extended by a social fiction to include vast numbers of individuals who have no traceable ancestors in common . . . This social fiction receives unequivocal expression in the terms of relationship which are used. Instead of distinguishing lineal from collateral kin as we do in the distinction between father and uncle, brother and cousin, one term means literally 'man of my father's group (relationship, locality, etc.) of his generation,' . . . Certain tribes of eastern Australia use an extreme form of this so-called classificatory kinship system. Those whom they call brothers and sisters are all those of their generation with whom they recognize any relationship.[8]

One anthropologist notes that "the family in all societies is distinguished by a stability that arises out of the fact that it is based on marriage, that is to say, on socially sanctioned mating entered into with the assumption of permanency."[9] If we extend the notion of socially sanctioned mating to embrace socially sanctioned procreation, it is evident that the new artificial means of reproduction call for careful thought about what should be socially sanctioned before policy decisions are made.

"Subjective Intention" as a determinant of family

This category is most heterogeneous and amorphous. It includes a variety of ways in which individuals – singly, in pairs, or as a group, consider themselves a family even if their arrangement is not recognized by law or custom. Without an accompanying analysis, I list here an array of examples, based on real people and their situations.

- A homosexual couple decides to solidify their relationship by taking matrimonial vows. Despite the fact that their marriage is not recognized by civil law, they find an ordained minister who is willing to perform the marriage ceremony. They are now a married couple, a family. Later they apply to be foster parents of children with AIDS whose biological parents have died or abandoned them. The foster agency accepts the couple. Two children are placed in foster care with them. They are now a family.

- A variation on this case: A lesbian couple has a long-term monogamous relationship. They decide they want to rear a child. Using "turkey-baster" technology, one of the women is inseminated, conceives, and gives birth to a baby. The three are now a family, with one parent genetically related to the child.
- Pat Anthony, a 47-year-old grandmother in South Africa, agreed to serve as gestational surrogate for her own daughter. The daughter had had her uterus removed, but could still produce eggs and wanted more children. The daughter's eggs were inseminated with her husband's sperm, and the resulting embryos implanted in her own mother, Pat Anthony. Mrs. Anthony gave birth to triplets when she was 48. She was the gestational mother and the genetic grandmother of the triplets.
- Linda Kirkman was the gestational mother of a baby conceived with a sister's egg and destined to live with the infertile sister and her husband. Linda Kirkman said, "I always considered myself her aunt." Carol Chan donated eggs so that her sister Susie could bear and raise a child. Carol Chan said: "I could never regard the twins as anything but my nephews." The two births occurred in Melbourne within weeks of each other.[10]

My point in elucidating this category of heterogeneous examples is to suggest that there may be entirely subjective yet valid elements that contribute to our understanding of the family, family membership, or family relationships. I believe it would be arbitrary and narrow to rule out all such examples by fiat. The open texture of our language leaves room for conceptions of family not recognized by law or pre-existing custom.

Posing the question "Who counts as family?", Carol Levine replies: "The answer to this apparently simple question is by no means easy. It depends on why the question is being asked and who is giving the answer."[11] Levine's observation, made in the context of AIDS, applies equally well to the context of artificial means of reproduction.

The Gestational versus the Genetic Mother

One critical notion rendered problematic by the new technological capabilities of artificial reproduction is the once simple concept of a mother. The traditional concept is complicated by the possibility that a woman can gestate a fetus genetically unrelated to her. This prospect has implications both for public policy and our understanding of the family. The central policy question is: How much should genetic relatedness count in disputed surrogacy arrangements?

A matter of discovery or decision?

Which criterion – genetic or gestational – should be used to determine who is the "real" mother? I contend that this question is poorly formulated. Referring to the "real" mother implies that it is a matter of discovery, rather than one calling for a decision. To speak of "the real x" is to assume that there is an underlying metaphysical structure to be probed by philosophical inquiry. But now that medical technology has separated the two biological contributions to motherhood, in place of the single conjoint role provided by nature, some decisions will have to be made.

One decision is conceptual, and a second is moral. The conceptual question is: Should a woman whose contribution is only gestational be termed a "mother" of the baby? We may assume, by analogy with our concept of paternity, that the woman who makes the genetic contribution in a surrogacy arrangement can properly be termed a "mother" of the baby. So it must be decided whether there can be only one "mother," conceptually speaking, or whether this technological advance calls for new terminology.

Conceptual decisions often have implications beyond mere terminology. A decision not to use the term "mother" (even when modified by the adjective "gestational") to refer to a woman who acts in this capacity can have important consequences for ethics and public policy. As a case in point, the Wayne County Circuit Court in Michigan issued an interim order declaring a gamete donor couple to be the biological parents of a fetus being carried to term by a woman hired to be the gestational mother . . . Upon birth, the court entered an order that the names of the ovum and sperm donors be listed on the birth certificate, rather than that of the woman who gave birth, who was termed by the court a "human incubator."[12]

The ethical question posed by the separation of biological motherhood into genetic and gestational components is: Which role should entitle a woman to a greater claim on the baby, in case of dispute? Since the answer to this question cannot be reached by discovery, but is, like the prior conceptual question, a matter for decision, we need to determine which factors are morally relevant and which have the greatest moral weight. In order to avoid begging any ethical questions by a choice of terminology, I use the terms "geneticmother" and "gestational mother" to refer to the women who make those respective contributions. And instead of speaking of the "real" mother, I'll use the phrase "primary mother" when referring to the woman presumed to have a greater claim on the child.

Morally relevant factors

The possibilities outlined below are premised on the notion that surrogacy contracts are voidable. I take this to mean that no legal presumption is set up by the fact that there has been a prior contract between the surrogate and the intended rearing parents. From an ethical perspective, that premise must be argued for independently, and convincing arguments have been advanced by a number of authors.[13] If we accept

the premise that a contractual provision to relinquish a child born of a surrogacy agreement has no legal force, the question then becomes: Is there a morally relevant distinction between the two forms of surrogacy with respect to a claim on the child? Who has the weightiest moral claim when a surrogate is unwilling to give the baby up after its birth? Where should the moral presumption lie?

Who most "deserves" or has a "right" to the child?

Three main views are outlined under this heading, each taking a different stance on which factor should be the criterion for having the greatest moral claim.

1. Gestation is the overriding factor

According to this position, whether a woman is merely the gestational surrogate, or also contributes her genetic material, makes no difference in determining moral priorities. In either case, the surrogate is the primary mother because the criterion is gestation.

This position is adopted by George Annas and others who have argued that the gestational mother should be legally presumed to have the right and responsibility to rear the child. One reason given in support of this presumption is (a) "the greater biological and psychological investment of the gestational mother in the child."[14] This is referred to as "sweat equity." A related yet distinct reason is (b) "the biological reality that the mother at this point has contributed more to the child's development, and that she will of necessity be present at birth and immediately thereafter to care for the child."[15]

Reason (a) focuses on what the gestational mother deserves, based on her investment in the child, while reason (b), though mentioning her contribution, also focuses on the interests of the child during and immediately after birth. Annas adds that "to designate the gestational mother, rather than the genetic mother, the legal or 'natural mother' would be protective of children."[16]

2. Genetics is the overriding factor

In surrogacy arrangements, it is the inseminating male who seen as the father, not the husband of the woman who acts as a surrogate. This is because the genetic contribution is viewed as determinative for fatherhood. By analogy, the woman who makes the genetic contribution is the primary mother. This position sharply distinguishes between the claim to the child made by the two different types of surrogate. It makes the surrogate who contributes her egg as well as her womb the primary (or sole) mother. But now recall the fact that in AID, the law recognizes the husband of the inseminated woman as the father. This shows that laws can be made to go either way.

This position was supported by the court in *Smith & Smith* v. *Jones & Jones*, on grounds of the analogy with paternity. The court said: "the donor of the ovum, the biological mother, is to be deemed, in fact, the natural mother of this infant, as is the biological father to be deemed the natural father of this child."[17]

Legal precedents aside, is there a moral reason that could be invoked in support of this position? One possibility is (a) "ownership" of one's genetic products. Since each individual has a unique set of genes, people might be said to have a claim on what develops from their own genes, unless they have explicitly relinquished any such claims. This may be a metaphorical sense of "ownership," but it reflects the felt desire to have genetically related children – the primary motivation behind all forms of assisted reproduction.

Another possible reason for assigning greater weight to the genetic contribution is (b) the child-centered position. Here it is argued that it is in children's best interest to be reared by parents to whom they are genetically related. Something like this position is taken by Sidney Callahan. She writes:

> The most serious ethical problems in using third party donors in alternative reproduction concern the well-being of the potential child . . . A child who has donor(s) intruded into its parentage will be cut off from its genetic heritage and part of its kinship relations in new ways. Even if there is no danger

of transmitting unknown genetic disease or causing physiological harm to the child, the psychological relationship of the child to its parents is endangered – with or without the practice of deception and secrecy about its origins.[18]

Additional considerations lending plausibility to this view derive from data concerning adopted children who have conducted searches for their biological parents, and similar experiences of children whose birth was a result of donor insemination and who have sought out their biological fathers. In the case of gestational surrogacy, the child is genetically related to both of the intended rearing parents. However, there is no data to suggest whether children born of gestational mothers might someday begin to seek out those women in a quest for their "natural" or "real" mothers.

3. Gestation and genetics both count

According to this position, the surrogate who contributes both egg and womb has more of a claim to being the "primary" mother than does the surrogate who contributes only her womb. Since the first type of surrogate makes both a genetic and a gestational contribution, in case of a dispute she gets to keep the baby instead of the biological father, who has made only one contribution. But this does not yet settle the question of who has a greater moral claim to the infant in cases where the gestational surrogate does not wish to give up the baby to the genetic parents. To determine that, greater weight must be given either to the gestational component or the genetic component.

Subsidiary views

One may reject the notion that the only morally relevant considerations are the respective contributions of each type of surrogate. Another possible criterion draws on the biological conception of family, and thus takes into account the contribution of the genetic father. According to this position, two genetic contributions count more than none. This leads to three subsidiary views, in addition to the three main positions outlined above.

4. Gestational surrogates have less of a moral claim to the infant than the intended parents, both of whom have made a genetic contribution. This is because two (genetic) contributions count more than one (gestational) contribution. This view, derived from "society's traditional respect for biological ties," gives greatest weight to the concept of family based on genetic inheritance.

5. A woman who contributes both egg and womb has a claim equal to that of the biological father, since both have made genetic contributions. If genetic contribution is what determines both "true" motherhood and fatherhood, the policy implications of this view are that each case in which a surrogate who is both genetic and gestational mother wishes to keep the baby would have to go to court and be settled in the manner of custody disputes.

As a practical suggestion, this model is of little value. It throws every case of this type of surrogacy – the more common variety – open to this possibility, which is to move backwards in public policy regarding surrogacy.

6. However, if genetic and gestational contributions are given equal weight, but it is simply the number of contributions that counts, the artificially inseminated surrogate has the greater moral claim since she has made two contributions – genetic and gestational – while the father has made only one, the genetic contribution.

Conclusions

What can we conclude from all this about the effects of artificial means of reproduction on the family and on our conception of the family? Several conclusions emerge, although each requires a more extended elaboration and defense than will be given here.

A broad definition of "family" is preferable to a narrow one. A good candidate is the working definition proposed by Carol Levine: "Family members are individuals who by birth, adoption, marriage, or declared commitment share deep personal connections and are mutually entitled to receive and obligated to provide support of various kinds to the extent possible, especially in times of need."[19]

Some of the effects of the new reproductive technologies on the family call for the development of public policy, while others remain private, personal matters to be decided within a given family. An example of the former is the determination of where the presumptions should lie in disputed surrogacy arrangements, whose rights and interests are paramount, and what procedures should be followed to safeguard those rights and interests. An example of the latter is disclosure to a child of the facts surrounding genetic paternity or maternity in cases of donor insemination or egg donation, including the identity of the donor when that is known. These are profound moral decisions, about which many people have strong feelings, but they are not issues to be addressed by public policy.

It is not at all clear that artificial modes of reproduction threaten to produce greater emotional difficulties for family members affected, or pose more serious ethical problems, than those already arising out of long-standing practices such as adoption and artificial insemination. The analogy is often made between the impact on women who serve as surrogates and those who have lost their biological offspring in other ways.

Warning of the dangers of surrogacy, defenders of birth mothers have related the profound emotional trauma and lasting consequences for women who have given their babies up for adoption. One such defender is Phyllis Chesler, a psychologist who has written about the mother-infant bond and about custody battles in which mothers have lost their children to fathers. Dr. Chesler reports that many women never get over having given up their child for adoption. Their decision "leads to thirty to forty years of being haunted."[20] Chesler contends that the trauma to women who have given up their babies for adoption is far greater than that of incest, and greater than that felt by mothers who have lost custody battles for their children.

Additional evidence of the undesirable consequences for birth mothers of adoption is provided by Alison Ward, a woman who serves as an adoption reform advocate. Having given up her own daughter for adoption in 1967, she found and was reunited with her in 1980. Ms. Ward said to an audience assembled to hear testimony on surrogacy:

> I think that you lack the personal experience I have: that of knowing what it is like to terminate your parental rights and go for years not knowing if your child is dead or alive. All the intellectual and philosophical knowledge in the world cannot begin to touch having to live your life as a birthparent. Last Sunday was Mother's Day. It seems ironic that, as our country gives such lip service to the values of motherhood and the sanctity of the bond between mother and child, that we even consider legalizing a process [surrogacy] which would destroy all that.[21]

The effects of these practices on children are alleged to be equally profound and damaging. Scholarly studies conducted in recent years have sought to evaluate the adjustment of children to adoption. One expert notes that "the pattern emerging from the more recent clinical and nonclinical studies that have sampled widely and used appropriate controls, generally supports the view that, on the average, adopted children are more likely to manifest psychological problems than nonadopted children."[22] The additional fact that numerous adopted children have sought to find their biological parents, despite their being in a loving family setting, suggests that psychological forces can intrude on the dictates of law or custom regarding what counts as a family. Although it is easier to keep secret from a child the circumstances surrounding artificial insemination and egg donation, such secrets have sometimes been revealed with terrible emotional consequences for everyone involved.

> Alison Ward compares the impact of surrogacy on children to both situations: There will always be pain for these children. Just as adoptive parents have learned that they cannot love the pain of their adopted children away, couples who raise children obtained through surrogacy will have to deal with a

special set of problems. Donor offspring . . . rarely find out the truth of their origins. But, some of them do, and we must listen to them when they speak of their anguish, of not knowing who fathered them; we must listen when they tell us how destructive it is to their self esteem to find out their father sold the essence of his lineage for $40 or so, without ever intending to love or take responsibility for them. For children born of surrogacy contracts, it will be even worse: their own mothers did this to them.[23]

Phyllis Chesler paints a similarly bleak picture of the effect on children of being adopted away from their birth mothers. She contends that this has "dramatic, extreme psychological consequences." She cites evidence indicating that adopted children seem more prone to mental and emotional disorders than other children, and concludes that "children need to know their natural origins."[24]

These accounts present only one side, and there is surely another, more positive picture of parents and children flourishing in happy, healthy families that would not have existed but for adoption or artificial insemination. Yet the question remains, what follows in any case from such evidence? Is it reasonable to conclude that the negative consequences of these practices, which have altered traditional conceptions of the family, are reasons for abolishing them? Or for judging that it was wrong to institute them in the first place, since for all practical purposes they cannot be reversed? A great deal more evidence, on a much larger scale, would be needed before a sound conclusion could be reached that adoption and artificial insemination have had such negative consequences for the family that they ought never to have been socially sanctioned practices.

Similarly, there is no simple answer to the question of how artificial means of reproduction affect our understanding of the family. We need to reflect on the variety of answers, paying special attention to what follows from answering the question one way rather than another. Since there is no single, univocal concept of the family, it is a matter for moral and social decision just which determinants of "family" should be given priority.

Notes

1 George J. Annas, "Redefining Parenthood and Protecting Embryos," *Judging Medicine* (Clifton, NJ: Humana Press, 1988), p. 59. Reprinted from *The Hastings Center Report*, October 1984.

2 William F. Bolan, Jr., Executive Director, New Jersey Catholic Conference, "Statement of New Jersey Catholic Conference in Connection with Public Hearing on Surrogate Mothering," Commission on Legal and Ethical Problems in the Delivery of Health Care, Newark, New Jersey, May 11, 1988.

3 Cited in Carol Levine, "AIDS and Changing Concepts of Family," *The Milbank Quarterly* 68, Supplement 1 (1990), p. 37.

4 A. M. Capron and M. J. Radin, "Choosing Family Law Over Contract Law as a Paradigm for Surrogate Motherhood," *Law, Medicine & Health Care* 16 (1988): 35.

5 Ibid.

6 Ruth Benedict, *Patterns of Culture* (New York: Mentor Books, 1934), p. 29.

7 Ibid., p. 30.

8 Melville J. Herskovits, *Cultural Anthropology* (New York: Alfred A. Knopf, 1955), p. 171.

9 R. Alta Charo, "Legislative Approaches to Surrogate Motherhood," *Law, Medicine & Health Care* 16 (1988): 104.

10 "AIDS and Changing Concepts of Family," p. 35.

11 O.T.A. report, Infertility: Medical and Social Choices, p. 284; case cited *Smith & Smith* v. *Jones & Jones*, 85–532014 DZ, Detroit MI, 3rd Dist. (March 15, 1986), as reported in *Bio Law*, J. Childress, P. Kin, K. Rothenberg, et al. (eds.) (Frederick, MD: University Publishers of America, 1986). See also Annas, "The Baby Broker Boom," *Hastings Center Report* 16 (June 1986): 30–1.

12 See, e.g., George J. Annas, "Death without Dignity for Commercial Surrogacy: The Case of Baby M," *Hastings Center Report* 18 (April/May 1 Bonnie Steinbock, "Surrogate Motherhood a natal Adoption ed. Larry Gostin, *Surrogate Moth hood: Politics and Privacy* (Bloomington, IN) Indiana University Press, 1990), pp. 123–35.

13 Sherman Elias and George J. Annas, "Noncoital Reproduction," *JAMA* 255, (January 3, 1986): 67.

14 George J. Annas, "Death without Dignity for Commercial Surrogacy: The Case of Baby M," p. 23.

15 Ibid., p. 24.

16 Annas, "The Baby Broker Boom," p. 31.

17 "The Ethical Challenge of the New Reproductive Technology," presentation before the Task Force on New Reproductive Practices; published in John F. Monagle and David C. Thomasma (eds.), *Medical Ethics: A Guide for Health Care Professionals* (Frederick, Maryland: Aspen Publishers, 1987) pp. 15–16, typescript.

18 "AIDS and Changing Concepts of Family," p. 36.

19 This statement and subsequent ones attributed to Phyllis Chesler are taken from her unpublished remarks made at a Public Hearing on Surrogacy conducted by the New Jersey Bioethics Commission, Newark, New Jersey, May 11, 1988, in which the author was a participant.

20 Written testimony, presented orally at the New Jersey Bioethics Commission public hearing on Surrogacy, May 11, 1988.

21 David M. Brodzinsky, "Adjustment to Adoption: A Psychosocial Perspective," *Clinical Psychology Review* 7 (1987): 29.

22 Ward, written testimony from New Jersey public hearing.

23 Chesler, oral testimony at New Jersey public hearing.

s Labor a Commodity?

Elizabeth S. Anderson

In the past few years the practice of commercial surrogate motherhood has gained notoriety as a method for acquiring children. A commercial surrogate mother is anyone who is paid money to bear a child for other people and terminate her parental rights, so that the others may raise the child as exclusively their own. The growth of commercial surrogacy has raised with new urgency a class of concerns regarding the proper scope of the market. Some critics have objected to commercial surrogacy on the ground that it improperly treats children and women's reproductive capacities as commodities.[1] The prospect of reducing children to consumer durables and women to baby factories surely inspires revulsion. But are there good reasons behind the revulsion? And is this an accurate description of what commercial surrogacy implies? This article offers a theory about what things are properly regarded as commodities which supports the claim that commercial surrogacy constitutes an unconscionable commodification of children and of women's reproductive capacities.

What Is a Commodity?

The modern market can be characterized in terms of the legal and social norms by which it governs the production, exchange, and enjoyment of commodities. To say that something is properly regarded as a commodity is to claim that the norms of the market are appropriate for regulating its production, exchange, and enjoyment. To the extent that moral principles or ethical ideals preclude the application of market norms to a good, we may say that the good is not a (proper) commodity.

Why should we object to the application of a market norm to the production or distribution of a good? One reason may be that to produce or distribute the good in accordance with the norm is to *fail to value it in an appropriate way*. Consider, for example, a standard Kantian argument against slavery, or the commodification of persons. Slaves are treated in accordance with the market norm that owners may use commodities to satisfy their own interests without regard for the interests of the commodities themselves. To treat a person without regard for her interests is to fail to respect her. But slaves are persons who may not be merely used in this fashion, since as rational beings they possess a dignity which commands respect. In Kantian theory, the problem with slavery is that it treats beings worthy of *respect* as if they were worthy merely of *use*. "Respect" and "use" in this context denote what we may call different *modes of valuation*.

We value things and persons in other ways than by respecting and using them. For example, love, admiration, honor, and appreciation constitute distinct modes of valuation. To value a thing or person in a distinctive way involves treating it in accordance with a particular set of norms. For example, courtesy expresses a mode of valuation we may call "civil respect," which differs from Kantian respect in that it calls for obedience to the rules of etiquette rather than to the categorical imperative.

Any ideal of human life includes a conception of how different things and persons should be valued. Let us reserve the term "use" to refer to the mode of valuation proper to commodities, which follows the market norm of treating things solely in accordance with the owner's nonmoral preferences. Then the Kantian argument against commodifying persons can be generalized to apply to many other cases. It can be argued that many objects which are worthy of a higher mode of valuation than use are not properly regarded as mere commodities.[2] Some current arguments against the colorization of classic black-and-white films take this form. Such films have been colorized by their owners in an attempt to enhance their market value by attracting audiences unused to black-and-white cinematography. But some opponents of the practice object that such treatment of the film classics fails to appreciate their aesthetic and historical value. True appreciation of these films would preclude this kind of crass commercial exploitation, which debases their aesthetic qualities in the name of profits. Here the argument rests on the claim that the goods in question are worthy of appreciation, not merely of use.

The ideals which specify how one should value certain things are supported by a conception of human flourishing. Our lives are enriched and elevated by cultivating and exercising the capacity to appreciate art. To fail to do so reflects poorly on ourselves. To fail to value things appropriately is to embody in one's life an inferior conception of human flourishing.

These considerations support a general account of the sorts of things which are appropriately regarded as commodities. Commodities are those things which are properly treated in accordance with the norms of the modern market. We can question the application of market norms to the production, distribution, and enjoyment of a good by appealing to ethical ideals which support arguments that the good should be valued in some other way than use. Arguments of the latter sort claim that to allow certain market norms to govern our treatment of a thing expresses a mode of valuation not worthy of it. If the thing is to be valued appropriately, its production, exchange, and enjoyment must be removed from market norms and embedded in a different set of social relationships.

The Case of Commercial Surrogacy

Let us now consider the practice of commercial surrogate motherhood in the light of this theory of commodities. Surrogate motherhood as a commercial enterprise is based upon contracts involving three parties: the intended father, the broker, and the surrogate mother. The intended father agrees to pay a lawyer to find a suitable surrogate mother and make the requisite medical and legal arrangements for the conception and birth of the child, and for the transfer of legal custody to himself. The surrogate mother agrees to become impregnated with the intended father's sperm, to carry the resulting child to term, and to relinquish her parental rights to it, transferring custody to the father in return for a fee and medical expenses. Both she and her husband (if she has one) agree not to form a parent–child bond with her child and to do everything necessary to effect the transfer of the child to the intended father. At current market prices, the lawyer arranging the contract can expect to gross $15,000 from the contract, while the surrogate mother can expect a $10,000 fee.[3]

The practice of commercial surrogacy has been defended on four main grounds. First, given the shortage of children available for adoption and the difficulty of qualifying as adoptive parents, it may represent the only hope for some people to be able to raise a family. Commercial surrogacy should be accepted as an effective means for realizing this highly significant good. Second, two fundamental human rights support commercial surrogacy: the right to procreate and freedom of contract. Fully informed autonomous adults should have the right to make whatever arrangements they wish for the use of their bodies and the reproduction of children, so long as the children themselves are not harmed. Third, the labor of tire of the surrogate mother is said to be a labor of love. Her altruistic acts should be permitted and encouraged.[4] Finally, it is argued that commercial surrogacy is no different in its ethical implications from many already accepted practices which separate genetic, gestational, and social parenting, such as artificial insemination by donor, adoption, wet-nursing, and day care. Consistency demands that society accept this new practice as well.[5]

In opposition to these claims, I shall argue that commercial surrogacy does raise new ethical issues, since it represents an invasion of the market into a new sphere of conduct, that of specifically women's labor – that is, the labor of carrying children to term in pregnancy. When women's labor is treated as a commodity, the women who perform it are degraded. Furthermore, commercial surrogacy degrades children by reducing their status to that of commodities. Let us consider each of the goods of concern in surrogate motherhood – the child, and women's reproductive labor – to see how the commercialization of parenthood affects people's regard for them.

Children as Commodities

The most fundamental calling of parents to their children is to love them. Children are to be loved and cherished by their parents, not to be used or manipulated by them for merely personal advantage. Parental love can be understood as a passionate, unconditional commitment to nurture one's child, providing it with the care, affection, and guidance it needs to develop its capacities to maturity. This under-

standing of the way parents should value their children informs our interpretation of parental rights over their children. Parents' rights over their children are trusts, which they must always exercise for the sake of the child. This is not to deny that parents have their own aspirations in raising children. But the child's interests beyond subsistence are not definable independently of the flourishing of the family, which is the object of specifically parental aspirations. The proper exercise of parental rights includes those acts which promote their shared life as a family, which realize the shared interests of the parents and the child.

The norms of parental love carry implications for the ways other people should treat the relationship between parents and their children. If children are to be loved by their parents, then others should not attempt to compromise the integrity of parental love or work to suppress the emotions supporting the bond between parents and their children. If the rights to children should be understood as trusts, then if those rights are lost or relinquished, the duty of those in charge of transferring custody to others is to consult the best interests of the child.

Commercial surrogacy substitutes market norms for some of the norms of parental love. Most importantly, it requires us to understand parental rights no longer as trusts but as things more like property rights – that is, rights of use and disposal over the things owned. For in this practice the natural mother deliberately conceives a child with the intention of giving it up for material advantage. Her renunciation of parental responsibilities is not done for the child's sake, nor for the sake of fulfilling an interest she shares with the child, but typically for her own sake (and possibly, if "altruism" is a motive, for the intended parents' sakes). She and the couple who pay her to give up her parental rights over her child thus treat her rights as a kind of property right. They thereby treat the child itself as a kind of commodity, which may be properly bought and sold.

Commercial surrogacy insinuates the norms of commerce into the parental relationship in other ways. Whereas parental love is not supposed to be conditioned upon the child having particular characteristics, consumer demand is properly responsive to the characteristics of commodities. So the surrogate industry provides opportunities to adoptive couples to specify the height, I.Q., race, and other attributes of the surrogate mother, in the expectation that these traits will be passed on to the child.[6] Since no industry assigns agents to look after the "interests" of its commodities, no one represents the child's interests in the surrogate industry. The surrogate agency promotes the adoptive parents' interests and not the child's interests where matters of custody are concerned. Finally, as the agent of the adoptive parents, the broker has the task of policing the surrogate (natural) mother's relationship to her child, using persuasion, money, and the threat of a lawsuit to weaken and destroy whatever parental love she may develop for her child.

All of these substitutions of market norms for parental norms represent ways of treating children as commodities which are degrading to them. Degradation occurs when something is treated in accordance with a lower mode of valuation than is proper to it. We value things not just, "more" or "less," but in qualitatively higher and lower ways. To love or respect someone is to value her in a higher way than one would if one merely used her. Children are properly loved by their parents and respected by others. Since children are valued as mere use-objects by the mother and the surrogate agency when they are sold to others, and by the adoptive parents when they seek to conform the child's genetic makeup to their own wishes, commercial surrogacy degrades children insofar as it treats them as commodities.

One might argue that since the child is most likely to enter a loving home, no harm comes to it from permitting the natural mother to treat it as property. So the purchase and sale of infants is unobjectionable, at least from the point of view of children's interests.[7] But the sale of an infant has an expressive significance which this argument fails to recognize. By engaging in the transfer of children by sale, all of the parties to the surrogate contract express a set of attitudes toward children which undermines the norms of parental love. They all agree in treating the

ties between a natural mother and her children as properly loosened by a monetary incentive. Would it be any wonder if a child born of a surrogacy agreement feared resale by parents who have such an attitude? And a child who knew how anxious her parents were that she have the "right" genetic makeup might fear that her parent's love was contingent upon her expression of these characteristics.

The unsold children of surrogate mothers are also harmed by commercial surrogacy. The children of some surrogate mothers have reported their fears that they may be sold like their half-brother or half-sister, and express a sense of loss at being deprived of a sibling.[8] Furthermore, the widespread acceptance of commercial surrogacy would psychologically threaten all children. For it would change the way children are valued by people (parents and surrogate brokers) – from being loved by their parents and respected by others, to being sometimes used as objects of commercial profit-making.[9]

Proponents of commercial surrogacy have denied that the surrogate industry engages in the sale of children. For it is impossible to sell to someone what is already his own, and the child is already the father's own natural offspring. The payment to the surrogate mother is not for her child, but for her services in carrying it to term.[10] The claim that the parties to the surrogate contract treat children as commodities, however, is based on the way they treat the *mother's* rights over her child. It is irrelevant that the natural father also has some rights over the child; what he pays for is exclusive rights to it. He would not pay her for the "service" of carrying the child to term if she refused to relinquish her parental rights to it. That the mother regards only her labor and not her child as requiring compensation is also irrelevant. No one would argue that the baker does not treat his bread as property just because he sees the income from its sale as compensation for his labor and expenses and not for the bread itself, which he doesn't care to keep.

Defenders of commercial surrogacy have also claimed that it does not differ substantially from other already accepted parental practices. In the institutions of adoption and artificial insemination by donor (AID), it is claimed, we already grant parents the right to dispose of their children.[11] But these practices differ in significant respects from commercial surrogacy. The purpose of adoption is to provide a means for placing children in families when their parents cannot or will not discharge their parental responsibilities. It is not a sphere for the existence of a supposed parental right to dispose of one's children for profit. Even AID does not sanction the sale of fully formed human beings. The semen donor sells only a product of his body, not his child, and does not initiate the act of conception.

Two developments might seem to undermine the claim that commercial surrogacy constitutes a degrading commerce in children. The first is technological: the prospect of transplanting a human embryo into the womb of a genetically unrelated woman. If commercial surrogacy used women only as gestational mothers and not as genetic mothers, and if it was thought that only genetic and not gestational parents could properly claim that a child was "theirs," then the child born of a surrogate mother would not be hers to sell in the first place. The second is a legal development: the establishment of the proposed "consent–intent" definition of parenthood.[12] This would declare the legal parents of a child to be whoever consented to a procedure which leads to its birth, with the intent of assuming parental responsibilities for it. This rule would define away the problem of commerce in children by depriving the surrogate mother of any legal claim to her child at all, even if it was hers both genetically and gestationally.

There are good reasons, however, not to undermine the place of genetic and gestational ties in these ways. Consider first the place of genetic ties. By upholding a system of involuntary (genetic) ties of obligation among people, even when the adults among them prefer to divide their rights and obligations in other ways, we help to secure children's interests in having an assured place in the world, which is more firm than the wills of their parents. Unlike the consent–intent rule, the principle of respecting genetic ties does not make the

obligation to care for those whom one has created (intentionally or not) contingent upon an arbitrary desire to do so. It thus provides children with a set of preexisting social sanctions which give them a more secure place in the world. The genetic principle also places children in a far wider network of associations and obligations than the consent–intent rule sanctions. It supports the roles of grandparents and other relatives in the nurturing of children, and provides children with a possible focus of stability and an additional source of claims to care if their parents cannot sustain a well-functioning household.

In the next section I will defend the claims of gestational ties to children. To deny these claims, as commercial surrogacy does, is to deny the significance of reproductive labor to the mother who undergoes it and thereby to dehumanize and degrade the mother herself. Commercial surrogacy would be a corrupt practice even if it did not involve commerce in children.

Women's Labor as a Commodity

Commercial surrogacy attempts to transform what is specifically women's labor – the work of bringing forth children into the world – into a commodity. It does so by replacing the parental norms which usually govern the practice of gestating children with the economic norms which govern ordinary production processes. The application of commercial norms to women's labor reduces the surrogate mothers from persons worthy of respect and consideration to objects of mere use.

Respect and consideration are two distinct modes of valuation whose norms are violated by the practices of the surrogate industry. To respect a person is to treat her in accordance with principles she rationally accepts – principles consistent with the protection of her autonomy and her rational interests. To treat a person with consideration is to respond with sensitivity to her and to her emotional relations with others, refraining from manipulating or denigrating these for one's own purposes.

Given the understanding of respect as a dispassionate, impersonal regard for people's interests, a different ethical concept – consideration – is needed to capture the engaged and sensitive regard we should have for people's emotional relationships. The failure of consideration on the part of the other parties to the surrogacy contract explains the judgment that the contract is not simply disrespectful of the surrogate mother, but callous as well.

The application of economic norms to the sphere of women's labor violates women's claims to respect and consideration in three ways. First, by requiring the surrogate mother to repress whatever parental love she feels for the child, these norms convert women's labor into a form of alienated labor. Second, by manipulating and denying legitimacy to the surrogate mother's evolving perspective on her own pregnancy, the norms of the market degrade her. Third, by taking advantage of the surrogate mother's noncommerical motivations without offering anything but what the norms of commerce demand in return, these norms leave her open to exploitation. The fact that these problems arise in the attempt to commercialize the labor of bearing children shows that women's labor is not properly regarded as a commodity.

The key to understanding these problems is the normal role of the emotions in noncommercialized pregnancies. Pregnancy is not simply a biological process but also a social practice. Many social expectations and considerations surround women's gestational labor, marking it off as an occasion for the parents to prepare themselves to welcome a new life into their family. For example, obstetricians use ultrasound not simply for diagnostic purposes but also to encourage maternal bonding with the fetus. We can all recognize that it is good, although by no means inevitable, for loving bonds to be established between the mother and her child during this period.

In contrast with these practices, the surrogate industry follows the putting-out system of manufacturing. It provides some of the raw materials of production (the father's sperm) to the surrogate mother, who then engages in production of the child. Although her labor is subject to periodic supervision by her doctors and by the surrogate agency, the agency does not have physical control over the product of her labor as firms using the factory system do. Hence, as in all putting-out systems, the surrogate industry faces the problem of extracting the final product from the mother. This problem is exacerbated by the fact that the social norms surrounding pregnancy are designed to encourage parental love for the child. The surrogate industry addresses this problem by requiring the mother to engage in a form of emotional labor.[13] In the surrogate contract, she agrees not to form or to attempt to form a parent–child relationship with her offspring.[14] Her labor is alienated, because she must divert it from the end which the social practices of pregnancy rightly promote – an emotional bond with her child. The surrogate contract thus replaces a norm of parenthood, that during pregnancy one create a loving attachment to one's child, with a norm of commercial production, that the producer shall not form any special emotional ties to her product.

The demand to deliberately alienate oneself from one's love for one's own child is a demand which can reasonably and decently be made of no one. Unless we were to remake pregnancy into a form of drudgery which is only performed for a wage, there is every reason to expect that many women who do sign a surrogate contract will, despite this fact, form a loving attachment to the child they bear. For this is what the social practices surrounding pregnancy encourage. Treating women's labor as just another kind of commercial production process violates the precious emotional ties which the mother may rightly and properly establish with her "product," the child, and thereby violates her claims to consideration.

Commercial surrogacy is also a degrading practice. The surrogate mother, like all persons, has an independent evaluative perspective on her activities and relationships. The realization of her dignity demands that the other parties to the contract acknowledge rather than evade the claims which her independent perspective makes upon them. But the surrogate industry has an interest in suppressing, manipulating, and trivializing her perspective, for there is an ever-present danger that she will see her involvement in her pregnancy from the perspective of a parent rather than from the perspective of a contract laborer.

How does this suppression and trivialization take place? The commercial promoters of surrogacy commonly describe the surrogate mothers as inanimate objects: mere "hatcheries," "plumbing," or "rented property" – things without emotions which could make claims on others.[15] They also refuse to acknowledge any responsibility for the consequences of the mother's emotional labor. Should she suffer psychologically from being forced to give up her child, the father is not liable to pay for therapy after her pregnancy, although he is liable for all other medical expenses following her pregnancy.[16]

The treatment and interpretation of surrogate mothers' grief raises the deepest problems of degradation. Most surrogate mothers experience grief upon giving up their children – in 10 percent of cases, seriously enough to require therapy.[17] Their grief is not compensated by the $10,000 fee they receive. Grief is not an intelligible response to a successful deal, but rather reflects the subject's judgment that she has suffered a grave and personal loss. Since not all cases of grief resolve themselves into cases of regret, it may be that some surrogate mothers do not regard their grief, in retrospect, as reflecting an authentic judgment on their part. But in the circumstances of emotional manipulation which pervade the surrogate industry, it is difficult to determine which interpretation of her grief more truly reflects the perspective of the surrogate mother. By insinuating a trivializing interpretation of her emotional responses to the prospect of losing her child, the surrogate agency may be able to manipulate her into accepting her fate without too much fuss, and may even succeed in substituting its interpretation of her emotions for her own. Since she has already signed a contract to perform an emotional labor – to express or repress emotions which are dictated by the interests of the surrogate industry – this might not be a difficult task.[18] A considerate treatment of the mothers'

grief, on the other hand, would take the evaluative basis of their grief seriously.

Some defenders of commercial surrogacy demand that the provision for terminating the surrogate mother's parental rights in her child be legally enforceable, so that peace of mind for the adoptive parents can be secured.[19] But the surrogate industry makes no corresponding provision for securing the peace of mind of the surrogate. She is expected to assume the risk of a transformation of her ethical and emotional perspective on herself and her child with the same impersonal detachment with which a futures trader assumes the risk of a fluctuation in the price of pork bellies. By applying the market norms of enforcing contracts to the surrogate mother's case, commercial surrogacy treats a moral transformation as if it were merely an economic change.[20]

The manipulation of the surrogate mother's emotions which is inherent in the surrogate parenting contract also leaves women open to grave forms of exploitation. A kind of exploitation occurs when one party to a transaction is oriented toward the exchange of "gift" values, while the other party operates in accordance with the norms of the market exchange of commodities. Gift values, which include love, gratitude, and appreciation of others, cannot be bought or obtained through piecemeal calculations of individual advantage. Their exchange requires a repudiation of a self-interested attitude, a willingness to give gifts to others without demanding some specific equivalent good in return each time one gives. The surrogate mother often operates according to the norms of gift relationships. The surrogate agency, on the other hand, follows market norms. Its job is to get the best deal for its clients and itself, while leaving the surrogate mother to look after her own interests as best she can. This situation puts the surrogate agencies in a position to manipulate the surrogate mothers' emotions to gain favorable terms for themselves. For example, agencies screen prospective surrogate mothers for submissiveness, and emphasize to them the importance of the motives of generosity and love. When applicants question some of the terms of the contract, the broker sometimes intimidates them by questioning their character and morality: if they were really generous and loving they would not be so solicitous about their own interests.[21]

Some evidence supports the claim that most surrogate mothers are motivated by emotional needs and vulnerabilities which lead them to view their labor as a form of gift and not a purely commercial exchange. Only 1 percent of applicants to surrogate agencies would become surrogate mothers for money alone; the others have emotional as well as financial reasons for applying. One psychiatrist believes that most, if not all, of the 35 percent of applicants who had had a previous abortion or given up a child for adoption wanted to become surrogate mothers in order to resolve their guilty feelings or deal with their unresolved loss by going through a process of losing a child again.[22] Women who feel that giving up another child is an effective way to punish themselves for past abortions, or a form of therapy for their emotional problems, are not likely to resist manipulation by surrogate brokers.

Many surrogate mothers see pregnancy as a way to feel "adequate," "appreciated," or "special." In other words, these women feel inadequate, unappreciated, or unadmired when they are not pregnant.[23] Lacking the power to achieve some worthwhile status in their own right, they must subordinate themselves to others' definitions of their proper place (as baby factories) in order to get from them the appreciation they need to attain a sense of self-worth. But the sense of self-worth one can attain under such circumstances is precarious and ultimately self-defeating. For example, those who seek gratitude on the part of the adoptive parents and some opportunity to share the joys of seeing their children grow discover all too often that the adoptive parents want nothing to do with them.[24] For while the surrogate mother sees in the arrangement some basis for establishing the personal ties she needs to sustain her emotionally, the adoptive couple sees it as an impersonal commercial contract, one of whose main advantages to them is that all ties between them and the surrogate are ended once the terms of the contract are fulfilled.[25] To them, her presence is a threat to marital unity and a competing object for the child's affections.

These considerations should lead us to question the model of altruism which is held up to women by the surrogacy industry. It is a strange form of altruism which demands such radical self-effacement, alienation from those whom one benefits, and the subordination of one's body, health, and emotional life to the independently defined interests of others.[26] Why should this model of "altruism" be held up to *women*? True altruism does not involve such subordination, but rather the autonomous and self-confident exercise of skill, talent, and judgment. (Consider the dedicated doctor.) The kind of altruism we see admired in surrogate mothers involves a lack of self-confidence, a feeling that one can be truly worthy only through self-effacement. This model of altruism, far from affirming the freedom and dignity of women, seems all too conveniently designed to keep their sense of self-worth hostage to the interests of a more privileged class.[27]

The primary distortions which arise from treating women's labor as a commodity – the surrogate mother's alienation from loved ones, her degradation, and her exploitation – stem from a common source. This is the failure to acknowledge and treat appropriately the surrogate mother's emotional engagement with her labor. Her labor is alienated, because she must suppress her emotional ties with her own child, and may be manipulated into reinterpreting these ties in a trivializing way. She is degraded, because her independent ethical perspective is denied, or demoted to the status of a cash sum. She is exploited, because her emotional needs and vulnerabilities are not treated as characteristics which call for consideration, but as factors which may be manipulated to encourage her to make a grave self-sacrifice to the broker's and adoptive couple's advantage. These considerations provide strong grounds for sustaining the claims of women's labor to its "product," the child. The attempt to redefine parenthood so as to strip women of parental claims to the children they bear does violence to their emotional engagement with the project of bringing children into the world.

Commercial Surrogacy, Freedom, and the Law

In the fight of these ethical objections to commercial surrogacy, what position should the law take on the practice? At the very least, surrogate contracts should not be enforceable. Surrogate mothers should not be forced to relinquish their children if they have formed emotional bonds with them. Any other treatment of women's ties to the children they bear is degrading.

But I think these arguments support the stronger conclusion that commercial surrogate contracts should be illegal, and that surrogate agencies who arrange such contracts should be subject to criminal penalties. Commercial surrogacy constitutes a degrading and harmful traffic in children, violates the dignity of women, and subjects both children and women to a serious risk of exploitation. But are these problems inherent in the practice of commercial surrogacy? Defenders of the practice have suggested three reforms intended to eliminate these problems: (1) give the surrogate mother the option of keeping her child after birth; (2) impose stringent regulations on private surrogate agencies; (3) replace private surrogate agencies with a state-run monopoly on surrogate arrangements. Let us consider each of these options in turn.

Some defenders of commercial surrogacy suggest that the problem of respecting the surrogate mother's potential attachment to her child can be solved by granting the surrogate mother the option to reserve her parental rights after birth.[28] But such an option would not significantly change the conditions of the surrogate mother's labor. Indeed, such a provision would pressure the agency to demean the mother's self-regard more than ever. Since it could not rely on the law to enforce the adoptive parents' wishes regardless of the surrogate's feelings, it would have to make sure that she assumed the perspective which it and its clients have of her: as "rented plumbing."

Could such dangers be avoided by careful regulation of the surrogate industry? Some have suggested that exploitation of women could be avoided by such measures as properly screening surrogates, setting low fixed fees (to avoid tempting women in financial duress), and requiring independent counsel for the surrogate mother.[29] But no one knows how to predict who will suffer grave psychological damage from surrogacy, and the main forms of duress encountered in the industry are emotional rather than financial. Furthermore, there is little hope that regulation would check the exploitation of surrogate mothers. The most significant encounters between the mothers and the surrogate agencies take place behind closed doors. It is impossible to regulate the multifarious ways in which brokers can subtly manipulate the emotions of the vulnerable to their own advantage. Advocates of commercial surrogacy claim that their failure rate is extremely low, since only five out of the first five hundred cases were legally contested by surrogate mothers. But we do not know how many surrogate mothers were browbeaten into relinquishing their children, feel violated by their treatment, or would feel violated had their perspectives not been manipulated by the other parties to the contract. The dangers of exploiting women through commercial surrogacy are too great to ignore, and too deep to effectively regulate.

Could a state-run monopoly on surrogate arrangements eliminate the risk of degrading and exploiting surrogate mothers? A nonprofit state agency would arguably have no incentive to exploit surrogates, and it would screen the adoptive parents for the sake of the best interests of the child. Nevertheless, as long as the surrogate mother is paid money to bear a child and terminate her parental rights, the commercial norms leading to her degradation still apply. For these norms are constitutive of our understanding of what the surrogate contract is for. Once such an arrangement becomes socially legitimized, these norms will govern the understandings of participants in the practice and of society at large, or at least compete powerfully with the rival parental norms. And what judgment do these norms make of a mother who, out of love for her child, decides that she cannot relinquish it? They blame her for commercial irresponsibility and flighty emotions. Her transformation of moral and emotional perspective, which she experiences as real but painful growth, looks like a capricious and selfish exercise of will from the standpoint of the market, which does not distinguish the deep commitments of love from arbitrary matters of taste.

The fundamental problem with commercial surrogacy is that commercial norms are inherently manipulative when they are applied to the sphere of parental love. Manipulation occurs whenever norms are deployed to psychologically coerce others into a position where they cannot defend their own interests or articulate their own perspective without being charged with irresponsibility or immorality for doing so. A surrogate contract is inherently manipulative, since the very form of the contract invokes commercial norms which, whether upheld by the law or by social custom only, imply that the mother should feel guilty and irresponsible for loving her own child.

But hasn't the surrogate mother decided in advance that she is not interested in viewing her relationship to her child in this way? Regardless of her initial state of mind, once she enters the contract, she is not free to develop an autonomous perspective on her relationship with her child. She is contractually bound to manipulate her emotions to agree with the interests of the adoptive parents. Few things reach deeper into the self than a parent's evolving relationship with her own child. To lay claim to the course of this relationship in virtue of a cash payment constitutes a severe violation of the mother's personhood and a denial of the mother's autonomy.

Two final objections stand in the way of criminalizing commercial surrogacy. Prohibiting the practice might be thought to infringe two rights: the right of procreation, and the right to freedom of contract. Judge Harvey Sorkow, in upholding the legality and enforceability of commercial surrogate parenting contracts, based much of his argument on an interpretation of the freedom to procreate. He argued that the protection of the right to procreate requires the protection of noncoital means of procreation, including commercial surrogacy. The interests upheld by the creation of the family are the same, regardless of the means used to bring the family into existence.[30]

Sorkow asserts a blanket right to procreate, without carefully examining the specific human interests protected by such a right. The interest protected by the right to procreate is that of being able to create and sustain a family life with some integrity. But the enforcement of surrogate contracts against the will of the mother destroys one family just as surely as it creates another. And the same interest which generates the right to procreate also generates an obligation to uphold the integrity of family life which constrains the exercise of this right.[31] To recognize the legality of commercial surrogate contracts would undermine the integrity of families by giving public sanction to a practice which expresses contempt for the moral and emotional ties which bind a mother to her children, legitimates the view that these ties are merely the product of arbitrary will, properly loosened by the offering of a monetary incentive, and fails to respect the claims of genetic and gestational ties to children which provide children with a more secure place in the world than commerce can supply.

The freedom of contract provides weaker grounds for supporting commercial surrogacy. This freedom is already constrained, notably in preventing the purchase and sale of human beings. Yet one might object that prohibiting surrogate contracts could undermine the status of women by implying that they do not have the competence to enter into and rationally discharge the obligations of commercial contracts. Insofar as the justification for prohibiting commercial surrogacy depends upon giving special regard to women's emotional ties to their children, it might be thought to suggest that women as a group are too emotional to subject themselves to the dispassionate discipline of the market. Then prohibiting surrogate contracts would be seen as an offensive, paternalistic interference with the autonomy of the surrogate mothers.

We have seen, however, that the content of the surrogate contract itself compromises the autonomy of surrogate mothers. It uses the norms of commerce in a manipulative way and commands the surrogate mothers to conform their emotions to the interests of the other parties to the contract. The surrogate industry fails to acknowledge the surrogate mothers as possessing an independent perspective worthy of consideration. And it takes advantage of motivations – such as self-effacing "altruism" – which women have formed under social conditions inconsistent with genuine autonomy. Hence the surrogate industry itself, far from expanding the realm of autonomy for women, actually undermines the external and internal conditions required for fully autonomous choice by women.

If commercial surrogate contracts were prohibited, this would be no cause for infertile couples to lose hope for raising a family. The option of adoption is still available, and every attempt should be made to open up opportunities for adoption to couples who do not meet standard requirements – for example, because of age. While there is a shortage of healthy white infants available for adoption, there is no shortage of children of other races, mixed-race children, and older and handicapped children who desperately need to be adopted. Leaders of the surrogate industry have proclaimed that commercial surrogacy may replace adoption as the method of choice for infertile couples who

wish to raise families. But we should be wary of the racist and eugenic motivations which make some people rally to the surrogate industry at the expense of children who already exist and need homes.

The case of commercial surrogacy raises deep questions about the proper scope of the market in modern industrial societies. I have argued that there are principled grounds for rejecting the substitution of market norms for parental norms to govern the ways women bring children into the world. Such substitutions express ways of valuing mothers and children which reflect an inferior conception of human flourishing. When market norms are applied to the ways we allocate and understand parental rights and responsibilities, children are reduced from subjects of love to objects of use. When market norms are applied to the ways we treat and understand women's reproductive labor, women are reduced from subjects of respect and consideration to objects of use. If we are to retain the capacity to value children and women in ways consistent with a rich conception of human flourishing, we must resist the encroachment of the market upon the sphere of reproductive labor. Women's labor is *not* a commodity.

Notes

1   See, for example, Gena Corea, *The Mother Machine* (New York: Harper and Row, 1985), pp. 216, 219; Angela Holder, "Surrogate Motherhood: Babies for Fun and Profit," *Case and Comment* 90 (1985): 3–11; and Margaret Jane Radin, "Market Inalienability," *Harvard Law Review* 100 (June 1987): 1849–937.

2   This account of higher and lower modes of valuation is indebted to Charles Taylor's account of higher and lower values. See Charles Taylor, "The Diversity of Goods," in *Utilitarianism and Beyond*, ed. Amartya Sen and Bernard Williams (Cambridge: Cambridge University Press, 1982), pp. 129–44.

3   See Katie Marie Brophy, "A Surrogate Mother Contract to Bear a Child," *Journal of Family Law* 20 (1981–2): 263–91, and Noel Keane, "The Surrogate Parenting Contract," *Adelphia Law Journal* 2 (1983): 45–53.

4   Mary Warnock, *A Question of Life* (Oxford: Blackwell, 1985), p. 45.

5   John Robertson, "Surrogate Mothers: Not So Novel After All," *Hastings Center Report*, October 1983,

pp. 28–34; John Harris, *The Value of Life* (Boston: Routledge and Kegan Paul, 1985).

6   See "No Other Hope for Having a Child," *Time*, January 19, 1987, pp. 50–1. Radin argues that women's traits are also commodified in this practice. See "Market Inalienability," pp. 1932–5.

7   See Elizabeth Landes and Richard Posner, "The Economics of the Baby Shortage," *Journal of Legal Studies* 7 (1978): 323–48, and Richard Posner, "The Regulation of the Market in Adoptions," *Boston University Law Review* 67 (1987): 59–72.

8   Kay Longcope, "Surrogacy: Two Professionals on Each Side of Issue Give Their Arguments for Prohibition and Regulation," *Boston Globe*, March 23, 1987, pp. 18–19; and Iver Peterson, "Baby M Case: Surrogate Mothers Vent Feelings," *New York Times*, March 2, 1987, pp. B1, B4.

9   Herbert Krimmel, "The Case against Surrogate Parenting," *Hastings Center Report*, October 1983, pp. 35–7.

10 *In Re Baby M*, 217 N.J. Super 313. Reprinted in *Family Law Reporter* 13 (1987): 2001–30; *In the Matter of Baby M*, 109 N.J. 396, 537 A. 2d 1227 (1988).

11 Robertson, "Surrogate Mothers: Not So Novel after All," p. 32; Harris, *The Value of Life*, pp. 144–5.

12 See Philip Parker, "Surrogate Motherhood: The Interaction of Litigation, Legislation and Psychiatry," *International Journal of Law and Psychiatry* 5 (1982): 341–54.

13 Arlie Hochschild, *The Managed Heart* (Berkeley and Los Angeles: University of California Press, 1983).

14 Noel Keane and Dennis Breo, *The Surrogate Mother* (New York: Everest House, 1981), p. 291; Brophy, "A Surrogate Mother Contract," p. 267.

15 Corea, *The Mother Machine*, p. 222.

16 Keane and Breo, *The Surrogate Mother*, p. 292.

17 Kay Longcope, "Standing Up for Mary Beth," *Boston Globe*, March 5, 1987, p. 83; Daniel Goleman, "Motivations of Surrogate Mothers," *New York Times*, January 20, 1987, p. Cl; Robertson, "Surrogate Mothers," p. 30, 34 n. 8.

18 See Hochschild, *The Managed Heart*.

19 Keane and Breo, *The Surrogate Mother*, pp. 236–7.

20 See Elizabeth Kane, *Birth Mother: The Story of America's First Legal Surrogate Mother* (San Diego: Harcourt Brace Jovanovich, 1988).

21 Susan Ince, "Inside the Surrogate Industry," in *Test-Tube Women*, ed. Rita Arditti, Ranate Duelli Klein, and Shelley Minden (Boston: Pandora Press, 1984), p. 110.

22 Philip Parker, "Motivation of Surrogate Mothers: Initial Findings," *American Journal of Psychiatry* 140 (1983): 117–18.

23 Keane and Breo, *The Surrogate Mother*, pp. 247ff.

24 See, for example, the story of the surrogate mother Nancy Barrass in Anne Fleming, "Our Fascination with Baby M," *New York Times Magazine*, March 29, 1987, p. 38.

25 Peterson, "Baby M Case," p. B4.

26 Brophy, "A Surrogate Mother Contract to Bear a Child"; Keane, "The Surrogate Parenting Contract"; and Ince, "Inside the Surrogate Industry."

27 See Corea, *The Mother Machine*, pp. 227–33, and Christine Overall, *Ethics and Human Reproduction* (Boston: Allen and Unwin, 1987), pp. 122–8.

28 Barbara Cohen, "Surrogate Mothers: Whose Baby Is It?" *American Journal of Law and Medicine* 10 (1984): 282; Peter Singer and Deane Wells, *Making Babies* (New York: Scribner, 1985), pp. 106–7, 111.

29 Harris, *The Value of Life*, pp. 143–4, 156.

30 *In Re Baby M*, P. 2022. See also Robertson, "Surrogate Mothers," p. 32.

31 Congregation for the Doctrine of the Faith, "Instruction on Respect for Human Life In Its Origin and on the Dignity of Procreation: Replies to Certain Questions of the Day," reproduced in *New York Times*, March 11, 1987, pp. A14–A17.

22

"Goodbye Dolly?" The Ethics of Human Cloning

John Harris

The recent announcement of a birth in the press heralds an event probably unparalleled for two millennia and has highlighted the impact of the genetic revolution on our lives and personal choices. More importantly perhaps, it raises questions about the legitimacy of the sorts of control individuals and society purport to exercise over something, which while it must sound portentous, is nothing less than human destiny. This birth, that of "Dolly" the cloned sheep, is also illustrative of the responsibilities of science and scientists to the communities in which they live and which they serve, and of the public anxiety that sensational scientific achievements sometimes provokes.

The ethical implications of human clones have been much alluded to, but have seldom, if ever, been examined with any rigour. Here I will examine the possible uses and abuses of human cloning and draw out the principal ethical dimensions, both of what might be done and its meaning, and of public and official responses.

There are two rather different techniques available for cloning individuals. One is by nuclear substitution, the technique used to create Dolly, and the other is by cell mass division or "embryo splitting". We'll start with cell mass division because this is the only technique for cloning that has, as yet, been used in humans.

Cell Mass Division

Although the technique of cloning embryos by cell mass division has, for some time been used extensively in animal models, it was used as a way of multiplying human embryos for the first time in October 1993 when Jerry Hall and Robert Stillman[1] at George Washington Medical Centre cloned human embryos by splitting early two to eight cell embryos into single embryo cells. Among other uses, cloning by cell mass division or embryo splitting could be used to provide a "twin" embryo for biopsy, permitting an embryo undamaged by invasive procedures to be available for implantation following the result of the biopsy on its twin, or to increase the number of embryos available for implantation in the treatment of infertility.[2] To what extent is such a practice unethical?

Individuals, Multiples and Genetic Variation

Cloning does not produce identical copies of the same individual person. It can only produce identical copies of the same genotype. Our experience of identical twins demonstrates that each is a separate individual with his or her own character, preferences and so on. Although there is some evidence of striking similarities with respect to these factors in twins, there is no question but that each twin is a distinct individual, as independent and as free as is anyone else. To clone Bill Clinton is not to create multiple Presidents of the United States. Artificial clones do not raise any difficulties not raised by the phenomenon of 'natural' twins. We do not feel apprehensive when natural twins are born, why should we when twins are deliberately created?

If the objection to cloning is to the creation of identical individuals separated in time (because the twin embryos might be implanted in different cycles, perhaps even years apart), it is a weak one at best. We should remember that such twins will be 'identical' in the sense that they will each have the same genotype, but they will never (unlike some but by no means all natural monozygotic twins) be identical in the more familiar sense of looking identical at the same moment in time. If we think of expected similarities in character, tastes and so on, then the same is true. The further separated in time, the less likely they are to have similarities of *character* (the more different the environment, the more different environmental influence on individuality).

The significant ethical issue here is whether it would be morally defensible, by outlawing the creation of clones by cell mass division, to deny a woman the chance to have the child she desperately seeks. If this procedure would enable a woman to create a sufficient number of embryos to give her a reasonable chance of successfully implanting one or two of them, then the objections to it would have to be weighty indeed. If pre-implantation testing by cell biopsy might damage the embryo to be implanted, would it be defensible to prefer this to testing a clone, if technology permits such a clone to be created without damage, by separating a cell or two from the embryonic cell mass? If we assume each procedure to have been perfected and to be equally safe, we must ask what the ethical difference would be between taking a cell for cell biopsy and destroying it thereafter, and taking a cell to create a clone, and then destroying the clone? The answer can only be that destroying the cloned embryo would constitute a waste of human potential. But this same potential is wasted whenever an embryo is not implanted.

Nuclear Substitution: the Birth of Dolly

This technique involves (crudely described) deleting the nucleus of an egg cell and substituting the nucleus taken from the cell of another individual. This can be done using cells from an adult. The first viable offspring produced from fetal and adult mammalian cells was reported from an Edinburgh based group in *Nature* on February 27, 1997.[3] The event caused an international sensation, was widely reported in the world press, with President Clinton of the United States calling for an investigation into the ethics of such procedures and announcing a moratorium on public spending on human cloning, the British Nobel Prize winner, Joseph Rotblat, describing it as science out of control creating "a means of mass destruction",[4] and the German newspaper *Die Welt*, evoking the Third Reich, commented: "The cloning of human beings would fit precisely into Adolph Hitler's world view."[5]

More sober commentators were similarly panicked into instant reaction. Dr Hiroshi Nakajima, Director General of the World Health Organisation said: "WHO considers the use of cloning for the replication of human individuals to be ethically unacceptable as it would violate some of the basic principles which govern medically assisted procreation. These include respect for the dignity of the human being and protection of the security of human genetic material".[6] WHO followed up the line taken by Nakajima with a resolution of the *Fiftieth World Health Assembly* which saw fit to affirm "that the use of cloning for the replication of human individuals is ethically unacceptable and contrary to human integrity and morality".[7] Federico Mayor of UNESCO, equally quick off the mark, commented: "Human beings must not be cloned under any circumstances. Moreover, UNESCO's International Bioethics Committee (IBC), which has been reflecting on the ethics of scientific progress, has maintained that the human genome must be preserved as common heritage of humanity."[8]

The European Parliament rushed through a resolution on cloning, the preamble of which asserted (Paragraph B):

> [T]he cloning of human beings . . . , cannot under any circumstances be justified or tolerated by any society, because it is a serious violation of fundamental human rights and is contrary to the principle of equality of human beings as it permits a eugenic and racist selection of the human race, it offends against human dignity and it requires experimentation on humans,

And which went on to claim that (Clause 1):

> each individual has a right to his or her own genetic identity and that human cloning is, and must continue to be, prohibited.[9]

These statements are, perhaps unsurprisingly, thin on argument and rationale; they appear to have been plucked from the air to justify an instant reaction. There are vague references to "human rights" or "basic principles" with little or no attempt to explain what these principles are, or to indicate how they might apply to cloning. The WHO statement for example refers to the basic principles which govern human reproduction and singles out "respect for the dignity of the human being" and "protection of the security of genetic material". How, we are entitled to ask, is the security of genetic material compromised? Is it less secure when inserted with precision by scientists, or when spread around with the characteristic negligence of the average human male?[10]

Human Dignity

Appeals to human dignity, on the other hand, while universally attractive, are comprehensively vague and deserve separate attention. A first question to ask when the idea of human dignity is invoked is: whose dignity is attacked and how? Is it the duplication of a large part of the genome that is supposed to constitute the attack on human dignity? If so we might legitimately ask whether and how the dignity of a natural twin is threatened by the existence of her sister? The notion of human dignity is often also linked to Kantian ethics. A typical example, and one that attempts to provide some basis for objections to cloning based on human dignity, was Axel Kahn's invocation of this principle in his commentary on cloning in *Nature*.[11]

> The creation of human clones solely for spare cell lines would, from a philosophical point of view, be in obvious contradiction to the principle expressed by Emmanuel Kant: that of human dignity. This principle demands that an individual – and I would extend this to read human life – should never be thought of as a means, but always also as an end. Creating human life for the sole purpose of preparing therapeutic material would clearly not be for the dignity of the life created.

The Kantian principle, crudely invoked as it usually is without any qualification or gloss, is seldom helpful in medical or bio-science contexts. As formulated by Kahn, for example, it would outlaw blood transfusions. The beneficiary of blood donation, neither knowing of, nor usually caring about, the anonymous donor uses the blood (and its donor) simply as a means to her own ends. It would also outlaw abortions to protect the life or health of the mother.

Instrumentalization

This idea of using individuals as a means to the purposes of others is sometimes termed "instrumentalization". Applying this idea coherently or consistently is not easy! If someone wants to have children in order to continue their genetic line do they act instrumentally? Where, as is standard practice in IVF, spare embryos are created, are these embryos created instrumentally? If not how do they differ from embryos created by embryo splitting for use in assisted reproduction?[12]

Kahn responded in the journal *Nature* to these objections.[13] He reminds us, rightly, that Kant's famous principle states: "respect for human dignity requires that an individual is *never* used . . . *exclusively* as a means" and suggests that I have ignored the crucial use of the term "exclusively". I did not of course, and I'm happy with Kahn's reformulation of the principle. It is not that Kant's principle does not have powerful intuitive force, but that it is so vague and so open to selective interpretation and it's scope for application is consequently so limited, that it's utility as one of the "fundamental principles of modern bioethical thought", as Kahn describes it, is virtually zero.

Kahn himself rightly points out that debates concerning the moral status of the human embryo are debates about whether embryos fall within the *scope* of Kant's or indeed any other moral principles concerning persons; so the principle itself is not illuminating in this context. Applied to the creation of individuals which are, or will become autonomous, it has limited application. True the Kantian principle rules out slavery, but so do a range of other principles based on autonomy and rights. If you are interested in the ethics of creating people then, so long as existence is in the created individual's own best interests, and the individual will have the capacity for autonomy like any other, then the motives for which the individual was created are either morally irrelevant or subordinate to other moral considerations. So that even where, for example, a child is engendered exclusively to provide "a son and heir" (as so often in so many cultures) it is unclear how or whether Kant's principle applies. Either other motives are also attributed to the parent to square parental purposes with Kant, or the child's eventual autonomy, and its clear and substantial interest in or benefit from existence, take precedence over the comparatively trivial issue of parental motives. Either way the "fundamental principle of modern

bioethical thought" is unhelpful and debates about whether or not an individual has been used *exclusively* as a means are sterile and usually irresolvable.

We noted earlier the possibility of using embryo splitting to allow genetic and other screening by embryo biopsy. One embryo could be tested and then destroyed to ascertain the health and genetic status of the remaining clones. Again, an objection often voiced to this is that it would violate the Kantian principle, and that "one twin would be destroyed for the sake of another".

This is a bizarre and misleading objection both to using cell mass division to create clones for screening purposes, and to creating clones by nuclear substitution to generate spare cell lines. It is surely ethically dubious to object to one embryo being sacrificed for the sake of another, but not to object to it being sacrificed for nothing. In *in vitro* fertilization, for example, it is, in the United Kingdom, currently regarded as good practice to store spare embryos for future use by the mother or for disposal at her direction, either to other women who require donor eggs, or for research, or simply to be destroyed. It cannot be morally worse to use an embryo to provide information about its sibling, than to use it for more abstract research or simply to destroy it. If it is permissible to use early embryos for research or to destroy them, their use in genetic and other health testing is surely also permissible. The same would surely go for their use in creating cell lines for therapeutic purposes.

It is Better to Do Good

A moral principle, that has at least as much intuitive force as that recommended by Kant, is that it is better to do some good than to do no good. It cannot, from the ethical point of view, be better or more moral to waste human material that could be used for therapeutic purposes, than to use it to do good. And I cannot but think that if it is right to *use* embryos for research or therapy then it is also right to *produce* them for such purposes.[14] Kant's prohibition does after all refer principally to use. Of course some will think that the embryo is a full member of the moral community with all the rights and protections possessed by Kant himself. While this is a tenable position, it is not one held by any society which permits abortion, post-coital contraception, or research with human embryos.

The UNESCO approach to cloning is scarcely more coherent than that of WHO; how does cloning affect "the preservation of the human genome as common heritage of humanity"? Does this mean that the human genome must be "preserved intact", that is without variation, or does it mean simply that it must not be "reproduced a-sexually"? Cloning cannot be said to impact on the variability of the human genome, it merely repeats one infinitely small part of it, a part that is repeated at a natural rate of about 3.5 per thousand births.[15]

Genetic Variability

So many of the fears expressed about cloning, and indeed about genetic engineering more generally, invoke the idea of the effect on the gene pool or upon genetic variability or assert the sanctity of the human genome as a common resource or heritage. It is very difficult to understand what is allegedly at stake here. The issue of genetic variation need not detain us long. The numbers of twins produced by cloning will always be so small compared to the human gene pool in totality, that the effect on the variation of the human gene pool will be vanishingly small. We can say with confidence that the human genome and the human population were not threatened at the start of the present millennium in the year AD 1, and yet the world population was then perhaps 1 percent of what it is today. Natural species are usually said to be endangered when the population falls to about one thousand breeding individuals; by these standards fears for humankind and it's genome may be said to have been somewhat exaggerated.[16]

The resolution of the European Parliament goes into slightly more detail; having repeated the, now mandatory, waft in the direction of fundamental human rights and human dignity, it actually produces an argument. It suggests that cloning violates the principal of equality, "as it permits a eugenic and racist selection of the human race". Well, so does prenatal, and pre-implantation screening, not to mention egg donation, sperm donation, surrogacy, abortion and human preference in choice of sexual partner. The fact that a technique could be abused does not constitute an argument against the technique, unless there is no prospect of preventing the abuse or wrongful use. To ban cloning on the grounds that it might be used for racist purposes is tantamount to saying that sexual intercourse should be prohibited because it permits the possibility of rape.

Genetic Identity

The second principle appealed to by the European Parliament states, that "each individual has a right to his or her own genetic identity". Leaving aside the inevitable contribution of mitochondrial DNA,[17] we have seen that, as in the case of natural identical twins, genetic identity is not an essential component of personal identity[18] nor is it necessary for 'individuality'. Moreover, unless genetic identity is required either for personal identity, or for individuality, it is not clear why there should be a right to such a thing. But if there is, what are we to do about the rights of identical twins?

Suppose there came into being a life-threatening (or even disabling) condition that affected pregnant women and that there was an effective treatment, the only side effect of which was that it caused the embryo to divide, resulting in twins. Would the existence of the supposed right conjured up by the European Parliament mean that the therapy should be outlawed? Suppose that an effective vaccine for HIV was developed which had the effect of doubling the natural twinning rate; would this be a violation of fundamental human rights? Are we to foreclose the possible benefits to be derived from human cloning on so flimsy a basis? We should recall that the natural occurrence of monozygotic (identical) twins is one in 270 pregnancies.

This means that in the United Kingdom, with a population of about 58 million, that over 200 thousand such pregnancies have occurred. How are we to regard human rights violations on such a grand scale?

A Right to Parents

The apparently overwhelming imperative to identify some right that is violated by human cloning sometimes expresses itself in the assertion of "a right to have two parents" or as "the right to be the product of the mixture of the genes of two individuals". These are on the face of it highly artificial and problematic rights – where have they sprung from, save from a desperate attempt to conjure some rights that have been violated by cloning? However, let's take them seriously for a moment and grant that they have some force. Are they necessarily violated by the nuclear transfer technique?

If the right to have two parents is understood to be the right to have two social parents, then it is of course only violated by cloning if the family identified as the one to rear the resulting child is a one-parent family. This is not of course necessarily any more likely a result of cloning, than of the use of any of the other new reproductive technologies (or indeed of sexual reproduction). Moreover if there is such a right, it is widely violated creating countless 'victims', and there is no significant evidence of any enduring harm from the violation of this supposed right. Indeed war widows throughout the world would find its assertion highly offensive.

If, on the other hand we interpret a right to two parents as the right to be the product of the mixture of the genes of two individuals, then the supposition that this right is violated when the nucleus of the cell of one individual is inserted into the de-nucleated egg of another, is false in the way this claim is usually understood. There is at least one sense in which a right expressed in this form might be violated by cloning, but not in any way which has force as an objection. Firstly it is false to think that the clone is the genetic child of the nucleus donor. It is not. The clone is the twin brother or sister of the nucleus donor and the genetic offspring of the nucleus donor's own parents. Thus this type of cloned individual is, and always must be, the genetic child of two separate genotypes, of two genetically different individuals, however often it is cloned or re-cloned.

Two Parents Good, Three Parents Better

However, the supposed right to be the product of two separate individuals is perhaps violated by cloning in a novel way. The de-nucleated egg contains mitochondrial DNA – genes from the female whose egg it is. The inevitable presence of the mitochondrial genome of a third individual, means that the genetic inheritance of clones is in fact richer than that of other individuals, richer in the sense of being more variously derived.[19] This can be important if the nucleus donor is subject to mitochondrial diseases inherited from his or her mother and wants a child genetically related to her that will be free of these diseases. How this affects alleged rights to particular combinations of 'parents' is more difficult to imagine, and perhaps underlines the confused nature of such claims.

What Good is Cloning?

One major reason for developing cloning in animals is said to be[20] to permit the study of genetic diseases and indeed genetic development more generally. Whether or not there would be major advantages in human cloning by nuclear substitution is not yet clear. Certainly it would enable some infertile people to have children genetically related to them, it offers prospect, as we have noted, of preventing some diseases caused by mitochondrial DNA, and could help 'carriers' of X-linked and autosomal recessive disorders to have their own genetic children without risk of passing on the disease. It is also possible that cloning could be used for the creation of 'spare parts' by for example, growing stem cells for particular cell types from non-diseased parts of an adult.

Any attempt to use this technique in the United Kingdom, is widely thought to be illegal. Whether it would in fact be illegal might turn on whether it is plausible to regard such cloning as the product of "fertilization". Apparently only fertilized embryos are covered by the Human Fertilisation and Embryology Act 1990.[21] The technique used in Edinburgh which involves deleting the nucleus of an unfertilized egg and then substituting a cell nucleus from an existing individual, bypasses what is normally considered to be fertilization completely and may therefore turn out not to be covered by existing legislation. On the other hand, if as seems logical we consider 'fertilization' as the moment when all 46 chromosomes are present and the zygote is formed the problem does not arise.

The unease caused by Dolly's birth may be due to the fact that it was just such a technique that informed the plot of the film "The Boys from Brazil" in which Hitler's genotype was cloned to produce a Fuehrer for the future. The prospect of limitless numbers of clones of Hitler is rightly disturbing. However, the numbers of clones that could be produced of any one genotype will, for the foreseeable future, be limited not by the number of copies that could be made of one genotype (using serial nuclear transfer techniques 470 copies of a single nuclear gene in cattle have been reported),[22] but by the availability of host human mothers.[23] Mass production in any democracy could therefore scarcely be envisaged. Moreover, the futility of any such attempt is obvious. Hitler's genotype might conceivably produce a "gonadically challenged" individual of limited stature, but reliability in producing an evil and vicious megalomaniac is far more problematic, for reasons already noted in our consideration of cloning by cell mass division.

Dolly Collapses the Divide Between Germ and Somatic Cells

There are some interesting implications of cloning by nuclear substitution (which have been clear since frogs were cloned by this method in the 1960s) which have not apparently been noticed.[24] There is currently a world-wide moratorium on manipulation of the human germ line, while therapeutic somatic line interventions are, in principal permitted.[25] However, inserting the mature nucleus of an adult cell into a de-nucleated egg turns the cells thus formed into germ line cells. This has three important effects. First, it effectively eradicates the firm divide between germ line and somatic line nuclei because each adult cell nucleus is in principle 'translatable' into a germ line cell nucleus by transferring it's nucleus and creating a clone. Secondly, it permits somatic line modifications to human cells to become germ line modifications. Suppose you permanently insert a normal copy of the adenosine deaminase gene into the bone marrow cells of an individual suffering from Severe Combined Immuno Deficiency (which affects the so-called "bubble boy" who has to live in a protective bubble of clean air) with obvious beneficial therapeutic effects. This is a somatic line modification. If you then cloned a permanently genetically modified bone marrow cell from this individual, the modified genome would be passed to the clone and become part of his or her genome, transmissible to her offspring indefinitely through the germ line. Thus a benefit that would have perished with the original recipient and not been passed on for the protection of her children, can be conferred on subsequent generations by cloning.[26] The third effect is that it shows the oft asserted moral divide between germ line and somatic line therapy to be even more ludicrous than was previously supposed.[27]

Immortality?

Of course some vainglorious individuals might wish to have offspring not simply with their genes but with a matching genotype. However, there is no way that they could make such an individual a duplicate of themselves. So many years later the environmental influences would be radically different, and since every choice, however insignificant, causes a life-path to branch with unpredictable consequences, the holy grail of duplication would be doomed to remain a fruitless quest. We can conclude that people who would clone themselves would probably be foolish and ill-advised, but would they be immoral and would their attempts harm society or their children significantly?

Whether we should legislate to prevent people reproducing, not 23 but all 46 chromosomes, seems more problematic for reasons we have already examined, but we might have reason to be uncomfortable about the likely standards and effects of child rearing by those who would clone themselves. Their attempts to mould their child in their own image would be likely to be more pronounced than the average.

Whether they would likely be worse than so many people's attempts to duplicate race, religion and culture, which are widely accepted as respectable in the contemporary world, might well depend on the character and constitution of the genotype donor. Where identical twins occur naturally we might think of it as "horizontal twinning", where twins are created by nuclear substitution we have a sort of "vertical twinning". Although horizontal twins would be closer to one another in every way, we do not seem much disturbed by their natural occurrence. Why we should be disturbed either by artificial horizontal twinning or by vertical twinning (where differences between the twins would be greater) is entirely unclear.

Suppose a woman's only chance of having 'her own' genetic child was by cloning herself; what are the strong arguments that should compel her to accept that it would be wrong to use nuclear substitution? We must assume that this cloning technique is safe, and that initial fears that individuals produced using nuclear substitution might age more rapidly have proved groundless.[28] We usually grant the so called "genetic imperative" as an important part of the right to found a family, of procreative autonomy.[29] The desire of people to have "their own" genetic children is widely accepted, and if we grant the legitimacy of genetic aspirations in so many cases, and using so many technologies to achieve it,[30] we need appropriately serious and weighty reasons to deny them here.

It is perhaps salutary to remember that there is no necessary connection between phenomena,

attitudes or actions that make us uneasy, or even those that disgust us, and those phenomena, attitudes, and actions that there are good reasons for judging unethical. Nor does it follow that those things we are confident *are* unethical must be prohibited by legislation or regulation.

We have looked at some of the objections to human cloning and found them less than plausible, we should now turn to one powerful argument that has recently been advanced in favour of a tolerant attitude to varieties of human reproduction.

Procreative Autonomy

We have examined the arguments for and against permitting the cloning of human individuals. At the heart of these questions is the issue of whether or not people have rights to control their reproductive destiny and, so far as they can do so without violating the rights of others or threatening society, to choose their own procreative path. We have seen that it has been claimed that cloning violates principles of human dignity. We will conclude by briefly examining an approach which suggests rather that failing to permit cloning might violate principles of dignity.

The American philosopher and legal theorist, Ronald Dworkin has outlined the arguments for a right to what he calls "procreative autonomy" and has defined this right as "a right to control their own role in procreation unless the state has a compelling reason for denying them that control".[31] Arguably, freedom to clone one's own genes might also be defended as a dimension of procreative autonomy because so many people and agencies have been attracted by the idea of the special nature of genes and have linked the procreative imperative to the genetic imperative.

> The right of procreative autonomy follows from any competent interpretation of the due process clause and of the Supreme Court's past decisions applying it . . . The First Amendment prohibits government from establishing any religion, and it guarantees all citizens free exercise of their own religion. The Fourteenth Amendment, which incorporates the First

Amendment, imposes the same prohibition and same responsibility on states. These provisions also guarantee the right of procreative autonomy.[32]

The point is that the sorts of freedoms which freedom of religion guarantees, freedom to choose one's own way of life and live according to one's most deeply held beliefs are also at the heart of procreative choices. And Dworkin concludes:

> that no one may be prevented from influencing the shared moral environment, through his own private choices, tastes, opinions, and example, just because these tastes or opinions disgust those who have the power to shut him up or lock him up.[33]

Thus it may be that we should be prepared to accept both some degree of offence and some social disadvantages as a price we should be willing to pay in order to protect freedom of choice in matters of procreation and perhaps this applies to cloning as much as to more straightforward or usual procreative preferences.[34]

The nub of the argument is complex and abstract but it is worth stating at some length. I cannot improve upon Dworkin's formulation of it.

> The right of procreative autonomy has an important place . . . in Western political culture more generally. The most important feature of that culture is a belief in individual human dignity: that people have the moral right – and the moral responsibility – to confront the most fundamental questions about the meaning and value of their own lives for themselves, answering to their own consciences and convictions . . . The principle of procreative autonomy, in a broad sense, is embedded in any genuinely democratic culture.[35]

In so far as decisions to reproduce in particular ways or even using particular technologies constitute decisions concerning central issues of value, then arguably the freedom to make them is guaranteed by the constitution (written or not) of any democratic society, unless the state has a compelling reason for denying them that control. To establish such a compelling reason the state (or indeed a federation or union of states, like the European Union for example) would have to show that more was at stake than the fact that a majority found the ideas disturbing or even disgusting.

As yet, in the case of human cloning, such compelling reasons have not been produced. Suggestions have been made, but have not been sustained, that human dignity may be compromised by the techniques of cloning. Dworkin's arguments suggest that human dignity and indeed democratic constitutions may be compromised by attempts to limit procreative autonomy, at least where greater values cannot be shown to be thereby threatened.

In the absence of compelling arguments against human cloning, we can bid Dolly a cautious "hello". We surely have sufficient reasons to permit experiments on human embryos to proceed, provided, as with any such experiments, the embryos are destroyed at an early stage.[36] While we wait to see whether the technique will ever be established as safe, we should consider the best ways to regulate its uptake until we are in a position to know what will emerge both by way of benefits and in terms of burdens.

Notes

This essay was presented to the UNDP/WHO/World Bank Special Programme of Research, Development and Research Training in Human Reproduction Review Group Meeting, Geneva, 25 April 1997 and to a hearing on cloning held by the European Parliament in Brussels, 7 May 1997. I am grateful to participants at these events for many stimulating insights. The arguments concerning human dignity are developed in my "Cloning and human dignity" in *Cambridge Quarterly of Healthcare Ethics* 7/2 (Spring 1998). I must also thank Justine Burley, Christopher Graham and Pedro Lowenstein for many constructive comments. The issues raised by cloning were discussed in a special issue of the *Kennedy Institute of Ethics Journal* 4/3 (September 1994) and in my *Wonderwoman and Superman: The Ethics of Human Biotechnology*, Oxford University Press, Oxford 1992, esp. ch.1.

1. "Human Embryo Cloning Reported", *Science* 262, (October 1993): 652–3.

2. Where few eggs can be successfully recovered or where only one embryo has been successfully fertilized, this method can multiply the embryos available for implantation to increase the chances of successful infertility treatment.

3. Wilmut, I. et al. "Viable offspring derived from fetal and adult mammalian cells," *Nature*, 27 February 1997.

4. J. Aridge, *The Guardian*, 26 February 1997.

5. T. Rodford, *The Guardian*, 28 February 1997.

6. WHO Press Release (WHO/20 11 March 1997).

7. WHO document (WHA50.37 14 May 1997). Despite the findings of a Meeting of the Scientific and Ethical Review Group (see note 1) which recommended that "the next step should be a thorough exploration and fuller discussion of the [issues]".

8. UNESCO Press Release No. 97–29.

9. The European Parliament, Resolution on Cloning, Motion dated 11 March 1997. Passed 13 March 1997.

10. Perhaps the sin of Onan was to compromise the security of his genetic material?

11. Axel Kahn, "Clone mammals . . . clone man", *Nature* 386 (13 March 1997). Page 119.

12. For use of the term and the idea of "instrumentalization" see Opinion of the group of advisers on the ethical implications of biotechnology to the European Commission No. 9, 28 May 1997. Rapporteur Dr. Anne McClaren.

13. Axel Kahn, "Cloning, dignity and ethical revisionism," *Nature* 388, 320 (24 July 1997) and John Harris, "Is cloning an attack on human dignity?" *Nature* 387 (19 June 1997): 754.

14. See my *Wonderwoman and Superman: The ethics of human biotechnology*. Oxford University Press, Oxford, 1992, ch. 2.

15. It is unlikely that 'artificial' cloning would ever approach such a rate on a global scale and we could, of course, use regulative mechanisms to prevent this without banning the process entirely. I take this figure of the rate of natural twinning from Keith L Moore and T. V. N. Persaud, *The Developing Human*, (fifth edition), W. B. Saunders, Philadelphia, 1993. The rate mentioned is 1 per 270 pregnancies.

16. Of course if all people were compulsorily sterilized and reproduced only by cloning, genetic variation would become fixed at current levels. This would halt the evolutionary process. How bad or good this would be could only be known if the course of future evolution and its effects could be accurately predicted.

17. Mitochondrial DNA individualizes the genotype even of clones to some extent.

18. Although of course there would be implications for criminal justice since clones could not be differentiated by so called "genetic fingerprinting" techniques.

19. Unless of course the nucleus donor is also the egg donor.

20. See note 4.

21. Margaret Brazier alerted me to this possibility.

22. Apparently Alan Trounson's group in Melbourne Australia have recorded this result. Reported in *The Herald Sun*, 13 March 1997.

23. What mad dictators might achieve is another matter; but such individuals are, almost by definition, impervious to moral argument and can therefore, for present purposes, be ignored.

24. Except by Pedro Lowenstein, who pointed them out to me.

25. See note 13.

26. These possibilities were pointed out to me by Pedro Lowenstein who is currently working on the implications for human gene therapy.

27. See note 13.

28. See "Science Technology", *The Economist*, 1 March 1997, 101–4.

29. *Universal Declaration of Human Rights* (Article 16), European Convention on Human Rights (Article 12). These are vague protections and do not mention any particular ways of founding families.

30. These include the use of reproductive technologies such as surrogacy and ICSI.

31. Ronald Dworkin, *Life's Dominion*, Harper Collins, London, 1993, p. 148.

32. See note 31. Page 160.

33. Ronald Dworkin, *Freedom's Law*, Oxford University Press, Oxford, 1996, pp. 237–38.

34. Ronald Dworkin has produced an elegant account of the way the price we should be willing to pay for freedom might or might not be traded off against the costs. See his *Taking Rights Seriously*, Duckworth, London, 1977, ch. 10. And his *A Matter of Principle*, Harvard University Press, Cambridge MA, 1985, ch. 17.

35. See note 30. Pages 166–7.

36. The blanket objection to experimentation on humans suggested by the European Parliament resolution would dramatically change current practice on the use of spare or experimental human embryos.

23

The Wisdom of Repugnance: Why We Should Ban the Cloning of Humans

Leon R. Kass

Our habit of delighting in news of scientific and technological breakthroughs has been sorely challenged by the birth announcement of a sheep named Dolly. Though Dolly shares with previous sheep the "softest clothing, woolly, bright," William Blake's question, "Little Lamb, who made thee?" has for her a radically different answer: Dolly was, quite literally, made. She is the work not of nature or nature's God but of man, an Englishman, Ian Wilmut, and his fellow scientists. What's more, Dolly came into being not only asexually – ironically, just like "He [who] calls Himself a Lamb" – but also as the genetically identical copy (and the perfect incarnation of the form or blueprint) of a mature ewe, of whom she is a clone. This long-awaited, yet not quite expected, success in cloning a mammal raised immediately the prospect – and the specter – of cloning human beings: "I a child and Thou a lamb," despite our differences, have always been equal candidates for creative making, only now, by means of cloning, we may both spring from the hand of man playing at being God . . . .

Taking Cloning Seriously, Then and Now

Cloning first came to public attention roughly 30 years ago, following the successful asexual production, in England, of a clutch of tadpole clones by the technique of nuclear transplantation. The individual largely responsible for bringing the prospect and promise of human cloning to public notice was Joshua Lederberg, a Nobel Laureate geneticist and a man of large vision. In 1966, Lederberg wrote a remarkable article in *The American Naturalist* detailing the eugenic advantages of human cloning and other forms of genetic engineering, and the following year he devoted a column in *The Washington Post*, where he wrote regularly on science and society, to the prospect of human cloning. He suggested that cloning could help us overcome the unpredictable variety that still rules human reproduction, and allow us to benefit from perpetuating superior genetic endowments. . . . [I thought then, and think now that] "the programmed reproduction of man will, in fact, dehumanize him. . . .

Cloning turns out to be the perfect embodiment of the ruling opinions of our new age. Thanks to the sexual revolution, we are able to deny in practice, and increasingly in thought, the inherent procreative teleology of sexuality itself. But, if sex has no intrinsic connection to generating babies, babies need have no necessary connection to sex. Thanks to feminism and the gay rights movement, we are increasingly encouraged to treat the natural heterosexual difference and its preeminence as a matter of "cultural construction." But if male and female are not normatively complementary and generatively significant, babies need not come from male and female complementarity. Thanks to the prominence and the acceptability of divorce and out-of-wedlock births, stable, monogamous marriage as the ideal home for procreation is no longer the agreed-upon cultural norm. For this new dispensation, the clone is the ideal emblem: the ultimate "single-parent child."

Thanks to our belief that all children should be wanted children (the more high-minded principle we use to justify contraception and abortion), sooner or later only those children who fulfill our wants will be fully acceptable. Through cloning, we can work our wants and wills on the very identity of our children, exercising control as never before. Thanks to modern notions of individualism and the rate of cultural change, we see ourselves not as linked to ancestors and defined by traditions, but as projects for our own self-creation, not only as self-made men but also man-made selves; and self-cloning is simply an extension of such rootless and narcissistic self-re-creation.

Unwilling to acknowledge our debt to the past and unwilling to embrace the uncertainties and the limitations of the future, we have a false relation to both: cloning personifies our desire fully to control the future, while being subject to no controls ourselves. Enchanted and enslaved by the glamour of technology, we have lost our awe and wonder before the deep mysteries of nature and of life. We cheerfully take our own beginnings in our hands and, like the last man, we blink . . . .

The State of the Art

If we should not underestimate the significance of human cloning, neither should we exaggerate its imminence or misunderstand just what is involved. The procedure is conceptually simple. The nucleus of a mature but unfertilized egg is removed and replaced with a nucleus obtained from a specialized cell of an adult (or fetal) organism (in Dolly's case, the donor nucleus came from mammary gland epithelium). Since almost all the hereditary material of a cell is contained within its nucleus, the renucleated egg and the individual into which this egg develops are genetically identical to the organism that was the source of the transferred nucleus. An unlimited number of genetically identical individuals – clones – could be produced by nuclear transfer. In principle, any person, male or female, newborn or adult, could be cloned, and in any quantity. With laboratory cultivation and storage of tissues, cells outliving their sources make it possible even to clone the dead . . . .

Exactly how soon someone will succeed in cloning a human being is anybody's guess. Wilmut's technique, almost certainly applicable to humans, makes attempting the feat an imminent possibility. Yet some cautions are in order and some possible misconceptions need correcting. For a start, cloning is not Xeroxing. As has been reassuringly reiterated, the clone of Mel Gibson, though his genetic double, would enter the world hairless, toothless and peeing in his diapers, just like any other human infant. Moreover, the success rate, at least at first, will probably not be very high: the British transferred 277 adult nuclei into enucleated sheep eggs, and implanted 29 clonal embryos, but they achieved the birth of only one live lamb clone. For this reason, among others, it is unlikely that, at least for now, the practice would be very popular, and there is no immediate worry of mass-scale production of multicopies. The need of repeated surgery to obtain eggs and, more crucially, of numerous borrowed wombs for implantation will surely limit use, as will the expense; besides, almost everyone who is able will doubtless prefer nature's sexier way of conceiving.

Still, for the tens of thousands of people already sustaining over 200 assisted-reproduction clinics in the United States and already availing themselves of in vitro fertilization, intracytoplasmic sperm injection, and other techniques of assisted reproduction, cloning would be an option with virtually no added fuss (especially when the success rate improves). Should commercial interests develop in "nucleus-banking," as they have in sperm-banking; should famous athletes or other celebrities decide to market their DNA the way they now market their autographs and just about everything else; should techniques of embryo and germline genetic testing and manipulation arrive as anticipated, increasing the use of laboratory assistance in order to obtain "better" babies – should all this come to pass, then cloning, if it is permitted, could become more than a marginal practice simply on the basis of free reproductive choice, even without any social encouragement to upgrade the gene pool or to replicate superior types. Moreover, if laboratory research on human cloning proceeds, even without any intention to produce cloned humans, the existence of cloned human embryos in the laboratory, created to begin with only for research purposes, would surely pave the way for later baby-making implantations.

In anticipation of human cloning, apologists and proponents have already made clear possible uses of the perfected technology, ranging from the sentimental and compassionate to the grandiose. They include: providing a child for an infertile couple; "replacing" a beloved spouse or child who is dying or has died; avoiding the risk of genetic disease; permitting reproduction for homosexual men and lesbians who want nothing sexual to do with the opposite sex; securing a genetically identical source of organs or tissues perfectly suitable for transplantation; getting a child with a genotype of one's own choosing, not excluding oneself; replicating individuals of great genius, talent, or beauty – having a child who really could "be like Mike"; and creating large sets of genetically identical humans suitable for research on, for instance, the question of nature versus nurture, or for special missions in peace and war (not excluding espionage), in which using identical humans would be an advantage. Most people who envision the cloning of human beings, of course, want none of these scenarios. That they cannot say why is not surprising. What is surprising, and welcome, is that, in our cynical age, they are saying anything at all.

The Wisdom of Repugnance

"Offensive." "Grotesque." "Revolting." "Repugnant." "Repulsive." These are the words most commonly heard regarding the prospect of human cloning. Such reactions come both from the man or woman in the street and from the intellectuals, from believers and atheists, from humanists and scientists. Even Dolly's creator has said he "would find it offensive" to clone a human being.

People are repelled by many aspects of human cloning. They recoil from the prospect of mass production of human beings, with large clones of look-alikes, compromised in their individuality; the idea of father–son or mother–daughter twins; the bizarre prospects of a woman giving birth to and rearing a genetic copy of herself, her spouse, or even her deceased father or mother; the grotesqueness of conceiving a child as an exact replacement for another who has died; the utilitarian creation of embryonic genetic duplicates of oneself, to be frozen away or created when necessary, in case of need for homologous tissues or organs for transplantation; the narcissism of those who would clone themselves and the arrogance of others who think they know who deserves to be cloned or which genotype any child-to-be should be thrilled to receive; the Frankensteinian hubris to create human life and increasingly to control its destiny; man playing God. Almost no one finds any of the suggested reasons for human cloning compelling; almost everyone anticipates its possible misuses and abuses. Moreover, many people feel oppressed by the sense that there is probably nothing we can do to prevent it from happening. This makes the prospect all the more revolting.

Revulsion is not an argument; and some of yesterday's repugnances are today calmly accepted – though, one must add, not always for the better. In crucial cases, however, repugnance is the emotional expression of deep wisdom, beyond reason's power fully to articulate it. Can anyone really give an argument fully adequate to the horror that is father–daughter incest (even with consent), or having sex with animals, or mutilating a corpse, or eating human flesh, or even just (just!) raping or murdering another human being? Would anybody's failure to give full rational justification for his or her revulsion at these practices make that revulsion ethically suspect? Not at all. On the contrary, we are suspicious of those who think that they can rationalize away our horror, say, by trying to explain the enormity of incest with arguments only about the genetic risks of inbreeding.

The repugnance at human cloning belongs in this category. We are repelled by the prospect of cloning human beings not because of the strangeness or novelty of the undertaking, but because we intuit and feel, immediately and without argument, the violation of things that we rightfully hold dear. Repugnance, here as elsewhere, revolts against the excesses of human willfulness, warning us not to transgress what is unspeakably profound. Indeed, in this age in which everything is held to be permissible so long as it is freely done, in which our given human nature no longer commands respect, in which our bodies are regarded as mere instruments of our autonomous rational wills, repugnance may be the only voice left that speaks up to defend the central core of our humanity. Shallow are the souls that have forgotten how to shudder.

The goods protected by repugnance are generally overlooked by our customary ways of approaching all new biomedical technologies. The way we evaluate cloning ethically will in fact be shaped by how we characterize it descriptively, by the context into which we place it, and by the perspective from which we view

it. The first task for ethics is proper description. And here is where our failure begins.

Typically, cloning is discussed in one or more of three familiar contexts, which one might call the technological, the liberal, and the meliorist. Under the first, cloning will be seen as an extension of existing techniques for assisting reproduction and determining the genetic makeup of children. Like them, cloning is to be regarded as a neutral technique, with no inherent meaning or goodness, but subject to multiple uses, some good, some bad. The morality of cloning thus depends absolutely on the goodness or badness of the motives and intentions of the cloners: as one bioethicist defender of cloning puts it, "the ethics must be judged [only] by the way the parents nurture and rear their resulting child and whether they bestow the same love and affection on a child brought into existence by a technique of assisted reproduction as they would on a child born in the usual way."

The liberal (or libertarian or liberationist) perspective sets cloning in the context of rights, freedoms, and personal empowerment. Cloning is just a new option for exercising an individual's right to reproduce or to have the kind of child that he or she wants. Alternatively, cloning enhances our liberation (especially women's liberation) from the confines of nature, the vagaries of chance, or the necessity for sexual mating. Indeed, it liberates women from the need for men altogether, for the process requires only eggs, nuclei, and (for the time being) uteri – plus, of course, a healthy dose of our (allegedly "masculine") manipulative science that likes to do all these things to mother nature and nature's mothers. For those who hold this outlook, the only moral restraints on cloning are adequately informed consent and the avoidance of bodily harm. If no one is cloned without her consent, and if the clonant is not physically damaged, then the liberal conditions for licit, hence moral, conduct are met. Worries that go beyond violating the will or maiming the body are dismissed as "symbolic" – which is to say, unreal.

The meliorist perspective embraces valetudinarians and also eugenicists. The latter were formerly more vocal in these discussions, but they are now generally happy to see their goals advanced under the less threatening banners of freedom and technological growth. These people see in cloning a new prospect for improving human beings – minimally, by ensuring the perpetuation of healthy individuals by avoiding the risks of genetic disease inherent in the lottery of sex, and maximally, by producing "optimum babies," preserving outstanding genetic material, and (with the help of soon-to-come techniques for precise genetic engineering) enhancing inborn human capacities on many fronts. Here the morality of cloning as a means is justified solely by the excellence of the end, that is, by the outstanding traits or individuals cloned – beauty, or brawn, or brains.

These three approaches, all quintessentially American and all perfectly fine in their places, are sorely wanting as approaches to human procreation. It is, to say the least, grossly distorting to view the wondrous mysteries of birth, renewal, and individuality, and the deep meaning of parent–child relations, largely through the lens of our reductive science and its potent technologies. Similarly, considering reproduction (and the intimate relations of family life!) primarily under the political-legal, adversarial, and individualistic notion of rights can only undermine the private yet fundamentally social, cooperative, and duty-laden character of childbearing, childrearing and their bond to the covenant of marriage. Seeking to escape entirely from nature (in order to satisfy a natural desire or a natural right to reproduce!) is self-contradictory in theory and self-alienating in practice. For we are erotic beings only because we are embodied beings, and not merely intellects and wills unfortunately imprisoned in our bodies. And, though health and fitness are clearly great goods, there is something deeply disquieting in looking on our prospective children as artful products perfectible by genetic engineering, increasingly held to our willfully imposed designs, specifications, and margins of tolerable error.

The technical, liberal, and meliorist approaches all ignore the deeper anthropological, social, and, indeed, ontological meanings of bringing forth new life. To this more fitting

and profound point of view, cloning shows itself to be a major alteration, indeed, a major violation, of our given nature as embodied, gendered, and engendering beings – and of the social relations built on this natural ground. Once this perspective is recognized, the ethical judgment on cloning can no longer be reduced to a matter of motives and intentions, rights and freedoms, benefits and harms, or even means and ends. It must be regarded primarily as a matter of meaning: Is cloning a fulfillment of human begetting and belonging? Or is cloning rather, as I contend, their pollution and perversion? To pollution and perversion, the fitting response can only be horror and revulsion; and conversely, generalized horror and revulsion are *prima facie* evidence of foulness and violation. The burden of moral argument must fall entirely on those who want to declare the widespread repugnances of humankind to be mere timidity or superstition.

Yet repugnance need not stand naked before the bar of reason. The wisdom of our horror at human cloning can be partially articulated, even if this is finally one of those instances about which the heart has its reasons that reason cannot entirely know.

The Profundity of Sex

To see cloning in its proper context, we must begin not, as I did before, with laboratory technique, but with the anthropology – natural and social – of sexual reproduction.

Sexual reproduction – by which I mean the generation of new life from (exactly) two complementary elements, one female, one male, (usually) through coitus – is established (if that is the right term) not by human decision, culture, or tradition, but by nature; it is the natural way of all mammalian reproduction. By nature, each child has two complementary biological progenitors. Each child thus stems from and unites exactly two lineages. In natural generation, moreover, the precise genetic constitution of the resulting offspring is determined by a combination of nature and chance, not by human design: each human child shares the common natural human species genotype, each child is genetically (equally) kin to each (both) parent(s), yet each child is also genetically unique.

These biological truths about our origins foretell deep truths about our identity and about our human condition altogether. Every one of us is at once equally human, equally enmeshed in a particular familial nexus of origin, and equally individuated in our trajectory from birth to death – and, if all goes well, equally capable (despite our mortality) of participating, with a complementary other, in the very same renewal of such human possibility through procreation. Though less momentous than our common humanity, our genetic individuality is not humanly trivial. It shows itself forth in our distinctive appearance through which we are everywhere recognized; it is revealed in our "signature" marks of fingerprints and our self-recognizing immune system; it symbolizes and foreshadows exactly the unique, never-to-be-repeated character of each human life.

Human societies virtually everywhere have structured child-rearing responsibilities and systems of identity and relationship on the bases of these deep natural facts of begetting. The mysterious yet ubiquitous "love of one's own" is everywhere culturally exploited, to make sure that children are not just produced but are well cared for and to create for everyone clear ties of meaning, belonging, and obligation. But it is wrong to treat such naturally rooted social practices as mere cultural constructs (like left- or right-driving, or like burying or cremating the dead) that we can alter with little human cost. What would kinship be without its clear natural grounding? And what would identity be without kinship? We must resist those who have begun to refer to sexual reproduction as the "traditional method of reproduction," who would have us regard as merely traditional, and by implication arbitrary, what is in truth not only natural but most certainly profound.

Asexual reproduction, which produces "single-parent" offspring, is a radical departure from the natural human way, confounding all normal understandings of father, mother, sibling, grandparent, etc., and all moral relations tied thereto. It becomes even more of a radical departure when the resulting offspring is a clone derived not from an embryo, but from a mature adult to whom the clone would be an identical twin; and when the process occurs not by natural accident (as in natural twinning), but by deliberate human design and manipulation; and when the child's (or children's) genetic constitution is preselected by the parent(s) (or scientists). Accordingly, as we will see, cloning is vulnerable to three kinds of concerns and objections, related to these three points: cloning threatens confusion of identity and individuality, even in small-scale cloning; cloning represents a giant step (though not the first one) toward transforming procreation into manufacture, that is, toward the increasing depersonalization of the process of generation and, increasingly, toward the "production" of human children as artifacts, products of human will and design (what others have called the problem of "commodification" of new life); and cloning – like other forms of eugenic engineering of the next generation – represents a form of despotism of the cloners over the cloned, and thus (even in benevolent cases) represents a blatant violation of the inner meaning of parent–child relations, of what it means to have a child, of what it means to say "yes" to our own demise and "replacement . . . ."

The response to this challenge broaches the ontological meaning of sexual reproduction. For it is impossible, I submit, for there to have been human life – or even higher forms of animal life – in the absence of sexuality and sexual reproduction. We find asexual reproduction only in the lowest forms of life: bacteria, algae, fungi, some lower invertebrates. Sexuality brings with it a new and enriched relationship to the world. Only sexual animals can seek and find complementary others with whom to pursue a goal that transcends their own existence. For a sexual being, the world is no longer an indifferent and largely homogeneous otherness, in part edible, in part dangerous. It also contains some very special and related and complementary beings, of the same kind but of opposite sex, toward whom one reaches out with special interest and intensity. In higher birds and mammals, the outward gaze keeps a lookout not only for food and predators, but also for prospective mates; the beholding of the many-splendored world is suffused with desire for union, the animal antecedent of human eros and the germ of sociality. Not by accident is the human animal both the sexiest animal – whose females do not go into heat but are receptive throughout the estrous cycle and whose males must therefore have greater sexual appetite and energy in order to reproduce successfully – and also the most aspiring, the most social, the most open, and the most intelligent animal.

The soul-elevating power of sexuality is, at bottom, rooted in its strange connection to mortality, which it simultaneously accepts and tries to overcome. Asexual reproduction may be seen as a continuation of the activity of self-preservation. When one organism buds or divides to become two, the original being is (doubly) preserved, and nothing dies. Sexuality, by contrast, means perishability and serves replacement; the two that come together to generate one soon will die. Sexual desire, in human beings as in animals, thus serves an end that is partly hidden from, and finally at odds with, the self-serving individual. Whether we know it or not, when we are sexually active we are voting with our genitalia for our own demise. The salmon swimming upstream to spawn and die tell the universal story: sex is bound up with death, to which it holds a partial answer in procreation.

The salmon and the other animals evince this truth blindly. Only the human being can understand what it means. As we learn so powerfully from the story of the Garden of Eden, our humanization is coincident with sexual self-consciousness, with the recognition of our sexual nakedness and all that it implies: shame at our needy incompleteness, unruly self-division, and finitude; awe before the eternal; hope in the self-transcending possibilities of children and a relationship to the divine. In the sexually self-conscious animal, sexual desire can become eros, lust can become love. Sexual desire humanly regarded is thus sublimated into erotic longing for wholeness, completion, and immortality, which drives us knowingly into the

embrace and its generative fruit – as well as into all the higher human possibilities of deed, speech, and song.

Through children, a good common to both husband and wife, male and female achieve some genuine unification (beyond the mere sexual "union," which fails to do so). The two become one through sharing generous (not needy) love for this third being as good. Flesh of their flesh, the child is the parents' own commingled being externalized, and given a separate and persisting existence. Unification is enhanced also by their commingled work of rearing. Providing an opening to the future beyond the grave, carrying not only our seed but also our names, our ways, and our hopes that they will surpass us in goodness and happiness, children are a testament to the possibility of transcendence. Gender duality and sexual desire, which first draws our love upward and outside of ourselves, finally provide for the partial overcoming of the confinement and limitation of perishable embodiment altogether.

Human procreation, in sum, is not simply an activity of our rational wills. It is a more complete activity precisely because it engages us bodily, erotically, and spiritually, as well as rationally. There is wisdom in the mystery of nature that has joined the pleasure of sex, the inarticulate longing for union, the communication of the loving embrace, and the deep-seated and only partly articulate desire for children in the very activity by which we continue the chain of human existence and participate in the renewal of human possibility. Whether or not we know it, the severing of procreation from sex, love, and intimacy is inherently dehumanizing, no matter how good the product.

We are now ready for the more specific objections to cloning.

The Perversities of Cloning

First, an important if formal objection: any attempt to clone a human being would constitute an unethical experiment upon the resulting child-to-be. As the animal experiments (frog and sheep) indicate, there are grave risks of mishaps and deformities. Moreover, because of what cloning means, one cannot presume a future cloned child's consent to be a clone, even a healthy one. Thus, ethically speaking, we cannot even get to know whether or not human cloning is feasible . . . .

Cloning creates serious issues of identity and individuality. The cloned person may experience concerns about his distinctive identity not only because he will be in genotype and appearance identical to another human being, but, in this case, because he may also be twin to the person who is his "father" or "mother" – if one can still call them that. What would be the psychic burdens of being the "child" or "parent" of your twin? The cloned individual, moreover, will be saddled with a genotype that has already lived. He will not be fully a surprise to the world. People are likely always to compare his performances in life with that of his alter ego. True, his nurture and his circumstance in life will be different; genotype is not exactly destiny. Still, one must also expect parental and other efforts to shape this new life after the original – or at least to view the child with the original version always firmly in mind. Why else did they clone from the star basketball player, mathematician, and beauty queen – or even dear old dad – in the first place?

Since the birth of Dolly, there has been a fair amount of doublespeak on this matter of genetic identity. Experts have rushed in to reassure the public that the clone would in no way be the same person, or have any confusions about his or her identity: as previously noted, they are pleased to point out that the clone of Mel Gibson would not be Mel Gibson. Fair enough. But one is shortchanging the truth by emphasizing the additional importance of the intrauterine environment, rearing, and social setting: genotype obviously matters plenty. That, after all, is the only reason to clone, whether human beings or sheep. The odds that clones of Wilt Chamberlain will play in the NBA are, I submit, infinitely greater than they are for clones of Robert Reich [former Secretary of Labor].

Curiously, this conclusion is supported, inadvertently, by the one ethical sticking point insisted on by friends of cloning: no cloning without the donor's consent. Though an orthodox liberal objection, it is in fact quite puzzling when it comes from people (such as Ruth Macklin) who also insist that genotype is not identity or individuality, and who deny that a child could reasonably complain about being made a genetic copy. If the clone of Mel Gibson would not be Mel Gibson, why should Mel Gibson have grounds to object that someone had been made his clone? We already allow researchers to use blood and tissue samples for research purposes of no benefit to their sources: my falling hair, my expectorations, my urine, and even my biopsied tissues are "not me" and not mine. Courts have held that the profit gained from uses to which scientists put my discarded tissues do not legally belong to me. Why, then, no cloning without consent – including, I assume, no cloning from the body of someone who just died? What harm is done the donor, if genotype is "not me"? Truth to tell, the only powerful justification for objecting is that genotype really does have something to do with identity, and everybody knows it. If not, on what basis could Michael Jordan object that someone cloned "him," say, from cells taken from a "lost" scraped-off piece of his skin? The insistence on donor consent unwittingly reveals the problem of identity in all cloning.

Genetic distinctiveness not only symbolizes the uniqueness of each human life and the independence of its parents that each human child rightfully attains. It can also be an important support for living a worthy and dignified life. Such arguments apply with great force to any large-scale replication of human individuals. But they are sufficient, in my view, to rebut even the first attempts to clone a human being. One must never forget that these are human beings upon whom our eugenic or merely playful fantasies are to be enacted.

Troubled psychic identity (distinctiveness), based on all-too-evident genetic identity (sameness), will be made much worse by the utter confusion of social identity and kinship ties. For, as already noted, cloning radically confounds lineage and social relations, for "offspring" as for "parents." As bioethicist James Nelson has pointed out, a female child cloned from her "mother" might develop a desire for a relationship to her "father," and might understandably seek out the father of her "mother," who is after all also her biological twin sister. Would "grandpa," who thought his paternal duties concluded, be pleased to discover that the clonant looked to him for paternal attention and support?

Social identity and social ties of relationship and responsibility are widely connected to, and supported by, biological kinship. Social taboos on incest (and adultery) everywhere serve to keep clear who is related to whom (and especially which child belongs to which parents), as well as to avoid confounding the social identity of parent-and-child (or brother-and-sister) with the social identity of lovers, spouses, and co-parents. True, social identity is altered by adoption (but as a matter of the best interest of already living children: we do not deliberately produce children for adoption). True, artificial insemination and in vitro fertilization with donor sperm, or whole embryo donation, are in some way forms of "prenatal adoption" – a not altogether unproblematic practice. Even here, though, there is in each case (as in all sexual reproduction) a known male source of sperm and a known single female source of egg – a genetic father and a genetic mother – should anyone care to know (as adopted children often do) who is genetically related to whom.

In the case of cloning, however, there is but one "parent." The usually sad situation of the "single-parent child" is here deliberately planned, and with a vengeance. In the case of self-cloning, the "offspring" is, in addition, one's twin; and so the dreaded result of incest – to be parent to one's sibling – is here brought about deliberately, albeit without any act of coitus. Moreover, all other relationships will be confounded. What will father, grandfather, aunt, cousin, sister mean? Who will bear what ties and what burdens? What sort of social identity will someone have with one whole side – "father's" or "mother's" – necessarily excluded? It is no answer to say that our society, with its high incidence of divorce, remarriage, adoption, extramarital childbearing, and the rest, already confounds lineage and confuses

kinship and responsibility for children (and everyone else), unless one also wants to argue that this is, for children, a preferable state of affairs.

Human cloning would also represent a giant step toward turning begetting into making, procreation into manufacture (literally, something "handmade"), a process already begun with in vitro fertilization and genetic testing of embryos. With cloning, not only is the process in hand, but the total genetic blueprint of the cloned individual is selected and determined by the human artisans. To be sure, subsequent development will take place according to natural processes; and the resulting children will still be recognizably human. But we here would be taking a major step into making man himself simply another one of the man-made things. Human nature becomes merely the last part of nature to succumb to the technological project, which turns all of nature into raw material at human disposal, to be homogenized by our rationalized technique according to the subjective prejudices of the day. How does begetting differ from making? In natural procreation, human beings come together, complementarily male and female, to give existence to another being who is formed, exactly as we were, by what we are: living, hence perishable, hence aspiringly erotic, human beings. In clonal reproduction, by contrast, and in the more advanced forms of manufacture to which it leads, we give existence to a being not by what we are but by what we intend and design. As with any product of our making, no matter how excellent, the artificer stands above it, not as an equal but as a superior, transcending it by his will and creative prowess. Scientists who clone animals make it perfectly clear that they are engaged in instrumental making; the animals are, from the start, designed as means to serve rational human purposes. In human cloning, scientists and prospective "parents" would be adopting the same technocratic mentality to human children: human children would be their artifacts.

Such an arrangement is profoundly dehumanizing, no matter how good the product. Mass-scale cloning of the same individual makes the point vividly; but the violation of human equality, freedom, and dignity are present even in a single planned clone. And procreation dehumanized into manufacture is further degraded by commodification, a virtually inescapable result of allowing baby-making to proceed under the banner of commerce. Genetic and reproductive biotechnology companies are already growth industries, but they will go into commercial orbit once the Human Genome Project nears completion. Supply will create enormous demand. Even before the capacity for human cloning arrives, established companies will have invested in the harvesting of eggs from ovaries obtained at autopsy or through ovarian surgery, practiced embryonic genetic alteration, and initiated the stockpiling of prospective donor tissues. Through the rental of surrogate-womb services, and through the buying and selling of tissues and embryos, priced according to the merit of the donor, the commodification of nascent human life will be unstoppable.

Finally, and perhaps most important, the practice of human cloning by nuclear transfer – like other anticipated forms of genetic engineering of the next generation – would enshrine and aggravate a profound and mischievous misunderstanding of the meaning of having children and of the parent–child relationship. When a couple now chooses to procreate, the partners are saying "yes" to the emergence of new life in its novelty, saying "yes" not only to having a child but also, tacitly, to having whatever child this child turns out to be. In accepting our finitude and opening ourselves to our replacement, we are tacitly confessing the limits of our control. In this ubiquitous way of nature, embracing the future by procreating means precisely that we are relinquishing our grip, in the very activity of taking up our own share in what we hope will be the immortality of human life and the human species. This means that our children are not our children: they are not our property, not our possessions. Neither are they supposed to live our lives for us, or anyone else's life but their own. To be sure, we seek to guide them on their way, imparting to them not just life but nurturing, love, and a way of life; to be sure, they bear our hopes that they

will live fine and flourishing lives, enabling us in small measure to transcend our own limitations. Still, their genetic distinctiveness and independence are the natural foreshadowing of the deep truth that they have their own and never-before-enacted life to live. They are sprung from a past, but they take an uncharted course into the future.

Much harm is already done by parents who try to live vicariously through their children. Children are sometimes compelled to fulfill the broken dreams of unhappy parents; John Doe Jr. or the III is under the burden of having to live up to his forebear's name. Still, if most parents have hopes for their children, cloning parents will have expectations. In cloning, such overbearing parents take at the start a decisive step that contradicts the entire meaning of the open and forward-looking nature of parent–child relations. The child is given a genotype that has already lived, with full expectation that this blueprint of a past life ought to be controlling of the life that is to come. Cloning is inherently despotic, for it seeks to make one's children (or someone else's children) after one's own image (or an image of one's choosing) and their future according to one's will. In some cases, the despotism may be mild and benevolent. In other cases, it will be mischievous and downright tyrannical. But despotism – the control of another through one's will – it inevitably will be. . . .

Ban the Cloning of Humans

What, then, should we do? We should declare that human cloning is unethical in itself and dangerous in its likely consequences. In so doing, we shall have the backing of the overwhelming majority of our fellow Americans, and of the human race, and (I believe) of most practicing scientists. Next, we should do all that we can to prevent the cloning of human beings. We should do this by means of an international legal ban if possible, and by a unilateral national ban, at a minimum. Scientists may secretly undertake to violate such a law, but they will be deterred by not being able to stand up proudly to claim the credit for their technological bravado and success. Such a ban on clonal baby-making, moreover, will not harm the progress of basic genetic science and technology. On the contrary, it will reassure the public that scientists are happy to proceed without violating the deep ethical norms and intuitions of the human community.

This still leaves the vexed question about laboratory research using early embryonic human clones, specially created only for such research purposes, with no intention to implant them into a uterus. There is no question that such research holds great promise for gaining fundamental knowledge about normal (and abnormal) differentiation, and for developing tissue lines for transplantation that might be used, say, in treating leukemia or in repairing brain or spinal cord injuries – to mention just a few of the conceivable benefits. Still, unrestricted clonal embryo research will surely make the production of living human clones much more likely. Once the genies put the cloned embryos into the bottles, who can strictly control where they go (especially in the absence of legal prohibitions against implanting them to produce a child)?

I appreciate the potentially great gains in scientific knowledge and medical treatment available from embryo research, especially with cloned embryos. At the same time, I have serious reservations about creating human embryos for the sole purpose of experimentation. There is something deeply repugnant and fundamentally transgressive about such a utilitarian treatment of prospective human life. This total, shameless exploitation is worse, in my opinion, than the "mere" destruction of nascent life. But I see no added objections, as a matter of principle, to creating and using cloned early embryos for research purposes, beyond the objections that I might raise to doing so with embryos produced sexually.

And yet, as a matter of policy and prudence, any opponent of the manufacture of cloned humans must, I think, in the end oppose also the creating of cloned human embryos. Frozen embryonic clones (belonging to whom?) can be shuttled around without detection. Commercial ventures in human cloning will be developed without adequate oversight. In order to build a fence around the law, prudence dictates that one oppose – for this reason alone – all production of cloned human embryos, even for research purposes. We should allow all cloning research on animals to go forward, but the only safe trench that we can dig across the slippery slope, I suspect, is to insist on the inviolable distinction between animal and human cloning . . . .

Sexuality

A few readers may be surprised to see essays discussing animals, the environment, and the virtues included in this volume. They may not think that all these are moral issues, or at least not especially important or interesting ones. However, virtually everyone recognizes that sex is a morally significant issue. In fact, some people talk as if sex were the only moral issue. They imply that the most important moral issue is with whom (when and how) we have sex. This view is not restricted to laypeople or preachers; I also find it in academics. Several years ago a respected professor at my former university listed what he saw as a dozen pressing moral issues. Nine concerned sex.

Such a view of morality is unacceptably narrow. The scope of morality is much broader. Nonetheless, sex does raise important moral questions, which essays in this section explore. Punzo claims that sexual intercourse should be limited to loving, committed relationships. Most people today fail to see the wisdom of this view, he claims, because they see the world through the lens of the "acquisitive society." Our social-political environment encourages us to think of having sex with someone in the same way we think about going out to dinner with them. If I ask you to dinner and you agree, then there is nothing morally wrong with

our sharing dinner. Likewise if I ask you to have sex and you agree, then there is nothing wrong with sharing our bodies.

Punzo – like Kass in the previous section (FAMILY AND REPRODUCTIVE TECHNOLOGY) – argues that this is a perverted conception of sex. In a healthier, non-acquisitive environment, we would see that sex is more than just physical contact. It is a unique physical union, "the most intimate physical expression of themselves." To treat sex as a simple exchange, as people in our society are wont to do, misunderstands its nature and role.

Goldman disagrees. He claims that sex is just the desire for a certain kind of physical contact with another's body. Sex is concerned with giving and receiving certain kinds of pleasure, nothing more. Perhaps sex is better between two people who love one another. Nevertheless, he might say, a fine dinner is also better when shared by two people who love one another. However, no one thinks only people who are in love should share dinner. So why should we think that only people who are in love (or still less, only people who are married) should share sex?

Goldman rejects any definition of "sex" that seeks to settle moral issues by fiat. For instance, if we define "sex" as "a form of physical interaction between people who have committed, long-term relationships," then, according to that definition, "casual sex" is a contradiction. Perhaps casual sex is not as meaningful as sex between people who deeply love one another. Nonetheless, that is something we should not settle by definition. We must first understand what sex is. Then, and only then, can we morally evaluate it.

Not surprisingly, this explains why Goldman thinks no analysis of "sex" can show that homosexuality is immoral. The last two authors in this section explicitly discuss this theme. Levin claims homosexuality is biologically unnatural. That is, he argues that homosexuality is not the result of evolution – it is not conducive to the survival of the organism or of the species. Although he does not think this shows that homosexuality is immoral, it does explain the "almost universal revulsion" toward the practice (seemingly akin to Kass's claims that repugnance is a good barometer of what is immoral). That explains why we can legitimately discriminate against homosexuals – especially male homosexuals – even though they are not immoral. Corvino disagrees. He argues that homosexuality is not unnatural, at least not in any sense that would lead us to conclude that it is immoral. He likewise dismisses another standard objection to homosexuality, namely, that sex's proper role is in the bonds of a loving, committed heterosexual relationship – a view akin to Punzo's.

No matter how we resolve this issue, the debate between Levin and Corvino raises a fascinating theoretical question. Does an action's biological nature determine (or even influence) its morality? Some people claim that humans are biologically inclined to favor humans over non-human animals. Does that morally justify favoring humans over non-human ANIMALS? Many authors (e.g., Frey) say "No." These authors argue that moral discussion may be informed by, but not entirely settled by, biological facts. Thus, we should not discriminate against animals, even if we are biologically prone to do so. Warren and Marquis (ABORTION) would agree. Both argue (although from different sides of the abortion debate) that we cannot determine that a fetus has moral status simply by knowing its species. Rather, we must determine what are morally relevant characteristics, and then decide if fetuses have them. For instance, we are likely to have some biological or natural tendency to favor our family, friends, and neighbors, over strangers. However, some philosophers, like Rachels (FAMILY AND REPRODUCTIVE TECHNOLOGY), argue that such favoritism would be immoral.

We see a similar dispute at play in the debate between Singer and Arthur over WORLD HUNGER. Arthur argues that we may reasonably favor family and friends, while Singer, like Rachels, thinks we must embrace the principle of equality, even if it means we cannot treat family with the sort of favoritism we might like. Once again we confront questions about the scope or and limits to morality.

Finally, it is interesting to compare Corvino's discussion of "the moral relevance of experience" with Kass's idea of "the wisdom of repugnance" (FAMILY AND REPRODUCTIVE TECHNOLOGY). Kass claims that if we are repulsed by some action, then we have good reason to think the act is immoral. This is the perspective of a third person observing someone else's action. Corvino proposes, in contrast, taking the first-person perspective. We should count the first-hand experiences of those who are homosexual, especially if we have no good arguments for why they are deceiving themselves or why homosexuality is immoral, despite their experiences. Since there are no such arguments, he claims, we should conclude that homosexuals have the same moral rights as heterosexuals.

Further Reading

Baker, R. and Elliston, F. (eds.) (1984) *Philosophy and Sex*. Buffalo, NY: Prometheus Books.

Mohr, R. (1988) *Gays/Justice: A Study of Ethics, Society, and Law*. New York: Columbia University Press.

Soble, A. (ed.) (1980) *The Philosophy of Sex: Contemporary Readings*. Totowa, NJ: Littlefield, Adams.

Taylor, R. (1982) *Having Loving Affairs*. Buffalo, NY: Prometheus Books.

Vannoy, R. (1980) *Sex without Love: A Philosophical Exploration*. Buffalo, NY: Prometheus Books.

24

Morality and Human Sexuality

Vincent C. Punzo

If one sees man's moral task as being simply that of not harming anyone, that is if one sees this task in purely negative terms, he will certainly not accept the argument to be presented in the following section. However, if one accepts the notion of the morality of aspiration, if one accepts the view that man's moral task involves the positive attempt to live up to what is best in man, to give reality to what he sees to be the perfection of himself as a human subject, the argument may be acceptable.

Sexuality and the Human Subject

[Prior discussion] has left us with the question as to whether sexual intercourse is a type of activity that is similar to choosing a dinner from a menu. This question is of utmost significance in that one's view of the morality of premarital intercourse seems to depend on the significance that one gives to the sexual encounter in human life. Those such as [John] Wilson and [Eustace] Chesser who see nothing immoral about the premarital character of sexual intercourse seem to see sexual intercourse as being no different from myriad other purely aesthetic

matters. This point is seen in Chesser's questioning of the reason for demanding permanence in the relationship of sexual partners when we do not see such permanence as being important to other human relationships.[1] It is also seen in his asking why we raise a moral issue about premarital coition when two people may engage in it, with the resulting social and psychological consequences being no different than if they had gone to a movie.[2]

Wilson most explicitly makes a case for the view that sexual intercourse does not differ significantly from other human activities. He holds that people think that there is a logical difference between the question "Will you engage in sexual intercourse with me?" and the question "Will you play tennis with me?" only because they are influenced by the acquisitive character of contemporary society.[3] Granted that the two questions may be identical from the purely formal perspective of logic, the ethician must move beyond this perspective to a consideration of their content. Men and women find themselves involved in many different relationships: for example, as buyer–seller, employer–employee, teacher–student, lawyer–client, and partners or competitors in certain games such as tennis or bridge. Is there any morally significant difference between these relationships and sexual intercourse? We cannot examine all the possible relationships into which a man and woman can enter, but we will consider the employer–employee relationship in order to get some perspective on the distinctive character of the sexual relationship.

A man pays a woman to act as his secretary. What rights does he have over her in such a situation? The woman agrees to work a certain number of hours during the day taking dictation, typing letters, filing reports, arranging appointments and flight schedules, and greeting clients and competitors. In short, we can say that the man has rights to certain of the woman's services or skills. The use of the word "services" may lead some to conclude that this relationship is not significantly different from the relationship between a prostitute and her client in that the prostitute also offers her "services."

It is true that we sometimes speak euphemistically of a prostitute offering her services to a man for a sum of money, but if we are serious about our quest for the difference between the sexual encounter and other types of human relationships, it is necessary to drop euphemisms and face the issue directly. The man and woman who engage in sexual intercourse are giving their bodies, the most intimate physical expression of themselves, over to the other. Unlike the man who plays tennis with a woman, the man who has sexual relations with her has literally entered her. A man and woman engaging in sexual intercourse have united themselves as intimately and as totally as is physically possible for two human beings. Their union is not simply a union of organs, but is as intimate and as total a physical union of two selves as is possible of achievement. Granted the character of this union, it seems strange to imply that there is no need for a man and a woman to give any more thought to the question of whether they should engage in sexual intercourse than to the question of whether they should play tennis.

In opposition to Wilson, I think that it is the acquisitive character of our society that has blinded us to the distinction between the two

activities. Wilson's and Chesser's positions seem to imply that exactly the same moral considerations ought to apply to a situation in which a housewife is bartering with a butcher for a few pounds of pork chops and the situation in which two human beings are deciding whether sexual intercourse ought to be an ingredient of their relationship. So long as the butcher does not put his thumb on the scale in the weighing process, so long as he is truthful in stating that the meat is actually pork, so long as the woman pays the proper amount with the proper currency, the trade is perfectly moral. Reflecting on sexual intercourse from the same sort of economic perspective, one can say that so long as the sexual partners are truthful in reporting their freedom from contagious venereal diseases and so long as they are truthful in reporting that they are interested in the activity for the mere pleasure of it or to try out their sexual techniques, there is nothing immoral about such activity. That in the one case pork chops are being exchanged for money whereas in the other the decision concerns the most complete and intimate merging of one's self with another makes no difference to the moral evaluation of the respective cases.

It is not surprising that such a reductionistic outlook should pervade our thinking on sexual matters, since in our society sexuality is used to sell everything from shave cream to underarm deodorants, to soap, to mouthwash, to cigarettes, and to automobiles. Sexuality has come to play so large a role in our commercial lives that it is not surprising that our sexuality should itself come to be treated as a commodity governed by the same moral rules that govern any other economic transaction.

Once sexuality is taken out of this commercial framework, once the character of the sexual encounter is faced directly and squarely, we will come to see that Doctor Mary Calderone has brought out the type of questions that ought to be asked by those contemplating the introduction of sexual intercourse into their relationships: "How many times, and how casually, are you willing to invest a portion of your total self, and to be the custodian of a like investment from the other person, without the sureness of knowing that these investments are being made for keeps?"[4] These questions come out of the recognition that the sexual encounter is a definitive experience, one in which the physical intimacy and merging involves also a merging of the nonphysical dimensions of the partners. With these questions, man moves beyond the negative concern with avoiding his or another's physical and psychological harm to the question of what he is making of himself and what he is contributing to the existential formation of his partner as a human subject.

If we are to make a start toward responding to Calderone's questions we must cease talking about human selfhood in abstraction. The human self is an historical as well as a physical being. He is a being who is capable of making at least a portion of his past an object of his consciousness and thus is able to make this past play a conscious role in his present and in his looking toward the future. He is also a being who looks to the future, who faces tomorrow with plans, ideals, hopes, and fears. The very being of a human self involves his past and his movement toward the future. Moreover, the human self is not completely shut off in his own past and future. Men and women are capable of consciously and purposively uniting themselves in a common career and venture. They can commit themselves to sharing the future with another, sharing it in all its aspects in its fortunes and misfortunes, in its times of happiness and times of tragedy. Within the lives of those who have so committed themselves to each other, sexual intercourse is a way of asserting and confirming the fullness and totality of their mutual commitment.

Unlike those who have made such a commitment and who come together in the sexual act in the fullness of their selfhood, those who engage in premarital sexual unions and who have made no such commitment act as though they can amputate their bodily existence and the most intimate physical expression of their selfhood from their existence as historical beings. Granting that there may be honesty on the verbal level in that two people engaging in premarital intercourse openly state that they are interested only in the pleasure of the activity, the fact remains that such unions are morally deficient because they lack existential integrity in that there is a total merging and union on a physical level, on the one hand, and a conscious decision not to unite any other dimension of themselves, on the other hand. Their sexual union thus involves a "depersonalization" of their bodily existence, an attempt to cut off the most intimate physical expression of their respective selves from their very selfhood. The mutual agreement of premarital sex partners is an agreement to merge with the other not as a self, but as a body which one takes unto oneself, which one possesses in a most intimate and total fashion for one's own pleasure or designs, allowing the other to treat oneself in the same way. It may be true that no physical or psychological harm may result from such unions, but such partners have failed to existentially incorporate human sexuality, which is at the very least the most intimate physical expression of the human self, into the character of this selfhood.

In so far as premarital sexual unions separate the intimate and total physical union that is sexual intercourse from any commitment to the self in his historicity, human sexuality, and consequently the human body, have been fashioned into external things or objects to be handed over totally to someone else, whenever one feels that he can get possession of another's body, which he can use for his own purposes.[5] The human body has thus been treated no differently from the pork chops spoken of previously or from any other object or commodity which human beings exchange and haggle over in their day-to-day transactions. One hesitates to use the word that might be used to capture the moral value that has been sacrificed in premarital unions because in our day the word has taken on a completely negative meaning at best, and, at worst, it has become a word used by "sophisticates" to mock or deride certain attitudes toward human sexuality. However, because the word "chastity" has been thus abused is no reason to leave it in the hands of those who have misrepresented the human value to which it gives expression.

The chaste person has often been described as one intent on denying his sexuality. The value of chastity as conceived in this section is in direct opposition to this description. It is the unchaste person who is separating himself from his sexuality, who is willing to exchange human bodies as one would exchange money for tickets to a baseball game honestly and with no commitment of self to self. Against this alienation of one's sexuality from one's self, an alienation that makes one's sexuality an object, which is to be given to another in exchange for his objectified sexuality, chastity affirms the integrity of the self in his bodily and historical existence. The sexuality of man is seen as an integral part of his subjectivity. Hence, the chaste man rejects depersonalized sexual relations as a reduction of man in his most intimate physical being to the status of an object or pure instrument for another. He asserts that man is a subject and end in himself, not in some trans-temporal, nonphysical world, but in the historical-physical world in which he carries on his moral task and where he finds his fellow man. He will not freely make of himself in his bodily existence a thing to be handed over to another's possession, nor will he ask that another treat his own body in this way. The total physical intimacy of sexual intercourse will be an expression of total union with the other self on all levels of their beings. Seen from this perspective, chastity is one aspect of man's attempt to attain existential integrity, to accept his body as a dimension of his total personality.

In concluding this section, it should be noted that I have tried to make a case against the morality of premarital sexual intercourse even in those cases in which the partners are completely honest with each other. There is reason to question whether the complete honesty, to which those who see nothing immoral in such unions refer, is as a matter of fact actually found very often among premarital sex partners. We may well have been dealing with textbook cases which present these unions in their best light. One may be pardoned for wondering whether sexual intercourse often occurs under the following conditions: "Hello, my name is Josiah. I am interested in having a sexual experience with you. I can assure you that I am good at it and that I have no communicable disease. If it sounds good to you and if you have taken the proper contraceptive precautions, we might have a go at it. Of course, I want to make it clear to you that I am interested only in the sexual experience and that I have no intention of making any long-range commitment to you." If those who defend the morality of premarital sexual unions so long as they are honestly entered into, think that I have misrepresented what they mean by honesty, then they must specify what they mean by an honest premarital union. . . .

Marriage as a Total Human Commitment

The preceding argument against the morality of premarital sexual unions was not based on the view that the moral character of marriage rests on a legal certificate or on a legal or religious ceremony. The argument was not directed against "preceremonial" intercourse, but against premarital intercourse. Morally speaking, a man and woman are married when they make the mutual and total commitment to share the problems and prospects of their historical existence in the world. . . .

. . . A total commitment to another means a commitment to him in his historical existence. Such a commitment is not simply a matter of words or of feelings, however strong. It involves a full existential sharing on the part of two beings of the burdens, opportunities, and challenges of their historical existence.

Granted the importance that the character of their commitment to each other plays in determining the moral quality of a couple's sexual encounter, it is clear that there may be nothing immoral in the behavior of couples who engage in sexual intercourse before participating in the marriage ceremony. For example, it is foolish to say that two people who are totally committed to each other and who have made all the arrangements to live this commitment are immoral if they engage in sexual intercourse the night before the marriage ceremony. Admittedly this position can be abused by those who have made a purely verbal commitment, a commitment which will be carried out in some vague and ill-defined future. At some time or other, they will unite their two lives totally by setting up house together and by actually undertaking the task of meeting the economic, social, legal, medical responsibilities that are involved in living this commitment. Apart from the reference to a vague and amorphous future time when they will share the full responsibility for each other, their commitment presently realizes itself in going to dances, sharing a box of popcorn at Saturday night movies, and sharing their bodies whenever they can do so without taking too great a risk of having the girl become pregnant.

Having acknowledged that the position advanced in this section can be abused by those who would use the word "commitment" to rationalize what is an interest only in the body of the other person, it must be pointed out that neither the ethician nor any other human being can tell two people whether they actually have made the commitment that is marriage or are mistaking a "warm glow" for such a commitment. There comes a time when this issue falls out of the area of moral philosophy and into the area of practical wisdom. . . .

The characterization of marriage as a total commitment between two human beings may lead some to conclude that the marriage ceremony is a wholly superfluous affair. It must be admitted that people may be morally married without having engaged in a marriage ceremony. However, to conclude from this point that the ceremony is totally meaningless is to lose sight of the social character of human beings. The couple contemplating marriage do not exist in a vacuum, although there may be times when they think they do. Their existences reach out beyond their union to include other human beings. By making their commitment a matter of public record, by solemnly expressing it before the law and in the presence of their respective families and friends and, if they are religious people, in the presence of God and one of his ministers, they sink the roots of their commitment more deeply and extensively in the world in which they live, thus taking steps to provide for the future growth of their commitment to each other. The public expression of this commitment makes it more fully and more explicitly a part of a couple's lives and of the world in which they live. . . .

Notes

1 Eustace Chesser, *Unmarried Love* (New York: Pocket Books, 1965), p. 29.
2 Ibid., pp. 35–6, see also p. 66.
3 John Wilson, *Logic and Sexual Morality* (Baltimore, MD: Penguin Books, 1965). See footnote 1, p. 67.
4 Mary Steichen Calderone, "The Case for Chastity," *Sex in America*, ed. Henry Anatole Grunwald (New York: Bantam Books, 1964), p. 147.
5 The psychoanalyst Rollo May makes an excellent point in calling attention to the tendency in contemporary society to exploit the human body as if it were only a machine. Rollo May, "The New Puritanism," *Sex in America*, pp. 161–4.

25

Plain Sex

Alan H. Goldman

I

Before we can get a sensible view of the relation of sex to morality, perversion, social regulation, and marriage, we require a sensible analysis of the concept itself; one which neither understates its animal pleasure nor overstates its importance within a theory or system of value. I say "before," but the order is not quite so clear, for questions in this area, as elsewhere in moral philosophy, are both conceptual and normative at the same time. Our concept of sex will partially determine our moral view of it, but as philosophers we should formulate a concept that will accord with its proper moral status. What we require here, as elsewhere, is "reflective equilibrium," a goal not achieved by traditional and recent analyses to-gether with their moral implications. Because sexual activity, like other natural functions such as eating or exercising, has become imbedded in layers of cultural, moral, and superstitious super-structure, it is hard to conceive it in its simplest terms. But partially for this reason, it is only by thinking about plain sex that we can begin to achieve this conceptual equilibrium.

I shall suggest here that sex continues to be misrepresented in recent writings, at least in philosophical writings, and I shall criticize the predominant form of analysis which I term "means-end analysis." Such conceptions attri-bute a necessary external goal or purpose to sexual activity, whether it be reproduction, the expression of love, simple communication, or interpersonal awareness. They analyze sexual activity as a means to one of these ends, imply-ing that sexual desire is a desire to reproduce, to love or be loved, or to communicate with others. All definitions of this type suggest false views of the relation of sex to perversion and morality by implying that sex which does not fit one of these models or fulfill one of these functions is in some way deviant or incomplete.

The alternative, simpler analysis with which I will begin is that sexual desire is desire for con-tact with another person's body and for the pleasure which such contact produces; sexual activity is activity which tends to fulfill such desire of the agent. Whereas Aristotle and Butler were correct in holding that pleasure is normally a byproduct rather than a goal of purposeful action, in the case of sex this is not so clear. The desire for another's body is, principally among other things, the desire for the pleasure that physical contact brings. On the other hand, it is not a desire for a particular sensation detachable from its causal context, a sensation which can be derived in other ways. This definition in terms of the general goal of sexual desire appears preferable to an attempt to more explicitly list or define specific sexual activities, for many activities such as kissing, embracing, massaging, or holding hands may or may not be sexual, depending upon the context and more specifically upon the purposes, needs, or desires into which such activities fit. The generality of the definition also represents a refusal (common in recent psychological texts) to overemphasize orgasm as the goal of sexual desire or genital sex as the only norm of sexual activity. . . .

Central to the definition is the fact that the goal of sexual desire and activity is the physical contact itself, rather than something else which this contact might express. By contrast, what I term "means–end analyses" posit ends which I take to be extraneous to plain sex, and they view sex as a means to these ends. Their fault lies not in defining sex in terms of its general goal, but in seeing plain sex as merely a means to other separable ends. I term these "means–end analyses" for convenience, although "means–separable–end analyses," while too cumbersome, might be more fully explanatory. The desire for physical contact with another person is a minimal criterion for (normal) sexual desire, but is both necessary and sufficient to qualify normal desire as sexual. Of course, we may want to express other feelings through sexual acts in various contexts; but without the desire for the physical contact in and for itself, or when it is sought for other reasons, activities in which contact is involved are not predominantly sexual. Furthermore, the desire for physical contact in itself, without the wish to express affection or other feelings through it, is sufficient to render sexual the activity of the agent which fulfills it. Various activities with this goal alone, such as kissing and caressing in certain contexts, qualify as sexual even without the presence of genital symptoms of sexual excitement. The latter are not therefore necessary criteria for sexual activity.

This initial analysis may seem to some either over- or underinclusive. It might seem too broad in leading us to interpret physical contact as sexual desire in activities such as football and other contact sports. In these cases, however, the desire is not for contact with another body per se, it is not directed toward a particular person for that purpose, and it is not the goal of the activity – the goal is winning or exercising or knocking someone down or displaying one's prowess. If the desire is purely for contact with another specific person's body, then to interpret it as sexual does not seem an exaggeration. A slightly more difficult case is that of a baby's desire to be cuddled and our natural response in wanting to cuddle it. In the case of the baby, the desire may be simply for the physical contact, for the pleasure of the caresses. If so, we may characterize this desire, especially in keeping with Freudian theory, as sexual or protosexual. It will differ nevertheless from full-fledged sexual desire in being more amorphous, not directed outward toward another specific person's body. It may also be that what the infant unconsciously desires is not physical contact per se but signs of affection, tenderness, or security, in which case we have further reason for hesitating to characterize its wants as clearly sexual. The intent of our response to the baby is often the showing of affection, not the pure physical contact, so that our definition in terms of action which fulfills sexual desire *on the part of the agent* does not capture such actions, whatever we say of the baby. (If it is intuitive to characterize our response as sexual as well, there is clearly no problem here for my analysis.) The same can be said of signs of affection (or in some cultures polite greeting) among men or women: these certainly need not be homosexual when the intent is only to show friendship, something extrinsic to plain sex although valuable when added to it.

Our definition of sex in terms of the desire for physical contact may appear too narrow in that a person's personality, not merely her or his body, may be sexually attractive to another, and in that looking or conversing in a certain way can be sexual in a given context without bodily contact. Nevertheless, it is not the contents of one's thoughts per se that are sexually appealing, but one's personality as embodied in certain manners of behavior. Furthermore, if a person is sexually attracted by another's personality, he or she will desire not just further conversation, but actual sexual contact. While looking at or conversing with someone can be interpreted as sexual in given contexts it is so when intended as preliminary to, and hence parasitic upon, elemental sexual interest. Voyeurism or viewing a pornographic movie qualifies as a sexual activity, but only as an imaginative substitute for the real thing (otherwise a deviation from the norm as expressed in our definition). The same is true of masturbation as a sexual activity without a partner.

That the initial definition indicates at least an ingredient of sexual desire and activity is too obvious to argue. We all know what sex is, at least in obvious cases, and do not need philosophers to tell us. My preliminary analysis is meant to serve as a contrast to what sex is not, at least, not necessarily. I concentrate upon the physically manifested desire for another's body, and I take as central the immersion in the physical aspect of one's own existence and attention to the physical embodiment of the other. One may derive pleasure in a sex act from expressing certain feelings to one's partner or from awareness of the attitude of one's partner, but sexual desire is essentially desire for physical contact itself: it is a bodily desire for the body of another that dominates our mental life for more or less brief periods. Traditional writings were correct to emphasize the purely physical or animal aspect of sex; they were wrong only in condemning it. This characterization of sex as an intensely pleasurable physical activity and acute physical desire may seem to some to capture only its barest level. But it is worth distinguishing and focusing upon this least common denominator in order to avoid the false views of sexual morality and perversion which emerge from thinking that sex is essentially something else.

II

We may turn then to what sex is not, to the arguments regarding supposed conceptual connections between sex and other activities which it is necessary to conceptually distinguish. The most comprehensible attempt to build an extraneous purpose into the sex act identifies that purpose as reproduction, its primary biological function. While this may be "nature's" purpose, it certainly need not be ours (the analogy with eating, while sometimes overworked, is pertinent here). While this identification may once have had a rational basis which also grounded the identification of the value and morality of sex with that applicable to reproduction and child-rearing, the development of contraception rendered the connection weak. Methods of contraception are by now so familiar and so widely used that it is not necessary to dwell upon the changes wrought by these developments in the concept of sex itself and in a rational sexual ethic dependent upon that concept. In the past, the ever present possibility of children rendered the concepts of sex and sexual morality different from those required at present. There may be good reasons, if the presence and care of both mother and father are beneficial to children, for restricting reproduction to marriage. Insofar as society has a legitimate role in protecting children's interests, it may be justified in giving marriage a legal status, although this question is complicated by the fact (among others) that children born to single mothers deserve no penalties. In any case, the point here is simply that these questions are irrelevant at the present time to those regarding the morality of sex and its potential social regulation. (Further connections with marriage will be discussed below.)

It is obvious that the desire for sex is not necessarily a desire to reproduce, that the psychological manifestation has become, if it were not always, distinct from its biological roots. There are many parallels, as previously mentioned, with other natural functions. The pleasures of eating and exercising are to a large extent independent of their roles in nourishment or health (as the junk-food industry discovered with a vengeance). Despite the obvious parallel with sex, there is still a tendency for many to think that sex acts which can be reproductive are, if not more moral or less immoral, at least more natural. These categories of morality and "naturalness," or normality, are not to be identified with each other, as will be argued below, and neither is applicable to sex by virtue of its connection to reproduction. The tendency to identify reproduction as the conceptually connected end of sex is most prevalent now in the pronouncements of the Catholic church. There the assumed analysis is clearly tied to a restrictive sexual morality according to which acts become immoral and unnatural when they are not oriented toward reproduction, a morality which has independent roots in the Christian sexual ethic as it derives from Paul. However, the means–end analysis fails to generate a consistent sexual ethic: homosexual and oral–genital sex is condemned while kissing or caressing, acts equally unlikely to lead in themselves to fertilization, even when properly characterized as sexual according to our definition, are not.

III

Before discussing further relations of means–end analyses to false or inconsistent sexual ethics and concepts of perversion, I turn to other examples of these analyses. One common position views sex as essentially an expression of love or affection between the partners. It is generally recognized that there are other types of love besides sexual, but sex itself is taken as an expression of one type, sometimes termed "romantic" love.[1] Various factors again ought to weaken this identification. First, there are other types of love besides that which it is appropriate to express sexually, and "romantic" love itself can be expressed in many other ways. I am not denying that sex can take on heightened value and meaning when it becomes a vehicle for the expression of feelings of love or tenderness, but so can many other usually mundane activities such as getting up early to make breakfast on Sunday, cleaning the house, and so on. Secondly, sex itself can be used to communicate many other emotions besides love, and, as I will argue below, can communicate nothing in particular and still be good sex.

On a deeper level, an internal tension is bound to result from an identification of sex, which I have described as a physical-psychological desire, with love as a long-term, deep emotional relationship between two individuals. As this type of relationship, love is permanent, at least in intent, and more or less exclusive. A normal person cannot deeply love more than a few individuals even in a lifetime. We may be suspicious that those who attempt or claim to love many love them weakly if at all. Yet, fleeting sexual desire can arise in relation to a variety of other individuals one finds sexually attractive. It may even be, as some have claimed, that sexual desire in humans naturally seeks variety, while this is obviously false of love. For this reason, monogamous sex, even if justified, almost always represents a sacrifice or the exercise of self-control on the part of the spouses, while monogamous love generally does not. There is no such thing as casual love in the sense in which I intend the term "love." It may occasionally happen that a spouse falls deeply in love with someone else (especially when sex is conceived in terms of love), but this is relatively rare in comparison to passing sexual desires for others; and while the former often indicates a weakness or fault in the marriage relation, the latter does not.

If love is indeed more exclusive in its objects than is sexual desire, this explains why those who view sex as essentially an expression of love would again tend to hold a repressive or restrictive sexual ethic. As in the case of reproduction, there may be good reasons for reserving the total commitment of deep love to the context of marriage and family – the normal personality may not withstand additional divisions of ultimate commitment and allegiance. There is no question that marriage itself is best sustained by a deep relation of love and affection; and even if love is not naturally monogamous, the benefits of family units to children provide additional reason to avoid serious commitments elsewhere which weaken family ties. It can be argued similarly that monogamous sex strengthens families by restricting and at the same time guaranteeing an outlet for sexual desire in marriage. But there is more force to the argument that recognition of a clear distinction between sex and love in society would help avoid disastrous marriages which result from adolescent confusion of the two when sexual desire is mistaken for permanent love, and would weaken damaging jealousies which arise in marriages in relation to passing sexual desires. The love and affection of a sound marriage certainly differs from the adolescent romantic variety, which is often a mere substitute for sex in the context of a repressive sexual ethic.

In fact, the restrictive sexual ethic tied to the means–end analysis in terms of love again has failed to be consistent. At least, it has not been applied consistently, but forms part of the double standard which has curtailed the freedom of women. It is predictable in light of this history that some women would now advocate using sex as another kind of means, as a political weapon or as a way to increase unjustly denied power and freedom. The inconsistency in the sexual ethic typically attached to the sex–love analysis, according to which it has generally been taken with a grain of salt when applied to men, is simply another example of the impossibility of tailoring a plausible moral theory in this area to a conception of sex which builds in conceptually extraneous factors.

I am not suggesting here that sex ought never to be connected with love or that it is not a more significant and valuable activity when it is. Nor am I denying that individuals need love as much as sex and perhaps emotionally need at least one complete relationship which encompasses both. Just as sex can express love and take on heightened significance when it does, so love is often naturally accompanied by an intermittent desire for sex. But again love is accompanied appropriately by desires for other shared activities as well. What makes the desire for sex seem more intimately connected with love is the intimacy which is seen to be a natural feature of mutual sex acts. Like love, sex is held to lay one bare psychologically as well as physically. Sex is unquestionably intimate, but beyond that the psychological toll often attached may be a function of the restrictive sexual ethic itself, rather than a legitimate apology for it. The intimacy involved

in love is psychologically consuming in a generally healthy way, while the psychological tolls of sexual relations, often including embarrassment as a correlate of intimacy, are too often the result of artificial sexual ethics and taboos. The intimacy involved in both love and sex is insufficient in any case in light of previous points to render a means–end analysis in these terms appropriate . . . .

I have now criticized various types of analysis sharing or suggesting a common means–end form. I have suggested that analyses of this form relate to attempts to limit moral or natural sex to that which fulfills some purpose or function extraneous to basic sexual desire. The attempts to brand forms of sex outside the idealized models as immoral or perverted fail to achieve consistency with intuitions that they themselves do not directly question. The reproductive model brands oral–genital sex a deviation, but cannot account for kissing or holding hands . . . .

The sex–love model makes most sexual desire seem degrading or base. These views condemn extramarital sex on the sound but irrelevant grounds that reproduction and deep commitment are best confined to family contexts. The romanticization of sex and the confusion of sexual desire with love operate in both directions: sex outside the context of romantic love is repressed; once it is repressed, partners become more difficult to find and sex becomes romanticized further, out of proportion to its real value for the individual.

What all these analyses share in addition to a common form is accordance with and perhaps derivation from the Platonic–Christian moral tradition, according to which the animal or purely physical element of humans is the source of immorality, and plain sex in the sense I defined it is an expression of this element, hence in itself to be condemned. All the analyses examined seem to seek a distance from sexual desire itself in attempting to extend it conceptually beyond the physical. The love and communication analyses seek refinement or intellectualization of the desire; plain physical sex becomes vulgar, and too straightforward sexual encounters without an aura of respectable cerebral communicative content are to be avoided. Solomon explicitly argues that sex cannot be a "mere" appetite, his argument being that if it were, subway exhibitionism and other vulgar forms would be pleasing.[2] This fails to recognize that sexual desire can be focused or selective at the same time as being physical. Lower animals are not attracted by every other member of their species, either. Rancid food forced down one's throat is not pleasing, but that certainly fails to show that hunger is not a physical appetite. Sexual desire lets us know that we are physical beings and, indeed, animals; this is why traditional Platonic morality is so thorough in its condemnation. Means–end analyses continue to reflect this tradition, sometimes unwittingly. They show that in conceptualizing sex it is still difficult, despite years of so-called revolution in this area, to free ourselves from the lingering suspicion that plain sex as physical desire is an expression of our "lower selves," that yielding to our animal natures is subhuman or vulgar.

VI

Having criticized these analyses for the sexual ethics . . . they imply, it remains to contrast my account along these lines. To the question of what morality might be implied by my analysis, the answer is that there are no moral implications whatever. Any analysis of sex which imputes a moral character to sex acts in themselves is wrong for that reason. There is no morality intrinsic to sex, although general moral rules apply to the treatment of others in sex acts as they apply to all human relations. We can speak of a sexual ethic as we can speak of a business ethic, without implying that business in itself is either moral or immoral or that special rules are required to judge business practices which are not derived from rules that apply elsewhere as well. Sex is not in itself a moral category, although like business it invariably places us into relations with others in which moral rules apply. It gives us opportunity to do what is otherwise recognized as wrong, to harm others, deceive them or manipulate them against their wills. Just as the fact that an act is sexual in itself never renders it wrong or adds to its wrongness if it is wrong on other grounds (sexual acts towards minors are wrong on other grounds, as will be argued below), so no wrong act is to be excused because done from a sexual motive. If a "crime of passion" is to be excused, it would have to be on grounds of temporary insanity rather than sexual context (whether insanity does constitute a legitimate excuse for certain actions is too big a topic to argue here). Sexual motives are among others which may become deranged, and the fact that they are sexual has no bearing in itself on the moral character, whether negative or exculpatory, of the actions deriving from them. Whatever might be true of war, it is certainly not the case that all's fair in love or sex.

Our first conclusion regarding morality and sex is therefore that no conduct otherwise immoral should be excused because it is sexual conduct, and nothing in sex is immoral unless condemned by rules which apply elsewhere as well. The last clause requires further clarification. Sexual conduct can be governed by particular rules relating only to sex itself. But these precepts must be implied by general moral rules when these are applied to specific sexual relations or types of conduct. The same is true of rules of fair business, ethical medicine, or courtesy in driving a car. In the latter case, particular acts on the road may be reprehensible, such as tail-gating or passing on the right, which seem to bear no resemblance as actions to any outside the context of highway safety. Nevertheless their immorality derives from the fact that they place others in danger, a circumstance which, when avoidable, is to be condemned in any context. This structure of general and specifically applicable rules describes a reasonable sexual ethic as well. To take an extreme case, rape is always a sexual act and it is always immoral. A rule against rape can therefore be considered an obvious part of sexual morality which has no bearing on nonsexual conduct. But the immorality of rape derives from its being an extreme violation of a person's body, of the right not to be humiliated, and of the general moral prohibition against using other persons against their wills, not from the fact that it is a sexual act.

The application elsewhere of general moral rules to sexual conduct is further complicated by the fact that it will be relative to the particular desires and preferences of one's partner (these may be influenced by and hence in some sense include misguided beliefs about sexual morality itself). This means that there will be fewer specific rules in the area of sexual ethics than in other areas of conduct, such as driving cars, where the relativity of preference is irrelevant to the prohibition of objectively dangerous conduct. More reliance will have to be placed upon the general moral rule, which in this area holds simply that the preferences, desires, and interests of one's partner or potential partner ought to be taken into account. This rule is certainly not specifically formulated to govern sexual relations; it is a form of the central principle of morality itself. But when applied to sex, it prohibits certain actions, such as molestaction of children, which cannot be categorized as violations of the rule without at the same time being classified as sexual. I believe this last case is the closest we can come to an action which is wrong *because* it is sexual, but even here its wrongness is better characterized as deriving from the detrimental effects such behavior can have on the future emotional and sexual life of the naive victims, and from the fact that such behavior therefore involves manipulation of innocent persons without regard for their interests. Hence, this case also involves violation of a general moral rule which applies elsewhere as well.

Aside from faulty conceptual analyses of sex and the influence of the Platonic moral tradition, there are two more plausible reasons for thinking that there are moral dimensions intrinsic to sex acts per se. The first is that such acts are normally intensely pleasurable. According to a hedonistic, utilitarian moral theory they therefore should be at least prima facie morally right, rather than morally neutral in themselves. To me this seems incorrect and reflects unfavorably on the ethical theory in question. The pleasure intrinsic to sex acts is a good, but not, it seems to me, a good with much positive moral signifi-

cance. Certainly I can have no duty to pursue such pleasure myself, and while it may be nice to give pleasure of any form to others, there is no ethical requirement to do so, given my right over my own body. The exception relates to the context of sex acts themselves, when one partner derives pleasure from the other and ought to return the favor. This duty to reciprocate takes us out of the domain of hedonistic utilitarianism, however, and into a Kantian moral framework, the central principles of which call for just such reciprocity in human relations. Since independent moral judgments regarding sexual activities constitute one area in which ethical theories are to be tested, these observations indicate here, as I believe others indicate elsewhere, the fertility of the Kantian, as opposed to the utilitarian, principle in reconstructing reasoned moral consciousness.

It may appear from this alternative Kantian viewpoint that sexual acts must be at least prima facie wrong in themselves. This is because they invariably involve at different stages the manipulation of one's partner for one's own pleasure, which might appear to be prohibited on the formulation of Kant's principle, which holds that one ought not to treat another as a means to such private ends. A more realistic rendering of this formulation, however, one which recognizes its intended equivalence to the first universalizability principle, admits no such absolute prohibition. Many human relations, most economic transactions for example, involve using other individuals for personal benefit. These relations are immoral only when they are one-sided, when the benefits are not mutual, or when the transactions are not freely and rationally endorsed by all parties. The same holds true of sexual acts. The central principle governing them is the Kantian demand for reciprocity in sexual relations. In order to comply with the second formulation of the categorical imperative, one must recognize the subjectivity of one's partner (not merely by being aroused by her or his desire, as Nagel describes). Even in an act which by its nature "objectifies" the other, one recognizes a partner as a subject with demands and desires by yielding to those desires, by allowing oneself to be a sexual object as well, by giving pleasure or ensuring that the pleasures of the acts are mutual. It is this kind of reciprocity which forms the basis for morality in sex, which distinguishes right acts from wrong in this area as in others. (Of course, prior to sex acts one must gauge their effects upon potential partners and take these longer-range interests into account.)

VII

I suggested earlier that in addition to generating confusion regarding the rightness or wrongness of sex acts, false conceptual analyses of the means–end form cause confusion about the value of sex to the individual. My account recognizes the satisfaction of desire and the pleasure this brings as the central psychological function of the sex act for the individual. Sex affords us a paradigm of pleasure, but not a cornerstone of value. For most of us it is not only a needed outlet for desire but also the most enjoyable form of recreation we know. Its value is nevertheless easily mistaken by being confused with that of love, when it is taken as essentially an expression of that emotion. Although intense, the pleasures of sex are brief and repetitive rather than cumulative. They give value to the specific acts which generate them, but not the lasting kind of value which enhances one's whole life. The briefness of these pleasures contributes to their intensity (or perhaps their intensity makes them necessarily brief), but it also relegates them to the periphery of most rational plans for the good life.

By contrast, love typically develops over a long-term relation; while its pleasures may be less intense and physical, they are of more cumulative value. The importance of love to the individual may well be central in a rational system of value. And it has perhaps an even deeper moral significance relating to the identification with the interests of another person, which broadens one's possible relationships with others as well. Marriage is again important in preserving this relation between adults and children, which seems as important to the adults as it is to the children in broadening concerns which have a tendency to become selfish. Sexual desire, by contrast, is desire for another which is nevertheless essentially self-regarding. Sexual pleasure is certainly a good for the individual, and for many it may be necessary in order for them to function in a reasonably cheerful way. But it bears little relation to those other values just discussed, to which some analyses falsely suggest a conceptual connection.

Notes

1 Even Bertrand Russell, whose writing in this area was a model of rationality, at least for its period, tends to make this identification and to condemn plain sex in the absence of love: "sex intercourse apart from love has little value, and is to be regarded primarily as experimentation with a view to love." *Marriage and Morals* (New York: Bantam, 1959), p. 87.

2 Robert Solomon, "Sex and Perversion," *Philosophy and Sex*, ed. R. Baker and F. Elliston (Buffalo: Prometheus, 1975), p. 285.

26

Why Homosexuality is Abnormal

Michael Levin

1 Introduction

This essay defends the view that homosexuality is abnormal and hence undesirable – not because it is immoral or sinful, or because it weakens society or hampers evolutionary development, but for a purely mechanical reason. It is a misuse of bodily parts. Clear empirical sense attaches to the idea of *the use* of such bodily parts as genitals, the idea that they are *for* something, and consequently to the idea of their misuse. I argue on grounds involving natural selection that misuse of bodily parts can with high probability be connected to unhappiness. I regard these matters as prolegomena to such policy issues as the rights of homosexuals, the rights of those desiring not to associate with homosexuals, and legislation concerning homosexuality, issues which I shall not discuss systematically here. However, I do in the last section draw a seemingly evident corollary from my view that homosexuality is abnormal and likely to lead to unhappiness . . . .

2 On "Function"

To bring into relief the point of the idea that homosexuality involves a misuse of bodily parts,

I will begin with an uncontroversial case of misuse, a case in which the clarity of our intuitions is not obscured by the conviction that they are untrustworthy. Mr Jones pulls all his teeth and strings them around his neck because he thinks his teeth look nice as a necklace. He takes puréed liquids supplemented by intravenous solutions for nourishment. It is surely natural to say that Jones is misusing his teeth, that he is not using them for what they are for, that indeed the way he is using them is incompatible with what they are for. Pedants might argue that Jones's teeth are no longer part of him and hence that he is not misusing any bodily parts. To them I offer Mr Smith, who likes to play "Old MacDonald" on his teeth. So devoted is he to this amusement, in fact, that he never uses his teeth for chewing – like Jones, he takes nourishment intravenously. Now, not only do we find it perfectly plain that Smith and Jones are misusing their teeth, we predict a dim future for them on purely physiological grounds; we expect the muscles of Jones's jaw that are used for – that *are* for – chewing to lose their tone, and we expect this to affect Jones's gums. Those parts of Jones's digestive tract that are for processing solids will also suffer from disuse. The net result will be deteriorating health and perhaps a shortened life. Nor is this all. Human beings enjoy chewing. Not only has natural selection selected in muscles for chewing and favored creatures with such muscles, it has selected in a tendency to find the use of those muscles reinforcing. Creatures who do not enjoy using such parts of their bodies as deteriorate with disuse will tend to be selected out. Jones, product of natural selection that he is, descended from creatures who at least tended to enjoy the use of such parts. Competitors who didn't simply had fewer descendants. So we expect Jones sooner or later to experience vague yearnings to chew something, just as we find people who take no exercise to experience a general listlessness. Even waiving for now my apparent reification of the evolutionary process, let me emphasize how little anyone is tempted to say "each to his own" about Jones or to regard Jones's disposition of his teeth as simply a deviation from a statistical norm. This sort of case is my paradigm when discussing homosexuality . . . .

3 Applications to Homosexuality

The application of this general picture to homosexuality should be obvious. There can be no reasonable doubt that one of the functions of the penis is to introduce semen into the vagina. It does this, and it has been selected in because it does this . . . . Nature has consequently made this use of the penis rewarding. It is clear enough that any proto-human males who found unrewarding the insertion of penis into vagina have left no descendants. In particular, proto-human males who enjoyed inserting their penises into each other's anuses have left no descendants. This is why homosexuality is abnormal, and why its abnormality counts prudentially against it. Homosexuality is likely to cause unhappiness because it leaves unfulfilled an innate and innately rewarding desire. And should the reader's environmentalism threaten to get the upper hand, let me remind him again of an unproblematic case. Lack of exercise is bad and even abnormal not only because it is unhealthy but also because one feels poorly without regular exercise. Nature made exercise

rewarding because, until recently, we had to exercise to survive. Creatures who found running after game unrewarding were eliminated. Laziness leaves unreaped the rewards nature has planted in exercise, even if the lazy man cannot tell this introspectively. If this is a correct description of the place of exercise in human life, it is by the same token a correct description of the place of heterosexuality.

It hardly needs saying, but perhaps I should say it anyway, that this argument concerns tendencies and probabilities. Generalizations about human affairs being notoriously "true by and large and for the most part" only, saying that homosexuals are bound to be less happy than heterosexuals must be understood as short for "Not coincidentally, a larger proportion of homosexuals will be unhappy than a corresponding selection of the heterosexual population." There are, after all, genuinely jolly fat men. To say that laziness leads to adverse affective consequences means that, because of our evolutionary history, the odds are relatively good that a man who takes no exercise will suffer adverse affective consequences. Obviously, some people will get away with misusing their bodily parts. Thus, when evaluating the empirical evidence that bears on this account, it will be pointless to cite cases of well-adjusted homosexuals. I do not say they are non-existent; my claim is that, of biological necessity, they are rare.

My argument might seem to show at most that heterosexual behavior is (self-) reinforcing, not that homosexuality is self-extinguishing – that homosexuals go without the built-in rewards of heterosexuality, but not that homosexuality has a built-in punishment. This distinction, however, is merely verbal. They are two different ways of saying that homosexuals will find their lives less rewarding than will heterosexuals. Even if some line demarcated happiness from unhappiness absolutely, it would be irrelevant if homosexuals were all happily above the line. It is the comparison with the heterosexual life that is at issue. A lazy man might count as happy by some mythic absolute standard, but he is likely to be less happy than someone otherwise like him who exercises . . . .

Talk of what is "in the genes" inevitably provokes the observation that we should not blame homosexuals for their homosexuality if it is "in their genes." True enough. Indeed, since nobody decides what he is going to find sexually arousing, the moral appraisal of sexual object "choice" is entirely absurd. However, so saying is quite consistent with regarding homosexuality as a misfortune, and taking steps – this being within the realm of the will – to minimize its incidence, especially among children. Calling homosexuality involuntary does not place it out-side the scope of evaluation. Victims of sickle-cell anemia are not blameworthy, but it is absurd to pretend that there is nothing wrong with them. Homosexual activists are partial to genetic explanations and hostile to Freudian environmentalism in part because they see a genetic cause as exempting homosexuals from blame. But surely people are equally blameless for indelible traits acquired in early childhood. And anyway, a blameless condition may still be worth trying to prevent. (Defenders of homosexuality fear Freud at another level, because his account removes homosexuality from the biological realm altogether and deprives it of whatever legitimacy adheres to what is "in the genes.")

My sociobiological scenario also finds no place for the fashionable remark that homosexuality has become fitness-enhancing in our supposedly overpopulated world. Homosexuality is said to increase our species' chances by easing the population pressure. This observation, however correct, is irrelevant. Even if homosexuality has lately come to favor species survival, this is no part of how homosexuality is created. Salvation of the human species would be at best a fortuitous byproduct of behavior having other causes. It is not easy, moreover, to see how this feature of homosexuality could get it selected in. If homosexuality enhances inclusive fitness precisely because homosexuals don't reproduce, the tendency to homosexuality cannot get selected for by a filtering process when it is passed to the next generation – it doesn't get passed to the next generation at all. The same applies, of course, to any tendency to find homosexuality rewarding.

The whole matter of the survival advantage of homosexuality is in any case beside the point. Our organs have the functions and rewards they do because of the way the world was, and what favored survival, many millions of years ago. *Then*, homosexuality decreased fitness and heterosexuality increased it; an innate tendency to homosexuality would have gotten selected out if anything did. We today have the tendencies transmitted to us by those other ancestors, whether or not the race is going to pay a price for this. That 50 years ago certain self-reinforcing behavior began to threaten the race's future is quite consistent with the behavior remaining self-reinforcing. Similarly, widespread obesity and the patent enjoyment many people experience in gorging themselves just show that our appetites were shaped in conditions of food scarcity under which gorging oneself when one had the chance was a good policy. Anyway, the instability created by abundance is, presumably, temporary. If the current abundance continues for 5,000 generations, natural gluttons will almost certainly disappear through early heart disease and unattractiveness to the opposite sex. The ways in which the populous human herd will be trimmed are best left to speculation.

I should also note that nothing I have said shows bisexuality or sheer polymorphous sexuality to be unnatural or self-punishing. One might cite the Greeks to show that only exclusive homosexuality conflicts with our evolved reinforcement mechanism. But in point of fact bisexuality seems to be a quite rare phenomenon – and animals, who receive no cultural conditioning, seem instinctively heterosexual in the vast majority of cases. Clinicians evidently agree that it is possible for a person to be homosexual at one period of his life and heterosexual at another, but not at the same time. . . .

Utilitarians must take the present evolutionary scenario seriously. The utilitarian attitude toward homosexuality usually runs something like this: even if homosexuality is in some sense unnatural, as a matter of brute fact homosexuals take pleasure in sexual contact with members of the same sex. As long as they don't hurt anyone else, homosexuality is as great a good as heterosexuality. But the matter cannot end here. Not even a utilitarian doctor would have words of praise for a degenerative disease that happened to foster a certain kind of pleasure (as sore muscles uniquely conduce to the pleasure of stretching them). A utilitarian doctor would presumably try just as zealously to cure diseases that feel good as less pleasant degenerative diseases. A pleasure causally connected with great distress cannot be treated as just another pleasure to be toted up on the felicific scoreboard. Utilitarians have to reckon with the inevitable consequences of pain-causing pleasure.

Similar remarks apply to the question of whether homosexuality is a "disease." A widely-quoted pronouncement of the American Psychiatric Association runs:

> Surely the time has come for psychiatry to give up the archaic practice of classifying the millions of men and women who accept or prefer homosexual object choices as being, by virtue of that fact alone, mentally ill. The fact that their alternative life-style happens to be out of favor with current cultural conventions must not be a basis in itself for a diagnosis.

Apart from some question-begging turns of phrase, this is right. One's taste for mutual anal intercourse is nothing "in itself" for one's psychiatrist to worry about, any more than a life of indolence is anything "in itself" for one's doctor to worry about. In fact, in itself there is nothing wrong with a broken arm or an occluded artery. The fact that my right ulna is now in two pieces is just a fact of nature, not a "basis for diagnosis." But this condition is a matter for medical science anyway, because it will lead to pain. Permitted to persist, my fracture will provoke increasingly punishing states. So if homosexuality is a reliable sign of present or future misery, it is beside the point that homosexuality is not "by virtue of that fact alone" a mental illness. High rates of drug addiction, divorce and illegitimacy are in themselves no basis for diagnosing social pathology. They support this diagnosis because of what else they signify about a society which exhibits them. Part of the problem here is the presence

of germs in paradigm diseases, and the lack of a germ for homosexuality (or psychosis). . . . Whether homosexuality is a disease is a largely verbal issue. If homosexuality is a self-punishing maladaptation, it hardly matters what it is called.

4 Evidence and Further Clarification

I have argued that homosexuality is "abnormal" in both a descriptive and a normative sense because – for evolutionary reasons – homosexuals are bound to be unhappy. In Kantian terms, I have explained how it is possible for homosexuality to be unnatural even if it violates no cosmic purpose or such purposes as we retrospectively impose on nature. What is the evidence for my view? For one thing, by emphasizing homosexual unhappiness, my view explains a ubiquitous fact in a simple way. The fact is the universally acknowledged unhappiness of homosexuals. Even the staunchest defenders of homosexuality admit that, as of now, homosexuals are not happy. . . .

The usual environmentalist explanation for homosexuals' unhappiness is the misunderstanding, contempt and abuse that society heaps on them. But this not only leaves unexplained why society has this attitude, it sins against parsimony by explaining a nearly universal phenomenon in terms of variable circumstances that have, by coincidence, the same upshot. Parsimony urges that we seek the explanation of homosexual unhappiness in the nature of homosexuality itself, as my explanation does. Having to "stay in the closet" may be a great strain, but it does not account for all the miseries that writers on homosexuality say are the homosexual's lot. . . .

One crucial test of my account is its prediction that homosexuals will continue to be unhappy even if people altogether abandon their "prejudice" against homosexuality. This prediction, that homosexuality being unnatural homosexuals will still find their behavior self-punishing, coheres with available evidence. It is consistent with the failure of other oppressed groups, such as American Negroes and

European Jews, to become warped in the direction of "cruising," sado-masochism and other practices common in homosexual life. It is consistent as well with the admission by even so sympathetic an observer of homosexuality as Rechy that the immediate cause of homosexual unhappiness is a taste for promiscuity, anonymous encounters and humiliation. It is hard to see how such tastes are related to the dim view society takes of them. Such a relation would be plausible only if homosexuals courted multiple anonymous encounters *faute de mieux*, longing all the while to settle down to some sort of domesticity. But, again, Europeans abhorred Jews for centuries, but this did not create in Jews a special weakness for anonymous, promiscuous sex. Whatever drives a man away from women, to be fellated by as many different men as possible, seems independent of what society thinks of such behavior. It is this behavior that occasions misery, and we may expect the misery of homosexuals to continue.

In a 1974 study, Weinberg and Williams found no difference in the distress experienced by homosexuals in Denmark and the Netherlands, and in the US, where they found public tolerance of homosexuality to be lower. This would confirm rather strikingly that homosexual unhappiness is endogenous, unless one says that Weinberg's and Williams's indices for public tolerance and distress – chiefly homosexuals' self-reports of "unhappiness" and "lack of faith in others" – are unreliable. Such complaints, however, push the social causation theory toward untestability. Weinberg and Williams themselves cleave to the hypothesis that homosexual unhappiness is entirely a reaction to society's attitudes, and suggest that a condition of homosexual happiness is positive endorsement by the surrounding society. It is hard to imagine a more flagrantly *ad hoc* hypothesis. Neither a Catholic living among Protestants nor a copywriter working on the great American novel in his off hours asks more of a society than tolerance in order to be happy in his pursuits.

It is interesting to reflect on a natural experiment that has gotten under way in the decade since the Weinberg–Williams study. A remarkable change in public opinion, if not private

sentiment, has occurred in America. For whatever reason – the prodding of homosexual activists, the desire not to seem like a fuddy-duddy – various organs of opinion are now hard at work providing a "positive image" for homosexuals. Judges allow homosexuals to adopt their lovers. The Unitarian Church now performs homosexual marriages. Hollywood produces highly sanitized movies like *Making Love* and *Personal Best* about homosexuality. Macmillan strongly urges its authors to show little boys using cosmetics. Homosexuals no longer fear revealing themselves, as is shown by the prevalence of the "clone look." Certain products run advertising obviously directed at the homosexual market. On the societal reaction theory, there ought to be an enormous rise in homosexual happiness. I know of no systematic study to determine if this is so, but anecdotal evidence suggests it may not be. The homosexual press has been just as strident in denouncing pro-homosexual movies as in denouncing Doris Day movies. Especially virulent venereal diseases have very recently appeared in homosexual communities, evidently spread in epidemic proportions by unabating homosexual promiscuity. One selling point for a presumably serious "gay rights" rally in Washington, DC, was an "all-night disco train" from New York to Washington. What is perhaps most salient is that, even if the changed public mood results in decreased homosexual unhappiness, the question remains of why homosexuals in the recent past, who suffered greatly for being homosexuals, persisted in being homosexuals.

But does not my position also predict – contrary to fact – that any sexual activity not aimed at procreation or at least sexual intercourse leads to unhappiness? First, I am not sure this conclusion is contrary to the facts properly understood. It is universally recognized that, for humans and the higher animals, sex is more than the insertion of the penis into the vagina. Foreplay is necessary to prepare the female and, to a lesser extent, the male. Ethologists have studied the elaborate mating rituals of even relatively simple animals. Sexual intercourse must therefore be understood to include the kisses and caresses that necessarily precede copulation, behaviors that nature has made rewarding. What my view does predict is that exclusive preoccupation with behaviors normally preparatory for intercourse is highly correlated with unhappiness. And, so far as I know, psychologists do agree that such preoccupation or "fixation" with, e.g., cunnilingus is associated with personality traits independently recognized as disorders. In this sense, sexual intercourse really is virtually necessary for well-being. Only if one is antecedently convinced that "nothing is more natural than anything else" will one confound foreplay as a prelude to intercourse with "foreplay" that leads nowhere at all. One might speculate on the evolutionary advantages of foreplay, at least for humans; by increasing the intensity and complexity of the pleasures of intercourse, it binds the partners more firmly and makes them more fit for child-rearing. In fact, such analyses of sexual perversion as Nagel's, which correctly focus on the interruption of mutuality as central to perversion, go wrong by ignoring the evolutionary role and built-in rewards of mutuality. They fail to explain why the interruption of mutuality is disturbing.

It should also be clear that my argument permits gradations in abnormality. Behavior is the more abnormal, and the less likely to be rewarding, the more its emission tends to extinguish a genetic cohort that practices it. The less likely a behavior is to get selected out, the less abnormal it is. Those of our ancestors who found certain aspects of foreplay reinforcing might have managed to reproduce themselves sufficiently to implant this strain in us. There might be an equilibrium between intercourse and such not directly reproductive behavior. It is not required that any behavior not directly linked to heterosexual intercourse lead to maximum dissatisfaction. But the existence of these gradations provides no entering wedge for homosexuality. As no behavior is more likely to get selected out than rewarding homosexuality – except perhaps an innate tendency to suicide at the onset of puberty – it is extremely unlikely that homosexuality can now be unconditionally reinforcing in humans to any extent.

Nor does my position predict, again contrary to fact, that celibate priests will be unhappy. My view is compatible with the existence of happy celibates who deny themselves as part of a higher calling which yields compensating satisfactions. Indeed, the very fact that one needs to explain how the priesthood can compensate for the lack of family means that people do regard heterosexual mating as the natural or "inertial" state of human relations. The comparison between priests and homosexuals is in any case inapt. Priests do not simply give up sexual activity without ill-effect; they give it up for a reason. Homosexuals have hardly given up the use of their sexual organs, for a higher calling or anything else. Homosexuals continue to use them, but, unlike priests, they use them for what they are not for. . . .

5 On Policy Issues

Homosexuality is intrinsically bad only in a prudential sense. It makes for unhappiness. However, this does not exempt homosexuality from the larger categories of ethics – rights, duties, liabilities. Deontic categories apply to acts which increase or decrease happiness or expose the helpless to the risk of unhappiness.

If homosexuality is unnatural, legislation which raises the odds that a given child will become homosexual raises the odds that he will be unhappy. The only gap in the syllogism is whether legislation which legitimates, endorses or protects homosexuality does increase the chances that a child will become homosexual. If so, such legislation is *prima facie* objectionable. The question is not whether homosexual elementary school teachers will molest their charges. Pro-homosexual legislation might increase the incidence of homosexuality in subtler ways. If it does, and if the protection of children is a fundamental obligation of society, legislation which legitimates homosexuality is a dereliction of duty. I am reluctant to deploy the language of "children's rights," which usually serves as one more excuse to interfere with the prerogatives of parents. But we do have obligations to our children, and one of them is to protect them from harm. If, as some have suggested, children have a right to protection from a religious education, they surely have a right to protection from homosexuality. So protecting them limits somebody else's freedom, but we are often willing to protect quite obscure children's rights at the expense of the freedom of others. There is a movement to ban TV commercials for sugar-coated cereals, to protect children from the relatively trivial harm of tooth decay. Such a ban would restrict the freedom of advertisers, and restrict it even though the last clear chance of avoiding the harm, and thus the responsibility, lies with the parents who control the TV set. I cannot see how one can consistently support such legislation and also urge homosexual rights, which risk much graver damage to children, in exchange for increased freedom for homosexuals. (If homosexual behavior is largely compulsive, it is falsifying the issue to present it as balancing risks to children against the freedom of homosexuals.) The right of a homosexual to work for the Fire Department is not a negligible good. Neither is fostering a legal atmosphere in which as many people as possible grow up heterosexual.

It is commonly asserted that legislation granting homosexuals the privilege or right to be firemen endorses not homosexuality, but an expanded conception of human liberation. It is conjectural how sincerely this can be said in a legal order that forbids employers to hire whom they please and demands hours of paperwork for an interstate shipment of hamburgers. But in any case legislation "legalizing homosexuality" cannot be neutral because passing it would have an inexpungeable speech-act dimension. Society cannot grant unaccustomed rights and privileges to homosexuals while remaining neutral about the value of homosexuality. Working from the assumption that society rests on the family and its consequences, the Judaeo-Christian tradition has deemed homosexuality a sin and withheld many privileges from homosexuals. Whether or not such denial was right, for our society to grant these privileges to homosexuals *now* would amount to declaring that it has rethought the matter and decided that homo-

sexuality is not as bad as it had previously supposed. And unless such rethinking is a direct response to new empirical findings about homosexuality, it can only be a revaluing. Someone who suddenly accepts a policy he has previously opposed is open to the same interpretation: he has come to think better of the policy. And if he embraces the policy while knowing that this interpretation will be put on his behavior, and if he knows that others know that he knows they will so interpret it, he is acquiescing in this interpretation. He can be held to have intended, meant, this interpretation. A society that grants privileges to homosexuals while recognizing that, in the light of generally known history, this act can be interpreted as a positive reevaluation of homosexuality, is signalling that it now thinks homosexuality is all right. Many commentators in the popular press have observed that homosexuals, unlike members of racial minorities, can always "stay in the closet" when applying for jobs. What homosexual rights activists really want, therefore, is not access to jobs but legitimation of their homosexuality. Since this is known, giving them what they want will be seen as conceding their claim to legitimacy. And since legislators know their actions will support this interpretation, and know that their constituencies know they know this, the Gricean effect or symbolic meaning of passing anti-discrimination ordinances is to declare homosexuality legitimate.

Legislation permitting frisbees in the park does not imply approval of frisbees for the simple reason that frisbees are new; there is no tradition of banning them from parks. The legislature's action in permitting frisbees is not interpretable, known to be interpretable and so on, as the reversal of long-standing disapproval. It is because these Gricean conditions are met in the case of abortion that legislation – or rather judicial fiat – permitting abortions and mandating their public funding are widely interpreted as tacit approval. Up to now, society has deemed homosexuality so harmful that restricting it outweighs putative homosexual rights. If society reverses itself, it will in effect be deciding that homosexuality is not as bad as it once thought.

Postscript Added 1995

I now see the foregoing argument as defective in two ways.

First, it is biased toward environmental explanations of homosexuality. Recent evidence from neuroanatomy and behavioral genetics has confirmed a significant biological factor in sexual orientation. The region of the hypothalamus which controls sexual arousal has been found to be twice as large in heterosexual as homosexual males. Identical twins reared apart are more concordant for homosexuality than fraternal twins reared apart or together, and, within families, concordance for homosexuality is greater than chance for males related on the mother's side but not the father's, suggesting sex-linkage.

However, a genetic basis for homosexuality does *not* imply that homosexuality is normal, for it does not imply that homosexuality has an adaptive function. The ostensible maladaptiveness of homosexuality suggests, rather, that the (poly)-gene for homosexuality survives through *pleiotropy*, expression in more than one phenotype. The (poly)gene that codes for homosexuality presumably also codes for some other trait(s) that strongly enhance(s) fitness, although no one now knows what that trait might be. But whatever version of the pleiotropy hypothesis may prove correct, it still counts homosexuality itself as abnormal, or at least non-normal. If the homosexual phenotype survives through an adaptive correlate, homosexuality would not explain the survival of the gene that codes for it – the gene would survive by expressing the correlate – and would therefore serve no function. Homosexuality would be a side-effect fatal to any gene that coded for it alone, resembling genetic diseases like sickle-cell anemia, which has survived because its gene also confers immunity to malaria. Homosexuality would also retain its negative aspect, on the pleiotropy hypothesis, since maladaptive side-effects are not expected to be reinforcing. Enjoyment of homosexuality would not increase fitness, so there would not have been selection for its being reinforcing.

My second error was to misconstrue the normative issues involved in the homosexuality debate. In effect I attacked an Equal Rights Amendment for homosexuals, defending some legal classifications based on sexual orientation on the grounds that overturning them would signal social acceptance of homosexuality and increase its prevalence. On one hand, emphasizing genes undercuts this argument; if homosexuality is largely biological in origin, this worry is empty. (I should add, however, that, if the central role of reproduction in society's continued existence gives the state a say in sexual relations, the state may and should reserve the privileges of marriage for heterosexuals.)

Ironically, the more ambitious goals of current homosexual liberationists make a biology *more* relevant than it was fifteen years ago. What is now being demanded is civil rights for homosexuals, that is, a legal ban on *private* discrimination based on sexual object choice.

This demand is often based upon the idea that it is wrong to discriminate on the basis of immutable traits, and homosexuality is involuntary and immutable if genetic. I contest the major premise: we discriminate every day on the basis of immutable traits. Reflex speed is unchosen, but the quickest shortstop makes the team. Going on the offensive, civil rights for homosexuals violates freedom of association, which, it seems to me, is an immediate corollary of the categorical imperative. It will be replied that, on my view, civil rights for blacks and women are also illicit; that indeed is my view, although, because others will find it a reductio, it is important to stress the difference between blacks and women, on one hand, and homosexuals on the other. There is nothing *abnormal* about being a black or a woman, and no one is made as profoundly uncomfortable by members of the opposite sex or other races as many people are made by homosexuals. This antipathy to homosexuals – which is not "hate," a desire to harm, but merely a desire to avoid – may itself have a biological basis. This being so, it strikes me as profoundly wrong to force association with homosexuals on anyone who does not want it.

These views are developed at length in "Homosexuality, Abnormality, and Civil Rights," *Public Affairs Quarterly* 10 (1996): 31–48, which expresses my current thinking on the subject.

27

Homosexuality and the Moral Relevance of Experience

John Corvino

Consider the following anecdote: Glenn and Stacy, a young couple who have been dating for several months, are driving home in a snowstorm after an enjoyable evening on the town. As they are crossing a bridge the traffic comes to a standstill, and they find themselves surrounded by blinding snow (though, fortunately, with a full tank of gas) waiting patiently for a clearing. Ten minutes pass, then twenty, and still there is no movement. So Glenn and Stacy do what any young lovebirds might do in such a situation: they start "making out" in the car. And despite the severe weather and the stalled traffic, they each think to themselves, "This is beautiful." For the snow is quite romantic, really, and the cold winter air is no match for the warmth of each other's touch. And so, for nearly an hour ("Were we stuck that long? Who's counting?") they snuggle and kiss and each silently concludes "Life is good."

Most of us have experiences that warrant the claim "Life is good." Not all of these are romantic, though many are. We believe human connection to be a valuable thing, and we desire it for ourselves and our loved ones. We are touched by Glenn and Stacy's story because it is familiar, and also because we long for it to be more familiar. We dream about finding "that special someone," and we typically hope that incidents like the above will not be isolated phenomena, but part of a larger picture. Perhaps Glenn and Stacy will eventually marry and spend their lives together, occasionally reminiscing about that sweet and tender moment on the bridge.

The above anecdote is based on a true story. Sadly, the real-life Glenn and Stacy split up a month later, just two days before Christmas. But the more salient feature of the real-life counterparts to my story is that they were both men – on their way home from celebrating Stacy's birthday at a gay bar in New York City's Greenwich Village, stuck on the Williamsburg Bridge. The only detail I altered was their names. Suddenly, what at first appeared to be a charming little story will now strike many as controversial, even revolting. "But that's just *wrong*," they counter, and they are not alone in that sentiment. Indeed, no matter how right and good and beautiful the experience felt to Glenn and Stacy at the time, there are countless others who will object that the two of them are simply deceiving themselves.

Some of these objectors even claim to have had relevant similar experiences. I am reminded, for example, of a speech given by a self-professed "ex-gay" – let's call him Charles – at a campus where I once taught. Charles, who knew first-hand what he called "the homosexual lifestyle," recounted an incident where he was engaged in a sexual experience with a stranger at a highway rest stop. There he stood, surrounded by the dreary lighting and horrible stench of a public restroom: "Suddenly I knew deep in my heart that what I was doing was wrong," he said almost tearfully, "and I vowed then and there that I would change." And when Glenn (who happened also to be in the audience listening to Charles's speech) stood up to counter with his own experiences, Charles looked him in the eye and said, "Come on, you *know* that it's wrong."

Two stories, two experiences, two very different moral conclusions. Glenn now claims that no amount of argument will ever convince him that what happened that day on the bridge was anything other than sublime; Charles is equally firm in his convictions. Both believe that their experiences offer moral insight into homosexuality: one sees it as a means of human connection and deep personal fulfillment; the other, as a misguided addiction leading to despair and hopelessness. This paper is not written for them, at least not primarily. Rather, I address myself to the many sincere individuals who have had neither experience and remain perplexed by the issue. What moral conclusions should we reach about Glenn, Charles, and those similar to them? And to what extent (if any) should their testimony be relevant to such conclusions? In what follows I explore these questions. Although my central aim is to defend Glenn and Stacy (and more generally, homosexuality), I hope in the process to shed some light on whether and how the experience of gays and lesbians is relevant to our moral theorizing about them.

The Prima Facie Argument for Homosexuality

Let us return to our happy gay couple on the bridge. They believe that this experience is beautiful and meaningful and *good*, by which term they mean to indicate a positive moral assessment. We might be tempted to reply, "So what?" Their believing it to be good doesn't make it so. People often approve of wrongful acts (slavery is an excellent historical example, though there are numerous contemporary ones). Moreover, the claim that "if it feels good, do it," has been justly criticized as a shoddy excuse for all kinds of objectionable behavior. One might even argue that the fact that homosexual behavior feels "good" or "right" or "natural" to Glenn and Stacy is just further evidence of their depravity. So if that's all we can say on their behalf, we have a fairly unconvincing case.

I think, however, that there's more to be said on their behalf. Recall the case as I initially described it. Most readers probably assumed that Glenn and Stacy were a man and a woman, even though both names are gender-ambiguous. (Consider Glenn Close and Stacy Keach, for example.) And under that assumption, most readers probably shared a positive reaction to the story, or at least experienced no negative one. What was it about the behavior that made it seem good? There are several relevant features, I think. First, as noted above, the behavior was pleasurable. This fact is not sufficient to justify it, but all else being equal, it is certainly a point in its favor. Pleasure is in itself a good thing, although sometimes (as with drug addiction or overeating) it can have long-term bad effects. Second, the behavior opened an avenue of communication, allowing them to express affection in a manner for which mere words would have been inadequate. Third, and related, the behavior facilitated a kind of connection between the two parties: their physical intimacy both manifested and enhanced their emotional intimacy. Finally, there were no relevant negative features mentioned: the activity wasn't coerced, nor did it seem – at least under the initial description – to put them at any risk. (It would have been quite different, for instance, if they had been engaging in the activity while one of them was attempting to drive.)

Let us generalize from these reactions to the assumed-heterosexual Glenn and Stacy and consider the moral value of heterosexual activity more broadly. One might want to claim that heterosexual activity is valuable because of its role in the production of children. This is one of its values, no doubt, but it certainly is not the whole of it. Indeed, to view heterosexual activity as valuable solely as a means to producing children would be to reduce sexual partners to mere baby-making machines. Rather, heterosexual activity is additionally valuable for many of the reasons mentioned in connection with Glenn and Stacy: it is pleasurable; it is a form of communication; it manifests and enhances intimacy between persons. These are reasons why activities such as kissing, cuddling, and caressing can be morally valuable even when they do not lead to intercourse. And they are reasons why heterosexual intercourse is valuable even when (as in the vast majority of cases) it does not lead to reproduction. There are a variety of concrete human goods that can be realized in sexual activity even between partners who cannot have children or choose not to do so. The Glenn and Stacy story (under the heterosexual assumption, at least) strikes a familiar chord precisely because these goods are so evident.

The analogy between the assumed-heterosexual Glenn and Stacy and the actual homosexual Glenn and Stacy suggests a prima facie argument in favor of homosexuality. To put it simply, homosexual activity can realize all of the concrete goods that non-procreative heterosexual activity does. It can be an avenue of intimacy, of pleasure, and of lasting interpersonal fulfillment. Over the long haul, it can play a role in building relationships that can be important sources of growth. Anyone who has been in a long-term relationship will understand how physical intimacy not only expresses but also facilitates deep emotional bonds. These bonds enrich human life and can make us better people – happier, more secure, more sensitive and more generous. They are the kinds of things that make us want to shout, "Life is good!"

Thus, even at first blush, there is more to be said in Glenn's and Stacy's favor than "if it feels good, do it." Yes, their romantic connection feels good, but it also has a much larger role to play in their lives. Of course, not every homosexual encounter will realize the various goods mentioned. Recall, for example, the story of Charles, whose experiences left him feeling empty and degraded. I do not wish to be dismissive of his experience, but instead to criticize the way in which he generalizes from that experience to make a claim about *all* homosexual experience. Just as it would be wrong for Glenn to claim, on the basis of his experience with Stacy, that all homosexual experience is deep and meaningful, it is wrong for Charles to claim, on the basis of his encounters at the rest stop, that none is. Sex is powerful, and like most other powerful things, it can have good and bad effects. This is as true for homosexual experience as for heterosexual experience. Analogously, it would be wrong to draw a blanket conclusion about heterosexuality from observations about the heterosexual couples portrayed on the Jerry Springer show, for example – though many people make precisely this sort of mistake with respect to homosexuality.

My point is that testimony like Glenn's demonstrates that homosexual experience can sometimes realize the very same concrete goods sometimes realized by non-procreative heterosexual experience. This evidence is especially powerful when it includes the testimony of homosexual people who have experienced long-term romantic relationships and the goods associated with them. Through our own experience with such goods we recognize them as valuable, and thus we would need a very strong reason to deny them to others or to judge others wrong for pursuing them. Yet moral opponents of homosexuality do precisely that. They are not simply making some theoretical claim about some abstract construct: they are claiming that actual persons (like Glenn and Stacy) are wrong to engage in concrete actions (like "making out" on the bridge). Given the prima facie argument just sketched, the burden of proof is on such opponents to explain some relevant difference between the case of the assumed-heterosexual Glenn and Stacy and that of the actual homosexual Glenn and

Stacy. Why, despite the apparently identical concrete goods realized in each case, is the one morally right and the other morally wrong?

Before proceeding, I should acknowledge a certain vagueness in my remarks thus far. I described Glenn and Stacy as "making out," which can comprise a rather wide variety of activities, depending on whom one asks. Opponents of homosexuality might suggest that whether the activity should be evaluated differently in the homosexual and heterosexual cases depends on what "making out" means. For instance, they might claim that if Glenn and his boyfriend were merely kissing, the activity was permissible, but if they were doing something "more than" that, it was not. I find this suggestion rather strange, but it is worth considering, if only briefly. When people condemn *homosexuality*, what activities are they condemning? Presumably, there are a wide variety of activities and choices that make up Glenn's romantic life. Some of these may be sexual, but most, presumably, are not. Indeed, Glenn's taking Stacy out for a romantic birthday dinner in some sense manifests Glenn's homosexuality, yet few would be prepared to condemn *that*.

Rather than settle this issue here, let me state my thesis as follows: whatever sort of activity is permissible for heterosexuals is permissible for homosexuals. Thus, if heterosexual kissing is permissible, then (all else being equal) homosexual kissing is permissible. If heterosexual oral sex is permissible, then homosexual oral sex is permissible – and so on. The reason is that the very same goods can be realized in the homosexual case as in the (non-procreative) heterosexual case. The burden of proof is on opponents to indicate some morally relevant difference between the two cases.

Some Counterarguments

I turn now to some attempts to indicate such a difference. For initial appearances may be misleading, and what seem at first glance to be similar cases may in fact be quite different. Perhaps the opponent of homosexuality is cor-rect in claiming that (the actual homosexual) Glenn and Stacy are simply deceived about the goods they're realizing.

Emotional risks and Levin's argument

In what ways might Glenn and Stacy be deceived? One possible answer is that although their activity seems good now, it will be regretted later. Here one might point to Charles's experience and claim that Glenn and Stacy will be left feeling similarly empty and alone over time. The problem with this claim is that the evidence suggests otherwise. While *some* gays and lesbians – just like some heterosexuals – experience their sex lives as largely negative, many do not. Indeed, one noteworthy result of the increasing number of "out" gays and lesbians is that it has provided mounting public evidence that homosexual relationships can be just as fulfilling as heterosexual ones. One might be tempted to dismiss such evidence as "mere testimony," but that dismissal applies equally to the case of Charles. If we are to take people's experience seriously, we must conclude that some people are happy engaging in homosexual activity even while others are miserable doing so.

Of course, if *most* people who engage in homosexual activity turn out to be miserable as a result, than there might be good reasons for society to discourage homosexuality (even if we do not conclude that it is immoral, strictly speaking). If nine out of ten friends report that Woody Allen's most recent film is wretched, their testimony might provide sufficient reason for declining to watch it (and for recommending that others not watch it) even if the tenth friend positively raves about it. Analogously, if the vast majority of people who engage in homosexual activity tell stories similar to Charles's, then one might have a good prudential reason, and perhaps even a good moral reason, to refrain from homosexual behavior and to encourage others to do the same. In a well-known article reprinted in this volume, Michael Levin offers a complex version of this kind of prudential argument.[1] Levin contends that homosexuality is likely to lead to unhappiness because it is "abnormal"; thus, it should be avoided and discouraged. Since Levin's argument includes the most rigorous attempt to date to articulate the view that homosexuality is a kind of "biological error," it merits some discussion.

In calling homosexuality "abnormal," Levin does not simply mean it is uncommon or rare. Being a philosophy professor is uncommon (in the sense that only a small minority of people do it), but it is not "abnormal" in Levin's sense. For Levin, an activity is abnormal in the relevant sense whenever it involves using an organ for purposes for which it was not intended. Levin argues that penises are for inserting into vaginas, not for inserting into mouths or other orifices; vaginas are for receiving penises, not for rubbing up against other vaginas.

One fortunate feature of Levin's claim about the purpose of genitalia is that it does not depend upon any controversial claims about divine intentions. (That matter is best left for theologians to debate, and in any case would take us too far afield here.[2]) Rather, he bases his argument on evolutionary theory. For Levin, an organ is *for* some function if and only if that function explains its existence through evolution. Our teeth are *for* chewing: we have teeth because our ancestors who used their teeth for chewing tended to survive and reproduce, creating progeny who also had teeth and used them for chewing. In a later article Levin illustrates further:

> Shark teeth are for tearing flesh, since primeval sharks with sharp teeth devoured prey more efficiently than less well-endowed competitors, and were thereby fitter. Thus, their ability to tear flesh explains why there are shark teeth. Shark teeth also impress aquarium visitors, but that is not what shark teeth are *for* because impressing aquarium visitors is not why today's sharks have sharp teeth.[3]

In a similar fashion, Levin argues that human beings have penises and vaginas because our ancestors who put their penises into vaginas (or put their vaginas around penises) tended to reproduce, passing along the tendency to have penises and vaginas and to use them in this way. That is what genitalia are *for*. Any other uses (such as homosexual acts) are abnormal.

Levin connects normality and happiness in the following way. Evolution tends to make us enjoy normal behaviors because in doing so it reinforces them:

> Evolution makes us like what makes us fit; it makes organisms not only seek food, but enjoy it, for organisms reinforced by eating are more apt to eat than competitors who are not, and therefore more apt to reproduce.[4]

Our ancestors who enjoyed using their teeth for chewing tended to use their teeth this way and thus lived longer and created more offspring, who in turn enjoyed using their teeth in this way. In a sense, we are "programmed" through evolution to enjoy using our organs in evolutionarily adaptive (i.e. normal) ways. Correspondingly, we are likely to be unhappy when we use them in abnormal ways. Levin uses the peculiar example of Mr. Jones, who removes all his teeth and wears them as a necklace. Because of the evolutionary processes of which he is a product, Jones is likely eventually to feel dissatisfaction at his inability to chew. For similar reasons, those who use their genitalia in abnormal ways are likely eventually to feel dissatisfied. We should thus not be surprised by testimony like that of Charles, who claimed that "the homosexual lifestyle" made him miserable. Evolutionary theory gives us reason to expect that abnormal behaviors will lead to unhappiness.

Herein lies Levin's justification for treating the homosexual Glenn and Stacy differently from their heterosexual counterparts. Homosexuals, insofar as they are engaging in abnormal behavior, are likely to be less happy than heterosexuals. Society has an interest in maintaining and promoting the happiness of its members. Therefore, society is justified in using legal and social sanctions to discourage homosexuality. Notably, Levin does not claim to have established that homosexuality is *immoral*. Rather, he claims to have shown that homosexuality is intrinsically bad in a prudential sense, much like smoking, or (to repeat an example) watching movies that have been widely panned. (Of course, given certain versions of utilitarianism, Levin's argument might have moral implications as well.)

There is much to be said about Levin's argument, and particularly about his account of evolution, which is problematic on several counts. For brevity's sake, however, I shall limit my response to the portion of his argument most relevant to my thesis – namely, his contentions about the connection between abnormality and unhappiness.[5] There are several points to be made here. First, it seems implausible to claim that people tend to enjoy using their organs only for those purposes that explain the organs' existence. Human beings have ears because the ability to hear helped our ancestors to detect approaching predators (and thus to survive and reproduce), but it does not follow that it will make us unhappy to use them to sport earrings, to listen to music, or to keep our eyeglasses from slipping off our noses. Indeed, although such uses are "abnormal" according to Levin's definition, they all seem to promote human happiness (and even, in the eyeglass case, survival) rather than to detract from it. Similarly, using the genital organs to express affection – even if that is not what they are *for*, in Levin's technical sense – seems clearly to promote happiness. Why else would people persist in doing it?

This brings me to a second important point. Levin's argument is a probabilistic one, in that it suggests that *most* of the time, we should *expect* that abnormal behaviors will correlate with unhappiness. But what should we do when our expectations are contradicted by the evidence – as in the case of Glenn and Stacy? Presumably, they engage in homosexual behavior precisely because such behavior makes them happy. Even if we don't expect or understand their preference, that is no reason to condemn it. Perhaps there is some complex evolutionary reason explaining why homosexuality (which admittedly seems to be a counterselective trait) continues to manifest itself across time and cultures. In any case, Levin's argument fails to explain the undeniable fact that some people – despite immense social pressure and even threat of prosecution – want to pursue homosexual relationships and enjoy doing so. As Andrew Koppelman writes, "People tend to want to do what will make them happy, and they don't

need Levin to tell them not to pull out their teeth and wear them as necklaces. Whatever it is that makes homosexual sex gratifying to some people is missing from his model."[6]

Levin might respond by claiming that although some people find homosexual sex gratifying, most do not. This claim is doubtless correct, but it still doesn't explain why we should condemn or discourage those who do find it gratifying. Nor do Levin's statistics about homosexual unhappiness provide much help. For even if we grant that homosexuals are on average less happy than heterosexuals, and even if we grant – what seems exceedingly implausible – that this supposed disparity has nothing to do with society's treatment of the groups in question, Levin's conclusion about how society should treat homosexuals still doesn't follow. For if one is concerned with promoting a happy society, the question to ask is not, "Who is happier – heterosexuals or homosexuals?" The question to ask is "Is society better off (i.e., happier overall) by supporting or discouraging homosexuality?"

Recall that we are talking about actual people here – people like Glenn and Stacy. There are at least three stances society could take toward them (if I may be permitted some oversimplification). First, it could condemn their relationships, perhaps encouraging them to seek heterosexual relationships instead. This approach does nothing for the general happiness; indeed, insofar as it interferes with these individuals' pursuit of happiness and perhaps even pressures them into relationships for which they are unsuited, it seems bound to promote misery.[7] (Even proponents of so-called "reparative" therapy" for homosexuals admit that it has scant success.[8]) Second, society could "tolerate" such relationships – a kind of "live and let live" attitude. Finally, it could encourage and support such relationships, much as it does with heterosexual relationships.

Without entering the thorny debate over gay marriage, I suggest that this third option – active support – is the one most likely to achieve Levin's expressed aim of promoting happiness. After all, it is widely recognized that romantic relationships, which are conducive to many important goods, require considerable effort to sustain. The support of friends, family, and society is invaluable in this regard. That the relationships in which Glenn and Stacy find fulfillment are homosexual is no reason to deny them such support. Indeed, insofar as these relationships make them not merely happier but also more stable, sensitive, and productive members of society, societal support of their relationship is not merely in their interest but in society's interest as well.

I conclude that Levin's argument gives us no reason to treat homosexuals any differently from non-procreating heterosexuals: the unhappiness that Levin alleges in connection with homosexuality is either non-existent or irrelevant. However, many people condemn homosexuality not because of its alleged emotional risks but instead because of its alleged physical risks – in particular, its connection with diseases like AIDS. I turn now to such arguments. (For simplicity's sake I will use the example of AIDS throughout, though the points made will apply, *mutatis mutandis*, to other diseases as well.)

Physical risks

Recall that the activity I initially described was Glenn's and Stacy's "making out" in the car – an activity that carries relatively little risk of disease and is probably safer than driving.[9] But what about oral and anal intercourse? These do in fact pose some risk of disease, and no amount of personal testimony from Glenn and Stacy can change this fact. I have two responses. First, it is important to remember that these activities pose a risk of disease only insofar as one's partner carries the disease. While this seems patently obvious, opponents of homosexuality often speak as if (male) homosexual sex *causes* AIDS in the same way that sparks cause fires. This view is simply naïve. AIDS is caused by the HIV-virus and cannot develop without it. If Glenn and Stacy are both virus-free, they can have intercourse with each other for days on end and not worry for a moment about contracting AIDS. (Fatigue, yes; AIDS, no.) It would be a different matter if Glenn were having sex with people whose

HIV status he didn't know, but this brings me to my second point. Insofar as oral and anal sex transmit bodily fluids, they are risky *regardless* of the gender of the participants. Prudence dictates that Glenn protect himself against AIDS whether Stacy is an unfamiliar man or an unfamiliar woman; sex with either could pose an AIDS risk.

Now it may be the case that in a given population a homosexual male is statistically more likely to carry the virus than a heterosexual female, and thus, that male homosexual sex in that population is statistically riskier than heterosexual sex. But what is the moral force of that? Under such circumstances, homosexual sex would be riskier for men than heterosexual sex in the same way that, in our own society, *heterosexual* sex is riskier for women than homosexual sex. (Lesbians have a remarkably low incidence of AIDS, not to mention cervical cancer.) Yet no one infers from these facts that the Surgeon General should recommend lesbianism, or that we should condemn women who decline to pursue it. It remains unclear how one justifies the move from claiming that an activity is risky to claiming that it is immoral. Being a coal miner is riskier than being a college professor, yet the latter profession carries no moral superiority as a result.

We can summarize the problems with the physical-risk argument as follows. The argument seems to be something like the following:

> Homosexual activity is risky.
> *Risky activity is immoral.*
> Therefore, homosexual activity is immoral.

Both premises are false, or at least ambiguous, as written. *Some* homosexual activity is risky, as is some heterosexual activity, not to mention some activities that are not sexual at all. *Some* risky activities may be immoral – particularly, if they put non-consenting parties at risk – but many are not. Moreover, even if risky activities were essentially immoral, they would be equally immoral for heterosexuals and homosexuals. The argument gives us no reason to distinguish morally between the assumed-heterosexual Glenn and Stacy and the actual homosexual ones.

Finnis and the PIB argument

At this point opponents of homosexuality might try a different tack. Thus far I have argued that homosexual behavior can realize the same goods as (non-procreative) heterosexual behavior. In doing so, I have focused on the effects of such behavior – in particular, its contribution to a happy and fulfilling life. But perhaps I have been missing something. Maybe there are certain other, less obvious goods which are realized by heterosexual activity – including non-procreative heterosexual activity – but not by homosexual activity. Such goods might constitute a relevant difference between the cases of the assumed-heterosexual Glenn and Stacy and the actual homosexual Glenn and Stacy.

John Finnis argues along such lines.[10] Understanding Finnis's argument requires understanding his natural law theory. As one of the "new natural lawyers," Finnis holds that there are certain basic goods that are intrinsically worthy of pursuit. By "basic," he means that they are irreducible to other goods such as happiness. One of these goods is what Finnis calls "the marital good." The marital good is the two-in-one-flesh union of a husband and wife. This union realizes two important values (though it is not reducible to either): procreation and friendship. Finnis claims that it would be wrong to engage in sexual activity as a *means* to either of these goods – including procreation – for to do so would be to treat one's body as an instrument for the satisfaction of desire. Rather, the good realized in (married heterosexual) intercourse is the intrinsic good of the marital union itself.

An analogy might be helpful here. Suppose a student were to ask me, "What good is reading philosophy?" In answering this question, I might point to various desirable effects that such reading might have: passing my class, earning a degree, getting a good job. These answers point to the *instrumental* value of reading philosophy. But I also might claim that reading philosophy is "valuable for its own sake," because knowledge is *intrinsically good*. Finnis makes this kind of claim with respect to marital intercourse. It is not good because of any subsequent result it produces, but rather because in itself it achieves a special union between husband and wife.

With admirable consistency, Finnis condemns all sexual acts that fall short of this marital good – including masturbation, contraception, and oral or anal sex by heterosexual partners. (For some readers, such prohibitions provide a sufficient *reductio ad absurdum* of his view. In any case, his arguments are not available for use by anyone who endorses one or more of the above.) Accordingly, Finnis would argue against my prima facie case by claiming that it is simply impossible for homosexual partners to engage in "whatever sexual acts are morally permissible for heterosexual partners," as I put it. Homosexual partners, by definition, cannot achieve the biological union that is required for sexual activity (even between heterosexual partners) to be morally permissible.

But what about sterile heterosexual partners? Finnis responds (controversially) that the biological union constitutive of the marital good is still possible in their case. A sexual act between such partners can still be of "the reproductive kind" – that is, of the sort normally suitable for reproduction. Such an act thus actualizes the union of the partners in a way that homosexual acts cannot. The problem with homosexuality, as Finnis sees it, is that it turns away from this basic good and instead involves treating the body as a mere instrument of pleasure, thus damaging the basic good of integrity. Finnis concludes that homosexual conduct is therefore unnatural, immoral, and worthy of condemnation.

Suppose, for the sake of argument, we were to grant that homosexual intercourse cannot achieve "the marital good." Finnis's argument nevertheless seems to depend on a false dichotomy: either sexual acts achieve the marital good or they fail to achieve any goods at all, instead counterfeiting the marital good while using the body as a mere instrument of pleasure. But what about the various concrete goods we described in the case of Glenn and Stacy? Their sexual acts realize intense emotional intimacy. They communicate affection in a manner for which mere words are inadequate. Such goods are at least as intelligible – and valuable – as Finnis's somewhat nebulous "marital good."

Finnis might reply that such acts instrumentalize our bodies for the sake of realizing the goods, but it is unclear why this must be so. Glenn and Stacy do not engage in their sexual act as a *means to* communication, which is as such a separable result of the act; rather, the act itself is an act of communication. It realizes communication intrinsically, not instrumentally. Moreover, it is unclear why the other allegedly good-making features of their act need involve their treating their bodies as "mere" instruments any more than does *any* sexual act – or for that matter, any bodily act at all. When I point to the blackboard I use my body as an instrument to facilitate the good of my students' education, but surely Finnis would not fault me for that.

In short, Finnis's "marital good" appears to be nothing but an *ad hoc* construction designed to distinguish between the sterile heterosexual couple and the homosexual couple, who are otherwise essentially similar. As such, it provides no compelling reason for treating the two differently – morally, socially, or legally.

Finnis and other similar theorists sometimes argue that in claiming that there is no relevant moral difference between homosexual acts and heterosexual acts (including non-procreative heterosexual acts), one abandons any principled reason for condemning various other sexual acts commonly regarded as vices. Because polygamy, incest, and bestiality are the standard examples, I refer to this as the "PIB" argument. According to this argument, if homosexual relationships are permissible then it seems PIB relationships could be permissible as well. After all, can't one use the same prima facie case for PIB relationships as for Glenn's and Stacy's relationship?

Not so fast. It is certainly true that defenders of PIB relationships can use the same *form* of argument that I used in defense of Glenn and Stacy. That is, they could claim that PIB relationships realize the same goods realized in non-procreative heterosexual relationships and possess no relevant drawbacks. But whether PIB relationships do in fact realize such goods and lack relevant drawbacks is an entirely separate issue, one that will not be settled by looking to homosexual relationships. I have argued this point at greater length elsewhere, but the quick response to the PIB argument is quite simple : *What does one thing have to do with the other?*[11] If there are plausible arguments against these other phenomena – and I believe that there are – they should remain unaffected by our defense of homosexuality.

Another – and perhaps more efficient – way to indicate the logical distance between homosexual relationships and PIB relationships is to point out that PIB relationships can be either homosexual or heterosexual. Proponents of the PIB argument must therefore explain why they group PIB relationships with homosexual relationships rather than heterosexual ones. There's only one plausible reason: PIB and homosexuality have traditionally been condemned. But that's also true of interracial relationships, which traditionalists (typically) no longer condemn. The question at hand is why we should group PIB relationships with homosexual relationships rather than heterosexual ones. Saying that "we've always grouped them together" doesn't answer that question; it begs it.

Conclusion

The testimony of people like Glenn and Stacy provides ample evidence that gay and lesbian relationships enhance people's lives in concrete and familiar ways. Justice demands that we give these relationships the same acceptance, approval, and support that we give to heterosexual relationships. The goods at stake are identical, and the pain that comes from our denying these goods is real.

Attempts to withhold such goods from gays and lesbians might even be partly responsible for the unfortunate experience of Charles. Deep, committed relationships require nurturing and support. The denial of legal marriage, the pressure to remain closeted, and the threat of verbal and physical attack faced by gays and lesbians are all more conducive to clandestine, transient encounters than to meaningful interpersonal unions. Surely, the development of satisfying relationships is challenging enough without such burdens. Perhaps in a more supportive environment Charles would have realized that his problem was not homosexuality *per se* but rather his misguided and destructive expressions of it.

In the course of this chapter I have suggested several ways in which experience is relevant to the moral conclusions we draw. First, our own experience reveals the value inherent in certain phenomena. We understand why Glenn and Stacy say "life is good" because we have had similar moments. Thus, second, experience can facilitate empathy, which is itself

an important human value. Finally, the testimony of others' experiences provides premises which, when combined with certain normative claims, yield moral conclusions. By misrepresenting – or perhaps merely misunderstanding – such experience, critics of homosexuality like Levin and Finnis draw erroneous conclusions about the lives of Glenn and Stacy and others like them. Indeed, the problem may be one of simple prejudice – literally, *pre-judging* the experience of a person or group rather than examining the evidence. If we want truly to understand Glenn and Stacy, we should begin by consulting *them*. Unless, of course, they're still busy on the bridge.

Notes

Over the years my work on this issue has benefited tremendously from the work of Richard Mohr, Stephen Macedo, and Andrew Koppelman. I am also indebted to Alessandro Giovannelli, Dallas S. Kelsey III, David Stylianou, Thomas Williams, and Daniel Wright Zalewski for their helpful comments and suggestions.

1 See Michael Levin, "Why Homosexuality is Abnormal," *Monist* 67 (1984): 251–83, reprinted as pp. 233–40 of this volume, and also "Homosexuality, Abnormality, and Civil Rights," *Public Affairs Quarterly* 10/1 (January 1996): 31–48. Portions of my remarks on Levin appear in different form in my "Justice for Glenn and Stacy: On Gender, Morality, and Gay Rights," in James P. Sterba, ed., *Social and Political Philosophy: Contemporary Perspectives* (Routledge, 2001), pp. 300–18.

2 For discussion of some religious arguments see Daniel Helminiak, *What the Bible Really Says About Homosexuality* (San Francisco: Alamo Square Press, 1994), and John Corvino, "The Bible Condemned Usurers, Too," *The Harvard Gay and Lesbian Review* 3/4 (Fall 1996): 11–12. For a discussion about how assumptions about divine intentions often appear in supposedly secular arguments regarding homosexuality see Andrew Koppelman, "Is Marriage Inherently Heterosexual?" 42 *Am. J. Juris.* 51 (1997), pp. 51–95.

3 "Homosexuality, Abnormality, and Civil Rights," p. 32.

4 Ibid., p. 34.

5 For fuller responses to Levin see Koppelman, "Is Marriage Inherently Heterosexual?"; Timothy F.

Murphy, "Homosexuality and Nature: Happiness and the Law at Stake," *Journal of Applied Philosophy* 4 (1987): 195–205; and Laurence M. Thomas, "Preferences and Equality: A Response to Levin," in Laurence M. Thomas and Michael E. Levin, *Sexual Orientation and Human Rights* (Lanham, MD: Rowman Littlefield, 1999), pp. 159–68.

6 See Koppelman, "Is Marriage Inherently Heterosexual?," p. 83.

7 The problems with such pressure are well-documented. See, for example, Richard M. Isay, "Heterosexually Married Homosexual Men: Clinical and Developmental Issues," *Am. J. Orthopsychiatry* 68/3 (1998): 424–32.

8 The success rate typically claimed, for those who are highly "motivated to change," is about 30 percent, but even this (rather unimpressive) figure is based on a skewed sample. For a recent (non-scientific) discussion of problems with reparative therapy see Andrew Sullivan, "They've Changed, So They Say," *New York Times*, July 26, 1998.

9 Recent studies suggest fairly conclusively that HIV is inactivated by saliva. See AIDS 2000, September 8; 14(13) pp. 1917–20; *Journal of Infectious Diseases*, May 2000; 181(5): pp. 1607–13; and *Arch. Oral Biology*, June 1999; 44(6), pp. 445–53. I am indebted to David Piontkowski, M.D., for pointing out these studies to me.

10 See John Finnis, "Law, Morality, and 'Sexual Orientation'," in John Corvino, ed., *Same Sex: Debating the Ethics, Science, and Culture of Homosexuality* (Lanham, MD: Rowman Littlefield, 1997), pp. 31–43. Portions of my remarks on Finnis appear in

different form in my "Justice for Glenn and Stacy: On Gender, Morality, and Gay Rights." See note 1. For fuller responses to Finnis see Stephen Macedo, "Homosexuality and The Conservative Mind," *Georgetown Law Journal*, 84/2 (December 1995)

and Andrew Koppelman, "Homosexual Conduct: A Reply to the New Natural Lawyers," in *Same Sex*.

11 For a fuller response see my "No Slippery Slope," *The Gay and Lesbian Review Worldwide* vii 7/3 (Summer 2000): 37–40.

PART IV

Liberty and Equality

Paternalism and Risk

When discussing how much freedom individuals should have, there is no better place to begin than by reading John Stuart Mill's *On Liberty*. This is the classic defense of individual liberty; arguably it is still the best. He crisply states the liberal credo: "that the sole end for which mankind are warranted, individually or collectively, in interfering with the liberty of action of any of their number is . . . to prevent harm to others." Interfering with the liberty of a rational person merely to prevent her from harming herself is never legitimate. If an action has no victim, then it should not be a crime.

Of course, as I noted in THEORIZING ABOUT ETHICS, we sometimes have difficulty deciding whether our actions harm others in a morally relevant sense. After all, virtually everything we do affects others to some degree or in some fashion. If nothing else, others may be bothered, upset, offended, or repulsed by our actions. The bare knowledge that I eat meat might offend a vegetarian. Does that mean that my actions harm the vegetarian in ways the law and society should recognize? Should the state legally prohibit me from pursuing my preferred eating habits *simply* because some other person is bothered by my culinary practices? Should society

criticize me if I continue? Not according to Mill. In setting social policy we should give no weight to such reactions to others' behavior. Otherwise, we unduly stretch the notion of harm.

Arthur (FREE SPEECH) would agree. We should not have an expansive notion of harm; otherwise, we would make virtually every action illegal. We should instead hold that an action harms others only if it *directly* diminishes their *long-term interests*. That is why he thinks we should not have speech codes. Hate speech may annoy or upset someone, but it does not harm them in this sense. If Arthur is correct, many actions people consider harmful are not, in fact, harmful – at least not in any sense that should concern the law. Not everyone agrees. Altman (in that same section) and May and Strikwerda (SEXUAL AND RACIAL DISCRIMINATION) think that Arthur's account of harm is too restrictive – even if they might agree about this particular case. This shows us that deciding how to define "harm" has momentous practical consequences.

Even if we refuse to make an action criminal simply because others are repulsed by it, we must still ask whether we should also forbid risky behaviors or behaviors that harm only the person doing the action. Let us briefly look at the second issue first. We have evidence that using some currently illegal drugs is dangerous to the person using them. Sometimes people die of drug overdoses; other times drug use may not kill them immediately but will lead to an early death. Wilson (PATERNALISM AND RISK) thinks this alone justifies the state's decision to legally prohibit the sale, possession, and use of these drugs. If drug use is illegal, fewer people will use the drugs; if fewer people use the drugs, fewer people will be harmed by them. Wilson also claims that drug use harms others as well: people who use (certain) drugs are more likely to abuse their children and less likely to fulfill their familial and social obligations. Consequently, he rejects the contention that drug use is a victimless crime. Husak is not so sure about either claim. He thinks we lack solid evidence that drug use harms either users or others, or, more precisely, that it causes more harm than the laws themselves.

We don't tend to think about the harm laws do. We should. We now assume that the burden of proof is on those who claim that drug use should be decriminalized. Husak claims the reverse is true. What we really need are arguments for criminalizing such drug use in the first place. Criminal laws exact enormous costs on both society and those individuals punished by them. Additionally, Husak, like Mill, thinks respect for autonomy gives us substantial reason to permit drug use even if it does harm the user. We permit people to engage in many behaviors that are dangerous to them: smoking, eating a bad diet, not exercising, etc. That is why showing that people are harmed by using drugs does not, by itself, justify making that use criminal.

We have seen that concern for personal freedom (autonomy) before. Most authors writing on EUTHANASIA argued that autonomy was exceedingly important. The problem, as I noted in that introduction, is that autonomy is a slippery notion. Although we might have no trouble deciding that a careful and seemingly reasonable choice by an unstressed, intelligent adult is fully autonomous, there are many cases about which we are far less sure.

Even if drug use does harm others, it does not harm them directly, for instance, in the same way that murder, assault, robbery, or rape does. Not every drug user harms others, and no user invariably harms others. So while most acts we make criminal directly harm others, drug use, at most, creates a *risk* of harm. Is that sufficient to make drug use illegal? Can we legitimately prohibit drug use because *some* drug users *sometimes* harm others?

This question sets the stage for the last two papers in this section. They ask whether the mere fact that allowing private ownership of guns is risky is sufficient reason to make gun ownership illegal (or to deem it immoral). Hughes and Hunt say "No." If we genuinely respect autonomy, they argue, then we should not prohibit people from owning guns unless we had compelling evidence of a significant causal relationship between owning guns and causing harm. Moreover, since guns can serve to equalize the differences between a strong aggressor and a weak (potential) victim, then there are positive reasons (guaranteeing equity and self-defense) for allowing people to own guns. LaFollette acknowledges that a proper respect for autonomy requires that we restrict guns only if the evidence indicates that it is dangerous to allow their private ownership. However, since guns are inherently dangerous, people do not have a fundamental right to own them. Moreover, if we have empirical evidence that allowing private citizens to own guns is harmful, then we are justified in abolishing or at least restricting who can own which guns, under what circumstances. He concludes there is reason to believe that guns are quite risky, and, therefore, that we should take some steps to control them.

Further Reading

Dworkin, R. (1977) *Taking Rights Seriously*. Cambridge, MA: Harvard University Press.

Feinberg, J. (1984) *The Moral Limits of the Criminal Law: Harm to Others*. New York: Oxford University Press.

—— (1984) *The Moral Limits of the Criminal Law: Harm to Self.* New York: Oxford University Press.

Husak, D. (2002) *Legalize This! The Case for Decriminalizing Drugs.* London: Verso Press.

—— (1992) *Drugs and Rights.* Cambridge: Cambridge University Press.

Kleinig, J. (1984) *Paternalism.* Totowa, NJ: Rowman & Allanheld.

LaFollette, H. (2001) "Controlling Guns," *Criminal Justice Ethics* 20: 34–9.

—— 1994: "Mandatory Drug Testing." In Luper-Foy, S. & Brown, C. (eds.) *Drugs, Morality, and the Law.* New York: Garland Press, pp. 283–99.

Mill, J. S. 1859/1978: *On Liberty.* Indianapolis, IN: Hackett.

28

Freedom of Action

John Stuart Mill

The object of this essay is to assert one very simple principle . . . to govern absolutely the dealings of society with the individual. . . . [It is to govern the] control [over individuals], whether the means used be physical force in the form of legal penalties, or the moral coercion of public opinion. That principle is, that the sole end for which mankind are warranted, individually or collectively in interfering with the liberty of action of any of their number, is self-protection. [T]he only purpose for which power can be rightfully exercised over any member of a civilized community, against his will, is to prevent harm to others. His own good, either physical or moral, is not a sufficient warrant. He cannot rightfully be compelled to do or forbear because it will be better for him to do so, because it will make him happier, because, in the opinions of others, to do so would be wise, or even right. These are good reasons for remonstrating with him, or reasoning with him, or persuading him, or entreating him, but not for compelling him, or visiting him with any evil, in case he do otherwise. To justify that, the conduct from which it is desired to deter him must be calculated to produce evil to some one else. The only part of the conduct of any one, for which he is amenable to society, is that which concerns others. In the part which merely concerns himself, his independence is, of right, absolute. Over himself, over his own body and mind, the individual is sovereign . . .

No society in which these liberties are not on the whole respected, is free, whatever may be its form of government; and none is completely free in which they do not exist absolute and unqualified. The only freedom which deserves the name, is that of pursuing our own good in our own way, so long as we do not attempt to deprive others of theirs, or impede their efforts to obtain it. . . . Mankind are greater gainers by suffering each other to live as seems good to themselves, than by compelling each to live as seems good to the rest. . . .

[Of course] no one pretends that actions should be as free as opinions. On the contrary, even opinions lose their immunity, when the circumstances in which they are expressed are . . . a positive instigation to some mischievous act. An opinion that corndealers are starvers of the poor, or that private property is robbery, ought to be unmolested when simply circulated through the press, but may justly incur punishment when delivered orally to an excited mob assembled before the house of a corndealer, or when handed about among the same mob in the form of a placard. Acts of whatever kind, which, without justifiable cause, do harm to others, may be, and in the more important cases absolutely require to be, controlled by the unfavourable sentiments, and, when needful, by the active interference of mankind. The liberty of the individual must be thus far limited; he must not make himself a nuisance to other people. But if he refrains from molesting others in what concerns them, and merely acts according to his own inclination and judgment in things which concern himself, [then] . . . he should be allowed, without molestation, to carry his opinions into practice at his own cost.

[A]s it is useful that while mankind are imperfect there should be different opinions, so is it that there should be different experiments of living. [We should give] free scope . . . to varieties of character, short of injury to others. [T]he worth of different modes of life should be proved practically, when any one thinks fit to try them. It is desirable, in short, that in things which do not primarily concern others, individuality should assert itself. Where not the person's own character, but the traditions of customs of other people are the rule of conduct, there is wanting one of the principle ingredients of human happiness, and quite the chief ingredient of individual and social progress.

[I]f it were felt that the free development of individuality is one of the leading essentials of well-being; that it is not only a coordinate element with all that is designated by the terms civilization, instruction, education, culture, but is itself a necessary part and condition of all those things; there would be no danger that liberty should be undervalued, and the adjustment of the boundaries between it and social control would present no extraordinary difficulty. But the evil is that individual spontaneity is hardly recognized by the common modes of thinking as having any intrinsic worth, or deserving any regard on its own account. The majority, being satisfied with the ways of mankind as they now are (for it is they who make them what they are), cannot comprehend why those ways should not be good enough for everybody. [W]hat is more, spontaneity forms no part of the ideal of the majority. . . .

[However,] no one's idea of excellence in conduct is that people should do absolutely nothing but copy one another. No one would assert that people ought not to put into their mode of life, and into the conduct of their concerns, any impress whatever of their own judgment, or of their own individual character. On the other hand, it would be absurd to pretend that people ought to live as if nothing whatever had been known in the world before they came into it; as if experience had as yet done nothing towards showing that one mode of existence, or of conduct, is preferable to another. Nobody denies that people should be so taught and trained in youth, as to know and benefit by the ascertained results of human experience. But it is the privilege and proper condition of a human being, arrived at the maturity of his faculties, to use and interpret experience in his own way. It is for him to find out what part of recorded experience is properly applicable to his own circumstances and character.

The traditions and customs of other people are, to a certain extent, evidence of what their experience has taught them . . . and as such, have a claim to this deference. [However,] their experience may be too narrow; or they may not have interpreted it rightly. [Moreover] their interpretation of experience may be correct but unsuitable to him. Customs are made for customary circumstances, and customary characters: and his circumstances or his character may be uncustomary. [Finally] though the customs be both good as customs, and suitable to him, yet to conform to custom, merely as custom, does not educate or develop in him any of the qualities which are the distinctive endowment of a human being. The human faculties of perception, judgment, discriminative feeling, mental activity, and even moral preference, are exercised only in making a choice. He who does anything because it is the custom, makes no choice. He gains no practice either in discerning or in desiring what is best. The mental and moral, like the muscular powers, are improved only by being used.

He who lets the word, or his own portion of it, choose his plan of life for him, has no need of any other faculty than the ape-like one of imitation. He who chooses his plan for himself, employs all his faculties. He must use observation to see, reasoning and judgment to foresee, activity to gather materials for decision, discrimination to decide, and when he has decided, firmness and self-control to hold to his deliberate decision. And these qualities he requires and exercises exactly in proportion as the part of his conduct which he determines according to his own judgment and feelings is a large one. It is possible that he might be guided in some good path, and kept out of harm's way, without any of these things. But what will be his comparative worth as a human being? It really is of importance, not only what men do, but also what manner of men they are that do it. Among the works of man, which human life is rightly employed in perfecting and beautifying, the first in importance surely is man himself. . . . Human nature is not a machine to be built after a model, and set to do exactly the work prescribed for it, but a tree, which requires to grow and develop itself on all sides, according to the tendency of the inward forces which make it a living thing . . .

It is not by wearing down into uniformity all that is individual in themselves, but by cultivating it and calling it forth, within the limits imposed by the rights and interests of others, that human beings become a noble and beautiful object of contemplation. [A]s the works partake the character of those who do them, by the same process human life also becomes rich, diversified, and animating. [Such a life furnishes] more abundant aliment to high thoughts and elevating feelings, and strengthens the tie which binds every individual to the race. [B]y making the race infinitely better worth belonging to [by developing] his individuality, each person becomes more valuable to himself, and is therefore capable of being more valuable to others. There is a greater fulness of life about his own existence, and when there is more life in the units there is more in the mass which is composed of them. As much compression as is necessary to prevent the stronger specimens of human nature

from encroaching on the rights of others, cannot be dispensed with. [F]or this there is ample compensation even in the point of view of human development. The means of development which the individual loses by being prevented from gratifying his inclinations to the injury of others, are chiefly obtained at the expense of the development of other people . . .

It will not be denied by anybody, that originality is a valuable element in human affairs. There is always need of persons not only to discover new truths, and point out when what were once truths are true no longer, but also to commence new practices, and set the example of more enlightened conduct, and better taste and sense in human life. This cannot well be gainsaid by anybody who does not believe that the world has already attained perfection in all its ways and practices. It is true that this benefit is not capable of being rendered by everybody alike: there are but few persons, in comparison with the whole of mankind, whose experiments, if adopted by others, would be likely to be any improvement on established practice. But these few are the salt of the earth; without them, human life would become a stagnant pool. Not only is it they who introduce good things which did not before exist; it is they who keep the life in those which already existed. If there were nothing new to be done, would human intellect cease to be necessary? . . .

Persons of genius, it is true, are, and are always likely to be, a small minority; but in order to have them, it is necessary to preserve the soil in which they grow. Genius can only breathe freely in an atmosphere of freedom. Persons of genius are . . . more individual than any other people, less capable, consequently, of fitting themselves, without hurtful compression, into any of the small number of moulds which society provides in order to save its members the trouble of forming their own character. If from timidity they consent to be forced into one of these moulds, and to let all that part of themselves which cannot expand under the pressure remain unexpanded, society will be little the better for their genius. . . .

I insist thus emphatically on the importance of genius. [We must allow it] to unfold itself freely both in thought and in practice, being well aware that no one will deny the position in theory, but knowing also that almost every one, in reality, is totally indifferent to it. People think genius a fine thing if it enables a man to write an exciting poem, or paint a picture. But in its true sense, that of originality in thought and action, though no one says that it is not a thing to be admired, nearly all, at heart, think they can do very well without it. Unhappily this is too natural to be wondered at. Originality is the one thing which unoriginal minds cannot feel the use of. They cannot see what it is to do for them: how should they? If they could see what it would do for them, it would not be originality. The first service which originality has to render them, is that of opening their eyes: which being once fully done, they would have a chance of being themselves original. . . .

In sober truth, whatever homage may be professed, or even paid, to real or supposed mental superiority, the general tendency of things throughout the world is to render mediocrity the ascendant power among mankind . . . . Those whose opinions go by the name of public opinion, are not always the same sort of public: in America, they are the whole white population; in England, chiefly the middle class. But they are always a mass, that is to say, collective mediocrity. And what is still greater novelty, the mass do not now take their opinions from dignitaries in Church or State, from ostensible leaders, or from books. Their thinking is done for them by men much like themselves, addressing them or speaking in their name, on the spur of the moment, through the newspapers.

I am not complaining of all this. I do not assert that anything better is compatible, as a general rule, with the present low state of the human mind. But that does not hinder the government of mediocrity from being mediocre government. No government by a democracy or a numerous aristocracy, either in its political acts or in the opinions, qualities, and tone of mind which it fosters, ever did or could rise above mediocrity, except in so far as the sovereign Many have let themselves be guided (which in their best times they always have

done) by the counsels and influence of a more highly gifted and instructed One or Few. . . .

I have said that it is important to give the freest scope possible to uncustomary things, in order that it may in time appear which of these are fit to be converted into customs. But independence of action, and disregard of custom are not solely deserving of encouragement for the chance they afford that better mode of action. [C]ustoms more worthy of general adoption, may be struck out; nor is it only persons of decided mental superiority who have a just claim to carry on their lives in their own way. There is no reason that all human existences should be constructed on some one, or some small number of patterns. If a person possesses any tolerable amount of common sense and experience, his own mode of laying out his existence is the best, not because it is the best in itself, but because it is his own mode. Human beings are not like sheep; and even sheep are not undistinguishably alike. A man cannot get a coat or a pair of boots to fit him, unless they are either made to his measure, or he has a whole warehouseful to choose from: and is it easier to fit him with a life than with a coat, or are human beings more like one another in their whole physical and spiritual conformation than in the shape of their feet? If it were only that people have diversities of taste that is reason enough for not attempting to shape them all after one model. But different persons also require different conditions for their spiritual development; and can no more exist healthily in the same moral, than all the variety of plants can in the same physical atmosphere and climate.

The same things which are helps to one person towards the cultivation of his higher nature, are hindrances to another. The same mode of life is a healthy excitement to one, keeping all his faculties of action and enjoyment in their best order, while to another it is a distracting burden, which suspends or crushes all internal life. Such are the differences among human beings in their sources of pleasure, their susceptibilities of pain, and the operation on them of different physical and moral agencies, that unless there is a corresponding diversity in their modes of life, they neither obtain their fair share of happiness, nor grow up to the mental, moral, and aesthetic stature of which their nature is capable. . . .

The despotism of custom is everywhere the standing hindrance to human advancement, being in unceasing antagonism to that disposition to aim at something better than customary, which is called, according to circumstances, the spirit of liberty, or that of progress or improvement. . . .

[Nonetheless] every one who receives the protection of society owes a return for the benefit, and the fact of living in society renders it indispensable that each should be bound to observe a certain line of conduct towards the rest. This conduct consists, first, in not injuring the interests of one another; or rather certain interests, which, either by express legal provision or by tacit understanding, ought to be considered as rights; and secondly, in each person's bearing his share (to be fixed on some equitable principle) of the labors and sacrifices incurred for defending the society or its members from injury and molestation. These conditions society is justified in enforcing, at all costs to those who endeavour to withhold fulfilment. Nor is this all that society may do. The acts of an individual may be hurtful to others, or wanting in due consideration for their welfare, without going the length of violating any of their constituted rights. The offender may then be justly punished by opinion, though not by law.

As soon as any part of a person's conduct affects prejudicially the interests of others, society has jurisdiction over it, and the question whether the general welfare will or will not be promoted by interfering with it, becomes open to discussion. But there is no room for entertaining any such question when a person's conduct affects the interests of no persons besides himself, or needs not affect them unless they like (all the persons concerned being of full age, and the ordinary amount of understanding). In all such cases there should be perfect freedom, legal and social, to do the action and stand the consequences. . . .

Note

This chapter has been abridged and edited from chapters 1 and 3 of *On Liberty*.

29

On Improving People by Political Means

Lester H. Hunt

Some writers have so confounded society with government, as to leave little or no distinction between them; whereas, they are not only different, but have different origins. Society is produced by our wants, and government by our wickedness; the former promotes our happiness positively by uniting our affections, the latter negatively by restraining our vices. . . . The first is a patron, the last is a punisher.

Thomas Paine, *Common Sense*[1]

Clearly, there are a number of ways in which one might think that Thomas Paine's remarks restrict too narrowly the ends that laws can legitimately be framed to serve. I will be concerned with one of them. It has been said that the law may be used not only to restrain our vices but to increase our virtue as well: it can make better people of us and thereby positively promote – if not our happiness, necessarily, then – what might be called "the quality of life." Perhaps the most familiar statement of this notion of the legislator as a moral educator is Aristotle's:

> we become just by the practice of just actions, self-controlled by exercising self-control, and courageous by performing acts of courage. This is corroborated by what happens in states. Lawgivers make the citizens good by inculcating habits in them, and this is

the aim of every lawgiver; if he does not succeed in doing that, his legislation is a failure.[2]

In other words, the law makes us good by compelling us to act as a good person acts. More specifically, I assume that Aristotle is putting forward the following position:[3] To be a good person is to possess certain virtues, such as courage. To each of these traits there corresponds a certain class of actions, such as courageous actions. The law instills these traits by making us perform the acts that correspond to them. This it does, I assume, by declaring what must be done and offering, by specifying punishments for noncompliance, some extra incentive for doing as it says. In complying with such declarations we gradually form certain habits that either are virtues or are naturally transformed into virtues when we reach a certain level of maturity and enlightenment.

Needing a name for it, I will call this model of how virtues arise "the Aristotelian paradigm." Since the method of moral education it recommends is perhaps the most obvious way in which the state might accomplish this aim, I will call it "the political means of improving character" or "the political means" for short. In what follows, I will argue that the Aristotelian paradigm is an incorrect picture of how character is changed for the better. I will also try to show that, for the same reasons, the political means suffers from certain crippling deficiencies as a means of imparting precisely those virtues it seems most likely to impart. These deficiencies should at least inspire caution in legislators who contemplate using it. If I am right, it is in some contexts misleading to call it an instrument of moral education at all.

I will not claim that what I call the political means is the only way in which the law and the state could possibly make us better.[4] Nor will I claim that it must not play a role in any program of moral education whatsoever. In this way, the case I will make will arrive at a less sweeping conclusion than the most familiar arguments against the political means, which always take the form of showing that the political means should never be used. We shall soon see that these arguments are inadequate, and the need to overcome the most obvious difficulties they encounter will take us directly to one of the most difficult questions of moral psychology: the question of how excellence of character is in fact instilled. Such arguments assume some answer to this question and, as we shall see, it is only by offering a true one that the political means can be plausibly criticized as a pedagogical method. I will offer an alternative answer in which something like the work the Aristotelian paradigm assigns to the state will be performed instead by what Paine called "society." As I do so, I will also offer reasons for rejecting a third alternative, which might be called "the Kantian paradigm," the notion that moral education is accomplished largely by means of the student's own purely autonomous insight. As far as specific policy recommendations are concerned, the case I will make will be unspectacular, but if I manage to shed light on the nature of moral education I think no one should complain.

Some Familiar Arguments

One objection to the political means is perhaps more obvious and more often heard than the others. A straightforward example of it may be found in the writings of the American anarchist Albert J. Nock.[5] According to Nock, to control human behavior by means of law is to control it "by force, by some form of outside compulsion." Thus it is incompatible with freedom. Freedom, however, is a necessary condition of "responsibility," because to be responsible, Nock believes, means "to rationalize, construct and adhere to a code of one's own." Responsibility, in turn, is a necessary condition of virtue. Thus the effort to create virtue by law destroys the very thing it is intended to bring about. The political means is therefore simply self-defeating.

This line of reasoning poses a number of problems, not the least of which arises from the remarkably narrow conception of responsibility it employs. If this is what responsibility is, it is surely practiced by very few of the people who actually exist in this world: most people do not live by a code they have constructed themselves, nor even by one they have thought about critically to any large extent. For the most part they accept the principles they live by as social conventions; that is, they accept them because they are accepted by others, who have accepted them for the same reason.[6] This fact presents anyone who holds Nock's position with a dilemma. On the one hand, if this is what responsibility is, social convention is at least as incompatible with it as law is. Thus if Nock's reasoning shows anything about the law it shows that social convention as such prevents people from being responsible. Since such conventions are in large part the basis of human life as we know it, this would seem to mean that most people are not responsible and, presumably, that they have no moral worth. Since such a conclusion must surely seem too harsh even to most cynics, it is a good reason for abandoning this notion of responsibility. But this would destroy the argument as a critique of attempts to create virtue by making it legally obligatory. The argument therefore proves both too much and too little.

We encounter a problem similar to the one confronting Nock's remarks in what is surely the most famous critique of the idea that virtue can be created by enforcing it legally. This is the "fugitive and cloistered virtue" passage in John Milton's *Areopagitica*. In it, he says:

> As therefore the state of man now is, what wisdom can there be to choose, what continence to forbear without the knowledge of evil? He that can apprehend and consider vice with all her baits and seeming pleasures, and yet abstain, and yet distinguish, and yet prefer that which is truly better, he is the true warfaring Christian. I cannot praise a fugitive and cloistered virtue, unexercised and unbreathed . . . . Assuredly we bring not innocence into the world, we bring impurity rather: that which purifies us is trial, and trial is by what is contrary.[7]

Like Nock's argument, Milton's assumes a moral theory: virtue requires a certain sort of knowledge, and this knowledge must include acquaintance with models of bad thought and conduct. Thus, it is precisely by attempting to "banish all objects of lust"[8] from the community that law defeats the purpose proposed by Aristotle, which is to make us more virtuous. Milton's alternative is the one expressed in the form of a paradox by the "revised motto" of Mark Twain's "The Man That Corrupted Hadleyburg": "Lead us into temptation."

Milton's argument suffers from a rather serious shortcoming. He wants to say, not merely that the political means of promoting virtue is a bad one, but that at least in some circumstances there is a better one. "Impurity and remissness, for certain, are the bane of a commonwealth; but there the great art lies, to discern in what the law is to bid restraint and punishment, and in what things persuasion only is to work."[9] But why is persuasion ever any better than the law in this respect? To the extent that it works at all, it eliminates temptation from our lives and will presumably produce the same problem he believes to be generated by the law. Indeed, Milton's argument settles on the one characteristic that *all* means to ethical improvement have in common, to the extent that they are successful.[10] If it proves anything about the law it therefore proves the same thing about all of them. It gives no reason for preferring one successful method over another. Since neither Milton nor anyone else wants to oppose all of them, his argument is at best incomplete. Those who like it as far as it goes can only

use it as a criticism of the political means if, at least, they find some feature of some alternative, such as convention, which compensates for the effect exposed by Milton, making it a superior method.[11]

A little reflection will show that the remarks of Nock and Milton indicate a problem that confronts any attempt to criticize the political means of improving character. It is obvious that social conventions resemble laws in a number of ways. Any attempt to criticize the political means is in some danger of going too far and opposing reliance on social convention as well. Perhaps, as I have suggested, we can only avoid this danger by indicating some relevant difference between these two ways of controlling behavior. I will try to indicate such a difference in what follows, but first I will attempt to diminish the plausibility of the paradigm suggested by Aristotle's remarks.

Virtuous Action

First, it is not difficult to see at least that actions (including abstentions from action) that are done because the law requires them are different in kind from virtuous actions. Whether an action is virtuous or not depends partly on the reason for which it is done: to give something to someone in order to curry their favor is not to be generous. When a lawgiver gives us a law requiring some action that was previously not required by law, he gives us two new reasons for performing that action, and it is for these reasons that it will be performed more frequently than before. First, laws that require us to act in certain ways are widely seen as commands issued by a body of persons having the authority to do so, and thus those who see it this way will see the fact that the law requires something of them as by itself a reason for doing what it requires. Second, such laws bring with them penalties that make it less desirable to omit the required action than it was before.

It is easy to see that neither of these reasons by themselves can make what we do virtuous. Consider the first one. Suppose that I am a member of a mass movement, an admirer of its charismatic leader. One day our leader issues an order that all members of the movement must give all they have to those in need, and I immediately begin to do it. If this makes me a generous person, then by the same token if my leader cancels his order and forbids us to give to the needy then I immediately cease being a generous person. If he replaces the order with another commanding that we fight the enemies of the movement in spite of the danger involved, I become courageous: if he reverses himself again and commands extreme prudence I become something else. Obviously, virtues – and vices – do not change as easily as authoritative directives do. Such traits are what Aristotle called *hexeis*, relatively permanent dispositions to act in certain ways. Obedience can give one a disposition to act in the same ways, but the disposition is apparently different in kind from those that constitute one's character. Obedience to authority does not generate any virtues by itself.

This is if anything more obvious in the case of the second reason for doing as the laws enjoin. Giving things to people in order to avoid a penalty is no more generous than doing it in order to curry favor.

Separately, neither obedience nor fear of retribution are the sort of reason that virtue requires and they will be equally insufficient when they are combined, as they often are, when one does something because the law requires it. What is perhaps more interesting is that what we have seen so far suggests that, in a limited way, Nock was right: virtue does seem to rest on a certain minimal sort of autonomy, if not on the extreme kind he describes. To have a trait like courage or generosity is to act on the basis of one's own notions about the right and the good. This would explain why virtue does not change as easily as the behavior of an obedient person: such notions are themselves relatively fixed characteristics of a person.[12] In acting obediently one acts on the basis of the directives of others, which change much more readily than one's own principles do.

The fact that virtuous conduct is quite different from actions that are done because the law requires them is not fatal to the Aristotelian

paradigm. Aristotle himself, in fact, seems to recognize the difference between them.[13] But if authoritative commands and the penalties attached to them can make us better persons by making us act as better persons act, then they must, by making us act that way, teach us the notions about what is right and good that make us better people. By considering an example, we can see that, in a way, such methods do teach us ideas of this sort, but we can also see that it does not appear to be true in the way that the Aristotelian paradigm requires.

Let us take an extreme case. Mary's son, Peter, is five years old and no more concerned with the welfare of others than most boys his age. She decides that he will not grow up to be a truly charitable person unless she guides him in that direction. She lays down a rule to the effect that he must give his best toy to any needy child he meets. She knows he is a good boy and generally does what she tells him to do, but to help make sure of it she hints that he will be punished if he disobeys. Eventually he forms a painful habit of doing what the rule says. Before long, though, something unforeseen happens: he conceives a powerful disliking for children who have something "wrong" with them. Children who are lame or blind or sick become more odious to him than broccoli or spinach. This odium is in a way quite rational in the present circumstances and is based on something he has learned: namely, that people with disabilities are bad. He has learned this because his mother *has made it true*. She has altered his situation in such a way that people with disabilities have become bad in the sense that they are now *bad for him*, like poison. Even if, due to a certain natural sympathy with the sufferings of others, he minds sacrificing his interests to theirs less than he would have without it, it remains true that they are destructive of his interests. Since all the most powerfully visible evidence he has on the matter leads to this conclusion, it would actually be irrational of him not to draw it. In a way, he has learned the principle she meant him to learn. She meant to teach him that he should act in a certain way and he has learned it. But she also wanted him to learn that others are worthy of respect and concern. This is shown by the fact that she wanted him to be a charitable person and not simply a compulsive giver. But somehow he has learned virtually the opposite of this.

In the Aristotelian paradigm, the formation of a virtue is the formation of a certain habit. We can see now that this is at best only part of the story of how such traits are formed. Mary has given Peter precisely that habit she would be giving him in teaching him to be charitable, but she has not taught him to be charitable. Peter consistently gives to those in need, but he does so with a resentful, teeth-gritting attitude which, as Aristotle tells us, is inconsistent with virtuous giving.[14] What is missing from this sort of account is an explanation of how the moral educator is to impart to the student an understanding, in terms of notions of what is right or good, of the *point* of the activity in which he is being drilled. Any activity, in order to qualify as a form of education, must give the instructor a certain measure of control over how the student sees things after the activity is completed. I have described Mary as using educational resources – namely, authoritative commands and punishments – which are precisely the ones that the political means employs. As I have described the situation so far, the control that the instructor exercises over how the point is taken seems very poor.

The problem remains even if we alter my admittedly extreme example in ways that make it more realistic. We might suppose, for instance, that Mary attempts to impart a rule about giving that is more reasonable than the one I have her trying to instill. But any rule which requires giving to others would ensure that to some extent Peter's interests come into conflict with the interests of others, thus opening the possibility of his drawing the conclusions I have him drawing. Again, we might introduce into the example the familiar fact that moral education proceeds by precept as well as habituation – that authoritative commands and punishments are not the only means employed. That is, we might have Mary telling her son that the point of all this is that others have dignity and importance as well as oneself, and that their welfare thus merits our concern.

But why would he believe this? It is true that her – to him – awesome parental authority helps to make her pronouncements credible, but all the *facts* she presents him with lead in another direction. So far, she does not seem to have an even minimally reliable method of influencing which way he will go. What is worse, nothing in all this suggests how he is even to understand what such precepts mean. Such assertions are not self-explanatory, and this one conflicts with all the palpable facts she has presented him with, since they point to the conclusion that others are dangerous to him and therefore to be avoided insofar as they need his concern.

Notice, finally, that the story I have told does not in any way assume that Peter possesses an ineradicable, natural instinct to be "selfish." I have made two psychological assumptions about him, neither of which commits me to a controversial theory about human nature. First, I have assumed that he has certain desires – whatever their nature and wherever they come from – which run contrary to the rule he has learned. If this were not so, there would be no point in laying down the rule at all. Second, I have assumed that he really believes the rule he has learned. Due to the regard he has for his mother's authority, he may even be quite incapable of doubting the correctness of the rule. Consequently, he believes that he really ought to give his toys to needy children he meets. This is precisely why they have become so odious to him: whenever one of them appears, he thinks he really must do something that is painful to him, something that is peculiarly painful because he does not see the point of it. Though he believes the rule he must, so far, find it more or less meaningless and even, in a way, absurd.

Rules and Understanding

So far, my efforts to undermine the Aristotelian paradigm rather obviously have something in common with the arguments I considered earlier. I have tried to show that the educational efficacy of the law is limited to the extent that its resources are those singled out by the theory I have attributed to Aristotle. It is already obvious, however, that the same resources are employed in the sort of instruction that occurs in the home, in which we make our initial acquaintance with social conventions. The problem I have posed for the law seems to afflict social convention as well. This is so despite the fact that I have applied a requirement of autonomous moral understanding that is considerably less drastic than the one applied by Nock. Later I will attempt to show that, in fact, such conventions make certain other resources available, in the home and elsewhere, which do meet my less drastic requirement while the political means does not. First, however, I will need to describe in somewhat more detail the problem I have posed.

Both law and social norms serve primarily to regulate our relations with others. Both contain rules which, like the one laid down by Mary in my example, propose that we promote the interests of others. Both also include rules that in various ways require us to refrain from doing things which damage the interests of others. It might be supposed that the difficulties encountered by Mary arise from the fact that she was teaching the first sort of rule, but in fact problems of the same kind are raised by the second sort as well. Rules that prevent us from harming others always either require that we forgo goods we could otherwise secure (by picking pockets, and so forth), or else they require us to give up some good we might otherwise keep (for instance, by refusing to pay our bills). On the whole, it costs us a great deal to observe such rules. In a way, they present other people as threats and obstacles to the pursuit of our own interests. Perhaps even a child can see that we are nonetheless all better off if we all obey rules of this sort. Yet it is rather more obvious that he can see that there is another situation in which he is still better off – namely, that in which everyone else obeys them and he does not. The rules are a help if others follow them and a hindrance if he does.

What is interesting, though, is the fact that, while this is in a way what the rules of morality are like, a moral person does not *see* them that way. If he believes in a rule prohibiting theft, he does not see it as an obstacle to his enriching himself by stealing the purse of the woman standing next to him at the subway station. To see a rule as an obstacle is, in itself, perfectly consistent with believing in the rightness of the rule. I can believe that I really ought to stop for all stop signs and yet be very irritated when one delays me in meeting an important appointment. Why does a moral person not see persons and the moral rules that protect them from harm in this light? The answer suggested by my remarks on the case of Peter is that he "respect" persons in a way that we do not normally "respect" stop signs. Yet the rules themselves do not support any positive attitude toward persons at all, while they do support a certain negative attitude – namely, seeing others as obstructions. On the other hand, while they do not *support* respect, they do *require* it. If we are to acquire any of the virtues expressed by following these rules – honesty, considerateness, and the like – we must somehow acquire respect for others.[15]

It appears that any institution that instills the virtues which both the law and social convention can most plausibly be thought to give us must somehow teach us respect for others. What we need, then, is some insight into what this respect amounts to and how such institutions might teach it. To this end, it will help to draw a distinction – an informal one will be sufficient – between two kinds of rules, one of which I have thus far ignored.

So far, I have treated social norms that are examples of a class of rules that also includes the kind of laws the political means employs: these are rules which tell us what to do and what not to do. In all the examples I have cited, they also, in one way or another, determine the distribution of various goods which, of course, exist independently of the rules that distribute them. Such rules, which might be called "substantive rules," can be contrasted with what I will call "ceremonial rules."[16] Ceremonial rules do not declare who shall have goods of this kind. Indeed, they do not even tell us what to do or not to do. They only specify *ways* in which we can engage in certain activities if we wish or need to. We are quite familiar with such rules in virtue of having observed them. We begin an encounter with others by saying "Hello" and asking how they are, we end it by saying "Goodbye." We make requests and ask permissions; if granted them, we give thanks. If we do not do such things at the time or place which some substantive rule requires, we make apologies and give excuses. As these examples suggest, the activities these rules might be said to regulate would not exist if rules of this kind did not exist. When we say "Hello" we are engaging in an activity called a "salutation" and, if it were not for the rule which says that we can accomplish it by saying "Hello," and other rules like it, there would be no such thing as a salutation. The same is true of making requests, giving thanks, and all other activities of this sort. Further, these activities are important to us only because of their expressive function and, although it is not always easy to say just what they express, it always has something to do with the agent's appreciation of the person to whom they are done. The lesson of ceremonial observances seems to be that others must be approached gingerly and left with a benediction: we must not assume too much or handle them too roughly.

It is not difficult to see how a child can be brought to learn this lesson by being taught to follow ceremonial rules. Consider the following story. Young Paul wants to play with a pair of binoculars belonging to his uncle John. John has let him use them in the past and, thinking that John wouldn't object to his having them now, Paul takes them. But his mother, Martha, makes it clear to him that this is not the way one goes about getting what someone else has already got: you must ask him for it first, and say "please." Paul asks his uncle if he can please use the binoculars and is immediately told he has done it wrong: one says "may," not "can." If your request is granted, you say "thank you." He soon masters these rules well enough. He cannot doubt their correctness, since he has them on the infallible authority of his mother. He even possesses evidence of their correctness: somehow, people become angry and unpleasant if you take something they have, even if they have no objection to giving it to you, without first saying words like "may," "please," and "thank you." If you say the

words, however, they are soothed and happy. There are many ways in which one must avoid jarring people's feelings, and this is one of them. He has learned his lesson.

Yet Paul is really in more or less the same position that Peter was in after Mary laid down her new rule: he has faith in certain principles but does not understand them. Why do people have such volatile feelings about such things in the first place, and why do these words have the apparently magic power to soothe these feelings? If Paul had the sophisticated intellectual resources of a social scientist or a philosopher there would be many answers he could give to these questions. For instance, he might suppose that people are proud of the things they possess because such things show that they have the power it takes to accumulate them. Thus, they hate to have things taken from them because it is a challenge to their power: they would rather give or lend things than have them taken, since giving or lending shows that they have the power to dispose of what they have according to their whims and without any hindrance. Alternatively, Paul might think that people simply want to keep in their possession as many things as possible, and that they insist on the practice of asking permission because it enables them to say "no," so that they can maintain the size of their hoard. Because he is only a child, however, Paul cannot indulge in such imaginative speculations. Fortunately, though, he does not need to. It is obvious to him that Martha and John understand the rules he has learned; for him, to understand them is simply to know how adults understand them.

This method of understanding rules, unlike the method in which one relies on one's own imagination, can only lead to one conclusion. These principles are related in definite ways to other ideas that adults use, including especially the notions of "yours" and "mine." The practices of asking, granting, and refusing permission are among those which mark the boundaries between what is yours and what is mine. Paul is aware that he need not seek permission to use something that already belongs to him; he also knows that he need not seek permission in order to come into possession of something which he is being given as a gift, or which he is taking in trade.

Sometimes, though, Paul wants to get to use, on his own initiative, something that is not his and for which he offers nothing in trade. The practices concerning permissions make it possible to accomplish this without simply taking what he wants. The use of this complicated apparatus makes sense to him when he realizes that it is one indication of the fact that, in the adult world, people are ordinarily seen as having a *right* to determine what happens to the things they possess: this is part of what it means to say that these things are *their* things. Asking permission is a practice that makes it possible for Paul to acquire something possessed by someone else without violating that right, which he would be violating if he were to simply take it. If he understands this, he can understand the moves in the game he has been taught in the way that adults understand them. By saying "may" rather than "can" he signifies that he is asking that a right be transferred from someone else to him rather than asking for information. By saying "please" and "thank you" he expresses an appreciation for the fact that the thing he is asking for is not already his by right – that it comes to him, if it does, as a gift. The entire activity, then, expresses a respect for the boundaries between "mine" and "yours" – it expresses a respect for the rights of others.[17] If he comes to see and to pursue the activity in this way, he has acquired in some degree the respect for others that I have said underlies decent relations between people.

The kind of training Paul has undergone is a more effective form of moral instruction than the sort to which Peter was subjected. It is possible, on the basis of what I have said, to explain this fact. The rule Peter learned was one of the substantive rules that regulate our relations with others. It was an example of the sort of substantive rule that governs the distribution of things which, independently of these rules, are regarded as good. Rules of this sort always require that we forgo or relinquish such goods. Consequently, they have a certain tendency to make us see others as threats or obstacles to the promotion of our interests. It was precisely

what Peter could see in light of his rule that prevented him from grasping what respect is.

In a limited way, Paul's circumstances were like Peter's; they also involved a substantive rule requiring him to forgo or relinquish something antecedently regarded as good. This is the rule prohibiting one from simply taking things which do not belong to oneself. But of course it was not from this rule that Paul learned respect. He learned it from a ceremonial rule and not from a substantive one. Ceremonial rules in general are are relatively costless to follow.[18] It is not in itself against one's interest to ask permission (rather the contrary, in fact). This is true even if one knows in advance that the request will probably be refused. These rules make possible an activity which obviously expresses something, and which is quite mysterious to someone in Paul's position because he does not yet understand what it expresses. As such it *invites* him to try to understand it. We have seen that the practice he is confronted with, and others associated with it, provide him with the materials he needs to succeed. Once he understands it, he also understands substantive rules like the one that prohibits him from simply taking things that do not belong to him: once he comes to see others as having rights, he can appreciate rules that specify what rights others have, and that is what rules like this one do. We have also seen that to understand this practice is, in part, to understand what it is to regard others with respect; it is also clear from what I have said that to come to understand such respect under the influence of a certain sort of authority is, to some extent, to come to possess it.

Conclusion

It is time to stop and review the argument I have laid down so far, to see what it has come to. Early on, I said Nock's argument has certain undesirable consequences because of a rather extreme assumption he makes regarding the sort of autonomy required for virtue. These consequences can be avoided if one replaces this assumption with the much more reasonable one that one must act on principles which one understands. The political means however cannot reliably impart this kind of understanding because of the nature of the class of rules of which the relevant kinds of laws are instances: such rules, in general, place barriers in the way of achieving this sort of understanding. There are certain conventions, however, which do have the capacity to impart this sort of understanding. This capacity is sufficient to deliver us from the difficulties that I said were entailed by the assumptions behind Milton's familiar criticism of the political means. It shows that not all ways of promoting decent behavior are equal in this respect; there is one that has virtues which compensate to some extent for whatever limitations they might have in common.

What may we conclude concerning the relative merits of these two kinds of rules as instruments of moral education? It is perhaps important to notice the difference here between what follows and what does not. What follows is that, if they are considered separately, one of them has the character of an instrument of education and the other does not: one tends to lead to the required sort of understanding and the other is apt to block it. However, it is obvious that such instruments are not used separately in the world we live in. As far as what I have said is concerned, it is possible that substantive rules can acquire such a character when they work in the context of a whole system of educational means. It is possible that such rules could contribute something worthwhile to such a system, while other parts of the system overcome the bad effects which, as I have claimed, they are likely to produce. Indeed, we have good reason to believe that such a system is possible, because the one we use to raise our children seems to be precisely of this sort: their behavior is held in place by all sorts of substantive rules while other means of moral education do their work. This is how I have described the case of Paul earlier. It is part of the value of the practices having to do with making requests that they enable Paul to understand certain substantive rules such as the one which prohibits him from simply taking what he wants. Presumably, by helping him to grasp the point of such rules it also enables him to follow them with greater alacrity than before.

As I said at the outset, my argument does not imply that the political means ought never to be used.[19] However, it does imply several other things which were not obvious in the beginning. First, even in the context of the sort of system I have just imagined, the political means has a rather peculiar status: if the system works, it is because the other means function as adequate *antidotes* to the political means. They overcome its ill effects. This in turn suggests a second point. If a legislator is pressing for a new use of the political means, if he is trying to pass a new law to instill a virtue that will improve the way his subjects treat one another, it is not enough for him to claim that the actions enjoined by the proposed law are indeed those which would spring from the neglected virtue itself. The measure he proposes is apt to have effects that run counter to his own purpose and they will be overcome, if at all, by a complex system of beliefs and practices over which he has little control. He must claim the undesirable effects of this measure are not too weighty to be overcome by this system. This is a kind of claim which is obviously capable of being false. It would be false, for instance, if it were made of the rule that I have imagined Mary laying down for Peter. The difficulties involved in making such a claim may not be serious in the parent–child relationship, where it is possible to see all the important effects and easy to change the rule if it does not appear to be a good one. For legislators, who in most states control the behavior of millions of people they can never know, they are much more likely to be formidable. Whether they can be surmounted or not, they should not be ignored.

What I have said here also implies a third and more metaphysical point, one which concerns the relative positions of society and the state in the foundations of the moral life. The Aristotelian paradigm, as I have defined it, depicts the process by which virtue is taught as being fundamentally like the one in which a drill instructor teaches his soldiers to march. I have tried to show that part of the process of acquiring the other-regarding virtues which the law seems most likely to instill is more like learning a language than it is like learning to march or stand at attention, and that ceremonial rules provide the materials for this crucial aspect of moral education. They provide the expressive actions the meaning of which the student must grasp. This suggests that legislators in fact cannot originate such rules. It is impossible for the same reason that it is impossible for the law to originate a new language. The resources of the political means – authoritative commands and punishments – can make people do what the legislator wants them to do, but they cannot make them mean what the legislator wants them to mean by what they do.

To the extent that what people mean is not a product of individual fiat, it seems to arise from social conventions like those which govern the use of language. We do not need to have a theory showing precisely how such rules originate in order to know that they are not made by a specialized social organ which, like the state,

imposes its rules on those outside it. They appear to arise somehow from voluntary relations among individuals. In a way, the position I have taken here can be seen as a variant of the theme, which appeared above, that virtue depends on freedom. But it is rather widely different from the variants I considered there. Specifically, I have avoided the assumption that virtue can only arise from purely autonomous individual insight. I have avoided suggesting that the individual must devise his principles himself (by deriving them, perhaps, from the dictates of pure practical reason), or even that he must subject them to critical examination. However, I have supposed that he must *understand* them, and I have tried to show that here the individual relies on the social background of his actions. On this point, Aristotle, with his insistence that man is a social being (*zoon politikon*), seems closer to the truth than an extreme individualist like Kant.

Notes

This essay was improved by comments from acquaintances, colleagues, and students too numerous to thank by name, but I should mention that Charles King, John Kekes, Gilbert Harman, Amelie Rorty, Michael Stocker, Morton Winston, and James D. Wallace were good enough to provide comments in writing. An earlier version was presented at the April 1980 Liberty Fund Conference on Virtue and Political Freedom. A fellowship from the Mellon Foundation made writing it much easier than it would have been otherwise.

1   In Merrill Jensen (ed.), *Tracts of the American Revolution* (Indianapolis: Bobbs-Merrill, 1977), pp. 402–3.
2   Aristotle, *Nicomachean Ethics*, trans. Martin Ostwald (Indianapolis: Bobbs-Merrill, 1962), 1103b2–5.
3   This is not an essay in Aristotle scholarship, and I do not insist that this is Aristotle's position. It seems attractive enough to be worth discussing on its own merits, even if he did not hold it.
4   For examples of other possible ways, see Aristotle's *Politics*, 7, chs. 13–15 and 17. I have argued elsewhere that the criminal law produces an effect of this kind by removing opportunities for vengeful thoughts and feelings on the part of the victims of crime. But this happens by means of a process that bears no resemblance to what I am now calling the political means. See "Punishment, Revenge, and the Minimal Functions of the State," in *Understanding*

Human Emotions, ed. Fred D. Miller, Jr, and Thomas W. Attig (Bowling Green, Ohio: Applied Philosophy Program, 1979).
5   All quotations in this paragraph are from his short essay, "On Doing the Right Thing," reprinted as an appendix to his *Our Enemy the State* (New York: Free Life Editions, 1973), pp. 93–9.
6   For a more complete account of what social conventions are and how they work, see my "Some Advantages of Social Control: An Individualist Defense," in *Public Choice*, 36 (1981): 3–16.
7   *Areopagitica*, in *John Milton: Complete Poems and Major Prose*, ed. Merrit Y. Hughes (New York: Odyssey, 1957), p. 728.
8   Ibid., p. 733.
9   Ibid.
10 It is worth noticing that, in Mark Twain's story, convention has precisely the effects Milton says the law has. It creates a sort of virtue which is not genuine and is easily corruptible, simply because it works too well in eliminating temptation. The virtue of Hadleyburg is exemplary only because it has never been subjected to a trial, but this means it is only apparent virtue, because it will fail any genuine trial it meets.
11 Perhaps I should point out in passing that the issue dealt with in these remarks of Nock and Milton is distinct from that of "the enforcement of morals" as it is presented in the writings of J. F. Stephen and

Patrick Devlin, although the two issues are connected in a way. Someone who believes in the enforcement of morals could conceivably agree with Nock and Milton that the law actually makes us worse – he might think for instance that, if we obey the strictures of morality because it is the law, we are doing it for *reasons* which are vicious rather than virtuous. Yet he might think that immoral *acts* are so horrible as such that it is worthwhile to debase people somewhat in order to reduce the frequency with which such acts are done. Where victimless crimes are concerned, this may be an uncomfortable position to hold, but it is not contradictory. It is possible to hold that "morals" should always be enforced while admitting that this would not improve anyone's character.

12 See my "Character and Thought," *American Philosophical Quarterly* (July 1978), where I argue at length that both virtues and vices rest on such notions. I also attempt to show that beliefs about the right and the good are in fact more difficult to change than other beliefs are.

13 See *Nicomachean Ethics*, 1144a13–18 and 1105a18–1105b18.

14 *Nicomachean Ethics*, 1120a30–31.

15 In addition, respect seems essential to the value we place upon having these rules observed by others in their conduct toward us. It is obvious that both laws and social norms serve to protect the conditions of our well-being – our property, our health, our "territories," and so forth – against destructive acts on the part of others. It has been pointed out, though, that damage of this kind is not the only evil we perceive in the offenses thus discouraged. Adam Smith remarked that "what chiefly enrages us against the man who injures or insults us, is the little account which he seems to make of us. . . . " We read offenses against us as expressive acts in which the offender shows that "he seems to imagine, that other people may be sacrificed at any time, to his convenience or his humour." Adam Smith, *The Theory of Moral Sentiments* (Indianapolis: Liberty Press, 1969), p. 181. A large part of the value of living in a community in which our rights are observed is the fact that it seems to show that our rights are *respected*. It may be possible for the social and political apparatus to secure such observance solely through fear of the penalties it imposes,

but order obtained i[n]
perfect, would be hollow an[d]

16 This distinction is a reformulatio[n]
Emile Durkheim. See chapter 2 of E[]
man's *Interaction Ritual* (Garden City, NY: D[]
day, 1967). The account of ceremonial norms in this
paragraph is largely drawn from Goffman. See also
his *Relations in Public* (New York: Harper, 1971),
chs. 2 and 4.

17 Paul can come to this conclusion because it explains
a coherent system of practices of which this activity
is a part. His reaching this conclusion is an instance
of what Gilbert Harman calls an inference to the
best explanation.

18 Of course, this generalization has exceptions, but
since the activities these rules make possible are
important only because of their expressive function,
the exceptions can only be cases in which the meaning of the act is one that one finds unpleasant to
express. An obvious case of this is the activity of
apologizing, in which we express a conviction that
we have wronged the person to whom the activity is
directed. Also, in some cultures, there are conventions for greeting religious and political leaders by
performing intrinsically self-abasing gestures, like
banging one's forehead on the ground. In addition,
there may be some conventions that some people
find abasing while others do not. It is conceivable,
for instance, that some people find it unpleasant to
say thank you because it includes an acknowledgment that people other than themselves have rights.
If this sort of unpleasantness were a common feature
of ceremonial observances then, naturally, the account of moral education I am offering would be no
good. However, I doubt that, in our culture at least,
they are very common.

19 It seems obvious that such a position could only be a
sensible one if applied to adults. It may turn out that
it can only be adequately supported by an argument
that is not pedagogical, like mine, but *moral*. It can
perhaps only be supported by defending a principle
like the one which H. L. Mencken called "Mencken's Law": "When A annoys or injures B on the
pretense of saving or improving X, A is a scoundrel." *Newspaper Days: 1899–1906* (New York:
Knopf, 1941), pref. This is the sort of argument
John Locke gives throughout the *First Letter Concerning Toleration*.

The Legalization of Drugs

James Q. Wilson

In 1972, the President appointed me chairman of the National Advisory Council for Drug Abuse Prevention. Created by Congress, the Council was charged with providing guidance on how best to coordinate the national war on drugs. (Yes, we called it a war then, too.) In those days, the drug we were chiefly concerned with was heroin. When I took office, heroin use had been increasing dramatically. Everybody was worried that this increase would continue. Such phrases as "heroin epidemic" were commonplace.

That same year, the eminent economist Milton Friedman published an essay in *Newsweek* in which he called for legalizing heroin. His argument was on two grounds: as a matter of ethics, the government has no right to tell people not to use heroin (or to drink or to commit suicide); as a matter of economics, the prohibition of drug use imposes costs on society that far exceed the benefits. Others, such as the psychoanalyst Thomas Szasz, made the same argument.

We did not take Friedman's advice. (Government commissions rarely do.) I do not recall that we even discussed legalizing heroin, though we did discuss (but did not take action on) legalizing a drug, cocaine, that many people then argued was benign. Our marching orders were to figure out how to win the war on heroin, not to run up the white flag of surrender.

That was 1972. Today, we have the same number of heroin addicts that we had then – half a million, give or take a few thousand. Having that many heroin addicts is no trivial matter, these people deserve our attention; but not having had an increase in that number for over fifteen years is also something that deserves our attention. What happened to the "heroin epidemic" that many people once thought would overwhelm us?

The facts are clear: a more or less stable pool of heroin addicts has been getting older, with relatively few new recruits. In 1976 the average age of heroin users who appeared in hospital emergency rooms was about twenty-seven; ten years later it was thirty-two. More than two-thirds of all heroin users appearing in emergency rooms are now over the age of thirty. Back in the early 1970s, when heroin got onto the national political agenda, the typical heroin addict was much younger, often a teenager. Household surveys show the same thing – the rate of opiate use (which includes heroin) has been flat for the better part of two decades. More fine-grained studies of inner-city neighborhoods confirm this. John Boyle and Ann Brunswick found that the percentage of young blacks in Harlem who used heroin fell from 8 percent in 1970–1 to about 3 percent in 1975–6.

Why did heroin lose its appeal for young people? When the young blacks in Harlem were asked why they stopped, more than half mentioned "trouble with the law" or "high cost" (and high cost is, of course, directly the result of law enforcement). Two-thirds said that heroin hurt their health; nearly all said they had had a bad experience with it. We need not rely, however, simply on what they said. In New York City in 1973–5, the street price of heroin rose dramatically and its purity sharply declined, probably as a result of the heroin shortage caused by the success of the Turkish government in reducing the supply of opium base and of the French government in closing down heroin-processing laboratories located in and around Marseilles. These were short-lived gains for, just as Friedman predicted, alternative sources of supply – mostly in Mexico – quickly emerged. But the three-year heroin shortage interrupted the easy recruitment of new users.

Health and related problems were no doubt part of the reason for the reduced flow of recruits. Over the preceding years, Harlem youth had watched as more and more heroin users died of overdoses, were poisoned by adulterated doses, or acquired hepatitis from dirty needles. The word got around: heroin can kill you. By 1974 new hepatitis cases and drug-overdose deaths had dropped to a fraction of what they had been in 1970.

Alas, treatment did not seem to explain much of the cessation in drug use. Treatment programs can and do help heroin addicts, but treatment did not explain the drop in the number of *new* users (who by definition had never been in treatment) nor even much of the reduction in the number of experienced users.

No one knows how much of the decline to attribute to personal observation as opposed to high prices or reduced supply. But other evidence suggests strongly that price and supply

played a large role. In 1972 the National Advisory Council was especially worried by the prospect that US servicemen returning to this country from Vietnam would bring their heroin habits with them. Fortunately, a brilliant study by Lee Robins of Washington University in St Louis put that fear to rest. She measured drug use of Vietnam veterans shortly after they had returned home. Though many had used heroin regularly while in Southeast Asia, most gave up the habit when back in the United States. The reason: here, heroin was less available and sanctions on its use were more pronounced. Of course, if a veteran had been willing to pay enough – which might have meant traveling to another city and would certainly have meant making an illegal contact with a disreputable dealer in a threatening neighborhood in order to acquire a (possibly) dangerous dose – he could have sustained his drug habit. Most veterans were unwilling to pay this price, and so their drug use declined or disappeared. . . .

Back to the Future

Now cocaine, especially in its potent form, crack, is the focus of attention. Now as in 1972 the government is trying to reduce its use. Now as then some people are advocating legalization. Is there any more reason to yield to those arguments today than there was almost two decades ago?[1]

I think not. If we had yielded in 1972 we almost certainly would have had today a permanent population of several million, not several hundred thousand, heroin addicts. If we yield now we will have a far more serious problem with cocaine.

Crack is worse than heroin by almost any measure. Heroin produces a pleasant drowsiness and, if hygienically administered, has only the physical side effects of constipation and sexual impotence. Regular heroin use incapacitates many users, especially poor ones, for any productive work or social responsibility. They will sit nodding on a street corner, helpless but at least harmless. By contrast, regular cocaine use leaves the user neither helpless nor harmless. When smoked (as with crack) or injected, cocaine produces instant, intense, and short-lived euphoria. The experience generates a powerful desire to repeat it. If the drug is readily available, repeat use will occur. Those people who progress to "bingeing" on cocaine become devoted to the drug and its effects to the exclusion of almost all other considerations – job, family, children, sleep, food, even sex. Dr Frank Gawin at Yale and Dr Everett Ellinwood at Duke report that a substantial percentage of all high-dose, binge users become uninhibited, impulsive, hypersexual, compulsive, irritable, and hyperactive. Their moods vacillate dramatically, leading at times to violence and homicide.

Women are much more likely to use crack than heroin, and if they are pregnant, the effects on their babies are tragic. Douglas Besharov, who has been following the effects of drugs on infants for twenty years, writes that nothing he learned about heroin prepared him for the devastation of cocaine. Cocaine harms the fetus and can lead to physical deformities or neurological damage. Some crack babies have for all practical purposes suffered a disabling stroke while still in the womb. The long-term consequences of this brain damage are lowered cognitive ability and the onset of mood disorders. Besharov estimates that about 30,000 to 50,000 such babies are born every year, about 7,000 in New York City alone. There may be ways to treat such infants, but from everything we now know the treatment will be long, difficult, and expensive. Worse, the mothers who are most likely to produce crack babies are precisely the ones who, because of poverty or temperament, are least able and willing to obtain such treatment. In fact, anecdotal evidence suggests that crack mothers are likely to abuse their infants.

The notion that abusing drugs such as cocaine is a "victimless crime" is not only absurd but dangerous. Even ignoring the fetal drug syndrome, crack-dependent people are, like heroin addicts, individuals who regularly victimize their children by neglect, their spouses by improvidence, their employers by lethargy, and their co-workers by carelessness. Society is not and could never be a collection of autonomous individuals.

We all have a stake in ensuring that each of us displays a minimal level of dignity, responsibility, and empathy. We cannot, of course, coerce people into goodness, but we can and should insist that some standards must be met if society itself – on which the very existence of the human personality depends – is to persist. Drawing the line that defines those standards is difficult and contentious, but if crack and heroin use do not fall below it, what does? . . .

Have We Lost?

Many people who agree that there are risks in legalizing cocaine or heroin still favor it because, they think, we have lost the war on drugs. "Nothing we have done has worked" and the current federal policy is just "more of the same." Whatever the costs of greater drug use, surely they would be less than the costs of our present, failed efforts.

That is exactly what I was told in 1972 – and heroin is not quite as bad a drug as cocaine. We did not surrender and we did not lose. We did not win, either. What the nation accomplished then was what most efforts to save people from themselves accomplish: the problem was contained and the number of victims minimized, all at a considerable cost in law enforcement and increased crime. Was the cost worth it? I think so, but others may disagree. What are the lives of would-be addicts worth? I recall some people saying to me then, "Let them kill themselves." I was appalled. Happily, such views did not prevail. . . .

It took about ten years to contain heroin. We have had experience with crack for only about three or four years. Each year we spend perhaps $11 billion on law enforcement (and some of that goes to deal with marijuana) and perhaps $2 billion on treatment. Large sums, but not sums that should lead anyone to say, "We just can't afford this any more."

The illegality of drugs increases crime, partly because some users turn to crime to pay for their habits, partly because some users are stimulated by certain drugs (such as crack or PCP) to act more violently or ruthlessly than they otherwise would, and partly because criminal organizations seeking to control drug supplies use force to manage their markets. These also are serious costs, but no one knows how much they would be reduced if drugs were legalized. Addicts would no longer steal to pay black-market prices for drugs, a real gain. But some, perhaps a great deal, of that gain would be offset by the great increase in the number of addicts. These people, nodding on heroin or living in the delusion-ridden high of cocaine, would hardly be ideal employees. Many would steal simply to support themselves, since snatch-and-grab, opportunistic crime can be managed even by people unable to hold a regular job or plan an elaborate crime. Those British addicts who get their supplies from government clinics are not models of law-abiding decency. Most are in crime, and though their per-capita rate of criminality may be lower thanks to the cheapness of their drugs, the total volume of crime they produce may be quite large. Of course, society could decide to support all unemployable addicts on welfare, but that would mean that gains from lowered rates of crime would have to be offset by large increases in welfare budgets.

Proponents of legalization claim that the costs of having more addicts around would be largely if not entirely offset by having more money available with which to treat and care for them. The money would come from taxes levied on the sale of heroin and cocaine.

To obtain this fiscal dividend, however, legalization's supporters must first solve an economic dilemma. If they want to raise a lot of money to pay for welfare and treatment, the tax rate on the drugs will have to be quite high. Even if they themselves do not want a high rate, the politicians' love of "sin taxes" would probably guarantee that it would be high anyway. But the higher the tax, the higher the price of the drug, and the higher the price the greater the likelihood that addicts will turn to crime to find the money for it and that criminal organizations will be formed to sell tax-free drugs at below-market rates. If we managed to keep taxes (and thus prices) low, we would get that much less money to pay for welfare and treatment and more people could afford to become

addicts. There may be an optimal tax rate for drugs that maximizes revenue while minimizing crime, bootlegging, and the recruitment of new addicts, but our experience with alcohol does not suggest that we know how to find it. . . .

The Benefits of Illegality

We are now investing substantially in drug-education programs in the schools. Though we do not yet know for certain what will work, there are some promising leads. But I wonder how credible such programs would be if they were aimed at dissuading children from doing something perfectly legal. We could, of course, treat drug education like smoking education: inhaling crack and inhaling tobacco are both legal, but you should not do it because it is bad for you. That tobacco is bad for you is easily shown: the Surgeon General has seen to that. But what do we say about crack? It is pleasurable, but devoting yourself to so much pleasure is not a good idea (though perfectly legal)? Unlike tobacco, cocaine will not give you cancer or emphysema, but will it lead you to neglect your duties to family, job, and neighborhood? Everybody is doing cocaine, but you should not?

Again, it might be possible under a legalized regime to have effective drug-prevention programs, but their effectiveness would depend heavily, I think, on first having decided that cocaine use, like tobacco use, is purely a matter of practical consequences; no fundamental moral significance attaches to either. But if we believe – as I do – that dependency on certain mind-altering drugs *is* a moral issue and that their illegality rests in part on their immorality, then legalizing them undercuts, if it does not eliminate altogether, the moral message.

That message is at the root of the distinction we now make between nicotine and cocaine. Both are highly addictive, both have harmful physical effects. But we treat the two drugs differently, not simply because nicotine is so widely used as to be beyond the reach of effective prohibition, but because its use does not destroy the user's essential humanity. Tobacco shortens one's life, cocaine debases it. Nicotine alters one's habits, cocaine alters one's soul. The heavy use of crack, unlike the heavy use of tobacco, corrodes those natural sentiments of sympathy and duty that constitute our human nature and make possible our social life. To say, as does Nadelmann, that distinguishing morally between tobacco and cocaine is "little more than a transient prejudice" is close to saying that morality itself is but a prejudice.

The Alcohol Problem

Now we have arrived where many arguments about legalizing drugs begin: is there any reason to treat heroin and cocaine differently from the way we treat alcohol?

There is no easy answer to that question because, as with so many human problems, one cannot decide simply on the basis either of moral principles or of individual consequences; one has to temper any policy by a commonsense judgment of what is possible. Alcohol, like heroin, cocaine, PCP, and marijuana, is a drug – that is, a mood-altering substance – and consumed to excess it certainly has harmful consequences: auto accidents, bar-room fights, bedroom shootings. It is also, for some people, addictive. We cannot confidently compare the addictive powers of these drugs, but the best evidence suggests that crack and heroin are much more addictive than alcohol.

Many people, Nadelmann included, argue that since the health and financial costs of alcohol abuse are so much higher than those of cocaine or heroin abuse, it is hypocritical folly to devote our efforts to preventing cocaine or drug use. But as Mark Kleiman of Harvard has pointed out, this comparison is quite misleading. What Nadelmann is doing is showing that a *legalized* drug (alcohol) produces greater social harm than *illegal* ones (cocaine and heroin). But of course. Suppose that in the 1920s we had made heroin and cocaine legal and alcohol illegal. Can anyone doubt that Nadelmann would now be writing that it is folly to continue our ban on alcohol because cocaine and heroin are so much more harmful? . . .

If I am Wrong . . .

No one can know what our society would be like if we changed the law to make access to cocaine, heroin, and PCP easier. I believe, for reasons given, that the result would be a sharp increase in use, a more widespread degradation of the human personality, and a greater rate of accidents and violence.

I may be wrong. If I am, then we will needlessly have incurred heavy costs in law enforcement and some forms of criminality. But if I am right, and the legalizers prevail anyway, then we will have consigned millions of people, hundreds of thousands of infants, and hundreds of neighborhoods to a life of oblivion and disease. To the lives and families destroyed by alcohol we will have added countless more destroyed by cocaine, heroin, PCP, and whatever else a basement scientist can invent.

Human character is formed by society; indeed, human character is inconceivable without society, and good character is less likely in a bad society. Will we, in the name of an abstract doctrine of radical individualism, and with the false comfort of suspect predictions, decide to take the chance that somehow individual decency can survive amid a more general level of degradation?

I think not. The American people are too wise for that, whatever the academic essayists and cocktail-party pundits may say. But if Americans today are less wise than I suppose, then Americans at some future time will look back on us now and wonder, what kind of people were they that they could have done such a thing?

Note

1   I do not here take up the question of marijuana. For a variety of reasons – its widespread use and its lesser tendency to addict – it presents a different problem from cocaine or heroin. For a penetrating analysis, see Mark Kleiman, *Marijuana: Costs of Abuse, Costs of Control* (Greenwood Press).

Paternalism and
drug would no
be a concept
here, that c
to state
that th
alize
ish

31

Why We Should Decrimin
Drug Use

Douglas Husak

Philosophers have been strangely silent about the topic of illicit drugs, even though it is a gold mine of philosophical questions. It is distressing to see how few of the dozens of books now available on current moral and social issues contain sections on drug issues. It seems far more pressing to question the punishment of drug users than the execution of murderers – mostly because there are so many more of them. Approximately 80 to 90 million people have used illicit drugs at some point in their lives. There are well over 400,000 drug offenders in jail, about 130,000 for possession alone. Unlike in the case of capital murderers, it is plausible to suppose that drug users should not be punished at all, and this is what I want to argue here.

I suspect that the best single explanation for the philosophical neglect of this topic is that it is has a considerable empirical content. When I raise this issue with my undergraduate classes, and ask why we should or should not punish drug users, less than a minute is needed before someone makes a controversial empirical claim about the effects of given drugs on users or on society in general. No one can hope to address the set of moral and legal issues about drug decriminalization without knowing a lot of facts about drugs and drug users. Contrast this with abortion, in which the relevant facts can be learned fairly quickly. Philosophers understandably tend to shy away from topics with a heavily empirical component.

Yet without the input of philosophers, the field has been left largely to scholars in criminal justice, nearly all of whom profess to have no theory of criminalization, but seem mostly to be consequentialists. They prepare cost-benefit analyses of the relative merits of criminalization and decriminalization. Many have concluded that our current drug laws are ineffective and counterproductive. They are probably correct, but that is not the line of inquiry I want to pursue here. As philosophers, I think we should be more interested in examining arguments of *principle*.

I The Meaning of Decriminalization

First, there is absolutely no consensus among those of us who work in criminal theory about the meaning of such terms as *legalization* or *decriminalization*. So I resort to stipulation. What I mean by the use of the term "decriminalization" in this context is that the *use* of a given

...be a criminal offense. I take it to
...al truth, for which I will not argue
...riminal offenses render persons liable
...unishment. Thus anyone who thinks
... use of a given drug should be decrimin-
... believes that persons should not be pun-
...d merely for using that drug.

I am aware that there is enormous confusion
about this topic. In polls, many respondents
report that they do not want to see a given
drug decriminalized, but do not favor punishing
people who merely use that drug. If my account
of decriminalization is accepted, this response is
incoherent.

For a number of reasons, this definition of
decriminalization is deceptively simple. First,
there really is little punishment for use today.
In most but not all jurisdictions, what is punished is possession rather than use. Technically,
then, drug use is generally not criminalized. But
I take the fact that statutes punish possession
rather than use to be relatively unimportant.
Possession is punished rather than use because
it is easier to prove. In what follows, I ignore
this complication and continue to suppose that
decriminalization pertains to drug use. Except
perhaps in fantastic cases, no one can use a drug
without possessing it.

Second, there is no clear understanding of
what kinds of state responses amount to punishments. Many reformers argue that drug users
should be fined rather than imprisoned, and
they call this idea decriminalization. Others
argue that drug users should be made to
undergo treatment, and they also call this idea
decriminalization. Whether these proposals are
compatible with what I mean by decriminalization depends on whether fines or coerced treatment are modes *of* punishment rather than
alternatives *to* punishment. I think both fines
and coerced treatment are modes of punishment. Even though they are probably preferable
to what we now do to drug users, these responses are ruled out by decriminalization as I
construe it. But that is a quibble I hope not to
worry about. Simply put, whatever you take
punishment to be, that is what decriminalization forbids the state from doing to people who
merely use drugs.

Third, decriminalization as I propose to define it has no implications for what should be
done to persons who *produce* or *sell* drugs.
Therefore, it is not really a comprehensive
drug policy that can rival the status quo. The
considerations that I think work in favor of
decriminalizing use are somewhat different
from those that apply to the decriminalization
of production and sale, so I propose to put
production and sale aside in this essay. This is
bound to disappoint some people. Many
thinkers are attracted to decriminalization, or
reluctantly driven to support it, because they
hope to end the violence, black market, and
involvement of organized crime in drug transactions today. These sound like worthwhile objectives, but drug decriminalization per se does
not achieve them. I think we should start by
clarifying what should happen to drug users,
and *then* move to the issue of whether or how
production and sale should be regulated. Again,
I am aware that many thoughtful people believe
that these topics should all be tackled simultaneously, but I think it is easier to proceed one
step at a time.

Finally, I admit that there is something odd
about my understanding of decriminalization.
What I call decriminalization in the context of
drugs is comparable to what was called prohibition in the context of alcohol from 1920 to
1933. During those memorable years, production and sale were banned, but not the use or
mere possession of alcohol. If we replicated that
approach in our drug policy, I would call it
decriminalization. That is admittedly odd, but
it underscores the fact that our response to illicit
drug users today is far more punitive than anything we ever did to drinkers.

II   The Best Reason to Decriminalize Drug Use

With these preliminaries out of the way, let me
proceed to the basic question to be addressed.
In my judgment, the fundamental issue is not
whether to *de*criminalize the use of any or all
drugs, but whether to *criminalize* the use of any
or all drugs. The status quo must be defended.

If this is the right question to ask, I would now like to offer what I believe to be the most plausible answer to it: The best reason *not* to criminalize drug use is that no argument in favor of criminalizing drug use is any good – no argument is good enough to justify criminalization. I want to make three points about this general strategy for decriminalization.

First, I recognize that this approach is not very exciting. My reason to oppose criminalization does not invoke any deep principle worth fighting about like freedom of speech or religion. I am not sure that there is any deep principle that *all* drug prohibitions violate. In particular, my approach does not invoke the principle that some libertarians cite: the "freedom to do whatever you want to your own body." I do not invoke this principle because I do not believe it is true. I am not a libertarian. Whether you have a right to do something you want to your body depends on what happens when you do it.

Then again, *some* drug prohibitions seem to violate deep principles that philosophers should care about. This becomes more apparent when you pause to consider exactly what it is that drug proscriptions are designed to prevent. Most drugs have a legitimate use, so drug consumption per se is rarely prohibited. Instead, the use of most drugs is prohibited only for a given purpose. To get directly to the heart of the matter, the proscribed purpose is usually to produce a state of intoxication or a drug "high." In case there is any doubt, let me cite the California criminal statute regulating nitrous oxide. This statute makes it a crime for "any person [to possess] nitrous oxide . . . with the intent to breathe [or] inhale . . . for purposes of causing a condition of intoxication, elation, euphoria, dizziness, stupefaction, or dulling of the senses or for the purpose of, in any manner, changing . . . mental processes"[1] The ultimate objective of this statute is to prevent persons from breathing something in order to change their mental processes. It is hard to see why this objective is legitimate in a state committed to freedom of thought and expression.[2] I am not sure that *all* drug prohibitions so transparently jeopardize our right to freedom of thought. In

any event, I do not believe we need to appeal to any deep principle to resist drug prohibitions generally.[3]

Second, my case is necessarily inconclusive. I am in the unenviable position of trying to prove a negative. How can I hope to show that no argument in favor of criminalizing drug use is good enough? All I can ever aspire to do is to respond to the best arguments that have been given. I am reminded of a remark made by Hume. "'Tis impossible to refute a system, which has never been explain'd. In such a manner of fighting in the dark, a man loses his blows in the air, and often places them where the enemy is not present."[4] This is the predicament someone faces in trying to defend drug decriminalization. I am usually asked to go first on panels convened to debate drug decriminalization, but I think I should go last so that I can respond to what others think are good reasons for criminalization.

Third, my case for decriminalization has the advantage of making minimal assumptions about justice. I assume that no one should be punished unless there are excellent reasons for doing so. Punishment, after all, is the worst thing our state can do to us. The imposition of punishment must satisfy a very demanding standard of justification.[5] It is hard to imagine that anyone would reject this assumption.

Thus my case against criminalization depends on the claim that no case for criminalization has been adequately defended. It is utterly astounding, I think, that no very good argument for drug prohibitions has ever been given. When I am asked to recommend the best book or article that makes a philosophically plausible case for punishing drug users, I am embarrassed to say that I have little to suggest.[6]

Let me then cut directly to my own conclusions. No single argument for decriminalization responds to all arguments for criminalization. We must respond argument-by-argument, and, I think, drug-by-drug. We may have good reasons to criminalize some drugs, but not others. For example, I do not know anyone who wants to punish persons who use caffeine. Surely this is because of empirical facts about caffeine – how it affects those who use it and society in general. I can certainly *imagine* a drug that people should be punished for using. Such drugs are easy to describe; they are vividly portrayed in great works of fiction. Consider the substance that transformed Dr. Jekyll into Mr. Hyde. If a drug literally turned users into homicidal monsters, we would have excellent reasons to prohibit its consumption. Fortunately, no such drug actually exists. In fact, I have never seen a persuasive argument for punishing persons who use any drug that I am aware is widely used for recreational purposes.

III Criminalization

Any good reason to criminalize a kind of behavior invokes a theory of criminalization. We cannot decide whether we have a good reason to punish persons who use drugs in particular unless we know what would count as a good reason to punish anyone for anything. We do not really have a theory of criminalization in the real world, unless "more is always better" qualifies for a theory.[7] I want to pause briefly to describe what passes for a theory of criminalization in our constitutional law today.[8] Most laws limit or restrict liberties. When the constitutionality of these laws is challenged, courts respond by dividing liberties into two kinds: *fundamental* and *non-fundamental*. The constitutionality of legislation that restricts a fundamental liberty is subjected to "strict scrutiny" and is evaluated by applying the onerous "compelling state interest" test. Virtually all criminal laws, however, limit non-fundamental liberties, and they are assessed by applying the much less demanding "rational basis" test. Under this test, the challenged law will be upheld if it is substantially related to a legitimate government purpose. The legitimate government purpose need not be the actual objective of the legislation – only its conceivable objective. Since only those laws that lack a conceivable legitimate purpose will fail this test, courts almost never find a law to be unconstitutional when non-fundamental liberties are restricted. As a result, the state needs only some conceivable legitimate purpose to enact the great

majority of criminal laws on the books today – most notably, drug prohibitions, which are always evaluated by applying the rational basis test. So persons who break these laws can be punished simply because the state has a rational basis to do so.

What is remarkable about this approach is its complete indifference to the distinction between criminal and non-criminal legislation.[9] It is one thing to enact non-criminal laws that pass the rational basis test. But it is quite another when criminal legislation is assessed by that same standard. Criminal law is different – it is importantly dissimilar from other kinds of law. Many of the arguments I have heard for drug prohibitions do a perfectly good job explaining why rational persons might well decide not to use illicit drugs, or why the state may have good reasons to discourage people from using drugs, but I fear they do not provide a justification for *punishing* drug users.

If our theory of criminalization in the real world is so bad, one would have thought that the most distinguished criminal theorists of our day would have had lots to say to rectify the situation. But they have said surprising little. They mostly continue to argue about the *harm principle*. But debates about whether to accept the harm principle in our theory of criminalization do not get us very far when trying to decide whether to punish drug users. We have excellent reasons to punish people who commit theft or rape. These offenses harm others by violating their rights. But this rationale cannot explain why drug users should be punished. I do not think there is any sense of harm or any theory of rights that can be invoked to show that I harm someone or violate his rights when I inject heroin or smoke crack. At most, I risk harm to myself or to others when I use a drug. I conceptualize offenses that create only a *risk* of harm that may or may not materialize as *inchoate* offenses – similar to attempt, solicitation, or conspiracy. If I am correct, the criteria we should apply to assess the justifiability of drug proscriptions are those we should apply to assess the justifiability of inchoate offenses. Unfortunately, we have no such criteria. Almost no theorist has tried very hard to extend a theory of criminalization to conduct that creates a risk of harm rather than harm itself.[10]

Notice, however, the enormous burden an argument for criminalization would have to bear. As I have said, there are about 80 or 90 million Americans who have used an illicit drug at some point in their lives. That is approximately 42 percent of our population aged 12 and over. About 15 million Americans used an illicit drug last year, on literally billions of occasions. Very few of these occasions produced any harm. Longitudinal studies do not indicate that the population of persons who ever have used illicit drugs is very different from the population of lifetime abstainers in any ways that seem relevant to criminalization. So any argument for punishment would have to justify punishing the many, whose behavior is innocuous, for the sake of some objective that results in a very tiny percentage of cases. Many attempted murders result in successful murders, which are harms, but very few instances of drug use bring about any result we should describe as significantly harmful.

When you cannot possibly punish *all* of the people who commit a crime, you can only punish *some*. Inevitably, those who get arrested, prosecuted, and sentenced are the least powerful. Drug prohibition would have vanished long ago had whites been sent to prison for drug offenses at the same rate as blacks. Although minorities are no more likely to use illicit drugs, they are far more likely to be arrested, prosecuted, and punished when they do. This is one of the features of drug prohibitions that should outrage us all. Some people try to package drug prohibitions as a benefit to minorities, but there is plenty of evidence that they devastate minority communities and will continue to do so as long as enforcement is so selective. And yet enforcement will always be selective, since every offender cannot possibly be punished.

If drug prohibitions are so bad for minority communities, one may wonder why minority leaders are not more outspoken about the drug war. In fact, blacks are more ambivalent than whites about drug policy.[11] Overall, blacks tend to have more negative opinions about drugs (both licit and illicit) than whites. At the same time, blacks are less likely than whites to believe that the solution to the problem is to enforce prohibition with severe punishments. Black mothers who are staunchly anti-drug are not enthusiastic about policies that lock up their sons and daughters for lengthy periods of time. But why are blacks not even more critical of the status quo? No one explanation can be given. But my own hypothesis cites the role of religion on attitudes about drugs. Although opinions about drug policy vary somewhat with age, education, income, and gender, no variable correlates with anti-drug attitudes more closely than religion and, at least in the United States, Protestant Christianity in particular.

IV   Predictions: A Bad Reason to Criminalize

I have space to provide a brief critique of only *one* argument, and I apologize in advance if I neglect the reader's own candidate for the best reason to criminalize drug use. I will not comment on drugs and kids, drugs and health, drugs and crime, or drugs and morality. But I think the argument I discuss here may be the most common. It rests on predictions that the use of drugs would soar if we stopped punishing persons who use them. This argument, I think, flounders on both empirical and normative grounds.

I begin with the empirical considerations. My conclusion is that we simply do not have any good basis to predict how the amount of harm caused by drugs would change if we did not punish those who use them. Many persons find my uncertainty to be unwarranted. Economic models indicate that the frequency of use is a function of costs: decriminalize use, and the monetary and non-monetary costs of drugs will go down. The trouble is that all predictions about how rates of consumption will rise after use is decriminalized assume that nothing else will change. One thing we can predict is that many other things will change if drug use is decriminalized. Let me mention just a few things that might very well change, and that make all such predictions perilous.

I'll begin by challenging the claim that de-criminalization will cause the monetary price of drugs to plummet. Why assume that decriminalization will make illicit drugs significantly more affordable? Decriminalization itself, as I have emphasized, need not allow illicit drugs to be sold with impunity. If decriminalization does not extend to sale, it need not have much effect on the monetary cost of drugs. But even were sale decriminalized, illicit drugs would become subject to taxation. I will not try to estimate the optimal rate of taxation. Whatever the exact amount, we can be sure that taxes would add enormously to the price of newly decriminalized drugs.

Another factor influencing the price of de-criminalized illicit drugs is very difficult to estimate. If illicit drugs are anywhere near as harmful as many people believe, some mechanism must be created to compensate victims for the harms they suffer when drugs are used. These harms might befall users themselves, or be suffered by others. One way to compensate victims for each of these kinds of harms is by allowing lawsuits against producers of illicit drugs. We have been reluctant to allow such lawsuits in the cases of tobacco, alcohol, or firearms; powerful lobbies have fought against them for years. But we need not be so reluctant if we establish a new system of sale for illicit drugs. Producers could be made to pay for the costs of the various harms that their customers cause to themselves or to others. Producers would be able to pay these costs, and remain in business, only if they could pass them along to buyers by raising their prices. How much of an increase in price would be needed to compensate all of the victims for the harms they suffer when illicit drugs are used? No one can be sure. We cannot begin to answer this question unless we know how dangerous illicit drugs really are. I believe that the dangers of illicit drugs tend to be grossly exaggerated. Even if I am mistaken about the dangers of illicit drugs today, we can be confident that illicit drugs would be less dangerous in a world in which production and sale had been decriminalized. In such a world, suppliers would have enormous incentives to make their drugs as safe as possible

in order to limit the amount of money they would be required to pay when harm was caused by the use of their product. If a given drug is very dangerous, we might even find that no company could hope to make a profit by selling it, and the drug would disappear from the lawful market. We simply do not know how dangerous illicit drugs will turn out to be after decriminalization – but financial incentives are bound to make them less harmful.

As a result of these two factors, we have almost no basis for estimating how the monetary price of decriminalized drugs would differ from their price in today's black market – if, that is, decriminalization were extended to production and sale. We do not know how much states will decide to tax the sale of drugs. In addition, we do not know how much sellers will have to charge in order to survive when lawsuits are brought against them. If this latter figure is high, drugs will be expensive, and fears about cheap drugs will be put to rest. If this figure is low, the price of drugs will decrease. But if the amount sellers must charge as a result of these lawsuits is low, it means that drugs will turn out to be less dangerous than we thought. If drugs turned out to be less dangerous than we thought, we will come to wonder why we were so worried about making them more affordable in the first place.

However uncertain we may be about how decriminalization will affect the monetary price of drugs, it will clearly eliminate the non-monetary cost of use. People will no longer fear arrest and prosecution. To the extent that this fear has helped to keep illicit drug use in check, we can anticipate that decriminalization would cause the incidence of drug use to rise. But to what extent? How will consumption change if drug users need not worry about punishment? No single piece of evidence on this point is decisive. But several factors suggest that the threat of punishment is not especially effective in curbing drug use. In what follows, I will describe a number of reasons to doubt that the removal of criminal penalties would cause a significant increase in the use of illicit drugs.

One source of evidence is obtained through surveys. People who have never used drugs are asked to explain their reasons for abstaining, and to speculate about how their willingness to experiment would be affected by a change in the law. Very few respondents cite their fear of punishment as a substantial factor in their decision not to try drugs.[12] The more dangerous the drug is perceived to be, the smaller the number of respondents who mention the law when asked to explain their reluctance to use it. Other surveys ask former users why they decided to quit. Those who once used drugs are asked why they do not continue to do so today, and to explain why their behavior has changed. Very few respondents report that fear of arrest and prosecution led them to stop using drugs. They cite a bad experience with a drug or some new responsibility, like a job or a newborn, but rarely mention the risk of punishment.[13] Of course, the value of these kinds of surveys is questionable. We may doubt that people have accurate insights into why they behave as they do, or what might lead them to behave differently. Surely, however, these surveys provide better evidence than mere conjecture. These surveys suggest that the fear of punishment is not a major factor in explaining why drug use is not more pervasive than it is.

For further evidence about how the fear of punishment affects the incidence of drug use, we might examine how trends in illicit drug use over the past 30 years are correlated with changes in law enforcement. If the fear of punishment were a significant factor in deterring illicit drug use, one would expect that rates of consumption would decline as punishments increased in frequency and severity. There is no correlation, however, between the frequency and severity of punishment and trends in drug use. If we look at the decade from 1980 to 1990, a case could be made that punishments were effective in deterring use. The incidence of illicit drug use, which peaked in 1979, steadily decreased throughout the 1980s. But frequent and severe punishments have not caused further declines during the 1990s; drug use has remained relatively flat in the past decade. We reach the same conclusion when we examine the data on a state-by-state basis. States with greater rates of incarceration for drug offenders

tend to experience higher rates of drug use. Prohibitionists who predict a massive increase in drug use after decriminalization must struggle to explain these data. If punitive drug policies keep drug use in check, why do actual trends in drug consumption prove so resistant to the massive efforts we have made to punish drug users?

Additional evidence can be gleaned from the experience of other countries, where the fear of arrest and prosecution for the use of given drugs is practically non-existent. Most European countries have lower rates of illicit drug use, even though given drugs are often higher in quality, lower in price, and less likely to result in punishments. American teenagers consume more marijuana and most other illicit drugs than their European counterparts, although European teens are more likely to smoke cigarettes and drink alcohol. Consider the Netherlands, which is known for its relatively permissive drug laws. Although marijuana prevalence rates are roughly comparable in the two countries, about twice as many residents of the United States have experimented with other kinds of illicit drugs. In general, data from other parts of the world provide better evidence for an inverse than for a positive correlation between severities of punishments and rates of illicit drug use. Admittedly, however, this evidence is inconclusive. No country in the world has implemented decriminalization as I have defined it here.

The history of the United States provides further reason to doubt that fear of punishment plays a major role in reducing the use of illicit drugs. We must keep in mind that, for all practical purposes, drug prohibition did not begin until the early part of the twentieth century. In the nineteenth century, purchases of opium, morphine, cocaine, and marijuana were subject to almost no restrictions. Americans could buy these drugs in many different varieties from several different sources, including by mail order. But even though criminal penalties were not imposed for the use of opiates and cocaine, these drugs were probably less popular than today. Admittedly, however, the verdict of history is mixed. Most Americans agree that our era of alcohol prohibition was a dismal failure. By most accounts, however, per capita consumption of alcohol decreased throughout prohibition, and did not return to pre-prohibition levels for many years. This finding has led some social scientists to conclude that prohibition "worked" after all – if a reduction in use is the most important criterion of success. Others are skeptical. Curiously, however, even those social scientists who insist that alcohol prohibition was effective almost never recommend that our country should reinstate that policy.

Trends in the use of *licit* drugs provide yet another source of evidence. Prohibitionists tend to point to a reduction in illicit drug use over the last 20 years as a reason to believe that severe punishments have been effective in curbing drug use. Comparable declines in the use of alcohol and tobacco, however, have taken place over this same period of time, even without the threat of criminal liability. Rates of monthly illicit drug use in the United States peaked at about 14 percent in 1979, steadily declined to a low of just above 5 percent in 1992, and slowly increased thereafter to about 6 percent in 2001. Trends in alcohol and tobacco use exhibit more similarities than dissimilarities with these patterns. The overall use of alcohol and tobacco declined throughout the 1980s, and rebounded somewhat during the 1990s. We have ample evidence that the use of licit drugs can be decreased without the need to resort to criminal sanctions. We should assume that the same is true of illicit drugs.

If changes in the certainty and severity of punishment are not major factors in explaining trends in illicit drug use, what *does* account for these patterns? This is one of the most fascinating and difficult questions that arises about drug use, and I confess to having no good answer to it. Trends in the use of both licit and illicit drugs are as baffling and mysterious as trends in fashion. Unless we have better theories to explain why people use drugs, our forecasts about the future are bound to be simplistic. No one has a convincing explanation of why the use of a given drug increases or decreases within a given group in a given place at a given time. By 2001, the popularity of crack

in inner cities had waned enormously. Crack is no longer regarded as "cool" or "hip." Why? No simple answer can be given. Most experts believe that a heightened consciousness about health contributed to the reduction in the use of licit drugs during the 1980s. But what caused this growing concern about health, and why did it not lead rates of drug use to fall still further throughout the 1990s? Again, no answer is clearly correct. But credibility is strained if we suppose that a factor is important in accounting for decreases in the consumption of alcohol and tobacco but unimportant in accounting for decreases in the consumption of illicit drugs, especially when the patterns of these decreases are roughly comparable. In any event, we have little reason to believe that punishments play a central role in explaining trends in drug use.

I have provided several reasons to doubt that punishment is needed to keep rates of illicit drug use within reasonable bounds. But skepticism about the efficacy of punishment as a deterrent to drug use is only a small part of the reason why predictions about drug use after decriminalization are so tenuous. Recall the terms of decriminalization that I have offered here. The only change that this policy requires is that the state would not *punish* anyone simply for using a drug for recreational purposes. The state may adopt any number of devices to discourage drug use, as long as these devices are not punitive. Even more important, institutions other than the state can and do play a significant role in discouraging drug use. After decriminalization, some of these institutions might exert even more influence. Private businesses, schools, insurance companies, and universities, to cite just a few examples, might adopt policies that discriminate against drug users. Suppose that employers fired or denied promotions to workers who use cocaine. Suppose that schools barred students who drink alcohol from participating in extracurricular activities. Suppose that insurance companies charged higher premiums to policyholders who smoke tobacco. Suppose that colleges denied loans and grants to undergraduates who use marijuana. I do not endorse any of these ideas; many seem unwise and destined to backfire.

Removing drug-using kids from schools, for example, seems destined to *increase* their consumption. I simply point out that such institutions could have a far greater impact than our criminal justice system on people's decisions to use drugs.

Predictions about drug use after decriminalization are confounded by yet another phenomenon – the "forbidden fruit" effect. Many people, adolescents in particular, are attracted to an activity precisely because it is forbidden or perceived as dangerous. Much of the thrill of illicit drug use stems from its illegality and the culture of deviance that surrounds it. Might the use of some illicit drugs actually *decrease* because they are no longer forbidden? If we change the law, the appeal of illicit drugs will be changed as well. To what extent? No one knows. Although many scholars have noted the forbidden fruit effect, serious research has yet to demonstrate its real significance.

Alarming predictions about future use assume that the drugs of tomorrow will resemble the drugs of today. This assumption seems extraordinarily naïve. The development of new and different substances makes predictions about consumption enormously speculative. Even though many illicit drugs – heroin and LSD, for example – were originally created by pharmaceutical companies, reputable corporations have tried hard to disassociate their drug products from illicit drugs. Decriminalization may lead pharmaceutical companies to expend their talent and ingenuity to create better and safer recreational drugs. One can only wonder about the products that might be developed if the best minds were put to the task. If more enjoyable and less dangerous drugs could be perfected, consumption might boom. But the development of better and safer drugs would make the increase in consumption less of a problem.

Whether or not better drugs appear on the market, no one can predict how users will substitute newly decriminalized drugs for existing licit drugs. After decriminalization, consumers will have lawful alternatives that we take for granted in other contexts. We simply do not know whether and to what extent users will substitute newly decriminalized drugs for those licit drugs they now tend to prefer. If a great deal of substitution takes place, the enormous social harm presently caused by tobacco and alcohol might decline considerably. So the total amount of harm caused by *all* categories of drugs might actually *decrease*, even if the consumption of illicit drugs were to *increase*. I do not find this conjecture so implausible. Over time, one would expect that users would tend to gravitate toward those drugs that could be integrated more easily into their lifestyles. In particular, we should welcome a possible reduction in alcohol use. As any college administrator knows, alcohol is the drug implicated in most of the date rapes, property damage, and violent behavior on campus. A possible decrease in alcohol consumption is one of the silver linings on the feared black cloud of drug decriminalization.

For all of these reasons, we should avoid predictions about how the decriminalization of drugs will affect rates of consumption. An even more important point is that these empirical conjectures are not especially relevant to the topic at hand. We are looking for a respectable reason to criminalize drug use. Predictions about how decriminalization will cause an increase in drug use simply do not provide such a reason. Indeed, this reason could be given against repealing virtually any law, however unjustified it may be. Let me illustrate this point by providing an example of an imaginary crime that I assume everyone would agree to be unjustified. Suppose that the state sought to curb obesity by prohibiting people from eating pizza – an offense that would pass the rational basis test, by the way. Suppose that a group of philosophers convened to discuss whether we should change this law and decriminalize pizza consumption. Someone would be likely to protest that repealing this law would cause the consumption of pizza to increase. I imagine they would be correct. But surely this prediction would not serve to justify retaining this imaginary prohibition. If we lacked a good reason to attack the problem of obesity by punishing pizza eaters in the first place, the effects of repeal on pizza consumption would not provide such a reason. And so with drugs. Unless we already *have* a reason to punish pizza consumption, the prediction does not provide a good reason to *continue* to punish it.

If there is a good reason to criminalize illicit drug use, we have yet to find it. We need a better reason to criminalize something other than predictions about how its frequency would increase if punishments were not imposed. These predictions are dubious both normatively and (in this case) empirically. Despite my uncertainty about the future, there is *one* prediction about which

we can be absolutely confident. After decriminalization, those who use illicit drugs will not face arrest and prosecution. The lives of drug users would not be devastated by a state that is committed to waging war against them. Punishment, we must always be reminded, is the worst thing a state can do to us. The single prediction we can safely make about decriminalization is that it will improve the lives of the hundreds of thousands of people who otherwise would be punished for the crime of using drugs for recreational purposes.

Notes

These comments are drawn from two books I have written about drug prohibitions. See Douglas Husak, *Drugs and Rights* (Cambridge: Cambridge University Press, 1992); and *Legalize This! The Case for Decriminalizing Drugs* (London: Verso Press, 2002).

1   *California State Penal Code*, §381(b) (2002).
2   This point is made nicely by Richard Boire. See his http://www.cognitiveliberty.org.
3   I would be happy to be mistaken about this. Anyone who is more confident in his ability to identify and defend deep principles that are violated by all drug prohibitions is welcome to enlighten and assist me.
4   David Hume, *A Treatise of Human Nature* (Selby-Bigge ed., 1968), Book III, Section 1, p. 464.
5   See Douglas Husak, "Limitations on Criminalization and the General Part of Criminal Law," in Stephen Shute and A. P. Simester (eds.), *Criminal Law Theory: Doctrines of the General Part* (Oxford: Oxford University Press, 2002), p. 13.
6   When I lecture about this topic, I try to anticipate and respond to an argument that I think people in the particular audience are likely to hold. Invariably, among the first points raised in the ensuing discussion is: You did a fine job with the argument you addressed, but you did not respond to some other argument. Of course, the argument to which I

did not respond is the very argument which I addressed in a previous lecture, when someone in the audience protested that I neglected the argument to which I am now responding. This is all very frustrating. Again, I find myself in the predicament described by Hume.

7   William Stuntz, "The Pathological Politics of Criminal Law," *Michigan Law Review* 100 (2001): 508, n. 5.
8   For a more detailed elaboration, see Erwin Chemerinsky, *Constitutional Law: Principles and Policies* (New York: Aspen, 1997), pp. 414–17, 533–45.
9   See Sherry Colb, "Freedom from Incarceration: Why is This Right Different from All Other Rights?" *New York University Law Review* 69 (1994): 781.
10 But see Douglas Husak, "The Nature and Justifiability of Nonconsummate Offenses," *Arizona Law Review* 37 (1995): 151.
11 US Department of Justice, Bureau of Justice Statistics, *Sourcebook of Criminal Justice*, 29th edn. (2001), Table 2.49.
12 See Robert J. MacCoun and Peter Reuter, *Drug War Heresies* (Cambridge: Cambridge University Press, 2001).
13 See Mitch Earlywine, *Understanding Marijuana* (New York: Oxford University Press, 2002), p. 247.

32

The Liberal Basis of the Right to Bear Arms

Todd C. Hughes and Lester H. Hunt

1 Some Liberal Constraints

Bans on guns are typically considered a "liberal" policy. We will argue, however, that broad bans on firearms are in fact not liberal policies at all. The policy of a state that disarms its citizenry conflicts with more than one of the fundamental principles of liberalism.

The degree and nature of the conflict between liberalism and gun bans depends, however, on how one conceives of liberalism. In this regard, gun bans serve as a means of illustrating the disparity between two fundamentally different versions of liberalism, which we shall call *wide* and *narrow* liberalism. We shall try to show that a complete ban on the private possession of firearms is impermissible on either view; in fact *any* meaningful restriction is difficult to justify in the context of wide liberalism. Narrow liberalism, on the other hand, permits more restriction, but, if applied consistently, is unlikely to allow ones that will result in a significant decrease in violent crime.

The assumption motivating most calls for bans on private possession of guns is that a causal relationship exists between the number of guns in the private sector and the number of victims of violent crime: an increase in the number of guns (in some sense) *causes* an increase in violent crime.[1] The empirical literature on this issue is baffling, at least to those not trained in mathematics and social science. Let us assume, for the sake of the argument, that the alleged causal relationship between guns and crime really exists. Is this sufficient to justify a government ban on firearms? In a liberal state, the answer is simple: it is *no*. In a consistently liberal system, it is considered highly problematic to dispose of the rights and liberties of citizens – where these rights and liberties are believed by their owners to be important – simply and solely because the community can extract a benefit from doing so.

Consider the following example. It is very obvious that we could prevent a great many deaths from AIDS by enacting a policy reputedly followed in Cuba: that of simply rounding up everyone known to have the disease and isolating them in special camps until they no longer carry the disease (presumably, because they are dead). We do not have such a policy, though we know perfectly well that thousands of people will die because we do not have it. The reason we do not have it is that we, or most of us, think that incarceration is a bad way to treat sick people. It violates their rights. Of course, there are many ways to explain why we tend to think this, and why we tend to find this thought so decisive. One perfectly good way to explain it, however, is to say that this country, unlike Cuba, is a liberal democracy: from a liberal point of view, the mere fact that a policy could save lives is not a sufficient reason for adopting it. The policy itself must be morally permissible. In a consistently liberal polity, the pursuit of all social goals, including the goal of saving thousands from dying horribly and pointlessly, is *constrained*.

Liberalism, however, is distinguished not merely by the fact that its pursuit of the good is constrained, but by the particular set of constraints it recognizes: an action, including a government policy, is considered unjust, and consequently unacceptable, if it violates one or more of these liberal constraints. There are a number of principles that could be included in this set, but our focus here will be on three of them – autonomy, neutrality, and equality – and most importantly on autonomy and equality.

The concept of *autonomy* can be formulated in many different ways, with many different degrees of stringency, but what the formulations have in common is the general notion that individuals should control their own lives and be the instruments of their own acts of will. The individual has certain fundamental rights against interference by others. One way to formulate a usable version of the autonomy principle is to define a part of the individual's life as "private," in virtue of the fact that it includes behavior that has no significant effects on others without their consent, and to declare that, within this private domain, individuals may do whatever they wish. This is the method used by Mill and many others after him. This way of interpreting the idea of autonomy can be called "minimal," in that it constrains government policy less than the other interpretations do. Probably the most "maximal" interpretation is the one associated with the Lockean notion of self-ownership.[2] On this view, a person owns his or her self and, by the same token, the product of the labor of that self.

The principle of autonomy is a major source of the familiar liberal animus against paternalism. Government acts paternalistically when it makes or restricts important choices for individuals in order to do those same individuals some good. Such a policy involves interfering with individual conduct even when it affects no one but the individual agent and, consequently, tends to run afoul of even the most minimal version of the autonomy constraint. Liberals have at times carved out exceptions to the autonomy principle, formulating "soft" forms of paternalism which allow interference when the individual conduct involved is seriously nonvoluntary, or when the rights and liberties disposed of are trivial.[3] Because liberalism rests on the principle of autonomy, however, it cannot go very far in justifying policies that are paternalistic.

The second liberal constraint is the principle of *neutrality*. It holds that the justification for state action must be neutral between particular conceptions of the good life. It is an indirect constraint on government action, in that what it constrains is not the actions but the reasons that are given for them. The policies of liberal states have many side-effects and, no doubt, some of them create conditions in which certain conceptions of the good can no longer be pursued. For instance, there may be values that can only be achieved by pursuing the way of life of a samurai warrior, an eighteenth century aristocrat, or a Medieval knight – ways of life that were extinguished by liberal institutions. From a liberal point of view, this effect can be just, but only if these policies can be defended on other grounds, apart from the fact that they tend to "stamp out" ways of life that liberals do not appreciate.

As was the case with the principle of autonomy, the *equality* constraint is open to widely different formulations, and substantially different ones tend to mark the differences between different sorts of liberalism. Common to all the versions of this principle is the idea that the state should treat its subjects as equals. At a minimum, it means that governments must respect equally the rights of its citizens. They must not discriminate against some citizens and in favor of others. No one is to be either above or below the law. It also means that government must not function as an instrument by which the strong take advantage of the weak.

This idea – that governments must take the rights of citizens equally seriously – can be called the minimal interpretation of the equality constraint. It states something that all liberals believe. For instance, if it could be shown that state lotteries tend to take money from the relatively poor and uneducated (perhaps because such people tend to have a comparatively shaky grasp of probability theory) and tend to put this money into the hands of the relatively rich and educated, all liberals would feel that this is a weighty argument against state lotteries. They would all see such an arrangement as unjust because of the way in which it arbitrarily discriminates against people who are less well endowed and in favor of those who already enjoy advantages.

It is possible, however, to interpret the principle of equality in ways that go beyond this minimal version of it: one can interpret it, as we shall say, *extra*minimally. There are many ways to do this, but all tend, to one degree or other, to claim that the liberal state is committed, not merely to respecting equally the rights of its citizens, but to equalizing the value of the rights that each person has. The forms that this idea takes range from the idea that inequalities in the distribution of goods, though allowable, are subject to egalitarian constraints, to the idea that resources available in a society should be divided equally among its members through some scheme of redistribution.

As we have already suggested, one can envision quite different varieties of liberalism depending on how one interprets the principles of autonomy and equality. On the one hand, one could adopt an extremely extraminimal interpretation of the principle of equality, which would allow extensive state efforts to equalize the conditions of its citizens. Expecting this state activity to cut into the liberties of the individual, one might then adopt a relatively minimal interpretation of the autonomy constraint. On the other hand, one might adopt an extremely extraminimal interpretation

of the principle of autonomy and, expecting this to limit aggressive redistribution policies, one could adopt a relatively minimal interpretation of the principle of equality. Because it allows wider liberty of action, we call the latter sort of position "wide liberalism." The former, for analogous reasons, we will call "narrow liberalism."[4]

As we shall see, it makes a difference, as far as the issue of bans on firearms is concerned, whether one is a wide or a narrow liberal. But we will also argue that it does not make as much difference as one might think. No position could be called liberal that did not accept, in one form or other, all three of the principles we have discussed. We will argue that all three of these areas of concern tend to militate, though in different degrees and in different ways, against bans on firearms.

2 Firearms and Autonomy

Today, the very idea that the possession of a gun – a mere technological device prized by hobbyists and lunatics – is a right, like freedom of speech, freedom of religion, and the right against self-incrimination, strikes many people as silly. Nonetheless, such a conclusion is more or less forced on us by *all* plausible extraminimal versions of the autonomy constraint, including even the mildest of them.

This may sound like a strange claim, but it becomes much less so when we clearly understand certain of its concrete implications. To this end, consider the case of Ms. Jackson of Atlanta, Georgia:

> A College Park woman shot and killed an armed man she says was trying to carjack her van with her and her one-year-old daughter inside, police said Monday. . . .
>
> Jackson told police that the gunman accosted her as she drove into the parking lot of an apartment complex on Camp Creek Parkway. She had planned to watch a broadcast of the Evander Holyfield–Mike Tyson fight with friends at the complex.
>
> She fired after the man pointed a revolver at her and ordered her to "move over," she told the police. She offered to take her daughter and give up the van, but the man refused, police said.

"She was pleading with the guy to let her take the baby and leave the van, but he blocked the door," said College Park Detective Reed Pollard. "She was protecting herself and the baby."

Jackson, who told the police she bought the .44 caliber handgun in September after her home was burglarized, said she fired a shot from the gun, which she kept concealed in a canvas bag beside her car seat. "She didn't try to remove it," Pollard said. "She just fired."[5]

Considering the fact that Ms. Jackson's would-be abductor was threatening her with lethal force at the time she killed him, and considering also what his most likely motive was for refusing to simply steal her car and let her go free, it seems obvious that she had a right to do what she did. She has a right to self-defense.

Though this right is not protected by the minimal interpretation of the autonomy constraint (since the effect her act has on her assailant puts it well outside the domain of privacy) the reasons for adding it to the rights that are protected by this constraint seem to be as great as any could be. The interest that is protected by Ms. Jackson's right to defend herself is life itself. The interests protected by other rights recognized by liberals – including not only freedom of speech, but also freedom of religion, the right against self-incrimination, and many others – are no more important than this one. In many cases, they are a good deal less important.

Of course, Ms. Jackson's action has an effect on her assailant, and effects on others can give rise to powerful claims from those others that their rights have been violated. Such claims are potential reasons for *not* adding the act to the list of rights that are protected by a fundamental principle. Here, however, the strength of such reasons are as low as they can be. Though the effect suffered by her assailant is a powerfully negative one, his attack on her clearly cancels any claims he might have had against her use of force against him.

If we suppose, then, that Ms. Jackson has *any* rights to act on her own volition, outside the domain of privacy, then she must have this right, a right of self-defense. Further, if this supposition settles the question of her right of self-defense, it also settles the question of whether she has a right to use her gun to shoot her assailant.[6]

So far, then, it would seem that, even a very modestly extraminimal interpretation of the autonomy constraint would have to imply that Ms. Jackson has a right to use her weapon to defend herself, a right of non-interference that would be violated by having her weapon confiscated. The case we have made for this claim does make a certain assumption. Though it may require a lengthy inquiry to determine precisely what form the assumption should be given, it clearly must include the idea that one violates a right (in this case, Ms. Jackson's right of self-defense) if one coercively prevents them from using the only, or the best, means to exercising that right (here, Ms. Jackson's handgun). It would be interesting to discuss whether (or why) such a principle is true, but it is not necessary to do so here, since the same principle is recognized by liberals in other contexts. Most of them would agree, for instance, that the government would be violating our rights to freedom of expression if it made possessing a computer modem a crime punishable by a term in prison. The same would be true if the law allowed the police to give out modem permits in the event that they decide an individual citizen has a "valid" reason to possess one. On the face of it, the same principle would seem to apply to an agent, including a representative of the state, who takes Ms. Jackson's gun from her.

Liberals who support gun bans would probably urge at this point that there is an obvious difference between a modem and a gun. A gun, unlike a modem, is a weapon, and advocates of gun bans argue that guns are substantially more dangerous than other weapons. Firearms allow people to commit offenses they could not commit with other weapons, such as knives, clubs, and fists. They enable persons normally in a position of weakness to use the threat of harm to take the money, possessions, and even lives of their victims.

If the presence of guns in one's environment does indeed increase such dangers, and it is at least *prima facie* plausible to say that it does, the liberal autonomy constraint itself seems to support banning some or all of them. All liberals agree that the principle of autonomy, unlike the principle of equality, applies fully to individuals as well as to states. It is permissible for individuals to treat others in substantially unequal ways, but serious violations of the autonomy of others (at least of sane, innocent adults) is not permissible. Obviously, killing or maiming others is ordinarily such an impermissible violation. Consequently, the conclusion, which we tentatively suggested a moment ago, that even a modest autonomy constraint would imply that Ms. Jackson has a right against having her weapon confiscated, stands in need of further support. More needs to be said before we can draw such a conclusion.

3   Risk

No one would deny that a liberal state, even the relatively constrained state of wide liberalism, may prohibit activities that kill or maim others. Of course, a state that bans firearms like the one used by Ms. Jackson would not merely be prohibiting actions that *actually* do that sort of harm: they would rather be prohibiting an activity (owning a gun, or a gun of a certain sort) on the grounds that it creates a *risk* that such harm will be done. However, prohibiting activities that create such risks is itself something that a wide liberal state may do. Such a state may prohibit me from storing dynamite in my basement or driving while intoxicated, even when (luckily) these activities do not kill or maim anyone. One reason for this, and a sufficient one for our purposes, is that such risky activities are themselves violations of the autonomy of others.

Having admitted this, however, we claim that the mere fact of owning a gun, at least a gun like Ms. Jackson's .44, does not belong in this category: it does not create the *sort* of risk that justifies prohibition in the context of wide liberalism. In particular, it is starkly different from the two examples of risky activities that we just mentioned.

First, just as a gun is obviously different from a modem, it is also, though perhaps less

obviously, different from dynamite. Dynamite is an unstable substance, which can be detonated, under some circumstances, by a mere tap. Its unpredictability, together with the sheer scale of the destruction caused when it does explode, justifies us in classifying dynamite as a substance that cannot be handled entirely safely.

In the relevant respect, guns are as different from dynamite as can be imagined. Like clocks, guns are (ignoring an exception which we will discuss shortly) precision instruments: they are designed to function precisely, and for more or less the same reasons that clocks are. People have clocks so that they will know exactly what time it is, and not approximately what time it is. Similarly, they have guns so they will be able to hit a target, and not nearby objects. The function of a gun is not simply to provide lethal force, but to provide precisely controlled lethal force. Partly because of this fact, it is a surprisingly simple matter to handle a gun safely. As millions of Americans know from their firearms safety training, there are a few easy to follow rules which, if they are followed, will guarantee that unplanned detonations will not occur.

The same sorts of considerations suffice to show that possessing a gun is utterly different from drunk driving. Unlike drunk driving, gun ownership is not behavior that creates a significant likelihood of accidental injury. In 1993 there were 0.656 accidental deaths due to firearms per 100,000 firearms in the United States: far less than the more than 21 accidental deaths attributable to motor vehicles for that year, per 100,000 motor vehicles.[7] According to one report, the total number of accidental gun deaths due to guns is smaller than the number attributable to medical error.[8]

However, there is a sense in which the rate of accidental deaths from guns is actually a minor issue: the alleged risk involved in gun ownership that most often inspires proposals to ban guns probably has little or nothing to do with accidental death. The most important problem raised in the scholarly debate concerning bans on guns is *intentional* death: most of the anti-gun literature is sharply focused on the idea that guns make deliberate acts of violence more likely. This is the sort of risk that makes them especially dangerous objects, allegedly justifying placing them under a ban of some sort.

We maintain, however, that, within the limits of wide liberalism, even of a very moderate conception of those limits, this sort of risk is not a legitimate reason for banning guns. To return to the case of Ms. Jackson: the notion that she might use her gun to attack someone impermissibly might conceivably justify confiscating her gun, but only if there is reason to think she will actually do so. It is very unlikely that such reasons exist. The overwhelming majority of gun owners are honest citizens who never use their weapons to commit crimes. Obviously, ownership of a gun does not destroy one's ability to make choices, turning gun owners into people who are likely to become violent criminals.

Some people would say that whether a gun is dangerous or not depends entirely on who is in control of it. A gun in the holster of an honest and competent security guard can make people much safer from intentional violence than they would be in its absence. At the moment she was under attack, Ms. Jackson's gun actually enhanced her safety and that of her daughter. There is, however, another way to understand the dangerousness of guns, one that has nothing to do with whether Ms. Jackson or any other individual gun owner will use their weapon for an impermissible act of violence. On this view, the risk of violence that belongs to guns is not a characteristic that attaches to particular guns. Rather, the idea is that guns in general, as a class, are dangerous, because of what *some* people can and will do with objects that are members of that class. Guns, as a class, can be dangerous on balance and on the whole, though individual guns may indeed by safety-enhancing.

Given this conception of the dangerousness of guns, the danger of intentional death and injury can furnish a reason for taking Ms. Jackson's gun away from her that actually has nothing to do with the idea that she will use it to do something wrong. It rests in part on the obvious fact that a liberal state, because it must treat individuals equally, can only permit her to keep her gun if it permits many other people to have

guns as well. In consequence of this, one might argue, we ought ban guns in general, as a class, on the grounds that they (again, as a class) are simply too dangerous to allow in a society like ours. The same argument can, with even greater plausibility, be made concerning some sub-class of guns that are thought to be especially dangerous in this way, such as handguns.

Some people might find the conception of danger on which this argument rests – what might be called type-danger, as opposed to token-danger – problematic. We assume, for the sake of the argument, that it is not. We maintain, however, that a very serious difficulty stands in the way of using this conception to justify state action under the liberal autonomy constraint. While, as we have noted, liberalism allows us to force individuals, as well as states, to conform to this constraint, there has always been in the liberal tradition a very powerful tendency to interpret this constraint individualistically. That is, the harm or risk which justifies us in using force against an individual is generally limited to harm or risk that is *caused by* the individual. In other words, only token danger will do.

Consider, for instance, the case of AIDS. AIDS is a disease with an extremely high degree of type-danger. It may nonetheless be true that an individual AIDS victim who adheres to a few simple rules poses no known danger to others. If this is actually the case – as, in fact, it seems very likely that it is – then the type-dangerousness of AIDS does not, on an individualist interpretation of the autonomy constraint, justify coercively interfering, to their detriment, with such harmless victims of the disease.

Part of the reason why this sort of thinking is part of political liberalism is the traditional liberal concern with fair play. To round up and incarcerate all members of a group, including those who are quite harmless, because other individual members of the group are dangerous, is from a liberal point of view grossly unfair to the harmless ones. We suggest that, from the same point of view, the same sort of reasoning must apply to Ms. Jackson. To disarm her, exposing her to mortal danger, because of behavior for which she apparently bears no causal responsibility at all, is grossly unfair to her. For a liberal, it is quite possible that we may sometimes have to live with a preventable epidemic, an epidemic of disease or of violence, because the only ways we have to prevent it involve state action that violates liberal constraints.

The autonomy constraint, we might say, prohibits us from inflicting harm, at least certain sorts of harm, but it does not in general prohibit possession of the *means* of harming others. The one possible exception to this can be founded on the claim that some guns simply cannot be used in ways that, under the autonomy constraint, are permissible. Arguably, the only relevant actions that a ban on these firearms would prevent would be violations of the autonomy constraint. Supposing such an argument can be made, then, even in the context of a fairly robust wide liberalism, it might serve as a justification for banning such weapons.

However, we would in that case need to take care to determine precisely what kinds of firearms this ban would affect. The criterion for deciding whether a certain firearm is eligible for government restriction would seem to be something like this: the government may permissibly ban a type of gun if it has impermissible uses but has no permissible uses. Perhaps one sort of gun that would be eligible is the sawed-off shotgun. This is the weapon that seems to be the exception to the generalization we made earlier, that guns are precision instruments. Except at fairly close range, it cannot be aimed at all, only pointed: it sprays destruction over a vaguely defined area. It seems to have no value for purposes of target shooting and, because it would often be impossible to fire such a weapon without harming the innocent, it would in those cases be irresponsible to use it (where there is any alternative) for self defense.

Nonetheless, even supposing such an argument can be rigorously made regarding short-barreled shotguns, very few types of guns seem to be like this: nearly all have permissible as well as impermissible uses. We suspect that even military-style assault weapons would fail to be eligible for banning under this criterion. There are many people – private militia groups, for instance – whose conception of the good life involves owning, shooting, and training with automatic weapons. Of course, liberals hold notions about the good that are deeply different from the those pursued by members of such groups. Liberals do not believe that proficiency in the use of deadly force is part of good citizenship or true "manhood," and they do not think it is healthy to view the world as full of menacing threats. It is probably difficult for them to see those who hold contrary views as pursuing a conception of the good at all, the conception involved is so deeply alien to their own. However, they clearly are, and, because of the neutrality constraint, liberals cannot raise such errors about the good as justifications for coercion. As long as these people are peacefully pursuing their strange activities, harming no one, a wide-liberal state cannot coercively deprive them of the means of pursuing them. In view of this, we find that the set of guns it is permissible to ban using the aforementioned criterion is likely to be a very small one.

Before leaving the subject of risk, we need to comment briefly on one more risk commonly attributed to firearms: this is the alleged fact that possessing a gun makes it more likely that the possessor will commit suicide.

The most obvious problem confronting liberals who might want to justify gun bans on the basis of this sort of reasoning lies in the fact that such reasoning is clearly paternalistic. Suicide belongs, if anything does, to the private domain that is protected even by the minimal interpretation of the autonomy constraint. Nonetheless, one might hope to justify some sort of ban by suitably extending the "soft paternalism" by which liberals sometimes justify measures like mandatory life jackets, seat belts, and motorcycle helmets.[9] The prospects of doing so, however, do not seem good. Requiring boaters to wear life jackets and drivers to wear seat belts does not prevent them from living lives in which boating and driving are important elements: it does not limit the liberty of individuals to choose activities that are really important to them. Boaters who are forced to use a life jacket might desire to go without it, but this desire is not crucial to their conception of the good life, in the way that their desire to go boating is. On the other hand, requiring gun owners to give up their guns does preclude the pursuit of various activities – namely, those that include using guns – that in many cases are very important to them and crucial to their notions of the good life.

More importantly, the desire to commit suicide is deeply felt and as important to those who experience it as any desire they could have. Further, supposing that they have carefully considered their decision to die, it is literally true that death is now part of their conception of the good, inasmuch as they have decided that being dead is (for them) better than being alive.

The autonomy constraint is a formidable obstacle to justifying a ban on firearms. To the extent that a particular variety of liberalism relies on this constraint – to the extent, in other words, that it is an instance of wide liberalism – we can expect it to be inhospitable to arguments for bans on firearms. If people own guns and use them in permissible ways, there seems to be no reason for limiting their liberty to own them. The government should, of course, legitimately restrict what people may use firearms *for*, but that is quite a different matter. The adage "Guns don't kill people, people kill people," while hackneyed, is appropriate here. For wide liberalism, it is important what people do, not who they are or what they own.

4   Firearms and Equality

As we have said, though, wide liberalism is not the only form that liberalism takes. Narrow liberalism, which places less stress on the principle of autonomy, assumes a greater license to interfere with individual freedom of choice than wide liberalism does. The emphasis that wide liberalism places on the autonomy principle creates a strong presumption in favor of liberty which makes it extremely difficult to justify almost any sort of ban on firearms, since such a ban would be an infringement on liberty. In its many varieties, however, narrow liberalism tends to accept no more than the minimal interpretation of the autonomy constraint.

Accordingly, narrow liberalism is probably unable to make a case for the right to bear arms that is based on notions of individual liberty.

We claim, however, that the narrow liberal commitment to equality, together with the neutrality constraint it shares with all forms of liberalism, strongly support the idea that gun ownership is a right that citizens must have. As was the case with the autonomy principle, it makes a difference whether one interprets the principle of equality minimally or extraminimally. Unlike the autonomy principle, however, equality can justify a substantial right to bear arms even under its minimal interpretations.

Recall that the minimal interpretation of the equality principle requires the state to respect equally the rights of its citizens. This means, broadly speaking, that it must not discriminate against some of its citizens and in favor of others and, in particular, it must not function as means by which the strong take advantage of the weak. So construed, the equality constraint has immediate implications for the right to own guns. To see this, consider the case of Ms. Johnson, a composite drawn from several news stories of a certain, far-too-familiar sort.

After enduring several years of increasingly severe physical abuse at his hands, Ms. Johnson divorced her husband, Mr. Johnson. Unfortunately, this was not enough to free her from him. After the divorce, he stalked her and beat her severely, for which he was sentenced to a term in prison. The punishment only seemed to make him more angry, and he repeatedly sent her death threats from prison. When his release was imminent, she called the police, but they had to tell her that, unfortunately, they cannot act as bodyguards for citizens in danger. Their role, they explained, is to help ensure that people are punished for crimes they have already committed and, if possible, to interrupt crimes in progress. "Call us right away if he comes to your apartment," was the best advice they could give her. When Mr. Johnson did come for her, he quickly beat down her door, shouting all the while that he had come to kill her. Fortunately, she owned a handgun and, before he had a chance to begin his attack in deadly earnest, she shot and killed him.

Suppose that, just before Mr. Johnson came to Ms. Johnson's apartment, someone (perhaps a confederate of his) interfered by disabling or taking away her gun. It would be obvious that they were acting as a means by which the strong take terrible advantage of the weak. Another way to put the same argument is this. At the moment that Ms. Johnson's former husband broke down her door, it became very likely that one of them would die violently. The question was, which one shall it be. As long as Ms. Johnson was able to use her handgun, it was very likely that the death will be his, Mr. Johnson's. If she were unable to use it, the death would very likely be hers. A government that disarms her is shifting the great burden of premature, violent death from the strong to the weak. According to the principle of equality, this shift is being made in the wrong direction.

This conclusion can easily be generalized. As one study has shown, men who batter their wives "average 45 pounds heavier and 4 to 5 inches taller" than their victims.[10] Such men do not need weapons to kill their wives. They can strangle them or simply beat them to death. If these women are disarmed by the government, relations between them and their batterers are made unequal in a way that any liberal would find extremely objectionable.

More generally still: the capacity of firearms to be a tool for self-defense promotes equality in general, and not merely between battered women and their male batterers. People in general can differ substantially in size, strength, and coordination. People who possess greater physical prowess have an advantage over others. Most especially, bigger people are more capable of harming others than smaller people are. The force of non-gun weapons such as knives and clubs is, like the force of bare hands, strongly contingent on the size, strength, and skill of their users: the weaker of two people equally armed with a non-gun weapon is still at a potentially fatal disadvantage. In typical self-defense situations, however, firearms are equally harmful in anyone's hands, provided the individuals handling them have the capacity to fire them and reasonably good aim at close

range. Two people equally armed with guns, then, are very likely to have equal harming and coercive power, regardless of their physical disparities. Firearms actually *equalize* the balance of power between persons who are naturally unequal.

The minimal interpretation of the equality principle, then, is a very formidable obstacle to the banning of at least some sorts of firearms. If we interpret it extraminimally, this obstacle only becomes more formidable. In its various different guises, extraminimal equality imposes on the state an even stronger commitment to equality than the minimal variety does. As the strength of this commitment increases, so does the stringency of the constraint against disarming the weak and exposing them to attack by the strong.

Clearly, then, a narrow liberal state ought to grant the liberty to own firearms. However, there remains the problem of specifying the *extent* of that liberty: which sorts of firearms should citizens have a right to own? The answer to this question is not as straightforward as it is in wide liberalism. As we have said, narrow liberalism typically includes no strong presumption in favor of freedom of choice outside the private domain. Outside that realm, there is considerable room in narrow liberalism for curtailing the scope of liberty, as long as this is done for neutral reasons, and as long as the principle of equality (whichever formulation might apply) is observed.

Partly for this reason, narrow liberalism does seem to allow for limitations on the ownership of firearms. One available reason for adopting such limitations, within narrow liberalism, is the supposed causal relationship between the number of guns in private hands and the quantity of violent crime. If the justification for a ban on some types of firearms is that it will reduce the rates of violent crime, then it certainly meets the neutrality constraint. This justification, after all, has no necessary connection with disapproval of someone's conception of the good.

The question, then, is whether a ban satisfies the autonomy and equality constraints: is it permissible to prohibit the ownership of significant classes of firearms without violating the minimal interpretation of the autonomy constraint, and without violating narrow liberalism's commitment to equality? The answer clearly seems to be *yes*. For example, consider a ban on the private possession of all firearms capable of killing several people in rapid succession or simultaneously, an extremely large category of firearms that includes automatic rifles, semiautomatic rifles, extremely high-powered handguns, grenade launchers, anti-tank weapons, and so on. Supposing that such weapons do increase the crime rate, the minimal version of the autonomy principle would not be violated by banning them. Further, it would not seem to violate the equality-based considerations we raised in defending Ms. Johnson's right to possess her handgun. These extremely advanced weapons are not practical for self-defense. Other firearms are much more useful for these purposes, and in many cases are less expensive and wasteful of ammunition. Banning them would not expose the weak to the doubtful mercies of the strong.

Of course, there are people, including members of private militia groups, whose conception of the good life includes training with and using these advanced firearms. They may find that marching about in the forest with mere facsimiles of military assault rifles does not fit their notions of what citizenship and manhood require of them. Their capacity to pursue their conception of the good, accordingly, will be diminished by banning such weapons. This fact, however, does not violate the neutrality constraint, which does not constrain the actions of the state directly, but only the reasons that are given for them. The reasons we are currently entertaining for banning these weapons do not rely on the idea that the conception of the good these people are pursuing must be fought, but only on the idea that violent crime must be fought: it is, in the requisite sense, quite neutral.

It would seem, then, that we can have a ban on a substantial range of firearms that is consistent with narrow liberalism. However, it is important to consider the kinds of guns the ban would *not* include, for the results are bound to disappoint some people. As mentioned, firearms that are useful for self-defense are not subject to the ban. There is a serious difficulty here for narrow

liberals who would like to use gun bans to significantly reduce crime: the guns that are most useful for self-defense are handguns, which are also most useful for committing crimes. If gunbans are to be an important tool in fighting crime, handguns are the most rational targets of such bans, perhaps the only sort of firearm in common use that is really worth banning. Certainly, the number of crimes committed with assault rifles is, by comparison, extremely small.[11] Thus, even though the narrow liberal state may permissibly restrict a large number of guns, the advocates of gun bans probably would not predict that these sorts of bans would actually bring about the state of affairs that they want to produce: a major reduction in violent crime. Those who believe the causal theory that closely links the number of guns in civilian hands with the level of violent crime would only expect to reduce such crime significantly by banning the sorts of weapons that are most often involved in the commission of crimes. Narrow liberalism cannot approve such bans without betraying its commitment to equality.

It is clear that narrow liberalism enjoys a greater license than wide liberalism does to ban firearms: the narrow liberal state can legitimately control a greater number of guns than the wide liberal state. However, the prospects are very poor that this distinction would make a great difference in the rates of violent crime.

5 Conclusion

The issue of bans on firearms brings to the surface the fundamental ideological differences between wide and narrow liberalism. Wide liberalism, having a stronger presumption in favor of liberty, is less receptive to bans than narrow liberalism is. Wide liberalism must allow a weapon if it has permissible uses to which it *can* be put, while narrow liberalism must allow it only if it is *necessary* for the permissible activity of self-defense, or if it has no effect on others. On the other hand, rather surprisingly, the fundamental principle of narrow liberalism is more immediately inimical to bans than that of wide liberalism, since it implies a serious right to bear arms even in its minimal form, while that does not seem to be true of the principle that is fundamental to wide liberalism. Autonomy is only inimical to bans if it is interpreted extraminimally. In addition, the possible risks associated with guns raised the issue of whether the banned behavior might itself have some general tendency to violate the principle of autonomy, which in turn raised the issue of whether the principle might actually *require* some sort of ban. We found no analogous sort of issue in the case of the principle of equality.

Passionate defenders of gun control may well be tempted to say that, if our argument is cogent, it is simply a *reductio ad absurdum* of liberalism. It certainly does bring into sharp relief the fact that liberalism is, unlike some competing ideologies, a *constrained* view of the political realm. As we have already suggested, to be a liberal is to decide, in advance, that there may be epidemics, whether of the moral or the physical realms, for which there are no permissible remedies.

This can be a distressing thing to hear. One can hope to reduce this distress by searching further for remedies that *are* permissible. One might wonder about the permissibility of other gun control measures, such as mandatory waiting periods, background checks, gun buy-backs, licensing laws, and mandatory gun safety training. Most of these kinds of regulations may be more nearly compatible with either wide or narrow liberalism than actual prohibitions of firearms. This seems to be likely, in fact. However, one must be careful not simply to assume that other gun control policies are permissible alternatives to gun bans without first subjecting them to the sort of scrutiny we have carried out here.

One should also be willing to entertain the possibility that, if guns are a major part of the problem of crime, they may also be part of the solution. Non-discretionary "right to carry" laws, which permit the law-abiding to carry concealed weapons, seem to be, if what we have said is correct, compatible with both wide and narrow liberalism. They are also worth considering as ways to reduce crime: a world in which a significant number of the potential victims of crime are armed may well be a world with less crime.

Epilogue: Liberal Neutrality

We have argued that the fundamental principle of narrow liberalism is more immediately inimical to bans than that of wide liberalism. If this is so, however, it seems odd that so many narrow liberals are so well-disposed toward confiscatory firearms policies, including, in many cases, bans on handguns. Indeed, to many who adhere to that sort of liberalism, certain aspects of the argument we have presented must have seemed not merely theoretically inadequate but personally offensive. Many would probably find it more or less horrifying that two academics would calmly suggest that wives should shoot and kill their husbands, or, more generally, that lethal force is part of the solution to pressing social problems. The fact that we suggest taking this position in the name of equality probably only compounds the horror.

This reaction to the position we have taken, a reaction of horror and not mere disagreement, suggests a possible explanation for the ease with which narrow liberals tend to support handgun confiscation. According to this explanation, this tendency has nothing to do with the principles of autonomy, neutrality, or equality, nor with the notion of individualism, nor any other part of the liberal conception of justice. It rests, rather, on the notion that such obviously personal and deep-seated reactions often arise from broad notions of what life is and should be like. As we suggested earlier, liberals tend to have a certain distinctive conception of the good. They believe in being reasonable and humane. To them, shooting people seems neither reasonable nor humane. They tend to view violence between human beings, especially lethal violence, as intrinsically bad. Even when it is necessary, it is always, due to the quality of evil that still clings to it, deeply regrettable.

From this point of view, a gun cannot be seen simply as a device for perforating objects, a sort of long-distance drill. A gun is made for the purpose of killing and maiming, and this fact alone makes guns intrinsically bad. This is especially true of the handgun, which is uniquely suited, and in fact intended, for the activity of killing and maiming *people*. To this technological device is transferred some of the horror that belongs to that horrifying activity. The thought of coercively stamping out this thing of horror is consequently deeply attractive.

We are suggesting that an important part of the reason why so many liberals favor the suppression of the private possession of handguns, despite the potential of the handgun for enhancing equality in situations were equality is desperately important, may well be a certain tension within the liberal view of the world. On the one hand, liberals have principles that constrain them from using certain methods in achieving their goals. On the other hand, like everyone else, they have their own conception

of the good. In principle, this conception might, like any other, be promoted by violating those constraints. However, as we have said repeatedly, to interfere coercively with others because of preferences of one's own, preferences based solely on one's conception of the good, violates the principle of neutrality, and this is as true of the liberal conception of the good as it is of any other. If the tendency that we see in some parts of the liberal community to ban guns is indeed based on such preferences, it is actually illiberal. In that case, it represents a sort of illiberalism of which only liberals can be guilty: the urge to force *liberal* values on those who do not accept them.

Notes

We would like to thank Hugh LaFollette and Samuel C. Wheeler for showing us their work in progress on the right to bear arms. They helped considerably to advance our thinking on this issue. Their comments on earlier drafts of this essay were also very helpful, as were those of Don B. Kates, C. B. Kates, Harry Brighouse, and Claudia Card.

1 John Lott has collected information on changes in gun ownership rates and changes in crime rates in all 3,054 US counties over eighteen years, and he appears to establish that concealed carry laws, which allow private citizens without criminal records to carry weapons, are highly cost-effective ways to reduce levels of violent crime. *More Guns, Less Crime* (Chicago: University of Chicago Press, 1998).

2 John Locke, *Second Treatise of Government* (New York: Bobbs-Merrill, 1965), chs. 2 and 5.

3 Joel Feinberg, "Legal Paternalism," *Canadian Journal of Philosophy* 1/1 (1971): 106–24. Gerald Dworkin, "Paternalism," *The Monist* 56/1 (January 1972): 64–84. See also Dworkin's "Paternalism: Some Second Thoughts," in R. Sartorius (ed.), *Paternalism* (Minneapolis: University of Minnesota Press, 1983), pp. 105–11.

4 When its distinctive features are sufficiently pronounced, wide liberalism becomes what is sometimes called "classical" liberalism. Narrow liberalism, in its more fully developed forms, becomes what is sometimes called "left" liberalism.

5 "Mom saves Self and Child with Handgun," *Atlanta Constitution*, November 12, 1996, p. E2. Quoted in Lott, *More Guns, Less Crime*, p. 3.

6 We assume, in what follows, that the question of whether Ms. Jackson's rights are violated by the act

of coercively preventing her from using her gun is independent of the coercer's motives.

7 Gary Kleck, *Targeting Guns: Firearms and Their Control* (New York: Aldine De Gruyter, 1997), p. 323. The number of handgun deaths per 100,000 guns was 1.087.

8 Morgan Reynolds and H. Sterling Burnett, "No Smoking Guns: Answering Objections to Right-to-Carry Laws," *National Policy Center Brief Analysis* No. 246, November 17, 1997. The authors also point out that, although gun ownership has increased dramatically in recent decades, accidental deaths from guns have decreased. In the decade before their article, such deaths decreased by 19 percent. Kleck reports that, in the two decades 1974–94, the all-time low in fatal accidents among children was 1994. *Targeting Guns*, p. 324.

9 See note 3, above.

10 D. G. Saunders, "When Battered Women Use Violence: Husband Abuse or Self-Defense," *Violence and Victims*, 47/1 (1986): 49.

11 Nationwide figures on this subject do not seem to be available, but such local statistics as are available certainly bear out the claim we have just made. For instance, in Massachusetts from 1985 to 1991 assault weapons accounted for only .7 of 1 percent of shootings. In New Jersey in 1991 they were involved in .16 of 1 percent of murders, armed robberies, and aggravated assaults. In the state of New York during 1992 they were involved in .8 of 1 percent of murders. For the sources of these figures, and for a great deal more information that tends to support the same conclusions, see Kleck, *Targeting Guns*, pp. 141–2.

33

Gun Control

Hugh LaFollette

Many of us assume we must either oppose or support gun control. Not so. We have a range of alternatives. Even this way of speaking oversimplifies our choices since there are two distinct scales on which to place alternatives. One scale concerns the degree (if at all) to which guns should be abolished. This scale moves from those who want no abolition (NA) of any guns, through those who want moderate abolition (MA) – to forbid access to some subclasses of guns – to those who want absolute abolition (AA). The second scale concerns the restrictions (if any) on those guns that are available to private citizens. This scale moves from those who want absolute restrictions (AR) through those who want moderate restrictions (MR) to those who want no restrictions (NR) at all. Restrictions vary not only in strength but also in content. We could restrict who owns guns, how they obtain them, where and how they store them, and where and how they can carry them.

Our options are further complicated by the union of these scales. On one extreme no private citizen can own any guns (AA, which is functionally equivalent to AR), while at the other extreme, every private citizen can own any gun, with no restrictions (NA+NR). But once we leave those extremes, which few people hold, the options are defined by a pair of coordinates along these distinct scales. While most people embrace positions on the "same" end of both scales, others embrace more exotic mixtures: some will want few weapons available to private citizens, but virtually no restrictions on those guns that are available (MA+NR), while others may prefer making most guns available, but want to seriously restrict them (NA+MR).

So our choice is not merely to support or oppose gun control, but to decide *who* can own *which* guns, under *what conditions*. Although I cannot pretend to provide a definitive account here, I can isolate the central issues and offer the broad outline of an appropriate solution. To simplify discussion, I adopt the following locutions: those opposed to most abolition and most restrictions advocate a "serious right to bear arms," while those supporting more widespread abolition and more substantial restrictions are "gun control advocates." This simplification, of course, masks significant disagreements among advocates of each position.

Justifying Private Ownership of Guns

A moral question

Do citizens have a "serious right to bear arms"? This is a moral question, not a Constitutional one. For even if the Constitution did grant this right, we should determine if there are sufficiently compelling arguments against private gun ownership to warrant changing the Constitution. On the other hand, if this were not a Constitutional right, we should determine if there are strong reasons why the state should not ban or control guns, and if these reasons are sufficiently compelling to make this a constitutional right. Most defenders of private gun ownership claim we do have a moral right – as well as a Constitutional one – and that this right is not an ordinary right, but a fundamental one.

(i) *A fundamental right*

If they are correct, they would have the justificatory upper hand. Were this a fundamental right, it would not be enough to show that society would benefit from controlling access to guns (Hughes and Hunt, 2000). The arguments for gun control would have to be overwhelming. Yet there is also a hefty cost in claiming that this is a fundamental right: the evidence for the right must meet especially rigorous standards.

What makes a right fundamental? A fundamental right is a non-derivative right protecting a *fundamental* interest. Not every interest we individually cherish is fundamental. Since most interests are prized by someone, such a notion of "fundamental interest" would be anemic, serving no special justificatory role. Fundamental interests are special: they are integrally related to a person's chance of living a good life, *whatever her particular interests, desires, and beliefs happen to be.* For example, living in a society that protects speech creates an environment within which each of us can pursue our particular interests, goals, needs, and development, whatever our interests happen to be. Is the purported right to bear arms like this paradigmatic fundamental right?

Even if it were, that would not straightforwardly establish that it is impermissible to abolish or restrict private ownership of guns. After all, fundamental rights standardly have conditions, boundaries, or restrictions on them. Some rights, like the right to vote, are *conditional* upon reaching a specified age, and they can be *forfeited* by emigrants and imprisoned felons. Additionally, most right tokens can be *restricted* or *overridden* when the exercise of that right harms others. For example, my right to free religious expression gives me wide discretion in how I exercise my religion. I can remove my kids from high school and exclude them from selected school activities (*Wisconsin* v. *Yoder*, 406 U.S. 205 [1972]; *Moody* v. *Cronin*, 484 F. Supp. 270 [1979]). I can sacrifice animals (*Church of the Lukumi Babalu Aye* v. *City of Hialeah*, 508 U.S. 520 [1993]). Nonetheless, it does not permit me to sacrifice humans. Nor does my right to free speech permit me to slander someone or to preach outside her window at 2:00 a.m. Tokens of fundamental rights may be restricted to protect others from serious harms arising from the exercise of those rights.

Of course rights would not be worth much if they were straightforwardly subject to the wishes of the majority. We fiercely defend fundamental right types although their tokens sometimes undercut society's interests. We cannot restrict or put conditions on fundamental rights except for compelling reasons, and individuals cannot forfeit their fundamental rights (if they can forfeit them at all) except for overwhelming reasons. Still, although tokens of a right sometimes run counter to the majority's wishes (Dworkin, 1977), we should not infer that rights standardly undermine the public interest. Fundamental rights (freedom of speech, freedom of association, etc.) benefit society as well as individuals. Permitting free speech, religion, and association is the best – and arguably the only – way for society to uncover the truth (Mill, 1985/1885). Of course, not every right has such a significant social payoff – although most fundamental rights do. Still, we minimally assume fundamental rights (right types) do not harm society.

This provides a framework for evaluating people's claims that a right is fundamental.

Advocates must show that and how granting the right protects individuals' fundamental interests, and they must be prepared to respond to objections that granting that right type will harm society. These are serious obstacles for gun advocates. It is difficult to see that a serious right to bear arms satisfies either of these requirements, let alone both.

First, I see no compelling reason to think that owning a gun is a *fundamental* interest. Other fundamental interests are necessary to one's flourishing no matter what her particular desires, interests, and beliefs. It is difficult to see how this is true of guns. Moreover, the interests protected by paradigmatic fundamental rights – our interests in unfettered speech, freedom of religion, and freedom of association – are not merely means to my flourishing, they are elements constituting it. By contrast, having a gun in my bed stand, in my closet, or on my person might be a means for me to achieve my ends, but they are not constitutive elements of my flourishing. Hence, owning guns is not a fundamental interest.

Wheeler disagrees. He argues that the right to bear arms is fundamental since guns are the best way to protect our fundamental interest in self-defense (1997). However, on his view, guns are not inherently valuable; they are valuable only as a means of self-defense (pp. 433–8). I fail to see how this could make the right to bear arms fundamental. Not every means to a fundamental interest is a fundamental right. That would arguably make most actions protected by fundamental rights. Nonetheless, the connection between owning guns and self-defense is an important issue that I address later.

Others might claim that gun ownership is an essential element for the flourishing of a proper citizen. A proper citizen, on this view, is one capable of providing for and defending his family. Although each citizen can (generally) fend for himself, citizens come together to form a limited government to provide those few needs they cannot easily satisfy on their own. However, this vision of the citizen is very controversial, more controversial than the interest in gun ownership it seeks to justify. It assumes each of us has far more control over our lives than we

arguably do have. Furthermore, even if this conception were defensible, it would not establish a fundamental right to bear arms since guns are mere means to independent citizenship; they are not constitutive of that citizenship. Hence, it is doubtful that the purported right to bear arms satisfies the first requirement of a fundamental right.

Second, we have evidence that granting this right type does harm society. If this evidence is at all credible, then granting this purported right would not satisfy the second requirement either.

But this does not resolve the issue. Although people do not have a fundamental right to own guns, gun control might be wrong because it violates some derivative right or simply because it is bad public policy.

(ii) *Derivative right*

Suppose we determined that "the right to bear arms" is not a fundamental right, but a derivative right. This would still be a significant finding since derivative rights, like fundamental ones, cannot be restricted without good evidence. *Prima facie*, I think we have such a derivative right. Each of us has a fundamental right of noninterference: we should be allowed to live our lives as we wish, so long as we do not thereby harm others. This is a right each of us needs, no matter what our particular interests. That general right derivatively protects personally important activities.

For instance, I would be furious if the state forbade me from sharing a pint with a friend. Nonetheless, although consuming alcohol is a particular interest and enjoyment I have, it is not a constitutive element of the good life in the way that the freedoms of speech, freedom, and association are. That is why I do not have a *fundamental* right to consume alcohol. Consequently, the conditions under which my consumption of alcohol can be legitimately restricted are more lax than they would be if the activity were a fundamental interest.

Nonetheless, since I have a *prima facie* derivative right to consume alcohol, the state can legitimately abolish or restrict alcohol consumption only if they can show that so doing is an effective means of protecting the public from harm. They can do that in some cases: people who consume substantial amounts of alcohol are dangerous drivers. Since this behavior is unacceptably risky to others, the state can legitimately restrict drinking while driving. Whether privately owning guns is similarly risky is something we must discover.

Bad public policy

If private gun ownership were not a derivative right, it might still be bad policy to substantially restrict or abolish guns. There are always costs of enforcing a law. Sometimes these costs are prohibitive, especially when the public does not support that law. If the public will not voluntarily comply with the law, then the state must try to force compliance. In their efforts to do so, they invariably employ excessively intrusive methods. Such methods never entirely succeed, and, to the extent that they do, they undermine public confidence in and support for all Law. Consider America's experience with Prohibition. Although one of Prohibition's aims – to protect innocents from harm caused by those under the influence – was laudable, the law was unenforceable and excessively costly. Consequently, less than two decades after Prohibition was passed via Constitutional amendment, it was repealed.

The cost of enforcing any law – and especially an unpopular law – weighs against making any behavior illegal unless we have solid evidence that the behavior is seriously harmful. If we adopt a weaker standard – if we criminalize every action type whose tokens occasionally lead to some harm – then we would criminalize most behavior. Consequently, even if there were no right to bear arms, we should still not seek to substantially limit private ownership of guns unless we have good reason to think that will prevent serious harm.

Summing up: justifying the private ownership of guns

The preceding analysis isolates three questions we must answer in deciding whether people

should be permitted to own guns: (1) How important is owning a gun to some people? (2) What are the consequences of private gun ownership? (3) Is abolishing or restricting private ownership of guns bad policy? Although gun ownership is not a fundamental interest, many people want to own guns and think they have good reason to do so. That is sufficient to show that serious gun control would undermine gun owners' interests. Moreover, there is some reason to think that serious gun control in countries with a strong tradition of gun ownership would be bad policy. Therefore, we should certainly not abolish, and arguably should not restrict, private ownership of guns without good reason. Are there good reasons? To answer this question, we must determine the effects of private gun ownership: (a) How likely is it that private gun ownership seriously harms others? (b) Are there substantial benefits of gun ownership that might counterbalance any harm?

Harm, Danger, and Risk

We must be careful when we say that guns cause harm. Guns kill people because agents use them to kill people (or misuse them in ways that cause people to be killed). As the National Rifle Association (NRA) puts it: "guns don't kill people, people do." In one sense their claim is uncontroversial: Murder is the act of an agent, and guns are not agents. In another way, their claim is irrelevant. No gun control advocate claims, hints, or suggests that guns are moral agents. Guns are objects and objects do no evil. But not all objects are created equal. Imagine the NNWA (National Nuclear Weapons Association) claiming that "tactical nuclear weapons don't kill people, people do." While in one sense their claim would be true, in a more profound way, it would be ludicrous.

Of course guns are not nuclear weapons. Guns are not as dangerous as nuclear weapons and some guns have seemingly legitimate uses. The question is whether the character of guns makes them especially harmful. We know that some objects – tactical nuclear weapons, biochemical weapons, live grenades, etc., are much more dangerous than feathers, ice cream, and butter knives. Where do guns fall along this continuum?

There are two distinct but related questions: (1) are guns "inherently dangerous"; and (2) what is the empirical probability that they cause serious harm? "Inherently dangerous" objects are those whose nature or design is sufficient to justify our prediction that they will cause harm, independently of any empirical evidence. We do not need double-blind empirical studies to know that nuclear weapons are inherently dangerous: they were designed to cause harm, and their nature is such that we can confidently predict they will cause harm. The two questions are intricately related since inherently dangerous objects are more likely to cause serious harm. Yet they are separable because some dangerous objects are not inherently so. Automobiles, alcohol, and cigarettes were not designed to cause harm, but all are causally implicated in many people's deaths. Other things being equal, we are more prone to control inherently dangerous objects than objects that merely have harm as an unwanted side-effect.

Guns, unlike autos, are inherently dangerous. Guns were invented for the military; they were designed to cause (and threaten) harm (Singer, Holmyard et al., 1956). The same aims determine the ways in which guns are redesigned: they are changed to make them more efficient at causing harm. In contrast, a significant aim of redesigning automobiles is to make them less dangerous. To some extent these efforts have succeeded. Although the absolute number of annual traffic fatalities has not noticeably declined, the number of fatalities per mile traveled has declined 75 percent since the '50s (Hemenway, 1995) We have enhanced the auto's original aim of efficient transportation while lessening harmful side effects. That is why we can sensibly say that the automobile is not inherently dangerous despite the fact that it causes harm. We cannot say the same for guns.

The literature of gun advocates supports my contention that guns are inherently dangerous. They advocate the private ownership of guns to prevent crime and to arm the militia. Guns can serve these purposes only because they are

effective means of inflicting and threatening harm. Even guns normally not used to harm humans have purposes that ride piggy-back on this fundamental purpose. Shotguns are used to kill animals, and target guns are designed to be especially accurate. Taken together, this evidence supports the common view that guns are inherently dangerous. That is why we have special reasons to regulate them.

Although inherently dangerous, guns are far less dangerous than weapons of mass destruction, and they do have seemingly legitimate uses. That is why we must show just how risky they are before we can legitimately abolish or seriously restrict them. We must also determine if they have sufficient benefits so that we should permit them, even if risky.

An intermediate conclusion

We have shown that owning guns is not a fundamental interest and that guns are inherently dangerous. That is why we cannot categorically dismiss all forms of gun control. However, this is a weak conclusion. For although guns are inherently dangerous, they may not be so dangerous as to justify more than a system of minimal registration. What seems clear is that their inherent dangerousness precludes the idea that guns cannot be subject to governmental control. Some form of gun control cannot be categorically dismissed. Before determining the actual danger that guns present, we should first determine how risky an action must be before we can justifiably restrict it.

Risk

Humans are notoriously bad at judging risk. Often we are unaware of, or are inattentive to, the seriousness of risks. For instance, we may drive inebriated. At other times we overestimate the risks. For instance, we may refuse to fly because we think it is too dangerous. A proper determination of risk would be based on a careful accounting of the action's costs and benefits. We should determine (1) the probability of harm, (2) the seriousness of harm (the product of the gravity and extent of the harm), (3) the probability of achieving the benefits, (4) the significance of the benefits (the product of the importance and extent of the benefit), and then act accordingly. Of course even if we reached the same determination to the above question, we might still disagree about whether to act: we might disagree about what risks are worth which benefits. Nonetheless, we can all agree that (a) as the likelihood and seriousness of harm increase, we have increased reason to refrain from acting, while (b) as the likelihood and importance of the benefits increase, we have increased reasons to act. We can import these lessons into the law.

Legal rules

But not straightforwardly. The issue is not whether we should own guns if they are legal, although that is a fascinating question. The question is whether the state should curtail private gun ownership. The foregoing considerations are relevant but not decisive. The decision to permit private ownership of guns is shaped by two factors pulling in opposite directions. First, even if we think Roger (an adult) stupidly engages in a dangerous activity (sky diving or boxing or racing), we might think Roger's autonomy requires that we permit it. Our commitment to individual liberty weighs against the government's abolishing or restricting the private ownership of guns as a way of limiting harm (Hughes and Hunt, 2000). Second, some actions (smoking in public places) that are acceptably risky to Roger might be unacceptably risky to others. Are guns also unacceptably risky to others?

Put differently, gun control does not concern what private individuals should do, but what governments should allow private individuals to do. We must determine the risk of permitting the private ownership of guns, constrained by these complicating considerations. To illustrate how this might work, consider the following example. We have evidence that a number of wrecks are caused by drivers using cell phones. Roger wants to use his cell phone while commuting to work. He decides the inconvenience of not using the cell phone is worse than the

small probability of personal harm. He might overestimate the inconvenience of not being able to use his cell phone or insufficiently appreciate the seriousness of the risk. However, since he is an adult, we might think we should not interfere with his decision to use a cell phone while driving. That is what autonomy requires. Yet Roger is not the only person at risk. Passengers in his or other cars may also be harmed. The seriousness of harm to them must also be considered in deciding to permit or restrict drivers' use of cell phones.

These judgments of risk must be further tempered by the costs of enforcement mentioned earlier. Although we know that using cell phones while driving may lead to accidents, we also know other activities may do the same. Drinking coffee while driving. Eating a donut. Looking at a map. Talking to a passenger. Driving more than two hours without stopping. Driving on less than six hours of sleep. Driving home after a bad day at the office. Presumably we should not make all these illegal. The probabilities of serious harm are small and enforcing such laws would require far-reaching intrusions into everyone's life. When the risks of an activity's causing grave harm to many others are small and the costs of interference are significant, then we should not criminalize the action. But as the probability of grave and widespread harm increases, then, other things being equal, we should criminalize the action.

For instance, when people are released from prison (and not just on parole) they have "paid their debt to society." Yet we do not permit them to own a gun. We judge that they are more likely to harm others. Of course not all of them – and likely not a majority of them – would harm others if they were permitted to own a gun. They are prevented from owning guns because they are members of a group statistically more likely to cause harm: we judge that allowing former felons to own guns is unacceptably risky. The National Rifle Association and most other gun advocates agree.

Someone might counter, though, that we deny felons the right to own guns not because we judge that permitting them to own guns is risky, but that they, by their actions, have *forfeited* the right to own guns. But that is not the best justification for our action. Why should felons forfeit their right after they have served their time and are free of all obligations to the state? For instance, while imprisoned in the United States felons do forfeit their right against unlawful searches and seizures. But once they are released from prison (and are no longer on parole or probation), a former felon has an unconditional right against unlawful searches and seizures – the same as every other United States resident.

At first glance, there is some reason to think felons who use guns in commission of a crime could forfeit their right to own a gun, in the same way that drunk drivers lose their licenses. However, drunk drivers do not lose their licenses forever, while in most jurisdictions felons are *never* permitted to own guns. Moreover the prohibition against former felons owning guns is not limited to those who used guns in the commission of a crime. Hence, it is more plausible to think that we can prevent released felons from owning guns because we judge that they are more likely to commit crimes with guns.

This is our rationale for all laws proscribing risky actions. Every drunk driver does not cause an accident. Most do not. Yet we do not flinch at laws forbidding drunk driving. For it is not merely that drunk divers are statistically more likely to cause harm, they are more likely to cause harm *because* they are inebriated. We can arguably use the same rationale to justify restricting access to guns. We restrict access not only because guns are inherently dangerous, but because – if gun control advocates are right – permitting private ownership of guns is very risky.

What We Need to Know

We can now specify what we must know to intelligently decide whether to prohibit or restrict gun ownership (or any other risky action): (1) Is there a statistically significant correlation between the action (private ownership of guns) and harm (homicides, accidental deaths, suicides, armed robbery)? (2) Do we have good reason to think this correlation indicates that the purportedly risky action causes the harm? (3) How serious are these resultant harms? (4) How important is the activity that the state wishes to control (a) to the individual agent and (b) to the society?

In deciding whether to restrict the behavior, we must balance these considerations using the following general guidelines:

(1) If we have evidence that the behavior causes harm, then we have some reason to limit the behavior. As the evidence increases, the reasons for prohibiting the behavior increase. As the probability that the behavior will lead to *serious* harm (the product of the gravity and extent of the harm) approaches certainty, then the reasons for forbidding the behavior become very strong. (2) The more grave and widespread the potential harm, the more reason we have to constrain the behavior. If the gravity and extent of the harm are substantial, we might constrain the behavior even if our evidence that the behavior causes the harm is moderate. (3) The higher the probability that allowing the action will have important benefits, the stronger the reason to permit it. The greater the benefits, the greater the reason to permit it.

Libertarians might claim that individuals' rights are so strong that the state cannot justifiably intervene, even to constrain those who put others at extreme risk. The state should not proscribe risky actions, although they can intervene after harm has occurred. This use of "risk" is misleading. If on one occasion I drive while inebriated, I engage in a risky action: there is some probability that I and others will be harmed. However, permitting people to drive inebriated will definitely cause harm, although we cannot specify in advance who will be harmed. A personal decision to own a gun is risky in the former sense. A decision to permit citizens to privately own guns is – depending on the evidence – risky in the latter sense. If gun control advocates are right about the evidence, then we have good grounds to constrain private gun use. The question is: are they right?

Assessing the Evidence

Armchair arguments

Debates over gun control typically begin, and sometimes end, with armchair arguments. Both sides offer armchair explanations of why (and how) the presence (or absence) of guns will increase (or decrease) violent crime. It is tempting to categorically dismiss armchair arguments since they seem to be poor substitutes for empirical evidence. However, it would be a mistake to assume we could devise sound empirical studies or understand their results without armchairrguments. In a study to discover if widespread availability of guns increases homicides or decreases crimes, we need armchair arguments to tell us which variables we should control (e.g., Lott, 1998: 21–4). Without them we would not know that we should control for the extent of poverty, the incidence of drug use, increases in the number of police officers, or the introduction of tougher (or more lax) penalties. Without them we would not know that we do not need to control for the price of mayonnaise, the criminal's eye color, or who won the World Series.

Armchair arguments also take center stage in evaluating empirical studies, in criticizing experimental design and in reinterpreting the reported findings (Black and Nagin, 1998; Cook and Ludwig et al., 1997; Cook and Mollinoni et al., 1995; Hemenway, 1998, 1997b; Lott, 1998; Wheeler, 1997). So before I discuss the empirical evidence, I summarize some significant armchair arguments employed by gun advocates and gun control advocates.

(i) *More weapons, more violence*
Gun control supporters offer empirical evidence of a positive correlation between murder rates and the availability of guns (especially handguns). Availability of guns is also positively correlated with suicide and accident rates. This empirical evidence is best understood against the background of the following armchair argument: (1) Guns (and especially handguns) are the easiest way to kill others or oneself. People can stand at a relatively safe distance and pull the trigger. (2) When people

are angry, they act in ways they do not normally act. They may strike out at others. If they have a gun close to hand, they are more likely to use that gun. Although they could resort to a knife or a baseball bat, they are less likely to do so, and, even if they do, those weapons are less likely to cause a serious or fatal injury. (3) When people are depressed, they act in ways they would not act normally. If they have a gun close to hand, they are more likely to kill themselves. Although they might slit their wrists or take pills, they are less likely to do so, and, even if they do, they are less likely to kill themselves. (4) When people handle guns, even for a legitimate purpose, the probability of serious or fatal injury to themselves or others increases. When children have access to guns, the likelihood of an accident increases still more.

The conclusion of the armchair argument is clear: the more widely available guns are, the more people will be murdered, will commit suicide, and will die of accidents. This is a plausible armchair prediction. Perhaps it is wrong. Maybe it is reasonable but overinflated. Or it might be that the prediction is well-founded, but that the widespread availability of guns is nonetheless justified. What is apparent is that the claim that widespread availability of guns increases the number of homicides, suicides, and accidental deaths is highly plausible. It is difficult to imagine it is false.

(ii) *Availability of guns prevents or stops crimes*
Pro-gun supporters offer empirical evidence supporting the claim that guns prevent crime; their armchair arguments undergird and explain those studies. The motivating idea is simple: most criminals want to minimize their risks when committing a crime. If they know that someone in a house is armed, they will be less likely to enter that house, at least when the person is home and awake. Potential criminals are also less likely to assault or rob someone whom they believe is carrying a weapon. Finally, when criminals try to rob or assault an armed person, the person is more likely to foil the crime. This, too, is a plausible armchair prediction. Perhaps it is wrong. Maybe the claim is overinflated. Perhaps guns have these

benefits, but there are other effects of owning guns – e.g., those mentioned above – which outweigh them. What is apparent is that the claim that the widespread availability of guns would prevent or thwart some crimes is highly plausible. It is difficult to imagine that it is false.

Of course we cannot stop with these armchair arguments. We must assess the empirical evidence.

The data

The empirical evidence is difficult to assess, and, to the extent that we can, it does not univocally support either side. You might not know that from listening to the public policy debate. Some gun control advocates imply that strict guns laws would all but eliminate murder, while some gun advocates imply that having a gun in every home would virtually end crime. Both claims are unfounded. Gun control will not virtually eliminate murder. Arming all citizens will not virtually eliminate crime. About that we can be confident. The problem is determining the precise effects of permitting or restricting guns. The available evidence is less than compelling. But we must make a judgment based on the best evidence we have.

(i) The connection between availability of guns and murder

Perhaps the most well-established statistic is this: the more widely available guns (especially handguns) are, the more people are murdered. The figures are duplicated time and again in country after country. Here is the bottom line: "the correlation between any-gun prevalence and the overall murder rate is .67, while it is .84 between handgun prevalence and overall murder rate . . . " (Carter, 1997: 3). These figures are significant to the .01 level; that is, the chance that these correlations could occur merely by chance is less than one out of 100. This correlation meets the statisticians' gold standard.

But this does not resolve the issue, for it does not establish what gun control advocates claim it shows, namely, that gun control is an effective way of substantially lessening the murder rate.

First, a statistical correlation shows that two things are linked, but it does not tell us if the first caused the second, the second caused the first, or if there is some third factor which caused both. Second, even if the items are causally related, we do not know that changing the cause will automatically and straightforwardly change the effect since another factor might intervene to sustain the effect.

Gun advocates proffer their own armchair explanation for the correlations: These correlations reflect the character of the respective social and political systems. The European countries where murder rates are lower have more social solidarity and are more heterogeneous than the United States. Whether these social factors explain all the correlation is debatable, but I am confident they explain some of it. Were the United States to regulate guns as tightly as most European countries, our murder rates would arguably fall, but they would not immediately plummet to their levels.

We might settle the issue if we conducted controlled experiments, randomly dividing our population in half, giving half of them guns, removing all the guns from the other half, and then monitoring the murder rate. Of course, that would be morally unacceptable, politically unrealistic, and probably even scientifically unachievable. Before we had enough time to exclude all possible intervening causes, sufficient time might have elapsed so that new intervening causes could have emerged. But we are not in the dark. We have empirical evidence that helps adjudicate between competing explanations of the correlation.

First, we have empirical evidence, bolstered by armchair arguments, that guns are more lethal than other weapons. Some claim the ratio is 5:1; no estimates are lower than 2:1 (Reiss and Roth, 1993: 260). This partly explains the strong correlation between guns and homicides. If people get angry the same number of times, those using the most lethal weapons are more likely to kill their victims.

Second, the nature of secondary gun markets helps explain how the widespread availability of guns increases crime in general, and homicides in specific. Various opponents of gun control claim that "If we outlaw guns, only outlaws will have guns." Armchair arguments suggest why this is a silly claim. Where, one might ask, do criminals get their guns? They often steal them or buy them from those who purchased them legally. Even guns obtained from other criminals are usually traceable to people who purchased them legally. Empirical evidence supports this armchair supposition. Most criminals report having stolen their guns, received them from a friend or family member, or purchased them from someone who had stolen it. At least half a million guns are stolen each year (Cook and Mollinoni et al., 1995: 81), and these swell the numbers of guns available illegally.

Not only does the primary (legal) market effect the availability of guns on secondary markets, it also affects the price of guns on those markets, much "like the analogous markets for motor vehicles or prescription drugs" (Cook and Mollinoni et al., 1995: 71). As we restrict availability of guns in the primary market, the supply of guns in the secondary markets decreases and their cost increases (Cook and Mollinoni et al., 1995: 73). This increase in cost will diminish teenagers' ability to obtain guns, since they are least able to afford hefty price. Since teenagers commit most deadly crimes, decreasing the availability of legal guns will thereby decrease the number of homicides. Conversely, having huge numbers of legally available guns increases the number of guns on secondary markets and typically lowers their price. This makes it easier for prospective criminals, including teenagers, to obtain guns.

Third, having a gun around the house (or on the person) – even for self-protection – apparently increases the chance that someone in the family will kill themselves with the gun, or will be the victim of a homicide or an accident. One study found that "for every time a gun in the home was involved in a self-protection homicide, they noted 1.3 unintentional deaths, 4.5 criminal homicides, and 37 firearm suicides" (Reiss and Roth, 1993: 267). This implies that for every case where someone in a gun-owning household kills an intruder to thwart a life-threatening attack, nearly 43 people in similar households will die from a gunshot. Taken

together the evidence does not prove that widespread availability of guns increases the number of homicides. However, that empirical evidence, bolstered by earlier armchair arguments, makes the claim highly plausible.

(ii) *The use of guns to prevent crime*

The biggest "gun" in the anti-gun control lobby is the claim that having (and perhaps carrying) a gun prevents crime. As I noted earlier, this is a sensible armchair claim. Someone contemplating a robbery is more likely to proceed if they think they can succeed with little risk to themselves. So if a prospective robber believes the tenants are at home and have a gun they know how to use, then he will likely seek another target. Two surveys support this belief. According to one survey, 4 percent of all Americans have used a handgun in the past five years to avert a crime. Given those figures, researchers estimates that there are at least 600,000 defensive uses of guns per year. Kleck uses these results, in conjunction with another survey, to claim that the number might be as high as 2.5 million (Kleck, 1991: 105–6). Given the number of violent crimes using guns, "the best evidence indicates that guns are used about as often for defensive purposes as for criminal purposes" (ibid. 107). If true, that is a powerful reason to resist attempts to limit availability of guns (Kleck, 1997). Such statistics, particularly when bolstered by moving anecdotes of those who have saved their lives by having a gun, cannot be cavalierly dismissed by gun control advocates.

However, these figures are inflated, likely dramatically so. First, Kleck's methodology is flawed. Surveys have an inherent tendency to overestimate rare events. Kleck made his estimates based on phone interviews with people in 5,000 dwelling units. One percent of those units claimed to have used a gun defensively in the past year. Kleck inferred from these responses that there are 2.5 million defensive handgun uses per year. However, since this inference is based on an affirmative answer by one person out of a hundred, that means for every chance for a false negative (someone who falsely denies using a gun defensively) there are ninety-nine chances for a false positive (someone who falsely claims to have used a gun defensively) (Hemenway, 1997b). The probability that this or some other bias skews the findings is substantial.

Second, Kleck's findings are inconsistent with findings by the National Crime Victimization Survey (United States Department of Justice, 1996), which interviewed far more people, and interviewed them more regularly. Kleck's estimates even clash with the NCVS findings on the incidence and circumstances of robberies (which seems less subject to reporting bias). If Kleck's figures were correct, then "Kleck asks us to believe that burglary victims in gun owning households use their guns in self-defense more than 100% of the time, even though most were initially asleep" (Hemenway, 1997a: 1442).

Finally, if there were 2.5 million defensive gun uses each year, how many of those were necessary? Given the negative results of private gun ownership, gun advocates should show not only that guns deter crime, but that they are the *best* way of doing so. Some people plausibly claim that owning a dog is an effective deterrent. If true, then a not insignificant percentage of those who used a gun defensively could have achieved the same results without the accompanying danger. In summary, there is no doubt that guns deter some crime and stop the completion of other crimes. Just not in the numbers that Kleck claims.

John Lott supplements Kleck's argument by claiming that the widespread use of concealed weapons would decrease the annual number of homicides by 1,400, rapes by 4,200, aggravated assaults by 60,000, and robberies by 12,000 (Lott, 1998: 54). If true, and if there were no countervailing costs, this would be a powerful reason not only to permit guns, but to encourage people to have and carry them. However, Lott's conclusions have also come under severe criticism.

The central problem is that crime moves in waves, yet Lott's analysis does not include variables that can explain these cycles. For example, he used no variables on gangs, on drug consumption, or community policing. As a result, many of Lott's findings make no sense. He finds for instance, that both increasing the

rate of unemployment and reducing income reduces the rate of violent crimes . . . (Hemenway, 1998: 2029)

Perhaps the most compelling critique comes from Jens Ludwig who compares the rate of violent crime toward youths and adults in states that passed shall-issue carrying permits. Most of these states issue gun permits only to people over 21. Armchair considerations predict that younger people, who cannot legally carry, will not receive the full benefits from the purported deterrent effect of shall-issue laws. Thus, those under 21 years of age are a natural control group to track general swings in crime. Once we include this factor, we find that shall-issue laws lead to higher – not lower – homicide and robbery rates (Ludwig, 1998).

I also have an overarching worry about Lott's conclusions. The one correlation in the gun control debate that is seemingly beyond dispute is the high correlation between the presence of guns – especially handguns – and homicide rates. Gun advocates offer explanations for the correlation, but no one I have seen seriously challenges it. I find it difficult to square this correlation with Kleck's and Lott's claims that having more guns – and toting them with us – will lower crime.

An overall assessment of the empirical evidence

The strong correlation between the presence of guns and higher murder rate is compelling. Since the correlation is statistically significant to a .01 level, it is difficult to believe that limiting private gun ownership will not have a noticeable effect on the number of murders. Gun advocates disagree: they claim that cultural factors explain the correlation. Although I think they are partly correct, they draw the wrong inference. For one crucial difference between European and American cultures is the widespread presence of guns. Each culture is the way it is, at least in part, because of the role guns (or their absence) played in its creation and maintenance. Therefore, curtailing the private possession of guns might well change the American culture so that it would be less violent. Consequently, it is not only that fewer guns would directly cause some decline in violent crimes – which it should. It is also likely to reshape the cultural values which, along with ready availability of deadly weapons, lead to such an extraordinarily high murder rate in America.

On the other hand, the statistical evidence that guns prevent or thwart crimes is suggestive and cannot be ignored, despite its identified weaknesses. In summary, the overall statistical evidence tilts in favor of gun control advocates, although the evidence is disputable. But we should not expect nor do we need indisputable evidence. We can act on the best evidence we have, while being open to new evidence. If widespread availability of guns were responsible for even one-fourth of the increase in the number of murders, that would be a significant harm the state should prevent if it could do so in a relatively unintrusive and morally acceptable way.

There is little doubt that we can do that, at least to some degree. If nothing else we could control some types of guns and ammunition. To take one obvious example, teflon-coated bullets are designed to pierce protective vests. People do not use these bullets to pierce the vests on a deer or a squirrel, on a target or a skeet. They use them to pierce the vests on people, usually law enforcement officers. This ammunition has *no* purpose except to cause harm. Hence, we are justified in abolishing teflon bullets and in establishing severe criminal penalties for those possessing them. This would not save large numbers of lives. But, assuming this ban's enforcement is not impractical, then, if it saved even a few lives, that would be a compelling reason to outlaw such bullets.

On the other hand, some guns have a much wider use, even if they are occasionally used for ill. People have seemingly legitimate uses for shotguns and single-shot rifles. Consequently, barring strong evidence to the contrary, we should not abolish them. We should, however, study their contributory role in causing harm, and explore ways we might lessen this harm in a relatively unintrusive way.

The central debate concerns handguns. The evidence we have shows that handguns are disproportionately used in homicides and in robberies. Although "there are approximately three

times as many long guns as handguns in the US, more than 80% of gun homicides and 90% of gun robberies involve handguns" (Hemenway, 1995: 60). The experience in Canada suggests that criminals will not switch to long guns if handguns are unavailable. Given the special role handguns play in causing harm, we have compelling reasons to extensively control, or perhaps even abolish, handguns. But, policy considerations, mentioned earlier, should give us pause.

A Third Way

In the past we not only assumed that we must either support or oppose gun control, we assumed that the only way to control guns is to legally proscribe access to them. We should consider other options. Although I find the idea of a world without handguns immensely appealing, there are reasons to seek alternatives, especially in countries like the United States with a deeply entrenched gun culture. In the present political climate, the abolition or serious control of guns in the United States is unlikely to work and less unlikely to happen. There are far too many people who desperately want guns. There are far too many people who own guns. Any attempt to disarm the society would be beset with the problems like those that plagued Prohibition. We have other possibilities.

We could employ elements of a policy we use to control another inherently dangerous object: dynamite. Dynamite has many beneficial uses. That is why we permit people to own it under specifiable conditions, e.g., to build a road. But it is also inherently dangerous. That is why we heavily restrict its purchase, storage, and use. I cannot own dynamite for recreation (I like the flash), for hunting (I am a lousy shot) or for protection (I would not hear an intruder). Owning dynamite is rarely a significant interest, and never a fundamental one. More important to the present point, even when we do permit people to own dynamite, we subject them to strict legal liability. The owner is financially liable for any harm caused by his dynamite, even if he was not negligent.

I propose we make handgun owners (and perhaps ultimately all gun owners) strictly liable for harm caused by the use of their guns. If Jones's child takes his gun and kills someone while committing a crime, then Jones will be financially responsible to those harmed. If Jones's child accidentally kills a neighbor's child, Jones will be financially responsible to the child's family. If someone steals Jones's gun and kills someone while robbing them, then Jones will owe the victim compensatory damages. And if Jones were negligent in the storing of the gun, he could be subject to punitive damages as well. Perhaps if he were grossly negligent in the storing the gun (he left it lying in his front yard, next to a school playground), we might even bring criminal charges against him.

This procedure is justified since guns are inherently dangerous, and it is only reasonable to expect people to take responsibility for their risky actions. The benefits are notable: many people would be disinclined to own guns, while those owning guns would likely take greater care in storing, handling, and using

them. This could arguably achieve the central aims of gun control without direct government intervention. Doubtless that means that some people will be forced to pay for the misdeeds or mistakes of others in ways we might dislike. However, that is a more attractive policy than continuing the current scheme in which guns are easily obtained in the United States or than in completely denying individuals' interest in owning guns.

To make this option more palatable, we could let gun owners purchase liability insurance to cover potential losses. We might even require them to purchase insurance. After all, most states require drivers to have automobile insurance. This insurance-backed system of strict liability would make people take more care with any guns they own, while providing financial remuneration to those harmed by the use of those guns.

Perhaps this will not work. Other proposals might work better. What seems clear to me is that we need to do something: we cannot continue with the status quo.

Acknowledgment

I wish to thank Nicholas Dixon, Lester H. Hunt, Eva LaFollette, members of philosophy departments at East Tennessee State University and the University of Western Michigan, as well as the editors and two anonymous readers of *Ethics* for helpful comments and criticisms on earlier drafts of this essay.

References

Black, D. and Nagin, D. (1998) "Do Right-to-Carry Laws Deter Violent Crime?" *The Journal of Legal Studies* XXVII 1: 209–20.

Carter, G. L. (1997) *The Gun Control Movement*. New York: Twayne Publishers.

Cook, P. J. and Ludwig, J., et al. (1997) "The Gun Debate's New Mythical Number: *How* Many Defensive Uses Per Year?" *Journal of Policy Analysis and Management* 16 (3): 463–9.

Cook, P. J. and Mollinoni, S., et al. (1995) "Regulating Gun Markets," *The Journal of Criminal Law and Criminology* 86 (1): 59–92.

Dworkin, R. M. (1977) *Taking Rights Seriously*. London: Duckworth.

Hemenway, D. (1998) "Review of *More Guns, Less Crime*," *New England Journal of Medicine* 339: 2029–30.

—— (1997a) "The Myth of Millions of Annual Self-Defense Gun Uses: A Case Study of Survey Overestimates of Rare Events," *Chance* 10 (3): 6–10.

—— (1997b) "Survey Research and Self-Defense Gun Use: An Explanation of Extreme Overestimates," *The Journal of Criminal Law and Criminology* 87 (4): 1430–45.

—— (1995) "Guns, Public Health, and Public Safety." In D. A. Henigan, E. B. Nicholson, and D. Hemenway (eds.), *Guns and the Constitution*. Northhampton, MA: Aletheia Press, pp. 49–82.

Hughes, T. C. and Hunt, L. H. (2000) "The Liberal Basis of the Right to Bear Arms," *Public Affairs Quarterly* 14 (1): 1–25.

Kleck, G. (1997) *Targeting Guns: Firearms and Their Control*. New York: Aldine De Gruyter.

—— (1991) *Point Blank: Guns and Violence in America.* New York: Aldine de Gruyter.

Lott, J. R. (1998) *More Guns, Less Crime: Understanding Crime and Gun-Control Laws.* Chicago: University of Chicago Press.

Ludwig, J. (1998) "Concealed Gun-Carrying Laws and Violent Crime: Evidence from State Panel Data," *International Review of Law and Economics* 18: 239–54.

Mill, J. S. (1985/1885) *On Liberty.* Indianapolis, IN: Hackett Publishing Company.

Reiss, A. J., Jr. and Roth, J. A. (eds.). (1993) *Understanding and Preventing Violence*, Washington, DC: National Academy Press.

Singer, C., Holmyard, E. J., et al. (1956) *A History of Technology* (vol. II). Oxford: Oxford University Press.

United States Department of Justice. (1996) *Criminal Victimization in the United States, 1993: A National Crime Victimization Survey.* Washington, DC: US Government Printing Office.

Wheeler, S. C., Jr. (1997) "Self-Defense: Rights and Coerced Risk Acceptance," *Public Affairs Quarterly* 11 (4): 431–43.

Free Speech

Should we be morally and legally permitted to say whatever we want, whenever we want? Or are there moral – and should there be legal – limits on the views that we can publicly express? As in the previous section, we begin with a selection from John Stuart Mill's *On Liberty*. Mill argues that we are never justified in silencing the expression of an opinion, even if the view is patently false. We can, however, control *when* and *how* someone expresses an opinion. If the opinion is expressed at a time or in a way that is likely to harm another – for instance, by prompting third parties to attack that person violently – then we can legitimately constrain the speech. In all other circumstances, restricting speech is inappropriate. Indeed, Mill argues, we should actively encourage and promote the expression of diverse views.

Is Mill correct? Is it legitimate to restrict speech only when that speech demonstrably harms others? Many people speak as if they agree with Mill. But we know better. Few people openly denounce free speech, but many loathe free and open discussion. How can this be? There are two answers – one psychological and one logical. The psychological explanation is simple: never underestimate the power of self-deception. Some individuals sincerely believe

they are staunch advocates of individual liberty while seeking every available opportunity to squelch speech they dislike. Somehow they are blind to what they do – and why they do it.

The logical explanation is more interesting and more complex. Many people agree that we should suppress speech only when it harms others. However, they have radically different views about when speech harms others. Therefore they disagree about when speech can be prohibited or restricted. Mill thinks speech can rarely harm others and, therefore, can rarely be justifiably restricted. Others think speech frequently harms others and, therefore, can often be legitimately restricted. This disagreement about the criteria for harm was central to the discussion of drugs in the previous section. The authors there had widely divergent views about what constitutes harm to oneself and risk of harm to others. In this section the authors are equally divided about which actions can harm others.

This is a common issue in ethical debate, one worth stressing. We tend to think of ethical disagreements as disagreements over principles. Often, though, moral disagreements are often disagreements about the principles' application to a particular practical problem. This exhibits a feature I identified in THEORIZING ABOUT ETHICS.

We should not assume all deontologists or all consequentialists will reach the same moral conclusions about a particular moral problem. Ethical theories do not determine exactly how an advocate will evaluate any particular moral issue. Instead, they accent what that person takes to be morally relevant, morally significant.

Disagreements over the meaning and application of the harm principle infuse the debate over free speech. Virtually no one contends we should cavalierly restrict speech. Everyone would claim to champion Millean liberalism. However, they disagree dramatically about whether some speech really does harm others; they therefore disagree about whether that speech can be legally forbidden.

Should the state restrict the showing of sexually explicit movies? A sizeable minority of people say "yes." Those who support legal restrictions on pornography usually fall into two camps. The most politically powerful opponents of "a right to pornography" are (typically religious) folk who are offended by public depictions of sex. The second group comprises feminists who are not especially concerned about the idea of public displays of sex. However, they are concerned about the ways that pornography harms women. Most so-called pornography, these feminists say, is not primarily depictions of sex, but rather a glorification of the rape of, and violence toward, women. Thus, Brison argues, pornography harms women not by portraying explicit sex, but by encouraging the abuse of, violence toward, and degradation of women.

Altman contends that both fundamentalists and feminists are mistaken. But they are mistaken, he says, in thinking of this as an issue of free speech. The right to view pornography is, instead, a right to get turned on as one wants; it is an instance of the right of sexual autonomy.

Even so, if we had compelling evidence that pornography demonstrably caused harm, we would then have an important reason to prohibit or at least constrain it. However, the claim that it causes serious harm is mere speculation at best. We could then describe the difference between Brison and Altman as a disagreement about how strong the evidence of harm must be before the state can legitimately intervene. Altman thinks the evidence of harm must be compelling and overwhelming, while many feminists and fundamentalists disagree.

These differences likewise pervade the debate over speech codes. Over the past two decades, several universities instituted "speech codes" forbidding inflammatory speech aimed at members of racial, sexual, ethnic, national, or religious groups. Arthur says that although he is sympathetic to the aims of speech codes, there is no evidence that hate speech harms anyone. Hence such codes cannot be justified. An action is harmful only if it interferes with someone's future interests. Hate speech, as uncomfortable as it might be, does not harm anyone's future interests.

Altman disagrees. For hate speech can not only sustain and encourage the continued mistreatment of blacks, women, and other minorities, it can also constitute what he calls "expressive harm" – an expression of racist or sexist hostile attitude that, at least in a country like the USA (with its history of discrimination), is harmful. This combination of harms would justify universities having such speech codes since these harms can undermine the aims of a university education. Here, Altman seems to employ a much weaker sense of harm than he did in his essay on pornography. Is there some way to show that these two forms of harm are compatible?

Further Reading

Arthur, J. and Shapiro, A. (eds.) (1995) *Campus Wars: Multi-culturalism and the Politics of Difference.* Boulder, CO: Westview Press.

Berger, F. (ed.) (1980) *Freedom of Expression.* Belmont, CA: Wadsworth.

Copp, D. and Wendell, S. (eds.) (1983) *Pornography and Censorship.* Buffalo, NY: Prometheus Books.

Donnerstein, E., Linz, D., and Penrod, S. (eds.) (1987) *The Question of Pornography: Research Findings and Policy Implications.* New York: Free Press.

Faludi, S. (1991) *Backlash: The Undeclared War against American Women.* New York: Crown.

MacKinnon, C. (1987) *Feminism Unmodified.* Cambridge, MA: Harvard University Press.

34

Freedom of Thought and Discussion

John Stuart Mill

If all mankind minus one, were of one opinion, and only one person were of the contrary opinion, mankind would be no more justified in silencing that one person, than he, if he had the power, would be justified in silencing mankind. Were an opinion a personal possession of no value except to the owner; if to be obstructed in the enjoyment of it were simply a private injury, it would make some difference whether the injury was inflicted only on a few persons or on many. But the peculiar evil of silencing the expression of an opinion is that it is robbing the human race. . . . [It robs] those who dissent from the opinion, still more than those who hold it. (1) If the opinion is right, they are deprived of the opportunity of exchanging error for truth: (2) if wrong, they lose, what is almost as great a benefit, the clearer perception and livelier impression of truth, produced by its collision with error. . . .

It is necessary to consider separately these two . . . [options], each of which has a distinct branch of the argument corresponding to it. We can never be sure that the opinion we are endeavouring to stifle is a false opinion; and if we were sure, stifling it would be an evil still.

First: the opinion which it is attempted to suppress by authority may possibly be true.

Those who desire to suppress it, of course deny its truth; but they are not infallible. They have no authority to decide the question for all mankind, and exclude every other person from the means of judging. To refuse a hearing to an opinion, because they are sure that it is false, is to assume that their certainty is the same thing as absolute certainty. All silencing of discussion is an assumption of infallibility. Its condemnation may be allowed to rest on this common argument, not the worse for being common.

Unfortunately for the good sense of mankind, the fact of their fallibility is far from carrying the weight in their practical judgment, which is always allowed to it in theory. . . . [W]hile every one well knows himself to be fallible, few think it necessary to take any precautions against their own fallibility. [Neither do they] admit the supposition that any opinion of which they feel very certain, may be one of the examples of the error to which they acknowledge themselves to be liable. . . .

[How can we take precautions against our own fallibility?] [T]he source of everything respectable in man, either as an intellectual or as a moral being, . . . [is] that his errors are corrigible. He is capable of rectifying his mistakes by discussion and experience. [However, we cannot correct ourselves] by experience alone. There must be discussion, to show how experience is to be interpreted. Wrong opinions and practices gradually yield to fact and argument: but facts and arguments, to produce any effect on the mind, must be brought before it. Very few facts are able to tell their own story, without comments to bring out their meaning. The whole strength and value, then, of human judgment, depends [on its being able to be] set right when it is wrong. . . . [R]eliance can be placed on it only when the means of setting it right are kept constantly at hand.

In the case of any person whose judgment is really deserving of confidence, how has it become so? Because he has kept his mind open to criticism of his opinions and conduct. Because it has been his practice to listen to all that could be said against him; to profit by as much of it as was just, and expound to himself, and upon occasion to others, the fallacy of what was fallacious. Because he has felt that the only way in which a human being can make some approach to knowing the whole of a subject is by hearing what can be said about it by persons of every variety of opinion, and studying [them all]. No wise man ever acquired his wisdom in any mode but this; nor is it in the nature of human intellect to become wise in any other manner. . . .

. . . [Thus] the beliefs which we have most warrant for, have no safeguard to rest on, but a standing invitation to the whole world to prove them unfounded. If the challenge is not accepted, or is accepted and the attempt fails, we are far enough from certainty still; but we have done the best that the existing state of human reason admits of; we have neglected nothing that could give the truth a chance of reaching us. . . . This is the amount of certainty attainable by a fallible being, and this the sole way of attaining it.

Strange it is, that men should admit the validity of the arguments for free discussion, but object to their being "pushed to an extreme"; not seeing that unless the reasons are good for an extreme case, they are not good for any case. Strange that they should imagine that they are not assuming infallibility when they

acknowledge that there should be free discussion on all subjects which can possibly be doubtful, but think that some particular principle or doctrine should be forbidden to be questioned because it is so certain, that is, because they are certain that it is certain. To call any proposition certain, while there is any one who would deny its certainty if permitted, but who is not permitted, is to assume that we ourselves, and those who agree with us, are the judges of certainty, and judges without hearing the other side. . . .

Let us now pass to the second division of the argument. . . . [L]et us assume [the received options] to be true. [Let us] examine into the worth of the manner in which they are likely to be held, when their truth is not freely and openly canvassed. However unwillingly a person who has a strong opinion may admit the possibility that his opinion may be false, he ought to be moved by the consideration that however true it may be, if it is not fully, frequently, and fearlessly discussed, it will be held as a dead dogma, not a living truth. . . .

. . . He who knows only his own side of the case, knows little of that. His reasons may be good, and no one may have been able to refute them. But if he is equally unable to refute the reasons on the opposite side; if he does not so much as know what they are, he has no ground for preferring either opinion. The rational position for him would be suspension of judgment, and unless he contents himself with that, he is either led by authority, or adopts, like the generality of the world, the side to which he feels most inclination.

Nor is it enough that he should hear the arguments of adversaries from his own teachers, presented as they state them, and accompanied by what they offer as refutations. This is not the way to do justice to the arguments, or bring them into real contact with his own mind. He must be able to hear them from persons who actually believe them; who defend them in earnest, and do their very utmost for them. He must know them in their most plausible and persuasive form; he must feel the whole force of the difficulty . . . else he will never really possess himself of the portion of truth which meets and removes that difficulty.

Ninety-nine in a hundred of what are called educated men are in this condition, even of those who can argue fluently for their opinions. Their conclusion may be true, but it might be false for anything they know: they have never thrown themselves into the mental position of those who think differently from them, and considered what such persons may have to say; and consequently they do not, in any proper sense of the word, know the doctrine which they themselves profess. . . . All that part of the truth which turns the scale, and decides the judgment of a completely informed mind, they are strangers to; nor is it ever really known, but to those who have attended equally and impartially to both sides, and endeavoured to see the reasons of both in the strongest light. So essential is this discipline to a real understanding of moral and human subjects, that if opponents of all important truths do not exist, it is indispensable to imagine them and supply them with the strongest arguments which the most skilful devil's advocate can conjure up. . . .

[Consider] the manner in which the majority of believers hold the doctrines of Christianity. By Christianity I here mean what is accounted such by all churches and sects – the maxims and precepts contained in the New Testament. These are considered sacred, and accepted as laws, by all professing Christians. Yet it is scarcely too much to say that not one Christian in a thousand guides or tests his individual conduct by reference to those laws.

The standard to which he does refer it, is the custom of his nation, his class, or his religious profession. He has thus, on the one hand, a collection of ethical maxims, which he believes to have been vouchsafed to him by infallible wisdom as rules for his government; and on the other, a set of every-day judgments and practices, which go a certain length with some of those maxims, not so great a length with others, stand in direct opposition to some, and are, on the whole, a compromise between the Christian creed and the interests and suggestions of worldly life. To the first of these standards he gives his homage; to the other his real allegiance. All Christians believe that the blessed are the poor and humble, and those who are ill-used by the world; that it is easier for a camel to pass through the eye of a needle than for a rich man to enter the kingdom of heaven; that they should judge not, lest they be judged; that they should swear not at all; that they should love their neighbour as themselves; that if one take their cloak, they should give him their coat also; that they should take no thought for the morrow; that if they would be perfect, they should sell all that they have and give it to the poor.

[Christians] are not insincere when they say that they believe these things. They do believe them, as people believe what they have always heard lauded and never discussed. But in the sense of that living belief which regulates conduct, they believe these doctrines just up to the point to which it is usual to act upon them. The doctrines in their integrity are serviceable to pelt adversaries with; and it is understood that they are to be put forward (when possible) as the reasons for whatever people do that they think laudable. But any one who reminded them that the maxims require an infinity of things which they never even think of doing would gain nothing but to be classed among those very unpopular characters who affect to be better than other people. The doctrines have no hold on ordinary believers – are not a power in their minds. They have an habitual respect for the sound of them, but no feeling which spreads from the words to the things signified, and forces the mind to take them in, and make them conform to the formula. Whenever conduct is concerned, they look round for Mr A and B to direct them how far to go in obeying Christ.

Now we may be well assured that the case was not thus, but far otherwise, with the early Christians. Had it been thus, Christianity never would have expanded from an obscure sect of the despised Hebrews into the religion of the Roman Empire. When their enemies said, "See how these Christians love one another" (a remark not likely to be made by anybody now), they assuredly had a much livelier feeling of the meaning of their creed than they have ever had since. And to this cause, probably, it is chiefly owing that Christianity now makes so little progress in extending its domain, and after eighteen centuries, is still nearly confined to Europeans and the descendants of Europeans. . . . The sayings of Christ coexist passively in their minds, producing hardly any effect beyond what is caused by mere listening to words so amiable and bland.

There are many reasons, doubtless, why doctrines which are the badge of a sect retain more of their vitality than those common to all recognized sects, and why more pains are taken by teachers to keep their meaning alive; but one reason certainly is, that the peculiar doctrines are more questioned, and have to be oftener defended against open gainsayers. Both teachers and learners go to sleep at their post, as soon as there is no enemy in the field. . . .

Before quitting the subject of freedom of opinion, it is fit to take notice of those who say that the free expression of all opinions should be permitted, on condition that the manner be temperate, and do not pass the bounds of fair discussion. Much might be said on the impossibility of fixing where these supposed bounds are to be placed. [I]f the test be offence to those whose opinion is attacked, I think experience testifies that this offence is given whenever the attack is telling and powerful, and that every opponent who pushes them hard, and whom they find it difficult to answer, appears to them, if he shows any strong feeling on the subject, an intemperate opponent. [T]his, though an important consideration in a practical point of view, merges in a more fundamental objection. Undoubtedly the manner of asserting an opinion, even though it be a true one, may be very objectionable, and may justly incur severe censure. But the principal offences of the kind are such as it is mostly impossible, unless by accidental self-betrayal, to bring home to conviction. The gravest of them is, to argue sophistically, to suppress facts or arguments, to misstate the elements of the case, or misrepresent the opposite opinion. [I]t is rarely possible on adequate grounds conscientiously to stamp [this kind of] misrepresentation as morally culpable; and still less could law presume to interfere with this kind of controversial misconduct.

With regard to what is commonly meant by intemperate discussion, namely, invective, sarcasm, personality, and the like, the denunciation of these weapons would deserve more sympathy if it were ever proposed to interdict them equally to both sides; but it is only desired to restrain the employment of them against the prevailing opinion: against the unprevailing they may not only be used without general disapproval, but will be likely to obtain for him who uses them the praise of honest zeal and righteous indignation. Yet whatever mischief arises from their use, is greatest when they are employed against the comparatively defenceless; and whatever unfair advantage can be derived by any opinion from this mode of asserting it, accrues almost exclusively to received opinions. . . .

[Hence, since we should not restrict speech if the opinion to be repressed is false or if it is true, then we should not repress speech.]

Note

This essay is abridged and edited from chapter 2 of *On Liberty*.

35

"The Price We Pay?" Pornography and Harm

Susan J. Brison

Defenders of civil liberties have typically held, with J. S. Mill, that governments may justifiably exercise power over individuals, against their will, only to prevent harm to others.[1] Until the 1970s, liberals and libertarians assumed that since producers and consumers of pornography clearly didn't harm anyone else, the only reasons their opponents had for regulating pornography were that they considered it harmful to the producers or consumers, they thought it an offensive nuisance, and they objected, on moral or religious grounds, to certain private sexual pleasures of others. None of these reasons was taken to provide grounds for regulating pornography, however, because (1) individuals are considered to be the best judges of what is in their own interest (and, in any case, they cannot be harmed by something to which they consent), (2) what is merely offensive may be avoided (with the help of plain brown wrappers and zoning restrictions), and (3) the private sexual activities, of consenting adults anyway, are no one else's, certainly not the state's, business.

In the 1970s, however, the nature of the pornography debate changed as feminists argued that what is wrong with pornography is not that it morally defiles its producers and

consumers, nor that it is offensive or sinful, but, rather, that it is a species of hate literature as well as a particularly insidious method of sexist socialization. Susan Brownmiller was one of the first to take this stance in proclaiming that "[p]ornography is the undiluted essence of anti-female propaganda" (1975, p. 443) On this view, pornography (of the violent degrading variety) harms women by sexualizing misogynistic violence. According to Catharine MacKinnon, "[p]ornography sexualizes rape, battery, sexual harassment, prostitution, and child sexual abuse; it thereby celebrates, promotes, authorizes, and legitimizes them" (1987, p. 171).

The claim that women are harmed by pornography has changed the nature of the pornography debate, which is, for the most part, no longer a debate between liberals who subscribe to Mill's harm principle and legal moralists who hold that the state can legitimately legislate against so-called "morals offenses" that do not harm any non-consenting adults. Rather, the main academic debates now take place among those who subscribe to Mill's harm principle, but disagree about what its implications are for the legal regulation of pornography. Some theorists hold that violent degrading pornography does not harm anyone and, thus, cannot justifiably be legally regulated, socially stigmatized, or morally condemned. Others maintain that, although it is harmful to women, it cannot justifiably be regulated by either the civil or the criminal law since that would cause even greater harms and/or violate the legal rights of pornography producers and consumers, but that, nevertheless, private individuals should do what they can (through social pressure, educational campaigns, boycotts, etc.) to put an end to it. Still others claim that such pornography harms women by violating their civil right to be free from sex discrimination and should, for that reason, be addressed by the law (as well as by other means), just as other forms of sex discrimination are. But others argue that restricting such pornography violates the moral rights of pornography producers and consumers and, thus, restrictions are morally impermissible. In this chapter, I will argue that there is no moral right to such pornography.

What is Pornography?

First, however, I need to articulate what is at issue, but this is hard to do, given various obstacles to describing the material in question accurately. There is too much at stake to be put off writing about issues of urgent import to women because of squeamishness or fear of academic impropriety – but how can one write about this particular issue without reproducing the violent degrading pornography itself? (Recall the labeling of Anita Hill as "a little nutty and a little slutty" because she repeated, in public, the sexually demeaning language that Clarence Thomas had uttered to her in private.) However, if one doesn't write graphically about the content of violent degrading pornography one risks being viewed as either crazy (she must be imagining things!) or too prudish to talk frankly about sex. And what tone should one adopt – one of scholarly detachment or of outrage? There is a double bind here, similar to that faced by rape victims on the witness stand: If they appear calm and rational enough for

their testimony to be credible, that may be taken as evidence that they cannot have been raped. But if they are emotional and out of control enough to appear traumatized, then their testimony is not considered reliable.

Any critic of violent degrading pornography risks being viewed not only as prudish (especially if the critic is a woman), but also as meddling in others' "private" business, since we tend not to see the harm in pornography – harm which is often made invisible and considered unspeakable. But "we" didn't used to see the harm in depriving women and minorities of their civil rights. And "we" didn't used to see the harm in distributing postcards depicting and celebrating lynchings. More recently, "we" didn't see the harm in marital or "date" rape, spousal battering, or sexual harassment.

A further problem arises in critically analyzing violent degrading pornography, deriving from precisely those harmful aspects of it being critiqued, which is that descriptions of it and quotations from it can themselves be degrading, or even retraumatizing, especially for women who have been victimized by sexual violence. But one thing that is clear is that feminist critics of such pornography are *not* criticizing it on the grounds that it is erotic, or sexually arousing, or that it constitutes "obscenity," defined by the Court as "works which, taken as a whole, appeal to the prurient interest in sex, which portray sexual conduct in a patently offensive way, and which, taken as a whole, do not have serious literary, artistic, political or scientific value" (*Miller v. California*, 413 U.S. 15 at 24 [1973]).

Those who work on this issue – and have familiarized themselves with the real world of the pornography industry – know all too well that pornography is not merely offensive. In contrast, here is how some of them define "pornography": "the graphic sexually explicit subordination of women through pictures or words that also includes women dehumanized as sexual objects, things, or commodities; enjoying pain or humiliation or rape; being tied up, cut up, mutilated, bruised, or physically hurt; in postures of sexual submission, servility or display; reduced to body parts, penetrated by objects or animals, or presented in scenarios of degradation, injury, torture; shown as filthy or inferior; bleeding, bruised, or hurt in a context that makes these conditions sexual"[2] (MacKinnon, 1987, p. 176).

I define "pornography," for the purposes of this chapter, as violent degrading misogynistic hate speech (where "speech" includes words, pictures, films, etc.). Of course, what is commonly referred to as "pornography" is a much broader category, but I am focusing on only this sub-category. I will argue that, if pornography (the sub-category I've just defined) unjustly harms women (as there is reason to suppose it does), then there is no moral right to produce, sell, or consume it. (I will not here be arguing for or against its legal restriction. If there is no moral right to pornography, then any purported legal right to pornography must be grounded in something else. There may well be other reasons to defend a legal right to pornography, and, in any case, no position on that issue is dictated by my arguments against the alleged moral right.)

Pornography and Harm

I cannot hope to adequately portray the harms inflicted on girls and women in the production of pornography (for the reasons given above), but there is plenty of research documenting them. One of the most powerful forms of evidence for such harms is the first-person testimony of "participants" in pornography. (Those who are interested in reading more about this are referred to the Attorney General's Commission on Pornography, 1986; Itzen, 1992; Lederer, 1980; Lederer and Delgado, 1995; MacKinnon, 1987; MacKinnon, 1993; MacKinnon and Dworkin, 1997; Russell, 1993.) A not uncommon scenario, in which a girl becomes trapped in the porngraphy industry, is described by Evelina Giobbe in her testimony to the US Attorney General's Commission on Pornography. After running away from home at age 13 and being raped her first night on the streets, Giobbe was befriended by a man who initially seemed kind and

concerned, but who, after taking nude photographs of her, sold her to a pimp who raped and battered her, threatening her life and those of her family until she "agreed" to work as a prostitute for him. Her "customers" knew she was an adolescent and sexually inexperienced. "So," she testified, "they showed me pornography to teach me and ignored my tears and they positioned my body like the women in the pictures, and used me." She tried on many occasions to escape, but, as a teenager with no resources, cut off from friends and family, who believed she was a criminal, she was an easy mark for her pimp: "He would drag me down streets, out of restaurants, even into taxis, all the while beating me while I protested, crying and begging passersby for help. No one wanted to get involved" (quoted in Russell 1993, p. 38) She was later sold to another pimp who "was a pornographer and the most brutal of all." According to her testimony, he recruited other girls and women into pornography by advertising for models. "When a woman answered his ad, he'd offer to put her portfolio together for free, be her agent, and make her a 'star.' He'd then use magazines like *Playboy* to convince her to pose for 'soft-core' porn. He'd then engage her in a love affair and smooth talk her into prostitution. 'Just long enough,' he would say, 'to get enough money to finance your career as a model.' If sweet talk didn't work, violence and blackmail did. She became one of us" (p. 39).

Giobbe escaped the pornography industry by chance, after "destroy[ing] herself with heroin" and becoming "no longer usable." She considers herself one of the lucky ones – "a rare survivor" (pp. 39–40). And this was *before* the AIDS epidemic.

It is not enough to say that the participants in pornography consent, *even* in the case of adult women who apparently do, given the road many have been led (or dragged) down, since childhood in some cases, to get to that point. Genuine autonomous consent requires the ability to critically evaluate and choose from a range of significant and worthwhile options. Even if all the participants genuinely consented to their use in the pornography industry, however, we would need to consider how pornography influences how *other* non-consenting women are viewed and treated. Compare the (thankfully imaginary) scenario in which there existed "slave clubs" where some Blacks allowed themselves to be brutalized and degraded for the pleasure of their white customers. Suppose the Black "performers" determined that, given the options, it was in their best interest to make money in this way. Their financial gain – imagine that they are highly paid – more than compensates for the social harm to them as individuals of being subjected to a (let's say) slightly increased risk (resulting from the prevalence of such clubs) of being degraded and brutalized outside their workplace. Some of them even enjoy the work, having a level of ironic detachment that enables them to view their customers as pathetic or contemptible. Some, who don't actually enjoy their work, don't suffer distress, since they manage to dissociate during it. Others are distressed by it, but they have determined that the financial benefit outweighs the psychic and physical pain. For those Blacks who did not work in the clubs, however, there would be nothing that compensated for their slightly increased risk of being degraded and brutalized as a result of it. They would be better off if the clubs did not exist. The work the Blacks in the clubs did would make it harder for other Blacks to live their lives free of fear.

The harms pornography causes to non-participants in its production – often called "indirect" or "diffuse" harms, which makes them sound less real and less serious than they actually are – include (1) harms to those who have pornography forced on them, (2) increased or reinforced discrimination against – and sexual abuse of – girls and women, (3) harms to boys and men whose attitudes towards women and whose sexual desires are influenced by pornography, and (4) harms to those who have already been victimized by sexual violence. The first three categories of harm have been amply documented. (See the Attorney General's Commision on Pornography, 1986; Itzen, 1992; Lederer, 1980; Lederer and Delgado, 1995; MacKinnon, 1987; MacKinnon, 1993; MacKinnon and Dworkin, 1997; Russell,

1993.) That the proliferation of pornography leads to attitudinal changes in men, which, in turn, leads to harmful behavior, should not be surprising, especially given the high rates of exposure of pre-teen and teenage boys.

One might object, though, that pornography is merely a symptom (of a misogynistic, patriarchal society), not a cause. Even if this were the case, however, that would not mean that we should not be concerned about it. The fact that there are so few female legislators in the US at the federal level is a symptom, not a cause, of patriarchy. But this does not mean that we should not do anything about the political status quo. In any case, pornography is more than a mere symptom: it fosters and perpetuates the sexist attitudes that are essential for its enjoyment, even if it does not create them.

It should be noted here that the fact that the *point* of pornography (from the standpoint of the producers) is to make money by giving pleasure does not mean that it cannot also be harmfully degrading. On the contrary, it is pleasurable (and profitable) *precisely because* it is degrading to others. And it is reasonable to expect a spillover effect in the public domain, since its enjoyment requires the adoption of certain attitudes. In fact, although it may be difficult to see the process of dehumanization at work when girls and women are routinely portrayed as being worthy of degradation, torture, and even death, empirical studies have shown that exposure to such portrayals increases the likelihood that people will take actual sexual violence less seriously – and even consider it to be justified in some cases. (See MacKinnon and Dworkin, 1997, pp. 46–60; Lederer and Delgado, 1995, pp. 61–112; Russell, 1993, pp. 113–213.)

There is another connection between the dehumanization of girls and women in pornography and their brutalization in rape, battering, forced prostitution, and sexual murder, which is that, in a society where women are victimized in these ways at an alarming rate, it shows a callous disregard for the actual victims to have depictions of sexual violence bought and sold as entertainment. For a short while, after 9/11, we empathized so much with the victims of the terrorist attacks that films of similarly horrifying attacks were withdrawn because they were no longer considered entertaining. But victims of sexual violence are given so little respect that many of us see nothing wrong with being entertained by depictions of what they have had to endure.

If we take seriously the harm of pornography, then we want to know what to do about it. Should the government intervene by regulating it? The standard debate over pornography has framed it as a free speech issue. The drafters of an anti-pornography ordinance adopted by the city of Indianapolis argued that pornography constitutes a violation of the civil rights of women. In response to those who asserted that the First Amendment protected pornography, they argued that pornography violated the First Amendment rights of women (by "silencing" them – depriving them of credibility and making "no" appear to mean "yes" in rape scenarios), as well as their Fourteenth Amendment rights to equal protection. In his opinion in *American Booksellers Association v. Hudnut*, which ruled unconstitutional the Indianapolis anti-pornography ordinance, Judge Frank Easterbrook acknowledged that pornography harms women in very significant and concrete ways: "Depictions of subordination tend to perpetuate subordination. The subordinate status of women in turn leads to affront and lower pay at work, insult and injury at home, battery and rape on the streets. In the language of the legislature, '[p]ornography is central in creating and maintaining sex as a basis of discrimination. Pornography is a systematic practice of exploitation and subordination based on sex which differentially harms women. The bigotry and contempt it produces, with the acts of aggression it fosters, harm women's opportunities for equality and rights [of all kinds].' Indianapolis Code §16-1(a)(2). Yet this simply demonstrates the power of pornography as speech."[3]

Easterbrook seems to take the harms of pornography seriously, but he then goes on to talk about its "unhappy effects" which he considers to be the result of "mental intermediation." He assumes that speech has no (or merely negligible) effects that are not under the conscious control of the audience, although this assumption is undermined not only by the widely acknowledged power of advertising, but also by recent work in cognitive neuroscience on the prevalence of unconscious imitation in human beings.[4] It might be argued, though, that, if we consider the producers of pornography to be even partially responsible for the violence perpetrated by some of its consumers, then we must consider the perpetrators *not* to be responsible or to be less than fully responsible for their crimes. But this does not follow. Even if the perpetrators are considered to be 100 percent responsible, some responsibility can still be attributed to the pornographers. (In fact, two or more people can each be 100 percent responsible for the same crime, as in the case of multiple snipers who simultaneously fire many shots, fatally wounding their victim.)

The courts have, for now, decided that even if serious harm to women results from it, pornography is, qua speech, protected (except for that material which also meets the legal definition of obscenity). That is, there is, currently, a *legal* right to it, falling under the right to free speech. But *should* there be?

A Moral Right to Pornography?

Of course we value freedom of speech. But how should we value it? What should we do when speech is genuinely harmful? Traditionally, in the US, the constitutionally protected right to free speech is held to be of such high importance that it trumps just about everything else. For example, in the *Hudnut* case, discussed above, it was acknowledged that the pornography producers' and consumers' legal right to free speech was in conflict with women's legal right to equal protection, but it was asserted (without argumentation) that the free speech right had priority. Acceptance of this claim without requiring a defense of it, however, amounts to adopting a kind of free speech fundamentalism. But to see how untenable such a view is, suppose that uttering the words "you're dead" caused everyone within earshot (but the speaker) to fall down dead. Would anyone seriously say that such speech deserved legal protection? Granted, the harms of pornography are less obvious and less severe, but there is sufficient evidence for them for it to be reasonable to require an argument for why the legal right to it should take priority over others' legal rights not to be subjected to such harms.

If we reject free speech fundamentalism, the question of whether pornography should be legally restricted becomes much more complicated. My aim in this article is not to articulate or defend a position on this question; rather, I aim to undermine the view that there is a moral right to pornography that undergirds a legal right to it.

In "The Right to Get Turned On: Pornography, Autonomy, Equality" (this volume), Andrew Altman shifts the debate over pornography in a promising way by arguing that there is a *moral* right to (even violent misogynistic) pornography, falling, not under a moral right to free speech, but, rather, under a moral right to sexual autonomy (that also covers the right to use contraceptives and the right to homosexual sex).[5] On this view, which Altman dubs "liberal sexual morality," whatever harms result from pornography are just the price we pay for the right to sexual autonomy. Sexuality is an important, arguably central, aspect of a flourishing human life. Sexual expression is one of the primary ways we define ourselves and our relations to others, and a healthy society should value and celebrate it. But what does it add to these claims to say that we have a moral *right* to sexual autonomy? And, if we do have such a right, does it include a right to produce, distribute, and consume pornography (defined, as above, as violent degrading misogynistic hate speech)?

Although philosophers disagree about the nature of rights (and indeed even about whether such things exist at all), most hold that to say that someone, x, has a moral right to do something, y, means that others are under a duty not to interfere with x's doing y. (Of course, x's right is limited by others' rights, as expressed by the saying "your right to swing your arm ends at my face.") But beyond this, there is

little agreement. Some hold that rights are natural, inalienable, God-given. Others hold that rights talk is just a shorthand for talk about those interests that are especially important to us (for example, because protecting them tends to increase our welfare). Some hold that we have positive rights, just by virtue of being human, such that other people are under an obligation to provide us with whatever we need to exercise those rights. (If there is a positive right to education, for example, then society has an obligation to provide free public education for all.) Others hold that we have only negative rights (unless individuals *grant* us positive rights by, for example, making promises to assist us), which require only that other people not interfere with our exercising those rights. (The right to privacy, if taken to be simply a right to be left alone, is an example of a negative right.)

On any account, the concept of a right is diffuse. To say that x has a moral right to do y does not, by itself, say very much, unless we specify what others are required to do (or to refrain from doing) in order not to violate that right. There is a wide range of different responses to x's doing y, given that x has a right to do y – from complete acceptance (or perhaps even positive support) to something just short of physical restraint or intervention. Where is the alleged right to pornography located on this spectrum of moral assessment?

Altman considers the right to pornography and the right to sexual orientation to have the same foundation in a right to sexual autonomy. What should our (society's) attitude be towards the exercising of that right? Should we tolerate it, that is, have no laws against it, while allowing private individuals to lobby against it or to try to dissuade people from it? Or should we actively embrace it? Assimilating the right to pornography to the right to sexual orientation muddies the waters here. Presumably, according to liberal sexual morality, the right to sexual orientation requires more than mere tolerance. It requires society's complete acceptance (and, I would argue, positive support, given that prejudice and violence against gays and lesbians persist in our society). It is wrong to hold that gays and lesbians have "bad characters" or to try to get them to "reform."

The right to pornography, however, does not lie on the same end of the spectrum, since Altman claims that getting off on pornography is a sign of a bad character. Some feminists and liberals who defend a legal right to pornography also hold that all sorts of private pressures – protests, boycotts, educational campaigns – should be brought to bear on the pornographers. Altman's position is that there is not just a legal right, but also a *moral* right to pornography, even if there is something bad about exercising it. There are persuasive reasons for holding that we have legal rights to do some things that are morally wrong, in cases in which enforcement would be impossible or would involve gross violations of privacy. But Altman seems to hold that we have a *moral* right to do some things that are morally wrong. What does this mean? It cannot mean that people have a right to do things that are wrong in that they harm others. It might mean that people have the right to do things that other people consider wrong (but that are not harmful to others), that is, people have the right to do harmless things that other people morally disapprove of. However, if the behavior, e.g. engaging in homosexual sex, is not unjustly harming others, then liberals who subscribe to Mill's harm principle have no grounds for considering it to be wrong.

So where should the right to pornography be located on the spectrum of moral assessment? There is no one answer to this question. We need to look at particular cases. Suppose I have a 21-year-old son – I'm assuming minors have no right to pornography – who is a heavy consumer of pornography (of the kind I've been talking about). What does his (alleged) right to pornography entail? Given my opposition to pornography, presumably I would not be under an obligation to positively support his pornography habit by buying it for him. But would I have to pretend that I'm not aware of it? Would I be under a duty not to try to dissuade him from viewing pornography? Would his sister be under a duty not to throw the magazines out when she saw them in common areas of the

house? Would it be wrong for his buddies to try to talk him out of it? Would his teachers have a duty to refrain from arguing against it? Would it be wrong for his neighbors to boycott the local convenience store that sold it? Would his girlfriend (or boyfriend) who became convinced it was ruining their relationship be under a moral duty not to rip it out of his hands? If the answer to each of the above questions is "no," which I think it is, then it's not clear what, if anything, his right entitles him to.[6] What is clear is that, if a right to pornography exists, it is quite unlike a right to engage in homosexual sex or to use contraceptives, and is located at the opposite end of the spectrum of moral assessment.

Perhaps there is, nevertheless, something special about sexual arousal ("getting turned on") that gives it special moral status. But Altman has not said what makes sexual arousal different (in a morally significant way) from other forms of arousal, for example, that of racial animus. It makes sense to say that there is a right to be turned on – not a special right, but, rather, one falling under a general right to liberty, but this general right to liberty is delimited by the harm principle. There is no general right to have pleasurable feelings (of any sort, sexual or otherwise) that overrides others' rights not to be harmed. There is no moral right to achieve a feeling of comfort by unjustly discriminating against homosexuals on the grounds that associating with them makes you uncomfortable. Likewise, there is no moral right to achieve a feeling of superiority (no matter how pleasurable such a feeling might be) by discriminating against those of a different race. And it doesn't matter how central to one's self-definition the feeling in question might be. For parents, the satisfaction of ensuring the good upbringing and education of one's children is of paramount importance, and yet this degree of importance does not give racist parents the right to racially segregated housing or schools.

It might be argued that sexual arousal is special in that it is a bodily pleasure and, thus, more natural, possibly even immutable. Even if this were so, it would not follow that one has a right to achieve it by any means necessary. To take an example of another kind of "bodily" pleasure, suppose that there are gustatory pleasures that can be achieved only in immoral ways, for example, by eating live monkey brains – which some people used to do – or organs or flesh "donated" by (or purchased from) living human beings, or food that has been stolen from the people on the verge of starvation. That there is a (general) right to enjoy eating what one chooses to eat – it would be (in general) wrong, for example, for me to force you to eat, or not to eat, something – does not mean that one has a right to eat whatever gives one pleasure.

But it is not the case that what people find sexually arousing is a simple biological fact about them, a given, something immutable. People can be conditioned to be aroused by any number of things. (In one study, men were conditioned to be aroused by a picture of a woman's boot; Russell, 1993, p. 129.) Emotions, especially ones with strong physiological components, such as sexual arousal, *feel* natural. They don't seem to be socially constructed, because we don't (at the time) consciously choose them: they just *are*. But emotions are, at least to some extent, learned reactions to things. There are gender differences in emotional reactions; for example, men tend to get angry in some situations in which women tend to feel, not angry, but hurt. But this does not mean that such differences are *natural*.

Given the wide variety of sexual fantasies and fetishes we know about, it's conceivable that just about *anything* could be a turn-on for someone – looking at photos of dead, naked bodies piled in mass graves in Nazi death camps, for example, or looking at photos of lynched Black men. According to liberal sexual morality, the only reason for supposing that there might not be a moral right to make a profit from and get off on such "pornography" would be that the photographed people are posthumously harmed by it (given that they did not consent to their images being used in this way). But suppose they had consented. Or suppose, more plausibly, that the images were computer-generated – completely realistic-looking, but not images *of* actual individuals. Liberal sexual morality would have to allow (some) people to make

money by others' getting turned on by these images. Not only that, but, given that sexual desires are malleable, the pornographer also has a right to make money by acculturating others to be turned on by such images. (In other words, the pornographer has a right to turn the world into a place where people get turned on by such images.) And, if our attitude towards this is grounded in the right to sexual autonomy, it should be similar to our attitude towards homosexuality: we shouldn't merely tolerate it, we should come to accept and support it.

While conceding that there are limits to the right to sexual autonomy – it is constrained by the harm principle – Altman assumes (as most liberals do) that one cannot be harmed by something to which one consents. I argued earlier that the way many models get lured into the pornography industry should make us at least question the extent to which they are consenting to what is being done to them. But suppose they do consent. Does that mean that we must tolerate the production and use of whatever pornography results? Unfortunately, one doesn't have to construct a thought experiment to test our intuitions about this. According to *The New York Times*, Armin Meiwes, "[a] German computer technician who killed and ate a willing victim he found through the Internet," was recently convicted of manslaughter. His "victim," Bernd-Jürgen Brandes, had "responded to an Internet posting by Mr. Meiwes seeking someone willing to be 'slaughtered'." "'Both were looking for the ultimate kick'," the judge said. It was "an evening of sexual role-playing and violence, much of it videotaped by Mr. Meiwes," enough to convince the court that the "victim" consented.[7] Does the right to sexual autonomy include the rights to produce, sell, and get turned on by the videotape of this "slaughter" – a real-life instance of a snuff film? If we cannot *prove* that there is a causal connection between the film and harm to others, the answer, according to liberal sexual morality, is "yes."

Altman claims that even if a causal connection between violent pornography and sexual violence were clearly established, it would still be insufficient to conclude that, in contemporary society, the production, distribution and viewing of violent pornography lay beyond the limits of an adult's right to sexual autonomy (p. 360) because *other* media – he cites slasher films – arguably "cause at least some amount of violence against women, sexual and otherwise. However, it is not reasonable to deny that adults have no right to produce, distribute and view such movies" (p. 356). Why, if one has established that, say, slasher films are harmful, we must hold that adults have a right to them is not explained. But even if we agree that adults have the right to produce/consume non-pornographic media even if it is as harmful as pornography, it does not follow that adults have the right to produce/consume pornography. To assume that it does would be like arguing against prohibiting driving while talking on cell phones on the grounds that this is not the *only* thing (or even the main thing) contributing to automobile accidents.

Altman accepts that "it is reasonable to hold that the existence of . . . pornography makes it more difficult for women to live their lives as the sexual equals of men, i.e., more difficult relative to a society which was ruled by a liberal sexual morality and had fewer women, or none at all, who were willing to engage in humiliating conduct as part of the production of pornographic materials" (14), but he notes that women are better off in a society with liberal sexual morality than in a society with traditional sexual morality (for example, Saudi Arabia). I agree, but surely these are not the only two possibilities. I would advocate the alternative

of a progressive sexual morality. What might that look like? We don't even know. Even our most deep-seated assumptions about sexuality may turn out to be mistaken. We used to view rape as motivated purely by lust (or, in wartime, by a desire to humiliate enemy men) and battering as a way of showing spousal love. Some of us still do. Gradually, however, we are breaking the link between sexuality and violence. Perhaps some day we'll have reached the point where sexual violence is no longer arousing, where it makes no sense to talk of killing and being killed as the "ultimate" sexual "kick."

According to liberal sexual morality, the harms of pornography are the price we pay for having the right to sexual autonomy in other areas, e.g. the right to have sex outside of marriage (including homosexual sex) and the right to use contraceptives. But this view (of the right to sexual autonomy as an all-or-nothing package) is formed in response to legal moralism, and makes sense only if one considers all these rights to be rights to do harmless things that some people nevertheless morally condemn. In such cases, proponents of liberal sexual morality say: "If you don't like it, don't look at it (or hear about it or think about it)." This is a satisfactory response only if the behavior in question isn't harming anyone. But as our views about what constitutes harm have changed, our views of what is our business have also changed. Just as we no longer look the other way in response to marital or "date" rape, domestic violence, and sexual harassment, we should no longer accept pornography's harms as the price we pay for sexual autonomy.

Acknowledgments

I would like to thank Ann Bumpus, Christopher Wellman, Thomas Trezise, and, especially, Margaret Little for helpful discussions of many issues in this article. I am grateful, also, to Hugh La Follette and Kristen Grauer, for their help with revising this for inclusion in the present volume.

Notes

1 John Stuart Mill, *On Liberty* (Indianapolis, IN: Hackett Publishing Co., 1978). Mill considered his harm principle to apply equally to governmental regulation and to "the moral coercion of public

opinion." The harm principle states that " . . . the only purpose for which power can be rightfully exercised over any member of a civilized community, against his will, is to prevent harm to others" (p. 9). Mill does not specify what counts as harm. Following Joel Feinberg, I consider it to be a wrongful setback to one's significant interests. See Joel Feinberg, *The Moral Limits of the Criminal Law*, Vol. 1, *Harm to Others* (New York: Oxford University Press, 1984).

2   This is the definition used in the anti-pornography ordinance drafted by Andrea Dworkin and Catharine MacKinnon, passed by the city of Indianapolis, but ruled unconstitutional by the courts.

3   *American Booksellers Association, Inc. v. Hudnut*, 771 F.2d 323 (1985), p. 329. This view can't consistently be held, however, by liberals and feminists who support laws against sex or race discrimination and segregation in schools, workplaces, and even private clubs. One doesn't hear the argument that if segregation harms minorities' opportunities for equal rights this simply demonstrates the power of freedom of association, which is also protected by the First Amendment.

4   The recent research discussed in Hurley (2004) suggests that the imitation of others' behavior, including others' violent acts, is not a consciously mediated process, under the autonomous control of the viewers/imitators.

5   Since some theorists ground the right to free speech in a right to autonomy, however, there may not be such a sharp distinction between these two approaches. See Brison (1998).

6   I also mean for the above thought experiment to illustrate the fact that the nature of the duty one has with respect to the holder of the alleged moral right to pornography depends on one's relationship to the right-holder. Presumably a neighbor would be under a duty not to snatch pornography out of the right-holder's hands. But if someone *else*, the right-holder's lover, say, is under no such duty, then it's not clear what the right amounts to.

7   Mark Landler, "German Court Convicts Internet Cannibal of Manslaughter," *The New York Times*, January 31, 2004, p. A3.

References

Altman, Andrew (2005) "The Right to Get Turned on: Pornography, Autonomy, Equality." In Andrew I. Cohen and Christopher Heath Wellman (eds.), *Contemporary Debates in Applied Ethics*. Oxford: Blackwell.

American Booksellers Association, Inc. v. Hudnut (1985). 771 F.2d 323.

Attorney General's Commission on Pornography (1986). *Final Report*. Washington, DC: US Department of Justice.

Brison, Susan J. (1998) "The Autonomy Defense of Free Speech," *Ethics* 108: 312–39.

Brownmiller, Susan (1975) *Against our Will: Men, Women and Rape*. New York: Bantam Books.

Feinberg, Joel (1984) *The Moral Limits of the Criminal Law*, Vol. 1: *Harm to Others*. New York: Oxford University Press.

Hurley, Susan L. (2004) "Imitation, Media Violence, and Freedom of Speech," *Philosophical Studies* 17/1–2 (January): 165–218.

Itzen, Catherine (ed.) (1992) *Pornography: Women, Violence and Civil Liberties*. New York: Oxford University Press.

Landler, Mark (2004) "German court convicts Internet cannibal of manslaughter," *New York Times* (January 31): A3.

Lederer, Laura (ed.) (1980) *Take Back the Night: Women on Pornography*. New York: William Morrow and Co., Inc.

Lederer, Laura J. and Richard Delgado (eds.) (1995) *The Price We Pay: The Case Against Racist Speech, Hate Propaganda, and Pornography*. New York: Hill and Wang.

MacKinnon, Catharine A. (1987) *Feminism Unmodified: Discourses on Life and Law*. Cambridge, MA: Harvard University Press.

MacKinnon, Catharine A. (1993) *Only Words*. Cambridge, MA: Harvard University Press.

MacKinnon, Catharine A. and Dworkin, Andrea (eds.) (1997). *In Harm's Way: The Pornography Civil Rights Hearings*. Cambridge, MA: Harvard University Press.

Mill, John Stuart (1978) *On Liberty*. Indianapolis, IN: Hackett Publishing CO. (Originally published 1859.)

Miller v. California (1973). 413 US 15.

Russell, Diana E. H. (ed.) (1993 *Making Violence Sexy: Feminist Views on Pornography*. Buckingham: Open University Press.

36

The Right to Get Turned On: Pornography, Autonomy, Equality

Andrew Altman

I   Introduction

Debates over whether adults have a right to produce, distribute, and view pornographic materials have typically proceeded on the premise that freedom of speech is the central liberty at stake. Those who argue that there is a moral "right to pornography" contend that it is part of a person's freedom of speech. Those who argue that there is no such right contend that pornographic material is "low value" speech or more like conduct than speech. They proceed to claim that some other value such as sexual equality between men and women overrides an individual's claim to have access to pornography.

I believe that the premise behind this debate is mistaken. While there are certain respects in which freedom of speech is at stake in the matter of pornography, such freedom is not the central liberty relevant to the issue. Rather, the right to pornography should be understood primarily as an element of another form of freedom: sexual autonomy. Individuals ought to have a broad liberty to define and enact their own sexuality. Persons who view pornography are exercising

their sexual autonomy, and the debate over pornography should be seen from the standpoint of that liberty.

When seen from such a standpoint, the claim that there is a right to pornography is analogous to claims that there is a right to use contraceptives, to engage in sexual relations outside of marriage, and to engage in homosexual activity. Freedoms that protect sexuality-defining decisions get closer to the heart of the pornography issue than freedoms that protect speech and other activities whose primary intent is to communicate ideas or attitudes.

The principle of sexual autonomy has its limits. The moral right to have sex without being married does not include the moral right to have sex with children or with an unconsenting adult. A moral right to pornography does not include the moral right to buy or possess photographs of children having sex, or of people who are actually being raped or sexually assaulted. However, I will argue that sexual autonomy does entail a moral right to buy and possess a wide range of pornographic materials, including those that depict sexual violence.

387

II What is Pornography?

It is not realistic to think that there is a succinct definition of pornography that would prove acceptable to the different sides in the debate and capture all of the material that might reasonably be thought pornographic. This does not mean that we should remain content with Justice Potter Stewart's attitude: "I know it when I see it" (*Jacobellis v. Ohio*, 1964, p. 197). Rather, we can formulate a concise description of a class of materials that includes much, if not all, of the materials which the different sides in the debate could agree are reasonably described as pornographic. The description would be a kind of starting point that could be qualified and expanded in various ways as the debate proceeded. The point is that we need some reasonable starting point that can be accepted without unfairly tilting the debate over the existence of a moral right to pornography.

My suggestion for such a starting point is this: pornography is sexually explicit material, in words or images, which is intended by its creators to excite sexually those who are willing viewers of the material. By a "willing viewer," I mean a person who voluntarily pays something – in time, effort, or money – to view the material and who is willing to pay because he expects to become sexually aroused by viewing it. Thus, pornography is a commodity which represents a kind of sexual meeting of the minds between producer and consumer: the producer intends that the consumer be sexually aroused by the product and the consumer pays for the product in the expectation of becoming aroused by it.

The intention to cause sexual arousal is clearly not the only one for which a producer of pornography may be acting. Commercial producers intend to make money. However, the intent to cause sexual arousal is central, even in the commercial case. The producers intend to make money by creating a product which causes sexual arousal and the buyer expects to be aroused by viewing the product.

In contrast, consider the authors or publishers of a medical textbook which contains photographs of sexual organs and their various diseases. Such persons intend to make money.

However, it is not their intention to make it by causing sexual arousal but rather by communicating medical information. Moreover, buyers of medical textbooks do not generally purchase them in order to stimulate themselves sexually: there is no sexual meeting of the minds between the authors or publishers and the consumers.

It is an important fact about human sexuality that different people are sexually excited by very different kinds of sexually explicit material. The makers of pornography know this fact well. Much hardcore pornography is explicitly addressed to the viewer's preference for particular types of sexual content: oral, anal, sadomasochist, gay, lesbian, and so on.

It seems clear that the vast majority of pornography in contemporary society is directed at males. Among all of the hours spent watching pornography, the vast majority of those hours belong to men. However, even within the group of heterosexual men, there are differences in the pornographic content which they willingly seek out. In addition, empirical studies show that a significant percentage of willing viewers of pornography are women (Slade, 2001, p. 967).

III Sexual Autonomy

Individuals have a right to a substantial degree of control over their own lives. This right does not mean that any individual has the liberty to do whatever she or he chooses: one person's liberty is limited by the duties that she has toward others. Moreover, individual control is invariably exercised within a social context created by the choices and actions of other people who are exercising control over their own lives. Yet, it would be mistaken to think that individual control is rendered factually impossible by the unchosen character of our social context or morally meaningless by the existence of duties we owe to others. Persons are not puppets of their social circumstances, nor are they smothered by moral duties owed to others. Rather, they are agents who have the broad right to decide for themselves how to live their lives. Other individuals and the government have a duty to respect those decisions.

Under the rules of traditional sexual morality, a person's sexual life was, to a large extent, not his or her own: the rules imposed a highly confining set of duties on sexual choices and actions. In particular, sexual activity was condemned as "unnatural" if it was outside of heterosexual marriage or if the activities were undertaken for purposes of other than procreation. Traditional sexual morality looked askance on pornography because such materials excite passions which do not stay neatly confined within the narrow channels of sexual activity that traditional morality deemed the only natural and acceptable way of expressing human sexuality. Accordingly, pornography was seen as corrupting individual character and subverting the proper order of society.

The sexual revolution of the 1960s replaced the traditional sexual morality with a liberal one. This liberal morality located a person's sexual life much more within his or her own dominion than did traditional morality. One way of characterizing the liberal rules is to say that they left adults morally free to engage in the sexual activities of their choice, so long as the activities had no direct unwilling victims. This characterization will require some qualification, but it does help to highlight the difference between traditional and liberal sexual morality.

From the liberal viewpoint, traditional sexual morality violated the rights of the individual by treating a person's sexual choices as if they belonged to society. Where the traditional morality reigned, sexuality was conscripted by society to promote its interest in procreation and in preserving a certain model of the family. Individuals were expected to follow the "appropriate" social scripts, which were defined by gender and restricted a person to marital (heterosexual) intercourse without the use of contraceptives. Liberal morality does not deny the importance of procreation or family, but it does assert that adult individuals have the right to decide for themselves when and whether to have children and when and whether to engage in sexual activity for purposes other than procreation. And the liberal view is that this right of sexual autonomy is possessed equally by each

adult. David Richards, a leading proponent of a liberal sexual morality, puts the central point plainly: "Legal enforcement of a particular sexual ideal fails . . . to accord due respect to individual autonomy" (Richards, 1982, p. 99).

The new liberal principles cast a very different light on pornography than did the traditional morality. There is nothing inherent to the activities of producing or consuming pornography which raises a presumption that there is some direct unwilling victim of the activities. Pornography does not necessarily involve children or any unwilling adult. The sole participants in the production and use of pornographic materials may be consenting adults, and, in such a situation, the strong liberal presumption is that those adults have a moral right to do what they are doing. The basis of this presumption is the idea that the sexuality-defining decisions of adults are up to them, and those decisions include ones that involve voluntary association for purposes of sexual pleasure or for profit from the manufacture of materials that help produce sexual arousal.

Accordingly, on the liberal sexual morality, a right to pornography is akin to the right to use contraceptives: adults must be free to manufacture and use pornographic materials, just as they must be free to make and use contraceptive devices, and others must not interfere with those choices. Other sexuality-defining activities, such as the right to engage in homosexual activity, are also central to the liberal sexual morality.[1] Some people may be revolted by homosexuality and regard it as depraved, just as some are revolted by pornography and regard it as depraved. But such attitudes are not adequate grounds, on the liberal view, for restricting a person's sexual activities.

At the same time, it is important to understand that any reasonable version of liberal sexual morality must go beyond the idea that there is an absolute right to choose one's sexual activities as long as there is no direct unwilling victim. Some room must be left for the possibility that, in some circumstances, such choices are outside the boundaries of the person's right to sexual autonomy. In the next two sections, we will examine some possible circumstances which mark the limits of an individual's right. For the present, the key point is that, for a reasonable version of liberal morality, any restriction on the right of sexual autonomy must rest on considerations which possess considerable weight and are supported by clear and convincing evidence.

It is also important to note that the liberal claim that individuals have a broad right to define their own sexual identity is compatible with the idea that some of the activities which individuals have a right to engage in are, nonetheless, morally deficient. For example, one may agree that an adult has the right to view violent pornography but still contend that any adult who does seek sexual arousal by viewing violent sexual images has a morally deficient character. Put another way, it is consistent for a liberal to assert that a person who has an impeccable character would refrain from certain activities, even though people have a right to do those activities.[2]

Liberal sexual morality has become the dominant morality of contemporary society, although the traditional morality still survives and exerts some influence. Defenders of traditional morality claim that liberal "permissiveness" leads to social disintegration. Thus, Robert George, a contemporary proponent of the traditional view, asserts that "it is plain that moral decay has profoundly damaged the morally valuable institutions of marriage and the family" (George, 1993, p. 36).

It is true that divorce rates are much higher than in past generations, and family life has taken on a much different shape. However, one cannot infer that profound moral damage has been done without making many unproven assumptions about how good family was in "the good old days," when marriages often were forcibly held together by the economic dependence of the wife and the powerful social stigma of divorce. While it would be wrong for liberals to presume that liberal society is, in every aspect, better than traditional society was, there are two important respects in which liberals should insist that people are better off under the liberal morality: (1) men and women are freer to define a central aspect of their existence,

their sexuality, in ways that fit their individual character, and (2) women are freer and more equal participants in society. Without attempting any full-scale assessment of the traditional morality, in sections V and VII, I will elaborate on these two considerations in favor of liberal sexual morality. However, the principal task of the remainder of this essay is to examine critically several feminist arguments that, if sound, would show that any liberal right to pornography must be far more limited than I have suggested.

IV   Sexual Violence

Suppose that the viewing of certain types of pornography has very harmful indirect effects on unwilling victims. For example, consider pornographic movies which depict the gang rape of a woman. Even assuming that all of the participants in such movies are consenting adults – so that the rapes are staged and not real – it is possible that the movies could lead some male viewers to "imitate" what they see and commit real rapes. Similar possibilities could obtain for other kinds of violent pornography.

Moreover, in contemporary society, there are many willing viewers of violent pornography: the material is commercially produced and widely distributed. Even if most viewers do not directly violate anyone's rights, some of them may be prompted to commit sexual violence as a result of their exposure to violent pornography. Accordingly, Helen Longino expresses the view of many feminist thinkers when she claims, "Pornography, especially violent pornography, is implicated in the committing of crimes of violence against women" (Longino, 1995, p. 41). Longino proceeds to argue on the basis of her claim that the access of adults to pornography made by adults should be legally restricted. In the light of such an argument, it is important to address the question of whether the right to view pornography reaches its limit when sexual violence is depicted.[3]

It is true that a willing viewer of violent pornography who becomes sexually aroused does not necessarily harm any unwilling victim. Under liberal principles, this means that there is a presumption that the viewer is simply exercising his right of sexual autonomy. But we should not ignore the societal consequences of the availability of violent pornography in deciding whether that presumption is overridden by countervailing considerations.

If the availability of violent pornography led to substantial increases in sexual violence, then the victims of this increased violence would be paying the price for the availability of violent pornography to all adults. And it seems wrong to make those victims pay such a steep price so that some can have ready access to violent sexual materials for purposes of sexually arousing themselves. In such a situation, it would appear that any presumptive right to violent pornography would be overridden by countervailing considerations.

Notice that the considerations here consist precisely of rights-based concerns to which a liberal sexual morality must give considerable weight. The victims of the criminals who commit pornography-inspired sex crimes have their basic liberal right to sexual autonomy violated egregiously by the perpetrators. However, there are obstacles which need to be surmounted before one can reasonably conclude that, in contemporary society, any right to pornography must stop short of including a right to pornographic materials depicting sexual violence.

First, there must be clear evidence of a causal connection between the production of violent pornography and sexual violence. In the absence of such evidence, there are insufficient grounds for limiting the right of sexual autonomy so as to leave out a right to make and view violent pornography. Yet, the evidence for the existence of a causal connection is, at best, mixed.

Experimental studies suggest that when males repeatedly view violence against women in films, they tend to undergo attitudinal changes making them desensitized to such violence and more accepting of it.[4] However, the films used in the studies were R-rated "slasher movies," such as *Texas Chain Saw Massacre*, lacking the sort of graphic depictions of sexual activity characteristic of paradigm cases of

pornography. Moreover, the extrapolation from the experimental studies to conclusions about sexual crimes is rather tenuous: no one knows how long the attitudinal changes measured by the studies persist or whether they produce behavioral changes leading to the perpetration of sex crimes.

Since the 1960s, violent pornography has become much more readily accessible in many countries, including the United States. The incidence of sexual crime has also increased in those countries. However, data collected over many decades in the US show that the number of rapes rises in virtual lockstep with the rate of non-sexual assaults (Kutchinsky, 1991, p. 55). It is not plausible to think that violent pornography causes a rise in non-sexual violence.[5] Indeed, much more reasonable is the hypothesis that sociological variables such as poverty rates and the extent of alcohol consumption explain the equal increases in both sexual and non-sexual violence.

On the other hand, there are studies that provide some evidence for the conclusion that sexual crimes increase as a result of an increase in the availability of pornography. One such study found that the rise in rape rates around the world was traceable to pornography. However, other studies have found no correlation and some have even concluded that rape drops as a result of the availability of pornography (Slade, 2001, pp. 997–8).

The existing state of the evidence, then, is quite far from clearly establishing any causal connection between violent pornography and sexual violence, and appears to weigh against any such connection. Yet, even if a causal connection between violent pornography and sexual violence were clearly established, it would still be insufficient to conclude that, in contemporary society, the production, distribution, and viewing of violent pornography lay beyond the limits of an adult's right of sexual autonomy. Additionally, one would need to justify selecting out such pornography and distinguishing it from the myriad of other forms of media violence that have the potential to cause violence.

Consider the slasher films mentioned earlier. It is reasonable to suspect that such films and much else in the mass media cause at least some amount of violence against women, sexual and otherwise. However, it is not reasonable to deny that adults have a right to produce, distribute, and view such movies, even if we were to assume the existence of an established causal relation between the films and sexual violence. Adults who find the films entertaining are subject to criticism for getting enjoyment from watching depictions of terrified women inhumanely attacked. However, these adults do not violate anyone's rights by getting their enjoyment in that way. The situation with respect to viewing violent pornography is different only in the respect that watching such pornography is typically an exercise of sexual autonomy. To the extent that viewing slasher films is seen as non-sexual entertainment, the right to see them would actually be *less* strong than the right to view violent pornography.

Accordingly, it is unclear how one could justify selecting out violent pornography as setting a limit to the individual's right of sexual autonomy, while at the same time conceding that there is a right to view forms of media which, as far as we know, could contribute just as much to sexual violence as does violent pornography. It might be argued that violent pornography is a more powerful stimulus to sexual violence. However, we have seen that the evidence of any causal connection between pornography and violence is mixed. And there is simply no evidence indicating the relative contribution which different factors make to the overall level of sexual violence in society.

It may seem that liberal sexual morality is indifferent to the actual violence that may be caused by the production and viewing of the depictions of sexual violence found in films and other media. However, we must be careful in our understanding of what the liberal right of sexual autonomy involves. I have argued that it does include the right to produce and view violent pornography. However, liberal sexual morality also holds that each adult has an equal right to sexual autonomy. If sexual violence is widespread in society, as it is in ours, then liberal morality cannot simply brush off that fact. Widespread sexual violence means

widespread violation of the equal right of sexual autonomy. Liberal morality demands that something be done about it. But there are ways of reducing levels of sexual violence without placing the production and viewing of violent pornography – or any other media depictions of violence against women – beyond the bounds of the right of autonomy.

The most straightforward ways involve more vigorous prosecution of, and more serious punishments for, crimes of sexual violence. In a similar vein, laws regarding rape and sexual assault can and should be changed, so that the women who are the victims of such crimes are treated in a respectful manner by the criminal justice system. Additionally, efforts at educating individuals – especially young men – about sexual violence should be more seriously pursued.[6] In sum, then, subscribing to a liberal sexual morality does not require that one ignore or exhibit indifference to the level of sexual violence in society and its harmful impact on women.

V Sexual Inequality

Even if we set aside the issue of whether violent pornography causes sexual violence, the question remains as to whether pornography in general helps to maintain many of the important social and economic inequalities that disadvantage females. Many feminists assert that pornography plays a pivotal role in maintaining such sexual inequalities, and they cast the issue of pornography as one that is "not a moral issue," but rather is a matter of the civil rights of women (MacKinnon, 1988, pp. 146–62).

For example, Catherine Itzin claims that "women are oppressed in every aspect of their public and private lives," and she sees pornography as playing a central role in maintaining the system of oppression. Itzin proceeds to defend "civil sex discrimination legislation against pornography [that] would enable women to take action on grounds of harm done to them by pornography" (Itzin, 1992, p. 424). The legislation is seen as a kind of civil rights law for women.[7]

There is little doubt that the vast bulk of pornography willingly viewed by heterosexual men – whether violent or not – involves women in positions of sexual servility or subordination: the women are there to serve the sexual pleasure of the men. And serve it they do, not only to the men who are their "co-stars" in the movie or photograph, but also to the men who masturbate to the scene or who have sex with their partners while using the scene to help arouse them. These facts are what lead some feminists to argue that pornography is unique in its power to create a psychological nexus between the social subordination of women and the sexual pleasure of men, and so is unique in its power to create and sustain patterns of sex inequality that severely disadvantage females. Catharine MacKinnon puts the matter plainly: "Pornography is masturbation material. . . . With pornography, men masturbate to women being exposed, humiliated, violated, degraded, mutilated, dismembered, bound, gagged, tortured and killed. . . . Men come doing this" (MacKinnon, 1993, p. 17).

MacKinnon is right to take the focus off of pornography as a form of speech and instead look at its role in sexual behavior. However, there is a crucial consideration which renders her line of thinking problematic as a viable basis for rejecting a right to pornography. The evidence does not support the idea of any robust correlation, much less a causal relation, between the level of sex inequality in a society and the availability of pornography in it. Quite the opposite; the most repressive countries in the world for women are ones where pornography is least available. Compared to Saudi Arabia, the United States is awash in pornography. Indeed, MacKinnon herself insists that the United States is "a society saturated with pornography" (MacKinnon, 1993, p. 7) – a description which might be arguably applied to the US but clearly does not apply to Saudi Arabia. Nonetheless, on the indices of sex inequality developed by the United Nations Development Programme, the United States and other Western countries where pornography circulates widely are the nations with the highest levels of *equality*, while Saudi Arabia and other sexu-

ally repressive regimes have among the highest levels of inequality (United Nations Development Programme, 2002, pp. 222–42). Thus, it is hard to credit the notion that pornography is a kind of causal linchpin in the creation and maintenance of large inequalities between males and females.

There is a certainly an analogy between the ways in which much pornography depicts women in relation to men and the ways in which social practices actually treat women in relation to men. In much pornography, there is a sexual hierarchy dominated by men; in much of society, there is a social hierarchy dominated by men. Moreover, it is plausible to think that pornography plays some causal role in the perpetuation of sexual hierarchy. But, as with the matter of sexual violence, any limitation of the right of adults to sexual autonomy requires more than a plausible belief that some indeterminate degree of connection exists between pornography and sexual hierarchy.

VI Making Pornography

Much pornography depicts the subordination of women. Even though the symbolic representation of inequality is not the same as the inequality that is represented, it may be argued that in making pornography, women humiliate and subordinate themselves. They get on their knees and suck on men's cocks. They let men ejaculate into their mouth and on their face and breasts. They have several men simultaneously penetrating their anus, vagina, and mouth. They are tied up and gagged. The humiliation seems all the more acute because it is done before cameras that will circulate the images to untold numbers of men to view. One might claim that this means that making pornography is making female inequality and not simply depicting it.

However, context counts in deciding whether a person's sexual conduct is a form of humiliation and subordination. It is difficult to see why fellatio is any more inherently degrading than cunnilingus, or why either form of oral sex has that feature. If the parties are adults and consent, the assessment of the activity as humiliating is highly contestable. Multiple penetration also seems inherently innocuous.

Nonetheless, the key point is this: even if we grant that much pornography does involve women performing humiliating or degrading sexual acts, it does not follow that the actors have no right to participate in making such material or that viewers have no right to see it. A willingness to sexually degrade oneself before a camera for commercial purposes may constitute a serious deficiency in one's character. A willingness to view such pornography may also reflect a character flaw. But the men and women who perform in such pornography have a right to make their choices, and consumers have a right to view the commercial product.

If women are intimidated by violent threats into performing in pornography, then their rights have been violated and their victimizers ought to be prosecuted and punished. But it is simply an ideological prejudice to assume a priori that any woman who performs humiliating or degrading sexual acts in pornography has been threatened or coerced in some way. Especially in matters of sex, the line between humiliation, on one side, and breaking the procrustean bed of traditional morality, on the other, is a very tricky one to draw.

Some feminist advocates of laws against pornography claim that physical threats, violence, and economic coercion against women pervade the actual operation of the pornography industry (Dworkin, 2000, pp. 27–9). It may be said that the only way to stop such threats is by closing down the industry. But even if that were true, it would not justify closing down the industry. It does not make sense to think that the only industries that should be allowed are those that can operate without anyone abusing them by threatening violence. Such abuse can be found in any industry. Criminal prosecution of the perpetrators should be the main remedy for physical abuse and coercion in the pornography industry.

Moreover, there are less draconian ways of diminishing violence in the industry than shutting the industry down. For example, some feminists have argued for the unionization of women who work in pornography and other sex-related industries (Cornell, 2000, p. 552). While unionization efforts may not have good prospects at present, especially in the US, the prospects for banning pornography under a civil rights approach are no better. And the unionization strategy has the decided advantage of treating women in the pornography industry as agents who are capable of exercising their own right of sexual autonomy.

Some of the females who get caught up in the pornography industry are legal minors. The industry executives who intentionally, or negligently, hire minors ought to be prosecuted and punished. Legal minors may have some aspects of the right of sexual autonomy (for example, a 17-year-old girl has the right to purchase and use contraceptives), but the law should rest on the premise that minors are too easily manipulated by industry executives and other adults with vested interests to have a right to decide for themselves to perform in commercial pornographic films or pose for pornographic pictures.

Some feminists contend that women accede to make pornography only because they have no other economic options (except perhaps prostitution, a close cousin of pornography). This contention may have some truth in countries of the underdeveloped world, where educational opportunities for women are highly restricted, rampant sexism operates in all quarters of life, and economic opportunities even for many men are bleak at best. However, in the economically advanced liberal democracies, the situation of almost all women is drastically better, and claims of economic coercion are considerably less plausible as a result.

The clear conclusion seems to be that uncoerced adults have a right to be legally free to make, market, and view pornography. However, it might be objected that if some women voluntarily choose to make pornography in which they are engaged in humiliating or degrading conduct, then their actions affect all women in a detrimental way. The idea here is that the manufacture and circulation of such pornography shapes the sex-role expectations of men and women in society at large, and it does so by showing women as the sexual servants of men. The result is that individuals are not free to control their sexual identities: just as much as in a society ruled by traditional sexual morality, sexual identities are controlled by social forces which are beyond their control and which are hostile to their basic interests.

VII Sexual Identity

It must be admitted that, even in a society governed by a liberal sexual morality, the sexual autonomy of a person is significantly circumscribed. There is a built-in tension between living in a society and possessing the autonomy to define oneself sexually or in any other way. Without connections to other people in an organized and ongoing system of relations, the life-options of the individual would be radically limited. But those connections also mean that a person's life-defining choices are not entirely her own. The patterns of behavior and attitude that other people adopt not only establish pathways through life which would not otherwise exist but also create barriers and limits on the individual's exercise of her autonomy. The ability of the individual to shape her own identity is both enabled by, and held hostage to, the actions and attitudes of other people.

There is no solution to this problem. The conditions of meaningful autonomy are also conditions that can inhibit the exercise of such autonomy. Nonetheless, even though this conflict cannot be eliminated, it can be mitigated. And some kinds of society do a much better job of mitigating it than others. Societies with a liberal sexual morality are much better in this respect than those with a traditional sexual morality, and that is the decisive consideration in favor of the liberal morality. Individuals have many more meaningful options in living out the sexual aspects of their lives: their sexuality is not held hostage to what other people do and think to nearly the extent that is found traditional societies. The grip of pre-existing social scripts that define a sexual identity for each person is dramatically weaker in liberal societies and the power of individuals to shape a centrally important aspect of their lives is correspondingly greater.

However, even in a liberal society, there is no escaping the fact that how other women act and think affects the opportunities and obstacles for any given woman's efforts to define her own sexual identity. The same is true, of course, for men, but the problem of concern here is the willingness of some women to participate in the creation of pornography in which they engage in conduct that is humiliating and servile. Such conduct may be voluntary on the part of the woman, but – the claim goes – it also makes it more difficult for other women to define their own sexual identities as the equals of men.

I think that it is reasonable to hold that the existence of such pornography makes it more difficult for women to live their lives as the sexual equals of men, i.e., more difficult relative to a society which was ruled by a liberal sexual morality and had fewer women, or none at all, who were willing to engage in humiliating conduct as part of the production of pornographic materials. However, women are far better off in societies where a liberal sexual morality dominates than in traditional societies, even when the liberal ones contain much pornography degrading to women. Although the freedom of women to humiliate or degrade themselves in making pornography creates costs that all women in a liberal society bear, the gains for women that have resulted from society moving to a liberal sexual morality from a traditional morality far outweighs the costs.

It might be argued that the costs are still too great, and I would not dissent. However, there are ways to lessen those costs without incursions on the right to sexual autonomy. Those ways are likely to be far more effective in promoting sexual equality than restricting the freedom of willing adults to view pornography made by willing adults.

VIII Conclusion

The recognition of a right to sexual autonomy is critical in adequately addressing the issue of pornography. There are other important dimensions of the issue, including the levels of sexual violence perpetrated against women and the social inequalities that systematically disadvantage women. Also relevant is the question of whether there is some character defect in those who make and enjoy pornographic materials.

However, liberal sexual morality correctly places the right of sexual autonomy at the center of the pornography issue. In doing so, the liberal morality places a substantial burden on those who argue for legal restrictions on the access of adults to pornography made by consenting adults. Those who argue for such restrictions tacitly concede that the burden is theirs, as they make claims aimed at meeting it, for example, that pornography causes sexual violence, reinforces sexual hierarchy, and involves unconsenting women who are forced to perform.

When examined carefully, though, we find that the burden has not been met. The empirical claims are insufficiently verified, and some of the empirical assertions, even if substantiated, would be inadequate to justify restricting an adult's right of sexual autonomy. We are left, then, with the claim that the producers and viewers of pornography exhibit a defect of moral character. Such a claim is consistent with a liberal sexual morality. However, it is also inadequate to justify restrictions on adults who willingly create and view pornography.

Notes

1 Cf. Richards (1982, pp. 29, 39).
2 Cf. Waldron (1993, chap. 3), and Driver (1992).
3 Longino also contends that pornography defames women by communicating falsehoods about them and reinforces the societal oppression of women. The oppression argument is considered in section V below. The defamation argument would license sweeping restrictions on communication, including political expression.
4 See, for example, Linz et al. (1984).
5 Kutchinsky (1991) also found that in West Germany, Denmark, and Sweden rape increased less than nonsexual assault, despite the greatly increased availability of violent pornography in those countries as well.

6 Many thinkers assert that pornography fosters the myth that women enjoy being forced to have sex (the rape myth) and some studies support the assertion. However, other studies show that better educating young men can counteract their acceptance of the rape myth. Moreover, mainstream movies in which rapes take place also appear to foster the rape myth. See Slade (2001, pp. 992–3).
7 Catharine MacKinnon and Andrea Dworkin helped draft anti-pornography, civil rights laws in the United States, but the courts have found them to be unconstitutional on free-speech grounds. See *American Booksellers v. Hudnut* 771 F.2d 323 (7th Cir. 1985).

References

American Booksellers v. Hudnut (1985) 771 F.2d 323 (7th Cir. 1985).
Cornell, Drucilla (2000) "Pornography's Temptation." In Drucilla Cornell (ed.), *Feminism and Pornography*. New York: Oxford University Press, pp. 552–68.
Driver, Julia (1992) "The Suberogatory," *Australasian Journal of Philosophy* 70: 286–95.
Dworkin, Andrea (2000) "Against the Male Flood." In Drucilla Cornell (ed.), *Feminism and Pornography*. New York: Oxford University Press, pp. 19–44.
George, Robert P. (1993) *Making Men Moral*. Oxford: Oxford University Press.
Itzin, Catherine (1992) "Legislating against Pornography without Censorship." In Catherine Itzin (ed.), *Pornography: Women, Violence, and Civil Liberties*. New York: Oxford University Press, pp. 401–34.

Jacobellis v. Ohio (1964) 378 US 184 (1964).
Kutchinsky, Bert (1991) "Pornography and Rape: Theory and Practice," *International Journal of Law and Psychiatry* 14: 47–64.
Linz, Daniel, Donnerstein, Edward, and Penrod, Stephen (1984) "The Effects of Multiple Exposures to Filmed Violence against Women," *Journal of Communication* 34: 130–47.
Longino, Helen (1995) "Pornography, Oppression, and Freedom: a Closer Look." In Susan Dwyer (ed.), *The Problem of Pornography*. Belmont, CA: Wadsworth Publishing, pp. 34–47.
MacKinnon, Catharine (1988) *Feminism Unmodified*. Cambridge, MA: Harvard University Press.
—— (1993) *Only Words*. Cambridge, MA: Harvard University Press.

Richards, David A. J. (1982) *Sex, Drugs, Death and the Law*. Totowa, NJ: Rowman and Littlefield.

Slade, Joseph W. (2001) *Pornography and Sexual Representation*, *vol.* III. Westport, CT: Greenwood Press.

United Nations Development Programme (2002) *Human Development Report 2002*. New York: Oxford University Press.

Waldron, Jeremy (1993) *Liberal Rights*. New York: Cambridge University Press.

37

Sticks and Stones

John Arthur

A recent *New York Times* article described the intense controversy surrounding a German court's decision that a bumper-sticker proclaiming "soldiers are murderers" is constitutionally protected, just as it would be under the First Amendment to the United States Constitution. Chancellor Helmut Kohl characterized himself as "outraged" at the court's decision, saying that "We cannot and must not stand by while our soldiers are placed on the same level with criminals." A leading German newspaper editorialized that "In a democracy, criticism of war and the military is naturally not forbidden. But among reasonable people, it must be done in a civilized way and not with brutal insults like 'murderers.' " And the judge in the case, who said he regretted having to decide as he did, complained that earlier decisions of the Constitutional Court "are steadily placing freedom of speech ahead of the protection of people's honor" (*New York Times*, January 15, 1996, p. A-5). As this event shows, hate speech occurs in a wide array of contexts; it can also be directed at many different targets, not just racial groups. It is also unclear, of course, whether and in what form hate speech should be censored.

Proponents of limiting hate speech on college campuses and elsewhere have generally taken one of two approaches. One is to pass a "speech code" that identifies which words or ideas are banned, the punishment that may be imposed, and (as at the University of Michigan) an interpretive "Guide" meant to explain how the rules will be applied. The other approach has been to treat hate speech as a form of harassment. Here the censorship is justified on anti-discrimination grounds: hate speech, it is argued, subjects its victims to a "hostile" work environment, which courts have held constitutes job discrimination (*Meritor Savings Bank* v. *Vinson*, 1986).

Advocates of banning hate speech do not usually include all expressions of hatred, however devastating and humiliating they may be. Few would ban such criticism of the military, for example. And words directed at another person because of what he has done are also not normally included: "You bastard, you murdered my father!" is not thought of as "hate speech," nor is an attack on a person simply for being stupid or incompetent. Rather than censoring all expressions of hatred, advocates of banning hate speech use the term narrowly, to refer to speech directed at people *in virtue of their membership in a (usually historically disadvantaged) racial, religious, ethnic, sexual or other group.*

Such a conception can be criticized, of course, on the ground that it arbitrarily narrows the field to one form of hate speech. Perhaps, however, there is reason to focus on a limited problem: if it turns out, for example, that hate speech directed against such groups is especially harmful, then it may seem reasonable to have created this special usage of the term. In this paper I consider some of the important issues surrounding hate speech and its regulation: the political and legal importance of free speech; the types of harm that might be attributed to it; and whether, even if no harm results, causing emotional distress and offense is by itself sufficient to warrant censorship.

1 Why Protect Freedom of Speech?

Respecting freedom of speech is important for a variety of reasons. First, as J. S. Mill argued long ago, free and unfettered debate is vital for the pursuit of truth. If knowledge is to grow, people must be free to put forth ideas and theories they deem worthy of consideration, and others must be left equally free to criticize them. Even false ideas should be protected, Mill argued, so that the truth will not become mere dogma, unchallenged and little understood. "However true [an opinion] may be," he wrote, "if it is not fully, frequently, and fearlessly discussed, it will be held as a dead dogma, not a living truth" (Mill, 1978, p. 34). It helps, of course, if the competition among ideas is fair and all sides have an equal opportunity to have their ideas expressed. Censorship is therefore only one of the dangers to the marketplace of ideas; unequal access to the media is another.

Free speech is also an essential feature of democratic, efficient and just government. Fair, democratic elections cannot occur unless candidates are free to debate and criticize each other's policies, nor can government be run efficiently unless corruption and other abuses can be exposed by a free press. But beyond that, there is an important sense in which freedom of speech provides a necessary precondition for the protection of other rights and therefore for justice. Free and open debate about the nature and limits of other rights to privacy, religion, equal treatment and the rest is vital if society is to reach sound and fair decisions about when and how those other rights must be defined and respected. We cannot expect sound political deliberation, including deliberation about rights themselves, without first securing freedom of speech.

A third value, individual autonomy, is also served by free speech. In chapter III of *On Liberty*, "Of Individuality, as One of the Elements of Well Being," Mill writes that "He who lets the world, or his own portion of it, choose his plan of life for him, has no need of any other faculty than the ape-like one of imitation. . . . Among the works of man, which human life is rightly employed in perfecting and beautifying, the first in importance surely is man himself" (Mill, 1978, p. 56). Mill's suggestion is that the best life does not result from being forced to live a certain way, but instead is freely chosen without coercion from outside. But if Mill is right, then freedom of speech as well as action are important to achieve a worthwhile life. Free and open discussion helps people exercise their capacities of reasoning and judgment, capacities that are essential for autonomous and informed choices.

Besides these important social advantages of respecting free speech, including learning the truth, securing efficient, democratic and just government, and promoting individual autonomy, freedom of expression is important for its own sake, because it is a basic human right. Not only does free speech *promote* autonomy, as Mill argued, but it is also a *reflection* of individual autonomy and of human equality. Censorship denigrates our status as equal, autonomous persons by saying, in effect, that some people simply cannot be trusted to make up their own minds about what is right or true. Because of the ideas they hold or the subjects they find interesting, they need not be treated with the same respect as other citizens with whom they disagree; only we, not they, are free to believe as we wish. Viewed that way, denying free speech is much like establishing an official religion: it says to some citizens that because of their beliefs they are less than equal members of society. So, unlike the previous arguments, which see speech as an instrument to realize other important values, here the claim is that free speech must be protected out of respect for the fact that each adult in the community is entitled to be treated as an equal among others (Dworkin, 1996, ch. 8).

Because it serves important social goals, and also must be respected in the name of equal citizenship, the right to speak and write freely is perhaps the most important of all rights. But beyond that, two further points also need to be stressed. Free speech is fragile, in two respects. The first is the chilling effect that censorship poses. Language banning hate speech will inevitably be vague and indeterminate, at least to some extent: words like "hate" and "denigrate" and "victimize," which often occur in such rules, are not self-defining. When such bans bring strict penalties, as they sometimes do, they risk sweeping too broadly, capturing valuable speech in their net along with the speech they seek to prohibit. Criminal or civil penalties therefore pose a threat to speech generally, and the values underlying it, as people consider the potential risks of expressing their opinions while threatened by legal sanctions. Censorship risks having a chilling effect.

The second danger of censorship, often referred to as the "slippery slope," begins with the historical observation that unpopular minorities and controversial ideas are always vulnerable to political repression, whether by authoritarian regimes hoping to remain in power, or elected officials desiring to secure reelection by attacking unpopular groups or silencing political opponents. For that reason, it is important to create a high wall of constitutional protection securing the right to speak against attempts to limit it. Without strong, politically resistant constraints on governmental efforts to restrict speech, there is constant risk – demonstrated by historical experience – that what begins as a minor breech in the wall can be turned by governmental officials and intolerant majorities into a large, destructive exception.

Protecting speech is essential if society is to protect truth, autonomy, efficiency, democracy, and justice; it also must be protected if we are to show equal respect for others with whom we differ. Censorship is also risky, I have argued, given the dangers of chilling effects and slippery slopes. Given all this, it is not surprising that the United States Supreme Court has sought ways to protect freedom of speech. So before considering hate-speech regulations, it will be helpful to look briefly at how the US Supreme Court has understood the First Amendment's guarantee of freedom of speech.

2 Free Speech and the Constitution

The Supreme Court has not always interpreted the First Amendment's free speech and press clauses in a manner consistent with speech's importance. Early in the twentieth century people were often jailed, and their convictions upheld, for expressing unpopular political views, including distributing pamphlets critical of American military intervention in the Russian revolution (*Abrams* v. *United States*, 1919). Then, in the McCarthy era of the 1950s, government prosecuted over a hundred people for what was in effect either teaching Marxism or belonging to the Communist Party (*Dennis* v. *United States*, 1951). Beginning in the 1960s, however, the US Supreme Court changed direction, interpreting the Constitution's command that government not restrict freedom of speech as imposing strict limits on governmental power to censor speech and punish speakers.

Pursuing this goal, the first defined "speech" broadly, to include not just words but other forms of expression as well. Free speech protection now extends to people who wear arm bands, burn the flag, and peaceably march. The Court has also made a critically important distinction, between governmental regulations aimed at the *content* or *ideas* a person wishes to convey and content-neutral restrictions on the *time, place, and manner* in which the speech occurs. Thus, government is given fairly wide latitude to curtail speakers who use bullhorns at night, spray-paint their ideas on public buildings, or invade private property in order to get their messages across. But when governmental censors object not to how or where the speech occurs, but instead to the content itself, the Constitution is far more restrictive. Here, the Supreme Court has held, we are at the very heart of the First Amendment and the values it protects. Indeed, said the Court, there is "no such thing as a false idea" under the US Constitution (*Gertz. v. Robert Welch, Inc.*, 1974).

Wary of the chilling effect and the slippery slope, the Supreme Court has therefore held that government cannot regulate the content of speech unless it falls within certain narrowly defined categories. These constitutionally "unprotected categories" include libel (but criticisms of public officials must not only be false but uttered "maliciously" to be libelous), incitement to lawlessness (if the incitement is "imminent," such as yelling "Let's kill the capitalist!" in front of an angry mob), obscenity (assuming that the speech also lacks substantial social value), and "fighting words" (like "fascist pig" that are uttered in a face-to-face context likely to injure or provoke immediate, hostile reaction). In that way, each of these unprotected categories is precisely defined so as not to endanger free expression in general. Like Ulysses tying himself to the mast, the Supreme Court uses the unprotected-categories approach to reduce the chance that we will return to a time when constitutional protections were vaguely defined and government was left free to issue vaguely worded sedition statutes, stifle dissent and lock up critics. Harmless advocacy of revolution, for example, is now constitutionally protected, as is virtually all criticism of public officials.

Applying these principles, the Supreme Court held in 1989 that a "flag desecration" is constitutionally protected (*Texas* v. *Johnson*, 1989). Texas's statute had defined "desecration" in terms of the tendency to "offend" someone who was likely to know of the act. But, said the Court in striking down the statute, not only does flag burning involve ideas, the statute is not viewpoint neutral. Because it singled out one side of a debate – those who are critical

of government – the law must serve an especially clear and important purpose. Mere "offense," the justices concluded, was insufficiently important to warrant intrusion into free expression.

In light of this constitutional history, it is not surprising that attempts to ban hate speech have fared poorly in American courts. Responding to various acts of racist speech on its campus, the University of Michigan passed one of the most far-reaching speech codes ever attempted at an American university; it prohibited "stigmatizing or victimizing" either individuals or groups on the basis of "race, ethnicity, religion, sex, sexual orientation, creed, national origin, ancestry, age, marital status, handicap or Vietnam-era veteran status." According to a "Guide" published by the University to help explain the code's meaning, conduct that violates the code would include a male student who "makes remarks in class like 'Women just aren't as good in this field as men,' thus creating a hostile learning atmosphere for female classmates." Also punishable under the code were "derogatory" comments about a person's or group's "physical appearance or sexual orientation, or their cultural origins, or religious beliefs" (*Doe* v. *University of Michigan*, 1989, pp. 857–8). To almost nobody's surprise, the Michigan Code was rejected as unconstitutional, on grounds that it violated rights both to free speech and to due process of law. The case was brought by a psychology instructor who feared that his course in developmental psychology, which discussed biological differences between males and females, might be taken by some to be "stigmatizing and victimizing." The Court agreed with the professor, holding that the Michigan code was both "over-broad" and "unconstitutionally vague." A second code at the University of Wisconsin soon met a similar fate, even though it banned only slurs and epithets (*UMV Post* v. *Board of Regents of the University of Wisconsin*, 1991).

Confirming these lower court decisions, the Supreme Court in 1992 ruled unconstitutional a city ordinance making it a misdemeanor to place on public or private property any "symbol, object, appellation, characterization or graffiti" that the person knows or has reasonable grounds for knowing will arouse "anger, alarm or resentment" on the basis of race, color, creed, religion or gender (*R.A.V.* v. *City of St Paul*, 1992, p. 2541). In overturning a juvenile's conviction for placing a burning cross on a black family's lawn, the majority held that even if the statute were understood very narrowly, to limit only "fighting words," it was nonetheless unconstitutional because it punished only some fighting words and not others. In so doing, argued one justice, the law violated the important principle of content neutrality: it censored some uses of fighting words, namely those focusing on race, color, creed, religion or gender, but not others. It prescribed political orthodoxy. Other justices emphasized that no serious harm had been identified that could warrant restrictions on speech. The law, wrote Justice White, criminalizes conduct that "causes only hurt feelings, offense, or resentment, and is protected by the First Amendment" (*R.A.V.* v. *City of St. Paul*, 1992, p. 2559).

Perhaps, however, the Court has gone too far in protecting hate speech. Advocates of banning hate speech commonly claim it harms its victims. "There is a great difference," writes Charles Lawrence, "between the offensiveness of words that you would rather not hear because they are labelled dirty, impolite, or personally demeaning and the injury [of hate speech]" (Lawrence, 1990, p. 74). Elsewhere he describes hate speech as "aimed at an entire group with the effect of causing significant *harm* to individual group members" (Lawrence, 1990, p. 57, emphasis added). Richard Delgado similarly claims that it would be rare for a white who is called a "dumb honkey" to be in a position to claim legal redress since, unlike a member of an historically oppressed group, it would be unlikely that a white person would "suffer *harm* from such an insult" (Delgado, 1982, p. 110, emphasis added).

But are these writers correct that various forms of hate speech cross the boundary from the distressing and offensive to the genuinely harmful? To weigh their claim, we will first ask how we are to understand the concept of harm. Once that is clear, we can then proceed to the question of whether hate speech is in fact harmful, and then to whether it should be banned on other grounds.

3 Harm and Offense

To claim that someone has been harmed is different from claiming she has been wronged. I can break into your house undetected, do no damage, and leave. While I have wronged you, I might not have harmed you, especially if you didn't know about it and I didn't take anything.

What then must be the case for wronging somebody to also constitute a harm? First, to be harmed is not merely to experience a minor irritation or hurt, nor is it simply to undergo an unwanted experience. Though unwanted, the screech of chalk on the blackboard, an unpleasant smell, a pinch or slap, a brief but frightening experience, and a revolting sight are not harms. Harms are significant events. Following Joel Feinberg, I will assume that harms occur not when we are merely hurt or offended, but when our "interests" are frustrated, defeated or set back (Feinberg, 1984, pp. 31–51). By interests he means something in which we have a stake – just as we may have a "stake" in a company. So while many of our interests are obviously tied to our wants and desires, a mere want does not constitute an interest. A minor disappointment is not a frustration of interests in the relevant sense. Feinberg thus emphasizes the "directional" nature of interests that are "set back" when one is harmed, pointing out that the interests are "ongoing concerns" rather than temporary wants. Genuine harms thus impede or thwart people's future objectives or options, which explains why the unpleasant memory or smell and the bite's itch are not harms while loss of a limb, of freedom, and of health are. Harms can therefore come from virtually any source: falling trees, disease, economic or romantic competitors, and muggers are only a few examples.

It seems clear therefore why government is concerned about harm and its prevention. Whether caused by other people or by nature, to be harmed is never trivial; it involves a setback or frustration of an interest of a person. For government to ignore genuinely harmful acts requires justification; sometimes such a justification is easy to see, as when competition causes economic harm or a person injures another in self-defense. But, absent such a justification, there is a *prima facie* case that harmful actions should not be allowed.

We now turn to the question of whether hate speech causes harm. In discussing this, we will consider various types of harm that might result, as well as making important distinctions between group and individual harm, between cumulative and individual harm and between direct and indirect harm.

4   Group Harm

One typical form of hate speech is directed not at any particular individual but at a group: fliers attacking racial and religious minorities are typical examples. But why might it be thought that attacks on groups are harmful? Here are some possibilities.

Larry May argues that attacks on groups harm people "vicariously." Because people care about others in their group, an attack on any one of them is in effect an attack on them all. He terms this state "solidarity." "If people are in a state of solidarity," he writes, "in which they identify the interests of others as their own interests, then . . . vicarious harm is possible" (May, 1987, p. 115). But that seems wrong: even assuming people are in a state of solidarity and identify strongly with the interests of others in the group, and also assuming that the hate speech harms the interests of its specific subject in some way, it still does not follow that others in the group are harmed by such an attack. Even such an attack on a family member might not result in such vicarious *harm*, though it could surely cause distress, anger, and resentment. Attacks on group members cause harm only if they also frustrate others' interests, understood as limiting ongoing objectives or options. But group "solidarity" is not normally like that; no doubt other group members are often distressed, but to suffer distress is not, by itself, a harm.

Perhaps, however, the harm caused by attacks aimed at a racial or other group is to the group itself rather than to any particular individual. But what sense can be made of such a claim, that the group itself is somehow harmed? It may seem that groups are not the sort of thing that *can* be harmed, only individual members. But consider corporations. Not only do they have duties and rights (they can sue and be sued, be held legally liable, and be fined) but they also have goals and objectives (namely to make a profit or to achieve some charitable goal if they are not-for-profit corporations). Nor is the corporation's goal reducible to the interests of its members: individuals involved with the corporation may care little or nothing about whether the corporation makes a profit, worrying instead about their salary, job security, work conditions, status among others, or whatever. So because corporations have independent goals, it seems that corporations can also be harmed. Exxon Corporation, for example, was probably harmed by the Alaskan oil spill, and certainly US auto makers were harmed by competition from the Japanese in the 1980s.

It is far from clear, however, how the analogy with corporations can be extended to religious, racial, or other groups. Consider the group of people on board an airplane. *Individuals* on the airplane can be harmed, of course, but it makes little sense to ask after a crash whether, in addition to all the deaths, the *group* itself was harmed. One reason that some groups, like corporations, can be harmed while others, such as people on airplanes, cannot is that corporations exist in a legal environment that provides them with their own, independent goal: both their charter and the legal context in which they function define their purpose as making profits for shareholders. A second point, besides legally defined purpose, is that corporations have an organizational structure whose purpose is to achieve the goal. For these reasons, sense can be made of a corporation being harmed in its pursuit of its goals. The situation is different, however, for racial, religious, ethnic, or cultural groups. These groups are socially, not legally created, and obviously do not have a charter defining their goals; nor do they have the organizational structures that allowed us to make sense of a corporation's goals. Lacking a purpose, they therefore cannot be harmed in its pursuit.

It might be argued in response, however, that at least some groups, like religious ones, *can* have defined goals: The goal of the Jewish people, it is sometimes said, is to be a "light unto the nations," and that of Evangelical Christians, to preach salvation. But again it is unclear how to make sense of these "group" goals without assuming there is somebody else, God, who has established the purpose for the groups. But then it would be God, and not the group itself, that has the goal. On the other hand, if God has not established such a purpose then it seems reasonable to think of the goal as residing in individual members, not in the group itself. Similarly, a people or nation are sometimes said to have goals such as creating "socialist man" or achieving "manifest destiny," but again this depends on an organizational structure, usually a government, that represents the people and pursues the objective. Take that structure away, and the "group" goal dissolves.

The claim that hate speech harms a racial, religious, or ethnic group is therefore best not taken literally. Group harm is best understood as a shorthand way of suggesting individual members have been harmed. What sort of harm is then at issue, exactly? And how might hate speech cause it?

5 Cumulative vs. Individual Harm

To give this argument its due, we must first distinguish between harms flowing from *individual* actions and *cumulative* harms. Often what is a singly harmless act can be damaging when added to other similar acts. One person walking across a lawn does little damage, but constant walking will destroy the lawn. Indeed the single act might be entirely without negative effect. Pollution, for instance, is often harmful only cumulatively, not singly. Though one car battery's lead may do no harm to those who drink the water downstream, when added to the

pollution of many others the cumulative harm can be disastrous.

Further, the fact that it was singly harmless is no justification for performing the act. The complete response to a person who insists that he had a right to pollute since his action did no damage is that if everyone behaved that way great harm would follow: once a legal scheme protecting the environment is in place, criminal law is rightly invoked even against individually harmless acts on grounds of cumulative harm.

It might then be argued that even if individual hate speech acts do not cause harm, it should still be banned because of its cumulatively harmful effects. What might that harm consist in? Defending hate speech codes, Mari J. Matsuda writes that "As much as one may try to resist a piece of hate propaganda, the effect on one's self-esteem and sense of personal security is devastating. To be hated, despised, and alone is the ultimate fear of all human beings. . . . [R]acial inferiority is planted in our minds as an idea that may hold some truth" (Matsuda, 1989, p. 25). Besides the distress caused by the hate speech, Matsuda is suggesting, hate speech victims may also be harmed in either of two ways: reduced self-esteem or increased risk of violence and discrimination. I will begin with self-esteem, turning to questions of violence and discrimination in the next section.

6 Cumulative Harm to Self-esteem

What then is self-esteem? Following Rawls, let us assume that by "self-esteem" or "self-respect" we mean the sense both that one's goals and life-plan are worthwhile and that one has talents and other characteristics sufficient to make their accomplishment possible (Rawls, 1971, pp. 440–6). Loss of self-esteem might therefore constitute harm because it reduces motivation and willingness to put forth effort. If hate-speech victims believe they have little or no chance of success, their future options will be reduced, rather as former slaves are sometimes said to have had their futures foreclosed as a result of the attitudes they inherited from slavery.

Assuming loss of self-esteem is a harm, how plausible is Matsuda's suggestion that hate speech has the (cumulative) effect of reducing it? Many factors can reduce self-esteem. Demeaning portrayals of one's group in the media, widespread antisocial behavior of others in the group, family breakdown, poor performance in school and on the job, drugs, and even well intended affirmative action programs all may lessen self-esteem. Indeed, I suggest that, absent those other factors, simply being subject to hate speech would not significantly reduce self-esteem. An otherwise secure and confident person might be made angry (or fearful) by racial or other attacks, feeling the speaker is ignorant, rude, or stupid. But without many other factors it is hard to see that hate speech by itself would have much impact on self-esteem. Gerald Gunther, who as a Jew was subjected to some of the worst hate speech imaginable, nevertheless opposes speech codes. While writing eloquently of the distress such speech caused, there is no suggestion that the speech had an impact on the self-esteem of an otherwise self-confident person (Gunther, 1990).

But even assuming hate speech does reduce self-esteem to some degree, notice how far the argument has strayed from the original, robust claim that hate speech should be banned because it causes harm. First each individual act must be added to other acts of hate speech, but then it must also be added to the many other, more important factors that together reduce self-esteem. Given the importance of protecting speech I discussed earlier, and the presumption it creates against censorship, Matsuda's argument that it reduces self-esteem seems far too speculative and indirect to warrant criminalizing otherwise protected speech.

7 Discrimination and Violence as Indirect Harms

But surely, it may be objected, the real issue is simply this: hate speech should be banned because it increases racial or other forms of hatred, which in turn leads to increased violence and discrimination – both of which are obviously harmful. That is a serious claim, and must be taken seriously. Notice first, however, that this effect of hate speech, if it exists, is only indirect; hate speech is harmful only because of its impact on others who are then led in turn to commit acts of violence or discrimination. The claim is not that the speech itself directly caused the harm, but instead that it encouraged attitudes in people who then, on their own, acted wrongly and harmed others.

There are important problems with this as an argument for banning hate speech. One, epistemological problem is whether we really know that the link exists between hate speech, increased hatred, and illegal acts. Suppose we discovered a close correlation between reading hate speech and committing acts of violence – what have we proved? Not, as might be thought, that hate speech causes violence. Rather, we would only know that *either* (A) reading such material increases hatred and violence, *or* (B) those who commit hate crimes also tend to like reading hate speech. The situation with respect to hate speech mirrors arguments about violence and pornography: the observation that rapists subscribe in greater proportion to pornographic magazines than do non-rapists does not show we can reduce rape by banning pornography. Maybe people who rape just tend also to like pornography. Similarly, reduction in hate speech might, or might not, reduce hate-related crime, even assuming that those who commit hate crimes are avid readers of hate literature.

Nor is it clear that hate speech has the effect on people's attitudes that the argument assumes. Consider an example reported recently in Mizzoula, Montana, where a vandal threw a brick through a window of the house of a Jewish family that had put a Menorah in their window to celebrate Hanukkah. In response, much of that overwhelmingly Christian city simply put pictures of a Menorah in their own windows, published in the local newspaper. Far from encouraging anti-Jewish hatred, this act seemed to have the opposite effect. Indeed it seems clear that members of groups whom hate-speech regulations are aimed to protect are themselves aware that hate speech can sometimes be beneficial. At my university alone, we have had two incidents in which acts of hate speech were perpetrated by members of the attacked group itself. Evidently, those students believed that rather than increasing hatred they could use hate speech to call attention to problems of racism and anti-semitism and increase people's sympathy, just as occurred in Mizzoula. We cannot assume, therefore, that censoring hate speech would reduce hatred. The reaction in Mizzoula, to meet racist speech with more speech, not only avoided censorship but also allowed people to make a powerful statement of their feelings about the importance of respecting the rights of others in their community.

It is unclear, I am suggesting, that regulating hate speech really would reduce hatred, let alone reduce hate crimes. And that uncertainty matters in the case of speech. Pollution, walking on the grass, and other activities that are less important than speech, and less threatened by governmental regulation, can be restricted without clear demonstration of their harmful effects. We need not wait to see for certain that a product is toxic to ban it; sometimes only a reasonable suspicion is enough if the product is relatively unimportant and the risks it may pose are significant. But speech, I have argued, is not like that. Freedom of expression is of great social value, enjoys the status as a basic right, and is in real danger due to slippery slopes and chilling effects.

There is a further problem, in addition to the epistemological one we have been discussing, with the argument that, by increasing hatred, hate speech in turn leads to more violence and discrimination. Any accused criminal, including one whose acts were motivated by racial or group hatred, must be shown to have *mens rea* or "guilty mind" in order to be convicted. That means, roughly, that the accused must have been aware of the nature of the act, aware that it was illegal or wrong, and was *able to have complied with the law*. But if the person could have complied with the law, then it follows that despite having read or heard the hate speech, and (we are now assuming) thereby had his hatred increased, he must still have been able

to ask himself whether he wished to *act* on the basis of that attitude. Between the desire and the action comes the decision. Criminals are not zombies, controlled by their desires and unable to reflect on the nature and quality of their actions. It is no excuse that the criminal acted on a strong desire, whether it was to be wealthy without earning money, have sex without another's consent, or express hatred of a group through violent acts or discrimination.

This means, then, that we have on hand two different ways of dealing with acts of violence and discrimination motivated by hatred: by using government censorship in an effort at thought control, trying to eliminate hatred and prejudice, or by insisting that whether people like somebody or not they cannot assault them or discriminate against them. My suggestion is that passing and vigorously enforcing laws against violence and discrimination themselves is a better method of preventing indirect harm than curtailing speech. Government should not be in the business of making people like each other; it should, however, insist that we treat each other fairly and respect each other's rights. Indeed, using the power of government to persuade people how they should live and whom they should like seem quite incompatible with Mill's claim, discussed earlier, that individual autonomy and freedom are part of the valuable life. Even if we could, through government, force people to share our attitudes it is not clear we should try.

8   Offensive Expression and Epithets

I have argued that hate speech should not be banned on the ground of preventing harm. But government often restricts behavior that is not strictly speaking harmful: it prevents littering, for instance, and limits how high we build our buildings, the drugs we take and the training our doctors receive, to mention only a few examples. Some of these restrictions are controversial, of course, especially ones that seem designed only to keep us from harming ourselves. But others, for example limiting alterations of historic buildings and preventing littering, are rarely disputed. Government also limits various forms of public behavior that are grossly offensive, revolting or shocking. An assault on the sense of smell and hearing, unusual or even common sexual activities in public, extreme provocations of anger, or threats that generate great anxiety or fear, are generally regarded as examples of behavior that can be restricted although they do not cause genuine harm.

Charles Lawrence suggests that this argument also applies to hate speech. The experience of being called "nigger," "spic," "Jap," or "kike," he writes, "is like receiving a slap in the face. The injury is instantaneous" (Lawrence, 1990, pp. 68–9). He describes the experience of a student who was called a "faggot" on a subway: "He found himself in a state of semi-shock, nauseous, dizzy, unable to muster the witty, sarcastic, articulate rejoinder he was accustomed to making" (Lawrence, 1990, p. 70).

Sometimes, of course, hate speech can be banned, even speech about important public issues. A Nazi yelling about the virtues of Fascism in a public bus or library, for example, can be asked to stop by a policeman. But that is not *content* regulation, unless somebody yelling just as loudly about the virtues of patriotism or of the Republican Party would be permitted to remain. Neutral regulations that prevent people from disturbing others, without regard to what is being said, do not raise the same constitutional and political issues as does content regulation of political speech.

But because of speech's critical importance and government's tendency to regulate and limit political discussion to suit its own ends, I have argued, it is important to limit governmental censorship to narrowly and precisely defined unprotected categories. This provides a more secure protection of speech than allowing officials to balance, case by case, the relative costs and benefits of individual laws government might wish to pass limiting free speech. Assuming that we might wish to keep this unprotected-categories approach, how might offensive hate speech be regulated? One possibility is to allow government to ban speech that "causes substantial distress and offense" to

those who hear it. Were we to adopt such a principle, however, we would effectively gut the First Amendment. All kinds of political speech, including much that we would all think must be protected, is offensive to somebody somewhere. "Fuck the draft" is but one of many examples of constitutionally protected offensive speech (*Cohen* v. *California*, 1971); burning the American Flag is another (*Texas* v. *Johnson*, 1989).

Nor would it work to limit the unprotected category to all speech that is distressing and offensive to members of historically stigmatized groups, for that too would sweep far too broadly. Speech critical of peoples, nations, and religious institutions and practices often offends group members, as do discussions of differences between the races and sexes. Social and biological scientists sometimes find themselves confronted by people who have been deeply wounded by their words, as the instructor who got in trouble at the University of Michigan over his comments about sex-linked abilities illustrates. Or what about psychologists who wish to do research into group IQ differences? Should only those who reach conclusions that are not offensive be allowed to publish? Or should we perhaps simply ban research into any topic that offends? Such examples can be repeated endlessly, of course; it is virtually impossible to predict what might be taken as offensive. Even Malcolm X's autobiography might be punishable; he says at one point that "I'd had too much experience that women were only tricky, deceitful, untrustworthy flesh" (Malcolm X, 1964, p. 226).

Others, however, have suggested another, less sweeping approach: why not at least ban racial or other *epithets* since they are a unique form of "speech act" that does not deserve protection. Unlike other forms of protected speech, it is claimed that epithets and name calling are constitutionally useless; they constitute acts of "subordination" that treat others as "moral inferiors" (Altmann, 1993). Racial, religious and ethnic epithets are therefore a distinct type of speech act in which the speaker is subordinating rather than claiming, asserting, requesting, or any of the other array of actions

we accomplish with language. So (it is concluded) while all the other types of speech acts
deserve protection, mere epithets and slurs
do not.

The problem with this argument, however, is
that epithets are *not* simply acts of subordination, devoid of social and political significance
or meaning, any more than burning a flag is
simply an act of heating cloth. Besides "subordinating" another, epithets can also express
emotion (anger or hatred, for example) or defiance of authority. And like burning or refusing
to salute the flag (both protected acts), epithets
also can be seen to express a political message,
such as that another person or group is less
worthy of moral consideration or is receiving
undeserved preferences. That means, then,
that however objectionable the content of such
epithets is they go well beyond mere acts of
"subordination" and therefore must be protected.

It is worth emphasizing, however, that although people have a political and constitutional *right* to use such language, it does not
follow that they *should* use it or that they are
behaving decently or morally when they exercise the right. A wrong remains a wrong, even if
government may for good reason choose not to
punish it. I am therefore in no way defending on
moral grounds those who utter hate speech – an
impossible task, in my view – but instead have
tried to show why meeting hatred with more
speech, as was done in Mizzoula, is a better
response than governmental censorship. Nor is
it correct to think that because government
allows people to speak it is thereby condoning
either the speech or the speaker. Government
doesn't condone Christians, Jews, Muslims and
atheists by merely allowing them to exercise
their religious freedom, as it would if it established and financed one religion. In religious
matters, as well as in the case of speech, government's job is to remain neutral.

What, finally, should be said when a university is seeking to prevent harassment by limiting
speech that creates a "hostile" environment
for faculty and students? Clearly, a university
could on aesthetic grounds prevent people from
hanging banners or other material from their

windows and doors, or pasting billboards on
public walls. But again such a regulation must
be content neutral; a state university cannot ban
some messages while leaving other students,
with different, less controversial and offensive
views, to express themselves. (Private universities, since they are not run by government and
therefore not bound by the First Amendment,
are free to impose whatever orthodoxy they
choose.)

More than most places, a university is committed to scholarship and the pursuit of knowledge. Freedom of inquiry is its life-blood. That
means, however, that nobody can be guaranteed
never to be offended or upset. (How often are
students in a religion class deeply offended by
what they hear? Or conservative Christians by
openly gay, or pro-choice speech?) Being forced
to confront people with widely different views
and attitudes, including those whom we dislike
and who dislike us, is rarely easy or pleasant;
but it can also be an important part of acquiring
an education. Once it is admitted that for purposes of regulating speech *content* there is no
such thing as a false idea, Nazi marches have as
much constitutional value as civil rights
marches, swastikas as much value as anti-war
or Israeli symbols, and emotionally charged
speeches by members of the Klan as much
value as Martin Luther King's "I Have a
Dream" speech. Indeed, it is rare that hate
speech is merely expressive and does not have
at least some political or social content. However offensive and stupid Louis Farrakhan's
description of Jews as "blood-sucking" may
be, it is more than contentless expression of
emotion.

None of this implies, however, that genuine
harassment, whether in the workplace or university, should be protected. But harassment is
not hate speech. For one thing, to suffer harassment requires more than hearing an offensive
remark. Genuine harassment requires a pattern
of behavior, not just a single event, and must
occur in a context in which its intended vic-
tim(s) are made to feel sufficiently intimidated
or distressed that their ability to perform is
impeded. Nor would verbal harassment be
limited to "hate speech" directed at women

and racial or ethnic minorities. Vulgar, sexually explicit language directed at a religiously conservative white male could be part of a pattern of harassment of him, for example, as could verbal attacks aimed at people for being short, or in a fraternity, or long haired, or even (a personal concern of mine) being bald. Nor, finally, are acts of harassment limited to speech; other actions (making late-night noise or dumping litter, for example) would also have to be included under a genuine anti-harassment regulation. The point, then, is not that people have a free speech right to harass others. Rather, it is that a ban on harassment would be both broader and narrower than a ban on hate speech. To avoid the charge that they are disguised censorship, harassment regulations must ban more than hate speech as well as avoid treating hate speech per se as harassment.

But how, then, should others respond to those, on a university or off, who are offended and distressed when others exercise their right to speak? When children call each other names and cruelly tease each other, the standard adult response is to work on both sides of the problem. Teasers are encouraged to be more sensitive to others' feelings, and victims are encouraged to ignore the remarks. "Sticks and stones can break my bones, but names can never hurt me" was a commonplace on the playground when I was a child. A minimum of self-assurance and toughness can be expected of people, including students at college.

Like the sexual freedoms of homosexuals, freedom of speech is often the source of great distress to others. I have argued, however, that because of the risks and costs of censorship there is no alternative to accepting those costs, or more precisely to imposing the costs on those who find themselves distressed and offended by the speech. Like people who are offended by homosexuality or interracial couples, targets of hate speech can ask why *they* should have to suffer distress. The answer is the same in each case: nobody has the right to demand that government protect them against distress when doing so would violate others' rights. Many of us believe that racists would be better people and lead more worthwhile lives if they didn't harbor hatred, but that belief does not justify restricting their speech, any more than the Puritans' desire to save souls would warrant religious intolerance, or Catholics' moral disapproval of homosexuality justify banning homosexual literature.

Acknowledgments

Earlier versions of this paper were read at the American Philosophical Association Pacific Meetings, St. Andrews College, Mansfield University, the University of Glasgow and St. Andrews University. I am grateful for the many helpful comments I received on all those occasions, and especially to Jacqueline Mariña and Amy Shapiro.

References

Abrams v. *United States*, 250 US 616 (1919).

Altmann, A. (1993) "Liberalism and Campus Hate Speech," *Ethics* 103.

Cohen v. *California*, 403 US 15 (1971).

Delgado, R. (1982) "Words that Wound: A Tort Action for Racial Insults, Epithets, and Name Calling," 17, *Harvard Civil Rights – Civil Liberties Law Review* 133 (1982); reprinted in Matsuda et al. (1993).

Dennis v. *United States*, 341 US 494 (1951).

Doe v. *University of Michigan*, 721 F. Supp. 852 (E. D. Mich. 1989).

Dworkin, R. (1996) *Freedom's Law: The Moral Reading of the American Constitution*. Cambridge, MA: Harvard University Press.

Feinberg, J. (1984) *The Moral Limits of the Criminal Law*, Volume I: *Harm to Others*. New York: Oxford University Press.

—— (1985) *The Moral Limits of the Criminal Law*, Volume II: *Offense to Others*. New York: Oxford University Press.

Gertz. v. *Robert Welch, Inc.*, 418 US 323, 339 (1974).

Gunther, G. (1990) "Good Speech, Bad Speech – No," *Stanford Lawyer*, 24.

Lawrence, C. (1990) "If He Hollers Let Him Go: Regulating Racist Speech on Campus," *Duke Law Journal*, 431; reprinted in Matsuda et al. (1993).

Malcolm X, and Haley, A. (1964) *The Autobiography of Malcolm X*. New York: Grove Press.

Matsuda, M. (1989) "Public Response to Racist Speech: Considering the Victim's Story," *Michigan Law Review*, 87, reprinted in Matsuda et al. (1993).

Matsuda, M., Lawrence, C. R., Delgado, R., and Crenshaw, K. W. (1993) *Words that Wound: Critical Race Theory, Assaultive Speech, and the First Amendment.* Boulder, CO: Westview Press.

May, L. (1987) *The Morality of Groups: Collective Responsibility, Group-Based Harm, and Corporate Rights.* Notre Dame: University of Notre Dame Press.

Meritor Savings Bank v. *Vinson*, 477 US 57 (1986).

Mill, J. S. (1978) *On Liberty*. Indianapolis, IN: Hackett.

R. A. V. v *City of St. Paul*, 50 US 377 (1992).

Rawls, J. (1971) *A Theory of Justice*. Cambridge, MA: Harvard University Press.

Texas v. *Johnson*, 491 US 397 (1989).

UMV Post v. *Board of Regents of the University of Wisconsin*, 774 F. supp. 1163 (1991).

38

Speech Codes and Expressive Harm

Andrew Altman

I Introduction

During the 1980s and early 1990s, many American colleges and universities adopted rules prohibiting speech that denigrates individuals on the basis of race, gender, ethnicity, religion, sexual orientation and similar categories of social identity. An apparent rash of racist and sexist incidents on campuses across the nation had led to the adoption of these 'speech codes'.[1] For example, at the University of Michigan, someone had written on a blackboard "A mind is a terrible thing to waste – especially on a nigger." (Lawrence, 1993: 55). The bigotry exhibited in such incidents was widely condemned. Yet, the codes designed to respond to this bigotry generated considerable controversy.

Critics argued that the codes violated the principle of free speech. They did not claim that all rules regulating speech on campus would be objectionable. Rules against rallies or demonstrations in the library would be unobjectionable. The aim of such rules would simply be to allow all students to use the library facilities without disruption, and no particular political beliefs or social attitudes would be singled out for suppression. But speech codes were entirely different, as the critics saw it: the

codes aimed to suppress the expression of certain beliefs and attitudes. And such an aim, the critics argued, was incompatible with any adequate understanding of free speech.

Advocates of the codes pointed to the harm caused to those targeted by 'hate speech': generalized psychic distress, feelings of anger and alienation, a sense of physical insecurity, and the various academic and social difficulties that naturally flow from such psychological disturbances. Treating the interests of all students with equal consideration, argued the advocates, required rules punishing hate speech. Code advocates also argued that restrictions on campus hate speech could help combat bigoted attitudes and practices in society at large.

American courts have uniformly sided with the critics of campus speech codes (Shiell, 1998, pp. 73–97). In a series of cases, courts struck down a variety of codes as unconstitutional. It might seem that these legal rulings would have put the controversy to rest. But that has not happened. Discussion and debate over the legitimacy of speech codes continues.

Because the US Supreme Court has not taken up a speech code case, there is some room to argue that the legal door has not been shut entirely on the question of the constitutionality of the codes. But the continuation of the controversy does not depend on expectations about future court action. It continues because the codes raise crucial ethical and political questions in a society committed both to freedom of speech and to equality under the law. What is the best way to understand the principle of free speech? Are there special aspects of the university context that must be taken into account by that understanding? Are there special aspects of American history and society that make a difference to the speech code debate? Legal cases can help shed light on such questions, but no court ruling can decisively settle them.[2]

In my view, it is difficult to justify speech codes solely on the basis of the harmful causal effects of hate speech. But I think that there is another type of harm to consider, what has been called "expressive harm" (Pildes and Niemi, 1993; Anderson and Pildes, 2000). Expressive harm is not a causal consequence of hate speech. Rather, it is a harm that derives from the kind of attitude expressed in the very act of hate speech, and it is independent of the causal effects of such a speech act.

In the next section, I explain why the causally harmful results of hate speech provide an insufficient basis on which to justify speech codes. Section III then gives an account of the nature of expressive harm, focusing on how symbolic speech by public officials can do expressive harm to an individual's right to be treated by government with equal respect and consideration. Section IV compares and contrasts private individuals with public officials when it comes to speech that does expressive harm. That section also formulates two main obstacles to justifying speech codes. In Sections V and VI, I seek to surmount those obstacles and present the case for speech codes. Section VII examines several campus speech policies, arguing for the superiority of a certain type of speech code.

II   Causal Harm

In an influential essay, Mari Matsuda writes: "When racist propaganda appears on campus, target-group students experience debilitated access to the full university experience. This is so even when it is directed at groups rather than at individuals" (1993, p. 45). And to those speech–code skeptics inclined to dismiss the harm of hate speech as merely psychological, Charles Lawrence points out: "Psychic injury is no less an injury than being struck in the face, and it often is far more severe. Racial epithets and harassment often cause deep emotional scarring and feelings of anxiety and fear that pervade every aspect of a victim's life" (1993, p. 74).

There is little doubt that hate speech can have psychologically debilitating effects and those effects in turn can interfere with a student's opportunities to enjoy the educational and social benefits of campus life. Black students who walk into a classroom in which the blackboard has written on it a vicious racial epithet directed against them will likely – and reasonably – respond with anger and even rage. Moreover, additional psychological injury is certainly possible: the students may come to think that they are unwelcome and even unsafe on campus. As Matsuda notes, hate speech often uses symbols, such as a burning crosses and swastikas, which are associated with violence against minorities.

Advocates of speech codes also argue that hate speech reinforces and perpetuates bigoted attitudes and practices in society at large. Thus Lawrence writes that "racist speech . . . distorts the marketplace of ideas by muting or devaluing the speech of Blacks and other despised minorities" (1993, p. 78). He contends that racist speech defames Blacks as a group: it causes a reputational injury to all Blacks, not simply to the immediate targets. Delgado and Stefancic also point to the general social effects of hate speech: "the racist insult remains one of the most pervasive channels through which discriminatory attitudes are imparted" (1997, p. 4).

The harms cited by the advocates of speech codes are real and serious. Undoubtedly, the members of society have a moral obligation to combat those harms. The issue is whether university speech codes are a justifiable way to proceed.

Some critics of speech codes argue that other means of combating the harms of hate speech should be pursued. Such means include 'counterspeech', i.e., speaking out against the bigoted attitudes of hate speakers. Also included are educational programs aimed at promoting equality and highlighting the harm caused by bigotry. Thomas Simon doubts that speech codes or educational programs make any significant impact on racism but suggests that universities can exert some substantial leverage in society's fight for racial equality by "carefully examining their employment practices, investment decisions, and community service" (1994, p. 186).

Advocates of speech codes claim that the remedies suggested by Simon and others should be pursued in addition to speech codes, not in place of them. But that claim is persuasive only if speech codes are a justifiable way to regulate speech. The prima facie plausibility of the claim that the codes seek to suppress the expression of certain viewpoints places a substantial burden of argument on those who contend that they are justifiable. That burden is only increased by the availability of other ways of combating the causal harms of hate speech.

The arguments that we have canvassed thus far have little chance of meeting that burden because they appear to license restrictions on speech that sweep too broadly. The arguments would not only license speech codes banning the use of racial epithets and slurs. Philosophical, literary, religious, and scientific works conveying racist, sexist or heterosexist ideas would be subject to prohibition. As Martin Golding says in his critique of speech codes, racist and anti-Semitic beliefs that are 'sanitized' and presented in the form of scholarly work is potentially more harmful that the slurs and epithets that students may hurl at one another (2000, p. 54). Such sanitized bigotry, e.g., the notorious anti-Semitic tract, "Protocols of the Elders of Zion," has the appearance of a work of scholarship and so may well have a greater psychological and reputational impact on the group it targets than the vulgar racist rant of a student.

Yet, a university is precisely where any work that purports to have objective validity should be available for critical assessment. As Golding has argued, the university is "a form of institutionalized rationality" that subjects knowledge-claims to the test of "critical examination . . . by competent inquirers" (2000, pp. 18, 22). The function of the university requires "communal discussion" and "the *organized* pursuit of knowledge," and it would be seriously compromised by the prohibition of works that convey bigoted ideas and views (Golding, 2000, pp. 17–18).

Moreover, there is a body of literature that is not the fraudulent work of vicious bigots but is regarded as racist by many and would be subject to prohibition under the arguments of Lawrence and Matsuda. Consider the work on race of the psychologist J. P. Rushton, who summarizes it this way:

> In new studies and reviews of the world literature, I consistently find that East Asians and their descendants average a larger brain size, greater intelligence, more sexual restraint, slower rates of maturation, and greater law abidingness and social organization than do Europeans and their descendants who average higher scores on these dimensions than do Africans and their descendants. I proposed a gene-based evolutionary origin for this pattern. (2000)

Rushton's views have the potential to cause much more reputational damage to Blacks than an undergraduate's drunken utterance of a racial slur. Moreover, regardless of Rushton's intent, it is reasonable to think that his views would reinforce the bigoted attitudes of those inclined to treat Blacks as moral inferiors. And the views would obviously provoke anger among Black students.

Yet, Rushton's work may not be legitimately banned from libraries, classrooms, and other campus forums by a speech code. The institutional rationality of the university demands that the work be available for the critical analysis of scholarly experts and for the study of interested students.

The university's role as a testing ground for claims to knowledge makes it difficult for advocates of speech codes to meet their burden of justification solely by pointing to the harmful causal consequences of hate speech. But this does not necessarily doom all efforts to justify the codes. There is another form of harm associated with hate speech – expressive harm. A justification that takes account of both causal and expressive harm has better prospects for success. Let us turn to some examples to illustrate the existence and nature of expressive harm.

III Expressive Harm: Public Actors

In the recent past, there was considerable controversy sparked by southern states that flew the Confederate flag over their capitols. On July 1, 2000, South Carolina became the last state to remove the flag from its site over the seat of the state government. Blacks and many others take the flag to be a symbol of slavery and racism, and they construed the display of the flag to be an expression of racist attitudes. Some southern whites rejected that interpretation and argued that the flag was a legitimate expression of reverence for the valor of their ancestors who suffered and died during the Civil War. But in the wake of protests, state legislators voted to take the flag down.

What was the harm of flying the flag over state capitols? In *NAACP* v. *Hunt* (1990), a federal appeals court rejected the claim that Alabama was violating the Equal Protection Clause of the Fourteenth Amendment by flying the confederate flag over its capitol. The court reasoned that the only harm done by the flying of the flag was the emotional distress of the plaintiffs and that such harm did not amount to a violation of the constitutional principle of equality.

However, the court's reasoning was flawed by its failure to see that there is another form of harm done by the flying of the flag, which did violate the equality principle. The flying of the flag did expressive harm to Blacks: aside from its causal consequences, the act of flying the flag was the expression of a racist attitude hostile, or at least grossly indifferent, to the interests of Blacks (Forman, 1991, p. 508). The official expression of such an attitude constituted a violation of the right to be treated by government with equal respect and consideration.

There are undoubtedly well-meaning individuals who take pride in the display of the Confederate flag. But they fail to realize that the nation is not sufficiently removed from its history of racial oppression for the flag to be a benign cultural symbol. The debilitating effects of past racism still severely hamper the life chances of Blacks, and current racism aggravates the wounds left by this history (Bobo, 1997). The meaning of the flag is still freighted with the history and legacy of racial oppression.

In such a context, flying the flag over the seat of government is, at best, an expression of a callous indifference toward the state's racial minorities and counts as an expressive harm to them. As Anderson and Pildes explain it, "a person suffers expressive harm when she is treated according to principles that express negative or inappropriate attitudes toward her" (2000, p. 1528). And Alabama was treating its Black citizens in exactly that way.

Another example of expressive harm is found in Amar's hypothetical variation of the Hunt case: suppose that Alabama adopted as its official motto the slogan "The White Supremacy State" (1998, 254). It would be strained to argue that non- White plaintiffs seeking a ruling that the state had violated the Equal Protection Clause would need to prove that the adoption of the motto had causal effects harmful to racial equality. Indeed, under certain scenarios, the motto might produce political backlash promoting equality. The fact is that the very adoption of the motto, apart from its causal consequences, is a harm to racial minorities. It is an expressive harm.

IV Expressive Harm: Private Actors

In the Confederate flag and state motto cases, public officials were the ones whose actions did expressive harm. Their status as officials made the harms ascribable to the state and so – the circuit court's ruling notwithstanding – a constitutional violation. But the expressive harm they did was independent of their official status. State officials can typically exert much more causal power in the world than private citizens. And what they express through their acts might well have much more widespread causal effects than the expressive activities of a private individual. Those causal effects may result in harms that most private individuals simply do not have the causal capacity to produce, for example, widespread loss of employment opportunities. But the private individual is capable of doing expressive harm. Just as a state official can express callous indifference or hostility to racial minorities, so can a private citizen. And expression of such an attitude can amount to a harm in both sorts of cases.

On the other hand, there is a big difference between the expressive harm to racial equality committed by a state official and the same sort of harm done by a private individual. When the expressive harm is done by the communicative act of a private individual, it is protected by free speech principles. It is unjustifiable for the law to allow state officials to fly the Confederate Flag above their capitols, but the law should protect private individuals who wish to display the flag outside their homes or on their car antennas. Such private actions can express indifference or hostility to racial equality, but it should be not subject to legal sanction.

Private hate speakers thus have a free-speech shield that protects them from liability for the expressive harm they may do, just as that same shield usually protects them from liability for the harmful causal effects of their speech. So it may seem that we have not really advanced the argument for speech codes. Moreover, one can claim that the argument has been made even more difficult by the difference between official and private speech.

When a university punishes a student for a speech code violation, it seems to be committing an expressive harm against him. Aside from any bad causal effects the punishment may have on the student, it is an expression of the emphatic moral condemnation of his social attitudes. And critics of restrictions on hate speech might contend that such condemnation by government violates the rights of hate speakers to equal consideration. Everyone should be permitted to express their views, without discrimination on the basis of what those views are (Dworkin, 1995, pp. 200–1). Accordingly, we appear to have two strong reasons against speech codes.

The campus hate speaker may do expressive harm, but that form of harm is no less protected by free speech principles that the causal harm he may do. And the university's punitive response to the hate speaker is a form of official moral condemnation that expressively harms the speaker. The challenge of justifying speech codes depends upon a cogent response to these two reasons. The next two sections seek to develop such a response.

V   Moral Contempt

The expressive harm of hate speech plays two related roles in the justification of speech codes. First, it helps explain why certain forms of hate speech should be regarded as "low value" speech in the university context. Second, it serves to distinguish those forms of hate speech that ought to be subject to official restriction from those that ought to be protected against such restriction. Let us begin with a look at how the meaning and use of racial epithets can be understood in terms of the idea of expressive harm.

Racial epithets and similar terms of abuse are communicative tools for expressing an extreme form of moral contempt.[3] Such contempt involves the attitude that the person targeted by the epithet belongs to a group whose members have a lower moral status than those in the group to which the speaker belongs. For those who think in such terms, it is appropriate to express such contempt when members of the morally subordinate groups seek to be treated as equals. The expression of extreme contempt is thought to be fitting because those who are moral inferiors are trying to act as equals: they are impostors who need to be treated as such. Racial epithets and similar terms of abuse are words whose use is to treat someone in a morally degrading way by expressing a certain form of moral contempt toward them. Racist or sexist speech in the form of scientific or philosophical discourse might also convey contempt, but that is not the principal purpose of those forms of discourse. Rather, the vocabulary of such discourse is for formulating and expressing ideas that claim to have objective validity. Any such validity-claim is subject to critical scrutiny and challenge by anyone who can raise such a challenge, even by those persons whom the claim might assert to be moral inferiors to the speaker. "Scientific racism" might explicitly assert that a certain racial group is inherently less intelligent or more prone to crime than other racial groups, but in making such claims it implicitly invites anyone to produce arguments and evidence to refute them.

It is true that the use of epithets can be part of assertions that claim objective validity. Anti–Semites can say "Kikes are all thieves." But hate speech couched in scientific or philosophical discourse does not employ such epithets because the discourse is meant to convey objective claims unadorned by the subjective feelings of the speaker. In contrast, the point of epithets is precisely to express the feelings of the speaker.

The contrast explains why hate speech couched in the discourse of science, philosophy, theology or other scholarly vocabularies should be protected. The claims that such speech makes are subject to the scrutiny, challenge and refutation of those operating within the institutional rationality of the university. As Golding has stressed, that rationality requires protection even for speech that claims or suggests some groups of humans are inherently inferior to others.

In contrast, speech using racist epithets and similarly abusive terms is "low value" speech in the university context because it contributes virtually nothing to the operation of the institutional rationality of the university at the same time that it is used to degrade members of the university community. The exercise of that rationality involves the critical assessment of claims to objective validity. It is difficult to see what role is played in that process by the use of epithets to express contempt for and degrade persons who are members of the university community on the basis of their race, gender, and other categories of social identity.

My argument might be rejected on the basis of the reasoning in the case of *Cohen* v. *California*. Writing for the Court, Justice Harlan said that the words on the jacket Cohen wore into a courthouse, "Fuck the Draft," conveyed a message in which the emotional and cognitive elements were inseparable. Protecting Cohen's message against the Vietnam War draft meant protecting the expletive in terms of which the message was expressed. And the Court held that the message must be protected as the expression of Cohen's political viewpoint.

It may be argued that Harlan's reasoning applies to the use of racist or sexist epithets. Such epithets convey a message in which emotional and cognitive elements are mixed and the message must be protected as the expression of certain viewpoint. However, there is an important difference between campus hate-speech cases and Cohen's case: the campus cases – but not Cohen's – are closely analogous to cases of verbal racial harassment in the workplace. And restrictions on such harassment at work are unobjectionable.

Cohen was not acting in an employment context but rather as a member of the general public, expressing his views in a building open to the public. And he caused no disturbance in courthouse operations. But imagine that he were an employee at a business with Black employees and that he wore a jacket in the workplace saying "Fuck niggers." Such expression could be justifiably prohibited on grounds of equal employment opportunity.

Campus speech cases are more like such an employment case than they are like the actual Cohen case. Students are not employees. But they do have a defined role within the university, and they should not be materially disadvantaged in their role on account of their race, gender, or sexual orientation. The use of racial epithets and similar terms of abuse in the campus context is reasonably thought to interfere with equal educational opportunity, just as the use of such terms can interfere with equal employment opportunity in the workplace.

It is also true that the principle of equal educational opportunity must be construed in a way that is responsive to the special role of the university in critically examining all ideas claiming objective validity. Hate speech in the mode of scientific or philosophical discourse can cause psychological distress sufficient to interfere with a student's ability to enjoy the opportunities of campus life. But in that case, it is the ideas expressed that are the grounds for the distress. And, unlike other institutions, the role of the university in critically assessing ideas requires that distress caused by the assertion of ideas be excluded as a reason for adopting a speech policy. However, that role does not require the university to ignore the causal effects of racist epithets on the student.

Sadurski has claimed that "insensitivity to many psychic harms is the price of a broadened scope for individual autonomy" (1999, 224). It is also true that a certain degree of such insensitivity is the price of a university's commitment to the free expression and critical testing of ideas claiming objective validity. But the causal harm of racial epithets is not the result of putting forth propositions that claim objective validity. Rather, the causal harm is the product of the extreme moral contempt that the epithets express. Thus, a university speech policy that takes account of the causal harms of such epithets is not subject to the same objection as a policy that takes account of the causal harm of statements that claim objective validity.

VI Official Condemnation

Let us now turn to the matter of whether a speech code treats hate speakers with less than equal consideration. After all, such a code makes them liable to punitive measures for the expression of their social and political attitudes, and "the significance of punishment is moral condemnation" (Kahan, 1996, p. 598). There is no circumventing the fact that a speech policy that employs punishment to express such condemnation seeks to suppress speech for the viewpoint it expresses. And in so doing, the policy violates the equal expressive rights of those who hold the disfavored viewpoints.

Any viewpoint-biased speech restriction should be troubling to those who value strong protections for freedom of speech. But it is important to place the speech code debate in its broader social and historical context in order to understand how a limited departure from viewpoint neutrality can be justifiable.

Consider again the Confederate flag dispute. Blacks and many others reasonably took the flag as symbolic of the state's indifference, or even antagonism, to racial equality. Removal of the flag was reasonably construed as an expressive affirmation of that value. The removal was hardly viewpoint-neutral and could not have been in the situation. But the expressive affirmation of racial equality was justifiable, and even mandatory, under the circumstances.

The flag was reasonably construed as standing for a set of values associated with the Confederacy, including white supremacy. In theory, the flag can stand for such virtues as courage and honor without the taint of the white supremacist regime those virtues in fact served. But in contemporary American society the display of the flag cannot be purified of such a taint. There is no way for a state to display the flag over its capitol without it being reasonably interpreted as callous indifference to interests of its black citizens.

Many advocates of speech codes appear to see the code controversy in similar terms: adopting a speech code is a way of symbolically affirming the value of racial equality but not adopting one amounts to the expressive repudiation of that value (Shiffrin, 1999, pp. 78–80). But the analogy is not quite right. The failure to have a code is not analogous to displaying a symbol whose meaning is still inextricably intertwined with racism. For that reason, it is wrong to think that it is morally, even if not legally, mandatory for any university to have a speech code. But having such a code still may be a justifiable option.

A speech code is an expressive affirmation of racial equality. So are other aspects of university life, such as the observance of the Martin Luther King holiday. Hate speakers may object to the holiday as a departure from viewpoint neutrality and a denigration of their right to equality. They don't get to have an official holiday for their favorite opponent of the civil rights movement. But the nation's commitment to racial equality means that hate speakers and advocates of racial equality simply are not treated in an absolutely evenhanded way, nor should they be. The history of racial injustice is so egregious, and its lingering effects still so troublesome, that some tilt away from strict expressive neutrality and in the direction of racial equality is entirely justifiable. The question is the degree and nature of the tilt.

Critics of speech codes may concede that symbolically affirming racial equality and condemning bigotry through official holidays is fine but then argue that it is an entirely different matter when it comes to using punitive measures for strictly symbolic purposes. But speech codes can be reasonably understood as more than a strictly symbolic gesture. Their condemnation of bigotry sends a strong educational message to the university community and arguably deters forms of verbal degradation that interfere with a student's opportunity to enjoy benefits of campus life.

It may be true that speech codes are not indispensable for providing equal educational opportunity: counterspeech that condemns instances of campus bigotry and other alternatives might work. But it is not unreasonable for a school to judge that a speech code would be of sufficient value to warrant its adoption. The question is how to formulate a code that serves equal opportunity while respecting the centrality of free expression to the role of the university.

VII   Speech Codes

Some advocates of speech codes defend bans on hate speech that sweep more broadly than the use of epithets (Matsuda, 1993, pp. 44–5; Lawrence, 1993, p. 70). Such broad codes would prohibit hate speech formulated in scientific, philosophical, or theological terms. It should be clear that my analysis rejects codes of that kind as inconsistent with the central place that free speech must play in the life of the university. A speech code must be narrowly drawn in order to be justifiable (Weinstein, 1999, pp. 52, 127; Cohen, 1996, pp. 212–14).

A typical version of a narrow code prohibits hate speech only when (a) it uses racial epithets

or analogously abusive terms based on sex, sexual orientation, and similar categories of social identity, (b) the speaker intends to degrade persons through his use of such terms, and (c) the terms are addressed directly to a specific person or small group of persons.

In criticizing narrow speech codes, some legal theorists have suggested that general rules against verbal harassment would be preferable to codes formulated in terms of race, gender, and so on (Golding, 2000, p. 60). Such general rules would not select out particular categories of verbal harassment, but would rather prohibit any verbal abuse that materially interfered with a (reasonable) student's ability to learn and enjoy the other benefits of campus life and that was intended to cause such interference. General harassment rules certainly have much to be said for them as an alternative to narrow speech codes. A student's opportunities to take advantage of the benefits of the university should not be materially interfered with by any form of verbal harassment. And if the speech policy of a university were restricted to racial epithets and the like, then students who were harassed for other reasons, e.g., their political affiliation, could rightly complain that the university was not adequately protecting their interest in equal educational opportunity. Accordingly, it is reasonable to think that general rules against all forms of verbal harassment would be preferable to a speech code limited to categories such as race and gender. Nonetheless, it is possible to give due recognition to the special expressive and causal harm of racial epithets within a set of general rules prohibiting any verbal harassment that interferes with a student's equal educational opportunity.

The capacity of racial epithets to express extreme moral contempt gives them an unusual power to interfere with a student's efforts to take advantage of her educational opportunities. General rules against verbal harassment can be interpreted and applied in a way that takes account of that fact. For instance, the use of anti-Semitic epithets could be judged a violation of the rules even in the case of just a single incident, while other forms of abusive speech, e.g., those targeting a person's political affiliation, would need to involve repeated episodes before they would rise to the level of a violation. Or the use of a racist epithet might be judged a violation when it is reasonably foreseeable that an individual in the targeted group would be exposed to the abusive term, even if the epithet were not specifically directed at her.[4] For other forms of verbal harassment, directly addressing the targeted individual might be required.

The basic standard for a violation would be the same in all cases of verbal harassment: Did the abusive speech materially interfere with a student's opportunity to take advantage of the benefits of campus life?[5] But in the interpretation and application of that standard, the distinctive expressive power of racist epithets and similar terms of abuse would be taken into account.[6]

A campus speech policy that took account of that special expressive power could do a better job of protecting equal opportunity than general rules against verbal harassment that failed to be responsive to expressive harm of hate speech. And the policy could also do a better job than speech codes limited to the prohibition of verbal abuse based on race, gender, sexual orientation, and similar categories of social identity. Taking account of the expressive power of racial epithets and analogous terms of abuse involves some departure from the principle that restrictions on speech should be viewpoint-neutral. But the departure is relatively minor and the value served – equal educational opportunity in our institutions of higher education – is an important one.

References

Amar, Akhil (1998). *The Bill of Rights*. New Haven, CT: Yale University Press.

Anderson, Elizabeth and Richard Pildes (2000). "Expressive Theories of Law: A General Restatement," *University of Pennsylvania Law Review* 148: 1503–75.

Bobo, Lawrence (1997). "Laissez-Faire Racism: The Crystallization of a Kinder, Gentler, Antiblack Ideology." In Steven Tuch and Jack Martin (eds.), *Racial Attitudes in the 1990s*. Westport: Praeger.

Cohen v. *California*. 1971. 403 U.S. 15.

Cohen, Joshua (1996). "Freedom of Expression." In David Heyd (ed.), *Toleration*. Princeton, NJ: Princeton University Press, pp. 173–225.

Delgado, Richard and Jean Stefancic (1997). *Must We Defend Nazis?* New York: New York University Press.

Dworkin, Ronald (1995). *Freedom's Law*. Cambridge, MA: Harvard University Press.

Forman, James (1991). "Driving Dixie Down: Removing the Confederate Flag from Southern State Capitols," *Yale Law Journal* 101: 505–26.

Golding, Martin (2000). *Free Speech on Campus*. Lanham, MD: Rowman and Littlefield.

Kahan, Daniel, (1996) "What Do Alternative Sanctions Mean?" *University of Chicago Law Review* 62: 591–653.

Lawrence, Charles (1993). "If He Hollers Let Him Go: Regulating Racist Speech on Campus." In Mari Masuda et al. (eds.), *Words that Wound*. Boulder, CO: Westview, pp. 53–88.

Matsuda, Mari (1993). "Public Response to Hate Speech: Considering The Victim's Story." In Mari Matsuda et al. (eds.), *Words that Wound*. Boulder, CO: Westview, pp. 17–51.

NAACP v. *Hunt*. 1990. 891 F.2d 1555 (11th Cir).

Pildes, Richard and Richard Niemi (1993). "Expressive Harms, 'Bizarre Districts' and Voting Rights," *Michigan Law Review* 92: 483–587.

Rushton, J. P. (2000). *http://www.sscl.uwo.ca/ psychology/faculty/rushton.html*

Sadurski, Wojcieck (1999). *Freedom of Expression and Its Limits*. Dordrecht: Kluwer.

Shiell, Timothy (1998). *Campus Hate Speech on Trial*. Lawrence: University Press of Kansas.

Shiffrin, Steven (1999). *Dissent, Injustice, and the Meanings of America*. Princeton NJ: Princeton University Press.

Simon, Thomas (1994) "Fighting Racism: Hate Speech Detours." In M. N. S. Sellers (ed.), *An Ethical Education*. Providence, RI: Berg, pp. 171–86.

Weinstein, James (1999) *Hate Speech, Pornography, and the Radical Attack on Free Speech Doctrine*. Boulder, CO: Westview.

Wisconsin v. *Mitchell*. 1993. 113 S.Ct. 2194.

Notes

1 In this essay, I use the term 'speech code' to refer to rules that punish individuals for speech that degrades or demeans others on the basis of race or the other listed features.

2   Under US constitutional law, there is an important distinction between state and private universities: the former, but not the latter, are subject to the free speech clause of the Constitution. For this essay, I will assume that most, if not all, private institutions of higher education place a high value on free speech and desire to respect free-speech principles.

3   My analysis of epithets is meant to capture a standard use of such terms. There are other uses.

4   Consider the case from the University of Michigan, cited in section I.

5   There should also be requirements that the speech intentionally interfere with the student's opportunities and that the response of the affected student be reasonable.

6   Delgado and Stefancic (1997) propose general rules against verbal harassment combined with provisions for extra punishment in cases where the harassment is based on race, gender, and the like. They point out that their proposal appears to be consistent with the Supreme Court ruling in *Wisconsin* v. *Mitchell* (1993), which permitted a state to enhance criminal penalties for crimes committed from racially discriminatory motives. It is unclear, though, whether the Court would extend that ruling to cases where the underlying "crime" is a speech offense. My proposal is not that extra punishment be given for hate speech, but rather that the expressive harm of such speech be factored into the question of whether an incident rises to the level of an offense. The two proposals are not incompatible, although I think that, aside from truly egregious cases, a university's punitive response to hate speech episodes should be relatively mild and mainly symbolic.

Sexual and Racial Discrimination

Several times in this volume I have pointed out that even when people embrace the same general moral principle, they may disagree dramatically over practical moral questions. For instance, in the previous section I explained that although most people assert that we should limit speech only if it demonstrably harms others, they often disagree about what counts as harm and whether some particular actions do, in fact, harm others. Knowing someone's stance on a practical issue does not necessarily reveal their theoretical commitments; knowing their theoretical commitments may not reveal how they will resolve any particular ethical issue.

In this section we see a similar gap between abstract principles and concrete judgments and behavior. Few people unabashedly champion racism or sexism – and those that do rarely populate courses like this one. That does not mean, however, that everyone agrees that racism and sexism are extinct; still less do they agree about how we should treat people of different races and genders. Only the most naive person would think that we are no longer a racist and sexist society. Many of us see within ourselves, much to our chagrin, remnants of our racist and sexist pasts. We all occasionally see

those tendencies in others. Finally, people often wildly disagree about whether some particular action is racist or sexist.

Thus, the real questions are not whether we are or should be racist or sexist, but (1) exactly what we mean by "racism" and "sexism," (2) just how pervasive racism and sexism are, (3) what forms current-day racism and sexism take, and (4) how, precisely, should people of different races and different genders relate? Moody-Adams offers tentative answers to each of these questions. In specifying racism, she insists that we cannot fully understand racism unless we understand the particular ways that it arose, the precise ways it functions in political and social practices.

Her discussion focuses our attention on important theoretical issues, especially (1) the extent to which we define ourselves and others by group membership, and (2) the nature and power of subconscious forces that lead people to discriminate against others, even when they claim to be neither racists or sexists. We often react and behave as racists and sexists, even when we are unaware (or only marginally aware) of what we do. This is not a new phenomenon. Many – arguably most – slaveholders did not think they were acting wrongly by holding slaves. Likewise, most of our great-great-grandparents did not think they were acting immorally when they denied women the right to vote. But regardless of what they thought, their acts were racist and sexist. No doubt we, too, act in racist ways, even if we deny it.

Hill's essay raises questions common to both racism and sexism. Both blacks and women have, at times, been servile to whites and to men. Sometimes those decisions were prudent. Slaves knew that if they were "uppity" they might endanger themselves and their families. In such extreme oppressive environments, servility was arguably not a vice. However, in the current environment, blacks and women should shed any remnants of servility. They should see themselves as valuable people whom others should respect. People with a healthy self-respect will, among other things, claim their rights. Otherwise, by their silence, they imply that the dominant group's behavior and attitudes toward them is justified.

Although the remaining selections focus on sexual discrimination, the authors do so in ways that also illuminate racial discrimination. The first topic – sexual harassment – has been widely discussed. The issue took center stage during the confirmation hearings for Clarence Thomas, a nominee to the United States Supreme Court. A former employee of Thomas's, Anita Hill, claimed he had sexually harassed her on numerous occasions. Thomas's main line of defense was that he did not intend to harass anyone and that many women who worked with him did not interpret his behavior as harassing. Thomas thereby embraced what Superson calls the "subjective view of harassment" – the view that an action is harassment only (a) if it is intended to harass and (b) if it, in fact, bothers women. Superson rejects this account in favor of an "objective view of harassment." This view states that one person harasses another if it perpetuates the view that men are superior to, and should have control over, women.

That explains why she thinks sexual harassment is a wrong not only to the specific women being harassed, but a wrong to all women. This contrasts with Arthur's rejection of the idea that groups can be harmed, and agrees with Altman's argument that groups can be harmed (Free Speech).

Pineau discusses a related topic: date rape. Evidence suggests that date rape is far more common than most of us would like to admit. Several significant trials in the United States – the trials of William Kennedy Smith (the nephew of former US President John Kennedy) and of heavyweight fighter Michael Tyson – made citizens aware of this phenomenon. These two trials accent conceptual, empirical, and moral quandaries about date rape. Virtually everyone agrees that rape is bad, even if, and perhaps especially if, the perpetrator and the victim know each other.

However, people disagree vehemently about how, in particular cases, to distinguish consensual sex from date rape. We can all agree about paradigm cases of consensual sex – when it is clear to everyone that both parties are eager participants. We can also agree about paradigm cases of rape – when a woman is taken forcibly from her home, physically assaulted, and raped. However, in the two aforementioned cases, the public was unsure how to evaluate events. Neither defendant denied that he had had sex with the victim. Both defended themselves by arguing that the woman had consented. Kennedy's jurors believed his account of events and acquitted him, while Tyson's jurors did not believe him; they convicted him of rape. The disputes over these verdicts reflect the public's uncertainty about how to distinguish consensual sex from rape.

The problems in deciding if date rape has occurred are twofold. Criminal law, which we discuss in the section on Punishment, typically holds that we should punish a person for a crime only if he has the appropriate *mens rea* or "guilty mind." On this view it seems that a man who is charged with rape but sincerely believes that the woman consented, would lack a guilty mind, and therefore would not be guilty of rape. Pineau rejects this reasoning. The relevant question, she claims, is not whether the man thought she consented, but whether his belief was reasonable. Pineau thus advocates an "objective view of rape" not unlike Superson's "objective view of sexual harassment."

The second (related) issue is what must a woman do to show (especially in court) that she did not consent. The legal assumption – at least for people who know each other (as in date rape) – is that the woman must give clear and strong evidence that she did not consent. Lacking such evidence, jurors often construe the fact that she dated the man as evidence that she did, in fact, consent. Pineau claims this presumption is founded on a series of myths about women, sex, and rape.

These ideas are explored further by May and Strikwerda, who argue that all men are, to some degree, guilty of rape, either by directly encouraging rape, by holding and promulgating attitudes that make rape more likely, or at least by failing to make serious efforts to end rape. They do not claim, of course, that every man actually is guilty of physically raping a woman. Rather they claim that men *as a group* contribute to rape, and thus that all men, as members of that group, bear at least some responsibility for it. Once again, we see just how important it is to decide if groups have moral status.

Further Reading

Card, C. (ed.) (1991) *Feminist Ethics*. Lawrence, KA: University of Kansas Press.

Friedman, M. and May, L. (1985) "Harming Women as a Group," *Social Theory and Practice* 11: 208–34.

Griffin, S. (1971) "Rape: The All-American Crime," *Ramparts*: 26–35.

Jaggar, A. (1983) *Feminist Politics and Human Nature*. Totowa, NJ: Rowman and Allenheld.

Kittay, E. and Myers, D. (eds.) (1987) *Women and Moral Theory*. Totowa, NJ: Rowman and Allenheld.

Mill, J. S. (1988/1869) *On the Subjection of Women*. Indianapolis, IN: Hackett Publishing Company.

Mills, C. (1997) *The Racial Contract*. Ithaca, NY: Cornell University Press.

—— (1999) *Blackness Visible*. Ithaca, NY: Cornell University Press.

Scully, D. (1990) *Understanding Sexual Violence*. Boston, MA: Unwin Hyman.

Vetterling-Braggin, M., Elliston, F., and English, J. (eds.) (1978) *Feminism and Philosophy*. Totowa, NJ: Rowman and Allenheld.

West, C. (1993) *Race Matters*. Boston, MA: Beacon Press.

39

Racism

Michele Moody-Adams

In several topics of importance to applied ethics it is frequently difficult to find uncontroversial propositions from which to begin a substantive discussion of the relevant ethical problems. This phenomenon is perhaps most familiar in discussions of abortion, where simply describing the competing positions to be analyzed and evaluated is an activity fraught with controversy. Less familiar, or at least less frequently acknowledged, is the extent to which substantive discussion of the ethical dimensions of racism must begin with assumptions that, to some, will seem as controversial as any assumptions shaping discussions of abortion. But consider three propositions that many, including the author, believe to be fundamental to any discussion of the ethical implications of racism.

1 Racism is morally wrong, and should not be embodied in the beliefs and actions of individuals, or in the practices and institutions of social groups, cultures, or nations.
2 Racism exists (even in many circumstances where it is the subject of official condemnation), and in its most virulent manifestations continues to have socially and economically important consequences for those unjustly affected by it.
3 The effects of even virulent forms of racism can be powerfully mitigated, and sometimes even eliminated, by collective, and sometimes individual, efforts of determined moral agents.

All three of these propositions have long been the source of intense discussion and debate. Yet given what seems to be their centrality to discussions of the ethical implications of racism, it is important to enquire about the nature and source of the disagreement that concerns these propositions, and then to consider whether there are any means for responding to the underlying disagreement in a constructive way.

Articulating the nature and source of the relevant disagreement is a relatively straightforward task. To begin with, those who appreciate the depth and breadth of moral disagreement will not be surprised at the contention that the normative claim contained in proposition (1) remains a subject of controversy. But it should be emphasized that this claim remains controversial despite the spread of legal, political, and social orthodoxies officially condemning racism.

It may be less widely recognized that, largely in response to the rise of official condemnations of racism, proposition (2), alleging the continued existence and effects of racism, is in many contexts as controversial as proposition (1). For instance, citing the legal prohibition of discrimination in the United States, an increasingly vocal group of social critics has confidently proclaimed the "end of racism" in America (D'Souza, 1995). According to such critics, wherever legal, political, and social orthodoxies officially condemn racism, any substantial lingering disparities between the social, economic, and political positions of groups "formerly" discriminated against and those of other social groups can be attributed primarily, or even solely, to some failure on the part of the complaining groups themselves. End-of-racism theorists allege that the less well-off groups frequently exhibit failures to take advantage of legally protected opportunities, as well as intrinsic "racially based" weaknesses and blameworthy cultural impoverishment, or some combination of these three causes.

Some opponents of this view construe its claims about the "end" of racism as manifestations of an entirely new form of racism. In a related vein, others worry that it may be impossible to mount a morally robust response to persistent racism without relying on "color-conscious" social policies. But they also expect any such reliance to generate, in response, demands for "color blind" policies that, ironically, rely on concepts and methods created by the anti-discrimination movement to give a renewed legitimacy to racial discrimination (Freeman, 1978; Crenwhaw, 1988). Taken together, these fears have given rise to a pessimistic assertion of the "permanence of racism" (Bell, 1992). It is thus that resistance to proposition (3), with its claim that the effects of racism can be eliminated or substantially mitigated, has developed largely in answer to complex controversies that have emerged in response to the claim of proposition (2).

But it is relatively easy to illuminate the grounds of various controversies on which discussions of the ethical dimensions of racism frequently founder. More concerted reflection

is required if we are to provide useful insights into the means by which we might move beyond the resultant ethical impasse created primarily by disagreement about propositions (2) and (3). Ethical thinkers have frequently failed to appreciate that the most promising path starts with a clear and detailed understanding of what racism actually is. Nor have they appreciated that it is impossible to make sense of racism, or its ethical dimensions, if they confine their analyses to the explicitly "evaluative" components of racism (that is, to claims about differences in the intrinsic value of different racialized groups). (For we scrutinize only the "purely" evaluative components of racist claims at the expense of the kind of substantive scrutiny of racism's purportedly "empirical," even "scientific," claims without which it is impossible to achieve any kind of analytical clarity about the nature of racism.) That is, only after a careful analysis of the central features of racist conceptions of reality will it be possible to articulate important elements of a robust response to controversies about the ethical dimensions of racism.

A robust response to racism must then provide a strong statement of the reasons for which racism must be rejected as morally wrong. The account must then discuss the circumstances in which it is possible to recognize the existence and persistence of racism. Finally, a robust challenge to racism must also suggest at least some reasons for believing that we can remedy the effects of racism without unintentionally reaffirming racism's worst moral excesses. It is to the details of this account that I now turn.

What Is Racism?

At the core of any instance of racism is the two-pronged notion that: (a) the human species can be divided into discrete "races" characterized by fairly consistently aligned bundles of essential attributes; and (b) the bundles of essential attributes possessed by some races make their "members," on balance, intrinsically more valuable (especially socially, economically, and morally more valuable) than members of other races. Racism may be manifested in the behavior of individual persons; it may also shape social practices and institutions, either by the deliberate action or the prolonged inaction of varied sets of social actors. But before it is ever expressed in the actions of individuals, or embodied in social practices and institutions, racism is essentially a distinctive conception of the nature of reality. Plausible efforts to articulate what might be required to mitigate or eliminate racism's effects must proceed from serious scrutiny of the complex ways in which racism, along with the human agents who (to varying degrees) accept it, attempts to construct reality.

Efforts to scrutinize racist conceptions are surely made more difficult by the fact that racism takes many complex and varied forms. It is important, first of all, to remember that different social contexts have produced quite varied systems of racial classification, and equally varied understandings of how (allegedly) intrinsic differences in the merits of particular groups will be expressed in experience. For instance, while North American racism in the second half of the twentieth century presumed the existence of two, possibly three, "major" races to which people were supposedly assignable by descent, twentieth-century Brazilian racism is widely believed to have relied on as many as 40 racial categories in which descent played a very small role (Marshall, 1993).

Second, historical developments within a given society can have profound consequences for any socially dominant structure of racial classification, as well as for any resultant racism linked with that structure. What this means is that racism and its effects can undergo significant changes in a single society over time – sometimes over a relatively short period of time. In a particularly vivid example of this, scholars have documented politically and economically influential changes in the structure of American racism. One of the most interesting changes concerns American descendants of populations who had immigrated to the United States in the late nineteenth and early twentieth centuries, from countries such as Ireland and Italy. In the middle of the twentieth century, members of these groups gradually went from being members of several distinct "white races"

(with varying amounts of allegedly desirable attributes) to being members of a single white or "Caucasian" race celebrated as "superior" to "non-Caucasians" (Jacobson, 1998).

Other difficulties tend to complicate the task of scrutinizing racist conceptions, especially for the ethical thinker seeking a socially neutral, historically unreflective answer to the question "What's wrong with racism?" A third, and especially intriguing, complication is that some classifications central to racist conceptions of human and social reality attempt to divide into racially distinct populations groups of human beings believed, by essentially disinterested observers, to be phenotypically, and apparently genotypically, pretty much the same. One such classification system, believed to have come into existence in eighth-century Japan, is a system which gradually created a separate "racially diverse" outcaste, known as the Eta, who are believed by many to be virtually indistinguishable from the social classes who exclude them (Marshall, 1993). Another such system, brought into existence primarily during the Belgian colonization of central Africa, created "racially distinct" Tutsi and Hutu groups in Rwanda out of people whose principal differences before colonization concerned ownership of various kinds of property. The classification systems in these two cases create diversity that does not really exist, but they have had consequences as profound as any systems that (as is more often the case) radically mischaracterize population diversity that does exist. Those who insist that racial classification systems essentially function to codify something deeply "obvious" about human diversity should reflect on the frequency with which some systems create the diversity they claim only to find, with potentially quite drastic consequences.

Whatever the potentially shifting details of particular classification systems, racism in all its varied manifestations involves an extraordinarily robust worldview that merits just as much philosophical scrutiny by applied ethicists as do the actions and practices which emanate from, and are claimed to be justified by, racist worldviews. Yet the task of making sense of racist conceptions is further complicated by the fact that, frequently, the essential components of racist conceptions – the idea that the species *Homo sapiens* can be divided into discrete "races," and that human races are intrinsically characterized by more and less valuable traits – are not fully articulated by those who accept and act on racist characterizations of the species. We can call this the problem of unarticulated racism. Moreover, the shaping presence of unarticulated racism is especially pronounced in contexts (like many contemporary contexts in "developed" nations) where there is at least some explicit social disapproval of racist actions and practices. In such contexts, it is not uncommon to find that various devices of self-deception, and related forms of affected ignorance, generate vigorous denials that actions and practices most reasonably interpreted to manifest racism are what reasonable interpreters rightly take them to be.

Of course, some such denials rightly generate more incredulity than others – even amongst relatively naive social observers. None but the most gullible observer is likely to believe a college fraternity member who claims that he attended a party in blackface, to the delight of his peers, really intending to "compliment" the black students he appears to mock. In contrast, the conduct of a philosophy professor who routinely discourages black students from majoring in the subject, claiming simply to appreciate the "special strengths and weaknesses" of her students, is less likely to be recognized, at least by the novice observer, as evidence of racism. It will be even more difficult if the professor cites purportedly statistical proof of her black students' weaknesses at analytical tasks, and insists that discouraging them from majoring in philosophy on this basis is surely well intentioned. The problem in such cases, of course, is that it is sometimes the instances of racism that can be excused by external observers as "well intentioned" that do the most harm to assignable individuals and groups. For instance, there are few contexts more important for reflection on the destructive consequences of racism than the complex relation between teachers and their fundamentally impressionable students (Moody-Adams, 1992–3).

However, perhaps the most important obstacle to careful philosophical scrutiny of racist conceptions is the fact that some who explicitly affirm racist views claim that their views have gradually been placed on an objective footing. In contemporary contexts, these claims are made most typically, though not only, by those who insist that psychometric methods allow them to prove the relative superiority and inferiority of different races, along with evidence allegedly showing that at least some of the attributes that make human populations "valuable" (especially intelligence) are, in large part, heritable. This move then underwrites a claim that, far from being a morally problematic stance, a racist worldview must surely be morally unimpeachable. The claim will be that it provides morally unimpeachable explanations of (and, ultimately, justifications for) differences in the economic and social positions of particular races, and even otherwise unacceptable differences in treatment (such as racial profiling, for instance).

Such assertions have become especially powerful weapons in socially divisive debates in the United States about several differences in social, economic, and political power that have frequently been the subject of moral criticism. Those who wield the psychometrician's axe in these debates claim to have an iron-clad method of supporting their case. They claim to be able to provide measurements of largely heritable traits that are crucial to economic and social success (in particular, a trait they describe as "general intelligence"). They claim, further, that the results of their measurements show that there is nothing unjust about existing distributions of social benefits and burdens (Herrnstein and Murray, 1994).

But these claims have been the subject of a vast body of literature that, more widely appreciated by philosophers, would surely call this confidence into question in discussions of applied ethics. Ethicists have frequently assumed that discussion of this literature, and its implications, might be most appropriate in contemporary critical race theory, and possibly in some pockets of work in the philosophy of science. But this assumption is to the detriment of work being done on the ethical implications of racism.

Several decades of work by influential evolutionary biologists, population geneticists, physical anthropologists, and social scientists strongly suggest that the psychometricians' claims are at best unreliable, and at worst entirely unsupportable. This work has produced important challenges to psychometric methods and assumptions – for instance, to assumptions that there is a single trait called "general intelligence" that can be measured in isolatable "units," as well as to the notion that the psychometrician can claim to have measured it, and to have done so reliably (Fischer et al., 1996). It has been noted, further, that even the allegedly most "scientific" versions of the relevant views rely on science to affirm the "reality" of racial typologies that not only precede the scientific enterprise, but seem to have evolved, and will no doubt continue to evolve, primarily in response to sociopolitical expediency (Marshall, 1993). One must ask whether there are any other domains of human concern in which sociopolitical expediency has proved to be an especially reliable source of scientific knowledge. More general resistance to the claims of racial science has noted even deeper difficulties with the idea that the effort to divide the human species into genetically discrete racial groups is itself fundamentally flawed. Thus, for instance, studies of gene differences between the major population groups in America reveal as much genetic variation between individuals from the same "racial group" as between individuals allowed to come from different racial groups (Livingstone, 1964; Nei and Roychoudhury, 1972; Cavalli-Sforza et al., 1996).

During the early development of philosophical work on racism and its effects, many philosophers simply ignored such discussions, despite their apparent relevance to the task of scrutinizing the ethical dimensions of racism. Part of the explanation for this inattention may simply be an unexamined acceptance of the notion that it is possible to challenge racism's evaluative claims while leaving its (purportedly) empirical assertions about races intact. But it is difficult to see how to understand racism's evaluative claims unless one understands them as responses to the underlying empirical assumptions with which they are typically joined.

It is true that racism's evaluative claims, especially in many "folk" versions of racist views, are not always based on the kind of falsifiable beliefs about the structure of the natural world likely to render scientific scrutiny of those beliefs an effective challenge to racism. The frequency with which non-rational, and sometimes profoundly irrational, attitudes about what it is to "belong" to a particular racial group tend to provide the basis for racism's evaluative claims has justly strengthened the pessimism of those who fear the permanence of racism. Yet a substantial number of socially influential racists claim to believe that racism's evaluative claims are based on scientifically supportable generalizations about human populations. They suggest, that is, that their racist convictions are essentially falsifiable and subject to revision if defeated. Thus it is not unimportant for philosophers interested in the ethical dimensions of racism to take seriously potentially plausible challenges to the generalizations that underwrite racist convictions.

Fortunately, there is increasing evidence that philosophers are now willing to debate the strengths and weaknesses of these challenges, and that they have finally recognized the crucial relevance of these challenges to applied ethics. Several useful and important philosophical discussions of the very idea of race have appeared in the past 15 years. Many such discussions have begun to tackle the potentially unsettling possibility that mainstream philosophy (effectively "taking sides" in sociopolitical controversies) may have played an especially unsavory role in helping to formulate ideas of race later taken up (sometimes wholesale) by the burgeoning science of the late eighteenth and early nineteenth centuries (Goldberg, 1990; Harding, 1993; West, 1994; Appiah and Gutmann, 1996; Mills, 1997; Bernasconi, 2001).

Why is Racism Morally Wrong?

Of course, generalizations about human populations are not in themselves morally wrong.

Moreover, there can be morally significant differences among human beings precisely as members of particular populations. For instance, people who steal the property of others, and are rightfully convicted of doing so, are plausibly assumed to have forfeited a portion of their liberty. Past conduct provides a morally significant basis on which to treat convicted thieves, as a group, differently from other people. In a different but potentially related kind of example, it is surely defensible to claim that, for some purposes – though obviously not for just any purpose – it can be morally acceptable to spend social resources differentially in response to certain kinds of differences in the abilities of those who stand to profit from social resources. Criteria on the basis of which decisions about such allocations should be made are extremely controversial. It is thus that most public school systems are constantly debating decisions to shift resources from "extremely gifted" students to "differently abled" students, and back again. What is clear, however, is that (at least morally) there will be some criteria that can license differential spending tied to differences in ability.

On a first reflection, what seems morally most problematic in such contexts about relying on racist worldviews to provide any criteria for disparities in treatment among groups is that racist worldviews are profoundly unreliable accounts of reality. They seem to divide the species up in conceptually problematic ways, and to make claims about the characteristics of those they classify that do not stand up to scrutiny. If the challenges to systems of racial classification are correct, the problem is that such systems rely on shifting, sociopolitically generated, and scientifically unsupportable, assignments to particular racial groups and that they pick out characteristics of human beings that have no genuine moral significance.

But let us, in fact, suppose that the challenges to many racist assertions about the nature of reality, and hence to racism's evaluative claims, are correct. Does accepting this supposition actually lead to a moral condemnation of racism as unavoidably as I have suggested? Suppose that a confirmed racist is ready to concede that racial classification systems frequently mask human complexity, including the complexity that occurs both within and across racial groups, as well as the complexity that occurs across societies and historical eras in the various racial classification systems that have held sway. We can surely imagine such a person ready to insist that these are "simple" failures of scientific rationality, but that holding on to racist beliefs – possibly on the strength of vaguely particularist notions about the moral value of group membership – is not so obviously morally wrong, whatever its potential intellectual shortcomings. This racist might even concede that, at least in some instances, racial classification systems incorrectly reify contingent correlations between racial assignments and the possessions of particular traits – as when individual members of certain groups turn out not to have the traits that would be assigned to them by the system, or even to possess an abundance of traits supposed to be "essential" to persons receiving quite different racial assignments. But we can surely imagine a "particularist" racist who would insist that there are always a few "anomalies," insisting all the while that the anomalies are simply exceptions that "prove the rule."

What is the best way to reply to someone whose racism remains resilient in the face of challenges to some of the underlying assumptions of racist worldviews? In many typical discussions of applied ethics, a reply to this stance might seek to apply influential contemporary moral theories to the problem – relying, most notably, on one or more theories from the familiar catalogue of Kantian deontological views, consequentialist (especially utilitarian) views, perhaps also on the "care" perspective, and certain kinds of communitarian views. Yet while there is much of interest in familiar efforts to show how currently influential views might illuminate contemporary moral problems, this method of moral reflection proves remarkably unhelpful on the matter of the ethical dimensions of racism. This is because the most compelling account of the moral wrong embodied in racist misperceptions of human reality is not a contemporary moral theory at all, but a particularly rich interpretation of how a Socratic (and ultimately Platonic) view of moral reasoning can best show what is wrong with racism. The most influential articulation of this stance is contained in Martin Luther King's development of the Socratic notion that racism is unjust because it "distorts the soul, and degrades the personality" (King, 1964). King's account is especially important for the subtle, but rich, way in which it reminds us of the psychologically and morally deleterious effects of racism on the personality of the racist, as much as on the personality of the object of racism, without diminishing the moral weight of the wrong done to those on the receiving end.

The Socratic account developed by King, in his classic apology for civil disobedience, is thus important for the way in which it forces us to recognize the moral usefulness of a device we might call "moral ethnography" (Moody-Adams, 1997). Unlike many other moral conceptions, the Socratic conception (rightly, in my view) requires that evaluations be rooted in an understanding of at least some details of historically significant interactions between an agent and those likely to be affected by action. Moreover, this is the standard for reflecting on evaluations of all sorts, whether to be embodied in action, or in reflection on the actions of others. In the case at hand, of course, a complete moral ethnography would need to reflect on and help illuminate specific details of important interactions between the racist and the object of her racism. King did not himself complete this kind of moral ethnography of racism in all its complexity, since he was concerned to concentrate critical attention on articulating the perspective of the victims of racism. Yet given the dearth of detailed moral reflection on the internal perspective of some of racism's victims, at least at the time of King's writings, it was perhaps morally sufficient for King to concentrate on illuminating the perspective of the objects of racism. Equally important, however, is that the Socratic view he defends quite explicitly points to the moral importance of the task of eventually supplying the ethnographic details on the other side. Those details will prove crucial, in fact, if we hope to understand the deleterious

effects of racism on the psyche of the racist as well as on those who are subjected to racism. Many Kantian thinkers might argue that the Kantian idea of "respect for persons," explicitly embodied in the second formulation of the Categorical Imperative, provides an equally (or even more) compelling response to the question about what constitutes the fundamental moral wrong of racism. After all, it might be urged, Kant's notion that morality demands fundamental respect for the dignity of humanity, whether in the agent's own person or in the person of the other, certainly contains an important part of the truth about morality. What is more, it is a truth that seems to have special relevance in this context. But Kant suggests that perhaps the most important way to understand the moral wrong of failing to respect human dignity is embodied in the idea that it is wrong to use the other merely as a means to an end she does not share. This stance fails, in my view, to show us how to understand the full scope of the moral damage done to the racist. There is, no doubt, a loss of dignity. But there is an impoverishment (often unacknowledged) of the conditions that make for a flourishing human life. The problem is that this undermining of the conditions for human flourishing is something we cannot see without some effort at a moral ethnography of racism. Kant's view cannot show why such an ethnography is crucial. In this instance, therefore, it fails to generate a complete account of the methods of moral reflection best able to open the details and implications of racism over time to scrutiny. The Socratic view, both as developed by Plato in the Socratic Dialogues and eventually by King in the "Letter from Birmingham Jail" (1964), sheds far more light on the question of how we might most profitably reflect on the moral implications of the practice of racism.

What Constitutes Racism and When is It Morally Wrong?

I have asserted the greater clarity and usefulness of a Socratic view of moral evaluation, generally, for constructive reflection on the moral status of racism. What the Socratic view suggests, most immediately in Plato's Socratic Dialogues but also in King's twentieth-century borrowings, is that it is frequently impossible to understand the moral nature of character and actions without reflecting on the way in which they are situated in various practices (one might even say embedding them in various "moral narratives") extended over time. It is thus, for instance, that we come to understand the character of Socrates only over the course of several dialogues, and only as a consequence of mundane conversations as well as elevated philosophical exchanges with many different kinds of persons in varied social settings.

This conception takes on special importance in the effort to understand what it means to characterize some action or practice as an instance of racism, particularly when the agent or agents in question have either explicitly denied any racist motivations, or may simply fail to articulate any motivations at all. It is equally important when, in such contexts, we confront social institutions and practices which may well continue to bear the stamp of quite powerful racist intentions and policies, whatever the official orthodoxies of the moment. It must not be forgotten that, even in official contexts in which racism is condemned, both individuals and groups sometimes celebrate the racist underpinnings of their conduct or the social practices supported by that conduct. The end-of-racism theorist is far too prone to ignore this fact. Yet sometimes people don't tell us that they are in fact attempting to put racism into practice, and sometimes institutions can embody racist assumptions about the nature of human populations in the absence of any kind of overt justification or explanation in terms of racist convictions. It is in these instances that we must turn to the Socratically inspired notion that moral understanding requires us to put actions, along with social practices and institutions, into their appropriate social and historical contexts.

What might reflection on social and historical context reveal? To begin with, we must appreciate that in some cases where individual actions or social institutions are not explicitly justified (or "explained") by reference to racist conceptions, history and social context provide compelling reasons to believe that the conduct or institutions are in fact deeply rooted in racism. The list of compelling reasons emerging from history and context can be indefinitely long, but two of the most important are (a) general consistency with other, similar actions or institutions known to be racist (whether or not they are performed by other agents, or rooted in the practices of this or other societies); and (b) good evidence that expressions of racial superiority would promote either the personal self-interest of the agent, or promote the collective self-interest of a particular racial group that clearly benefits from the social practice in question. The actions of the ("white") college fraternity member who dresses up in blackface, for instance, have a compelling consistency with past actions or practices known in the relevant society to embody humiliating racist attitudes.

But consider more complicated cases. We might wonder what history and social context should tell us about cases in which, even though we have a strong intuition that the action, practice, or institution in question is an instance of racism, they are not explicitly justified by reference to racist conceptions and there are strong *prima facie* reasons not to interpret the action or practice in question as an expression of racism. For some, a social context in which discrimination in employment, college admissions, and housing have been officially outlawed will seem to provide just the right kind of *prima facie* reasons against finding racism to be the appropriate explanation of persistent racial disparities in employment, college admission, and housing. Indeed, "end-of-racism" theorists tend to assume that many of the actions, practices, or institutions that contemporary critics tend to describe as racism are best construed as cases where what they see as *prima facie* reasons against finding "racism" turn out to be overwhelming (or "all things considered") reasons against doing so.

Yet there are surely circumstances in which even though there are indeed *prima facie* reasons suggesting an absence of racism, rationality nonetheless demands reflection on a number of other considerations that might serve to complicate our reflections. Of course, wherever there are strong *prima facie* reasons against calling something racism, the standard for defeating claims of moral innocence must be relatively high. But it seems obvious that there can actually be compelling considerations capable of defeating claims of moral innocence, even in these cases. For instance, if it is impossible to attribute moral innocence to some action or practice without seriously falsifying important historical details, or without requiring acceptance of implausible assumptions about the nature and sources of human motivation, then it seems unreasonable to assume that the action or practice in question is genuinely morally innocent. An unexpectedly resilient social practice that seems to fall into this category is the allegedly purely "statistical" phenomenon in banking whereby black loan-seekers are either denied loans at a rate higher than non-black applicants with relevantly similar profiles, or given the loans at higher interest rates than applicants with relevantly similar profiles. The end-of-racism theorist wants to view this kind of practice as morally innocent. Yet at many points in recent United States history, anti-discrimination officials have rejected his stance, and sought legal action to challenge claims of innocence (moral, as well as legal).

Much depends on the specific context of the action or practice in question, and on the moral narrative in which the action or practice is embedded. It is virtually impossible, for instance, to make reliable determinations about the racist or morally benign character of the actions of the concerned philosophy professor, who selectively discourages black students from pursuing philosophy, without a fuller picture of the complex moral context of the conduct. Yet, it must be reiterated that the social and historical rootedness of moral evaluation should never be overlooked. Perhaps the most problematic characteristic of writings proclaiming the end of racism is the tendency to assume that the end of legally sanctioned racism somehow brings with it a newfound moral innocence, even for those whose upbringing and social interactions continue to bear the stain of racist conceptions. The end-of-racism theorist simply ignores obvious and important facts of social,

and especially historical, complexity that make racism a potentially fair and rational explanation in far too many social contexts.

To be fair, opponents of the end-of-racism views (especially the permanence-of-racism theorists) can be as inattentive to causal complexity as the end-of-racism theorists are to historical complexity. Moreover, their inattention can issue in unconvincing accounts of socially complex phenomena. This problem is especially pronounced in discussions of crime, a phenomenon for which racism appears to be at best only a partial explanation (or, more precisely, to be only part of their proximate cause). Such unhelpful accounts, in turn, will then frequently figure in unnecessarily controversial and unhelpful discussions of the American criminal justice system. The problem, as many knowledgeable commentators observe, is that there is very good evidence, in some American jurisdictions, of racial profiling of black motorists that discriminates unfairly against them solely on the basis of race. Yet the fact that there is evidence of the unfair use of racial profiling cannot license the blanket assumption that any racial disparity in the criminal justice system counts as evidence of disparate treatment on the basis of race (Kennedy, 1997).

The causes of crime are complex. It is no doubt true that one may be more likely to commit certain kinds of crimes, or to commit those crimes in certain settings, if one has been subject to the social and economic deprivation traceable to the lingering effects of racial discrimination than if one has not been so subject. The fact remains, however, that there is no evidence that racism is necessarily more than a proximate cause of the crime rate in certain social contexts, or that racism (in the criminal justice system, or outside of it) is the primary cause of some of the troubling social realities concerning conviction and imprisonment rates for African-American offenders. Not everyone who has suffered, or continues to suffer, from racism's effects engages in criminal activity (Moody-Adams, 1992–3). It is thus simplistic and dangerous to attempt to trace the cause of every racial disparity in the American legal system to the direct effects of racism.

Must We Believe in the "Permanence of Racism?"

But if it is disingenuous and destructive to deny that a variety of causal phenomena may intensify the effects of lingering racism, it is equally disingenuous and destructive for those who seek to proclaim the end of racism to deny the continuing impact of history. In this context, it helps to recall the reasonableness of H. L. A. Hart's contention that non-authoritarian legal systems can command extended obedience to law only because they gradually give rise to a complex "internal perspective" on their rules. The internal perspective on rules, according to Hart, is that perspective from which agents come to treat demands for conformity to legal rules (and criticisms for non-conformity) as fundamentally justified (Hart, 1961). If Hart is right about the gradual emergence of the internal perspective on the law, and I think he is, it is surely implausible to suggest that merely changing the law of discrimination could magically and immediately end all socially influential attempts to discriminate on the basis of race. This conceptual sleight of hand is especially unreasonable in reflecting on the American national context, given the fact that legally sanctioned segregation in America lasted for so long and was more than once reconfigured and revived just as some optimists hoped it might be about to end.

Yet while affirming the plausibility of Hart's view suggests pessimism about the possibility that legal change might bring an immediate end to racism, it is surely compatible with holding the optimistic conviction that influential social actors can have extraordinary influence (actual, as well as symbolic) over all but the most non-authoritarian legal systems. It is also consistent with the assertion that, at important points in American history, such influential actors –

whether individually or collectively – have successfully managed to exercise that influence responsibly in social protest. The success of non-violent civil disobedience in the American civil rights movement of the 1950s and 1960s, in particular, is powerful evidence of the moral possibilities available to those who take concerted "direct action" against persistent discrimination. This fact surely gives special weight to King's Socratic analysis of the moral wrong of racism.

Yet we must not ignore the fact that the successes of the civil rights movement gradually gave way to a number of quite different tactics, some of which seem to have far more mixed success. The verdict is still out, for example, on the "color-conscious" social policies that critics have come to see as "reverse racism," even as their supporters view them as the only way to remedy subordination and oppression that they trace to unjust racial discrimination. Equally important, it is far from clear whether those countries (including, quite recently, Brazil) which have emulated America's experiment with color-conscious practices as an effort to remedy social injustice will manage to avoid the socially divisive debates that they tend to generate. Yet the debates over color-conscious policies – over their fairness, their effectiveness, even the likelihood that they will generate unwanted backlashes however fair or effective they might ever be – are an unexpectedly hopeful sign. For they show that the citizens of several modern nation-states stand ready and willing to engage in difficult, but crucially important, discussions about the nature and implications of racism, instead of simply taking its persistence for granted. Whatever the "permanence-of-racism" theorists say, this is surely a reason for genuine, if cautious, optimism about the moral progress of the human species.

References

Appiah, Anthony and Gutmann, Amy (1996) *Color Conscious: The Political Morality of Race*. Princeton, NJ: Princeton University Press.

Bell, Derrick (1992) *Faces at the Bottom of the Well: The Permanence of Racism*. New York: Basic Books.

Bernasconi, Robert (2001) "Who Invented the Concept of Race? Kant's Role in the Enlightenment Construction of Race." In R. Bernasconi (ed.), *Race*. Oxford: Blackwell.

Cavalli-Sforza, L. L., Menozzi, P., and Piazza, A. (1996) *The History and Geography of Human Genes*, abridged edn. Princeton, NJ: Princeton University Press.

Crenwhaw, Kimberly W. (1988) "Race, Reform, and Retrenchment," *Harvard Law Review* 101: 1331.

D'Souza, Dinesh (1995) *The End of Racism: Principles for a Multi-racial Society*. New York: Free Press.

Fischer, Claude S., Hout, M., Swindler, A., et al. (1996) *Inequality by Design: Cracking the Bell Curve Myth*. Princeton, NJ: Princeton University Press.

Freeman, Alan (1978) "Legitimizing Racial Discrimination through Anti-discrimination Law: a Critical Review of Supreme Court Doctrine," *Minnesota Law Review* 62: 1049.

Goldberg, David T. (ed.) (1990) *The Anatomy of Racism*. Minneapolis: University of Minnesota Press.

Harding, Sandra (ed.) (1993) *The "Racial" Economy of Science: Toward a Democratic Future*. Bloomington, IN: Indiana University Press.

Hart, H. L. A. (1961) *The Concept of Law*. Oxford: Oxford University Press.

Herrnstein, Richard J. and Murray, Charles (1994) *The Bell Curve: Intelligence and Class Structure in American Life*. New York: Free Press.

Jacobson, Matthew F. (1998) *Whiteness of a Different Color: European Immigrants and the Alchemy of Race*. Cambridge, MA: Harvard University Press.

Kennedy, Randall (1997) *Race, Crime, and the Law*. New York: Pantheon.

King, Martin Luther (1964) "Letter from Birmingham Jail." In *Why We Can't Wait*. New York: New American Library.

Livingstone, Frank B. (1964) "On the Non-existence of Human Races." In A. Montagu (ed.), *The Concept of Race*. New York: Free Press of Glencoe.

Marshall, Gloria A. (1993) "Racial Classifications: Popular and Scientific." In Sandra Harding (ed.), *The "Racial" Economy of Science: Toward a Democratic Future*. Bloomington, IN: Indiana University Press, pp. 116–27.

Mills, Charles S. (1997) *The Racial Contract*. Ithaca, NY: Cornell University Press.

Moody-Adams, Michele (1992–3) "Race, Class, and the Social Construction of Self-respect," *The Philosophical Forum* 24: 251–6.

—— (1997) *Fieldwork in Familiar Places: Morality, Culture and Philosophy*. Cambridge, MA: Harvard University Press.

Nei, Masatoshi and Roychoudhury, Arun K. (1972) "Gene Differences between Individuals from Different Ethnic Groups," *Science* 177: 434–6.

West, Cornell (1994) *Race Matters*. New York: Vintage Books.

40

Servility and Self-Respect

Thomas E. Hill, Jr.

NO!

Several motives underlie this essay. In the first place, I am curious to see if there is a legitimate source for the increasingly common feeling that servility can be as much a vice as arrogance is. There seems to be something morally defective about the Uncle Tom and the submissive housewife; and yet, on the other hand, if the only interests they sacrifice are their own, it seems that we should have no right to complain. Secondly, I have some sympathy for the now unfashionable view that each person has duties to himself as well as to others. It does seem absurd to say that a person could literally violate his own rights or owe himself a debt of gratitude, but I suspect that the classic defenders of duties to oneself had something different in mind. If there are duties to oneself, it is natural to expect that a duty to avoid being servile would have a prominent place among them. . . .

I

Three examples may give a preliminary idea of what I mean by *servility*. Consider, first, an extremely deferential black, whom I shall call

the *Uncle Tom*. He always steps aside for white men; he does not complain when less qualified whites take over his job; he gratefully accepts whatever benefits his all-white government and employers allot him, and he would not think of protesting its insufficiency. He displays the symbols of deference to whites, and of contempt toward blacks: he faces the former with bowed stance and a ready "Sir" and "Ma'am"; he reserves his strongest obscenities for the latter. Imagine, too, that he is not playing a game. He is not the shrewdly prudent calculator, who knows how to make the best of a bad lot and mocks his masters behind their backs. He accepts without question the idea that, as a black, he is owed less than whites. He may believe that blacks are mentally inferior and of less social utility, but that is not the crucial point. The attitude which he displays is that what he values, aspires for, and can demand is of less importance than what whites value, aspire for, and can demand. He is far from the picture book's carefree, happy servant, but he does not feel that he has a right to expect anything better.

Another pattern of servility is illustrated by a person I shall call the *Self-deprecator*. Like the Uncle Tom, he is reluctant to make demands.

435

He says nothing when others take unfair advantage of him. When asked for his preferences or opinions, he tends to shrink away as if what he said should make no difference. His problem, however, is not a sense of racial inferiority but rather an acute awareness of his own inadequacies and failures as an individual. These defects are not imaginary: he has in fact done poorly by his own standards and others'. But, unlike many of us in the same situation, he acts as if his failings warrant quite unrelated maltreatment even by strangers. His sense of shame and self-contempt makes him content to be the instrument of others. He feels that nothing is owed him until he has earned it and that he has earned very little. He is not simply playing a masochist's game of winning sympathy by disparaging himself. On the contrary, he assesses his individual merits with painful accuracy.

A rather different case is that of the *Deferential Wife*. This is a woman who is utterly devoted to serving her husband. She buys the clothes *he* prefers, invites the guests *he* wants to entertain, and makes love whenever *he* is in the mood. She willingly moves to a new city in order for him to have a more attractive job, counting her own friendships and geographical preferences insignificant by comparison. She loves her husband, but her conduct is not simply an expression of love. She is happy, but she does not subordinate herself as a means to happiness. She does not simply defer to her husband in certain spheres as a trade-off for his deference in other spheres. On the contrary, she tends not to form her own interests, values, and ideals; and, when she does, she counts them as less important than her husband's. She readily responds to appeals from Women's Liberation that she agrees that women are mentally and physically equal, if not superior, to men. She just believes that the proper role for a woman is to serve her family. As a matter of fact, much of her happiness derives from her belief that she fulfills this role very well. No one is trampling on her rights, she says; for she is quite glad, and proud, to serve her husband as she does.

Each one of these cases reflects the attitude which I call servility.[1] It betrays the absence of a certain kind of self-respect. What I take this attitude to be, more specifically, will become clearer later on. It is important at the outset, however, not to confuse the three cases sketched above with other, superficially similar cases. In particular, the cases I have sketched are not simply cases in which someone refuses to press his rights, speaks disparagingly of himself, or devotes himself to another. A black, for example, is not necessarily servile because he does not demand a just wage; for, seeing that such a demand would result in his being fired, he might forbear for the sake of his children. A self-critical person is not necessarily servile by virtue of bemoaning his faults in public; for his behavior may be merely a complex way of satisfying his own inner needs quite independent of a willingness to accept abuse from others. A woman need not be servile whenever she works to make her husband happy and prosperous; for she might freely and knowingly choose to do so from love or from a desire to share the rewards of his success. If the effort did not require her to submit to humiliation or maltreatment, her choice would not mark her as servile. There may, of course, be grounds for objecting to the attitudes in these cases; but the defect is not servility of the sort I want to consider. It should also be noted that my cases of servility are not simply instances of deference to superior knowledge or judgment. To defer to an expert's judgment on matters of fact is not to be servile; to defer to his every wish and whim is. Similarly the belief that one's talents and achievements are comparatively low does not, by itself, make one servile. It is no vice to acknowledge the truth, and one may in fact have achieved less, and have less ability, than others. To be servile is not simply to hold certain empirical beliefs but to have a certain attitude concerning one's rightful place in a moral community.

II

Are there grounds for regarding the attitudes of the Uncle Tom, the Self-deprecator, and the Deferential Wife as morally objectionable? Are there moral arguments we could give them to show that they ought to have more self-respect? None of the more obvious replies is entirely satisfactory.

One might, in the first place, adduce utilitarian considerations. Typically the servile person will be less happy than he might be. Moreover, he may be less prone to make the best of his own socially useful abilities. He may become a nuisance to others by being overly dependent. He will, in any case, lose the special contentment that comes from standing up for one's rights. A submissive attitude encourages exploitation, and exploitation spreads misery in a variety of ways. These considerations provide a *prima facie* case against the attitudes of the Uncle Tom, the Deferential Wife, and the Self-deprecator, but they are hardly conclusive. Other utilities tend to counterbalance the ones just mentioned. When people refuse to press their rights, there are usually others who profit. There are undeniable pleasures in associating with those who are devoted, understanding, and grateful for whatever we see fit to give them – as our fondness for dogs attests. Even the servile person may find his attitude a source of happiness, as the case of the Deferential Wife illustrates. There may be comfort and security in thinking that the hard choices must be made by others, that what I would say has little to do with what ought to be done. Self-condemnation may bring relief from the pangs of guilt even if it is not deliberately used for that purpose. On balance, then, utilitarian considerations may turn out to favor servility as much as they oppose it.

For those who share my moral intuitions, there is another sort of reason for not trying to rest a case against servility on utilitarian considerations. Certain utilities seem irrelevant to the issue. The utilitarian must weigh them along with others, but to do so seems morally inappropriate. Suppose, for example, that the submissive attitudes of the Uncle Tom and the Deferential Wife result in positive utilities for those who dominate and exploit them. Do we need to tabulate *these* utilities before conceding that servility is objectionable? The Uncle Tom, it seems, is making an error, a moral error, quite apart from consideration of how much others in

fact profit from his attitude. The Deferential Wife may be quite happy; but if her happiness turns out to be contingent on her distorted view of her own rights and worth as a person, then it carries little moral weight against the contention that she ought to change that view. Suppose I could cause a woman to find her happiness in denying all her rights and serving my every wish. No doubt I could do so only by nonrational manipulative techniques, which I ought not to use. But is this the only objection? My efforts would be wrong, it seems, not only because of the techniques they require but also because the resultant attitude is itself objectionable. When a person's happiness stems from a morally objectionable attitude, it ought to be discounted. That a sadist gets pleasure from seeing others suffer should not count even as a partial justification for his attitude. That a servile person derives pleasure from denying her moral status, for similar reasons, cannot make her attitude acceptable. These brief intuitive remarks are not intended as a refutation of utilitarianism, with all its many varieties; but they do suggest that it is well to look elsewhere for adequate grounds for rejecting the attitudes of the Uncle Tom, the Self-deprecator, and the Deferential Wife.

III

Why, then, is servility a moral defect? There is, I think, another sort of answer which is worth exploring. The first part of this answer must be an attempt to isolate the objectionable features of the servile person; later we can ask why these features are objectionable. As a step in this direction, let us examine again our three paradigm cases. The moral defect in each case, I suggest, is a failure to understand and acknowledge one's own moral rights. I assume, without argument here, that each person has moral rights. Some of these rights may be basic human rights; that is, rights for which a person needs only to be human to qualify. Other rights will be derivative and contingent upon his special commitments, institutional affiliations, etc. Most rights will be *prima facie* ones; some may be absolute. Most can be waived under appropriate conditions; perhaps some cannot. Many rights can be forfeited; but some, presumably, cannot. The servile person does not, strictly speaking, violate his own rights. At least in our paradigm cases he fails to acknowledge fully his own moral status because he does not fully understand what his rights are, how they can be waived, and when they can be forfeited.

The defect of the Uncle Tom, for example, is that he displays an attitude that denies his moral equality with whites. He does not realize, or apprehend in an effective way, that he has as much right to a decent wage and a share of political power as any comparable white. His gratitude is misplaced; he accepts benefits which are his by right as if they were gifts. The Self-deprecator is servile in a more complex way. He acts as if he has forfeited many important rights which in fact he has not. He does not understand, or fully realize in his own case, that certain rights to fair and decent treatment do not have to be earned. He sees his merits clearly enough, but he fails to see that what he can expect from others is not merely a function of his merits. The Deferential Wife *says* that she understands her rights *vis-à-vis* her husband, but what she fails to appreciate is that her consent to serve him is a valid waiver of her rights only under certain conditions. If her consent is coerced, say, by the lack of viable options for women in her society, then her consent is worth little. If socially fostered ignorance of her own talents and alternatives is responsible for her consent, then her consent should not count as a fully legitimate waiver of her right to equal consideration within the marriage. All the more, her consent to defer constantly to her husband is not a legitimate setting aside of her rights if it results from her mistaken belief that she has a moral duty to do so. (Recall: "The *proper* role for a woman is to serve her family.") If she believes that she has a *duty* to defer to her husband, then, whatever she may say, she cannot fully understand that she has a *right* not to defer to him. When she says that she freely gives up such a right, she is confused. Her confusion is rather like that of a person who has been persuaded by an unscrupulous lawyer that

it is legally incumbent on him to refuse a jury trial but who nevertheless tells the judge that he understands that he has a right to a jury trial and freely waives it. He does not really understand what it is to have and freely give up the right if he thinks that it would be an offense for him to exercise it.

Insofar as servility results from moral ignorance or confusion, it need not be something for which a person is to blame. . . . Suppose, however, that our servile persons come to know their rights but do not substantially alter their behavior. Are they not still servile in an objectionable way?

The answer, I think, should depend upon why the deferential role is played. If the motive is a morally commendable one, or a desire to avert dire consequences to oneself, or even an ambition to set an oppressor up for a later fall, then I would not count the role player as servile. The Uncle Tom, for instance, is not servile in my sense if he shuffles and bows to keep the Klan from killing his children, to save his own skin, or even to buy time while he plans the revolution. Similarly, the Deferential Wife is not servile if she tolerates an abusive husband because he is so ill that further strain would kill him, because protesting would deprive her of her only means of survival, or because she is collecting atrocity stories for her book against marriage. If there is fault in these situations, it seems inappropriate to call it *servility*. The story is quite different, however, if a person continues in his deferential role just from laziness, timidity, or a desire for some minor advantage. He shows too little concern for his moral status as a person, one is tempted to say, if he is willing to deny it for a small profit or simply because it requires some effort and courage to affirm it openly. A black who plays the Uncle Tom merely to gain an advantage over other blacks is harming them, of course; but he is also displaying disregard for his own moral position as an equal among human beings. Similarly, a woman throws away her rights too lightly if she continues to play the subservient role because she is used to it or is too timid to risk a change. A Self-deprecator who readily accepts what he knows are violations of his rights may be indulging his peculiar need for punishment at the expense of denying something more valuable. In these cases, I suggest, we have a kind of servility independent of any ignorance or confusion about one's rights. The person who has it may or may not be blameworthy, depending on many factors; and the line between servile and nonservile role-playing will often be hard to draw. Nevertheless, the objectionable feature is perhaps clear enough for present purposes: it is a willingness to disavow one's moral status, publicly and systematically, in the absence of any strong reason to do so.

IV

The objectionable feature of the servile person, as I have described him, is his tendency to disavow his own moral rights either because he misunderstands them or because he cares little for them. The question remains: why should anyone regard this as a moral defect? After all, the rights which he denies are his own. He may be unfortunate, foolish, or even distasteful; but why *morally* deficient? One sort of answer, quite different from those reviewed earlier, is suggested by some of Kant's remarks. Kant held that servility is contrary to a perfect nonjuridical duty to oneself.[2] To say that the duty is perfect is roughly to say that it is stringent, never overridden by other considerations (e.g., beneficence). To say that the duty is nonjuridical is to say that a person cannot legitimately be coerced to comply. Although Kant did not develop an explicit argument for this view, an argument can easily be constructed from materials which reflect the spirit, if not the letter, of his moral theory. The argument which I have in mind is prompted by Kant's contention that respect for persons, strictly speaking, is respect for moral law.[3] If taken as a claim about all sorts of respect, this seems quite implausible. If it means that we respect persons only for their moral character, their capacity for moral conduct, or their status as "authors" of the moral law, then it seems unduly moralistic. My strategy is to construe the remark as saying that at least one sort of respect for persons is respect for the

rights which the moral law accords them. If one respects the moral law, then one must respect one's own moral rights; and this amounts to having a kind of self-respect incompatible with servility.

The premises for the Kantian argument, which are all admittedly vague, can be sketched as follows:

First, let us assume, as Kant did, that all human beings have equal basic human rights. Specific rights vary with different conditions, but all must be justified from a point of view under which all are equal. Not all rights need to be earned, and some cannot be forfeited. Many rights can be waived but only under certain conditions of knowledge and freedom. These conditions are complex and difficult to state; but they include something like the condition that a person's consent releases others from obligation only if it is autonomously given, and consent resulting from underestimation of one's moral status is not autonomously given. Rights can be objects of knowledge, but also of ignorance, misunderstanding, deception, and the like.

Second, let us assume that my account of servility is correct; or, if one prefers, we can take it as a definition. That is, in brief, a servile person is one who tends to deny or disavow his own moral rights because he does not understand them or has little concern for the status they give him.

Third, we need one formal premise concerning moral duty, namely, that each person ought, as far as possible, to respect the moral law. In less Kantian language, the point is that everyone should approximate, to the extent that he can, the ideal of a person who fully adopts the moral point of view. Roughly, this means not only that each person ought to do what is morally required and refrain from what is morally wrong but also that each person should treat all the provisions of morality as valuable – worth preserving and prizing as well as obeying. One must, so to speak, take up the spirit of morality as well as meet the letter of its requirements. To keep one's promises, avoid hurting others, and the like, is not sufficient; one should also take an attitude of respect towards the principles, ideals, and goals of morality. A respectful attitude towards a system of rights and duties consists of more than a disposition to conform to its definite rules of behavior; it also involves holding the system in esteem, being unwilling to ridicule it, and being reluctant to give up one's place in it. The essentially Kantian idea here is that morality, as a system of equal fundamental rights and duties, is worthy of respect, and hence a completely moral person would respect it in word and manner as well as in deed. And what a completely moral person would do, in Kant's view, is our duty to do so far as we can.

The assumptions here are, of course, strong ones, and I make no attempt to justify them. They are, I suspect, widely held though rarely articulated. In any case, my present purpose is not to evaluate them but to see how, if granted, they constitute a case against servility. The objection to the servile person, given our premises, is that he does not satisfy the basic requirement to respect morality. A person who fully respected a system of moral rights would be disposed to learn his proper place in it, to affirm it proudly, and not to tolerate abuses of it lightly. This is just the sort of disposition that the servile person lacks. If he does not understand the system, he is in no position to respect it adequately. This lack of respect may be no fault of his own, but it is still a way in which he falls short of a moral ideal. If, on the other hand, the servile person knowingly disavows his moral rights by pretending to approve of violations of them, then, barring special explanations, he shows an indifference to whether the provisions of morality are honored and publicly acknowledged. This avoidable display of indifference, by our Kantian premises, is contrary to the duty to respect morality. The disrespect in this second case is somewhat like the disrespect a religious believer might show towards his religion if, to avoid embarrassment, he laughed congenially while nonbelievers were mocking the beliefs which he secretly held. In any case, the servile person, as such, does not express disrespect for the system of moral rights in the obvious way by violating the rights of others. His lack of respect is more subtly manifested by his acting before others as if he did not know or care about his position of equality under that system.

The central idea here may be illustrated by an analogy. Imagine a club, say, an old German dueling fraternity. By the rules of the club, each member has certain rights and responsibilities. These are the same for each member regardless of what titles he may hold outside the club. Each has, for example, a right to be heard at meetings, a right not to be shouted down by the others. Some rights cannot be forfeited: for example, each may vote regardless of whether he has paid his dues and satisfied other rules. Some rights cannot be waived: for example, the right to be defended when attacked by several members of the rival fraternity. The members show respect for each other by respecting the status which the rules confer on each member. Now one new member is careful always to allow the others to speak at meetings; but when they shout him down, he does nothing. He just shrugs as if to say, "Who am I to complain?" When he fails to stand up in defense of a fellow member, he feels ashamed and refuses to vote. He does not deserve to vote, he says. As the only commoner among illustrious barons, he feels that it is his place to serve them and defer to their decisions. When attackers from the rival fraternity come at him with swords drawn, he tells his companions to run and save themselves. When they defend him, he expresses immense gratitude – as if they had done him a gratuitous favor. Now one might argue that our new member fails to show respect for the fraternity and its rules. He does not actually violate any of the rules by refusing to vote, asking others not to defend him, and deferring to the barons, but he symbolically disavows the equal status which the rules confer on him. If he ought to have respect for the fraternity, he ought to change his attitude. Our servile person, then, is like the new member of the dueling fraternity in having insufficient respect for a system of rules and ideals. The difference is that everyone ought to respect morality whereas there is no comparable moral requirement to respect the fraternity.

The conclusion here is, of course, a limited one. Self-sacrifice is not always a sign of servility. It is not a duty always to press one's rights. Whether a given act is evidence of servility will depend not only on the attitude of the agent but also on the specific nature of his moral rights, a matter not considered here. Moreover, the extent to which a person is responsible, or blameworthy, for his defect remains an open question. Nevertheless, the conclusion should not be minimized. In order to avoid servility, a person who gives up his rights must do so with a full appreciation for what they are. A woman, for example, may devote herself to her husband if she is uncoerced, knows what she is doing, and does not pretend that she has no decent alternative. A self-contemptuous person may decide not to press various unforfeited rights but only if he does not take the attitude that he is too rotten to deserve them. A black may demand less than is due to him provided he is prepared to acknowledge that no one has a right to expect this of him. Sacrifices of this sort, I suspect, are extremely rare. Most people, if they fully acknowledged their rights, would not autonomously refuse to press them.

An even stronger conclusion would emerge if we could assume that some basic rights cannot be waived. . . .

Even if there are no specific rights which cannot be waived, there might be at least one formal right of this sort. This is the right to some minimum degree of respect from others. No matter how willing a person is to submit to humiliation by others, they ought to show him some respect as a person. By analogy with self-respect, as presented here, this respect owed by others would consist of a willingness to acknowledge fully, in word as well as action, the person's basically equal moral status as defined by his other rights. To the extent that a person gives even tacit consent to humiliations incompatible with this respect, he will be acting as if he waives a right which he cannot in fact give up. To do this, barring special explanations, would mark one as servile.

Kant suggests that duties to oneself are a precondition of duties to others. On our account of servility, there is at least one sense in which this is so. Insofar as the servile person is ignorant of his own rights, he is not in an adequate position to appreciate the rights of others. Misunderstanding the moral basis for his equal status with others, he is necessarily liable to underestimate the rights of those with whom he classifies himself. On the other hand, if he plays the servile role knowingly, then, barring special explanation, he displays a lack of concern to see the principles of morality acknowledged and respected and thus the absence of one motive which can move a moral person to respect the rights of others. In either case, the servile person's lack of self-respect necessarily puts him in a less than ideal position to respect others. Failure to fulfill one's duty to oneself, then, renders a person liable to violate duties to others. This, however, is a consequence of our argument against servility, not a presupposition of it.

Notes

1 Each of the cases is intended to represent only one possible pattern of servility. I make no claims about how often these patterns are exemplified, nor do I mean to imply that only these patterns could warrant the labels "Deferential Wife," "Uncle Tom," etc. All the more, I do not mean to imply any comparative judgments about the causes or relative magnitude of the problems of racial and sexual discrimination. One person, e.g. a self-contemptuous woman with a sense of racial inferiority, might exemplify features of several patterns at once; and, of course, a person might view her being a woman the way an Uncle Tom views his being black, etc.

2 See Immanuel Kant, *The Doctrine of Virtue*, Part II of *The Metaphysics of Morals*, ed. M. J. Gregor (New York: Harper & Row, 1964), pp. 99–103; Prussian Academy edition, vol. VI, pp. 434–7.

3 Immanuel Kant, *Groundwork of the Metaphysics of Morals*, ed. H. J. Paton (New York: Harper & Row, 1964), p. 69; Prussian Academy edition, vol. IV, p. 401; *The Critique of Practical Reason*, ed. Lewis W. Beck (New York: Bobbs-Merrill, 1956), pp. 81, 84; Prussian Academy edition, vol. V, pp. 78, 81. My purpose here is not to interpret what Kant meant but to give a sense to his remark.

41

Sexual Harassment

Anita M. Superson

I   Introduction

By far the most pervasive form of discrimination against women is sexual harassment (SH). Women in every walk of life are subject to it, and I would venture to say, on a daily basis. Even though the law is changing to the benefit of victims of SH, the fact that SH is still so pervasive shows that there is too much tolerance of it, and that victims do not have sufficient legal recourse to be protected.

The main source for this problem is that the way SH is defined by various Titles and other sources does not adequately reflect the social nature of SH, or the harm it causes all women. As a result, SH comes to be defined in subjective ways. One upshot is that when subjective definitions infuse the case law on SH, the more subtle but equally harmful forms of SH do not get counted as SH and thus are not afforded legal protection. . . .

II   The Social Nature of Sexual Harassment

Sexual harassment, a form of sexism, is about domination, in particular, the domination of the group of men over the group of women.[1] Domination involves control or power which can be seen in the economic, political, and social spheres of society. Sexual harassment is not simply an assertion of power, for power can be used in beneficial ways. The power men have over women has been wielded in ways that oppress women. The power expressed in SH is oppression, power used wrongly.

Sexual harassment is integrally related to sex roles. It reveals the belief that a person is to be relegated to certain roles on the basis of her sex, including not only women's being sex objects, but also their being caretakers, motherers, nurturers, sympathizers, etc. In general, the sex roles women are relegated to are associated with the body (v. mind) and emotions (v. reason).

When A sexually harasses B, the comment or behavior is really directed at the group of all women, not just a particular woman, a point often missed by the courts. After all, many derogatory behaviors are issued at women the harasser does not even know (e.g., scanning a stranger's body). Even when the harasser knows his victim, the behavior is directed at the particular woman because she happens to be "available" at the time, though its message is for all women. For instance, a catcall says not (merely) that the perpetrator likes a woman's body, but that he thinks women are at least primarily sex objects and he – because of the power he holds by being in the dominant group – gets to rate them according to how much pleasure they give him. The professor who refers to his female students as "chicks" makes a statement that women are intellectually inferior to men as they can be likened to non-rational animals, perhaps even soft, cuddly ones that are to serve as the objects of (men's) pleasure. Physicians using Playboy centerfolds in medical schools to "spice up their lectures" sends the message that women lack the competence to make it in a "man's world" and should perform the "softer tasks" associated with bearing and raising children.[2]

These and other examples make it clear that SH is not about dislike for a certain person; instead, it expresses a person's beliefs about women as a group on the basis of their sex, namely, that they are primarily emotional and bodily beings. Some theorists – Catherine MacKinnon, John Hughes and Larry May – have recognized the social nature of SH. Hughes and May claim that women are a disadvantaged group because (1) they are a social group having a distinct identity and existence apart from their individual identities, (2) they occupy a subordinate position in American society, and (3) their political power is severely circumscribed.[3] They continue:

> Once it is established that women qualify for special disadvantaged group status, all practices tending to stigmatize women as a group, or which contribute to the maintenance of their subordinate social status, would become legally suspect.[4]

This last point, I believe, should be central to the definition of SH.

Because SH has as its target the group of all women, this *group* suffers harm as a result of the behavior. Indeed, when any one woman is in any way sexually harassed, all women are harmed. The group harm SH causes is different from the harm suffered by particular women as individuals: it is often more vague in nature as it is not easily causally tied to any particular incident of harassment. The group harm has to do primarily with the fact that the behavior reflects

and reinforces sexist attitudes that women are inferior to men and that they do and ought to occupy certain sex roles. For example, comments and behavior that relegate women to the role of sex objects reinforce the belief that women *are* sex objects and that they *ought to* occupy this sex role. Similarly, when a female professor's cogent comments at department colloquia are met with frowns and rolled eyes from her colleagues, this behavior reflects and reinforces the view that women are not fit to occupy positions men arrogate to themselves.

The harm women suffer as a group from any single instance of SH is significant. It takes many forms. A Kantian analysis would show what is wrong with being solely a sex object. Though there is nothing wrong with being a caretaker or nurturer, etc., *per se*, it is sexist – and so wrong – to assign such roles to women. In addition, it is wrong to assign a person to a role she may not want to occupy. Basically women are not allowed to decide for themselves which roles they are to occupy, but this gets decided for them, no matter what they do. Even if some women occupy important positions in society that men traditionally occupy, they are still viewed as being sex objects, caretakers, etc., since all women are thought to be more "bodily" and emotional than men. This is a denial of women's autonomy, and degrading to them. It also contributes to women's oppression. The belief that women must occupy certain sex roles is both a cause and an effect of their oppression. It is a cause because women are believed to be more suited for certain roles given their association with body and emotions. It is an effect because once they occupy these roles and are victims of oppression, the belief that they *must* occupy these sex roles is reinforced.

Women are harmed by SH in yet another way. The belief that they are sex objects, caretakers, etc., gets reflected in social and political practices in ways that are unfair to women. It has undoubtedly meant many lost opportunities that are readily available to men. Women are not likely to be hired for jobs that require them to act in ways other than the ways the sex roles dictate, and if they are, what is expected of them is different from what is expected of men. Mothers are not paid for their work, and caretakers are not paid well in comparison with people in jobs traditionally held by men. Lack of economic reward is paralleled by lack of respect and appreciation for those occupying such roles. Certain rights granted men are likely not to be granted women (e.g., the right to bodily self-determination, and marriage rights).

Another harm SH causes all women is that the particular form sex stereotyping takes promotes two myths: (1) that male behavior is normally and naturally predatory, and (2) that females naturally (because they are taken to be primarily bodily and emotional) and even willingly acquiesce despite the appearance of protest.[5] Because the behavior perpetuated by these myths is taken to be normal, it is not seen as sexist, and in turn is not counted as SH.

The first myth is that men have stronger sexual desires than women, and harassment is just a natural venting of these desires which men are unable to control. The truth is, first, that women are socialized *not* to vent their sexual desires in the way men do, but this does not mean these desires are weaker or less prevalent. Masters and Johnson have "decisively established that women's sexual requirements are no less potent or urgent than those of men."[6] But secondly, SH has nothing to do with men's sexual desires, nor is it about seduction; instead, it is about oppression of women. Indeed, harassment generally does not lead to sexual satisfaction, but it often gives the harasser a sense of power.

The second myth is that women either welcome, ask for, or deserve the harassing treatment. Case law reveals this mistaken belief. In *Lipsett* v. *Rive-Mora*[7] (1987), the plaintiff was discharged from a medical residency program because she "did not react favorably to her professor's requests to go out for drinks, his compliments about her hair and legs, or to questions about her personal and romantic life."[8] The court exonerated the defendant because the plaintiff had initially reacted favorably by smiling when shown lewd drawings of herself and when called sexual nicknames as she thought she had to appease the physician. The court said that "given the plaintiff's admittedly favorable responses to these flattering comments, there was no way anyone could consider them as 'unwelcome.' "[9] The court in *Swentek* v. *US Air*[10] (1987) reacted similarly when a flight attendant who was harassed with obscene remarks and gestures was denied legal recourse because previously she had used vulgar language and openly discussed her sexual encounters. The court concluded that "she was the kind of person who could not be offended by such comments and therefore welcomed them generally."[11]

The idea that women welcome "advances" from men is seen in men's view of the way women dress. If a woman dresses "provocatively" by men's standards, she is said to welcome or even deserve the treatment she gets. One explanation harassing professors give for their behavior is that they are bombarded daily with the temptation of physically desirable young women who dress in what they take to be revealing ways.[12] When the case becomes public, numerous questions arise about the attractiveness of the victim, as if she were to blame for being attractive and the consequences thereof. Catcallers often try to justify their behavior by claiming that the victim should expect such behavior, given her tight-fitting dress or shorts, low-cut top, high heels, etc. This way of thinking infests discussions of rape in attempts to establish that women want to be raped, and it is mistaken in that context, too. The myth that women welcome or encourage harassment is designed "to keep women in their place" as men see it. The truth of the matter is that the perpetrator alone is at fault.

Both myths harm all women as they sanction SH by shifting the burden onto the victim and all members of her sex: women must either go out of their way to avoid "natural" male behavior, or establish conclusively that they do not in any way want the behavior. Instead of the behavior being seen as sexist, it is seen as women's problem to rectify.

Last, but certainly not least, women suffer group harm from SH because they come to be stereotyped as victims.[13] Many men see SH as something they can do to women, and in many cases, get away with. Women come to see themselves as victims, and come to believe that the roles they *can* occupy are only the sex roles men have designated for them. Obviously these harms are quite serious for women, so the elimination of all forms of SH is warranted.

I have spoken so far as if it is only men who can sexually harass women, and I am now in a position to defend this controversial view. When a woman engages in the very same harassing behavior men engage in, the underlying message implicit in male-to-female harassment is missing. For example, when a woman scans a man's body, she might be considering him to be a sex object, but all the views about domination and being relegated to certain sex roles are absent. She cannot remind the man that he is inferior because of his sex, since given the way things are in society, he is not. In general, women cannot harm or degrade or dominate men *as a group*, for it is impossible to send the message that one dominates (and so cause group harm) if one does not dominate. Of course, if the sexist roles predominant in our society were reversed, women *could* sexually harass men. The way things are, any bothersome behavior a woman engages in, even though it may be of a sexual nature, does not constitute SH because it lacks the social impact present in male-to-female harassment. Tort law would be sufficient to protect against this behavior, since it is unproblematic in these cases that tort law fails to recognize group harm.

III Subjective vs. Objective Definitions of Sexual Harassment

Most definitions of "sexual harassment" make reference to the behavior's being "unwelcome" or "annoying" to the victim. *Black's Law Dictionary* defines "harassment" as a term used "to describe words, gestures and actions which tend to annoy, alarm and abuse (verbally) another person."[14] The *American Heritage Dictionary* defines "harass" as "to disturb or irritate persistently," and states further that "[h]arass implies systematic persecution by besetting with annoyances, threats, or demands."[15] The

EEOC *Guidelines* state that behavior constituting SH is identified as "unwelcome sexual advances, requests for sexual favors, and other verbal or physical conduct of a sexual nature."[16] In their philosophical account of SH, Hughes and May define "harassment" as "a class of annoying or unwelcome acts undertaken by one person (or group of persons) against another person (or group of persons)."[17] And Rosemarie Tong takes the feminists' definition of noncoercive SH to be that which "denotes sexual misconduct that merely annoys or offends the person to whom it is directed."[18]

The criterion of "unwelcomeness" or "annoyance" is reflected in the way the courts have handled cases of SH, as in *Lipsett*, *Swentek*, and *Meritor*, though in the latter case the court said that the voluntariness of the victim's submission to the defendant's sexual conduct did not mean that she welcomed the conduct.[19] The criterion of unwelcomeness or annoyance present in these subjective accounts of harassment puts the burden on the victim to establish that she was sexually harassed. There is no doubt that many women *are* bothered by this behavior, often with serious side-effects including anything from anger, fear, and guilt,[20] to lowered self-esteem and decreased feelings of competence and confidence,[21] to anxiety disorders, alcohol and drug abuse, coronary disturbances, and gastro-intestinal disorders.[22]

Though it is true that many women are bothered by the behavior at issue, I think it is seriously mistaken to say that whether the victim is bothered determines whether the behavior constitutes SH. This is so for several reasons.

First, we would have to establish that the victim was bothered by it, either by the victim's complaints, or by examining the victim's response to the behavior. The fact of the matter is that many women are quite hesitant to report being harassed, for a number of reasons. Primary among them is that they fear negative consequences from reporting the conduct. As is often the case, harassment comes from a person in a position of institutional power, whether he be a supervisor, a company president, a member of a dissertation committee, the chair of the department, and so on. Unfortunately for many women, as a review of the case law reveals, their fears are warranted.[23] Women have been fired, their jobs have been made miserable, forcing them to quit, professors have handed out unfair low grades, and so on. Worries about such consequences mean that complaints are not filed, or are filed years after the incident, as in the *Anita Hill* v. *Clarence Thomas* case. But this should not be taken to imply that the victim was not harassed.

Moreover, women are hesitant to report harassment because they do not want anything to happen to the perpetrator, but just want the behavior to stop.[24] Women do not complain because they do not want to deal with the perpetrator's reaction when faced with the charge. He might claim that he was "only trying to be friendly." Women are fully aware that perpetrators can often clear themselves quite easily, especially in tort law cases where the perpetrator's intentions are directly relevant to whether he is guilty. And most incidents of SH occur without any witnesses – many perpetrators plan it this way. It then becomes the harasser's word against the victim's. To complicate matters, many women are insecure and doubt themselves. Women's insecurity is capitalized upon by harassers whose behavior is in the least bit ambiguous. Clever harassers who fear they might get caught or be reported often attempt to get on the good side of their victim in order to confuse her about the behavior, as well as to have a defense ready in case a charge is made. Harassers might offer special teaching assignments to their graduate students, special help with exams and publications, promotions, generous raises, and the like. Of course, this is all irrelevant to whether he harasses, but the point is that it makes the victim less likely to complain. On top of all this, women's credibility is very often questioned (unfairly) when they bring forth a charge. They are taken to be "hypersensitive." There is an attitude among judges and others that women must "develop a thick skin."[25] Thus, the blame is shifted off the perpetrator and onto the victim. Given this, if a woman thinks she will get no positive response – or, indeed, will get a negative one – from complaining, she is unlikely to do so.

Further, some women do not recognize harassment for what it is, and so will not complain. Sometimes this is because they are not aware of their own oppression, or actually seem to endorse sexist stereotypes. I recall a young woman who received many catcalls on the streets of Daytona Beach, Florida, during spring break, and who was quite proud that her body could draw such attention. Given that women are socialized into believing their bodies are the most important feature of themselves, it is no surprise that a fair number of them are complacent about harassing behavior directed at them. Sandra Bartky provides an interesting analysis of why every woman is not a feminist, and I think it holds even for women who understand the issue.[26] Since for many women having a body felt to be "feminine" is crucial to their identity and to their sense of self "as a sexually desiring and desirable subject," feminism "may well be apprehended by a woman as something that threatens her with desexualization, if not outright annihilation."[27] The many women who resist becoming feminists are not likely to perceive harassing behavior as bothersome. It would be incorrect to conclude that the behavior is not harassment on the grounds that such victims are not bothered. What we have is a no-win situation for victims: if the behavior bothers a woman she often has good reason not to complain; and if it does not bother her, she will not complain. Either way, the perpetrator wins. So we cannot judge whether women are bothered by the behavior on the basis of whether they *say* they are bothered.

Moreover, women's *behavior* is not an accurate indicator of whether they are bothered. More often than not, women try to ignore the perpetrator's behavior in an attempt not to give the impression they are encouraging it. They often cover up their true feelings so that the perpetrator does not have the satisfaction that his harassing worked. Since women are taught to smile and put up with this behavior, they might actually appear to enjoy it to some extent. Often they have no choice but to continue interacting with the perpetrator, making it very difficult to assert themselves. Women often make up excuses for not "giving in" instead of telling the perpetrator to stop. The fact that their behavior does not indicate they are bothered should not be used to show they were not bothered. In reality, women are fearful of defending themselves in the face of men's power and physical strength. Given the fact that the courts have decided that a lot of this behavior should just be tolerated, it is no wonder that women try to make the best of their situation.

It would be wrong to take a woman's behavior to be a sign that she is bothered also because doing so implies the behavior is permissible if she does not seem to care. This allows the *perpetrator* to be the judge of whether a woman is harassed, which is unjustifiable given the confusion among men about whether their behavior is bothersome or flattering. Sexual harassment should be treated no differently than crimes where harm to the victim is assessed in some objective way, independent of the perpetrator's beliefs. To give men this power in the case of harassment is to perpetuate sexism from all angles.

An *objective* view of SH avoids the problems inherent in a subjective view. According to the objective view defended here, what is decisive in determining whether behavior constitutes SH is not whether the victim is bothered, but whether the behavior is an instance of a practice that expresses and perpetuates the attitude that the victim and members of her sex are inferior because of their sex. Thus the Daytona Beach case counts as a case of SH because the behavior is an instance of a practice that reflects men's domination of women in that it relegates women to the role of sex objects.[28]

The courts have to some extent tried to incorporate an objective notion of SH by invoking the "reasonable person" standard. The EEOC *Guidelines*, as shown earlier, define SH partly as behavior that "has the purpose or effect of *unreasonably* interfering with an individual's work performance . . . ".[29] The *Restatement of Torts*, referring to the tort of intentional infliction of emotional distress, states that the emotional distress must be "so severe that no *reasonable* man could be expected to endure it."[30]

In various cases the courts have invoked a reasonable man (or person) standard, but *not*

to show that women who are not bothered still suffer harassment. Instead, they used the standard to show that even though a particular woman *was* bothered, she would have to tolerate such behavior because it was behavior a reasonable person would not have been affected by. In *Rabidue* v. *Osceola Refining Co.*[31] (1986), a woman complained that a co-worker had made obscene comments about women in general and her in particular. The court ruled that "a reasonable person would not have been significantly affected by the same or similar circumstances,"[32] and that "women must expect a certain amount of demeaning conduct in certain work environments."[33]

But the reasonable man standard will not work, since men and women perceive situations involving SH quite differently. The reasonable person standard fares no better as it becomes the reasonable man standard when it is applied by male judges seeing things through male eyes. Studies have shown that sexual overtures that men find flattering are found by women to be insulting. And even when men recognize behavior as harassment, they think women will be flattered by it.[34] The difference in perception only strengthens my point about the group harm that SH causes all women: unlike women, men can take sexual overtures directed at them to be complimentary because the overtures do not signify the stereotyping that underlies SH of women. A reasonable man standard would not succeed as a basis upon which to determine SH, as its objectivity is outweighed by the disparity found in the way the sexes assess what is "reasonable."

Related to this last topic is the issue of the harasser's intentions. In subjective definitions this is the counterpart to the victim's being bothered. Tort law makes reference to the injuror's intentions: in battery tort, the harasser's intent to contact, in assault tort, the harasser's intent to arouse psychic apprehension in the victim, and in the tort of intentional emotional distress, the harasser's intent or recklessness, must be established in order for the victim to win her case.

But like the victim's feelings, the harasser's intentions are irrelevant to whether his behavior is harassment. As I just pointed out, many men do not take their behavior to be bothersome, and sometimes even mistakenly believe that women enjoy crude compliments about their bodies, ogling, pinching, etc. From perusing cases brought before the courts, I have come to believe that many men have psychological feelings of power over women, feelings of being in control of their world, and the like, when they harass. These feelings might be subconscious, but this should not be admitted as a defense of the harasser. Also, as I have said, many men believe women encourage SH either by their dress or language, or simply by the fact that they tolerate the abuse without protest (usually out of fear of repercussion). In light of these facts, it would be wrongheaded to allow the harasser's intentions to count in assessing harassment, though they might become relevant in determining punishment. I am arguing for an objective definition of SH: it is the attitudes embedded and reflected *in the practice* the behavior is an instance of, not the attitudes or intentions *of the perpetrator*, that makes the behavior SH.

Yet the idea that the behavior must be directed at a certain person in order for it to count as harassment, seems to suggest that intentions *do* count in assessing harassment. This feature is evident both in my definition, as well as in that found in *Black's Law Dictionary*, which takes harassment to be conduct directed against a specific person causing substantial emotional distress. If conduct is directed at a particular individual, it seems that the person expressing himself must be intentionally singling out that individual, wanting to cause her harm.

I think this is mistaken. Since the harasser can subconsciously enjoy the feeling of power harassing gives him, or might even consider his behavior to be flattering, his behavior can be directed at a specific person (or group of persons) without implying any ill intention on his part. By "directed at a particular individual," I mean that the behavior is in some way observed by a particular person (or persons). This includes, for example, sexist comments a student hears her professor say, pornographic pictures a worker sees, etc. I interpret it loosely enough to

include a person's overhearing sexist comments even though the speaker has no idea the person is within earshot (sometimes referred to as "nondirected behavior"). But I interpret it to exclude the bare knowledge that sexist behavior is going on (e.g., female employees knowing that there are pornographic pictures hidden in their boss's office). If it did not exclude such behavior it would have to include knowledge of *any* sexist behavior, even if no person who can be harmed by it ever observes it (e.g., pornographic magazines strewn on a desert island). Though such behavior is sexist, it fails to constitute SH.

IV Implications of the Objective Definition

One implication of my objective definition is that it reflects the correct way power comes into play in SH. Traditionally, SH has been taken to exist only between persons of unequal power, usually in the workplace or an educational institution. It is believed that SH in universities occurs only when a professor harasses a student, but not *vice versa*. It is said that students can cause "sexual hassle," because they cannot "destroy [the professor's] self-esteem or endanger his intellectual self-confidence," and professors "seldom suffer the complex psychological effects of sexual harassment victims."[35] MacKinnon, in her earlier book, defines SH as "the unwanted imposition of sexual requirements in the context of a relationship of unequal power."[36]

Though it is true that a lot of harassment occurs between unequals, it is false that harassment occurs *only* between unequals: equals and subordinates can harass. Indeed, power is irrelevant to tort law, and the courts now recognize harassment among co-workers under Title VII.

The one sense in which it is true that the harasser must have power over his victim is that men have power – social, political, and economic – over women as a group. This cannot be understood by singling out individual men and showing that they have power over women or any particular woman for that matter. It is power that all men have, in virtue of being men. Defining SH in the objective way I do allows us to see that *this* is the sense in which power exists in SH, in *all* of its forms. The benefit of not restricting SH to cases of unequal institutional power is that *all* victims are afforded protection.

A second implication of my definition is that it gives the courts a way of distinguishing SH from sexual attraction. It can be difficult to make this distinction, since "traditional court-ship activities" are often quite sexist and fre-quently involve behavior that is harassment. The key is to examine the practice the behavior is an instance of. If the behavior reflects the attitude that the victim is inferior because of her sex, then it is SH. Sexual harassment is not about a man's attempting to date a woman who is not interested, as the courts have tended to believe; it is about domination, which might be reflected, of course, in the way a man goes about trying to get a date. My definition allows us to separate cases of SH from genuine sexual attraction by forcing the courts to focus on the social nature of SH.

Moreover, defining SH in the objective way I do shifts the burden and the blame off the victim. On the subjective view, the burden is on the victim to prove that she is bothered significantly enough to win a tort case; or under Title VII, to show that the behavior unreasonably interfered with her work. In tort law, where the perpet-rator's intentions are allowed to figure in, the blame could easily shift to the victim by showing that she in some way welcomed or even encour-aged the behavior, thereby relinquishing the per-petrator from responsibility. By focusing on the practice the behavior is an instance of, my def-inition has nothing to do with proving that the victim responds a certain way to the behavior, nor does it in any way blame the victim for the behavior.

Finally, defining SH in a subjective way means that the victim herself must come forward and complain, as it is her response that must be assessed. But given that most judges, law enforcement officers, and even superiors are men, it is difficult for women to do so. They are embarrassed, afraid to confront some-one of the same sex as the harasser, who is likely not to see the problem. They do not feel their voices will be heard. Working with my definition will, I hope, assuage this. Recognizing SH as a group harm will allow women to come to each other's aid as co-complainers, thereby alleviating the problem of reticence. Even if the person the behavior is directed at does not feel bothered, other women can complain, as they suffer the group harm associated with SH.

V Conclusion

The definition of SH I have defended in this paper has as its main benefit that it acknow-ledges the group harm SH causes all women, thereby getting to the heart of what is wrong with SH. By doing so, it protects all victims in all cases from even the most subtle kinds of SH, since all cases of SH have in common group harm.

Of course, as with any definition, problems exist. Though space does not allow that I deal with them, a few are worth mentioning. One is that many behaviors will count as SH, leading perhaps to an unmanageable number of claims. Another is that it will still be a matter of inter-pretation whether a given behavior meets the criteria for SH. Perhaps the most crucial objec-tion is that since so many kinds of behavior count as SH, the right to free speech will be curtailed in unacceptable ways.[37]

I believe there are at least partial solutions to these problems. My proposal is only pro-grammatic, and a thorough defense of it would include working through these and other prob-lems. Such a defense will have to wait.

Notes

I would like to thank John Exdell and Lois Pineau for helpful discussions and many insightful comments on an earlier draft of this paper.

1 This suggests that only men can sexually harass women. I will defend this view later in the paper.

2 Frances Conley, a 50-year-old distinguished neuro-physician at Stanford University, recently came forward with this story. Conley resigned after years of putting up with sexual harassment from her colleagues. Not only did they use *Playboy* spreads during their lectures, but they routinely called her "hon," invited her to bed, and fondled her legs under the operating table. *Chicago Tribune*, Sunday, June 9, 1991, Section 1, p. 22.

3 Hughes, J. and May, L. "Sexual Harassment," *Social Theory and Practice* no. 3 (Fall 1980), pp. 264–5.

4 Ibid., p. 265.

5 These same myths surround the issue of rape. This is discussed fruitfully by Lois Pineau in "Date Rape: A Feminist Analysis," *Law and Philosophy* 8 (1989): 217–43.

6 Catherine MacKinnon, *Sexual Harassment of Working Women: A Case of Sex Discrimination* (New Haven: Yale University Press, 1979), p. 152.

7 *Lipsett* v. *Rive-Mora*, 669 F. Supp. 1188 (D. Puerto Rico 1987).

8 Dawn D. Bennett-Alexander, "Hostile Environment Sexual Harassment: A Clearer View," *Labor Law Journal* 42. 3 (March 1991): 135.

9 *Lipsett*, ibid., Sec. 15.

10 *Swentek* v. *US Air*, 830 F. 2d 552 (4th Cir. 1987).

11 *Swentek* v. *US Air*, ibid., 44 EPd at 552.

12 Billie Wright Dziech and Linda Weiner, *The Lecherous Professor: Sexual Harassment on Campus* (Boston: Beacon Press, 1984), p. 63.

13 This harm is similar to the harm Ann Cudd finds with rape. Since women are the victims of rape, "they come to be seen as in need of protection, as weak and passive, and available to all men." See Ann E. Cudd, "Enforced Pregnancy, Rape, and the Image of Woman," *Philosophical Studies*, vol. 60 (1990), pp. 47–59.

14 *Black's Law Dictionary* (6th edn) (St Paul, MN: West Publishing, 1990), p. 717.

15 *American Heritage Dictionary of the English Language* (New York: American Heritage Publishing, 1973), p. 600.

16 EEOC *Guidelines on Discrimination because of Sex*, 29, C.F.R. Sec 1604.11(a) (1980).

17 Hughes and May, "Sexual Harassment," p. 250.

18 Rosemarie Tong, *Women, Sex, and the Law* (Savage, MD: Rowman Littlefield, 1984), p. 67.

19 *Meritor Savings Bank, FSB* v. *Vinson*, 477 US 57 (1986). 1113–16.

20 MacKinnon, *Sexual Harassment of Working Women*, p. 83.

21 Stephanie Riger, "Gender Dilemmas in Sexual Harassment Policies and Procedures," *American Psychologist* 46 (1991): 497–505.

22 Martha Sperry, "Hostile Environment Sexual Harassment and the Imposition of Liability Without Notice: A Progressive Approach to Traditional Gender Roles and Power Based Relationships," *New England Law Review* 24 (1980): 942, fns. 174 and 175.

23 See Catherine MacKinnon, *Feminism Unmodified: Discourses on Life and Law* (Cambridge, MA: Harvard University Press, 1987), ch. 9, for a nice discussion of the challenges women face in deciding whether to report harassment. See also Ellen Frankel Paul, "Sexual Harassment as Sex Discrimination: A Defective Paradigm," *Yale Law Policy Review* 8. 2 (1990) for an excellent summary of the case law on sexual harassment.

24 MacKinnon, *Sexual Harassment of Working Women*, p. 83.

25 See Frankel Paul, "Sexual Harassment," pp. 333–65. Frankel Paul wants to get away from the "helpless victim syndrome," making women responsible for reporting harassment, and placing the burden on them to develop a tough skin so as to avoid being seen as helpless victims (pp. 362–3). On the contrary, what Frankel Paul fails to understand is that placing these additional burdens on women *detracts* from the truth that they *are* victims, and implies that they deserve the treatment if they do not develop a "tough attitude."

26 Sandra Bartky, "Foucault, Femininity, and the Modernization of Patriarchal Power," in Sandra Bartky, *Femininity and Domination: Studies in the Phenomenology of Oppression* (New York: Routledge, Chapman, and Hall, 1990), pp. 63–82. See especially pp. 77–8.

27 Ibid., p. 77.

28 This case exemplifies my point that the behavior need not be persistent in order to constitute harassment, despite the view of many courts. One catcall, for example, will constitute SH if catcalling is shown to be practice reflecting domination.

29 EEOC *Guidelines*, Sec. 1604.11(a), my emphasis.

30 *Restatement (Second) of Torts*, Sec. 146, (1965), comment i, my emphasis.

31 *Rabidue* v. *Osceola Refining Co.*, 805 F2d (1986), Sixth Circuit Court.

32 Ibid., at 662.

33 Ibid., at 620–22.

34 Stephanie Riger, "Gender Dilemmas in Sexual Harassment Policies and Procedures," *American Psychologist* 46. 5 (May 1991): 499, is where she cites the relevant studies.

35 Wright Dziech and Weiner, *The Lecherous Professor*, p. 24.

36 MacKinnon, *Sexual Harassment of Working Women*, p. 1. It is actually not clear that MaçKinnon endorses this definition throughout this book, as what she says seems to suggest that harassment can occur at least between equals. In her most recent book, she recognizes that harassment "also happens among coworkers, from third parties, even by subordinates

in the workplace, men who are women's hierarchical inferiors or peers." Catherine A. MacKinnon, *Feminism Unmodified: Discourses on Life and Law* (Cambridge, MA: Harvard University Press, 1987), p. 107.

37 For an excellent analysis on sexist speech and the limits of free speech as guaranteed by the Constitution, see March Strauss, "Sexist Speech in the Workplace," *Harvard Civil Rights and Civil Liberties Law Review* 25 (1990), pp. 1–51. She cites the relevant case law concerning sexist speech that is not protected by First Amendment rights. She defends the view that the Constitution can prohibit speech demanding or requesting sexual relationships, sexually explicit speech directed at the woman, and degrading speech directed at the woman, but not sexually explicit or degrading speech that the woman employee knows exists in the workplace, even though it is not directed at her (p. 43). She employs an interesting and useful distinction between speech that discriminates, and speech that merely advocates discrimination, recognizing that the state has an interest in regulating the former, given the harm it can cause.

42

Date Rape

Lois Pineau

Date rape is nonaggravated sexual assault, non-consensual sex that does not involve physical injury, or the explicit threat of physical injury. But because it does not involve physical injury, and because physical injury is often the only criterion that is accepted as evidence that *actus reas* is nonconsensual, what is really sexual assault is often mistaken for seduction. The replacement of the old rape laws with the new laws on sexual assault have done nothing to resolve this problem.

Rape, defined as nonconsensual sex, usually involving penetration by a man of a woman who is not his wife, has been replaced in some criminal codes with the charge of sexual assault. This has the advantage both of extending the range of possible victims of sexual assault, the manner in which people can be assaulted, and replacing a crime which is exclusive of consent, with one for which consent is a defence. But while the consent of a woman is now consistent with the conviction of her assailant in cases of aggravated assault, nonaggravated sexual assault is still distinguished from normal sex solely by the fact that it is not consented to. Thus the question of whether someone has consented to a sexual encounter is still important, and the

criteria for consent continue to be the central concern of discourse on sexual assault.

However, if a man is to be convicted, it does not suffice to establish that the *actus reas* was nonconsensual. In order to be guilty of sexual assault a man must have the requisite *mens rea*, i.e., he must have believed either that his victim did not consent or that she was probably not consenting. In many common law jurisdictions a man who sincerely believes that a woman consented to a sexual encounter is deemed to lack the required *mens rea*, even though the woman did not consent, and even though his belief is not reasonable. Recently, strong dissenting voices have been raised against the sincerity condition, and the argument made that *mens rea* be defeated only if the defendant has a reasonable belief that the plaintiff consented. The introduction of legislation which excludes "honest belief" (unreasonable sincere belief) as a defence, will certainly help to provide women with greater protection against violence. But while this will be an important step forward, the question of what constitutes a reasonable belief, the problem of evidence when rapists lie, and the problem of the entrenched attitudes of the predominantly male police, judges, lawyers, and jurists who handle sexual assault cases, remains.

The criteria for *mens rea*, for the reasonableness of belief, and for consent are closely related. For although a man's sincere belief in the consent of his victim may be sufficient to defeat *mens rea*, the court is less likely to believe his belief is sincere if his belief is unreasonable. If his belief is reasonable, they are more likely to believe in the sincerity of his belief. But evidence of the reasonableness of his belief is also evidence that consent really did take place. For the very things that make it reasonable for *him* to believe that the defendant consented are often the very things that incline the court to believe that she consented. What is often missing is the voice of the woman herself, an account of what it would be reasonable for *her* to agree to, that is to say, an account of what is reasonable from *her* standpoint.

Thus, what is presented as reasonable has repercussions for four separate but related concerns: (1) the question of whether a man's belief in a woman's consent was reasonable; (2) the problem of whether it is reasonable to attribute *mens rea* to him; (3) the question of what could count as reasonable from the woman's point of view; (4) the question of what is reasonable from the court's point of view. These repercussions are of the utmost practical concern. In a culture which contains an incidence of sexual assault verging on epidemic, a criterion of reasonableness which regards mere submission as consent fails to offer persons vulnerable to those assaults adequate protection.

The following statements by self-confessed date rapists reveal how our lack of a solution for dealing with date rape protects rapists by failing to provide their victims with legal recourse:

> All of my rapes have been involved in a dating situation where I've been out with a woman I know. . . . I wouldn't take no for an answer. I think it had something to do with my acceptance of rejection. I had low self-esteem and not much self-confidence and when I was rejected for something which I considered to be rightly mine, I became angry and I went ahead anyway. And this was the same in any situation, whether it was rape or it was something else.

> When I did date, when I was younger, I would pick up a girl and if she didn't come across I would threaten her or slap her face then tell her she was going to fuck – that was it. But that's because I didn't want to waste time with any come-ons. It took too much time. I wasn't interested because I didn't like them as people anyway, and I just went with them just to get laid. Just to say that I laid them.

There is, at this time, nothing to protect women from this kind of unscrupulous victimization. A woman on a casual date with a virtual stranger has almost no chance of bringing a complaint of sexual assault before the courts. One reason for this is the prevailing criterion for consent. According to this criterion, consent is implied unless some emphatic episodic sign of resistance occurred, and its occurrence can be established. But if no episodic act occurred, or if it did occur, and the defendant claims that it didn't, or if the defendant threatened the plaintiff but won't admit it in court, it is almost impossible to find any evidence that would support the plaintiff's word against the defendant. This difficulty is exacerbated by suspicion on the part of the courts, police, and legal educators that even where an act of resistance occurs, this act should not be interpreted as a withholding of consent, and this suspicion is especially upheld where the accused is a man who is known to the female plaintiff.

In Glanville Williams's classic textbook on criminal law we are warned that where a man is unknown to a woman, she does not consent if she expresses her rejection in the form of an episodic and vigorous act at the "vital moment". But if the man is known to the woman she must, according to Williams, make use of "all means available to her to repel the man". Williams warns that women often welcome a "mastery advance" and present a token resistance. He quotes Byron's couplet,

> A little still she strove, and much repented
> And whispering 'I will ne'er consent' – consented

by way of alerting law students to the difficulty of distinguishing real protest from pretence. Thus, while in principle a firm unambiguous stand, or a healthy show of temper ought to be sufficient, if established, to show nonconsent, in practice the forceful overriding of such a stance is apt to be taken as an indication that the resistance was not seriously intended, and that the seduction had succeeded. The consequence of this is that it is almost impossible to establish the defendant's guilt beyond a reasonable doubt.

Thus, on the one hand, we have a situation in which women are vulnerable to the most exploitive tactics at the hands of men who are known to them. On the other hand, almost nothing will count as evidence of their being assaulted, including their having taken an emphatic stance in withholding their consent. The new laws have done almost nothing to change this situation. Yet clearly, some solution must be sought. Moreover, the road to that solution presents itself clearly enough as a need for a reformulation of the criterion of consent. It is patent that a criterion that collapses whenever the crime itself succeeds will not suffice. . . .

The reasoning that underlies the present criterion of consent is entangled in a number of mutually supportive mythologies with see sexual assault as masterful seduction, and silent submission as sexual enjoyment. Because the prevailing ideology has so much informed our conceptualization of sexual interaction, it is extraordinarily difficult for us to distinguish between assault and seduction, submission and enjoyment, or so we imagine. At the same time, this failure to distinguish has given rise to a network of rationalizations that support the conflation of assault with seduction, submission and enjoyment. . . .

Rape Myths

The belief that the natural aggression of men and the natural reluctance of women somehow makes date rape understandable underlies a number of prevalent myths about rape and human sexuality. These beliefs maintain their force partly on account of a logical compulsion exercised by them at an unconscious level. The only way of refuting them effectively, is to excavate the logical propositions involved, and to expose their misapplication to the situations to which they have been applied. In what

follows, I propose to excavate the logical support for popular attitudes that are tolerant of date rape. These myths are not just popular, however, but often emerge in the arguments of judges who acquit date rapists, and policemen who refuse to lay charges.

The claim that the victim provoked a sexual incident, that "she asked for it", is by far the most common defence given by men who are accused of sexual assault. Feminists, rightly incensed by this response, often treat it as beneath contempt, singling out the defence as an argument against it. On other fronts, sociologists have identified the response as part of an overall tendency of people to see the world as just, a tendency which disposes them to conclude that people for the most part deserve what they get. However, an inclination to see the world as just requires us to construct an account which yields this outcome, and it is just such an account that I wish to examine with regard to date rape.

The least sophisticated of the "she asked for it" rationales, and in a sense, the easiest to deal with, appeals to an injunction against sexually provocative behaviour on the part of women. If women should not be sexually provocative, then, from this standpoint, a woman who is sexually provocative deserves to suffer the consequences. Now it will not do to respond that women get raped even when they are not sexually provocative, or that it is men who get to interpret (unfairly) what counts as sexually provocative. The question should be: Why shouldn't a woman be sexually provocative? Why should this behaviour warrant any kind of aggressive response whatsoever?

Attempts to explain that women have a right to behave in sexually provocative ways without suffering dire consequences still meet with surprisingly tough resistance. Even people who find nothing wrong or sinful with sex itself, in any of its forms, tend to suppose that women must not behave sexually unless they are prepared to carry through on some fuller course of sexual interaction. The logic of this response seems to be that at some point a woman's behaviour commits her to following through on the full course of a sexual encounter as it is defined by her assailant. At some point she has made an agreement, or formed a contract, and once that is done, her contractor is entitled to demand that she satisfy the terms of that contract. Thus, this view about sexual responsibility and desert is supported by other assumptions about contracts and agreement. But we do not normally suppose that casual nonverbal behaviour generates agreements. Nor do we normally grant private persons the right to enforce contracts. What rationale would support our conclusion in this case?

The rationale, I believe, comes in the form of a belief in the especially insistent nature of male sexuality, an insistence which lies at the foot of natural male aggression, and which is extremely difficult, perhaps impossible to contain. At a certain point in the arousal process, it is thought, a man's rational will gives way to the prerogatives of nature. His sexual need can and does reach a point where it is uncontrollable, and his natural masculine aggression kicks in to ensure that this need is met. Women, however, are naturally more contained, and so it is their responsibility not to provoke the irrational in the male. If they do go so far as that, they have both failed in their responsibilities, and subjected themselves to the inevitable. One does not go into the lion's cage and expect not to be eaten. Natural feminine reluctance, it is thought, is no protection against a sexually aroused male.

This belief about the normal aggressiveness of male sexuality is complemented by common knowledge about female gender development. Once, women were taught to deny their sexuality and to aspire to ideals of chastity. Things have not changed so much. Women still tend to eschew conquest mentalities in favour of a combination of sex and affection. Insofar as this is thought to be merely a cultural requirement, however, there is an expectation that women will be coy about their sexual desire. The assumption that women both want to indulge sexually, and are inclined to sacrifice this desire for higher ends, gives rise to the myth that they want to be raped. After all, doesn't rape give them the sexual enjoyment they *really* want, at the same time that it relieves them of the responsibility for admitting to and acting upon what they want? And how then can we blame

men, who have been socialized to be aggressively seductive precisely for the purpose of overriding female reserve? If we find fault at all, we are inclined to cast our suspicions on the motives of the woman. For it is on her that the contradictory roles of sexual desirer and sexual denier have been placed. Our awareness of the contradiction expected of her makes us suspect her honesty. In the past, she was expected to deny her complicity because of the shame and guilt she felt at having submitted. This expectation persists in many quarters today, and is carried over into a general suspicion about her character, and the fear that she might make a false accusation out of revenge, or some other low motive.

But if women really want sexual pleasure, what inclines us to think that they will get it through rape? This conclusion logically requires a theory about the dynamics of sexual pleasure that sees that pleasure as an emergent property of overwhelming male insistence. For the assumption that a raped female experiences sexual pleasure implies that the person who rapes her knows how to cause that pleasure independently of any information she might convey on that point. Since her ongoing protest is inconsistent with requests to be touched in particular ways in particular places, to have more of this and less of that, then we must believe that the person who touches her knows these particular ways and places instinctively, without any directives from her.

Thus, we find, underlying and reinforcing this belief in incommunicative male prowess, a conception of sexual pleasure that springs from wordless interchanges, and of sexual success that occurs in a place of meaningful silence. The language of seduction is accepted as a tacit language: eye contact, smiles, blushes, and faintly discernible gestures. It is, accordingly, imprecise and ambiguous. It would be easy for a man to make mistakes about the message conveyed, understandable that he should mistakenly think that a sexual invitation has been made, and a bargain struck. But honest mistakes, we think, must be excused.

In sum, the belief that women should not be sexually provocative is logically linked to several other beliefs, some normative, some empirical. The normative beliefs are (1) that people should keep the agreements they make, (2) that sexually provocative behaviour, taken beyond a certain point, generates agreements, (3) that the peculiar nature of male and female sexuality places such agreements in a special category, one in which the possibility of retracting an agreement is ruled out, or at least made highly unlikely, (4) that women are not to be trusted, in sexual matters at least. The empirical belief, which turns out to be false, is that male sexuality is not subject to rational and moral control.

Dispelling the Myths

The "she asked for it" justification of sexual assault incorporates a conception of a contract that would be difficult to defend in any other context and the presumptions about human sexuality which function to reinforce sympathies rooted in the contractual notion of just deserts are not supported by empirical research.

The belief that a woman generates some sort of contractual obligation whenever her behaviour is interpreted as seductive is the most indefensible part of the mythology of rape. In law, contracts are not legitimate just because a promise has been made. In particular, the use of pressure tactics to extract agreement is frowned upon. Normally, an agreement is upheld only if the contractors were clear on what they were getting into, and had sufficient time to reflect on the wisdom of their doing so. Either there must be a clear tradition in which the expectations involved in the contract are fairly well known (marriage), or there must be an explicit written agreement concerning the exact terms of the contract and the expectations of the persons involved. But whatever the terms of a contract, there is no private right to enforce it. So that if I make a contract with you on which I renege, the only permissible recourse for you is through due legal process.

Now it is not clear whether sexual contracts can be made to begin with, or if so, what sort of sexual contracts would be legitimate. But assuming that they could be made, the terms of those contracts would not be enforceable. To allow public enforcement would be to grant the State the overt right to force people to have sex, and this would clearly be unacceptable. Granting that sexual contracts are legitimate, state enforcement of such contracts would have to be limited to ordering nonsexual compensation for breaches of contract. So it makes no difference whether a sexual contract is tacit or explicit. There are no grounds whatsoever that would justify enforcement of its terms.

Thus, even if we assume that a woman has initially agreed to an encounter, her agreement does not automatically make all subsequent sexual activity to which she submits legitimate. If during coitus a woman should experience pain, be suddenly overcome with guilt or fear of pregnancy, or simply lose her initial desire, those are good reasons for her to change her mind. Having changed her mind, neither her partner nor the State has any right to force her to continue. But then if she is forced to continue she is assaulted. Thus, establishing that consent occurred at a particular point during a sexual encounter should not exclusively establish the legitimacy of the encounter. What is needed is a reading of whether she agreed throughout the encounter.

If the "she asked for it" contractual view of sexual interchange has any validity, it is because there is a point at which there is no stopping a sexual encounter, a point at which that encounter becomes the inexorable outcome of the unfolding of natural events. If a sexual encounter is like a slide on which I cannot stop halfway down, it will be relevant whether I enter the slide of my own free will, or am pushed.

But there is no evidence that the entire sexual act is like a slide. While there may be a few seconds in the "plateau" period just prior to orgasm in which people are "swept" away by sexual feelings to the point where we could justifiably understand their lack of heed for the comfort of their partner, the greater part of a sexual encounter comes well within the bounds of morally responsible control of our own actions. Indeed, the available evidence shows that most of the activity involved in sex has to do with building the requisite level of desire, a task that involves the proper use of foreplay, the possibility of which implies control over the form that foreplay will take. Modern sexual therapy assumes that such control is universally accessible, and so far there has been no reason to question that assumption. Sexologists are unanimous, moreover, in holding that mutual sexual enjoyment requires an atmosphere of comfort and communication, a minimum of pressure, and an ongoing check-up on one's partner's state. They maintain that different people have different predilections, and that what is pleasurable for one person is very often anathema to another. These findings show that the way to achieve sexual pleasure, at any time at all, let alone with a casual acquaintance, decidedly does not involve overriding the other person's express reservations and providing them with just any kind of sexual stimulus. And while we do not want to allow science and technology a voice in which the voices of particular women are drowned, in this case science seems to concur with women's perception that aggressive incommunicative sex is not what they want. But if science and the voice of women concur, if aggressive seduction does not lead to good sex, if women do not like it, or want it, then it is not rational to think that they would agree to it. Where such sex takes place, it is therefore rational to presume that the sex was not consensual.

The myth that women like to be raped is closely connected, as we have seen, to doubt about their honesty in sexual matters, and this suspicion is exploited by defence lawyers when sexual assault cases make it to the courtroom. It is an unfortunate consequence of the presumption of innocence that rape victims who end up in court frequently find that it is they who are on trial. For if the defendant is innocent, then either he did not intend to do what he was accused of, or the plaintiff is mistaken about his identity, or she is lying. Often the last alternative is the only plausible defence, and as a result, the plaintiff's word seldom goes unquestioned. Women are frequently accused of having made a false accusation, either as a defensive mechanism for dealing with guilt and shame, or out of a desire for revenge.

Now there is no point in denying the possibility of false accusation, though there are probably better ways of seeking revenge on a man than accusing him of rape. However, we can now establish a logical connection between the evidence that a woman was subjected to high-pressure aggressive "seduction" tactics, and her claim that she did not consent to that encounter. Where the kind of encounter is not the sort to which it would be reasonable to consent, there is a logical presumption that a woman who claims that she did not consent is telling the truth. Where the kind of sex involved is not the sort of sex we would expect a woman to like, the burden of proof should not be on the woman to show that she did not consent, but on the defendant to show that contrary to every reasonable expectation she did consent. The defendant should be required to convince the court that the plaintiff persuaded him to have sex with her even though there are not visible reasons why she should.

In conclusion, there are no grounds for the "she asked for it" defence. Sexually provocative behaviour does not generate sexual contracts. Even where there are sexual agreements, they cannot be legitimately enforced either by the state, or by private right, or by natural prerogative. Secondly, all the evidence suggests that neither women nor men find sexual enjoyment in rape or in any form of noncommunicative sexuality. Thirdly, male sexual desire is containable, and can be subjected to moral and rational control. Fourthly, since there is no reason why women should not be sexually provocative, they do not "deserve" any sex they do not want. This last is a welcome discovery. The taboo on sexual provocativeness in women is a taboo both on sensuality and on teasing. But sensuality is a source of delight, and teasing is playful and inspires wit. What a relief to learn that it is not sexual provocativeness, but its enemies, that constitute a danger to the world. . . .

In thinking about sex we must keep in mind its sensual ends, and the facts show that aggressive high-pressure sex contradicts those ends. Consensual sex in dating situations is presumed to aim at mutual enjoyment. It may not always do this, and when it does, it might not always succeed. There is no logical incompatibility between wanting to continue a sexual encounter, and failing to derive sexual pleasure from it.

But it seems to me that there is a presumption in favour of the connection between sex and sexual enjoyment, and that if a man wants to be sure that he is not forcing himself on a woman, he has an obligation either to ensure that the encounter really is mutually enjoyable, or to know the reasons why she would want to continue the encounter in spite of her lack of enjoyment. A closer investigation of the nature of this obligation will enable us to construct a more rational and more plausible norm of sexual conduct.

Onora O'Neill has argued that in intimate situations we have an obligation to take the ends of others as our own, and to promote those ends in a non-manipulative and non-paternalistic manner. Now it seems that in honest sexual encounters just this is required. Assuming that each person enters the encounter in order to seek sexual satisfaction, each person engaging in the encounter has an obligation to help the other seek his or her ends. To do otherwise is to risk acting in opposition to what the other desires, and hence to risk acting without the other's consent.

But the obligation to promote the sexual ends of one's partner implies that obligation to know what those ends are, and also the obligation to know how those ends are attained. Thus, the problem comes down to a problem of epistemic responsibility, the responsibility to know. The solution, in my view, lies in the practice of a communicative sexuality, one which combines the appropriate knowledge of the other with respect for the dialectics of desire. . . .

Cultural Presumptions

Now it may well be that we have no obligation to care for strangers, and I do not wish to claim that we do. Nonetheless, it seems that O'Neill's point about the special moral duties we have in certain intimate situations is supported by a conceptual relation between certain kinds of personal relationships and the expectation that it should be a communicative relation. Friendship is a case in point. It is a relation that is

greatly underdetermined by what we usually include in our sets of rights and obligations. For the most part, rights and obligations disappear as terms by which friendship is guided. They are still there, to be called upon, in case the relationship breaks down, but insofar as the friendship is a friendship, it is concerned with fostering the quality of the interaction and not with standing on rights. Thus, because we are friends, we share our property, and property rights between us are not invoked. Because we are friends, privacy is not an issue. Because we are friends we may see to each other's needs as often as we see to our own. The same can be said for relations between lovers, parents and dependent children, and even between spouses, at least when interaction is functioning at an optimal level. When such relations break down to the point that people must stand on their rights, we can often say that the actors ought to make more of an effort, and in many instances fault them for their lack of charity, tolerance, or benevolence. Thus, although we have a right to end friendships, it may be a reflection on our lack of virtue that we do so, and while we cannot be criticized for violating other people's rights, we can be rightfully deprecated for lacking the virtue to sustain a friendship.

But is there a similar conceptual relation between the kind of activity that a date is, and the sort of moral practice that it requires? My claim is that there is, and that this connection is easily established once we recognize the cultural presumption that dating is a gesture of friendship and regard. Traditionally, the decision to date indicates that two people have an initial attraction to each other, that they are disposed to like each other, and look forward to enjoying each other's company. Dating derives its implicit meaning from this tradition. It retains this meaning unless other aims are explicitly stated, and even then it may not be possible to alienate this meaning. It is a rare woman who will not spurn a man who states explicitly, right at the onset, that he wants to go out with her solely on the condition that he have sexual intercourse with her at the end of the evening, and that he has no interest in her company apart from gaining that end, and no concern for mutual satisfaction.

Explicit protest to the contrary aside, the conventions of dating confer on it its social meaning, and this social meaning implies a relationship which is more like friendship than the cutthroat competition of opposing teams. As such, it requires that we do more than stand on our rights with regard to each other. As long as we are operating under the auspices of a dating relationship, it requires that we behave in the mode of friendship and trust. But if a date is more like a friendship than a business contract, then clearly respect for the dialectics of desire is incompatible with the sort of sexual pressure that is inclined to end in date rape. And clearly, also, a conquest mentality which exploits a situation of trust and respect for purely selfish ends is morally pernicious. Failure to respect the dialectics of desire when operating under the auspices of friendship and trust is to act in flagrant disregard of the moral requirement to avoid manipulative, coercive, and exploitive behaviour. Respect for the dialectics of desire is *prima facie* inconsistent with the satisfaction of one person at the expense of the other. The proper end of friendship relations is mutual satisfaction. But the requirement of mutuality means that we must take a communicative approach to discovering the ends of the other, and this entails that we respect the dialectics of desire.

But now that we know what communicative sexuality is, and that it is morally required, and that it is the only feasible means to mutual sexual enjoyment, why not take this model as the norm of what is reasonable in sexual interaction. The evidence of sexologists strongly indicates that women whose partners are aggressively uncommunicative have little chance of experiencing sexual pleasure. But it is not reasonable for women to consent to what they have little chance of enjoying. Hence it is not reasonable for women to consent to aggressive noncommunicative sex. Nor can we reasonably suppose that women have consented to sexual encounters which we know and they know they do not find enjoyable. With the communicative model as the norm, the aggressive contractual model should strike us as a model of deviant sexuality, and sexual encounters patterned on that model should strike us as encounters to which *prima facie* no one would reasonably agree. But if acquiescence to an encounter counts as consent only if the acquiescence is reasonable, something to which a reasonable person, in full possession of knowledge relevant to the encounter, would agree, then acquiescence to aggressive noncommunicative sex is not reasonable. Hence, acquiescence under such conditions should not count as consent.

Thus, where communicative sexuality does not occur, we lack the main ground for believing that the sex involved was consensual. Moreover, where a man does not engage in communicative sexuality, he acts either out of reckless disregard, or out of wilful ignorance. For he cannot know, except through the practice of communicative sexuality, whether his partner has any sexual reason for continuing the encounter. And where she does not, he runs the risk of imposing on her what she is not willing to have. All that is needed then, in order to provide women with legal protection from "date rape" is to make both reckless indifference and wilful ignorance a sufficient condition of *mens rea* and to make communicative sexuality the accepted norm of sex to which a reasonable woman would agree. Thus, the appeal to communicative sexuality as a norm for sexual encounters accomplishes two things. It brings the aggressive sex involved in "date rape" well within the realm of sexual assault, and it locates the guilt of date rapists in the failure to approach sexual relations on a communicative basis.

43

Men in Groups: Collective Responsibility for Rape

Larry May and Robert Strikwerda

As teenagers, we ran in a crowd that incessantly talked about sex. Since most of us were quite afraid of discovering our own sexual inadequacies, we were quite afraid of women's sexuality. To mask our fear, of which we were quite ashamed, we maintained a posture of bravado, which we were able to sustain through mutual reinforcement when in small groups or packs. Riding from shopping mall to fast food establishment, we would tell each other stories about our sexual exploits, stories we all secretly believed to be pure fictions. We drew strength from the camaraderie we felt during these experiences. Some members of our group would yell obscenities at women on the street as we drove by. Over time, conversation turned more and more to group sex, especially forced sex with women we passed on the road. To give it its proper name, our conversation turned increasingly to rape. At a certain stage, we tired of it all and stopped associating with this group of men, or perhaps they were in most ways still boys. The reason we left was not that we disagreed with what was going on but, if this decision to leave was reasoned at all, it was that the posturing (the endless attempts to impress one another by our daring ways) simply became very tiresome. Only much later in life did we think that there was anything wrong, morally, socially, or politically, with what went on in that group of adolescents who seemed so ready to engage in rape. Only later still did we wonder whether we shared in responsibility for the rapes that are perpetrated by those men who had similar experiences to ours.

This is an essay about the relationship between the shared experiences of men in groups, especially experiences that make rape more likely in western culture, and the shared responsibility of men for the prevalence of rape in that culture. The claim of the essay is that in some societies men are collectively responsible for rape in that most if not all men contribute in various ways to the prevalence of rape, and as a result, these men should share in responsibility for rape.

Most men do very little at all to oppose rape in their societies; does this make them something like co-conspirators with the men who rape? In Canada, a number of men have founded the "White Ribbon Campaign." This is a program of fund-raising, consciousness raising, and symbolic wearing of white ribbons during the week ending on December 6th, the anniversary of the murder of 14 women at a Montreal engineering school by a man shouting "I hate feminists." Should men in US society start a similar campaign? If they do not, do they deserve the "co-conspirator" label? If they do, is this symbolic act enough to diminish their responsibility? Should men be speaking out against the program of rape in the war in Bosnia? What should they tell their sons about such rapes, and about rapes that occur in their home towns? If men remain silent, are they not complicitous with the rapists?

We will argue that insofar as male bonding and socialization in groups contributes to the prevalence of rape in western societies, men in those societies should feel responsible for the prevalence of rape and should feel motivated to counteract such violence and rape. In addition, we will argue that rape should be seen as something that men, as a group, are collectively responsible for, in a way which parallels the collective responsibility of a society for crimes against humanity perpetrated by some members of their society. Rape is indeed a crime against humanity, not merely a crime against a particular woman. And rape is a crime perpetrated by men as a group, not merely by the individual rapist.

To support our claims we will criticize four other ways to understand responsibility for rape. First, it is sometimes said that only the rapist is responsible since he alone intentionally committed the act of rape. Secondly, it is sometimes said that no one is responsible since rape is merely a biologically oriented response to stimuli that men have little or no control over. Thirdly, it is sometimes said that everyone, women and men alike, contribute to the violent environment which produces rape so both women and men are equally responsible for rape, and hence it is a mistake to single men out. Fourthly, it is sometimes said that it is "patriarchy," rather than individual men or men as a group, which is responsible for rape. After examining each of these views we will conclude by briefly offering our own positive reasons for thinking that men are collectively responsible for the prevalence of rape in western society.

I The Rapist as Loner or Demon

Joyce Carol Oates has recently described the sport of boxing, where men are encouraged to violate the social rule against harming one another, as "a highly organized ritual that violates taboo."

> The paradox of the boxer is that, in the ring, he experiences himself as a living conduit for the inchoate, demonic will of the crowd: the expression of their collective desire, which is to pound another human being into absolute submission. (Oates, 1992, p. 60)

Oates makes the connection here between boxing and rape. The former boxing heavyweight champion of the world, Mike Tyson, epitomizes this connection both because he is a convicted rapist, and also because, according to Oates, in his fights he regularly used the prefight taunt "I'll make you into my girlfriend," clearly the "boast of a rapist" (Oates, 1992, p. 61).

Just after being convicted of rape, Mike Tyson gave a twisted declaration of his innocence.

> I didn't rape anyone. I didn't hurt anyone, no black eyes, no broken ribs. When I'm in the ring, I break their ribs, I break their jaws. To me, that's hurting someone. (*St Louis Post Dispatch*, 1992)

In the ring, Tyson had a license to break ribs and jaws; and interestingly he understood that this was a case of hurting another person. It was just that in the ring it was acceptable. He knew that he was not supposed to hurt people outside the ring. But since he didn't break any ribs or jaws, how could anyone say that he hurt his accuser, Desiree Washington? Having sex with a woman could not be construed as having hurt her, for Tyson apparently, unless ribs or jaws were broken.

Tyson's lawyer, attempting to excuse Tyson's behavior, said that the boxer grew up in a "male-dominated world." And this is surely true. He was plucked from a home for juvenile delinquents and raised by boxing promoters. Few American males had been so richly imbued with male tradition, or more richly rewarded for living up to the male stereotype of the aggressive, indomitable fighter. Whether or not he recognized it as a genuine insight, Tyson's lawyer points us toward the heart of the matter in American culture: misbehavior, especially sexual misbehavior of males toward females is, however mixed the messages, something that many men condone. This has given rise to the use of the term "the rape culture" to describe the climate of attitudes that exists in the contemporary American male-dominated world (see Griffin, 1971).

While noting all of this, Joyce Carol Oates ends her *Newsweek* essay on Tyson's rape trial by concluding that "no one is to blame except the perpetrator himself." She absolves the "culture" at large of any blame for Tyson's behavior. Oates regards Tyson as a sadist who took pleasure in inflicting pain both in and out of the boxing ring. She comes very close to demonizing him when, at the end of her essay, she suggests that Tyson is an outlaw or even a sociopath. And while she is surely right to paint Tyson's deed in the most horrific colors, she is less convincing when she suggests that Tyson is very different from other males in our society. In one telling statement in her essay, however, Oates opens the door for a less individualistic view of rape by acknowledging that the boxing community had built up in Tyson a "grandiose sense of entitlement, fueled by the insecurities and emotions of adolescence" (Oates, 1992, p. 61).

Rape is normally committed by individual men; but, in our view, rape is not best understood in individualistic terms. The chief reasons for this are that individual men are more likely to engage in rape when they are in groups, and men receive strong encouragement to rape from the way they are socialized as men, that is, in the way they come to see themselves as instantiations of what it means to be a man. Both the "climate" that encourages rape and the "socialization" patterns which instill negative attitudes about women are difficult to understand or assess when one focuses on the isolated individual perpetrator of a rape. There are significant social dimensions to rape that are best understood as group-oriented.

As parents, we have observed that male schoolchildren are much more likely to misbehave (and subsequently to be punished by being sent to "time out") than are female schoolchildren. This fact is not particularly remarkable, for boys are widely believed to be more active than girls. What is remarkable is that school teachers, in our experience, are much more likely to condone the misbehavior of boys than the misbehavior of girls. "Boys will be boys" is heard as often today as it was in previous times. (See Robert Lipsyte's essay about the Glen Ridge, New Jersey rape trial where the defense attorney used just these words to defend the star high school football players who raped a retarded girl.) From their earliest experience with authority figures, little boys are given mixed signals about misbehavior. Yes, they are punished, but they are also treated as if their misbehavior is expected, even welcome. It is for some boys, as it was for us, a "badge of honor" to be sent to detention or "time out." From older boys and from their peers, boys learn that they often will be ostracized for being "too goody-goody." It is as if part of the mixed message is that boys are given a license to misbehave.

And which of these boys will turn out to be rapists is often as much a matter of luck as it is a matter of choice. The data on date rape suggest that young men in our society engage in much more rape than anyone previously anticipated. It is a serious mistake in psychological categorization to think that all of these rapes are committed by sadists. (Studies by Amir, cited in Griffin, 1971, p. 178, show that the average rapist is not psychologically "abnormal.") Given our own experiences and similar reports from others, it is also a serious mistake to think that those who rape are significantly different from the rest of the male population. (Studies by Smithyman, cited in Scully, 1990, p. 75, indicate that rapists "seemed not to differ markedly from the majority of males in our culture.") Our conclusion is that the typical rapist is not a demon or sadist, but, in some sense, could have been many men.

Most of those who engage in rape are at least partially responsible for these rapes, but the question we have posed is this: are those who perpetrate rape the *only* ones who are responsible for rape? Contrary to what Joyce Carol Oates contends, we believe that it is a serious mistake to think that only the perpetrators are responsible. The interactions of men, especially in all-male groups, contribute to a pattern of socialization that also plays a major role in the incidence of rape. In urging that more than the individual perpetrators be seen as responsible for rape, we do not mean to suggest that the responsibility of the perpetrator be diminished. When responsibility for harm is shared it need not be true that the perpetrators of harm find their responsibility relieved or even diminished. Rather, shared responsibility for harms merely means that the range of people who are implicated in these harms is extended. (More will be said on this point in the final section.)

II The Rapist as Victim of Biology

The most recent psychological study of rape is that done by Randy Thornhill and Nancy Wilmsen Thornhill (1992). In this work, any contention that coercion or rape may be socially or culturally learned is derisively dismissed, as is any feminist argument for changing men's attitudes through changing especially group-based socialization. The general hypothesis they support is that:

> sexual coercion by men reflects a sex-specific, species-typical psychological adaptation to rape: Men have certain psychological traits that evolved by natural selection specifically in the context of coercive sex and made rape adaptive during human evolution. (p. 363)

They claim that rape is an adaptive response to biological differences between men and women.

Thornhill and Thornhill contend that the costs to women to engage in sex ("nine months of pregnancy") greatly exceed the costs to men ("a few minutes of time and an energetically cheap ejaculate"). As a result women and men came very early in evolutionary time to adapt quite differently sexually.

> Because women are more selective about mates and more interested in evaluating them and delaying

copulation, men, to get sexual access, must often break through feminine barriers of hesitation, equivocation, and resistance. (p. 366)

Males who adapted by developing a proclivity to rape and thus who "solved the problem" by forcing sex on a partner, were able to "out-reproduce" other more passive males and gain an evolutionary advantage.

In one paragraph, Thornhill and Thornhill dismiss feminists who support a "social learning theory of rape" by pointing out that males of several "species with an evolutionary history of polygyny" are also "more aggressive, sexually assertive and eager to copulate." Yet, in "the vast majority of these species there is no sexual training of juveniles by other members of the group." This evidence, they conclude, thoroughly discredits the social learning theory and means that such theories "are never alternatives to evolutionary hypotheses about psychological adaptation" (p. 364). In response to their critics, Thornhill and Thornhill go so far as to say that the feminist project of changing socialization patterns is pernicious.

> The sociocultural view does seem to offer hope and a simple remedy in that it implies that we need only fix the way that boys are socialized and rape will disappear. This naive solution is widespread. . . . As Hartung points out, those who feel that the social problem of rape can be solved by changing the nature of men through naive and arbitrary social adjustments should "get real about rape" because their perspective is a danger to us all. (p. 416)

According to the Thornhills, feminists and other social theorists need to focus instead on what are called the "cues that affect the use of rape by adult males" (p. 416).

The evolutionary biological account of rape we have rehearsed above would seemingly suggest that no one is responsible for rape. After all, if rape is an adaptive response to different sexual development in males and females, particular individuals who engage in rape are merely doing what they are naturally adapted to do. Rape is something to be controlled by those who control the "cues" that stimulate the natural rapist instincts in all men. It is for this reason that the Thornhills urge that more attention be given to male arousal and female stimulation patterns in laboratory settings (p. 375). Notice that even on the Thornhills' own terms, those who provide the cues may be responsible for the prevalence of rape, even if the perpetrators are not. But Thornhill and Thornhill deny that there are any normative conclusions that follow from their research, and criticize those who wish to draw out such implications as committing the "naturalistic fallacy" (p. 407).

In contrast to the Thornhills, a more plausible sociobiological account is given by Lionel Tiger. Tiger is often cited as someone who attempted to excuse male aggression. In his important study he defines aggression as distinct from violence, but nonetheless sees violence as one possible outcome of the natural aggressive tendencies, especially in men.

> Aggression occurs when an individual or group see their interest, their honor, or their job bound up with coercing the animal, human, or physical environment to achieve their own ends rather than (or in spite of) the goals of the object of their action. Violence may occur in the process of interaction. (Tiger [1969] 1984, pp. 158–9)

For Tiger, aggression is intentional behavior which is goal-directed and based on procuring something which is necessary for survival. Aggression is a " 'normal' feature of the human biologically based repertoire" (p. 159). Violence, "coercion involving physical force to resolve conflict" (p. 159), on the other hand, is not necessarily a normal response to one's environment, although in some circumstances it may be. Thus, while human males are evolutionarily adapted to be aggressive, they are not necessarily adapted to be violent.

Tiger provided an account that linked aggression in males with their biological evolution.

> Human aggression is in part a function of the fact that hunting was vitally important to human evolution and that aggression is typically undertaken by males in the framework of a unisexual social bond of which participants are aware and with which they are concerned. It is implied, therefore, that aggression is "instinctive" but also must occur within an explicit social context varying from culture to culture and to

be learned by members of any community. . . . Men in continuous association aggress against the environment in much the same way as men and women in continuous association have sexual relations. (pp. 159–60)

And while men are thus predisposed to engage in aggression, in ways that women are not, it is not true in Tiger's view that a predisposition to engage in violent acts is a normal part of this difference.

Thornhill and Thornhill fail to consider Tiger's contention that men are evolutionarily adapted to be aggressive, but not necessarily to be violent. With Tiger's distinction in mind it may be said that human males, especially in association with other males, are adapted to aggress against women in certain social environments. But this aggressive response need not lead to violence, or the threat of violence, of the sort epitomized by rape; rather it may merely affect non-coercive mating rituals. On a related point, Tiger argues that the fact that war has historically been "virtually a male monopoly" (p. 81) is due to both male bonding patterns and evolutionary adaptation. Evolutionary biology provides only part of the story since male aggressiveness need not result in such violent encounters as occur in war or rape. After all, many men do not rape or go to war; the cultural cues provided by socialization must be considered at least as important as evolutionary adaptation.

We side with Tiger against the Thornhills in focusing on the way that all-male groups socialize their members and provide "cues" for violence. Tiger has recently allied himself with feminists such as Catherine MacKinnon and others who have suggested that male attitudes need to be radically altered in order to have a major impact on the incidence of rape. (See the preface to the second edition of Tiger [1969] 1984.) One of the implications of Tiger's research is that rape and other forms of male aggressive behavior are not best understood as isolated acts of individuals. Rather than simply seeing violent aggression as merely a biologically predetermined response, Tiger places violent aggressiveness squarely into the group dynamics of men's interactions, a result of his research not well appreciated.

In a preface to the second edition of his book, Tiger corrects an unfortunate misinterpretation of his work.

> One of the stigmas which burdened this book was an interpretation of it as an apology for male aggression and even a potential stimulus of it after all, boys will be boys. However I clearly said the opposite: "This is not to say that . . . hurtful and destructive relations between groups of men are inevitable . . . It may be possible, as many writers have suggested, to alter social conceptions of maleness so that gentility and equivocation rather than toughness and more or less arbitrary decisiveness are highly valued." (p. 191)

If Tiger is right, and the most important "cues" are those which young boys and men get while in the company of other boys and men, then the feminist project of changing male socialization patterns may be seen as consistent with, rather than opposed to, the socio-biological hypotheses. Indeed, other evidence may be cited to buttress the feminist social-learning perspective against the Thornhills. Different human societies have quite different rates of rape. In her anthropological research among the Minangkabau of West Sumatra, Peggy Reeves Sanday has found that this society is relatively rape-free. Rape does occur, but at such a low rate – 28 per three million in 1981–2, for example – as to be virtually nonexistent (Sanday, 1986, p. 85; also see Sanday, 1990, and Lepowsky, 1990). In light of such research, men, rather than women, are the ones who would need to change their behavior. This is because it is the socialization of men by men in their bonding-groups, and the view of women that is engendered, that provides the strongest cues toward rape. Since there may indeed be something that males could and should be doing differently that would affect the prevalence of rape, it does not seem unreasonable to continue to investigate the claim that men are collectively responsible for the prevalence of rape.

III   The Rapist as Victim of Society

It is also possible to acknowledge that men are responsible for the prevalence of rape in our society but nonetheless to argue that women are equally responsible. Rape is often portrayed as a sex crime perpetrated largely by men against women. But importantly, rape is also a crime of violence, and many factors in our society have increased the prevalence of violence. This prevalence of violence is the cause of both rape and war in western societies. Our view, that violence of both sorts is increased in likelihood by patterns of male socialization, which then creates collective male responsibility, may be countered by pointing out that socialization patterns are created by both men and women, thereby seemingly implicating both men and women in collective responsibility for rape and war.

Sam Keen has contended that it is violence that we should be focusing on rather than sex or gender, in order to understand the causes and remedies for the prevalence of rape. According to Keen,

> Men are violent because of the systematic violence done to their bodies and spirits. Being hurt they become hurters. In the over-all picture, male violence toward women is far less than male violence toward other males . . . these outrages are a structural part of a warfare system that victimizes both men and women. (Keen, 1991, p. 47)

Keen sees both men and women conspiring together to perpetuate this system of violence, especially in the way they impart to their male children an acceptance of violence.

Women are singled out by Keen as those who have not come to terms with their share of responsibility for our violent culture. And men have been so guilt-tripped on the issue of rape that they have become desensitized to it. Keen thinks that it is a mistake to single out men, and not women also, as responsible for rape.

> Until women are willing to weep for and accept equal responsibility for the systematic violence done to the male body and spirit by the war system, it is not likely that men will lose enough of their guilt and regain enough of their sensitivity to accept responsibility for women who are raped. (p. 47)

Even though women are equally responsible for the rape culture, in Keen's view, women should be singled out because they have not previously accepted their share of responsibility for the creation of a violent society.

Keen is at least partially right insofar as he insists that issues of rape and war be understood as arising from the same source, namely the socialization of men to be violent in western cultures. We agree with Keen that rape is part of a larger set of violent practices that injure both men and women. He is right to point out that men are murdering other men in our society in increasing numbers, and that this incidence of violence probably has something to do with the society's general condoning, even celebrating, of violence, especially in war.

Keen fails to note though that it is men, not women, who are the vast majority of both rapists and murderers in our society. And even if some women do act in ways which trigger violent reactions in men, nevertheless, in our opinion this pales in comparison with the way that men socialize each other to be open to violence. As Tiger and others have suggested, aggressive violence results primarily from male-bonding experiences. In any event, both fathers and mothers engage in early childhood socialization. Men influence the rape culture both through early childhood socialization and through male-bonding socialization of older male children. But women only contribute to this culture, when they do, through individual acts of early childhood socialization. For this reason Keen is surely wrong to think that women share responsibility *equally* with men for our rape culture.

In our view, some women could prevent some rapes; and some women do contribute to the patterns of socialization of both men and women that increase the incidence of rape. For these reasons, it would not be inappropriate to say that women share responsibility for rape as well as men. But we believe that it is a mistake to think that women share equally in this responsibility with men. For one thing, women are different from men in that they are, in general, made worse off by the prevalence of rape in our society. As we will next see, there is a sense in which men, but not women, benefit from the prevalence of rape, and this fact means that men have more of a stake in the rape culture, and hence have more to gain by its continued existence.

In general, our conclusion is that women share responsibility, but to a far lesser extent than men, for the prevalence of rape. We do not support those who try to "blame the victim" by holding women responsible for rape because of not taking adequate precautions, or dressing seductively, etc. Instead, the key for us is the role that women, as mothers, friends and lovers, play in the overall process of male socialization that creates the rape culture. It should come as no surprise that few members of western society can be relieved of responsibility for this rape culture given the overwhelming pervasiveness of that culture. But such considerations should not deter us from looking to men, first and foremost, as being collectively responsible for the prevalence of rape. The women who do contribute to aggressive male-socialization do so as individuals; women have no involvement parallel to the male-bonding group.

IV   The Rapist as Group Member

Popular literature tends to portray the rapist as a demonic character, as the "Other". What we find interesting about the research of Thornhill and Thornhill is that it operates unwittingly to support the feminist slogan that "all men are rapists," that the rapist is not male "Other" but male "Self." What is so unsettling about the tens of thousands of rapes in Bosnia is the suggestion that what ordinary men have been doing is not significantly different from what the "sex-fiends" did. The thesis that men are adapted to be predisposed to be rapists, regardless of what else we think of the thesis, should give us pause and make us less rather than more likely to reject the feminist slogan. From this vantage point, the work of Tiger as well as Thornhill and Thornhill sets the stage for a serious reconsideration of the view that men are collectively responsible for rape.

There are two things that might be meant by saying that men are collectively responsible for the prevalence of rape in western culture. First, seeing men as collectively responsible may mean that men as a group are responsible in that they form some sort of super-entity that causes, or at least supports, the prevalence of rape. When some feminists talk of "patriarchy," what they seem to mean is a kind of institution that operates through, but also behind the backs of, individual men to oppress women. Here it may be that men are collectively responsible for the prevalence of rape and yet no men are individually responsible. We call this nondistributive collective responsibility. Second, seeing men as collectively responsible may mean that men form a group in which there are so many features that the members share in common, such as attitudes or dispositions to engage in harm, that what holds true for one man also holds true for all other men. Because of the common features of the members of the group men, when one man is responsible for a particular harm, other men are implicated. Each member of the group has a share in the responsibility for a harm such as rape. We call this distributive collective responsibility. (See May, 1992, especially chapter 2.) In what follows we will criticize the first way of understanding men's collective responsibility, and offer reasons to support the second.

When collective responsibility is understood in the first (nondistributive) sense, this form of responsibility is assigned to those groups that have the capacity to act. Here there are two paradigmatic examples: the corporation and the mob. (See May, 1987, especially chapters 2 and 4.) The corporation has the kind of organizational structure that allows for the group to form intentions and carry out those intentions, almost as if the corporation were itself a person. Since men, *qua* men, are too amorphous a group to be able to act in an organized fashion, we will not be interested in whether they are collectively responsible in this way. But it may be that men can act in the way that mobs act, that is, not through a highly organized structure but through something such as like-mindedness. If there is enough commonality of belief, disposition and interest of all men, or at least all men within a particular culture, then the group may be able to act just as a mob is able to respond to a commonly perceived enemy.

It is possible to think of patriarchy as the oppressive practices of men coordinated by the common interests of men, but not organized intentionally. It is also productive to think of rape as resulting from patriarchy. For if there is a "collective" that is supporting or creating the prevalence of rape it is not a highly organized one, since there is nothing like a corporation that intentionally plans the rape of women in western culture. If the current Serbian army has engaged in the systematic and organized rape of Muslim women as a strategy of war, then this would be an example of nondistributive responsibility for rape. But the kind of oppression characterized by the prevalence of rape in most cultures appears to be systematic but not organized. How does this affect our understanding of whether men are collectively responsible for rape?

If patriarchy is understood merely as a system of coordination that operates behind the backs of individual men, then it may be that no single man is responsible for any harms that are caused by patriarchy. But if patriarchy is understood as something which is based on common interests, as well as common benefits, extended to all or most men in a particular culture, then it may be that men are collectively responsible for the harms of patriarchy in a way which distributes out to all men, making each man in a particular culture at least partially responsible for the harms attributable to patriarchy. This latter strategy is consistent with our own view of men's responsibility for rape. In the remainder of this essay we will offer support for this conceptualization of the collective responsibility of men for the prevalence of rape.

Our positive assessment, going beyond our criticism of the faulty responses in earlier sections of our paper, is that men in western culture are collectively responsible in the distributive sense, that is, they each share responsibility, for the prevalence of rape in that culture. This claim rests on five points. (1) Insofar as most perpetrators of rape are men, then these men are responsible, in most cases, for the rapes they committed. (2) Insofar as some men, by the way they interact with other (especially younger) men, contribute to a climate in our society where rape is made more prevalent, then they are collaborators in the rape culture and for this reason share in responsibility for rapes committed in that culture. (3) Also, insofar as some men are not unlike the rapist, since they would be rapists if they had the opportunity to be placed into a situation where their inhibitions against rape were removed, then these men share responsibility with actual rapists for the harms of rape. (4) In addition, insofar as many other men could have prevented fellow men from raping, but did not act to prevent these actual rapes, then these men also share responsibility along with the rapists. (5) Finally, insofar as some men benefit from the existence of rape in our society, these men also share responsibility along with the rapists.

It seems to us unlikely that many, if any, men in our society fail to fit into one or another of these categories. Hence, we think that it is not unreasonable to say that men in our society are collectively responsible (in the distributive sense) for rape. We expect some male readers to respond as follows:

> I am adamantly opposed to rape, and though when I was younger I might have tolerated rape-conducive comments from friends of mine, I don't now, so I'm not a collaborator in the rape culture. And I would never be a rapist whatever the situation, and I would certainly act to prevent any rape that I could. I'm pretty sure I don't benefit from rape. So how can I be responsible for the prevalence of rape?

In reply we would point out that nearly all men in given western society meet the third and fifth conditions above (concerning similarity and benefit). But women generally fail to meet either of these conditions, or the first. So, the involvement of women in the rape culture is much less than is true for men. In what follows we will concentrate on the benefit issue.

We believe that Lionel Tiger's work illustrates the important source of strength that men derive from the all-male groups they form. There is a strong sense in which men benefit from the all-male groups that they form in our culture. What is distinctly lacking is any sense that men have responsibility for the social conditions, especially the socialization of younger men which diminishes inhibitions toward rape, that are created in those groups. Male bonding is made easier because there is

an "Other" that males can bond "against." And this other is the highly sexualized stereotype of the "female." Here is a benefit for men in these groups but there is a social cost: from the evidence we have examined there is an increased prevalence of rape. Men need to consider this in reviewing their own role in a culture that supports so much rape.

There is another sense in which benefit is related to the issue of responsibility for rape. There is a sense in which many men in our society benefit from the prevalence of rape in ways of which many of us are quite unaware. Consider this example:

> Several years ago, at a social occasion in which male and female professors were present, I asked off-handedly whether people agreed with me that the campus was looking especially pretty at night these days. Many of the men responded positively. But all of the women responded that this was not something that they had even thought about, since they were normally too anxious about being on campus at night, especially given the increase in reported rapes recently.

We men benefitted in that, relative to our female colleagues, we were in an advantageous position *vis-à-vis* travel around campus. And there were surely other comparative benefits that befell us as a result of this advantage concerning travel, such as our ability to gain academically by being able to use the library at any hour we chose.

In a larger sense, men benefit from the prevalence of rape in that many women are made to feel dependent on men for protection against potential rapists. It is hard to overestimate the benefit here for it potentially affects all aspects of one's life. One study found that 87 percent of women in a borough of London felt that they had to take precautions against potential rapists, with a large number reporting that they never went out at night alone (Radford, 1987, p. 33). Whenever one group is made to feel dependent on another group, and this dependency is not reciprocal, then there is a strong comparative benefit to the group that is not in the dependent position. Such a benefit, along with the specific benefits mentioned above, supports the view that men as a group have a stake in perpetuating the rape culture in ways that women do not. And just as the benefit to men distributes throughout the male population in a given society, so the responsibility should distribute as well.

V Conclusions

The feminist slogan "all men are rapists" seems much stronger than the claim "all men contribute to the prevalence of rape." Is the feminist slogan merely hyperbole? It is if what is meant is that each time a rape occurs, every man did it, or that only men are ever responsible for rape. But, as we have seen, each time a rape occurs, there is a sense in which many men could have done it, or made it more likely to have occurred, or benefitted from it. By direct contribution, or by negligence or by similarity of disposition, or by benefitting, most if not all men do share in each rape in a particular society. This is the link between being responsible for the prevalence of rape and being responsible, at least to some extent, for the harms of each rape.

The purpose of these arguments has been to make men aware of the various ways that they are implicated in the rape culture in general as well as in particular rapes. And while we believe that men should feel some shame for their group's complicity in the prevalence of rape, our aim is not to shame men but rather to stimulate men to take responsibility for changing the socialization of boys and men. How much should any particular man do? Answering this question would require another paper, although participating in the Canadian White Ribbon Campaign, or in anti-sexism education programs, would be a good first step. Suffice it to say that the status quo, namely doing nothing, individually or as a group, is not satisfactory, and will merely further compound our collective and shared responsibility for the harms caused by our fellow male members who engage in rape.

References

Griffin, Susan (1971) "Rape: The All-American Crime." *Ramparts*, September: 26–35. Reprinted in *Women and Values: Readings in Feminist Philosophy*, ed. Marilyn Pearsall. (Belmont, CA: Wadsworth, 1986), pp. 176–88.

Keen, Sam (1991) *Fire in the Belly*. New York: Bantam Books.

Lepowsky, Maria (1990) "Gender in an Egalitarian Society." In *Beyond the Second Sex*, ed. Peggy Reeves Sanday and Ruth Gallagher Goodenough. Philadelphia: University of Pennsylvania Press.

Lipsyte, Robert (1993) "An Ethics Trial: Must Boys Always be Boys," *New York Times*, March 12: B-11.

May, Larry (1987) *The Morality of Groups*. Notre Dame, IN: University of Notre Dame Press.

—— (1992) *Sharing Responsibility*. Chicago: University of Chicago Press.

Oates, Joyce Carol (1992) "Rape and the Boxing Ring," *Newsweek*, February 24: 60–1.

Radford, Jill (1987) "Policing Male Violence, Policing Women." In *Women, Violence and Social Control*, ed. Jalna Hanmer and Mary Maynard. Atlantic Highlands, NJ: Humanities Press.

St Louis Post Dispatch, March 22, 1992: 20A.

Sanday, Peggy Reeves (1986) "Rape and the Silencing of the Feminine." In *Rape: An Historical and Social Enquiry*, ed. Sylvana Tomaselli and Roy Porter. Oxford: Blackwell.

—— (1990) "Androcentric and Matrifocal Gender Representation in Minangkabau Ideology." In *Beyond the Second Sex*, ed. Peggy Reeves Sanday and Ruth Gallagher Goodenough. Philadelphia: University of Pennsylvania Press.

Scully, Diana (1990) *Understanding Sexual Violence*. Boston: Unwin Hyman.

Thornhill, Randy and Nancy Wilmsen Thornhill (1992) "The Evolutionary Psychology of Men's Coercive Sexuality," *Behavioral and Brain Sciences*, vol. 15: 363–75.

Tiger, Lionel [1969] (1984) *Men in Groups*. New York: Marion Boyars Publishers.

Affirmative Action

Affirmative action – the practice of giving special consideration to minorities and women in hiring and school placement – once enjoyed widespread support in the United States. Now many people think the practice, even if it were once justified, no longer serves a useful purpose. In fact, many people see affirmative action of any form as a positive evil that we must purge from public life. Many states in the United States have passed laws or even constitutional amendments forbidding affirmative action by governmental agencies.

Louis Pojman clearly articulates the most common objections to the practice. He argues that (1) it is simply a form of reverse discrimination, which is (2) unfair to more qualified white males who are passed over because of their sex or race. He also avers that (3) these programs disadvantage males and whites who are not themselves responsible for the harm historically done to women and blacks. Finally, he claims that (4) these programs encourage mediocrity among minorities and women.

The case against affirmative action thus rests on two theoretical moral claims. The first denies that groups have any (or at least any significant) moral status. On this view individuals

are responsible only for acts that they, as specific individuals, do, and, as a corollary, that we should compensate individuals only for wrongs they specifically suffered. The second asserts that a society should distribute its goods according to merit. That is, we should always give jobs and school positions to the persons with the best qualifications.

Dworkin explicitly disavows both principles. Group membership – in this case race or gender – can have moral significance. If some individuals have been mistreated because of their membership in a group, then we must now compensate them because they are members of that group. However, as we have seen, there is considerable disagreement about the moral status of groups. Arthur (FREE SPEECH) explicitly rejects the idea that groups have moral status or significance, while May and Strikwerda (SEXUAL AND RACIAL DISCRIMINATION) argue that members of groups are collectively responsible for what other members of their group do.

Dworkin likewise rejects the second linchpin of Pojman's argument: Pojman implies that employers should hire (and school officials should admit) the best-qualified candidates. Dworkin disagrees. He argues that no one has a right to be judged *solely* on their merits – at least not in any sense that would support Bakke's case. The problem is that there is no such thing as merit per se. Having high grades in college chemistry does not automatically mean that I am the most qualified prospective medical student; certainly it does not mean that I would be a better doctor than some student with less stellar grades. Consequently, it does not justify the claim that I deserve a seat in medical school. Rather, an individual "deserves" the seat if school officials reasonably decide that she could be the best doctor they think we need. For instance, if, in the school officials' best judgment, we need to increase the number of black and female physicians (because blacks and women are more likely to seek medical care from someone of the same race and sex), then race and sex would be qualifications for seats in medical school, and blacks or females would be, in these circumstances, better qualified.

Although Harris and Narayan challenge Pojman's conclusions, they reject Dworkin's arguments as well. That is, even though they think affirmative action is justified, they think Dworkin's arguments for that conclusion are seriously flawed, indeed, positively dangerous. Calling affirmative action "preferential treatment" suggests that we give blacks and women some benefit withheld from whites and males. However, they argue, affirmative action does not involve preference of any kind. Rather, it is a program to promote equality of opportunity for people who have been, and continue to be, victims of systematic discrimination.

Discrimination is not merely a relic of past civilizations. Blacks and women continue to suffer the effects of previous discrimination. Moreover, Harris and Narayan argue, blacks and women continue to be effectively excluded from many jobs, simply because of their race or gender. Therefore, the purpose of affirmative action is not to discriminate against whites and men, nor is it to bestow benefits on blacks and women. Rather, its aim is to level the playing field, to provide genuine equality of opportunity.

Of course, not everyone agrees that equality is desirable. Still less do people agree about what we must do to guarantee "equality of opportunity." Clearly, though, this is a significant theoretical concern that weaves through many practical issues discussed in this volume. It underlines every essay in the section on SEXUAL AND RACIAL DISCRIMINATION – after all, discrimination is, by definition, an unjust denial of equal treatment. Equality likewise plays a pivotal role in determining what is an equal PUNISHMENT for an equal crime. Are all murders equal? Should we punish them equally? Or are some murders (say, the torture and killing of a young child) sufficiently different from others (a fight between two drunks) that we should punish the first more severely?

Questions about equality were also central in the discussion about ANIMALS. Humans and non-human animals are indisputably different. The question, though, is: Are they different in *relevant* ways, in ways that justify their being treated differently (THEORIZING ABOUT ETHICS)? Finally, we will see the issue discussed in the later sections on ECONOMIC JUSTICE and WORLD HUNGER. Does equality require that we financially help those in need, whether they be residents of our country or foreigners?

If we are to think carefully about affirmative action, we must also attend to the ways in which institutional structures constrain our choices and shape our moral understanding. Defenders of affirmative action claim that discrimination is not simply, or even primarily, a result of conscious choice. Most racists and sexists do not consciously advocate discrimination. Many of them would vehemently deny they are racists or sexists. Therefore, most discrimination toward, and mistreatment of, minorities and women is probably best explained as the result of well-entrenched institutional structures. These structures have a life of their own: they undermine the opportunities of blacks and women even when no one actively tries to discriminate against them. Perhaps that explains why white males passed over by such programs feel wronged by this system: since they have not intentionally discriminated against minorities or women, they don't feel responsible for their plight. The role of the centrality of institutions plays an important role in Pogge's discussion in WORLD HUNGER.

Further Reading

Cohen, M., Nagel, T., and Scanlon, T. (eds.) (1977) *Equality and Preferential Treatment*. Princeton, NJ: Princeton University Press.

Eastland, T. (1996) *Ending Affirmative Action: The Case for Colorblind Justice*. New York: Basic Books.

Feinberg, W. (1998) *On Higher Ground: Education and the Case for Affirmative Action*. New York: Teachers College Press.

Glazer, N. (1978) *Affirmative Discrimination: Ethnic Inequality and Public Policy*. New York: Basic Books.

Goldman, A. (1979) *Justice and Reverse Discrimination*. Princeton, NJ: Princeton University Press.

Wasserstrom, R. (1977) "Racism, Sexism, and Preferential Treatment: An Approach to the Topic," *UCLA Law Review* 24 (3): 581–622.

44

The Case Against Affirmative Action

Louis P. Pojman

Each person possesses an inviolability founded on justice that even the welfare of society cannot override.

John Rawls, A Theory of Justice

On June 23, 2003 in two 5–4 decisions involving admissions policies at the University of Michigan, the US Supreme Court decided on the constitutionality of Affirmative Action programs. In one of the cases, *Grutter v. Bollinger*, it ruled that some forms of reverse discrimination are constitutional. This settled the legal issue for the moment, but it did not settle the moral issue, which is what I will address in this essay.

Hardly a week goes by but that the subject of Affirmative Action (AA) does not come up. Whether in the form of preferential hiring, non-traditional casting, quotas, "goals and time tables," minority scholarships, race norming, reverse discrimination, or employment of members of underutilized groups, the issue confronts us as a terribly perplexing problem. Affirmative action was one of the issues that divided the Democratic and Republican parties during the 1996 election, the Democrats supporting it ("Mend it, don't end it") and many of the Republicans opposing it ("affirmative action

is reverse racism"). During the general election of November 7, 1996, California voters by a 55 percent to 45 percent vote approved Proposition 209 (called the "California Civil Rights Initiative"), which made it illegal to discriminate on the basis of race or gender, hence ending Affirmative Action in public institutions in California. The Supreme Court subsequently refused to rule on the appeal, thus leaving it to the individual states to decide how they would deal with this issue. Both sides have reorganized for a renewed battle. During the 2000 presidential election campaigns both the Democrats and the Republican Party leaders endorsed AA, though Vice President Gore claimed that if Governor Bush were elected, he would abolish AA and reduce African-Americans to 3/5ths of a citizen.[1] Meanwhile the University of Michigan was sued by white students for unjust discrimination at the undergraduate college and the Law School. As already noted, in June 2003 the Supreme Court ruled that the Law School's policy of using race as one factor in admissions was permissible, but the undergraduate program was not permissible because it gave race too much weight. The debate has now taken on international dimensions, being fought over in Brazil, India, Malaysia, and the European Union.[2]

Let us agree that despite the evidence of a booming economy, the poor are suffering grievously, with children being born into desperate material and psychological poverty, for whom the ideal of "equal opportunity for all" is a cruel joke. Many feel that the federal government has abandoned its guarantee to provide the minimum necessities for each American, so that the pace of this tragedy seems to be worsening daily. Add to this, the fact that in our country African-Americans have a legacy of slavery and unjust discrimination to contend with, and we have the makings of an inferno and, perhaps, in the worst-case scenario, the downfall of a nation. What is the answer to our national problem? Is it increased welfare? more job training? more support for education? required licensing of parents to have children? negative income tax? more support for families or for mothers with small children? All of these have merit and should be part of the national debate. However, my thesis is: however tragic the situation may be (and we may disagree on just how tragic it is), one policy is *not* a legitimate part of the solution and that is, *unjust reverse discrimination* against young white males or any other group of people (e.g., white women, Asians, Jews, or Mormons). Strong Affirmative Action, which implicitly advocates reverse discrimination, while no doubt well intentioned, is morally heinous, asserting, by implication, that *two wrongs make a right*.

The *Two Wrongs Make a Right* thesis goes like this: Because *some* whites once enslaved some blacks, the descendants of those slaves, some of whom may now enjoy high incomes and social status, have a right to opportunities and offices over better qualified whites who had nothing to do with either slavery or the oppression of blacks, and who in some cases may even have suffered hardship comparable to that of poor blacks. In addition, Strong Affirmative Action creates a new Hierarchy of the Oppressed: blacks get primary preferential treatment, women second, native Americans third, Hispanics fourth, and handicapped fifth, and so on until white and sometimes, Asian, males, no matter how needy or well qualified, must accept the leftovers. Naturally, combinations of oppressed classes (e.g., a one-eyed, black Hispanic female) trump all single classifications. The equal protection clause of the Fourteenth Amendment becomes reinterpreted as, "Equal protection for all equals, but some equals are more equal than others."

Before analyzing arguments concerning Affirmative Action, I must define my terms.

By *Weak Affirmative Action* I mean policies that will increase the opportunities of disadvantaged people to attain social goods and offices. It includes the dismantling of segregated institutions, widespread advertisement to groups not previously represented in certain privileged positions, special scholarships for the disadvantaged classes (e.g., the poor, regardless of race or gender), and even using diversity or underrepresentation of groups or history of past discrimination as a tiebreaker when candidates for these goods and offices are relatively equal. The goal of *Weak Affirmative Action* is *equal opportunity* to compete, not *equal results*. We seek to provide each citizen regardless of race or gender a fair chance to the most favored positions in society. There is no more moral requirement to guarantee that 12 percent of professors at American universities are black than to guarantee that 85 percent of the players in the National Basketball Association are white.

By *Strong Affirmative Action* I mean preferential treatment on the basis of race, ethnicity, or gender (or some other morally irrelevant criterion), discriminating in favor of underrepresented groups against overrepresented groups, aiming at roughly equal results. *Strong Affirmative Action* is reverse discrimination. It says it is right to do wrong to correct a wrong. It is the policy that is currently being promoted under the name of *Affirmative Action*, so I will use that term or "AA" for short throughout this essay to stand for this version of Affirmative Action. I will not argue for or against the principle of *Weak Affirmative Action*. Indeed, I think it has considerable moral weight. *Strong Affirmative Action* has none, or so I will argue. But it is this type of AA that is the dominant form in college admissions and university hiring, the two areas with which I am most familiar.

In what follows I will mainly concentrate on Affirmative Action policies with regard to race, but the arguments can be extended to cover ethnicity and gender. I think that if a case for Affirmative Action can be made it will be as a corrective to racial oppression. I will examine seven arguments regarding Affirmative Action. The first four will be *negative*, attempting to show that the best arguments for Affirmative Action fail. The last three will be *positive* arguments for policies opposing Affirmative Action. My treatment will necessarily be brief, setting forth the central features of the arguments and challenging those who disagree to show where my arguments are unsound.

I Arguments for Affirmative Action

1 The need for role models

This argument is straightforward. We all have need of role models, and it helps to know that others like us can be successful. We learn and are encouraged to strive for excellence by emulating our heroes and "our kind of people" who have succeeded.

In the first place it's not clear that role models of one's own racial or sexual type are necessary (let alone sufficient) for success. One of my heroes was Gandhi, an Indian Hindu, another was my grade school science teacher, Miss DeVoe, and another Martin Luther King Jr., behind whom I marched in Civil Rights demonstrations. More important than having role models of one's "own type" is having genuinely good people, of whatever race or gender, to emulate. Our common humanity should be a sufficient basis for us to see the possibility of success in people of virtue and merit. To yield to the demand, however tempting it may be to do so, for "role-models-just-like-us" is to treat people like means not ends. It is a policy of disrespect for the individual as a person. It elevates morally irrelevant particularity over relevant traits, such as ability and integrity. We don't need people exactly like us to find inspiration. As Steve Allen once quipped, "If I had to follow a role model exactly, I would have become a nun." If we are to achieve the

reality of a color-blind society, we need to find heroes and role models in people who have the requisite virtues, regardless of race, ethnicity, or gender.

Furthermore, even if it is of some help to people with low self-esteem to gain encouragement from seeing others of their particular kind in successful positions, it is doubtful whether this need is a sufficient reason to justify preferential hiring or reverse discrimination. What good is a role model who is inferior to other professors or physicians or business personnel? The best way to create role models is not to promote people because of race or gender but because they are the best qualified for the job. It is the violation of this fact that is largely responsible for the widespread whisper in the medical field (at least in New York), "Never go to a black physician under 40" (referring to the fact that AA has affected the medical system during the past 20 years). Fight the feeling however hard I try, I cannot help wondering on seeing a black or woman in a position or honor, "Is she in this position because she merits it or because of Affirmative Action?" Where Affirmative Action is the policy, the "figment of pigment" creates a stigma of undeservedness, whether or not it is deserved.

Finally, entertain this thought experiment. Suppose we discovered that tall handsome white males somehow made the best role models for the most people, especially poor people. Suppose even large numbers of minority people somehow found inspiration in their sight. Would we be justified in hiring tall handsome white males over better-qualified short Hispanic women?

2 The compensation argument

The argument goes like this: blacks have been wronged and severely harmed by whites. Therefore white society should compensate blacks for the injury caused them. Reverse discrimination in terms of preferential hiring, contracts, and scholarships is a fitting way to compensate for the past wrongs.[3]

This argument actually involves a distorted notion of compensation. Normally, we think of compensation as owed by a specific person A to another person B whom A has wronged in a specific way C. For example, if I have stolen your car and used it for a period of time to make business profits that would have gone to you, it is not enough that I return your car. I must pay you an amount reflecting your loss and my ability to pay. If I have only made $5,000 and only have $10,000 in assets, it would not be possible for you to collect $20,000 in damages – even though that is the amount of loss you have incurred.

Sometimes compensation is extended to groups of people who have been unjustly harmed by the greater society. For example, the United States government has compensated the Japanese-Americans who were interred during the Second World War, and the West German government has paid reparations to the survivors of Nazi concentration camps. But here, a specific group of people have been identified who were wronged in an identifiable way by the government of the nation in question. We normally think there should be a statute of limitation. Otherwise, Jews might sue the Egyptians for being held in slavery some 4,000 years ago (see Exodus 1).[4]

On the face of it, demands by blacks for compensation do not fit the usual pattern. Perhaps Southern States with Jim Crow laws could be accused of unjustly harming blacks, but slavery, regrettably, was legal and the United States government was not directly involved in promoting slavery. Much of the harm done to blacks was the result of private discrimination, not state action. So the Germany/US analogy doesn't hold. Furthermore, it is not clear that all blacks were harmed in the same way or whether some were *unjustly* harmed or harmed more than poor whites and others (e.g. short people). Most "blacks" are partially Caucasian or Native American, mulattos or quadroons, so that, if even if we accepted some form of the compensation argument, determining how much compensation each "black" is owed would be a Herculean task. If compensation is to be paid by the descendants of those who participated in slavery, then the present members of the nations of West Africa, whose ancestors sold their

own people into slavery, should bear a large part of the burden. Finally, even if identifiable blacks were harmed by identifiable social practices, it is not clear that most forms of Affirmative Action are appropriate to restore the situation. The usual practice of a financial payment seems more appropriate than giving a high-level job to someone unqualified or only minimally qualified, who, speculatively, might have been better qualified had he not been subject to racial discrimination. If John is the star tailback of our college team with a promising professional future, and I accidentally (but culpably) drive my pick-up truck over his legs, and so cripple him, John may be due compensation, but he is not due the tailback spot on the football team.

Still, there may be something intuitively compelling about compensating members of an oppressed group who are minimally qualified. Suppose that the Hatfields and the McCoys are enemy clans and some youths from the Hatfields go over and steal diamonds and gold from the McCoys, distributing it within the Hatfield economy. Even though we do not know which Hatfield youths did the stealing, we would want to restore the wealth, as far as possible, to the McCoys. One way might be to tax the Hatfields, but another might be to give preferential treatment in terms of scholarships and training programs and hiring to the McCoys.

This is perhaps the strongest argument for Affirmative Action, and it may well justify some weaker versions, but it is doubtful whether the *Compensation Argument* is sufficient to justify strong versions with quotas and "goals and timetables" (really a euphemism for *quotas*) in skilled positions or even preferential treatment in admission to universities and law schools. There are at least two reasons for this. First, we have no way of knowing how many people of any given group would have achieved some given level of competence had the world been different. Secondly, the normal criterion of merit is a strong *prima facie* consideration when the most important positions are at stake. There are three reasons for this: (1) treating people according to their merits respects them as persons, as ends in themselves, rather than as means to social ends. In the words of John Rawls, "Each person possesses an inviolability founded on justice that even the welfare of society cannot override."[5] If we believe that individuals possess a dignity which deserves to be respected, then we ought to treat that individual on the basis of his or her merits, not as a mere instrument for social policy. (2) Society has given people expectations that if they attain certain levels of excellence they will be awarded appropriately; and (3) filling the most important positions with the best qualified is the best way to insure efficiency in job-related areas and in society in general. These reasons are not absolutes. They can be overridden.[6] But there is a strong presumption in their favor so that a burden of proof rests with those who would override them.

Further, we do know who the Hatfields were: Southern slave owners and the West African tribal leaders who sold their neighbors into slavery, not the United States government or all the people of the United States. The freed slaves may have had a case against the slave owners, but none against the government. A civil war was fought to free the slaves, in which 6,000,000 soldiers lost their lives. For that sacrifice all Americans, black and white, must be grateful.

At this point we get into the problem of whether innocent non-blacks should have to pay a penalty in terms of preferential hiring of blacks. We turn to that argument.

3 The argument for compensation from those who innocently benefited from past injustice

Young white males as innocent beneficiaries of unjust discrimination against blacks and women have no grounds for complaint when society seeks to level the tilted field. They may be innocent of oppressing blacks, other minorities, and women, but they have unjustly benefited from that oppression or discrimination. So it is perfectly proper that less qualified women and blacks be hired before them.

The operative principle is: He who knowingly and willingly benefits from a wrong must help pay for the wrong. Judith Jarvis Thomson puts it this way. "Many [white males] have been direct beneficiaries of policies which have downgraded blacks and women . . . and even those who did not directly benefit . . . had, at any rate, the advantage in the competition which comes of the confidence in one's full membership [in the community], and of one's right being recognized as a matter of course."[7] That is, white males obtain advantages in self-respect and self-confidence deriving from a racist/sexist system which denies these to blacks and women.

Here is my response to this argument. As I noted in the previous section, compensation is normally individual and specific. If A harms B regarding x, B has a right to compensation from A in regards to x. If A steals B's car and wrecks it, A has an obligation to compensate B for the stolen car, but A's son has no obligation to compensate B. Furthermore, if A dies or disappears, B has no moral right to claim that society compensate him for the stolen car – though if he has insurance, he can make such a claim to the insurance company. Sometimes a wrong cannot be compensated, and we just have to make the best of an imperfect world.

Suppose my parents, divining that I would grow up to have an unsurpassable desire to be a basketball player, bought an expensive growth hormone for me. Unfortunately, a neighbor stole it and gave it to little Michael, who gained the extra 13 inches – my 13 inches – and shot up to an enviable 6 feet 6 inches. Michael, better known as Michael Jordan, would have been a runt like me but for his luck. As it is, he profited from the injustice and excelled in basketball, as I would have done had I had my proper dose.

Do I have a right to the millions of dollars that Jordan made as a professional basketball player – the unjustly innocent beneficiary of my growth hormone? I have a right to something from the neighbor who stole the hormone, and it might be kind of Jordan to give me free tickets to the Bull's basketball games, and perhaps I should be remembered in his will. As far as I can see, however, he does not *owe* me anything, either legally or morally.

Suppose further that Michael Jordan and I are in high school together and we are both qualified to play basketball, only he is far better than I. Do I deserve to start in his position because I would have been as good as he is had someone not cheated me as a child? Again, I think not. But if being the lucky beneficiary of wrongdoing does not entail that Jordan (or the coach) owes me anything in regards to basketball, why should it be a reason to engage in preferential hiring in academic admissions or highly coveted jobs? If minimal qualifications are not adequate to override excellence in basketball, even when the minimality is a consequence of wrongdoing, why should they be adequate in other areas?

4   The diversity argument

The argument put forth by the administrators of the University of Michigan in its defense of its AA policy was based on the need for diversity. It argued that racial diversity was beneficial in promoting the educational process.

It is important that we learn to live in a pluralistic world, learning to get along with those of other races and cultures, so we should have fully integrated schools and employment situations. We live in a shrinking global village and need to appreciate each other's culture and specific way of looking at life. Diversity is an important symbol and educative device. As Barbara Bergmann argues, "Diversity has positive value in many situations, but in some its value is crucial. To give an obvious example, a racially diverse community needs a racially diverse police force if the police are to gain the trust of all parts of the community and if one part of the community is not to feel dominated by the other part."[8] Thus preferential treatment is warranted to perform this role in society.

Once again, there is some truth in these concerns. Diversity of ideas challenges us to scrutinize our own values and beliefs, and diverse customs have aesthetic and moral value, helping us to appreciate the novelty and beauty in life. Diversity may expand our moral horizons. But, again, while we can admit the value of diversity, it hardly seems adequate to override the moral requirement to treat each person with equal respect. *Diversity for diversity's sake is moral*

promiscuity, since it obfuscates rational distinctions, undermines the moral principle of treating individuals as ends, treating them, instead, as mere means (to the goals of social engineering), and, furthermore, unless those hired are highly qualified, the diversity factor threatens to become a fetish. Each person is a unique individual, different from every other. Perhaps it is a sad commentary of our shallow conformist society, that we are turning out look-alike, act-alike, Barbie dolls, instead of eccentric gems who cannot be put into a mold, but stand out, offering their own unique contribution. It's not diversity of race or gender that is important but diversity of ideas, of perspective and personality. At the same time we want a uniformity in some areas. We want a highly unified commitment to the moral point of view, to tolerance of individual difference, and to the goals of a democratic society. The motto of the Unitarian Church is, "We don't have to think alike to love alike." That seems a worthy motto for a culturally diverse society, where difference is accepted, but depends on considerable cooperation.

There may be times when diversity may seem to be "crucial" to the well-being of a diverse community, such as a diverse police force. Suppose that white policemen overreact to young black males and the latter group then come to distrust white policemen. Hiring more "less qualified" (by formal standards) black policemen, who would relate better to these youth, may have overall utilitarian value. If the black policeman, though lacking certain formal skills of the white policeman, really is able to do a better job in the black community, this might constitute a case of merit, not Affirmative Action. This is similar to the legitimacy of hiring Chinese men to act as undercover agents in Chinatown. Indeed, this would only involve revising our criteria for job performance, not a radical move of reverse discrimination. Our ultimate goal is to hire the best police, that is, those who can perform in a disciplined, intelligent manner, regardless of their race. A white policeman must be able to arrest a black burglar, even as a black policeman must be able to arrest a white rapist. The quality of the policeman or - woman, not their race or gender, is what counts.

So much for a critique of the major arguments for Affirmative Action. I now turn to three positive arguments for why AA is wrong.

II Arguments against Affirmative Action

5 Affirmative action requires discrimination against a different group

Weak Affirmative Action weakly discriminates against new minorities, mostly innocent young white males, and Strong Affirmative Action strongly discriminates against these new minorities. As I argued in I. 4, this discrimination is unwarranted, since, even if some compensation to blacks were indicated, it would be unfair to make innocent young white males bear the whole brunt of the payments. Albert Mosley has asserted that my arguments against AA are straw men, because the Strong AA I'm arguing against almost never happens and isn't really defended.[9] Recently I had this experience. I knew a brilliant philosopher, with outstanding publications in first-level journals, who was having difficulty getting a tenure-track position. For the first time in my life I offered to make a phone call on his behalf to a university to which he had applied. When I got the Chair of the Search Committee, he offered that the committee was under instructions from the Administration to hire a woman or a black. They had one of each on their short-list, so they weren't even considering the applications of white males. At my urging he retrieved my friend's file, and said, "This fellow looks far superior to the two candidates we're interviewing, but there's nothing I can do about it." Cases like these come to my attention regularly. In fact, it is poor and middle-class white youth who become the new pariahs on the job market. The children of the wealthy have no trouble getting into the best private grammar schools and, on the basis of superior early education, into the best universities, graduate schools, managerial and professional positions. Affirmative Action simply shifts injustice, setting blacks, Hispanics, Native Americans, Asians and women

against young white males, especially ethnic and poor white males. It makes no more sense to discriminate in favor of a rich black or female who had the opportunity of the best family and education available against a poor white, than it does to discriminate in favor of white males against blacks or women. It does little to rectify the goal of providing equal opportunity to all.

Early in my career I was invited for an interview for a position at a prominent state university. Because my references and dossier showed that I had been a Black Studies major, had been the minister of a black church in Bedford-Stuyvesant, and had publications on Civil Rights, the Search Committee assumed that I was black and would serve as their representative black. The consternation on the faces of the Search Committee was most memorable, as they discovered their error. Being only another white philosopher, I didn't get the job, which went to a more qualified white male. I discovered that there were many candidates more qualified than myself, but since they were operating under Affirmative Action guidelines, I was the only candidate they had seriously considered until the Great Awakening. Cases like this regularly come to my attention, leaving resentment in their wake.

At the end of his essay supporting AA, Albert Mosley points out that other groups besides blacks have been benefited by AA, "women, the disabled, the elderly."[10] He's correct in including the elderly, for through powerful lobbies, such as the AARP, they do get special benefits, including Medicare, and may sue on the grounds of being discriminated against due to *Agism*, prejudice against older people. Might this not be a reason to reconsider Affirmative Action? Consider the sheer rough percentages of those who qualify for Affirmative Action programs.

The elderly can bring litigation on the grounds of *Agism*, receive entitlements in terms of Social Security and Medicare, and have the AARP lobbying on their behalf. Recently, it has been proposed that homosexuals be included in oppressed groups deserving Affirmative Action.[11] At Northeastern University in 1996 the faculty governing body voted to

Table 44.1

Group	Percentage %
1 Women	52
2 Blacks	12
3 Hispanics	9
4 Native Americans	2
5 Asians	4
6 Physically disabled	10
7 Welfare recipients	6
8 The elderly	25 (est. adults over 60)
9 Italians (in New York City)	10 (estimate)
Totals	**130**

grant homosexuals Affirmative Action status. How many more percentage points would this add? Several authors have advocated putting all poor people on the list.[12] And if we took handicaps seriously would we not add ugly people, obese people, and, especially, short people, for which there is ample evidence of discrimination? How about left-handed people (about 9 percent of the population) – they can't play shortstop off third base and have to put up with a right-handedly biased world. The only group not the list is that of white males. Are they, especially healthy, middle-class young white males, becoming the new "oppressed class"? Should we add them to our list?

Respect for persons entails that we treat each person as an end in him- or herself, not simply as a means to be used for social purposes. What is wrong about discrimination against blacks is that it fails to treat black people as individuals, judging them instead by their skin color rather than their merit. What is wrong about discrimination against women is that it fails to treat them as individuals, judging them by their gender, not their merit. What is equally wrong about Affirmative Action is that it fails to treat white males with dignity as individuals, judging them by *both their race and gender*, instead of their merit. Affirmative Action, as presently practiced, *is both racist and sexist*.

Along these same lines, note how indignant members of minority groups become at instances of racial profiling. Innocent black males are often stopped and inconvenienced by policemen simply because black males are overrepresented in some classes of crime. We can appreciate their resentment. But how is this different from Affirmative Action, where innocent white young people are discriminated against simply because they're members of a group that is overrepresented in college or high-profile professions?

6 Affirmative action encourages mediocrity and incompetence

A few years ago Jesse Jackson joined protesters at Harvard Law School in demanding that the Law School faculty hire black women. Jackson dismissed Dean of the Law School, Robert C. Clark's standard of choosing the best-qualified person for the job as "cultural anemia." "We cannot just define who is qualified in the most narrow vertical academic terms," he said. "Most people in the world are yellow, brown, black, poor, non-Christian and don't speak English, and they can't wait for some white males with archaic rules to appraise them."[13] It might be noted that if Jackson is correct about the depth of cultural decadence at Harvard, blacks might be well advised to form and support their own more vital law schools and leave places like Harvard to their archaism.

Stories of the deleterious effects of Affirmative Action abound. The philosopher Sidney Hook writes that, "At one Ivy League university, representatives of the Regional HEW demanded an explanation of why there were no women or minority students in the Graduate Department of Religious Studies. They were told that a reading knowledge of Hebrew and Greek was presupposed. Whereupon the representatives of HEW advised orally: 'Then end those old fashioned programs that require irrelevant languages. And start up programs on relevant things which minority group students can study without learning languages.' "[14]

Nicholas Capaldi notes that the staff of HEW itself was one-half women, three-fifths members of minorities, and one-half black – a clear case of racial overrepresentation.

In 1972 officials at Stanford University discovered a proposal for the government to monitor the curriculum in higher education: the

"Summary Statement . . . Sex Discrimination Proposed HEW Regulation to Effectuate Title IX of the Education Amendment of 1972" to "establish and use internal procedure for reviewing curricula, designed both to ensure that they do not reflect discrimination on the basis of sex and to resolve complaints concerning allegations of such discrimination, pursuant to procedural standards to be prescribed by the Director of the office of Civil Rights." Fortunately, Secretary of HEW Caspar Weinberger discovered the intrusion and assured Stanford University that he would never approve of it.[15]

Government programs of enforced preferential treatment tend to appeal to the lowest possible common denominator. Witness the 1974 HEW Revised Order No. 14 on Affirmative Action expectations for preferential hiring: "Neither minorities nor female employees should be required to possess higher qualifications than those of the lowest qualified incumbents." Furthermore, no test may be given to candidates unless it is *proved* to be relevant to the job.

> No standard or criteria which have, by intent or effect, worked to exclude women or minorities as a class can be utilized, unless the institution can demonstrate the necessity of such standard to the performance of the job in question.
>
> Whenever a validity study is called for . . . the user should include . . . an investigation of suitable alternative selection procedures and suitable alternative methods of using the selection procedure which have as little adverse impact as possible . . . Whenever the user is shown an alternative selection procedure with evidence of less adverse impact and substantial evidence of validity for the same job in similar circumstances, the user should investigate it to determine the appropriateness of using or validating it in accord with these guidelines.[16]

But if we are going this far in allowing for mediocrity, why not race-norm in grading and SAT scores, and other standardized tests? We could make a grade of 80 a B− for a white or Asian, but a B+ for an Hispanic and an A for a black. This seems in line with the logic of Affirmative Action, and it is what is happening at our universities. Black scores are, in the name of diversity, given more weight than equivalent white scores. But the process must continue through grading and passing standardized tests through the whole of the university experience. A black student admitted at my college on the basis of AA recently failed a necessary condition for graduation, his Writing Exam. In fact he was allowed to retake the exam eight times (whites and other students are only allowed to retake the exam four times). He failed each time, but an exception was made for him, and he was allowed to graduate anyway. This is not an isolated incident. Mediocrity takes on a life of its own.

And it can backfire even on its most ardent proponents. It is remarkable that none of the media has noticed that Vice President Al Gore, an advocate of AA, if there ever was one, essentially had his chances for the presidency in December of 2000 crushed by a Supreme Court Justice, Clarence Thomas, who was undoubtedly an Affirmative Action appointee. Poetic Justice!

At the same time, Americans are wondering why standards in our country are falling and the Japanese and Koreans are getting ahead. Affirmative Action with its twin idols, Sufficiency and Diversity, is the enemy of excellence. I will develop this thought in the next section.

7 An argument from the principle of merit

Traditionally, we have believed that the highest positions in society should be awarded to those who are best qualified. The Koran states that, "A ruler who appoints any man to an office, when there is in his dominion another man better qualified for it, sins against God and against the State." Rewarding excellence both seems just to the individuals in the competition and makes for efficiency. Note that one of the most successful acts of racial integration, the Brooklyn Dodgers' recruitment of Jackie Robinson in the late 1940s, was done in just this way, according to merit. If Robinson had been brought into the major league as a mediocre player or had batted .200 he would have been scorned and sent back to the minors where he belonged.

As I mentioned earlier, merit is not an absolute value, but there is are strong *prima facie* reasons for awarding positions on its basis, and it should enjoy a weighty presumption in our social practices.

In a celebrated article, Ronald Dworkin says that "Bakke had no case," because society did not owe Bakke anything. That may be, but then why does it owe anyone anything? Dworkin puts the matter in Utility terms, but if that is the case, society may owe Bakke a place at the University of California/Davis, for it seems a reasonable rule-utilitarian principle that achievement should be rewarded in society. We generally want the best to have the best positions, the best-qualified candidate to win the political office, the most brilliant and competent scientist to be chosen for the most challenging research project, the best-qualified pilots to become commercial pilots, only the best soldiers to become generals. Only when little is at stake do we weaken the standards and content ourselves with sufficiency (rather than excellence) – there are plenty of jobs where "sufficiency" rather than excellence is required. Perhaps we have even come to feel that medicine or law or university professorships are so routine that they can be performed by minimally qualified people – in which case AA has a place.

Note! No one is calling for quotas or proportional representation of *underutilized* groups in the National Basketball Association, where blacks make up 80 percent of the players. But, surely, if merit and merit alone reigns in sports, should it not be valued at least as much in education and industry?

The case for meritocracy has two pillars. One pillar is a deontological argument, which holds that we ought to treat people as ends and not merely means. By giving people what they deserve as *individuals*, rather than as members of *groups*, we show respect for their inherent worth. If you and I take a test, and you get 95 percent of the answers correct and I only get 50 percent correct, it would be unfair to you to give both of us the same grade, say an A, and even more unfair to give me a higher grade, A+, than your B+. Although I have heard cases where teachers have been instructed to "race norm" in grading (giving blacks and Hispanics higher grades for the same numerical

scores), most proponents of AA stop short of advocating such a practice. But, I would ask them, what's really the difference between taking the overall average of a white and a black and "race norming" it? If teachers shouldn't do it, why should administrators?

The second pillar for meritocracy is utilitarian. In the end, we will be better off by honoring excellence. We want the best leaders, teachers, policemen, physicians, generals, lawyers, and airplane pilots that we can possibly produce in society. So our program should be to promote equal opportunity, as much as is feasible in a free market economy, and reward people according to their individual merit.

Conclusion

Let me sum up my discussion. The goal of the Civil Rights movement and of moral people everywhere has been justice for all, including equal opportunity. The question is: how best to get there? Civil Rights legislation removed the legal barriers, opening the way towards equal opportunity, but it did not tackle the deeper causes that produce differential results. Weak Affirmative Action aims at encouraging minorities in striving for the highest positions without unduly jeopardizing the rights of majorities. The problem of Weak AA is that it easily slides into Strong AA, where quotas, "goals and timetables," "equal results," – in a word – reverse discrimination prevails and is forced onto groups, thus promoting mediocrity, inefficiency, and resentment. Furthermore, Affirmative Action aims at the higher levels of society – universities and skilled jobs – but if we want to improve our society, the best way to do it is to concentrate on families, children, early education, and the like, so all are prepared to avail themselves of opportunity. Affirmative Action, on the one hand, is too much, too soon and on the other hand, too little, too late.

I have not had space to consider all the objections to my position or discuss the issue of freedom of association, which, I think, should be given much scope in private but not in public institutions. Barbara Bergmann[17] and others argue that we already allow preferential treatment for athletes and veterans, especially in university admissions, so, being consistent, we should provide it for women and minorities. My response is that I am against giving athletic scholarships; I regard scholarships to veterans as a part of a contractual relationship, a reward for service to one's country. But I distinguish entrance programs from actual employment. I don't think that veterans should be afforded special privilege in hiring practices, unless it be as a tiebreaker.

I should also mention that my arguments from merit and respect apply more specifically to public institutions than private ones, where issues of property rights and freedom of association carry more weight. If a university unfairly discriminated against blacks or women, it would soon find its federal funds withdrawn. But it can discriminate against better-qualified whites and Asians and enjoy full support. It doe not seem fair or, I have argued, morally justifiable.

In addition to the arguments I have offered, Affirmative Action, rather than uniting people of good will in the common cause of justice, tends to balkanize us into segregation-thinking. Professor Derrick Bell of Harvard Law School recently said that Clarence Thomas, the African-American Supreme Court Judge, who opposes Affirmative Action, "doesn't think black."[18] Does Bell really claim that there is a standard and proper "black" (and presumably a white) way of thinking? Ideologues like Bell, whether radical blacks like himself, or Nazis who advocate "think Aryan," both represent the same thing: cynicism about rational debate, the very antithesis of the quest for impartial truth and justice. People who believe in reason to resolve our differences will oppose this kind of balkanization of the races.

Finally, ask yourself, in general, have individuals of any group ever succeeded in the long run by being given special privilege? Hasn't the American way (indeed the way of every successful culture) been equal opportunity, keeping the standards high and encouraging individuals to work hard, to take responsibility for their actions, and eventually reaching such a high level of excellence that we can't help admiring them? It could be argued, as Thomas Sowell does, that AA has actually hindered many blacks in their quest towards success.

Martin Luther said that humanity is like a man mounting a horse who always tends to fall off on the other side of the horse. This seems to be the case with Affirmative Action. Attempting to redress the discriminatory inequities of our history, our well-intentioned social engineers now engage in new forms of discriminatory inequity and thereby think that they have successfully mounted the horse of racial harmony. They have only fallen off on the other side.

Notes

An earlier version of this essay appeared in the *International Journal of Applied Philosophy* 12 (1998). I am indebted to Mary Gilbertson, Stephen Kershnar, James Kellenberger, Michael Levin, Wallace Matson, Bill Shaw, Max Hocutt, Elliot Cohen, and Bill Shaw for comments on earlier versions of this paper.

1   See Andrew Sullivan on Gore's "Race Card," *The New Republic* December 18, 2000. Both George W. Bush and Albert Gore have spoken in favor of Affirmative Action. Gore's Vice President choice, Joel Lieberman, had strongly opposed Affirmative Action as reverse discrimination in the Senate. Here is an excerpt of his speech made on the Senate floor in 1995:

Affirmative Action is dividing us in ways its creators could never have intended because most Americans who do support equal opportunity and are not biased don't think it is fair to discriminate against some Americans as a way to make up for historic discrimination against other Americans. For after all, if you discriminate in favor of one group on the basis of race, you thereby discriminate against another group on the basis of race.
(Quoted in the *New York Times*, August 8, 2000)

However, during the Democratic Convention in August 2000, upon meeting with Jesse Jackson, Maxine Waters, and the Black Caucus, he did an about-face and maintained that he had always supported Affirmative Action. Since then, he has been politically correct. By the time the 2004 primary campaign had started Lieberman had become a true believer, proclaiming his longstanding support for Affirmative Action.

2 See the report in *The Chronicle of Higher Education* (February 13, 2004).

3 For a good discussion of this argument see Boxill, "The Morality of Reparation" in *Social Theory and Practice* 2:1 (1972) and Mosley, *op. cit.*, pp. 23–7.

4 Note, in this regard, that although Yahweh set about freeing the people of Israel because of His covenant relationship, slavery itself is never condemned in the Bible. Although our moral conscience has developed to see slavery as an evil, and regret that it was ever used, economic conditions might have made it more excusable in ages past. Note that even Aristotle accepted it as permissible (*Politics* 2).

5 John Rawls, *A Theory of Justice* (Cambridge, MA: Harvard University Press, 1971), p. 3.

6 Merit sometimes may be justifiably overridden by need, as when parents choose to spend extra earnings on special education for their disabled child rather than for their gifted child. Sometimes we may override merit for utilitarian purposes. For example, suppose you are the best shortstop on a baseball team but are also the best catcher. You'd rather play shortstop, but the manager decides to put you at catcher because, while your friend can do an adequate job at short, no one else is adequate at catcher. It's permissible for you to be assigned the job of catcher. Probably, some expression of appreciation would be due you.

7 Judith Jarvis Thomson, "Preferential Hiring," in Marshall Cohen, Thomas Nagel, and Thomas Scanlon (eds.), *Equality and Preferential Treatment* (Princeton, NJ: Princeton University Press, 1977).

8 Barbara Bergmann, *In Defense of Affirmative Action* (New York: Basic Books, 1996), pp. 9–10.

9 Albert Mosley, "Pojman's Strawman Arguments Against Affirmative Action," *International Journal of Applied Philosophy* 12.2 (1998). See my response in that same issue. *The Center for Equal Opportunity* has documented that many state and private universities use race-norming criteria in admissions, generally admitting blacks with SAT scores 200 or more points lower than whites and Asians.

10 Albert Mosley, "Affirmative Action: Pro," in Albert Mosley and Nicholas Capaldi, *Affirmative Action: Social Justice or Unfair Preference?* (Rowman & Littlefield, 1997), p. 53.

11 J. Sartorelli, "The Nature of Affirmative Action, Anti-Gay Oppression, and the Alleviation of Enduring Harm," *International Journal of Applied Philosophy* 11(2) (1997).

12 For example, Iddo Landau, "Are You Entitled to Affirmative Action?" *International Journal of Applied Philosophy* 11(2) (1997) and Richard Kahlenberg, "Class Not Race," *The New Republic* April 3, 1995.

13 *New York Times*, May 10, 1990.

14 Quoted by Nicholas Capaldi, *Out of Order: Affirmative Action and the Crisis of Doctrinaire Liberalism* (Buffalo, NY: Prometheus, 1985).

15 Ibid., p. 95.

16 Ibid.

17 Ibid., p. 122–5.

18 See L. Gordon Crovitz, "Borking Begins, but Mudballs Bounce Off Judge Thomas," *The Wall Street Journal*, July 17, 1991.

45

The Rights of Allan Bakke

Ronald Dworkin

On October 12, 1977 the Supreme Court heard oral argument in the case of *The Regents of the University of California v. Allan Bakke*. No lawsuit has ever been more widely watched or more thoroughly debated in the national and international press before the Court's decision. Still, some of the most pertinent facts set before the Court have not been clearly summarized.

The medical school of the University of California at Davis has an affirmative action program (called the "task force program") designed to admit more black and other minority students. It sets sixteen places aside for which only members of "educationally and economically disadvantaged minorities" compete. Allan Bakke, white, applied for one of the remaining eighty-four places; he was rejected but, since his test scores were relatively high, the medical school has conceded that it could not prove that he would have been rejected if the sixteen places reserved had been open to him. Bakke sued, arguing that the task force program deprived him of his constitutional rights. The California Supreme Court agreed, and ordered the medical school to admit him. The university appealed to the Supreme Court.

The Davis program for minorities is in certain respects more forthright (some would say cruder) than similar plans now in force in many other American universities and professional schools. Such programs aim to increase the enrollment of black and other minority students by allowing the fact of their race to count affirmatively as part of the case for admitting them. Some schools set a "target" of a particular number of minority places instead of setting aside a flat number of places. But Davis would not fill the number of places set aside unless there were sixteen minority candidates it considered clearly qualified for medical education. The difference is therefore one of administrative strategy and not of principle.

So the constitutional question raised by *Bakke* is of capital importance for higher education in America, and a large number of universities and schools have entered briefs *amicus curiae* urging the Court to reverse the California decision. They believe that if the decision is affirmed then they will no longer be free to use explicit racial criteria in any part of their admissions programs, and that they will therefore be unable to fulfill what they take to be their responsibilities to the nation.

It is often said that affirmative action programs aim to achieve a racially conscious society divided into racial and ethnic groups, each entitled, as a group, to some proportionable share of resources, careers, or opportunities. That is a perverse description. American society is currently a racially conscious society; this is the inevitable and evident consequence of a history of slavery, repression, and prejudice. Black men and women, boys and girls, are not free to choose for themselves in what roles – or as members of which social groups – others will characterize them. They are black, and no other feature of personality or allegiance or ambition will so thoroughly influence how they will be perceived and treated by others, and the range and character of the lives that will be open to them.

The tiny number of black doctors and professionals is both a consequence and a continuing cause of American racial consciousness, one link in a long and self-fueling chain reaction. Affirmative action programs use racially explicit criteria because their immediate goal is to increase the number of members of certain races in these professions. But their long-term goal is to *reduce* the degree to which American society is overall a racially conscious society.

The programs rest on two judgments. The first is a judgment of social theory: that America will continue to be pervaded by racial divisions as long as the most lucrative, satisfying, and important careers remain mainly the prerogative of members of the white race, while others feel themselves systematically excluded from a professional and social elite. The second is a calculation of strategy: that increasing the number of blacks who are at work in the professions will, in the long run, reduce the sense of frustration and injustice and racial self-consciousness in the black community to the point at which blacks may begin to think of themselves as individuals who can succeed like others through talent and initiative. At that future point the consequences of nonracial admissions programs, whatever these consequences might be, could be accepted with no sense of racial barriers or injustice.

It is therefore the worst possible misunderstanding to suppose that affirmative action programs are designed to produce a Balkanized America, divided into racial and ethnic subnations. They use strong measures because weaker ones will fail; but their ultimate goal is to lessen not to increase the importance of race in American social and professional life.

According to the 1970 census, only 2.1 percent of US doctors were black. Affirmative action programs aim to provide more black doctors to serve black patients. This is not because it is desirable that blacks treat blacks and whites treat whites, but because blacks, for no fault of their own, are now unlikely to be well served by whites, and because a failure to provide the doctors they trust will exacerbate rather than reduce the resentment that now leads them to trust only their own. Affirmative action tries to provide more blacks as classmates for white doctors, not because it is desirable that a medical school class reflect the racial makeup of the community as a whole, but because professional association between blacks and whites will decrease the degree to which whites think of blacks as a race rather than as people, and thus the degree to which blacks think of themselves that way. It tries to provide "role models" for future black doctors, not because it is desirable for a black boy or girl to find adult models only among blacks, but because our history has made them so conscious of their race that the success of whites, for now, is likely to mean little or nothing for them.

The history of the campaign against racial injustice since 1954, when the Supreme Court decided *Brown* v. *Board of Education*, is a history in large part of failure. We have not succeeded in reforming the racial consciousness of our society by racially neutral means. We are therefore obliged to look upon the arguments for affirmative action with sympathy and an open mind. Of course, if Bakke is right that such programs, no matter how effective they may be, violate his constitutional rights then they cannot be permitted to continue. But we must not forbid them in the name of some mindless maxim, like the maxim that it cannot be right to fight fire with fire, or that the end cannot justify the means. If the strategic claims for affirmative action are cogent, they cannot be dismissed simply on the ground that racially explicit tests are distasteful. If such tests are distasteful it can only be for reasons that make the underlying social realities the programs attack more distasteful still.

The New Republic, in a recent editorial opposing affirmative action, missed that point. "It is critical to the success of a liberal pluralism," it said, "that group membership itself is not among the permissible criteria of inclusion and exclusion." But group membership is in fact, as a matter of social reality rather than formal admission standards, part of what determines inclusion or exclusion for us now. If we must choose between a society that is in fact liberal and an illiberal society that scrupulously avoids formal racial criteria, we can hardly appeal to the ideals of liberal pluralism to prefer the latter.

Professor Archibald Cox of Harvard Law School, speaking for the University of California in oral argument, told the Supreme Court that this is the choice the United States must make. As things stand, he said, affirmative action programs are the only effective means of increasing the absurdly small number of black doctors. The California Supreme Court, in approving Bakke's claim, had urged the university to pursue that goal by methods that do not explicitly take race into account. But that is unrealistic. We must distinguish, as Cox said, between two interpretations of what the California court's recommendation means. It might mean that the university should aim at the same immediate goal, of increasing the proportion of black and other minority students in the medical school, by an admissions procedure that on the surface is not racially conscious.

That is a recommendation of hypocrisy. If those who administer the admissions standards, however these are phrased, understand that their immediate goal is to increase the number of blacks in the school, then they will use race as a criterion in making the various subjective judgments the explicit criteria will require, because that will be, given the goal, the only right way to make those judgments. The recommendation might mean, on the other hand, that the school should adopt some nonracially conscious goal, like increasing the number of disadvantaged

students of all races, and then hope that that goal will produce an increase in the number of blacks as a by-product. But even if that strategy is less hypocritical (which is far from plain), it will almost certainly fail because no different goal, scrupulously administered in a nonracially conscious way, will in fact significantly increase the number of black medical students.

Cox offered powerful evidence for that conclusion, and it is supported by the recent and comprehensive report of the Carnegie Council on Policy Studies in Higher Education. Suppose, for example, that the medical school sets aside separate places for applicants "disadvantaged" on some racially neutral test, like poverty, allowing only those disadvantaged in that way to compete for these places. If the school selects these from that group who scored best on standard medical school aptitude tests, then it will take almost no blacks, because blacks score relatively low even among the economically disadvantaged. But if the school chooses among the disadvantaged on some basis other than test scores, just so that more blacks will succeed, then it will not be administering the special procedure in a nonracially-conscious way.

So Cox was able to put his case in the form of two simple propositions. A racially conscious test for admission, even one that sets aside certain places for qualified minority applicants exclusively, serves goals that are in themselves unobjectionable and even urgent. Such programs are, moreover, the only means that offer any significant promise of achieving these goals. If these programs are halted, then no more than a trickle of black students will enter medical or other professional schools for another generation at least.

If these propositions are sound, then on what ground can it be thought that such programs are either wrong or unconstitutional? We must notice an important distinction between two different sorts of objections that might be made. These programs are intended, as I said, to decrease the importance of race in the United States in the long run. It may be objected, first, that the programs will in fact harm that goal more than they will advance it. There is no way now to prove that that is so. Cox conceded, in his argument, that there are costs and risks in these programs.

Affirmative action programs seem to encourage, for example, a popular misunderstanding, which is that they assume that racial or ethnic groups are entitled to proportionate shares of opportunities, so that Italian or Polish ethnic minorities are, in theory, as entitled to their proportionate shares as blacks or Chicanos or American Indians are entitled to the shares the present programs give them. That is a plain mistake: the programs are not based on the idea that those who are aided are entitled to aid, but only on the strategic hypothesis that helping them is now an effective way of attacking a national problem. Some medical schools may well make that judgment, under certain circumstances, about a white ethnic minority. Indeed it seems likely that some medical schools are even now attempting to help white Appalachian applicants, for example, under programs of regional distribution.

So the popular understanding is wrong, but so long as it persists it is a cost of the program because the attitudes it encourages tend to a degree to make people more rather than less conscious of race. There are other possible costs. It is said, for example, that some blacks find affirmative action degrading; they find that it makes them more rather than less conscious of prejudice against their race as such. This attitude is also based on a misperception, I think, but for a small minority of blacks at least it is a genuine cost.

In the view of the many important universities who have such programs, however, the gains will very probably exceed the losses in reducing racial consciousness overall. This view is hardly so implausible that it is wrong for these universities to seek to acquire the experience that will allow us to judge whether they are right. It would be particularly silly to forbid these experiments if we know that the failure to try will mean, as the evidence shows, that the status quo will almost certainly continue. In any case, this first objection could provide no argument that would justify a decision by the Supreme Court holding the programs unconstitutional. The Court has no business substituting

its speculative judgment about the probable consequences of educational policies for the judgment of professional educators.

So the acknowledged uncertainties about the long-term results of such programs could not justify a Supreme Court decision making them illegal. But there is a second and very different form of objection. It may be argued that even if the programs *are* effective in making our society less a society dominated by race, they are nevertheless unconstitutional because they violate the individual constitutional rights of those, like Allan Bakke, who lose places in consequence. In the oral argument Reynold H. Colvin of San Francisco, who is Bakke's lawyer, made plain that his objection takes this second form. Mr Justice White asked him whether he accepted that the goals affirmative action programs seek are important goals. Mr Colvin acknowledged that they were. Suppose, Justice White continued, that affirmative action programs are, as Cox had argued, the only effective means of seeking such goals. Would Mr Colvin nevertheless maintain that the programs are unconstitutional? Yes, he insisted, they would be, because his client has a constitutional right that the programs be abandoned, no matter what the consequences.

Mr Colvin was wise to put his objections on this second ground; he was wise to claim that his client has rights that do not depend on any judgment about the likely consequences of affirmative action for society as a whole, because if he makes out that claim then the Court must give him the relief he seeks.

But can he be right? If Allan Bakke has a constitutional right so important that the urgent goals of affirmative action must yield, then this must be because affirmative action violates some fundamental principle of political morality. This is not a case in which what might be called formal or technical law requires a decision one way or the other. There is no language in the Constitution whose plain meaning forbids affirmative action. Only the most naïve theories of statutory construction could argue that such a result is required by the language of any earlier Supreme Court decision or of the Civil Rights Act of 1964 or of any other congressional enactment.

If Mr Colvin is right it must be because Allan Bakke has not simply some technical legal right but an important moral right as well.

What could that right be? The popular argument frequently made on editorial pages is that Bakke has a right to be judged on his merit. Or that he has a right to be judged as an individual rather than as a member of a social group. Or that he has a right, as much as any black man, not to be sacrificed or excluded from any opportunity because of his race alone. But these catch phrases are deceptive here, because, as reflection demonstrates, the only genuine principle they describe is the principle that no one should suffer from the prejudice or contempt of others. And that principle is not at stake in this case at all. In spite of popular opinion, the idea that the *Bakke* case presents a conflict between a desirable social goal and important individual rights is a piece of intellectual confusion.

Consider, for example, the claim that individuals applying for places in medical school should be judged on merit, and merit alone. If that slogan means that admissions committees should take nothing into account but scores on some particular intelligence test, then it is arbitrary and, in any case, contradicted by the long-standing practice of every medical school. If it means, on the other hand, that a medical school should choose candidates that it supposes will make the most useful doctors, then everything turns on the judgment of what factors make different doctors useful. The Davis Medical School assigned to each regular applicant, as well as to each minority applicant, what it called a "benchmark score." This reflected not only the results of aptitude tests and college grade averages, but a subjective evaluation of the applicant's chances of functioning as an effective doctor, in view of society's present needs for medical service. Presumably the qualities deemed important were different from the qualities that a law school or engineering school or business school would seek, just as the intelligence tests a medical school might use would be different from the tests these other schools would find appropriate.

There is no combination of abilities and skills and traits that constitutes "merit" in the abstract; if quick hands count as "merit" in the case of a prospective surgeon, this is because quick hands will enable him to serve the public better and for no other reason. If a black skin will, as a matter of regrettable fact, enable another doctor to do a different medical job better, then that black skin is by the same token "merit" as well. That argument may strike some as dangerous; but only because they confuse its conclusion – that black skin may be a socially useful trait in particular circumstances – with the very different and despicable idea that one race may be inherently more worthy than another.

Consider the second of the catch phrases I have mentioned. It is said that Bakke has a right to be judged as an "individual," in deciding whether he is to be admitted to medical school and thus to the medical profession, and not as a member of some group that is being judged as a whole. What can that mean? Any admissions procedure must rely on generalizations about groups that are justified only statistically. The regular admissions process at Davis, for example, set a cutoff figure for college grade-point averages. Applicants whose averages fell below that figure were not invited to any interview, and were therefore rejected out of hand.

An applicant whose average fell one point below the cutoff might well have had personal qualities of dedication or sympathy that would have been revealed at an interview, and that would have made him or her a better doctor than some applicant whose average rose one point above the line. But the former is excluded from the process on the basis of a decision taken for administrative convenience and grounded in the generalization, unlikely to hold true for every individual, that those with grade averages below the cutoff will not have other qualities sufficiently persuasive. Indeed, even the use of standard Medical College Aptitude Tests (MCAT) as part of the admissions procedure requires judging people as part of groups because it assumes that test scores are a guide to medical intelligence, which is in turn a guide to medical ability. Though this judgment is no doubt true statistically, it hardly holds true for every individual.

Allan Bakke was himself refused admission to two other medical schools, not because of his race but because of his age: these schools thought that a student entering medical school at the age of thirty-three was likely to make less of a contribution to medical care over his career than someone entering at the standard age of twenty-one. Suppose these schools relied, not on any detailed investigation of whether Bakke himself had abilities that would contradict the generalization in his specific case, but on a rule of thumb that allowed only the most cursory look at applicants over (say) the age of thirty. Did these two medical schools violate his right to be judged as an individual rather than as a member of a group?

The Davis Medical School permitted whites to apply for the sixteen places reserved for members of "educationally or economically disadvantaged minorities," a phrase whose meaning might well include white ethnic minorities. In fact several whites have applied, though none has been accepted, and the California Court found that the special committee charged with administering the program had decided, in advance, against admitting any. Suppose that decision had been based on the following administrative theory: it is so unlikely that any white doctor can do as much to counteract racial imbalance in the medical professions as a well-qualified and trained black doctor can do that the committee should for reasons of convenience proceed on the presumption no white doctor could. That presumption is, as a matter of fact, more plausible than the corresponding presumption about medical students over the age of thirty, or even the presumption about applicants whose grade-point averages fall below the cutoff line. If the latter presumptions do not deny the alleged right of individuals to be judged as individuals in an admissions procedure, then neither can the former.

Mr Colvin, in oral argument, argued the third of the catch phrases I mentioned. He said that his client had a right not to be excluded from medical school because of his race alone, and this as a statement of constitutional right sounds more plausible than claims about the right to be judged on merit or as an individual. It sounds plausible, however, because it suggests the following more complex principle. Every citizen has a constitutional right that he not suffer disadvantage, at least in the competition for any public benefit, because the race or religion or sect or region or other natural or artificial group to which he belongs is the object of prejudice or contempt.

That is a fundamentally important constitutional right, and it is that right that was systematically violated for many years by racist exclusions and anti-Semitic quotas. Color bars and Jewish quotas were not unfair just because they made race or religion relevant or because they fixed on qualities beyond individual control. It is true that blacks or Jews do not choose to be blacks or Jews. But it is also true that those who score low in aptitude or admissions tests do not choose their levels of intelligence. Nor do those denied admission because they are too old, or because they do not come from a part of the country underrepresented in the school, or because they cannot play basketball well, choose not to have the qualities that made the difference.

Race seems different because exclusions based on race have historically been motivated not by some instrumental calculation, as in the case of intelligence or age or regional distribution or athletic ability, but because of contempt for the excluded race or religion as such. Exclusion by race was in itself an insult, because it was generated by and signaled contempt.

Bakke's claim, therefore, must be made more specific than it is. He says he was kept out of medical school because of his race. Does he mean that he was kept out because his race is the object of prejudice or contempt? That suggestion is absurd. A very high proportion of those who were accepted (and, presumably, of those who run the admissions program) were members of the same race. He therefore means simply that if he had been black he would have been accepted, with no suggestion that this would have been so because blacks are thought more worthy or honorable than whites.

That is true: no doubt he would have been accepted if he were black. But it is also true, and in exactly the same sense, that he would have been accepted if he had been more intelligent, or made a better impression in his interview, or, in the case of other schools, if he had been younger when he decided to become a doctor. Race is not, in *his* case, a different matter from these other factors equally beyond his control. It is not a different matter because in his case race is not distinguished by the special character of public insult. On the contrary the program presupposes that his race is still widely if wrongly thought to be superior to others.

In the past, it made sense to say that an excluded black or Jewish student was being sacrificed because of his race or religion; that meant that his or her exclusion was treated as desirable in itself, not because it contributed to any goal in which he as well as the rest of society might take pride. Allan Bakke is being "sacrificed" because of his race only in a very artificial sense of the word. He is being "sacrificed" in the same artificial sense because of his level of intelligence, since he would have been accepted if he were more clever than he is. In both cases he is being excluded not by prejudice but because of a rational calculation about the socially most beneficial use of limited resources for medical education.

It may now be said that this distinction is too subtle, and that if racial classifications have been and may still be used for malign purposes, then everyone has a flat right that racial classifications not be used at all. This is the familiar appeal to the lazy virtue of simplicity. It supposes that if a line is difficult to draw, or might be difficult to administer if drawn, then there is wisdom in not making the attempt to draw it. There may be cases in which that is wise, but those would be cases in which nothing of great value would as a consequence be lost. If racially conscious admissions policies now offer the only substantial hope for bringing more qualified black and other minority doctors into the profession, then a great loss is suffered if medical schools are not allowed voluntarily to pursue such programs.

We should then be trading away a chance to attack certain and present injustice in order to gain protection we may not need against speculative abuses we have other means to prevent. And such abuses cannot, in any case, be worse than the injustice to which we would then surrender.

We have now considered three familiar slogans, each widely thought to name a constitutional right that enables Allan Bakke to stop programs of affirmative action no matter how effective or necessary these might be. When we inspect these slogans, we find that they can stand for no genuine principle except one. This is the important principle that no one in our society should suffer because he is a member of a group thought less worthy of respect, as a group, than other groups. We have different aspects of that principle in mind when we say that individuals should be judged on merit, that they should be judged as individuals, and that they should not suffer disadvantages because of their race. The spirit of that fundamental principle is the spirit of the goal that affirmative action is intended to serve. The principle furnishes no support for those who find, as Bakke does, that their own interests conflict with that goal.

It is of course regrettable when any citizen's expectations are defeated by new programs serving some more general concern. It is regrettable, for example, when established small businesses fail because new and superior roads are built; in that case people have invested more than Bakke has. And they had more reason to believe their businesses would continue than Bakke had to suppose he could have entered the Davis Medical School at thirty-three even without a task-force program.

There is, of course, no suggestion in that program that Bakke shares in any collective or individual guilt for racial injustice in America; or that he is any less entitled to concern or respect than any black student accepted in the program. He has been disappointed, and he must have the sympathy due that disappointment, just as any other disappointed applicant – even one with much worse test scores who would not have been accepted in any event – must have sympathy. Each is disappointed because places in medical schools are scarce resources and must be used to provide what the more general society most needs. It is hardly Bakke's fault that racial justice is now a special need – but he has no right to prevent the most effective measures of securing that justice from being used.

46

Affirmative Action as Equalizing Opportunity: Challenging the Myth of "Preferential Treatment"

Luke Charles Harris and Uma Narayan

Introduction

Affirmative action is an issue on which there has been considerable public debate. We think, however, that it is a policy that has often been misunderstood and mischaracterized, not only by those opposed to it, *but even by its defenders* (Harris and Narayan, 1994). In this essay, we intend to describe these misconceptions, to explain why we consider them misconceptions, and to offer a much stronger defense of affirmative action policies than is usually offered. In the first section, we examine and challenge prevalent misrepresentations of the *scope* of affirmative action policies – misconceptions about the groups of people these policies are designed to benefit, and about the benefits they are intended to achieve. In the second section, we address misunderstandings about the *rationale* for affirmative action policies, and take issue with those who regard affirmative action as bestowing "preferential treatment" on its beneficiaries. We argue that affirmative action policies should be understood as attempts to *equalize opportunity* for groups of people who confront ongoing forms of institutional discrimination and a lack of equal opportunity. In the third and fourth sections respectively, we take issue with those who defend affirmative action on the grounds that it is a form of *compensation*, and with those who defend it on the grounds that it promotes *diversity* and a range of other long-term goals. We argue that such rationales mischaracterize affirmative action as providing justifiable "preferences" to its beneficiaries. In the final section, we argue that the "stigma argument" against affirmative action dissolves if affirmative action is understood as equalizing opportunities, and not as *bestowing preferences*.

Clarifying the Scope of Affirmative Action Policies

The debate on affirmative action often misrepresents the scope of these policies in several important ways. The most perturbing of these misrepresentations is the widespread tendency to construe these policies as *race-based policies alone*, and further, to talk about African Americans as the only racial group they are intended to benefit. This picture of affirmative action policies is, to put it bluntly, false. Even when these policies were first initiated, they were designed to benefit members of other disadvantaged racial minorities besides African Americans. For example, almost two-thirds of the students admitted under the affirmative action program of the Davis Medical School that was challenged in the landmark *Bakke* case in 1978 were Latino or Asian American. Nonetheless, almost the entire public debate surrounding the case discussed it in terms of Blacks and Whites only. Even more oddly, the opinions of the Justices of the Supreme Court that considered this case – the majority opinions as well as the dissenting opinions – discussed affirmative action only as benefitting African Americans. In the context of the racial politics of the United States, we believe such a misrepresentation of the scope of these policies is not only false, but also dangerous since it is easier to negatively stereotype these policies when African Americans are viewed as their only beneficiaries.

Thus, even at their inception, when affirmative action policies were predominantly race-based, they were designed to remedy the institutional exclusion of *a number of racially-disadvantaged groups*. In many institutional contexts, they have long since expanded to cover other grounds on which groups of people face discrimination and unequal opportunity. A great many educational institutions, professions and trades have opened their doors to *women* as a result of affirmative action, promoting the entry of women into a range of formerly male domains, from law schools to corporations to police departments. This has benefitted not only women of color, but many middle-class White women. Affirmative action policies in some institutions such as professional schools have also promoted the entry of working-class applicants, including working-class White men, a fact that is seldom discussed and little known. Derrick Bell points out that "special admissions criteria have been expanded to encompass disadvantaged but promising White applicants," and that, for example, the open admissions program of New York's City University system, which was initiated by minority pressure, has benefitted even greater numbers of lower-middle-class and working-class Whites than Blacks (Bell, 1979).

We need to remember that the world in which affirmative action policies were initiated was a world where a great many prestigious institutions and professions were almost exclusively enclaves of upper-class White men, and where many of the blue-collar trades were predominantly the preserve of White working-class men. Affirmative action has been crucial in opening up the former to women, to members of racial minorities, and to working-class Whites, and in opening up the latter to women and members of racial minorities. We are not arguing that each and every instance of affirmative action does or should consider each category of class, race, and gender. Which factors should be considered depends on the patterns of exclusion within a particular occupation and institution. For instance, affirmative action policies in the blue-collar trades and police and fire departments need to affirmatively promote the entry of women of all races and of minority men, since they were the groups who faced obstacles to entry, not White working-class men. On the other hand, student admissions policies at institutions that used to be women's colleges attended predominantly by White upper-class women such as our institution, Vassar College, should seek to affirmatively recruit students of color and students from working-class backgrounds, including White working-class men. What we are arguing is that, taken as a whole, affirmative action policies in many contexts have long operated on multiple criteria of inclusion, even though they continue to be portrayed as policies that either only benefit or principally benefit African Americans.

The prevalent failure to consider the range of people that affirmative action policies have benefitted breeds a number of misplaced objections to these policies. For instance, many people argue that affirmative action policies should be class-based instead of race-based, since they believe that middle-class African Americans do not need or "deserve" affirmative action (Carter, 1991). This view is problematic in a number of ways. First, many proponents of this view pose the issue as *a choice between race and class*, ignoring the fact that affirmative action policies have been *both* class-based and race-based. Secondly, proponents of this view believe that middle-class Blacks do not suffer from the effects of discrimination despite substantial evidence to the contrary.

In 1985, independent studies by the Grier Partnership and the Urban League revealed striking disparities in the employment levels of Blacks and Whites in Washington, DC, an area that constitutes one of the "best markets" for Blacks (Pyatt, 1985). Both studies cite racial discrimination as the major factor that accounts for this difference. A 1991 study by the Urban Institute examined employment practices in the Chicago and Washington, DC areas by sending equally qualified and identically dressed White and Black applicants to newspaper-advertised positions. The testers were also matched for speech patterns, age, work experience, physical build and personal characteristics. The study found repeated discrimination that increased with the level of the advertised position, and revealed that Whites received job offers three times more often than *equally qualified* Blacks (Turner et al., 1991).

Finally, the limitation of the view that middle-class Blacks do not suffer racial discrimination becomes clear when we attend to gender-based affirmative action policies. No one has seriously suggested that the sexism and gender-based discrimination women face in a variety of institutions is merely a product of their class status, or that middle-class status shields White women from these effects. Just as affirmative action policies that attend only to class disadvantages are unlikely to remedy the institutional exclusions faced by women, they would surely fail to remedy race-based exclusions faced by members of several racial minority groups. In short, the effects of gender and race bias would be only partially curtailed by purely class-based policies. Indeed, purely class-based policies would mostly benefit working-class White men, whose race and gender are not the sources of invidious discrimination. As some recent feminist works teach us, we must, therefore, pay particular attention to the interconnected ways in which factors such as class, race, gender and sexual orientation work together to sustain disparities between different groups of Americans in a variety of institutional and social contexts.

There is, then, no need to pit class against race (or against gender) as the only valid basis for affirmative action. An array of factors that contribute to institutional discrimination – such as class, race, gender and disability – should be taken into account. When several factors intersect and jointly contribute to a process of discrimination, as in the case of a working-class Black woman, each factor should be considered. When only one aspect of a person's identity adversely affects his or her opportunities in a given setting – for instance, class status in the case of working-class White men, or race in the case of middle-class Black men – then only that factor should be taken into account.

Another prevalent objection to affirmative action policies that seems connected to misunderstanding its actual scope is the objection that *truly disadvantaged* poor Blacks have not benefitted from these policies. The impression that affirmative action benefits only the Black middle class and that few working-class or poor Blacks benefit from these programs is mistaken. For the vast majority of Blacks were working-class prior to the Civil Rights Era and the promulgation of civil rights laws and affirmative action initiatives. These efforts have combined to play a major role in the creation of the Black middle class that exists today. Bob Blauner points out that due to occupational mobility that is in part a product of affirmative action, nearly 25 percent of Black families had incomes of more than $25,000 (in constant dollars) in 1982, compared with 8.7 percent in 1960. Moreover, the proportion of employed Blacks who hold middle-class jobs rose from 13.4 percent in 1960 to 37.8 percent in 1981. The number of Black college students rose from 340,000 in 1966 to more than one million in 1982 (Blauner, 1989). From sanitation departments to university departments, from the construction industry to corporate America, these programs have helped to open doors once tightly sealed.

An empirically accurate assessment of affirmative action policies shows that they have not only benefitted poor and working-class Blacks, but poor and working-class people of all races, including some White working-class men and women. White working-class people's opposition to these policies based on the belief that they are "victims" of such programs is based on a mistake, a mistake facilitated by discussions of these policies that portray them as only benefitting Blacks.

Lastly, some people also argue against affirmative action on the grounds that it has not solved a host of problems pertaining to poverty, the inner-city and the "underclass" (Steele, 1990). It is entirely true that affirmative action has not solved these problems. Neither has it solved problems such as rape, domestic violence and sexual harassment. However, we do not think these are legitimate objections, since they more obviously over-inflate the scope of what these policies were intended to accomplish. Affirmative action polices cannot be, and were not intended to be, a magic solution to *all* our social problems; indeed no single policy can solve every social problem we confront. Their purpose is a limited though important one – to partially counter the ways in which factors such as class, race, gender and disabilities function in our society to impede equal access and opportunity, thereby promoting greater inclusion of diverse Americans in a range of institutions and occupations. They have clearly succeeded in this goal, and should not be condemned for failing to solve problems they were not intended to solve.

Re-envisioning the Rationale for Affirmative Action: from "Preferential Treatment" to "Equal Opportunity"

We believe that many mistaken views about affirmative action result from misunderstandings about the justification or rationale for such policies. Unfortunately, the debate on affirmative action has largely been a dialogue between two broadly characterizable positions. On the one hand, its critics describe it as a form of "reverse discrimination" that bestows "undeserved preferences" on its beneficiaries. On the other hand, its defenders continue to characterize the policy as "preferential treatment,"

but argue that these preferences are justified, either as "compensation" or on grounds of "social utility." Few question the assumption that affirmative action involves the "bestowal of preferences," or challenge the premise that it marks a sudden deviation from a system that, until its advent, operated strictly and clearly on the basis of merit. Setting out a view of affirmative action that rejects these ideas is our central task here.

In our view, affirmative action is not a matter of affording "preferential treatment" to its beneficiaries. Our position is that affirmative action is best understood as an attempt to promote *equality of opportunity* in a social context marked by pervasive inequalities, one in which many institutional criteria and practices work to impede a fair assessment of the capabilities of those who are working-class, women or people of color. Thus, affirmative action is an attempt to equalize opportunity for people who continue to face institutional obstacles to equal consideration and equal treatment. These obstacles include not only continuing forms of blatant discrimination, but, more importantly, a variety of subtle institutional criteria and practices that unwarrantedly circumscribe mobility in contemporary America. These criteria and practices are often not deliberately designed to discriminate and exclude; the fact remains, however, that they nevertheless function to do so, as our subsequent examples demonstrate. Thus, in countering such forms of discrimination, affirmative action policies attempt only to "level the playing field." They do not "bestow preferences" on their beneficiaries; rather, they attempt to undo the effects of institutional practices and criteria that, however unintentionally, amount in effect to "preferential treatment" for Whites.

Those who believe that affirmative action constitutes "preferential treatment" assume (a) that the criteria and procedures generally used for admissions and hiring are neutral indicators of "merit," unaffected by factors such as class, race, or gender, and (b) that such criteria are fairly and impartially applied to all individuals at each of the stages of the selection process. In the rest of this section, we will try to show why these two assumptions are seriously open to question.

Although test scores on standardized tests are often "taken as absolute by both the public and the institutions that use the scores in decision making," there is ample evidence that they do not predict equally well for men and women. A study of three college admissions tests (the SAT, the PSAT/NMSQT, and the ACT) reveals that although women consistently earn better high school and college grades, they receive lower scores on all three tests. Rosser argues that "if the SAT predicted equally well for both sexes, girls would score about 20 points higher than the boys, not 61 points lower" (Rosser, 1987). Standardized test scores adversely affect women's chances for admission to colleges and universities, their chances for scholarships, and entry into "gifted" programs, as well as their academic self-perceptions. Similarly, James Crouse and Dale Trusheim argue, on the basis of statistical evidence, that the scores are not very useful indicators for helping to "admit black applicants who would succeed and reject applicants who would fail" (Crouse and Trusheim, 1988).

The literature on such standardized tests demonstrates that they are often inaccurate indicators even with respect to their *limited stated objective* of predicting students' first-year grades in college and professional school. Yet, they are often used as if they measured a person's overall intelligence and foretold long-term success in educational institutions and professional life. As a result of these unsupported beliefs, affirmative action policies that depart from strict considerations of these test scores are often taken to constitute the strongest evidence for institutional deviation from standards of merit, and constitutive elements of the "preference" thought to be awarded to women and minority applicants.

There are also many other examples of established rules, practices and policies of institutions that, no matter how benign their intention, have the effect of discriminating against the members of relatively marginalized groups. For instance, word-of-mouth recruitment where the existing labor pool is predominantly White male reduces the chances of women or people of color

applying for the jobs in question, as do unions that influence or control hiring in well-paid jobs in the construction, transportation and printing industries when they recruit through personal contacts. A 1990 study reports that over 80 percent of executives find their jobs through networking, and that about 86 percent of available jobs do not appear in the classifieds (Ezorsky, 1991). "Last hired, first fired" rules make more recently hired women and minorities more susceptible to lay-offs. The "old boy network" that results from years of social and business contacts among White men, as well as racially or sexually segregated country clubs or social organizations, often paid for by employers, also have discriminatory impacts on women and minorities. Furthermore, stereotyped beliefs about women and minorities often justify hiring them for low-level, low-paying jobs, regardless of their qualifications for higher-level jobs (Kantor and Stein, 1976).

Indeed, some empirical studies show that many Black candidates for jobs are rated more negatively than White candidates with identical credentials. Other studies demonstrate that the same résumé with a woman's name on it receives a significantly lower rating than when it has a man's name on it, showing that gender-bias operates even when there is no direct contact with the persons evaluated. Still other problematic practices include evaluations where subjective assessments of factors such as "fitting in," "personality," and "self-confidence" serve class, race and gender prejudice.

Personal interviews, job evaluations, and recommendations all have an inescapable subjective element which often works in the favor of better-off White men. As Lawrence A. Blum (1988) writes:

> Persons can fail to be judged purely on ability because they have not gone to certain colleges or professional schools, because they do not know the right people, because they do not present themselves in a certain way. And, again, sometimes this sort of discrimination takes place without either those doing the discriminating or those being discriminated against realizing it. . . . Often these denials of equal opportunity have a lot to do with class background, as well as race or sex, or with a combination of these.

Interview processes that precede being selected or hired are often not as "neutral" as assumed. A two-step experiment done at Princeton University began with White undergraduates interviewing both White and Black job applicants. Unknown to the interviewers, the applicants in the first stage of the experiment were all confederates of the experimenters and were trained to behave consistently from interview to interview. This study reported that interviewers spent less time with Black applicants and were less friendly and outgoing than with the White applicants. In the second stage of the experiment, confederates of the experimenters were trained to approximate the two styles of interviewing observed during the first stage of the study when they interviewed two groups of White applicants. A panel of judges who reviewed tapes of these interviews reported that White applicants subjected to the style previously accorded Blacks performed noticeably worse in the interviews than other White applicants. In this respect, there is also substantial evidence that women are asked inappropriate questions and subject to discrimination in interviews.

None of the discriminatory institutional structures and practices we have detailed above necessarily involve conscious antipathy toward women and minorities or the operation of conscious sexist or racist stereotypes. Some discriminatory structures and practices involve unconscious stereotypes at work, from which women and people of color are hardly immune in their evaluations of other women and minorities. Many of the examples we discuss involve practices central to hiring and promotion that work to disadvantage many marginalized Americans even when all persons involved sincerely believe themselves to be fair and impartial. Because the processes of getting through an educational program, or being hired, retained and promoted in a job involve the possibility, for example, of women and minority applicants being subject to a variety of such practices, it seems likely that few, if any, women or people of color are apt to escape the cumulative adverse effects of these practices. In the context of these structures and practices that systematically disadvantage some Americans, it would be naive, at best, to believe that our society is a well-functioning meritocracy.

The problem is far more complicated than is captured by the common perspective that working-class people, women and minorities have generally not had equal advantages and opportunities to acquire qualifications that are on par with those of their better-off, White male counterparts, and so we should compensate them by awarding them preferences even though they are less well qualified. Their qualifications, in fact, tend to be under-valued and under-appraised in many institutional contexts. Moreover, many of the criteria that are unquestioningly taken to be important impartial indicators of people's competencies, merit and potential, such as test scores, not only fail to be precise measurements of these qualities, but systematically stigmatize these individuals within institutions in which these tests function as important criteria of admission.

We do not however wish to deny that factors such as class, race and gender often impede persons from acquiring qualifications. A 1981 study, for instance, showed that Black school districts received less funding and inferior educational resources compared with similar White districts, often as a result of decision-making by Whites. There is also increasing evidence of disadvantaging practices in the pre-college advising offered to minority students. Evidence suggests that teachers often interpret linguistic and cultural differences as indications of low potential or a lack of academic interests on the part of minority students; and guidance counselors often steer female and minority students away from "hard" subjects, such as mathematics and science, which are often paths to high-paying jobs.

In such contexts, even if the criteria used to determine admission and hiring were otherwise unproblematic, it is not at all clear that taking them simply "at face value" would fairly or accurately gauge the talents and potential of disparate individuals. When some candidates have to overcome several educational and social obstacles that others do not, similarity of credentials may well amount to a significant difference in talent and potential. Thus, treating identical credentials as signs of identical capabilities and effort may, under prevailing conditions of inequality, significantly devalue the worth of credentials obtained in the teeth of such obstacles. We would argue that individuals who obtained their credentials in the face of severe obstacles are likely to do better than those who have similar or even somewhat better credentials obtained without coping with such obstacles, especially over a period of years, where they have opportunities to remedy their handicaps. Affirmative action policies with respect to admissions and hiring recruit individuals for positions where "success" depends on the nature of one's performance over several years. Such recruitment should rightly concern itself with a person's evidenced *potential* for success rather than simply assess what their capabilities appear to be, based on the comparison of credentials acquired by individuals under distinctly different circumstances.

We are not arguing, however, that affirmative action policies are, or can be, magical formulas that help us determine with perfect precision in every case the exact weights that must be accorded a person's class background, gender, and minority status so as to afford him or her perfect equality of opportunity. Particular institutions must use practical wisdom and good-faith efforts to determine the exact measures that they will undertake to promote equality within their frameworks, as well as monitor and periodically reassess the parameters and scope of their institutional policies. Nor do we wish to deny that some persons recruited as a result of affirmative action policies might turn out to be incompetent or demonstrate significant limitations in their ability to meet requirements. After all, the same incompetencies and limitations are manifested by some who are recruited by "regular" channels. No recruitment policies are immune to these problems. What we do argue is that in contexts where, for example, class, race, and gender operate to impede equality of opportunity, affirmative action policies have enabled many talented and promising individuals to have their talent and promise more fairly evaluated by the

institutions in question than would otherwise have been the case.

The Limitations of the Compensation Rationale for Affirmative Action

Affirmative action has frequently been defended on the grounds that it provides preferential treatment to members of marginalized groups as reparation or compensation for injustices they have suffered. The term *compensation* draws heavily on the model of recompense or payment of damages that is found in tort law. In the context of tort remedies, the particular agent who is responsible for injuring another compensates the specific person injured by paying what is judged to be an appropriate sum of money for the actual extent of the injury he or she has caused. This rationale tends to raise a number of questions precisely at those points where affirmative action policies seem to differ from the practice of tort-based compensation. Some argue that those who are "paying the price" for affirmative action have no direct responsibility for any harms or injuries suffered by any of its beneficiaries. Others raise the question of why the specific form of payment involved – construed as preferences for jobs or preferential entry to educational institutions – is the appropriate form of compensation, rather than monetary awards. Such critics reinforce these arguments by pointing out that affirmative action policies do not seem to be the most equitable form of compensation because those who have been most injured are probably not the ones receiving the compensation since their injuries have resulted in their not having "the qualifications even to be considered."

There have been attempts to defend the compensation rationale against these objections (Boxhill, 1978). However, we believe that it remains an inadequate and problematic rationale for affirmative action. In suggesting that affirmative action compensates individuals for damage done by phenomena such as racism or sexism, this rationale implies that the problem is one of "damaged individuals" rather than a problem due to structures, practices and institutional criteria within our institutions that continue to impede a fair assessment of the capabilities of some Americans. We have argued in the previous section that there is ample evidence to show that many prevalent criteria and procedures do not fairly gauge the capabilities of members of marginalized groups. The compensation model, however, does not question the normative criteria used by our institutions or encourage critical reflection about the processes of assessment used to determine these "qualifications"; and, as a result, it fails to question the view that affirmative action involves "preferential treatment." We consider this a serious weakness, since it does not challenge the view that affirmative action policies promote the entry of "less qualified" individuals. Rather it merely insists that "preferences" bestowed on less qualified individuals are justified as a form of compensation.

The compensation literature also conflates the rationale for race- and gender-based affirmative action policies with that for policies that promote institutional access for veterans. Policies based on veteran status may indeed be understood as compensation for their risks, efforts, and injuries sustained in the service of the nation, which may also have impeded or detracted from their employment or educational goals. However, it does not necessarily follow that a rationale that works best to explain one type of special assistance program works equally well to explain all others. In this respect, not only is a person's veteran status usually less visible than their race or gender, veteran status *per se* does not very often render persons targets of prejudice and institutional discrimination.

The Limitations of the Social Utility Rationales for Affirmative Action

We believe that our rationale for affirmative action is stronger than the "social utility" arguments that have been proffered in its defense. To illuminate our perspective, we will focus on one of the best known of such defenses, that offered by Ronald Dworkin. Dworkin understands affirmative action to involve

"preferential treatment" and discusses affirmative action policies only as pertaining to Blacks. His argument can be summarized as follows. First, he argues that affirmative action policies that "give preferences" to minority candidates do not violate the "right to equal treatment" or the "right to equal consideration and respect" of White male applicants. Dworkin argues that these rights would be violated if a White male suffers disadvantage when competing with Blacks because his race is "the object of prejudice or contempt," but that this is not the case with affirmative action policies. Secondly, Dworkin argues that the "costs" that White male applicants suffer as a result of affirmative action policies are justified because such policies promote several beneficial social ends, the most important of which is their long-term impact in making us a less race-conscious society. Other beneficial social ends that Dworkin argues are served by affirmative action include providing role models for Blacks, providing more professionals such as doctors and lawyers willing to serve the Black community, reducing the sense of frustration and injustice in the Black community, and alleviating social tensions along racial lines.

Whereas Dworkin focuses on the negative claim that affirmative action policies do not violate the right to treatment as an equal, or the right to equal consideration and respect for the interests of White men, we make the positive and much stronger claim that affirmative action policies are justified because *they are necessary to ensure the right to treatment as an equal for the members of marginalized groups*, in a social context where a variety of social structures and institutional practices conspire to deny their interests equal consideration and respect. While we have no quarrel with Dworkin's claims about the social benefits of affirmative action, we do not rest our case for affirmative action on such *consequentialist arguments* about its long-term effects, arguments that are notoriously vulnerable to counter-arguments that project a set of more negative consequences as the long-term results. Since we do not believe that affirmative action bestows "preferential treatment" on its beneficiaries or imposes "costs" on White male applicants, as Dworkin does, we do not need to rely on Dworkin-type arguments that the long-term social "benefits" of these "preferences" justify imposing these "costs."

Our rationale for affirmative action also differs from social utility arguments that justify these policies on the ground that they contribute to a greater diversity of backgrounds and perspectives within academic institutions, thereby enhancing the learning process. First, "diversity" on a campus can be enhanced by admitting people from a wide variety of backgrounds, and with a wide range of special talents. A commitment to "diversity" *per se* could justify policies that promoted the recruitment of students from abroad, from remote areas of the country, and those with artistic skills or unusual interests. While there might well be institutional reasons for, and benefits from, promoting diversity in these forms, none of these students need necessarily have suffered from the systematic effects of social and institutional forms of discrimination within the United States. Thus, many students who would provide "diversity" would not qualify for affirmative action, even though there might be other reasons for admitting them. Secondly, while admitting greater numbers of working-class people, women, and minorities into institutions in which they are significantly underrepresented would also increase institutional diversity in meaningful ways, we see such beneficial consequences as supplemental benefits of affirmative action rather than its central goal.

While we believe affirmative action has in fact had beneficial consequences in making many areas of work and education more integrated along class, race and gender lines, we see these consequences as the results of treating people more equally, and not as benefits that have resulted from "imposing costs" on non-beneficiaries of affirmative action. Our central objection to both the "compensation" and "social utility" rationales for affirmative action is that neither questions the related assumptions that affirmative action "bestows preferences" on some, and imposes "costs" on others, even as they regard these "preferences" and "costs"

as justified. In short, we insist that affirmative action policies that attempt to foster equal treatment do not constitute "preferential treatment" and that such attempts to undo the effects of institutional practices and criteria that privilege the capacities of some people over others are not "costs" that need to be justified by pointing to the "benefits" of the long-term consequences of these policies.

Challenging the "Stigma" of Affirmative Action

Affirmative action has been criticized on the grounds that it "stigmatizes" its participants because both they themselves as well as others regard the beneficiaries of affirmative action as "less qualified" than non-beneficiaries. Affirmative action policies are also criticized on the grounds that they cause resentment among the "more qualified" people who are denied entry as a result of these policies and thereby forced to pay its "costs." We believe that both criticisms are often the results of failing to accurately understand the rationale for affirmative action. Furthermore, we believe that these arguments about "stigma" and "resentment" are unwittingly reinforced by those who defend affirmative action on the basis of the "compensation" or "social utility" arguments, since these arguments fail to challenge the claims that affirmative action promotes the "less qualified" and imposes "costs" on those who are "better qualified" for the positions in question. Instead they merely insist that such "preferences" and "costs" are justified either as "compensation" or as a means to promote a range of long-term goals.

Our view of affirmative action as a policy to foster equality of opportunity rejects the claim that its beneficiaries are "less qualified." We argue instead that there is good reason to believe that their capabilities are not *accurately gauged or fairly evaluated* by prevailing selection criteria and procedures. Without affirmative action policies, as we see it, those who are its beneficiaries would not be given equal consideration, or have their qualifications and capabilities assessed fairly. Given our rationale for affirmative action, the "stigma problem" disappears since we see nothing demeaning or stigmatizing in being given equal consideration or in being treated as fairly as one's peers. Thus, from our perspective, not only do the beneficiaries of affirmative action have no valid reason to feel "inferior," the non-beneficiaries of it have no good reason to regard themselves as "more qualified" than affirmative action beneficiaries.

Our account of affirmative action, then, also helps to illuminate why resentment by non-beneficiaries is unjustified. We believe that such resentment is based on the *false* belief that the "better qualified" are being burdened by having to bear the "costs" of "preferences" bestowed on others, a sentiment reinforced by views that see affirmative action as preferential treatment. Since we do not believe affirmative action bestows preferences we do not think that affirmative action imposes any corresponding costs or burdens on non-beneficiaries. On the contrary, we believe that it should be understood as an attempt to counteract a variety of procedures and criteria that work to *unfairly privilege* those who are middle-class, White and male. We believe that the only costs to non-beneficiaries that result from affirmative action policies are the loss of these privileges, privileges that are the results of a lack of fairness to and opportunity for others.

Neither affirmative action policies, nor a fair and judicious assessment of the performance of their various beneficiaries, are the central causes of the prevailing negative stereotypes about the competencies of women, working-class people, or people of color. Critiques of affirmative action along these lines often suggest that the world was once a fairer place, which has only recently become tainted with new stereotypes about the capabilities of women or members of racial minorities as a result of affirmative action policies infusing large numbers of its "underqualified" and "unqualified" beneficiaries into American institutions. Such critiques suggest that affirmative action has exacerbated the old negative stereotypes about women and people of color which had begun to wane. In fact, however, it was racist and sexist stereotypes, and the

institutional practices that worked to perpetuate and reinforce them, that made affirmative action policies necessary.

One of the ways in which racist and sexist stereotypes function is to obstruct our ability to see women and people of color as individuals. Thus, an individual woman or minority person's inadequacies can be generalized and seen as signs of the incompetence of whole groups, whereas the failures of White men remain personal limitations. Moreover, success stories involving women or minorities often tend to be interpreted as exceptions, and not as examples of the capabilities of women or people of color generally (Harris, 1994). Much of the discourse on affirmative action reveals this pattern: instances of women and people of color who have failed to meet the requirements of a profession or institution are taken to be testimony to the grand failure of affirmative action policies and the incompetence of the bulk of its beneficiaries. No nuanced account is given of the possible causes of these failures. The fact that no set of admissions or promotion criteria can guarantee that everyone who manifests potential for success will in fact succeed gets lost amidst anxious rumors of incompetence. Seldom dwelt upon are the numerous stories of those who have succeeded as a result of affirmative action.

As far back as the debate over the admission of minority applicants to the Davis Medical School in the *Bakke* case, little attention was paid to the success stories of people admitted as a result of affirmative action. Yet four years after the admission of the sixteen "affirmative action" candidates to Davis in 1978, thirteen had graduated in good standing, several had excelled, and one of their number had earned the school's most prestigious senior class award for "the qualities most likely to produce an outstanding physician." Much of the debate in 1978, however, *presumed*, just as it does now, that affirmative action's departure from the traditional admissions criteria represented a departure from objective criteria of "excellence."

There are a number of additional troublesome assumptions that underlie the stigma arguments. For example, for decades, almost all of our elite institutions and professions, as well as many non-elite career paths, were domains that permitted entry to a very small, and extremely privileged segment of the population. Yet there were millions of equally talented individuals who, because they were working-class, or women, or members of racial minority groups, were deprived of the chances to develop their talents and capabilities, which may well have exceeded those of many of their privileged White male counterparts. Rarely, if ever, in all these decades, have privileged White men who benefitted from such "undeserved privileges" ever castigated themselves or publicly expressed the feeling that they were not "really talented" or "really deserving of their positions" because they had acquired them in a context that had eliminated most of their fellow citizens, including the female members of their own families, from the competitive pool. We are unaware of a body of literature from these individuals filled with anxiety and self-doubt about their capabilities and merit. Indeed, one of the unnerving effects of privilege is that it permits the privileged to feel so entitled to their privileges that they often fail to see them as privileges at all. In such a setting, it is more than a little ironic that the beneficiaries of affirmative action programs designed to counteract the effect of institutional discrimination are now expected to wear the hair-shirt of "stigma."

Many who complain about the preferential treatment they believe affirmative action accords to women and minorities in academia assume that everyone other than its beneficiaries is admitted purely as a result of merit. Yet, paradoxically, policies that favor relatives of alumni, and children of faculty members or donors to the university, have not created a storm of legal or social controversy, or even been objected to. Perhaps this is because such policies tend to benefit predominantly White middle-class individuals. Our point is not simply to claim, however, that people who accept preferential policies that benefit middle-class Whites are often outraged by "preferences" rooted in affirmative action policies. Our point is in fact a much stronger one that hinges on the profound differences between affirmative action

and these other policies. Policies that favor children of alumni or donors are policies that may serve some useful goals for a particular institution, but they are genuinely "favors" or "preferences" with respect to the individuals admitted, in that such policies are in no way intended to equalize the opportunities of those thus admitted. We therefore insist on a conceptual distinction between affirmative action and policies that are genuinely tantamount to bestowing preferences.

Our point, however, is not to endorse a "purely meritocratic society" as the ideal society, but rather to highlight the reality that many existing institutional structures not only fail to function as pure meritocracies, but also serve to systematically disadvantage whole groups of people including working-class people, women, and people of color. To those strongly committed to traditional meritocratic ideals, we suggest that when close attention is paid to the systematically disadvantaging effects of many institutional procedures, they may have reason to see affirmative action policies as conducive to their ideal rather than as deviations from it.

Conclusion

The intellectual confusion surrounding affirmative action transcends ideological categories. Critics and supporters, of all political stripes, have underestimated the significance of these policies, collaborated in equating affirmative action with "preferential treatment," and permitted important assumptions about how institutions function, to lie unchallenged. We argue that affirmative action policies do not involve preferential treatment but should rather be understood as attempts to promote fairness, equality and full citizenship by affording members of marginalized groups a fair chance to enter significant social institutions.

The fact that formal legal equality seems commonplace and obviously justified to many today, should not obscure how recently formal equality has been a reality for many nor the struggles it took to make it a reality. More importantly, we should not imagine that the achievement of formal legal equality erased the consequences of centuries of inequality, making the promise of equality and full citizenship an immediate reality for those previously excluded. The institutional consequences of such historically group-based exclusions in significant domains of occupational and social life still remain. Class, race, and gender, for example, continue to deprive people of the opportunities to participate in numerous forms of association and work that are crucial to the development of talents and capabilities that enable people to contribute meaningfully to, and benefit from, the collective possibilities of national life.

Only since the latter part of the nineteenth century and the early decades of the twentieth century have some democratic political communities, such as the United States, sought to embrace the members of certain marginalized groups they had once excluded from the rights and privileges of citizenship. Only in the latter part of the twentieth century has there dawned the recognition that laws and policies that promote formal equality do not necessarily ensure substantive equality or genuine equal opportunity for all citizens to participate in all spheres of American life. In this respect, affirmative action policies are a significant historic achievement, for they constitute an attempt to transform our legacy of unequal treatment with respect to certain marginalized groups of Americans. They symbolize our political commitment to ensuring substantive participation in all domains of life for various groups of our diverse citizenry. Thus, we believe that affirmative action programs warrant a much more favorable evaluation, both as an historic achievement and in terms of their positive effects within contemporary American institutions, than they are usually accorded.

References

Bell, Derrick A. Jr. (1979) "Bakke, Minority Admissions and the Usual Price of Racial Remedies," 67 q. L. Rev. 3, 13 (1988).

Blum, Lawrence A. (1988) "Opportunity and Equality of Opportunity," *Public Affairs Quarterly*.

Bennets, Leslie (1988) "Carnegie Study Finds Status, Not Brains, Makes a Child's Future," in *Racism and Sexism: An Integrated Study*, ed. Paula Rothenberg, pp. 54, 55.

Blauner, Robert (1989) *Black Lives, White Lives: Three Decades of Race Relations* (1989).

Boxhill, Bernard R. (1978) "The Morality of Preferential Hiring," *Philosophy and Public Affairs* 7, 246–68.

Carter, Stephen L. (1991) *Reflections of an Affirmative Action Baby*.

Crouse, James and Trusheim, Dale (1988) *The Case Against the SAT* (1985).

Dworkin, Ronald (1985) "Why Bakke Has No Case," in *Today's Moral Problems*, ed. Richard Wasserstrom, pp. 138, 145–6.

Ezorsky, Gertrude (1991) *Racism and Justice: The Case for Affirmative Action* p. 72.

Harris, Luke Charles (1994) "Affirmative Action and the White Backlash: Notes from a Child Apartheid," in *Picturing Us: African American Identity in Photography*, ed. Deborah Willis.

Harris, Luke Charles and Narayan, Uma (1994) "Affirmative Action and the Myth of Preferential Treatment: A Transformative Critique of the Terms of the Affirmative Action Debate," *Harvard BlackLetter Law Journal* 11/1.

Kantor, R. M. and Stein, B. A. (1976) "Making a Life at the Bottom," in *Life in Organizations, Workplaces as People Experience Them*, pp. 176–90.

Pyatt, Rudolf A. Jr. (1985) "Significant Job Studies," *Washington Post*, April 30, at D1–D2 (cited in Tom Beauchamp, "Goals and Quotas in Hiring and Promotion," in *Ethical Theory and Business*, ed. Tom Beauchamp and Norman E. Borire (1993), p. 384).

Turner, Margery Austin et al. (1991) *Opportunities Denied, Opportunities Diminished: Racial Discrimination in Hiring* (1991), pp. 91–9.

Phyllis, Rosser (1987) *Sex Bias in College Admissions Tests: Why Women Lose Out*, 2nd edn.

Steele, Shelby (1990) *The Content of our Character: A New Vision of Race in America*.

PART V

Justice

Punishment

Public opinion polls suggest that people in the Western world are increasingly worried about crime. In the United States the public thinks crime is out of control, and that it is out of control because the state has not punished criminals as often or as severely as it should. Thus, for many people, deciding what to do about crime is not a minor technical problem that criminologists or the police should solve. It is a practical problem with momentous consequences. However, it is also imperative that we be responsible citizens. We should not let fear lead us to embrace immoral policies. Harming another person without compelling reasons is wrong, and criminal punishment most assuredly harms the person punished. Therefore, before we blindly embrace a "get tough" policy toward criminals, we should be confident that our system is morally justified. That is, (1) we must determine the circumstances under which the state can justifiably deprive someone of her life or liberty, and (2) we must decide what the morally appropriate punishment would be.

Historically there have been three dominant theories of punishment: deterrence, retribution, and rehabilitation. The deterrence theorist holds that the overriding reason to punish someone is to deter future crime. Thus, the deterrence theory is primarily forward-looking: it is concerned about what will happen in the future, not what has happened in the past.

In contrast, the retributive theory is backward-looking: it emphasizes not the deterrence of future crimes, but punishment for past crimes. Punishing people for their crimes may deter future crimes. However, if it does deter, that is an unexpected benefit of retributive punishment, not its justification.

Finally, the rehabilitative theory, like the deterrence theory, is forward-looking. However, unlike the deterrence theory, its primary aim is not to prevent future crime, but to rehabilitate criminals so that they can return to society as responsible and productive citizens. Of course, rehabilitated criminals are less likely to commit further crimes. Nonetheless, although that may be a desirable consequence of rehabilitation, it is not its purpose.

All three theories often lead to the same practical conclusions. Normally they would agree about whom we should punish, and about how severely we should punish them. For instance, severely punishing an armed robber may be, from the retributivist stand-point, exactly what the criminal deserves, and, for the deterrence theorist, the action most likely to prevent future crime. Moreover, if we carry out the punishment correctly, we might also expect that the criminal would be rehabilitated.

It would be a mistake, however, to infer that since these theories often offer the same practical advice, they are really the same theory dressed differently. Despite their similarities, they will sometimes disagree over whether, when, and how we should punish someone. The severity of punishment required to deter a criminal (and others) is, I suspect, often greater (and other times less) than what we might, on retributive grounds, think the criminal deserves. Perhaps the person has committed a monstrous crime (torture), yet we know that this criminal and others would probably be deterred by only a few months in prison. Or, conversely, someone may have committed an insignificant crime (jaywalking), which we could deter only by a severe punishment (chopping off the offender's legs).

Moreover, even when these theorists do agree about whom we should punish (and how severely we should punish them), they will disagree about why we should punish them. The difference in rationale is likely to lead to important, though perhaps barely perceptible, differences in punishment. Even if both retributive and deterrence theorists conclude that we should send a child molester to prison for 20 years, we will be likely to communicate something different to the criminal (and to others) if we think we are giving the criminal what he deserves, or if we think we are deterring potential child molesters.

It is illuminating to note the striking parallels between these theories of punishment and the consequentialist and deontological ethical theories (THEORIZING ABOUT ETHICS, ETHICAL THEORY). Consequentialist theories are forward-looking; deontological theories tend to be backward-looking. Even when both tell us to refrain from lying, to feed our starving neighbors, or to care for our ailing parents, their reasons for so acting invariably differ. We tend to think

different ethical theories give different practical advice. Sometimes they do, sometimes they don't. What they invariably do is direct us to attend to different features of an action, or to evaluate those features differently. They disagree about which features of an action are morally relevant. Likewise, the principal difference between deterrent and retributive theories is not necessarily that they disagree about whom we should punish, or how we should punish them, but rather *why* we should punish them.

Rachels advocates a backward-looking stance toward punishment. He argues that the key to our ordinary moral understanding is that we should give people what they deserve, and that what people deserve is based on their freely chosen actions. If you work hard, you deserve to get that promotion. If you perform well in school, you deserve good grades. Conversely, if you are a slacker, you do not deserve either a promotion or good grades. This premium on individual responsibility undergirds the retributive theory of punishment.

Retributive theories standardly explain "what people deserve" by reference to not only what the person did (the *actus reus*), but by the state of her mind (the *mens rea*). On this view, it is not appropriate to severely punish someone who did a forbidden action if they lacked the requisite guilty mind. The problem, Doris argues, is that this view typically rests on empirically dubious accounts of human character and motivation. That is, they – along with virtue theory (ETHICAL THEORY) – assume that people have stable characters leading people to act in the same ways, regardless of the circumstances. Such a view cannot be sustained by the evidence. What we find instead, Doris claims, is that people's actions are more frequently determined by small – indeed, seemingly trivial – changes in the environment.

Wright et al. would agree with elements of this proposal, even if they disagree with many of the details. They are criminologists who study the empirical evidence for various forms of punishment. That evidence, they claim, requires the United States (and any country relying on similar approaches to punishment) to seriously rethink current penal practice. The United States now has the highest incarceration rate in the world despite the fact that we have had decreasing crime rates for more than a decade.

A critical account of the evidence to hand, they claim, shows that deterrence just does not work, and may even be counterproductive. Incapacitation (trying to lower crime by getting criminals off the street) works to some degree, but only if it is directed toward a select group of criminals. As a general strategy, it shows no ability to lower crime, and yet comes at a very high cost. All elements of the criminal justice system now consume 10 percent of the country's Gross National Product. The only form of punishment proven to work is rehabilitation. Well-designed rehabilitation programs do lessen crime and decrease the chance for recidivism (returning to crime after release). These programs are especially likely to work with juveniles, and rehabilitating juveniles is especially likely to lower crime.

The last two essays in this section move from a general discussion of punishment to a contentious debate about one form of punishment: the death penalty. Pojman argues that (at least certain) murderers deserve death – that it is the only appropriate response to their heinous crimes. He also claims that we have both empirical and armchair evidence that the death penalty deters murder. Even if one doubts this evidence, it is better to risk being wrong by using the death penalty (and needlessly killing some murderers) than to be wrong by not using it (and failing to save the lives of innocent people who would be their victims). Hence, we should have and use the death penalty.

Reiman agrees that *in principle* the death penalty seems to be an appropriate response for especially heinous murderers. However, the death penalty, at least in our world, is unjustified. For although it might be appropriate to put such people to death, it is not inappropriate to give them a less severe punishment – especially if, as he argues, it is unnecessary as a means of deterring other potential murderers. Moreover, were the state to refrain from using the death penalty – in the same way and for the same reason that they refrain from state-sanctioned torture – it could lessen our tolerance for cruelty, and thus advance human civilization. Finally, we should not use the death penalty because it is applied arbitrarily and discriminatorily.

The contrast here is illuminating. For although these authors seem to agree about some very basic moral principles, they end up giving completely different evaluations of the practice. This shows that what often matters in moral debate is not merely what principles one embraces, but the way in which one interprets and applies them. Moreover, it reveals, once again, the role that empirical evidence plays in many moral debates; for instance, the role it plays in LaFollette's discussion of "Gun Control" (PATERNALISM AND RISK) and Pogge's discussion of WORLD HUNGER.

Further Reading

Duff, R. A. (1986) *Trials and Punishments*. Cambridge: Cambridge University Press.

—— (2003) "Punishment." In H. LaFollette (ed.), *Oxford Handbook of Practical Ethics*. Oxford: Oxford University Press, pp. 331–57.

Duff, R. A. and Garland, D. (1994) *A Reader on Punishment*. Oxford: Oxford University Press.

Gorr, M. and Harwood, S. (eds.) (1995) *Crime and Punishment*. Boston, MA: Jones and Bartlett.

Gross, H. (1979) *Theory of Criminal Punishment*. New York: Oxford University Press.

Hart, H. (1968) *Punishment and Responsibility*. New York: Oxford University Press.

Hondrerich, T. (1984) *Punishment: The Supposed Justification*. New York: Penguin.

Morris, H. (1994/1981) "A Paternalistic Theory of Punishment." In R. A. Duff and D. Garland (eds.), *A Reader on Punishment*. Oxford: Oxford University Press, pp. 92–111.

Murphy, J. (ed.) (1995) *Punishment and Rehabilitation*, 3rd edn. Belmont, CA: Wadsworth Press.

47

Punishment and Desert

James Rachels

When someone who delights in annoying and vexing peace-loving folk receives at last a right good beating, it is certainly an ill, but everyone approves of it and considers it as good in itself, even if nothing further results from it.

Immanuel Kant, *Critique of Practical Reason* (1788)[1]

Retributivism – the idea that wrongdoers should be "paid back" for their wicked deeds – fits naturally with many people's feelings. They find it deeply satisfying when murderers and rapists "get what they have coming," and they are infuriated when villains "get away with it." But others dismiss these feelings as primitive and unenlightened. Sometimes the complaint takes a religious form. The desire for revenge, it is said, should be resisted by those who believe in Christian charity. After all, Jesus himself rejected the rule of "an eye for an eye,"[2] and St Paul underscored the point, saying that we should not "return evil for evil" but we should "overcome evil with good."[3] To those who adopt this way of thinking, whether on secular or religious grounds, vengeance cannot be an acceptable motive for action.

This objection is, for the most part, misguided. The idea that wrongdoers should be "paid back" for their wickedness is not merely a demand for primitive vengeance. It is part of a moral view with a subtle and complicated structure, that can be supported by a surprisingly strong array of arguments. The key idea is that people deserve to be treated in the same way that they voluntarily choose to treat others. If this were only a view about punishment, it would not be very compelling. But the idea that people should be treated according to their deserts is a central component of our general moral understanding. It has applications in many areas of life. Retributivism is just the application of this idea to the special case of punishment.

In what follows we will begin by asking what it means to treat people as they deserve. What does the practice of "treating people as they deserve" involve? We can describe this practice without making any judgement about whether it is a good thing. Then we will consider, as a separate matter, the normative question: Should we treat people as they deserve? Are there any compelling reasons in favor of such a practice? Finally, we will turn to the special case of punishment.

Treating People as They Deserve

Desert and past actions

What people deserve always depends on what they have done in the past. The familiar lament, "What have I done to deserve this?" is not just an idle remark; when desert is at issue, it asks exactly the right question. Consider this case:

> *The two candidates for promotion.* The owner of a small business must decide which of two employees to promote. The first is a man who has been a loyal and hard-working member of the staff for many years. He has frequently taken on extra work without complaint, and in the company's early days, when its future was in doubt, he would put in overtime without demanding extra pay. His efforts are one reason that the company survived and prospered. The other candidate is a man who has always done the least he could get by with, avoiding extra duties and quitting early whenever he could. We may call them Worker and Slacker. Which should the owner promote?

Clearly, Worker deserves the promotion. He has earned it and Slacker has not.

Deserving the promotion is not the same as needing it or wanting it. Both Worker and Slacker might benefit from the promotion; perhaps both could use the extra money and status it would bring. But this has nothing to do with desert. Although Slacker might benefit just as much from being promoted, he does not have the same claim to it as Worker because he has not earned it in the same way.

Nor is the question of desert the same as the question of who would perform better in the new position. Obviously there is reason to think Worker would do better, because he has shown himself to be more diligent. But again, that is not the basis of Worker's claim. Even if we knew that Slacker would reform and do just as well in the new position – the promotion may be just the prod he needs – Worker would still have an independent claim on the promotion, based simply on his past performance.

Does anything other than past performance affect what a person deserves? Sometimes it is assumed that people deserve things because of their superior native endowments. If Slacker is naturally smarter or more talented than Worker, it might be suggested that this makes him

deserving of the promotion. This sort of idea was once commonplace, but it is no longer very popular among those who systematically study ethics. It has fallen into disrepute since the publication of John Rawls's *A Theory of Justice*. Rawls writes that:

> Perhaps some will think that the person with greater natural endowments deserves those assets and the superior character that made their development possible. Because he is more worthy in this sense, he deserves the greater advantages that he could achieve with them. This view, however, is surely incorrect. It seems to be one of the fixed points of our considered judgments that no one deserves his place in the distribution of native endowments, any more than one deserves one's initial starting place in society.[4]

Rawls refers to "our considered judgments," but there is something more here than an appeal to our beliefs. There is also an implicit argument, namely that native endowments are not deserved because no one *does anything* to deserve them: they are the result of a "natural lottery" over which we have no control. If you are naturally smarter or more talented than other people, you are just luckier; and you do not deserve better merely on that account. This fits well with the idea that people deserve things because and only because of their past actions.

What else might plausibly be thought to provide a basis for desert? It has sometimes been suggested that *achievements* are pertinent. It may be argued that Slacker could deserve the promotion, despite Worker's greater effort, if Slacker had succeeded in contributing more to the company. (Maybe Slacker's puny efforts had a big payoff.) But achievements are only the products of native endowments combined with work – often with a good bit of luck thrown in – and if one cannot deserve things because of one's native endowments, neither can one deserve things because of the achievements that those endowments make possible. To see what someone deserves we have to separate the two components (native endowments and work) and identify the contribution made by each. The maximally deserving man or woman is not simply the one who achieves the most, but the one who achieves the most he or she can given the abilities with which he or she is endowed. The key idea, as far as desert is concerned, is "doing the best you can with what you have."

Moral deserts

Moral deserts are deserts that one has, not in virtue of one's performance in a special type of activity (such as working at a job), but in virtue of one's more general way of dealing with other people. We can choose to treat others well or badly, and what we deserve from them in return depends on the choice we make. Consider this example:

> *The ride to work*. Suppose you, Smith, and Jones all work at the same place. One morning your car won't start and you need a ride to work, so you call Smith and ask him to come by for you. But Smith refuses. It is clear that he could do it, but he doesn't want to be bothered, so he makes up some excuse. Then you call Jones, and he gives you the ride you need. A few weeks later, you get a call from Smith. Now he is having car trouble and he asks you for a ride. Should you accommodate him?

Perhaps you will think you should help Smith, despite his own unhelpfulness – after all, it would be little trouble for you, and by helping him you might teach him a lesson in generosity. But if we focus on what he *deserves* a different answer seems obvious: he deserves to be left to fend for himself. Jones, on the other hand, is an entirely different matter. If Jones should ask you for a ride, you have every reason to give it: not only will it help him, he deserves it. This is especially clear when we consider the case of a forced choice:

> *The simultaneous requests*. Smith calls and asks for a ride. Meanwhile, Jones is on the other line also needing a ride. But they live in opposite directions, so it is impossible for you to help both. Which do you help?

If we did not concede that Jones's past conduct makes him more deserving, we would be hard put to explain why it seems so obvious that helping Jones is the mandatory choice.

Particular people may be especially obligated in this way. If someone has done you a favor, *you* are indebted to them and you specifically owe it

to them to return the favor. It is you, and not someone else, who owes Jones the ride. Sometimes this is thought to end the matter: if someone has helped you, it is said, you are indebted to them; otherwise you have no obligation. But it is short-sighted to view things in this way. Anyone at all can justifiably take it as a good reason for treating someone well if that person has treated others well. Suppose Jones is habitually helpful to people, while Smith is not; but you personally have never had much interaction with either of them. Now suppose you must choose which to help, and you cannot help both. Surely their respective histories is a reason, even for you, to prefer Jones. Thus we have:

> *The principle of desert*. People deserve to be treated in the same way that they have (voluntarily) treated others. Those who have treated others well deserve to be treated well in return, while those who have treated others badly deserve to be treated badly in return.

This principle has both a positive and a negative side. Those with a generous temperament may find one appealing but recoil from the other: they may like the idea that some people deserve good treatment but dislike the companion idea that others deserve bad treatment. After all, it seems ungrateful to say that someone who has treated others well does not deserve to be treated well in return; but to say that someone deserves to be treated badly seems, on the face of it, mean-spirited and unsympathetic. So it might be suggested that we keep the idea of positive desert and discard the idea of negative desert.

But this won't work. If we jettison one we will surely have to jettison the other. Superficially it may appear that we could split them apart. We could *say* that some people deserve good treatment but that no one ever deserves ill, and if we go no further this might seem consistent. But the inconsistency would emerge when we tried to provide a rationale for this combination of beliefs. What reasoning could justify holding that good performance merits a positive response that would not also imply that bad performance merits a negative response? The answer, so far as I can tell, is none.

Why People Should Be Treated as They Deserve

So far we have merely described, in a rough-and-ready way, what it means to treat people as they deserve. But we have given no reason whatever for thinking this is a good thing. Should we treat people as they deserve? Or, having seen what the practice involves, should we reject the whole business? There are at least three reasons for treating people according to their deserts. Together they add up to a compelling case.

First, acknowledging deserts is a way of granting people the power to determine their own fates. Because we live together in mutually cooperative societies, how each of us fares depends not only on what we do but on what others do as well. So, if we are to flourish, we need to obtain the good treatment of other people. A system of understandings in which desert is acknowledged gives us a way of doing that. Thus, if you want to be promoted, you may earn it by working hard at your job; and if you want others to treat you decently, you can treat them decently.

Absent this, what are we to do? We might imagine a system in which the only way for a person to secure good treatment by others is somehow to coerce that treatment from them – Worker might try threatening his employer. Or we might imagine that good treatment always comes as charity – Worker might simply hope the employer will be nice to him. But the practice of acknowledging deserts is different. The practice of acknowledging deserts gives people control over whether others will treat them well or badly, by saying to them: if you behave well, you will be *entitled* to good treatment from others because you will have earned it. Without this control people would be impotent, unable to affect how others will treat them and dependent on coercion or charity for any decent treatment they might receive.

I believe this is the deepest reason why desert is important, but there are others. A second reason is connected with the egalitarian idea that social burdens and benefits should be equally distributed. In working harder, Worker had to forgo benefits that Slacker was able to enjoy. While Worker was tied down on the job, Slacker was free to do things that Worker might have liked to do but was unable to. (This, of course, will be typical of any situation in which one person chooses to expend time and effort on a disagreeable task, while another person – faced with the same choice – opts for a more enjoyable alternative.) This suggests a simple argument for rewarding the harder worker: Slacker has had a benefit (more leisure time) that Worker has not had, while Worker has had a burden (more work) that Slacker has not had. Giving Worker a benefit now (the promotion) may therefore be seen as nothing more than righting the balance. Contrary to superficial appearances, then, giving Worker the promotion does not make their respective situations less equal. On the contrary, it alters things in the direction of greater equality. This is a reason why even egalitarians might favor treating people according to their deserts.

These arguments apply equally well to moral deserts. Acknowledging moral desert permits people, who are after all largely dependent for their welfare on what other people do, to control their own fates by allowing them to earn good treatment at the hands of others. They do not have to rely on coercion or charity. Moreover, those who treat others well will have, in the course of doing so, forgone benefits for themselves. There are costs involved in helping others – in giving you the ride, Jones was inconvenienced in a way that Smith was not. So once again, reciprocating is a way of making the distribution of burdens and benefits more nearly equal.

To these reasons a third may be added. Morality includes (some would say it consists in) how we choose to treat other people in our myriad interactions with them. But if reciprocity could not be expected, the morality of treating others well would come to occupy a less important place in people's lives. Morality would have no reward, and immorality would have no bad consequences; so there would be less reason for one to be concerned with it. If people were perfectly benevolent, of course, such incentives would not be needed. But for imperfectly benevolent beings such as ourselves the acknowledgment of deserts provides the reason for being moral that is required for the whole system to be effective.

Punishment

Retributivism is the application of the Principle of Desert to the special case of criminal punishment: it is the view that people who commit crimes such as murder and rape deserve to be punished and that this alone is sufficient to justify punishing them. It is not merely that punishing them satisfies certain sorts of vengeful feelings. On the contrary, it is a violation of justice if murderers and rapists are allowed to walk away as if they had done nothing wrong. It is a matter of justice for the same reason that promoting Worker is a matter of justice or that preferring to help Jones rather than Smith is a matter of justice.

As we have seen, acknowledging deserts is part of a moral system that allows people, by their own behavior, to determine how others will respond to them. Those who treat others well elicit good treatment in return, while those who treat others badly provoke ill treatment in return. That is why, when a criminal is punished, it may be said that "He brought it on himself." The argument concerning equality is also commonly invoked when punishment is at issue. There are costs associated with law-abidance. Law-abiding people bear a burden – inconvenient constraints on their conduct – that the lawbreaker has not shouldered. Meanwhile the lawbreaker has had benefits denied to others (assuming that his illegal conduct was not entirely irrational, and that there was profit of *some* kind in it for him). Punishment corrects things in the direction of greater equality.[5] That is why it is commonly said that crime "upsets the scales of justice" and that punishing wrongdoers "restores the balance."

But the charge that retributivism is a mere rationalization of vengeful feelings is not the only objection that has been made against it. Philosophers have faulted retributivism on other, weightier grounds. Bentham, who believed that social policies should promote the general welfare, noted that retributivism approves of *increasing the amount of suffering in the world* – if a miscreant harms someone, and we "pay him back" by harming him in return, we have only added to the total misery. Bentham did not see how this could be right. In his *Principles of Morals and Legislation*, published only one year after Kant's remark about the "right good beating," Bentham wrote: "All punishment is mischief: all punishment in itself is evil." Therefore, he concluded, "if it ought at all to be admitted, it ought only to be admitted in as far as it promises to exclude some greater evil."[6]

How can punishment "exclude some greater evil"? The obvious answer is by preventing crime. If there were no rules against murder, assault, and theft, no one would be safe; we would live in a Hobbesian State of Nature in which life would be "solitary, poor, nasty, brutish, and short." To avoid this, it is not enough to ask people politely if they would mind behaving themselves. Murder, theft, and the like cannot be left as matters of individual discretion. So, to ensure compliance with such rules, we attach sanctions to them. We do not say "Please do not murder"; we say "You must not murder, *or else*."

The idea that punishment is justified as a means of preventing crime is so natural and appealing that we might expect it would dominate social-scientific thinking about the criminal justice system. Surprisingly, however, it has not been that influential. During the past 150 years a different sort of conception has prevailed. In the latter half of the nineteenth century it was argued that, if we are serious about preventing crime, we should try to identify its causes and do something about them. Crime, it was said, results from poverty, ignorance, and unemployment; therefore, social energy should be directed toward eliminating those blights. Moreover, when individuals commit crimes, rather than simply punishing them, we should address the problems that caused their aberrant behavior. People turn to crime because they are uneducated, lack job skills, and have emotional problems. So they should be educated, trained, and treated, with an eye to making them into "productive members of society" who will not repeat their offenses. In enlightened circles this came to be regarded as the only sensible approach. As Bertrand Russell once put it:

> No man treats a motorcar as foolishly as he treats another human being. When the car will not go, he does not attribute its annoying behavior to sin; he does not say, "You are a wicked motorcar, and I shall not give you any more petrol until you go." He attempts to find out what is wrong and to set it right.[7]

Today people are often skeptical about efforts to rehabilitate criminals. Those efforts have not been notably successful, and there is reason to doubt whether they could be successful – for one thing, we do not know nearly enough about the individual causes of crime or the nature of personality or motivation to design effective ways to control them. Nevertheless, rehabilitationist ideas have been the single most important force in shaping the modern criminal justice system.[8] In the United States prisons are not even called prisons; they are called "correctional facilities," and the people who work in them are called "corrections officers."

Here, then, are three theories about punishment: retributivism, deterrence, and rehabilitation. What are we to make of them? We have already seen that retributivism is more plausible than its critics suppose. But the other theories are also plausible. As for the deterrence theory, there is no doubt that sanctions are useful. They ensure massive, if imperfect, compliance with the social rules. That would probably be enough to justify punishment even if there was no other argument available. Moreover, it is hard to deny that rehabilitating criminals would be a good thing, if only we knew how to do it. Yet it can still be argued that the criminal justice system should not be designed primarily to promote deterrence or rehabilitation. Rather, it should be designed along lines suggested by the retributive theory.

The argument for this is that a system of punishment based on retributive principles is fairer and more just than systems fashioned after those other ideas. This may be shown by considering the following four principles:

1 *Guilt*: Only the guilty may be punished.

This is perhaps the most fundamental of all rules of justice: if you have committed no crime, the law should leave you alone.

2 *Equal Treatment*: People who have committed the same crime should get the same punishment.

It is not fair for one person to be sent to prison for five years, while another is incarcerated for only eighteen months, if they are charged and convicted for exactly the same offense.

3 *Proportionality*: The punishment should be proportional to the crime.

Sometimes it is not easy to say what punishment "fits" a particular crime; nevertheless, the basic idea is clear enough. Serious crimes merit severe punishments, while minor infractions should receive only mild punishments. People should not be sent to prison for jay-walking; nor should they be fined five dollars for murder.

4 *Excuses*: People who have good excuses should not be punished, or at the very least, they should not be punished as severely as if they had no excuse.

Excuses include, for example, accident (the child ran in front of the car and there was no way the driver could stop), coercion (the man was forced to help the criminals because they were holding a gun to his head), and ignorance of fact (that nurse had been told by the child's mother that the child was not allergic to penicillin). In each case, if there was no excuse (the driver deliberately ran over the child, the man willingly participated in the crime, the nurse knowingly gave the child a harmful drug), the person would be fully blameworthy. But the excuse relieves the person of responsibility and so he or she should not be punished.

Any system of punishment is unjust if it departs from these four principles. But now suppose we were to design a system of punishment with deterrence in mind – that is to say, suppose we were to give the system just those features it would need to motivate people not to break the law. Would such a system satisfy these four principles?

(1) *Guilt* – No. There is no reason, if we are concerned only with deterrence, to punish only the guilty. As far as deterrence is concerned, what matters is not whether the person punished is guilty, but whether he or she is generally *believed* to be guilty. If people believe she is guilty, the deterrent effect will be the same as if she really were guilty. Moreover, from this point of view, it would be much better to convict an innocent person (who is generally believed to be guilty) than for the crime to go "unsolved," because when crimes are unsolved people get the idea that the law is ineffective and the deterrent effect of the law is diminished.

(2) *Equal Treatment* – Yes. A system of punishment designed solely to maximize the deterrent effect would need to be consistent in meting out similar punishments for similar crimes. This would be necessary to assure people who are tempted to violate the law that they will also get the full penalty. If in some cases lesser penalties had been imposed, then they might reasonably hope for the lesser penalty, and the deterrent effect would thereby be diminished.

(3) *Proportionality* – No. How severe should punishments be? If we are concerned only to deter crime, we will want to make penalties severe enough that the unlawful behavior really will be discouraged. This is a very different standard from the idea that punishments should "fit the crime." For example, a penalty that would actually stop people from jay-walking might have to be much more severe than we would think appropriate given the trivial nature of the offense.

(4) *Excuses* – No. For purposes of deterrence, it is best to have a "no excuses accepted" policy. If excuses are allowed, people might hope to avoid punishment by pleading special circumstances. A system that relentlessly punishes all offenders will offer less hope of avoiding punishment and so will have greater deterrent power.

A deterrence-based system of punishment will therefore violate three of the four principles. What about a system of rehabilitation? Rehabilitation fares no better.

(1) *Guilt* – No. The basic aim of such a system is to transform people who are inclined to commit crimes into people who are not inclined to commit crimes. The fact that someone *has* committed a crime is simply the best evidence we currently have of the inclination. But if it were possible to identify such people in advance, why should we wait until a crime has actually been committed? Why not go ahead and pick up individuals who are deemed likely to commit crimes and subject them to the rehabilitative routines? Of course this seems unjust, but there is nothing in the basic idea of such a system to preclude bringing people who have not committed crimes within its grasp.

(2) *Equal Treatment* – No. In a system designed to rehabilitate, individuals who have committed similar crimes will not receive similar treatments. What will happen to a particular lawbreaker will depend on his or her particular circumstances. Typically, a convicted person will be sentenced to prison for an indefinite period of time – say, "not less than ten nor more than twenty years" – and then he or she will be released when the authorities (the prison officials, a parole board) decide they are "ready" to be released. Since it takes people different amounts of time to be rehabilitated, the amount of time served will vary from prisoner to prisoner.

As we have already noted, the American criminal justice system has largely been shaped by the rehabilitationist ideal, in theory if not in fact. The widespread use of indefinite sentencing, the parole system, and the like, are manifestations of this. But the rehabilitationist character of the system has implications that are frequently misunderstood. Often critics point out that an affluent white offender is likely to serve less time in prison than a black kid from the ghetto, even if they have committed the same crime (say, a drug-related crime); and this disparity is attributed to racism. Racism no doubt has something to do with it.

But it should not be overlooked that the prevailing rehabilitationist ideology also contributes decisively to such outcomes. When a "white-collar criminal" is well-educated, psychologically healthy, and has a good job, there's not much for a rehabilitationist system to do with him. He may as well be given an early release. But a surly, uneducated kid with no job skills is another matter – he is just the sort of person for whom the system is designed.

(3) *Proportionality* – No. It should now be clear why a rehabilitative system will not respond proportionately to the crimes committed. It will respond instead to the offender's psychological or educational needs. More concretely, in most US jurisdictions today, the length of one's stay in prison will depend on a parole board's judgment about when one is ready to be released, not on the seriousness of one's offense.

(4) *Excuses* – Yes. This is the only one of our four principles with which the rehabilitationist ideology is in accord. People need to be rehabilitated only if something in their character inclines them to commit crimes. But if someone violated the law only because of an unavoidable accident, coercion, or the like, then they do not need to be rehabilitated – or at least, the fact that they violated the law in this manner provides no evidence of it. So, in a rehabilitationist scheme, offenders with a good excuse would be let off the hook.

Once again, three of our four principles are violated.

When we turn to retributivism, however, things are entirely different. Retributivism incorporates all four principles in the most natural way possible. (1) Only the guilty should be punished, because innocent people have not done anything to deserve punishment. (2) People who committed the same crime should receive the same punishment, because what one deserves depends only on what one has done. It is a trivial consequence of the Principle of Desert that those who have behaved in the same way deserve the same response. (3) The Principle of Desert also requires proportionate responses, because what people deserve de-

Table 47.1

	Deterrence	Rehabilitation	Retribution
Guilt	No	No	Yes
Equal Treatment	Yes	No	Yes
Proportionality	No	No	Yes
Excuses	No	Yes	Yes

pends on how well, or how badly, they have behaved. A murderer has treated another person very badly indeed, and so deserves a very severe response. (That is why retributivists are inclined to support capital punishment in principle, although they might have other reasons for opposing it in practice.) A thief, on the other hand, has done something less wicked, and so deserves a more moderate response. (4) Finally, a retributivist system of punishment would have to accept excuses, because what people deserve depends only on their *voluntary* behavior. Acceptable excuses show that behavior was not voluntary; that is why the demonstration that one was coerced, or that it was all an unavoidable accident, and the like, gets one off the hook.

We have now asked a number of questions about the three theories and four principles, and we might summarize our results as is shown in the table below. The upshot is that retribution is the only idea that provides the basis of a just system of punishment. The other ideas do not even come close.

Does all this mean that Kant was right? Unlike Bentham, who believed that, to be justified, the pains of punishment must "exclude some greater evil," Kant believed that a villain's punishment is "good in itself, even if nothing further results from it." The arguments we have examined seem to support Kant, but they do so only up to a point. To justify punishing someone, we may refer simply to what he or she has done – we may point out that they deserve it. But when we examine the arguments that support the general practice of treating people as they deserve, it turns out that those arguments all refer to ways in which people are *better off* under such a practice. So, at least as far as anything said here is concerned, the ultimate justifications could all be utilitarian.

Thus we might understand our overall situation as follows. The best social practices are the ones that maximize welfare. The practice of treating people as they deserve is like this – people are on the whole better off if deserts are taken into account than if decisions are made solely on other grounds. One consequence of this is that we end up with a retributive understanding of punishment. Our feelings – our sense of justice, which requires that the four principles be satisfied, and our retributive feelings, which cause us to be happy when villains are punished and outraged when they are not – are useful because they reinforce the useful social practice. So Kant's description of our attitudes is correct: when the annoying fellow gets at last a right good beating, we approve of it even if there are no further results. But in the larger accounting, it is a good thing that we have such attitudes only because they reinforce social practices that do have further results.

Notes

1 Immanuel Kant, *Critique of Practical Reason*, translated by Lewis White Beck (Chicago: University of Chicago Press, 1949; but originally published in 1788), p. 170.
2 Matthew 5: 38–41.
3 Romans 12: 17, 21.
4 John Rawls, *A Theory of Justice* (Cambridge, MA: Harvard University Press, 1971) pp. 103–4.
5 Philosophical discussions of justice frequently distinguish "retributive justice" from "distributive justice" and treat them as altogether different topics. But if this argument is correct, the two are closely related.
6 Jeremy Bentham, *An Introduction to the Principles of Morals and Legislation* (New York: Hafner, 1948; but first published in 1789), p. 170.
7 Bertrand Russell, *Why I Am Not a Christian* (New York: Simon and Schuster, 1967), p. 40.
8 *Struggle for Justice: A Report on Crime and Punishment in America*, by the American Friends Service Committee (New York: Hill & Wang, 1971), is still one of the best discussions of the rehabilitationist idea ever produced.

48

Out of Character: On the Psychology of Excuses in the Criminal Law

John M. Doris

In Western cultures, personality appraisals structure social interaction: affections and aversions are regularly cued to perceptions of character.[1] This way of thinking is not limited to us ordinary folks; it is articulated in the philosophical tradition of "virtue ethics," where qualities of character, rather than qualities of action, are the primary focus of ethical reflection (e.g., MacIntyre, 1984; Williams, 1985; Annas, 1993; Hursthouse, 1999). Recently, critics have argued that both folk and philosophers are misguided: familiar understandings of character, they contend, are undercut by empirical investigation in the human sciences (Flanagan, 1991; Doris, 1998, 2002, forthcoming; Harman, 1999, 2000; Merritt, 2000; Vranas, 2005). The critics have themselves drawn spirited criticism, but I won't here attempt resolving the debate (see Miller, 2003; Montmarquet, 2003; Kamtekar, 2004; Sabini and Silver, 2005; Annas, forthcoming). Instead, I reflect on how a question there embodied – *What is the most perspicuous understanding of human psychology?* – might impact the theory of punishment and excuses in the criminal law.

Just as some moral philosophers have argued that a psychology of character is indispensable to ethical reflection, numerous legal theorists argue that punishment and excuse are best justified by reference to the wrongdoer's character (e.g., Pincoffs, 1973; Brandt, 1985; Vuoso, 1987; Arenella, 1990; Tadros, 2001, 2005).[2] These "character theorists" offer a *theoretical reconstruction* of legal practice; while they recognize that criminal law frequently focuses on properties of actions more than properties of persons, they insist that the deeper rationale for determining criminal liability relies on character assessment (Vuoso, 1987, p. 1662). I want to ask whether such a reconstruction is sustainable: while there is much to commend it, character theory has not – like all but the most recent moral philosophy – been articulated with sufficient attention to highly relevant empirical research, particularly that found in experimental social psychology.[3] When this omission is corrected, I argue, there emerges good reason to doubt the role of character in criminal law.

Preliminaries

I'll understand punishment as applying penalty in response to wrongdoing, and I'll assume a retributivist, or "backward-looking" approach.

For the retributivist, punishment is justified "on the grounds that wrongdoing merits punishment" (Rawls, 1955, p. 4); as one might put it, the individual may be justly punished when she *deserves* to incur penalty for something she has done (or failed to do). When I say a person is entitled an excuse I'll mean that although what she did was criminal, it is not appropriate to subject her to punishment (see Tadros, 2001, pp. 498–9); to put it another way, when an individual has an excuse she does not deserve to be punished for her action. Although matters are rather more complicated than is sometimes supposed, I'll follow the custom of distinguishing excuses, such as duress, from justifications, such as self-defense, which assert that no wrongdoing occurred (see Husak, forthcoming). The question of whether punishing a particular wrongdoer is warranted, then, can be approached through the question of whether they are entitled an excuse, and that is exactly how I will approach it.

Character Theory

According to the character theorist, the proper focus of a criminal proceeding is not the particular criminal act, but the character trait manifested in that act. For example, criminal property damage might be understood as flowing from "the absence of an adequate aversion" to infringing property rights, and it is the personal deficiency, rather than the action itself, to which criminal liability attaches (Brandt, 1985, p. 174). But if criminal liability fixes to character rather than actions, why shouldn't courts preemptively punish deficiencies of character, rather than waiting until wrongful action has occurred (see Duff, 1993, p. 371)?

A more plausible way for character to enter the picture is through the notion of excuse: in a view perhaps attributable to Hume (1978/1740, p. 411, cf. 575), character theorists maintain that people are responsible for their actions insofar as these actions are expressions of their character, so that "an excuse will be available to the defendant to the extent that her action was no manifestation of her character" (Tadros,

2001, pp. 495–6, cf. 501; Duff, 1993, p. 367).[4] Thus, if the wrongful action is not the proper expression of the agent's character – "out of character," it is sometimes said – legal penalty is not appropriately imposed. It is this proposal that I will attempt to explicate and assess in what follows.

That the law must account for the psychological condition of the actor is not a novel suggestion – that is the gist of *mens rea*, the requirement of a "guilty mind" for criminal liability.[5] What makes character theory distinctive is the contention that the requisite psychological assessment cannot be undertaken without evaluation of the actor's character. I will not explore this contention as it relates to the general issue of *mens rea*, but will limit myself to the theory of excuses. As an expository convenience, I focus on duress.

Witness intimidation and the suborning of perjury are, according to the United States Department of Justice, among the most serious obstacles to the prosecution of organized crime (Finn and Healy, 1996). At the Boston trial of gang members accused of killing a ten-year old girl, spectators came to the courtroom wearing "Stop Snitching" T-shirts, while a witness to another Boston shooting found copies of his grand jury testimony posted in the apartment building where he lived (Butterfield, 2005). The American mafia, of course, has long set the standard: one FBI informant was disemboweled as a warning to others who might "spill their guts," while a murder victim with wires driven into his head illustrated the hazards of "wearing a wire" (Earley and Shur, 2003).

Prescinding from the horror of authentic detail, consider Citizen and Criminal, two rather wooden characters who have, to my dismay, insinuated themselves throughout this paper. Both testify in a high-profile mafia trial, and both commit perjury subsequent to some especially impressive witness intimidation. Ordinarily, Citizen is an upstanding citizen, but in this instance, the threats did their work; facing unspeakable consequences, Citizen dissembles on the stand. Criminal, on the other hand, is a mafia soldier of the old school, and hasn't a thought of breaking *omertà* by testifying truthfully. It's not that he's unimpressed by the threats; in the past, he's been the instrument rather than the object, so he knows better than most what the penalties are. But he doesn't perjure himself *because* of the intimidation; he does so because he is, as his old-school colleagues like to say, a "man of honor."

It's tempting to suppose that Citizen is entitled a duress excuse, and Criminal not; we'd like to hold Criminal, but not Citizen, criminally liable for his perjury. But both Citizen and Criminal experience the same, undeniably impressive, threat; what's wanted, if we are to preserve the tempting distinction, is a way of making out the thought that one may *occupy excusing conditions* without being *entitled an excuse*. The natural thought is that Criminal *would have done it anyway*, regardless of the threat, so the threat is somehow irrelevant (compare Tadros, 2005, p. 299). But what could justify confidence in this counterfactual? A likely answer proceeds in terms of character: Criminal is the sort of person who can be reliably expected to give false testimony in court, while Citizen is the sort of person who can be reliably expected to tell the truth.

Tadros (2001, p. 518, cf. 507–8; cf. Vuoso, 1987, pp. 1673, 1682) puts the excuse like this:

> [A]lthough I behaved wrongly, I was in a state where my actions did not reflect my settled character. And I was either not responsible for or justified for being in that state. In short, I did it but I was really not myself, and for good reason.

This seems a fair way to describe the case at hand. Citizen's threat-induced perjury did not reflect his "settled character"; when he did what he did, he "wasn't himself." Criminal's perjury, on the other hand, well reflects his (criminal) character; when he perjured himself, he *just was* being himself. As I'll eventually argue, much turns on whether we can make the needed sense of "settled character," but for now, the point is that the character theory allows an attractive distinction between occupying excusing conditions and being entitled to an excuse.

Compare a "choice theory" of criminal liability, such as that associated with Hart (1968,

p. 22; cf. Moore, 1990): a person is justly punished only if "he broke the law by an action which was the outcome of his free choice." Famously, duress is problematic for such accounts: cases of coercion, under familiar descriptions, often *do* have the look of choices, at least in the "minimal" sense that the victim acted knowingly and wanted to do as she did (Duff, 1993, p. 352). It's natural to suppose that the well-armed thug coerces me when he relieves me of my wallet, yet it's equally natural to suppose that my donation was a paradigm of choice: all things considered, I prefer my life to my money. So also, one is tempted to think, in the case of Citizen; he'd rather lie under oath than go the ghastly way of other mafia witnesses. Citizen's action looks to be knowingly chosen, even as he wishes to not face such a choice. Something looks to have gone wrong here, since the conviction that Citizen didn't *really* choose lingers; the choice account apparently offers too "skimpy" an account of criminal liability (Duff, 1993, p. 368).

In attempt to enrich the account of choice, we might proceed as follows. While it is true that Citizen chooses to perjure himself, his choice is not a reflection of his "rational judgment." Making a rough start on "rational judgment," we might say his choice was not a reflection of his values, or *evaluative commitments*, just as we might say that Criminal's choice *was* an expression of his. Citizen firmly values truth telling and cooperating with the authorities, while Criminal values neither of these things. The threat counts as an excuse for Citizen because it precluded Citizen from choosing in accordance with his values; his behavior was not a reflection of his rational "plan of life." While Citizen and Criminal both choose to perjure themselves, in the skimpy sense of "choose," only Criminal's choice was the sort to which criminal liability properly attaches.

Fleshed out this way, choice theory is slouching into character theory. To explicate choice along in terms of rational judgment, and rational judgment in terms of evaluative commitments, is to construe choice in terms of character, insofar as to describe a person's character is, at least in substantial measure, to describe their evaluative commitments (Duff, 1993, pp. 352–3).[6] So the character theorist's reconstruction goes: to preserve the thought that Citizen's perjury is to be excused and Criminal's not, we need to understand their behavior in terms of their characters. The strategy may be supposed to generalize: character evaluation is the key to explicating psychological notions, such as choice, central in the criminal law.

The Character in Character Theory

To fairly assess character theory, we need to develop the operative conception of character. On standard views, character is made up of *enduring* character traits that issue in *reliable patterns* of thought and action (e.g., Duff, 1993, p. 365; Tadros, 2001, pp. 503–4). Of course, not all character traits are a proper concern for the law, at least in a liberal democracy. Those of interest are typically referenced in the language of virtue and vice, particularly the virtues and vices implicated in observing or disregarding the criminal law: honesty/dishonesty, generosity/meanness, compassion/callousness (Duff, 1993, p. 364; Tadros, 2001, p. 497). It is tempting to understand these traits as dispositions (e.g., Duff, 1993, p. 365), and say that to have a character trait is to have a persisting disposition behave in certain ways: Citizen is reliably disposed to behave honestly, while Criminal is reliably disposed to behave dishonestly, and so on. This way of talking seems sensible enough, but we must proceed cautiously, lest talk of dispositions misleadingly suggest that character traits can be fully specified by reference to overt behavioral manifestations, without consideration of underlying psychological processes (Doris, 2002, pp. 16–17, forthcoming). While it is uncontroversial that character traits are associated with *action* (Duff, 1993, p. 365), they are also associated with *reason*: as Tadros (2001, p. 503; cf. Arenella, 1990, p. 79; Duff, 1993, p. 366) has it, "[o]ne's character is made up, at least to a significant degree, by the reasons that commonly move one." We might say, then, that character traits involve *settled patterns of reason-responsiveness*; some of these responses take the form of actions, but others take the form of thoughts, judgments, emotions, and the like.

In saying such things, we are saying things that embody a venerable tradition: as Aristotle said in the *Ethics* (1105a30–b1), for an action to count as virtuous, the actor must act knowingly choose the action for its own sake, and act from "a firm and unchangeable character." Aristotle's classical picture resonates with influential contemporary expositors such as Nussbaum (1999, p. 170), who writes that virtue ethics is typically concerned with the "settled patterns of motive, emotion, and reasoning that lead us to call someone a person of a certain sort (courageous, generous, moderate, just, etc.)."[7] This venerable tradition, as we'll now see, has lately become controversial – in ways that have implications for the character theory of excuses.

Unsettled Characters

There exists a long experimental tradition in social psychology that unsettles the notion of "settled character" central in character theory (Ross and Nisbett, 1991; Doris, 2002; Vranas, 2005). For example:

- Isen and Levin (1972, p. 387) discovered that subjects who had just found a dime were 22 times more likely to help a woman who had dropped some papers than subjects who did not find a dime (88 percent v. 4 percent).
- Haney et al. (1973) describe how college students role playing as "guards" in a simulated prison began, over the course of only a few days, to systematically abuse students playing the role of "prisoners."
- Darley and Batson (1973, p. 105) report that passersby not in a hurry were six times more likely to help an unfortunate who appeared to be in significant distress than were passersby in a hurry (63 percent v. 10 percent).
- Milgram (1974) found that subjects would repeatedly "punish" a screaming "victim" with realistic (but simulated) electric shocks at the polite request of an experimenter.

- Mathews and Canon (1975, pp. 574–5) reported subjects were five times more likely to help an apparently injured man who had dropped some books when ambient noise was at normal levels than when a power lawnmower was running nearby (80 percent v. 15 percent).

These experiments are not aberrational, but *representative*: social psychologists have *repeatedly* found that both disappointing omissions and appalling actions are *readily* induced through seemingly minor situational manipulations. What makes these findings so striking is just how insubstantial the situational influences effecting troubling moral failures seem to be; it is not that people fail standards for good conduct that they themselves appear to endorse, but that they can be induced to do so with such ease. At the same time, research predicated on the attribution of character and personality traits has enjoyed uneven success in the prediction of behavior; standard measures of personality traits have very often been found to be tenuously related to behavior in particular situations where the expression of that trait is expected.[8] In short, the record indicates that situational influences often appear to do their work with little regard to the character or personality of the person in the situation. Viewing this very substantial experimental tradition, we should begin to question whether behavior is appropriately understood as "flowing" from "settled character."

It is important to see that this difficulty obtains whether psychological or behavioral aspects of character are emphasized. The studies just cited were in the first instance concerned with overt behavior, but the workings of what philosophers like to call "reason" has been shown to be similarly susceptible to situational flux. For example, a wealth of empirical work indicates that people experience remarkable difficulty "transferring" cognitive skills across even closely related domains, such as from job training to actual work situations; they may solve problems effectively in one context and fail to solve similar problems in another (Detterman, 1993; Ceci, 1996). Additionally, quantities of experimental work indicate that even slight variations in problem formulation may affect judgment. Perhaps most famous are the "framing effects" documented by Tversky and Kahneman (1981); in their well-known "Asian Disease" case, couching proposed public health interventions in terms of numbers "saved" or numbers that will "die" affected subject assessments of which interventions were best, even though the fatality estimates for the different "framings" of the problem were *identical*. Many such framing effects look to be *ethically irrelevant* influences on ethical responses, just as whether or not one has found a dime is unrelated to whether one is morally obligated to help.[9] Our habits of reason are not in every case responsive to the most appropriate considerations.

Another suggestive line of research indicates that the salience of different values is highly sensitive to seemingly minor variations in the cognitive environment. For example, Gardner et al. (1999; cf. Brewer and Gardner, 1996; Gardner et al., 2002) found that subjects "primed" by searching for first personal *plural* pronouns (e.g., *we*, *ours*) in a writing sample were subsequently more likely to report that "interdependent" values such belongingness, friendship, and family security were a "guiding principle in their lives" than were subjects primed by searching for first personal *singular* pronouns (e.g., *I*, *mine*). Apparently, what evaluative commitments people are willing to affirm can be influenced by trivialities; values drift on the waters of circumstance.

Of course, "reason" and "action" cannot be easily disentangled; indeed, the situational variability of cognitive processes can be invoked to explain behavioral variability. For example, Darley and Batson (1973, pp. 107–8) observe that some of their hurried subjects may have failed to help the apparently ailing "victim" because haste impeded their ability to see the situation as an "occasion for ethical decision." How one behaviorally responds to one's environment depends on how one codes it, and this coding is itself highly dependent on environmental factors. "Reason-responsiveness" is likely to be no less situationally variable than is overt behavior.

As indicated above, commentators have drawn pointed conclusions from such research, arguing that (1) familiar conceptions of character, like the "settled character" of the present discussion, are *empirically inadequate*, and (2) ethical reflection would benefit from reduced reliance on such conceptions. Moreover, it has been suggested that such arguments, if sound, have radical implications; for example, Kamtekar (2004; cf. Doris, forthcoming) asserts that they threaten a far-reaching skepticism about "the power of practical reasoning."

I won't now agitate for such contentions: the issues are both complex and contested, and space here precludes the *detailed* empirical discussion required to responsibly join the debate (see Doris and Stich, 2005; Doris, forthcoming). More importantly, making headway on the present issue does not require pressing a radical skepticism, for the empirical literature indicates that the notion of "out of character" required by character theory is epistemically unsustainable, whether or not one favors a strong skepticism about character. In short, the situational sensitivity of human behavior makes it impracticable to determine, in the bulk of particular cases, whether an "out of character" excuse is warranted.

The Epistemological Problem

How is it to be established that a criminal act is out of character? We might start by saying that an action is out of character when it is uncharacteristic, or not the sort of thing the agent typically does. We could then attempt to explicate "uncharacteristic" statistically: if the actor has not previously, or has seldom (exercising the philosophical prerogative to remain vague on the numbers) acted in this way, that action is out of character.

This won't do. Unless one is a mafia turncoat, government official, or the like, one does not often testify in court; moreover, many criminal actions, such as homicide, are relatively rare, and serial offenders are still rarer; but surely one need not be a career recidivist to be liable for their crime. (We might be justly con-

fident that a particular crime committed by a career recidivist or serial offender is in character, but acknowledging such limited cases does not establish the general applicability of character theory.) A possible fix proceeds in terms of frequency, so that an act is out of character if it is seldom undertaken relative to available opportunities. But adverting to frequencies won't do either, even supposing they could be meaningfully estimated; that I pass on countless opportunities to kill my rival before working up the nerve to do him in doesn't present the makings of a promising excuse.

Here, the character theorist will say, is where the dangers of focusing on actions at the expense of reasons loom large. Even habitual behaviors may emerge as novel when described in sufficient detail; behaviorally speaking, one can't step in the same river twice. What is "settled" is not our ever-varying behaviors, but the reasons for which we so behave: your brushing your teeth (and, of course, your flossing!) is variously performed, but it consistently expresses your abiding commitment to the value of good oral hygiene.

This won't do, either. Doesn't Citizen's perjury express a characteristic reason? If he's an averagely prudent man, won't he consistently be impressed by impressive threats? Maybe something turns on how we specify the action: under one description Citizen acts on characteristic (prudential) reason of *his own*, but under another, he acts on the characteristic (criminal) reason of *someone else*, namely his threatener. While his "complying with a threat" expresses his settled character, his "perjuring himself" does not. He is therefore to be excused for perjuring himself, even though he is responsible for complying with the threat. On the other hand, Criminal's perjuring himself does reflect his settled character; he does so for reasons, like fealty to *omertà*, that are his own. (Indeed, it is therefore not obvious that Criminal can be aptly said to *comply* with the threat, even if his actions conform to it.)

There's still trouble. Suppose Citizen had been *unfailingly* honest, and then did something mendacious. We here have strong *prima facie* evidence of an action being "out of character";

simply put, it's the sort of thing Citizen has *never* done before. But how do we decide that this anomaly is a case of circumstances forcing a "fundamental shift" in character (Tadros, 2001, p. 504), and is not an "in character" response to a novel confluence of circumstances? This point requires emphasis: for the character theorist, it's not that something is *merely* out of character that indicates an excuse, but the fact that the out-of-character behavior reflects a *situationally induced destabilization of character* (cf. Tadros, 2005, pp. 296–8). But we can't simply cross-examine Citizen to establish the absence or presence of destabilization, given the well-known (and well-documented) schisms between what we say we care about and what we do; testimony about one's self is very often, intentionally or not, unreliable testimony.[10]

Then we'd better get cracking, because there's a lot of poking about on offer: Does Citizen, being of sound body, park in handicap spaces? Pull the appropriate permits when working on his house? And to the extent that honesty and not mere lawfulness is relevant to the character assessment at issue, we might want to dig deeper: Does Citizen cheat on his spouse? Cheat at cards? Lie in confession? This seems a lot of work for the courts, but there's still more required, since we need to establish the habits of reason-responsiveness that inform the behavioral patterns we identify; we must catalog not only behavior, but also cognition, affect, and motivation.

What will the patterns look like, once we've endured the required toil? What is the likely result, if a court could open Citizen's book of days? Far the best bet, based on the empirical evidence, is a very mixed bag. Remember what the evidence indicated: it is rather easy to get people to behave in morally undesirable ways, even people there is every reason to think are more or less ordinary folk; for example, there is no reason to think that the subjects in the above-mentioned obedience and prison experiments were possessed of aberrant personalities, their appalling behavior notwithstanding (Haney et al., 1973, pp. 71–3; Milgram, 1974, p. 205; Miller, 1986, pp. 238–42; Blass, 1991, pp. 402–3). While there is some controversy

about how strongly such claims should be stated, there is little doubt that *it is very often ordinary people who do terrible things* (for discussion, see Doris, 2002, ch. 3). This is not to describe a laboratory artifact; controversy again duly noted, it represents a standard interpretation of perpetrator psychology in atrocity (Arendt, 1964, p. 25; cf. 276; Levi, 1965, p. 228; Browning, 1992, pp. 159ff.; Todorov, 1996, pp. 121ff.).

However unsettling this thesis is, with its implications for our own fragile decency, the alternative is to suppose that certain places at certain times – be it 1940s Germany, 1990s Rwanda, or "Frontier" America – are home to remarkably high percentages of individuals exhibiting abnormalities like psychopathy. If we accept the altogether plausible assumption that Citizen, like most of us, has experienced a wide variety of subtly and not so subtly various situations, we should conclude that his behavior has also been widely various, even if it does not manifest extremes of the sort marking totalitarian states and other social degradations.

Most human organisms are responsive to an impressively large suite of evaluatively conflicting stimuli, such as incentives to break and obey the law, so that it will be near impossible to say whether that reason is or is not "theirs" in the sense required. And this will be true even if we suppose that there are often individual differences sufficient to ground fairly confident comparisons, such as, "Citizen is a better citizen than Criminal." For instance, many of the obedient – and normal – Milgram subjects apparently manifested tendencies *both* towards deference to authority *and* to resist inflicting suffering on others. Such conflict is a persistent feature of experimental and historical study of moral failure (Doris, 2002, pp. 42–4, 53, 56), and it raises an awkward question: Given that tendencies of widely variable moral status may be manifested by a single individual, how do we decide that one tendency is more that individual's "own" than another? (Of course, dispositional conflict may be resolved in favor of one action over another, but if action is sufficient for ownership, we've no need of character theory.) To put it glibly, *tendencies to act out of character are part of every character*. Again, this is not to advocate a skepticism about character. Indeed, it grants that people have characters in a sense that allows comparative moral evaluations, but insists that in *particular* cases, the "fragmented" nature of character will make it impossible to settle, with confidence, whether an action is "out of character."[11] That is the epistemological difficulty faced by character theory, and for real-world courts with real-world resource limitations, it is likely to be a serious difficulty indeed.

Interestingly, the character theorist cannot avail herself of an expedient popular in the virtue ethics literature. In response to the charge that virtue ethics trades on a conception of character that is (at most) seldom instantiated in actual human beings, virtue ethicists have responded that on their view virtue is *expected* to be rare, observing – quite rightly – that the empirical evidence is compatible with there being some number of fully virtuous individuals, even as it suggests that many (or most) people fall depressingly short of full-blooded virtue (e.g., Kupperman, 2001, pp. 242–3). The appeal of this picture is debated (Doris, 2002, pp. 149–52; Doris and Stich, 2005, pp. 120–23), but that won't detain us here. For however attractive, it is of little help for the character theory of excuses.

In the case of the fully virtuous person, one *does* have a good sense of what it is for them to act out of character, for they quite reliably, if perhaps not exceptionlessly, act appropriately, on appropriate reasons. If a person we know to be virtuous acts badly, or anyway, *really* badly, we know straightaway that they have acted out of character, and we will start casting about for the unsettling influence. (A question for this view: Do we want to say that King's untoward academic habits, or Gandhi's untoward sleeping arrangements, are out of character?) But the criminal courts are not an institution intended, or needed, to celebrate the virtuous; such impressive specimens should not often find themselves as grist for the legal mill. In the usual course of things, the criminal courts are concerned with whether more ordinary persons should be punished or excused for their

wrongdoings; the courts take over, if you like, where good character breaks off. And for the ordinary person it will very often be quite unclear whether a particular action is in or out of character, *even if* we can distinguish, with considerable confidence, the pretty good eggs from the not so good. Perhaps the character theory of excuses is adequate to those (presumably rare) cases where the fully virtuous are defendants. But these are not the cases on which to model the day-to-day practice of criminal law.

Conclusion

How are we to understand excuses, if not by appealing to character? Of course, there exist familiar alternatives, such as the *Model Penal Code's* suggestion that a defendant may be entitled a duress excuse when "a person of reasonable firmness in his situation would have been unable to resist" the coercion he suffered.[12] The "reasonable person" standard is a famously nebulous one, and has endured considerable criticism (see Simmons, 2003, esp. 185–7; Tadros, 2005, ch. 13). My aim is not to defend it here – supposing it may be successfully defended. I wish only to illustrate the observation that there exist alternatives to character theory that may evade some of its difficulties – even as they contend with difficulties of their own. Here, as elsewhere, theory choice is comparative, and I am highlighting only one dimension of comparison.

It is often said that most people will yield to a sufficiently determined torturer. On the other hand, many people have been able to endure embarrassment without catastrophic consequences; accordingly, humiliation is not a likely excuse, while torture is. Taking our cue from the *Model Penal Code*, we might say that a person of ordinary fortitude and cognitive ability can resist humiliation, but not torture, so the person who commits a crime under torture (or threat of torture) may escape criminal liability, but the person who does so to escape humiliation will not. Such observations should not be taken to indicate that excuses are determined simply by reference to population "base rates";

observing, "everyone's doing it" does not have the makings of an excuse (Doris, 2002, pp. 134–5).[13] Still, reflection on base rates helps determine what can fairly be expected of a particular individual in particular circumstances; surely it is partly because most people yield under torture that it seems unfair to hold victims liable for failing to resist it.

But as the reference to unabashedly evaluative notions like fairness indicates, the discussion will inevitably be "normative" as well as "statistical," adverting to such factors as the actor's circumstances, obligations, and social role.[14] Thus, we might demand more fortitude from a soldier than a civilian, expect officers to be more assiduous than ordinary soldiers in determining the legality of orders, and expect soldiers under fire to be less critical of orders than soldiers who are not (see Osiel, 1999). Such discriminations do not make the law insensitive to the details of particular cases; on the contrary, close attention to particulars is precisely what is being commended. Nor do they suggest that psychological evaluation is irrelevant to establishing excuses. Nothing I have said requires – implausibly – that the law ignore psychological antecedents of behavior, such as knowledge or intention, or psychopathologies, such as severe mental disorders. Eschewing character assessment is not to eschew the doctrine of *mens rea*.

I *am* suggesting the criminal law do without the kind of psychological evaluation associated with character assessment. Perhaps this carries

costs: returning a last time to our fictional defendants, we now seem to have lost our way of distinguishing between Citizen and Criminal, and may find ourselves forced to say that they are both, by virtue of being under credible threat, entitled to an excuse. In this instance, the unwanted result may be avoidable, because courts have held that gang members may be denied a duress excuse, if the intimidation comes from violent gang members with whom they knowingly associated (e.g. Cowley, 1987). Such a judgment gets Criminal back where we want him, but I won't here argue for it. What is important for my purposes is that the gang exception exemplifies a general approach, where courts look to a defendant's circumstances, rather than delving the uncertain depths of his character. Neglecting character may sometimes seem morally insensitive; by ignoring individual differences of personality or psychological constitution, the better may suffer equally under the law with the worse when they have acted in similar circumstances, despite the fact that we may take very different moral views of the deficiencies implicated in their crime.[15] This may seem a hard result, and I don't know how to soften it. Unfortunately, courts will not often be epistemically able to inform the assignment of excuses with confident distinctions of character. A justice that does not attend to such distinctions may at times be a rough justice, but it is all the justice we are in a position to have.

Notes

I am grateful for the patience of two legal theorists, Doug Husak and Victor Tadros, in helping me with this paper, and regret that time and space prevents me from taking fuller account of their suggestions. I also wish timing permitted full consideration of Tadros (2005), an especially compelling exposition of the position I discuss here.

1 Apparently, such appraisals are less prominent in other cultures, notably East Asian ones (see Doris, 2002: 105–6, forthcoming; Nisbett, 2003), but this will not detain me here, given my focus on Western criminal law.

2 The application of character theory may be highly general or limited. Tadros (2005, p. 294) is skeptical about aspirations to a highly general, theoretically simple, theory of excuses, but thinks character theory offers *one kind* of viable excuse claim. My observations are meant to apply to both general and limited permutations, since I will argue that character excuses are never, or very seldom, viable.

3 There is some relevant discussion in legal quarters (see Rhode, 1985; Luban, 2003; Nadler, 2003), but little directly pertaining to the theory of punishment and excuse. See Luban (2003) for particularly illuminating observations on the experimental work.

4 For criticisms of the Humean view related to those offered here, see Doris (2002, ch. 7).

5 I here ignore cases of "strict liability," where criminal liability may be established without establishing *mens rea*. Strict liability is controversial, but for present purposes, I need only note that the doctrine is not widely applied (see Leonard, 2002).

6 Note that Duff, although he apparently endorses some character-theoretical criticisms of choice theory, does not in the end endorse character theory (e.g., 1993, pp. 378–80).

7 Notions akin to "settled character" are commonplace in the ethics literature (see Doris, 2002, pp.15–20; cf. Brandt, 1970, p. 27; Aristotle, 1984: 1105a28–b1, 1100b32–4, 1128b29; Blum, 1994, pp. 178–80; Hursthouse, 1999, p. 140).

8 There is a history of personality psychologists expressing skepticism about notions of personality akin to that at issue here (e.g., Mischel, 1968, 1999; Pervin, 1994). For personality psychologists dissenting from this skeptical view, see Funder (1991) and Goldberg (1995).

9 For fuller discussion, see Baron (1994).

10 Arguably, the "unreliability of self-reports" is among the most challenging methodological difficulties in the social sciences; it has been a particularly vexing issue in the study of personality (Mischel, 1968, p. 25; Ross and Nisbett, 1991, pp. 98–9; McClelland, 1985, pp. 818–20).

11 Compare Vranas (2005) on the "indeterminacy" of character.

12 *Model Penal Code and Commentaries*, Section 209 (1), at p. 367.

13 For a challenging argument to the contrary, see Husak (1996).

14 Gardner (1998, pp. 578–81) develops this sort of suggestion in his critique of character theory.

15 Interestingly, courts have not always been eager to make such distinctions in evaluating duress defenses; personal characteristics such as neuroticism or timidity that leave individuals especially susceptible to threat are often held to be irrelevant in establishing duress. See *R v Hegarty* (1994) Crim LR 353, *R v Horne* (1994) Crim LR 584, and *R v Bowen* (1996) Crim LR 577. Tadros (2005, pp. 359–65) argues against the "impersonal" approach.

References

Annas, J. (forthcoming) "Comments on Doris' *Lack of Character*," *Philosophy and Phenomenological Research*.

—— (1993) *The Morality of Happiness*. New York and Oxford: Oxford University Press.

Arendt, H. (1964) *Eichmann in Jerusalem: A Report on the Banality of Evil*. New York: Penguin Books.

Arenella, P. (1990) "Character, Choice and Moral Agency: The Relevance of Character to Our Moral Culpability Judgments," *Social Philosophy and Policy* 7: 59–83.

Aristotle (1984) *The Complete Works of Aristotle*, ed. J. Barnes. Princeton, NJ: Princeton University Press.

Athanassoulis, N. (2000) "A Response to Harman: Virtue Ethics and Character Traits," *Proceedings of the Aristotelian Society* 100: 215–22.

Baron, J. (1994) "Nonconsequentialist Decisions," *Behavioral and Brain Sciences* 17: 1–42.

Blass, T. (1991) "Understanding Behavior in the Milgram Obedience Experiment: The Role of Personality, Situations, and Their Interactions," *Journal of Personality and Social Psychology* 60: 398–413.

Blum, L. A. (1994) *Moral Perception and Particularity*. Cambridge: Cambridge University Press.

Brandt, R. B. (1970) "Traits of Character: A Conceptual Analysis," *American Philosophical Quarterly* 7: 23–37.

—— (1985) "A Motivational Theory of Excuses in Criminal Law," *Nomos* 27: 195–8.

Brewer, M. B., and Gardner, W. L. (1996) "Who Is This 'We'? Levels of Collective Identity and Self Representations," *Journal of Personality and Social Psychology* 71: 83–93.

Browning, C. R. (1992) *Ordinary Men: Reserve Police Battalion 101 and the Final Solution in Poland*. New York: Harper Collins.

Butterfield, F. (2005) "Guns and Jeers Used by Gangs to Buy Silence," *The New York Times*, January 16.

Ceci, S. J. (1996) *On Intelligence: A Bioecological Treatise on Intellectual Development* (Expanded Edition). Cambridge, MA and London: Harvard University Press.

Cowley, D. (1987) "Defense of Duress: Not Available to Gangsters," *Great Britain Journal of Criminal Law* 51: 390–2.

Darley, J. M., and Batson, C. D. (1973) "From Jerusalem to Jericho: A Study of Situational and Dispositional Variables In Helping Behavior," *Journal of Personality and Social Psychology* 27: 100–8.

Detterman, D. K. (1993) "The Case for the Prosecution: Transfer as Epiphenomenon." In D. K. Detterman and R. J. Sternberg (eds.), *Transfer on Trial: Intelligence, Cognition, and Instruction*. Norwood, NJ: Ablex.

Doris, J. M. (1998) "Persons, Situations, and Virtue Ethics," *Noûs* 32: 504–30.

—— (2002) *Lack of Character: Personality and Moral Behavior*. New York: Cambridge University Press.

—— (forthcoming) "Replies: Evidence and Sensibility," *Philosophy and Phenomenological Research*.

Doris, J. M., and Stich, S. P. (2005) "As a Matter of Fact: Empirical Perspectives on Ethics." In F. Jackson and M. Smith (eds.), *The Oxford Handbook of Contemporary Philosophy*. Oxford University Press.

Duff, R. A. (1993) "Choice, Character, and Criminal Liability," *Law and Philosophy* 12: 345–83.

Earley, P, and Shur, G. (2003) *WITSEC: Inside the Federal Witness Protection Program*. New York: Bantam.

Finn, P., and Healy, K. M. (1996) "Preventing Gang- and Drug-Related Witness Intimidation." *National Institute of Justice Report: Issues and Practices in Criminal Justice*. Washington DC: US Department of Justice.

Flanagan, O. (1991) *Varieties of Moral Personality: Ethics and Psychological Realism*. Cambridge, MA: Harvard University Press.

Funder, D. C. (1991) "Global Traits: A Neo-Allportian Approach to Personality," *Psychological Science* 2: 31–9.

Gardner, J. (1998) "The Gist of Excuses," *Buffalo Criminal Law Review* 1: 575–98.

Gardner, W. L., Gabriel, S., and Hochschild, L. (2002) "When You and I Are 'We,' You Are No Longer Threatening: The Role of Self-expansion in Social Comparison Processes," *Journal of Personality and Social Psychology* 83: 239–51.

Gardner, W. L., Gabriel, S., and Lee, A. Y. (1999) "'I' Value Freedom But 'We' Value Relationships: Self-construal Priming Mirrors Cultural Differences in Judgment," *Psychological Science* 10: 321–6.

Goldberg, L. R. (1995) "What the Hell Took So Long? Donald W. Fiske and the Big-Five Factor Structure." In P. E. Shrout and S. T. Fiske (eds.), *Personality Research, Methods, and Theory: A Festschrift Honoring Donald W. Fiske*. Hillsdale, NJ: Lawrence Erlbaum Associates.

Haney, C., Banks, W., and Zimbardo, P. (1973) "Interpersonal Dynamics of a Simulated Prison," *International Journal of Criminology and Penology* 1: 69–97.

Harman, G. (1999) "Moral Philosophy Meets Social Psychology: Virtue Ethics and the Fundamental Attribution Error," *Proceedings of the Aristotelian Society* 99: 315–31.

—— (2000) "The Nonexistence of Character Traits," *Proceedings of the Aristotelian Society* 100: 223–6.

Hart, H. L. A. (1968) *Punishment and Responsibility*. Oxford: Clarendon Press.

Hume, D. (1978) *A Treatise of Human Nature*, 2nd edn. Oxford: Oxford University Press. (Originally published, 1740.)

Hursthouse, R. (1999) *On Virtue Ethics*. Oxford and New York: Oxford University Press.

Husak, D. (1996) "The 'But Everybody Does That!' Defense," *Public Affairs Quarterly* 10: 307–34.

—— (forthcoming) "On the Supposed Priority of Justification to Excuse."

Isen, A. M. and Levin, P. F. (1972) "Effect of Feeling Good on Helping: Cookies and Kindness," *Journal of Personality and Social Psychology* 21: 384–8.

Kamtekar, R. (2004) "Situationism and Virtue Ethics on the Content of Our Character," *Ethics* 114: 458–91.

Kupperman, J. J. (2001) "The Indispensability of Character," *Philosophy* 76: 239–50.

Leonard, G. (2002) "Towards a Legal History of American Criminal Theory: Culture and Doctrine from Blackstone to the Model Penal Code." *Research Paper Series, Public Law and Legal Theory*: No. 02-19. Boston, MA: Boston University School of Law.

Levi, P. (1965) "Afterword," trans. R. Feldman. In P. Levi, *The Reawakening*, trans. S. Woolf. New York: Collier-Macmillan.

Luban, D. (2003) "Integrity: Its Causes and Cures," *Fordham Law Review* 72: 279–310.

MacIntyre, A. (1984) *After Virtue*, 2nd edn. Notre Dame, IN: University of Notre Dame Press.

Mathews, K. E., and Cannon, L. K. (1975) "Environmental Noise Level as a Determinant of Helping Behavior," *Journal of Personality and Social Psychology* 32: 571–7.

McClelland, D. C. (1985) "How Motives, Skills, and Values Determine What People Do," *American Psychologist* 40: 812–25.

Merritt, M. (2000) "Virtue Ethics and Situationist Personality Psychology," *Ethical Theory and Moral Practice* 3: 365–83.

Milgram, S. (1974) *Obedience to Authority*. New York: Harper and Row.

Miller, A. G. (1986) *The Obedience Experiments: A Case Study of Controversy in Social Science*. New York: Praeger Publishers.

Miller, C. (2003) "Social Psychology and Virtue Ethics," *The Journal of Ethics* 7: 365–92.

Mischel, W. (1968) *Personality and Assessment*. New York: John J. Wiley and Sons.

—— (1999) "Personality Coherence and Dispositions in a Cognitive-Affective Personality System (CAPS) Approach." In D. Cervone and Y. Shoda (eds.), *The Coherence of Personality: Social-Cognitive Bases of Consistency, Variability, and Organization*. New York and London: Guilford Press.

Montmarquet, J. (2003) "Moral Character and Social Science Research," *Philosophy* 78: 355–68.

Moore, M. S. (1990) "Choice, Character, and Excuse," *Social Philosophy and Policy* 7: 29–58.

Nadler, J. (2003) "No Need to Shout: Bus Sweeps and the Psychology of Coercion," *2002 The Supreme Court Review* 153-222.

Nisbett, R. E. (2003) *The Geography of Thought: How Asians and Westerners Think Differently . . . and Why*. New York: Free Press.

Nussbaum, M. C. (1999) "Virtue Ethics: A Misleading Category?" *The Journal of Ethics* 3: 163–201.

Osiel, M. J. (1999) *Obeying Orders: Atrocity, Military Discipline, and the Law of War*. New Brunswick and London: Transaction Publishers.

Pervin, L. A. (1994) "A Critical Analysis of Current Trait Theory," *Psychological Inquiry* 5: 103–13.

Pincoffs, E. L. (1973) "Legal Responsibility and Moral Character," *Wayne Law Review* 19: 905–23.

Rawls, J. (1955) "Two Concepts of Rules," *Philosophical Review* 64: 3–32.

Rhode, D. L. (1985) "Moral Character as a Professional Credential," 94 *Yale Law Journal* 491.

Ross, L., and Nisbett, R. E. (1991) *The Person and the Situation: Perspectives of Social Psychology*. Philadelphia, PA: Temple University Press.

Sabini, J., and Silver, M. (2005) "Lack of Character? Situationism Critiqued," *Ethics* 115: 535–62.

Simmons, K. W. (2003) "Should the Model Penal Code's *Mens Rea* Provisions Be Amended?" *Ohio State Journal of Criminal Law* 1: 179–205.

Tadros, V. (2001) "The Characters of Excuse," *Oxford Journal of Legal Studies* 21: 495–519.

—— (2005) *Criminal Responsibility*. Oxford: Oxford University Press.

Todorov, T. (1996) *Facing the Extreme: Moral Life in the Concentration Camps*. New York: Metropolitan Books.

Tversky, A, and Kahneman, D. (1981) "The Framing of Decisions and the Psychology of Choice," *Science* 211: 453–63.

Vranas, P. B. M. (2005) "The Indeterminacy Paradox: Character Evaluations and Human Psychology," *Noûs* 39: 1–42.

Vuoso, G. (1987) "Background, Responsibility, and Excuse," *Yale Law Journal* 96: 1661–86.

Williams, B. A. O. (1985) *Ethics and the Limits of Philosophy*. Cambridge, MA: Harvard University Press.[CR3]

49

Does Punishment Work?

John Paul Wright, Francis T. Cullen, and Kevin M. Beaver

Introduction

At the turn of the twenty-first century, the United States again made history. It was not the mapping of the human genome and all the promises for new and better medical interventions; it was not the discovery of planets in a far-away galaxy; nor was it the coming of age of the Internet and instantaneous worldwide communication. This historical event did not generate front-page headlines or receive the awards and accolades that come along with great achievement. Instead, this achievement passed by with little notice: the United States generated the highest incarceration rate in the world. At the turn of the century, over 6.9 million US citizens were under some form of correctional control; probation, jail/prison, or parole – with a record 2.0 million citizens locked away (Bureau of Justice Statistics, 2004).

Today, the United States has one of the lowest crime rates since records have been kept. As shown in Figure 49.1, crime rates in America have decreased year by year from the late 1990s through 2005. Even serious crimes such as non-negligent homicide and rape have declined. Yet prisons and jails in the United States continued to grow by an average of 900 inmates each week from 2003 to 2004. By June of 2004 there were 48,000 more inmates than the previous year.

Data from the Bureau of Justice Statistics graphically depict the accelerated growth in inmate population across the United States. From 1980 through 2003, the number of adult individuals on some form of probation soared to over 4 million (see Figure 49.2), while prison, jail, and parole populations continued to climb.

Across states, prison populations have increased dramatically since 1980. By the end of 2001, over 600,000 violent inmates had entered state prisons. These dramatic gains were followed by increases in the number of property offenders and drug offenders being sent to institutions. As evidence of the trend to use incarceration more frequently, even the number of individuals sent to prison for public order offenses has increased significantly (see Figure 49.3).

The Great Punishment Experiment

There are various explanations for America's two-decade-long experiment, but it can be

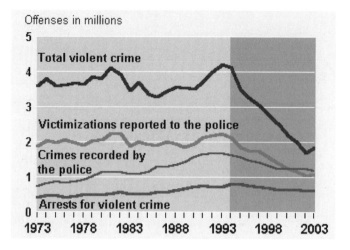

Figure 49.1   Trends in serious violent crime, 1973–2003

generally attributed to at least three fundamental social facts. First, from the late 1980s to the mid-1990s crime, especially serious juvenile crime, increased precipitously. Murder increased 117 percent overall, for youth 15 to 17 years old it increased a staggering 183 percent, and for youth 12 to 14, it escalated 111 percent. Crime became an immediate and pivotal social concern.

Second, progressives' faith in rehabilitation – that is, in changing offenders – dwindled. From their point of view, rehabilitation allowed the state too much power over the lives of inmates, and it allowed the state to justify any sort of punitive and inhumane treatment of prisoners

as "rehabilitative." Instead of trying to change offenders, progressives turned to the vague notion of "doing justice" – that is, in limiting the injustice found in criminal penalties.

When progressives abandoned rehabilitation, they inadvertently left open a policy gap that conservatives were happy to fill. Conservatives had always decried the "laxness" of the criminal justice system and had always favored harsher penalties for lawbreakers. In the war of ideas, the "war on crime" emerged as a potent framework from which highly punitive policies were enacted. "Three strikes" laws, where third-time felons are incarcerated for 25 years to life, entered the public vernacular; truth-in-sentencing laws

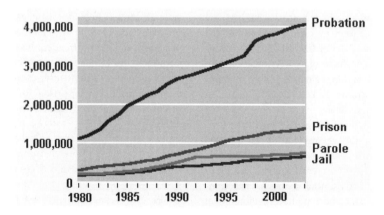

Figure 49.2   Adult correctional populations, 1980–2003

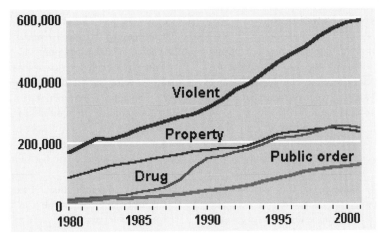

Figure 49.3   State prison populations by offense type, 1980–2001

increased drastically the amount of time offenders would have to serve before being eligible for parole; and at least 37 states altered their constitutions to emphasize punishment or social protection over rehabilitation (Cullen and Wright, 2002).

Third, advocates of punishment articulated a simple, widely understandable set of principles. Criminal behavior, they argued, was the product of choice; a choice that involved the weighing of benefits of a behavior against the potential costs (Wilson, 1975; Cullen and Gilbert, 1982; Logan and Gaes, 1993). This view of human agency resonated with the public and with officials within the justice system. No longer would they have the burden of combating "root causes" of crime, such as disorganized neighborhoods or poverty. With the widespread acceptance of a "crime as choice" theory of human action, lawmakers and justice officials could focus on elevating the sanctions associated with criminal behavior. Punishment, they reasoned, had to outweigh any gains from criminal conduct.

Out of the potent mix of increases in crime, the death of rehabilitation as a goal of corrections, and the widely accepted view that criminal behavior could be deterred only by elevating the punishment of offenders, emerged the punishment experiment. The experiment represents a hodgepodge of sanctions across various states and the federal government. Mandatory sentencing replaced the more flexible indeterminate sentence; some states abolished parole; while in others a new set of "intermediate sanctions" came into fruition. With no credible evidence that these new forms of punishment would be effective, states and the federal system invested heavily in boot camps, Intensive Supervision Probation/Parole (ISP), and electronic monitoring (Cullen et al., 1996).

Perhaps not surprisingly, but not foreseen by punishment advocates, the justice system became the "Pacman" of state budgets – eating away all discretionary income and eating into the budgets of schools, universities, and other social programs (Cullen et al., 1996). From 1982 to 2001, federal spending on the justice system increased to $167 billion. In addition, spending on policing increased 494 percent; on the judiciary spending went up 636 percent; and on corrections it went up 861 percent. States too increased their spending on the justice system. From 1977 to 2001, spending on policing went up 470 percent, on corrections 1101 percent, and on the judiciary an amazing 1766 percent (Bureau of Justice Statistics, 2001). Today, our system of punishment costs roughly 10 percent of our gross domestic product (GDP) – the value of all goods and services produced in the United States.

Justifications for Punishment

Before we can evaluate the effectiveness of punishment delivered by the criminal justice system, we first need to know the justifications of punishment. That is, what purposes are served when the state intervenes in the life of a criminal offender? This issue is one of critical importance for at least two reasons. First, certain justifications serve a utilitarian, measurable purpose. These goals, such as reducing crime, can be empirically assessed. In this way, scholars can estimate the practical and financial costs associated with specific criminal justice sanctions. Second, other justifications serve a utilitarian purpose, but do not lend themselves easily to empirical validation, such as balancing the scales of justice.

We examine briefly four justifications for punishment: deterrence, incapacitation, just deserts, and rehabilitation. The four are not mutually exclusive, as they function together every day in contemporary penal systems throughout America. While some scholars argue for "pure" correctional models that favor one justification over all others (Logan and Gaes, 1993), history has shown that it is very difficult to operate a system of criminal penalties absent other justifications. Indeed, contemporary philosophers have made the distinction between a practice that can be justified by its consequences, such as making society safer, and acts that fall within that justification. The decision of who to punish may be driven, for example, by retributivist concerns, but the methods used to punish may include a mix of deterrent and rehabilitative efforts (Rawls, 1971). Modern corrections, whether at the juvenile or adult level, tend to integrate these justifications to varying degrees – and as we will see, with varying success.

Deterrence

Advocates of punishment often rely heavily on the supposed ability of punishment, defined broadly, to deter unwanted social behavior. Invoking the "crime as choice" explanation for criminal conduct, deterrence theorists maintain that increasing the social costs associated with the choice to engage in crime will reduce crime.

Two types of deterrence are typically recognized: specific deterrence and general deterrence. Specific deterrence refers to criminal sanctions applied to individuals convicted of violating the law. The purpose of specific deterrence is to increase the costs associated with the offender's behavior so that they overshadow any gains. In this way, specific deterrence should deter the individual's future conduct – that is, to reduce their recidivism upon release.

Specific deterrence relies not only on the theory that crime emerges out of a weighing of costs and benefits, it also assumes that criminals learn from their behavior the same way that relatively prosocial individuals do. It also assumes that offenders experience punishment as "punishing." The costs that accompany many criminal sanctions, such as loss of liberty and the loss of independence and autonomy, are thought to be punishing – especially in a democracy that places a premium on individual freedoms.

Just as specific deterrence recognizes, correctly or incorrectly, that human beings learn from their experiences, general deterrence recognizes that humans also learn by observation. Vicarious experience with punishment, such as seeing an individual convicted and incarcerated, ought to have potent effects on relatively prosocial individuals.

Deterrence theorists believe that the imposition of the criminal sanction and the resulting punishment can reduce wayward behavior. For them, the justification for punishment is one of utility; by punishing offenders, society will benefit through lower recidivism rates (specific deterrence) and through reduced crime rates (general deterrence). Criminologists, however, differ substantially on how well potential sanctions that occur in the distant future can deter individuals high in criminal propensity.

Incapacitation

The use of incapacitation as a form of punishment has its roots in America. The Progressive movement that paved the way for the inception of the juvenile justice system, for workplace safety laws, and for our first environmental laws also gave us the creation of the penitentiary (Rothman, 1980). The original justification supporting the use of incapacitation as a form of punishment differs from today's justification. Progressives were strong environmentalists, meaning they viewed the environment that offenders came from as responsible for producing criminal proclivities. Removing an offender from a criminogenic environment and placing him within an institution where he could contemplate his salvation was thought to be a worthwhile enterprise. In this sense, incapacitation was designed to help rehabilitate an offender.

Today, however, advocates of incapacitation make no such claim, or they see rehabilitation as "something nice," as something on the periphery, or as something tangential that might emerge from the experience of incapacitation. Modern justifications for institutionalizing offenders inevitably make the point that at least while an offender is imprisoned he/she is not committing crime against free citizens (DiIulio and Piehl, 1991).

Some will point out that our investments in punishment have been associated with substantial drops in crime rates and in the number of crime events. At one level, it is difficult to argue that removing 2.0 to 2.2 million people from society will not have an influence on rates of crime, or, in a more perverse sense, that greater imposition of the death penalty does not reduce crimes committed by those subject to this form of punishment. It would strain credulity to argue otherwise. Moreover, the evidence indicates that sending *certain* people to jail or prison saves innocent lives. Still, there is ample reason to suspect that the hundreds of billions of dollars spent on punishment have not had the desired social effect of improving society.

As we mentioned before, it is difficult to argue with this justification. Individuals locked away in institutions usually cannot offend in free society. However, all is not as clear or as simple as those who advocate for greater use of incapacitation want us to believe. For our purposes, let us differentiate between mass incapacitation and selective incapacitation. On the one hand, mass incapacitation refers to the use of institutionalization for minor to severe transgressions. Whether you sell a small amount of drugs or commit murder, you serve time. The main assumption is that the more people you incarcerate, the lower the crime rate. Selective incapacitation, on the other hand, reserves incarceration for only the most severe and most active offenders (Wilson, 1975). Offenders with lengthy criminal records or who commit relatively serious crimes are "selected" from the population of offenders to face imprisonment.

Scholars estimating the "incapacitation effect," or the amount of crime reduced through the use of incarceration, recognized that crime savings through incarceration depended primarily on the type of offender being incarcerated (Cook, 1980). For this reason, numerous studies sought to estimate how much crime an offender commits during his offending career. Estimates of lambda, or an individual's offense rate, varied tremendously (Nagin, 1998); some offenders committed very few crimes over the course of their criminal career, while others committed hundreds (Petersilia and Honig, 1980).

The effectiveness of incapacitation thus came down to the type of offender being incarcerated. If the state utilized mass incarceration, which did not differentiate between types of offenders, little would be gained in the way of crime reduction. Moreover, at an average cost of $23,000 per year, incarcerating low-risk individuals seemed economically disadvantageous. Still, selectively incarcerating high-rate offenders has been found to reduce crime – about 10–15 percent (Spelman, 2000). The question that ultimately emerges from this line of research, however, is whether the criminal justice system can become more selective. Already, research consistently shows that the best predictors of being incarcerated are the seriousness of the charged offense and the number of prior convictions. To a certain degree then, the system already practices a form of selective incarceration. Moreover, it is important to keep in mind that the majority of individuals that come before a court are not subject to detention or incarceration. They may be fined, placed on probation, or at worst placed on some form of community control, but most are not candidates for long-term incarceration.

Just Deserts and Retribution

Few events can change a life like being a victim of a crime. Whether it is the loss of life that occurs needlessly and without provocation, the loss of property that one has worked to obtain, or the frustration and loss of trust that emerges from being conned, being a victim of crime can have devastating effects. Being a victim of crime can bring with it emotional trauma, depression, anxiety, anger, resentment, and feelings of helplessness. It can bring financial hardship and bankruptcy. And it can bring calls for revenge.

Retribution, or exacting a toll on the offender, is a common human desire. It connotes a sense of restoration in the balance of justice, as well as providing the victim with a sense of retaliation or empowerment. Also called "just deserts," this justification for punishment is one of the most elemental and, for better or for worse, one of the most human. In all societies, even in higher-order primates, deviation from acceptable social norms can lead to banishment, the loss of property, and even the loss of life.

Under this model, punishment is the public's response to criminal behavior. This justification has no expectation to reform an offender, nor does it aim to reduce crime – it seeks merely to "repay" the offender for the harm he/she has caused. Even so, a just-deserts model relies on the social perception of harm – or what society deems to be harmful at that moment in history. During prohibition, for example, the production and distribution of alcohol was linked to various social maladies, including addiction, crime, gambling, divorce, and adultery. The supposed "harm" from the widespread use of alcohol was seen as a justification for the state to confiscate personal property and to imprison offenders. More recently, just deserts has been used as a justification to expand the war on drugs, the number of crimes eligible for capital punishment, and the increased use of determinate sentencing laws.

Rehabilitation

Of all the justifications for punishment, rehabilitation is the most socially utilitarian and empirically measurable. This justification seeks to make punishment functional – that is, to use punishment as a mechanism to change the likelihood that an offender will commit crime in the future.

As a justification for the state intervening in the life of an offender, rehabilitation has had a long and troubled history. Just as the Progressives of the nineteenth century sought to use incarceration as a form of punishment, they also sought to help offenders deviate from their criminal pathways. At the beginning of the Progressive movement, little was known about criminal behavior or about psychological adjustment; hence rehabilitation efforts typically involved reading the Bible and living in total silence (Rothman, 1980).

The death of rehabilitation as a correctional goal occurred with the publication and wide circulation of Robert Martinson's (1974) now infamous study. Summarizing his review of rehabilitation programs, Martinson stated that "with few and isolated exceptions," rehabilitation programs do not work. For the next 20 years, rehabilitation was a paradigm with few admirers. On closer inspection of Martinson's findings, however, scholars found that at least 40 percent of the programs reviewed by Martinson were found to significantly reduce recidivism. With this evidence in hand, Martinson (1979) eventually repudiated his initial claim. The damage, however, had been done.

Although the majority of states and the federal government abandoned rehabilitation as a core justification for punishment, rehabilitation would not die. Scholars from Canada and the US began an intensive investigation into "what works" in correctional programming. They linked knowledge on human and criminal behavior to findings from psychology that shed light on how individuals change their behavior.

Out of this body of research, several principles of effective correctional intervention were established. For instance, effective rehabilitation programs have to target high-risk offenders – that is, offenders with the highest risk of continuing to commit crime. They have to use cognitive-behavioral treatment approaches to attack antisocial values and beliefs, while at the same time modeling appropriate behavior. They have to tailor their treatment to individual factors, such as intelligence and motivation, and they have to have fidelity in their delivering of services and treatment (Andrews and Bonta, 1998).

Reviews of the research literature, largely through meta-analytic methods that used the study as the focal point of the analysis, began to show numerous positive findings. Effective correctional programs reduce recidivism nearly 20 percent: if the recidivism of the control group equals 55 percent, the recidivism of the experimental group would equal 45 percent. However, programs that modestly adhered to the principles of effective intervention could reduce recidivism up to 35 percent; those that adhered strictly to the principles achieved even more dramatic reductions of over 50 percent (Andrews, 1995; Gendreau, 1996; Andrews and Bonta, 1998).

Today, rehabilitation is being revived as a correctional goal. Numerous states have sought to ensure they are offering the most effective programming public monies can buy and they are holding programs accountable for results. Rehabilitation as a justification for punishment, as a justification to intervene in the life of an offender, is now seen as a method to save the state money and to reduce the number of victims of crime.

As we mentioned before, no single justification for punishment dominates the criminal justice or juvenile justice system. Instead what exists is a complex mix of overlapping justifications. To be certain, there is still widespread debate of the purpose of the criminal justice sanctions. Yet one thing remains true, not a single meta-analytic review of the research literature has found that punishment reduces recidivism (Andrews et al., 1990; Lipsey, 1992,

1999; Cullen et al., 1996; Lipsey and Wilson, 1998; Redondo et al., 1999). To the contrary, some programs, like Scared Straight, and some criminal justice interventions, such as being incarcerated, are associated with *increases* in recidivism (Lipsey, 1992, 1999). With this in mind, we progress to the next stage of evaluating the effectiveness of punishment.

What Does It Take for Punishment to Be Effective?

Most people have an inherent and simplistic understanding of punishment. Psychologists, however, inform us that for punishment to be effective it must follow specific guidelines – guidelines that the criminal justice system cannot in most situations meet. While the subject of making punishment effective is undoubtedly complicated, we offer four elements that must be present.

First, for punishment to change behavior, it must occur very soon after the behavioral transgression (swiftness) and it must be predictable (certainty). Most crimes, however, go undetected by authorities. We can take drug dealing as an example. Dealers can complete hundreds of transactions a day, and, if they are not operating in an open-air drug market that is readily visible to the police, the likelihood of detection is minimal. For the vast majority of criminal events then, the offender is never apprehended and consequently never punished.

Second, on the chance occasion that their behavior is detected they must still be arrested, prosecuted, convicted, and sentenced. The process that will ultimately impose the punishment can break down at any point: police may not make the arrest, the prosecutor may not wish to charge the individual, or the jury may find the individual innocent of the charges. Needless to say, if the process is followed through to its completion, it can take years, in some cases, between the time of the initial event and the imposition of the punishment. Years hardly qualify as swift, and being able to commit multiple crimes before being apprehended hardly qualifies as being certain. We should also add that 95 percent of all criminal cases are plea-bargained before ever going to trial.

Third, the offender has to view the intervention as punishing and as somewhat legitimate. Offenders, in general, and serious offenders specifically, view the world through a fairly distorted lens. Research into social information processing, for example, consistently reveals that aggressive youth and adults are significantly more likely to view the world in aggressive terms, are more likely to infer aggression where there is none, and are more likely to infer hostile intent from the actions of others (Dodge et al., 2003). More importantly, they are significantly more likely to rationalize away their behavior, to place blame on sources outside of their control, and to deny responsibility. Consequently, they are also more likely to deny that any punishment of them is just or is an appropriate consequence of their illegal behavior.

Finally, many of the most serious offenders have long criminal records that date back to their adolescence. They have been punished by the state and society for years, if not decades. These experiences have a tendency to accumulate and to diminish the capacity for future punishments to have an effect. This is another point that psychologists offer: when individuals are punished too frequently, they adapt to it and anticipate its likelihood. In essence, they learn that they can handle the most the state can offer.

Life-course Development of Offending: Why Punishment Most Often Fails

One of the core findings to emerge from empirical investigations into the development of offending behavior is that the roots of serious criminal behavior are traceable all the way back to the womb. Evidence pointing to this fact comes from at least five consistent criminological findings. First, criminologists have long known that there is strong intergenerational continuity in crime; youth born to criminal parents are at a three- to fivefold increased risk for serious and violent behavior later in life (Huesmann et al., 1984; Lipsey and Derzon, 1998; Wright and Cullen, 2001).

Second, behavioral genetic studies demonstrate consistently that antisocial, delinquent, and criminal behavior is modestly to strongly heritable (Reiss et al., 2000; Walsh, 2002). Heritability should not be confused with "inherited." All humans inherit the genetic code for the development of two eyes, a nose, and lips. Heritability, however, reflects the degree to which genes influence variation in phenotypic characteristics, such as behavior. Estimates of heritability range from 0, showing no genetic influence, to 1, indicating that the outcome of interest is 100 percent genetic (Plomin, 1990).

Using primarily samples of monozygotic and dyzygotic twins reared together and apart, researchers consistently find that genetic processes influence serious behavioral problems. Behavioral genetic studies estimate that genetic influences account for 40 percent to 85 percent of the variation in childhood aggression and conduct disorders, delinquency, and adult criminal behavior (Mason and Frick, 1994; Rhee and Waldman, 2002; Arseneault et al., 2003; Hudziak et al., 2003). These estimates, however, depend on a range of factors, including environmental factors that allow or promote certain behaviors.

Third, the induction of neurotoxins in utero and during infancy can have long-term debilitating effects on the developing central nervous system. The brain is composed of ~100 billion nerve cells (neurons), and each neuron can have as many as 1,000 to 10,000 connections (synapses) to other neurons (Drubach, 2000). During embryonic and postnatal development, the number of synaptic pathways multiplies at a rate of 250,000 connections per *second*. Indeed, the brain of a two-year-old is 40 times more active than the brain of an adult (Siegel, 1999).

Fourth, numerous studies have found that antisocial behavior emerges very early in the life-course. Studies of toddlers, for example, reveal that young children regularly engage in behaviors that include hitting, kicking, and punching others, pulling hair, and biting. Young children are also capable of intentionally deceptive behavior, such as theft (Tremblay et al., 1999).

According to Tremblay and his colleagues, physical aggression in young children peaks at

24 months and declines precipitously thereafter. Approximately 80 percent of children eliminate their use of aggression altogether by the age of seven (Tremblay et al., 1999). A small percentage, however, continue to utilize physical aggression. Estimates vary, but typically between 4 to 10 percent of youth will continue to use direct physical aggression (Campbell, 1995). Using a much broader definition of problem behavior, a large-scale study conducted in Dunedin, New Zealand found that about 10 percent of sample three-year-olds were rated as uncontrollable – impulsive, emotionally unstable, irritable and restless (Moffitt et al., 2001).

Finally, the hallmark of serious antisocial behavior is that it can be highly stable over long swaths of the life-course (Olweus, 1979; Loeber, 1982; Gottfredson and Hirschi, 1990; Sampson and Laub, 1993). Difficult, temperamental infants can grow into children with oppositional defiance disorder (ODD) (Campbell, 1995; Keenan and Wakschlag, 2000). In turn, children with ODD are substantially more likely to evolve into adolescents who are conduct disordered (CD) and then into adults with diagnosable antisocial personality disorder (ASP) (White et al., 1990; Tremblay et al., 1994; Barkley, 1997; Raine, 2002; Keenan and Shaw, 2003).

Fortunately, only a small fraction of youth at each developmental period will continue along the pathway that leads to life-course persistent offending (Tremblay et al., 1999). These individuals, however, will be responsible for the majority of all crimes (Elliott, 1994). Along the developmental pathway, they are also at an increased risk for being rejected by conventional peers (Dodge et al., 2003), for substance abuse and addiction, and for dropping out of high school, arrest, and imprisonment (Huizinga and Jakob-Chien, 1998).

Serious, violent offenders thus generally progress along an identifiable pathway from conception to adulthood. While not all offenders fall within this pathway, many of the most active and serious offenders will. They are differentially born to parents who have a history of behavioral problems, to mothers who smoke or use drugs while they are pregnant, and into areas where environmental neurotoxins are prevalent. They experience a range of problems early in life and elevate the seriousness of their misbehavior as they grow older. Throughout their development, they are likely to be sanctioned severely and repeatedly. They are likely to be punished by their parents, sometimes very harshly, by teachers and school administrators, and by local systems of justice. Indeed, a close inspection of their life reveals that they are punished frequently for their behavior; far more frequently and more severely than prosocial individuals.

Unlike adaptive individuals, highly aggressive youth and adults do not tend to learn from their prior behaviors. Instead, empirical data indicate that antisocials are highly capable of psychologically neutralizing the harm they have committed and of rationalizing their behavior (Andrews and Bonta, 1998). Subsequently, they also have a strong tendency to view punishment as undeserved, as unnecessary, and as unfair (Sherman, 1993). In general, they do not cognitively or emotionally experience punishment the same as prosocial people – which helps to explain why deterrence does not work.

Understanding the complex developmental pathways that lead some individuals into serious crime and social pathology helps us further understand why punishment is so ineffective with most offenders. Punishment alone does nothing to change a person. It does not attack criminal values and beliefs, nor does it demonstrate to an offender proper ways to act or how to avoid situations where misbehavior is more likely. This is not to say that criminal behavior does not warrant some form of response from the state; it is to say, though, that the effectiveness of the response should be understood and should not be over- or underestimated.

Putting It All Together: Empirical Evidence for the Justifications of Punishment

Any intervention, whether taking a prescription drug or going through an alcohol abuse program, can have one of three potential outcomes. It can have no effect, it can work as predicted, or it can have a harmful effect. Punishment is no different. As we mentioned earlier, no meta-analytic review has found that punishment reduces recidivism. To the contrary, punishment oriented programs – those programs where the primary goal is to embarrass, humiliate, or impose a cost on an offender – can generate unforeseen negative consequences: that is, they can actually *increase* recidivism (Gendreau et al., 2000). While criminologists are just now investigating why and how this happens, current theories maintain that for some offenders, being punished cuts them off further from prosocial institutions, like work and marriage (Sampson and Laub, 1993). Other offenders seemingly rebel at the idea of being sanctioned, while others psychologically equate being punished as a sign of their toughness (Sherman, 1993).

In general, we remain skeptical that the criminal justice system can be made more efficient, or that punishment can be made to reduce criminal conduct absent a strong rehabilitative effort. For punishment to work, it must be linked to empirically verified mechanisms that promote offender change. Enacting a toll or cost on an offender does nothing to change his or her criminal behavior, criminal values, or criminal associates.

Of all the justifications for punishment, we view rehabilitation as the most empirically supported, incapacitation next, followed by deterrence and just deserts. However, we must caution the reader that the efficacy of punishment outcomes depends in part on the type of offender. Low-risk offenders, for example, can be somewhat deterred, while high-risk offenders remain unresponsive to sanctions aimed at deterring their future behavior. Similarly, intensive interventions with low-risk offenders can increase their offending, while those same interventions applied to high-risk offenders stand a better chance of reducing recidivism.

Unlike the other justifications for punishment, rehabilitation is the most amenable to scientific evaluation. This allows knowledge about how best to change criminal offenders to

continue to develop and to build, with more effective interventions possible as the state of the art matures. The other justifications do not hold out this possibility and, in some instances, such as with just-deserts models, they do not even make an attempt. We also favor rehabilitation because it is more aligned with the current knowledge on the development of offending trajectories over time. Unlike incapacitation, where the effort is merely to warehouse offenders, rehabilitation transforms the knowledge of offending into practices and interventions that can be put into place within institutions or communities. This knowledge helps practitioners know who to target with the most invasive interventions and it helps to identify the variables that must be addressed to reduce offending. Deterrence, with its simplistic notion of the cause of crime, fails to offer insight capable of making these types of important, if not critical, distinctions.

Finally, rehabilitation demands accountability from the justice system, and ultimately it will demand that the system employ the most empirically sound programs. Without rehabilitation, the criminal justice system is free to simply warehouse prisoners, to offer programs that haven't a shred of hope of being effective, or worse, to engage in practices that increase the number of crimes and victims upon an offender's release. An empirically driven focus on rehabilitation provides policy makers and practitioners with a body of knowledge from which useful decisions can be made and positive results expected. Moreover, with the cost associated with incarcerating a large number of individuals continuing to rise, states will demand more evidence that correctional interventions work.

To be certain, there are limits to every justification to punishment. Rehabilitation is not perfect, but perfection is not the standard. Unlike the other justifications, rehabilitation at least guides research into what works and what doesn't work. For those individuals that remain unresponsive to treatment interventions, incapacitation may be the only intervention remaining. Even so, there is something purposive and worthwhile about trying, about making an effort to reduce the harm that offenders create. Deterrence has not proven effective; just deserts remains silent on the issue; incapacitation makes no attempt. If rehabilitation hastens desistance in criminal involvement, then eventually fewer prison cells will be needed, lengthier and more severe conditions of confinement will become unnecessary, and our collective will to punish may be reduced. With continued research into "what works" in correctional programming, the "Good Society" envisioned by the Progressives may be one step closer.

References

Andrews, D. A. (1995) "The Psychology of Criminal Conduct and Effective Correctional Treatment." In J. McGuire (ed.), *What Works: Reducing Reoffending.* London: John Wiley, pp. 35–62.

Andrews, D. A. and Bonta, J. (1998) *The Psychology of Criminal Conduct*, 2nd edn. Cincinnati, OH: Anderson.

Andrews, D. A., Zinger, I., Hoge, R. D., Bonta, J., Gendreau, P., and Cullen F. T. (1990) "Does Correctional Treatment Work? A Clinically-relevant and Psychologically-informed Meta-analysis," *Criminology* 28: 369–404.

Arseneault, L., Moffitt, T. E., Caspi, A., Taylor, A., Rijsdijk, F. V., Jaffee, S. R., Ablow, J. C., and Measell, J. R. (2003) "Strong Genetic Effects on Cross-situational Antisocial Behaviour among 5-year-old Children According to Mothers, Teachers, Examiner-observers, and Twins' Self-reports," *Journal of Child Psychology and Psychiatry* 44: 832–48.

Barkley, R. A. (1997) *ADHD and the Nature of Self-Control.* New York: Guilford Press.

Bureau of Justice Statistics (2004) *Key Crime and Justice Facts at a Glance.* Available online at: http://www.ojp.usdoj. gov/bjs/glance.htm#Crime.

Campbell, S. B. (1995) "Behavior Problems in Preschool Children: A Review of Recent Research," *Journal of Child Psychology and Psychiatry* 36: 113–49.

Cook, P. (1980) "Research in Criminal Deterrence: Laying the Groundwork for the Second Decade." In N. Morris and M. Tonry (eds.), *Crime and Justice: A Review of Research*, Vol. 2. Chicago, IL: University of Chicago Press.

Cullen, F. T. and Gilbert K. E. (1982) *Reaffirming Rehabilitation.* Cincinnati, OH: Anderson Publishing Company.

Cullen, F. T. and Wright, J. P. (2002) "Criminal Justice in the Lives of American Adolescents." In J. Mortimer and R. Larson (eds.), *The Future of Adolescent Experience: Societal Trends and the Transition to Adulthood in the 21st Century.* New York: Cambridge University Press, pp. 88–128.

Cullen, F. T., Wright, J. P., and Applegate, B. K. (1996) "Control in the Community: The Limits of Reform?" In A. T. Harland (ed.), *Choosing Correctional Interventions that Work: Defining the Demand and Evaluating the Supply.* Newbury Park, CA: Sage, pp. 69–116.

DiIulio, J. J. and Piehl, A. M. (1991) "Does Prison Pay?" *The Bookings Review* 9: 28–35.

Dodge, K. A., Lansford, J. E., Burks, V. S., Bates, J. E., Pettit, G. S., Fontaine, R., and Price, J. M. (2003) "Peer Rejection and Social Information-processing Factors in the Development of Aggressive Behavior Problems in Children," *Child Development* 74: 374–93.

Drubach, D. (2000) *The Brain Explained.* Upper Saddle River, NJ: Prentice Hall.

Elliott, D. S. (1994) "Serious Violent Offenders: Onset, Developmental Course, and Termination: The American Society of Criminology 1993 Presidential Address," *Criminology* 32: 1–21.

Gendreau, P. (1996) "The Principles of Effective Intervention with Offenders." In A. T. Harland (ed.), *Choosing Correctional Options that Work.* Thousand Oaks, CA: Sage, pp. 117–30.

Gendreau, P., Goggin, C., Cullen, F. T., and Andrews, D. A. (2000) "The Effects of Community Sanctions and Incarceration on Recidivism," *Forum on Corrections Research* 12: 10–13.

Gottfredson, M. R. and Hirschi, T. (1990) *A General Theory of Crime.* Stanford, CA: Stanford University Press.

Hudziak, J. J., van Beijsterveldt, C. E., Bartels, M., Rietveld, M. J., Rettew, D. C., Derks, E. M., and Boomsma, D. I. (2003) "Individual Differences in Aggression: Genetic Analyses by Age, Gender, and Informant in 3-, 7-, and 10-year-old Dutch Twins," *Behavior Genetics* 33: 575–89.

Huesmann, L. R., Eron, L. D., Lefkowitz, M. M., and Walder, L. O. (1984) "The Stability of Aggression over Time and Generations," *Developmental Psychology* 20: 1120–34.

Huizinga, D., and Jakob-Chien, C. (1998) "The Contemporaneous Co-occurrence of Serious and Violent Juvenile Offending and Other Problem Behaviors." In R. Loeber and D. P. Farrington (eds.), *Serious and Violent Juvenile Offenders: Risk Factors and Successful Interventions.* Thousand Oaks, CA: Sage, pp. 47–67.

Keenan, K. and Shaw, D. (2003) "Starting at the Beginning: Exploring the Etiology of Antisocial Behavior in the First Years of Life." In B. Lahey, T. Moffett, and A. Caspi (eds.), *Causes of Conduct Disorder and Juvenile Delinquency.* New York: Guilford, pp. 153–81.

Keenan, K., Shaw, D., Delliquadri, E., Giovannelli, J., and Walsh, B. (1998) "Evidence for the Continuity of Early Problem Behaviors: Application of a Developmental Model," *Journal of Abnormal Child Psychology* 26: 441–54.

Keenan, K., and Wakschlag, L. S. (2000) "More than the Terrible Twos: The Nature and Severity of Behavior Problems in Clinic-referred Preschool Children," *Journal of Abnormal Child Psychology* 28: 33–46.

Lipsey, M. W. (1992) "Juvenile Delinquency Treatment: A Meta-analytic Inquiry into the Variability of Effects." In T. D. Cook, H. Cooper, D. S. Cordray, H. Hartmann, L. V. Hedges, R. J. Light, T. A. Lewis, and F. Mosteller (eds.), *Meta-analysis for Explanation: A Casebook*. New York: Russell Sage.

—— (1999) "Can Intervention Rehabilitate Serious Delinquents?" *Annals of the American Academy of Political and Social Science* 564: 142–66.

Lipsey, M. W. and J. H. Derzon (1998) "Predictors of Violent or Serious Delinquency in Adolescence and Early Adulthood." In R. Loeber and D. P. Farrington (eds.), *Serious and Violent Juvenile Offenders: Risk Factors and Successful Interventions*. Thousand Oaks, CA: Sage, pp. 86–105.

Lipsey, M. W. and Wilson, D. B. (1998) "Effective Intervention for Serious Juvenile Offenders: A Synthesis of Research." In R. Loeber and D. P. Farrington (eds.), *Serious and Violent Juvenile Offenders: Risk Factors and Successful Interventions*. Thousand Oaks, CA: Sage, pp. 313–66.

Loeber, R. (1982) "The Stability of Antisocial and Delinquent Child Behavior: A Review," *Child Development* 53: 1431–46.

Logan, C. H. and Gaes, G. G. (1993) "Meta-analysis and the Rehabilitation of Punishment," *Justice Quarterly* 10: 245–63.

Martinson, R. (1974) "What Works? – Questions and Answers about Prison Reform," *The Public Interest* 35: 22–54.

—— (1979) "New Findings, New Views: A Note of Caution Regarding Sentencing Reform," *Hofstra Law Review* 7: 243–58.

Mason, D. A. and Frick P. J. (1994) "The Heritability of Antisocial Behavior: A Meta-analysis of Twin and Adoption Studies," *Journal of Psychopathology and Behavioral Assessment* 16: 131–45.

Moffitt, T. E., Caspi, A., Rutter, M., and Silva, P. A. (2001) *Sex Differences in Antisocial Behaviour: Conduct Disorder, Delinquency, and Violence in the Dunedin Longitudinal Study*. Cambridge: Cambridge University Press.

Nagin, D. S. (1998) "Criminal Deterrence Research at the Outset of the Twenty-first Century." In M. Tonry (ed.), *Crime and Justice: A Review of Research*, Vol. 23. Chicago, IL: University of Chicago Press, pp. 1–42.

Olweus, D. (1979) "Stability of Aggressive Reaction Patterns in Males: A Review," *Psychological Bulletin* 86: 852–75.

Petersilia, J. and Honig, P. (1980) "The Prison Experience of Career Criminals." R-2511-DOJ, The RAND Corporation.

Plomin, R. (1990) *Nature and Nurture: An Introduction to Human Behavioral Genetics*. Belmont, CA: Wadsworth.

Raine, A. (2002) "Biosocial Studies of Antisocial and Violent Behavior in Children and Adults: A Review," *Journal of Abnormal Child Psychology* 30: 311–26.

Rawls, J. (1971) *A Theory of Justice*. The Belknap Press of Harvard University Press

Redondo, S., Sanchez-Meca, J., and Garrido, V. (1999) "The Influence of Treatment Programmes on the Recidivism of Juvenile and Adult Offenders: A European Meta-analytic Review," *Psychology, Crime and Law* 5: 251–78.

Reiss, D., Neiderhiser, N., Hetherington, E. M., and Plomin, R. (2000) *The Relationship Code: Deciphering Genetic and Social Influences on Adolescent Development*. Cambridge: Cambridge University Press.

Rhee, S. H. and Waldman, I. D. (2002) "Genetic and Environmental Influences on Antisocial Behavior: A Meta-analysis of Twin and Adoption Studies," *Psychological Bulletin* 128: 490–529.

Rothman, D. J. (1980) *Conscience and Convenience: The Asylum and Its Alternatives in Progressive America*. Boston, MA: Little Brown.

Sampson, R. J. and Laub, J. H. (1993) *Crime in the Making: Pathways and Turning Points through Life*. Cambridge, MA: Harvard University Press.

Sherman, L. W. (1993) "Defiance, Deterrence, and Irrelevance: A Theory of the Criminal Sanction," *Journal of Research in Crime and Delinquency* 30: 445–73.

Siegel, D. J. (1999) *The Developing Mind: Toward a Neurobiology of Interpersonal Experience*. New York: Guilford Press.

Spelman, W. (2000) "What Recent Studies Do (and Don't) Tell Us about Imprisonment and Crime." In M. Tonry (ed.), *Crime and Justice: A Review of Research*, Vol. 27. Chicago, IL: University of Chicago Press, pp. 419–94.

Tremblay, R. E., Japel, C., Perusse, D., Boivin, M., Zoccolillo, M., Montplaisir, and McDuff, P. (1999) "The Search for the Age of "Onset" of Physical Aggression: Rousseau and Bandura Revisited," *Criminal Behavior and Mental Health* 9: 24–39.

Tremblay, Phil, R. O., Vitaro, F., and Dobkin, P. L. (1994) "Predicting Early Onset of Male Antisocial Behavior from Preschool Behavior," *Archives of General Psychiatry* 51: 732–9.

Walsh, A. (2002) *Biosocial Criminology: Introduction and Integration*. Cincinnati, OH: Anderson.

White, J., Moffitt, T. E., Earls, F., Robins, L. N., and Silva, P. A. (1990) "How Early Can We Tell? Predictors of Childhood Conduct Disorder and Adolescent Delinquency," *Criminology* 28: 507–33.

Wilson, J. Q. (1975) *Thinking about Crime*. New York: Vintage Books.

Wright, J. P. and Cullen F. T. (2001) "Parental Efficacy and Delinquent Behavior: Do Control and Support Matter?" *Criminology* 39: 677–706.

50

In Defense of the Death Penalty

Louis P. Pojman

In June 1941 the Nazis under the German Führer Adolf Hitler set out to exterminate European Jewry, a program now known as the Holocaust. The slaughter lasted four years by which time some six million of Europe's eight million Jews had been systematically murdered. Another six million non-Jews – Poles, Catholics, Gypsies, homosexuals, and political enemies – were also destroyed. We are all aware of the atrocities committed at Auschwitz, Birkenau, Buchenwald, Chelmno, Dachau, Treblinka, Bergen-Belsen and Majdanek.

At the Nuremberg Trials, which took place after the War in late 1945, 21 German leaders were put on trial for war crimes and crimes against humanity. Eighteen were found guilty and 11 were sentenced to death, including Herman Göring, Hitler's chosen successor, and Julius Streicher, the ardent Jew-baiter. Hitler, Himmler and Goebbels would have also have been condemned to death had they not already committed suicide.

What is particularly interesting – and problematic – in this case is that the Nazi criminals broke no German laws in their treatment of the Jews. The plaintiffs appealed to a higher law, the universal moral law that forbids killing the innocent, a minimal version of natural law. As Supreme Court Justice Robert Jackson, the US Prosecutor, stated,

> The wrongs which we seek to condemn and punish have been so calculated, so malignant, and so devastating, that civilization cannot tolerate their being ignored, because it cannot survive their being repeated. . . . Against their opponents, including Jews, Catholics, and free labor, the Nazis directed such a campaign of arrogance, brutality, and annihilation as the world has not witnessed since the pre-Christian era. . . . At length bestiality and bad faith reached such excess that they aroused the sleeping strength of imperiled civilization.

Were the judges at Nuremberg justified in condemning the Nazi war criminals to death for their extermination policies? I think they were. Death was too good for these moral monsters. The gravity of their crime defies quantification, but they deserved no less punishment than death.

But perhaps you will demur on the grounds that the Nazis were being judged by ex post facto law, so that the trial had no legal standing. Suppose we accept that point. Then my question becomes: if there had been a law that forbad genocide, then, given due process, would the

Nazi criminals have deserved the death penalty? If German law attached the death penalty to such crimes against humanity, would the legal system have been immoral for violating the rights of Hitler, Himmler, Goebbels and Goring in sentencing them to death? Would it have been wrong even if such a sentence would deter others from embarking on genocidal policies? I would like to ask each of my panelists whether they think that the Nazi leaders – Hitler, Himmler and Göring – deserved the death penalty. Do you think they did?

If you agree that under conditions like these the death penalty is morally permissible (or required), then we have one clear case where it is acceptable. Absolute Abolitionism is defeated and the only question is where to draw the line between cases where the death penalty is morally permissible and where it ceases to be so. Do those who bombed the Murrah Federal Building in Oklahoma in April 1995, killing 168 men, women, and children deserve to be executed? Why is killing 168 innocent people relevantly different than killing a million? Isn't the same malice aforethought present in both cases? How about the serial killers Jeffrey Dahmer and Ted Bundy? Do they merit the death penalty? How about the cold blooded murder of one's spouse, one's parent, a helpless woman, a store keeper, a child, any one of us? If you accept the judgment of Nuremberg regarding the Nazis, the reasons that warrant the death penalty there may turn out to be applicable to other cases.

Here are my grounds for supporting the death penalty.

The Retributivist Argument

Let me say a word about my notion of desert. Historically, a component of justice, going back to Plato, Aristotle, Kant, the Biblical tradition, and virtually every major religion, holds that people ought to get what they deserve. Those who work hard for worthy goals deserve reward, those who do not make the effort deserve nothing, while those who purposefully do evil deserve punishment. The virtuous deserve to flourish to the degree of their virtue and the

vicious deserve to suffer to the degree of their vice. "Whatsoever a man soweth, that shall he reap," is an ancient adage, perhaps as old as its metaphysical counterpart of eternal judgment (Jewish/Christian tradition) or karma (Hindu/Buddhist tradition) – that what one does in this life will be part of one's essential constitution in the next life. This notion presumes the principle of responsibility, that people are accountable for their actions and should be rewarded and punished accordingly. In this sense, the Nuremberg Trials were only carrying out our idea of universal justice as desert. Only in contemporary liberalism, such as John Rawls's theory of justice as fairness, has the notion of natural desert been seriously undermined. But Rawls is wrong here. Though we may not deserve our initial endowments or capacities, we do deserve what we make with them. Our effort and contribution is worthy of moral assessment, and as agents we can be held accountable for our effort and contributions. That is, without the concept of desert, responsibility has no validity, and without the notion of responsibility, neither morality nor law has a foundation.

Suppose, we assume, as most of us do, that each person has a right to life. That right, however, is not absolute, but conditional (otherwise we could not kill even in self-defense). Like our right to property and liberty, it can be overridden for weighty moral reasons. When an offender threatens or attempts to kill the innocent person, the offender deserves a punishment appropriate to the severity of the crime. When the offender with malice aforethought takes the life of an innocent person, he or she forfeits his or her own right to life. But the main idea in the retributivist theory is that not only is the death penalty permissible for the murderer; he *deserves* it. For the guilty deserve punishment and that punishment should be proportional to the severity of their crime. A complete retributivist like Kant holds that all and only those who are guilty should be so punished. The moderate retributivist holds that only the guilty should be so punished – but not necessarily all the guilty. Mitigating circumstances, the external costs of punishment, the possibility of reform, and so forth may prescribe lesser degrees of punishment than are deserved. Hell itself may be a just desert for Hitler, but morality doesn't require that we torture him. The moderate retributivist holds that giving people what they deserve (positive and negative) is a prima facie duty – not an absolute, non-overridable one.

Some have objected that the death penalty is itself murder. To quote the eighteenth-century abolitionist, Cesare di Beccaria, "Putting the criminal to death only compounds evil. If killing is an evil, then the State actually doubles the evil by executing the murderer. The State violates the criminal's right to life. It carries out *legalized murder*. The death penalty cannot be useful because of the example of barbarity it gives to men . . . it seems to me absurd that the laws which punish homicide should themselves commit it." But there is a difference. The murderer volunteered for his crime. The victim didn't volunteer for his fate. The murderer had reason to believe that he would be justly and severely punished for his crime, so he has no reason to complain when the state executes him. The murderer violated the right to life of the victim, thereby forfeiting his own prima facie right to life. The fifth and fourteenth amendments of our Bill of Rights state that no one should be deprived of life, liberty or property without due process of the law, implying that so long as due process of the law has been observed, condemning a murderer to death is both legally and morally justified.

Society may rank punishments roughly corresponding to the gravity of the crime. That is, it draws up two lists. The first list consists of a list of crimes from the worst to the least serious. The second is a list of punishments that it considers acceptable from the most severe to the least severe. So long as there is a rough correspondence between the two lists, a society is permitted to consult its own sense of justice in linking the various punishments with each crime in question. The death penalty, it would seem, would be at the head of the list of severe punishments, linked retributively with the worst crimes. Whether torture is also permitted for the torturer, mutilation for the rapist, and so forth, may be debated. Strictly speaking I have no argument against their appropriate use,

though I think torture is not necessary. It seems to me that death is a sufficient punishment for the most heinous crimes, but it's not part of my thesis to sort out these matters. Where to put the limit of harm to be imposed on the murderer is partly a cultural matter, as the history of legal punishment indicates.[1] Our notion of what is or is not "humane," connected with repulsion against torture and corporal punishment in general is largely a cultural matter. It has to do with how we have been socialized, torture shocks our sensibilities, but not those of our ancestors, and not necessarily our moral principles. Although I am a moral objectivist, holding that moral truth exists, part of morality is relative to culture, to the sensibilities of the majority of its members.

One objection to the retributivist argument is that while the criminal may deserve the death penalty, the justification of the State's execution of the criminal is another matter. It needs a separate justification. My response is: justice consists of giving people what they deserve. As Locke noted, in the state of nature we would each have the right and duty to punish the offender, but in organizing society we surrender that right and duty to the State. We may override justice because of mitigating circumstances, but in so far as the State has duty to dispense justice, it is justified in executing those who commit murder.

The Utilitarian Argument

The utilitarian argument for capital punishment is that it deters would-be offenders from committing first degree murder. If the death penalty deters, we have an auxiliary argument for its use. It may supplement (but not replace) the retributivist argument. Isaac Ehrlich's study, to my knowledge the most thorough study to date, takes into account the complex sociological data and concludes that over the period 1933–69 "an additional execution per year . . . may have resulted on the average in 7 or 8 fewer murders." Ehrlich's findings have been challenged by many opponents with the result that the issue is left in doubt. It seems an enormous

after Reiman

undertaking to prove either that the death penalty deters or that it does not deter. The statistical evidence is inconclusive – which is different from saying it is "zero," as the abolitionist sometimes claims.

There are common sense reasons for believing that the death penalty deters some would-be murderers from murdering. Richard Herrnstein and James Q. Wilson in *Crime and Human Nature* have argued that a great deal of crime is committed on a cost–benefit scheme, wherein the criminal engages in some form of risk assessment as to his or her chances of getting caught and punished in some manner. If the would-be criminal estimates the punishment to be mild, the crime becomes inversely attractive, and vice versa. So if the potential murderer judges that he may be punished by imprisonment or death, he will be more deterred from committing a crime than if he judges he will be punished only by imprisonment. Doesn't the fact that those condemned to death do everything in their power to postpone it and to get their sentences reduced to long-term prison sentences, show that the death penalty is feared as an evil to be avoided? The potential criminal need not go through deliberate cost–benefit analysis. The awful association of murder with the penalty of death may have embedded a powerful deterrence in the subconscious mind of the potential criminal. Perhaps the abolition of the death penalty from the 1960s until the late 1970s, and the fact that it is only recently being carried out with any regularity, has eroded the awful association, accounting for the increased murder rate from 1980 until 1993. The fact that it is beginning to be carried out, may partially account for the decrease of homicides in the past two years.

Former Prosecuting Attorney for the State of Florida, Richard Gernstein, has set forth the common-sense case for deterrence. First of all, the death penalty certainly deters the murderer from any further murders, including those he or she might commit within the prison where he is confined. Secondly, statistics cannot tell us how many potential criminals have refrained from taking another's life through fear of the death penalty. As Hyman Barshay puts it:

> The death penalty is a warning, just like a lighthouse throwing its beams out to sea. We hear about shipwrecks, but we do not hear about the ships the lighthouse guides safely on their way. We do not have proof of the number of ships it saves, but we do not tear the lighthouse down.

Some of the common sense evidence is anecdotal as reported by the British member of parliament, Arthur Lewis, who was converted from being an abolitionist to a retentionist:

> One reason that has stuck in my mind, and which has proved to me beyond question, is that there was once a professional burglar in my constituency who consistently boasted of the fact that he had spent about one-third of his life in prison . . . he said to me, "I am a professional burglar. Before we go out on a job we plan it down to every detail. Before we go into the boozer to have a drink we say, 'Don't forget, no shooters' " – shooters being guns. He adds, "We did our job and didn't have shooters because at that time there was capital punishment. Our wives, girlfriends and our mums said, 'Whatever you do, do not carry a shooter because if you are caught you might be topped.' If you do away with capital punishment they will all be carrying shooters."

It's difficult to know how widespread this kind of reasoning is. My own experience, growing up in a neighborhood where some of my acquaintances were criminals, corroborates this testimony. These criminals admitted being constrained in their behavior by the possibility of the death penalty. No doubt some crimes are committed in the heat of passion or by the temporally insane, but not all crime fits that mold. Perhaps rational risk assessment which involves the cost–benefit analysis of crime, is mainly confined to certain classes of potential and professional criminals, including burglars and kidnappers. It probably applies to people who are tempted to kill their enemies. We simply don't know how much capital punishment deters, but this sort of common sense, anecdotal evidence cannot be dismissed as worthless. Common sense tells us that people will be deterred by greater punishments like death than by lesser ones like imprisonment.

I have been arguing that we do have some statistical and common–sense evidence that the death penalty deters would-be killers. But, even if you are skeptical about that evidence, another

Table 50.1 The Wager

	CP works	CP doesn't work
We bet	We win: some murderers die & innocents are saved	We lose: some murderers die for no purpose
We bet against CP	We lose: murderers live & innocents needlessly die.	We win: murderers live & some lives of others are unaffected.

argument based on the mere *possibility* that it deters is available to us. This is the argument set forth by Ernest van den Haag, which he calls the "Best Bet Argument."[2] Van den Haag argues that even though we don't know for certain whether the death penalty deters or prevents other murders, we should bet that it does. Indeed, due to our ignorance, any social policy we take is a gamble. Not to choose capital punishment for first degree murder is as much a bet that capital punishment doesn't deter as choosing the policy is a bet that it does. There is a significant difference in the betting, however, in that to bet against capital punishment is to bet against the innocent and for the murderer, while to bet for it is to bet against the murderer and for the innocent.

The point is this: We are accountable for what we let happen as well as what we actually do. If I fail to bring up my children properly, so that they are a menace to society, I am to some extent responsible for their bad behavior. I could have caused it to be somewhat better. If I have good evidence that a bomb will blow up the building you are working in, and fail to notify you (assuming I can), I am partly responsible for your death, if and when the bomb explodes. So we are responsible for what we omit doing, as well as what we do. Purposefully to refrain from a lesser evil which we know will allow a greater evil to occur, is to be, at least partially responsible for the greater evil.

This responsibility for our omissions underlies van den Haag's argument, to which we now return. Suppose that we choose a policy of capital punishment for capital crimes. In this case we are betting that the death of some murderers will be more than compensated for by the lives of some innocents not being murdered (either by these murderers or others who

would have murdered). If we're right, we have saved the lives of the innocent. If we're wrong, unfortunately, we've sacrificed the lives of some murderers. But what if we choose not to have a social policy of capital punishment? If capital punishment doesn't work as a deterrent, we've come out ahead, but if it does, then we've missed an opportunity to save innocent lives. If we value the saving of innocent lives more highly than the loss of the guilty, then to bet on a policy of capital punishment turns out to be rational. The reasoning goes like this. Let "CP" stand for "Capital Punishment":

Suppose that we estimate that the utility value of a murderer's life is 5 while the value of an innocent's life is 10 (although we cannot give lives exact numerical values, we can make rough comparative estimates of value – e.g., Mother Teresa's life is greater than Adolf Hitler's – all things being equal, the life of an innocent person is at least twice the value of the murderer's life. My own sense is that the murderer has forfeited most, if not all of his worth, but if I had to put a figure on it, it would be 1000 to 1). Given van den Haag's figures, the sums work out this way:

A murderer saved + 5
A murderer executed − 5
An innocent saved + 10
An innocent murdered − 10

Suppose that for each execution only two innocent lives are spared. Then the outcomes read as follows:

(a) −5 + 20 = +15
(b) −5
(c) +5 − 20 = −15
(d) +5

If all the possibilities are roughly equal, we can sum their outcomes like this.

If we bet on capital punishment, (a) and (b) obtain = +10

If we bet against capital punishment, (c) and (d) obtain = −10.

So we optimize value by betting in favor of capital punishment. If, as I believe, the difference between an innocent life and a murderer's life is more than double, it becomes even more value enhancing to bet on capital punishment for murderers. To abolish the death penalty for convicted murderers would be a bad bet. We unnecessarily put the innocent at risk.

Even if we only value the utility of an innocent life slightly more than that of the murderers, it is still rational to execute convicted murderers. As van den Haag writes, "Though we have no proof of the positive deterrence of the penalty, we also have no proof of zero or negative effectiveness. I believe we have no right to risk additional future victims of murder for the sake of sparing convicted murderers; on the contrary, our moral obligation is to risk the possible ineffectiveness of executions."[3]

Objections to Capital Punishment

Let us examine three major objections to capital punishment, as well as the retentionist's responses to those objections.

1 Objection: Capital punishment is a morally unacceptable thirst for revenge. As former British Prime Minister Edward Heath put it:

The real point which is emphasized to me by many constituents is that even if the death penalty is not a deterrent, murderers deserve to die. This is the question of revenge. Again, this will be a matter of moral judgment for each of us. I do not believe in revenge. If I were to become the victim of terrorists, I would not wish them to be hanged or killed in any other way for revenge. All that would do is deepen the bitterness which already tragically exists in the conflicts we experience in society, particularly in Northern Ireland.[4]

Response: Retributivism is not the same thing as revenge, although the two attitudes are often intermixed in practice. Revenge is a personal response to a perpetrator for an injury.

Retribution is an impartial and impersonal response to an offender for an offense done against someone. You cannot desire revenge for the harm of someone to whom you are indifferent. Revenge always involves personal concern for the victim. Retribution is not personal but based on objective factors: the criminal has deliberately harmed an innocent party and so deserves to be punished, whether I wish it or not. I would agree that I or my son or daughter deserves to be punished for our crimes, but I don't wish any vengeance on myself or my son or daughter.

Furthermore, while revenge often leads us to exact more suffering from the offender than the offense warrants, retribution stipulates that the offender be punished in proportion to the gravity of the offense. In this sense, the *lex talionis* which we find in the Old Testament is actually a progressive rule, where retribution replaces revenge as the mode of punishment. It says that there are limits to what one may do to the offender. Revenge demands a life for an eye or a tooth, but Moses provides a rule that exacts a penalty equal to the harm done by the offender.

2 Objection: Miscarriages of justice occur. Capital punishment is to be rejected because of human fallibility in convicting innocent parties and sentencing them to death. In a survey done in 1985 Hugo Adam Bedau and Michael Radelet found that of the 7,000 persons executed in the United States between 1900 and 1985, 25 were innocent of capital crimes.[5] While some compensation is available to those unjustly imprisoned, the death sentence is irrevocable. We can't compensate the dead. As John Maxton, a member of the British Parliament puts it, "If we allow one innocent person to be executed, morally we are committing the same, or, in some ways, a worse crime than the person who committed the murder."[6]

Response: Mr. Maxton is incorrect in saying that mistaken judicial execution is morally the same or worse than murder, for a deliberate intention to kill the innocent occurs in a murder, whereas no such intention occurs in wrongful capital punishment.

Sometimes this objection is framed this way: It is better to let ten criminals go free than to execute one innocent person. If this dictum is a call for safeguards, then it is well taken; but somewhere there seems to be a limit on the tolerance of society towards capital offenses. Would these abolitionists argue that it is better that 50 or 100 or 1,000 murderers go free than that one guilty person be executed? Society has a right to protect itself from capital offenses even if this means taking a finite chance of executing an innocent person. If the basic activity or process is justified, then it is regrettable, but morally acceptable, that some mistakes are made. Fire trucks occasionally kill innocent pedestrians while racing to fires, but we accept these losses as justified by the greater good of the activity of using fire trucks. We judge the use of automobiles to be acceptable even though such use causes an average of 50,000 traffic fatalities each year. We accept the morality of a defensive war even though it will result in our troops accidentally or mistakenly killing innocent people.

The fact that we can err in applying the death penalty should give us pause and cause us to build an appeals process into the judicial system. Such a process is already in the American and British legal systems. That occasional error may be made, regrettable though this is, is not a sufficient reason for us to refuse to use the death penalty, if on balance it serves a just and useful function.

Furthermore, aboliltionists are simply misguided in thinking that prison sentences are a satisfactory alternative here. It's not clear that we can always or typically compensate innocent parties who waste away in prison. Jacques Barzun has argued that a prison sentence can be worse than death and carries all the problems that the death penalty does regarding the impossibility of compensation:

> In the preface of his useful volume of cases, *Hanged in Error*, Mr. Leslie Hale refers to the tardy recognition of a minor miscarriage of justice – one year in jail: "The prisoner emerged to find that his wife had died and that his children and his aged parents had been removed to the workhouse. By the time a small payment had been assessed as 'compensation' the victim was incurably insane." So far we are as indignant with the law as Mr. Hale. But what comes next? He cites the famous Evans case, in which it is very probable that the wrong man was hanged, and he

exclaims: "While such mistakes are possible, should society impose an irrevocable sentence?" Does Mr. Hale really ask us to believe that the sentence passed on the first man, whose wife died and who went insane, was in any sense *revocable*? Would not any man rather be Evans dead than that other wretch "emerging" with his small compensation and his reason for living gone?[7]

The abolitionist is incorrect in arguing that death is different than long-term prison sentences because it is irrevocable. Imprisonment also take good things away from us that may never be returned. We cannot restore to the inmate the freedom or opportunities he or she lost. Suppose an innocent 25-year-old man is given a life sentence for murder. Thirty years later the mistake is discovered and he is set free. Suppose he values three years of freedom to every one year of life. That is, he would rather live ten years as a free man than thirty as a prisoner. Given this man's values, the criminal justice system has taken the equivalent of ten years of life from him. If he lives until he is 65, he has, as far as his estimation is concerned, lost ten years, so that he may be said to have lived only 55 years.[8]

The numbers in this example are arbitrary, but the basic point is sound. Most of us would prefer a shorter life of higher quality to a longer one of low quality. Death prevents all subsequent quality, but imprisonment also irrevocably harms one in diminishing the quality of life of the prisoner.

3 Objection: The death penalty is unjust because it discriminates against the poor and minorities, particularly, African Americans, over against rich people and whites. Former Supreme Court Justice William Douglas wrote that "a law which reaches that [discriminatory] result in practice has no more sanctity than a law which in terms provides the same."[9] Stephen Nathanson argues that "in many cases, whether one is treated justly or not depends not only on what one deserves but on how other people are treated."[10] He offers the example of unequal justice in a plagiarism case. "I tell the students in my class that anyone who plagiarizes will fail the course. Three students plagiarize papers, but I give only one a failing grade. The other two, in describing their motivation, win my sympathy, and I give them passing grades." Arguing that this is patently unjust, he likens this case to the imposition of the death penalty and concludes that it too is unjust.

Response: First of all, it is not true that a law that is applied in a discriminatory manner is unjust. Unequal justice is no less justice, however, uneven its application. The discriminatory application, not the law itself, is unjust. A just law is still just even if it is not applied consistently. For example, a friend of mine once got two speeding tickets during a 100-mile trip (having borrowed my car). He complained to the police officer who gave him his second ticket that many drivers were driving faster than he was at the time. They had escaped detection, he argued, so it wasn't fair for him to get two tickets on one trip. The officer acknowledged the imperfections of the system but, justifiably, had no qualms about giving him the second ticket. Unequal justice is still justice, however regrettable. So Justice Douglas is wrong in asserting that discriminatory results invalidate the law itself. Discriminatory practices should be reformed, and in many cases they can be. But imperfect practices in themselves do not entail that the laws engendering these practices are themselves are unjust.

With regard to Nathanson's analogy with the plagiarism case, two things should be said against it. First, if the teacher is convinced that the motivational factors are mitigating factors, then he or she may be justified in passing two of the plagiarizing students. Suppose that the one student did no work whatsoever, showed no interest (Nathanson's motivation factor) in learning, and exhibited no remorse in cheating, whereas the other two spent long hours seriously studying the material and, upon apprehension, showed genuine remorse for their misdeeds. To be sure, they yielded to temptation at certain – though limited – sections of their long papers, but the vast majority of their papers represented their own diligent work. Suppose, as well, that all three had C averages at this point. The teacher gives the unremorseful, gross plagiarizer an F but relents and gives

the other two D's. Her actions parallel the judge's use of mitigating circumstances and cannot be construed as arbitrary, let alone unjust.

The second problem with Nathanson's analogy is that it would lead to disastrous consequences for all law and benevolent practices alike. If we concluded that we should abolish a rule or practice, unless we treated everyone exactly by the same rules all the time, we would have to abolish, for example, traffic laws and laws against imprisonment for rape, theft, and even murder. Carried to its logical limits, we would also have to refrain from saving drowning victims if a number of people were drowning but we could only save a few of them. Imperfect justice is the best that we humans can attain. We should reform our practices as much as possible to eradicate unjust discrimination wherever we can, but if we are not allowed to have a law without perfect application, we will be forced to have no laws at all.

Nathanson acknowledges this latter response but argues that the case of death is different. "Because of its finality and extreme severity of the death penalty, we need to be more scrupulous in applying it as punishment than is necessary with any other punishment."[11] The retentionist agrees that the death penalty is a severe punishment and that we need to be scrupulous in applying it. The difference between the abolitionist and the retentionist seems to lie in whether we are wise and committed enough as a nation to reform our institutions so that they approximate fairness. Apparently, Nathanson is pessimistic here, whereas I have faith in our ability to learn from our mistakes and reform our systems. If we can't reform our legal system, what hope is there for us?

More specifically, the charge that a higher percentage of blacks than whites are executed was once true but is no longer so. Many states have made significant changes in sentencing procedures, with the result that currently whites convicted of first-degree murder are sentenced to death at a higher rate than blacks.[12]

One must be careful in reading too much into these statistics. While great disparities in statistics should cause us to examine our judicial procedures, they do not in themselves prove injustice. For example, more males than females are convicted of violent crimes (almost 90 percent of those convicted of violent crimes are males – a virtually universal statistic), but this is not strong evidence that the law is unfair, for there are psychological explanations for the disparity in convictions. Males are on average and by nature more aggressive (usually tied to testosterone) than females. Likewise, there may be good explanations why people of one ethnic group commit more crimes than those of other groups, explanations which do not impugn the processes of the judicial system.

Conclusion

Both abolitionists and retentionists agree that punishment for crime is intended to deter (1) the criminal and (2) potential criminals from future crimes. We could deter people from crimes by framing and punishing the innocent, but that would violate justice. The innocent don't deserve to be punished, but the guilty do. So we ground punishment on retributive foundations. The strong (Kantian) version of retributivism holds that the guilty must be punished equivalently or, if that's not possible, in proportion to the gravity of their offense. It is a moral absolute. The moderate retributivist holds that the guilty ought to be punished in a manner proportionate to the gravity of the crime, but the punishment may be mitigated or even overridden for other moral reasons. The weakest version of retributivism holds that guilt is only a necessary (but not a sufficient) condition for punishment, and that it does not necessitate proportionality. In each of these retributivist theories capital punishment remains an option. When we add utilitarian reasons to the retributivist position, the case for capital punishment

becomes even stronger. Common sense tells us that the death penalty deters potential murderers. If by executing murderers who deserve the death penalty we can prevent future murders, we should do so. Finally, I have dealt with three prominent objections to the death penalty: (1) that it is a form of revenge; (2) that it sometimes executes innocent people; and (3) that it discriminates against minorities. I have argued that these objections can be met.

Many good people would still object to my arguments, intending that they show a lack of regard for human life. But I think that the fact is just the opposite – that capital punishment respects the worth of the victim – is bluntly articulated by the newspaper columnist, Mike Royko:

> When I think of the thousands of inhabitants of Death Rows in the hundreds of prisons in this country, I don't react the way the kindly souls do – with revulsion that the state would take these lives. My reaction is: What's taking us so long? Let's get that electrical current flowing. Drop the pellets now!
>
> Whenever I argue this with friends who have opposite views, they say that I don't have enough regard for that most marvelous of miracles – human life.
>
> Just the opposite: It's because I have so much regard for human life that I favor capital punishment. Murder is the most terrible crime there is. Anything less than the death penalty is an insult to the victim and society. It says, in effect, that we don't value the victim's life enough to punish the killer fully.

It's just because the victim's life is sacred that I favor the death penalty as fitting punishment for first degree murder. I too regret the use of capital punishment and am in favor of its elimination. I would vote in favor of the abolition of capital punishment today but on one condition – that those contemplating murder would set an example for me. Otherwise, it is better that the murderer should perish than their innocent victims should be cut down by their knife or bullets.

Notes

A more complete set of notes and references is found in my jointly authored book (with Jeffrey Reiman), *The Death Penalty: For and Against* (Rowman & Littlefield, 1999).

1   Michael Davis has a excellent discussion of "humane punishment" in "Death, Deterrence, and the Method of Common Sense" in *Social Theory and Practice* (summer 1981).

2   Ernst van den Haag, "On Deterrence and the Death Penalty," *Ethics* 78 (July 1968).

3   Ibid.

4   British Parliamentary Debates, 1982, quoted in Sorrell, *Moral Theory and Anomoly* Oxford: Blackwell, 1999, 43.

5   Hugo Adam Bedau and Michael Radelet, *Miscarriages of Justice in Potential Capital Cases* (1st draft October 1985, on file at Harvard Law School Library), quoted in E. van den Haag "The Ultimate Punishment: A Defense" *Harvard Law Review*, vol. 99, no. 7 (May 1986): 1664.

6   Ibid., 47.

7   Jacques Barzun, "In Favor of Capital Punishment" *The American Scholar*, vol 31, no. 2, Spring 1962.

8   I have been influenced by similar arguments by Michael Levin (unpublished manuscript) and Michael Davis, "Is the Death Penalty Irrevocable?" *Social Theory and Practice*, vol 10:2 (Summer 1984).

9   Justice William Douglas in *Furman* v *Georgia* 408 U.S. 238 (1972).

10 Stephen Nathanson, *An Eye for an Eye?* Totowa, NJ: Rowman & Littlefield, 1987, 62.

11 Ibid., 67.

12 The Department of Justice's *Bureau of Justice Statistics Bulletin* for 1994 reports that between 1977 and 1994 2,336 (51%) of those arrested for murder were white, 1838 (40%) were black, 316 (7%) were Hispanic. Of the 257 who were executed, 140 (54%) were white, 98 (38%) were black, 17 (7%) were Hispanic and 2 (1%) were other races. In 1994, 31 prisoners, 20 white men and 11 black men, were executed although whites made up only 7,532 (41%) and blacks 9,906 (56%) of those arrested for murder. Of those sentenced to death in 1994, 158 were white men, 133 were black men, 25 were Hispanic men, 2 were Native American men, 2 were white women, and 3 were black women. Of those sentenced, relatively more blacks (72%) than whites (65%) or Hispanics (60%), had prior felony records. Overall the criminal justice system does not seem to favor white criminals over black, though it does seem to favor rich defendants over poor ones. Furthermore, one sometimes gets the impression that whites kill blacks more than vice versa, but actually the reverse is true. In 1997 Federal arrest records show that approximately 1,100 whites were killed by blacks, and 480 blacks were killed by whites, indicating that blacks are about 15 times more likely to kill a white than a white to kill a black.

51

Against the Death Penalty

Jeffrey Reiman

My position about the death penalty as punishment for murder can be summed up in the following four propositions:

1 though the death penalty is a just punishment for some murderers, it is not unjust to punish murderers less harshly (down to a certain limit);
2 though the death penalty would be justified if needed to deter future murders, we have no good reason to believe that it is needed to deter future murders; and
3 in refraining from imposing the death penalty, the state, by its vivid and impressive example, contributes to reducing our tolerance for cruelty and thereby fosters the advance of human civilization as we understand it.

Taken together, these three propositions imply that we do no injustice to actual or potential murder victims, and we do some considerable good, in refraining from executing murderers. This conclusion will be reinforced by another argument, this one for the proposition:

4 though the death penalty is *in principle* a just penalty for murder, it is unjust *in practice* in America because it is applied in arbitrary and discriminatory ways, and this is likely to continue into the foreseeable future.

This fourth proposition conjoined with the prior three imply the overall conclusion *that it is good in principle to avoid the death penalty and bad in practice to impose it.* In what follows, I shall state briefly the arguments for each of these propositions.[1] For ease of identification, I shall number the first paragraph in which the argument for each proposition begins.

1 Before showing that the death penalty is just punishment for some murders, it is useful to dispose of a number of popular but weak arguments against the death penalty. One such popular argument contends that, if murder is wrong, then the death penalty is wrong as well. But this argument proves too much! It would work against *all* punishments since all are wrong if done by a regular citizen under normal circumstances. (If I imprison you in a little jail in my basement, I am guilty of kidnaping; if I am caught and convicted, the state will lock me up in jail and will not have committed the same wrong that I did.) The point here is that what is

wrong about murder is not merely that it is killing per se, but the killing of a legally innocent person by a nonauthorized individual – and this doesn't apply to executions that are the outcome of conviction and sentencing at a fair trial.

Another argument that some people think is decisive against capital punishment points to the irrevocability of the punishment. The idea here is that innocents are sometimes wrongly convicted and if they receive the death penalty there is no way to correct the wrong done to them. While there is some force to this claim, its force is at best a relative matter. To be sure, if someone is executed and later found to have been innocent, there is no way to give him back the life that has been taken. But, if someone is sentenced to life in prison and is found to have been innocent, she can be set free and perhaps given money to make up for the years spent in prison – but those years cannot be given back. On the other hand, the innocent person who has been executed can at least be compensated in the form of money to his family and he can have his named cleared. So, it's not that the death penalty is irrevocable and other punishments are revocable; rather, all punishments are irrevocable though the death penalty is, so to speak, relatively more irrevocable than the rest. In any event, this only makes a difference in cases of mistaken conviction of the innocent, and the evidence is that such mistakes – particularly in capital cases – are quite rare.[2] And, further, since we accept the death of innocents elsewhere, on the highways, as a cost of progress, as a necessary accompaniment of military operations, and so on, it is not plausible to think that the execution of a small number of innocent persons is so terrible as to outweigh all other considerations, especially when every effort is made to make sure that it does not occur.

Finally, it is sometimes argued that if we use the death penalty as a means to deter future murderers, we kill someone to protect others (from different people than the one we have executed), and thus we violate the Kantian prohibition against using individuals as means to the welfare of others. But the Kantian prohibition is not against using others as means, it is against using others as *mere* means (that is, in total disregard of their own desires and goals). Though you use the busdriver as a means to your getting home, you don't use him as a mere means because the job pays him a living and thus promotes his desires and goals as it does yours. Now, if what deters criminals is the existence of an effective system of deterrence, then criminals punished as part of that system are not used as mere means since their desires and goals are also served, inasmuch as they have also benefited from deterrence of other criminals. Even criminals don't want to be crime victims. Further, if there is a right to threaten punishment in self- defense, then a society has the right to threaten punishment to defend its members, and there is no more violation of the Kantian maxim in imposing such punishment then there is in carrying out any threat to defend oneself against unjust attack.[3]

One way to see that the death penalty is a just punishment for at least some murders (the cold-blooded, premeditated ones) is to reflect on the *lex talionis*, an eye for an eye, a tooth for a tooth, and all that. Some regard this as a primitive rule, but it has I think an undeniable element of justice. And many who think that the death penalty is just punishment for murder are responding to this element. To see what the element is consider how similar the *lex talionis* is to the Golden Rule. The Golden Rule tells us to do unto others what we would have others do unto us, and the *lex talionis* counsels that we do to others what they have done to us. Both of these reflect a belief in the equality of all human beings. Treating others as you *would* have them treat you means treating others as equal to you, because it implies that you count their suffering to be as great a calamity as your own suffering, that you count your right to impose suffering on them as no greater than their right to impose suffering on you, and so on. The Golden Rule would not make sense if it were applied to two people, one of whom was thought to be inherently more valuable than the other. Imposing a harm on the more valuable one would be worse than imposing the same harm on the less valuable one – and neither could judge her actions by what she would have the other do to her.

Since *lex talionis* says that you are rightly paid back for the harm you have caused another with a similar harm, it implies that the value of what of you have done to another is the same as the value of having it done to you – which, again, would not be the case, if one of you were thought inherently more valuable than the other. Consequently, treating people according to the *lex talionis* (like treating them according to the Golden Rule) affirms the equality of all concerned – and this supports the idea that punishing according to *lex talionis* is just.

Furthermore, on the Kantian assumption that a rational individual implicitly endorses the universal form of the intention that guides his action, a rational individual who kills another implicitly endorses the idea that he may be killed, and thus, he authorizes his own execution thereby absolving his executioner of injustice. What's more, much as above we saw that acting on *lex talionis* affirms the equality of criminal and victim, this Kantian-inspired argument suggests that acting on *lex talionis* affirms the rationality of criminal and victim. The victim's rationality is affirmed because the criminal only authorizes his own killing if he has intended to kill another rational being like himself – then, he implicitly endorses the universal version of that intention, thereby authorizing his own killing. A person who intentionally kills an animal does not implicitly endorse his own being killed; only someone who kills someone like himself authorizes his own killing. In this way, the Kantian argument also invokes the equality of criminal and victim.

On the basis of arguments like this, I maintain that the idea that people deserve having done to them roughly what they have done (or attempted to do) to others affirms both the equality and rationality of human beings and for that reason is just. Kant has said: "no one has ever heard of anyone condemned to death on account of murder who complained that he was getting too much [punishment] and therefore was being treated unjustly; everyone would laugh in his face if he were to make such a statement."[4] If Kant is right, then even murderers recognize the inherent justice of the death penalty.

However, while the justice of the *lex talionis* implies the justice of executing some murderers, it does not imply that punishing less harshly is automatically unjust. We can see this by noting that the justice of the *lex talionis* implies also the justice of torturing torturers and raping rapists. I am certain and I assume my reader is as well that we need not impose these latter punishments to do justice (even if there were no other way of equaling the harm done or attempted by the criminal). Otherwise the price of doing justice would be matching the cruelty of the worst criminals, and that would effectively price justice out of the moral market. It follows that justice can be served with lesser punishments. Now, I think that there are two ways that punishing less harshly than the *lex talionis* could be unjust: it could be unjust to the actual victim of murder or to the future victims of potential murderers. It would be unjust to the actual victim if the punishment we mete out instead of execution were so slight that it trivialized the harm that the murderer did. This would make a sham out of implicit affirmation of equality that underlies the justice of the *lex talionis*. However, life imprisonment, or even a lengthy prison sentence – say, twenty years or more without parole – is a very grave punishment and not one that trivializes the harm done by the murderer. Punishment would be unjust to future victims if it is so mild that it fails to be a reasonable deterrent to potential murderers. Thus, refraining from executing murderers could be wrong if executions were needed to deter future murderers. In the following section, I shall say why there is no reason to think that this is so.

2 I grant that, if the death penalty were needed to deter future murderers, that would be a strong reason in favor of using the death penalty, since otherwise we would be sacrificing the future victims of potential murderers whom we could have deterred. And I think that this is a real injustice to those future victims, since the we in question is the state. Because the state claims a monopoly on the use of force, it owes its citizens protection, and thus does them injustice when it fails to provide the level of protection it reasonably could provide.

However, there is no reason to believe that we need the death penalty to deter future murderers. The evidence we have strongly supports the idea that we get the same level of deterrence from life imprisonment, and even from substantial prison terms, such as twenty years without parole.

Before 1975, the most important work on the comparative deterrent impact of the capital punishment versus life in prison was that of Thorsten Sellin. He compared the homicide rates in states with the death penalty to the rates in similar states without the death penalty, and found no greater incidence of homicide in states without the death penalty than in similar states with it. In 1975, Isaac Ehrlich, a University of Chicago econometrician, reported the results of a statistical study which he claimed proved that, in the period from 1933 to 1969, each execution deterred as many as eight murders. This finding was, however, widely challenged. Ehrlich found a deterrent impact of executions in the period from 1933 to 1969, which includes the period of 1963 to 1969, a time when hardly any executions were carried out and crime rates rose for reasons that are arguably independent of the existence or nonexistence of capital punishment. When the 1963–9 period is excluded, no significant deterrent effect shows. This is a very serious problem since the period from 1933 through to the end of the 1930s was one in which executions were carried out at the highest rate in American history – before or after. That no deterrent effect turns up when the study is limited to 1933 to 1962 almost seems evidence *against* the deterrent effect of the death penalty!

Consequently, in 1978, *after Ehrlich's study*, the editors of a National Academy of Sciences' study of the impact of punishment wrote: "In summary, the flaws in the earlier analyses (i.e., Sellin's and others) and the sensitivity of the more recent analyses to minor variation in model specification and the serious temporal instability of the results lead the panel to conclude that the available studies provide no useful evidence on the deterrent effect of capital punishment."[5] Note that, while the deterrence research commented upon here generally compares the deterrent impact of capital punishment with that of life imprisonment, the failure to prove that capital punishment deters murder more than does incarceration goes beyond life in prison. A substantial proportion of people serving life sentences are released on parole before the end of their sentences. Since this is public knowledge, we should conclude from these studies that we have no evidence that capital punishment deters murder more effectively than prison sentences that are less than life, though still substantial, such as twenty years.

Another version of the argument for the greater deterrence impact of capital punishment compared to lesser punishments is called *the argument from common sense*. It holds that, whatever the social science studies do or don't show, it is only common sense that people will be more deterred by what they fear more, and since people fear death more than life in prison, they will be deterred more by execution than by a life sentence. This argument for the death penalty, however, assumes without argument or evidence that deterrence increases continuously and endlessly with the fearfulness of threatened punishment rather than leveling out at some threshold beyond which increases in fearfulness produce no additional increment of deterrence. That being tortured for a year is worse than being tortured for six months doesn't imply that a year's torture will deter you from actions that a half-year's torture would not deter – since a half-year's torture may be bad enough to deter you from all the actions that you can be deterred from doing. Likewise, though the death penalty may be worse than life in prison, that doesn't imply that the death penalty will deter acts that a life sentence won't because a life sentence may be bad enough to do all the deterring that can be done – and that is precisely what the social science studies seem to show. And, as I suggested above, what applies here to life sentences applies as well to substantial prison sentences.

I take it then that there is no reason to believe that we save more innocent lives with the death penalty than with less harsh penalties such as life in prison or some lengthy sentence, such as twenty years without parole. But then we do no injustice to the future victims of potential murderers by refraining from the death penalty. And, in conjunction with the argument of the previous section, it follows that we do no injustice to actual or potential murder victims if we refrain from executing murderers and sentence them instead to life in prison or to some substantial sentence, say, twenty or more years in prison without parole. But it remains to be seen what good will be served by doing the latter instead of executing.

3 Here I want to suggest that, in refraining from imposing the death penalty, the state, by its vivid and impressive example, contributes to reducing our tolerance for cruelty and thereby fosters the advance of human civilization as we understand it. To see this, note first that it has long been acknowledged that the state, and particularly the criminal justice system, plays an educational role in society as a model of morally accepted conduct and an indicator of the line between morally permissible and impermissible actions. Now, consider the general repugnance that is attached to the use of torture – even as punishment for criminals who have tortured their victims. It seems to me that, by refraining from torturing even those who deserve it, our state plays a role in promoting that repugnance. That we will not torture even those who have earned it by their crimes conveys a message about the awfulness of torture, namely, that it is something that civilized people will not do even to give evil people their just deserts. Thus it seems to me that in this case the state advances the cause of human civilization by contributing to a reduction in people's tolerance for cruelty. I think that the modern state is uniquely positioned to do this sort of thing because of its size (representing millions, even hundreds of millions of citizens) and its visibility (starting with the printing press that accompanied the birth of modern nations, increasing with radio, television and the other media of instantaneous communication). And because the state can do this, it should. Consequently, I contend that if the state were to put execution in the same category as torture, it would contribute yet further to reducing our

tolerance for cruelty and to advancing the cause of human civilization. And because it can do this, it should.

To make this argument plausible, however, I must show that execution is horrible enough to warrant its inclusion alongside torture. I think that execution is horrible in a way similar to (though not identical with) the way in which torture is horrible. Torture is horrible because of two of its features, which also characterize execution: intense pain and the spectacle of one person being completely subject to the power of another.[6] This latter is separate from the issue of pain, since it is something that offends people about unpainful things, such as slavery (even voluntarily entered) and prostitution (even voluntarily chosen as an occupation). Execution shares this separate feature. It enacts the total subjugation of one person to his fellows, whether the individual to be executed is strapped into an electric chair or bound like a laboratory animal on a hospital gurney awaiting lethal injection.

Moreover, execution, even by physically painless means, is characterized by a special and intense psychological pain that distinguishes it from the loss of life that awaits us all. This is because execution involves the most psychologically painful features of death. We normally regard death from human causes as worse than death from natural causes, since a humanly caused shortening of life lacks the consolation of unavoidability. And we normally regard death whose coming is foreseen by its victim as worse than sudden death because a foreseen death adds to the loss of life the terrible consciousness of that impending loss. An execution combines the worst of both: Its coming is foreseen, in that its date is normally already set, and it lacks the consolation of unavoidability, in that it depends on the will of one's fellow human beings not on natural forces beyond human control. It was on just such grounds that Albert Camus regarded the death penalty as itself a kind of torture: "As a general rule, a man is undone by waiting for capital punishment well before he dies. Two deaths are inflicted on him, the first being worse than the second, whereas he killed but once. Compared to such torture, the penalty of retaliation [the *lex talionis*] seems like a civilized law."[7]

Consequently, if a civilizing message is conveyed about torture when the state refrains from torturing, I believe we can and should try to convey a similar message about killing by having the state refrain from killing even those who have earned killing by their evil deeds. Moreover, if I am right about this, then it implies further that refraining from executing murderers will have the effect of deterring murder in the long run and thereby make our society safer. This much then shows that it would be good in principle to refrain from imposing capital punishment. I want now to show why it would be good in practice as well.

4 However just in principle the death penalty may be, it is applied unjustly in practice in America and is likely to be so for the foreseeable future. The evidence for this conclusion comes from various sources. Numerous studies show that killers of whites are more likely to get the death penalty than killers of blacks, and that black killers of whites are far more likely to be sentenced to death than white killers of blacks. Moreover, just about everyone recognizes that poor people are more likely to be sentenced to death and to have those sentences carried out than well-off people. And these injustices persist even after all death penalty statutes were declared unconstitutional in 1972[8] and only those death penalty statutes with provisions for reducing arbitrariness in sentencing were admitted as constitutional in 1976.[9] In short, injustice in the application of the death penalty persists even after legal reform, and this strongly suggests that it is so deep that it will not be corrected in the foreseeable future.

It might be objected that discrimination is also found in the handing out of prison sentences and thus that this argument would prove that we should abolish prison as well as the death penalty. But I accept that we need some system of punishment to deter crime and mete out justice to criminals, and for that reason even a discriminatory punishment system is better than none. Then, the objection based on discrimination works only against those elements of the punishment system that are not

needed either to deter crime or to do justice, and I have shown above that this is true of the death penalty. Needless to say we should also strive to eliminate discrimination in the parts of the criminal justice that we cannot do without.

Other, more subtle, kinds of discrimination also affect the way the death penalty is actually carried out. There are many ways in which the actions of well-off people lead to death which are not counted as murder. For example, many more people die as a result of preventable occupational diseases (due to toxic chemicals, coal and textile dust, and the like, in the workplace) or preventable environmental pollution than die as a result of what is treated legally as homicide.[10] So, in addition to all the legal advantages that money can buy a wealthy person accused of murder, the law also helps the wealthy by not defining as murder many of the ways in which the wealthy are responsible for the deaths of fellow human beings. Add to this that many of the killings that we do treat as murders, the ones done by the poor in our society, are the predictable outcome of remediable social injustice – the discrimination and exploitation that, for example, have helped to keep African Americans at the bottom of the economic ladder for centuries. Those who benefit from injustice and who could remedy it bear some of the responsibility for the crimes that are the predictable outcome of injustice – and that implies that plenty of well-off people share responsibility with many of our poor murderers. But since these more fortunate folks are not likely to be held responsible for murder, it is unfair to hold only the poor victims of injustice responsible – and wholly responsible to boot!

Finally, we already saw that the French existentialist, Albert Camus, asserted famously that life on death row is a kind of torture. Recently, Robert Johnson has studied the psychological effects on condemned men on death row and confirmed Camus' claim. In his book *Condemned to Die*, Johnson recounts the painful psychological deterioration suffered by a substantial majority of the death row prisoners he studied.[11] Since the death row inmate faces execution, he is viewed as having nothing to lose and thus is treated as the most dangerous of criminals. As a result, his confinement and isolation are nearly total. Since he has no future for which to be rehabilitated, he receives the least and the worst of the prison's facilities. Since his guards know they are essentially warehousing him until his death, they treat him as something less than human – and so he is brutalized, taunted, powerless and constantly reminded of it. The effect of this on the death row inmate, as Johnson reports it, is quite literally the breaking down of the structures of the ego – a process not unlike that caused by brainwashing. Since we do not reserve the term "torture" only for processes resulting in physical pain, but recognize processes that result in extreme psychological suffering as torture as well (consider sleep deprivation or the so-called Chinese water torture), Johnson's and Camus' application of this term to the conditions of death row confinement seems reasonable.

It might be objected that some of the responsibility for the torturous life of death row inmates is the inmates's own fault, since in pressing their legal appeals, they delay their executions and thus prolong their time on death row. Capital murder convictions and sentences, however, are reversed on appeal with great frequency, nearly ten times the rate of reversals in noncapital cases. This strongly supports the idea that such appeals are necessary to test the legality of murder convictions and death penalty sentences. To hold the inmate somehow responsible for the delays that result from his appeals, and thus for the (increased) torment he suffers as a consequence, is effectively to confront him with the choice of accepting execution before its legality is fully tested or suffering torture until it is. Since no just society should expect (or even want) a person to accept a sentence until its legal validity has been established, it is unjust to torture him until

it has and perverse to assert that he has brought the torture on himself by his insistence that the legality of his sentence be fully tested before it is carried out.

The worst features of death row might be ameliorated, but it is unlikely that its torturous nature will be eliminated, or even that it is possible to eliminate it. This is, in part, because it is linked to an understandable psychological strategy used by the guards in order to protect themselves against natural, painful, and ambivalent feelings of sympathy for a person awaiting a humanly inflicted death. Johnson writes: "I think it can also be argued . . . that humane death rows will not be achieved in practice because the purpose of death row confinement is to facilitate executions by de-humanizing both the prisoners and (to a lesser degree) their executioners and thus make it easier for both to conform to the etiquette of ritual killing."[12]

If conditions on death row are and are likely to continue to be a real form of psychological torture, if Camus and Johnson are correct, then it must be admitted that the death penalty is in practice not merely a penalty of death – it is a penalty of torture until death. Then the sentence of death is more than the *lex talionis* allows as a just penalty for murder – and thus it is unjust in practice.

I think that I have proven that it would be good in principle to refrain from imposing the death penalty and bad in practice to continue using it. And, I have proven this while accepting the two strongest claims made by defenders of capital punishment, namely, that death is just punishment for at least some murderers, and that, if the death penalty were a superior deterrent to murder than imprisonment that would justify using the death penalty.

Notes

1   The full argument for these propositions, along with supporting data, references and replies to objections is in Louis Pojman and Jeffrey Reiman, *The Death Penalty: For and Against* (Lanham, MD: Rowman Littlefield Publishers, Inc., 1998), pp. 67–132, 151–63. That essay in turn is based upon and substantially revises my "Justice, Civilization, and the Death Penalty: Answering van den Haag," *Philosophy and Public Affairs* 14, no. 2 (Spring 1985): 115–48, and my "The Justice of the Death Penalty in an Unjust World," in *Challenging Capital Punishment: Legal and Social Science Approaches*, ed. K. Haas J. Inciardi (Beverly Hills, CA: Sage, 1988), pp. 29–48.

2 Some recent developments, most notably the use of DNA testing to exonerate a number of death row inmates, suggest that this claim may be overly optimistic. In that case, the risk of condemning the innocent would become a stronger argument against capital punishment and, in fact, has recently led to calls for a moratorium on executions. In January 2000, Illinois Governor George Ryan, "a Republican who supports capital punishment, cited the exoneration of 13 death row inmates since Illinois re-adopted the death penalty in 1977 and said he would permit no more executions until a study was completed of a system he described as 'fraught with error' " (Sara Rimer, "U.S. Cities Call for Death Penalty Moratorium," *International Herald Tribune*, November 1, 2000, p. 7). Philadelphia, Atlanta, Baltimore, San Francisco and Charlotte, North Carolina, are among two dozen cities that have recently passed non-legally binding moratorium resolutions, and polls show that support for the death penalty among Americans is at its lowest in 20 years – down to two-thirds from a high of 75 percent in 1994.

3 Elsewhere I have argued at length that punishment needed to deter reasonable people is deserved by criminals. See Pojman and Reiman, *The Death Penalty*, pp. 79–85.

4 Immanuel Kant, "The Metaphysical Elements of Justice," pt. 1 of *The Metaphysics of Morals*, trans. J. Ladd (Indianapolis, IN: Bobbs-Merrill, 1965; originally published 1797), p. 104, see also p. 133.

5 Alfred Blumstein, Jacqueline Cohen, and Daniel Nagin, eds., *Deterrence and Incapacitation: Estimating the Effects of Criminal Sanctions on Crime Rates* (Washington, DC: National Academy of Sciences, 1978), p. 9.

6 Hugo Bedau has developed this latter consideration at length with respect to the death penalty. See Hugo A. Bedau, "Thinking about the Death Penalty as a Cruel and Unusual Punishment," *U.C. Davis Law Review* 18 (Summer 1985): 917ff. This article is reprinted in Hugo A. Bedau, *Death Is Different: Studies in the Morality, Law, and Politics of Capital Punishment* (Boston: Northeastern University Press, 1987); and Hugo A. Bedau, ed., *The Death Penalty in America: Current Controversies* (New York: Oxford University Press, 1997).

7 Albert Camus, "Reflections on the Guillotine," in Albert Camus, *Resistance, Rebellion, and Death* (New York: Knopf, 1961), p. 205.

8 *Furman v Georgia*, 408 U.S. 238 (1972).

9 *Gregg v Georgia*, 428 U.S. 153 (1976).

10 Jeffrey Reiman, *The Rich Get Richer and the Poor Get Prison: Ideology, Class, and Criminal Justice*, 6th edn. (Needham Heights, MA: Allyn Bacon, 2001), pp. 79–85, 88–94.

11 Robert Johnson, *Condemned to Die: Life under Sentence of Death* (New York: Elsevier, 1981), pp. 129ff.

12 Robert Johnson, personal correspondence to author.

Economic Justice

Philosophers have historically distinguished between three types of justice. In the previous section on PUNISHMENT the authors discussed retributive justice. In the section on AFFIRMATIVE ACTION, two authors discussed compensatory justice. In the current section, the authors focus on the third: distributive justice. Distributive justice concerns how we should distribute the products of social cooperation among the community's citizens. Some of the most important goods a society distributes are economic. The first two selections articulate the most widely discussed contemporary theories of economic justice. The essay by Rawls outlines the economic implications of his theory of justice. Before I describe his economic views (captured in his "second principle of justice"), I must briefly mention his "first principle of justice," namely, that the first responsibility of government is to guarantee equal civil liberties for all citizens. According to Rawls, governments should protect liberties such as those granted in the *United States Constitution*: freedom of speech, freedom of religion, freedom of the press, etc. These liberties are essential to any just society; we cannot sacrifice them to increase economic well-being. Nor may we sacrifice any particular individual's civil liberties for the benefit of others, not even the majority. Rawls's emphasis on individual freedom is reminiscent of the views of several authors in the sections on drugs (PATERNALISM AND RISK) and FREE SPEECH.

After these individual liberties are secure, we must then agree on a system for distributing economic goods. He proposes that we adopt his "second principle of justice," namely, that the state should distribute economic goods to maximize the advantage of the least advantaged members of society. This principle will permit some people to have more economic goods than others, but only if their having more goods will promote the well-being of the least well-off members of society. By following this principle, we know that even the most disadvantaged members of society will have a tolerably decent life – the best life they could reasonably expect.

Rawls's argument for these two principles has important theoretical implications, and is therefore worthy of mention. We should arrive at principles of justice from behind "the veil of ignorance." That is, we should ask not, "What principle of justice would I adopt if I knew my talents, interests, and station in life?" but "What principles of justice would I adopt if I were ignorant of my talents, interests, and station in life?" He offers both practical and moral reasons for claiming that we should select principles of justice in this way. The practical reason is simple: if we ask the first question, we lose any chance for consensus. Each of us will, intentionally or unintentionally, strive to design principles that will benefit us, given our particular array of interests and talents. However, if we asked the second question, we would be likely to select principles of justice that promote our interests, no matter what our specific interests and talents happened to be. We are more likely to identify principles on which all rational people (who go through this reasoning process) could agree.

Rawls also offers moral reasons for selecting principles from behind the veil of ignorance. Reasoning behind the veil of ignorance will lead us to minimize the influence of luck in determining people's life prospects. Rawls claims that the circumstances of one's birth – one's natural talents, social status, family influences, etc. – are matters of luck that should not unduly influence our chances in life. A central task of morality is to constrain the detrimental effects of luck.

Is he correct? That is clearly a theoretical question with profound practical consequences. Those who embrace a retributive theory of PUNISHMENT would likely sympathize with Rawls's claim. For if justice requires that we give people what they deserve, and what they deserve is determined by their freely chosen actions, then it is difficult to see why someone who was born intelligent deserves more than someone who was born retarded. We will also see disagreements about the appropriate role of luck in the discussion of WORLD HUNGER. Children in developed countries have better life prospects than children in Third World countries for one reason alone: luck in the circumstances of their birth. I did not deserve to be born to parents who could provide for me, in a developed country with an educational system; certainly I did not deserve it more than a poor child in Addis Ababa, Khartoum, or Jakarta. So why should I have a relatively cushy life, while

they fight to stay alive, simply because of luck? Should luck play such a large role in determining our fates? Or should morality seek to limit luck's influence?

Nozick thinks not. The job of morality is not to eliminate the detrimental effects of luck. In fact, the aim of justice is not to strive for any particular economic distribution. The state does not have the right to distribute economic goods. Particular individuals already own those goods. The role of a theory of economic justice is simply to set down rules that everyone should follow in acquiring and transferring those goods. The ideal theory, according to Nozick, would go something like this: If someone acquires her goods justly, that is, by initially acquiring them fairly, or by receiving the goods via transfer from someone who justly owned them, then there is nothing else we need know. What makes a distribution just is not the final outcome, but the rules followed in determining that outcome.

Nozick further argues that we can achieve and maintain an ideal distribution only by constantly interfering with individual liberty. If people have liberty, then they will, through private transfers, inevitably alter the distribution so that it no longer satisfies the ideal – no matter what the ideal. Perhaps we can best understand Nozick's view if we assume that he imports Mill's emphasis on individual liberty (FREE SPEECH and PATERNALISM AND RISK) into the economic arena. For Nozick, all liberty – whether civil or economic – is created equal. If he is correct, then that has important implications for other practical issues.

For instance, if we embrace Nozick's view about the sanctity of individual property rights, then individuals should be able to keep their property, even if, by so doing, other people die. Indeed, that is precisely the thrust of Arthur's arguments about WORLD HUNGER.

Young rejects this entire way of describing and discussing the issue of justice. Although distribution is an important element of justice, it is not, she claims, the only or even the most important element. For instance, the state should provide educational and employment opportunities for all citizens. We cannot use a purely distributive model to adequately evaluate whether the state has provided for these fundamental needs. Distributive justice is concerned with handing out consumable goods in a fair and reasonable manner. However, equality of opportunity is not so much a matter of what we have, as what we do. The distributive paradigm simply ignores these crucial elements of justice.

Moreover, the "standard" ways of framing issues about justice mask the powerful role social institutions play not only in determining who gets what, but also in determining how we define and evaluate jobs and positions. Why do we describe some positions as professional jobs and other jobs as "white-collar?" Is there any intrinsic reason why physicians should make more money than astrophysicists, even if both positions require similar training, talent, and expertise? And how, exactly, do we best guarantee equality of opportunity?

The distributive paradigm does not give us a plausible response to any of these questions. That is why, Young argues, we should abandon the distributive paradigm, and focus instead on relationships of power, especially relationships of domination and oppression. Other authors raised these concerns earlier, for example, in the discussions of SEXUAL AND RACIAL DISCRIMINATION and AFFIRMATIVE ACTION.

Wolff's discussion of and worries about competition shares some of Young's misgivings about standard views of distributive justice. In particular, he fears that we become so accustomed to using competition to distribute economic goods that we do not pay attention to the ways in which some forms of competition harm those who lose. Admittedly not all forms of competition are objectionable; participants may actually enjoy it. But in our economic world, some people do not enjoy it and are regularly harmed by it.

Here again we see deep disagreements about what constitutes harm. On Nozick's view, competition does not *harm* anyone, even though some people are most assuredly losers. The losers are not harmed because they are not *wronged* by the winners. Wolff, however, contends this is an unduly narrow conception of harm. Defenders of capitalism do claim that the losers are not harmed since the economic system benefits everyone (by presumably lowering prices and raising quality). However, although this may be true, Wolff argues, it still exploits some workers by using them for the benefits of others. Such use is morally acceptable only if those who lose are properly said to benefit by that system. That would seem to require that we erect a safety net to insure that the losers don't fall too far. Moreover, we should change our economic relations with other countries so that we do not exploit Third World workers just so we can have cheaper and more plentiful goods.

Further Reading

Feinberg, J. (1980) *Rights, Justice, and the Bounds of Liberty*. Princeton, NJ: Princeton University Press.

Goodin, R. and Pettit, P. (1993) *A Companion to Contemporary Political Philosophy*. Oxford: Blackwell Publishers.

Locke, J. (1963) *Two Treatises of Government*, ed. Peter Laslett. New York: Cambridge University Press.

Nozick, R. (1974) *Anarchy, State, and Utopia*. New York: Basic Books.

Rawls, J. (1970) *A Theory of Justice*. Cambridge, MA: Harvard University Press.

Waldron, J. (1986) "Welfare and the Images of Charity," *Philosophical Quarterly* 36: 463–82.

Wolff, J. (2000) "Economic Justice." In H. LaFollette (ed.), *Oxford Handbook of Practical Ethics*. Oxford: Oxford University Press, pp. 433–58.

52

A Theory of Justice

John Rawls

The Main Idea of the Theory of Justice

My aim is to present a conception of justice which generalizes and carries to a higher level of abstraction the familiar theory of the social contract as found, say, in Locke, Rousseau, and Kant.[1] In order to do this we are not to think of the original contract as one to enter a particular society or to set up a particular form of government. Rather, the guiding idea is that the principles of justice for the basic structure of society are the object of the original agreement. They are the principles that free and rational persons concerned to further their own interests would accept in an initial position of equality as defining the fundamental terms of their association. These principles are to regulate all further agreements; they specify the kinds of social cooperation that can be entered into and the forms of government that can be established. This way of regarding the principles of justice I shall call justice as fairness.

Thus we are to imagine that those who engage in social cooperation choose together, in one joint act, the principles which are to assign basic rights and duties and to determine the division of social benefits. Men are to decide in advance how they are to regulate their claims against one another and what is to be the foundation charter of their society. Just as each person must decide by rational reflection what constitutes his good, that is, the system of ends which it is rational for him to pursue, so a group of persons must decide once and for all what is to count among them as just and unjust. The choice which rational men would make in this hypothetical situation of equal liberty, assuming for the present that this choice problem has a solution, determines the principles of justice.

In justice as fairness the original position of equality corresponds to the state of nature in the traditional theory of the social contract. This original position is not, of course, thought of as an actual historical state of affairs, much less as a primitive condition of culture. It is understood as a purely hypothetical situation characterized so as to lead to a certain conception of justice.[2] Among the essential features of this situation is that no one knows his place in society, his class position or social status, nor does any one know his fortune in the distribution of natural assets and abilities, his intelligence, strength, and the like. I shall even assume that the parties do not know their conceptions of the good or their special psychological propensities.

The principles of justice are chosen behind a veil of ignorance. This ensures that no one is advantaged or disadvantaged in the choice of principles by the outcome of natural chance or the contingency of social circumstances. Since all are similarly situated and no one is able to design principles to favor his particular condition, the principles of justice are the result of a fair agreement or bargain. For given the circumstances of the original position, the symmetry of everyone's relations to each other, this initial situation is fair between individuals as moral persons, that is, as rational beings with their own ends and capable, I shall assume, of a sense of justice. The original position is, one might say, the appropriate initial status quo, and thus the fundamental agreements reached in it are fair. This explains the propriety of the name "justice as fairness": it conveys the idea that the principles of justice are agreed to in an initial situation that is fair. The name does not mean that the concepts of justice and fairness are the same, any more than the phrase "poetry as metaphor" means that the concepts of poetry and metaphor are the same.

Justice as fairness begins, as I have said, with one of the most general of all choices which persons might make together, namely, with the choice of the first principles of a conception of justice which is to regulate all subsequent criticism and reform of institutions. Then, having chosen a conception of justice, we can suppose that they are to choose a constitution and a legislature to enact laws, and so on, all in accordance with the principles of justice initially agreed upon. Our social situation is just if it is such that by this sequence of hypothetical agreements we would have contracted into the general system of rules which defines it. Moreover, assuming that the original position does determine a set of principles (that is, that a particular concept of justice would be chosen), it will then be true that whenever social institutions satisfy these principles those engaged in them can say to one another that they are cooperating on terms to which they would agree if they were free and equal persons whose relations with respect to one another were fair. They could all view their arrangements as

meeting the stipulations which they would acknowledge in an initial situation that embodies widely accepted and reasonable constraints on the choice of principles. The general recognition of this fact would provide the basis for a public acceptance of the corresponding principles of justice. No society can, of course, be a scheme of cooperation which men enter voluntarily in a literal sense; each person finds himself placed at birth in some particular position in some particular society, and the nature of this position materially affects his life prospects. Yet a society satisfying the principles of justice as fairness comes as close as a society can to being a voluntary scheme, for it meets the principles which free and equal persons would assent to under circumstances that are fair. In this sense its members are autonomous and the obligations they recognize self-imposed.

One feature of justice as fairness is to think of the parties in the initial situation as rational and mutually disinterested. This does not mean that the parties are egoists, that is, individuals with only certain kinds of interests, say in wealth, prestige, and domination. But they are conceived as not taking an interest in one another's interests. They are to presume that even their spiritual aims may be opposed, in the way that the aims of those of different religions may be opposed. Moreover, the concept of rationality must be interpreted as far as possible in the narrow sense, standard in economic theory, of taking the most effective means to given ends. I shall modify this concept to some extent, as explained later, but one must try to avoid introducing into it any controversial ethical elements. The initial situation must be characterized by stipulations that are widely accepted.

In working out the conception of justice as fairness one main task clearly is to determine which principles of justice would be chosen in the original position. To do this we must describe this situation in some detail and formulate with care the problem of choice which it presents. These matters I shall take up later. It may be observed, however, that once the principles of justice are thought of as arising from an original agreement in a situation of equality, it is an open question whether the principle of utility would be acknowledged. Offhand it hardly seems likely that persons who view themselves as equals, entitled to press their claims upon one another, would agree to a principle which may require lesser life prospects for some simply for the sake of a greater sum of advantages enjoyed by others. Since each desires to protect his interests, his capacity to advance his conception of the good, no one has a reason to acquiesce in an enduring loss for himself in order to bring about a greater net balance of satisfaction. In the absence of strong and lasting benevolent impulses, a rational man would not accept a basic structure merely because it maximized the algebraic sum of advantages irrespective of its permanent effects on his own basic rights and interests. Thus it seems that the principle of utility is incompatible with the conception of social cooperation among equals for mutual advantage. It appears to be inconsistent with the idea of reciprocity implicit in the notion of a well-ordered society. Or, at any rate, so I shall argue.

I shall maintain instead that the persons in the initial situation would choose two rather different principles: the first requires equality in the assignment of basic rights and duties, while the second holds that social and economic inequalities, for example inequalities of wealth and authority, are just only if they result in compensating benefits for everyone, and in particular for the least advantaged members of society. These principles rule out justifying institutions on the grounds that the hardships of some are offset by a greater good in the aggregate. It may be expedient but it is not just that some should have less in order that others may prosper. But there is no injustice in the greater benefits earned by a few provided that the situation of persons not so fortunate is thereby improved. The intuitive idea is that since everyone's well-being depends upon a scheme of cooperation without which no one could have a satisfactory life, the division of advantages should be such as to draw forth the willing cooperation of everyone taking part in it, including those less well situated. Yet this can be expected only if reasonable terms are

proposed. The two principles mentioned seem to be a fair agreement on the basis of which those better endowed, or more fortunate in their social position, neither of which we can be said to deserve, could expect the willing cooperation of others when some workable scheme is a necessary condition of the welfare of all.[3] Once we decide to look for a conception of justice that nullifies the accidents of natural endowment and the contingencies of social circumstance as counters in the quest for political and economic advantage, we are led to these principles. They express the result of leaving aside those aspects of the social world that seem arbitrary from a moral point of view.

The problem of the choice of principles, however, is extremely difficult. I do not expect the answer I shall suggest to be convincing to everyone. It is, therefore, worth noting from the outset that justice as fairness, like other contract views, consists of two parts: (1) an interpretation of the initial situation and of the problem of choice posed there, and (2) a set of principles which, it is argued, would be agreed to. One may accept the first part of the theory (or some variant thereof), but not the other, and conversely. The concept of the initial contractual situation may seem reasonable although the particular principles proposed are rejected. To be sure, I want to maintain that the most appropriate conception of this situation does lead to principles of justice contrary to utilitarianism and perfectionism, and therefore that the contract doctrine provides an alternative to these views. Still, one may dispute this contention even though one grants that the contractarian method is a useful way of studying ethical theories and of setting forth their underlying assumptions.

Justice as fairness is an example of what I have called a contract theory. Now there may be an objection to the term "contract" and related expressions, but I think it will serve reasonably well. Many words have misleading connotations which at first are likely to confuse. The terms "utility" and "utilitarianism" are surely no exception. They too have unfortunate suggestions which hostile critics have been willing to exploit; yet they are clear enough for those prepared to study utilitarian doctrine. The same should be true of the term "contract" applied to moral theories. As I have mentioned, to understand it one has to keep in mind that it implies a certain level of abstraction. In particular, the content of the relevant agreement is not to enter a given society or to adopt a given form of government, but to accept certain moral principles. Moreover, the undertakings referred to are purely hypothetical: a contract view holds that certain principles would be accepted in a well-defined initial situation.

The merit of the contract terminology is that it conveys the idea that principles of justice may be conceived as principles that would be chosen by rational persons, and that in this way conceptions of justice may be explained and justified. The theory of justice is a part, perhaps the most significant part, of the theory of rational choice. Furthermore, principles of justice deal with conflicting claims upon the advantages won by social cooperation; they apply to the relations among several persons or groups. The word "contract" suggests this plurality as well as the condition that the appropriate division of advantages must be in accordance with principles acceptable to all parties. The condition of publicity for principles of justice is also connoted by the contract phraseology. Thus, if these principles are the outcome of an agreement, citizens have a knowledge of the principles that others follow. It is characteristic of contract theories to stress the public nature of political principles. Finally there is the long tradition of the contract doctrine. Expressing the tie with this line of thought helps to define ideas and accords with natural piety. There are then several advantages in the use of the term "contract." With due precautions taken, it should not be misleading.

A final remark. Justice as fairness is not a complete contract theory. For it is clear that the contractarian idea can be extended to the choice of more or less an entire ethical system, that is, to a system including principles for all the virtues and not only for justice. Now for the most part I shall consider only principles of justice and others closely related to them; I make no attempt to discuss the virtues in a

systematic way. Obviously if justice as fairness succeeds reasonably well, a next step would be to study the more general view suggested by the name "rightness as fairness." But even this wider theory fails to embrace all moral relationships, since it would seem to include only our relations with other persons and to leave out of account how we are to conduct ourselves toward animals and the rest of nature. I do not contend that the contract notion offers a way to approach these questions, which are certainly of the first importance; and I shall have to put them aside. We must recognize the limited scope of justice as fairness and of the general type of view that it exemplifies. How far its conclusions must be revised once these other matters are understood cannot be decided in advance.

The Original Position and Justification

I have said that the original position is the appropriate initial status quo which insures that the fundamental agreements reached in it are fair. This fact yields the name "justice as fairness." It is clear, then, that I want to say that one conception of justice is more reasonable than another, or justifiable with respect to it, if rational persons in the initial situation would choose its principles over those of the other for the role of justice. Conceptions of justice are to be ranked by their acceptability to persons so circumstanced. Understood in this way the question of justification is settled by working out a problem of deliberation: we have to ascertain which principles it would be rational to adopt given the contractual situation. This connects the theory of justice with the theory of rational choice.

If this view of the problem of justification is to succeed, we must, of course, describe in some detail the nature of this choice problem. A problem of rational decision has a definite answer only if we know the beliefs and interests of the parties, their relations with respect to one another, the alternatives between which they are to choose, the procedure whereby they make up their minds, and so on. As the circumstances are presented in different ways, correspondingly different principles are accepted. The concept of the original position, as I shall refer to it, is that of the most philosophically favored interpretation of this initial choice situation for the purposes of a theory of justice.

But how are we to decide what is the most favored interpretation? I assume, for one thing, that there is a broad measure of agreement that principles of justice should be chosen under certain conditions. To justify a particular description of the initial situation one shows that it incorporates these commonly shared presumptions. One argues from widely accepted but weak premises to more specific conclusions. Each of the presumptions should by itself be natural and plausible; some of them may seem innocuous or even trivial. The aim of the contract approach is to establish that taken together they impose significant bounds on acceptable principles of justice. The ideal outcome would be that these conditions determine a unique set of principles; but I shall be satisfied if they suffice to rank the main traditional conceptions of social justice.

One should not be misled, then, by the somewhat unusual conditions which characterize the original position. The idea here is simply to make vivid to ourselves the restrictions that it seems reasonable to impose on arguments for principles of justice, and therefore on these principles themselves. Thus it seems reasonable and generally acceptable that no one should be advantaged or disadvantaged by natural fortune or social circumstances in the choice of principles. It also seems widely agreed that it should be impossible to tailor principles to the circumstances of one's own case. We should ensure further that particular inclinations and aspirations, and persons' conceptions of their good, do not affect the principles adopted. The aim is to rule out those principles that it would be rational to propose for acceptance, however little the chance of success, only if one knew certain things that are irrelevant from the standpoint of justice. For example, if a man knew that he was wealthy, he might find it rational to advance the principle that various taxes for welfare measures be counted unjust; if he knew that he was poor, he would be most likely to propose the contrary principle. To represent the desired restrictions one imagines a situation in which everyone is deprived of this sort of information. One excludes the knowledge of those contingencies which sets men at odds and allows them to be guided by their prejudices. In this manner the veil of ignorance is arrived at in a natural way. This concept should cause no difficulty if we keep in mind the constraints on arguments that it is meant to express. At any time we can enter the original position, so to speak, simply by following a certain procedure, namely, by arguing for principles of justice in accordance with these restrictions.

It seems reasonable to suppose that the parties in the original position are equal. That is, all have the same rights in the procedure for choosing principles; each can make proposals, submit reasons for their acceptance, and so on. Obviously the purpose of these conditions is to represent equality between human beings as moral persons, as creatures having a conception of their good and capable of a sense of justice. The basis of equality is taken to be similar in these two respects. Systems of ends are not ranked in value; and each man is presumed to have the requisite ability to understand and to act upon whatever principles are adopted. Together with the veil of ignorance, these conditions define the principles of justice as those which rational persons concerned to advance their interests would consent to as equals when none are known to be advantaged or disadvantaged by social and natural contingencies.

There is, however, another side to justifying a particular description of the original position. This is to see if the principles which would be chosen match our considered convictions of justice or extend them in an acceptable way. We can note whether applying these principles would lead us to make the same judgments about the basic structure of society which we now make intuitively and in which we have the greatest confidence; or whether, in cases where our present judgments are in doubt and given with hesitation, these principles offer a resolution which we can affirm on reflection. There are questions which we feel sure must be answered in a certain way. For example, we are confident that religious intolerance and racial discrimination are unjust. We think that we have examined these things with care and have reached what we believe is an impartial judgment not likely to be distorted by an excessive attention to our own interests. These convictions are provisional fixed points which we presume any conceptions of justice must fit. But we have much less assurance as to what is the correct distribution of wealth and authority. Here we may be looking for a way to remove our doubts. We can check an interpretation of the initial situation, then, by the capacity of its principles to accommodate our firmest convictions and to provide guidance where guidance is needed.

In searching for the most favored description of this situation we work from both ends. We begin by describing it so that it represents generally shared and preferably weak conditions. We then see if these conditions are strong enough to yield a significant set of principles. If not, we look for further premises equally reasonable. But if so, and these principles match our considered convictions of justice, then so far well and good. But presumably there will be discrepancies. In this case we have a choice. We can either modify the account of the initial situation or we can revise our existing judgments, for even the judgments we take provisionally as fixed points are liable to revision. By going back and forth, sometimes altering the conditions of the contractual circumstances, at others withdrawing our judgments and conforming them to principle, I assume that eventually we shall find a description of the initial situation that both expresses reasonable conditions and yields principles which match our considered judgments duly pruned and adjusted. This state of affairs I refer to as reflective equilibrium.[4] It is an equilibrium because at last our principles and judgments coincide; and it is reflective since we know to what principles our judgments conform and the premises of their derivation. At the moment everything is in order. But this equilibrium is not necessarily stable. It is liable to be upset by further examination of the conditions which should be imposed on the contractual situation and by particular cases which may lead us to revise our judgments. Yet for the time being we

have done what we can to render coherent and to justify our convictions of social justice. We have reached a conception of the original position.

I shall not, of course, actually work through this process. Still, we may think of the interpretation of the original position that I shall present as the result of such a hypothetical course of reflection. It represents the attempt to accommodate within one scheme both reasonable philosophical conditions on principles as well as our considered judgments of justice. In arriving at the favored interpretation of the initial situation there is no point at which an appeal is made to self-evidence in the traditional sense either of general conceptions or of particular convictions. I do not claim for the principles of justice proposed that they are necessary truths or derivable from such truths. A conception of justice cannot be deduced from self-evident premises or conditions on principles; instead, its justification is a matter of the mutual support of many considerations, of everything fitting together into one coherent view.

A final comment. We shall want to say that certain principles of justice are justified because they would be agreed to in an initial situation of equality. I have emphasized that this original position is purely hypothetical. It is natural to ask why, if this agreement is never actually entered into, we should take any interest in these principles, moral or otherwise. The answer is that the conditions embodied in the description of the original position are ones that we do in fact accept. Or if we do not, then perhaps we can be persuaded to do so by philosophical reflection. Each aspect of the contractual situation can be given supporting grounds. Thus what we shall do is to collect together into one conception a number of conditions on principles that we are ready upon due consideration to recognize as reasonable. These constraints express what we are prepared to regard as limits on fair terms of social cooperation. One way to look at the idea of the original position, therefore, is to see it as an expository device which sums up the meaning of these conditions and helps us to extract their consequences. On the other hand, this conception is also an intuitive notion that suggests its own elaboration, so that led on by it we are drawn to define more clearly the standpoint from which we can best interpret moral relationships. We need a conception that enables us to envision our objective from afar: the intuitive notion of the original position is to do this for us. . . .

Two Principles of Justice

I shall now state in a provisional form the two principles of justice that I believe would be chosen in the original position. In this section I wish to make only the most general comments, and therefore the first formulation of these principles is tentative. As we go on I shall run through several formulations and approximate step by step the final statement to be given much later [in the book]. I believe that doing this allows the exposition to proceed in a natural way.

> The first statement of the two principles reads as follows.
>
> First: each person is to have an equal right to the most extensive basic liberty compatible with a similar liberty for others.
>
> Second: social and economic inequalities are to be arranged so that they are both
> (a) reasonably expected to be to everyone's advantage, and (b) attached to positions and offices open to all.

By way of general comment, these principles primarily apply, as I have said, to the basic structure of society. They are to govern the assignment of rights and duties and to regulate the distribution of social and economic advantages. As their formulation suggests, these principles presuppose that the social structure can be divided into two more or less distinct parts, the first principle applying to the one, the second to the other. They distinguish between those aspects of the social system that define and secure the equal liberties of citizenship and those that specify and establish social and economic inequalities. The basic liberties of citizens are roughly speaking, political liberty (the right to vote and to be eligible for public office) together with freedom of speech and assembly; liberty of conscience and freedom of

thought; freedom of the person along with the right to hold (personal) property; and freedom from arbitrary arrest and seizure as defined by the concept of the rule of law. These liberties are all required to be equal by the first principle, since citizens of a just society are to have the same basic rights.

The second principle applies, in the first approximation, to the distribution of income and wealth and to the design of organizations that make use of differences in authority and responsibility, or chains of command. While the distribution of wealth and income need not be equal, it must be to everyone's advantage, and at the same time, positions of authority and offices of command must be accessible to all. One applies the second principle by holding positions open, and then, subject to this constraint, arranges social and economic inequalities so that everyone benefits.

These principles are to be arranged in a serial order with the first principle prior to the second. This ordering means that a departure from the institutions of equal liberty required by the first principle cannot be justified by, or compensated for by, greater social and economic advantages. The distribution of wealth and income, and the hierarchies of authority, must be consistent with both the liberties of equal citizenship and equality of opportunity.

It is clear that these principles are rather specific in their content, and their acceptance rests on certain assumptions that I must eventually try to explain and justify. A theory of justice depends upon a theory of society in ways that will become evident as we proceed. For the present, it should be observed that the two principles (and this holds for all formulations) are a special case of a more general conception of justice that can be expressed as follows.

> All social values – liberty and opportunity, income and wealth, and the bases of self-respect – are to be distributed equally unless an unequal distribution of any, or all, of these values is to everyone's advantage.

Injustice then, is simply inequalities that are not to the benefit of all. Of course, this conception is extremely vague and requires interpretation.

As a first step, suppose that the basic structure of society distributes certain primary goods, that is, things that every rational man is presumed to want. These goods normally have a use whatever a person's rational plan of life. For simplicity, assume that the chief primary goods at the disposition of society are rights and liberties, powers and opportunities, income and wealth. (Later on in Part Three [of the book] the primary good of self-respect has a central place.) These are the social primary goods. Other primary goods such as health and vigor, intelligence and imagination, are natural goods; although their possession is influenced by the basic structure, they are not so directly under its control. Imagine, then, a hypothetical initial arrangement in which all the social primary goods are equally distributed: everyone has similar rights and duties, and income and wealth are evenly shared. This state of affairs provides a benchmark for judging improvements. If certain inequalities of wealth and organizational powers would make everyone better off than in this hypothetical starting situation, then they accord with the general conception.

Now it is possible, at least theoretically, that by giving up some of their fundamental liberties men are sufficiently compensated by the resulting social and economic gains. The general conception of justice imposes no restrictions on what sort of inequalities are permissible; it only requires that everyone's position be improved. We need not suppose anything so drastic as consenting to a condition of slavery. Imagine instead that men forgo certain political rights when the economic returns are significant and their capacity to influence the course of policy by the exercise of these rights would be marginal in any case. It is this kind of exchange which the two principles as stated rule out; being arranged in serial order they do not permit exchanges between basic liberties and economic and social gains. The serial ordering of principles expresses an underlying preference among primary social goods. When this preference is rational, so likewise is the choice of these principles in this order.

In developing justice as fairness I shall, for the most part, leave aside the general conception of justice and examine instead the special case of the two principles in serial order. The advantage of this procedure is that from the first the matter of priorities is recognized and an effort made to find principles to deal with it. One is led to attend throughout to the conditions under which the acknowledgment of the absolute weight of liberty with respect to social and economic advantages, as defined by the lexical order of the two principles, would be reasonable. Offhand, this ranking appears extreme and too special a case to be of much interest; but there is more justification for it than would appear at first sight. Or at any rate, so I shall maintain. Furthermore, the distinction between fundamental rights and liberties and economic and social benefits marks a difference among primary social goods that one should try to exploit. It suggests an important division in the social system. Of course, the distinctions drawn and the ordering proposed are bound to be at best only approximations. There are surely circumstances in which they fail. But it is essential to depict clearly the main lines of a reasonable concept of justice; and under many conditions anyway, the two principles in serial order may serve well enough. When necessary we can fall back on the more general conception.

The fact that the two principles apply to institutions has certain consequences. Several points illustrate this. First of all, the rights and liberties referred to by these principles are those which are defined by the public rules of the basic structure. Whether men are free is determined by the rights and duties established by the major institutions of society. Liberty is a certain pattern of social forms. The first principle simply requires that certain sorts of rules, those defining basic liberties, apply to everyone equally and that they allow the most extensive liberty compatible with a like liberty for all. The only reason for circumscribing the rights defining liberty and making men's freedom less extensive than it might otherwise be is that these equal rights as institutionally defined would interfere with one another.

Another thing to bear in mind is that when principles mention persons, or require that everyone gain from an inequality, the reference is to representative persons holding the various social positions, or offices, or whatever, established by the basic structure. Thus in applying the second principle I assume that it is possible to assign an expectation of well-being to representative individuals holding these positions. This expectation indicates their life prospects as viewed from their social station. In general, the expectations of representative persons depend upon the distribution of rights and duties throughout the basic structure. When this changes, expectations change. I assume, then, that expectations are connected: by raising the prospects of the representative man in one position we presumably increase or decrease the prospects of representative men in other positions. Since it applies to institutional forms, the second principle (or rather the first part of it) refers to the expectations of representative individuals. As I shall discuss below, neither principle applies to distributions of particular goods to particular individuals who may be identified by their proper names. The situation where someone is considering how to allocate certain commodities to needy persons who are known to him is not within the scope of the principles. They are meant to regulate basic institutional arrangements. We must not assume that there is much similarity from the standpoint of justice between an administrative allotment of goods to specific persons and the appropriate design of society. Our common-sense intuitions for the former may be a poor guide to the latter.

Now the second principle insists that each person benefit from permissible inequalities in the basic structure. This means that it must be reasonable for each relevant representative man defined by this structure, when he views it as a going concern, to prefer his prospects with the inequality to his prospects without it. One is not allowed to justify differences in income or organizational powers on the ground that the disadvantages of those in one position are outweighed by the greater advantages of those in another. Much less can infringements of liberty be counterbalanced in this way. Applied to the basic structure, the principle of utility would have us maximize the sum of expectations of

representative men (weighted by the number of persons they represent, on the classical view); and this would permit us to compensate for the losses of some by the gains of others. Instead, the two principles require that everyone benefit from economic and social inequalities. It is obvious, however, that there are indefinitely many ways in which all may be advantaged when the initial arrangement of equality is taken as a benchmark. How then are we to choose among these possibilities? The principles must be specified so that they yield a determinate conclusion. I now turn to this problem. . . .

The Reasoning Leading to the Two Principles of Justice

In this section I take up the choice between the two principles of justice and the principle of average utility. Determining the rational preference between these two options is perhaps the central problem in developing the conception of justice as fairness as a viable alternative to the utilitarian tradition. I shall begin in this section by presenting some intuitive remarks favoring the two principles. I shall also discuss briefly the qualitative structure of the argument that needs to be made if the case for these principles is to be conclusive.

It will be recalled that the general conception of justice as fairness requires that all primary social goods be distributed equally unless an unequal distribution would be to everyone's advantage. No restrictions are placed on exchanges of these goods and therefore a lesser liberty can be compensated for by greater social and economic benefits. Now looking at the situation from the standpoint of one person selected arbitrarily, there is no way for him to win special advantages for himself. Nor, on the other hand, are there grounds for his acquiescing in special disadvantages. Since it is not reasonable for him to expect more than an equal share in the division of social goods, and since it is not rational for him to agree to less, the sensible thing for him to do is to acknowledge as the first principle of justice one requiring an equal distribution. Indeed, this principle is so obvious that we would expect it to occur to anyone immediately.

Thus, the parties start with a principle establishing equal liberty for all, including equality of opportunity, as well as an equal distribution of income and wealth. But there is no reason why this acknowledgment should be final. If there are inequalities in the basic structure that work to make everyone better off in comparison with the benchmark of initial equality, why not permit them? The immediate gain which a greater equality might allow can be regarded as intelligently invested in view of its future return. If, for example, these inequalities set up various incentives which succeed in eliciting more productive efforts, a person in the original position may look upon them as necessary to cover the costs of training and to encourage effective performance. One might think that ideally individuals should want to serve one another. But since the parties are assumed not to take an interest in one another's interests, their acceptance of these inequalities is only the acceptance of the relations in which men stand in the circumstances of justice. They have no grounds for complaining of one another's motives. A person in the original position would, therefore, concede the justice of these inequalities. Indeed, it would be short-sighted of him not to do so. He would hesitate to agree to these regularities only if he would be dejected by the bare knowledge or perception that others were better situated; and I have assumed that the parties decide as if they are not moved by envy. In order to make the principle regulating inequalities determinate, one looks at the system from the standpoint of the least advantaged representative person. Inequalities are permissible when they maximize, or at least all contribute to, the long-term expectations of the least fortunate group in society.

Now this general conception imposes no constraints on what sorts of inequalities are allowed, whereas the special conception, by putting the two principles in serial order (with the necessary adjustments in meaning), forbids exchanges between basic liberties and economic and social benefits. I shall not try to justify this ordering here. But roughly, the idea underlying this ordering is that if the parties assume that their basic liberties can be effectively exercised, they will not exchange a lesser liberty for an improvement in economic well-being. It is only when social conditions do not allow the effective establishment of these rights that one can concede their limitation; and these restrictions can be granted only to the extent that they are necessary to prepare the way for a free society. The denial of equal liberty can be defended only if it is necessary to raise the level of civilization so that in due course these freedoms can be enjoyed. Thus in adopting a serial order we are in effect making a special assumption in the original position, namely, that the parties know that the conditions of their society, whatever they are, admit the effective realization of the equal liberties. The serial ordering of the two principles of justice eventually comes to be reasonable if the general conception is consistently followed. This lexical ranking is the long-run tendency of the general view. For the most part I shall assume that the requisite circumstances for the serial order obtain.

It seems clear from these remarks that the two principles are at least a plausible conception of justice. The question, though, is how one is to argue for them more systematically. Now there are several things to do. One can work out their consequences for institutions and note their implications for fundamental social policy. In this way they are tested by a comparison with our considered judgments of justice. . . . But one can also try to find arguments in their favor that are decisive from the standpoint of the original position. In order to see how this might be done, it is useful as a heuristic device to think of the two principles as the maximin solution to the problem of social justice. There is an analogy between the two principles and the maximin rule for choice under uncertainty.[6] This is evident from the fact that the two principles are those a person would choose for the design of a society in which his enemy is to assign him his place. The maximin rule tells us to rank alternatives by their worst possible outcomes: we are to adopt the alternative the worst outcome of which is superior to the worst outcomes of the others. The persons in the original position do not, of course, assume that their initial place in society is decided by a malevolent opponent. As I note below, they should not reason from false premises. The veil of ignorance does not violate this idea, since an absence of information is not misinformation. But that the two principles of justice would be chosen if the parties were forced to protect themselves against such a contingency explains the sense in which this conception is the maximin solution. And this analogy suggests that if the original position has been described so that it is rational for the parties to adopt the conservative attitude expressed by this rule, a conclusive argument can indeed be constructed for these principles. Clearly the maximin rule is not, in general, a suitable guide for choices under uncertainty. But it is attractive in situations marked by certain special features. My aim, then, is to show that a good case can be made for the two principles based on the fact that the original position manifests these features to the fullest possible degree, carrying them to the limit, so to speak.

Consider the gain-and-loss table shown below. It represents the gains and losses for a situation which is not a game of strategy. There is no one playing against the person making the decision; instead he is faced with several possible circumstances which may or may not obtain. Which circumstances happen to exist does not depend upon what the person choosing decides or whether he announces his moves in advance. The numbers in the table are monetary values (in hundreds of dollars) in comparison with some initial situation. The gain (g) depends upon the individual's decision (d) and the circumstances (c). Thus $g = f(d,c)$. Assuming that there are three possible decisions and three possible circumstances, we might have this gain-and-loss table.

The maximin rule requires that we make the third decision. For in this case the worst that can happen is that one gains 500 dollars, which is better than the worst for the other actions. If we adopt one of these we may lose either 800 or 700 dollars. Thus, the choice of d_3 maximizes

Table 52.1

Decisions	Circumstances		
	c_1	c_2	c_3
d_1	-7	8	12
d_2	-8	7	14
d_3	5	6	8

$f(d, c)$ for that value of c, which for a given d, minimizes f. The term "maximin" means the *maximum minimorum*; and the rule directs our attention to the worst that can happen under any proposed course of action, and directs us to decide in the light of that.

Now there appear to be three chief features of situations that give plausibility to this unusual rule.[7] First, since the rule takes no account of the likelihoods of the possible circumstances, there must be some reason for sharply discounting estimates of these probabilities. Offhand, the most natural rule of choice would seem to be to compute the expectation of monetary gain for each decision and then to adopt the course of action with the highest prospect. (This expectation is defined as follows: let us suppose that g_{ij} represents the numbers in the gain-and-loss table, where i is the row index and j is the column index; and let p_j, $j = 1, 2, 3$, be the likelihoods of the circumstances, with $\hat{\Sigma}p_j = 1$. Then the expectation for the ith decision is equal to $\hat{\Sigma}p_j g_{ij}$.) Thus it must be, for example, that the situation is one in which a knowledge of likelihoods is impossible, or at best extremely insecure. In this case it is unreasonable not to be skeptical of probabilistic calculations unless there is no other way out, particularly if the decision is a fundamental one that needs to be justified to others.

The second feature that suggests the maximin rule is the following: the person choosing has a conception of the good such that he cares very little, if anything, for what he might gain above the minimum stipend that he can, in fact, be sure of by following the maximin rule. It is not worthwhile for him to take a chance for the sake of a further advantage, especially when it may turn out that he loses much that is important to him.

This last provision brings in the third feature, namely, that the rejected alternatives have outcomes that one can hardly accept. The situation involves grave risks. Of course these features work most effectively in combination. The paradigm situation for following the maximin rule is when all three features are realized to the highest degree. This rule does not, then, generally apply, nor of course is it self-evident. Rather, it is a maxim, a rule of thumb, that comes into its own in special circumstances. Its application depends upon the qualitative structure of the possible gains and losses in relation to one's conception of the good, all this against a background in which it is reasonable to discount conjectural estimates of likelihoods.

It should be noted, as the comments on the gain-and-loss table say, that the entries in the table represent monetary values and not utilities. This difference is significant since for one thing computing expectations on the basis of such objective values is not the same thing as computing expected utility and may lead to different results. The essential point though is that in justice as fairness the parties do not know their conception of the good and cannot estimate their utility in the ordinary sense. In any case, we want to go behind de facto preferences generated by given conditions. Therefore expectations are based upon an index of primary goods and the parties make their choice accordingly. The entries in the example are in terms of money and not utility to indicate this aspect of the contract doctrine.

Now, as I have suggested, the original position has been defined so that it is a situation in which the maximin rule applies. In order to see this, let us review briefly the nature of this situation with these three special features in mind. To begin with, the veil of ignorance excludes all but the vaguest knowledge of likelihoods. The parties have no basis for determining the probable nature of their society, or their place in it. Thus they have strong reasons for being wary of probability calculations if any other course is open to them. They must also take into account the fact that their choice of principles should seem reasonable to others, in particular their descendants, whose rights will be deeply affected by it.

There are further grounds for discounting that I shall mention as we go along. For the present it suffices to note that these considerations are strengthened by the fact that the parties know very little about the gain-and-loss table. Not only are they unable to conjecture the likelihoods of the various possible circumstances, they cannot say much about what the possible circumstances are, much less enumerate them and foresee the outcome of each alternative available. Those deciding are much more in the dark than the illustration by a numerical table suggests. It is for this reason that I have spoken of an analogy with the maximin rule.

Several kinds of arguments for the two principles of justice illustrate the second feature. Thus, if we can maintain that these principles provide a workable theory of social justice, and that they are compatible with reasonable demands of efficiency, then this conception guarantees a satisfactory minimum. There may be, on reflection, little reason for trying to do better. Thus much of the argument, . . . is to show, by their application to the main questions of social justice, that the two principles are a satisfactory conception. These details have a philosophical purpose. Moreover, this line of thought is practically decisive if we can establish the priority of liberty, the lexical ordering of the two principles. For this priority implies that the persons in the original position have no desire to try for greater gains at the expense of the equal liberties. The minimum assured by the two principles in lexical order is not one that the parties wish to jeopardize for the sake of greater economic and social advantages.

Finally, the third feature holds if we can assume that other conceptions of justice may lead to institutions that the parties would find intolerable. For example, it has sometimes been held that under some conditions the utility principle (in either form) justifies, if not slavery or serfdom, at any rate serious infractions of liberty for the sake of greater social benefits. We need not consider here the truth of this claim, or the likelihood that the requisite conditions obtain. For the moment, this contention is only to illustrate the way in which conceptions of justice may allow for outcomes which the parties may not be able to accept. And having the ready alternative of the two principles of justice which secure a satisfactory minimum, it seems unwise, if not irrational, for them to take a chance that these outcomes are not realized. . . .

Notes

1 As the text suggests, I shall regard Locke's *Second Treatise of Government*, Rousseau's *The Social Contract*, and Kant's ethical works beginning with *The Foundations of the Metaphysics of Morals* as definitive of the contract tradition. For all of its greatness, Hobbes's *Leviathan* raises special problems. A general historical survey is provided by J. W. Gough, *The Social Contract*, 2nd edn. (Oxford: Clarendon Press, 1957); and Otto Gierke, *Natural Law and the Theory of Society*, trans. with an introduction by Ernest Barker (Cambridge: Cambridge University Press, 1934). A presentation of the contract view as primarily an ethical theory is to be found in G. R. Grice, *The Grounds of Moral Judgment* (Cambridge: Cambridge University Press, 1967).

2 Kant is clear that the original agreement is hypothetical. See *The Metaphysics of Morals*, pt. I (*Rechtslehre*), especially paragraphs 47, 52; and pt. II of the essay "Concerning the Common Saying: This May Be True in Theory but It Does Not Apply in Practice," in *Kant's Political Writings*, ed. Hans Reiss and trans. H. B. Nisbet (Cambridge: Cambridge University Press, 1970), pp. 73–87. See Georges Vlachos, *La Pensée politique de Kant* (Paris: Presses Universitaires de France, 1962), pp. 326–35; and J. G. Murphy, *Kant: The Philosophy of Right* (London: Macmillan, 1970), pp. 109–12, 133–6, for a further discussion.

3 For the formulation of this intuitive idea I am indebted to Allan Gibbard.

4 The process of mutual adjustment of principles and considered judgments is not peculiar to moral philosophy. See Nelson Goodman, *Fact, Fiction, and Forecast* (Cambridge: MA: Harvard University Press, 1955), pp. 65–8, for parallel remarks concerning the justification of the principles of deductive and inductive inference.

5 For a similar view, see B. A. O. Williams, "The Idea of Equality," *Philosophy, Politics, and Society*, Second Series, ed. Peter Laslett and W. G. Runciman (Oxford: Basil Blackwell, 1962), p. 113.

6 An accessible discussion of this and other rules of choice under uncertainty can be found in W. J. Baumol, *Economic Theory and Operations Analysis*, 2nd edn. (Englewood Cliffs, NJ: Prentice-Hall, 1965), ch. 24. Baumol gives a geometric interpretation of these rules, including the diagram used in paragraph 13 to illustrate the difference principle. See pp. 558–62. See also R. D. Luce and Howard Raiffa, *Games and Decisions* (New York: John Wiley and Sons, 1957), chapter XIII, for a fuller account.

7 Here I borrow from William Fellner, *Probability and Profit* (Homewood, IL: R. D. Irwin, 1965), pp. 140–2, where these features are noted.

53

The Entitlement Theory of Justice

Robert Nozick

The minimal state is the most extensive state that can be justified. Any state more extensive violates people's rights. Yet many persons have put forth reasons purporting to justify a more extensive state. It is impossible [here] to examine all the reasons that have been put forth. Therefore, I shall focus upon those generally acknowledged to be most weighty and influential, to see precisely wherein they fail. In this chapter we consider the claim that a more extensive state is justified, because necessary (or the best instrument) to achieve distributive justice . . .

The term "distributive justice" is not a neutral one. Hearing the term "distribution," most people presume that some thing or mechanism uses some principle or criterion to give out a supply of things. Into this process of distributing shares some error may have crept. So it is an open question, at least, whether *re*distribution should take place; whether we should do again what has already been done once, though poorly. However, we are not in the position of children who have been given portions of pie by someone who now makes last minute adjustments to rectify careless cutting. There is no *central* distribution, no person or group entitled to control all the resources, jointly deciding how they are to be doled out. What each person gets, he gets from others who give to him in exchange for something, or as a gift. In a free society, diverse persons control different resources, and new holdings arise out of the voluntary exchanges and actions of persons. There is no more a distributing or distribution of shares than there is a distributing of mates in a society in which persons choose whom they shall marry. The total result is the product of many individual decisions which the different individuals involved are entitled to make. Some uses of the term "distribution," it is true, do not imply a previous distributing appropriately judged by some criterion (for example, "probability distribution"): nevertheless, despite the title of this chapter, it would be best to use a terminology that clearly is neutral. We shall speak of people's holdings; a principle of justice in holdings describes (part of) what justice tells us (requires) about holdings. I shall state first what I take to be the correct view about justice in holdings, and then turn to the discussion of alternate views.

The subject of justice in holdings consists of three major topics. The first is the *original acquisition of holdings*, the appropriation of unheld things. This includes the issues of how unheld things may come to be held, the process, or processes, by which unheld things may come to be held, the things that may come to be held by these processes, the extent of what comes to be held by a particular process, and so on. We shall refer to the complicated truth about this topic, which we shall not formulate here, as the principle of justice in acquisition.

The second topic concerns the *transfer of holdings* from one person to another. By what processes may a person transfer holdings to another? How may a person acquire a holding from another who holds it? Under this topic come general descriptions of voluntary exchange, and gift and (on the other hand) fraud, as well as reference to particular conventional details fixed upon in a given society. The complicated truth about this subject (with placeholders for conventional details) we shall call the principle of justice in transfer. (And we shall suppose it also includes principles governing how a person may divest himself of a holding, passing it into an unheld state.)

If the world were wholly just, the following inductive definition would exhaustively cover the subject of justice in holdings.

1 A person who acquires a holding in accordance with the principle of justice in acquisition is entitled to that holding.
2 A person who acquires a holding in accordance with the principle of justice in transfer, from someone else entitled to the holding, is entitled to the holding.
3 No one is entitled to a holding except by (repeated) applications of 1 and 2.

The complete principle of distributive justice would say simply that a distribution is just if everyone is entitled to the holdings they possess under the distribution.

A distribution is just if it arises from another just distribution by legitimate means. The legitimate means of moving from one distribution to another are specified by the principle of justice in transfer. The legitimate first "moves" are specified by the principle of justice

in acquisition.[1] Whatever arises from a just situation by just steps is itself just. The means of change specified by the principle of justice in transfer preserve justice. As correct rules of inference are truth-preserving, and any conclusion deduced via repeated application of such rules from only true premises is itself true, so the means of transition from one situation to another specified by the principle of justice in transfer are justice-preserving, and any situation actually arising from repeated transitions in accordance with the principle from a just situation is itself just. The parallel between justice-preserving transformations and truth-preserving transformations illuminates where it fails as well as where it holds. That a conclusion could have been deduced by truth-preserving means from premises that are true suffices to show its truth. That from a just situation a situation *could* have arisen via justice-preserving means does *not* suffice to show its justice. The fact that a thief's victims voluntarily *could* have presented him with gifts does not entitle the thief to his ill-gotten gains. Justice in holdings is historical; it depends upon what actually has happened. We shall return to this point later.

Not all actual situations are generated in accordance with the two principles of justice in holdings: the principle of justice in acquisition and the principle of justice in transfer. Some people steal from others, or defraud them, or enslave them, seizing their product and preventing them from living as they choose, or forcibly exclude others from competing in exchanges. None of these are permissible modes of transition from one situation to another. And some persons acquire holdings by means not sanctioned by the principle of justice in acquisition.

The existence of past injustice (previous violations of the first two principles of justice in holdings) raises the third major topic under justice in holdings: the rectification of injustice in holdings. If past injustice has shaped present holdings in various ways, some identifiable and some not, what now, if anything, ought to be done to rectify these injustices? What obligations do the performers of injustice have toward those whose position is worse than it would

Economic Justice

have been had the injustice not been done? Or, than it would have been had compensation been paid promptly? How, if at all, do things change if the beneficiaries and those made worse off are not the direct parties in the act of injustice, but, for example, their descendants? Is an injustice done to someone whose holding was itself based upon an unrectified injustice? How far back must one go in wiping clean the historical slate of injustices? What may victims of injustice permissibly do in order to rectify the injustices being done to them, including the many injustices done by persons acting through their government? I do not know of a thorough or theoretically sophisticated treatment of such issues. Idealizing greatly, let us suppose theoretical investigation will produce a principle of rectification. This principle uses historical information about previous situations and injustices done in them (as defined by the first two principles of justice and rights against interference), and information about the actual course of events that flowed from these injustices, until the present, and it yields a description (or descriptions) of holdings in the society. The principle of rectification presumably will make use of its best estimate of subjunctive information about what would have occurred (or a probability distribution over what might have occurred, using the expected value) if the injustice had not taken place. If the actual description of holdings turns out not to be one of the descriptions yielded by the principle, then one of the descriptions yielded must be realized.[2]

The general outlines of the theory of justice in holdings are that the holdings of a person are just if he is entitled to them by the principles of justice in acquisition and transfer, or by the principle of rectification of injustice (as specified by the first two principles). If each person's holdings are just, then the total set (distribution) of holdings is just. To turn these general outlines into a specific theory we would have to specify the details of each of the three principles of justice in holdings: the principle of acquisition of holdings, the principle of transfer of holdings, and the principle of rectification of violations of the first two principles. I shall not attempt that task here.

Historical Principles and End-result Principles

The general outlines of the entitlement theory illuminate the nature and defects of other conceptions of distributive justice. The entitlement theory of justice in distribution is *historical*; whether a distribution is just depends upon how it came about. In contrast, *current time-slice principles* of justice hold that the justice of a distribution is determined by how things are distributed (who has what) as judged by some *structural* principle(s) of just distribution. A utilitarian who judges between any two distributions by seeing which has the greater sum of utility and, if the sums tie, applies some fixed equality criterion to choose the more equal distribution, would hold a current time-slice principle of justice. As would someone who had a fixed schedule of trade-offs between the sum of happiness and equality. According to a current time-slice principle, all that needs to be looked at, in judging the justice of a distribution, is who ends up with what; in comparing any two distributions one need look only at the matrix presenting the distributions. No further information need be fed into a principle of justice. It is a consequence of such principles of justice that any two structurally identical distributions are equally just. (Two distributions are structurally identical if they present the same profile, but perhaps have different persons occupying the particular slots. My having ten and your having five, and my having five and your having ten are structurally identical distributions.) Welfare economics is the theory of current time-slice principles of justice. The subject is conceived as operating on matrices representing only current information about distribution. This, as well as some of the usual conditions (for example, the choice of distribution is invariant under relabeling of columns), guarantees that welfare economics will be a current time-slice theory, with all of its inadequacies.

Most persons do not accept current time-slice principles as constituting the whole story about distributive shares. They think it relevant in assessing the justice of a situation to consider not only the distribution it embodies, but also how that distribution came about. If some persons are in prison for murder or war crimes, we do not say that to assess the justice of the distribution in the society we must look only at what this person has, and that person has, and that person has, . . . at the current time. We think it relevant to ask whether someone did something so that he *deserved* to be punished, deserved to have a lower share. Most will agree to the relevance of further information with regard to punishments and penalties. Consider also desired things. One traditional socialist view is that workers are entitled to the product and full fruits of their labor; they have earned it; a distribution is unjust if it does not give the workers what they are entitled to. Such entitlements are based upon some past history. No socialist holding this view would find it comforting to be told that because the actual distribution A happens to coincide structurally with the one he desires D, A therefore is no less just than D; it differs only in that the "parasitic" owners of capital receive under A what the workers are entitled to under D, and the workers receive under A what the owners are entitled to under D, namely very little. This socialist rightly, in my view, holds onto the notions of earning, producing, entitlement, desert, and so forth, and he rejects current time-slice principles that look only to the structure of the resulting set of holdings. (The set of holdings resulting from what? Isn't it implausible that how holdings are produced and come to exist has no effect at all on who should hold what?) His mistake lies in his view of what entitlements arise out of what sorts of productive processes.

We construe the position we discuss too narrowly by speaking of *current* time-slice principles. Nothing is changed if structural principles operate upon a time sequence of current time-slice profiles and, for example, give someone more now to counterbalance the less he has had earlier. A utilitarian or an egalitarian or any mixture of the two over time will inherit the difficulties of his more myopic comrades. He is not helped by the fact that *some* of the information others consider relevant in assessing a distribution is reflected, unrecoverably, in past matrices. Henceforth, we shall refer to such unhistorical principles of distributive justice, including the current time-slice principles, as *end-result principles* or *end-state principles*.

In contrast to end-result principles of justice, *historical principles* of justice hold that past circumstances or actions of people can create differential entitlements or differential deserts to things. An injustice can be worked by moving from one distribution to another structurally identical one, for the second, in profile the same, may violate people's entitlements or deserts; it may not fit the actual history.

Patterning

The entitlement principles of justice in holdings that we have sketched are historical principles of justice. To better understand their precise character, we shall distinguish them from another subclass of the historical principles. Consider, as an example, the principle of distribution according to moral merit. This principle requires that total distributive shares vary directly with moral merit; no person should have a greater share than anyone whose moral merit is greater. (If moral merit could be not merely ordered but measured on an interval or ratio scale, stronger principles could be formulated.) Or consider the principle that results by substituting "usefulness to society" for "moral merit" in the previous principle. Or instead of "distribute according to moral merit," or "distribute according to usefulness to society," we might consider "distribute according to the weighted sum of moral merit, usefulness to society, and need," with the weights of the different dimensions equal. Let us call a principle of distribution *patterned* if it specifies that a distribution is to vary along with some natural dimension, weighted sum of natural dimensions, or lexicographic ordering of natural dimensions. And let us say a distribution is patterned if it accords with some patterned principle. (I speak of natural dimensions, admittedly without a general criterion for them, because for any set of holdings some artificial dimensions can be gimmicked up to vary along with the distribution of the set.) The principle of distribution in accordance with moral merit is a patterned historical principle, which specifies a patterned distribution. "Distribute according to IQ" is a patterned principle that looks to information not contained in distributional matrices. It is not historical, however, in that it does not look to any past actions creating differential entitlements to evaluate a distribution; it requires only distributional matrices whose columns are labeled by IQ scores. The distribution in a society, however, may be composed of such simple patterned distributions, without itself being simply patterned. Different sectors may operate different patterns, or some combination of patterns may operate in different proportions across a society. A distribution composed in this manner, from a small number of patterned distributions, we also shall term "patterned." And we extend the use of "pattern" to include the overall designs put forth by combinations of end-state principles.

Almost every suggested principle of distributive justice is patterned: to each according to his moral merit, or needs, or marginal product, or how hard he tries, or the weighted sum of the foregoing, and so on. The principle of entitlement we have sketched is *not* patterned.[3] There is no one natural dimension or weighted sum or combination of a small number of natural dimensions that yields the distributions generated in accordance with the principle of entitlement. The set of holdings that results when some persons receive their marginal products, others win at gambling, others receive a share of their mate's income, others receive gifts from foundations, others receive interest on loans, others receive gifts from admirers, others receive returns on investment, others make for themselves much of what they have, others find things, and so on, will not be patterned. Heavy strands of patterns will run through it; significant portions of the variance in holdings will be accounted for by pattern-variables. If most people most of the time choose to transfer some of their entitlements to others only in exchange for something from them, then a large part of what many people hold will vary with what they held that others wanted. More

details are provided by the theory of marginal productivity. But gifts to relatives, charitable donations, bequests to children, and the like, are not best conceived, in the first instance, in this manner. Ignoring the strands of pattern, let us suppose for the moment that a distribution actually arrived at by the operation of the principle of entitlement is random with respect to any pattern. Though the resulting set of holdings will be unpatterned, it will not be incomprehensible, for it can be seen as arising from the operation of a small number of principles. These principles specify how an initial distribution may arise (the principle of acquisition of holdings) and how distributions may be transformed into others (the principle of transfer of holdings). The process whereby the set of holdings is generated will be intelligible, though the set of holdings itself that results from this process will be unpatterned.

The writings of F. A. Hayek focus less than is usually done upon what patterning distributive justice requires. Hayek argues that we cannot know enough about each person's situation to distribute to each according to his moral merit (but would justice demand we do so if we did have this knowledge?); and he goes on to say, "our objection is against all attempts to impress upon society a deliberately chosen pattern of distribution, whether it be an order of equality or of inequality." However, Hayek concludes that in a free society there will be distribution in accordance with value rather than with moral merit; that is, in accordance with the perceived value of a person's actions and services to others. Despite his rejection of a patterned conception of distributive justice, Hayek himself suggests a pattern he thinks justifiable: distribution in accordance with the perceived benefits given to others, leaving room for the complaint that a free society does not realize exactly this pattern. Stating this patterned strand of a free capitalist society more precisely, we get "To each according to how much he benefits others who have the resources for benefiting those who benefit them." This will seem arbitrary unless some acceptable initial set of holdings is specified, or unless it is held that the operation of the system over time washes out any significant effects from the initial set of holdings is specified, or unless it is held that the operation of the system over time washes out any significant effects from the initial set of holdings. As an example of the latter, if almost anyone would have bought a car from Henry Ford, the supposition that it was an arbitrary matter who held the money then (and so bought) would not place Henry Ford's earnings under a cloud. In any event, *his* coming to hold it is not arbitrary. Distribution according to benefits to others *is* a major patterned strand in a free capitalist society, as Hayek correctly points out, but it is only a strand and does not constitute the whole pattern of a system of entitlements (namely, inheritance, gifts for arbitrary reasons, charity, and so on) or a standard that one should insist a society fit.

Will people tolerate for long a system yielding distributions that they believe are unpatterned? No doubt people will not long accept a distribution they believe is *unjust*. People want their society to be and to look just. But must the look of justice reside in a resulting pattern rather than in the underlying generating principles? We are in no position to conclude that the inhabitants of a society embodying an entitlement conception of justice in holdings will find it unacceptable. Still, it must be granted that were people's reasons for transferring some of their holdings to others always irrational or arbitrary, we would find this disturbing. (Suppose people always determined what holdings they would transfer, and to whom, by using a random device.) We feel more comfortable upholding the justice of an entitlement system if most of the transfers under it are done for reasons. This does not mean necessarily that all deserve what holdings they receive. It means only that there is a purpose or point to someone's transferring a holding to one person rather than to another; that usually we can see what the transferrer thinks he's gaining, what cause he thinks he's serving, what goals he thinks he's helping to achieve, and so forth. Since in a capitalist society people often transfer holdings to others in accordance with how much they perceive these others benefiting them, the fabric constituted by the individual

transactions and transfers is largely reasonable and intelligible.[4] (Gifts to loved ones, bequests to children, charity to the needy also are non-arbitrary components of the fabric.) In stressing the large strand of distribution in accordance with benefit to others, Hayek shows the point of many transfers, and so shows that the system of transfer of entitlements is not just spinning its gears aimlessly. The system of entitlements is defensible when constituted by the individual aims of individual transactions. No overarching aim is needed, no distributional pattern is required.

To think that the task of a theory of distributive justice is to fill in the blank in "to each according to his –" is to be predisposed to search for a pattern; and the separate treatment of "from each according to his –" treats production and distribution as two separate and independent issues. On an entitlement view these are *not* two separate questions. Whoever makes something, having bought or contracted for all other held resources used in the process (transferring some of his holdings for these cooperating factors), is entitled to it. The situation is *not* one of something's getting made, and there being an open question of who is to get it. Things come into the world already attached to people having entitlements over them. From the point of view of the historical entitlement conception of justice in holdings, those who start afresh to complete "to each according to his –" treat objects as if they appeared from nowhere, out of nothing. A complete theory of justice might cover this limit case as well; perhaps here is a use for the usual conceptions of distributive justice.

So entrenched are maxims of the usual form that perhaps we should present the entitlement conception as a competitor. Ignoring acquisition and rectification, we might say:

> From each according to what he chooses to do, to each according to what he makes for himself (perhaps with the contracted aid of others) and what others choose to do for him and choose to give him of what they've been given previously (under this maxim) and haven't yet expended or transferred.

This, the discerning reader will have noticed, has its defects as a slogan. So as a summary and great simplification (and not as a maxim with any independent meaning) we have:

From each as they choose, to each as they are chosen.

How Liberty Upsets Patterns

It is not clear how those holding alternative conceptions of distributive justice can reject the entitlement conception of justice in holdings. For suppose a distribution favored by one of these non-entitlement conceptions is realized. Let us suppose it is your favorite one and let us call this distribution D_1; perhaps everyone has an equal share, perhaps shares vary in accordance with some dimension you treasure. Now suppose that Wilt Chamberlain is greatly in demand by basketball teams, being a great gate attraction. (Also suppose contracts run only for a year, with players being free agents.) He signs the following sort of contract with a team: In each home game, twenty-five cents from the price of each ticket of admission goes to him. (We ignore the question of whether he is "gouging" the owners, letting them look out for themselves.) The season starts, and people cheerfully attend his team's games; they buy their tickets, each time dropping a separate twenty-five cents of their admission price into a special box with Chamberlain's name on it. They are excited about seeing him play; it is worth the total admission price to them. Let us suppose that in one season one million persons attend his home games, and Wilt Chamberlain winds up with $250,000, a much larger sum than the average income and larger even than anyone else has. Is he entitled to this income? Is this new distribution D_2, unjust? If so, why? There is *no* question about whether each of the people was entitled to the control over the resources they held in D_1; because that was the distribution (your favorite) that (for the purposes of argument) we assumed was acceptable. Each of these persons *chose* to give twenty-five cents of their money to Chamberlain. They could have spent it on going to the movies, or on candy bars, or on copies of *Dissent* magazine, or of *Monthly Review*. But they all, at least one million of them, converged on giving it to Wilt

Chamberlain in exchange for watching him play basketball. If D_1 was a just distribution, and people voluntarily moved from it to D_2, transferring parts of their shares they were given under D_1 (what was it for it not to do something with?), isn't D_2 also just? If the people were entitled to dispose of the resources to which they were entitled (under D_1), didn't this include their being entitled to give it to, or exchange it with, Wilt Chamberlain? Can anyone else complain on grounds of justice? Each other person already has his legitimate share under D_1. Under D_1, there is nothing that anyone has that anyone else has a claim of justice against. After someone transfers something to Wilt Chamberlain, third parties *still* have their legitimate shares; *their* shares are not changed. By what process could such a transfer among two persons give rise to a legitimate claim of distributive justice on a portion of what was transferred, by a third party who had no claim of justice on any holding of the others *before* the transfer?[5] To cut off objections irrelevant here, we might imagine the exchanges occurring in a socialist society, after hours. After playing whatever basketball he does in his daily work, or doing whatever other daily work he does, Wilt Chamberlain decides to put in *overtime* to earn additional money. (First his work quota is set; he works time over that.) Or imagine it is a skilled juggler people like to see, who puts on shows after hours.

Why might someone work overtime in a society in which it is assumed their needs are satisfied? Perhaps because they care about things other than needs. I like to write in books that I read, and to have easy access to books for browsing at odd hours. It would be very pleasant and convenient to have the resources of Widener Library in my back yard. No society, I assume, will provide such resources close to each person who would like them as part of his regular allotment (under D_1). Thus, persons either must do without some extra things that they want, or must be allowed to do something extra to get some of these things. On what basis could the inequalities that would eventuate be forbidden? Notice also that small factories would spring up in a socialist society, unless forbidden. I melt down some of my personal possessions (under D_1) and build a machine out of the material. I offer you, and others, a philosophy lecture once a week in exchange for your cranking the handle on my machine, whose products I exchange for yet other things, and so on. (The raw materials used by the machine are given to me by others who possess them under D_1, in exchange for hearing lectures.) Each person might participate to gain things over and above their allotment under D_1. Some persons even might want to leave their job in socialist industry and work full time in this private sector. I wish merely to note how private property even in means of production would occur in a socialist society that did not forbid people to use as they wished some of the resources they are given under the socialist distribution D_1. The socialist society would have to forbid capitalist acts between consenting adults.

The general point illustrated by the Wilt Chamberlain example and the example of the entrepreneur in a socialist society is that no end-state principle or distributional patterned principle of justice can be continuously realized without continuous interference with people's lives. Any favored pattern would be transformed into one unfavored by the principle, by people choosing to act in various ways; for example, by people exchanging goods and services with other people, or giving things to other people, things the transferrers are entitled to under the favored distributional pattern. To maintain a pattern one must either continually interfere to stop people from transferring resources as they wish to, or continually (or periodically) interfere to take from some persons resources that others for some reason chose to transfer to them. (But if some time limit is to be set on how long people may keep resources others voluntarily transfer to them, why let them keep these resources for *any* period of time? Why not have immediate confiscation?) It might be objected that all persons voluntarily will choose to refrain from actions which would upset the pattern. This presupposes unrealistically (1) that all will most want to maintain the pattern (are those who don't, to be

"reeducated" or forced to undergo "self-criticism"?), (2) that each can gather enough information about his own actions and the on-going activities of others to discover which of his actions will upset the pattern, and (3) that diverse and far-flung persons can coordinate their actions to dovetail into the pattern. Compare the manner in which the market is neutral among persons' desires, as it reflects and transmits widely scattered information via prices, and coordinates persons' activities.

It puts things perhaps a bit too strongly to say that every patterned (or end-state) principle is liable to be thwarted by the voluntary actions of the individual parties transferring some of their shares they receive under the principle. For perhaps some *very* weak patterns are not so thwarted. Any distributional pattern with any egalitarian component is overturnable by the voluntary actions of individual persons over time; as is every patterned condition with sufficient content so as actually to have been proposed as presenting the central core of distributive justice. Still, given the possibility that some weak conditions or patterns may not be unstable in this way, it would be better to formulate an explicit description of the kind of interesting and contentful patterns under discussion, and to prove a theorem about their instability. Since the weaker the patterning, the more likely it is that the entitlement system itself satisfies it, a plausible conjecture is that any patterning either is unstable or is satisfied by the entitlement system. . . .

Redistribution and Property Rights

Apparently, patterned principles allow people to choose to spend upon themselves, but not upon others, those resources they are entitled to (or rather, receive) under some favored distributional pattern D_1. For if each of several persons chooses to expend some of his D_1 resources upon one other person, then that other person will receive more than his D_1 share, disturbing the favored distributional pattern. Maintaining a distributional pattern is individualism with a vengeance! Patterned distributional principles do not give people what entitlement principles do, only better distributed. For they do not give the right to choose what to do with what one has; they do not give the right to choose to pursue an end involving (intrinsically, or as a means) the enhancement of another's position. To such views, families are disturbing; for within a family occur transfers that upset the favored distributional pattern. Either families themselves become units to which distribution takes place, the column occupiers (on what rationale?), or loving behavior is forbidden. We should note in passing the ambivalent position of radicals toward the family. Its loving relationships are seen as a model to be emulated and extended across the whole society, at the same time that it is denounced as a suffocating institution to be broken and condemned as a focus of parochial concerns that interfere with achieving radical goals. Need we say that it is not appropriate to enforce across the wider society the relationships of love and care appropriate within a family, relationships which are voluntarily undertaken?[6] Incidentally, love is an interesting instance of another relationship that is historical, in that (like justice) it depends upon what actually occurred. An adult may come to love another because of the other's characteristics; but it is the other person, and not the characteristics, that is loved. The love is not transferable to someone else with the same characteristics, even to one who "scores" higher for these characteristics. And the love endures through changes of the characteristics that gave rise to it. One loves the particular person one actually encountered. Why love is historical, attaching to persons in this way and not to characteristics, is an interesting and puzzling question.

Proponents of patterned principles of distributive justice focus upon criteria for determining who is to receive holdings; they consider the reasons for which someone should have something, and also the total picture of holdings. Whether or not it is better to give than to receive, proponents of patterned principles ignore giving altogether. In considering the distribution of goods, income, and so forth, their theories are theories of recipient justice; they

completely ignore any right a person might have to give something to someone. Even in exchanges where each party is simultaneously giver and recipient, patterned principles of justice focus only upon the recipient role and its supposed rights. Thus discussions tend to focus on whether people (should) have a right to inherit, rather than on whether people (should) have a right to bequeath or on whether persons who have a right to hold also have a right to choose that others hold in their place. I lack a good explanation of why the usual theories of distributive justice are so recipient oriented; ignoring givers and transferrers and their rights is of a piece with ignoring producers and their entitlements. But why is it *all* ignored?

Patterned principles of distributive justice necessitate *re*distributive activities. The likelihood is small that any actual freely-arrived-at set of holdings fits a given pattern; and the likelihood is nil that it will continue to fit the pattern as people exchange and give. From the point of view of an entitlement theory, redistribution is a serious matter indeed, involving, as it does, the violation of people's rights. (An exception is those takings that fall under the principle of the rectification of injustices.) From other points of view, also, it is serious.

Taxation of earnings from labor is on a par with forced labor.[7] Some persons find this claim obviously true: taking the earnings of n hours labor is like taking n hours from the person; it is like forcing the person to work n hours for another's purpose. Others find the claim absurd. But even these, *if* they object to forced labor, would oppose forcing unemployed hippies to work for the benefit of the needy.[8] And they would also object to forcing each person to work five extra hours each week for the benefit of the needy. But a system that takes five hours' wages in taxes does not seem to them like one that forces someone to work five hours, since it offers the person forced a wider range of choice in activities than does taxation in kind with the particular labor specified. (But we can imagine a gradation of systems of forced labor, from one that specifies a particular activity, to one that gives a choice among two activities, to . . . ; and so on up.) Furthermore, people envisage a system with something like a proportional tax on everything above the amount necessary for basic needs. Some think this does not force someone to work extra hours, since there is no fixed number of extra hours he is forced to work, and since he can avoid the tax entirely by earning only enough to cover his basic needs. This is a very uncharacteristic view of forcing for those who *also* think people are forced to do something *whenever* the alternatives they face are considerably worse. However, *neither* view is correct. The fact that others intentionally intervene, in violation of a side constraint against aggression, to threaten force to limit the alternatives, in this case to paying taxes or (presumably the worse alternative) bare subsistence, makes the taxation system one of forced labor and distinguishes it from other cases of limited choices which are not forcings.

The man who chooses to work longer to gain an income more than sufficient for his basic needs prefers some extra goods or services to the leisure and activities he could perform during the possible nonworking hours; whereas the man who chooses not to work the extra time prefers the leisure activities to the extra goods or services he could acquire by working more. Given this, if it would be illegitimate for a tax system to seize some of a man's leisure (forced labor) for the purpose of serving the needy, how can it be legitimate for a tax system to seize some of a man's goods for that purpose? Why should we treat the man whose happiness requires certain material goods or services differently from the man whose preferences and desires make such goods unnecessary for his happiness? Why should the man who prefers seeing a movie (and who has to earn money for a ticket) be open to the required call to aid the needy, while the person who prefers looking at a sunset (and hence need earn no extra money) is not? Indeed, isn't it surprising that redistributionists choose to ignore the man whose pleasures are so easily attainable without extra labor, while adding yet another burden to the poor unfortunate who must work for his pleasures? If anything, one would have expected the reverse. Why is the person with the nonmaterial or nonconsumption desire allowed to proceed unimpeded to his most

favored feasible alternative, whereas the man whose pleasures or desires involve material things and who must work for extra money (thereby serving whomever considers his activities valuable enough to pay him) is constrained in what he can realize? Perhaps there is no difference in principle. And perhaps some think the answer concerns merely administrative convenience. (These questions and issues will not disturb those who think that forced labor to serve the needy or to realize some favored end-state pattern is acceptable.) In a fuller discussion we would have (and want) to extend our argument to include interest, entrepreneurial profits, and so on. Those who doubt that this extension can be carried through, and who draw the line here at taxation of income from labor, will have to state rather complicated patterned *historical* principles of distributive justice, since end-state principles would not distinguish *sources* of income in any way. It is enough for now to get away from end-state principles and to make clear how various patterned principles are dependent upon particular views about the sources or the illegitimacy or the lesser legitimacy of profits, interest, and so on; which particular views may well be mistaken.

What sort of right over others does a legally institutionalized end-state pattern give one? The central core of the notion of a property right in X, relative to which other parts of the notion are to be explained, is the right to determine what shall be done with X; the right to choose which of the constrained set of options concerning X shall be realized or attempted. The constraints are set by other principles or laws operating in the society; in our theory, by the Lockean rights people possess (under the minimal state). My property rights in my knife allow me to leave it where I will, but not in your chest. I may choose which of the acceptable options involving the knife is to be realized. This notion of property helps us to understand why earlier theorists spoke of people as having property in themselves and their labor. They viewed each person as having a right to decide what would become of himself and what he would do, and as having a right to reap the benefits of what he did.

This right of selecting the alternative to be realized from the constrained set of alternatives may be held by an *individual* or by a *group* with some procedure for reaching a joint decision; or the right may be passed back and forth, so that one year I decide what is to become of X, and the next year you do (with the alternative of destruction, perhaps, being excluded). Or, during the same time period, some types of decisions about X may be made by me, and others by you. And so on. We lack an adequate, fruitful, analytical apparatus for classifying the *types* of constraints on the set of options among which choices are to be made, and the *types* of ways decision powers can be held, divided, and amalgamated. A *theory* of property would, among other things, contain such a classification of constraints and decision modes, and from a small number of principles would follow a host of interesting statements about the *consequences* and effects of certain combinations of constraints and modes of decision.

When end-result principles of distributive justice are built into the legal structure of a society, they (as do most patterned principles) give each citizen an enforceable claim to some portion of the total social product; that is, to some portion of the sum total of the individually and jointly made products. This total product is produced by individuals laboring, using means of production others have saved to bring into existence, by people organizing production or creating means to produce new things or things in a new way. It is on this batch of individual activities that patterned distributional principles give each individual an enforceable claim. Each person has a claim to the activities and the products of other persons, independently of whether the other persons enter into particular relationships that give rise to these claims, and independently of whether they voluntarily take these claims upon themselves, in charity or in exchange for something.

Whether it is done through taxation on wages or on wages over a certain amount, or through seizure of profits, or through there being a big *social pot* so that it's not clear what's coming from where and what's going where, patterned principles of distributive justice involve

appropriating the actions of other persons. Seizing the results of someone's labor is equivalent to seizing hours from him and directing him to carry on various activities.

If people force you to do certain work, or unrewarded work, for a certain period of time, they decide what you are to do and what purposes your work is to serve apart from your decisions. This process whereby they take this decision from you makes them a *part-owner* of you; it gives them a property right in you. Just as having such partial control and power of decision, by right, over an animal or inanimate object would be to have a property right in it.

End-state and most patterned principles of distributive justice institute (partial) ownership by others of people and their actions and labor. These principles involve a shift from the classical liberals' notion of self-ownership to a notion of (partial) property rights in *other* people.

Considerations such as these confront end-state and other patterned conceptions of justice with the question of whether the actions necessary to achieve the selected pattern don't themselves violate moral side constraints. Any view holding that there are moral side constraints on actions, that not all moral considerations can be built into end states that are to be achieved, must face the possibility that some of its goals are not achievable by any morally permissible available means. An entitlement theorist will face such conflicts in a society that deviates from the principles of justice for the generation of holdings, if and only if the only actions available to realize the principles themselves violate some moral constraints. Since deviation from the first two principles of justice (in acquisition and transfer) will involve other persons' direct and aggressive intervention to violate rights, and since moral constraints will not exclude defensive or retributive action in such cases, the entitlement theorist's problem rarely will be pressing. And whatever difficulties he has in applying the principle of rectification to persons who did not themselves violate the first two principles are difficulties in balancing the conflicting considerations so as correctly to formulate the complex principle of rectification itself; he will not violate moral side constraints by applying the principle. Proponents of patterned conceptions of justice, however, often will face head-on clashes (and poignant ones if they cherish each party to the clash) between moral side constraints on how individuals may be treated and their patterned conception of justice that presents an end state or other pattern that *must* be realized.

May a person emigrate from a nation that has institutionalized some end-state or patterned distributional principle? For some principles (for example, Hayek's) emigration presents no theoretical problem. But for others it is a tricky matter. Consider a nation having a compulsory scheme of minimal social provision to aid the neediest (or one organized so as to maximize the position of the worst-off group); no one may opt out of participating in it. (None may say, "Don't compel me to contribute to others and don't provide for me via this compulsory mechanism if I am in need.") Everyone above a certain level is forced to contribute to aid the needy. But if emigration from the country were allowed, anyone could choose to move to another country that did not have compulsory social provision but otherwise was (as much as possible) identical. In such a case, the person's *only* motive for leaving would be to avoid participating in the compulsory scheme of social provision. And if he does leave, the needy in his initial country will receive no (compelled) help from him. What rationale yields the result that the person be permitted to emigrate, yet forbidden to stay and opt out of the compulsory scheme of social provision? If providing for the needy is of overriding importance, this does militate against allowing internal opting out; but it also speaks against allowing external emigration. (Would it also support, to some extent, the kidnapping of persons living in a place without compulsory social provision, who could be forced to make a contribution to the needy in your community?) Perhaps the crucial component of the position that allows emigration solely to avoid certain arrangements, while not allowing anyone internally to opt out of them, is a concern for fraternal feelings within the country. "We don't want anyone here who doesn't contribute, who doesn't care enough about the others to contribute." That concern, in this case, would have to be tied to the view that forced aiding tends to produce fraternal feelings between the aided and the aider (or perhaps merely to the view that the knowledge that someone or other voluntarily is not aiding produces unfraternal feelings).

Notes

1 Applications of the principle of justice in acquisition may also occur as part of the move from one distribution to another. You may find an unheld thing now and appropriate it. Acquisitions also are to be understood as included when, to simplify, I speak only of transitions by transfers.

2 If the principle of rectification of violations of the first two principles yields more than one description of holdings, then some choice must be made as to which of these is to be realized. Perhaps the sort of considerations about distributive justice and equality that I argue against play a legitimate role in *this* subsidiary choice. Similarly, there may be room for such considerations in deciding which otherwise arbitrary features a statute will embody, when such features are unavoidable because other considerations do not specify a precise line; yet a line must be drawn.

3 One might try to squeeze a patterned conception of distributive justice into the framework of the entitlement conception, by formulating a gimmicky obligatory "principle of transfer" that would lead to the pattern. For example, the principle that if one has more than the mean income one must transfer everything one holds above the mean to persons below the mean so as to bring them up to (but not over) the mean. We can formulate a criterion for a "principle of transfer" to rule out such obligatory transfers, or we can say that no correct principle of transfer, no principle of transfer in a free society will be like this. The former is probably the better course, though the latter also is true. Alternatively, one might think to make the entitlement conception instantiate a pattern, by using matrix entries that express the relative strength of a person's entitlements as measured by some real-valued function. But even if the limitation to natural dimensions failed to exclude this function, the resulting edifice would *not* capture our system of entitlements to *particular* things.

4 We certainly benefit because great economic incentives operate to get others to spend much time and energy to figure out how to serve us by providing things we will want to pay for. It is not mere paradox mongering to wonder whether capitalism should be criticized for most rewarding and hence encouraging,

not individualists like Thoreau who go about their own lives, but people who are occupied with serving others and winning them as customers. But to defend capitalism one need not think businessmen are the finest human types. (I do not mean to join here the general maligning of businessmen, either.) Those who think the finest should acquire the most can try to convince their fellows to transfer resources in accordance with *that* principle.

5 Might not a transfer have instrumental effects on a third party, changing his feasible options? (But what if the two parties to the transfer independently had used their holdings in this fashion?) I discuss this question below, but note here that this question concedes the point for distributions of ultimate intrinsic noninstrumental goods (pure utility experiences, so to speak) that are transferrable. It also could be objected that the transfer might make a third party more envious because it worsens his position relative to someone else. I find it incomprehensible how this can be thought to involve a claim of justice. . . .

Here and elsewhere in this chapter, a theory which incorporates elements of pure procedural justice might find what I say acceptable, *if* kept in its proper place; that is, if background institutions exist to ensure the satisfaction of certain conditions on distributive shares. But if these institutions are not themselves the sum or invisible-hand result of people's voluntary (nonaggressive) actions, the constraints they impose require justification. At no point does our argument assume any background institutions more extensive than those of the minimal night-watchman state, a state limited to protecting persons against murder, assault, theft, fraud, and so forth.

6 One indication of the stringency of Rawls's difference principle, which we attend to in the second part of this chapter, is its inappropriateness as a governing principle even within a family of individuals who love one another. Should a family devote its resources to maximizing the position of its least well off and least talented child, holding back the other children or using resources for their education and development only if they will follow a policy through their lifetimes of maximizing the position of their least fortunate sibling? Surely not. How then can this even be considered as the appropriate policy for enforcement in the wider society? (I discuss below what I think would be Rawls's reply: that some principles apply at the macro-level which do not apply to micro-situations.)

7 I am unsure as to whether the arguments I present below show that such taxation merely *is* forced labor; so that "is on a par with" means "is one kind of." Or alternatively, whether the arguments emphasize the great similarities between such taxation and forced labor, to show it is plausible and illuminating to view such taxation in the light of forced labor. This latter approach would remind one of how John Wisdom conceives of the claims of metaphysicians.

8 Nothing hangs on the fact that here and elsewhere I speak loosely of *needs*, since I go on, each time, to reject the criterion of justice which includes it. If, however, something did depend upon the notion, one would want to examine it more carefully. For a skeptical view, see Kenneth Minogue, *The Liberal Mind* (New York: Random House, 1963), pp. 103–12.

54

Displacing the Distributive Paradigm

Iris Marion Young

It was in general a mistake to make a fuss about so-called distribution and put the principal stress on it. Any distribution whatever of the means of consumption is only a consequence of the distribution of the conditions of production themselves. The latter distribution, however, is a feature of the mode of production itself.

Karl Marx

Thousands of buses converge on the city, and tens of thousands of people of diverse colors, ages, occupations, and life styles swarm onto the mall around the Washington Monument until the march begins. At midday people move into the streets, chanting, singing, waving wild papier-mâché missiles or effigies of government officials. Many carry signs or banners on which a simple slogan is inscribed: "Peace, Jobs, and Justice."

This scene has occurred many times in Washington, DC, in the last decade, and many more times in other US cities. What does "justice" mean in this slogan? In this context, as in many other political contexts today, I suggest that social justice means the elimination of institutionalized domination and oppression. Any aspect of social organization and practice relevant to domination and oppression is in principle subject to evaluation by ideals of justice.

Contemporary philosophical theories of justice, however, do not conceive justice so broadly. Instead, philosophical theories of justice tend to restrict the meaning of social justice to the morally proper distribution of benefits and burdens among society's members. In this essay I define and assess this distributive paradigm. While distributive issues are crucial to a satisfactory conception of justice, it is a mistake to reduce social justice to distribution.

I find two problems with the distributive paradigm. First, it tends to focus thinking about social justice on the allocation of material goods such as things, resources, income, and wealth, or on the distribution of social positions, especially jobs. This focus tends to ignore the social structure and institutional context that often help determine distributive patterns. Of particular importance to the analyses that follow are issues of decision-making power and procedures, division of labor, and culture.

One might agree that defining justice in terms of distribution tends to bias thinking about justice toward issues concerning wealth,

591

income, and other material goods, and that other issues such as decision-making power or the structure of the division of labor are as important, and yet argue that distribution need not be restricted to material goods and resources. Theorists frequently consider issues of the distribution of such nonmaterial goods as power, opportunity, or self-respect. But this widening of the concept of distribution exhibits the second problem with the distributive paradigm. When metaphorically extended to nonmaterial social goods, the concept of distribution represents them as though they were static things, instead of a function of social relations and processes.

In criticizing distributively oriented theories I wish neither to reject distribution as unimportant nor to offer a new positive theory to replace the distributive theories. I wish rather to displace talk of justice that regards persons as primarily possessors and consumers of goods to a wider context that also includes action, decisions about action, and provision of the means to develop and exercise capacities. The concept of social justice includes all aspects of institutional rules and relations insofar as they are subject to potential collective decision. The concepts of domination and oppression, rather than the concept of distribution, should be the starting point for a conception of social justice . . .

The Distributive Paradigm Presupposes and Obscures Institutional Context

Most theorizing about social justice focuses on the distribution of material resources, income, or positions of reward and prestige. Contemporary debates among theorists of justice, as Charles Taylor (1985) points out, are inspired largely by two practical issues. First, is the distribution of wealth and income in advanced capitalist countries just, and if not, does justice permit or even require the provision of welfare services and other redistributive measures? Second, is the pattern of the distribution of positions of high income and prestige just, and if not, are affirmative action policies just means to rectify that injustice? Nearly all writers who

define justice in distributive terms identify questions of the equality or inequality of wealth and income as the primary questions of social justice (see also Arthur and Shaw, 1978). They usually subsume the second set of questions, about the justice of the distribution of· social positions, under the question of economic distribution, since "more desirable" positions usually correspond to those that yield higher income or greater access to resources.

Applied discussions of justice too usually focus on the distribution of material goods and resources. Discussions of justice in medical care, for example, usually focus on the allocation of medical resources such as treatment, sophisticated equipment, expensive procedures, and so on (e.g., Daniels, 1985, esp. chapters 3 and 4). Similarly, issues of justice enter discussion in environmental ethics largely through consideration of the impact that alternative policies might have on the distribution of natural and social resources among individuals and groups (see, e.g., Simon, 1984). . . .

The social context of welfare capitalist society helps account for this tendency to focus on the distribution of income and other resources. Public political dispute in welfare corporate society is largely restricted to issues of taxation, and the allocation of public funds among competing social interests. Public discussions of social injustice tend to revolve around inequalities of wealth and income, and the extent to which the state can or should mitigate the suffering of the poor.

There are certainly pressing reasons for philosophers to attend to these issues of the distribution of wealth and resources. In a society and world with vast differences in the amount of material goods to which individuals have access, where millions starve while others can have anything they want, any conception of justice must address the distribution of material goods. The immediate provision of basic material goods for people now suffering severe deprivation must be a first priority for any program that seeks to make the world more just. Such a call obviously entails considerations of distribution and redistribution.

But in contemporary American society, many public appeals to justice do not concern primarily the distribution of material goods. Citizens in a rural Massachusetts town organize against a decision to site a huge hazardous waste treatment plant in their town. Their leaflets convince people that state law has treated the community unjustly by denying them the option of rejecting the plant (Young, 1983). Citizens in an Ohio city are outraged at the announcement that a major employer is closing down its plant. They question the legitimacy of the power of private corporate decision-makers to throw half the city out of work without warning, and without any negotiation and consultation with the community. Discussion of possible compensation makes them snicker; the point is not simply that we are out of jobs and thus lack money, they claim, but that no private party should have the right to decide to decimate the local economy. Justice may require that former workers and other members of the community have the option of taking over and operating the plant themselves (Schweickart, 1984). These two cases concern not so much the justice of material distributions as the justice of decision-making power and procedures.

Black critics claim that the television industry is guilty of gross injustice in its depictions of Blacks. More often than not, Blacks are represented as criminals, hookers, maids, scheming dealers, or jiving connivers. Blacks rarely appear in roles of authority, glamour, or virtue. Arab Americans are outraged at the degree to which television and film present recognizable Arabs only as sinister terrorists or gaudy princes, and conversely that terrorists are almost always Arab. Such outrage at media stereotyping issues in claims about the injustice not of material distribution, but of cultural imagery and symbols.

In an age of burgeoning computer technology, organizations of clerical workers argue that no person should have to spend the entirety of her working day in front of a computer terminal typing in a set of mindless numbers at monitored high speeds. This claim about injustice concerns not the distribution of goods, for the claim would still be made if VDT operators earned $30,000 annually. Here the primary issues of justice concern the structure of the division of labor and a right to meaningful work.

There are many such claims about justice and injustice in our society which are not primarily about the distribution of income, resources, or positions. A focus on the distribution of material goods and resources inappropriately restricts the scope of justice, because it fails to bring social structures and institutional contexts under evaluation. Several writers make this claim about distributive theories specifically with regard to their inability to bring capitalist institutions and class relations under evaluation. In his classic paper, for example, Allen Wood (1972) argues that for Marx justice refers only to superstructural juridical relations of distribution, which are constrained by the underlying mode of production. Because they are confined to distribution, principles of justice cannot be used to evaluate the social relations of production themselves (cf. Wolff, 1977, pp. 199–208).

Other writers criticize distributive theories of justice, especially Rawls's (the first selection), for presupposing at the same time that they obscure the context of class inequality that the theories are unable to evaluate (Macpherson, 1973; Nielsen, 1978). A distributive conception of justice is unable to bring class relations into view and evaluate them, Evan Simpson suggests, because its individualism prevents an understanding of structural phenomena, the "macroscopic transfer emerging from a complicated set of individual actions" (Simpson, 1980, p. 497) which cannot be understood in terms of any particular individual actions or acquisitions.

Many who make this Marxist criticism of the distributive focus of theories of justice conclude that justice is a concept of bourgeois ideology and thus not useful for a socialist normative analysis. Others disagree, and this dispute has occupied much of the Marxist literature on justice. I will argue later that a criticism of the distributive paradigm does not entail abandoning or transcending the concept of justice. For the moment I wish to focus on the point on which both sides in this dispute agree, namely, that predominant approaches to justice tend to presuppose and uncritically accept the relations of production that define an economic system.

The Marxist analysis of the distributive paradigm provides a fruitful starting point, but it is both too narrow and too general. On the one hand, capitalist class relations are not the only phenomena of social structure or institutional context that the distributive paradigm fails to evaluate. Some feminists point out, for example, that contemporary theories of justice presuppose family structure, without asking how social relations involving sexuality, intimacy, child-rearing, and household labor ought best to be organized (see Okin, 1986; Pateman, 1988, pp. 41–3). Like their forebears, contemporary liberaleral theorists of justice tend to presume that the units among which basic distributions take place are families, and that it is as family members, often heads of families, that individuals enter the public realm where justice operates (Nicholson, 1986, ch. 4). Thus they neglect issues of justice within families – for example, the issue of whether the traditional sexual division of labor still presupposed by much law and employment policy is just.

While the Marxist criticism is too narrow, it is also too vague. The claim that the distributive paradigm fails to bring class relations under evaluation is too general to make clear what specific nondistributive issues are at stake. While property is something distributed, for example, in the form of goods, land, buildings, or shares of stock, the legal relations that define entitlement, possible forms of title, and so on are not goods to be distributed. The legal framework consists of rules defining practices and rights to make decisions about the disposition of goods. Class domination is certainly enacted by agents deciding where to invest their capital – a distributive decision; but the social rules, rights, procedures, and influences that structure capitalist decision-making are not distributed goods. In order to understand and evaluate the institutional framework within which distributive issues arise, the ideas of "class" and "mode of production" must be concretized in terms of specific social processes and relations.

The general criticism I am making of the predominant focus on the distribution of wealth, income, and positions is that such a focus ignores and tends to obscure the institutional context within which those distributions

take place, and which is often at least partly the cause of patterns of distribution of jobs or wealth. Institutional context should be understood in a broader sense than "mode of production." It includes any structures or practices, the rules and norms that guide them, and the language and symbols that mediate social interactions within them, in institutions of state, family, and civil society, as well as the workplace. These are relevant to judgments of justice and injustice insofar as they condition people's ability to participate in determining their actions and their ability to develop and exercise their capacities.

Many discussions of social justice not only ignore the institutional contexts within which distributions occur, but often presuppose specific institutional structures whose justice they fail to bring under evaluation. Some political theories, for example, tend to assume centralized legislative and executive institutions separated from the day-to-day lives of most people in the society, and state officials with the authority to make and enforce policy decisions. They take for granted such institutions of the modern state as bureaucracies and welfare agencies for implementing and enforcing tax schemes and administering services (see, e.g., Rawls, 1971, pp. 274–84). Issues of the just organization of government institutions, and just methods of political decision-making, rarely get raised.

To take a different kind of example, when philosophers ask about the just principles for allocating jobs and offices among persons, they typically assume a stratification of such positions. They assume a hierarchical division of labor in which some jobs and offices carry significant autonomy, decision-making power, authority, income, and access to resources, while others lack most of these attributes. Rarely do theorists explicitly ask whether such a definition and organization of social positions is just.

Many other examples of ways in which theorizing about justice frequently presupposes specific structural and institutional background conditions could be cited. In every case a clear understanding of these background conditions can reveal how they affect distribution – what there is to distribute, how it gets distributed, who distributes, and what the distributive outcome is. With Michael Walzer, my intention here is "to shift our attention from distribution itself to conception and creation: the naming of the goods, the giving of meaning, and the collective making" (Walzer, 1983, p. 7). I shall focus most of my discussion on three primary categories of nondistributive issues that distributive theories tend to ignore: decision-making structure and procedures, division of labor, and culture.

Decision-making issues include not only questions of who by virtue of their positions have the effective freedom or authority to make what sorts of decisions, but also the rules and procedures according to which decisions are made. Discussion of economic justice, for example, often deemphasizes the decision-making structures which are crucial determinants of economic relations. Economic domination in our society occurs not simply or primarily because some persons have more wealth and income than others, as important as this is. Economic domination derives at least as much from the corporate and legal structures and procedures that give some persons the power to make decisions about investment, production, marketing, employment, interest rates, and wages that affect millions of other people. Not all who make these decisions are wealthy or even privileged, but the decision-making structure operates to reproduce distributive inequality and the unjust constraints on people's lives that I name exploitation and marginalization. As Carol Gould (1988, pp. 133–4) points out, rarely do theories of justice take such structures as an explicit focus. In the chapters that follow I raise several specific issues of decision-making structure, and argue for democratic decision-making procedures as an element and condition of social justice.

Division of labor can be understood both distributively and nondistributively. As a distributive issue, division of labor refers to how pregiven occupations, jobs, or tasks are allocated among individuals or groups. As a nondistributive issue, on the other hand, division of labor concerns the definition of the occupations themselves. Division of labor as an institutional structure involves the range of tasks performed in a given position, the definition of the nature, meaning, and value of those tasks, and the relations of cooperation, conflict, and authority among positions. Feminist claims about the justice of a sexual division of labor, for example, have been posed both distributively and nondistributively. On the one hand, feminists have questioned the justice of a pattern of distribution of positions that finds a small proportion of women in the most prestigious jobs. On the other hand, they have also questioned the conscious or unconscious association of many occupations or jobs with masculine or feminine characteristics, such as instrumentality or affectivity, and this is not itself a distributive issue . . .

Overextending the Concept of Distribution

The following objection might be made to my argument thus far. It may be true that philosophical discussions of justice tend to emphasize the distribution of goods and to ignore institutional issues of decision-making structure and culture. But this is not a necessary consequence of the distributive definition of justice. Theories of distributive justice can and should be applied to issues of social organization beyond the allocation of wealth, income, and resources. Indeed, this objection insists, many theorists explicitly extend the scope of distributive justice to such nonmaterial goods.

Rawls, for example, regards the subject of justice as "the way in which the major social institutions distribute fundamental rights and duties" (Rawls, 1971, p. 7), and for him this clearly includes rights and duties related to decision-making, social positions, power, and so on, as well as wealth or income. Similarly, David Miller specifies that "the 'benefits' the distribution of which a conception of justice evaluates should be taken to include intangible benefits such as prestige and self-respect" (Miller, 1976, p. 22). William Galston, finally, insists that "issues of justice involve not only the distribution of property or income, but also such non-material goods as productive tasks, opportunities for development, citizenship, authority, honor, and so on" (Galston, 1980, p. 6; cf. p. 116).

The distributive paradigm of justice may have a bias toward focusing on easily identifiable distributions, such as distributions of things, income, and jobs. Its beauty and simplicity, however, consist in its ability to accommodate any issue of justice, including those concerning culture, decision-making structures, and the division of labor. To do so the paradigm simply formulates the issue in terms of the distribution of some material or nonmaterial good among various agents. Any social value can be treated as some thing or aggregate of things that some specific agents possess in certain amounts, and alternative end-state patterns of distribution of that good among those agents can be compared. For example, neo-classical economists have developed sophisticated schemes for reducing all intentional action to a matter of maximizing a utility function in which the utility of all conceivable goods can be quantified and compared.

But this, in my view, is the main problem with the distributive paradigm: it does not recognize the limits to the application of a logic of distribution. Distributive theorists of justice agree that justice is the primary normative concept for evaluating all aspects of social institutions, but at the same time they identify the scope of justice with distribution. This entails applying a logic of distribution to social goods which are not material things or measurable quantities. Applying a logic of distribution to such goods produces a misleading conception of the issues of justice involved. It reifies aspects of social life that are better understood as a function of rules and relations than as things. And it conceptualizes social justice primarily in terms of end-state patterns, rather than focusing on social processes. This distributive paradigm implies a misleading or incomplete social ontology.

But why should issues of social ontology matter for normative theorizing about justice? Any normative claims about society make assumptions about the nature of society, often only implicitly. Normative judgments of justice

are about something, and without a social ontology we do not know what they are about. The distributive paradigm implicitly assumes that social judgments are about what individual persons have, how much they have, and how that amount compares with what other persons have. This focus on possession tends to preclude thinking about what people are doing, according to what institutionalized rules, how their doings and havings are structured by institutionalized relations that constitute their positions, and how the combined effect of their doings has recursive effects on their lives. Before developing this argument further, let us look at some examples of the application of the distributive paradigm to three nonmaterial goods frequently discussed by theorists of justice: rights, opportunity, and self-respect.

I quoted Rawls earlier to the effect that justice concerns the distribution of "rights and duties," and talk of distributing rights is by no means limited to him. But what does distributing a right mean? One may talk about having a right to a distributive share of material things, resources, or income. But in such cases it is the good that is distributed, not the right. What can it mean to distribute rights that do not refer to resources or things, like the right of free speech, or the right of trial by jury? We can conceive of a society in which some persons are granted these rights while others are not, but this does not mean that some people have a certain "amount" or "portion" of a good while others have less. Altering the situation so that everyone has these rights, moreover, would not entail that the formerly privileged group gives over some of its right of free speech or trial by jury to the rest of society's members, on analogy with a redistribution of income.

Rights are not fruitfully conceived as possessions. Rights are relationships, not things; they are institutionally defined rules specifying what people can do in relation to one another. Rights refer to doing more than having, to social relationships that enable or constrain action.

Talk of distributing opportunities involves a similar confusion. If by opportunity we mean "chance," we can meaningfully talk of distributing opportunities, of some people having more opportunities than others, while some have none at all. When I go to the carnival I can buy three chances to knock over the kewpie doll, and my friend can buy six, and she will have more chances than I. Matters are rather different, however, with other opportunities. James Nickel (1988, p. 110) defines opportunities as "states of affairs that combine the absence of insuperable obstacles with the presences of means – internal or external – that give one a chance of overcoming the obstacles that remain." Opportunity in this sense is a condition of enablement, which usually involves a configuration of social rules and social relations, as well as an individual's self-conception and skills.

We may mislead ourselves by the fact that in ordinary language we talk about some people having "fewer" opportunities than others. When we talk that way, the opportunities sound like separable goods that can be increased or decreased by being given out or withheld, even though we know that opportunities are not allocated. Opportunity is a concept of enablement rather than possession; it refers to doing more than having. A person has opportunities if he or she is not constrained from doing things, and lives under the enabling conditions for doing them. Having opportunities in this sense certainly does often entail having material possessions, such as food, clothing, tools, land, or machines. Being enabled or constrained refers more directly, however, to the rules and practices that govern one's action, the way other people treat one in the context of specific social relations, and the broader structural possibilities produced by the confluence of a multitude of actions and practices. It makes no sense to speak of opportunities as themselves things possessed. Evaluating social justice according to whether persons have opportunities, therefore, must involve evaluating not a distributive outcome but the social structures that enable or constrain the individuals in relevant situations (cf. Simpson, 1980; Reiman, 1987).

Consider educational opportunity, for example. Providing educational opportunity certainly entails allocating specific material resources – money, buildings, books, computers,

and so on – and there are reasons to think that the more resources, the wider the opportunities offered to children in an educational system. But education is primarily a process taking place in a complex context of social relations. In the cultural context of the United States, male children and female children, working-class children and middle-class children, Black children and white children often do not have equally enabling educational opportunities even when an equivalent amount of resources has been devoted to their education. This does not show that distribution is irrelevant to educational opportunity, only that opportunity has a wider scope than distribution.

Many writers on justice, to take a final example, not only regard self-respect as a primary good that all persons in a society must have if the society is to be just, but also talk of distributing self-respect. But what can it mean to distribute self-respect? Self-respect is not an entity or measurable aggregate, it cannot be parceled out of some stash, and above all it cannot be detached from persons as a separable attribute adhering to an otherwise unchanged substance. Self-respect names not some possession or attribute a person has, but her or his attitude toward her or his entire situation and life prospects. While Rawls does not speak of self-respect as something itself distributed, he does suggest that distributive arrangements provide the background conditions for self-respect (Rawls, 1971, pp. 148–50). It is certainly true that in many circumstances the possession of certain distributable material goods may be a condition of self-respect. Self-respect, however, also involves many nonmaterial conditions that cannot be reduced to distributive arrangements (cf. Howard, 1985).

People have or lack self-respect because of how they define themselves and how others regard them, because of how they spend their time, because of the amount of autonomy and decision-making power they have in their activities, and so on. Some of these factors can be conceptualized in distributive terms, but others cannot. Self-respect is at least as much a function of culture as it is of goods, for example, and in later chapters I shall discuss some elements of cultural imperialism that undermine the self-respect of many persons in our society. The point here is that none of the forms and not all of the conditions of self-respect can meaningfully be conceived as goods that individuals possess; they are rather relations and processes in which the actions of individuals are embedded.

These, then, are the general problems with extending the concept of distribution beyond material goods or measurable quantities to nonmaterial values. First, doing so reifies social relations and institutional rules. Something identifiable and assignable must be distributed. In accord with its implicit social ontology that gives primacy to substance over relations, moreover, the distributive paradigm tends to conceive of individuals as social atoms, logically prior to social relations and institutions. As Galston makes clear in the passage I quoted earlier (Galston, 1980, p. 112), conceiving justice as a distribution of goods among individuals involves analytically separating the individuals from those goods. Such an atomistic conception of the individual as a substance to which attributes adhere fails to appreciate that individual identities and capacities are in many respects themselves the products of social processes and relations. Societies do not simply distribute goods to persons who are what they are apart from society, but rather constitute individuals in their identities and capacities (Sandel, 1982; Taylor, 1985). In the distributive logic, however, there is little room for conceiving persons' enablement or constraint as a function of their relations to one another. . . . Such an atomistic social ontology ignores or obscures the importance of social groups for understanding issues of justice.

Secondly, the distributive paradigm must conceptualize all issues of justice in terms of patterns. It implies a static social ontology that ignores processes. In the distributive paradigm individuals or other agents lie as points in the social field, among whom larger or smaller packets of goods are assigned. One evaluates the justice of the pattern by comparing the size of the packages individuals have and comparing the total pattern to other possible patterns of assignment.

Robert Nozick (1974; chapter 52, in this volume) argues that such a static or end-state approach to justice is inappropriately ahistorical. End-state approaches to justice, he argues, operate as though social goods magically appear and get distributed. They ignore the processes that create the goods and produce distributive patterns, which they find irrelevant for evaluating justice. For Nozick, only the process is relevant to evaluating distributions. If individuals begin with holdings they are justly entitled to, and undertake free exchanges, then the distributive outcomes are just, no matter what they are. This entitlement theory shares with other theories a possessively individualist social ontology. Society consists only of individuals with "holdings" of social goods which they augment or reduce through individual production and contractual exchange. The theory does not take into account structural effects of the actions of individuals that they cannot foresee or intend, and to which they might not agree if they could. Nevertheless, Nozick's criticism of end-state theories for ignoring social processes is apt. . . .

This identification of a weakness in traditional social theory can be applied to the distributive paradigm of justice. I disagree with Nozick that end-state patterns are irrelevant to questions of justice. Because they inhibit the ability of some people to live and be healthy, or grant some people resources that allow them to coerce others, some distributions must come into question no matter how they came about. Evaluating patterns of distribution is often an important starting point for questioning about justice. For many issues of social justice, however, what is important is not the particular pattern of distribution at a particular moment, but rather the reproduction of a regular distributive pattern over time.

For example, unless one begins with the assumption that all positions of high status, income, and decision-making power ought to be distributed in comparable numbers to women and men, finding that very few top corporate managers are women might not involve any question of injustice. It is in the context of a social change involving more acceptance of women in corporate management, and a considerable increase in the number of women who obtain degrees in business, that a question of injustice becomes most apparent here. Even though more women earn degrees in business, and in-house policies of some companies aim to encourage women's careers, a pattern of distribution of managerial positions that clusters women at the bottom and men at the top persists. Assuming that justice ultimately means equality for women, this pattern is puzzling, disturbing. We are inclined to ask: what's going on here? Why is this general pattern reproduced even in the face of conscious efforts to change it? Answering that question entails evaluation of a matrix of rules, attitudes, interactions, and policies as a social process that produces and reproduces that pattern. An adequate conception of justice must be able to understand and evaluate the processes as well as the patterns.

One might object that this account confuses the empirical issue of what causes a particular distribution with the normative issue of whether the distribution is just. As will be apparent, however, in the spirit of critical social theory I do not accept this division between empirical and normative social theory. While there is a distinction between empirical and normative statements and the kinds of reasons required for each, no normative theory meant to evaluate existing societies can avoid empirical inquiry, and no empirical investigation of social structures and relations can avoid normative judgments. Inquiry about social justice must consider the context and causes of actual distributions in order to make normative judgments about institutional rules and relations.

The pattern orientation of the distributive paradigm, then, tends to lead to abstraction from institutional rules and relations and a consequent failure to bring them into evaluation. For many aspects of social structure and institutional context cannot be brought into view without examining social processes and the unintended cumulative consequences of individual actions. Without a more temporal approach to social reality, a theory of justice cannot conceptualize exploitation, as a social process by which

the labor of some unreciprocally supports the privilege of others. . . .

Defining Injustice as Domination and Oppression

Because distributive models of power, rights, opportunity, and self-respect work so badly, justice should not be conceived primarily on the model of the distribution of wealth, income, and other material goods. Theorizing about justice should explicitly limit the concept of distribution to material goods, like things, natural resources, or money. The scope of justice is wider than distributive issues. Though there may be additional nondistributive issues of justice, my concerns in this book focus on issues of decision-making, division of labor, and culture.

Political thought of the modern period greatly narrowed the scope of justice as it had been conceived by ancient and medieval thought. Ancient thought regarded justice as the virtue of society as a whole, the well-orderedness of institutions that foster individual virtue and promote happiness and harmony among citizens. Modern political thought abandoned the notion that there is a natural order to society that corresponds to the proper ends of human nature. Seeking to liberate the individual to define "his" own ends, modern political theory also restricted the scope of justice to issues of distribution and the minimal regulation of action among such self-defining individuals (Heller, 1987, ch. 2; cf. MacIntyre, 1981, ch. 17).

While I hardly intend to revert to a full-bodied Platonic conception of justice, I nevertheless think it is important to broaden the understanding of justice beyond its usual limits in contemporary philosophical discourse. Agnes Heller (1987, ch. 5) proposes one such broader conception in what she calls an incomplete ethico-political concept of justice. According to her conception, justice names not principles of distribution, much less some particular distributive pattern. This represents too narrow and substantive a way of reflecting on justice.

Instead, justice names the perspectives, principles, and procedures for evaluating institutional norms and rules. Developing Habermas's communicative ethics, Heller suggests that justice is primarily the virtue of citizenship, of persons deliberating about problems and issues that confront them collectively in their institutions and actions, under conditions without domination or oppression, with reciprocity and mutual tolerance of difference. She proposes the following test of the justice of social or political norms:

> Every valid social and political norm and rule (every law) must meet the condition that the foreseeable consequences and side effects the general observance of that law (norm) exacts on the satisfaction of the needs of each and every individual would be accepted by everyone concerned, and that the claim of the norm to actualize the universal values of freedom and/or life could be accepted by each and every individual, regardless of the values to which they are committed. (Heller, 1987, pp. 240–1).

. . . I endorse and follow this general conception of justice derived from a conception of communicative ethics. The idea of justice here shifts from a focus on distributive patterns to procedural issues of participation in deliberation and decision-making. For a norm to be just, everyone who follows it must in principle have an effective voice in its consideration and be able to agree to it without coercion. For a social condition to be just, it must enable all to meet their needs and exercise their freedom; thus justice requires that all be able to express their needs.

As I understand it, the concept of justice coincides with the concept of the political. Politics includes all aspects of institutional organization, public action, social practices and habits, and cultural meanings insofar as they are potentially subject to collective evaluation and decision-making. Politics in this inclusive sense certainly concerns the policies and actions of government and the state, but in principle can also concern rules, practices, and actions in any other institutional context (cf. Mason, 1982, pp. 11–24).

The scope of justice, I have suggested, is much wider than distribution, and covers everything political in this sense. This coheres with the meaning of justice claims of the sort mentioned at the outset of this chapter. When people claim that a particular rule, practice, or cultural meaning is wrong and should be changed, they are often making a claim about social injustice. Some of these claims involve distributions, but many also refer to other ways in which social institutions inhibit or liberate persons. . . .

Persons certainly are possessors and consumers, and any conception of justice should presume the value of meeting material needs, living in a comfortable environment, and experiencing pleasures. Adding an image of people as doers and actors (Macpherson, 1973; Gintis and Bowles, 1986) helps to displace the distributive paradigm. As doers and actors, we seek to promote many values of social justice in addition to fairness in the distribution of goods: learning and using satisfying and expansive skills in socially recognized settings; participating in forming and running institutions, and receiving recognition for such participation; playing and communicating with others, and expressing our experience, feelings, and perspective on social life in contexts where others can listen. Certainly many distributive theorists of justice would recognize and affirm these values. The framework of distribution, however, leads to a deemphasizing of these values and a failure to inquire about the institutional conditions that promote them.

This, then, is how I understand the connection between justice and the values that constitute the good life. Justice is not identical with the concrete realization of these values in individual lives; justice, that is, is not identical with the good life as such. Rather, social justice concerns the degree to which a society contains and supports the institutional conditions necessary for the realization of these values. The values comprised in the good life can be reduced to two very general ones: (1) developing and exercising one's capacities and expressing one's experience (cf. Gould, 1988, ch. 2; Galston, 1980, pp. 61–9), and (2) participating in determining one's action and the conditions of one's action (cf. Young, 1979). These are universalist values, in the sense that they assume the equal moral worth of all persons, and thus justice requires their promotion for everyone. To these two general values correspond two social conditions that define injustice: oppression, the institutional constraint on self-development; and domination, the institutional constraint on self-determination.

Oppression consists in systematic institutional processes which prevent some people from learning and using satisfying and expansive skills in socially recognized settings, or institutionalized social processes which inhibit people's ability to play and communicate with others or to express their feelings and perspective on social life in contexts where others can listen. While the social conditions of oppression often include material deprivation or maldistribution, they also involve issues beyond distribution.

Domination consists in institutional conditions which inhibit or prevent people from participating in determining their actions or the conditions of their actions. Persons live within structures of domination if other persons or groups can determine without reciprocation the conditions of their action, either directly or by virtue of the structural consequences of their actions. Thorough social and political democracy is the opposite of domination.

References

Arthur, John and William Shaw (eds.) (1978) *Justice and Economic Distribution*. Englewood Cliffs, NJ: Prentice-Hall.

Daniels, Norman (1985) *Just Health Care*. Cambridge: Cambridge University Press.

Galston, William (1980) *Justice and the Human Good*. Chicago: University of Chicago Press.

Gintis, Herbert and Samuel Bowles (1986) *Capitalism and Democracy*. New York: Basic Books.

Gould, Carol (1988) *Rethinking Democracy: Freedom and Political Cooperation in Politics, Economics, and Society*. Cambridge: Cambridge University Press.

Heller, Agnes (1987) *Beyond Justice*. New York: Basic Books.

Howard, Michael (1985) "Worker Control, Self-Respect, and Self-Esteem," *Philosophy Research Archives*, 10: 455–72.

MacIntyre, Alasdair (1981) *After Virtue*. Notre Dame: University of Notre Dame Press.

Macpherson, C. B. (1973) *Democratic Theory: Essays in Retrieval*. Oxford: Oxford University Press.

Mason, Ronald (1982) *Participatory and Workplace Democracy*. Carbondale: Southern Illinois University Press.

Miller, David (1976) *Social Justice*. Oxford: Clarendon Press.

Nicholson, Linda (1986) *Gender and History*. New York: Colombia University Press.

Nickel, James (1988) "Equal Opportunity in a Pluralistic Society." In Ellen Frankel Paul, Fred D. Miller, Jeffrey Paul, and John Ahrens (eds.), *Equal Opportunity*. Oxford: Blackwell.

Nielsen, Kai (1978) "Class and Justice." In John Arthur and William Shaw (eds.), *Justice and Economic Distribution*. Englewood Cliffs, NJ: Prentice-Hall.

Nozick, Robert (1974) *Anarchy, State, and Utopia*. New York: Basic Books.

Okin, Susan (1986) "Are our Theories of Justice Gender-Neutral?" In Robert Fullinwider and Claudia Mills (eds), *The Moral Foundations of Civil Rights* Totowa, NJ: Rowman and Little-field.

Pateman, Carole (1988) *The Sexual Contract*. Stanford: Stanford University Press.

Rawls, John (1971) *A Theory of Justice*. Cambridge, MA: Harvard University Press.

Reiman, Jeffrey (1987) "Exploitation, Force, and the Moral Assessment of Capitalism: Thoughts on Roemer and Cohen," *Philosophy and Public Affairs* 16 (Winter): 3–41.

Sandel, Michael (1982) *Liberalism and the Limits of Justice*. Cambridge: Cambridge University Press.

Schweickart, David (1984) "Plant Relocations: A Philosophical Reflection," *Review of Radical Political Economics* 16 (Winter): 32–51.

Simon, Robert (1984) "Troubled Waters: Global Justice and Ocean Resources." In Tom Regan (ed.), *Earthbound*. New York: Random House.

Simpson, Evan (1980) "The Subject of Justice," *Ethics* 90 (July): 490–501.

Taylor, Charles (1985) "The Nature and Scope of Distributive Justice." In *Philosophy and the Human Sciences*. Cambridge: Cambridge University Press.

Walzer, Michael (1983) *Spheres of Justice*. New York: Basic Books.

Wolff, Robert Paul (1977) *Understanding Rawls*. Princeton: Princeton University Press.

Wood, Allen (1972) "The Marxian Critique of Justice" *Philosophy and Public Affairs* 1 (Spring): 244–82.

Young, Iris (1979) "Self-Determination as a Principle of Justice," *Philosophical Forum* 11 (Fall): 172–82.

—— (1983). "Justice and Hazardous Waste." In Michael Bradie (ed.), *The Applied Turn in Contemporary Philosophy*. Bowling Green, OH: Applied Philosophy Program, Bowling Green State University.

55

Economic Competition: Should We Care about the Losers?

Jonathan Wolff

Suppose you own and run a small shop. One night an unauthorised stranger enters your premises and removes your stock. This way of harming your economic interests is called theft, and your legal rights protect you against it. If the thief is caught, he will be punished and will be made to compensate you for your loss.

Imagine that he is, indeed, caught, and you receive compensation. With this money you restock. A month later another stranger sets fire to your store. The premises are saved but the stock is lost. This way of harming your economic interests is called arson, and your legal rights protect you against it. If the arsonist is caught, she will be punished and will be made to compensate you for your loss.

Once more an arrest is made, and you are compensated. Once more you restock. Or, at least, try to. But the deliveries never arrive. You find out that another stranger has written letters to all your suppliers, on a copy of your notepaper, saying that deliveries are be made to a different address. This way of harming your economic interests is called fraud, and your legal rights protect you against it. If the fraudster is caught, he will be punished and will be made to compensate you for your loss.

Finally you sort out the mess and try again. But now you find that a big company has opened up a shiny new store right next to you, selling exactly the same products as you. But in a calculated ploy to put you and others like you out of business they sell their goods very cheap indeed, at prices you can't hope to match. Your customers desert you. This way of harming your economic interests is called competition. It is celebrated the world over. Those who are particularly good at it receive honours, and dine with government ministers, who listen attentively to their advice. You are finished.

Theft, arson, fraud and economic competition can all cause economic harm, of apparently very similar forms and magnitudes. Yet theft, arson and fraud are illegal, while competition is encouraged. You have rights that protect you against the first three, but not the fourth. Why is this? And why is this question so seldom asked?

I don't say that questions about the moral acceptability of economic competition are never asked. Marx, and others in the Marxist/socialist tradition, have pointed out that a society of individuals all struggling to get the upper hand, at whatever cost to each other, is a deeply unappealing spectacle. John Stuart Mill, summarising the socialist case said:

> Morally speaking [the evils of individual competition] are obvious. It is the parent of envy, hatred, and all uncharitableness; it makes every one the natural enemy of all others who cross his path, and every one's path is liable to be crossed. Under the present system hardly any one can gain except by the loss or disappointment of one or of many others.[1]

In *On Liberty* he famously expands on that last remark:

> Whoever succeeds in an overcrowded profession, or in a competitive examination; whoever is preferred to another in any contest for an object which both desire, reaps benefit from the loss of others, from their wasted exertion and their disappointment.[2]

Once we get ourselves in this frame of mind we come to realise that competition – economic and non-economic – is one of the few areas of life where people are actively encouraged to embark on courses of action that can do grave harm to others. Why do we permit it, let alone encourage it?

My experience is that people often express irritation at this question in the belief that the answer is blindingly obvious. Free competition, it is said, is required by a proper respect for liberty. To restrict competition is to stop some people doing what they want to do, and this, so it is said, reduces their liberty. Thus we permit economic competition for the sake of liberty. But this is a terrible argument. We do not generally believe that people should be free to harm each other. At best liberty is the right to act as you wish provided that you do not harm others. Thus it is not a restriction on my legitimate liberty if I am prohibited from defrauding you. Yet, it seems, harm suffered in economic competition can be just as serious. What we need to know is why we treat one of these harms as illegitimate and the other as entirely respectable. No simple appeal to liberty can provide the answer.

A more promising solution is to point out the great overall benefits that can flow from a system of economic competition. Even if competition requires 'private vices' the 'public virtues' are so evident that we can forgive all. So perhaps we take the moral argument against economic competition to have been answered long ago, in consequentialist terms. We cannot deny that the argument is impressive. Competition keeps prices down, quality up, and facilitates efficient deployment of resources. Few will deny that this is an impressive track record: the consequentialist argument looks unanswerable.

But appearances can be deceptive, and we cannot allow the argument to rest here. Even if it is true that economic competition can be defended in consequentialist terms, this only settles the question if we are prepared to accept consequentialist arguments in unqualified form. But very few people will endorse the sort of absolute consequentialist reasoning implied here; reasoning that allows us to inflict severe harm on some for the greater good it makes available for others. This is the sort of reasoning that allows the torture of innocent children if it saves enough lives. But if you think this abhorrent then you don't accept uncompromising consequentialist reasoning; perhaps you think that the innocent should be protected. But this, then, returns us to the starting point, for many of those damaged by economic competition will claim to be innocent, and thus in need of protection. At the least, then, the consequentialist argument for economic competition requires considerable qualification. Where else can we turn?

Many readers may still think that this is a lot of fuss about nothing. In many walks of life competition is taken for granted, even enjoyed, and those who lose do not even begin to think of themselves as harmed. Those who play in a squash ladder, or play Sunday league football, and do badly, rarely complain that they have suffered harm at the hands of the winners. Rather, they vow to do better next time, or, if they are not enjoying it, stop. For most people who are voluntarily involved in competitive sport, competition is a way of adding spice to an activity that they enjoy in any case. It enhances this enjoyment. Competition, then, is plausibly part of the good life for these people, at least for a time.

No doubt some people view economic competition in this light; maybe even some for whom losing in economic competition means losing everything. But for others, this suggestion is a vast distortion of their position. They may feel forced into competition, and have no option but to swim or sink. The importance of this observation is that it makes us aware that there are different forms of competition – or at least ways of viewing competition. Before we try to say anything in general about the harms and benefits of competition, we should become aware of its forms.

Forms of Competition

All forms of competition have some features in common. A number of people (or groups, or teams) engage in an activity in which there can be differing levels of achievement, normally measured on a scale, which is often broadly correlated with some underlying trait which the scale is designed to capture. Whoever achieves at the highest level of this scale is the winner, and is awarded by some sort of prize, honour or other recognition.

It is possible to distinguish several forms of competition, or, at least, reasons why we have practices of competition:[3] Here I will distinguish seven reasons. The first five, I hope, should be easy to understand, but the last two, being unfamiliar when stated in abstract terms, may seem obscure. However, illustrations later in the essay should make things much clearer.

> **Pure Lottery**. This may well be the limit case of competition. A scarce good is to be allocated and a competition of pure luck is held as a means of fair allocation. Here one may only win or lose, and the result is not intended to be sensitive to any underlying trait of the participants. Any example would be the coin toss, as a way of deciding who will be first in a game.
> **Weighted Lottery**. Consider the example of a marathon, run for a valuable prize. Here, once more, a competition is held at least in part to allocate a scarce resource, but this time different levels of skill, effort, or other input, are possible. In general such competitions are designed so that the greater the input, the greater chance of winning.

> **Pure competition**. Consider two people who decide to have a bet on the colour of the next car to come round the corner. Here competitive behaviour is considered desirable in itself, and so turns an activity of no value into an activity of some value.
> **Constitutive competition**. Here an activity can only exist if it involves competition (chess, for example).
> **Activity enhancement**. A competition for a prize is used to add enjoyment to an activity that is already valued for itself. Competitive sport is the most obvious example.
> **Side-effect of award**. A weighted lottery is held for the sake of the external effects of awarding the reward to someone of a certain type. (As I mentioned above, examples of this will be given shortly.)
> **Side-effect of activity**: A competition is held because of the value of individuals acting (or the value of individuals preparing to act) in the manner required by the competition. (Once again: illustrations to follow.)

These categories are not exclusive. That is, a particular episode of competition could be valued for more than one reason. Consider the example of a parent who is asked to arbitrate a dispute between two children, who, at 4.30 p.m., declare that they wish to watch different television channels at 5.00 p.m. In the absence of a second TV or video recorder the parent declares that whichever child has the tidier bedroom at 4.55 p.m. gets to choose what to watch.

At one level this could have been intended as a pure lottery; simply a way of breaking a tie, or finding a fair means of distributing a scarce resource; assuming, of course, that the bedrooms were in an equal state of untidiness to start with. But at least at the back of the parent's mind might have been the thought that this is a weighted lottery. That is, they may believe that the child with the more intense preference should have their way, and a good way of attempting to see which child cares most is to see which is prepared to make the greater effort. Of course this example makes various assumptions, such as neither child detests tidying more than the other, but against such a background it is quite likely that the child with the stronger desire will be moved to put in a winning performance.

Furthermore, although the children certainly won't view things this way, the parent may hope to bring about a degree of 'activity enhancement'; perhaps if the children get used to tidying their rooms in a competition they will come to see the value of a tidy room. (Of course, it may backfire: the children may be reinforced in their view that tidying up is such a useless way of spending time that it should only be done for the sake of an external goal.) Finally, and most obviously, the parent is almost certain considering the 'side-effects of activity'. By getting the children to act this way, the parent's own burdens are likely to be significantly reduced. Thus this case illustrates the seventh category (side-effect of activity) above, and also shows that one competition can serve several goals.

The idea of side-effect of activity may, as I noted, be hard to grasp, and so some further examples may help. Consider a publisher who sets a literary quiz, largely based on its own books, in order to stimulate sales to those who want to take part. Or a farmer who sets a ploughing competition, in order to get his field ploughed. In both cases the main objective of the person setting the competition (although not of those taking part, who simply want to win) is to reap the benefits of people engaging in the competitive activity. The competition is valued not because it allows us to allocate a scare resource, but because of some external effect of people behaving in the manner required or encouraged by the competition.

Other examples can demonstrate the point already made that a competition can be valued for more than one reason. In *On Liberty* Mill briefly discusses two examples of competition; not only economic competition but also competitive examinations for the civil service. In this latter case, we can see it as aiming to satisfy a number of goals. First, it is a weighted lottery, giving desirable jobs to those who put in the most effort or have the highest ability. Second, this provides an illustration of the idea of 'side-effect of award'. It is for the good of us all if jobs in government offices are put in the hands of those with the most appropriate talents, and the competition will tend to have this effect, to the benefit of us all. Finally, there is an indirect side-effect of activity. If rewards go to those who do best in examinations then everyone has

an incentive to educate themselves in order to do as well as possible in those examinations. This will raise the general educational level of society as a whole, to the benefit both of the participants and the rest of society. Here, then, the benefit stems from people behaving competitively, rather than the effect of awarding the prize to one person rather than another. Interestingly neither of these arguments appeal to the idea that the most talented deserve to have the best jobs, although we might also believe this.

But let us change the example, so that the costs of receiving an education much outweigh the benefits, unless you happen to get one of the scarce jobs, which, let us also now say, don't really require any special talents. Nevertheless we continue to have the competition (rather than some other way of allocating the jobs) because we think the economy will benefit from an educated workforce, and realise that this is the best way of encouraging people to educate themselves. So now we are encouraging people to take a large risk of loss, purely for the good it does for others. Might, then, we begin to have some doubts about this practice? Note that in this case, like both the literary competition and the ploughing competition, the people setting the competition were using it simply as a way of a way of achieving goals that had nothing to do with the competition in itself. They either wanted a field ploughed, or books sold, or the economy boosted, and were prepared to use the competition as a means to that end. This sounds sneaky; maybe even exploitative, and should put us on our guard. Are there moral grounds for objecting to competitions valued for side-effect of activity? Maybe. But to give a proper answer I will have to introduce an analysis of exploitation.

Exploitation

For present purposes I can be brief.[4] The core of exploitation is making some sort of wrongful or unfair use of another person purely for your own benefit. This is normally only possible if that person is vulnerable in some way; if they are weak, poor, ignorant, or dependent, economically, emotionally or psychologically. Traits like ambition or avarice can also make you vulnerable. Just as in judo, it is said, you can turn your opponent's strength against them, a skilled exploiter can turn what is often thought of as a strength of character into a weakness. Typically, then, an exploiter is someone who uses another's weakness for their own ends. Yet what does it mean to use another for your own ends? Don't we all use each other for our own ends all the time? When I buy a ticket to watch a play I have only my own ends in mind, and not those of the actors, investors or even the ticket seller. But I want to get at another idea. To use another person for your own ends, in the sense I am interested in, is to act without sufficient regard for how the other person may be affected. It is this lack of regard that makes you an exploiter. Now you may reply that in this case that still leaves us as exploiters in much of what we do, and this cannot be true. But in response I would say, first, that we are likely to have at least some regard for the other parties to these transactions without realising it. If we found that the ticket seller was chained to her desk, and the actors blackmailed into performing for no pay, we may decide not to go to the theatre at all. Now if you continue to contend that even after making such discoveries you would go to the theatre, I would respond that then you *are* treating these people merely as means to your own ends; that you are an exploiter. In sum, then, an exploiter is someone who uses another person as you might a tool or instrument; that is, without regard to the effect your behaviour might be having on them.

Before leaving the analysis of exploitation I should make clear that while it may always be wrong to act without sufficient regard for others, it is not always exploitative. A drunk driver is negligent but not exploitative. Exploitation requires not mere impact – actual or possible – on others, but that in the circumstances as they are, they or their action should be an essential component in the achievement of my goals. Thus an exploiter in some way relies on the exploited person, but does so without worrying about how that person will be affected.

Let us return to the idea of side-effect of activity. Are there cases where this turns out to be exploitative, by the definition just given? We have four examples so far: the tidying competition, competitive examinations, the ploughing competition, and the literary quiz. In the case of the tidying competition it seems reasonable to say that the parent was being opportunistic, but not exploitative. He probably has his children's best interests in mind, and, in any case, children ought to keep their rooms tidy. But imagine parents who managed to get all the household chores done by setting competition after competition, simply so they can spend every evening in the pub. Surely we would conclude that this has crossed the line into exploitation.

In each of the other cases as they are described, we might think it is going too far to say that those setting the competition are exploiters. After all the ploughers voluntarily enter the competition and all they lose is a little time; those who enter the literary quiz are probably intelligent enough to understand what is going on and don't mind it too much; and finally it is good to get an education. But as we have seen, we can adjust the examples to make them appear exploitative. In the last version of the competitive examination example we considered, getting an education is extremely costly in terms of time and money. And suppose that while a population of educated people is generally more prosperous, there is no particular advantage for the educated person, unless they happen to win one of the high-status jobs (for which the education is, we assumed, not really necessary). Here, I think, we could reasonably describe the set-up as exploitative. A competition has been set up for the general good, but without sufficient regard to how this affects the people who are enticed into the competition by the promise of victory.

Now it might be said that even this cannot be exploitative because the competitors voluntarily entered the competition. Yet we should note that it is a general feature of exploitation that the victims are, in some sense, willing. Because individuals are in a vulnerable position, others can take advantage of this. Consequently the exploited person is offered an opportunity which while it might seem to be the best thing to do, is in some sense 'low-grade' or carries at least some risk of harm. So generally, those who are exploited do, in some sense, agree to take part in the exploitative situation. Thus the fact that the exploited people consent to the exploitative situation is not, in general, a sufficient defence to the charge of exploitation.

However there do are several factors that can be used as a defence against the charge that people who benefit from a system are exploiters:

- That the victims are also part of the group that benefits.
- That those who benefit have no influence or control over the system.
- That the interests of the victims have been taken into account to a sufficient degree.

The last of these, I think, would simply show that the system is not exploitative. The second would show that the beneficiaries are not to blame for the exploitation. The first would possibly make the system less exploitative, but not necessarily remove the claim entirely. These possible defences will become relevant shortly, when we look at the question of whether economic activity is exploitative. But let us say, for the moment, that any activity that is primarily valued for the side-effects of people engaging in competitive activity is *potentially* exploitative. Whether it is *actually* exploitative depends on the presence or absence of the factors just mentioned.

Economic Competition and Exploitation

It is time, finally, to return to the issue of economic competition. Why is it valued? Which of the categories set out above does it fall into? It may, of course, like the tidying competition, fall into more than one.

It is clear that economic competition is rarely, if ever, valued as a pure lottery; as a fair way of distributing scarce resources. What about a weighted lottery; a way of putting resources in the hands of those with particular traits? Often

competition is defended in these terms. The winners in economic competition are more deserving, hard-working and resourceful than others. Sometimes, of course, they are also more greedy, deceitful, manipulative, and double-faced than the losers too. But more often they are just plain lucky. They might have been born with the talents or money to give them a headstart, or simply got a lucky break along the way. Still, we need not settle the question of desert here. All we need say is that some people will try to defend economic competition in terms of desert, and hence in terms of a weighted lottery.

The, next category, 'activity enhancement' is less plausible as a general defence of economic competition. To use this argument would be to claim that economic competition enhances an activity that is otherwise desirable in itself; that competition adds spice to commerce. This may be true for some, but surely most producers or traders would feel more comfortable with a monopoly position. Competition is seen as a fact of life, not a life enhancer. Note also that this shows that the 'constitutive' approach is also unavailable. Trade is possible without competition. Even if no one has a monopoly, cartels may form in which, say, members of trade associations agree not to undercut each other.

This leaves us with the two instrumental justifications. The idea I called 'side-effect of award' would require us to value economic competition because we find it socially useful for the enterprising to have more money than the less enterprising. Remember that this is distinct from any considerations of desert, which were discussed in connection with the idea of the weighted lottery. And indeed it is sometimes said that the enterprising can make better use of resources than the rest of us, and this is for the good of all. This may well be true. But even so, 'side-effect of activity' is a more common defence. This is the idea that, from the point of view of social utility, the important thing about economic competition is not who wins or loses but that enough people are playing the game. Competitive activity is what we want, for it is this that keeps prices down and quality up. For this reason we don't actually want anyone to win the competition, for that would end the competition and leave us with monopoly. We want the competition to go on indefinitely. The inescapable conclusion is that we value economic competition primarily because the process or activity of competition benefits people outside the competition.

It should not now be too difficult now to see how the anti-competition argument runs. First I argued that when a form of competition is valued primarily because of the side-effects of people engaging in that competition, then there is something morally dubious about setting such competitions. It is potentially exploitative. And then I suggested that this is precisely why we value economic competition. So now we find ourselves with the conclusion that there is something morally suspect about economic competition; that it is potentially exploitative.

Note, however, we must be clear about the nature of this suggestion. Although the winning competitor may well harm the losing competitor, I would not claim that the winner exploits the loser. Not at all. Rather, the exploiter, if there is one, is you, or me: the consumer. Why? Because we, the ordinary voters or consumers, benefit from the process of economic competition and are quite happy to acquiesce in a system where people potentially do a great deal of harm to each other for our benefit.

Now this is not, of course, enough to show that we are actually exploiters. We benefit from all sorts of things without being exploiters. Rather exploitation involves gaining a benefit from other people without giving sufficient regard to their interests. As consumers we are potentially exploiters, but will be actual exploiters only if we do not pay sufficient attention to the interests of those who may be harmed in the process of creating cheaper or better goods for us. If we use economic competitors for our own ends, without concern for how they are affected, then we are exploiters.

I can well anticipate the reluctance many will have to accepting the idea that consumers exploit producers. Isn't it just absurd to say that I, and others like me, exploit mighty multinational retailers, or enormous agribusinesses, or even the small shopkeeper at the end of the road?

What harm do I actually do? Now there may be an answer to this, but before getting there we will do well to remind ourselves that exploitation does not require actual harm to anyone. Just as a drunk driver has acted wrongly even if she doesn't harm anyone, an exploiter may similarly be guilty of a form of reckless endangerment. But I still anticipate resistance to this conclusion, so let us try to isolate its source.

First it might be said that there is no alternative to economic competition. But this is patently false. Most industries are protected in some ways, if only by such things as health and safety legislation. Legally you can't enter the trade if you don't comply. It is possible to increase the degree of regulation to the point where, by law or fact, every existing producer is protected from competition and becomes a monopoly supplier. This may be an awful economy, from the point of view of the consumer, and so this is why we encourage competition. But none of this shows that competition is not a form of exploitation.

However, I did lay out some excusing conditions which will prevent a potentially exploitative situation becoming actually exploitation. One was that if the exploited group is part of the group that benefits then although they may still have some complaint it seems mitigated. And, indeed, those who take part in economic competition often benefit from the fact that others do too. So this will often apply. A second was that if an individual had no control at all over the existence of the activity then blame seems to disappear. Yet even if this is what we think, it cannot be true of us. Surely as members of an electorate, and as consumers who could make different purchasing decisions, we bear a collective responsibility. We could vote for governments that act differently, or only buy from certain types of producers Thus we cannot excuse ourselves this way. However the final mitigating circumstance is the trump card: if those who benefit also sufficiently take into account the interests of those who may suffer then there is no exploitation. It is only where there is disregard that the charge of exploitation bites.

Does this get us off the hook? Possibly. All developed countries have fairly sophisticated measures to protect people from falling 'too' low. Although it is hard to say where the distinction between unconcern and sufficient concern should be set, it is plausible that in many countries sufficient concern is shown for those who lose in economic competition. We have bankruptcy laws that allow people to draw a line under their failure. We have social security to feed and shelter them when they cannot otherwise survive. In these and other ways we stop the weak from going to the wall, and so it turns out that we might not be exploiters after all. Collectively we show more concern than we might have realised. Not only do these measures provide a financial safety net for those who fail, but they also provide a moral safety net for the rest of us. By protecting others in this way, we are protecting ourselves from being exploiters.

Can we stand back satisfied that, although economic competition is potentially exploitative, it is not actually so? So are earlier impressions correct: this *is* a lot of fuss about nothing? Not so fast. I have not, to this point, been very explicit about who falls into the category of 'producer'. Examples have been small traders and large companies. But we cannot overlook the people who work for those companies. They too are producers, sucked into a process of competition which is for the benefit of others. These are people who engage in a process of economic competition not out of greed, or ambition, but simply because they have no other sensible alternative. Now it will be correctly pointed out that on the analysis presented here this doesn't make them exploited. After all, we voted for governments that put in place minimum wage legislation; that regulate the workplace in various ways; and that provide for people if they are thrown out of work. Surely we can take comfort in this.

Well, we do take care of our compatriots in these ways, at least to some degree, and so we don't exploit them. But this is not the end of the story. We are part of a global market place and many of the goods we purchase are now produced in the developing world precisely because it is cheaper to do this. It is cheaper partly because the safeguards to protect the vulnerable that we have grown used to simply do not exist in these territories. Think of the competitive

advantages of producing in countries where wages are minimal, health and safety legislation, and social security virtually non-existent. Thus we benefit without providing a safety-net. And we cannot rely on the other mitigating circumstances set out above. Exploited third world workers barely benefit from the system that exploits them. We as consumers could decide only to purchase goods from countries with good social legislation, even if this puts prices up. But most of us don't, and, typically, we act with little or no regard to any harms that may be suffered by those engaging in production overseas for our benefit. Now it has to be said that not all of the harms suffered by producers in poor conditions are the result of economic competition. But nevertheless it is the need to keep prices down, and quality up, that often explains poor pay and conditions. So although we may console ourselves with the thought that we no longer exploit our fellow citizens, even though we set them in competition, this argument does not generalize. In importing goods we are exporting exploitation. Putting our heads in the sand is part of the problem; not the answer.

Conclusion

In sum, then, there is something morally suspect about economic competition, but not what we first thought. The problem is not so much that the winners harm the losers – even though they do – but that we, as voters and consumers, benefit from a system which allows people to harm each other. Potentially, we who benefit are exploiters. I conceded, however, that as long as there are safeguards in place that show sufficient regard for the interests of those engaged in competition, there is no significant moral wrong, no actual exploitation. But if we derive benefits from a system which does not contain such safeguards then the situation differs. And this does seem to be our position with regard to international trade, in many cases. We encourage others to risk, and to suffer, harm for our benefit. Thus, to the degree that this is true, we are exploiters. This may not be a comfortable conclusion, but it is not so easy to see how it is to be avoided.

Notes

For their comments on earlier versions of this paper I am very grateful to Veronique Munoz Dardè, Ian Carter, Hillel Steiner, and Hugh LaFollette.

1 J. S. Mill, Chapters on Socialism, in *On Liberty and Other Writings*, ed. S. Collini, (Cambridge: Cambridge University Press, 1989), p. 233.

2 J. S. Mill, *On Liberty* in *Utilitarianism and Other Writings*, ed. Mary Warnock (Glasgow: Collins, 1962), p. 277.

3 I first set out these distinctions in 'The Ethics of Competition', in *The Legal and Moral Aspects of International Trade, Freedom and Trade*, volume III, ed. A. Qureshi, G. Parry, and H. Steiner (London: Routledge 1998), pp. 82–96. This essay also makes use of several arguments made there.

4 A fuller account is set out in my 'Marx and Exploitation', *Journal of Ethics* 3 (1999): 105–20.

World Hunger

Do we have any obligations to, or moral responsibility for, people living in other countries? If so, are we responsible only to our political allies or those countries we think can benefit us? Or are we also obligated to countries with which we have few, no, or even antagonistic, relations? Most people acknowledge that we are obligated not to harm others, even if they do not live within our country, and even if they are not our allies. Thus, I should not embezzle money from my boss – whether my boss is a foreigner or a fellow citizen. Are we obligated to do more than not harm foreigners? Should we also prevent harm that is about to befall them? Must we, for example, feed starving children in Thailand or promote the economy of Zimbabwe? If so, how much should we help them, and under what circumstances?

Even if we decide that we should feed starving children living in other countries, we must still address two theoretical questions. First, are our obligations to foreigners as strong as our obligations to fellow citizens? Second, do we have obligations to prevent harm, as well as obligations not to do harm directly? Singer claims the answer to both is "Yes."

Let us look at each question in turn. First, Singer claims there is no fundamental difference between our obligations to someone near us and to someone geographically remote. It may be more difficult to help a foreigner than a neighbor. If so, we have a practical reason to favor the neighbor: our intervention is more likely to help. However, if we can help distant people (roughly) as effectively as we can help our neighbors, then we have the same general obligation – whatever it is – to both.

Questions about the precise scope of our moral obligations lie at the base of virtually every issue discussed in this volume. Most people recognize that they should care for their children and family. Nevertheless, exactly how much further do our obligations go? That issue, which first raised its head in the essay by Rachels (FAMILY AND REPRODUCTIVE TECHNOLOGY), keeps cropping up, albeit in a different guise. In the previous section we discussed our obligations to fellow citizens. Here we are discussing obligations to citizens of other countries. Earlier we asked whether our obligations extend to non-human ANIMALS. In the following section, the authors will ask whether we are also obligated to the ENVIRONMENT. Then, in WAR AND TERRORISM, we will explore the moral constraints on using military might to protect ourselves from terrorist threats, or to prevent genocide and other human rights atrocities.

The second theoretical issue also intersects most issues in this book: the *act/omission* or the *doing/allowing* distinction. The act/omission distinction first appeared in the essays on EU-THANASIA, and has lurked in the background of most issues. Everyone acknowledges that we must make serious personal sacrifices to stop from actively harming others. For instance, I should crash my expensive car rather than run over a child who strays into the road in front of me.

However, many people claim that whereas I may have to make a considerable sacrifice so that I do not directly harm another, I need not make similar sacrifices to keep a comparable harm from occurring – unless, of course, I created the conditions that led to that harm. We can see the force of the act/omission distinction in the current debate. Those who think the distinction is morally significant claim that whereas I should not kill a young child in a distant country simply to increase my wealth, I need not give up my wealth to keep that same child from starving to death.

Singer denies the moral force of this distinction. He claims not only that those of us in affluent nations have an obligation to feed the starving of the world, but that the obligation is sufficiently strong that we must be willing to make substantial sacrifices for them. Arthur disagrees. We are not morally required to make substantial (and perhaps not even minor) sacrifices to help others. After all, he says, each of us has a right to our life and our property. These rights are sufficiently strong to show that it is often the case that we may keep our property, even if that means others die of starvation. This view would be very similar to – but weaker than – the position advocated by Nozick (ECONOMIC JUSTICE), but rather at odds with that recommended by Young and Wolff in that same section.

Pogge thinks these ways of describing the factual and moral issues blind us to our role in global institutions that advantage those of us living in the West, and disadvantage those in the Third World. Our financially superior position is not an accident – it emerged from a historical process permeated by grievous moral wrongs. Hence, it is not enough to merely offer aid to those who are starving. We must make recompense for our injustice in creating and sustaining their poverty.

Further Reading

Aiken, W. and LaFollette, H. (1996) *World Hunger and Morality*. Englewood Cliffs, NJ: Prentice-Hall.

Brown, P. and Shue, H. (eds.) (1977) *Food Policy: The Responsibility of the United States in the Life and Death Choices*. New York: Free Press.

Drèze, J. and Sen, A. (eds.) (1989) *Hunger and Public Action*. Oxford: Clarendon Press.

—— (1990) *The Political Economy of Hunger. Entitlement and Well-Being*. Oxford: Clarendon Press.

Food and Agricultural Organization (FAO) (1992) *World Food Supplies and Prevalence of Chronic Undernutrition in Developing Regions as Assessed in 1992*. Rome: FAO Press.

Goodin, R. E. (1985) *Protecting the Vulnerable: A Reanalysis of Our Social Responsibilities*. Chicago, IL: University of Chicago Press.

LaFollette, H. (2002) "World Hunger." In R. Frey and C. H. Wellman (eds.), *Blackwell Companion to Applied Ethics*. Oxford: Blackwell Publishers, pp. 238–53.

Nussbaum, M. and Sen, A. (eds.) (1993) *The Quality of Life*. Oxford: Clarendon Press.

Pogge, T. W. (2002) *World Hunger and Human Rights: Cosmopolitan Responsibilities and Reforms*. Cambridge: Polity Press.

United Nations Children's Fund (UNICEF) (1993) *The State of the World's Children 1993*. Oxford: Oxford University Press.

56

Famine, Affluence, and Morality

Peter Singer

As I write this, in November 1971, people are dying in East Bengal from lack of food, shelter, and medical care. The suffering and death that are occurring there now are not inevitable, not unavoidable in any fatalistic sense of the term. Constant poverty, a cyclone, and a civil war have turned at least nine million people into destitute refugees; nevertheless, it is not beyond the capacity of the richer nations to give enough assistance to reduce any further suffering to very small proportions. The decisions and actions of human beings can prevent this kind of suffering. Unfortunately, human beings have not made the necessary decisions. At the individual level, people have, with very few exceptions, not responded to the situation in any significant way. Generally speaking, people have not given large sums to relief funds; they have not written to their parliamentary representatives demanding increased government assistance; they have not demonstrated in the streets, held symbolic fasts, or done anything else directed toward providing the refugees with the means to satisfy their essential needs. At the government level, no government has given the sort of massive aid that would enable the refugees to survive for more than a few days.

Britain, for instance, has given rather more than most countries. It has, to date, given £14,750,000. For comparative purposes, Britain's share of the nonrecoverable development costs of the Anglo-French Concorde project is already in excess of £275,000,000, and on present estimates will reach £440,000,000. The implication is that the British government values a supersonic transport more than thirty times as highly as it values the lives of the nine million refugees. Australia is another country which, on a per capita basis, is well up in the "aid to Bengal" table. Australia's aid, however, amounts to less than one-twelfth of the cost of Sydney's new opera house. The total amount given, from all sources, now stands at about £65,000,000. The estimated cost of keeping the refugees alive for one year is £464,000,000. Most of the refugees have now been in the camps for more than six months. The World Bank has said that India needs a minimum of £300,000,000 in assistance from other countries before the end of the year. It seems obvious that assistance on this scale will not be forthcoming. India will be forced to choose between letting the refugees starve or diverting funds from her own development program, which will mean that more of her own people will starve in the future.[1]

These are the essential facts about the present situation in Bengal. So far as it concerns us here, there is nothing unique about this situation except its magnitude. The Bengal emergency is just the latest and most acute of a series of major emergencies in various parts of the world, arising both from natural and from man-made causes. There are also many parts of the world in which people die from malnutrition and lack of food independent of any special emergency. I take Bengal as my example only because it is the present concern, and because the size of the problem has ensured that it has been given adequate publicity. Neither individuals nor governments can claim to be unaware of what is happening there.

What are the moral implications of a situation like this? In what follows, I shall argue that the way people in relatively affluent countries react to a situation like that in Bengal cannot be justified; indeed, the whole way we look at moral issues – our moral conceptual scheme – needs to be altered, and with it, the way of life that has come to be taken for granted in our society.

In arguing for this conclusion I will not, of course, claim to be morally neutral. I shall, however, try to argue for the moral position that I take, so that anyone who accepts certain assumptions, to be made explicit, will, I hope, accept my conclusion.

I begin with the assumption that suffering and death from lack of food, shelter, and medical care are bad. I think most people will agree about this, although one may reach the same view by different routes. I shall not argue for this view. People can hold all sorts of eccentric positions, and perhaps from some of them it would not follow that death by starvation is in itself bad. It is difficult, perhaps impossible, to refute such positions, and so for brevity I will henceforth take this assumption as accepted. Those who disagree need read no further.

My next point is this: if it is in our power to prevent something bad from happening, without thereby sacrificing anything of comparable moral importance, we ought, morally, to do it.

By "without sacrificing anything of comparable moral importance" I mean without causing anything else comparably bad to happen, or doing something that is wrong in itself, or failing to promote some moral good, comparable in significance to the bad thing that we can prevent. This principle seems almost as uncontroversial as the last one. It requires us only to prevent what is bad, and to promote what is good, and it requires this of us only when we can do it without sacrificing anything that is, from the moral point of view, comparably important. I could even, as far as the application of my argument to the Bengal emergency is concerned, qualify the point so as to make it: if it is in our power to prevent something very bad from happening, without thereby sacrificing anything morally significant, we ought, morally, to do it. An application of this principle would be as follows: if I am walking past a shallow pond and see a child drowning in it, I ought to wade in and pull the child out. This will mean getting my clothes muddy, but this is insignificant, while the death of the child would presumably be a very bad thing.

The uncontroversial appearance of the principle just stated is deceptive. If it were acted upon, even in its qualified form, our lives, our society, and our world would be fundamentally changed. For the principle takes, firstly, no account of proximity or distance. It makes no moral difference whether the person I can help is a neighbor's child ten yards from me or a Bengali whose name I shall never know, ten thousand miles away. Secondly, the principle makes no distinction between cases in which I am the only person who could possibly do anything and cases in which I am just one among millions in the same position.

I do not think I need to say much in defense of the refusal to take proximity and distance into account. The fact that a person is physically near to us, so that we have personal contact with him, may make it more likely that we *shall* assist him, but this does not show that we *ought* to help him rather than another who happens to be further away. If we accept any principle of impartiality, universalizability, equality, or whatever, we cannot discriminate against someone merely because he is far away from us (or we are far away from him). Admittedly, it is possible that we are in a better position to judge what needs to be done to help a person near to us than one far away, and perhaps also to provide the assistance we judge to be necessary. If this were the case, it would be a reason for helping those near to us first. This may once have been a justification for being more concerned with the poor in one's town than with famine victims in India. Unfortunately for those who like to keep their moral responsibilities limited, instant communication and swift transportation have changed the situation. From the moral point of view, the development of the world into a "global village" has made an important, though still unrecognized, difference to our moral situation. Expert observers and supervisors, sent out by famine relief organizations or permanently stationed in famine-prone areas, can direct our aid to a refugee in Bengal almost as effectively as we could get it to someone in our own block. There would seem, therefore, to be no possible justification for discriminating on geographical grounds.

There may be a greater need to defend the second implication of my principle – that the fact that there are millions of other people in the same position, in respect to the Bengali refugees, as I am, does not make the situation significantly different from a situation in which I am the only person who can prevent something very bad from occurring. Again, of course, I admit that there is a psychological difference between the cases; one feels less guilty about doing nothing if one can point to others, similarly placed, who have also done nothing. Yet this can make no real difference to our moral obligations.[2] Should I consider that I am less obliged to pull the drowning child out of the pond if on looking around I see other people, no further away than I am, who have also noticed the child but are doing nothing? One has only to ask this question to see the absurdity of the view that numbers lesson obligation. It is a view that is an ideal excuse for inactivity; unfortunately most of the major evils – poverty, overpopulation, pollution – are problems in which everyone is almost equally involved.

The view that numbers do make a difference can be made plausible if stated in this way: if everyone in circumstances like mine gave £5 to the Bengal Relief Fund, there would be enough to provide food, shelter, and medical care for the refugees; there is no reason why I should give more than anyone else in the same circumstances as I am; therefore I have no obligation to give more than £5. Each premise in this argument is true, and the argument looks sound. It may convince us, unless we notice that it is based on a hypothetical premise, although the conclusion is not stated hypothetically. The argument would be sound if the conclusion were: if everyone in circumstances like mine were to give £5, I would have no obligation to give more than £5. If the conclusion were so stated, however, it would be obvious that the argument has no bearing on a situation in which it is not the case that everyone else gives £5. This, of course, is the actual situation. It is more or less certain that not everyone in circumstances like mine will give £5. So there will not be enough to provide the needed food, shelter, and medical care. Therefore by giving more than £5 I will prevent more suffering than I would if I gave just £5.

It might be thought that this argument has an absurd consequence. Since the situation appears to be that very few people are likely to give substantial amounts, it follows that I and everyone else in similar circumstances ought to give as much as possible, that is, at least up to the point at which by giving more one would begin to cause serious suffering for oneself and one's dependants – perhaps even beyond this point to the point of marginal utility, at which by giving more one would cause oneself and one's dependants as much suffering as one would prevent in Bengal. If everyone does this, however, there will be more than can be used for the benefit of the refugees, and some of the sacrifice will have been unnecessary. Thus, if everyone does what he ought to do, the result will not be as good as it would be if everyone did a little less than he ought to do, or if only some do all that they ought to do.

The paradox here arises only if we assume that the actions in question – sending money to the relief funds – are performed more or less simultaneously, and are also unexpected. For if it is to be expected that everyone is going to contribute something, then clearly each is not obliged to give as much as he would have been obliged to had others not been giving too. And if everyone is not acting more or less simultaneously, then those giving later will know how much more is needed, and will have no obligation to give more than is necessary to reach this amount. To say this is not to deny the principle that people in the same circumstances have the same obligations, but to point out that the fact that others have given, or may be expected to give, is a relevant circumstance: those giving after it has become known that many others are giving and those giving before are not in the same circumstances. So the seemingly absurd consequence of the principle I have put forward can occur only if people are in error about the actual circumstances – that is, if they think they are giving when others are not, but in fact they are giving when others are. The result of everyone doing what he really ought to do cannot be worse than the result of everyone doing less than he ought to do, although the result of everyone doing what he reasonably believes he ought to do could be.

If my argument so far has been sound, neither our distance from a preventable evil nor the number of other people who, in respect to that evil, are in the same situation as we are, lessens our obligation to mitigate or prevent that evil. I shall therefore take as established the principle I asserted earlier. As I have already said, I need to assert it only in its qualified form: if it is in our power to prevent something very bad from happening, without thereby sacrificing anything else morally significant, we ought, morally, to do it.

The outcome of this argument is that our traditional moral categories are upset. The traditional distinction between duty and charity cannot be drawn, or at least, not in the place we normally draw it. Giving money to the Bengal Relief Fund is regarded as an act of charity in our society. The bodies which collect money are known as "charities." These organizations see themselves in this way – if you send them a check, you will be thanked for your "generosity." Because giving money is regarded as an act of charity, it is not thought that there is anything wrong with not giving. The charitable man may be praised, but the man who is not charitable is not condemned. People do not feel in any way ashamed or guilty about spending money on new clothes or a new car instead of giving it to famine relief. (Indeed, the alternative does not occur to them.) This way of looking at the matter cannot be justified. When we buy new clothes not to keep ourselves warm but to look "well-dressed" we are not providing for any important need. We would not be sacrificing anything significant if we were to continue to wear our old clothes, and give the money to famine relief. By doing so, we would be preventing another person from starving. It follows from what I have said earlier that we ought to give money away, rather than spend it on clothes which we do not need to keep us warm. To do so is not charitable, or generous. Nor is it the kind of act which philosophers and theologians have called "supererogatory" – an act which it would be good to do, but not wrong not to do. On the contrary, we ought to give the money away, and it is wrong not to do so.

I am not maintaining that there are no acts which are charitable, or that there are no acts which it would be good to do but not wrong not to do. It may be possible to redraw the distinction between duty and charity in some other place. All I am arguing here is that the present way of drawing the distinction, which makes it an act of charity for a man living at the level of affluence which most people in the "developed nations" enjoy to give money to save someone else from starvation, cannot be supported. It is beyond the scope of my argument to consider whether the distinction should be redrawn or abolished altogether. There would be many other possible ways of drawing the distinction – for instance, one might decide that it is good to make other people as happy as possible, but not wrong not to do so.

Despite the limited nature of the revision in our moral conceptual scheme which I am proposing, the revision would, given the extent of both affluence and famine in the world today, have radical implications. These implications may lead to further objections, distinct from those I have already considered. I shall discuss two of these.

One objection to the position I have taken might be simply that it is too drastic a revision of our moral scheme. People do not ordinarily judge in the way I have suggested they should. Most people reserve their moral condemnation for those who violate some moral norm, such as the norm against taking another person's property. They do not condemn those who indulge in luxury instead of giving to famine relief. But given that I did not set out to present a morally neutral description of the way people make moral judgments, the way people do in fact judge has nothing to do with the validity of my conclusion. My conclusion follows from the principle which I advanced earlier, and unless that principle is rejected, or the arguments are shown to be unsound, I think the conclusion must stand, however strange it appears. It might, nevertheless, be interesting to consider why our society, and most other societies, do judge differently from the way I have suggested they should. In a wellknown article, J. O. Urmson suggests that the imperatives of duty, which tell us what we must do, as distinct from what it would be good to do but not wrong not to do, function so as to prohibit behavior that is intolerable if men are to live together in society.[3] This may explain the origin and continued existence of the present division between acts of duty and acts of charity. Moral attitudes are shaped by the needs of society, and no doubt society needs people who will observe the rules that make social existence tolerable. From the point of view of a particular society, it is essential to prevent violations of norms against killing, stealing, and so on. It is quite inessential, however, to help people outside one's own society.

If this is an explanation of our common distinction between duty and supererogation, however, it is not a justification of it. The moral point of view requires us to look beyond the interests of our own society. Previously, as I have already mentioned, this may hardly have been feasible, but it is quite feasible now. From the moral point of view, the prevention of the starvation of millions of people outside our society must be considered at least as pressing as the upholding of property norms within our society.

It has been argued by some writers, among them Sidgwick and Urmson, that we need to have a basic moral code which is not too far beyond the capacities of the ordinary man, for otherwise there will be a general breakdown of compliance with the moral code. Crudely stated, this argument suggests that if we tell people that they ought to refrain from murder and give everything they do not really need to famine relief, they will do neither, whereas if we tell them that they ought to refrain from murder and that it is good to give to famine relief but not wrong not to do so, they will at least refrain from murder. The issue here is: Where should we draw the line between conduct that is required and conduct that is good although not required, so as to get the best possible result? This would seem to be an empirical question, although a very difficult one. One objection to the Sidgwick–Urmson line of argument is that it takes insufficient account of the effect that moral standards can have on the decisions we make. Given a society in which a wealthy man who gives 5 percent of his income to famine relief is regarded as most generous, it is not surprising that a proposal that we all ought to give away half our incomes will be thought to be absurdly unrealistic. In a society which held that no man should have more than enough while others have less than they need, such a proposal might seem narrow-minded. What it is possible for a man to do and what he is likely to do are both, I think, very greatly influenced by what people around him are doing and expecting him to do. In any case, the possibility that by spreading the idea that we ought to be doing very much more than we are to relieve famine we shall bring about a general breakdown of moral behavior seems remote. If the stakes are an end to widespread starvation, it is worth the risk. Finally, it should be emphasized that these considerations are relevant only to the issue of what we should require from others, and not to what we ourselves ought to do.

The second objection to my attack on the present distinction between duty and charity is one which has from time to time been made against utilitarianism. It follows from some forms of utilitarian theory that we all ought, morally, to be working full time to increase the balance of happiness over misery. The position I have taken here would not lead to this conclusion in all circumstances, for if there were no bad occurrences that we could prevent without sacrificing something of comparable moral importance, my argument would have no application. Given the present conditions in many parts of the world, however, it does follow from my argument that we ought, morally, to be working full time to relieve great suffering of the sort that occurs as a result of famine or other disasters. Of course, mitigating circumstances can be adduced – for instance, that if we wear ourselves out through overwork, we shall be less effective than we would otherwise have been. Nevertheless, when all considerations of this sort have been taken into account, the conclusion remains: we ought to be preventing as much suffering as we can without sacrificing something else of comparable moral importance. This conclusion is one which we may be reluctant to face. I cannot see, though, why it should be regarded as a criticism of the position for which I have argued, rather than a criticism of our ordinary standards of behavior. Since most people are self-interested to some degree, very few of us are likely to do everything that we ought to do. It would, however, hardly be honest to take this as evidence that it is not the case that we ought to do it.

It may still be thought that my conclusions are so wildly out of line with what everyone else thinks and has always thought that there must be something wrong with the argument somewhere. In order to show that my conclusions, while certainly contrary to contemporary Western moral standards, would not have seemed so extraordinary at other times and in other places, I would like to quote a passage from a writer not normally thought of as a way-out radical, Thomas Aquinas.

Now, according to the natural order instituted by divine providence, material goods are provided for the satisfaction of of human needs. Therefore the division and appropriation of property, which proceeds from human law, must not hinder the satisfaction of man's necessity from such goods. Equally, whatever a man has in superabundance is owed, of natural right, to the poor for their sustenance. So Ambrosius says, and it is also to be found in the *Decretum Gratiani*: "The bread which you withhold belongs to the hungry; the clothing you shut away, to the naked; and the money you bury in the earth is the redemption and freedom of the penniless."[4]

I now want to consider a number of points, more practical than philosophical, which are relevant to the application of the moral conclusion we have reached. These points challenge not the idea that we ought to be doing all we can to prevent starvation, but the idea that giving away a great deal of money is the best means to this end.

It is sometimes said that overseas aid should be a government responsibility, and that therefore one ought not to give to privately run charities. Giving privately, it is said, allows the government and the noncontributing members of society to escape their responsibilities.

This argument seems to assume that the more people there are who give to privately organized famine relief funds, the less likely it is that the government will take over full responsibility for such aid. This assumption is unsupported, and does not strike me as at all plausible. The opposite view – that if no one gives voluntarily, a government will assume that its citizens are uninterested in famine relief and would not wish to be forced into giving aid – seems more plausible. In any case, unless there were a definite probability that by refusing to give one would be helping to bring about massive government assistance, people who do refuse to make voluntary contributions are refusing to prevent a certain amount of suffering without being able to point to any tangible beneficial consequence of their refusal. So the onus of showing how their refusal will bring about government action is on those who refuse to give.

I do not, of course, want to dispute the contention that governments of affluent nations should be giving many times the amount of genuine, no-strings-attached aid that they are giving now. I agree, too, that giving privately is not enough, and that we ought to be campaigning actively for entirely new standards for both public and private contributions to famine relief. Indeed, I would sympathize with someone who thought that campaigning was more important than giving oneself, although I doubt whether preaching what one does not practice would be very effective. Unfortunately, for many people the idea that "it's the government's responsibility" is a reason for not giving which does not appear to entail any political action either.

Another, more serious reason for not giving to famine relief funds is that until there is effective population control, relieving famine merely postpones starvation. If we save the Bengal refugees now, others, perhaps the children of these refugees, will face starvation in a few years' time. In support of this, one may cite the now well-known facts about the population explosion and the relatively limited scope for expanded production.

This point, like the previous one, is an argument against relieving suffering that is happening now, because of a belief about what might happen in the future; it is unlike the previous point in that very good evidence can be adduced in support of this belief about the future. I will not go into the evidence here. I accept that the earth cannot support indefinitely a population rising at the present rate. This certainly poses a problem for anyone who thinks it important to prevent famine. Again, however, one could accept the argument without drawing the conclusion that it absolves one from any obligation to do anything to prevent famine. The conclusion that should be drawn is that the best means of preventing famine, in the long run, is population control. It would then follow from the position reached earlier that one ought to be doing all one can to promote population control (unless one held that all forms of population control were wrong in themselves, or would have significantly bad consequences). Since there are organizations working specifically for population control, one would then support

them rather than more orthodox methods of preventing famine.

A third point raised by the conclusion reached earlier relates to the question of just how much we all ought to be giving away. One possibility, which has already been mentioned, is that we ought to give until we reach the level of marginal utility – that is, the level at which, by giving more, I would cause as much suffering to myself or my dependants as I would relieve by my gift. This would mean, of course, that one would reduce oneself to very near the material circumstances of a Bengali refugee. It will be recalled that earlier I put forward both a strong and a moderate version of the principle of preventing bad occurrences. The strong version, which required us to prevent bad things from happening unless in doing so we would be sacrificing something of comparable moral significance, does seem to require reducing ourselves to the level of marginal utility. I should also say that the strong version seems to me to be the correct one. I proposed the more moderate version – that we should prevent bad occurrences unless, to do so, we had to sacrifice something morally significant – only in order to show that, even on this surely undeniable principle, a great change in our way of life is required. On the more moderate principle, it may not follow that we ought to reduce ourselves to the level of marginal utility, for one might hold that to reduce oneself and one's family to this level is to cause something significantly bad to happen. Whether this is so I shall not discuss, since, as I have said, I can see no good reason for holding the moderate version of the principle rather than the strong version. Even if we accepted the principle only in its moderate form, however, it should be clear that we would have to give away enough to ensure that the consumer society, dependent as it is on people spending on trivia rather than giving to famine relief, would slow down and perhaps disappear entirely. There are several reasons why this would be desirable in itself. The value and necessity of economic growth are now being questioned not only by conservationists, but by economists as well.[5] There is no doubt, too, that the consumer society has had a distorting effect on the goals and purposes of its members. Yet looking at the matter purely from the point of view of overseas aid, there must be a limit to the extent to which we should deliberately slow down our economy; for it might be the case that if we gave away, say, 40 percent of our Gross National Product, we would slow down the economy so much that in absolute terms we would be giving less than if we gave 25 percent of the much larger GNP that we would have if we limited our contribution to this smaller percentage.

I mention this only as an indication of the sort of factor that one would have to take into account in working out an ideal. Since Western societies generally consider 1 percent of the GNP an acceptable level for overseas aid, the matter is entirely academic. Nor does it affect the question of how much an individual should give in a society in which very few are giving substantial amounts.

It is sometimes said, though less often now than it used to be, that philosophers have no special role to play in public affairs, since most public issues depend primarily on an assessment of facts. On questions of fact, it is said, philosophers as such have no special expertise, and so it has been possible to engage in philosophy without committing oneself to any position on major public issues. No doubt there are some issues of social policy and foreign policy about which it can truly be said that a really expert assessment of the facts is required before taking sides or acting, but the issue of famine is surely not one of these. The facts about the existence of suffering are beyond dispute. Nor, I think, is it disputed that we can do something about it, either through orthodox methods of famine relief or through population control or both. This is therefore an issue on which philosophers are competent to take a position. The issue is one which faces everyone who has more money than he needs to support himself and his dependants, or who is in a position to take some sort of political action. These categories must include practically every teacher and student of philosophy in the universities of the Western world. If philosophy is to deal with matters that are relevant to both teachers and students, this is an issue that philosophers should discuss.

Discussion, though, is not enough. What is the point of relating philosophy to public (and personal) affairs if we do not take our conclusions seriously? In this instance, taking our conclusion seriously means acting upon it. The philosopher will not find it any easier than anyone else to alter his attitudes and way of life to the extent that, if I am right, is involved in doing everything that we ought to be doing. At the very least, though, one can make a start. The philosopher who does so will have to sacrifice some of the benefits of the consumer society, but he can find compensation in the satisfaction of a way of life in which theory and practice, if not yet in harmony, are at least coming together.

Postscript

The crisis in Bangladesh that spurred me to write the above article is now of historical interest only, but the world food crisis is, if anything, still more serious. The huge grain reserves that were then held by the United States have vanished. Increased oil prices have made both fertilizer and energy more expensive in developing countries, and have made it difficult for them to produce more food. At the same time, their population has continued to grow. Fortunately, as I write now, there is no major famine anywhere in the world; but poor people are still starving in several countries, and malnutrition remains very widespread. The need for assistance is, therefore, just as great as when I first wrote, and we can be sure that without it there will, again, be major famines.

The contrast between poverty and affluence that I wrote about is also as great as it was then. True, the affluent nations have experienced a recession, and are perhaps not as prosperous as they were in 1971. But the poorer nations have suffered as least as much from the recession, in reduced government aid (because if governments decide to reduce expenditure, they regard foreign aid as one of the expendable items, ahead of, for instance, defense or public construction projects) and in increased prices for goods and materials they need to buy. In any case, compared with the difference between the affluent nations and the poor nations, the whole recession was trifling; the poorest in the affluent nations remained incomparably better off than the poorest in the poor nations.

So the case for aid, on both a personal and a governmental level, remains as great now as it was in 1971, and I would not wish to change the basic argument that I put forward then.

There are, however, some matters of emphasis that I might put differently if I were to rewrite the article, and the most important of these concerns the population problem. I still think that, as I wrote then, the view that famine relief merely postpones starvation unless something is done to check population growth is not an argument against aid, it is only an argument against the *type* of aid that should be given. Those who hold this view have the same obligation to give to prevent starvation as those who do not; the difference is that they regard assisting population control schemes as a more effective way of preventing starvation in the long run. I would now, however, have given greater space to the discussion of the population problem; for I now think that there is a serious case for saying that if a country refuses to take any steps to slow the rate of its population growth, we should not give it aid. This is, of course, a very drastic step to take, and the choice it represents is a horrible choice to have to make; but if, after a dispassionate analysis of all the available information, we come to the conclusion that without population control we will not, in the long run, be able to prevent famine or other catastrophes, then it may be more humane in the long run to aid those countries that are prepared to take strong measures to reduce population growth, and to use our aid policy as a means of pressuring other countries to take similar steps.

It may be objected that such a policy involves an attempt to coerce a sovereign nation. But since we are not under an obligation to give aid unless that aid is likely to be effective in reducing starvation or malnutrition, we are not under an obligation to give aid to countries that make no effort to reduce a rate of population growth that will lead to catastrophe. Since we do not force any nation to accept our aid, simply making it clear that we will not give aid where it is not going to be effective cannot properly be regarded as a form of coercion.

I should also make it clear that the kind of aid that will slow population growth is not just assistance with the setting up of facilities for dispensing contraceptives and performing sterilizations. It is also necessary to create the conditions under which people do not wish to have so many children. This will involve, among other things, providing greater economic security for people, particularly in their old age, so that they do not need the security of a large family to provide for them. Thus, the requirements of aid designed to reduce population growth and aid designed to eliminate starvation are by no means separate; they overlap, and the latter will often be a means to the former. The obligation of the affluent is, I believe, to do both. Fortunately, there are now many people in the foreign aid field, including those in the private agencies, who are aware of this.

One other matter that I should now put forward slightly differently is that my argument does, of course, apply to assistance with development, particularly agricultural development, as well as to direct famine relief. Indeed, I think the former is usually the better long-term investment. Although this was my view when I wrote the article, the fact that I started from a famine situation, where the need was for immediate food, has led some readers to suppose that the argument is only about giving food and not about other types of aid. This is quite mistaken, and my view is that the aid should be of whatever type is most effective.

On a more philosophical level, there has been some discussion of the original article which has been helpful in clarifying the issues and pointing to the areas in which more work on the argument is needed. In particular, as John Arthur has shown in "Famine Relief and the Ideal Moral Code" (included in this volume), something more needs to be said about the notion of "moral significance." The problem is that to give an account of this notion involves nothing less than a full-fledged ethical theory; and while I am myself inclined toward a utilitarian view, it was my aim in writing "Famine, Affluence, and Morality" to produce an argument which would appeal not only to utilitarians, but also to anyone who accepted the initial premises of the argument, which seemed to me likely to have a very wide acceptance. So I tried to get around the need to produce a complete ethical theory by allowing my readers to fill in their own version – within limits – of what is morally significant, and then see what the moral consequences are. This tactic works reasonably well with those who are prepared to agree that such matters as being fashionably dressed are not really of moral significance; but Arthur is right to say that people could take the opposite view without being obviously irrational. Hence, I do not accept Arthur's claim that the weak principle implies little or no duty of benevolence, for it will imply a significant duty of benevolence for those who admit, as I think most nonphilosophers and even off-guard philosophers will admit, that they spend considerable sums on items that by their own standards are of no moral significance. But I do agree that the weak principle is nonetheless too weak, because it makes it too easy for the duty of benevolence to be avoided.

On the other hand, I think the strong principle will stand, whether the notion of moral significance is developed along utilitarian lines, or once again left to the individual reader's own sincere judgment. In either case, I would argue against Arthur's view that we are morally entitled to give greater weight to our own interests and purposes simply because they are our own. This view seems to me contrary to the idea, now widely shared by moral philosophers, that some element of impartiality or universalizability is inherent in the very notion of a moral judgment. (For a discussion of the different formulations of this idea, and an indication of the extent to which they are in agreement, see R. M. Hare, "Rules of War and Moral Reasoning," *Philosophy and Public Affairs* 1, no. 2, 1972.) Granted, in normal circumstances, it may be better for everyone if we recognize that each of us will be primarily responsible for running our own lives and only secondarily responsible for others. This, however, is not a moral ultimate, but a secondary principle that derives from consideration of how a society may best order its affairs, given the limits of altruism in human beings. Such secondary principles are, I think, swept aside by the extreme evil of people starving to death.

Notes

1 There was also a third possibility: that India would go to war to enable the refugees to return to their lands. Since I wrote this essay, India has taken this way out. The situation is no longer that described above, but this does not affect my argument, as the next paragraph indicates.

2 In view of the special sense philosophers often give to the term, I should say that I use "obligation" simply as the abstract noun derived from "ought," so that "I have an obligation to" means no more, and no less, than "I ought to." This usage is in accordance with the definition of "ought" given by the *Shorter Oxford English Dictionary*: "the general verb to express duty or obligation." I do not think any issue of substance hangs on the way the term is used; sentences in which I use "obligation" could all be rewritten, although somewhat clumsily, as sentences in which a clause containing "ought" replaces the term "obligation."

3 J. O. Urmson, "Saints and Heroes," in *Essays in Moral Philosophy*, ed. Abraham I. Melden (Seattle: University of Washington Press, 1958), p. 214. For a related but significantly different view see also Henry Sidgwick, *The Methods of Ethics*, 7th edn (London: Dover Press, 1907), pp. 220–1, 492–3.

4 *Summa Theologica*, II–II, Question 66, Article 7, in *Aquinas, Selected Political Writings*, ed. A. P. d'Entrèves, trans. J. G. Dawson (Oxford: Basil Blackwell, 1948), p. 171.

5 See, for instance, John Kenneth Galbraith, *The New Industrial State* (Boston: Houghton Mifflin, 1967); and E. J. Mishan, *The Costs of Economic Growth* (New York: Praeger, 1967).

57

Famine Relief and the Ideal Moral Code

John Arthur

Introduction

What do those of us who are relatively affluent owe, from a moral standpoint, to those who are hungry, sick, and may die without assistance? Peter Singer claims that we ought to prevent evil whenever we can do so without sacrificing something of comparable moral significance. In doing so, he argues there is a duty to provide aid whenever others are in greater need and will suffer without our help.[1] Other philosophers, relying on the principle that all human life is of equal value, have reached similar conclusions.[2] My first concern, then, is to assess such arguments on their own terms, asking whether these argument do, in fact, establish a duty to give aid. I will argue, in response, that our moral "intuitions" include not only the commitments they emphasize, but also entitlements, which suggests that people who deserve or have rights to their earnings may be allowed to keep them.

But the fact that our accepted social moral code includes entitlements is not a complete answer, for it is possible that contemporary moral attitudes are mistaken and our current code is defective. So in the final sections I ask whether an "ideal" moral code would reject entitlements and desert in favor of Singer's principle, arguing that in fact it would not.

A Duty to Prevent Evil?

Some have argued that the ideal of treating people equally requires that we do much more to aid others than is usually supposed. Richard Watson, for example, emphasizes what he calls the "principle of equity." Since "all human life is of equal value," and difference in treatment should be "based on freely chosen actions and not accidents of birth or environment," he thinks that we have "equal rights to the necessities of life."[3] To distribute food unequally assumes that some lives are worth more than others, an assumption which, he says, we do not accept. Watson claims the "equity principle" should not be violated even to stop annihilation.

Is Watson correct that all life is of equal value? Did Adolfh Hitler and Martin Luther King, for example, lead equally valuable lives? Clearly one did far more good, the other far more harm; and who would deny that while King fought for people's rights, Hitler violated them on a massive scale? Nor are moral virtues like courage, kindness, and trustworthiness equally distributed among people. So there are many important senses in which people are not, in fact, morally equal: some lives are more valuable to others, and some people are just, generous and courageous while others are unjust, cheap, and cowardly.

Yet all the same the ideal of equality is often thought to be a cornerstone of morality and justice. But what does it mean to say all people are "equal?" It seems to me that we might have in mind one of two things. First is an idea that Thomas Jefferson expressed in the *Declaration of Independence*. "All men are created equal" meant, for him, that no man is the moral inferior of another, that, in other words, there are certain rights which all men share equally, including life and liberty. We are entitled to pursue our own lives without interference from others, just as no person is the natural slave of another. But, as Jefferson also knew, equality in that sense does not require equal distribution of the necessities of life, only that we not interfere with one another, allowing instead every person the liberty to pursue his own affairs, so long as he does not violate the rights of others.

Some people, however, have something different in mind when they speak of human equality. To develop this second idea, we will turn to Singer's argument in "Famine, Affluence, and Morality." In that essay, Singer argues that two general moral principles are widely accepted, and then that those principles imply an obligation to eliminate starvation.

The first of the two principles he thinks we accept is that "suffering and death from lack of food, shelter and medical care are bad." Some may be inclined to think that the mere existence of such an evil in itself places an obligation on others, but that is, of course, the problem which Singer addresses. I take it that he is not begging the question in this obvious way and will *argue* from the existence of evil to the obligation of others to eliminate it. But how, exactly, does he establish this? He claims the *greater moral evil principle* shows the connection. That principle states that:

> If it is in our power to prevent something bad from happening, without thereby sacrificing anything of

comparable moral importance, we ought, morally, to do it."[4]

In other words, people are entitled to keep their earnings only if there is no way for them to prevent a greater evil by giving them away. Providing others with food, clothing, and housing would generally be of more importance than buying luxuries, so the greater moral evil principle now requires substantial redistribution of wealth.

Certainly few of us live by that principle, although as Singer emphasizes that hardly shows we are *justified* in behaving that way. We often fail to live up to our own standards. Why does Singer think our shared morality requires that we follow the greater moral evil principle?

He begins with an analogy. Suppose you came across a child drowning in a shallow pond. Certainly we feel it would be wrong not to help. Even if saving a child meant we must dirty our clothes, we would emphasize that those clothes are not of comparable significance to the child's life. The greater moral evil principle thus seems a natural way of capturing why we think it would be wrong not to help.

But the argument for the greater moral evil principle is not limited to Singer's claim that it explains our feelings about the drowning child or that it appears "uncontroversial." Moral equality also enters the picture, in the following way.[5] Besides the Jeffersonian idea that we share certain rights equally, most of us are also attracted to another conception of equality, namely that like amounts of suffering (or happiness) are of equal significance, no matter who is experiencing them. I cannot reasonably say that, while my pain is no more severe than yours, I am somehow special and it's more objectively important that mine be alleviated.

But if we fail to give to famine relief and instead purchase a new car when the old one will do, or buy fancy clothes for a friend when his or her old ones are perfectly good, are we not assuming that the relatively minor enjoyment we or our friends may get is as important as another person's life? And that, it seems, is a form of prejudice; we are acting as if people were not equal in the sense that their interests deserve equal consideration. We are giving special consideration to ourselves or to our group, rather like a racist does. Equal consideration of interests thus leads naturally to the greater moral evil principle.

Entitlements

Equal consideration seems to require that we should prevent harm to others if in doing so we do not sacrifice anything of comparable moral importance. But there is also another idea which Singer ignores: the idea of entitlements – that I have rights or may justly deserving something – and these are also morally significant. For example, we could help others is by giving away body parts. While your life may be shortened by the loss of a kidney or less enjoyable if lived with only one eye, those costs are probably not comparable to the loss experienced by a person who will die without any kidney or who is totally blind. Or perhaps somebody needs to remain hooked up to you for an extended period of time while awaiting a transplant.[6] However, our code does not *require* such heroism; you are entitled to your second eye and kidney and to control who uses your body, and that entitlement blocks the inference from the fact you could prevent harm to the conclusion you ought to let others have or use your body.

We express these ideas in terms of rights; it's your body, you have a right to it, and that weighs against whatever duty you have to help. To give up your right to your kidney for a stranger is more than not required, it is heroic. Unless, of course, you have agreed to let the person use your body, which brings us to the next point.

There are two types of rights, negative and positive. Negative rights are rights against interference by others. The right to life, for example, is a right not to be killed by others; the right against assault is a right not to be physically harmed by others. Other negative rights include the right to one's body, to property, to privacy, and to religious freedom. These require only that others not interfere. Positive rights, however, are rights to receive some benefit. I agree to work for Jones. If Jones does then not pay me, then my right to receive a paycheck has been violated.

Negative rights are also natural or human, that is, they depend on what you are, not what you've done. For instance, all persons have the right to life. But any positive rights you have are not natural in this sense. They arise because others have promised, agreed, or contracted to do something for you. Consequently, the right not to be killed does not depend on anything you or anybody else has done; however, the right to be paid a wage arises only from prior agreements.

None of that is to say that rights, whether negative or positive, are beyond controversy. Rights come in a variety of shapes and sizes, and people often disagree about both their shape and size. And while some rights are part of our generally shared moral code and widely accepted, others are controversial and hotly disputed.

Normally, then, we seem to think that a duty to help strangers in need is not based on any *right* that person has, but rather on the general duty all people have to aid those in need. The person would have a right to aid only if someone had contracted or promised to protect the child, for instance, a baby sitter or lifeguard who had agreed to care for the child. If the child is harmed, then the parent would be doubly wronged. First, the sitter, like everybody else, should not cruelly or thoughtlessly let it drown. Second, unlike in Singer's example, the sitter has also violated the child's rights since the sitter promised to care for the child, and hence, assumed special obligations.

In deciding what to do, we must consider moral rights. Unfortunately, the greater moral evil principle ignores them. But that is not all we need consider, for our moral code expects us to help people in need *as well as* to respect negative and positive rights. My claim here is simply that we are sometimes entitled to invoke our own rights to justify our inaction. It we did not promise to help, and are in no way responsible for the person's situation, then we need not ignore our own rights and give away our savings to help distant strangers.

A second form of entitlement are "just deserts": sometimes people *deserve* to keep what they have acquired. Suppose an industrious farmer works hard and produces a surplus of food for the winter while a lazy neighbor spends the summer relaxing. Must our hard working farmer give the surplus away because that neighbor, who refused to work, will suffer? In some circumstances our normal moral attitudes would direct the farmer to help – but not necessarily. We must consider not only suffering and rights, but also just deserts. And even if the farmer's just desert is outweighed in some cases by the greater need of a neighbor, being outweighed is not the same as weighing nothing!

Just deserts can be negative (unwanted) as well as positive (desired). Nazi war criminals *deserved* punishment. In some cases other considerations – the fact that nobody will be deterred or that the criminal is old and harmless – might weigh against punishing them. However, that does not mean that just deserts are irrelevant, just that we've decided for other reasons to ignore them in this case. But again: a principle's being outweighed is not the same as its having no importance.

Our social moral code thus honors both the greater moral evil principle and entitlements. The former emphasizes equality, that comparable suffering is equally significant. It encourages us to impartially discern all the effects of our actions, to be forward looking. Entitlements, though, direct our attention to the past. Whether we have rights to money, property, or even our body depends on how we came to possess them. A thief may possess the money he has stolen, but that does not give him a right to it. Or perhaps a person has promised to trade something, which would again (under normal circumstances) mean loss of entitlement. Like rights, just desert is also backward-looking, emphasizing past effort or past transgressions that now warrant responses such as reward, gratitude, or punishment.

I am suggesting, then, that in acknowledging both equality and entitlements as well as the importance of preventing harm to others our social moral code pulls in different directions. But unless we are moral relativists, the mere fact that equality and entitlements are both part of our moral code does not in itself justify a person who relies on them, any more than the fact that our moral code once condemned racial mixing while condoning sexual discrimination and slavery should convince us that *those* principles are justified. We all assume (I trust) that the more enlightened moral code – the one we now subscribe to – is better in part just because it condemns discrimination and slavery. Because we know the rules defining acceptable behavior are continually changing, and sometimes changing for the better, we must allow for the replacement of inferior principles with more reasonable guidelines (and must also allow the possibility that our current moral views are mistaken).

Viewed in this way, Singer is urging us to reform our current social moral code – to reject entitlements, at least when they conflict with the greater moral evil principle. He is claiming that we cannot justify our practice of evaluating actions by looking backward to rights and just desert, rather than looking forward to the consequences of our action. Consequently, we should ask how we might justify the moral rules and principles comprising a society's moral code. Then we can determine whether entitlements are part of an ideal moral code.

The Concept of a Social Moral Code

I suggest that we understand a social moral code as a system of principles, rules and other standards designed to guide people's conduct. It is akin to other systems of rules and standards, like the rules of organizations. Social clubs, sports leagues, corporations, bureaucracies, professional associations, even *The* Organization all have standards governing the behavior of members. These rules also serve a purpose, though their functions will vary depending on the nature of the organization. Sanctions will also vary: violation of a university's code of conduct leads to one sort of punishment, while social clubs or the American Bar Association may impose different sanctions. And while some standards of conduct are limited to members of an organization, others, like law, etiquette and customs apply more broadly.

Let's look at these issues more closely, comparing morality with other rule-governed practices like law and etiquette. First, as I suggested, the form sanctions take vary among the different types of social practices.[7] While in our legal system transgressions are punished by fines, jail, or even execution, we encourage conformity to morality and etiquette through informal sanctions like praise, criticism, and ostracism. Moreover, while violation of a moral principle is always a serious affair, this is not necessarily so for violations of law, etiquette, or custom. Many of us think it unimportant whether a fork is on the left side of a plate or whether an outmoded and widely ignored Sunday closing law is violated. But we do not think that someone's violating a moral principle is trivial. Indeed, when moral principles lose their importance, they are "demoted" to mere custom.

Third, legal rules differ from morality, custom, and etiquette in that they include "constitutional" rules governing how laws are to be created, modified and eliminated.[8] Under the US Constitution, for instance, if Congress acts to change the tax laws, then the rules are effective as of the date stated in the statute. Socially accepted moral rules, etiquette, and customs may also change, of course, but not according to any specified procedure.

So far, then, we've noted that different codes and standards of behavior can vary widely, along a number of dimensions. Some apply narrowly, only to members of a specific organization, while others extend broadly. And while all codes include rules or other standards to guide conduct, the sanctions that are imposed by different codes differ widely, as do the ways rules change and the importance assigned to violations of the different codes.

Finally, standards and norms serve a purpose, although their purposes will vary with the organization or practice in question. Rules governing games, for example, are often changed, either informally among players or by a governing organization like the National Football League. This is done to more effectively achieve the game's goals, although even the goals are sometimes open to dispute. Sometimes, for example, rules may be changed to improve safety (car design in auto racing) but at other times the changes may represent at attempt to make the sport less safe – but more exciting, or again, rules might be changed to accommodate younger players, such as abolishing the walk in kid's baseball.

Rules of games and organizations, like legal and moral rules and principles, can change to serve their purposes more effectively. However – and this is crucial – since there can be deep disagreement about the purposes of these practices, people may disagree about the rules: about what the rules require, about when there should be exceptions and about when the rules can be ignored. Disputes about rules governing a social group, for instance, may rest on deeper, sometimes hidden disagreements about the purposes of the organization, just as differences between fundamentalists and liberals over religious rules and principles can reveal disagreements about the purposes of religious practices.

This is crucial for understanding disagreements about morality. Consider the moral rule that forbids homosexual behavior. If people could agree that the rule serves no useful purpose, but only increases the guilt, shame, and social rejection borne by a significant portion of society, then we would have good reason to abandon this rule condemning homosexuality. However, others may think morality serves to encourage behavior compatible with God's will or with "natural" law. These people would likely oppose such a change and regard their attitudes toward homosexuality as warranted.

So I am suggesting that there is a connection between what we ought to do and how well a code serves its purposes. If we agree about the purpose of a practice, then we will have reason to follow any rule that serves the goals of that practice. Conversely, if a rule frustrates the purposes of an institution or practice, we should not support it, teach it, or to follow it. Applying this to morality, I can now state a conception of a right action: Any action is right if and only if it conforms with an ideal moral code for our society. Before we say precisely what this requires, we must consider what, exactly, an *ideal* moral code is. That requires knowing what we hope to accomplish by creating, teaching and enforcing a social moral code.

The Ideal Social Moral Code

One possibility, already mentioned, is that morality's purpose depends on God – that morality serves to encourage people to act in accord with God's will. However, I will suggest, and briefly defend, the view that the ideal moral code is the one that, when recognized and taught by members of society, would have the best consequences. By best consequences, I mean that it would most effectively promote the collective well-being of those living under it. (It's worth noting that a religious person need not reject this conception. She might reason that God would want to promote the general well-being.)

This idea – that the code serves the purpose of promoting well-being – seems central to both law and morality. Both *discourage* many of the same acts – killing, robbing, and beating – while *encouraging* other actions – repaying debts, keeping important agreements, and providing for one's children. The reason for rules discouraging killing and assault are clear enough; a society without such rules could not survive let alone provide a valuable life for its members. This approach is further substantiated when we think about the ways children are taught it is wrong to hit a baby brother or sister. Parents typically explain the rules in terms of their purposes: hitting brother hurts him. In short, these rules of morality and law function to keep people from unjustifiably harming one another, and ultimately to promote the well-being of people living under them. That is why we teach these rules to children, and why we follow them as adults.

Likewise for the rules encouraging certain behavior. The well-being of ourselves, our friends, our family, and indeed, our society depends on people generally keeping promises and fulfilling their agreements. Without laws and moral rules to encourage this behavior, the institutions of promising and contracting would likely be unsustainable, and without those institutions, we would be much worse-off.

Moral rules thus promote our welfare by discouraging acts of violence and other damaging behavior and by creating and maintaining valuable social conventions. They also perform the same service for our family, friends, and indeed all of us. A society wholly *without* legal and moral codes would likely deteriorate into a Hobbesian state of nature in which life is "solitary, poor, nasty, brutish and short."

Many people will find this uncontroversial, thinking that they have reason to support and follow a moral code that promotes the general welfare. But what more might be said to those who remain skeptical? One suggestion, from David Hume, emphasizes the importance of sentiment and feeling in human actions. Hume claimed humans can be moved to act only by feelings and sentiment. On this view people are moral because human nature is not simply selfish, but also exhibits a sentimental attachment to the well-being of others. This is apparent, he reasoned, from the fact that we

> frequently bestow praise on virtuous actions, performed in very distant ages and remote countries; where the utmost subtlety of imagination would not discover any appearance of self-interest, or find any connexion with our present happiness and security with events so widely separated from us.[9]

Hume's claim makes sense. We have evidence that sympathy and concern for others' well-being are a natural part of our biological heritage. Some biologists, for example, think altruism encourages the survival of many higher animals.[10] Other biologists claim we acquire the sentiments through learning. Benevolence originates naturally, via classical conditioning: we first experience our own pain, and then associate it with the pain of others.[11]

But whatever the explanation for sympathy, Hume concludes from this that we must renounce any moral theory "which accounts for every moral sentiment by the principle of self-love. We must adopt a more public affection, and allow, that the interests of society are not, even on their own account, indifferent to us."[12] Moral approval and condemnation, Hume is claiming, rest finally on sentiments rather than reason, and our sentiments lead us to be concerned not merely with our own happiness, but the happiness of all humanity. Given this universal sympathy for others, he concludes that it is natural to understand a social moral code as promoting everybody's well-being.

But suppose that some people do not share these sympathies for others. Such an egoist might claim that the best code would be one maximizing *his own* welfare. He might think that this "ideal" code, which he would support, would give him absolute power over the lives and property of others. How should others, who think the ideal code is the one that would have the best consequences for everybody, respond to that person? One might simply acknowledge that we cannot reason with, let alone refute, him. But it would be nice to have a further response. And we do.

Suppose we asked this rational egoist concerned only to secure his own welfare whether he could *publicly* support a moral code benefiting only himself? Could he expect others to accept the idea that society should recognize and teach a code serving only his interest? Would he be rational to spend time advocating that such a code be taught in schools, or advocating it to others? Of course not. An egoist could not rationally advocate such a code. Thus, even the egoist would be driven toward a conception of the ideal moral code that would not promote merely his own well-being. Even the egoist's conception of the ideal moral code will look more like the one that other people with more normal, sympathetic feelings would find ideal, namely the one that would have the best consequences for everybody. That is because a social moral code must be one that could function in the world, which requires that it be able to win general public support by people who propose to teach and enforce the code for society as a whole.

Now we are in the position to assess the issue with which we began: Would an ideal moral code include principles respecting rights and just deserts, or would it, as Singer suggested, reject them completely in favor of the greater moral evil principle? The answer depends on the fact that an ideal moral code must not only be one that can win public support but must

also be workable and practical. That is, the ideal code must be one that works for people as they are, or at least as they can be reasonably encouraged to become.

Are Rights Part of the Ideal Code?

Initially, it might seem that rights and just desert would not be part of an ideal code. After all, some would claim a code which included only the greater moral evil principle would have the best overall consequences. I will argue, however, that the ideal code would not ignore rights for two reasons, each of which arises from the fact that the code must employ realistic, accurate assumptions about human beings and our life in this world.

Recall the earlier discussion of self-love and altruism. Although I did suggest, following Hume, that we ought not ignore people's altruistic side, it is also important that we not assume people are *more* altruistic than they are. Moral (or legal) rules that would work only for angels are not the ideal ones for human beings. While we do care about others' well-being, we care especially about those we love; and we also care deeply about own lives. It will therefore be difficult, to put it mildly, to get people to accept and support a code requiring that they give away their savings or extra organs to a stranger simply because doing so would avoid substantial evil. Many people would simply ignore this rule. They care too deeply about their own lives and welfare, as well as the welfare of loved ones.

More precisely, were the moral code to expect such saintliness, three results would likely follow. First, since few would live up to the rules, people would feel guilty. Second, the code would encourage conflict between those who meet these moral expectations and those who do not. Finally, a realistic code that doesn't demand too much might actually result in more giving. Consider the following analogy. People might well buy less candy if they are permitted to buy it occasionally – but are praised for spending on other things – than if they are prohibited from buying candy altogether. We cannot assume that making what is now treated as charity into a moral requirement will always encourage such behavior. By giving people the right to keep their property, yet praising those who do not exercise the right but help others instead, we have found a good balance.

Furthermore, an ideal moral code must not assume people are more objective, informed, and unbiased than they are. People often rationalize their behavior when their interests are at stake. For example, we might think we should encourage people to break promises whenever doing so would have the best consequences on the ground that such a rule would lead to more well-being. However, this ignores people's tendency to give special weight to their own welfare, and their inability to be unbiased when tracing the effects of different actions. So while an ideal code would not teach that promises must never be broken no matter what the consequences, we also would not want to encourage breaking promises whenever people can convince themselves it would produce less evil to do so.

Similar considerations apply to property. Suppose someone contemplates preventing an evil to herself or himself by stealing from a large store where the object wouldn't be missed. Such theft could easily be rationalized by the greater moral evil principle. So although a particular act of theft may sometimes be welfare maximizing, it does not follow that a *principle* like Singer's should respect the right to property. To recognize and teach that theft is right whenever the robber is preventing greater evil, even to himself, would work only if people were far more objective, less liable to self-deception, and more knowledgeable about the long-term consequences of their actions than we are. So here again, including rights in our moral code serves a useful role – it discourages the tendency to underestimate the harm we may cause to others and to exaggerate the benefits that may accrue to ourselves.

Is Just Desert Part of the Ideal Moral Code?

Similar practical considerations suggest the ideal moral code would also include just desert.

Recall the case of the farmers. Most of us feel that while it would be nice of the hard worker to help out a lazy neighbor, the worker also has reason – based on his past effort – to refuse. As in the previous discussion of rights, our ideal code must be realistic and practical, and should not assume people are more altruistic, informed, or objective than they are. For instance, we know that many people do not especially enjoy working and earning a living; they would often prefer to do something else. Yet we must work if we hope to have a decent life. Therefore, the ideal moral code should include incentives to work. A moral code can encourage hard work by allowing people to keep a large part of what they earn, both by respecting their rights and acknowledging the principle of just desert.

Suppose we eliminated the notion of deserving what we work for from our code, and asked people to follow the greater moral evil rule instead. What might happen? There are three possibilities. One is that they continue to produce as before, only this time motivated by the desire – derived from their social moral code – to prevent whatever evil they can, as long as the cost to them is not a greater evil. But that seems unrealistic. Although people are not egoists, neither are they that altruistic.

Consequently, we could expect one of the other outcomes. One is that people would stop working as hard, feeling that it is no longer worth the effort if they are morally required to give away all but what they can use without producing a greater evil. For instance, suppose the tax system took away all income that could be used to prevent a greater evil befalling others. People would likely work less and produce fewer useful commodities, with the result that everyone's well-being would decline. The other possibility is that people would fail to follow the moral code. This would lead to widespread guilt among those who don't contribute, and heightened resentment by those (few?) who do follow the code. In either case, replacing the principle of just desert with the greater moral evil principle would lead to worse consequences. Like rights, the principle of just desert is also part of an ideal code.

Conclusion

Initially I tried to show that our moral code is a bit schizophrenic. It pulls us in opposite directions, sometimes toward helping people who are in need and other times toward the view that rights and desert justify keeping things we have even if giving it away would avert a greater evil. This apparent inconsistency led us to ask if our emphasis on rights and desert are really defensible. To pursue that question, I suggested we think about the idea of a social moral code and the purposes it serves. In the last sections I argued that our current code's emphasis on rights and desert is defensible once we understand that the ideal moral code must be practical, for only then could it really have the overall best consequences. Understood in this way, the ideal code would not reject entitlements in favor of the greater moral evil rule. Our moral code should encourage effort and should not fail by unrealistically assuming that people are more altruistic, informed, or objective than they are. Hence, an ideal code recognizes people's rights and encourages distribution according to desert. The ideal moral code would therefore not teach people to seek the best consequences in each case. But neither would an ideal moral code allow people to overlook those in desperate need by making entitlements absolute.

But where would it draw the line? Although it is hard to know the following seems a plausible answer: we should require people to help strangers when there is no *substantial* cost to themselves, that is, when what they are sacrificing would not mean *significant* reduction in their own or their family's welfare. Since most people's savings accounts and nearly everybody's second kidney are not insignificant, entitlements would in those cases outweigh another's need. But if what is at stake is truly trivial, as dirtying one's clothes would normally be, then an ideal moral code would not allow rights to override the greater evil that can be prevented.

That code might also plausibly distinguish between cases in which the evil is directly present (as in the drowning child) and in those in which it isn't present (as with distant people). The reason, of course, is again practical: people will be more likely to help those with whom they have direct contact and can see immediately the evil they will prevent than they are to help distant strangers. So while such a distinction may seem morally arbitrary, viewed from the perspective of an ideal moral code it makes good sense.

Despite our code's unclear and sometimes schizophrenic posture, these conclusions about the requirements of an ideal moral code that we would be rational to support are in line with our current moral attitudes. We tend to fault selfish people who give little or nothing to charity, and expect those with more to give more. Yet we do not ask people to make large sacrifices of their own or their family's well-being in order to aid distant strangers. What Singer's arguments do remind us of, however, is that entitlements are not absolute and we all have some duty to help. But the greater moral evil rule expresses only part of the story, and is not needed to make that point.

Notes

This is a slightly abridged version of an earlier paper by the same name. Copyright © 1996 by John Arthur.

1 Peter Singer, "Famine, Affluence, and Morality," *Philosophy and Public Affairs* 1/3 (1972): 229–43.
2 For example Richard Watson, "Reason and Morality in a World of Limited Food" in William Aiken and Hugh LaFollette, eds., *World Hunger and Moral Obligation* (Englewood Cliffs, NJ: Prentice-Hall, 1977).
3 Ibid., pp. 117–18.

4 Singer also offers a "weak" version of this principle that, it seems to me, is too weak. It requires giving aid only if the gift is of no moral significance to the giver. But since even minor embarrassment or small amounts of unhappiness are not completely without moral importance, this weak principle would imply no obligation to aid, even to the drowning child.
5 See Singer's, "Postscript" to "Famine, Affluence and Morality" in Aiken and LaFollette, *World Hunger and Moral Obligation*, p. 36.

6   Judith Jarvis Thomson, "A Defense of Abortion," *Philosophy and Public Affairs* 1/1 (1971).

7   H. L. A. Hart, *The Concept of Law*, 2nd edition (Oxford: Oxford University Press, 1995).

8   But Ronald Dworkin has argued that legal interpretation is partly moral and normative, making this claim more difficult to make in that context. See, for example, *Law's Empire* (Cambridge: Harvard University Press, 1986), chs. 2 and 7.

9   David Hume, *An Enquiry Concerning the Principles of Morals*, Sect. V, Part I, 175.

10 Stephen Jay Gould, "So Cleverly Kind an Animal" in *Ever Since Darwin* (New York: W. W. Norton Co., 1977).

11 Richard B. Brandt, *A Theory of the Good and the Right* (New York: Oxford University Press, 1979).

12 Hume, *An Enquiry Concerning the Principles of Morals*, Sect. V, Part II, 178.

58

Eradicating Systemic Poverty: Brief for a Global Resources Dividend

Thomas W. Pogge

Article 25: Everyone has the right to a standard of living adequate for the health and well-being of himself and of his family, including food, clothing, housing and medical care.

Article 28: Everyone is entitled to a social and international order in which the rights and freedoms set forth in this Declaration can be fully realized.

Universal Declaration of Human Rights

1 Introduction: Radical Inequality and Our Responsibility

One great challenge to any morally sensitive person today is the extent and severity of global poverty. Among six billion human beings, 790 million lack adequate nutrition, one billion lack access to safe water, 2.4 billion lack basic sanitation (UNDP, 2000, p. 30); more than 880 million lack access to basic health services (UNDP, 1999, p. 22); one billion are without adequate shelter and two billion without electricity (UNDP, 1998, p. 49). 250 million children between 5 and 14 do wage work outside their household – often under harsh or cruel conditions – as soldiers, prostitutes, or domestic servants, or in agriculture, construction, textile or carpet production (World Bank, 2000, p. 62).

About one billion adults are illiterate (UNDP, 2000, p. 30). Roughly one third of all human deaths, some 50,000 daily, are due to poverty-related causes and thus avoidable insofar as poverty is avoidable (UNICEF, 1999; WHO 2000). If the US had its proportional share of these deaths, poverty would kill some 820,000 of its citizens a year – more each month than were killed during the entire Vietnam War.

There are two ways of conceiving global poverty as a moral challenge to us: We may be failing to fulfill our *positive* duty to help persons in acute distress. And we may be failing to fulfill our more stringent *negative* duty not to uphold injustice, not to contribute to or profit from the unjust impoverishment of others.

These two views differ in important ways. The positive formulation is easier to substantiate. It need be shown only that they are very badly off, that we are very much better off, and that we could relieve some of their suffering without becoming badly-off ourselves. But this ease comes at a price: Some who accept the positive formulation think of the moral reasons it provides as weak and discretionary and thus do not feel obligated to promote worthy causes, especially costly ones. Many feel entitled, at least, to support good causes of their choice – their church or alma mater, cancer research or the environment – rather than putting themselves out for total strangers half a world away, with whom they share no bond of community or culture. It is of some importance, therefore, to investigate whether existing global poverty involves our violating a *negative* duty. This is important for us, if we want to lead a moral life, and important also for the poor, because it will make a great difference to them whether we affluent do or do not see global poverty as an injustice we help maintain.

Some believe that the mere fact of *radical inequality* shows a violation of negative duty. Radical inequality may be defined as involving five elements (extending Nagel, 1977):

1 The worse-off are very badly off in absolute terms.
2 They are also very badly off in relative terms – very much worse off than many others.
3 The inequality is impervious: It is difficult or impossible for the worse-off substantially to improve their lot; and most of the better-off never experience life at the bottom for even a few months and have no vivid idea of what it is like to live in that way.
4 The inequality is pervasive: It concerns not merely some aspects of life, such as the climate or access to natural beauty or high culture, but most aspects or all.
5 The inequality is avoidable: The better-off can improve the circumstances of the worse-off without becoming badly off themselves.

The phenomenon of global poverty clearly exemplifies radical inequality as defined. But I doubt that these five conditions suffice to invoke more than a merely positive duty. And I suspect most citizens of the developed west would also find them insufficient. They might appeal to the following parallel: Suppose we discovered people on Venus who are very badly off, and suppose we could help them at little cost to ourselves. If we did nothing, we would surely violate a positive duty of beneficence. But we would not be violating a negative duty of justice, because we would not be *contributing* to the perpetuation of their misery.

This point could be further disputed. But let me here accept the Venus argument and examine what *further* conditions must be satisfied for radical inequality to manifest an injustice that involves violation of a negative duty by the better-off. I see three plausible approaches to this question, invoking three different grounds of injustice: the *effects of shared institutions, the uncompensated exclusion from the use of natural resources*, and *the effects of a common and violent history*. These approaches exemplify distinct and competing political philosophies. We need nevertheless not decide among them here if, as I will argue, the following two theses are true. First, *all three approaches classify the existing radical inequality as unjust and its coercive maintenance as a violation of negative duty*. Second, *all three approaches can agree on the same feasible reform of the status quo as a major step toward justice*. If these two theses can be supported, then it may be possible to gather adherents of the dominant strands of western normative political thought into a coalition focused on eradicating global poverty through the introduction of a Global Resources Dividend or GRD.

2   Three Grounds of Injustice

2.1   The effects of shared institutions

The first approach (suggested in O'Neill, 1985; Nagel, 1977; and Pogge, 1989, §24) puts forward three additional conditions:

6 There is a shared institutional order that is shaped by the better-off and imposed on the worse-off.
7 This institutional order is implicated in the reproduction of radical inequality in that there is a feasible institutional alternative under which so severe and extensive poverty would not persist.
8 The radical inequality cannot be traced to extra-social factors (such as genetic handicaps or natural disasters) which, as such, affect different human beings differentially.

Present radical global inequality meets Condition 6 in that the global poor live within a worldwide states system based on internationally recognized territorial domains, interconnected through a global network of market trade and diplomacy. The presence and relevance of shared institutions is shown by how dramatically we affect the circumstances of the global poor through investments, loans, trade, bribes, military aid, sex tourism, culture exports, and much else. Their very survival often crucially depends on our consumption choices, which may determine the price of their foodstuffs and their opportunities to find work. In sharp contrast to the Venus case, we are causally deeply involved in their misery. This does not mean that we should hold ourselves responsible for the remoter effects of our economic decisions. These effects reverberate around the world and interact with the effects of countless other such decisions and thus cannot be traced, let alone predicted. Nor need we draw the dubious and utopian conclusion that global interdependence must be undone by isolating states or groups of states from one another. But we must be concerned with how the rules structuring international interactions foreseeably affect the incidence of extreme poverty. The developed countries, thanks to their vastly superior military and economic strength, control these rules and therefore share responsibility for their foreseeable effects.

Condition 7 involves tracing the poverty of individuals in an explanatory way to the structure of social institutions. This exercise is familiar in regard to national institutions, whose explanatory importance has been powerfully illustrated by domestic regime changes in China, Eastern Europe, and elsewhere. In regard to the global economic order, the exercise is unfamiliar and shunned even by economists. This is due in part, no doubt, to powerful resistance against seeing oneself as connected to the unimaginable deprivations suffered by the global poor. This resistance biases us against data, arguments, and researchers liable to upset our preferred world view and thus biases the competition for professional success against anyone exploring the wider causal context of global poverty. This bias is reinforced by our cognitive tendency to overlook the causal significance of stable background

factors (e.g., the role of atmospheric oxygen in the outbreak of a fire), as our attention is naturally drawn to geographically or temporally variable factors. Looking at the incidence of poverty worldwide, we are struck by dramatic local changes and international variations, which point to local explanatory factors. The heavy focus on such local factors then encourages the illusion, succumbed to by Rawls (1999, p. 108), for example, that they completely explain global poverty.

This illusion conceals how profoundly local factors and their effects are influenced by the existing global order. Yes, a culture of corruption pervades the political system and the economy of many developing countries. But is this culture unrelated to the fact that most affluent countries have, until quite recently, allowed their firms to bribe foreign officials and even made such bribes tax-deductible?[1] – Yes, developing countries have shown themselves prone to oppressive government and to horrific wars and civil wars. But is the frequency of such brutality unrelated to the international arms trade, and unrelated to international rules that entitle anyone holding effective power in such a country to borrow in its name and to sell ownership rights in its natural resources (Wantchekon, 1999)? – Yes, the world is diverse, and poverty is declining in some countries and worsening in others. But the larger pattern is quite stable, reaching far back into the colonial era: "The income gap between the fifth of the world's people living in the richest countries and the fifth in the poorest was 74 to 1 in 1997, up from 60 to 1 in 1990 and 30 to 1 in 1960. [Earlier] the income gap between the top and bottom countries increased from 3 to 1 in 1820 to 7 to 1 in 1870 to 11 to 1 in 1913" (UNDP, 1999, p. 3). The affluent countries have been using their power to shape the rules of the world economy according to their own interests and thereby have deprived the poorest populations of a fair share of global economic growth (Pogge, 2001) – quite avoidably so, as the GRD proposal shows.

Global poverty meets Condition 8 insofar as the global poor, if only they had been born into different social circumstances, would be just as able and likely to lead healthy, happy, and productive lives as the rest of us. The root cause of their suffering is their abysmal social starting position which does not give them much of a chance to become anything but poor, vulnerable, and dependent – unable to give their children a better start than they had had themselves.

It is because the three additional conditions are met that existing global poverty has, according to the first approach, the special moral urgency we associate with negative duties, why we should take it much more seriously than otherwise similar suffering on Venus. The reason is that the citizens and governments of the affluent countries – whether intentionally or not – are imposing a global institutional order that foreseeably and avoidably reproduces severe and widespread poverty. The worse-off are not merely poor and often starving, but are *being* impoverished and starved under our shared institutional arrangements, which inescapably shape their lives.

The first approach can be presented in a consequentialist guise, as in Bentham, or in a contractualist guise, as in Rawls or Habermas. In both cases, the central thought is that social institutions are to be assessed in a forward-looking way, by reference to their effects. In the present international order, billions are born into social starting positions that give them extremely low prospects for a fulfilling life. Their misery could be justified only if there were no institutional alternative under which such massive misery would be avoided. If, as the GRD proposal shows, there is such an alternative, then we must ascribe this misery to the existing global order and therefore ultimately to ourselves. As, remarkably, Charles Darwin wrote in reference to his native Britain: "If the misery of our poor be caused not by laws of nature, but by our own institutions, great is our sin" (quoted in Gould, 1991, p. 19).

2.2 Uncompensated exclusion from the use of natural resources

The second approach adds (in place of Conditions 6–8) only one condition to the five of radical inequality:

9 The better-off enjoy significant advantages in the use of a single natural resource base from whose benefits the worse-off are largely, and without compensation, excluded.

Currently, appropriation of wealth from our planet is highly uneven. Affluent people use vastly more of the world's resources, and they do so unilaterally, without giving any compensation to the global poor for their disproportionate consumption. Yes, the affluent often pay for the resources they use, such as imported crude oil. But these payments go to other affluent people, such as the Saudi family or the Nigerian kleptocracy, with very little, if anything, trickling down to the global poor. So the question remains: What entitles a global elite to use up the world's natural resources on mutually agreeable terms while leaving the global poor empty-handed?

Defenders of capitalist institutions have developed conceptions of justice that support rights to unilateral appropriation of disproportionate shares of resources while accepting that all inhabitants of the earth ultimately have equal claims to its resources. These conceptions are based on the thought that such rights are justified if all are better off with them than anyone would be if appropriation were limited to proportional shares.

This pattern of justification is exemplified with particular clarity in John Locke (cf. also Nozick, 1974, ch. 4). Locke is assuming that, in a state of nature without money, persons are subject to the moral constraint that their unilateral appropriations must always leave "enough, and as good" for others, that is, must be confined to a proportional share (Locke, 1689, §27 §33). This so-called Lockean Proviso may however be lifted with universal consent (ibid., §36). Locke subjects such a lifting to a second-order proviso, which requires that the rules of human coexistence may be changed only if all can *rationally* consent to the alteration, that is, only if everyone will be better off under the new rules than anyone would be under the old. And he claims that the lifting of the enough-and-as-good constraint through the general acceptance of money does satisfy this second-order proviso: A day laborer in England feeds, lodges, and is clad better than a king of a large fruitful territory in the Americas (ibid., §41 §37).

It is hard to believe that Locke's claim was true in his time. In any case, it is surely false on the global plane today. Billions are born into a world where all accessible resources are already owned by others. It is true that they can rent out their labor and then buy natural resources on the same terms as the affluent can. But their educational and employment opportunities are almost always so restricted that, no matter how hard they work, they can barely earn enough for their survival and certainly cannot secure anything like a proportionate share of the world's natural resources. The global poor get to share the burdens resulting from the degradation of our natural environment while having to watch helplessly as the affluent distribute the planet's abundant natural wealth amongst themselves. With average annual per capita income of about $82, corresponding to the purchasing power of $326 in the US, the poorest fifth of humankind are today just about as badly off, economically, as human beings could be while still alive.[2] It is then not true, what according to Locke and Nozick would need to be true, that all are better off under the existing appropriation and pollution rules than anyone would be with the Lockean Proviso. According to the second approach, the citizens and governments of the affluent states are therefore violating a negative duty of justice when they, in collaboration with the ruling elites of the poor countries, coercively exclude the poor from a proportional resource share.

2.3 The effects of a common and violent history

The third approach adds one condition to the five of radical inequality:

10 The social starting positions of the worse-off and the better-off have emerged from a single historical process that was pervaded by massive grievous wrongs.

The present circumstances of the global poor are significantly shaped by a dramatic period of conquest and colonization, with severe oppression, enslavement, even genocide, through which the native institutions and cultures of four continents were destroyed or severely traumatized. This is not to say (or to deny) that affluent descendants of those who took part in these crimes bear some special restitutive responsibility toward impoverished descendants of those who were victims of these crimes. The thought is rather that we must not uphold extreme inequalities in social starting positions when the allocation of these positions depends upon historical processes in which moral principles and legal rules were massively violated. A morally deeply tarnished history should not be allowed to result in *radical* inequality.

This third approach is independent of the others. For suppose we reject the other two approaches and affirm that radical inequality is morally acceptable when it comes about pursuant to rules of the game that are morally at least somewhat plausible and observed at least for the most part. The existing radical inequality is then still condemned by the third approach on the ground that the rules were in fact massively violated through countless horrible crimes whose momentous effects cannot be surgically neutralized decades and centuries later (cf. Nozick, 1974, p. 231).

Friends of the present distribution sometimes claim that standards of living, in Africa and Europe for instance, would be approximately the same if Africa had never been colonized. Even if this claim were both clear and true, it would still be ineffective because the argument I have sketched applies to persons, not to societies or continents. If world history had transpired without colonization and enslavement, then there would perhaps now be affluent people in Europe and poor ones in Africa, much like in the Venus scenario. But these would be persons and populations quite different from the ones who are now actually living there. So we cannot tell starving Africans that *they* would be starving and *we* would be affluent even if the crimes of colonialism had never occurred. Without these crimes there would not be the actually existing radical inequality which consists in *these* persons being affluent and *those* being extremely poor.

So the third approach, too, leads to the conclusion that the existing radical inequality is unjust, that coercively upholding it violates a negative duty, and that we have urgent moral reason to eradicate global poverty.

3 A Moderate Proposal

The reform proposal now to be sketched is meant to support my second thesis: that the status quo can be reformed in a way that all three approaches would recognize as a major step toward justice. But it is also needed to close gaps in my argument for the first thesis: The proposal should show that the existing radical inequality can be traced to the structure of our global economic order (Condition 7). And it should also show that Condition 5 is met; for, according to all three approaches, the status quo is unjust only if we can improve the circumstances of the global poor without thereby becoming badly-off ourselves.

I am formulating my reform proposal in line with the second approach, because the other two would support almost any reform that would improve the circumstances of the global poor. The second approach narrows the field by suggesting a more specific idea: Those who make more extensive use of our planet's resources should compensate those who, involuntarily, use very little. This idea does not require that we conceive of global resources as the common property of humankind, to be shared equally. My proposal is far more modest by leaving each government in control of the natural resources in its territory. Modesty is important if the proposed institutional alternative is to gain the support necessary to implement it and is to be able to sustain itself in the world as we know it. I hope that the GRD satisfies these two desiderata by staying reasonably close to the global order now in place and by being evidently responsive to each of the three approaches.

The GRD proposal envisions that states and their citizens' governments shall not have full libertarian property rights with respect to the natural resources in their territory, but can be required to share a small part of the value of any resources they decide to use or sell. This payment they must make is called a dividend because it is based on the idea that the global poor own an inalienable stake in all limited natural resources. As in the case of preferred stock, this stake confers no right to participate in decisions about whether or how natural resources are to be used and so does not interfere with national control over resources, or eminent domain. But it does entitle its holders to a share of the economic value of the resource in question, if indeed the decision is to use it. This idea could be extended to limited resources that are not destroyed through use but merely eroded, worn down, or occupied, such as air and water used for discharging pollutants or land used for farming, ranching, or buildings.

In light of the vast extent of global poverty today, one may think that a massive GRD would be necessary to solve the problem. But I doubt this is so. Present radical inequality is the cumulative result of decades and centuries in which the more affluent societies and groups have used their advantages in capital and knowledge to expand these advantages ever further. This inequality demonstrates the power of long-term compounding more than powerful centrifugal tendencies of our global market system. It is then quite possible that, if radical inequality has once been eradicated, quite a small GRD may, in the context of a fair and open global market system, be sufficient continuously to balance those ordinary centrifugal tendencies of markets enough to forestall its reemergence. The great magnitude of the problem does suggest, however, that initially more, perhaps as much as one percent of the global product, may be needed so that it does not take all too long until severe poverty is erased and an acceptable distributional profile is reached.[3] To get a concrete sense of the magnitudes involved, let us then consider this higher figure. While affluent countries now provide $52 billion annually in official development assistance (UNDP, 2000, 218), a one-percent GRD would currently raise about $300 billion annually.[4] This is $250 a year for each person below the international poverty line, over three times their present average annual income. More broadly spread, $300 billion is $107 a year for each person below the doubled poverty line, 82 percent of their present average annual income. Such an amount, if well targeted and effectively spent, would make a phenomenal difference to the poor even within a few years. On the other hand, the amount is rather small for the rest of us: close to the annual defense budget of just the US alone, significantly less than the annual 'peace dividend', and less than half the market value of the current annual crude oil production.[5]

Let us stay with the case of crude oil for a moment and examine the likely effects of a $2 per barrel GRD on crude oil extraction. This dividend would be owed by the countries in which oil is extracted, though most of this cost would be passed along, through higher world market prices, to the end-users of petroleum products. At $2 per barrel, over 18 percent of the high initial revenue target could be raised from crude oil alone – and comfortably so: at the expense of raising the price of petroleum products by about a nickel per gallon. It is thus clearly possible – without major changes to our global economic order – to eradicate world hunger within a few years by raising a sufficient revenue stream from a limited number of resources and pollutants. These should be selected carefully, with an eye to all collateral effects. This suggests the following desiderata: The GRD should be easy to understand and to apply. It should, for instance, be based on resources and pollutants whose extraction or discharge is easy to monitor or estimate, in order to ensure that every society is paying its fair share and to assure everyone that this is so. Such transparency also helps fulfill a second desideratum of keeping overall collection costs low. The GRD should, thirdly, have only a small impact on the price of goods consumed to satisfy basic needs. And it should, fourth, be focused on resource uses whose discouragement is especially important for conservation and environmental protection. In this last respect, the GRD reform can produce great ecological benefits that are hard to secure in a less concerted way because of familiar collective-action problems: Each society has little incentive to restrain its consumption and pollution, because the opportunity cost of such restraint falls on it alone while the costs of depletion and pollution are spread worldwide and into the future.

Proceeds from the GRD are to be used toward ensuring that all human beings will be able to meet their own basic needs with dignity. The goal is not merely to improve the nutrition, medical care, and sanitary conditions of the poor, but also to make it possible that they can themselves effectively defend and realize their basic interests. This capacity presupposes that they are freed from bondage and other relations of personal dependence, that they are able to read and write and to learn a profession, that they can participate as equals in politics and in the labor market, and that their status is protected by appropriate legal rights which they can understand and effectively enforce through an open and fair legal system.

The scheme for disbursing GRD funds is to be designed so as to make these funds maximally effective toward those ends. Such design must draw upon the expertise of economists and international lawyers. Let me nonetheless make some provisional suggestions to give more concreteness to the proposed reform. Disbursement should be made pursuant to clear and straightforward general rules whose administration is cheap and transparent. Transparency is important to exclude political favoritism and the appearance thereof. It is important also for giving the government of any developing country clear and strong incentives toward eradicating domestic poverty. To optimize such incentive effects, the disbursement rules should reward progress: by allocating more funds to this country and/or by assigning more of its allocation directly to its government.

This incentive may not always prevail. In some poor countries, the rulers care more about keeping their subjects destitute, uneducated, docile, dependent, and hence exploitable. In such cases, it may still be possible to find other ways of improving the circumstances and opportunities of the domestic poor: by making cash payments directly to them or to their organizations or by funding development programs administered through UN agencies or effective non-governmental organizations. When, in extreme cases, GRD funds cannot be used effectively in a particular country, then there is no reason to spend them there rather than in those many other places where these funds can make a real difference in reducing poverty and disadvantage.

Even if the incentives provided by the GRD disbursement rules do not always prevail, they will shift the political balance of forces in the right direction: A good government brings enhanced prosperity through GRD support and thereby generates more popular support which in turn will tend to make it safer from coup attempts. A bad government will find the poor harder to oppress when they receive GRD funds through other channels and when all strata of the population have an interest in realizing GRD-accelerated economic improvement under a different government more committed to poverty eradication. With the GRD in place, reforms will be pursued more vigorously and in more countries, and will succeed more often and sooner, than would otherwise be the case. Combined with suitable disbursement rules, the GRD can stimulate a peaceful international competition in effective poverty eradication.

This rough and revisable sketch has shown, I hope, that the GRD proposal deserves serious examination as an alternative to conventional development aid. While the latter has an aura of hand-outs and dependence, the GRD avoids any appearance of arrogant generosity: It merely incorporates into our global institutional order the moral claim of the poor to partake in the benefits from the use of planetary resources. It implements a moral right – and one that can be justified in multiple ways: namely also forward-lookingly, by reference to its effects, and backward-lookingly, by reference to the evolution of the present economic distribution. Moreover, the GRD would also be vastly more efficient. The disbursement of conventional development aid is heavily influenced by political considerations as is shown by the fact that only 21 percent of these $52 billion go to the least developed countries (UNDP, 2000, p. 218). A mere 8.3 percent ($4.3 billion) are spent on meeting

basic needs (UNDP, 2000, p. 79), less than one cent a day for each person in the poorest quintile. The GRD, by contrast, would initially raise 70 times as much exclusively toward meeting the basic needs of the global poor.

Since the GRD would cost more and return less in direct political benefits, many of the wealthier and more powerful states might be tempted to refuse compliance. Wouldn't the GRD scheme then require a global enforcement agency, something like a world government? In response, I agree that the GRD would have to be backed by sanctions. But sanctions could be decentralized: Once the agency facilitating the flow of GRD payments reports that a country has not met its obligations under the scheme, all other countries are required to impose duties on imports from, and perhaps also similar levies on exports to, this country to raise funds equivalent to its GRD obligations plus the cost of these enforcement measures. Such decentralized sanctions stand a very good chance of discouraging small-scale defections. Our world is now, and is likely to remain, highly interdependent economically. Most countries export and import between ten and fifty percent of their gross domestic product. No country would profit from shutting down foreign trade for the sake of avoiding its GRD obligation. And each would have reasons to fulfill its GRD obligation voluntarily: to retain control over how the funds are raised, to avoid paying extra for enforcement measures, and to avoid the adverse publicity associated with noncompliance.

To be sure, such a scheme of decentralized sanctions could work only so long as both the US and the European Union (EU) continue to comply and continue to participate in the sanction mechanism. I assume that both will do this, provided they can be brought to commit themselves to the GRD scheme in the first place. This prerequisite, which is decisive for the success of the proposal, is addressed in Section 5. It should be clear however that a refusal by the US or the EU to participate in the eradication of global poverty would not affect the implications of the present section. The feasibility of the GRD suffices to show that massive and severe poverty is avoidable at moderate cost (Condition 5), that the existing global order plays an important role in its persistence (Condition 7) and that we can take what all three approaches would recognize as a major step toward justice (second thesis).

4 The Moral Argument for the Proposed Reform

By showing that Conditions 1–10 are met, I hope to have demonstrated that present global poverty manifests a grievous injustice that can and should be abolished through institutional reform – involving the GRD scheme, perhaps, or some superior alternative. To make this train of thought as transparent and criticizable as possible, I restate it now as an argument in six steps. The first two steps involve new formulations, so I comment on them briefly at the end.

1 If a society or comparable social system, connected and regulated by a shared institutional order (Condition 6), displays radical inequality (Conditions 1–5), then this institutional order is *prima facie* unjust and requires justification. Here the burden of proof is on those who wish to defend this order and its coercive imposition as compatible with justice.

2 Such a justification of an institutional order under which radical inequality persists would need to show either

2a that Condition 10 is not met, perhaps because the existing radical inequality came about fairly: through an historical process that transpired in accordance with morally plausible rules that were generally observed; or

2b that Condition 9 is not met, because the worse-off can adequately benefit from the use of the common natural resource base through access to a proportional share or through some at least equivalent substitute; or

2c that Condition 8 is not met, because the existing radical inequality can be traced to extra-social factors (such as genetic handicaps or natural disasters) which, as such, affect different persons differentially; or

2d that Condition 7 is not met, because any proposed alternative to the existing institutional order either

- is impracticable, that is, cannot be stably maintained in the long run; or
- cannot be instituted in a morally acceptable way even with good will by all concerned; or
- would not substantially improve the circumstances of the worse-off; or
- would have other morally serious disadvantages that offset any improvement in the circumstances of the worse-off.

3 Humankind is connected and regulated by a shared global institutional order under which radical inequality persists.

4 This global institutional order therefore requires justification [from 1 and 3].

5 This global institutional order can be given no justification of forms 2a, 2b, or 2c. A justification of form 2d fails as well, because a reform involving introduction of a GRD provides an alternative that is practicable, can (with some good will by all concerned) be instituted in a morally acceptable way, would substantially improve the circumstances of the worse-off, and would not have disadvantages of comparable moral significance.

6 The existing global order cannot be justified [from 4, 2 and 5] and hence is unjust [from 1].

In presenting this argument, I have not attempted to satisfy the strictest demands of logical form, which would have required various qualifications and repetitions. I have merely tried to clarify the structure of the argument so as to make clear how it can be attacked.

One might attack the first step. But this moral premise is quite weak, applying only if the existing inequality occurs within a shared institutional order (Condition 6) *and* is radical, that is, involves truly extreme poverty and extreme differentials in standards of living (Conditions 1–5). Moreover, the first premise does not flatly exclude any institutional order under which radical inequality persists, but merely demands that it be justified. Since social institutions are created and upheld, perpetuated or reformed by human beings, this demand cannot plausibly be refused.

One might attack the second step. But this moral premise, too, is weak, in that it demands of the defender of the status quo only one of the four possible showings (**2a–2d**), leaving him free to try each of the conceptions of economic justice outlined in Section 2 even though he can hardly endorse all of them at once. Still, it remains open to argue that an institutional order reproducing radical inequality can be justified in a way that differs from the four (**2a–2d**) I have described.

One might try to show that the existing global order does not meet one of the ten conditions. Depending on which condition is targeted, one would thereby deny the third premise or give a justification of forms **2a** or **2b** or **2c**, or show that my reform proposal runs into one of the four problems listed under **2d**.

The conclusion of the argument is reached only if all ten conditions are met. Existing global poverty then manifests a *core injustice*: a phenomenon that the dominant strands of western normative political thought jointly – albeit for diverse reasons – classify as unjust and can jointly seek to eradicate. Insofar as advantaged and influential participants in the present international order grant the argument, we acknowledge our shared responsibility for its injustice: We are violating a negative duty of justice insofar as we contribute to (and fail to mitigate) the harms it reproduces and insofar as we resist suitable reforms.

5   Is the Reform Proposal Realistic?

Even if the GRD proposal is practicable, and even if it could be implemented with the good will of all concerned, there remains the problem of generating this good will, especially on the part of the rich and mighty. Without the support of the US and the EU, massive global poverty and starvation will certainly not be eradicated in our lifetimes. How realistic is the hope of mobilizing such support? I have two answers to this question.

First. Even if this hope is not realistic, it is still important to insist that present global poverty manifests a grievous injustice according to western normative political thought. We are not merely distant witnesses of a problem unrelated to ourselves, with a weak, positive duty to help. Rather we are, both causally and morally, intimately involved in the fate of the poor by imposing upon them a global institutional order that regularly produces severe poverty and/or by effectively excluding them from a fair share of the value of exploited natural resources and/or by upholding a radical inequality that evolved through an historical process pervaded by horrendous crimes. We can realistically end our involvement in their severe poverty not by extricating ourselves from this involvement, but only by ending such poverty through economic reform. If feasible reforms are blocked by others, then we may in the end be unable to do more than mitigate some of the harms we also help produce. But even then a difference would remain, because our effort would fulfill not a duty to help the needy, but a duty to protect victims of any injustice to which we contribute. The latter duty is, other things equal, much more stringent than the former, especially when we can fulfill it out of the benefits we derive from this injustice.

My second answer is that the hope may not be so unrealistic after all. My provisional optimism is based on two considerations. The first is that moral convictions can have real effects even in international politics – as even some political realists admit, albeit with regret. Sometimes these are the moral convictions of politicians. But more commonly politics is influenced by the moral convictions of citizens. One dramatic example of this is the abolitionist movement which, in the nineteenth century, pressured the British government into suppressing the slave trade (Drescher, 1986). A similar moral mobilization may be possible also for the sake of eradicating global poverty – provided the citizens of the more powerful states can be convinced of a moral conclusion that really can be soundly supported and a path can be shown that makes only modest demands on each of us.

The GRD proposal is morally compelling. It can be broadly anchored in the dominant strands of western normative political thought outlined in Section 2. And it also has the morally significant advantage of shifting consumption in ways that restrain global pollution and resource depletion for the benefit of future generations in particular. Because it can be backed by these four important and mutually independent moral rationales, the GRD proposal is well-positioned to benefit from the fact that moral reasons can have effects in the world. If some help can be secured from economists, political scientists and lawyers, then moral acceptance of the GRD may gradually emerge and become widespread in the developed west.

Eradicating global poverty through a scheme like the GRD also involves more realistic demands than a solution through private initiatives and conventional development aid. Continual mitigation of poverty leads to fatigue, aversion, even contempt. It requires the more affluent citizens and governments to rally to the cause again and again while knowing full well that most others similarly situated contribute nothing or very little, that their own contributions are legally optional, and that, no matter how much they give, they could for just a little more always save yet further children from sickness or starvation.

The inefficiency of conventional development aid is also sustained by the competitive situation among the governments of the donor countries, who feel morally entitled to decline to do more by pointing to their even less generous competitors. This explanation supports the optimistic assumption that the affluent societies would be prepared, in joint reciprocity, to commit themselves to more than what they tend to do each on its own. Analogous considerations apply to environmental protection and conservation, with respect to which the GRD also contributes to a collective solution: When many parties decide separately in this matter, then the best solution for all is not achieved, because each gets almost the full benefit of its pollution and wastefulness while the resulting harms are shared by all ('tragedy of the commons'). An additional point is that national development-aid and environmental-protection measures must be politically fought for or defended year after year, while acceptance of the GRD regime would require only one – albeit rather more far-reaching – political decision.

The other optimistic consideration has to do with prudence. The times when we could afford to ignore what goes on in the developing countries are over for good. Their economic growth will have a great impact on our environment and their military and technological gains are accompanied by serious dangers, among which those associated with nuclear, biological, and chemical weapons and technologies are only the most obvious. The transnational imposition of externalities and risks will ever more become a two-way street as no state or group of states, however rich and mighty, will be able effectively to insulate itself from external influences: from military and terrorist attacks, illegal immigrants, epidemics and the drug trade, pollution and climate change, price fluctuations, and scientific–technological and cultural innovations. It is then increasingly in our interest, too, that stable democratic institutions shall emerge in the developing countries – institutions under which governmental power is effectively constrained through procedural rules and basic rights. So long as large segments of these peoples lack elementary education and have no assurance that they will be able to meet even their most basic needs, such democratic institutions are much less likely than explosive mixtures of religious and ideological fanaticism, violent opposition movements, death squads, and corrupt and politicized militaries. To expose ourselves to the occasional explosions of these mixtures would be increasingly dangerous and also more costly in the long run than the proposed GRD.

This prudential consideration has a moral side as well. A future that is pervaded by radical inequality and hence unstable would endanger not only the security of ourselves and our progeny, but also the long-term survival of our society, values, and culture. Not only that: Such a future would, quite generally, endanger the security of all other human beings and their descendants as well as the survival of their societies, values, and cultures. And so the interest in peace – in a future world in which different societies, values, and cultures can coexist and interact peacefully – is obviously also, and importantly, a moral interest.

Realizing our prudential and moral interest in a peaceful and ecologically sound future will – and here I go beyond my earlier modesty – require supranational institutions and organizations that limit the sovereignty rights of states more severely than is the current practice. The most powerful states could try to impose such limitations upon all the rest while exempting themselves. It is doubtful, however, that today's great powers will summon the political will to make this attempt before it is too late. And it is doubtful also whether they could succeed. For such an attempt would provoke the bitter resistance of many other states, which would simultaneously try very hard, through military build-up, to gain access to the club of great powers. For such a project, the 'elites' in many developing countries could probably mobilize their populations quite easily, as the recent examples of India and Pakistan illustrate.

It might then make more sense for all to work toward supranational institutions and organizations that limit the sovereignty rights of all states equally. But this solution can work only if at least a large majority of the states participating in these institutions and organizations are stable democracies, which presupposes, in turn, that their citizens are assured that they can meet their basic needs, and can attain a decent level of education and social position.

The current geopolitical development drifts toward a world in which militarily and technologically highly advanced states and groups, growing in number, pose an ever greater danger for an ever larger subset of humankind. Deflecting this development in a more reasonable direction realistically requires considerable support from those other eighty-five percent of humankind who want to reduce our economic hegemony and achieve our high standard of living.

Through the introduction of the GRD or some similar reform we can gain such support by showing concretely that our relations to the rest of the world are not solely devoted to cementing our economic hegemony and that the global poor will be able peacefully to achieve a considerable improvement in their circumstances. In this way and only in this way can we refute the conviction, understandably widespread in the poor countries, that we will not give a damn about their misery until they will have the economic and military power to do us serious harm. And only in this way can we undermine the popular support that aggressive political movements of all kinds can derive from this conviction.

6 Conclusion

We are familiar, through charity appeals, with the assertion that it lies in our hands to save the lives of many or, by doing nothing, to let these people die. We are less familiar with the here examined assertion of a weightier responsibility: that most of us do not merely let people starve but also participate in starving them. It is not surprising that our initial reaction to this more unpleasant assertion is indignation, even hostility – that, rather than think it through or discuss it, we want to forget it or put it aside as plainly absurd.

I have tried to respond constructively to the assertion and to show its plausibility. I don't pretend to have proved it conclusively, but my argument should at least raise grave doubts about our commonsense prejudices, which we must in any case treat with suspicion on account of how strongly our self-interest is engaged in this matter. The great moral importance of reaching the correct judgment on this issue also counsels against lightly dismissing the assertion here defended. The essential data about the lives and deaths of the global poor are, after all, indisputable. In view of very considerable global interdependence, it is extremely unlikely that their poverty is due exclusively to local factors and that no feasible reform of the present global order could thus affect either that poverty or these local factors. No less incredible is the view that ours is the best of all possible global orders, that any modification of it could only aggravate poverty. So we should work together across disciplines to conceive a comprehensive solution to the problem of global poverty, and across borders for the political implementation of this solution.

Notes

A longer version of this essay was published in David A. Crocker and Toby Linden, eds.: *Ethics of Consumption: The Good Life, Justice, and Global Stewardship* (Lanham, MD: Rowman Littlefield 1998), 501–36. With help from Hugh LaFollette and Ling Tong, I have revised that version and shortened it by nearly one half.

1 *A Convention on Combating Bribery of Foreign Officials in International Business Transactions*, which requires signatory states to criminalize the bribery of foreign officials, was finally drafted within the OECD under public pressure generated by the new non-governmental organization Transparency International (*www.transparency.de*). The Convention went into effect in February 1999. Thirty-three states have ratified it at last count (*http://www.oecd.org/ daf/ nocorruption/ annex2.htm*).

2 The World Bank estimates that 1.2 out of six billion human beings live below the international poverty line, which it currently defines in terms of $32.74 PPP 1993 per month or $1.08 PPP 1993 per day (World Bank, 2001, pp. 17, 23). 'PPP' stands for 'purchasing power parity', so people count as poor by this standard when their income per person per year has less purchasing power than $393 had in the US in 1993 or less purchasing power than $466 have in the US in the year 2000 (*http://stats.bls.gov/ cpihome.htm*). Those living below this poverty line, on average, fall 30 percent below it (Chen and Ravallion, 2000, tables 2 and 4, dividing the poverty gap index by the headcount index). So they live on $326 PPP 2000 per person per year on average. Now the $PPP incomes the World Bank ascribes to people in poor developing countries are on average about four times higher than their actual incomes at market exchange rates. Thus the World Bank equates China's per capita GNP of $780 to $3,291 PPP, India's $450 to $2,149 PPP, Indonesia's $580 to $2,439 PPP, Nigeria's $310 to $744 PPP, and so on (World Bank, 2001, pp. 274–5). Since virtually all the global poor live in such poor developing countries, we can then estimate that their average annual per capita income of $326 PPP 2000 corresponds to about $82 at market exchange rates. The aggregate annual income of the poorest fifth of humankind is then about $100 billion at market exchange rates or about one third of one percent of the global product.

3 In the face of 18 million poverty-related deaths per year, the go-slow approach governments have non-bindingly endorsed at the 1996 World Food Summit in Rome – halving world hunger within 19 years – is morally unacceptable. I also think that the World Bank's poverty line is far too low to define an acceptable goal. The World Bank provides statistics also for a more adequate poverty line that is twice as high: $786 PPP 1993 ($932 PPP or roughly $233 in the year 2000) per person per year. There are 2.8 billion persons – nearly half of humankind – who are said to live below this higher poverty line, falling 44.4 percent below it on average (Chen and Ravallion, tables 3 and 4, again dividing the poverty gap index by the headcount index). The aggregate annual income of these persons is then about $363 billion at market exchange rates or less than $1\frac{1}{4}$ percent of the global product.

4 The global product (sum of all gross national products) is currently about $30 trillion per year; 78.4 percent thereof belongs to the 'high-income economies', including 33 countries plus Hong Kong, which contain 14.9 percent of world population (World Bank, 2001, p. 275). The US, with 4.6 percent of world population, accounts for 28.6 percent of global product (ibid. – and has just managed to renegotiate its share of the UN budget from 25 down to 22 percent).

5 The end of the Cold War enabled the high-income countries to cut their aggregate military expenditure from 4.1 percent of their combined gross domestic product in 1985 to 2.2 percent in 1998 (UNDP, 1998, p. 197; UNDP, 2000, p. 217). The peace dividend these countries reap can then be estimated at $420 billion annually (1.9 percent of their current aggregate GDP of over $22 trillion – UNDP, 2000, p. 209). Crude oil production is currently about 77 million barrels daily or about 28 billion barrels annually. At $25 per barrel, this comes to $700 billion per year.

Bibliography

Aiken, Will, and Hugh LaFolette, (eds) (1977) *World Hunger and Moral Obligation*. Englewood Cliffs: Prentice Hall.

Barry, Brian (1982) "Humanity and Justice in Global Perspective," in J. R. Pennock and J. W. Chapman, (eds), *Ethics, Economics, and the Law*. New York: New York University Press.

Beitz, Charles (1979) *Political Theory and International Relations*. Princeton, Princeton University Press.

Chen, Shaohua, and Martin Ravallion (2000) "How Did the World's Poorest Fare in the 1990s?," *www.econ. worldbank.org/ docs/ 1164.pdf*

Dasgupta, Partha (1993) *An Inquiry into Well-Being and Destitution*. Oxford: Oxford University Press.

Drescher, Seymour (1986) *Capitalism and Antislavery: British Mobilization in Comparative Perspective*. Oxford: Oxford University Press.

Eichengreen, Barry, James Tobin, and Charles Wyplosz (1995) "Two Cases for Sand in the Wheels of International Finance," *Economic Journal* 105: 162–72.

Gould, Stephen Jay (1991) "The Moral State of Tahiti – and of Darwin" *Natural History* 10: 12–19.

Locke, John (1689) "An Essay Concerning the True Original, Extent, and End of Civil Government" in Peter Laslett, ed., *John Locke Two Treatises of Government*. Cambridge: Cambridge University Press.

Murphy, Liam (2000) *Moral Demands in Non-Ideal Theory*. Oxford: Oxford University Press.

Nagel, Thomas (1977) "Poverty and Food: Why Charity Is Not Enough," in Peter Brown and Henry Shue (eds), *Food Policy: The Responsibility of the United States in Life and Death Choices*. New York: Free Press, pp. 54–62.

Nozick, Robert (1974) *Anarchy, State, and Utopia*. New York: Basic Books.

O'Neill, Onora (1985) "Lifeboat Earth" (1974) reprinted in Charles Beitz, Marshall Cohen, Thomas Scanlon, and A. John Simmons (eds), *International Ethics*. Princeton: Princeton University Press, pp. 262–81.

Pogge, Thomas (1989) *Realizing Rawls*. Ithaca: Cornell University Press.

—— (1998) "The Bounds of Nationalism," in Jocelyne Couture et al. (eds), *Rethinking Nationalism, Canadian Journal of Philosophy*, Supplementary Volume 22 (Calgary: University of Calgary Press 1998), pp. 463–504.

—— (2001) "Priorities of Global Justice," *Metaphilosophy* 32: 6–24.

Rawls, John (1999) *The Law of Peoples*. Cambridge MA: Harvard University Press.

Sen, Amartya (1981) *Poverty and Famines*. Oxford: Oxford University Press.

Shue, Henry (1980) *Basic Rights*. Princeton: Princeton University Press.

Singer, Peter (1972) "Famine, Affluence and Morality," *Philosophy and Public Affairs* 1: 229–43.

Tobin, James (1978) "A Proposal for International Monetary Reform," *Eastern Economic Journal* 4: 153–9.

Unger, Peter (1996) *Living High and Letting Die: Our Illusion of Innocence*. Oxford: Oxford University Press.

United Nations Children's Fund (UNICEF 1999) *The State of the World's Children 1999*. New York: Oxford University Press.

United Nations Development Programme (UNDP), *Human Development Report*, New York: Oxford University Press (annual publication).

United States Department of Agriculture (USDA 1999) *U.S. Action Plan on Food Security, www.fas.usda. gov:80/ icd/ summit/ usactplan.pdf*.

Wantchekon, Leonard (1999) "Why do Resource Dependent Countries Have Authoritarian Governments?," Working Paper, Yale University, *www.yale.edu/ leitner/ pdf/ 1999–11.pdf*.

World Bank (2000), *World Development Report 1999/ 2000*, New York: Oxford University Press, *www.worldbank.org/ wdr/ 2000/ fullreport.html*.

World Bank (2001), *World Development Report 2000/ 2001*, New York: Oxford University Press, *www. worldbank.org/ poverty/ wdrpoverty/ report/ index.htm*.

World Health Organization (WHO 2000), *The World Health Report 2000, Health Systems: Improving Performance*, Geneva: WHO Publications, *www.who.int/ whr/ 2000*.

59

Feeding People versus Saving Nature

Holmes Rolston III

A bumper sticker reads: Hungry loggers eat spotted owls. That seems to pinpoint an ethical issue, and often one where the humanist protagonist, taking high moral ground, intends to put the environmentalist on the defensive. You wouldn't let the Ethiopians starve to save some butterfly, would you? "Human beings are at the centre of concerns for sustainable development." So the *Rio Declaration* begins. Once this was to be an *Earth Charter*, but the developing nations were more interested in getting their poor fed: "All States and all people shall cooperate in the essential task of eradicating poverty as an indispensable requirement."[1] Can we fault them for putting poor people first?

We have to be circumspect. If, in the abstract, we are asked whether we should feed hungry people or save nature, most people will favor people; nature be damned. However, that question misrepresents the choices we actually face. Moral questions only make sense in context; asking the questions outside the context is invariably misleading. So before we can reasonably decide whether to favor people or nature, we must analyze the choices we face, in the actual context, with all its richness.

Humans win? Nature loses? We must not forget, of course, that humans do not really win if they sacrifice their life support system. "In order to achieve sustainable development, environmental protection shall constitute an integral part of the development process and cannot be considered in isolation from it."[2] After all, food has to be grown in some reasonably healthy natural system, and the clean water that the poor need is also good for fauna and flora. Extractive reserves, where people can hunt, gather medicinal plants, or nuts, or latex from rubber trees, leaving the forests healthy and largely intact, give people an incentive to conserve. Tourism can benefit the local poor as well as the wildlife. When possible, we should seek solutions that benefit both humans and nature. Practically, these are often the only kind likely to work; and, where possible, they will be most satisfying.

Yet there are times when we sacrifice nature for human development – most development requires that some nature be sacrificed. Most people think this is an acceptable trade-off. After all, people seem supremely important; and food is their most urgent need. People should always win, even if nature loses? Perhaps.

Can we ever say that we ought save nature rather than feed people?

1 Feed People First? Do We? Ought We?

"Feed people first!" That has a ring of righteousness. In the biblical parable of the great judgment, Jesus welcomes the righteous to their reward. "I was hungry and you gave me food, I was thirsty and you gave me drink." Those who refused to help are damned (Matthew 2: 31–46). The vision of those in heaven is that "they shall hunger no more, neither thirst any more" (Revelation 7: 16). Jesus teaches his disciples to pray, "Give us this day our daily bread" (Matthew 6: 11). Food is such a basic value, if there is to be any ethics at all, surely food comes first.

Does it always? A woman washed Jesus's feet with expensive ointment. When the disciples complained that it should have been sold and given to the poor, Jesus replied, "you always have the poor with you." He commended her: "She has done a beautiful thing" (Matthew 26: 10–11). While the poor are a continuing concern, with whom Jesus demonstrated ample solidarity, if we did nothing else of value until there were no more poor, we would have to postpone everything else indefinitely. Christians would never have built a sanctuary with an organ and stained glass, but rather would always have given the poor their daily bread. Eradicating poverty is one vital goal, but at the same time, set this commendable ideal beside the plain fact that we all daily prefer other values. Every time we buy a Christmas gift, or go to a symphony concert, or take a college education, we spend money that might have helped to eradicate poverty. We mostly choose to do things we value more than feeding the hungry.

An ethicist may reply, yes, that is the fact of the matter. But no normative ought follows from the description of this behavior. We ought not to behave so. Such widespread behavior, however, engaged in almost universally by persons who regard themselves as being

ethical, including readers of this article, is strong evidence that we in fact not only have these norms but think we ought to have them. To be sure, charity is appropriate, and we censure those who are wholly insensitive to the plight of others. Concern for the poor is indispensable, but we do not, and ought not, dispense with all these other values we pursue, while yet some people are starving.

If one were to advocate doing nothing else until no one in the world is hungry, this would paralyze civilization. People would not have invented writing, or smelted iron, or written music, or invented airplanes. Plato would not have written his dialogues, or Aquinas the *Summa Theologica*; Edison would not have discovered the electric light bulb. Einstein could not have discovered the theory of relativity, because he would have been working for Bread for the World. We both do and ought to devote ourselves to various worthy causes, while yet persons go hungry.

Our moral systems in fact do not teach us to feed the poor first. The Ten Commandments do not say that; the Golden Rule does not; Kant did nor say that; nor does the utilitarian greatest good for the greatest number imply that. Eradicating poverty may be indispensable but not always prior to all other cultural values. It may not always be prior to conserving natural values either.

2 Choosing for People to Die

But food is absolutely vital. "Thou shalt not kill" is one of the commandments. Next to the evil of taking life is taking the sustenance for life. Is not saving nature, thereby preventing hunting, harvesting, or development by those who need the produce of that land to put food in their mouths, almost like killing? Surely one ought not to choose for someone else to die; everyone has a right to life. To fence out the hungry is choosing that people will die. That can't be right.

Or can it? In broader social policy we make many decisions that cause people to die. When in 1988 we increased the US national speed limit on rural Interstate highways from 55 to 65 miles per hour, we chose for 400 persons to die each year.[3] We decide against hiring more police, though if we did, some murders would be avoided. The city council spends that money on a new art museum, or to give schoolteachers a raise. Congress decides not to pass a national healthcare program that would subsidize medical insurance for some who cannot otherwise afford it; and some, in result, fail to get timely medical care and die of preventable diseases.

We may decide to leave existing air pollution standards in place because it is expensive for industry to install new scrubbers, even though there is statistical evidence that a certain number of persons will contract diseases and die prematurely. All money budgeted for the National Endowment for the Humanities, and almost all that for the National Science Foundation, could be spent to prevent the deaths of babies from malnutrition. We do not know exactly who will die, but we know that some will; we often have reasonable estimates how many. The situation would be similar, should we choose to save nature rather than to feed people.

Wealthy and poverty-stricken nations alike put up borders across which the poor are forbidden to pass. Rich nations will not let them in; their own governments will not let them out. We may have misgivings about this on both sides, but if we believe in immigration laws at all, we, on the richer side of the border, think that protecting our lifestyle counts more than their betterment, even if they just want to be better fed. If we let anyone who pleased enter the United States, and gave them free passage, hundreds of millions would come. Already 30 percent of our population growth is by immigration, legal and illegal. Sooner or later we must fence them out, or face the loss of prosperity that we value. We may not think this is always right, but when one faces the escalating numbers that would swamp the United States, it seems sometimes right. Admitting refugees is humane, but it lets such persons flee their own national problems and does not contribute to any long-term solutions in the nations from which they emigrate. Meanwhile, people die as a result of such decisions.

Some of these choices address the question whether we ought to save nature if this causes people to die. Inside our US boundaries, we have a welfare system. Fortunately, we are wealthy enough to afford this as well as nature conservation. But if it came to this, we would think it wrong-headed to put animals (or art, or well-paid teachers) over starving people. Does that not show that, as domestic policy, we feed people first? Yet we let foreigners die, when we are not willing to open up our five hundred wilderness areas, nearly 100 million acres, to Cubans and Ethiopians.

3   Hunger and Social Justice

The welfare concept introduces another possibility, that the wealthy should be taxed to feed the poor. We should do that first, rather than losing our wildlife, or wilderness areas, or giving up art, or underpaying the teachers. In fact, there is a way greatly to relieve this tragedy. Few persons would need to go without enough if we could use the produce of the already domesticated landscape justly and charitably. It is better to try to fix this problem where it arises, within society, than to try to enlarge the sphere of society by the sacrifice of remnant natural values, by, say, opening up the wilderness areas to settlement. That only postpones the problem.

Peoples in the South (a code word for the lesser developed countries, or the poor) complain about the overconsumption by peoples in the North (the industrial rich), often legitimately so. But Brazil has within its own boundaries the most skewed income distribution in the world. The US ratio of personal income for the top 20 percent of people to the bottom 20 percent is 9 to 1; the ratio in Brazil is 26 to 1. Just 1 percent of Brazilians control 45 percent of the agricultural land. The biggest 20 landowners own more land between them than the 3.3 million smallest farmers. With the Amazon still largely undeveloped, there is already more arable land per person in Brazil than in the United States. The top 10 percent of Brazilians spend 51 percent of the national income.[4] This anthropocentric inequity ought to be put "at the center of concern" when we decide about saving nature versus feeding people.

Save the Amazon! No! The howler monkeys and toucans may delight tourists, but we ought not to save them if people need to eat. Such either–or choices mask how marginalized peoples are forced onto marginal lands; and those lands become easily stressed, both because the lands are by nature marginal for agriculture, range, and life support, and also because by human nature marginalized peoples find it difficult to plan for the long-range. They are caught up in meeting their immediate needs.

Prime agricultural lands can also be stressed to produce more and more, because there is a growing population to feed, or to grow an export crop, because there is an international debt to pay. Prime agricultural lands in southern Brazil, formerly used for growing food and worked by tenants who lived on these lands and ate their produce, as well as sending food into the cities, have been converted to growing coffee as an export crop, using mechanized farming, to help pay Brazil's massive debt, contracted by a military government since overthrown. Peoples forced off these lands were resettled in the Amazon basin, aided by development schemes fostered by the military government, resettled on lands really not suitable for agriculture. The integrity of the Amazon, to say nothing of the integrity of these peoples, is being sacrificed to cover for misguided loans. Meanwhile the wealthy in Brazil pay little or no income tax that might be used for such loan repayment.

The world is full enough of societies that have squandered their resources, inequitably distributed wealth, degraded their landscapes, and who will be tempted to jeopardize what natural values remain as an alternative to solving hard social problems. The decision about poor people over nature usually lies in the context of another decision, often a tacit one, to protect vested interests, wealthy people over poor people, wealthy people who are exploiting nature. En route to any conclusion such as let-people-starve, we regularly reach an if-then, go-to decision point in our logic, where before we face the people-over-nature choice we have to reaffirm or let stand the wealthy-over-poor choice.

In the more fortunate nations, we may distribute wealth more equitably, perhaps through taxes or minimum wage laws, or by labor unions, or educational opportunities, and we do have in place the welfare systems referred to earlier, refusing to let anyone starve. But lest we in the US seem too righteous, we also recall that we have such policies only domestically. The international picture puts this in a different light. There are two major blocs, the G-7 nations (the Group of 7, the big nations of North America, Europe, and Japan, "the North"), and the G-77 nations, once 77 but now including some 128 less developed nations, often south of the industrial North. The G-7 nations hold about one-fifth of the world's five billion persons, and they produce and consume about four-fifths of all goods and services. The G-77 nations, with four-fifths of the world's people, produce and consume one-fifth. (See figure 59.1, which diagrams this as a sort of pie chart.) For every person added to the population of the North, twenty are added in the South. For every dollar of economic growth per person in the South, twenty dollars accrue in the North.[5]

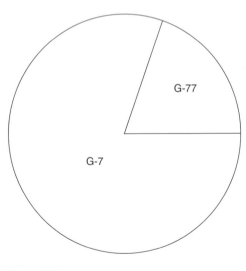

Figure 59.1

The distribution problem is complex. Earth's natural resources are unevenly distributed by nature. Diverse societies have often taken different directions of development; they have different governments, ideologies, and religions; they have made different social choices, valued material prosperity differently. Typically, where there is agricultural and industrial development, people think of this as an impressive achievement. Pies have to be produced before they can be divided, and who has produced this pie? Who deserves the pie? People ought to get what they earn. Fairness nowhere commands rewarding all parties equally; justice is giving each his or her due. We treat equal equally; we treat unequals equitably, and that typically means unequal treatment proportionately to merit. There is nothing evidently unfair in the pie diagram, not, at least, until we have inquired about earnings. Some distribution patterns reflect achievement. Not all of the asymmetrical distribution is a result of social injustice.

Meanwhile, it is difficult to look at the distribution chart and not think that something is unfair. Is some of the richness on one side related to the poverty on the other? Regularly, the poor come off poorly when they bargain with the rich; and wealth that originates as impressive achievement can further accumulate through exploitation. Certainly many of the hungry people have worked just as hard as many of the rich.

Some will say that what the poorer nations need to do is to imitate the productive people. Unproductive people need to learn how to make more pie. Then they can feed themselves. Those in the G-7 nations who emphasize the earnings model tend to recommend to the G-77 nations that they produce more, often offering to help them produce by investments which can also be productive for the G-7 nations. Those in the G-77 nations do indeed wish to produce, but they also realize that the problem is one of sharing as well as producing. Meanwhile the growth graphs caution us that producing can be as much part of the problem as part of the solution. One way to think of the circular pie chart is that this is planet Earth, and we do not have any way of producing a bigger planet. We

could, though, feed more people by sacrificing more nature.

Meanwhile too, any such decisions take place inside this 1/5-gets-4/5ths, 4/5ths-gets-1/5 picture. So it is not just the Brazilians, but all of us in the United States, Europe, and Japan as well that have to face an if-then, go-to decision point, reaffirming and/or letting stand the wealthy-over-poor division of the Earth's pie that we enjoy. This is what stings when we see the bumper-sticker ethical injunction: "Live simply that others may simply live."

4   Escalating Human Populations

Consider human population growth (see figure 59.2). Not only have the numbers of persons grown, their expectations have grown, so that we must superimpose one exploding curve on top of another. A superficial reading of such a graph is that humans really start winning big in the twentieth century. There are lots of them, and they want, and many get, lots of things. If one is a moral humanist, this can seem a good thing. Wouldn't it be marvelous if all could get what they want, and none hunger and thirst any more?

But when we come to our senses, we realize that this kind of winning, if it keeps on escalating, is really losing. Humans will lose, and nature will be destroyed as well. Cultures have become consumptive, with ever-escalating insatiable desires, overlaid on ever-escalating

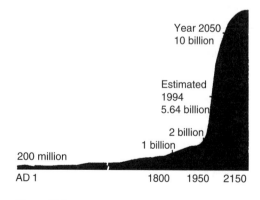

Figure 59.2

population growth. Culture does not know how to say "Enough!" and that is not satisfactory. Feeding people always seems humane; but, by just feeding people, without attention to the larger social results, we could be feeding a kind of cancer, that is, an explosion of unregulated growth.

One can say that where there is a hungry mouth, one should put food into it. But when there are two mouths there in result the next day, and four the day after that, and sixteen the day after that, one needs a more complex answer. The population of Egypt was less than three million for over five millennia, fluctuating between 1.5 and 2.5 million, even into the 1800s. Today the population of Egypt is about 55 million. Egypt has to import more than half its food. The effects on nature, both on land health and on wildlife, have been adversely proportional.

If, in this picture, we look at individual persons, caught up in this uncontrolled growth, and if we try to save nature, some persons will go hungry. Surely that is a bad thing. Would anyone want to say that such persons ought not to sacrifice nature, if needs be, to alleviate such harm as best they can? From their perspective, they are only doing what humans have always done, making a resourceful use of nature to meet their own needs. Regardless of whether such persons ought to have been born, they have been born; and now that they are here, for better or worse, it is unlikely that they are going to adopt the heroic course of starving in order to save nature. Even if a person should do this for himself voluntarily, it would be wrong for a mother to impose starvation on her children. And it is wrong, and hypocritical, for us to impose starvation on them.

But here we face a time-bound truth, where too much of a good thing becomes a bad thing. We have to figure in where such persons are located on the population curve, and realize that a good thing when human numbers are manageable is no longer a good thing when such a person is really another cell of cancerous growth. That sounds cruel, and it is tragic, but it does not cease to be true for these reasons. For a couple to have two children may be a

blessing; but the tenth child is a tragedy. When the child comes, one has to be as humane as possible, but one will only be making the best of a tragic situation, and if the tenth child is reared, and has ten children in turn, that will only multiply the tragedy. The quality of humans' lives deteriorates; the poor get poorer. Natural resources are further stressed; ecosystem health and integrity degenerate; and this compounds the losses again – a lose–lose situation. In a social system misfitted to its landscape, one's wins can only be temporary in a losing human ecology.

Even if there were an equitable distribution of wealth, the human population cannot go on escalating without people becoming all equally poor. Of the 90 million new people who will come on board planet Earth this year, 85 million will appear in the Third World, the countries least able to support such population growth. At the same time, the five million new people in the industrial countries will put as much strain on the environment as the 85 million new poor. There are three problems: overpopulation, overconsumption, and underdistribution. Sacrificing nature for development does not solve any of these problems, none at all. It only brings further loss. The poor, after a meal for a day or two, perhaps a decade or two, are soon hungry all over again, only now poorer still because their natural wealth is also gone.

To say that we ought always to feed the poor first commits a good–better–best fallacy. If feeding some humans is good, feeding more is better. And more. And more! Feeding all of them is best? That sounds right. We can hardly bring ourselves to say that anyone ought to starve. But we reach a point of diminishing returns, when the goods put at threat lead us to wonder. Once you agree that we ought always to feed people first, the existence of all other values is reduced to a contingency, to be promoted if and only if nobody can be fed by its sacrifice, value that can be permitted only when everyone has been lifted out of the bottomless pit of the poor. There can be no values above the poverty line. This is true of instrumental and intrinsic values in culture, and as well of instrumental and intrinsic values in nature.

5 When Nature Comes First

Humans now control 40 percent of the planet's landbased primary net productivity, that is, the basic plant growth which captures the energy on which everything else depends.[6] If the human population doubles, the capture will rise to 60–80 percent, and little habitat will remain for natural forms of life that cannot be accommodated after we have put people first. Humans do not use the lands they have domesticated effectively. A World Bank study found that 35 percent of the Earth's land has now become degraded.[7] Daniel Hillel, in a soils study, concludes, "Present yields are extremely low in many of the developing countries, and as they can be boosted substantially and rapidly, there should be no need to reclaim new land and to encroach further upon natural habitats."[8]

Africa is a case in point, and Madagascar epitomizes Africa's future. Its fauna and flora evolved independently from the mainland continent; there are 30 primates, all lemurs; the reptiles and amphibians are 90 percent endemic, including two-thirds of all the chameleons of the world, and 10,000 plant species, of which 80 percent are endemic. Humans came there about 1,500 years ago and, although there were some losses, they lived with the fauna and flora more or less intact until the twentieth century. Now an escalating population of impoverished Malagasy people rely heavily on slash-and-burn agriculture, and the forest cover is one-third of the original (27.6 million acres to 9.4 million acres), most of the loss occurring since 1950.[9] Madagascar is the most eroded nation on Earth, and little or none of the fauna and flora is safely conserved. The population is expanding at 3.2 percent a year; remaining forest is shrinking at 3 percent, almost all to provide for the expanding population. Are we to say that none ought to be conserved until after no person is hungry?

Tigers are sliding toward extinction. Populations have declined 95 percent in the twentieth century; the two main factors are loss of habitat and a ferocious black market in bones and other body parts used in traditional medicine, uses that are given no medical credence. Ranthambhore National Park in Rajasthan, India, is a tiger sanctuary; there were 40 tigers during the late 1980s, reduced in a few years by human pressures – illicit cattle grazing and poaching – to 20–25 tigers today. There are 200,000 Indians within three miles of the core of the park – more than double the population when the park was launched, 21 years ago. Most depend on wood from the 150 square miles of park to cook their food. They graze in and around the park some 150,000 head of scrawny cattle, buffalo, goats, and camels. The cattle impoverish habitat and carry diseases to the ungulates that are the tiger's prey base. In May 1993, a young tigress gave birth to four cubs; that month 316 babies were born in the villages surrounding the park.[10]

Hungry people will take what they need. So it is futile to think we can save tigers on habitat that hungry people could use. One will have to fix the hunger first, else one can save no nature. Yes, but what we are contending here is that sacrificing nature is no fix whatever for this hunger; it can at best alleviate it for a few years, after which the hunger will be back worse than ever. People have a right to access to the means of life? Yes, but the tigers have not threatened any such access. People did the overreproducing; they maldistribute resources between rich and poor. It cannot follow that the innocent tigers ought to be sacrificed of their access to the means of life to fix this people problem.

The tigers may be doomed, but ought they to be? Consider, for instance, that there are minimal reforestation efforts, or that cattle dung can be used for fuel with much greater efficiency than is being done, or that, in an experimental herd of jersey and holstein cattle there, the yield of milk increased to ten times that of the gaunt, freeranging local cattle, and that a small group of dairy producers has increased milk production 1,000 percent in just three years. In some moods we may insist that people are more important than tigers. But in other moods these majestic animals seem the casualties of human inabilities to manage themselves and their resources intelligently, a tragic story that leaves us wondering whether the tigers should always lose and the people win.

Ought we to save nature if this results in people going hungry? In people dying? Regrettably, sometimes, the answer is yes. In twenty years Africa's black rhinoceros population declined from 65,000 to 2,500, a loss of 97 percent; the species faces imminent extinction. Again, as with the tigers, there has been loss of habitat due to human population growth; but the primary direct cause is poaching, this time for horns. People cannot eat horns; but they can buy food with the money from selling them. Zimbabwe has a hardline shoot-to-kill policy for poachers, and over 150 poachers have been killed.[11]

So Zimbabweans do not always put people first; they are willing to kill some, and to let others go hungry. Otherwise, there will be no rhinos at all. Always too, we must guard against inhumanity, and take care, so far as we can, that poachers have other alternatives for overcoming their poverty. Still, if it comes to this, the Zimbabwean policy is right. Given the fact that rhinos have been so precipitously reduced, given that the Zimbabwean population is escalating (the average married woman there *desires* to have six children),[12] one ought to put the black rhino as a species first.

What about ordinary people, who are not breaking any laws? Even when the multiple causal factors are known, and lamented, should we not factor out overpopulation, overconsumption, and maldistribution, none of which are the fault of the particular individuals who may wish to develop their lands? "I did not ask to be born; I am poor, not overconsuming; I am not the cause but rather the victim of the inequitable distribution of wealth. I only want enough to eat, is that not my right?" Human rights must include, if anything at all, the right to subsistence.

So even if particular persons are located at the wrong point on the global growth graph, even if they are willynilly part of a cancerous and consumptive society, even if there is some better social solution than the wrong one that is in fact happening, have they not a right that will override the conservation of natural value? Will it not just be a further wrong to them to deprive them of their right to what little they have? Can

basic human rights ever be overridden by a society that wants to do better by conserving natural value?

This requires some weighing of the endangered natural values. If one concludes that the natural values at stake are quite high, and that the opportunities for development are low, because the envisioned development is inadvisable, then a possible answer is: No, there will be no development of these reserved areas, even if, with escalating populations, they become more poor. We are not always obligated to cover human mistakes with the sacrifice of natural values.

Does this violate human rights? Anywhere that there is legal zoning, persons are told what they may and may not do, in order to protect various social and natural values. Land ownership is limited when the rights of use conflict with the rights of other persons. One's rights are constrained by the harm one does to others, and we legislate to enforce this. Environmental policy may and ought to regulate the harms that people do on the lands on which they live, and it is perfectly appropriate to set aside conservation reserves to protect the cultural, ecological, scientific, economic, historical, aesthetic, religious, and other values people have at stake here, as well as for values that the fauna and flora have intrinsically in themselves. Indeed, unless there is such reserving of natural areas, counterbalancing the high pressures for development, there will be almost no conservation at all. Every person on Earth is told that he or she cannot develop some areas.

Persons are not told that they must starve, but they are told that they cannot save themselves from starving by sacrificing the nature set aside in reserves – not at least beyond the traditional kinds of uses that did leave the biodiversity on the landscape. If one is already residing in a location where development is constrained, this may seem unfair. Human rights to development, even by those who are poor, though they are to be taken quite seriously, are not everywhere absolute, but have to be weighed against the other values at stake. An individual sees at a local scale; the farmer wants only to graze cattle or plant crops on the now forested land. But environmental ethics sees that the actions of individuals cumulate and produce larger-scale changes that go on over the heads of these individuals. This ethic will regularly be constraining individuals in the interest of some larger ecological and social goods. That will regularly seem cruel, unfair to the individual caught in such constraints. This is the tragedy of the commons; individuals cannot see far enough ahead, under the pressures of the moment, to operate at intelligent ecological scales. Social policy must be set synoptically. This invokes both ecology and ethics, and blends them, if we are to respect life at all relevant scales.

These poor may not have so much a right to develop in any way they please, as a right to a more equitable distribution of the goods of the Earth that we, the wealthy, think we absolutely own.

Our traditional focus on individuals, and their rights, can blind us to how the mistakes (as well as the wisdom) of the parents can curse (and bless) the children, as the Ten Commandments put it, how "the iniquity of the fathers is visited upon the children to the third and fourth generation" (cf. Exodus 20: 5). All this has a deeply tragic dimension, made worse by the coupling of human foibles with ecological realities. We have little reason to think that misguided compassion that puts food into every hungry mouth, be the consequences whatever they may, will relieve the tragedy. We also have no reason to think that the problem will be solved without wise compassion, balancing a love for persons and a love for nature.

Ought we to feed people first, and save nature last? We never face so simple a question. The practical question is more complex:

- If persons widely demonstrate that they value many other worthwhile things over feeding the hungry (Christmas gifts, college educations, symphony concerts)
- and if developed countries, to protect what they value, post national boundaries across which the poor may not pass (immigration laws)

- and if there is unequal and unjust distribution of wealth, and if just redistribution to alleviate poverty is refused
- and if charitable redistribution of justified unequal distribution of wealth is refused
- and if one-fifth of the world continues to consume four-fifths of the production of goods and four-fifths consumes one-fifth
- and if escalating birthrates continue so that there are no real gains in alleviating poverty, only larger numbers of poor in the next generation
- and if low productivity on domesticated lands continues, and if the natural lands to be sacrificed are likely to be low in productivity
- and if significant natural values are at stake, including extinctions of species, then one ought not always to feed people first, but rather one ought sometimes to save nature.

Many of the "ands" in this conjunction can be replaced with "ors" and the statement will remain true, though we cannot say outside of particular contexts how many. The logic is not so much that of implication as of the weighing up of values and disvalues, natural and human, and of human rights and wrongs, past, present, and future.

Some will complain that all this is veiled cultural imperialism, the wealthy North imposing its newfound environmental values on the South, as if the South destroying its biodiversity were not also a form of cultural imperialism sacrificing nature. Our argument is really counter-imperialist: culture ought not always to triumph over nature, but ought at times to be constrained to solutions within culture, saving nature. Some will complain that it is easy to be generous about nature at somebody else's expense, to let their babies starve; but no one who so complains has availed himself or herself of the opportunities for generosity that he or she already has.

Some will protest that this risks becoming misanthropic and morally callous. The Ten Commandments order us not to kill, and saving nature can never justify what amounts to killing people. Yes, but there is another kind of killing here, one not envisioned at Sinai, where humans are superkilling species. Extinction kills forms (*species*) – not just individuals; it kills collectively, not just distributively. Killing a natural kind is the death of birth, not just of an individual life. The historical lineage is stopped forever. Preceding the Ten Commandments is the Noah myth, when nature was primordially put at peril as great as the actual threat today. There, God seems more concerned about species than about the humans who had then gone so far astray. In the covenant reestablished, the beasts are specifically included. "Keep them alive with you . . . according to their kinds" (Genesis 6: 19–20). There is something ungodly about an ethic by which the late-coming *Homo sapiens* arrogantly regards the welfare of his own species as absolute, with the welfare of all the other five million species sacrificed to that. The commandment not to kill is as old as Cain and Abel, but the most archaic commandment of all is the divine, "Let the earth bring forth" (Genesis 1). Stopping that genesis is the most destructive event possible, and we humans have no right to do that. Saving nature is not always morally naive; it can deepen our understanding of the human place in the scheme of things entire, and of our duties on this majestic home planet.

Notes

1 *Rio Declaration on Environment and Development,* Principles 1, 5, UNCED document A/CONF. 151/26, vol. 1, pp. 15–25.

2 *Rio Declaration,* Principle 4.

3 Insurance Institute for Highway Safety (Arlington, Virginia), *Status Report,* vol. 29, no. 10 (September 10, 1994): 3.

4 Jonathan Power, 1992. "Despite Its Gifts, Brazil Is a Basket Case," *Miami Herald,* June 22, p. 10A.

5 The pie chart summarizes data in the *World Development Report 1991* (New York: Oxford University Press, 1991).

6 Peter M. Vitousek, Paul R. Ehrlich, Anne H. Ehrlich, and Pamela A. Matson, "Human Appropriation of the Products of Biosynthesis," *Bio Science* 36 (1986): 368–73.

7 Robert Goodland, "The Case that the World has Reached Limits," in Robert Goodland, Herman E. Daly, and Salah El Serafy (eds.), *Population, Technology, and Lifestyle* (Washington, DC: Island Press, 1992), pp. 3–22.

8 Daniel Hillel, *Out of the Earth* (New York: Free Press, Macmillan, 1991), p. 279.

9 E. O. Wilson, *The Diversity of Life* (Cambridge, MA: Harvard University Press, 1992), p. 267; Alison Jolly, *A World Like Our Own: Man and Nature in Madagascar* (New Haven: Yale University Press, 1980).

10 Geoffrey C. Ward, "The People and the Tiger," *Audubon* 96, 4 (July–August 1994): 62–9.

11 Joel Berger and Carol Cunningham, "Active Intervention and Conservation: Africa's Pachyderm Problem," *Science* 263 (1994): 1241–2.

12 John Bongaarts, "Population Policy Options in the Developing World," *Science* 263 (1994): 771–6.

Environment

In the previous section, we discussed world hunger. Rolston's essay bridges between the issues in the previous section and the issues here. He wants to know what we should do when forced to choose between feeding people and saving nature. Do people always win? Do we feed the starving even if it means we must destroy nature (e.g., by clearing ground to plant more food)? To assume that we should ignores (a) the long-term costs of damaging the environment, (b) the fact that many people deeply value nature for its own sake, and (c) that morality does not require that we abandon things we value simply to help others. To that extent, Rolston's argument parallels Arthur's: neither claims we should cavalierly ignore the starving. However, both claim that morality does not require that we abandon things we deeply value. The other essays in this section further explore questions about our obligations to the environment.

Most people understand the claim that we have obligations and responsibilities to other humans, even strangers – even if they disagree about the scope and strength of these obligations. Many people also understand the claim that we have obligations and responsibilities to animals – even if they think that our obligations

to animals are considerably less stringent than our obligations to humans. However, the claim that we have substantial obligations to or responsibilities for "the environment" befuddles many people. It irritates more than a few people who rave about "those tree huggers."

Yet that is precisely what most authors in this section claim, at least to some degree. Aldo Leopold, the father of the modern environmental movement, claims we must abandon the old anthropocentric (human-centered) conception of ethics and replace it with a non-anthropocentric (environment-centered) ethic. This is in sharp contrast to most people's view. They think ethics is concerned only about the needs and interests of humans (and then, only some humans!). Thus, they never question whether using the environment for our purposes is morally acceptable. Those few who do worry about the environment tend to worry only because they fear that by damaging the environment, we ultimately harm ourselves and our progeny (polluted water, toxic wastes, etc.). For the masses, at least in the United States, the environment's value is wholly instrumental.

That, Leopold claims, must change. We must begin to see the land not as an economic utensil, but as something with intrinsic value. Leopold here voices a common complaint of most environmentalists: that far too many people see and treat the environment is a mere commodity. In different ways the remaining three papers each address this issue. Schmidtz asks about the proper use of cost-benefit analysis (CBA) when deciding whether to undertake a policy that affects the environment. According to CBA, we should weigh both the costs and the benefits of available actions, and then choose the best outcome.

However, he says, we know from experience that businesses who claim to be doing CBA often make dreadful decisions with disastrous consequences for the public and for the environment. Does that show that CBA should be jettisoned? No. These businesses err not because they use CBA but because they focus narrowly on their own corporate interests. They should, instead, do a Full Cost Accounting which considers not only the effects of their actions on the business, but also all relevant human costs as well – including any costs on the environment. If we do, then we have made the best decision we can.

Hill would not be so sure. For he thinks we rightly feel some unease at some destruction of the natural environment, even if it could be justified on some reasonable cost-benefit analysis. Sometimes – perhaps often – this discomfort reflects our belief that CBA usually ignores the long-term effects of destroying a habitat or eliminating a species. This would not be surprising since humans have a penchant for narrow and short-term thinking. However, this does not exhaust our discomfort with such uses of the environment. He thinks that treating the environment as a *mere* resource also fails to live up to the highest ideals of human excellence. Those ideals understand humans' place

in the world, and proceed with an appropriate moral humility. This concept is important on its own, and also because such an attitude is deeply connected with a range of moral virtues we want to cultivate in ourselves and in others. It rejects the idea of human self-importance; it reflects an awareness that we are not all that matters in the world. Understanding our proper place in the world is the first step in being moral.

Carter takes a similar tack to explain why we should be concerned about the environment. David Hume's moral theory provides a mechanism for understanding humans' proper place in the world, the ability to explain why we should care about the environment in general, and non-human animals in particular. Hume claims that human knowledge is built upon our natural tendency to associate ideas. One such tendency is especially important for understanding morals: our tendency to feel sympathy when we see the pain and suffering of others. Of course sympathetic reactions can sometimes be inappropriate or misplaced, and that is where the role of reason enters: to help us remove biases that skew our moral evaluations of the world. Once we recognize that we can critique these evaluations, we can see how they might be fruitfully extended to showing concern for animals, entire species, and even an entire ecological system. For instance, just as humans are naturally moved to feel sympathy for humans, we can be moved to feel sympathy for non-human animals.

It would be worthy to speculate how Carter's views about sympathy arising naturally from experience might resemble Corvino's claims about the role of experience in moral judgment (SEXUALITY), and they might resemble or differ from Kass's claim that our spontaneous repugnance toward some actions is a good indication that the action is immoral.

Further Reading

Callicott, J. (1989) *In Defense of the Land Ethic: Essays in Environmental Philosophy*. Albany, NY: State University of New York Press.

Dower, N. (ed.) (1989) *Ethics and the Environmental Concern*. Aldershot, UK: Avebury Press.

Regan, T. (1984) *Earthbound: New Introductory Essays in Environmental Ethics*. New York: Random House.

Rolston, H. (1986) *Philosophy Gone Wild: Essays in Environmental Ethics*. Buffalo, NY: Prometheus Books.

Sterba, J. (ed.) (1995) *Earth Ethics: Environmental Ethics, Animal Rights, and Practical Applications*. Englewood Cliffs, NJ: Prentice-Hall.

VanDeVeer, D. and Pierce, C. (eds.) (1986) *People, Penguins, and Plastic Trees: Basic Issues in Environmental Ethics*. Belmont, CA: Wadsworth.

—— (1994) *The Environmental Ethics and Policy Book*. Belmont, CA: Wadsworth.

Wenz, P. (2001) *Environmental Ethics*. Oxford: Oxford University Press.

60

The Land Ethic

Aldo Leopold

When god-like Odysseus returned from the wars in Troy, he hanged all on one rope a dozen slave-girls of his household whom he suspected of misbehavior during his absence.

This hanging involved no question of propriety. The girls were property. The disposal of property was then, as now, a matter of expediency, not of right and wrong.

Concepts of right and wrong were not lacking from Odysseus' Greece: witness the fidelity of his wife through the long years before at last his blackprowed galleys clove the wine-dark seas for home. The ethical structure of that day covered wives, but had not yet been extended to human chattels. During the three thousand years which have since elapsed, ethical criteria have been extended to many fields of conduct, with corresponding shrinkages in those judged by expediency only.

The Ethical Sequence

This extension of ethics, so far studied only by philosophers, is actually a process in ecological evolution. Its sequences may be described in ecological as well as in philosophical terms. An ethic, ecologically, is a limitation on freedom of action in the struggle for existence. An ethic, philosophically, is a differentiation of social from anti-social conduct. These are two definitions of one thing. The thing has its origin in the tendency of interdependent individuals or groups to evolve modes of cooperation. The ecologist calls these symbioses. Politics and economics are advanced symbioses in which the original free-for-all competition has been replaced, in part, by cooperative mechanisms with an ethical content.

The complexity of cooperative mechanisms has increased with population density, and with the efficiency of tools. It was simpler, for example, to define the anti-social uses of sticks and stones in the days of the mastodons than of bullets and billboards in the age of motors.

The first ethics dealt with the relation between individuals; the Mosaic Decalogue is an example. Later accretions dealt with the relation between the individual and society. The Golden Rule tries to integrate the individual to society; democracy to integrate social organization to the individual.

There is as yet no ethic dealing with man's relation to land and to the animals and plants which grow upon it. Land, like Odysseus' slave-girls, is still property. The land-relation is still strictly economic, entailing privileges but not obligations.

The extension of ethics to this third element in human environment is, if I read the evidence correctly, an evolutionary possibility and an ecological necessity. It is the third step in a sequence. The first two have already been taken. Individual thinkers since the days of Ezekiel and Isaiah have asserted that the despoliation of land is not only inexpedient but wrong. Society, however, has not yet affirmed their belief. I regard the present conservation movement as the embryo of such an affirmation.

An ethic may be regarded as a mode of guidance for meeting ecological situations so new or intricate, or involving such deferred reactions, that the path of social expediency is not discernible to the average individual. Animal instincts are modes of guidance for the individual in meeting such situations. Ethics are possibly a kind of community instinct in-the-making.

The Community Concept

All ethics so far evolved rest upon a single premise: that the individual is a member of a community of interdependent parts. His instincts prompt him to compete for his place in the community, but his ethics prompt him also to cooperate (perhaps in order that there may be a place to compete for).

The land ethic simply enlarges the boundaries of the community to include soils, waters, plants, and animals, or collectively: the land.

This sounds simple: do we not already sing our love for and obligation to the land of the free and the home of the brave? Yes, but just what and whom do we love? Certainly not the soil, which we are sending helter-skelter downriver. Certainly not the waters, which we assume have no function except to turn turbines, float barges, and carry off sewage. Certainly not the plants, of which we exterminate whole communities without batting an eye. Certainly not the animals, of which we have already extirpated many of the largest and most beautiful

species. A land ethic of course cannot prevent the alteration, management, and use of these "resources," but it does affirm their right to continued existence, and, at least in spots, their continued existence in a natural state.

In short, a land ethic changes the role of *Homo sapiens* from conqueror of the land-community to plain member and citizen of it. It implies respect for his fellow-members, and also respect for the community as such.

The Land Pyramid

An ethic to supplement and guide the economic relation to land presupposes the existence of some mental image of land as a biotic mechanism. We can be ethical only in relation to something we can see, feel, understand, love, or otherwise have faith in.

The image commonly employed in conservation education is "the balance of nature." For reasons too lengthy to detail here, this figure of speech fails to describe accurately what little we know about the land mechanism. A much truer image is the one employed in ecology: the biotic pyramid. I shall first sketch the pyramid as a symbol of land, and later develop some of its implications in terms of landuse.

Plants absorb energy from the sun. This energy flows through a circuit called the biota, which may be represented by a pyramid consisting of layers. The bottom layer is the soil. A plant layer rests on the soil, an insect layer on the plants, a bird and rodent layer on the insects, and so on up through various animal groups to the apex layer, which consists of the larger carnivores.

The species of a layer are alike not in where they came from, or in what they look like, but rather in what they eat. Each successive layer depends on those below it for food and often for other services, and each in turn furnishes food and services to those above. Proceeding upward, each successive layer decreases in numerical abundance. Thus, for every carnivore there are hundreds of his prey, thousands of their prey, millions of insects, uncountable plants. The pyramidal form of the system reflects this numerical progression from apex to base. Man shares an intermediate layer with the bears, raccoons, and squirrels, which eat both meat and vegetables.

The lines of dependency for food and other services are called food chains. Thus soil-oak-deer-Indian is a chain that has now been largely converted to soil-corn-cow-farmer. Each species, including ourselves, is a link in many chains. The deer eats a hundred plants other than oak, and the cow a hundred plants other than corn. Both, then, are links in a hundred chains. The pyramid is a tangle of chains so complex as to seem disorderly, yet the stability of the system proves it to be a highly organized structure. Its functioning depends on the co-operation and competition of its diverse parts.

In the beginning, the pyramid of life was low and squat; the food chains short and simple. Evolution has added layer after layer, link after link. Man is one of thousands of accretions to the height and complexity of the pyramid. Science has given us many doubts, but it has given us at least one certainty: the trend of evolution is to elaborate and diversify the biota.

Land, then, is not merely soil; it is a fountain of energy flowing through a circuit of soils, plants, and animals. Food chains are the living channels which conduct energy upward; death and decay return it to the soil. The circuit is not closed; some energy is dissipated in decay, some is added by absorption from the air, some is stored in soils, peats, and long-lived forests; but it is a sustained circuit, like a slowly augmented revolving fund of life. There is always a net loss by downhill wash, but this is normally small and offset by the decay of rocks. It is deposited in the ocean and, in the course of geological time, raised to form new lands and new pyramids.

The velocity and character of the upward flow of energy depend on the complex structure of the plant and animal community, much as the upward flow of sap in a tree depends on its complex cellular organization. Without this complexity, normal circulation would presumably not occur. Structure means the characteristic numbers, as well as the characteristic kinds and functions, of the component species. This interdependence between the complex structure of the land and its smooth functioning as an energy unit is one of its basic attributes.

When a change occurs in one part of the circuit, many other parts must adjust themselves to it. Change does not necessarily obstruct or divert the flow of energy; evolution is a long series of self-induced changes, the net result of which has been to elaborate the flow mechanism and to lengthen the circuit. Evolutionary changes, however, are usually slow and local. Man's invention of tools has enabled him to make changes of unprecedented violence, rapidity, and scope.

One change is in the composition of floras and faunas. The larger predators are lopped off the apex of the pyramid; food chains, for the first time in history, become shorter rather than longer. Domesticated species from other lands are substituted for wild ones, and wild ones are moved to new habitats. In this worldwide pooling of faunas and floras, some species get out of bounds as pests and diseases, others are extinguished. Such effects are seldom intended or foreseen; they represent unpredicted and often untraceable readjustments in the structure. Agricultural science is largely a race between the emergence of new pests and the emergence of new techniques for their control.

Another change touches the flow of energy through plants and animals and its return to the soil. Fertility is the ability of soil to receive, store, and release energy. Agriculture, by over-drafts on the soil, or by too radical a substitution of domestic for native species in the superstructure, may derange the channels of flow or deplete storage. Soils depleted of their storage or of the organic matter which anchors it, wash away faster than they form. This is erosion.

Waters, like soil, are part of the energy circuit. Industry, by polluting waters or obstructing them with dams, may exclude the plants and animals necessary to keep energy in circulation.

Transportation brings about another basic change: the plants or animals grown in one region are now consumed and returned to the soil in another. Transportation taps the energy stored in rocks, and in the air, and uses it elsewhere; thus we fertilize the garden with nitrogen gleaned by the guano birds from the fishes of seas on the other side of the Equator. Thus the formerly localized and self-contained circuits are pooled on a worldwide scale.

The process of altering the pyramid for human occupation releases stored energy, and this often gives rise, during the pioneering period, to a deceptive exuberance of plant and animal life, both wild and tame. These releases of biotic capital tend to becloud or postpone the penalties of violence.

This thumbnail sketch of land as an energy circuit conveys three basic ideas:

Environment

1 That land is not merely soil.
2 That the native plants and animals kept the energy circuit open; others may or may not.
3 That manmade changes are of a different order than evolutionary changes, and have effects more comprehensive than is intended or foreseen.

These ideas, collectively, raise two basic issues: Can the land adjust itself to the new order? Can the desired alterations be accomplished with less violence?

Biotas seem to differ in their capacity to sustain violent conversion. Western Europe, for example, carries a far different pyramid than Caesar found there. Some large animals are lost; swampy forests have become meadows or plowland; many new plants and animals are introduced, some of which escape as pests; the remaining natives are greatly changed in distribution and abundance. Yet the soil is still there and, with the help of imported nutrients, still fertile; the waters flow normally; the new structure seems to function and to persist. There is no visible stoppage or derangement of the circuit.

Western Europe, then, has a resistant biota. Its inner processes are tough, elastic, resistant to strain. No matter how violent the alterations, the pyramid, so far, has developed some new *modus vivendi* which preserves its habitability for man, and for most of the other natives.

Japan seems to present another instance of radical conversion without disorganization.

Most other civilized regions, and some as yet barely touched by civilization, display various stages of disorganization, varying from initial symptoms to advanced wastage. In Asia Minor and North Africa diagnosis is confused by climatic changes, which may have been either the cause or the effect of advanced wastage. In the United States the degree of disorganization varies locally; it is worst in the Southwest, the Ozarks, and parts of the South, and least in New England and the Northwest. Better land-uses may still arrest it in the less advanced regions. In parts of Mexico, South America, South Africa, and Australia a violent and accelerating wastage is in progress, but I cannot assess the prospects.

This almost worldwide display of disorganization in the land seems to be similar to disease in an animal, except that it never culminates in complete disorganization or death. The land recovers, but at some reduced level of complexity, and with a reduced carrying capacity for people, plants, and animals. Many biotas currently regarded as "lands of opportunity" are in fact already subsisting on exploitative agriculture, i.e., they have already exceeded their sustained carrying capacity. Most of South America is overpopulated in this sense.

In arid regions we attempt to offset the process of wastage by reclamation, but it is only too evident that the prospective longevity of reclamation projects is often short. In our own West, the best of them may not last a century.

The combined evidence of history and ecology seems to support one general deduction: the less violent the manmade changes, the greater the probability of successful readjustment in the pyramid. Violence, in turn, varies with human population density; a dense population requires a more violent conversion. In this respect, North America has a better chance for permanence than Europe, if she can contrive to limit her density.

This deduction runs counter to our current philosophy, which assumes, because a small increase in density enriched human life, that an indefinite increase will enrich it indefinitely.

Ecology knows of no density relationship that holds for indefinitely wide limits. All gains from density are subject to a law of diminishing returns.

Whatever may be the equation for men and land, it is improbable that we as yet know all its terms. Recent discoveries in mineral and vitamin nutrition reveal unsuspected dependencies in the up-circuit: incredibly minute quantities of certain substances determine the value of soils to plants, of plants to animals. What of the down-circuit? What of the vanishing species, the preservation of which we now regard as an esthetic luxury? They helped build the soil; in what unsuspected ways may they be essential to its maintenance? Professor Weaver proposes that we use prairie flowers to reflocculate the wasting soils of the dust bowl; who knows for what purpose cranes and condors, otters and grizzlies may some day be used?

The Outlook

It is inconceivable to me that an ethical relation to land can exist without love, respect, and admiration for land, and a high regard for its value. By value, I of course mean something far broader than mere economic value; I mean value in the philosophical sense.

Perhaps the most serious obstacle impeding the evolution of a land ethic is the fact that our educational and economic system is headed away from, rather than toward, an intense consciousness of land. Your true modern is separated from the land by many middlemen, and by innumerable physical gadgets. He has no vital relation to it; to him it is the space between cities, on which crops grow. Turn him loose for a day on the land, and if the spot does not happen to be a golf links or a "scenic" area, he is bored stiff. If crops could be raised by hydroponics instead of farming, it would suit him very well. Synthetic substitutes for wood, leather, wool, and other natural land products suit him better than the originals. In short, land is something he has "outgrown."

Almost equally serious as an obstacle to a land ethic is the attitude of the farmer for whom the land is still an adversary, or a taskmaster that keeps him in slavery. Theoretically, the mechanization of farming ought to cut the farmer's chains, but whether it really does is debatable.

One of the requisites for an ecological comprehension of land is an understanding of ecology, and this is by no means coextensive with "education"; in fact, much higher education seems deliberately to avoid ecological concepts. An understanding of ecology does not necessarily originate in courses bearing ecological labels; it is quite as likely to be labeled geography, botany, agronomy, history, or economics. This is as it should be, but whatever the label, ecological training is scarce.

The case for a land ethic would appear hopeless but for the minority which is in obvious revolt against these "modern" trends.

The "key-log" which must be moved to release the evolutionary process for an ethic is simply this: quit thinking about decent landuse as solely an economic problem. Examine each question in terms of what is ethically and esthetically right, as well as what is economically expedient. A thing is right when it tends to preserve the integrity, stability, and beauty of the biotic community. It is wrong when it tends otherwise.

It of course goes without saying that economic feasibility limits the tether of what can or cannot be done for land. It always has and it always will. The fallacy the economic determinists have tied around our collective neck, and which we now need to cast off, is the belief that economics determines *all* landuse. This is simply not true. An innumerable host of actions and attitudes, comprising perhaps the bulk of all land relations, is determined by the landuser's tastes and predilections, rather than by his purse. The bulk of all land relations hinges on investments of time, forethought, skill, and faith rather than on investments of cash. As a land-user thinketh, so is he.

I have purposely presented the land ethic as a product of social evolution because nothing so important as an ethic is ever "written." Only the most superficial student of history supposes that Moses "wrote" the Decalogue; it evolved in the minds of a thinking community, and Moses wrote a tentative summary of it for a "seminar." I say tentative because evolution never stops.

The evolution of a land ethic is an intellectual as well as emotional process. Conservation is paved with good intentions which prove to be futile, or even dangerous, because they are devoid of critical understanding either of the land, or of economic land-use. I think it is a truism that as the ethical frontier advances from the individual to the community, its intellectual content increases.

The mechanism of operation is the same for any ethic: social approbation for right actions: social disapproval for right actions: social disapproval for wrong actions.

By and large, our present problem is one of attitudes and implements. We are remodeling the Alhambra with a steam-shovel, and we are proud of our yardage. We shall hardly relinquish the shovel, which after all has many good points, but we are in need of gentler and more objective criteria for its successful use.

Conservation as a Moral Issue

Thus far we have considered the problem of conservation of land purely as an economic issue. A false front of exclusively economic determinism is so habitual to Americans in discussing public questions that one must speak in the language of compound interest to get a hearing. In my opinion, however, one cannot round out a real understanding of the situation in the Southwest without likewise considering its moral aspects.

In past and more outspoken days conservation was put in terms of decency rather than dollars. Who cannot feel the moral scorn and contempt for poor craftsmanship in the voice of Ezekiel when he asks: *Seemeth it a small thing unto you to have fed upon good pasture, but ye must tread down with your feet the residue of your pasture? And to have drunk of the clear waters, but ye must foul the residue with your feet?*

In these two sentences may be found an epitome of the moral question involved. Ezekiel

seems to scorn waste, pollution, and unnecessary damage as something unworthy – as something damaging not only to the reputation of the waster, but to the self-respect of the craft and the society of which he is a member. We might even draw from his words a broader concept – that the privilege of possessing the earth entails the responsibility of passing it on, the better for our use, not only to immediate posterity, but to the Unknown Future, the nature of which is not given us to know. It is possible that Ezekiel respected the soil, not only as a craftsman respects his material, but as a moral being respects a living thing.

Many of the world's most penetrating minds have regarded our so-called "inanimate nature" as a living thing, and probably many of us who have neither the time nor the ability to reason out conclusions on such matters by logical processes have felt intuitively that there existed between man and the earth a closer and deeper relation than would necessarily follow the mechanistic conception of the earth as our physical provider and abiding place.

Of course, in discussing such matters we are beset on all sides with the pitfalls of language. The very words *living thing* have an inherited and arbitrary meaning derived not from reality, but from human perceptions of human affairs. But we must use them for better or for worse.

A good expression of this conception of an organized animate nature is given by the Russian philosopher Onpensky, who presents the following analogy:

> Were we to observe, from the inside, one cubic centimetre of the human body, knowing nothing of the existence of the entire body and of man himself, then the phenomena going on in this little cube of flesh would seem like elemental phenomena in inanimate nature.

He then states that it is at least not impossible to regard the earth's parts – soil, mountains, rivers, atmosphere, etc. – as organs, or parts of organs, of a coordinated whole, each part with a definite function. And, if we could see this whole, as a whole, through a great period of time, we might perceive not only organs with coordinated functions, but possibly also that process of consumption and replacement which in biology we call the metabolism, or growth. In such a case we would have all the visible attributes of a living thing, which we do not now realize to be such because it is too big, and its life processes too slow. And there would also follow that invisible attribute – a soul, or consciousness – which not only Onpensky, but many philosophers of all ages, ascribe to all living things and aggregations thereof, including the "dead" earth.

There is not much discrepancy, except in language, between this conception of a living earth, and the conception of a dead earth, with enormously slow, intricate, and interrelated functions among its parts, as given us by physics, chemistry, and geology. The essential thing for present purposes is that both admit the interdependent functions of the elements. But "anything indivisible is a living being," says Onpensky. Possibly, in our intuitive perceptions, which may be truer than our science and less impeded by words than our philosophies, we realize the indivisibility of the earth – its soil, mountains, rivers, forests, climate, plants, and animals, and respect it collectively not only as a useful servant but as a living being, vastly less alive than ourselves in degree, but vastly greater than ourselves in time and space – a being that was old when the morning stars sang together, and, when the last of us has been gathered unto his fathers, will still be young.

Philosophy, then, suggests one reason why we cannot destroy the earth with moral impunity; namely, that the "dead" earth is an organism possessing a certain kind and degree of life, which we intuitively respect as such. Possibly, to most men of affairs, this reason is too intangible to either accept or reject as a guide to human conduct. But philosophy also offers another and more easily debatable question: was the earth made for man's use, or has man merely the privilege of temporarily possessing an earth made for other and inscrutable purposes? The question of what he can properly do with it must necessarily be affected by this question.

Most religions, insofar as I know, are premised squarely on the assumption that man is the end and purpose of creation, and that not only the dead earth, but all creatures thereon, exist solely for his use. The mechanistic or scientific philosophy does not start with this as a premise, but ends with it as a conclusion and hence may be placed in the same category for the purpose in hand. This high opinion of his own importance in the universe Jeanette Marks stigmatizes as "the great human impertinence." John Muir, in defense of rattlesnakes, protests: "as if nothing that does not obviously make for the benefit of man had any right to exist; as if our ways were God's ways." But the noblest expression of this anthropomorphism is Bryant's "Thanatopsis":

> . . . The hills
> Rock-ribbed and ancient as the sun, – the vales
> Stretching in pensive quietness between;
> The venerable woods – rivers that move
> In majesty, and the complaining brooks
> That make the meadows green, and, poured round all
> Old oceans gray and melancholy waste, –
> *Are but the solemn decorations all*
> Of the great tomb of man.

Since most of mankind today profess either one of the anthropomorphic religions or the scientific school of thought which is likewise anthropomorphic, I will not dispute the point. It just occurs to me, however, in answer to the scientists, that God started his show a good many million years before he had any men for audience – a sad waste of both actors and music – and in answer to both, that it is just barely possible that God himself likes to hear birds sing and see flowers grow. But here again we encounter the insufficiency of words as symbols for realities.

Granting that the earth is for man – there is still a question: what man? Did not the cliff dwellers who tilled and irrigated these our valleys think that they were the pinnacle of creation – that these valleys were made for them? Undoubtedly. And then the Pueblos? Yes. And then the Spaniards? Not only thought so, but said so. And now we Americans? Ours beyond a doubt! (How happy a definition is that one of Hadley's which states, "Truth is that which prevails in the long run"!)

Five races – five cultures – have flourished here. We may truthfully say of our four predecessors that they left the earth alive, undamaged. Is it possibly a proper question or us to consider what the sixth shall say about us? If we are logically anthropomorphic, yes. We and

> . . . all that tread
> The globe are but a handful to the tribes
> That slumber in its bosom. Take the wings
> Of morning; pierce the Barcan wilderness
> Or lose thyself in the continuous woods
> Where rolls the Oregon, and hears no sound
> Save his own dashings – yet the dead are there,
> And millions in those solitudes, since first
> The flight of years began, have laid them down
> In their last sleep.

And so, in time, shall we. And if there be, indeed, a special nobility inherent in the human race – a special cosmic value, distinctive from and superior to all other life – by what token shall it be manifest?

By a society decently respectful of its own and all other life, capable of inhabiting the earth without defiling it? Or by a society like that of John Burrough's potato bug, which exterminated the potato, and thereby exterminated itself? As one or the other shall we be judged in "the derisive silence of eternity."

Thinking Like a Mountain

A deep chesty bawl echoes from rimrock to rimrock, rolls down the mountain, and fades into the far blackness of the night. It is an outburst of wild defiant sorrow, and of contempt for all the adversities of the world.

Every living thing (and perhaps many a dead one as well) pays heed to that call. To the deer it is a reminder of the way of all flesh, to the pine a forecast of midnight scuffles and of blood upon the snow, to the coyote a promise of gleanings to come, to the cowman a threat of red ink at the bank, to the hunter a challenge of fang against bullet. Yet behind these obvious and immediate hopes and fears there lies a deeper meaning, known only to the mountain itself. Only the mountain has lived long enough to listen objectively to the howl of a wolf.

Those unable to decipher the hidden meaning know nevertheless that it is there, for it is felt in all wolf country, and distinguishes that country from all other land. It tingles in the spine of all who hear wolves by night, or who scan their tracks by day. Even without sight or sound of wolf, it is implicit in a hundred small events: the midnight whinny of a pack horse, the rattle of rolling rocks, the bound of a fleeing deer, the way shadows lie under the spruces. Only the ineducable tyro can fail to sense the presence or absence of wolves, or the fact that mountains have a secret opinion about them.

My own conviction on this score dates from the day I saw a wolf die. We were eating lunch on a high rimrock, at the foot of which a turbulent river elbowed its way. We saw what we thought was a doe fording the torrent, her breast awash in white water. When she climbed the bank toward us and shook out her tail, we realized our error: it was a wolf. A half-dozen others, evidently grown pups, sprang from the willows and all joined in a welcoming mêlée of wagging tails and playful maulings. What was literally a pile of wolves writhed and tumbled in the center of an open flat at the foot of our rimrock.

In those days we had never heard of passing up a chance to kill a wolf. In a second we were pumping lead into the pack, but with more excitement than accuracy: how to aim a steep downhill shot is always confusing. When our rifles were empty, the old wolf was down, and a pup was dragging a leg into impassable slide-rocks.

We reached the old wolf in time to watch a fierce green fire dying in her eyes. I realized then, and have known ever since, that there was something new to me in those eyes – something known only to her and to the mountain. I was young then, and full of trigger-itch; I thought that because fewer wolves meant more deer, that no wolves would mean hunters' paradise. But after seeing the green fire die, I sensed that neither the wolf nor the mountain agreed with such a view.

Since then I have lived to see state after state extirpate its wolves. I have watched the face of many a newly wolfless mountain, and seen the south-facing slopes wrinkle with a maze of new deer trails. I have seen every edible bush and seedling browsed, first to anaemic desuetude, and then to death. I have seen every edible tree defoliated to the height of a saddlehorn. Such a mountain looks as if someone had given God a new pruning shears, and forbidden Him all other exercise. In the end the starved bones of the hoped-for deer herd, dead of its own too-much, bleach with the bones of the dead sage, or molder under the high-lined junipers.

I now suspect that just as a deer herd lives in mortal fear of its wolves, so does a mountain live in mortal fear of its deer. And perhaps with better cause, for while a buck pulled down by wolves can be replaced in two or three years, a range pulled down by too many deer may fail of replacement in as many decades.

So also with cows. The cowman who cleans his range of wolves does not realize that he is taking over the wolf's job of trimming the herd to fit the range. He has not learned to think like a mountain. Hence we have dustbowls, and rivers washing the future into the sea.

We all strive for safety, prosperity, comfort, long life, and dullness. The deer strives with his supple legs, the cowman with trap and poison, the statesman with pen, the most of us with machines, votes, and dollars, but it all comes to the same thing: peace in our time. A measure of success in this is all well enough, and perhaps is a requisite to objective thinking, but too much safety seems to yield only danger in the long run. Perhaps this is behind Thoreau's dictum: In wildness is the salvation of the world. Perhaps this is the hidden meaning in the howl of the wolf, long known among mountains, but seldom perceived among men.

61

A Place for Cost-Benefit Analysis

David Schmidtz

How do we decide? Often, we weigh pros and cons. Occasionally, we make the weighing explicit, listing pros and cons and assigning numerical weights. What could be wrong with that? In fact, things sometimes go terribly wrong. This paper considers what cost-benefit analysis can do, and also what it cannot.

1 What is CBA, and What is it For?

Here is an example of how things go wrong. Ontario Hydro is a Canadian government-owned utility company (a Crown Corporation, on a par with Canada Post). Ten years ago, Ontario Hydro was expecting to become a hugely profitable provider of electricity to consumers all over the continent. At that time, Ontario circulated a report explaining how it planned to meet projected demand. Of interest to us is the report's admission that, "The analysis conducted in the development of the Demand/Supply Plans includes those costs which are borne directly by Hydro. It is these costs which can properly be included in Hydro's rates. Costs and benefits for the Ontario community, beyond these direct costs, are not

factored into the cost comparisons." Why not? Because "even if desirable, these costs are difficult to estimate in monetary terms given the diffuse nature of the impacts and wide variety of effects." The costs that Ontario Hydro proposed to take into account "include the social and environmental costs incurred by Hydro but do not include social and environmental costs external to Hydro. This reflects normal business practice. In Hydro's judgment, including additional costs and benefits on an equitable basis would be impracticable."[1]

It is amazing that people would defend such a patently unethical stance by describing it as "normal business practice." Sadly, though, appealing to "normal business practice" is itself normal business practice, and Ontario Hydro is not especially guilty in that regard. Indeed, it is notable that Ontario Hydro was not duplicitous, since it did, after all, express its policy bluntly and publicly. Those who wrote the report evidently had no idea that what they were saying was wrong.

Environmentalists have their own "normal business practices," though, and it is too easy to condemn organizations like Ontario Hydro without thinking things through. Many critics of cost–benefit analysis (henceforth CBA) seem driven by a gut feeling that CBA is heartless. They think that, in denouncing CBA, they are taking a stand against heartlessness. This is unfortunate. The fact is, weighing costs and benefits does not make you a bad person. What makes you a bad person is *ignoring* costs – the costs you impose on others.

The problem with Ontario Hydro arose, not when Ontario Hydro took costs and benefits into account, but rather when it decided *not* to do so. The problem in general terms is a problem of *external* costs. External costs are costs that decision makers ignore, leaving them to be paid by someone else. Ontario Hydro makes a decision that has certain costs. Some of the costs will fall not on Ontario Hydro but on innocent bystanders; following normal business practice, Ontario Hydro seems to say, "That's not our problem."

Decision makers naturally are tempted to ignore external costs. It is only human. Almost everyone does the same sort of thing in one context or another. Every time you leave an empty popcorn box in a theater rather than dispose of it properly, you are doing the same sort of thing as the person who dumps industrial waste in the river rather than dispose of it properly. Every time you drive a car, you are risking other people's lives, and you probably have never wasted a minute feeling guilty about it. And just like you, industrial polluters defend themselves by saying, "But everybody does it!" Part of the problem is simple laziness, when we think no one is watching. Another part of the problem is the normal human desire to conform, even when "normal practice" is unconscionable.

2 Is CBA Anti-Environmentalist?

CBA comes in many variations, and there are many that no ethicist would defend. Needless to say, no ethicist would defend conventional CBA, that is, CBA in the narrowly focused way that Ontario Hydro used it in the 1980s. All sides agree: there can be no general justification for foisting costs on innocent bystanders.

Any controversy concerns whether there are other more justifiable forms of CBA.

Full Cost Accounting, for example, attempts to perform CBA in a way that takes *all* known costs, external as well as internal, into account.[2] Except where otherwise noted, when I speak of CBA, I will be referring to cost–benefit analysis with Full Cost Accounting. As E. J. Mishan's influential text defines it, "in cost–benefit analysis we are concerned with the economy as a whole, with the welfare of a defined society, and not any smaller part of it."[3] Ontario Hydro, perhaps having learned some environmental ethics, changed its stance in 1993 and now trumpets its use of Full Cost Accounting.

Understood in this way, CBA is more than an accounting method. It is a commitment to take responsibility for the consequences of one's actions. That is why environmentalists were once among the most vocal *advocates* of CBA as a vehicle for making industries and governments answerable for the full cost of their decisions.

When, then, should we want policy makers to employ CBA? Two answers come to mind:

- when one group pays the cost of a piece of legislation while another group gets the benefit;
- more generally, whenever decision makers have an incentive not to take full costs into account.

Where benefits of political decisions are concentrated while costs are dispersed, special interest groups can push through favorable policies even when costs to the population at large outweigh benefits. To contain the proliferation of unconscionable policies, we might require that policies be justified by the lights of a proper CBA. Requiring decision makers to provide a CBA, which is then made available for public scrutiny, is one way of teaching decision makers to take environmental costs into account. We do not want upstream people ignoring costs they impose on downstream people.[4] We want cultural and legal arrangements that encourage people to be aware of the full cost of what they do.

The most fundamental argument in favor of CBA has to do with CBA's role as a means of introducing accountability into decisions that affect whole communities. Think about it. If a business pollutes, would it be wrong to insist that the business should be paying the true full cost of its operation? As a mechanism for holding decision makers publicly accountable, CBA has the potential to constrain activities that are not worthwhile when external costs are taken into account. Accordingly, the National Policy Act of 1969 required CBA of environment-related federal projects. To that extent, CBA is a friend of the environment. Or so it seemed at one time.

The tables seemingly have been turning, though. Throughout the 1970s, the Council on Wage and Price Stability and the Office of Management and Budget pressured the Environmental Protection Agency to pay more attention to the costs of complying with standards it was imposing on industry. Finally, in 1981, President Reagan issued an Executive Order requiring government agencies to justify new regulations by submitting a formal CBA (of which an environmental impact statement would be only one part) to the Office of Management and Budget. Why? Why force agencies to perform CBA of their regulatory proposals? The point, very generally, was to force agencies to take into account costs they otherwise would have preferred to ignore. The Reagan administration reputedly felt some regulations were being pushed through by environmental zealots who did not care what their proposals cost in human terms. Accordingly, the Executive Order mandating CBA was perceived as having an anti-environmental thrust. Perhaps partly because of that bit of recent history, current environmentalist opinion remains, on the whole, anti-CBA. The following sections consider reasons (some cogent, some not) for distrusting CBA.

3 Is CBA Anthropocentric?

Is it only the interests of human persons that can be taken into account in a CBA? If so, then isn't CBA essentially anthropocentric? The answer is no. CBA as construed here is partly an accounting procedure, and partly a way of organizing public debate. In no way is it a substitute for philosophical debate. Animal liberationists who think full costs must (by definition?) include pain suffered by animals, for example, must argue for that point in philosophical debate with those who think otherwise. If CBA presupposed one or the other position, thereby preempting philosophical debate, that would be a flaw.

4 Must CBA Treat All Values as Mere Commodities?

As Mark Sagoff nicely expresses the point, "There are some who believe on principle that worker safety and environmental quality ought to be protected only insofar as the benefits of protection balance the costs. On the other hand, people argue – also on principle – that neither worker safety nor environmental quality should be treated as a commodity to be traded at the margin for other commodities, but rather each should be valued for its own sake."[5] The second argument (Sagoff might agree) is a false dichotomy. Valuing worker safety and environmental quality, each for its own sake, is perfectly compatible with recognizing that we cannot have either for free. They have costs, and therefore investing in them is a tradeoff.

For example, suppose a certain recycling process is risky to the workers involved. The process improves environmental quality, but inevitably workers risk getting their hands caught in the machines, and so on. Notice: although we value both environmental quality and worker safety for their own sake, we still have to weigh the operation's costs and benefits. Is recycling's environmental benefit worth the risk? It is a good question, and we are missing the point if we try to end the conversation by saying we value environmental quality for its own sake.

Note: We do not need to imagine different values (worker safety and environmental quality) coming into conflict. The need for CBA can arise even when environmental quality is the only thing at stake. For example, suppose the recycling process in question saves paper (and therefore trees), but saving trees comes at a cost of all the water and electricity used in the process; gasoline is used by trucks that collect the paper from recycling bins, and so on. Therefore, the very recycling process that reduces pollution and natural resource consumption also increases pollution and natural resource consumption in other respects. In this case, our reason to do CBA is precisely that we care about environmental quality.

In a nutshell, we sometimes find ourselves in situations of conflicting values, where the values at stake are really important. Critics of CBA sometimes seem to say, when values at stake are really important, that that is when we should *not* think hard about the costs and benefits of resolving the conflict in one way rather than another. They seem to have things backwards.

Sagoff asserts: "It is the characteristic of cost-benefit analysis that it treats all value judgments other than those made on its behalf as nothing but statements of preference, attitude, or emotion."[6] There are several things going on in this passage. I will mention three. First, the phrase "other than those made on its behalf" is a jest at the pseudo-scientific posturing of radical subjectivists, and the jest is on target. Second, Sagoff is insinuating that it is a mistake simply to assume that all values are reducible to costs and benefits, and here too, Sagoff is on target. On the one hand, it is an economist's job to go as far as possible in treating values as preferences, and within economics narrowly construed, the reductionist bias serves a purpose. On the other hand, when we explore value in more philosophical terms, we cannot treat all values as mere preferences, as if valuing honesty were on a par with valuing chocolate. Accordingly, there is a problem with jumping from economic to philosophical discussion without stopping to remind ourselves that what we take for granted in one discussion cannot be taken for granted in the other.

The third thing Sagoff is saying is that CBA characteristically treats all values as mere preferences. Now, if Sagoff means to say that CBA *typically* does so, he may be right. But if Sagoff

were saying CBA *necessarily* does so, he would be wrong. CBA is about weighing costs and benefits. CBA does not presume everything is either a cost or a benefit. We have to decide which values to treat as mere preferences, costs, or benefits, and which to treat separately, as falling outside the scope of CBA. CBA itself does not make that decision for us. It is true by definition that to care about X is to have a preference regarding X, but we can care about X without thinking X is *merely* a preference. CBA assumes nothing about the nature of values, other than (1) they sometimes come into conflict and (2) no matter what we do, we will in effect be trading them off. CBA does not assume trading off values is unproblematic; it assumes only that we sometimes have no choice.

"Recycling" is a politically correct word, to be sure, but does that mean we should support any operation that uses the word in its title, even if the operation is environmentally catastrophic? Or should we instead stop to think about the operation's costs and benefits? Contra Sagoff, if we stop to think, that does not mean we are treating environmental quality as a mere "preference, attitude, or emotion." Stopping to think can be a way of showing respect.

5   Can CBA Handle Qualitative Values?

Steven Kelman says that CBA presupposes the desirability of being able to express all values as dollar values.[7] However, as Kelman correctly notes, converting values to dollars can be a problem. It can distort the true nature of the values at stake. It is a mistake, though, to think CBA *requires* us to represent every value as a dollar value. For example, if we care about Atlantic Green Turtles and do a CBA of alternative ways of protecting them, nothing in that process even suggests we have reduced the value of turtles to dollars. I admit that a sufficiently crude form of CBA will seem to license ignoring the view that sea turtles are priceless. To a more enlightened environmentalist, though (and in the policy arena, any environmentalist who fails to acknowledge that environmental protection has costs cannot count as enlightened), the very pricelessness of sea turtles is our best reason to insist on asking what will provide the best protection available within our not unlimited budget.

An object's *intrinsic* value is the value it has in and of itself, beyond any value it has as a means to further ends. Note that an object's having intrinsic value does not imply that the object is priceless. There is such a thing as limited intrinsic value. A painting can have an intrinsic value that is real without being infinite, or even particularly large. The value I would get from selling it is its instrumental value to me. The value it has to me in and of itself, simply because it is a beautiful painting, is its intrinsic value to me. Both values are real, but one is instrumental and the other is intrinsic. Neither is necessarily large.

More generally, we sometimes put dollar values on things even when their value to us is essentially different from the value of dollars. Incommensurability of different values is not generally an insurmountable obstacle to CBA. Still, there often is no point in trying to convert a qualitative balancing into something that *looks* like a precise quantitative calculation and thus *looks* scientific but in fact remains the same qualitative balancing, only now its qualitative nature is disguised by the attaching of made-up numbers.

Policy decisions can be like that. We can make up numbers when assessing the value of a public library we could build on land that otherwise will remain a public park. Maybe the numbers will mean something, maybe not. More often, even when we can accurately predict a policy's true costs and benefits, that does not entail that there will be any bottom line from which we simply read off what to do. When competing values cannot be reduced to a common measure without distortion, that makes it harder to know the bottom line. It may even mean there is no unitary bottom line to be known. Sometimes the bottom line is simply that one precious and irreplaceable thing is gained while another precious and irreplaceable thing is lost.

Neither should we expect to be able to arrive at a bottom line by any simple algorithm.

Ontario Hydro (since its reorganization) now tries to be sensitive to vague non-monetized costs, but in practice such sensitivity means their bottom line will reflect not (or not only) numerical inputs so much as their version of informed common sense.[8] Consider an analogy. A computer program can play chess by algorithm. Human chess players cannot. Human chess players need creativity, experience, alertness to unintended consequences, and other skills and virtues that are not algorithmic. People who formulate policy need similar skills and virtues, and interpersonal skills as well. Employing CBA cannot change that.

6 The Structure of CBA

Does CBA presuppose utilitarian moral theory?

Utilitarian moral theory holds roughly that X is right if and only if X maximizes utility, where maximizing utility is a matter of producing the best possible balance of benefits over costs. It may seem obvious that CBA presupposes the truth of utilitarian moral theory. In fact, it does not. CBA is a way of organizing a public forum expressing respect for persons: persons present at the meeting and other persons as well, on whose behalf those present can speak (citizens of faraway countries, future generations, etc.). For that matter, those present at the forum will speak not only on behalf of other persons but on behalf of whatever they care about: animals, trees, canyons, historic sites, and so on.

The forum therefore is defensible on utilitarian grounds, but it does not depend on utilitarian moral theory, for this sort of CBA could and probably should be advocated by deontologists. A conventional CBA that ignored external costs would be endorsed neither by deontologists nor by utilitarians, but CBA with Full Cost Accounting, defended in a public forum, could be endorsed by either.

Does CBA tell us to sacrifice the one for the sake of the many?

We can imagine advocates of CBA jumping to the conclusion that policies are justified whenever benefits exceed costs. That would be a mistake. We need to be more circumspect than that. When benefits exceed costs, the conclusion should be that the policy has passed one crucial test and therefore further discussion is warranted. On the other hand, when a proposal *fails* the test of CBA (when costs exceed benefits), the implication is more decisive, namely that further discussion is not warranted. If enacting a certain proposal would help some people and hurt others, then showing that winners are gaining more than losers are losing counts for something, but it is not decisive. One must then argue that the gain is so great for some people that it justifies imposing a loss on other people. In contrast, to show that losers are losing more than winners are gaining should pretty much end the conversation. Failing CBA is a fairly reliable test of when something is wrong. Passing CBA, however, is not a reliable test of when something is right.

Consider the following case:

> Hospital: Five patients lie on operating tables about to die for lack of suitable organ donors. A UPS delivery person just walked into the office. She is a suitable organ donor for all five patients. If you kidnap her and harvest her organs, you will be saving five and killing one.[9]

Suppose we perform CBA in that case, and it yields the conclusion that, well, five is more than one. Would that imply that taking the delivery person's life is permissible? Required, even? No. Of course, we could quibble about how the calculation works out, but that would miss the fundamental point, which is that when we are talking about killing people, costs and benefits are not the only issue. CBA offers us guidance when our objective is to promote the best possible balance of costs and benefits, but not all situations call on us to maximize what is valuable. Promoting value is not always the best way of respecting it. There are times when morality calls on us not to maximize value but simply to respect it.

I argued that CBA does not presume the truth of utilitarian moral theory. Now it may seem that what I call CBA presumes that utilitarian moral theory is false! On the contrary, even from a broadly utilitarian perspective, we do not want ordinary citizens to have a license to kill whenever they think they can do a lot of good in the process.[10] Some institutions have their utility precisely by *prohibiting* decisions based on utilitarian calculation. Hospitals, for example, cannot serve their purpose if they are a menace to innocent bystanders. Hospitals cannot serve their purpose unless people can trust hospitals to treat people as rights-bearers. Respecting people's rights is part of what helps make it safe to visit hospitals. And making it safe to visit the hospital is a prerequisite of hospitals' functioning properly. Accordingly, we cannot justify cutting up one patient to save five simply by saying five is more than one. Sometimes, numbers do not count.

Therefore, there are limits to the legitimate scope of CBA, and must be, even from a utilitarian perspective. Consider the case of *Peeveyhouse v. Garland Coal.*[11] Having completed a strip-mining operation on the Peeveyhouse property, Garland Coal refused to honor its contractual promise to restore the land to its original condition. The restored land would have been worth only $300 and it would have cost $29,000 to restore it. Still, Peeveyhouse wanted the land restored and Garland Coal had promised to do it.

Incredibly, the Oklahoma court awarded Peeveyhouse only the $300, judging that Garland Coal could not be held financially liable for a restoration when such restoration would not be cost-effective. The Court's verdict generally is regarded as utterly mistaken, though, and one way of understanding the mistake is to see it as a case of failing to understand the limits of CBA's legitimate scope. We live in a society where hospitals cannot take organs without consent. We live in a society where Garland Coal normally would have to honor its contract with Peeveyhouse. Thus, we know where we stand. We need not be perpetually preparing to prove before a tribunal that strip-mining our land or harvesting our internal organs without consent is not cost-effective. Instead, we have a right simply to say "no." In giving us moral space that we govern by right, our laws limit the energy we have to waste: trying to influence public regulators, fighting to keep what belongs to us, fighting to gain what belongs to others. In treating us as rights-bearers, our laws enable us simply to decline proposals that would benefit others at our expense.

Crucially, our being able to say "no" teaches people to search for ways of making progress that benefit everyone. CBA in its simplest form allows some to be sacrificed for the sake of the greater good of others, and therefore CBA in its simplest form is morally problematic. In contrast, CBA as a framework for public discussion, in a regime that treats people as rights-bearers, creates at least some pressure to craft proposals that promise benefits for all.

Again, part of the message here is that the proper purpose of CBA is not to show when a taking is permissible. If we see CBA as indicating when takings are permissible, we will have a problem, because breaking contracts, or taking things from people (including their lives) whenever the benefit is worth the cost is not a way of respecting people. But if we treat CBA as a *constraint* on takings, ruling out inefficient takings without licensing efficient takings, then it is not disrespectful.

Therefore, it would be a mistake to see CBA as an *alternative* to treating people as ends in themselves. On the contrary, when CBA is working properly, and in particular when treated not as a seal of approval for good proposals but rather as a means of filtering out bad proposals, CBA becomes a way of preventing people from treating each other as mere means. In other words, requiring people to offer an accounting of the true costs and benefits of their operations is a way of holding them publicly accountable for failing to treat fellow citizens as ends in themselves. CBA will not filter out every proposal that ought to be filtered out, but it will help to filter out many of the most flagrantly disrespectful proposals, and that is its proper purpose.

Some things are priceless: so what?

Critics of CBA think they capture the moral high ground when they say some things are beyond price. They miss the point. Even if Atlantic Green Turtles are a priceless world heritage, we still have to decide how to save them. We still need to look at costs and benefits of trying to protect them in one way rather than another, for two reasons. First, we need to know whether a certain approach will be effective, given available resources. Dollar for dollar, an effective way of protecting them is better than an ineffective way. Second, we need to know whether the cost of saving them involves sacrificing something else we consider equally priceless.

If baby Jessica has fallen into an abandoned well in Midland, Texas and it will cost nine million dollars to rescue her, is it worth the cost? It seems somehow wrong even to ask the question; after all, it is only money. But it is not wrong. If it would cost nine million dollars to save Jessica's life, what would the nine million dollars otherwise have purchased? Could it have been sent to Africa where it might have saved nine thousand lives? Consider an even more expensive case. If a public utility company in Pennsylvania (in the wake of a frivolous lawsuit blaming its high-voltage power lines for a child's leukemia) calculates that burying its power lines underground will cost two billion dollars, in the process maybe preventing one or two deaths from leukemia, is it only money? If the two billion dollars could have been sent to Africa where it might have saved two million lives, is it obvious we should *not* stop to think about it?

Critics like to say not all values are economic values. They are right, but no values whatsoever are purely economic values in that sense. Even money itself is never only money. In a small town in Texas in 1987, a lot of money was spent to save a baby's life – money that took several lifetimes to produce. It was not only money. It did after all save a baby's life. It also gave a community a chance to show the world what it stands for. These are not trivial things. Neither are many of the other things on which nine million dollars could have been spent.

There are things so valuable to us that we think of them as beyond price. Some economists might disagree, but it is, after all, a fact.

What does this fact imply? When we have no choice but to make tradeoffs, should we ignore items we consider priceless, or should we take them into account? The hard fact is, priceless values sometimes come into conflict. When that happens, and when we try rationally to weigh our options, we are in effect putting a price on that which is priceless.

Note in passing that although critics often speak of incommensurable values, incommensurability is not quite the issue, strictly speaking. Consider the central dilemma of the novel, *Sophie's Choice*.[12] Sophie's two children are about to be executed by a concentration camp commander. The commander says he will kill both children unless Sophie picks one to be killed, in which case the commander will spare the other one. Now, to Sophie, both children are beyond price. She does not value one more than the other. In some sense, she values each of them more than anything. Nevertheless, she does in the end pick one for execution, thereby saving the other one's life. The point is, although her values were incommensurate, she was still able to rank them in a situation where failing to rank them would have meant losing both. The values were incommensur*ate*, but not incommensur*able*. To Sophie, both children were beyond price, but when forced to put a price on them, she could.

Of course, the decision broke her heart. As the sadistic commander foresaw, the process of ranking her previously incommensurate values was psychologically devastating. At some level, commensuration is *always* possible, but there are times when something (our innocence, perhaps) is lost in the process. Perhaps that explains why some critics want to reject CBA; they see it as a mechanism for ranking values that should not be ranked. Unfortunately, although we can wish people like Sophie never had to rank their children and could instead go on thinking of each child as having infinite value, and although we can wish we never had to choose between worker safety and environmental quality, or between different aspects of environmental quality, the real world sometimes requires tradeoffs.

Must CBA measure valuations in terms of willingness to pay?

CBA often is depicted as requiring us to measure a good's value by asking how much people would pay for it. Such a requirement is indeed problematic. One problem: willingness to pay is a function not only of values but also of resources available for bidding on those values. Poorer people show up as less willing to pay even if, in some other sense, they value the good as much. Thus, we might contrive to justify building a waste treatment plant in a poorer neighborhood by determining that poorer people would not pay as much as richer people would to have the plant built elsewhere. Critics call this environmental racism (because minorities tend to live in poorer neighborhoods).[13] Whatever we call it, it looks preposterous.

Is there an alternative that would be more respectful of neighborhoods that provide the most likely building sites? Suppose we initially choose a site by random lottery, and suppose that by luck of the draw, Beverly Hills is selected as the site of the new waste treatment plant. Suppose we then ask Beverly Hills's rich residents what they are willing to pay to site the plant elsewhere. Suppose they say they jointly would pay 50 million dollars to locate the plant elsewhere. Suppose we then announce that the people of Beverly Hills are actually, not just hypothetically, offering 50 million to any neighborhood willing to make room for a waste treatment facility that otherwise will be built in Beverly Hills. Suppose a poor neighborhood votes to accept the bid. Would that be more respectful? Or, suppose no one accepts the Beverly Hills offer, and therefore the plant is built in Beverly Hills. Is there anything wrong with richer residents moving out, selling their houses to poorer people willing to live near the plant in order to live in better houses than they otherwise could afford? If siting a waste treatment plant drives down property values so that poorer people can afford to live in Beverly Hills, while rich people take their money elsewhere, is that a problem?

The implication is that even a random lottery will produce non-random results. No matter where we build a waste treatment facility, people who can afford to move away from waste treatment plants tend to be richer than the people who cannot. Home buyers who move in, accepting the nuisance in order to have a nicer house at a lower price, will tend to be poorer than buyers who opt to pay higher prices to live farther from the nuisance. One thing will never change: waste treatment facilities will tend to be found in poorer neighborhoods. Not even putting them all in Beverly Hills could ever change that.

Must future generations be discounted?

In financial markets, a dollar acquired today is worth more than a dollar we will acquire in a year. The dollar acquired today can be put to work immediately. At worst, it can be put in the bank, and thus be worth perhaps $1.05 in a year. Therefore, if you ask me how much I would pay today to be given a dollar a year from now, I certainly would not pay as much as a dollar. I would pay something less, perhaps about 95 cents. Properly valued, then, the future dollar sells at a discount. Therefore, there is nothing irrational about borrowing against the future to get a profitable project off the ground, even though the cost of borrowing a thousand dollars now will be more than a thousand dollars later.

But here is the catch. There is nothing wrong with taking out a loan, so long as we *pay it back*. But there is something obviously wrong with taking out a loan we have no intention of repaying. In other words, discounting is one thing when the cost of raising capital is internalized; it is something else when we borrow against *someone else's* future rather than our own. We have no right to discount the price that *others* will have to pay for our projects. We have no right to discount externalities. *Redistributive* discounting is objectionable: morally, economically, and sometimes ecologically as well.

7 Does CBA Work?

When individuals engage in CBA, they typically are asking themselves how much they should be willing to pay. That is an obvious and legitimate question because they are, after all, constrained by their budget. In contrast, legislators ask themselves how much they are willing to make *other* people pay, and that is a problem. In that case, paying has become an external cost, and it is no surprise if legislators seem cavalier about how much they are making other people pay. I said earlier that if the analysis shows that losers are losing more than winners are gaining, that should pretty much end the conversation. Unfortunately, the conversation does not always stop there. When a program's benefits are concentrated within influential constituencies, legislators conceal how costly the program is to taxpayers at large. Similarly, owners of dogs that bark all night ignore the costs they impose on neighbors. Again, it is not because people are evil. They are only human. Situations where we are not accountable tend not to bring out the best in us. CBA with Full Cost Accounting is a way of trying to introduce accountability.

In theory, then, CBA is a way of organizing agenda for public debates that respect all persons, and valuable non-persons, too. How does it work in practice? An effective resolution to hold decision makers and policy makers accountable for all costs would, in theory, make for a cleaner, safer, more prosperous society. The prospect of a public accounting can make corporations and governments rethink what they owe to the environment, and in Ontario Hydro's case, it seems to have done exactly that. Still, there is much corruption in the world and nothing like CBA will ever put an end to it. As with any other accounting method, the quality of the output typically will be only as good as the quality of the inputs. The valuations we supply as inputs drive the results, so how to avoid biased valuations? Biased inputs generate biased outputs. CBA, then, has the potential to be a smokescreen for the real action that takes place before numbers get added.

Can anything guarantee that the process of CBA will not itself be subject to the same political piracy that CBA was supposed to limit? Probably not. As I said earlier, the verdict in *Peevevhouse* generally is regarded as mistaken. What I did not mention is that, as Andrew Morriss notes, "Shortly after the *Peeveyhouse* decision, a corruption investigation uncovered more than thirty years of routine bribery of several of the court's members."[14] CBA per se does not correct for corrupted inputs. Neither does CBA stop people from applying CBA to cases where CBA has no legitimate role. However, if the process is public, with affected parties having a chance to protest when their interests are ignored, public scrutiny will have some tendency to correct for biased inputs. It also will encourage planners to supply inputs that can survive scrutiny in the first place. If the process is public, people will step forward to scrutinize not only valuations, but also the list of options, suggesting possibilities that planners may have concealed or overlooked. Still, the most we can hope for is that CBA done in public view helps to give democracies a fighting chance to operate as democracies are supposed to operate.

Even if we know the costs and benefits of any particular factor, that does not guarantee that we have considered everything. In the real world, we must acknowledge that for any actual calculation we perform, there could be some cost or benefit or risk we have overlooked. What can we do to avoid overlooking what in retrospect will become painfully obvious? Although it is no guarantee, the best thing I can think of is to open the process to public scrutiny.

Conclusions

I talked about doing CBA with Full Cost Accounting, but no mechanical procedure can be guaranteed to take all costs into account. For any mechanical procedure we devise, there will be situations where that procedure overlooks something important. Moreover, CBA with Full Cost Accounting is only one form of CBA. Many other forms of CBA are indefensible, and no ethicist would defend them. We do well not to conflate different forms of CBA, though, and we do well not to demonize the general idea of weighing costs and benefits. CBA has been subject to enormous philosophical scrutiny, and many critics have found it wanting. I do not dismiss the criticisms. In my experience, no form of collective decision making really works, and CBA cannot fix all the faults inherent in collective decision making. If and when collective decision making is unavoidable, CBA can, to some extent, put the onus on representatives to produce a balance of reasons open to public examination.

However, CBA is not magic. There is a limit to what it can do. CBA is a way of organizing information. It can be a forum for eliciting further information. It can be a forum for correcting biased information. It can be a forum for giving affected parties a voice in community decision making, thereby leading to better understanding of, and greater acceptance of, the tradeoffs involved in running a community.

CBA can be all of these good things, but it is not necessarily so. CBA can constrain a system's tendency to invite abuse, but CBA is prone to the same abuse that infects the system as a whole. It is no panacea. It is an antidote to abuse that is itself subject to abuse.

Notes

Originally published in *Philosophical Issues* (*Noûs* annual supplement) 11(2001): 148–71. Reprinted with permission of Blackwell Publishers.

1 Michael McDonald, J. T. Stevenson, and Wesley Craig, *Finding a Balance of Values: An Ethical Assessment of Ontario Hydro's Demand/Supply Plan*, Report to Aboriginal Research Coalition of Ontario, 1992, pp. 33–4.
2 The terms are not quite standardized. What I call Full Cost Accounting is what some people call Multiple Accounts Analysis or Life Cycle Analysis. Whatever term we use, though, I have in mind a kind of CBA that does not deliberately ignore any cost whatever, including costs imposed on future generations.
3 E. J. Mishan, (1976) *Elements of Cost-Benefit Analysis*, 2nd edn (London: George Allen & Unwin, 1976), p. 11.
4 Donald Scherer, *Upstream/Downstream: Issues in Environmental Ethics* (Philadelphia: Temple University Press, 1990).

5 Mark Sagoff, "At the Shrine of Our Lady of Fatima, or Why Political Questions Are Not All Economic," *Arizona Law Review* 23 (1981): 1283–98, at 1288–89.

6 Sagoff, "At the Shrine of Our Lady of Fatima, or Why Political Questions Are Not All Economic," pp. 1290–91.

7 Steven Kelman, "Cost-Benefit Analysis: An Ethical Critique," *Regulation* (January/February 1981): 33–40, at 33.

8 As gleaned from case studies: "Full Cost Accounting for Decision Making at Ontario Hydro," prepared by ICF Incorporated for the Environmental Protection Agency, and "Environmentally Sustainable Development Guidelines for Southeast False Creek," prepared by Sheltair Inc. for the City of Vancouver, 1998.

9 Judith Jarvis Thomson, "Killing, Letting Die, and the Trolley Problem," *Monist* 59 (1976): 204–17.

10 So, while I expect that any plausible moral theory will uphold a fairly strong version of the intuitively powerful distinction between doing and allowing, a moral theory need not treat the distinction as foundational. Any good Millian consequentialist recognizes that a fairly sweeping legal distinction between killing and letting die is morally justifiable.

11 382 P.2d 109 Oklahoma, 1962. For a discussion of what the case shows about relative merits of statutory versus common law, see Mishan, *Elements of Cost-Benefit Analysis*.

12 William Styron, *Sophie's Choice* (New York: Random House, 1979).

13 Robert Bullard, *Dumping In Dixie: Race, Class, and Environmental Quality* (Boulder, CO: Westview Press, 1990).

14 Andrew Morriss, "Lessons for Environmental Law from the American Codification Debate," in *The Common Law and the Environment*, ed. Roger Meiners and Andrew Morriss (Lanham, MD: Rowman & Littlefield, 2000), pp. 130–57, at p. 144.

Further Reading

Schmidtz, David and Willott, Elizabeth (2001) *Environmental Ethics: What Really Matters. What Really Works*. New York: Oxford University Press.

62

Ideals of Human Excellence and Preserving Natural Environments

Thomas E. Hill Jr.

I

A wealthy eccentric bought a house in a neighborhood I know. The house was surrounded by a beautiful display of grass, plants, and flowers, and it was shaded by a huge old avocado tree. But the grass required cutting, the flowers needed tending, and the man wanted more sun. So he cut the whole lot down and covered the yard with asphalt. After all it was his property and he was not fond of plants.

It was a small operation, but it reminded me of the strip mining of large sections of the Appalachians. In both cases, of course, there were reasons for the destruction, and property rights could be cited as justification. But I could not help but wonder, "What sort of person would do a thing like that?"

Many Californians had a similar reaction when a recent governor defended the leveling of ancient redwood groves, reportedly saying, "If you have seen one redwood, you have seen them all."

Incidents like these arouse the indignation of ardent environmentalists and leave even apolitical observers with some degree of moral discomfort. The reasons for these reactions are mostly obvious. Uprooting the natural environment robs both present and future generations of much potential use and enjoyment. Animals too depend on the environment; and even if one does not value animals for their own sakes, their potential utility for us is incalculable. Plants are needed, of course, to replenish the atmosphere quite aside from their aesthetic value. These reasons for hesitating to destroy forests and gardens are not only the most obvious ones, but also the most persuasive for practical purposes. But, one wonders, is there nothing more behind our discomfort? Are we concerned solely about the potential use and enjoyment of the forests, etc., for ourselves, later generations, and perhaps animals? Is there not something else which disturbs us when we witness the destruction or even listen to those who would defend it in terms of cost/benefit analysis?

Imagine that in each of our examples those who would destroy the environment argue elaborately that, even considering future generations of human beings and animals, there are benefits in "replacing" the natural environment which outweigh the negative utilities which environmentalists cite.[1] No doubt we could press the argument on the facts, trying to show that the destruction is shortsighted and that its defenders have underestimated its potential harm or ignored some pertinent rights or interests. But is this all we could say? Suppose we grant, for a moment, that the utility of destroying the redwoods, forests, and gardens is equal to their potential for use and enjoyment by nature lovers and animals. Suppose, further, that we even grant that the pertinent human rights and animal rights, if any, are evenly divided for and against destruction. Imagine that we also concede, for argument's sake, that the forests contain no potentially useful endangered species of animals and plants. Must we then conclude that there is no further cause for moral concern? Should we then feel morally indifferent when we see the natural environment uprooted?

II

Suppose we feel that the answer to these questions should be negative. Suppose, in other words, we feel that our moral discomfort when we confront the destroyers of nature is not fully explained by our belief that they have miscalculated the best use of natural resources or violated rights in exploiting them. Suppose, in particular, we sense that part of the problem is that the natural environment is being viewed exclusively as a natural *resource*. What could be the ground of such a feeling? That is, what is there in our system of normative principles and values that could account for our remaining moral dissatisfaction?[2]

Some may be tempted to seek an explanation by appeal to the interests, or even the rights, of plants. After all, they may argue, we only gradually came to acknowledge the moral importance of all human beings, and it is even more recently that consciences have been aroused to give full weight to the welfare (and rights?) of animals. The next logical step, it may be argued, is to acknowledge a moral requirement to take into account the interests (and rights?) of plants. The problem with the strip miners, redwood cutters, and the like, on this view, is not just that they ignore the welfare and rights of people and animals; they also fail to give due weight to the survival and health of the plants themselves.

The temptation to make such a reply is understandable if one assumes that all moral questions are exclusively concerned with whether *acts* are right or wrong, and that this, in turn, is determined entirely by how the acts impinge on the rights and interests of those directly affected. On this assumption, if there is cause for moral concern, some right or interest has been neglected; and if the rights and interests of human beings and animals have already been taken into account, then there must be some other pertinent interests, for example, those of plants. A little reflection will show that the assumption is mistaken; but, in any case, the conclusion that plants have rights or morally relevant interests is surely untenable. We do speak of what is "good for" plants, and they can "thrive" and also be "killed." But this does not imply that they have "interests" in any morally relevant sense. Some people apparently believe that plants grow better if we talk to them, but the idea that the plants suffer and enjoy, desire and dislike, etc., is clearly outside the range of both common sense and scientific belief. The notion that the forests should be preserved to avoid *hurting* the trees or because they have a *right* to life is not part of a widely shared moral consciousness, and for good reason.[3]

Another way of trying to explain our moral discomfort is to appeal to certain religious beliefs. If one believes that all living things were created by a God who cares for them and entrusted us with the use of plants and animals only for limited purposes, then one has a reason to avoid careless destruction of the forests, etc., quite aside from their future utility. Again, if one believes that a divine force is immanent in all nature, then too one might have reason to care for more than sentient things. But such arguments require strong and controversial premises, and, I suspect, they will always have a restricted audience.

Early in this century, due largely to the influence of G. E. Moore, another point of view developed which some may find promising.[4] Moore introduced, or at least made popular, the idea that certain states of affairs are intrinsically valuable – not just valued, but valuable, and not necessarily because of their effects on sentient beings. Admittedly Moore came to believe that in fact the only intrinsically valuable things were conscious experiences of various sorts, but this restriction was not inherent in the idea of intrinsic value.[5] The intrinsic goodness of something, he thought, was an objective, nonrelational property of the thing, like its texture or color, but not a property perceivable by sense perception or detectable by scientific instruments. In theory at least, a single tree thriving alone in a universe without sentient beings, and even without God, could be intrinsically valuable. Since, according to Moore, our duty is to maximize intrinsic value, his theory could obviously be used to argue that we have reason not to destroy natural environments independently of how they affect human beings and animals. The survival of a forest might have worth beyond its worth *to* sentient beings.

This approach, like the religious one, may appeal to some but is infested with problems. There are, first, the familiar objections to intuitionism, on which the theory depends. Metaphysical and epistemological doubts about nonnatural, intuited properties are hard to suppress, and many have argued that the theory rests on a misunderstanding of the words *good*, *valuable*, and the like.[6] Second, even if we try to set aside these objections and think in Moore's terms, it is far from obvious that everyone would agree that the existence of forests, etc., is intrinsically valuable. The test, says Moore, is what we would say when we imagine a universe with just the thing in question, without any effects or accompaniments, and then we ask, "Would its existence be better than its nonexistence?" Be careful, Moore would remind us, not to construe this question "Would you *prefer* the existence of that universe to its nonexistence?" The question is, "Would its existence have the objective, non-relational property, intrinsic goodness?"

Now even among those who have no worries about whether this really makes sense, we might well get a diversity of answers. Those prone to destroy natural environments will doubtless give one answer, and nature lovers will likely give another. When an issue is as controversial as the one at hand, intuition is a poor arbiter.

The problem, then, is this. We want to understand what underlies our moral uneasiness at the destruction of the redwoods, forests, etc., even apart from the loss of these as resources for human beings and animals. But I find no adequate answer by pursuing the questions, "Are rights or interests of plants neglected," What is God's will on the matter?" and "What is the intrinsic value of the existence of a tree or forest?" My suggestion, which is in fact the main point of this paper, is that we look at the problem from a different perspective. That is, let us turn for a while from the effort to find reasons why certain *acts* destructive of natural environments are morally wrong to the ancient task of articulating our ideals of human excellence. Rather than argue directly with destroyers of the environment who say, "Show me why what I am doing is *immoral*," I want to ask, "What sort of person would want to do what they propose?" The point is not to skirt the issue with an *ad hominem*, but to raise a different moral question, for even if there is no convincing way to show that the destructive acts are wrong (independently of human and animal use and enjoyment), we may find that the willingness to indulge in them reflects the absence of human traits that we admire and regard morally important.

This strategy of shifting questions may seem more promising if one reflects on certain analogous situations. Consider, for example, the Nazi who asks, in all seriousness, "Why is it wrong for me to make lampshades out of human skin – provided, of course, I did not myself kill the victims to get the skins?" We would react more with shock and disgust than with indignation, I suspect, because it is even more evident that the question reveals a defect in the questioner than that the proposed act is itself immoral. Sometimes we may not regard an act wrong at all though we see it as reflecting something objectionable about the person who does it. Imagine, for example, one who laughs spontaneously to himself when he reads a newspaper account of a plane crash that kills hundreds. Or, again, consider an obsequious grandson who, having waited for his grandmother's inheritance with mock devotion, then secretly spits on her grave when at last she dies. Spitting on the grave may have no adverse consequences and perhaps it violates no rights. The moral uneasiness which it arouses is explained more by our view of the agent than by any conviction that what he did was immoral. Had he hesitated and asked, "Why shouldn't I spit on her grave?" it would seem more fitting to ask him to reflect on the sort of person he is than to try to offer reasons why he should refrain from spitting.

III

What sort of person, then, would cover his garden with asphalt, strip mine a wooded mountain, or level an irreplaceable redwood grove? Two sorts of answers, though initially appealing, must be ruled out. The first is that persons who would destroy the environment in these ways are either shortsighted, underestimating the harm they do, or else are too little concerned for the well-being of other people. Perhaps too they have insufficient regard for animal life. But these considerations have been set aside in order to refine the controversy. Another tempting response might be that we count it a moral virtue, or at least a human ideal, to love nature. Those who value the environment only for its utility must not really love nature and so in this way fall short of an ideal. But such an answer is hardly satisfying in the present context, for what is at issue is *why* we feel moral discomfort at the activities of those who admittedly value nature only for its utility. That it is ideal to care for nonsentient nature beyond its possible use is really just another way of expressing the general point which is under controversy.

What is needed is some way of showing that this ideal is connected with other virtues, or human excellences, not in question. To do so is difficult and my suggestions, accordingly, will be tentative and subject to qualification. The main idea is that, though indifference to nonsentient nature does not *necessarily* reflect the absence of virtues, it often signals the absence of certain traits which we want to encourage because they are, in most cases, a natural basis for

the development of certain virtues. It is often thought, for example, that those who would destroy the natural environment must lack a proper appreciation of their place in the natural order, and so must either be ignorant or have too little humility. Though I would argue that this is not necessarily so, I suggest that, given certain plausible empirical assumptions, their attitude may well be rooted in ignorance, a narrow perspective, inability to see things as important apart from themselves and the limited groups they associate with, or reluctance to accept themselves as natural beings. Overcoming these deficiencies will not guarantee a proper moral humility, but for most of us it is probably an important psychological preliminary. Later I suggest, more briefly, that indifference to nonsentient nature typically reveals absence of either aesthetic sensibility or a disposition to cherish what has enriched one's life and that these, though not themselves moral virtues, are a natural basis for appreciation of the good in others and gratitude.[7]

Consider first the suggestion that destroyers of the environment lack an appreciation of their place in the universe.[8] Their attention, it seems, must be focused on parochial matters, on what is, relatively speaking, close in space and time. They seem not to understand that we are a speck on the cosmic scene, a brief stage in the evolutionary process, only one among millions of species on Earth, and an episode in the course of human history. Of course, they know that there are stars, fossils, insects, and ancient ruins; but do they have any idea of the complexity of the processes that led to the natural world as we find it? Are they aware how much the forces at work within their own bodies are like those which govern all living things and even how much they have in common with inanimate bodies? Admittedly scientific knowledge is limited and no one can master it all; but could one who had a broad and deep understanding of his place in nature really be indifferent to the destruction of the natural environment?

This first suggestion, however, may well provoke a protest from a sophisticated anti-environmentalist.[9] "Perhaps *some* may be indifferent to nature from ignorance," the critic may object, "but *I* have studied astronomy, geology, biology, and biochemistry, and I still unashamedly regard the nonsentient environment as simply a resource for our use. It should not be wasted, of course, but what should be preserved is decidable by weighing long-term costs and benefits." "Besides," our critic may continue, "as philosophers you should know the old Humean formula, 'You cannot derive an *ought* from an *is*.' *All* the facts of biology, biochemistry, etc., do not entail that I ought to love nature or want to preserve it. What one understands is one thing; what one values is something else. Just as nature lovers are not necessarily scientists, those indifferent to nature are not necessarily ignorant."

Although the environmentalist may concede the critic's logical point, he may well argue that, as a matter of fact, increased understanding of nature tends to heighten people's concern for its preservation. If so, despite the objection, the suspicion that the destroyers of the environment lack deep understanding of nature is not, in most cases, unwarranted, but the argument need not rest here.

The environmentalist might amplify his original idea as follows: "When I said that the destroyers of nature do not appreciate their place in the universe, I was not speaking of intellectual understanding alone, for, after all, a person can *know* a catalog of facts without ever putting them together and seeing vividly the whole picture which they form. To see oneself as just one part of nature is to look at oneself and the world from a certain perspective which is quite different from being able to recite detailed information from the natural sciences. What the destroyers of nature lack is this perspective, not particular information."

Again our critic may object, though only after making some concessions: "All right," he may say, "*some* who are indifferent to nature may lack the cosmic perspective of which you speak, but again there is no *necessary* connection between this failing, if it is one, and any particular evaluative attitude toward nature. In fact, different people respond quite differently when they move to a wider perspective. When *I* try

to picture myself vividly as a brief, transitory episode in the course of nature, I simply get depressed. Far from inspiring me with a love of nature, the exercise makes me sad and hostile. You romantics think only of poets like Wordsworth and artists like Turner, but you should consider how differently Omar Khayyam responded when he took your wider perspective. His reaction, when looking at his life from a cosmic viewpoint, was 'Drink up, for tomorrow we die.' Others respond in an almost opposite manner with a joyless Stoic resignation, exemplified by the poet who pictures the wise man, at the height of personal triumph, being served a magnificent banquet, and then consummating his marriage to his beloved, all the while reminding himself, 'Even this shall pass away.' "[10] In sum, the critic may object, "Even if one should try to see oneself as one small transitory part of nature, doing so does not dictate any particular normative attitude. Some may come to love nature, but others are moved to live for the moment; some sink into sad resignation; others get depressed or angry. So indifference to nature is not necessarily a sign that a person fails to look at himself from the larger perspective."

The environmentalist might respond to this objection in several ways. He might, for example, argue that even though some people who see themselves as part of the natural order remain indifferent to nonsentient nature, this is not a common reaction. Typically, it may be argued, as we become more and more aware that we are parts of the larger whole we come to value the whole independently of its effect on ourselves. Thus, despite the possibilities the critic raises, indifference to nonsentient nature is still in most cases a sign that a person fails to see himself as part of the natural order.

If someone challenges the empirical assumption here, the environmentalist might develop the argument along a quite different line. The initial idea, he may remind us, was that those who would destroy the natural environment fail to *appreciate* their place in the natural order. "Appreciating one's place" is not simply an intellectual appreciation. It is also an attitude, reflecting what one values as well as what one knows. When we say, for example, that both the servile and the arrogant person fail to *appreciate* their place in a society of equals, we do not mean simply that they are ignorant of certain empirical facts, but rather that they have certain objectionable attitudes about their importance relative to other people. Similarly, to fail to appreciate one's place in nature is not merely to lack knowledge or breadth of perspective, but to take a certain attitude about what matters. A person who *understands* his place in nature but still views nonsentient nature merely as a resource takes the attitude that nothing is *important* but human beings and animals. Despite first appearances, he is not so much like the pre-Copernican astronomers who made the intellectual error of creating the Earth as the "center of the universe" when they made their calculations. He is more like the racist who, though well aware of other races, treats all races but his own as insignificant.

So construed, the argument appeals to the common idea that awareness of nature typically has, and should have, a humbling effect. The Alps, a storm at sea, the Grand Canyon, towering redwoods, and "the starry heavens above" move many a person to remark on the comparative insignificance of our daily concerns and even of our species, and this is generally taken to be a quite fitting response.[11] What seems to be missing, then, in those who understand nature but remain unmoved is a proper humility.[12] Absence of proper humility is not the same as selfishness or egoism, for one can be devoted to self-interest while still viewing one's own pleasures and projects as trivial and unimportant.[13] And one can have an exaggerated view of one's own importance while grandly sacrificing for those one views as inferior. Nor is the lack of humility identical with belief that one has power and influence, for a person can be quite puffed up about himself while believing that the foolish world will never acknowledge him. The humility we miss seems not so much a belief about one's relative effectiveness and recognition as an attitude which measures the importance of things independently of their relation to oneself or to some narrow group with which one identifies. A paradigm of a

person who lacks humility is the self-important emperor who grants status to his family because it is *his*, to his subordinates because *he* appointed them, and to his country because *he* chooses to glorify it. Less extreme but still lacking proper humility is the elitist who counts events significant solely in proportion to how they affect his class. The suspicion about those who would destroy the environment, then, is that what they count important is too narrowly confined insofar as it encompasses only what affects beings who, like us, are capable of feeling.

This idea that proper humility requires recognition of the importance of nonsentient nature is similar to the thought of those who charge meat eaters with species-ism. In both cases it is felt that people too narrowly confine their concerns to the sorts of beings that are most like them. But, however intuitively appealing, the idea will surely arouse objections from our anti-environmentalist critic. "Why," he will ask, "do you suppose that the sort of humility I *should* have requires me to acknowledge the importance of nonsentient nature aside from its utility? You cannot, by your own admission, argue that nonsentient nature *is* important, appealing to religious or intuitionist grounds. And simply to assert, without further argument, that an ideal humility requires us to view nonsentient nature as important for its own sake begs the question at issue. If proper humility is acknowledging the relative importance of things as one should, then to show that I must lack this you must first establish that one *should* acknowledge the importance of nonsentient nature."

Though some may wish to accept this challenge, there are other ways to pursue the connection between humility and response to nonsentient nature. For example, suppose we grant that proper humility requires only acknowledging a due status to sentient beings. We must admit, then, that it is logically possible for a person to be properly humble even though he viewed all nonsentient nature simply as a resource. But this logical possibility may be a psychological rarity. It may be that, given the sort of beings we are, we would never learn humility before persons without developing the general capacity to cherish, and regard important, many things for their own sakes. The major obstacle to humility before persons is self-importance, a tendency to measure the significance of everything by its relation to oneself and those with whom one identifies. The processes by which we overcome self-importance are doubtless many and complex, but it seems unlikely that they are exclusively concerned with how we relate to other people and animals. Learning humility requires learning to feel that something matters besides what will affect oneself and one's circle of associates. What leads a child to care about what happens to a lost hamster or a stray dog he will not see again is likely also to generate concern for a lost toy or a favorite tree where he used to live.[14] Learning to value things for their own sake, and to count what affects them important aside from their utility, is not the same as judging them to have some intuited objective property, but it is necessary to the development of humility and it seems likely to take place in experiences with nonsentient nature as well as with people and animals. If a person views all nonsentient nature merely as a resource, then it seems unlikely that he has developed the capacity needed to overcome self-importance.

IV

This last argument, unfortunately, has its limits. It presupposes an empirical connection between experiencing nature and overcoming self-importance, and this may be challenged. Even if experiencing nature promotes humility before others, there may be other ways people can develop such humility in a world of concrete, glass, and plastic. If not, perhaps all that is needed is limited experience of nature in one's early, developing years; mature adults, having overcome youthful self-importance, may live well enough in artificial surroundings. More importantly, the argument does not fully capture the spirit of the intuition that an ideal person stands humbly before nature. That idea is not simply that experiencing nature tends to

foster proper humility before other people; it is, in part, that natural surroundings encourage and are appropriate to an ideal sense of oneself as part of the natural world. Standing alone in the forest, after months in the city, is not merely good as a means of curbing one's arrogance before others; it reinforces and fittingly expresses one's acceptance of oneself as a natural being.

Previously we considered only one aspect of proper humility, namely, a sense of one's relative importance with respect to other human beings. Another aspect, I think, is a kind of *self-acceptance*. This involves acknowledging, in more than a merely intellectual way, that we are the sort of creatures that we are. Whether one is self-accepting is not so much a matter of how one attributes *importance* comparatively to oneself, other people, animals, plants, and other things as it is a matter of understanding, facing squarely, and responding appropriately to who and what one is, e.g., one's powers and limits, one's affinities with other beings and differences from them, one's unalterable nature and one's freedom to change. Self-acceptance is not merely intellectual awareness, for one can be intellectually aware that one is growing old and will eventually die while nevertheless behaving in a thousand foolish ways that reflect a refusal to acknowledge these facts. On the other hand, self-acceptance is not passive resignation, for refusal to pursue what one truly wants within one's limits is a failure to accept the freedom and power one has. Particular behaviors, like dying one's gray hair and dressing like those twenty years younger, do not *necessarily* imply lack of self-acceptance, for there could be reasons for acting in these ways other than the wish to hide from oneself what one really is. One fails to accept oneself when the patterns of behavior and emotion are rooted in a desire to disown and deny features of oneself, to pretend to oneself that they are not there. This is not to say that a self-accepting person makes no value judgments about himself, that he likes all facts about himself, wants equally to develop and display them; he can, and should feel remorse for his past misdeeds and strive to change his current vices. The point is that he does not disown them, pretend that they do not exist or are facts about something other than himself. Such pretense is incompatible with proper humility because it is seeing oneself as better than one is.

Self-acceptance of this sort has long been considered a human excellence, under various names, but what has it to do with preserving nature? There is, I think, the following connection. As human beings we are part of nature, living, growing, declining, and dying by natural laws similar to those governing other living beings; despite our awesomely distinctive human powers, we share many of the needs, limits, and liabilities of animals and plants. These facts are neither good nor bad in themselves, aside from personal preference and varying conventional values. To say this is to utter a truism which few will deny, but to accept these facts, as facts about oneself, is not so easy – or so common. Much of what naturalists deplore about our increasingly artificial world reflects, and encourages, a denial of these facts, an unwillingness to avow them with equanimity.

Like the Victorian lady who refuses to look at her own nude body, some would like to create a world of less transitory stuff, reminding us only of our intellectual and social nature, never calling to mind our affinities with "lower" living creatures. The "denial of death," to which psychiatrists call attention, reveals an attitude incompatible with the sort of self-acceptance which philosophers, from the ancients to Spinoza and on, have admired as a human excellence.[15] My suggestion is not merely that experiencing nature causally promotes such self-acceptance, but also that those who fully accept themselves as part of the natural world lack the common drive to disassociate themselves from nature by replacing natural environments with artificial ones. A storm in the wilds helps us to appreciate our animal vulnerability, but, equally important, the reluctance to experience it may *reflect* an unwillingness to accept this aspect of ourselves. The person who is too ready to destroy the ancient redwoods may lack humility, not so much in the sense that he exaggerates his importance relative to others, but rather in the sense that he tries to avoid seeing himself as one among many natural creatures.

V

My suggestion so far has been that, though indifference to nonsentient nature is not itself a moral vice, it is likely to reflect either ignorance, a self-importance, or a lack of self-acceptance which we must overcome to have proper humility. A similar idea might be developed connecting attitudes toward nonsentient nature with other human excellences. For example, one might argue that indifference to nature reveals a lack of either an aesthetic sense or some of the natural roots of gratitude.

When we see a hillside that has been gutted by strip miners or the garden replaced by asphalt, our first reaction is probably, "How ugly!" The scenes assault our aesthetic sensibilities. We suspect that no one with a keen sense of beauty could have left such a sight. Admittedly not everything in nature strikes us as beautiful, or even aesthetically interesting, and sometimes a natural scene is replaced with a more impressive architectural masterpiece. But this is not usually the situation in the problem cases which environmentalists are most concerned about. More often beauty is replaced with ugliness.

At this point our critic may well object that, even if he does lack a sense of beauty, this is no moral vice. His cost/benefit calculations take into account the pleasure others may derive from seeing the forests, etc., and so why should he be faulted?

Some might reply that, despite contrary philosophical traditions, aesthetic and morality are not so distinct as commonly supposed. Appreciation of beauty they may argue, is a human excellence which morally ideal persons should try to develop. But, setting aside this controversial position, there still may be cause for moral concern about those who have no aesthetic response to nature. Even if aesthetic sensibility is not itself a moral virtue, many of the capacities of mind and heart which it presupposes may be ones which are also needed for an appreciation of other people. Consider, for example, curiosity, a mind open to novelty, the ability to look at things from unfamiliar perspectives, empathetic imagination, interest in details, variety, and order, and emotional freedom from the immediate and the practical. All these, and more, seem necessary to aesthetic sensibility, but they are also traits which a person needs to be fully sensitive to people of all sorts. The point is not that a moral person must be able to distinguish beautiful from ugly people; the point is rather that unresponsiveness to what is beautiful, awesome, dainty, dumpy, and otherwise aesthetically interesting in nature probably reflects a lack of the openness of mind and spirit necessary to appreciate the best in human beings.

The anti-environmentalist, however, may refuse to accept the charge that he lacks aesthetic sensibility. If he claims to appreciate seventeenth-century miniature portraits, but to abhor natural wildernesses, he will hardly be convincing. Tastes vary, but aesthetic sense is not *that* selective. He may, instead, insist that he *does* appreciate natural beauty. He spends his vacations, let us suppose, hiking in the Sierras, photographing wildflowers, and so on. He might press his argument as follows: "I enjoy natural beauty as much as anyone, but I fail to see what this has to do with preserving the environment independently of human enjoyment and use. Nonsentient nature is a resource, but one of its best uses is to give us pleasure. I take this into account when I calculate the costs and benefit of preserving a park, planting a garden, and so on. But the problem you raised explicitly set aside the desire to preserve nature as a means to enjoyment. I say let us enjoy nature fully while we can, but if all sentient beings were to die tomorrow, we might as well blow up all plant life as well. A redwood grove that no one can use or enjoy is utterly worthless."

The attitude expressed here, I suspect, is not a common one, but it represents a philosophical challenge. The beginnings of a reply may be found in the following. When a person takes joy in something, it is a common (and perhaps natural) response to come to cherish it. To cherish something is not simply to be happy with it at the moment, but to care for it for its own sake. This is not to say that one necessarily sees it as having feelings and so wants it to feel good nor does it imply that one judges the thing to have Moore's intrinsic value. One simply wants the thing to survive and (when appropriate) to thrive, and not simply for its utility. We see this attitude repeatedly regarding mementos. They are not simply valued as a means to remind us of happy occasions; they come to be valued for their own sake. Thus, if someone really took joy in the natural environment, but was prepared to blow it up as soon as sentient life ended, he would lack this common human tendency to cherish what enriches our lives. While this response is not itself a moral virtue, it may be a natural basis of the virtue we call "gratitude." People who have no tendency to cherish things that give them pleasure may be poorly disposed to respond gratefully to persons who are good to them. Again the connection is not one of logical necessity, but it may nevertheless be important. A nonreligious person unable to "thank" anyone for the beauties of nature may nevertheless feel "grateful" in a sense; and I suspect that the person who feels no such "gratitude" toward nature is unlikely to show proper gratitude toward people.

Suppose these conjectures prove to be true. One may wonder what is the point of considering them. Is it to disparage all those who view nature merely as a resource? To do so, it seems, would be unfair, for, even if this attitude typically stems from deficiencies which affect one's attitudes toward sentient beings, there may be exceptions and we have not shown that their view of nonsentient nature is itself blameworthy. But when we set aside questions of blame and inquire what sorts of human traits we want to encourage, our reflections become relevant in a more positive way. The point is not to insinuate that all anti-environmentalists are defective, but to see that those who value such traits as humility, gratitude, and sensitivity to others have reason to promote the love of nature.

Notes

The author thanks Gregory Kavka, Catherine Harlow, the participants at a colloquium at the University of Utah, and the referees for *Environmental Ethics*, Dale Jamieson and Donald Scherer, for helpful comments on earlier drafts of this paper.

1 When I use the expression "the natural environment," I have in mind the sort of examples with which I began. For some purposes it is important to distinguish cultivated gardens from forests, virgin forests from replenished ones, irreplaceable natural phenomena from the replaceable, and so on; but these distinctions, I think, do not affect my main points here. There is also a broad sense, as Hume and Mill noted, in which all that occurs, miracles aside, is "natural." In this sense, of course, strip mining is as natural as a beaver cutting trees for his dam, and, as parts of nature, we cannot destroy the "natural" environment but only alter it. As will be evident, I shall use *natural* in a narrower, more familiar sense.

2 This paper is intended as a preliminary discussion in *normative* ethical theory (as opposed to *metaethics*). The task, accordingly, is the limited, though still difficult, one of articulating the possible basis in our beliefs and values for certain particular moral judgments. Questions of ultimate justification are set aside. What makes the task difficult and challenging is not that conclusive proofs from the foundation of morality are attempted; it is rather that the particular judgments to be explained seem at first not to fall under the most familiar moral principles (e.g., utilitarianism, respect for rights).

3 I assume here that having a right presupposes having interests in a sense which in turn presupposes a capacity to desire, suffer, etc. Since my main concern lies in another direction, I do not argue the point, but merely note that some regard it as debatable. See, for example, W. Murray Hunt, "Are *Mere Things* Morally Considerable?" *Environmental Ethics* 2 (1980): 59–65; Kenneth E. Goodpaster, "On Stopping at Everything," *Environmental Ethics* 2 (1980): 288–94; Joel Feinberg, "The Rights of Animals and Unborn Generations," in William Blackstone, ed., *Philosophy and Environmental Crisis* (Athens: University of Georgia Press, 1974), pp. 43–68; Tom Regan, "Feinberg on What Sorts of Beings Can Have Rights," *Southern Journal of Philosophy* (1976): 485–98; Robert Elliot, "Regan on the Sort of Beings that Can Have Rights," *Southern Journal of Philosophy* (1978): 701–5; Scott Lehmann, "Do Wildernesses Have Rights?" *Environmental Ethics* 2 (1981): 129–46.

4 G. E. Moore, *Principia Ethica* (Cambridge: Cambridge University Press, 1903); *Ethics* (London: H. Holt, 1912).

5 G. E. Moore, "Is Goodness a Quality?" *Philosophical Papers* (London. George Allen and Unwin, 1959), 95–7.

6 See, for example, P. H. Nowell-Smith, *Ethics* (New York: Penguin Books, 1954).

7 The issues I raise here, though perhaps not the details of my remarks, are in line with Aristotle's view of moral philosophy, a view revitalized recently by Philippa Foot's *Virtue and Vice* (Berkeley: University of California Press, 1979), Alasdair McIntyre's *After Virtue* (Notre Dame: Notre Dame Press, 1981), and James Wallace's *Virtues and Vices* (Ithaca and London: Cornell University Press, 1978), and other works. For other reflections on relationships between character and natural environments, see John Rodman, "The Liberation of Nature," *Inquiry* (1976): 83–131 and L. Reinhardt, "Some Gaps in Moral Space: Reflections on Forests and Feelings," in Mannison, McRobbie, and Routley, eds., *Environmental Philosophy* (Canberra: Australian National University Research School of Social Sciences, 1980).

8 Though for simplicity I focus upon those who do strip mining, etc., the argument is also applicable to those whose utilitarian calculations lead them to preserve the redwoods, mountains, etc., but who care for only sentient nature for its own sake. Similarly the phrase "indifferent to nature" is meant to encornpass those who are indifferent *except* when considering its benefits to people and animals.

9 For convenience I use the labels *environmentalist* and *anti-environmentalist* (or *critic*) for the opposing sides in the rather special controversy I have raised. Thus, for example, my "environmentalist" not only favors conserving the forests, etc., but finds something objectionable in wanting to destroy them even aside from the costs to human beings and animals. My "anti-environmentalist" is not simply one who wants to destroy the environment; he is a person who has no qualms about doing so independent of the adverse effects on human beings and animals.

10 "Even this shall pass away," by Theodore Tildon, in *The Best Loved Poems of the American People*, ed., Hazel Felleman (Garden City, NY: Doubleday Co., 1936).

11 An exception, apparently, was Kant, who thought "the starry heavens" sublime and compared them with "the moral law within," but did not for all that see our species as comparatively insignificant.

12 By "proper humility" I mean that sort and degree of humility that is a morally admirable character trait. How precisely to define this is, of course, a controversial matter; but the point for present purposes is just to set aside obsequiousness, false modesty, underestimation of one's abilities, and the like.

13 I take this point from some of Philippa Foot's remarks.

14 The causal history of this concern may well depend upon the object (tree, toy) having given the child pleasure, but this does not mean that the object is then valued only for further pleasure it may bring.

15 See, for example, Ernest Becker, *The Denial of Death* (New York: Free Press, 1973).

63

Hume and Nature

Alan Carter

Would it be morally wrong for the last sentient being to engage in deliberate environmental destruction when little would be gained by it? Many of us think that it would be. And through posing a similar question, Richard Routley persuasively argues that species and ecosystems, for example, must be taken to possess intrinsic value.[1] This, Routley claims, is not only why it would be wrong for the last person to so act but also why our present moral theories, in omitting to ascribe intrinsic value to nonhuman, natural entities, fail to explain why the destructive action would be wrong. Hence, what seems to be urgently required is a new, environmental ethic – one that is consistent with widely held moral intuitions concerning the wrongness of treating individual nonhuman animals in certain ways, and that is equally consistent with the intuition that intentionally causing the extinction of species or destroying ecosystems is wrong.

Unfortunately, this has proved to be far easier said than done. Indeed, perhaps the most enduring, and seemingly intractable, problem within the field of environmental ethics is the apparent irreconcilability between: (i) granting moral weight to the preservation of ecosystems

and various species of fauna and flora; and (ii) viewing a disregard for animal welfare or animal rights as immoral. For as J. Baird Callicott has infamously argued, if one accords rights to individual nonhumans,[2] or extends utilitarianism to include within its calculus the pains and pleasures of nonhuman sentient life,[3] then '[t]he lynx, cougar, and other wild feline predators . . . should be regarded as merciless, wanton, and incorrigible murderers of their fellow creatures, who not only kill, it should be added, but cruelly toy with their victims, thus increasing the measure of pain in the world.'[4] Alternatively, if one subscribes to Aldo Leopold's land ethic, which holds that a 'thing is right when it tends to preserve the integrity, stability, and beauty of the biotic community',[5] then 'predators generally should be nurtured and preserved as critically important members of the biotic communities to which they are native'.[6] Callicott sides squarely with Leopold, and seeks to employ the moral philosophy of David Hume in support. However, it could be argued that a less partisan reading of Hume[7] actually allows environmental ethicists to make sense of the pull many of them feel towards a concern for animal welfare or a respect for animal rights and, simultaneously, towards the preservation of ecosystems and of the species within them. In other words, it can be argued that Hume's moral philosophy, when applied to environmental ethics, should not be viewed as responsible for the divide between environmentalism and animal liberation, but rather as the means by which they may be re-united. But for such an ambitious claim to be established, we would first need an appropriate interpretation of Hume's moral philosophy.

1   Humean Metaethics

In drawing a distinction between the 'offices of *reason* and of *taste*',[8] Hume is able to enquire whether moral properties are 'matters of fact' and discoverable by reason, or simply a matter of personal taste. And he is in no doubt about the answer:

> can there be any difficulty in proving, that vice and virtue are not matters of fact, whose existence we can infer by reason? Take any action allow'd to be vicious: Wilful murder, for instance. Examine it in all lights, and see if you can find that matter of fact, or real existence, which you call *vice*. In which-ever way you take it, you find only certain passions, motives, volitions and thoughts. There is no other matter of fact in the case. The vice entirely escapes you, as long as you consider the object. You never can find it, till you turn your reflexion into your own breast, and find a sentiment of disapprobation, which arises in you, towards this action. Here is a matter of fact; but 'tis the object of feeling, not of reason.[9]

And Hume later concludes that reason, in ascertaining truth and falsehood, 'discovers objects as they really stand in nature, without addition or diminution', while taste, which is responsible for the 'sentiments' of vice and virtue and of beauty and deformity, 'has a productive faculty, and guilding or staining all natural objects with the colours, borrowed from internal sentiment, raises in a manner a new creation'.[10] In other words, it appears that moral 'properties', such as virtue, and aesthetic 'properties', such as beauty, 'are not qualities in objects, but perceptions in the mind'.[11] Nevertheless, there remains a sense in which we 'see' how virtuous a

certain person is and a sense in which we 'see' how beautiful certain landscapes are – for in viewing them, we 'guild' and 'stain' them. And this suggests that we 'project'[12] moral and aesthetic 'properties' onto objects.

Further support for the view that Hume thinks that we can 'see' moral 'properties' is provided by his explicit comparison of vice and virtue with colour.[13] The colours that we see appear, at least in part, to be dependent upon our sense organs and upon their present condition. For whenever one spends a long time in a room lit only by a tungsten filament lightbulb and then walks outside into the daylight, the world appears blue for a few moments. Clearly, the world isn't blue. We temporarily 'stain' it that colour, as it were. But as no one else sees the blueness, then, it would seem, it must be a private, individual 'projection'. But then, one might argue, is there any good reason for not concluding that all colour vision is a projection? And if it is a projection, that would not mean that we were not 'seeing' colours (though it would have significant implications for what 'to see' actually means).[14]

Moreover, even if 'seeing' colours actually consists in projecting them onto the world, that would not entail that we cannot, at times, get the colour wrong. For temporarily seeing the world as blue and then thinking it to be blue is as clear a case a case as any of getting it wrong. And thinking the world to be blue is mistaken because, as Hume insists, how objects appear in daylight to everyone with normal eyesight and in a normal condition (for example, not having been exposed exclusively to yellow light for too long) 'is denominated their true and real colour, even while colour is allowed to be merely a phantasm of the senses'.[15] Most importantly, therefore, if we can get the colour wrong, and if 'seeing' vice is like seeing colours, then even if moral 'properties' are projections, we could still, in principle, make incorrect moral judgements.

However, it might well be asked, if 'seeing' moral 'properties' really is comparable to projecting colours onto the world, and if they are 'merely a phantasm of the senses', why do we take moral 'properties' as seriously as we do?

One reason might be that even if the colours we see are 'merely a phantasm of the senses', we nevertheless take them to be the cause of what we see. For example, we ordinarily assume that blue light is what causes us to see blue. Similarly, if we 'see' vice and virtue, then it is likely that we would take such moral 'properties' to be the cause of our moral responses. But in order to understand precisely why the 'perception' of vice and virtue might motivate us, we first need to consider some other aspects of Hume's philosophy.

Occupying a central role within his general philosophy is his theory of the association of ideas – a psychological theory which is premised upon a distinction between what Hume calls 'ideas' and what he calls 'impressions'. Impressions include the perceptions we derive from our senses, the pleasures and pains we experience, and our 'sentiments', 'passions' or 'feelings'. Our ideas are, as it were, 'copies' of our impressions. Ordinarily they are weaker and less motivating than impressions. For example, the mere idea of pain would usually affect our behaviour less dramatically than would a painful sensation.

What Hume observes is that we have a psychological propensity towards associating ideas, and that upon thinking of one idea we tend to think of an idea associated with it. He also holds that the 'force' of one idea can be transferred to an associated idea, and that the force of an impression can be transferred to the idea we have of it. Indeed, he holds that an idea can acquire so much force through association with an especially forceful impression or idea that it can become an impression itself.

One important product of the human tendency to associate ideas is, in Hume's view, the tendency to feel sympathy. Painful sensations can be extremely 'forceful'. Hence, one quickly acquires a very forceful idea of pain. One also associates whatever causes pain – sustaining an injury, for example – with that forceful idea. And one further associates certain effects pain has on one – such as uncontrollable screaming and squirming – with the forceful idea one has of pain. Because other human beings resemble one closely, then when one

sees others sustain some injury and cry out in pain, one will tend to associate such causes and effects with one's own pain. And because the idea of one's own pain is so forceful, one will tend to have a forceful idea of another's pain. Moreover, because pain is something one dislikes intensely and ardently seeks to avoid, then one will tend to dislike others being in pain, and will wish for them to avoid being subject to it. Hence, behaviour traits that tend to be harmful in their consequences for those with whom we sympathise will therefore be despised, and ones that tend to be beneficial will be highly valued.

However, because of this tendency to associate ideas, we will have a tendency to feel most sympathy towards those with whom we most 'associate'. And because we 'associate' more with some people than with others, this can lead to partiality. But partiality can create difficulties for social interaction. As Hume writes:

> every particular man has a peculiar position with regard to others; and it is impossible we could ever converse together on any reasonable terms, were each of us to consider characters and persons, only as they appear from his particular point of view. In order, therefore, to prevent those continual *contradictions*, and arrive at a more *stable* judgement of things, we fix on some *steady* and *general* points of view; and always, in our thoughts, place ourselves in them, whatever may be our present situation.[16]

To arrive at a 'steady' and 'general' point of view, we must employ our reason to abstract from any prejudices or biases we might be susceptible to. Consequently, we come to value behaviour traits which are *generally* beneficial, and not merely of benefit to our family and friends. Such behaviour traits constitute the 'natural' virtues. And behaviour traits which are generally harmful, we come to regard as despicable. Such behaviour traits constitute the 'natural' vices. In a word, given (a) our dislike of and motivation to avoid pain, and our like of and motivation to seek pleasure, (b) our tendency to move from one idea to an associated one, and (c) the social necessity of adopting a general standpoint, then we will disdain and be repelled by vicious characters, and we will value and be attracted to virtuous ones.

But, for Hume, the story doesn't end here. Society provides numerous benefits – which makes it valuable to us in terms of our own individual self-interest. Society also profits those with whom we sympathize. And in order for a social existence to remain valuable, people need to act according to certain rules: the rules of justice. These prescribe ways of behaving that are generally beneficial. Moreover, they are such that it is considered wrong to break them even in those rare instances where more benefit would flow from their infringement. The rules of justice arise by means of convention – hence they are 'artificial'. And because of their 'artificiality', the tendency to abide by them is an 'artificial virtue', while the tendency to break them is an 'artificial vice'. However, while the rules of justice are conventional, they are not merely conventional. For, ideally, they benefit all within a society, and persist because they do so.

Thus we see that, while the rules of justice might be valued because they benefit us and those we sympathize with, reason is essential for discovering the appropriate rules. It was necessary to reason carefully about which rules would, in actual fact, have beneficial effects when universally, or at least generally, adhered to. Furthermore, while 'moral properties' – such as vice and virtue – originate in the human tendency to feel sympathy, reason is essential if they are to be determined accurately. For reason is required in order to arrive at the general standpoint from which the virtues and vices may be clearly 'discerned'. Nevertheless, as we noted earlier, such 'properties' remain projections – or 'phantasms', as Hume puts it.

But all this seems to generate a problem. If, at the sight of the injury and writhing of a person one closely 'associates' with, the association of ideas leads to one feeling pain (a forceful idea becoming an impression), then the motivation to remove the source of that pain is quite understandable. But why should an assessment of character based upon a general standpoint or the appraisal of behaviour according to a general rule (a rule of justice) motivate anyone? Neither appears, at first sight, to be intimately connected with a personally motivating pain or pleasure.

It is not clear that Hume provides a compelling answer. However, it is not impossible to supply one on his behalf. Consider the following: Imagine Amy and her friends coming across a man beating with a heavy stick a severely over-ladened boy in order to force him to continue climbing with his heavy load, and without rest, to the top of a long and steep incline. Amy immediately 'sees' how vicious is the man's behaviour, as does Bob and Cathy. Dan, however, sees nothing wrong in the man mercilessly beating the boy. But when Amy, Bob and Cathy later remark on how vicious was the man's behaviour, Dan comes to think that he was mistaken in not seeing the viciousness. He thinks he should have seen it, but was suffering from 'moral blindness' due to his partiality – a moral blindness resulting from the fact that the 'vicious' man is a close and dear friend. And in now thinking that he 'should' have seen the viciousness that he now presumes was there to be seen, Dan is now motivated to avoid mimicking such 'vicious' behaviour and to prevent his friend from acting in that way again.

Why? Because, while the 'vice' Amy projects is a different token to that projected by Bob or Cathy, all three, in 'seeing' the same type, presume that they are all seeing the same token. And it is to that seemingly objective 'property' of the stick-wielding man's behaviour that each presumes he or she is referring. In other words, the supposed referents of certain varieties of moral discourse are not individual projections, but seemingly objective properties. Moreover, it is precisely such a 'property' that Dan now believes he should have perceived. And it is further presumed that it is the 'vice' which was responsible for the boy's having to endure such torment. Amy, Bob and Cathy feel a strong antipathy towards the boy's pain because of their associating his pain with their own. And by means of the association of ideas, that strong antipathy is transferred onto the seemingly objective property of viciousness, which is taken to have caused the boy's suffering. As pain is to be avoided, then the apparent cause of that pain is equally to be avoided. As pain is repellent, then the apparent cause of that pain is equally repellent. In short, vice is the sort of thing to avoid and to disapprove of emphatically. And as Dan now thinks that vice was there to be seen, then he thinks that he should have seen it, that in some way he was defective in failing to see it, and that in future he *will* see it and will disapprove of and be repelled by such 'vicious' behaviour. Moreover, if he doesn't see it, he will be viewed as abnormal and subject to censure. Indeed, *he* will be viewed as repellent.

Now, one advantage of construing moral 'properties' – the supposed referents of moral discourse – as seemingly objective properties which we presume all are equally capable of perceiving directly, rather than construing them simply as individual feelings, is that we can engage in arguments about such supposed referents. We cannot engage in similar arguments about opinions which merely result from personal tastes. If Amy likes something and Bob dislikes it, there is no inconsistency. But if Amy says that it is good and Bob says that it is not, then there is a clear disagreement between them. Indeed, they are contradicting each other. Construing the supposed referents of moral discourse as seemingly objective properties makes intelligible the arguments we frequently have about what is and what is not good – arguments that would be unintelligible if we were merely expressing our personal tastes.

Additionally, if one believes that one 'perceives' a moral 'property' correctly, then one is more likely to attempt to persuade others to 'see' it the same way than if one simply thinks that the differing assessments are due to differences in personal taste. Moreover, if there is reason to think that one might be in error because everyone else agrees that the moral 'property' is other than how one 'perceives' it, then there is reason to try to 'see' it differently – to try to 'see' it correctly. And given that moral disagreement is usually regarded as a serious matter, it seems a mistake, therefore, simply to reduce moral 'properties' to personal tastes.

Earlier we noted that Hume holds that an idea can acquire so much force through association with an especially forceful impression or idea that it, too, can become an impression. Given how much social pressure one can feel

when one fails to 'see' things the way others 'see' them, given how forceful the idea this pressure gives rise to can thus become, and given that one would like to perceive an objective moral property correctly, then it is quite understandable, from a Humean standpoint, how Dan could come to acquire an impression of his friend's vice – in other words, of how he could come to 'see' it for himself. And when he comes to 'see' the vice, it is quite understandable how he might come to view the vice, presumed to be the cause of pain, as 'objectively' repellent, and how he would then be motivated to avoid it. In a word, *the idea of 'vice' comes to be so associated with such forceful ideas and impressions that it, too, becomes an impression.* And because this impression is intimately connected to our passions, it is highly motivating.

2 Humean Normative Ethics

What moral principles might be thought to follow from the discussion so far? Behavioural traits which, in general, minimize suffering and maximize well-being would be expected to constitute the virtues, and virtuous behaviour would be expected to include a tendency to abide by social rules which, ideally, serve to minimize the suffering and maximize the well-being of all within one's society.

But there is no reason why we could not go further than Hume was prepared to go. And we might go beyond Hume in two ways. First, if we are to employ our reason in order to avoid prejudice, then there seems to be no good reason for stopping at the boundaries of our own society when seeking a general standpoint. A Humean ethic should therefore be cosmopolitan. But we could go further still. If we employ reason so as to be impartial, then in order to regard certain individuals as not meriting an equal appraisal or equal treatment, we would need to identify some morally relevant factor which differentiated them from the rest. For, *ceteris paribus*, any property of A which justifies treating or judging A in a certain manner will equally justify treating or judging B in a similar manner if B also possesses that property. Hence, unless there is a morally relevant difference which separates humans from nonhuman animals, it seems that it would be inconsistent of us not to count in our moral calculations their welfare alongside that of humans.

Second, not only do we dislike physical pain, we also greatly dislike our goals being frustrated. In short, each of us values our own freedom. And there is no reason why the association of ideas cannot underpin a general valuing of freedom paralleling the way in which it underpins a general valuing of welfare. For just as we dislike our own freedom being restricted in certain ways, by means of the association of ideas we can come to dislike those sorts of restrictions being placed upon others' freedom. Furthermore, in order to reach agreement we can adopt a general standpoint with respect to evaluating restrictions on freedom. Hence, behavioural traits which are consistent with safeguarding everyone's freedom can also be expected to be considered virtuous. And social rules which serve to safeguard individual freedom can equally be expected to be 'seen' to be extremely valuable. Put another way, there is nothing to prevent a Humean from insisting on freedom-safeguarding rights as well as on rules which serve to maximize welfare. And unless there is a morally relevant difference which separates humans from nonhuman animals, it seems that we should respect animal rights along with human rights.

3   An Application of Humean Moral Philosophy to Environmental Concerns

What, then, would follow from applying a Humean approach to environmental problems? We have seen that, although Hume ultimately bases morality on sympathy, reason plays an essential role in identifying an impartial standpoint and in ascertaining the rules of justice. And we have observed that unless there is a morally relevant difference which separates humans from nonhuman animals, then it would be inconsistent of us not to count their welfare alongside human welfare in our moral

calculations or not to respect their rights alongside human rights.

However, there *is* a morally significant difference between humans and nonhuman animals: with some possible exceptions, the latter do not 'perceive' moral 'properties'. And as nonhuman animals do not 'perceive' moral 'properties', then it is wholly inappropriate to view them as moral agents bearing moral responsibility for their actions. Consequently, we cannot, with justification, condemn predators for catching their prey. But unless nonhuman animals differ with respect to some other morally significant property that would justify their being treated by moral agents differently from how humans are treated, and insofar as they feel pain just as we do, then to disregard animal welfare is no less immoral than disregarding the welfare of humans.[17] Moreover, unless nonhuman animals differ with respect to some other morally significant property that would justify their being treated by moral agents differently from how humans are treated, and insofar as they feel frustration, as we do, in being confined or restricted, then to disregard the rights of animals is no less immoral than disregarding human rights.[18] In a word, the essential role played by reason in Hume's philosophy is sufficient for it to be amenable to cooption by promoters of both animal welfare and animal rights.

But what of the preservation of species and ecosystems? The stability and integrity of an ecosystem is essential for the well-being of the sentient beings dependent upon it. And if their well-being matters morally, so does the stability and integrity of the ecosystems they inhabit. Moreover, its stability and integrity requires the preservation of a large number of the species found within it. Furthermore, although predators harm the prey they catch, they ordinarily increase the well-being of those who escape their clutches, for predators prevent the numbers of their prey rising to a point where a great many would starve by overshooting the carrying capacity of their environment.

It should also be noted that evolution ordinarily serves to benefit the members of a species, even though it has been claimed that what is in the interests of a species is not what is in the interests of its members.[19] The latter has been advanced because, it has been argued, it is in the interests of the species to evolve, and evolution requires a large turnover of individual lives. For given an environment's finite carrying capacity with respect to the species in question, the shorter time individual members of the species live after producing offspring, then the greater the number of 'generations' that can appear within any given period of time, and the faster the process of evolution. But it would not seem to be in the interests of individuals to die relatively young.

However, evolution of the species would ordinarily mean that its future individual members were better adapted to their environment and would therefore flourish within it to a greater extent than less evolved individuals would have done. And surely it is in the interests of an individual to flourish. Moreover, if members of a species do not flourish to a greater extent than previous 'generations' because their predators have also evolved, then less evolved members would have fared far worse. Furthermore, if the species had remained unchanged, other species could be expected to have evolved in a manner that made them better adapted to occupying its niche, and thus less evolved members of the species would be far worse off than more evolved ones would have been. And it is surely not in an individual's interests to find that other species are now better adapted to surviving within its niche. So, it would seem that maintaining the conditions for the evolution of any species is indeed in the interests of individual members of that species: namely, future members of that species.[20]

Nevertheless, while all the above goes some way towards a moral recognition of most environmentalist concerns, there are some remaining gaps. Many environmentalists are concerned with preserving species that have so few remaining members that it seems clear that their role within an ecosystem is inessential for its stability.[21] Many environmentalists are also concerned to preserve 'unspoilt' inanimate natural entities (such as mountains or rivers), and not merely because of the habitats which they

provide for sentient beings. The most likely explanation for these concerns is the great aesthetic value which landscapes, species and ecosystems are 'perceived' to possess. And the 'perception' of such a value provides no insurmountable difficulty for a Humean, because aesthetic 'properties', on a Humean account, are projections of a similar kind to moral 'properties'.

However, it might be objected that all this seems to fail to take into account Routley's Last Person Argument, with which we began. Now, Peter Singer suspects – as I do – that one of the more promising avenues for justifying concern for species preservation may well be that 'the destruction of a whole species is the destruction of something akin to a great work of art'.[22] But he doubts that this avenue would actually lead to the promised land. For if Singer found himself, genuinely, to be the last sentient being, he doubts that it would really matter if he were to amuse himself 'by making a bonfire of all the paintings in the Louvre'.[23] No one would ever enjoy those paintings again, so why should their destruction matter?

But there is some reason to think that this might not be the most appropriate response to the Last Person Argument. If one happened to be the last sentient being, then no significant moral problems would seem to result from one's viewing the last member of a non-sentient species as the sort of thing that it would be wrong to destroy needlessly. For instance, so viewing the last member of a species would not cause any harm to other sentient beings. Yet viewing the rarity of a species as greatly increasing the value of any surviving members of that species would, ordinarily, greatly aid the preservation of species. And because a species might play an essential role within an ecosystem, and because ecosystems provide the conditions for our collective survival, then viewing rare species and stable ecosystems as extremely valuable generally serves a highly useful, social purpose. Indeed, given the extent of the environmental crises we seem to have induced and whose continuation, never mind extension, is most likely to be to our considerable detriment, such a perspective now appears to serve the most socially useful purpose imaginable. Consequently, it seems that it is currently in all our interests to keep viewing rare species and stable ecosystems as extremely valuable.

But what especially needs to be borne in mind – and this is crucial if we are to make sense of our response to the Last Person Argument – is that when we ask 'Would it be wrong for the last sentient being intentionally to engage in environmental destruction from which little was to be gained?', we are not addressing that question to the last sentient being. *We are asking ourselves that question.* And we are doing so in order to ascertain *our* values. And even if no one were ever to experience the loss of whatever was destroyed, *we* would only think that the destructive act would be of no moral significance if the seemingly objective property that demanded whatever it is be preserved had lost its hold over us. Put another way, we are, in effect, asking *now* how we should behave if we were the last sentient beings. But if we were to reply *now* that destructive acts performed at some future time would be irrelevant morally, then the relevant projected 'properties' – one's which demand that certain entities be preserved or left unharmed – would *now* have lost their social utility. They would be failing in their present social function. Hence, for the relevant projected 'properties' to retain their usefulness, it is necessary for us to think *now* that environmental destruction by the last sentient being would be wrong. It is far from surprising, therefore, that environmentalists should 'see' the viciousness in the last person's intentionally extinguishing a species.

Further light might be shed on the problem posed by the Last Person Argument by distinguishing between two 'levels' of moral thinking.[24] We could distinguish between thinking at the 'everyday level' – when we think in terms of those practical principles which we, by and large, unquestioningly apply in making our everyday moral judgements – and thinking at a 'higher level' – when we think in terms of the ultimate moral principle or principles, which must be consulted directly in unusual circumstances (for example, in the face of moral dilemmas), and which ordinarily justify everyday

principles. A projectivist could view everyday moral judgements as remaining within the grip of projected moral 'properties'. However, were one actually to find oneself in the highly unusual situation occupied by the last person, then the social utility of those 'properties' would be a thing of the past. And then it would be necessary to think very carefully from first principles about what is required of one in such a situation – in other words, to think like an 'Archangel',[25] as it were. But when *we* respond to the Last Person Argument *now* – i.e., while we are not, in actual fact, the last sentient beings – we think it wrong to extinguish a species because of the hold 'everyday' projected moral 'properties' retain over us. In other words, the common environmentalist response to the Last Person Argument could be argued to result from allowing 'everyday' moral thinking to affect 'higher level' moral principles. And it might be because he spends all his time thinking like an Archangel that Singer fails to see anything wrong with the last person burning Grand Masters.

Of course, given the plausibility of a Humean metaethic, we may well proceed to entertain doubts about the reality of moral 'properties' – especially while we remain within our studies. But rather than worry that we tend to continue 'seeing' value as a real property even after we have left our armchair theorizing behind, we should, instead, welcome that fact. For our continuing to 'perceive' moral 'properties' is precisely how it is that they have the social usefulness they undoubtedly have. And in today's world, amongst the most important values to 'perceive' if human societies are to survive would appear to be environment ones: the value of each sentient being, the value of each species, and the value of each ecosystem. Recognizing a plurality of values does, of course, create numerous difficulties, at least at times, for deciding how to act. It requires some method for trading off those values. But why should anyone presume in advance that morally acceptable environmental decisions must always be simple to make?[26]

Before closing, there is one objection to a projectivist approach that I must briefly respond to, for it is advanced by one of the leading environmental ethicists: Holmes Rolston, III. Rolston complains that

> the anthropogenic account of intrinsic value is a strained saving of what is really an inadequate paradigm, that of the subjectivity of value conferral. For all the kindly language about intrinsic value in nature, the cash value is that, 'Let the flowers live!' really means, 'Leave the flowers for humans to enjoy' . . . , because the flowers are valuable – able to be valued – only by humans even though when properly sensitive humans come along they do value these flowers for what they are in themselves.[27]

But this objection either begs the question in simply presuming that there is more to value than projectivism implies,[28] or, worse, if it is an objection worth stating, it is because of an implicit suggestion that any projectivist metaethic reduces the preservation of non-sentient life to the satisfaction of human interests. But we have just seen that the latter is not the case, for a projectivist approach is quite capable of accommodating Routley's Last Person Argument. Certain projected 'properties' are 'seen' as action guiding. If a species is 'seen' to be valuable, then its seeming 'intrinsic value' will appear to demand of us that we do not intentionally cause its extinction needlessly, and that apparent demand can, at that instant, be quite divorced from the satisfaction of human interests. Moreover, we have also seen that a Humean metaethic is wholly compatible with both animal welfarism and animal rights, neither of which can be reduced to the furthering of human interests.

In addition, if one is supposed to infer from Rolston's critique that projectivism reduces environmental values merely to some form of 'human value', then even if this is so, it is not necessarily a bad thing. For humans, if they are anything really distinctive, are value-driven beings. Humans have sacrificed their lives for their values, whether the value in question is freedom, democracy, human rights or whatever. Were environmental preservation a more widely held 'human value', like that of human freedom or democracy, I, for one, would not complain.

By way of conclusion, it is perhaps worth nothing that H. J. N. Horsburgh, while reflecting on the possibility of nuclear annihilation, once remarked that 'only the non-violent can inherit the earth', adding that 'the violent can only deny them a world to inherit.'[29] We could similarly argue that only those adhering to an environmental ethic can inherit the earth. And if, as many environmentalists have argued, the very survival of *our* species is in doubt because of the environmental crises we seem to have engendered,[30] then it would appear to be the case that the only ethic that can survive is an environmental one. Non-environmental ethics would spell 'species suicide', as it were, and would face extinction along with those practising them.[31] And the possibility of 'species suicide' does, at the very least, seem to provide some reason for why environmentalists should not abandon their moral views, nor cease 'perceiving' moral and aesthetic 'properties', even if dwelling on a Humean metaethic[32] might appear, at first glance, to undermine them.

Notes

1 See Richard Routley (later Sylvan), 'Is There A Need for A New, An Environmental, Ethic?', *Proceedings of the XVth World Congress of Philosophy*, Vol. 1 (Sophia: Sophia Press, 1973), pp. 205–10, especially p. 207. For similar arguments attempting to establish that certain non-sentient forms possess intrinsic value, see Robin Attfield, 'The good of trees', *Journal of Value Inquiry* 15 (1981): 51, Mary Anne Warren, 'The rights of the nonhuman world' in R. Elliot and A. Gare (eds), *Environmental Philosophy* (Milton Keynes: Open University Press, 1983), pp. 128–9, and Holmes Rolston III, 'Are Values in Nature Sub-

jective Or Objective?' in *Philosophy Gone Wild* (Buffalo: Prometheus Books, 1989), p. 114.

2 Tom Regan is the most famous exponent of animal rights. For a brief summary of his views, see Tom Regan, 'The case for animal rights' in Peter Singer (ed.), *In Defence of Animals* (Oxford: Blackwell, 1985).

3 This approach is most associated with Peter Singer. For his earlier hedonistic position, see Peter Singer, *Animal Liberation: A New Ethic for Our Treatment of Animals* (New York: Avon Books, 1977). For his later position, which deploys preference utilitarianism, see

Peter Singer, *Practical Ethics* (Cambridge: Cambridge University Press, 1979).

4 J. Baird Callicott, 'Animal Liberation: A Triangular Affair' in his *In Defense of the Land Ethics: Essays in Environmental Philosophy* (Albany, New York: State University of New York Press, 1989), p. 21.

5 Aldo Leopold, *A Sand County Almanac* (Oxford: Oxford University Press, 1949), p. 224.

6 Callicott, 'Animal Liberation: A Triangular Affair', p. 21.

7 For some objections to Callicott's reading of Hume, see Alan Carter, 'Humean Nature', *Environmental Values* 9/1 (2000): 3–37.

8 David Hume, *A Treatise of Human Nature*, ed. L. A. Selby-Bigge (Oxford: Clarendon Press, 1978), p. 468.

9 Ibid., pp. 468–9.

10 David Hume, 'An Enquiry Concerning the Principles of Morals' in *Enquiries concerning Human Understanding and concerning the Principles of Morals*, ed. L. A. Selby-Bigge, revised by P. H. Nidditch (Oxford: Clarendon Press, 1975), p. 294.

11 Hume, *A Treatise of Human Nature*, p. 469.

12 See J. L. Mackie, *Hume's Moral Theory* (London: Routledge, 1980), pp. 71–2.

13 See Hume, *A Treatise of Human Nature*, p. 469.

14 Hence, when Hume claims that, 'according to modern philosophy, [colours] are not qualities in objects, but perceptions in the mind' (ibid.), he should not be taken as meaning that colours cannot be 'seen' in some sense, otherwise he would simply be talking nonsense. For irrespective of what actually happens when we see colour, seeing in colour, along with seeing in monochrome, is precisely what gives content to our notion of 'seeing'.

15 David Hume, 'Of the Standard of Taste' in *Essays Moral, Political and Literary* (London: Oxford University Press, 1963), pp. 238–9.

16 Hume, *A Treatise of Human Nature*, pp. 581–2.

17 In other words, the role played by reason in Hume's moral philosophy allows a Humean to employ Singer's welfarist arguments.

18 And this means that the role played by reason in Hume's moral philosophy also allows a Humean to employ Regan's arguments for ascribing rights to nonhuman animals.

19 See Holmes Rolston III, *Environmental Ethics: Duties to and Values in the Natural World* (Philadelphia: Temple University Press, 1988), pp. 147–8.

20 However, given how much evolution may resemble an arms race, whether or not it is in the interests of the members of all species is, perhaps, open to question.

21 'One could argue "that lichens, which were once ubiquitous, might play some arcane but vital role in the long-term ecology of forests". But the same claim could not seriously be made for the furbish lousewort, a small member of the snapdragon family which has probably never been other than a rare constituent of the forests of Maine.' David Ehrenfeld, *The Arrogance of Humanism* (Oxford: Oxford University Press, 1981), p. 188.

22 Peter Singer, 'Not for Humans Only: the Place of Nonhumans in Environmental Issues' in K. E. Goodpaster and K. M. Sayre (eds), *Ethics and the Problems of the 21st Century* (London: University of Notre Dame Press, 1979), p. 203. As he amplifies: 'On this view, to exterminate a species is to commit an act of vandalism, like setting about Michelangelo's Pietà with a hammer; while allowing an endangered species to die out without taking steps to save it is like allowing Angkor Wat to fall into ruins and be obliterated by the jungle.' Ibid.

23 Ibid., p. 204.

24 See R. M. Hare, *Moral Thinking: Its Levels, Method and Point* (Oxford: Clarendon Press, 1981). Also see R. M. Hare, 'Ethical Theory and Utilitarianism' in A. Sen and B. Williams (eds), *Utilitarianism and Beyond* (Cambridge: Cambridge University Press, 1982).

25 See Hare, *Moral Thinking*.

26 For one argument which implies that value pluralism does not have to lead to indeterminacy, see Alan Carter, 'Moral Theory and Global Population', *Proceedings of the Aristotelian Society* 99/3 (1999): 289–313.

27 Rolston, *Environmental Ethics*, p. 116.

28 Rolston observes that the perception of value in nature somehow arises as we learn more about individual species and ecosystems. See Holmes Rolston III, 'Is There An Ecological Ethic?' in *Philosophy Gone Wild*, p. 20. Also see Rolston, *Environmental Ethics*, p. 232. But this observation tells us nothing about the ontology of value. For a projectivist has no difficulty in accepting that, phenomenologically, value 'appears' to arise and intensify as we study certain things. Remarkably, Rolston later writes: 'Humans value natural things for what they are in themselves – for example, enjoying a field of wild flowers, listening to loons call, or experiencing the sublime fury of a storm at sea.' Ibid., p. 331. And the storm's 'fury' isn't a projection?

29 H. J. N. Horsburgh, 'Reply to Kai Nielsen', *Inquiry* 24 (1981): 73.

30 See, for example, Alan Carter, *A Radical Green Political Theory* (London: Routledge, 1999).

31 I am, of course, here parodying Garrett Hardin's argument for the ascendancy of his notorious lifeboat ethic. See Garrett Hardin, 'Living on A Lifeboat' in Jan Narveson (ed.), *Moral Issues* (Toronto: Oxford University Press, 1983).

32 For a fuller account of Hume's metaethic, see Carter, 'Humean Nature'.

War and Terrorism

According to best estimates, more than 40 million people have been killed in wars since World War II. The number of people seriously injured is much larger. The damage to the ENVIRONMENT and to valuable cultural artifacts is nigh incalculable. If there was ever any human activity more appropriately subject to moral scrutiny than war I cannot imagine what it would be. Yet it is rarely discussed in moral terms. Indeed, those who deign to raise moral objections to war are commonly derided as unpatriotic or even immoral.

Events of September 11, 2001 magnified these tendencies. In our shock at the tragic loss of life in New York and Washington, many US citizens wanted to strike back, both as a form of retribution (PUNISHMENT) and to protect themselves from future terrorist attacks. However, as we have seen throughout this book, in order to act morally we must often step back from our initial reactions to make sure that we are acting morally. The need to do so here is especially acute. For the wars in Afghanistan and Iraq are each, in different ways, at odds with traditional just war theory. The invasion of Afghanistan runs afoul of the idea that one nation can militarily defend itself only against an attack by another *nation*. The invasion of Iraq runs afoul of the idea that one country cannot militarily attack except in self-defense. Does that mean we must rethink the principles of just war? Or are there other ways of using those principles to justify these (and similar) wars?

The essays in this section offer a variety of answers to these and related questions. Boyle explores the questions raised by the invasion of Afghanistan. He asks if it can ever be permissible to militarily attack a group that is not a nation. Although this possibility clearly stretches the moral and legal idea of a "just war," he thinks we can use just war standards to evaluate these military activities. Boyle employs St. Thomas Aquinas's account of a "just war." Aquinas says a war is justified only if it is proclaimed by a proper authority, has a just cause, and is conducted with right intent. Boyle argues that these principles could justify some military action against terrorist groups, even if they are not themselves nations. Whether these principles actually justify such actions in any specific case, he says, is always up for debate.

Lackey addresses a related, but somewhat broader question. Just war theory allows nations to use their militaries for self-defense. Historically that has meant only that states could repel overt attacks against them ("responsive force"). The United Nations Charter also appears to permit (or at least not explicitly prohibit) preemptive attacks against countries preparing for an imminent attack. Still, just war theory and international law has forbidden one country's (D) attacking another country (A) merely to stop the bare possibility of an attack by A. The reason for this prohibition is clear. If one country's fear that they *might* be attacked by another is sufficient to justify the first in militarily attacking the second, then just war theory would seem to justify many countries attacking many other countries. That most assuredly would not serve the cause of international peace.

The problem, Lackey notes, is whether we can draw a sufficiently clear line between preventive and preemptive war so that we legitimately allow the latter while forbidding the former. Lackey thinks we can. Indeed, he thinks we must. There are serious epistemological problems with trying to judge another country's intentions. We should be wary of claiming that others are about to attack us unless we can show that they have taken clear steps (e.g., massing troops on our joint border) to attack us. Finally, we must be aware that in responding – even when it might be justified – we inevitably kill and maim many innocent individuals. Those costs must be included in any moral evaluation of our actions.

Beitz takes the discussion in a slightly different direction. He specifically asks whether military force can be used to defend others against genocide and human rights atrocities. He acknowledges that it is not obvious that such actions can be justified according to current international law. However, that is not his question. He is concerned whether such intervention could ever be *morally* justified.

If it can be, it would have to be justified in the same ways that wars are. Beitz's principles of just war theory resemble Boyle's in many ways, but differ in at least one important respect. Beitz includes three elements not explicitly mentioned by Boyle: (a) that the war is pursued only as a last resort (other, less drastic

options were tried first); (b) that there is a reasonable chance of success; and (c) that the war is conducted in a way that is itself just. Boyle's account could be construed as including these elements, even if they are not specifically mentioned. However, even if they can be, Boyle and Beitz disagree whether "right intention" is a genuine requirement. Boyle thinks it is; Beitz does not. It would be worthwhile to explore the respective arguments about this last criterion.

Beitz's conclusion is that, in principle, humanitarian intervention could be justified. However, he (like Lackey) worries about our ability to accurately predict not only others' intentions, but our chances for success. That is why it may be that such intervention is rarely justified.

Despite their differences, each of the previous authors buy the claim that war is sometimes justified. Hawk thinks they are all mistaken. War involves the intentional killing of other humans. We generally think that killing others is grossly immoral. Yet somehow in times of war we think that it is not only permissible to kill, but that it is immoral to not support or participate in war. This, he thinks, is a topsy-turvy moral world that could have been concocted by Lewis Carroll.

Pacifism is the view that war is never, in fact, morally justified. There are various forms of pacifism, which he briefly catalogues. However, pacifists are united in thinking that war is a morally inappropriate means of achieving one's goals, no matter how laudable. They believe that human life is inherently valuable. In taking that stance the pacifist need not be – and usually is not – passive. She often finds a variety of ways to resist evil. For example, although many citizens of Le Chambon (France) refused to use violence to repel the Nazis or to protect Jews, they were not passive; they willingly risked their own lives to help Jews escape Europe, and, in other ways, to resist the Nazi occupation.

The idea of just war theory doubtless seems morally appealing: it requires that people be justified before they engage in the war. But that, Hawk suggests, is not the way the theory functions. It is standardly used more to permit wars than to prohibit them. These attempts to justify war fail to acknowledge the bias, self-deception, and propaganda that often generate our supposed justifications for war.

Further Reading

Frey, R. and Morris, C. W. (eds.) (1991) *Violence, Terrorism, and Justice*. Cambridge: Cambridge University Press.

Gray, J. G. (1998/1958) *The Warriors: Reflections on Men in Battle*. Lincoln, NE: University of Nebraska Press.

Leitenberg, M. (2001) "Deaths in Wars and Conflicts between 1945 and 2000." Conference on Data Collection in Armed Conflict: Uppsala, Sweden, June 8–9.

Shue, H. (2000) "War." In H. LaFollette (ed.), *Oxford Handbook of Practical Ethics*. Oxford: Oxford University Press, pp. 734–62.

64

Just War Doctrine and the Military Response to Terrorism

Joseph Boyle

Defining Terms and Formulating Issues

In this article, I will articulate a traditional version of just war theory and apply it to the case of a polity's response to terrorist actions by groups that are not themselves polities. I will argue that, according to just war theory, defending against this sort of terrorism is a just cause; that within significant constraints sovereign political authorities can have authority to undertake military actions for the sake of this just cause, notwithstanding the nature of organization of the terrorists; and that a political community can pursue such a cause with right intention, even though in the world as it is military efforts to defend against terrorism may well not meet this condition.

In this introduction I will define key terms; in the second section I will provide a formulation of just war theory; and in the last section I will apply its conditions for the permissibility of waging war to the case of responding to terrorism by groups that are not states.

Just war theory

The just war doctrine that I will discuss is reasonably named "traditional just war theory."

By this expression I refer to the doctrine and rationale concerning the moral permissibility of engaging in warfare that was developed by medieval canonists and moral theologians chiefly from the work of St. Augustine, and articulated by St. Thomas Aquinas in a pithy summary that has become its classic formulation.

I follow traditional just war theory in understanding the kind of action it evaluates to be simply "contending with arms." On this understanding, a polity's participation in violent conflict need not be formally declared as a war to be making war. More important to the current inquiry, a polity can make war on brigands, terrorists, or other groups lacking legitimate or recognized government and a legal system. This broad description is not meant to establish the moral permissibility of a polity's making war against a group that is not a polity.

As the previous paragraph suggests, an important component of the concept of war in the just war tradition is that waging war is a group action – something individuals cannot do acting alone, but only in concert with others. Therefore, it requires the coordination of individuals' contributing actions by means of social authority. The authority directs and coordinates the multiplicity of actions that comprise making war, and thereby unifies them into a single social act of the community. This does not imply that individuals can surrender responsibility for their own part in a war.[1] It does imply as a condition for a war's permissibility that the authority coordinating the bellicose action be of the right kind.

The form of war to be discussed is a polity's military response to terrorist actions directed against it, its citizens, or allies by groups that are not polities. Military action is the use of force outside the framework of domestic and international criminal law enforced by police and the criminal justice system.

Responding to terrorist activities is reasonably understood to presuppose that those activities actually exist, that is, that they are not simply planned actions or actions a group has ability and reason to undertake. So, I am not addressing preventive war against terrorists, but only defensive and punitive responses to terrorism. Setting aside preventive war against terrorism does not assume that there is a clear and easily recognized distinction between preventive war and defensive or punitive war. For preemption against bellicose actions begun but not fully executed can be defensive or punitive.

Terrorism

The notion of terrorism at work in current discussions of international relations is difficult to characterize with precision. I will, therefore, try to specify a core idea of a terrorist action, recognizing that there will be actions having only some of its defining features, and that terrorist actions will usually have other morally relevant features as well.

I begin by distinguishing the terrorist actions I will discuss from those military actions in which one group seeks to overwhelm an enemy by force, or simply to destroy or displace a population by genocide or ethnic cleansing. In such cases the intended goals are achieved – or could be – completely by force. Except incidentally, they involve no effort to persuade the targeted enemy, but only efforts to overwhelm or destroy it. Thus, if an army going down to military defeat decides on surrender in the face

of the prospect of an enemy's continued battlefield victories, that decision could be no more than a response to the prospect of being overwhelmed. This decision might be ignored by the powerful opponent, who might also accept it only as completely shaped by the weaker opponent's prospect of destruction.

By contrast, terrorist actions fall within the category of violent actions that do not include the intent to displace decision making by violence; they are violent acts intended to influence decisions. Terrorist actions are undertaken to cause fear and demoralization, and thereby to lead to changes in policy on the part of the terrorized party. Vengeful, destructive acts having no further purpose than destruction certainly cause terror in those being destroyed, but these are not the core cases of terrorism. Terrorist acts are like deterrence, which is undertaken to affect the decision making of the deterred party by threatening to bring about what the deterred party does not want if it acts in ways the deterring party wants to prevent.

Plainly, there are important differences between terrorism and deterrence. Terrorist actions are not, as such, threats, although terrorist undertakings ordinarily involve the threat of further terrorism. Moreover, the very idea of deterrence does not connote something morally wrong or questionable, as the idea of terrorism surely does. For it is possible to deter by threatening only what one may rightfully do, as happens in the formation and execution of provisions of the criminal law, at least partially for the sake of deterring future criminal acts.

But one can also threaten precisely terrorist action to deter, as seems to have been the case in the nuclear deterrence by the great powers during the Cold War. This possibility suggests that the designation of an action as terrorist, and so as generally morally suspect, is triggered not by the persuasive or political structure terrorist actions share with deterrence and many other actions involving violence, but by the particular ways in which violence is used. What is it that makes an action terrorist and so wrongful, or at least presumptively so?

It seems that terrorist actions are wrong because those who do them seek to affect others' behavior and decisions by directly or indirectly harming people whom they have no right to harm. The bad means whose use defines actions as terrorist are the intentional harms inflicted on some people to cause fear (often on the part of others than those harmed). Those harms are wrongs because the targets of the terrorist harms are in the relevant sense "innocent." Even if some are oppressors who may be attacked, they may not be killed by terrorist acts because these are acts seeking to cause politically effective fear, and so do not kill the oppressor to defend but as a means of causing fear, and most such acts are "indiscriminate" in a strong sense: anyone who can be harmed and whose harming will cause the hoped-for fear is a reasonable target, and so those who might be harmed only as a side-effect of other actions are harmed intentionally in terrorist actions.

Any person or group performs a terrorist act, therefore, when he, she, or they intentionally harm someone they have no right to harm to get a person or group to choose differently than she or they otherwise would.

There will, of course, be borderline cases in which it is unclear independently of careful inquiry whether the harms are intentionally inflicted and whether those on whom they are inflicted should be immune from such harm. For example, freedom fighters in a justified war of independence need not terrorize the group with whom they contend. However, in their efforts to persuade those who oppress them, freedom fighters may be tempted to use terrorism. In such situations, actions that are impermissible by the traditional *in bello* conditions for carrying out warfare justly are likely to be terrorist. Strategies that involve indiscriminately harming those who are not carrying out the oppression fought, intentionally harming them, and so on ordinarily contribute to the persuasion of the oppressors only in virtue of the terror they cause.

Terrorist actions, as I have defined them, can be performed by individuals or groups and their targets can be individuals or groups. For example, a person could terrorize a neighbor by wronging someone she cares about (although this would likely provoke a response from police

if the matter were serious), a criminal gang can terrorize a neighborhood by killing or maiming some of its residents, a nation can terrorize another by bombing some of its cities. For simplicity, however, I will use the expressions "terrorism" and "terrorist actions" to refer to terrorist actions as the action of a group that is not organized as a polity. Al-Qaeda seems to be a clear example of such an agent; other terrorist groups in the Middle East, and perhaps the IRA, appear to be somewhat more closely connected to political communities, even if these groups do not have, or do not clearly have, responsibility for the common goods of these communities.

The Conditions for the Permissibility of Waging War

Thomas Aquinas gathered the teachings of Augustine on the morality of war, by his day widely interpreted and incorporated into canon law, and in a short, clear statement provided what is probably the classic statement of traditional just war theory. This treatment is in Aquinas' best-known and most mature work, the *Summa Theologiae*, in the second part of the second part, which deals with moral problems. The discussion falls within the sins against the virtue of charity, since war is presumptively a sin against charity.

Aquinas maintains that a war can be morally justified if and only if three conditions are met. Those conditions are proper authority, just cause, and right intent. His concern is plainly with conditions for what came to be called *jus ad bellum*, the moral permissibility of going to war (or continuing in fighting a war already begun).[2] But Aquinas made plain in the discussion of killing, no one can be authorized to intentionally kill innocents.[3]

Proper authority

The first of Aquinas' conditions is proper authority; that is, only the head of a polity (*princeps*, often translated as "sovereign"), can properly command the waging of war. Two reasons are given: first, private persons have no business waging war and other lesser political leaders can appeal to higher authority to settle disputes and to remedy injustices. Second, only the head of the polity is authorized to bring together the community to fight.

What grounds the sovereign's authority in both these relationships is the fact that the care of the republic is entrusted to the sovereign, who has the responsibility to look after the welfare of the city, province, or kingdom. This responsibility includes authority to use force not only internally against domestic criminals but against outsiders who harm the polity.

Augustine and, following him, Aquinas clearly make an inference here from the domestic situation in which the magistrate is justified in using force for the common good, to the international situation in which the sovereign is justified in using force to respond to externally based wrongs. This inference is required because the biblical text cited by Augustine is understood as referring to the domestic authority of leaders.[4] But the inference is passed over as if straightforward. This inference seems justified, and it can be construed as an analogy from the domestic to the international sphere. It is not, however, an analogy from a private right of self-defense to a national right of self-defense, but from authority exercised within a polity to that same authority exercised against outsiders, for the same reason as it is exercised internally. Indeed, Augustine was suspicious of a private right of self-defense, and this suspicion led Aquinas to develop his complex story about killing in self-defense, an account which provided the elements for the later doctrine of double effect.

In short, war waged without public authority is not permissible. And not any kind of public authority qualifies. Only the authority of one who has the final say for the welfare of a political community may rightly take it to war; by implicit definition a leader has "final say" when there is no higher authority capable of and authorized to deal with the harm to the polity without commanding and carrying out violent action. The idea seems to be that the welfare of a political community, which includes the just protection of its subjects' liberties and other aspects of its common good, requires care and protection; and that care sometimes requires violent action. Those who are in charge of the community's welfare are the legitimate primary agents of this violent action. Those leaders who can invoke higher authority within the community are not in this ultimate way in charge of its welfare.

Presumably there is nothing in this analysis that requires the leader of a polity to be a single individual and not a constitutionally empowered group operating according to some fixed decision procedure, such as a parliament or a president and congress. Nor is there anything in it which prohibits the relevant leader or group from having worldwide jurisdiction.

However, such worldwide authority as exists in the world today is not the authority of a great polity. Such worldwide leaders as exist, in the UN and perhaps in the international courts, do serve a genuine common good that has global reach, but that common good appears to be less than an all-encompassing common good which contains the proper goods of polities as subordinate parts. The treaties, covenants, customs, and technology which bind the nations and peoples of the world together do not appear to create a super-polity that might allow worldwide leaders the interest or the capacity to care for the welfare of every polity. In other words, neither in terms of capacity nor of normative considerations are world leaders authorized for and capable of definitively settling all things pertaining to all human interactions and so capable of generating law and so being a general court of last resort.

My point here is only that the proper authority of the sovereign in undertaking war, which Aquinas took to be a necessary condition for a permissible war, now belongs to the leaders of a polity, not to leaders of transnational organizations. If a transnational organization developed the capacity to coordinate the actions of all in the world for a global common good, and if such leaders had the capacity to protect the common goods of the various political communities around the world, then such a government would have the essential features of sovereignty and there would always be this final court of appeal. Until these conditions obtain, some residue of the right of a polity to respond to unjust attacks from beyond its borders must remain. Still, that authority may be qualified by treaty, vested in an international authority, or rightly limited by the development of a renewed *jus gentium*. On just war grounds such limitations can be significant.

Just cause

Aquinas' second necessary condition for the permissibility of a war is that there be a just cause. He gives little justification for what he rightly takes to be an obvious ethical condition; that any action should be done only for a good purpose is for him a fundamental requirement of moral life. Nor does he provide a list or a set of examples of just reasons for undertaking warfare; such a list shows up only later in Vitoria.

But Aquinas does provide something more than the obvious moral requirement. He specifies the just cause needed for a permissible war as arising only in the face of the wrongdoing of outsiders, and further specifies it as being essentially punitive. He thus goes beyond the self-evident ethical point that a just cause is necessary, and beyond the intuitive requirement that a just war responds to wrongdoing, and adds the punitive understanding of that response, bolstering his claim with a reference to Augustine's authority.

He says that those who are rightly attacked must deserve it on account of some wrong they have done. Augustine's text makes plain that this response to wrongdoing is understood to be punitive: "We usually describe a just war as one that avenges wrongs, that is, when a nation or state has to be punished either for refusing to make amends for outrages done by its subjects or to restore what has been seized injuriously."

One of the major developments of just war thinking in the twentieth century is the rejection of the legitimacy of this punitive conception of just cause, and the limitation of just cause to defense. Recent Catholic thinking – both ecclesiastical and scholarly – has moved towards a more defensive conception, very much in line with the broader international tendency to treat aggression, even if justified for punitive reasons, as completely out of line.

The relationships between punishment, the common good of a polity, and the authority of the leaders who serve it are such that the punitive conception of just cause is not justifiable; in a word, leaders lack the authority to punish outsiders.

The reasoning is as follows: political leaders have authority over their subjects and authority to punish malefactors. That authority is rooted in the common good of the polity and the special role of service which political leaders have to that good. The care for that good sometimes requires the use of force to stop and deter domestic criminals, those who share in the life of a political community but violate its just regulations. This reasonably includes the right to punish them as a means of restoring justice, which also enhances the fulfillment of the deterrent and defensive responsibilities of leaders. For the same reason, political leaders also have authority to lead and command defensive measures against externally based threats to the welfare of the polity. Defending subjects from injuries inflicted by outsiders plainly is a responsibility of those entrusted with the care of a polity's common good. That defensive action is for the sake of that common good.

What is needed at this point is a justification of the authority of the leaders of a polity not simply to command and organize defense from outside attack but precisely to punish those who are not its citizens or voluntary residents, namely, other polities and the subjects of other polities. The condition of hostility does not make individual enemies participants in the common lives of the opposing communities, but only mutual external threats to those lives; similarly, the state of war does not collapse the common goods of the belligerents into one, or the authority of leaders into a kind of bloody election.

Yet that status of citizenship, that participation in the life of a community, is necessary if those who punish are to have the authority to do so. This is so because the authority to organize and command defense is not the stronger authority to punish, which involves imposing further burdens on those against whom defense is mounted than defense itself implies.

Punishment can be a means to defense, insofar as it deters some from actions for which punishments are prescribed, and sometimes prevents the punished persons from continuing in their criminal activity. But it is possible to choose to defend without choosing to inflict any further harm on the attacker that might constitute punishment. The negative effects on those against whom one defends can perhaps be understood as punishment, but that sort of injury to the attacker is an unavoidable aspect of defense. Just as a private self-defender may ward off an attack with no punitive authority and no interest in punishing, so may a community. The stronger authority to punish is rooted in the leaders' coordination of the actions of community members for common action for the sake of a community's common good. That basis sets its limits. They may punish those over whom they have authority, not outsiders against whom they may authoritatively organize and defend. Consequently, the only ground for extending this authority beyond community members is instrumental.

But, given the difference between punishment and defense, a justification of defense is not thereby a justification of punishment instrumental to it. Even the necessity of punishment for defense in some situations does not justify it, since plainly some forms of defense are wrongful, and, in the face of a lack of authority, more is needed than an instrumental justification of extending the authority to punish.

This is not to affirm that the relationship between attacker and defender is simply a matter of power. It is true that attackers sometimes suffer the ill effects of the violent, defensive action of the polity they injure. And when the attacker acts wrongfully, there is more to the forceful defense than simply its power; just as any fair-minded observer could address the attacker in moral terms, so too can those who are injured. But this appeal to general moral norms – "You are out of line in attacking and we are within our rights in defending" – is not

sufficient to render the attacker part of the community in a way that justifies anything like legal punishment. The truth of that moral judgment does not imply the cooperative relationship of membership in a common polity.

To sum up this line of reasoning: the defensive rather than punitive understanding of just cause which has developed in just war thinking in the twentieth century is a proper development of traditional just war doctrine.

Reflecting on this development makes clear that the authority to make war is constrained in important ways, and plainly the exact shape of these limitations will be important for assessing the permissibility of responding to terrorist actions by groups that are not organized as a polity.

Right intention

Aquinas argues that waging war can be wrong even if there is proper authority and just cause because a community can wage war with a perverse intention. The citations from Augustine make clear that the kind of bad motives Aquinas has in mind are hatred, revenge, a desire to dominate and so on. The idea seems to be that the presence of a just cause must not be a pretext for fighting for other morally questionable purposes, but rather the just cause must function as the practical principle of the bellicose action. The normative ground for this exclusion can be inferred from the Augustinian texts cited by Aquinas: war is presumptively immoral; its evils can be justified only on the narrow grounds that war justly serves peace, and any hostile action not completely controlled by that objective falls under the presumptive immorality of war.

This condition seems to rule out the practical influence of any other motives on war-making – even good ones which a polity might rightly pursue by non-violent means, but which are not included within the set of reasons encompassed by the just cause. The reason for this interpretation is that the condition of right intention serves to lock tightly together the just cause and the actions taken for that cause. Intention in Aquinas' view is a volition bearing on the end and making it not simply the object of a wish, but a practical goal. Intention is practical because it exists only when the person links the goal to something he or she can do about it – the means he or she can choose for its sake. In short, in a just war one can take actions only for the sake of the just cause, and not for any other end. Since the violent activities of warfare would be wrong except when done for the sake of the just cause, doing them for any other purpose is wrong.

Another aspect of this condition emerges by considering whose intentions are being evaluated. The motives of revenge and hatred which are often in the hearts of those who fight morally compromise their own involvement in a war. But surely the inevitable but essentially private sins of soldiers – unless sanctioned or overlooked – do not necessarily flaw an otherwise justified war. Therefore, the intention Aquinas has in mind here is that of the social act of undertaking war. This intention is revealed by the concrete war aims sought as goals in a war, and by the actions undertaken to realize these goals.

Right intention, therefore, gives concrete shape to the condition of just cause. If there is a just cause, and if that is the reason for making war – not a pretext – then there will be war aims, concrete goals, namely, a just state of affairs which can be produced by the military action, and which satisfies the just cause. That concrete goal, in turn, strictly controls the actions for its sake; violence for other goals or destruction in ways not required by the war aims is excluded.

Any action to serve a further goal remains unjustified, and that plainly includes the other legitimate interests a state might have within the international community. To pursue them by war is wrong.

The limitation of legitimate warfare to actions taken for and required by goals in which the just cause is realized does not mean that the war aims must be pursued as ends in themselves insofar as they realize the just cause. A just war aims at peace, as Aquinas, quoting Augustine, holds.[5] Surely, therefore, the intrinsic benefit of the fair and friendly relationships definitive of

genuine peace, and the further advantages that come from peace, may be hoped for as a result of succeeding in achieving morally defensible war aims. But peace is a good which war is never alone sufficient to achieve, and which war cannot rightly advance, except by seeking to bring about the just state of affairs satisfying the just cause.

This further horizon of human purposes that can be served by war in a limited way raises further questions about right intent and just cause. Since warfare undertaken for a just cause and fought with right intent must aim for peace, even though warfare is not sufficient for realizing this good, it is possible that a polity's warfare can fail to meet the condition of right intention because of its failure properly to pursue peace. This could happen if a state pursued policies incompatible with the peace achievable by the successful realization of just war aims; for example, a polity might continue its own unjust policies that provoke terrorist responses while making otherwise justified defensive war on the terrorists.

I return now to the defensive limit on just cause: Let us suppose that the intent of a morally justified war is simply to defend, to repel invasion, to stop ongoing violation of property and other rights, and other similar action to stop, limit, or block international wrongdoing. Such a conception limits the steps a defending state may take beyond such as these to punish enemies. As noted in the previous subsection, this limits the kind of rectification of grievances a state can rightly seek by warfare, and avoids a mysterious conception of political authority that allows the leaders of one community to punish outsiders.

But it also makes it much easier to determine whether or not the condition of right intent is met, since the defensive intention does not allow punitive actions beyond what is immediately involved in defense. Punitive acts are difficult in practice to distinguish from acts of vengeance. Just punishment should not seek precisely to injure the punished person, but all punishment imposes odious limitations on freedom, and often intentional injuries besides. Punishing in this context seems to me incompatible with the further goal of international peace, particularly in the absence of clear authority to punish. Moreover, at the deepest level, aiming precisely to harm people, especially kill them, is morally problematic. A defensive conception of war avoids that intention, and instead reasonably can regard the harms inflicted in defense as a side-effect of the defensive action, in a kind of strategic application of double effect to the social act of undertaking violent defense.

Applying Just War Conditions to Warfare Responsive to Terrorism

Is there legitimate authority to make war on terrorists?

Plainly, the leaders of a sovereign political community have the responsibility and so the authority to respond in some way to terrorist acts against their community, its subjects, or its allies. Since terrorist actions harm innocent people in ways serious enough to create fear in them or others that is sufficient to change their behavior and policies, such actions profoundly harm the common good of the affected community. Both the wrongs to innocents and the use of the fear these wrongs create for political purposes are of profound public concern. Those responsible for the welfare of the community are duty-bound to respond.

Depending upon the seriousness of the terrorist action and the capacity of police action, domestic and international, to provide a realistic response to terrorism, leaders may exercise this responsibility by commanding or requesting appropriate police action. Such action seems essential in dealing with terrorist acts having global reach by groups that are not polities. But where police action is insufficient to respond to terrorism, and military action likely to be effective, it appears to fall within the legitimate authority of political leaders.

This legitimacy has limitations. There are treaties and international law that may prohibit or constrain a state from taking unilateral military action in response to terrorism, or may require UN approval or action instead.

Traditional just war theory assumes that treaties are solemn promises to be kept, and that procedures and prohibitions that are widely agreed upon internationally should be followed. Consequently, there likely exists a presumption against a state's taking unilateral military action without appropriate international approval. Whether or not contending militarily with terrorists who do not form a political community qualifies as a war in international law, a state so contending is bound by the requirements of just war. And there is no basis in just war theory for thinking that the fact that a state contends with a non-political group removes its authority to wage war.

But other complications abound. In particular, making war on terrorists ordinarily involves crossing the borders of other countries, presumptively, the crime of aggression unless invited. Border crossings without the consent of the country entered will be aggression, unless approved by the UN, or unless the state invaded can be justly invaded to make war on the terrorists, in other words, if the refusal to consent is itself rightly understood to be a just cause for war. Thus, for example, the Taliban rulers of Afghanistan may have been so involved in al-Qaeda activities that there was just cause for the USA and its allies to cross Afghanistan's borders and attack Taliban soldiers and assets. But that condition seems exceptional and, consequently, permission of states in whose territory military action is conducted is a general limit on the authority of leaders to make war on terrorists.

Is responding to terrorism a just cause?

According to Aquinas' conception of just cause, military actions to defend against terrorism are for the sake of a just cause. According to the twentieth-century limitation of just cause, military actions for the sake of punishing terrorists for their action, or for preventing terrorism not actually under way, are not for the sake of a just cause. The justice of military defense against terrorism arises from the wrongfulness of the terrorist actions. As noted above, this is not only the wrongfulness of harming innocents but also the political wrong of using the terror this causes to change a polity's behavior and policy.

Two other wrong-making factors exist in the kind of terrorism under consideration: first, that terrorists do not act for a just cause; and second, that the leaders of the terrorist organizations lack the proper authority to wage war. Terrorists may act in response to wrongs on the part of other groups; for example, they may be acting in response to unjust oppression by powerful countries. But that is not sufficient for a just cause, since that is defined not simply by the wrong addressed but includes what the group means to do about it. This requires that the goal for which bellicose action is taken be just and terrorist goals are not. Similarly, terrorist leaders are not the persons finally responsible for the common good of a political society, and seem to have such authority as they do only within the terrorist group. They have recourse to higher courts of appeal. Of course, leaders of a community engaged in a civil war or succession may have proper authority, even if not formally recognized as leaders of a polity; their tolerance of or use of terrorism would not be flawed in this way.

The idea of defending from terrorism, when that excludes punishing terrorists or preventing their acts, needs some explaining. A definite terrorist act, once carried out, cannot be the object of defense. It seems that all that can be done here is to prevent or to punish. The response is that the social act of a terrorist group directed against a polity is not ordinarily a single discrete terrorist action but a coordinated set of actions, since a single act of terrorism, understood as such by terrorists and their victims, could hardly cause the fear needed to change a polity's behavior. So, the terrorist action ordinarily is not a single discrete performance but a complex, interlocked set of behaviors unified by the intention of a common goal – at least the goal of causing the change in policy the terrorist action seeks.

It is possible to defend against actions such as this. One can do this by preventing those who are engaged in the action from carrying out their part in it, by apprehending or incapacitating them, by destroying the assets needed and

so on. This is certainly prevention, but not prevention of the kind modern just war and international law theory finds morally questionable. For in this case, one is defending against an ongoing social act by preventing the carrying out of some of its elements. This is different from preventing a group from what they may have the capacity or motive or plans to do but are not evidently doing.

Analogous observations apply in the case of punishment: the effects of defense on terrorists are likely to be bad, and likely to be seen by them as punishments. But if the defensive actions are designed only to thwart ongoing terrorism, punishing them is not part of the rationale for waging war against terrorists. This is not to deny that terrorists can be punished and should be. The internationally organized criminal justice system can rightly do that, if they are apprehended in war or by police action. But that is distinct from war being waged to punish or to allow for later punishment.

Can a state respond to terrorism with right intent?

This condition is difficult to apply to defending against terrorism, and raises the most difficult questions about it from a just war perspective. Recall that this condition addresses not the individual motives of soldiers and leaders in making war but the intention involved in the social act of making war. That intention, as noted above in the section "The Conditions for the Permissibility of Waging War," is revealed in the war aims a state adopts, the relation of its bellicose actions to those war aims, and, ultimately, by whether the state removes obstacles to peace that are of its own making.

There are war aims that would reasonably satisfy the just cause of defending against terrorism, and would reveal the war effort as defensive but not punitive, vengeful, or inappropriately preventive. The state of affairs in which the prospect of terrorist activity is not a serious threat to people's conduct of their lives but part of the disagreeable but acceptable risks of modern life is a reasonable public goal in relationship to terrorism generally, as it is in relation to criminal activity more generally. A more ambitious goal for dealing with terrorism seems utopian, and seems motivated by punitive intent or vengeance against terrorists who have been successful in prior actions.

Much of the effort to put the prospect of terrorism within acceptable levels of risk will be carried out by police work and by addressing the conditions and grievances that give rise to terrorism. But if military action is called for to defend against an ongoing terrorist campaign, there will be a component of this larger public goal that military action can aim to secure. That component will be the war aim of reasonable military defense against terrorist action. Consequently, the war aim must be concrete – the violence is justified only by an ongoing terrorist initiative. Stopping that is what is justified – not anything so grand as ridding the world of terrorism. And only the violence needed for precisely that defensive effort is justified. Such things as the destruction of the command and control system of a terrorist group by focused bombing, or capture or isolation of leaders and soldiers are perhaps not by themselves sufficient to define the war aims of a defense against terrorism, but some list of such things considered in the light of what military action can do to defend against terrorism without itself turning to punishment, vengeance, or terror certainly seems to specify the kind of war aim that can rightly be sought. War aims including greater destruction of terrorists than such as these – for example, killing them all – appear vengeful.

I have not attended to the many moral questions about the proper conduct of war, but, as I noted above in "The Conditions for the Permissibility of Waging War," just war theory is reasonably understood as assuming that norms prohibiting murderous activity in war, both by individuals acting on their own and as a matter of state policy, must be observed. If they are not observed as a matter of the policy of a state making war, then the war is to that extent immoral to conduct. Consequently, I am taking for granted that non-combatants must not be harmed intentionally, that there must be a fair-minded assessment of the harms imposed on them as side-effects, and that it is possible to act in ways that discriminate between those who may be attacked and others.

Indeed, the need to address the conditions and grievances leading to terrorism suggests that anti-terrorist military action cannot contribute to peace without avoiding indiscriminate harming – either recklessly or intentionally – anyone other than those engaged in the terrorism against which it is right to defend.

The requirement of last resort, that war is legitimate only if all other practical remedies are unavailable, is more tightly connected to the conditions for going to or continuing in war: an abstractly just cause can be pursued with right intent only if the violence is as limited as possible, and that will not happen if military force is used before other steps are exhausted. Likewise, the authority of political leaders to command and lead war is reasonably limited by the requirement that they proceed as pacifically as possible in securing their polity's interests.

The relationship between an abstractly just cause, such as defense against terrorism, and the good of peace, which should be served by realizing the goals set by that just cause, raises the most difficult practical question about using force against terrorism. For it is plain that the good of peace includes more than the absence of war or the desolation which Tacitus said the Romans called peace: namely, some form of fair and friendly relationships between peoples. And polities, even those otherwise reasonably defending against terrorism, can have committed themselves to international policies that make impossible peace with the terrorists and the people they represent.

For example, a state engaged in or supporting unjust oppression which provokes terrorism can use military force against terrorism because it is terrorist and, to that extent, its actions are just. Indeed, the leaders of any polity attacked by terrorism will be gravely malfeasant unless they do what they can to allow their citizens to carry on the normal business of life. But, assuming the evil of terrorism, it is by no means clear that such a polity intends only what is right in defending from terrorism unless it stops its unjust oppression.

For a just cause must serve peace and not simply protect an unjust status quo. The refusal to stop oppression, since the oppression is the action of the defending polity, is fully within its power. Many conflicts within which terrorism plays a role are thought, at least by those who believe themselves oppressed and on whose behalf terrorism is done, to share this structure. Those who believe this are likely to tolerate the evil of terrorism and be unsupportive of efforts to defend from it.

My effort to sort out the ethical issues raised by conflicts structured in this way is as follows: any polity must do what it can to protect its members going lawfully about their ordinary, daily business. Since most terrorist activities aim at harming people in going about living their lives and to get terrorist results from the fear that induces, there seems to be a straightforward responsibility for leaders to deal with such actions. That responsibility seems basic for political leaders, and appears to exist independently of their foreign policy.

At the same time, leaders create for themselves and their subjects a moral dilemma if they refuse to take steps to remove the blocks to peace that exist because of their own national commitments. The dilemma arises from this refusal, and so that must be abandoned. In short, this is not a case of strict moral perplexity but of one created by wrongdoing. Here, as elsewhere, desisting from the wrongdoing is likely to be difficult but is morally required not only because any wrong should be repented, but because persisting in it makes immoral the carrying out of the basic responsibility to protect citizens lawfully going about their business.

Of course, many leaders will not recognize the moral ambiguity of their situations. They can recognize, however, that others see their carrying out of their social responsibilities as maintaining a status quo wrongful to them. That recognition perhaps will lead to a very strict application of the defensive conception of waging war to fight terrorism.

Notes

1 The question of the personal responsibility of members of a society for its warfare is complex, and there is much in traditional just war theory to criticize on this score, as David Rodin, *War and Self-Defense* (Oxford: Oxford University Press), pp. 165–73, indicates. These complexities can be sorted out in a traditional way; for example, see John Finnis et al., *Nuclear Deterrence, Morality and Realism* (Oxford: Oxford University Press, 1987), pp. 342–60, for the responsibilities of various parties holding various beliefs in the context of Cold War deterrence.

2 The exposition and interpretation of Aquinas in this section follow closely that of my "Traditional Just War and Humanitarian Intervention," presented at the annual meeting of the Association for Political and Legal Philosophy, Boston, August 30, 2002.

3 *Summa Theologiae*, 2–2, q. 64.

4 Romans 13: 4.

5 See John Finnis, "The Ethics of War and Peace in the Catholic Just War Tradition," *The Ethics of War and Peace: Religious and Secular Perspectives*, ed. T. Nardin (Princeton, NJ: Princeton University Press, 1996), pp. 15–17 for more on the relationship between war and peace in traditional just war theory.

65

Nipping Evil in the Bud: The Questionable Ethics of Preventive Force

Douglas P. Lackey

1 Introduction: Preventive, Preemptive, and Responsive Force

In this essay I want to discuss the moral permissibility of using *preventive force*: that is, the use of force against some individual, not because of anything the person has so far done, but because of some evil that person *might* do in the future. I will consider two types of preventive force: preventive military force, and preventive police force. Preventive military force is often referred to as *preventive war*; preventive police force is often referred to as *preventive detention*.

In the decades following World War II, preventive war and preventive detention were unpopular concepts. Preventive war is contrary to the Charter of the United Nations (Section 51), signed, ratified, and therefore binding on the United States. Preventive detention is contrary to the "due process" clause of the United States Constitution, and is prohibited under various international protocols of civil and political rights. (In 1988 the American Congress formally apologized for the preventive detention of American citizens of Japanese descent during World War II, an action now viewed as morally abominable.) But in the wake of the attacks of

September 11, 2001 the ideas of preventive war and preventive detention have been revived. Some now consider them necessary and legitimate instruments in the war against terrorism. So the problem is this: do the events of 9/11 require us to revise our moral ideas? Should we reject the old view, that preventive war and preventive detention are always wrong, for the new view that preventive war and preventive detention are sometimes right?

Before we begin the discussion, distinctions must be introduced between *preventive* force, *preemptive* force, and *responsive* force. Preventive force is force used against a person who *might* do an evil act, where "might" means "having some probability of doing the act." Preemptive force is force used against a person who *will* do an evil act, unless the preemptive force is applied. Responsive force is force used against someone who has *already* perpetrated an evil act.

The Charter of the United Nations authorizes an individual nation state to use force only "in the event of an armed attack." Thus, for individual nation states, only responsive force is permitted. But the Charter also authorizes the Security Council to use force when the Council determines that there is an imminent "threat to peace." Thus the UN Charter permits the use of preemptive force by the collective body.

International law is more liberal than the UN charter: it sanctions the use of preemptive military force by *individual* nation states in clear cases of imminent threat. Neither the UN Charter nor international law cross the line and sanction the use of preventive force. The problem, however, is whether a clear moral line can be drawn between preventive force and preemptive force.

2 An Argument for Preventive Force: the Distinction between Prevention and Preemption is Bogus

Suppose that a certain event E is a very evil thing: it involves, like the attacks on 9/11, the deaths of thousands of people. Suppose that E can only be produced by a four-step plan that unfolds through stages A, B, C, and D. Each stage is almost a necessary condition for E. Stop any one of them, and you are very likely to stop E. Furthermore, D is almost a sufficient condition for E; that is, if things reach stage D, then you are very likely to get E. If we use force to try to stop steps A, B, and C from happening, we have a preventive use of force. If we use force to try to stop step D from happening, we have a preemptive use of force. (Check the definitions to verify this.) Is there a moral difference between the use of force to stop A, B, and C, and the use of force to stop step D? Isn't the morally important thing stopping E and saving lives? And if the important thing is to stop E, isn't it better to nip the evil plan in the bud rather than to wait until it grows to stage D? So far as ethics is concerned, the distinction between preventive force and preemptive force seems to be a distinction without a moral difference.

As the evil plan unfolds, the chance that E will be reached increases step by step. When we are at stage A, there is some probability p that E will occur. When we are at stage C, there is some greater probability q that E will occur. So, if we use preemptive force after stage A, we are addressing a risk that has a size expressed by (E x probability p). If we use preventive force after stage C, we are addressing larger risk of size (E x probability q). Can a difference between the sizes of the risks here amount to a moral difference? After all, isn't the main problem preventing the big evil, E? If so, don't the small differences between p and q fade into insignificance? If the only difference between preventive force and preemptive force is that preemptive force addresses slightly bigger risk, isn't this a distinction without a moral difference?

Notice, furthermore, that preemptive force is not guaranteed to succeed, so a certain probability remains that the evil act will occur even after preemptive force is applied. Likewise the use of preventive force is not guaranteed to succeed, and a certain probability remains that the evil act will occur even after preventive force is applied. Since preventive force is used against an earlier stage in the unfolding of an evil plan, it has a greater chance of succeeding against the threat than preemptive force, which is applied only when all of an evil agent's forces are assembled and ready for use. Preemptive force has a smaller chance of success against a bigger threat, and preventive force has a bigger chance of success against a smaller threat. Can these differences between higher and lower probabilities of success amount to a moral difference?

Imagine, for example, that terrorists are engaged in a plan, which will take six months to complete, to blow up the Indian Point nuclear power plant on the Hudson River, contaminating Westchester County and New York City. In January, the first month of the plan, they have a 10 percent chance of success, and this chance increases by 10 percent each month, so that by May, the chances of success are 50 percent. If preventive force is applied in January, it addresses a 10 percent chance of disaster, but it will have caught the plan "in the bud," and for this reason there is a high probability that the terrorists will be thwarted in the effort the blow up Indian Point. If preemptive force is applied in May, it addresses a 50 percent chance of disaster, but since the terrorists are caught late in the game, they may have devised redundancies and "Plan B" scenarios that reduce the chance the preemptive force will succeed against the terrorists.

In short, the distinction between preventive force and preemptive is a matter of "more or less." Preemptive force has some probability of success in the struggle against evil. Preventive force has some probability of success in the struggle against evil. If is morally acceptable to use force to neutralize a 50 percent chance of a terrorist attack, then it is morally acceptable to use force to neutralize a 40 percent chance of terrorist attack. If it is morally acceptable to use force against terrorists that has a 50 percent chance of succeeding, then it is morally acceptable to use force against terrorists that has a 40 percent chance of succeeding. What we have here are differences in degree, not differences of kind, and even the differences of degree cut every which way.

If it makes little sense to base sharp moral distinctions on a blur of probabilities, it makes even less sense to base a moral distinction on a difference in timing of the use of force. Preemption catches an evil plan late in the process. Prevention catches an evil plan early in the process. What's the moral difference? Suppose that a terrorist plants a bomb under an office building with a very long fuse, so long that it will be six months before the bomb goes off. If he plants it in January, it will go off in June. Suppose the bomb is discovered in February, and the bomb squad is called to defuse the bomb. Wouldn't it be silly, at this point, for some morally minded person to say, "look, the bomb won't go off for five more months. To disable the bomb at this point would be the use of preventive force, contrary to our international law and our standard moral beliefs. We must wait until June, when the bomb is *about* to go off. Then if we disable the bomb, that is a use of preemptive force, and preemptive force is morally acceptable." Surely, if it permissible to disable the bomb in June, it is permissible to disable the bomb in February. Time itself, the philosophers say, does nothing. It cannot be that what is morally unacceptable on Tuesday becomes morally acceptable on Wednesday, simply because some time has passed.

If this is true of the planted bomb, shouldn't it also be true of the suicide bomber? Suppose a suicide bomber plans to blow himself up in January, but is instructed, for some propaganda purpose, to wait until June before blowing himself up. If it is permissible to apprehend the bomber in May, isn't it permissible to apprehend him in January? After all, all he is doing is *waiting*. He is no more evil in May than he was in January.

In sum, the moral distinction between preventive force and preemptive force is bogus. To be consistent, we must either accept them both or reject them both. Most people think that preemptive force is acceptable. If so, they should think that preventive force is acceptable as well.

Let's call this the "Preventive Force Argument." It is a serious argument, worthy of serious thought. Nevertheless, I reject it, and I will spend much of the rest of this essay criticizing it. The argument fails on three grounds. First, contrary to the argument, the distinction between preventive force and preemptive force is real: the two correspond to interventions at two different and morally distinct stages in the evolution of a human action. Second, the argument presumes knowledge that the users of force do not necessarily have – for example, knowledge of the moral character of the agents involved, knowledge of their plans and intentions, and knowledge of what their preliminary acts point to. Third, the argument ignores the problem of justifying the side-effects of preventive force; in particular, the fact that deployment of preventive force usually results in the killing of civilians and the violation of their rights.

3 The Structure of Acts and Plans

The Preventive Force Argument assumes that plans as they unfold do not have morally distinct stages. The argument speaks of "an evil plan unfolding," as if plans as they unfold just grow. In the "January to June" examples in the Preventive Force Argument, what we see is a gradually increasing probability that the evil act will be consummated at the end of the process.

But let us consider a crime from inception to consummation. Consider the murder of a certain Dr. Y.

(a) *Ideation*. Imagine that in American town, there is an abortion clinic, run by Dr. Y., that has functioned quietly for years without anyone paying much attention to it. The people in the town are neither pro-life nor pro-choice: they just haven't thought about the issue. On January 1, a pro-life speaker comes to town and gives a pro-life speech arguing that the clinic is a slaughterhouse and that Dr. Y is the murderer of children. Within a few days, the town is divided into people who are pro-life and people who are pro-choice, engaged in heated arguments.

Other things being equal, the pro-life people are more likely to murder Dr. Y than the pro-choice people. Furthermore, the probability that Dr. Y will be murdered has dramatically increased between December 31 and January 2. If an "increase in the probability of crime" is an argument for preventive force, then the police should start rounding up the pro-life people to forestall the murder of Dr. Y. If you think this is absurd, you should start worrying about the Preventive Force Argument.

Now enters into the story Mr. X, a long-time town resident, who has been convinced by the pro-life speaker that Dr. Y is evil. On February 1, X thinks that if someone murders Dr. Y, the abortion clinic will be shut down and evil driven from the town.

We are here at the stage of general ideation. X is not even thinking that he should be the one who murders Dr. Y., only that evil will be stopped if someone does. Nevertheless, by February 2, the probability that Dr. Y will be murdered has taken another upward leap. Should Mr. X be arrested?

Mr. X continues to ponder the problem. On March 1, it occurs to him that *he* might be the one to murder Dr. Y. We are now on the level of specific ideation. X ponders the problem from various angles. Killing Dr. Y would be a good thing. On the other hand, if he kills Dr. Y, he probably will be arrested and convicted for

murder, not a good thing. He is also puzzled by the thought that if he dislikes abortion because he values life, killing Dr. Y contradicts his own values.

(b) *Mere preparations*. All through March, X thinks about killing Dr. Y. He recalls that he has a pistol in the closet, and checks to see if it is still there, in working order. When he passes by the abortion clinic, he checks the sign on the door to see what days the clinic is open and what the closing time is. He does these things not because he has decided to commit murder, but because he wants to consider the factors involved. In April, he rejects his wife's idea of moving to some other town, because he wants to stay near the abortion clinic.

X has moved beyond ideation, but he has not yet decided to kill Y. He has acted, but only to keep his options open. In the law, such acts are called "mere preparations." All these actions in March raise the probability that Y will die at X's hands. But X has not decided to kill Y, and X in March cannot be said to be intending to kill Y. Do we want to use force against people because they might decide to do some crime, at a time when they are not intending to do it?

(c) *Deciding and intending*. On May 1, X weighs all the pros and cons and decides that he will kill Y. But Y is away on vacation for a month, and for the whole month of May, X does absolutely nothing that is overtly related to the plan to kill Dr. Y. At the same time, he does not change his mind, which is now properly described as an evil mind. And it is in his evil mind that the intention to commit murder is lodged. Should preventive force be used against X because of what is in his mind? He hasn't taken a single step to carry out his plan. And it is possible that he will change his mind about this before he takes a single step.

(d) *Substantial steps*. On June 1, X goes to the general store and buys bullets for his gun. For the next week he does nothing. Then, starting on June 7, each day for seven days, X (without his gun) positions himself opposite the abortion clinic, takes note Dr. Y's comings and goings, determines his routine, and locates his parking space. At this point, X is going to murder Y unless he is stopped. It would not be reasonable to rely on the hope that X will change his mind, or that other facts besides arrest and detention will stop X. If so, arresting Mr. X would count as a *preemptive* use of force, not just a *preventive* use of force.

(e) *Accidental non-consummation.* On June 15, X lies in wait for Y with a loaded gun. As Y walks to his parking space, X approaches, draws his gun, and fires. In that exact moment, Y bends over, and the bullet flies over his head. Before X can get off a second shot, he is apprehended by a passing police officer.

Look now at steps (a) through (e). Aren't the distinctions between these steps morally significant? There is a particularly vivid difference between steps (b) and (c). If we call for the use of preventive force in stage (b), we are calling for the use of force against a person who has not formed an evil intention, who has not committed himself to evil. To ignore the factor of intention would wipe out many deep distinctions of criminal law – for example, the distinction between murder and manslaughter.

There is a difference between a person who has evil thoughts and a person who is committed to evil plans. There is a difference between a person who has evil plans and a person who takes substantial steps to carry them out. All of these differences are wiped out in the abstract example of the "evil plan that unfolds from A to E."

4   The Problem of Knowledge

The story of Mr. X and Dr. Y is told from a "God's eye view." When the story says, "X decides to kill Y," you are to assume that it is a fact that X has decided to kill Y. But the political leaders and police officers who must decide at what point force is to be used against Mr. X are not God. They cannot see things from a God's eye view. In particular, they cannot see into Mr. X's mind. They must develop their own story of what is going on with Mr. X,

and they must develop the story on the basis of rational evidence and act only on what in the law is called "probable cause." In the story, X decides to kill Dr. Y on May 1, but, for the entire month of May, X does nothing that expresses or fulfills this intention. The intention is within his mind, and telepathy and mind reading are not recognized as a source of evidence in the law. So the police cannot legitimately proceed against X for the month of May. They must wait for X to perform an "overt act."

On June 1, X buys bullets for his gun, an overt act. We, the God-like readers, know that he has bought the bullets as part of his plan to kill Dr. X. We are inferring the purpose of the overt act from the intention. But the police are working the other way around. They must infer X's intentions from his overt acts. X has bought bullets for his gun. Many people buy bullets without intending to kill physicians who perform abortions. If the police ask X why he bought the bullets, X will tell them he intends to go hunting. Given all they know about X, this is as reasonable an interpretation of his overt act as the idea that he is going to murder someone. They might arrest X for attempted murder, but it is not likely that the charge will stick. Nor should it, given the evidence.

From June 7 to June 14, X keeps watch on the abortion clinic, but he does not carry his gun. Once again, we know what X's intentions are, but the police must infer them from his pattern of conduct. There are many fewer interpretations of these overt acts than there are interpretations of the purchase of bullets. X can be arrested, charged, and convicted of the crime of "stalking." But it is not likely, given these facts, that he could be arrested for intended murder, even though he has taken substantial steps towards the commission of a crime. The trouble is that X has not brought the murder weapon to the scene. The police cannot predict on June 14 that X will bring the weapon on June 15. That is a choice X will make freely and in his own home.

On June 15, having stalked Dr. Y for seven days, X waits at Y's parking place with a loaded gun. At this point, the range of interpretation of X's overt act is very limited. That he means to do harm is by far the most plausible interpretation.

Some states even make "lying in wait" sufficient evidence for attempted murder. And certainly, when X fires the gun at Y, we have indisputable evidence of full-fledged attempt.

It is important to note that in judging whether the condition of "probable cause" has been met, the police are *not* allowed to rely on *statistical* evidence. Suppose that Mr. Jones's wife has been murdered in circumstances C, and the police have a database that shows that in 80 percent of cases in which a wife has been murdered in circumstances C, the husband has turned out to be the murderer. Before they begin their investigation, the police can conclude from the database that there is an 80 percent chance that Jones is the killer. But at the moment, even with this statistically derived probability of guilt, there is (so far) no *real* evidence against Jones. Real evidence must have a cause-and-effect relation to what Jones has done, and the statistical evidence does not talk about Jones, but about *other* people like Jones. If Jones's hand motion causes a fingerprint on the murder weapon, that is real evidence. But the database of past crimes does not tell us whether or not Jones has or has not left such fingerprints.

In the case of Mr. Jones, we are talking about evidence for a murder that has been committed. In the case of Mr. X, we are talking about an attempted murder. The rules of evidence are the same: only real evidence justifies the use of force against either Jones or X. Of course, Mr. X is a "crime risk" once he starts thinking about murdering Dr. Y. The police might have statistics that show that persons who have gone through stage (b) preparations are 25 times more likely to commit murder than the average person. This information might be used to make X a legitimate object of police surveillance. But it cannot make X a legitimate object of force, detainable by the police.[1]

5 The Problem of Knowledge in International Affairs

Speculating about intentions

I have argued that the legitimate use of preventive police force requires mental powers possessed only by God. The same problem arises on the international scene as regards preventive war. Suppose that political leaders in the US believe that a certain foreign head of state poses a threat to peace. The foreign leader has already expressed certain ideas that could develop along dangerous lines. Some advocate a preventive strike against this allegedly evil enemy. But if all the foreign leader has done is express ideas, he may be at stage (a) or stage (b) or stage (c). If he is only at stage (a) or stage (b), he is not yet evil. And who can tell if he is at stage (c), the stage of intention formation? Henry Kissinger was once asked, during the Paris Peace Talks, about the intentions of the North Vietnamese. "I cannot comment on the intentions of the North Vietnamese," he said. "I have too much difficulty understanding our own."

Uncovering overt acts

But now suppose that the American advocates of preventive war say that the foreign leader has done *more* than think evil thoughts: he has performed overt acts that show that he has an evil plan unfolding towards an evil goal. We have two barriers to knowledge: first, do these overt acts exist? Second, if they exist, how should we interpret them?

Nation states, the United States most of all, spend billions of dollars a year on intelligence gathering. Yet the record shows that they have a difficult time discovering facts about the activities of foreign powers. The explosion of the first Soviet atomic bomb in 1949 was an unanticipated shock; the same was true of the first Indian nuclear detonation in 1974. The CIA reported to President Nixon in October 1973 that military action in the Middle East was "not likely" – two days later three nations launched large-scale military attacks against Israel. In October 2002, American officials at the highest levels believed that Saddam Hussein had built and hidden weapons of mass destruction. Colin Powell declared this before the United Nations. Yet the weapons had not been constructed and were not hidden anywhere.

The problem of government misinformation is not sporadic but pervasive. Governments, even in democracies, are hierarchies, and government workers, like most workers in hierarchies, are intensely concerned with moving up the career ladder. One good way to advance your career is to please your boss, and one pleases the boss by telling the boss what he or she wants to hear. What the boss wants to hear is something that will please the *next* boss up the chain of command. By the time reports reach the top level, they are full of wishful thinking. And remember that what leaders sometimes wish for is war, or at least a new line item in the defense budget.

Interpreting overt acts

The problem of wishful thinking clouds the uncovering of overt acts; it also clouds the interpretation of those acts.

In 2003 United States officials discovered that the government of Iran had constructed a number of gas centrifuges for the purpose of producing enriched uranium. The centrifuges existed: that was not in dispute. What was in dispute was the interpretation of the centrifuges. One thing enriched uranium can be used for is nuclear weapons. Another thing that enriched uranium can be used for is nuclear power. Naturally, the Americans claimed that the centrifuges were for nuclear weapons. Naturally, the Iranians claimed that the centrifuges were for nuclear power. The act of constructing the centrifuges was irreducibly ambiguous; there are two plausible interpretations of Iranian intentions. Given the centrifuges, some Americans called for military action against Iran. But if the centrifuges were intended for peaceful purposes, or if the Iranians had not yet made up their minds as to how to use the centrifuges, this would be an act of war against an innocent party.

In the case of overt acts that have two equally plausible interpretations, some might argue that it is legitimate to proceed on the basis of either interpretation. In the case of the Iranian centrifuges, it is as plausible to assume that the centrifuges are for nuclear weapons as it is plausible to assume that they are for nuclear power. Rational considerations being balanced, we can, if

we choose, decide that they are for nuclear weapons. In fact (the argument continues), since nuclear weapons are a serious threat, this is the interpretation that we *should* adopt, and having adopted it, we should act prudently and launch a preemptive strike.

I reject this view. It is not prudent to always think the worst of your opponents. If your opponent knows that you will think the worst of whatever he does, he will have no incentive to do less than his worst. It is not prudent, on the basis of "worst case" scenarios, to commit oneself to preventive uses of force. Commitment to preventive force introduces deep instabilities into international affairs detrimental to all parties.

This relation between instability and preventive force was well noted during the Cold War. Soviet missiles obviously posed a threat to the United States. Some advocated preemptive strikes against the Soviet Union, to "take out" Soviet weapons before they were used against us. But to the degree that the Soviets believed they would be subject to a preemptive strike, to that degree they were encouraged to "take out" American missiles before they could be used in a preemptive strike: to preempt our preemption. In turn, the Americans felt pressured to preempt their preemption of our preemption, and so forth.

The logic of what is said here about preemption carries over to preventive strikes. The possibility of a preventive strike encourages opponents to explore evil options before preventive action occurs. For example, when President Bush in January 2002 identified North Korea as part of an "axis of evil," it was clear to the North Koreans that they had become a possible target for a preventive strike by the United States. As a result, North Korea speeded up its nuclear weapons development program, so as to have its nuclear weapons in hand before any preventive strikes were launched. In the end, the belief that the United States was prepared to use preventive force forced the North Koreans to take steps that made the entire region less secure.

On the international scene, nations often have little real evidence to interpret the intentions and plans of foreign governments. Lacking real evidence, they fall back on what earlier in this paper was described as statistical evidence: judgments developed by projecting patterns from previous cases. Does Saddam have weapons of mass destruction? We don't have pictures, but we do know what kind of person Saddam is. He is evil, and evil people are the kind of people who build weapons of mass destruction. These patterns of reasoning are precisely the patterns that do not provide, in the law, evidence of intent or evidence of guilt, and the law provides better counsel about these problems than talk about what "these kinds of people are likely to do." That is why, if you suspect that an evil plan is unfolding, it is better to wait until the plan is a certain way along before taking action. Waiting may make the difference between acting on real evidence, and acting on hunch, speculation, and prejudice.

6 The Innocent Victims of Preventive Force

In all our previous discussion, we have concentrated on the use of preventive force without reference to side-effects. But preventive force is force, force is controlled violence, and violence in the world always produces side-effects – most of them unwanted, some of them tragic. Preventive detention can deprive completely innocent persons of liberty – remember, innocent Japanese-Americans were deprived of liberty *for years* – and make them objects of social suspicion for the rest of their lives. Preventive war has the even more troubling side-effect that preventive war, like all war, inevitably results in the killing of civilians.

The problem of justifying the killing of civilians in war is a deep moral puzzle. In normal circumstances, it is just plain wrong to kill innocent people, even if some good result will come from the killing. What is so special about the circumstances of war, so that in war the killing of civilians in war is *sometimes* right? It can't be merely that the war is fought for a good cause, since "good results" by themselves don't justify killing the innocent.

One way of getting a grip on the problem is to consider other "abnormal" cases in which the killing of the innocent seems justified. One such case, much discussed in contemporary ethics, is the Trolley Case. Imagine a trolley running loose down its track. Further down the track, ten children are playing, and if it continues down the track, the trolley will run over them. Fortunately there is a switch, and the switchman can divert the trolley to a sidetrack. But (unfortunately!) there is a little child playing on the sidetrack. Should the switchman divert the trolley onto the sidetrack? Most people say yes, but if the trolley is switched, the small child playing alone is killed.

The justification for killing the small child can't merely be that the ten other children are saved. You could not, for example, morally kill one child to save ten if ten children needed organ transplants and an eleventh healthy child could be chopped to pieces in order to make up for a lack of organ donors. There must be some other factor involved. Many philosophers say that the extra factor in the Trolley Case is that if the trolley is switched, you are not creating evil, but merely redirecting it, whereas if you kill a child to harvest his internal organs, you are not just diverting an evil. You are the source.

The distinction between "creating" evil and "diverting" evil requires much elaboration and analysis, but I think that the distinction is basically sound. If so, the distinction provides us with some clue as to why it is permissible to kill some civilians in some wars. In most modern theories of just war, war is just only if it is a *response* to evil: the paradigm case of just war is defense of one's country against attack. The aggressor nation *creates* evil; the defending nation merely *deflects* it back towards the aggressor, sometimes onto the heads of civilians in the aggressor's country. A blitzkrieg is like a runaway trolley. A just response to blitzkrieg loops the trolley back towards the enemy.

If this is right, it is important to show that one's use of force is a deflection of evil and not a creation of evil. In the trolley story, the trolley is dangerous; it is already in motion, and it will run over the children unless it is diverted onto the sidetrack. This is clearly a case of deflection, and relative to our initial example of an unfolding plan it corresponds to intervention after (c) and before (d). The actions of the switchman are more than just preventive; they are preemptive.

What would correspond to a *preventive* use of force in the Trolley Case? Suppose (Trolley Problem #2) the trolley gets loose five blocks away from the ten children. On each block there is a siding, and on each siding one child is playing. Furthermore, at the end of each block, the main track forks, and the trolley can take either the right fork or the left fork, with a 50 percent chance of going each way. Suppose the trolley will run over the ten children only if it takes the right fork four blocks in a row. Now, if you divert the trolley onto the siding on the first block, the children five blocks down the road are safe. But in so doing you kill one child for sure, and if you let the trolley go, there is a good chance that the trolley won't hit any children at all. Most people, confronted with Trolley Story #2, feel that it is not morally permissible to throw the switch in block 1. You must wait until the trolley has reached block 5, and is heading straight for the children with no more forks in the road. Then you can throw the switch.

In Trolley Problem #2, we do not feel that throwing the switch in the first block is a "deflection" of evil. (If we did, we would approve throwing the switch.) Why not? Because in the first block, the trolley is not yet an actual evil. It is only a potential evil. It will become an actual evil only if it takes the right fork in each of the next four blocks. A mirror can reflect only actual light, not possible light.

Diverting the trolley on block 1 is an example of the preventive use of force. But diverting the trolley on block 1 is not a case of deflecting evil. If the child on the siding on block 1 is killed after the switch is thrown, that killing is morally wrong. If civilians are killed by a preventive war, that killing of civilians is morally wrong. This is so no matter how admirable the goal, how desirable the result, of preventive war. In short, preemptive force deflects evil; preventive

force creates it. This draws a clear moral line between preemptive war and preventive war.

7 Preventive Measures and Liberty

We have already considered, with our story of Mr. X and Dr. Y, the point at which a series of thoughts and actions turns into an attempt at crime, and when it can be known that this point is reached. The use of force at an earlier point in the evolution of a crime is an intrusion on liberty, because it uses force to control what people think, not what they do. There are two related cases that have to be considered. Crimes can result from solicitation: prevent the solicitation and you prevent the crime. Crimes can require conspiracies: prevent the conspiracy and you prevent the crime. But stopping solicitation is not an example of preemption, and breaking up conspiracies is not a case of preemption. Are these acceptable uses of preventive force? It all depends, as philosophers say, on how you define "solicitation" and "conspiracy."

Go back to the story of Mr. X. The trouble started when the pro-life speaker came to town and stirred up the residents with a pro-life speech. If you are for nipping trouble in the bud, you are for stopping speeches of this sort. But suppose that the speaker says: "Abortionists are child murderers," "Abortion clinics are baby-slaughterhouses," and similar sentences. There is nothing in such sentences that describes a crime and asks people to do it. "Such butcher shops ought to be blown up," the speaker continues. Now the speaker is describing a crime and indicating that he would approve of people doing the crime. But in my view, this is not yet solicitation, since a person can say, "X ought to be done," without intending that X be done. We often say, when we see people doing what we don't like, that "they ought to be arrested," but we don't think that they will be arrested and we have not formed an intention that they be arrested. What we mean when we say "X ought to happen" is merely that "the world would be a better place if X happened."

But now suppose the speaker says, "Someone should get a bomb and blow the place up." At this point, I think, we have solicitation (or what in some states is called "incitement"), and the reason that we have solicitation is that a person who says such a thing has formed an intention to do things that will lead to the clinic being blown up. The speaker cannot know that there is no one in the crowd who will follow his suggestion. If someone does, that is what the speaker intended by saying those words. The words correspond to the "substantial steps" and "overt acts" that form the core of the crime of attempt.

Now let us consider conspiracy. If a number of people agree to commit a crime, then they are involved in a criminal conspiracy, even if it turns out that only a fraction of those involved take any concrete steps towards consummation of the crime. The "agreement" that forms the conspiracy need not be stated verbally or written down. What is required is some kind of *understanding*.

But now let us consider what is required in order for me to enter into an understanding. My wife is a night owl and I am a morning person. She used to disturb me with late-night TV and I would disturb her with early-morning stereo. We both realized that this was a problem, so I stopped playing music in the morning and she stopped playing the television at night. I don't play music on the understanding that she won't play the TV. My intention in not playing music is to induce her into not putting on the TV. And where is my intention? Not hidden in my soul, but in the overt verifiable act of not playing the stereo.

The formation of intentions, then, is part of the structure of an understanding between persons, just as it is part of the structure of solicitation and the structure of attempt. With attempt, force cannot be legitimately applied until the intention is formed and until there is some real evidence that the intention is there. Likewise force cannot be legitimately applied to prevent solicitation and break up conspiracy until the intention is formed and until there is real evidence that the intention is there. Even with solicitation and conspiracy, the police must

wait for overt acts that will be found in the later stages of the evolution of actions.

These considerations have implications for the domestic war on terrorism. In a case decided in April 2005 in Virginia, the Muslim cleric Ali al-Tamimi was convicted on six counts, including counseling others to wage war against the United States and to use firearms in furtherance of violent crimes (*New York Times*, April 27, 2005). In the course of the trial the prosecution introduced as evidence against Mr. Tamimi the fact that he described the crash of the space shuttle *Columbia* in 2003 as a "good omen" for Muslims. "This is a strong signal," he wrote to his followers, "that Western supremacy (especially that of America) that began 500 years ago is coming to an end."

It is not possible in this article to reach a judgment as to whether Mr. Tamimi was guilty as charged. But if specific intentions are required for solicitation or conspiracy, then the statement quoted here is no evidence that Mr. Tamimi was guilty of those crimes. It is a statement about what he thinks would be a better world, not a statement of intention expressed in steps towards creating that world. If this statement were the sole basis for jailing Mr. Tamimi, this would be an illegitimate application of preventive force and a violation of his liberty.

Most Americans, myself included, are appalled by Mr. Tamimi's interpretation of the destruction of the *Columbia* space shuttle and the death of our astronauts. Mr. Tamimi does not share our ideals. Relative to our values he is a heretic. But if there is to be liberty, there must be liberty for the heretics as well as for the believers. And if preventive measures are taken against heretics, there is less liberty left for the rest of us.

8 Conclusion

The new debate about preventive force began when various parties after 9/11 claimed that preventive detention and preventive war were necessary tools in the war against terrorism. What is evil about terrorists is that they are the enemies of liberty and murderers of civilians.

This essay argues that preventive detention is the enemy of liberty and that preventive war requires the murder of civilians. Thus, these tools against terrorism transform their users into terrorists. Terrorists used to believe that victory required the completion of their plans. Now all they need do is begin to plan. The application of preventive force will do the rest.

Note

1 There are cases, of course, where the police are involved in the removal of dangers to the community, on the mere basis of probability of risk and without reference to intentions. They will shoot a rabid dog, for example, even if rabid dogs are not evil, and they may have to use force in those rare cases where a mentally ill individual becomes violent. But these are not cases in which the police are dealing with those who, at least for the moment, are capable of forming intentions. In dealing with individuals who are capable of forming intentions, the scope of police action is limited by the rights of intention-forming individuals, which are discussed in section 5 below.

66

The Justifiability of Humanitarian Intervention

Charles R. Beitz

Humanitarian intervention is the threat or use of force by a state or group of states intended to stop or prevent the violation of human rights in another state. It is hardly a new phenomenon – the French intervention in Syria of 1860–61 and the US intervention in Cuba of 1898 are prominent nineteenth-century instances. But the end of the Cold War brought with it a dramatic increase in the frequency and ambition of humanitarian interventions – for example, in Somalia (to end famine), in Haiti (to restore a democratically elected government), and in Bosnia, Kosovo, and East Timor (to end ethnic killing and displacement). At the same time, other cases of massive human rights violations were allowed to occur unimpeded – most notoriously, the Rwandan genocide of 1994, when as many as 500,000 Tutsi were killed by militia-led Hutu while the international community failed to act.

Several aspects of this record of action and inaction were troubling. None of the interventions were completely successful. Most had unanticipated costs, not only for the intervening parties but also for the populations on whose behalf they were carried out. Not all were unambiguously clearly permissible under international law. The failure to act in Rwanda, where, arguably, the humanitarian stakes were higher than in any of the other cases, raised the question whether the international community is capable of purely humanitarian action at all.

Provoked by this ambiguous record, Kofi Annan, the Secretary General of the UN (United Nations), challenged the international community to work out a coherent doctrine of humanitarian intervention. Looking back on the Kosovo intervention, he wrote: "I believe it is essential that the international community reach consensus – not only on the principle that massive and systematic violations of human rights must be checked, wherever they take place, but also on ways of deciding what action is necessary, and when, and by whom."[1] At least two international commissions and a variety of academic studies responded to the challenge.[2]

In the aftermath of the attacks of September 11, 2001, the subject of concern about humanitarian intervention was eclipsed by the concern to prevent further acts of international terrorism. Some people believe this will be a lasting change in the international agenda – that humanitarian interventions were possible in the 1990s only because strong states had spare military capacity, a condition not likely to be replicated any time soon.[3] I suspect this will turn out to be false. Severe human rights violations will continue to take place and there will continue to be appeals by and on behalf of their victims for international help. The global humanitarian constituency will continue to amplify these appeals. In some cases the violations will endanger regional security. International actors will have reasons of both principle and prudence to take these facts seriously. The subject of concern about humanitarian intervention is not likely to go away.

The problem has legal, political, and ethical dimensions. As a matter of international law, for example, it is arguably not clear whether humanitarian intervention per se is *ever* justified – the UN Charter forbids the use of force by states except in self-defense and allows the Security Council to authorize armed intervention only when international peace and security are at risk (a condition that humanitarian disasters may not always satisfy). There is, perhaps, room for argument that international law, properly understood, is more permissive than the Charter provisions indicate, but there is no question that a legal cloud hangs over humanitarian intervention.[4] If the international community wishes to reconcile its humanitarian intervention with the law of the Charter, new legislation may be required.

There are also political issues, of which the most pressing is the absence of any standing international capacity to authorize and carry out interventions. Like the pope, the UN has no divisions – it must depend on member states to contribute troops and other military resources, which means that its capacity to intervene in any particular case will always be hostage to the willingness of one or more states to accept the risks of foreign military operations. This means, in turn, that the UN may be limited to intervening in cases where a small number of powerful countries believe themselves to have independent interests in the intervention – hardly a recipe for principled, consistent international action.

Both the legal and the political dimensions of the problem are important, but for the most part I will leave them aside. I shall concentrate instead on the ethical aspects of humanitarian intervention, for these are fundamental to our understanding of the problem and will influence our views about the other dimensions. Reduced to essentials, the most basic questions we must answer are: When, if ever, is humanitarian intervention morally justified? And, who should decide when these conditions are satisfied?

Humanitarian Intervention in the Perspective of the Charter

Let me begin by putting these questions in the context of the evolution of international doctrine, saying more about why these questions are especially pressing. Why is the problem of humanitarian intervention before us now? As I suggested, one answer looks to the experience of the 1990s. On the one hand, we were more aware of situations where human rights were gravely threatened, and with the end of the Cold War the chances of effective collaboration to resist these threats seemed greater than ever. On the other hand, the international experience with humanitarian intervention was frustrating both politically and operationally; with the possible exception of Haiti, it would be hard to argue that any of the 1990s interventions were completely successful in meeting their objectives. As a result, perceptions of humanitarian intervention oscillated from hopefulness to despair as it became clear that the international community's aspirations had run far in advance of its capabilities.

But the problem is hardly a creature of the 1990s and we understand it better by looking at the innovations in the political doctrine of international society that resulted from World War II. The United Nations Charter, promulgated in 1946, was a turning point in the constitution of international relations. It combined two principles, neither of which was, strictly speaking, an innovation, but whose combination in the "fundamental law" of the international community had far-reaching consequences. First, in proscribing war as an instrument of national policy, the Charter substituted collective for unilateral action as the preferred mechanism for protecting fundamental values in international affairs. It described a world order in which the responsibility for maintaining peace was transferred from individual states (and alliances) to the international level. Second, by incorporating a doctrine of human rights, the Charter embraced the idea that the domestic conduct of governments was a legitimate subject of international concern. The explicit commitment of the international community to the protection of human rights meant that individual states were not free to conduct their internal affairs as they saw fit; henceforth every state would be responsible for treating its people according to common, minimal standards of decency.

The problem is that the Charter did not connect these two principles. There was no mechanism through which concern about the domestic conduct of governments could be enforced through the collective action of the international community. This is basically what the experience of the 1990s demonstrates. The recent anxieties about humanitarian intervention are really reflections of a doctrinal tension within the Charter conception of world order. During much of the post-World War II period, this tension was obscured by a different set of international issues arising from the Cold War. What was special about the 1990s was that the political environment changed in ways that enabled the consequences of the tension in international doctrine to be played out in practice. Looked at from this perspective, the challenge today is to complete some unfinished business in the Charter's conception of world order.

Before turning directly to this challenge, let me make three preliminary observations that occur to me as a political theorist about humanitarian intervention as a problem in political theory. First, there are two levels at which the problem of humanitarian intervention might be discussed – the level of regime building and the level of immediate policy. If the basic problem is that the international community's aspirations have developed faster than its capabilities for action, then the obvious response is to develop the missing capabilities (e.g., by codifying

causes of action, establishing a standing international interventionary force, enabling the Security Council, or some alternate body, to act quickly and decisively to authorize the deployment of forces, etc.) But changes like these are unlikely come about quickly (or perhaps at all). So – this is the second level – we must also think about political action in the "non-ideal world" of today, in which individual states and alliances of states may be confronted with the unhappy choice of acting unilaterally to stave off a humanitarian disaster or sitting idly by while it takes place.

Second, the central moral question about humanitarian intervention is not what it used to be. Looking back over the last several years of international thought, it is striking (and perhaps surprising) to see that the main question that used to be posed about intervention – namely, whether considerations of sovereignty should be a bar, *in principle*, to intervention for humanitarian purposes – seems to be more or less settled, at least as a matter of political theory.[5] When gross abuses are imminent or when they are already taking place, and when an external actor is in a position to prevent or stop the abuses, there is a clear *prima facie* justification to act arising from our common duties of humanity, principally the duty to protect the innocent and vulnerable people from harms to which they are vulnerable. This justification is not stopped by the invocation of a state's right of sovereignty because this right itself is conditioned on the state's effective discharge of the duties of humanity owed to its people.[6]

But it hardly follows that humanitarian intervention is not morally problematic. (This is the third observation.) There is a difference between saying that considerations of sovereignty do not rule out humanitarian intervention and that humanitarian intervention is acceptable, all things considered, as a matter of policy, either for international institutions or for states and alliances or regional organizations. What I called the "non-ideal world" is distinctively a realm of instrumental judgment – specifically, judgment about the means that are best used to protect a value which, in a better world, would be protected by some institution that does not now exist. The large space for instrumental judgment means that one can consistently believe that whereas intervention is permissible in theory, it is virtually never a good idea in practice.[7] For example, one might be skeptical that the resources likely to be available for an intervention would be sufficient to accomplish the intervention's humanitarian goals. Or one might think it is rarely possible to foresee with enough confidence that intervention will do more good than harm. Although I do not share the skeptical view, I believe that any plausible account of conditions for justified humanitarian intervention should make room for, and give structure to, these kinds of instrumental judgments.

Intervention and the Just War

We cannot, therefore, avoid the two basic questions mentioned earlier: When, if ever, is humanitarian intervention morally justified? And, who should decide when these conditions are satisfied? Because humanitarian intervention involves the use or threat of military force,[8] I think the most helpful way to respond to these questions is to consider them under headings familiar from the theory of the just war.[9] A comprehensive just war analysis of humanitarian intervention is impossible here, so I shall focus on five specific conditions drawn from this tradition under which I believe intervention would be justified.

Some brief prefatory comments. First, I do not mean to suggest that the just war categories themselves settle anything morally; the tradition is open to enough different interpretations that its categories are better regarded as the beginning than as the end of moral reasoning. This is an especially important caution in connection with humanitarian intervention, which is different from standard cases of just war involving self-defense against aggression. Second, I intend these five conditions to be jointly sufficient to justify intervention; I leave it open whether they are necessary (possibly humanitarian intervention could be justified in other ways as well). Third, in saying that intervention would be permissible under these conditions I do not mean that it would be required; whether there is a *duty* to intervene when these conditions are satisfied is a further question. (I comment briefly about this later.) Finally, these comments are only a sketch of a view about the justification of humanitarian intervention. They leave open many questions. I note some of these at the end.

When would humanitarian intervention be morally justified and who should decide? Here are five conditions that help answer both questions.

1 *Intervention should have a just, humanitarian purpose.* The problem, of course, is to say what counts as such a purpose. It is tempting to frame a reply in terms of the defense and advancement of human rights. Thus, for example, the Secretary General says that, "massive and systematic violations of human rights must be checked." But this is not much help. The Universal Declaration of Human Rights (1948) contains 30 articles listing at least as many human rights. Virtually all of these might conceivably be violated in a "massive and systematic" way but it is implausible that the violation of *any* human right, even if the violation is "massive and systematic," could justify intervention.

If we look back over the range of recent cases of humanitarian intervention, we see that intervention was used to attain six kinds of goals, which can be summarized crudely as follows:

- to stop or prevent genocide and large-scale enslavement or expulsion of populations;
- to alleviate acute material distress (e.g., in cases of widespread, remediable starvation);
- to restore a constitutional, democratic government that was removed by force;
- to support an insurgent movement committed to human rights in an attempt to remove an authoritarian regime;
- to support a constitutional, democratic government fighting a rebellion;
- to help an oppressed or subjugated group to achieve political self-determination.

It is significant that all of these goals, except possibly the last, involve protecting a very limited class of human rights. These are what Henry Shue calls "basic rights" – rights to personal security, material subsistence, and political liberty.[10] These rights, as Shue argues, are particularly urgent because their enjoyment is necessary for the enjoyment of any other right: in this sense they are strategic. As a first approximation, we might say that intervention has a just, humanitarian purpose when its goal is to protect people against massive and systematic threats to or deprivations of their basic rights.

Earlier I said that such acts are warranted by considerations of humanity. Two aspects about this might be controversial. First, the causes of action I have listed may not seem to stand on the same ethical footing as justifications of intervention. Some people might argue, for example, that intervention is acceptable to combat massive violations of rights to personal security (like those involved in the Rwandan genocide) but not to establish or restore a democratic regime (as in Haiti), and perhaps not to deliver famine relief (as in Somalia). This is not an easy question, but my own view is that there are no relevant differences, in principle, among the values that stand behind the three basic rights. I accept Shue's argument that these rights are comparable in moral urgency; in principle, threats to each of these rights are equally capable of justifying humanitarian intervention. The relevant considerations in any particular case involve the extent of the threat and the probability that intervention can succeed in defeating it. These considerations are important and I return to them below.

The second controversial issue is whether considerations of humanity *require* us to act in every case where they *permit* us to do so. Is there always a *duty* to intervene in cases of the kinds I have described? The answer must be no. Humanitarian duties provide us with reasons to act. But, as a general matter, reasons for action come in two forms, which we may call *pro tanto* and *conclusory*. A conclusory reason is an overriding reason: if the reason applies under the circumstances, it overrides whatever other considerations there might be and requires us to

act. A pro tanto reason, on the other hand, is a consideration that argues in favor of action but does not rule out that there might be other, competing considerations that should also be taken into account. As a general matter, humanitarian duties yield pro tanto reasons, not conclusory ones. It could not be otherwise, since we have no way of knowing what other moral considerations might be in play in any particular case. Of course, pro tanto reasons may be very strong reasons – there may be few competing reasons strong enough to defeat them. Still, we can only know if a pro tanto reason *requires* us to act by taking account of all the reasons for and against acting that arise under the circumstances we face. Injudicious talk about a "duty to intervene" obscures this important fact.

2 *Intervention should be supported, or at least not opposed, by competent international authority.* The classical writers in the just war tradition insisted on the requirement of "competent authority" in order to maintain the distinction between war and violent crime. This can seem anachronistic to modern readers, who sometimes interpret it as merely a formal concern or perhaps as motivated by an obsolete belief in the divine right of princes. But it is a mistake to dismiss the requirement on these grounds. A just war, as opposed to an act of violent crime, involves a regulated use of deadly force for legitimate political ends. Both the legitimacy of the ends and the efficiency with which the use of force is regulated are essential to the justice of the war. The requirement of competent authority is a way of assigning responsibility for the decision to go to war so as to ensure attention to the legitimacy of the war's ends and to the proportionality of these ends to the damage likely to be done in their pursuit.

If we understand the "competent authority" requirement this way, we can see why some parallel condition should be imposed on humanitarian intervention. The motivating concerns are the well-known dangers of unilateralism. These include the temptation to rationalize self-serving conduct by claiming that it has humanitarian purposes, the possibility that conduct genuinely motivated by humanitarian concerns can be distorted by a state's strategic and political interests, and the potential for damage to emerging international law-enforcement processes.

The problem, of course, is that there is no international government that can act on behalf of the international community with the same legitimacy as the government of a state can act on behalf of its own people. The Security Council is an obvious surrogate, but we know that it is hardly a representative body and that the great-power veto could slow down or frustrate a majority that desires to act to avert a humanitarian disaster. If the question posed is, "Should this intervention take place?" then, if the Council's explicit prior assent is required, some interventions which are justified on the merits would almost certainly be blocked and some people whose lives are threatened with disaster would not be helped.

In the long run the solution would be to establish a method by which the international community can authorize humanitarian intervention. But for various reasons this is unlikely in the short run, so we must ask what might satisfy the goals of the "competent authority" requirement in the absence of an adequate international process.

The circumstances under which NATO forces intervened in Kosovo may be suggestive. NATO did not seek the prior authorization of the Security Council because it feared that at least one permanent member would veto the intervention. This means that the intervention was illegal. However, it was reasonable to suppose that the intervention would have had the support of the Council's majority and, in the event, the Council approved it after the fact. I leave it to others to judge the legality of this approach under the Charter. This example suggests the following condition, in the spirit of the just war requirement of competent authority: intervention should have the endorsement of either the Security Council or the appropriate regional organization which takes responsibility on behalf of its members; in the latter case the intervention should not be opposed by the Security Council.[11]

3 *Intervention should be a last resort.* All versions of just war theory agree that war should not be used to attain a political end if there are less harmful means available for attaining the end. This constraint seems to me self-evidently valid, and it applies as plausibly to humanitarian interventions as to other uses of force for political ends.

Some commentators disagree. They hold that there may be circumstances in which non-violent processes such as negotiations and sanctions would invite disaster – for example, by delaying action until after the damage has been done. It would be better, in the sense of minimizing human harm, for intervention to take place quickly and firmly as soon as the danger of serious human rights abuses becomes apparent. On this view obeying the "last resort" condition in some circumstances might be directly at odds with the value that underlies the condition, which these commentators therefore reject.

I believe, however, that this misunderstands the condition. Intervention is not a last resort when there are less harmful means available which could reasonably be expected to accomplish the same purpose. Whether such means actually exist in any situation depends on the context and is a matter for political judgment (and inevitably so). If, for example, there was reason to believe that a government would use negotiations as a delaying tactic while atrocities are carried out, then military intervention might be a "last resort" in the morally significant sense even if there had been no prior negotiations. The aim of the "last resort" condition is to avoid unnecessary harm. It makes no sense to interpret it in a way that frustrates this aim.

4 *There should be a reasonable chance of success.* We are only justified in doing harm by the prospect of the good expected to come of it. If you are going to intervene by force in order to accomplish a legitimate purpose, you must choose your tactics, and bring to bear sufficient resources, so that there is a reasonable chance of accomplishing that purpose. Moreover (to anticipate the next condition), you must do so within the constraints of the *jus in*

bello – a condition that bears not only on the choice of tactics but also on the resource requirements of success. Otherwise the harm imposed by force is not justified.

Taken seriously, the "reasonable chance" condition is a demanding one, and under contemporary circumstances, its practical effect may be to constrain humanitarian intervention more severely than any other condition. This is for several reasons, among which I note two. First, in most cases of systematic violations of human rights it will be possible to distinguish, if crudely, between immediate and underlying causes of the violations. It will often be unrealistic, both ethically and politically, to consider an intervention successful if it alleviates the immediate causes of distress but leaves the underlying causes intact, so that the violations recur after the interventionary force departs. But if a "successful" interventionary strategy must address underlying causes as well, then the costs of success may raise to a prohibitive level or there may simply be no strategy available that is really capable of succeeding.[12] Either way, the intervention would not be justified.

Second, it is essential to remember that political will is a component of success. Any realistic judgment about the chances of success will have to take into account the challenge of sustaining the political will required to see an intervention through to a conclusion, in spite of its predictable costs, in circumstances in which a society's vital interests are probably not implicated.[13] The fact that political will is not entirely an exogenous variable does not reduce the importance of the point.

5 *The conventional limitations of the* jus in bello *apply.* These are primarily the principles of discrimination and proportionality. As a first approximation, these principles hold that an intervention's tactics should be chosen so as to protect innocent life to the greatest extent possible and that any unavoidable damage to civilian targets should be proportional to the importance of the tactical objective sought.

It is important to see that these limitations – because they restrict the tactical alternatives available to those responsible for carrying out an intervention – feed back into a judgment about the chances of the intervention's success. An intervention is not justified unless there is a reasonable chance that it can succeed within the constraints of discrimination and proportionality.

The point is familiar in just war theory, but it has special relevance in connection with humanitarian intervention. This is for a slightly complex reason. In the absence of a standing UN force, any intervention must be carried out by units of national military forces acting under their own flag(s) or that of a regional or international organization. Because the vital interests of the intervening state(s) are not likely to be under threat, it is a serious question how, and for how long, political support for the intervention can be maintained, particularly after the intervening forces begin to take casualties. This means that political and military leaders will face even greater temptations than they would under normal wartime circumstances to make tactical choices that minimize the chances of casualties to their own forces – and therefore, perhaps, choices that pose a greater risk of harm to civilians on the other side than would be strictly necessary, absent domestic political constraints, to accomplish the tactical objectives of the intervention. Something like this dynamic was at work in the Kosovo mission, when NATO bombers struck urban targets in Serbia from high altitudes so that pilots could be kept out of range of anti-aircraft fire. I leave aside, for now, the moral questions raised there to emphasize the general point. If the only way an intervention can be successfully carried out, without losing domestic political support, is by means of tactics that pose a disproportionate and otherwise unnecessary risk to innocent lives, then the "reasonable chance of success" condition has not been met and the intervention is not justified. This may be what Michael Walzer means when he writes, "*You can't kill unless you are prepared to die.*"[14]

Further Questions

I believe these five conditions are jointly sufficient to justify humanitarian intervention. There is much more that might be said about these conditions and about various other considerations that some people have thought should figure in an analysis of the morality of humanitarian intervention. To conclude, let me frame three questions that might be evoked by what I have said and say briefly how they might be answered. I do not pretend to defend my answers here.

Must humanitarian intervention be motivationally pure? That is, is intervention only acceptable when the intervening party is motivated entirely by humanitarian concerns and acts without self-interest? Perhaps it is understandable why someone might ask such a question. If we are considering whether an apparently humanitarian action is praiseworthy, the discovery of a self-interested motive seems to cancel out the humanitarianism of the act, and it no longer appears praiseworthy. But praiseworthiness is one thing, justifiability is another. Political action is virtually always the outcome of mixed motives. As a practical matter this seems unavoidable. It is true, of course, that motives of self-interest can distort humanitarian concerns. It is also true that political leaders are given to ascribing humanitarian motives to actions which are actually motivated by considerations of self-interest. But neither possibility rules out the chance that motives of self-interest and those of humanitarianism may be compatible. They might even reinforce each other. Either way the intervention would be justified, provided it adhered to the moral constraints we have discussed. To act from mixed motives may not always be praiseworthy, but it is not for that reason wrong.

Must a policy of humanitarian intervention be even-handed or consistent? The question of consistency arises from the contrast of the Bosnia or Kosovo interventions with the failure to intervene to stop the genocide in Rwanda, where the death toll was much larger. Assuming for the moment that there was a strategy available in Rwanda with a reasonable chance of success, it is hard to see how the failure to intervene can be defended. But it does not follow that intervention where the stakes are not as great would be wrong: for example, even if intervention in Rwanda had a chance of success, and even if the stakes there were higher than in Bosnia, the failure to intervene in Rwanda, though on these assumptions tragic, does not by itself make intervention in Bosnia wrong. "Half a loaf is better than none" may be a sound principle of political morality.

Is humanitarian intervention the best use of scarce resources? Thomas Pogge has pointedly asked: "If it makes sense to spend billions and to endanger thousands of lives in order to rescue a million people from Serb oppression, would it not make more sense to spend similar sums, without endangering any lives, on leading many millions out of life-threatening poverty?"[15] It is a serious question. If we grant Pogge's assumptions, the answer is probably "yes." But it is also a serious question what we should conclude from this. The fact that A is more desirable than B does not entail that B is not desirable on its own merits; and if the chances that A can be made to occur are decidedly less than for B, opting for B rather than A is in no way objectionable.

To conclude: This essay has concentrated on moral rather than legal and political questions about humanitarian intervention – that is, on only one dimension of the challenge to work out a clearer view about the subject than can be found in contemporary international doctrine. As I observed earlier, the legal and political dimensions are enormously important and I regret not being able to consider them here. But the moral dimension is the most important and if there is a reason to concentrate on it to the exclusion of these other matters, it is that without a clear view of the moral justification of humanitarian intervention, we would not know how to think about the others.

Notes

This paper derives from "When to Intervene?," *The Bowdoin Forum* (Bowdoin College, 2001). A much-revised version was discussed at Merton College, Oxford, in November 2003. I am grateful to the participants in that discussion for comments.

1   Kofi Annan, "Two Concepts of Sovereignty," *The Economist*, September 18, 1999, p. 49.

2   Independent International Commission on Kosovo, *The Kosovo Report: Conflict, International Response, Lessons Learned* (Oxford: Oxford University Press, 2000); International Commission on Intervention and State Sovereignty, *The Responsibility to Protect* (Ottawa, Ontario: International Development Research Centre, 2001); *Humanitarian Intervention: Ethical, Legal and Political Dilemmas*, ed. J. L. Holzgrefe and Robert O. Keohane (Cambridge: Cambridge University Press, 2003).

3   Michael Ignatieff, "Is the Human Rights Era Ending?" *The New York Times*, February 5, 2002, p. A25.

4   For a discussion, see Tom J. Farer, "Humanitarian Intervention Before and After 9/11: Legality and Legitimacy," in *Humanitarian Intervention: Ethical, Legal and Political Dilemmas*, ed. J. L. Holzgrefe and R. O. Keohane, Keohane (Cambridge: Cambridge University Press, 2003), pp. 53–89.

5   Michael Walzer's critique of intervention in his *Just and Unjust Wars* (New York: Basic Books, 1977) is often taken to exemplify the liberal non-interventionist view. But even Walzer allows for humanitarian intervention in exceptional cases. For reflections, see his "The Politics of Rescue," *Dissent* (Winter 1995): 35–41.

6   The most prominent statement of this position can be found in the report of the International Commission on Intervention and State Sovereignty, *The Responsibility to Protect*, ch. 2.

7   C. A. J. Coady, "War for Humanity: A Critique," in *Ethics and Foreign Intervention*, ed. Deen K. Chatterjee and Don E. Scheid (Cambridge: Cambridge University Press, 2003), pp. 274–95.

8   There are also lesser forms of interference in a state's internal affairs – for example, economic sanctions and support for forces favoring political reform. Given the constraints of space I must leave them aside, even though in some circumstances these mechanisms would obviously be preferable to military intervention as ways to influence the internal conduct of states.

9   The best general source on the theory is James Turner Johnson, *Just War Tradition and the Restraint of War: a Moral and Historical Inquiry* (Princeton, NJ: Princeton University Press, 1981).

10 Henry Shue, *Basic Rights: Subsistence, Affluence, and U.S. Foreign Policy*, 2nd edn (Princeton, NJ: Princeton University Press, 1996), chs. 1, 3.

11 A similar condition was suggested by Winrich Kühne. See Chantal de Jonge Oudraat, "Intervention in Internal Conflicts: Legal and Political Conundrums," Carnegie Endowment for International Peace *Working Papers* no. 15 (August 2000): 8.

12 The second condition could rule out intervention to establish a democratic government in cases where suitable background conditions for democracy are missing. This is one way of understanding Mill's famous argument against intervention to remove a local tyranny, in "A Few Words on Non-intervention" (*Fraser's Magazine*, 1859).

13 Again, the need to do so within the limits of the *jus in bello* puts extra pressure on the point.

14 Michael Walzer, "Kosovo," *Dissent* (Summer 1999): 6 (emphasis in original).

15 Thomas Pogge, "Priorities of Global Justice," *Metaphilosophy* 32 (2001): 7.

67

Pacifism: Reclaiming the Moral Presumption

William J. Hawk

Pacifism: Refusing to Participate in War

Pacifism holds that because war is morally unjustified persons ought not participate in it. In this essay I hope to reclaim the moral presumption *for* pacifism.

Pacifists are persons who refuse to fight because wars are immoral. If their native country provides for conscientious objection, pacifists may perform alternative national service instead of fighting. If alternative service is not available, pacifists may be forced into war contrary to their will, exiled, imprisoned, physically assaulted, or even killed.

Typically pacifists are tolerated in peacetime. What is perceived as their moral "peculiarity" poses no real threat. But in times of war their treatment is frequently quite harsh. Sometimes they are roundly condemned as common criminals or enemy infiltrators.[1] To governments pacifists may appear naïve nuisances or domestic threats. Citizens see them as anti-patriots who don't fulfill their political duties – or worse, who aid and abet the enemy. Many moral theorists take pacifist reasoning to be simplistically wrong-headed. According to some accounts the failure to endorse and participate in war when innocent others are wrongly threatened makes the pacifist position positively immoral. By not fighting, pacifists are said to wrong their nation, undermine important ideals, subvert moral values, and fail their fellow citizens and those innocents who may be threatened and in need of assistance.

Refusing to kill other human beings does not immediately strike us as being morally wrong, naïve, or misguided. Far from it. Not killing others is ethically required and supported by moral theory. But what is standard morality for times of peace – namely, refusing to kill others – becomes unacceptable or immoral in times of international conflict. At least, this is commonly said. The task of the just war or right killing theorist is to explain how warfare makes immorality, namely killing others, morally acceptable, and standard morality, refusing to kill others, morally unacceptable. From pacifist vantage points those who attempt to morally justify war and intentional killing confront massive countervailing moral presumptions. When added to the usual epistemic limitations accompanying evaluations of war, along with the commonly observed tendency for seeing one's own side as always in the right, prudence, moral wisdom, and reason converge to say "no" to war.

This essay explores moral perspectives and arguments associated with a pacifist approach to war and life. Contrary to the usual condescending attitude of political strategists and the smug dismissal by many moral theorists, I contend that pacifism presents a rational, prudent, and ethically sound response to war. First, to a morally sensitive human being dealing with how to live her life in an increasingly morally complex world, it provides a workable guide for dealing with the atrocities of modern war. Second, for the moral philosopher investigating moral duties and obligations, pacifism offers a consistent platform that rejects all killings of human beings as morally unjustified. Before presenting these perspectives and arguments, it will prove beneficial to look at one historical example of pacifism in practice.

A Pacifist City of Refuge

During World War II the small town of Le Chambon in France became a city of refuge. There, hundreds, perhaps thousands, passed seeking to escape Nazi arrest and deportation to concentration camps and almost certain death. Le Chambon operated a highly successful clandestine rescue portage much like the Underground Railroad in the United States. Villagers, acting in secret consort, resisted intimidations by their own countrymen and government officials, often at grave personal and familial peril, to aid unknown Jews seeking asylum. Villagers were imprisoned. Some were killed. They risked death to save others.

The leader of the Le Chambon community was Andre Trocme, a pacifist pastor. Trocme served the local Huguenot congregation because his own Reformed Church would not permit his preaching pacifism.[2] Pacifism was so essential to who and what he was that Trocme could not lay it aside for the sake of better employment. Neither would he conceal it when surrounded by foreign warriors and French collaborators. Trocme's pacifism enabled a "miracle" to happen at Le Chambon – many innocent human lives were saved.

Pacifism for Trocme involved living out his commitment to the preciousness of human life. Because life is precious, sacred, Trocme vowed to value it, celebrate it, and never intentionally take it or aid in its being taken by others. Grounding this moral commitment were previous experiences with death, including his mother's, and his reading of New Testament scriptures, especially Jesus' teachings about peace. In *Lest Innocent Blood Be Shed*, philosopher Philip Hallie accounted for Trocme's pacifism this way:

> The attitude of nonviolence toward all human beings came to Andre Trocme from many sources . . . . But in its depths his nonviolence stayed . . . simple . . . ; it was an attitude toward people, not a carefully argued theological position. In its depths it was personal; it had to do with the persons he had known, ... Years later, he would study theology in Paris and New York, and he would work to develop persuasive arguments for pacifism. But this work would be primarily for the sake of convincing others. In his own mind, nonviolence was completely expressed in words as simple and direct as . . . , 'One must refuse to shoot. Christ taught us to love our enemies. That is His good news, that we should help, not hurt each other, . . . '[3]

Trocme's, and by extension Le Chambon's, pacifism involved harboring and shuttling to safety those who came seeking assistance. The difference between these historical pacifists and their critics is not whether morality demands that we assist others. The dispute concerns whether killing others or participating in war is morally permitted to prevent evil from occurring. Trocme's conscience would not permit him to kill Nazis or join the French resistance in order to save those who came to him for help. But through his actions many lives were saved.

The Pacifist Way of Life: More than Rejecting War and Intentional Killing

Pacifists point to historical examples such as Andre Trocme to indicate a fairer expression of the full implications of their moral commitments. Critics often focus exclusively on what pacifists don't do, namely their *refusal* to participate in war. This ignores the many morally responsible activities pacifists perform. Working for the common human good can be an all-consuming life-long occupation. Many who reject war live to improve the human condition. They work for justice, respond to human need, and champion the cause of those who suffer. Unfortunately, the critics usually overlook the "pacifist way of life" and instead notice pacifists only in times of war and then only for what they are *not* doing.

Those who live a "pacifist way of life" view critics as inconsistent and morally incoherent on this score. Pacifist actions and attitudes that arouse ire in times of war invoke moral praise in peacetime. For example, during World War II many criticized Trocme and his followers for not taking up arms. Some called for them to fight against the Nazis while others called for collaboration with the Nazis to turn over Jews. Trocme's pacifist way of life prohibited both killing Nazis and sending Jews to death camps. His pacifism mandated risky attempts to save Jews caught in the crossfire. The care and concern which guided his prewar activity of running a school for orphaned children motivated Trocme to open an underground passageway for orphaned human beings in the midst of war. His was a life of moral consistency. Unlike opponents for whom the presence or absence of war determines whether to praise or blame killing, pacifists remain consistent. The same coherence and consistency in life that demands humanitarian efforts in times of peace strengthened Trocme's character to say "No" in times of war.

The principal purpose of this essay is to reclaim the moral presumption of pacifism and respond to pacifism's critics. In defending pacifism I give some sense of the pacifist's life-affirming commitments, a "pacifist way of life," and how these benefit others. Philip Hallie's description of the life and work of Andre Trocme offers a glimpse into what a fuller treatment of pacifism should include. A "pacifist way of life" fully expressed involves a humanitarian, life-affirming, justice-seeking approach which, because of these commitments, rejects war.

Just War and Right Killing: the Open Question

Pacifists hold that war is not morally justified and that individual moral agents should not kill others. However, pacifists differ on which is the more basic moral claim. For some, the primary justification for not participating in war is a moral rejection of warfare. For others, war's immorality derives from their personal ethic, one proclaiming the moral impermissibility of killing others. Most committed pacifists see these two elements in one comprehensive vision. War's patent immorality and the moral sanction against killing others imply each other. While moral judgments against war and against killing others are frequently held together, they provide independent reasons for pacifism.

Against these core moral claims stand two traditions: (1) just war and (2) right killing (the permissible or obligatory killing of other human beings). For centuries theorists have engaged in careful reflection to clarify the conditions, if any, under which war may be just or justifiable and killing another human being against her will may be morally permitted. Just war theory looks at conditions for initiating war (*jus ad bellum*) and assesses the conduct of the war (*jus in bello*). Right killing theorists identify types of persons that may justifiably be killed, e.g. tyrants, murderers, or terrorists; or situations in which agents find themselves in which their killing of others may be made permissible, e.g. self-defense or defense of innocent others. The pacifist response to these enterprises is that they fail.

In outline, pacifists view the presumption against killing another human being as being very high. For some it is unconditional, absolute, while for others it is a *prima facie* presumption much stronger than that usually observed. Just war and right killing theorists fail to overcome the presumption that pacifists (along with other moral agents in times of peace) recognize against killing others. But even if the presumption against killing others could be overcome, there are additional factors advocating for pacifism. These factors are many (some will be detailed later) and include things such as: (1) limitations on knowledge when faced with choices involving killing or war, (2) inability to accurately predict war's outcomes, (3) failures to recognize the bias or prejudice in one's own reasoning (and obvious bias observed in the moral reasoning of others), (4) the operation of highly sophisticated propaganda systems, (5) self-deception, (6) the oft-observed tendency of ethical reasoning to align with self- or national interest, and finally (7) the fact that, so far as I know, just war analysis never results in finding that the war of the analyst's nation state is unjust, i.e. just war reasoning seems to condemn no wars except those fought by others.

In order to justify a pacifist position, however, it is not necessary to claim or to demonstrate that just war theory fails or that morally permissible killings of the unwilling are impossible. This is good fortune for pacifists because just war theorizing and right killing justifications appear to operate in such a context that all actual wars and most killings satisfy their vague criteria. Vagueness in the criteria or application make difficult disproving either just war or right killing.

To gain its moral footing pacifism needs to show that just war and morally permissible killing of the unwilling remain *open questions*. To the question, "Is war ever morally justified?" pacifists and just war theorists offer contradictory answers. Pacifists say "no" and just war theorists say "yes." Both sides provide reasons to support their claim. Because there are reasons for both sides we must conclude that whether war is morally justifiable is technically an open question. Similarly, to the question, "Is killing persons against their will ever morally justified?" there are contradictory answers. The fact of conflicting answers from different moral perspectives provides evidence for the openness of that question as well. Because pacifism represents one alternative response to a genuinely open question it comes to the debate as a tenable position, i.e. one plausible alternative.

But if just war and right killing remain genuinely open questions, then, I believe, pacifism rapidly becomes the superior position. With the moral quandaries and epistemic limitations that

must trouble any would-be "just warrior," and the availability of unambiguously ethical alternative pacifist actions such as Trocme's, the pacifist position becomes prudent, credible, reasonable, and ultimately preferable. Given the moral significance and ethical implications of a decision to embark on war, pacifism gains credibility as the limitations associated with just war and right killing are exposed. To ask pacifism to prove itself by disproving just war and right killing fundamentally misplaces the burden of proof. Pacifism's refusing to kill observes the moral presumption. Those who violate the presumption must make their case in light of pacifist alternatives. In light of real alternatives that pacifism offers, the burden on just war and right killing becomes onerous.

The Pacifist Moral Vision: Two Constitutive Elements

Accepting, for the purposes of philosophical inquiry, justifiable war and killing of human beings against their will as genuinely "open questions" means that just war and right killing must overcome strong moral presumptions against their views. Pacifism, on the other hand, reinforces the presumption against killing and offers alternative courses of conduct. Somehow, in the popular mind, these respective burdens of proof have been inverted. For pacifist critics it seems killing is presumed permissible and not killing problematic. It is not particularly helpful to point out all the "interests" (e.g., economic, political, technological, and personal) at work in this otherwise puzzling upside-down world. But it is important to point out that culturally in America the burden of proof has been misapplied. Instead of the forces of war and killing having to make their case, they are assumed legitimate. The forces of peace and humanitarian concern are wrongly required to justify themselves.

Earlier I argued that there are at least two different general "grounding" reasons for pacifism – a moral rejection of warfare or refusal to kill another human being. These two reasons constitute different emphases – one global and corporate, the other personal and individual – which prompt a pacifist response. They provide the ethical insights that inform a "pacifist moral vision."

1 *War is egregiously morally bad.* The beginning point for many who align with the community of pacifists starts with a thorough moral evaluation of the nature and consequences of war. Any empirical assessment shows war to be morally horrific; it is a horrendous demonstration of human ill intention and technological capability. It represents the lowest moral benchmark for the human species. During the twentieth century, for example, more than 100 million human beings, most of them non-combatants, were killed directly as a result of wars. In addition to this carnage and loss, millions of men, women, and children were wounded, raped, tortured, mutilated, scarred, or traumatized; countless non-human lives suffered and died; the environment was damaged; and priceless art and human habitats were destroyed. In terms of the utter destruction of moral values, arguably there is no worse institution or set of practices than warfare.

Exacerbating the moral egregiousness of warfare is the often-neglected fact that wars are a matter of human intention and policy. Unlike natural disasters, wars are fully preventable. Men (not always, but usually) make wars. Wars result from planning and preparation, technological innovation and investment, allocations of resources and decisions about priorities and policies. For any particular war, World War II to the war in Iraq, things could have gone otherwise. The war might not have occurred. Bertrand Russell personally intervened and some members of John F. Kennedy's war strategy group apparently prevented a possible world war during the Cuban missile crisis.[4] Conversely, with respect to any peacetime, because of continuous preparation, war is possible. War is a morally egregious, preventable phenomenon.

There is irony in the fact that the ranks of pacifists are continually expanded by new recruits with first-hand personal experience with war. This is true for civilian victims of war as well as military participants. Pacifism reached global proportions after World War I; it is widespread in Japan; and recently the majority of draft-age German youth registered as conscientious objectors.[5] Frequently, there is a greater affinity between pacifists and those who have seen combat, yet have not been totally hardened by it, than there is between returning soldiers and those who cheer them home. One element of the pacifist moral vision begins with concrete familiarity with moral costs, human and otherwise, of warfare. Those with an abstract familiarity with warfare are more likely to view it as morally justifiable. Many of those who know war personally reject it as atrocity.

2 *Human life is ultimately valuable (sacred) and, accordingly, intentionally killing human beings against their will is morally wrong.* Another element of the pacifist moral vision begins personally with a view of other human beings as the ultimate source of moral value. This may be articulated in different ways depending upon, for example, if one's moral stance is religious or secular, and if secular, deontological, virtue theory, or consequentialist. Religious pacifists, for example, may talk of each human life being sacred, a manifestation, instantiation, or gift of God. As a consequence of being morally precious, human lives must not be intentionally taken.

Secular or philosophically based pacifists use different vocabularies and rationales. They speak of life as being inviolable or of human beings as having an inalienable right to life or of human life being the grounding of moral value. A Kantian, for example, following the respect principle as captured in the Categorical Imperative (which enjoins treating human life always as an end), resists the idea of justified intentional killing of other human beings. This is especially true given the number and character of non-combatants or innocents who are routinely killed as a part of modern warfare. Perpetual peace is a consistent Kantian aspiration. Similarly, intentional killing of others may become habituated through warfare. Any serious virtue theorist must be cautious in justifying a particular intentional killing lest vicious habits develop. Finally, even if one's moral reasoning strategies tend toward consequentialism, anyone who considers carefully the actual wars that have been fought, the prospect of unforeseen and untoward consequences, including the possibilities of mistakes of every variety, and the destructive capabilities of current and future technologies of warfare, must pause before endorsing war. Any fair-minded consequentialist accounting of the wars of the twentieth century must reckon them unjustifiable. Their costs were higher than the presumed benefits. Within each of the dominant ethical traditions, religious or secular, there are considerations which counsel against justifying intentional killing of human beings contrary to their will. Pacifists use these varying traditions with their rationales as justification for refusing to intentionally kill others.

Two Types of Pacifism

Although there are many varieties of religious and secularly based pacifism, for purposes of analysis I identify and distinguish two general types. These versions are differentiated chiefly by the element of the moral vision (egregious war or inviolable human life) that grounds them. One of these might be termed anti-warism or *anti-warist pacifism*. The other is more difficult to characterize because it is grounded in the view that human life is sacred, inviolable, or an inalienable value. This is the view that most critics have in mind when they challenge or attempt to discredit pacifism. I call it *personal pacifism*.

Pacifist anti-warism

One need not view all human life as equally inviolable or sacred or reject all morally legitimate intentional killing of human beings against their will to be a pacifist. Needless to say, one need not be committed to the more strenuous moral stance of non-violence. The "nuclear pacifists" of a previous generation, i.e. those who rejected the ethical justifiability of a nuclear exchange between superpowers, are properly considered *anti-war pacifists*. Their refusal to participate in war stems from a moral judgment about one particular type of war, namely, one in which nuclear weapons, with their vast capacity for destruction, are employed.

Anti-war pacifists reject the moral justifiability of all wars because of one or more ethical considerations. One could hold this view based on the fact that the wrongs obviously done in war are so great that a strong *prima facie* case against war is created. Couple this *prima facie* case with a determination that (a) just war conditions fail to overcome the *prima facie* presumption against war or (b) it is not certain that just war considerations defeat the presumption, and, in cases where the stakes are as high as they are in warfare, one morally ought to defer to the presumption against war. From either of these considerations one generates a reasonable moral account for rejecting participation in all wars.

Many *anti-war pacifists* have come to their position because of warfare's failure to discriminate between innocent or guilty, combatant or non-combatant persons. The killing, intentional or not, of relatively innocent and dramatically defenseless human beings may prove sufficient to prompt a moral rejection of war. This, even if it were possible to satisfy every other moral consideration implicated in war. Similarly, the moral failure of warfare need not be stated so specifically as regarding failure to discriminate morally proper from improper targets. It may be a matter of the totality of destruction that is invariantly involved in modern warfare. Through many of his writings and much of his life it appears that the late philosopher Bertrand Russell fits this "totality of war's evils" category of *anti-war pacifists*.

Besides the direct loss of human life there may be any number of other moral reasons to reject all warfare. (1) Anyone who knows firsthand the experiences of war knows that women often pay a disproportionate price. The moral price varies. For instance, sometimes rape is rationalized as a tactic in combat. At other times, rape becomes an all-too-common accepted reality under the exigencies of combat. Frequently, along with fighting comes a dehumanizing of women, making them into objects of personal violence acted out sexually. The disfigurement of sexual relations is not an inconsequential moral cost associated with warfare. Focusing on this cost alone may be sufficient to lead some to reject all war.

(2) Secondly, the natural environment suffers as well. Anyone with any moral sensitivity for the welfare of the planet, both natural ecosystems and non-human life forms, may on that basis become an *anti-war pacifist*. Even were a conflict to be severely restricted in scope and focus, the environmental costs of war's destruction and a fragile ecological balance may give sufficient reason for rejecting war.

(3) Thirdly, anyone who prizes personal autonomy may not be able to perform as a soldier. People say that the first casualty of war is the truth. But the first casualty of joining the war effort, at least in modern nation states with standing armies, is moral autonomy. Military effectiveness is inversely relational to making one's own judgment, moral or otherwise. This lesson comes prominently to the fore in military training and preparation. The success of the military unit increases as personal choice ceases. Particularly deadly actions become a matter of trained reaction rather than moral reflection.[6] Although this may not represent a large number, as it seems that most people may be easily distanced from their personal moral responsibility, some *anti-war pacifists* arrive at their positions by considerations having to do with the moral preconditions and not the actual conduct of war. The extinguishing of moral autonomy may be one such determinative precondition.

One who announces oneself an *anti-war pacifist*, who goes on to explain the rationale of their pacifism as moral concern for the totality of destruction coming from nuclear weapons, the intentional deaths of relatively innocent and defenseless citizens, the mistreatment of women, the ruination of the environment, or their inalienable commitment to moral autonomy, will likely encounter many opponents with whom to debate. They are not, however, likely to be subjected to the disdain directed at those who espouse what I term *personal pacifism*.

Personal pacifism

Personal pacifism stems from a personal commitment to never intentionally kill another human being. Andre Trocme represented this variety of pacifism. To refuse to intentionally kill another human being is extraordinary. I believe, however, that this moral constraint on one's own conduct, even when one is faced with war, is reasonable and arguably morally preferable to other available options.

Most moral thinkers and theories endorse a *prima facie* obligation against killing others. For them, the prohibition against killing, while strong, is defeasible, i.e. it can be overridden by other moral considerations or values. Self-defense and the defense of innocent others are two standard cases where it is broadly agreed that the presumptive prohibition against taking another human life may be overridden. Ethicists of various theoretical frameworks spend a considerable amount of time specifying the conditions for such "right killing."

Personal pacifism, i.e. a refusal to participate in war because it involves killing other human beings, affirms the inviolable value of human life and rejects *right killing*. Another way to put this is to say that the presumption against killing human beings (recognized by other moral agents and theories) is (1) never defeated or (2) is never defeated with certainty. Given conditions of uncertainty, i.e. where the justifiability of the killing is an open question and where the stakes are someone's life, one morally ought to defer to the presumption against killing.

Critics, those who espouse right killing and just war, demand that *personal pacifism* offer a justification for refusing to accept right killing. However, since the *prima facie* case is against intentional killing, the burden of proof must fall to those who intend to justify killing. Many moral theorists take up this burden, showing, in their various ways, that in this instance or that, the *prima facie* prohibition against intentional killing is rightly overridden. Utilitarians and other consequentialists offer calculations and predictions of the future that effectively extinguish the *prima facie* case against killing. What results from attempting to justify killing is a vast array of various scenarios in which right killing purportedly occurs. However, there is very little agreement between moral theories or theorists about which killings, if any, are right. This reinforces the *personal pacifist's* reliance upon the *prima facie* case against killing.

Furthermore, for any observer of the human situation it comes as no surprise that those who intentionally kill others believe they are justified in what they have done. In addition to the human tendency to justify our conduct to ourselves and others, there are at least three factors diminishing our confidence in claims of right killing. First, we make simple mistakes and misperceptions and sometimes claim justified killing based on these mistakes, e.g. thinking someone poses a threat when they don't. Secondly, we sometimes have been deceived about what is taking place around us and our "right killing" results from such deception, e.g. we have been subjected to and victimized by propaganda. And, thirdly, there are elements within us that may produce self-deception. We frequently observe others purportedly killing for good reason when we know that self-deception is involved. How can we possibly know that we are not ourselves victims of our own deceptions? When the *personal pacifist* considers (1) these many epistemic problems which reduce confidence in right killing, (2) the significance of the stakes involved, namely, someone's life, and (3) the strong moral presumption against intentional killing, steadfastness in observing the presumption against killing becomes not merely prudent but obligatory

Human Life: the Ultimate Basis of Moral Value

That human life is sacred or inviolable finds expression in many historical proclamations. Religious leaders and texts, the Declaration of Independence, and orthodox moral theory frequently sound as if they take human life to be inviolable. For instance, pacifists take seriously the sixth commandment of the Decalogue, "Thou Shalt Not Kill." Or they pattern their

lives after the Golden Rule, which requires one to do unto others as he would have them do unto him. When the Declaration of Independence affirms life, liberty, and the pursuit of happiness to be inalienable rights, the pacifist takes this seriously and acts as if the right to life really were inalienable. Kant's Categorical Imperative disallows ever treating someone as a means solely but always as an end. The personal pacifist notices that anyone who intentionally kills has difficulty passing Kantian moral muster. Furthermore, pacifists stand ready and willing to observe Kant's demand to universalize their position. "I will there to be a world in which everyone refuses to kill another or participate in war." In all these instances personal pacifists understand themselves to be consistently applying basic moral claims about human life and its value. Their treating human life as inviolable (sacred) derives from the best of religious teaching and ethical theory. Critics of pacifists who endorse just war and right killing must, in terms of consistency with their efforts to justify homicide, treat these many religious and foundational expressions as merely "rhetoric" or manifesto-style aspirations of human life.

The majority perspective assumes that human lives may be intentionally taken, given a satisfactory reason. Personal pacifists see with equal clarity and intuitive obviousness the profound moral truth that no reason is ever sufficient to justify intentionally killing another human being. This is a bedrock moral difference. There seems to be an impasse between pacifists and the majority. One particular historical example, framed from a pacifist perspective, may shed light on what happens when fundamental moral values differ.

During the years of slavery in the United States, some abolitionists must have found incomprehensible the practices of their slave-owning fellow countrymen. For the abolitionists it was intuitively obvious that all persons had dignity and could not, for that reason, be treated as property. Alternatively, for the slave-owning community it was equally intuitively obvious that their slaves were not "persons" in the full sense of that word. The slaves were, both in terms of providential dictate and their own personal welfare, made better by enslavement. Between these conflicting moral positions there was no common ground.

Pacifists frequently view themselves as comparable to abolitionists and their adversaries as slaveholders. For a pacifist, just war and right killing theorists have not yet come to see the full humanity of the victims of war. The moral project is to constantly reaffirm that humanity until the evil of war is apparent to all.

A Response to the Chief Criticism of Pacifism

Critics claim that Hitler had to be stopped. Pol Pot and the Rwandan or Serbian genocides should have been stopped. Innocent persons are sometimes in need of protection and defense. Those in a position to do something are morally obligated to prevent evil from taking place. If a pacifist wants to sacrifice his own life because of his moral principles, that is fine, but it is immoral to neglect persons who are powerless against aggressive and violent assailants. It will not do to stand by while evil succeeds. To do so is to become responsible for the evil as though one had actually done it.

Just war and right killing strategists are surprised to discover that most pacifists agree with every statement in the above standard criticism. Neglecting the needs and harms done to others is morally wrong. Innocents, the powerless, and the victims of injustice must be protected. The weak and those who suffer make moral demands on us. One must attempt to stop Hitler, Pol Pot, or the Rwandan genocide.

What separates pacifists from their critics is not that one group observes and the other does not a moral duty to alleviate suffering, to promote justice, and to prevent evil. The "pacifist way of life" and "pacifist moral vision" are built upon obligations for justice and preventing suffering. What differentiates pacifists from their critics is (1) whether killing others can be made ethical by the evil it attempts to prevent and (2)

whether viable alternatives to killing others exist. Pacifists such as Andre Trocme contend that because there are alternatives to warfare and because killing others is itself immoral, killing and war must be rejected.

One strategy of anti-pacifists is (1) to deny a morally relevant difference between acting and refraining, (2) to assert a version of negative responsibility, i.e. that one is responsible for what one fails to prevent as much as for what one does, and then (3) claim that there are instances where the only options are to do nothing or engage in war. I contend that most actual pacifists agree, generally, with the sentiment behind the attempt to defeat an acting/refraining distinction (1); they wholeheartedly accept negative responsibility (2); but they refuse to reduce the complex realities of the world to only two options, war or doing nothing (3).

As critics suggest, some personal pacifists build a high wall between responsibility for acting and no responsibility for refraining. They appear to be motivated primarily by a concern for personal purity or avoiding "dirty hands." Most of these personal pacifists are religiously motivated and use an action/refraining distinction to (1) accurately describe their own moral sensibility and/or (2) deal with the issue of guilt for not intervening to assist others. However, the anti-war pacifists and many personal pacifists are not motivated by this concern for moral purity.

The fact is that far from recoiling from claims derived from negative responsibility, pacifists should and frequently do endorse the concept. Pacifists usually display a heightened awareness of their total responsibility. They tend to reject an acting/refraining distinction and hold themselves and others responsible for bad things that happen which could have been prevented. This means that doing nothing or "tending one's own garden" is an immoral response to the suffering and injustices of the world.

Because of their concern for suffering and injustices, pacifists do everything within their power to prevent warfare. They preach peace, they teach justice, they work to achieve human betterment in every way that they know. In times of war, instead of joining the fray, they do things like smuggle Jews to safety and render aid and assistance wherever there is humanitarian need.

Even when, as judged by the relative moral merits, a war is less unjustified than others, pacifists align against it. When their efforts fail and nation states go to war anyway, they do not concede defeat. Their efforts on behalf of humanity and against war operate under dual moral obligations to attempt to stop existing wars and prevent future ones.

Pacifists generally accept responsibility for the broad and lasting consequences of their actions and self-restraint. To their critics who endorse just war and right killing, they return the challenge of negative responsibility. Those who justify, plan, and prepare for wars have been directly responsible for millions of deaths and immense destruction. They are indirectly responsible for the totality of moral losses coming from the perpetuation of warfare. Instead of expending their precious energy, time, and effort in diplomacy, economic justice, trade and exchange, and communication with different nations in the world, all of which would minimize the likelihood of war, just war and right killing agents and theorists prepare for war, develop war's technology, and spend considerable intellectual skills justifying rather than critiquing the conditions for warfare. War justifiers, according to pacifists, are directly responsible for wars because of their moral justifications. They are grossly negatively responsible because of other things they could have been doing to prevent war but didn't.

Instead of building larger military arsenals and developing greater technological firepower, those in command and control positions could have dedicated themselves to peace. Wars may have been avoided. What is absent in just war and right killing is a real will to eliminate war. Such a will requires more than rhetoric. It eventuates in preparation, hard work, risk assessment, and imagination as nation states drastically alter their international relations and objectives and reallocate resources. Imagine a

twentieth century in which the resources and efforts dedicated to war had been spent in achieving peace. Such a century could have been much more humane.

Furthermore, to use negative responsibility to charge pacifists with immorality misses very important considerations. Genuine pacifists demonstrate a "pacifist way of life" that aims to alleviate suffering and advance justice. They reject war either because of the moral atrocities of war and/or because of the intentional and unjustified killing that takes place. They maintain their resistance even during popular wars because they affirm negative responsibility. Their actions affect the prospects of future wars. Pacifism's commitment is a witness and symbol of hope against all intentional killing and future wars. If only their critics believed in negative responsibility they would see that justifying and preparing for war have made wars and their evils more acceptable.

Conclusion

Personal pacifists accept human life as precious, sacred, inviolable. They represent a fundamental shift in moral perspective, taking human life as the ground of moral value. Anti-war pacifists highlight the moral shortcomings of war. To accept the legitimacy of right killing and just war opens the door to tremendous moral losses. When the sound moral presumption against killing is overridden, humanity pays the price. The argument from negative responsibility, often employed against pacifists, may be turned back on critics, showing their complicity in and preparation for war. Just war and right killing advocates share responsibility for all of war's harms, especially for failing to achieve peace when it may have been possible. Although pacifists are routinely criticized for their moral commitments they demonstrate a consistent and coherent ethic that reverences human life and rejects the most egregious violations of it. By living consistently with that tradition pacifists hope to eradicate war, the most horrible affront to humanity.

Notes

I owe much to the editor, Hugh LaFollette, for his encouragement to write this essay and his many helpful questions along the way. The problems that remain, alas, are of my own doing.

1   In the United States during World War I, 17 pacifist conscientious objectors were sentenced to death.
2   Philip Hallie, *Lest Innocent Blood Be Shed* (New York: Harper and Row, 1979), p. 71.
3   Hallie, *Lest Innocent Blood Be Shed*, p. 61.
4   For an account of his intervention see Bertrand Russell, *Unarmed Victory* (New York: Simon and Schuster, 1963).
5   See Charles C. Moskos and John Whiteclay Chambers, II(eds.), *The New Conscientious Objection: From Sacred to Secular Resistance* (New York: Oxford University Press, 1993).
6   For an analysis of changes in military training that turned decisions into reactions see Dave Grossman, *On Killing* (Boston, MA: Little, Brown and Company, 1995).